WHITE
SEA

...LAND

...AND

L. Onega

L. Ladoga

L. Peipus

Ob R.

URAL MTS.

$995

W9-CEQ-173

Volga R.

Kama R.

U.S.S.R.

Moscow •

Don R.

Volga R.

ARAL
SEA

Dnieper R.

SEA OF
AZOV

Crimea

CAUCASUS MTS.

CASPIAN SEA

OMANIA

...AN

• Bucharest

...ube R.

...LGARIA

...KAN MTS.

BLACK SEA

...E

...hens

AEGEAN
SEA

Crete

Ankara •

TURKEY

TAURUS MTS.

Rhodes

Cyprus

Euphrates R.

Tigris R.

SYRIA

Beirut
LEBANON

Damascus •

ISRAEL

JORDAN

• Tehran

IRAN

• Baghdad

IRAQ

Persian
Gulf

0   100   200   300

Scale of Miles

EUROPEAN SOCIETY AND POLITICS

Stanley Rothman

EUROPEAN
SOCIETY AND POLITICS

The Bobbs-Merrill Company, Inc.
Indianapolis and New York

To my mother and my wife

Preface

This book is an interpretation—or rather a series of interpretations—of the social and political life of four European nations. It begins with a discussion of the forces that have shaped European history and then turns to the particular fusion of these forces responsible for the different courses taken by each of the four countries.

Throughout the volume, European social and political institutions are treated as patterns of relationships that have been continuously changing and will probably continue to change. The section on political parties, for example, is concerned first with their general development in Europe and then with the party systems of England, France, Germany, and the Soviet Union. In each instance, the analysis relates the character of the party system to other institutions and emphasizes that contemporary patterns are part of an ever-evolving political process. Other sections of the book are arranged in the same way, moving always from the general European experience to more specific national phenomena. This arrangement allows the reader to view contemporary European politics as the prod-

uct of a complex interplay between indigenous cultural and social patterns and the forces that have transformed a specific type of traditional society into a number of modern industrial states.

As the explicitly theoretical sections of the text will indicate, my approach to the study of politics is highly eclectic. I have drawn whatever ideas seemed useful from various functionalist approaches, but I have combined these with more traditional kinds of analysis. The theoretical sections do not attempt to develop a systematic conceptual framework; they merely indicate what I consider to be some of the pivotal categories of political analysis, demonstrating how these categories relate to each other and developing a few general propositions. I am skeptical that at the present state of development of our discipline any more than this can usefully be done. Further, I have attempted to keep technical language at a minimum; whatever may be the advantages of a precise vocabulary, I think that an excessive emphasis on theoretical distinctions, in a text of this nature, would be more confusing than helpful.

In writing this book I have been keenly aware of the author's persistent problem of not being able to say everything at once. The text, therefore, is quite deliberately and consciously organized and will best be read in the order in which the material is presented. I suspect that the relevance of some of the points made in early chapters cannot be fully appreciated until later on; similarly, much of the material in the later chapters cannot be properly evaluated without reading the earlier chapters. In short, the text builds on itself.

Some of the conclusions I have reached in the text are undoubtedly controversial; while I have attempted to be as fair as I can, I have not hesitated to evaluate the actions of men or the consequences of institutions where I have deemed such evaluations to be germane. While ethical and factual statements are analytically distinct and cannot be derived from each other, one's ethical position is related in important ways to one's empirical analysis, and the social scientist can legitimately draw moral inferences from his understanding of politics.

A number of colleagues have offered me assistance in the writing of this book. Professor Samuel Beer of Harvard, my former teacher, read an earlier version of the manuscript and made a number of very valuable suggestions, most of which I have incorporated. Professor Peter Merkl of the University of California at Santa Barbara also read large sections of the manuscript and enabled me to correct errors of fact and interpretation. In addition, I received substantial help from Professor Bernard Brown of Brooklyn College, Professor Arnold J. Heidenheimer of Washington University, Professor Gerard Braunthal of the University of Massachusetts, Professor Steven Goldstein and Professor Charles L. Robertson of Smith College, and Professor Lewis Edinger of Columbia University. Dr. Charles E. McClelland, University of Pennsylvania, Dr. N. David Milder, Ohio State University, Messrs. Slava Lubomudrov and Arlo Mike Murray, both of the Graduate School of Indiana University, Department of Political Science, read galley proof for factual errors in particular regard to the countries of Germany, France, Russia and the Soviet Union, and England, respectively. Mr. Murray, in addition, made helpful suggestions in regard to the graphic illustrations.

A special word of thanks should go to my typist, Mrs. Esther Lanzello, who has been with this book just about as long as I have.

AUGUST 16, 1969

Contents

Introduction

1. THE STUDY OF COMPARATIVE POLITICS

Plato's *Republic* begins just after Socrates has returned from the Piraeus, the seaport for Athens. At the harbor mingle men from many lands of differing customs, beliefs, and values, and after attending a public procession, Socrates is persuaded by several young men to visit the home of an old friend. It is then that the philosophic speculation begins, for in comparing the customary Athenian methods of doing things with those of other peoples, his audience is forced to think in general terms about social and political life and to raise questions about values, about behavior, and about the structure of the model state.

The study of comparative politics is, in some sense, the social scientist's equivalent of the laboratory. It not only offers him the opportunity to develop new perspectives on his own society but it forces him to think in more general and systematic terms about the forces that shape the politics of any nation. With the exception of the Marxists, European political scientists, for example, have generally couched their analyses of politics in terms of

legal institutions, stressing such variables as the nature of electoral systems and the formal structure of legislatures in trying to explain the dynamics of particular political systems. It is only in the past 15 years that they have been forced to recognize that political institutions are an integral part of a society's culture and social structure, and that new approaches to the study of politics are necessary if one wishes to compare various European countries or to explain the differences between Europe and other areas of the world.

For many years American political scientists tended to analyze the politics of the United States as if it represented nothing more than a struggle among competing interest groups, each seeking to maximize its own economic position. The importance of economics and the role of special interests in the political process are undeniable, but the study of other political cultures makes it quite clear that such a restrictive analysis is inadequate. Both the kinds of interest groups that emerge in any society and the goals they regard as vital must be explained in terms of other variables.

1

THE IMPORTANCE OF THEORY: An awareness that "common-sense" views, derived from our own experience, cannot explain a wide range of facts may lead us to broaden our perspectives. But the matter is not as simple as that, for a "fact" often becomes significant to us only in the context of a theoretical framework which guides our observations. How to determine which facts are important is not an easy task, and while an instinctive feeling for politics is useful, it is also true that our knowledge of any subject depends largely upon our ability to develop more or less well-articulated theories. To medieval philosophers it seemed obvious that the sun circled the earth and that heavy bodies fell more rapidly than light ones; these were propositions confirmed by observation. It was only when the founders of modern science developed theories that contradicted common sense and, in addition, developed a whole set of new concepts, such as mass and velocity, that the revolution began which was to completely transform European society. So, too, the development of the various social sciences in the past hundred years, while in no way comparable with that of the natural sciences, has been a factor of some importance in leading students of politics to seek new ways of looking at the political process.

The next three sections of this introduction will very briefly present certain concepts that political scientists are finding more and more useful for the understanding of the political system. Each of the points discussed will be treated again, and in more detail, in the introductory sections of relevant chapters.

2. THE POLITICAL SYSTEM

Man's increasing ability to dominate the world may be explained by the fact that he has hands containing opposable thumbs or by the size and intricacy of his brain. The development of a highly complex civilization, however, has been possible only through the creation of social and political communities. It is by means of social organization that human beings have been able to mobilize sufficient resources to attain common goals and to create a culture that has grown increasingly complicated. Language itself, the basic tool of all but the most elementary thinking, is social in origin.

It is for this reason that philosophers as different in their views as Aristotle and Rousseau defined man as the "political" animal, for the first requisite of social order is the development of mechanisms by which men can govern their relations with each other. The existence of any complex society certainly calls for institutions that enable a community to define its goals—including that of survival—and to decide how best to achieve them.[1] These institutions, in turn, cannot function without some agreement as to what constitutes legitimate authority and on what basis this authority is to be delegated. They also require the development of a system of positive and negative sanctions designed to secure compliance with the established authority as well as the creation of devices to permit the implementation of authoritative decisions.

The political system of any society, then, consists of those institutions whose primary function is to enable the society to achieve what it—or at least the dominant groups within it—considers its primary ends.[2] The political institutions of any partial society (an interest group, a church, a fraternal organization) perform the same functions. The difference between these partial systems and the society or social system as a whole is that the

[1] Institutions—or structures—are to be conceived of as systems of interrelated roles. The family as an institution consists of the roles of mother, father, husband and wife, sibling and sibling; legal institutions consist of such roles as judge, prosecuting attorney, and defense attorney. A description of the legal institutions of any society requires not only a discussion of the formal content of the law, but also an analysis of the way in which the roles of judge and attorney and policeman, and so forth, are related to each other and to the society of which they are a part in terms of actual behavior.

[2] This is by no means the only function of a political system; a fuller discussion of this point will be found in later chapters.

latter generally claims a monopoly of legitimate force, is relatively self-sufficient, and occupies a determinate geographic boundary.

Other functions must be performed within any society if its members are to achieve both individual and collective goals. Citizens must be motivated to fulfill their roles and to accept the society's norms of behavior. Institutions must be developed to resolve the inevitable conflicts that emerge among individuals and groups, to reduce the inevitable tensions that social life produces, and to control the inevitable deviants who refuse to accept the society's basic values. These functions are the responsibility of familial, religious, legal, and educational institutions, among others. Finally, structures must exist that enable the society to adapt itself to its environment—a function performed in large part by the economic system.

All these institutions—the family, the church, the school—may be grouped into separate systems, although it should be stressed that any one of them may execute a variety of functions, and, as we shall see, all of those mentioned thus far are closely interrelated. For example, the political system of a society like the United States, which legitimizes private property and a relatively free market system, is likely to be quite different from one like the Soviet Union, in which economic life is explicitly a political matter and basic economic decisions are still made by a political elite.

POLITICAL INSTITUTIONS: Every political system must evolve its own methods for making political decisions—and for carrying them out. This in turn requires that machinery be set up for effectively mobilizing the resources of the community, for communicating the problems faced by the society—including the demands of its members—to those responsible for making decisions, and for enforcing the commands of those vested with authority.

In Western Europe the authority to make binding political decisions has gradually fallen to elective officials—parliamentary representatives, presidents, and prime ministers. And in most of these countries today, it is expected that these officials, responding to the demands of their constituents and the requirement that the society adapt successfully to its environment, will deliberate and then determine which policies are likely to be most effective in securing the general well-being of the population. Interest groups in the United States, England, France, and Germany theoretically fulfill the function of articulating the demands of the public, while political parties serve to aggregate these demands into more general policies and to provide the public with alternative choices of leadership to put them into effect.

The pattern is not a universal one by any means. Depending on the power structure and values of the community, the most significant decisions may be made by individuals or groups of individuals who enjoy hereditary status—as has been true for most political systems for most of human history—or else by individuals and organizations that claim authority for the community on the basis of superior knowledge or extraordinary insight. Religious leaders have been responsible for political decisions in theocratic societies, the Communist Party for decisions in the Soviet Union. Thus, the Soviet Communist Party discharges, albeit in different fashion, some of the functions that the congress and the president perform in the United States. On the other hand, the Communist Party has not, theoretically, attempted to aggregate the demands of community members, although the importance of this activity is increasing. Rather, the goal of the party has been to change the *nature* of these demands with the avowed aim of eliminating *political* decisions altogether.

If the functions which, in the United States, are relegated to interest groups and to political parties are not altogether universal, others are, or at least have been thus far in human history. Resources must be mobilized and decisions implemented—two tasks that are universally the concern of bureaucratic organizations, whether political or commercial. Furthermore, important social rules must be enforced, largely through legal institutions and a police apparatus.[3] All these activities and, indeed, the decision-making process itself require the development of communications networks. Only in this way can those with authority assess community problems and determine the optimal uses of resources for their solution; and only through a system of communications can the leadership make its decisions known and check upon their implementation. Communications networks in modern political systems consist not only of the mass media and professional journals but also of such widely diverse activities as face-to-face encounters and the shuffling of innumerable documents from office to office within bureaucratic organizations. The revolution in communications associated with the rise of a mass press, radio, and television has had important effects upon every aspect of social and political life. They have not, even so, replaced more traditional patterns of communications.

POWER AND AUTHORITY: The mobilization of resources and the implementation of political decisions require the creation of power. Political power may be defined provisionally as the capacity to induce people to act in a particular way. *A* has power over *B* if he can change the behavior of *B*. In extreme instances, power can be created by the use or threatened use of force. However, in most societies power is created by persuading key segments of the community to accept rules specifying which groups or which individuals can legitimately make decisions that others must obey. Legitimate power is referred to as *authority*. Whatever may be the differences in the capacities of the men who fill that office, the potential power of the American president, for instance, is very great simply because it is accepted as legitimate, and any

incumbent has at his disposal resources that no other single American political figure can command.

Insofar as societies consist of groups and individuals pursuing their own goals or their own conceptions of what the society's goals should be, competition for the control of institutions which confer power, such as the presidency, is the meat of politics. It should be stressed, however, that while power relations are basically asymmetrical, the amount of power available in a society is not a fixed quantity. In fact, the role of power in any political system is roughly analogous to that of money in the economic system. With marginal exceptions, its creation presupposes an organized political community wherein at least some values are shared. For the location of power as well as the amount of power available depends very much on the orientations that characterize members of the society. A highly industrialized society has more power available to it than a nomadic society, partly because it is more highly organized and its capacity for organization is very much dependent on the norms accepted by its population.

3. SOCIAL AND CULTURAL VARIABLES

The values, expressive symbols, and empirical beliefs that characterize a society and orient man to his environment constitute its culture. These values, symbols, and beliefs include not only forms of expression that are considered acceptable—the cultural "style" —but also the whole body of organized knowledge that is a society's inheritance. Perhaps the main function of the cultural system of any society is to legitimize its normative order—that is, to define the reasons for the rights and obligations assigned to members of the society. Historically, this legitimation has been based on some religious discipline which, in attempting to give meaning to the cosmos and man's place in it, defined the nature of good and evil. Even in contemporary secular societies, ideas of right and

---

[3] This has been true for all societies except small tribal groups with a relatively primitive technology.

wrong are based ultimately on conceptions of the "natural order of things."

In advanced societies, the major elements of the cultural system tend to become integrated: the rules governing the use of language form a coherent whole, organized knowledge in the sciences becomes a set of laws and propositions, and values become part of a hierarchically ordered system to help insure that behavior in specific cases can be justified by reference to more general norms. This ordering, of course, is psychological rather than logical, although a strain toward logical consistency can be detected in the development of the value system of any society.

The professed belief, for example, in the natural equality of all men as citizens—always taken by Americans as a public article of faith—has been contradicted in practice by the actual position of blacks in the United States. The moral issue for white Americans was always difficult—Gunnar Myrdal referred to it as "An American Dilemma." How could one justify depriving Negroes of the rights of citizenship to which all men are entitled by virtue of their humanity? At one time the issue was partially resolved by claiming that somehow blacks were not men, and for generations this assumption was accepted by many Negroes. The resolution, of course, was inherently unstable, and under the impact of social scientific analysis, as well as the decline of European power, the rationalizations for treating blacks as second-class citizens have crumbled. Whatever prejudices many white Americans may still feel against blacks, the absence of any scientific support for theories of racial superiority forces them to accept the legitimacy of Negro demands. The ability of America's black community to obtain concessions from the white majority has depended only in part on its own militancy; to a much larger degree it has reflected an increasing awareness on the part of this majority that the manner in which black citizens have been treated is incompatible with the American credo of equality.

Most complex societies have a number of subcultures that develop from the life experiences of their occupational groups. In nineteenth-century Europe, working- and middle-class values differed considerably in important ways, the differences varying with the nature of the stratification system. Such differences have tended to diminish with the advent of mass communications. Nevertheless, class differences in values still contribute to social conflict—even though they ultimately pose less of a threat to stability than the existence of religious, ethnic, or racial groups whose value structures differ sharply. On the Indian subcontinent, the tensions between Hindu and Muslim eventually resulted in the formation of two independent states. In the United States, tensions between Catholics and Protestants have been appreciably reduced by adherence to the higher norm of "tolerance" and by the subordination of both faiths to a broader *American* religion. Even today, however, religious differences continue to be of political importance in Europe and the United States. Catholics, whose religious beliefs have led most of them to desire a specifically Catholic education for their children, find themselves in conflict with groups that believe in an essentially secular school system. The source of the political controversy lies ultimately in differing views on the existence or nonexistence of God and the nature of religious knowledge. The issue has also been one involving conceptions of political goals, because it is the political system that determines how the society's resources shall be distributed.

In recent years the term "political culture" has come into use as a means of describing a society's general attitudes concerning the political process—its conceptions of legitimate authority and its disposition regarding the style of political action or the proper role of both the state and its institutions. This concept can be helpful, provided it is recognized that a society's political culture cannot be excised from the broader patterns of values and beliefs adopted by its members. The legitimation of a theocratic political system among the early Hebrews stemmed from the nature of their religious institutions, and attitudes toward political authority are usually derived from a more generalized feeling about how people relate or should relate to one another.

IDEOLOGY: The word "ideology" has been used in an infinite number of ways. For our purposes it may be defined as a relatively well-integrated system of values and beliefs which is critical of significant aspects of the society in terms of some ideal standard, or which represents a reaction to attacks upon the status quo. Ideologues are invariably polemical. Their aim is to galvanize individuals into action, and to achieve this they almost always distort or oversimplify the world they purport to describe by emphasizing its "bad" features or its "good" ones. Radical ideologists seek to chart new courses for the society, conservatives to resist any changes whatsoever, and reactionaries to bring about the return of some past, idealized condition.

Ideologies may reflect class position or ethnic identity, or may serve as rationalizations for economic self-interest. But whatever their purpose, their nature is partially determined by the cultural inheritance of the society of which they are a part. Sharp ideological divisions within any society are generally symptomatic of underlying strains and represent attempts to cope with them by redefining the society's character.

Cultural systems and ideologies are never created in a vacuum. We have considerable evidence from primitive societies that values and beliefs are closely related to problems of environmental adaptation. Thus, tribes whose subsistence was based on the cultivation of rice institutionalized social values quite different than those engaged in other forms of agriculture. On a more complex level, both the religious values and the political institutions of ancient Egyptian society were linked to the imperatives of a river civilization requiring extensive irrigation.

Neither values nor social institutions, however, are merely a reflection of economic needs or concerns. A society can adapt to its environment in many ways, each of which may be successful; and a particular adaptation may develop an inner logic of its own, leading either to stagnation or to greater complexity, once the basic problem of survival is solved reasonably satisfactorily. The Chinese created a highly complex civilization which, after a certain point, ceased to progress further until contact was made with the West. European culture and social institutions, on the other hand, continued to develop and to lead to the increasing domination of the natural environment. Both cultures represented, at least in some of their initial components, comparatively successful adaptations to a particular environment, or else they would not have survived; the point is that their later development was not merely adaptational.

THE ECONOMY AND SOCIAL STRATIFICATION: If the relationship among cultural, economic, and political variables is not as simple as theorists such as Marx have often believed, certainly the cultural and political systems of any society are closely related to economic factors—factors which have been, and in the foreseeable future will continue to be, among the most important sources of ideological and social conflict.

The interrelatedness is not surprising. Requirements for effectively adapting to the environment almost automatically set the limits of cultural and political variation even for relatively advanced societies and even though, as has been indicated, different paths may be taken toward survival and growth. In economies of scarcity—and all economies to date have been economies of scarcity—the allocation of economic resources will always be a source of some friction. And since in most societies until now labor has been, for all but a few, the most significant human experience, it is not surprising that the manner in which work is organized should have a profound effect upon the cultural, social, and political structure of the society.

The particular qualities of contemporary government in Western Europe, or in the Soviet dictatorship, could not have developed the way they did without the communication networks, industrial plants, transportation systems, and urban centers so typical of advanced societies. For one thing, the extent of political involvement in areas as large as, say, the United States, or of central control in areas as vast as the Soviet Union, was not possible in previous epochs. The commercial bourgeoisie in the late middle ages and, later, an industrial proletariat were partially responsible for the creation of centralized national states capable of keeping the peace and fashioning a common body of commercial law. It is also true that the hostility of the bourgeoisie to traditional feudal values was related to its economic activity, just as the values of the feudal aristocracy had been functionally related to that aristocracy's economic and political role during the middle ages. The clash, then, between bourgeois and aristocrat, which led eventually to the development of parliamentary regimes in Europe, was not without its economic ramifications. The economic factor was by no means the only important one, and feudalism itself had its origins in political imperatives, such as the lack of order that followed the destruction of the Roman Empire.

Historically, too, the economic organization of any society has been among the most significant sources of its system of social stratification—that is to say, its class system. Social classes are generally absent in the most primitive societies; they begin to evolve as the group masters its environment. The division of labor that contributes so immeasurably to productive efficiency leads to the development of differential rewards for these occupations which are more important to the society and for which the available supply of talent is limited. The need for coordination and effective authority leads to the creation of a political elite. It can be argued that stratification and the system of differential rewards associated with it have been historically necessary if men are to be motivated to undertake activities requiring greater effort of one kind or another. Of course, force has often been an important source of one group's domination by another, and frequently those elite groups whose positions have been institutionalized have accumulated both power and wealth beyond any functional justification.

Economic rewards are not necessarily the only kind that can serve to produce necessary motivations, but to date they have proved the most persuasive. This fact is recognized even in the Soviet Union. Whether or not money will always talk is a debatable question; Marx argued that social stratification based on *economic* classes would continue until scarcity and the division of labor had been eliminated.

Whatever Marx may have thought, however, control over economic resources has not been the only source of social or political power. True, the fact that money can be used to satisfy a wide variety of needs and to acquire a wide variety of facilities enables those who have it to translate it readily into social power; but other resources can also be used in this manner. Military power can be used to obtain control over either economic or political resources, or both, and political power can be used for economic purposes. In modern societies, the system of social stratification and the relationship of social class to political power have both become highly complicated. Many professional or quasi-professional elites have appeared— lawyers, the military, journalists, scientists— whose power is based in part upon the skills they practice even when their economic rewards are not as attractive as those of, say, businessmen.

The emergence in the West of mass societies based on the democratic suffrage has placed limits on the use of wealth for social and political ends, although differentials in income remain reasonably great in many countries, including the United States. In the Soviet Union, of course, economic power is of little political value. The example of the Soviet experience, and others, indicates that the extent of stratification in any society is, in the last analysis, a political matter—as is the very structure of the economy itself. That is, it is a question of what goals the community desires and how it intends to organize its various resources in order to achieve them. The "free" economy in the United States was built on a specific legal order that allowed the owner of property wide latitude. But this latitude was just as much a political decision, or rather a series of political decisions, as was the decision on the part of the leadership of the Soviet Communist Party to develop tight control over economic activities.

4. SOCIAL CONFLICT AND POLITICAL AND SOCIAL CHANGE

Some traditional societies of the past remained quite stable, in terms of basic structure, for long periods of time.[4] Yet from an overall viewpoint, cultural, social, and political change has been one of the major phenomena of human society. The sources of change have differed; alterations in the external environment, such as climate, have caused the fundamental restructuring of many communities. So, too, has conquest by other societies, or the advance of technology.

[4] The term "traditional society" has become a residual category which lumps together primitive societies, archaic societies, and what Talcott Parsons has called "historic intermediate empires." The use of the term poses a good many difficulties, as does that of its opposite, "modern society." In this volume a traditional society is conceived as one in which social institutions are relatively undifferentiated, in which science and technology are at relatively low levels of development, and in which "mythological" elements play a relatively large role in ordering human action. See Talcott Parsons, *Societies* (New York: Prentice-Hall, 1966), and Reinhard Bendix, "Tradition and Modernity Reconsidered," in *Comparative Studies in Society and History*, IX (1966–1967), 292–346.

Social change is usually accompanied by and often is the result of social and political conflict among groups and individuals. And the sources of conflict, like the sources of social change, are numerous. For instance, the question of how the available resources should be distributed has rarely been settled for an extended period, at least in modern societies. All the strategic elites vie for a larger portion of those resources they consider important, or the mass of the population comes, for one reason or another, to reject the norms that have justified existing inequalities.

Frequently, groups that owed their elite status to particular functions they performed maximized their advantages to a point far beyond any utilitarian justification. Aristocracies became hereditary, and their wealth accumulated to a point where traditional values could no longer be used to justify its magnitude. In other instances, elites have continued to receive rewards without fulfilling previous functions, as was the case in France and Russia before the revolutions that transformed both societies.

Both internal and external changes may lead to the rise of new social classes with competing claims for economic rewards or political authority. The Industrial Revolution and the consequent rise of an entrepreneurial class, as well as a working class, and their joint attack upon aristocratic privilege, constitute a prime example of this phenomenon in Europe. To be sure, such striking changes in class structure may weaken the position of some other groups in the society, and they may attempt to use political power to slow down or reverse changes. Depending upon the circumstances, such groups can be mobilized for either revolutionary or counterrevolutionary purposes. An example of this process is the ambiguous position of skilled artisans and peasants during the different stages of the Industrial Revolution in Europe. Artisans and even peasants played a significant and radical role in the French Revolution. At other times, as in Germany in the

1920's, they provided a major source of support for essentially reactionary movements.

Social and political conflict is more likely to take a violent turn when the system is not flexible enough to accommodate new demands. Violence most often occurs when the demands for change are too urgent to be "processed" by existing social and political arrangements. Under such circumstances, a potentially revolutionary situation is likely to develop.[5] Here three elites—the intellectual, the communications, and the military—are extremely important. The first two are crucial because they are the source of new systems of values and beliefs which undermine the legitimacy of the existing political order; and the military elite is always significant because, in modern societies at least, no violent revolution has been successful unless the loyalty of the military to the Establishment has been sapped or its effectiveness impaired in some way. The leadership of revolutionary movements is usually taken by disaffected members of the elite groups—in recent history, the intellectuals. In fact, it can be argued that a genuine revolution, as the term has been defined, never takes place unless at least a portion—and an influential portion at that—of the intellectual class has become alienated from the traditional system and has laid the groundwork for the formulation of new social and political norms.

The existence of a potentially revolutionary situation does not mean that a revolution will occur. The transformation of the potential into the actual requires the existence of a strong insurgent leadership and, often, a turn

of events that seriously threatens the existing structure of authority. Thus the revolution in Russia might never have occurred without Russia's entry into World War I, the severe defeats suffered by its armies, and the headlong deterioration of the economy.

The extent of social change that occurs in the wake of a revolution is often directly related to the sense of alienation from the old system felt by the revolutionary elite. Millenarian—or utopian—revolutions, which desire to replace the old society with social arrangements promising plenty for all and the elimination of all social conflict, are in part psychological reactions to an existing world considered to represent the depths of evil. At least this would seem to be a plausible hypothesis from recent studies of the history of millenarian movements. The particular form such millenarianism takes, however, will be determined by the stock of values and beliefs that are part of the cultural tradition out of which it springs. Certain tribes among the Plains Indians of the United States became convinced, in the last period before their total defeat, that leaders would appear who through special kinds of magic would permit them to become impervious to the white man's bullets and to restore an idealized version of the old ways of doing things. In Europe, both Marxism and the Soviet Revolution cannot be understood except in terms of the whole European heritage out of which they sprang.

In the past, most attempts to produce rapid, basic social changes have led to the use of force. As Marx argued, the normative patterns of any social system become so firmly established among groups ensconced in a satisfactory position that any significant change appears as unmitigated evil. Revolutionary violence itself, of course, contributes to the breakdown of old patterns of authority as well as the polarization of those groups that seek and oppose change. Hence the very fact of revolution tends to radicalize those who participate in it.

It is well to emphasize again that social

[5] A revolution may be defined as any rapid and fundamental change—involving violence—in the social or political structure of a society. Political revolutions may be distinguished from rebellions, which have as their goal the elimination of "bad" rulers rather than producing fundamental changes, and from coups d'etat, which represent conflicts within an existing elite group as to which individuals should occupy positions of power, rather than an attempt to fundamentally alter the social or political structure of the societies. The peasant Jacqueries of the middle ages were rebellions; the so-called "revolutions" in Latin America during the nineteenth century were primarily coups d'etat.

and political tension and conflict are inevitable concomitants of social life. It is difficult to conceive of any society so fully integrated that the distribution of resources is completely satisfactory to all. It can be argued that tension is not without value: the most creative periods of European history have been those marked by a high degree of social conflict.

Social scientists today are once again turning to the question of directionality in social change; is there, in other words, a discernible "evolutionary pattern" in human history? The answer seems to be yes. Human history has been marked by a gradual increase in man's capacity to control his environment through the creation of power. And power has been created through both the development of scientific theories that permit the more effective use of natural resources and the creation of forms of social organization that permit the more effective coordination of human action.

The German sociologist Max Weber argued that the essential element in this process was greater rationalization. On the level of social structure, rationalization has involved the slow differentiation of institutions in ways that enhance the society's ability to adapt to its environment. In traditional societies, for instance, legal, political, and economic institutions were generally fused. In more complex societies, these institutions, while related to each other in intricate ways, are more or less autonomous structures, each of which is charged with a particular set of problems. One consequence of such differentiation has been the emergence of large-scale bureaucratic organizations.

On the cultural level, rationalization has involved the grouping of societal values into hierarchical patterns of general applicability. Thus, in contrast to traditional societies, with their profusion of specific rules of behavior applicable to tribal or lineage groups, individual villages, or even individual families, modern legal systems usually consist of rules that pertain to general classes of persons and

acts, from which specific rules may be deduced.

One can also detect an evolutionary pattern of social change in the legitimation of authority. In most traditional societies, the authority of various elites was accepted because it had always been so or because of certain religious myths. The demythologizing of the world has resulted in the substitution of utilitarian standards. Authority can be justified only when individuals and groups believe their goals are furthered by its acceptance. Rules governing the society, therefore, are legitimized by their consequences for the well-being of the population—not because of tradition or religious sanction. Political leadership is accepted because it is thought to be pursuing policies whose consequences will benefit the individual or the larger group— not because those in power are descended from a hereditary ruling elite. The ultimate justification of democratic regimes lies in the assumption that the threat of withdrawing popular support will cause those elected to pursue policies designed to further the interests of the community. This cause-and-effect assumption is contingent on the further assumption that all citizens should participate in creating the rules by which they are governed. And more and more frequently in the contemporary world, efforts are made to create the illusion that this is, indeed, happening; in fact, the spread of literacy and communications networks has brought the masses into the political process in ways that were inconceivable in the past.

Taken together, these and other evolutionary social changes have resulted in what has come to be called "modernization." It is well to remember, however, that while many of them are becoming characteristic of other areas of the world, the process of rationalization began in Europe, and generalizations about the nature of modernization are usually drawn from the European experience. It is well to remember, too, that "modern" and "traditional" are merely shorthand terms for describing very complex phenomena, and that all societies exhibit at least some characteristics on both sides of a traditional-modern continuum. Finally, it should be remembered that our image of a modern society is derived from a mid–twentieth-century perspective; a number of thinkers have argued that the next stage in human development may involve a shifting of orientations away from the "rational instrumental" to the emotional, esthetic, and mythic, now that mankind is entering what has come to be called the post-industrial stage of human development. This was certainly the vision of Karl Marx, who, in fact, predicted an end to the division of labor and specialization, once productive capacity had reached certain levels.

5. THE LIMITS OF SOCIAL SCIENCE

Thus far we have concentrated on creating a frame of reference for the study of political systems. The emphasis has been on outlining a method of looking at political phenomena. Few laws of politics have been proposed—certainly none that would allow us to make even reasonably good predictions in concrete situations. A number of generalizations which resemble laws in the natural sciences have been suggested, but they have, on the whole, been either tautological or trivial as compared with what can be done by the chemist or physicist.

The limits of the social sciences stem partially from a lack of applicable data, but they also have their source in more basic difficulties. Social scientists work under the same general rules as physical scientists. Ideally, they seek to develop propositions that can be subject to empirical testing—and then they attempt to test them. Further, they strive to create a discipline that is an integrated whole, eliminating logical inconsistencies in their arguments. They labor, however, under very severe handicaps not encountered to the same degree in the natural sciences. The major and obvious problem, of course, is the difficulty of conducting experiments under conditions approaching those that exist

in a laboratory. It is true that astronomers have not been able to conduct experiments on the stars, but most laws applied to the study of the universe have been discovered, or at least can be tested, under laboratory conditions—for instance, propositions specifying the effects of gravity or the speed or nature of light.

The analysis of political systems does not lend itself to such experimentation. Insofar as any system is a relatively integrated whole, a laboratory experiment that sought to understand it would have to be the exact replica of the system itself, and the very fact of its being an experiment would change the whole structure of the system. The study of how American school children react to different types of authority in a laboratory situation may tell us something about how they may react to authority in a "real" situation, but it does not tell us too much about how they might have reacted fifty years ago, and even less about how German or French children will react today.

This limitation is closely tied in with the "openness" of any society. External elements are always impinging, so much so that experiments or models that attempt to ignore them are far more likely to be removed from reality than the controlled experiments in the physical sciences. For example, the victory of William, duke of Normandy, over the Saxon King Harold in 1066 had an enormous impact upon the whole course of English social and political development. This victory was, partially at least, accidental; tides were such that William delayed sailing from France for several days, during which time Harold rushed north to stem another invasion. When William finally did land, he was unopposed initially, and at Hastings he faced a decimated army of tired soldiers who had come south by forced march after their earlier victory. To take a more recent example, the success of the Communist revolution in Russia, and the course it took, were directly related to the role played by Lenin and Trotsky. Yet the fact that the talent and drive of both these men were available cannot be fully explained in terms of the categories of social analysis. Certainly none of the other leaders of the Bolshevik Party possessed their qualities, and other countries with similar revolutionary potential have not developed such leadership. Attempts, then, to develop general propositions on which to base predictions of the success or direction of invasions or revolutions—or even a nation's individual course of development—are likely to be less than completely successful.

Political and social systems are open in other ways. If there are certain basic biological variables that determine the pattern of the human personality, it might be possible to come up with certain general propositions about human action. One of the most significant factors about human society, however, is that it is constantly changing, and that these changes involve the institutionalization of new patterns of behavior. For this reason, generalizations about international politics within the context of a system of national states are valid only for a world composed of national states, and the nature of even this world has changed since the explosion of atomic and hydrogen weapons. Similarly, generalizations about voting behavior are useful only within political systems in which people vote. Indeed, the range of such generalizations is probably even narrower, as proved by the long-held axiom of American politics that a Catholic could never be elected president. Changes in both the composition and attitudes of the electorate made the proposition obsolete. All that can be said now is that the generalization was correct within a certain society at a certain time.

It is true that the differences between the social and the natural sciences in this connection are primarily a matter of degree. Generalizations about different forms of animal and plant life are limited to the period during which such forms exist—when they have not disappeared or evolved into other forms. Even the laws of physics are bound to our universe. We have no way of knowing whether they are applicable to all time, whatever our conception of time.

In fact, the areas in which the natural sciences are weakest are those that are of central concern to the social sciences: the areas that appertain to such problems as the origin and evolution of the universe and the direction of its continuing development, or even the evolution of life forms. Beyond some very general statements, both physics and biology have very little to say predictively about future changes in the systems they study. All sciences, then, are bound by a framework of time during which the fundamental constituents of their subject do not change. Unfortunately, in the social sciences this time span is, with some important exceptions, extremely short.

The social sciences have yet to develop categories of analysis that permit quantification and the precision which quantification can yield. Again, the natural sciences have progressed rather far in some areas without quantification, and economics, in general, and the use of game theory and new forms of mathematics in other disciplines provide an exception in the social sciences. Aside from economics, however, the attempt to use mathematical techniques in the social sciences has yet to bear any real fruit, and while the possibility of future developments cannot be foreclosed, these would appear to be a long way off.

Many, if not all, of the difficulties listed above would be reduced if sociological and political explanations could be replaced by categories derived from the biological or even physical sciences. Under such circumstances, political science would disappear and the study of social phenomena would be incorporated into other disciplines, as certain areas of genetics are becoming part of chemistry. But whether or not such reductionism is possible or even desirable, it is not likely to occur in the immediate future.

Other factors limiting both the precision and the generality of propositions in the social sciences could be listed, but those mentioned should be enough to indicate that for the foreseeable future, at least, we shall have to be satisfied with rather modest achievements in the study of politics. The problems involved, however, should not be a source of despair. We can certainly go some distance in attempting to develop a systematic body of material relating to our subject, and we can reject some explanations as obviously untenable. Just as important, perhaps, an awareness of the difficulties facing the scientific study of politics will make us more suspicious of overly simple formulas.

6. HISTORY, SOCIOLOGY, POLITICAL SCIENCE

Properly speaking, political science as a discipline is primarily concerned with the structure and dynamics of the political system of any society and with its relations to other subsystems of that society. The political scientist, in the kinds of concepts he uses, draws heavily upon the work of sociologists. Bearing in mind the functions performed by the political system in any society, the political scientist must of necessity place his examination of politics within the framework of an analysis of the society as a whole.

A society's political culture, including its ideas of legitimate authority, cannot be understood apart from a more general appraisal of the values held by groups within it. And the import of political conflicts within a society cannot be understood without an analysis of the demands of interest groups, demands which, in turn, are related to the society's economic and political structures.

If the political scientist must be something of a sociologist, he must also be something of a historian. The present can be understood only in terms of the past—in terms of the particular relationship of the forces that brought it into existence; a full description of any set of political or social institutions can only be one which delineates the conditions under which it emerged and the ways in which it is constantly changing. To say, for example, that the British political order functions the way it does because of a disciplined two-party system is only part of an explanation; it must also be added that this particular political configuration began to develop only late in the nineteenth century as the result of a particular configuration of social, cultural, economic and political forces, and, further, that this system is changing as British social and political life continues to change.

As noted in the preface, I believe that the most fruitful way of examining European countries is to deal with them in terms of their transition from a certain kind of traditional society to a certain kind of modern industrial society; the differences among them are the result of differing combinations of essentially similar European ingredients. Part One of this volume will discuss the overall social, economic, and political evolution of Europe, describing European feudalism and the forces that transformed it. Emphasis will be placed on the importance of Europe's Christian heritage, the emergence of nation states, the character of European industrialization, and the social conflicts and social and political ideologies that appeared in the nineteenth century. We shall then examine in detail the social and political transformation of each of the four countries with which we are concerned, demonstrating as we proceed that the social and political life of each nation represents a variation on a European theme.

Part Two will take up the social and cultural bases of European politics, considering in some detail how economic, social, and cultural variables have interacted, and what their total impact has been on political life. The structure of groups within European nations will be described, as well as patterns of communication and socialization. Each chapter will be preceded by a theoretical discussion which expands upon the material offered in this introduction. Once again the material will be presented developmentally, although as the volume proceeds the historical discussions will be shortened. Parts Three, Four, and Five will be concerned with the political system proper—the role of parties and of formal political institutions and, finally, the implementation of public policy.

The fact that we will be investigating social variables before we touch on political institutions does not constitute an insistence on their primacy as causal factors: historically, causation has run in both directions. Rather, the text can best be compared to the construction of a jigsaw puzzle. The first stage is to demarcate the general bounds, and each succeeding stage fills in further details. The puzzle is not complete until the very last piece has been put into place. Our analysis of the dynamics of European society and politics will not be complete until the last chapter.

part I

20

intellectual revolutions that created the modern world began in Europe. We are interested in why these revolutions took place, and in the relationship between the social changes involved and the ideological and social conflicts that occurred in the nineteenth century and that have a continuing impact today. We also want to understand why the United States, which is essentially a European country, developed along a somewhat different path. As we later discuss the institutions in each of the nations under study, the profound effect of these historical events upon every aspect of social and political life will be made clear and often will be presented in more detail.

2. EUROPEAN FEUDALISM

With the administrative collapse of the Roman Empire in the West following the barbarian invasions, economic, social, and political life in most of Western Europe regressed to a more primitive level than that achieved under Roman influence. Large-scale commerce dropped off sharply; the heritage of classical thought and literature all but disappeared; and tribal Germanic law tended to replace the urban Roman legal system.

The major problem for society was controlling violence. Coastal areas were continually harassed by Viking invasions from the north and Muslim invasions from the south, and the marauders moved far inland, once even crossing all of Russia from the north to the Black Sea. More importantly, the disappearance of Roman legal authority left a vacuum that could not be satisfactorily filled by the traditional tribal organization. Rather, a new form of political organization, European feudalism, evolved to provide rudimentary domestic peace and security. The essence of feudalism was vassalage. More powerful persons granted the use of land or the benefits of offices (fiefs) sufficient for decent livelihood to persons who in turn became their vassals and vowed homage and fealty. The relationship between lord and vas-

sal was not a simple one; deemed honorable by both parties, it was fundamentally one involving mutual defense and service. From its beginnings in Norman France as a series of local, petty arrangements, feudalism became in a few centuries a political or administrative device used by monarchs to extend their authority indirectly over larger and larger areas. The vassal, in addition to serving at his own expense in his lord's military forces upon call and paying customary dues for his fief, also served as his lord's administrative agent in dispensing justice and collecting taxes. When a lord's vassals granted the use of land or offices to other men, making them vassals of their own in a process we have come to call "subinfeudation," the patterns of authority and administration became more intricate—and security and order became less certain.

As a set of political institutions, feudalism attained its modest ends. Over several hundred years it provided some civil peace; paradoxically, this very fact led to the decline of the local feudal system as monarchies grew more powerful by adapting feudal arrangements to their purposes. For several centuries, however, before the rise of the national monarchies, much of Europe was divided into feudalities with only tenuous obligations to any higher level of authority.

The fundamental elements of the economic life of Europe during the feudal period revolved about the manor of the lord. Physically, it consisted of lands, fields, streams, woods, the lord's great house, its mills and barns, its animals, and the persons attached to it in varying degrees of bondage. Psychologically, it represented the whole world to the peasants and laborers who were bound to it by customary law. Serfs, whose children were inherited as chattels by the manor, and even freemen, though custom protected their rights against abuse by the lord of the manor, could not leave it without their lord's consent. Because feudalism in Europe was closely associated with manorialism, Marxists, especially, have tended to confuse the

THE EUROPEAN INHERITANCE

Alsatian Farmer. Clemens Kalisher

Sculpture on Chartres Cathedral. Editions-Tel

London Slums. Photoworld, Inc.

The Berlin State Opera House. Camera Press-Pix

Worshippers in Pokrousky Cathedral, Moscow. Dan Weiner

T

Development

Modern Eur

1. THE PROBLEM

Europe is a large triangular peninsula attached to Asia along a wide base on the east and narrowing down as it juts westward to the Atlantic Ocean. It is, even including European Russia, the smallest of the world's continents, covering an area of less than four million square miles. With the exception of the Soviet Union, each of the European powers is smaller than Texas.

As our awareness of the world has grown in recent years, it has become increasingly apparent that the nations of Western Europe partake of a common heritage (much of which is shared by Russia, although, because of certain special problems, it will be considered separately) that has sharply differentiated them from the civilizations of the Far and Middle East and of Africa. This heritage derives largely from Greek and Roman sources as these sources fused with Christianity, and the institutional patterns that have developed on the continent in the past thousand years are modifications of the same basic inheritance. Consequently, while other areas

of the world went through periods re
European feudalism, the Europea
generated qualities that were uni
and while modern industrial societi
resemble one another more and m
icant cultural and social difference
to exist between any European co
say, Japan.

It is important to outline some
cipal factors that have distingui
pean societies, if only because cor
European experience with thos
societies can prevent us from a
natural what must be explained.
historical view is also importa
events take place in time and ea
currence has effects that limit l
tives. Neither France nor the S
today can be understood, for ex
one examines the different pol
tions that transformed both sc

The next several chapters
transformation of Europe from
society of a certain type to a "n
trial society—and the conseq
transformation. The scientific,

two. It is well to stress again that feudalism was a political system; manorialism, as a set of economic institutions, has been associated with other political orders.

The manor was a comparatively self-sufficient unit. Life revolved about the land and its cultivation. Time was ordered about the seasons, religious feast days, and the cycle of birth and death. One was born, lived, and died in a single community on a certain piece of land, the use of which was to be handed on to one's heirs. Of all things, land was the most valuable since it was the immediate source of life itself.

Individuals were born into their stations in life; they fulfilled the tasks of those stations and trained their children to fulfill them. Even after the revival of trade and the growth of towns that accompanied the high middle ages, tradesmen and artisans, theoretically, at least, charged only a "just price" for their goods or services, and the production and distribution of goods was regulated by a detailed set of customary rules enforced by the Roman Catholic Church, by guilds, and by local and regional—later, national—authorities. These regulations were derived from conceptions of the community as an organic unit to which each person contributed according to his fixed station; each person's rights, obligations and rewards were restricted to those appropriate to his station.

Nevertheless, social mobility was never completely absent. In the later middle ages the aristocracy became a relatively closed class, but peasants and artisans could and did migrate to towns where social organization was more fluid. The Roman church always accepted men from any station, and occasionally the low-born rose within it to heights of power and influence. Yet compared with the societies of nineteenth- and twentieth-century America and Europe, it is the static character of social classes, their obvious differences before the law, and the rigidity of an individual's social status that are most striking in feudal Europe.

By the late middle ages, Europe, except for Spain, was Christian Europe. Spreading out from the center of the Roman Empire, Christianity had finally been adopted, although considerably modified, by the Germanic and Slavic peoples of the north. And as is true in all traditional societies, religious or magical ideas and customs dominated much of life. The Christian might find secular history meaningless or directionless, but secular history would some day end, to be replaced by the millennium.

It was unquestioned that the world and man in it had been created in six days by God for an ultimate purpose. Man had fallen from grace into sin and had thereby incurred the penalty of eternal damnation. Salvation was possible only because of the sacrifice of God's son. Life on earth was but a means to the desired end of salvation, a temporary probation for God's children. In God's appointed time the earthly city would come to an end and the earth itself would be swallowed up by flames. On that last day, good and evil men would be separated—the evil to burn in hell forever, the good to dwell in eternal bliss.

The structure and content of Western Christianity were to have profound effects upon later European development; the elements of which it was composed provided European society with a dynamic impetus that was not present in other societies. First, Christianity was both universalistic and individualistic. The purpose of the Catholic Church was the salvation of all men, and man's relation to God was individual rather than communal. Western Christianity, therefore, was far less likely to become identified with a single community or state than were Judaism or Byzantine Christianity.

Out of the nature of Christianity sprang both the individualism that became an integral part of Western European culture and the tension between religious and secular authority that played so important a role in Europe's political development. Theocracy, or the fusion of religious and secular authority in the hands of a political figure (caesaropapism), has historically been far less characteristic of Western Europe than of other cultures, even during those periods when the papacy claimed substantial secular authority.

Second, Christianity paralleled many other religious creeds in stressing the sinfulness of the flesh and the corruption of the world. But its emphasis was on "practical" or "inner-worldly" asceticism, not on mystical or "other-worldly" asceticism. Rather than counseling withdrawal from the world, as did a number of Eastern religions, it called for fulfilling one's appointed function in the world by mastering and ordering it. Complete withdrawal from the world, whether ascetic or mystical, was only a minor aspect of Western Christianity's broader tradition.

Third, Christianity set God above the world as its creator and stressed the importance of human reason in enabling man to understand the laws by which God ruled the world. In this way, Christian doctrine officially discouraged belief in magic. Whatever the sources of this view (the classical and Jewish heritages of Christianity were certainly significant), it clearly contributed to the development of modern science in the West.

3. THE EMERGENCE OF MODERN EUROPE

In the eight centuries following the collapse of the Roman Empire, the population of Europe grew steadily, if slowly. New methods of plowing were discovered which permitted the more effective use of the heavier soils of northern Europe. Trade and commerce gradually expanded; after the eleventh century, towns increased rapidly in size and number. Elements of the classical heritage, including Roman law, were rediscovered and incorporated into Christian and secular thought, a process that culminated in the Italian Renaissance of the fifteenth century.

These changes contributed to a revolution which was to transform European society and which consisted of four interrelated developments: the emergence of the modern nation state; the schism in Christianity and the development of the Protestant sects; the growth of modern science and technology and an industrial civilization; and the secularization of European society.

Despite the decline of central authority during the early middle ages, the memory of the Roman Empire (later the Holy Roman Empire) did not disappear; nor did traditional conceptions of royal authority. As stability returned to Europe, monarchs established their authority over more and more territory, and the peoples of Europe began to manifest a national consciousness. England was the first country to achieve the national unity that was crucial for her later development; this process began in the eleventh century under William the Conqueror and was consummated by the Tudors in the sixteenth. France achieved effective nationhood by the late sixteenth century, and Germany in the late nineteenth century. In general, the pattern of national self-consciousness moved from west to east, with national boundaries tending to follow ethnic or linguistic lines. The sense of national unity in Eastern Europe, including Russia, was and still is complicated by the self-consciousness of ethnic groups living in a geographic interrelationship that precludes satisfying the territorial aspirations of all of them. Even as the growth of the nation state resulted in a central authority replacing local authority, it weakened the medieval sense of being part of a common Christian community coextensive with Europe. Moreover, the growth of the nation state contributed to the secularization of political authority, since in the process individual rulers had to wrest power from the church.

The rise of the nation state also helped induce, and was supported by, economic changes. The unified nation states constituted larger economic units in which, for the first time since the Roman Empire, centralized governments took some responsibility for establishing transportation networks, uniform systems of weights and coinage, and uniform systems of enforceable law. In return, the drive toward unity and centralized control won the endorsement of the new commercial strata of the cities, who saw in the destruction of the feudal order by the new monarchs the best means of achieving their own ends.

The Protestant revolt, too, had a far-reaching effect upon the creation of nation states by weakening the authority of a transnational church. In turn, the Protestants received support from the secular authority in many cases for just this reason. The Protestant churches themselves represented a schism within Christianity, and neither their nature nor their development can be comprehended apart from the Christian tradition out of which they sprang. In the eyes of the reformers, Protestantism was a return to the purity of the early church, a disavowal of its later "corruption." Protestantism's emphasis on faith and on the individual's relation to God is certainly rooted in the earlier history of Christianity.

Whatever the degree of success, or failure, of the Reformation as a religious movement in the nations with which we are concerned —the subject will be treated later—its consequences for Europe were enormous. Protestantism was a vital factor in the secularization of political authority and of life in general; it was instrumental to the development of an industrial society and to the origin and growth of political liberalism and the idea of democracy.

The contribution of Protestantism, especially of the Calvinist sects, to secularization reversed the intention of the reformers, who saw in their break with Rome a return to a society dominated by religious values. The breakdown of a central religious authority and the extreme individualism of the Protestant sects, however, helped to spawn a multiplicity of sects; and this very multiplicity undoubtedly diminished the influence of religious ideals, producing an ideological ferment that

had to undermine the credibility of any particular doctrine. Social stability required toleration; and toleration, in the Christian world at least, entailed the gradual dilution of the content of Christian belief.

Insofar as Protestantism fostered secularization, it also had an effect on the development of a scientific world view, at least by weakening the barriers inhibiting its acceptance. And insofar as Protestantism furthered the growth of modern science, it was an important agent in the creation of an industrial technology. The relations between Protestantism and both science and industrialization were, however, more complex than this. Calvinism's insistence that one must fulfill one's calling, and its identification of salvation with success in rationally ordering the environment through hard work, make up the "Protestant ethic." Even though Calvin himself, and early Calvinists, were as antagonistic to commercialism as was the Catholic Church, the ethos of Protestantism provided the cultural basis for an industrial order, especially after the initial religious fervor had waned.

The significance of Protestantism for the development of capitalism in Western Europe was first advanced as a hypothesis by Max Weber. His hypothesis is by no means universally accepted; on the contrary, it has provoked extensive study and debate. Our argument here is merely that Protestantism was *one* important factor in the growth of European capitalism.

The legacy of Protestantism to democracy and liberalism is even more difficult to delineate. Certainly the diversity of sects, along with the idea of toleration, were important; so, too, was the primacy assigned self-government in the Calvinist congregation. Moreover, sectarian diversity and toleration abetted the fragmentation of religious and political authority; the idea of self-government for each congregation was closely associated with an individualism that stressed a personal relationship with God and rejected the idea of a religious governing hierarchy. Small wonder, then, that James I of England was suspicious of the Puritans and pointed out that their attacks upon the authority of bishops would ultimately lead to attacks upon the authority of kings; and it is no accident that the first really democratic theorists of the modern world were the extreme left-wing Levelers and Diggers of England's Puritan revolution. These relationships were not one-way affairs. For example, if Protestantism contributed to the establishment of an industrial middle class with certain values, the industrial middle classes found in Protestantism a religious orientation that satisfied their emotional needs. There is no need here to decide which influenced the other first or more.

Modern science and industry profoundly influenced European society after 1800. Because we are accustomed to vast and rapid changes in technology, we cannot appreciate fully the impact of science and technology in the nineteenth century; but though change was slower then, its effects were in some ways comparable to developments in India or Africa today. The material life of the European peasant had remained almost unchanged from Roman times to the nineteenth century. Then, in a period of not much more than a generation, his world was altered radically. In 1800, England was still basically a traditional agricultural society; by 1900 it was a fully industrialized one. In the 1700's the population of London was eight hundred thousand; it had trebled by 1850, and doubled again by 1900. In 1800 Europe included only 18 cities with more than a hundred thousand residents; together these amounted to no more than three per cent of the total population. By 1930 Europe included 248 cities of more than a hundred thousand people, totaling about thirty per cent of the population. (See Table 1.1.) In 1806 England produced less than a quarter of a million tons of pig iron; by 1910 it was producing more than nine million tons— roughly 36 times as much in about one cen-

tury. England's gross national product in 1913 was at least fifty times greater than it had been in 1720, and almost twenty times greater than it had been in 1800. Agricultural production made similar gains.[1]

The improvement of the material circumstances of life, the elimination of plagues, and the control of disease through advances in medical science and sanitation led to a sudden drop in the death rate and an astounding increase in population. It is estimated that in about A.D. 500 the population of Europe was about twenty million persons. By 1600 Europe had some 100 million inhabitants, a general growth of approximately one per cent a decade. By 1800 its population had risen to 200 million, and by 1900 to 400 million. In other words, between 1700 and 1900 the rate of increase averaged five per cent a decade.

This geometric rate of population increase (see Table 1.2) revolutionized the entire Continent and ultimately the entire world. Urbanization and industrialization gave time and distance new meanings and produced vast changes in the class and power structures of Europe and in the content of European culture. An industrial middle and working class replaced a landed gentry and a peasantry as the dominant social classes; increasingly, life became regulated by the rhythm of the machine and measured by the clock instead of the calendar. The enlargement of communication and the growth of literacy brought new strata into politics. By the early nineteenth century the annual sale of newspapers in England was about 24 million copies. Sales of newspapers rose by 33 per cent between 1816 and 1836, by seventy per cent between 1836 and 1856 and by some six hundred per cent between 1856 and 1882. By 1850 daily papers were being read by one adult in

1 Estimates of production or population in earlier periods are only approximate. Data from W. S. Woytinsky and E. S. Woytinsky, *World Population and Production* (New York: The Twentieth Century Fund, 1953), and Colin Clark, *The Conditions of Economic Progress* (London: Macmillan, 1950).

TABLE 1.1. THE GROWTH OF SELECTED EUROPEAN CITIES

Population in thousands

Country and city	1800	1850	1900	1930	1950's	1960's[4]
United Kingdom						
London (excluding suburbs)	959	2,363	4,537	4,397	8,348[1]	7,913
Birmingham	71	242	522	1,003	2,237[1]	2,437
Manchester	77	336	544	766	2,422[1]	2,453
Germany						
Berlin	172	419	1,889	4,243	2,146[2]	2,190[2]
Hamburg	130	132	706	1,129	1,605	1,851
Cologne	50	97	373	757	595	861
France						
Paris	547	1,053	2,714	2,830	4,823[1]	7,369
Marseilles	111	195	491	914	661[1]	807
Lyons	110	177	459	571	650[1]	885
U.S.S.R.						
Moscow	250	365	612	3,100[3]	4,847	6,507
Leningrad	220	485	877	2,300[3]	3,182[1]	3,706
Kiev		61	247	625	991	1,413
Other countries						
Rome	153	175	423	931	1,651[1]	2,485
Amsterdam	201	224	511	757	838[1]	1,043
Warsaw	100	160	638	1,179	804	1,261

[1] For the 1950's and 1960's the figures are for urban agglomerates.
[2] Figures for West Berlin only for 1950 and 1962.
[3] Estimated.
[4] United Kingdom and Germany figures are for 1966; France, for 1962;
U.S.S.R., for 1967.

Sources: To 1930, W.S. and E.S. Woytinsky, *World Population and Production* (New York: The Twentieth Century Fund, 1953), pp. 120–121; reprinted by permission of the publisher. Figures for 1950's and 1960's, *U.N. Demographic Yearbook, 1960*, pp. 327–348; 1967, 224–230.

eighty; by 1900 they were being read by one adult in five or six.[2]

More than any other single factor, the revolution in science and technology was responsible for the secularization of life. The scientific world view seemed to demolish substantial portions of Christian dogma. Protestantism accommodated itself to the new outlook far more easily than did the Catholic Church, whose rigidly structured organization and large body of well-defined dogma made adaptation more troublesome. Reformers,

therefore, especially in Catholic nations, saw the church as an obstacle not only to the reorganization of society but to the achievement of a personal happiness that increasing wealth seemed to promise.

4. THE NINETEENTH CENTURY

The industrialization of Europe was accompanied by a series of social and political upheavals and the explosion of new ideologies, both of which reached their greatest intensity in the nineteenth century. The three most important ideologies that matured during this period were liberalism, conservatism, and socialism. To a considerable, although de-

[2] Data from Raymond Williams, *Britain in the Sixties: Communications* (Baltimore: Penguin Books, 1962).

TABLE 1.2. COMPARATIVE POPULATION DATA:
EUROPE AND THE UNITED STATES

In millions

	France	Germany	United Kingdom	Italy	Russia	United States
Ca. 1800	27	25	11	18	39	5
Ca. 1850	36	35	27	23	62	23
Ca. 1900	38	56	37	32	129	76
Pre–World War I (1910–1913)	40	68	41	35	—	92
Pre–World War II (1936–1940)	41	70	46	43	170	132
Ca. 1950	42	70	49	47	201	151
Ca. 1963	48	75	54	51	225	189
Ca. 1967	48	77	55	52	236	199
Approximate increase,						
1850–1950	6	35	22	24	139	128
1950–1967	6	7	6	5	35	48

Adapted from Jesse H. Wheeler, Jr., J. Trenton Kostbade, and Richard S. Thomas, *Regional Geography of the World* (New York: Henry Holt and Co., 1955), p. 109; reprinted by permission of the publisher. Figures for 1963 and 1967 from the United Nations, *Statistical Yearbook, 1968*, pp. 78–86.

creasing, extent, these ideologies still dominate political rhetoric in Europe.

LIBERALISM: As a system of thought, liberalism is primarily associated with Adam Smith and with Jeremy Bentham and his followers, the Philosophical Radicals in England. Its source can be traced to John Locke, Thomas Hobbes, and the Protestant sects. In general, nineteenth-century liberals regarded the state as a watchman whose function was to enforce the basic rules necessary to permit the individual's powers of self-government and self-control to produce a reasonable, just, and peaceful society. The removal of traditional restrictions upon behavior would enable individual energies to be channeled in directions that would contribute to the heightened well-being of all citizens.

The state was expected to perform only a limited role in the economic sphere. Aside from keeping the peace, its major functions were the protection of property rights and the defense of the nation. Within this framework, and pushed and pulled by their desires to achieve pleasure and avoid pain, men would pursue their economic self-interest. In so doing, however, they would, through the mechanism of the market place, contribute to the wealth of all, and the greater rewards would go to the more industrious and skillful. The state should by no means regulate wages and prices as it had in the past; such policies, enforced by the restrictive guild system as well as by the state, had only hampered the effective operation of the economy.

In a free market encouraged by the state, relations between employer and employee would be purely contractual, each using the other to his own advantage and hence to the mutual advantage of both. The employer would hire the worker at the lowest possible wage, and the worker would sell his labor as dearly as possible. In this contractual association, the authority of the employer and the obligations of the worker would extend no further than their specific economic relationship.

Institutions were to be judged by whether they served the interest of the majority of the community. All institutions that contributed to ordered liberty were of value, because they permitted the individual the widest range of choice in his goals. All institutions that substituted rational principles for custom and tradition were of value, both because they were rational and because individuals should be evaluated on the basis of their actions rather than the accident of birth.

Representative government came to be considered superior to other forms because political institutions should be designed to reflect the wishes of the community. Men could be assured that their own interests would be furthered by their governors only if it was in the interest of the governors to do so; the elective principle was the most effective means of achieving this assurance. While all men were not necessarily equal in talent, they were considered equally entitled to pursue their own interests, and each certainly knew this interest better than any hereditary monarch or social class.

Liberal thought was characterized by a faith in man's burgeoning capacity to master the physical world and to take an enlightened and social view of his own interests. As poverty and superstition were eliminated, one could look forward to a world mastered by science, a world in which war and other conflicts would be reduced if not eliminated altogether. This enlightened view would evolve from the free competition of ideas, a competition in which truth would eventually triumph. Restrictions on the expression of ideas, the liberals believed, only inhibited innovation and prevented both the community and individuals from discovering where their true interest lay. Restrictions also deprived the individual not only of his right to choose how he would act but of the chance to be responsible for that free choice—rights which were essential to his humanity.

Liberal intellectuals were often hostile to organized religion. As "reformers" who welcomed the new industrial society, they equated religion with superstition, arguing that science offers no evidence for the existence of God and that religious beliefs merely uphold erroneous customs. The Catholic Church, particularly, came under attack as representing all that was wrong with the religious outlook, fostering backwardness and inequality, and it was considered authoritarian and intolerant.

Liberal groups, and later political parties, found membership and support in the urban commercial and industrial classes, and in those elements of the skilled working class that by the middle of the nineteenth century were beginning to obtain the vote.

This description of liberalism, like those of conservatism and socialism which follow, pertains to "ideal types" in that it has dealt with the essential implications of liberal thought in a manner that will enable us to account for its development.[3] In actuality, groups included under the generic term "liberal" held a variety of views depending, among other factors, on the country and the period under consideration. English Whigs, for instance, were hesitant about extending the suffrage to the "masses"; in the middle of the nineteenth century it was only the "radicals" who favored such measures. The nature of the divisions among liberals and the reasons for them will be spelled out more fully in later chapters.

CONSERVATISM: European conservatism essentially represented an attempt to rationalize tradition—to justify retaining the customary arrangements of the past. Conservatism was a reaction against both industrialization and liberalism, and in European intellectual history its foremost advocates were Edmund Burke in England, Louis de Bonald and Joseph de Maistre in France, and Georg Wilhelm Friedrich Hegel in Germany, although Hegel's position is, in some ways, quite ambiguous.

[3] See "ideal type analysis" in Julius Gould and William L. Kolb, eds., A Dictionary of the Social Sciences (New York: The Free Press, 1964), pp. 311–313.

Conservatives de-emphasized the role of reason and assailed the individualistic and egalitarian premises of liberalism. They condemned the liberals' faith in science and reason as utopian, regarded the new conceptions of knowledge as restrictive and self-contradictory, and denied that one could successfully construct a society based on self-interest. Tradition and religion, they claimed, were necessary for cohesion. The emphasis upon man's rationality would only accentuate irrationality; to reduce social life to a calculus of pains and pleasures would destroy the reality of life. Generally, conservatives supported established religion, whichever church it might be (the Catholic Church in France, the Church of England, the Lutheran Church in Germany); they supported hereditary, even absolute, monarchies; they supported tradition for the sake of tradition; and they supported the need for a society grounded in respect for authority.

Conservatives argued that the individualism of liberalism contributed to social dissolution and injustice. They re-emphasized that the purpose of the community was to achieve a just social order within the bounds of the community. And as a just social order involved the mutual responsibilities and rights of various estates, so it necessarily involved an ordered hierarchy. Again, the achievement of social justice—indeed of an ordered society—required a governing class that by inheritance and breeding was fit to govern. The emphasis on equality, they argued, could only lead to chaos. Thus, the conservatives rejected both the idea of the democratic state and the idea of the minimum state. The state, governed by the better elements in the community, would take an active part in social affairs in order to bring about social cohesion and justice.

The conservatives attacked industrialism and the values of capitalism as being egoistic and philistine. These attacks merged with the English and Continental Romantic movement, which contrasted the bucolic joys of an agricultural society with the filth, dirt, and general unhealthiness of industrial society, and the contentment and balance of rural society with the frenzied life of the masses in the growing industrial centers.

SOCIALISM: In the latter part of the nineteenth century, another and equally sharp critique was leveled against the values of liberal capitalism. This time the attack came from Socialist intellectuals.

Socialist ideas can be traced back at least as far as the early Christian community; and throughout the medieval and early modern periods, Christian sects arose that espoused a communal ownership of property in accordance with Christian doctrine and scripture. Modern European socialism, however, is primarily a post-industrial movement and forms an integral part of Europe's transition from a traditional to a modern industrial society. Socialist movements of considerable size appeared almost simultaneously throughout Western Europe in the nineteenth century.

On the ideological level, socialism involved, first of all, a basic criticism of the values of capitalist society. Socialists condemned capitalism's egoistic individualism, its acquisitive materialism, its denial of mutual responsibility, its dehumanization of man into types identifiable with economic function. In this sense, the Socialist and the conservative critique of capitalism were at one: a protest against the process of industrialization itself. The Socialists' solutions to the problems of industrialization, however, differed profoundly from those of the conservatives, for Socialists, on the whole, accepted the liberal faith in science, progress, and equality. Their critique of industrialism was directed solely against capitalist industrialization. They maintained that liberal capitalism worshiped false ideals, and that even those of its goals that were humane could not be achieved in a capitalistic society. Only under a Socialist organization of society was it possible to direct the fruits of science toward a fully human existence.

The manner in which socialism drew upon the conservative critique of capitalism and industrialization and on the values of liberal capitalism itself can be observed in the writings of Karl Marx, whose towering genius dominated European political and social thinking during the latter part of the nineteenth century and whose work inspired every major European Socialist party except the English.

Marx regarded historical change as the result of the violent collision of social classes, each limited in its awareness by ideological blinders. The position of each class in the prevailing economic system limited its perspective on society. Hence, once the time was ripe, the transformation of a capitalist society into a Communist society could be effected only through the revolutionary efforts of the working class. When Socialist parties developed on the Continent, the Marxist ones were invariably the most militant and the most strongly committed to a violent course of action.

5. INTERLUDE

Western Europe provided the initial setting for the industrialization that has changed the face of the world. The question of why the process of modernization began there rather than in some other civilizations to which it has since been imported has long interested historians and sociologists. Aside from racial explanations, now largely discredited, the first answer usually advanced bears upon environmental variables. Europe enjoys a temperate climate; it has, especially in the north, a soil that allows the intensive cultivation of any number of food crops. Many large harbors and river systems afford easy transportation of goods from shore to shore and easy access to the interior. Coal and iron, which were crucial resources at a certain phase of the Industrial Revolution, were found in convenient proximity.

While these factors may help to explain why Europe industrialized more rapidly than did areas where a harsh climate and a lack of resources inhibited development, they do not explain the primacy of Europe as a whole as against China, for example, or of England as against France and France as against Italy. The superiority of northern European soils only became an advantage when the special tools necessary to exploit them became available; and in the early years of English industrialization iron ore was imported from Sweden. It may be well to remember that northern Europe was inhabited by primitive migratory tribes long after civilizations of a very high order had flourished in other parts of the globe, and it might have remained uncivilized for a long time had it not been for the influence of Rome.

Further, it is difficult to argue that the European environment was far more conducive to industrialization than that of the Asiatic mainland. While ecological conditions may have been of some significance in setting the broad limits within which a modern civilization could grow, a full explanation must take into account other factors. It seems reasonable to suggest that what was decisive was Europe's particular cultural variables, including the Christian tradition which provided the underlying values for an industrial civilization and which explains much of the contemporary structure of European social and political life.

The United States, on the other hand, is essentially a European nation. Europeans make up the great bulk of its population; its principal social, political, and cultural institutions are European in origin.[4] Its differences from Western Europe have to do with the tone set by the initial immigration, which was largely Calvinist. Having no earlier tradition with which to contend, the logic of the Calvinist orientation unfolded naturally in the

[4] The two major non-European peoples are Indians, and the Africans who were brought over as slaves; insofar as the following discussion ignores these groups, it oversimplifies reality. However, until recently neither has had an important, direct impact on the dominant values of American society. They have been subject peoples rather than equal participants in the community.

New World. The United States, consequently, began its national life as a "liberal" nation, less affected by the strains that Europe experienced during its transition to an industrial society. Having no feudal heritage, the United States lacked both a genuine aristocracy and a genuine peasantry; it therefore never developed a powerful conservative movement. Lacking a religious establishment, it also never developed a strong tradition of anticlericalism. Despite signs of change, the two major American political parties are still essentially liberal parties dedicated, at least rhetorically, to democracy, capitalism, and the separation of church and state. While Richard Nixon and Eugene McCarthy differ on many issues, in Europe they would, until very recently, have merely represented the conservative and reform wings of the same political party—a liberal party—and they would be united in their opposition to both European conservatism and European socialism. The limits of the American political tradition are defined by the cultural symbols that all Americans accept unquestioningly as basic. Politically, these are the Declaration of Independence and the Constitution, essentially liberal documents, drawn from but one of the streams of modern European thought.

In Europe, both peasants and aristocrats remained conservative because, for different reasons, they felt threatened by the new society and new ideas associated with industrialization. In the United States, almost from the very beginning the vast majority of those Europeans who tilled the soil were independent farmers who adapted with relative ease to a liberal capitalist society.

There were other differences between the two continents. The European middle class, for example, remained highly self-conscious. It was aware of itself as a separate estate, and it accepted some aristocratic norms even as it reacted against them. In the United States, the middle class accepted a society in which European immigrants, at least, could eventually become social equals and in which achievement, not birth, was theoretically the measure of a man's worth. Social equality and

equality of opportunity were never as real in the United States as the official mythology of the nation claimed, but compared with the old world, it is the egalitarianism of American society that has always impressed European observers.

In Europe, the working class, migrating to the cities from a peasant background, was drawn to Socialist parties by both class consciousness and the trauma of having to adjust to an urban industrial environment. Criticism of the new society by Socialist intellectuals was taken seriously because of the constant tensions involved in the transition to modernity—and because the new society could be contrasted with an older one which, in retrospect, seemed to have placed much more stress on community life. In the United States, the very fluidity of the class system inhibited the development of class consciousness, and intellectuals who censured the dominant patterns of American society never received serious attention. America defined itself in terms of liberal capitalist values, and these values represented the logical culmination of the Calvinist ethos of its founders.

Obviously, other factors were important also in shaping American history: the impact of the frontier, the abundance of land, the waves of immigrants. Yet England had a frontier in America, and both Russian and French Canadian peasants, while influenced in their behavior by the existence of a frontier, retained more of the institutions of their parent societies. Further, the Spanish and Portuguese migrants to Latin America created, in their New World frontier, a quasi-feudal society based on their Iberian inheritance. In the last analysis, the frontier was significant to the development of American society only because English Protestants settled a new country that was free of the old country's traditional institutions.

Nineteenth-century American politics was distinguished by considerable conflict—and a good deal of violence. But this conflict took place within a rather narrow set of social and political premises. Even today when the "liberal" values characteristic of American society are rejected, at least verbally, by a segment of the university community and for different reasons by a growing number of black militants, the vast majority of the population—both black and white—still continues to honor them.

6. CONTEMPORARY EUROPE

The development of all Western European nations during the nineteenth century was in certain ways fundamentally similar. Industrial capitalist society was associated both with social stresses of varying intensity and with the birth of liberal democracy and even more radical movements. By the end of the century, many of these stresses were being alleviated. Liberal capitalist ideas became subject to amendment as working-class demands expressed through revolutionary action and the ballot box combined with the traditional concepts of community to modify extreme individualism. Liberal parties produced socially responsible programs and conservative parties accepted democratic and industrial ideals. The aristocracy, as a class of landowners, was disappearing, and Socialist parties became more moderate as they grew more popular.

In the meantime, Europe was expanding beyond its borders. The motives underlying this expansion were mixed: they stemmed partly from the desire for trading opportunities and for power and prestige, partly from missionary zeal. Europe's ability to expand its influence and to control countries of far greater size and population was based on a technological superiority that manifested itself in the creation of ever more effective military weapons. Europe's political suzerainty, however, was short-lived: the European empire crumbled no more than fifty or sixty years after it achieved its maximum extent. Compared with the Roman attainment it was fleeting indeed.

Contemporary Europe can probably best be dated from World War I, which, along with its aftermath, served to accelerate previous trends and to create new tensions that altered the direction of European development. The first consequence of the war was the founding of the Soviet state.

By the end of the nineteenth century, Socialist parties in the West had begun to lose their revolutionary élan. However, within almost all of them there remained powerful revolutionary factions, usually the more "orthodox" Marxists, though many who called themselves Marxists had accepted both gradualism and the democratic state. With a newly proclaimed revolutionary Marxist state in Russia and the chaos and slaughter of World War I, these factions quickly grew in strength immediately after the war. To the more radical Socialists, the war had been a capitalist enterprise and the slaughter it entailed offered justification for their doctrines. Soviet communism provided not only a solid base for organizing an international Communist movement but also the expectation that the millennium was at hand. The inflation and unemployment that accompanied postwar adjustments made the promises of radical Marxism even more appealing.

All the Socialist movements of Western Europe, except the British one, were split as a result, and powerful national Communist parties owing allegiance to the Comintern, or Third International, which had been set up in Moscow, were created. The Communists expected the immediate outbreak of revolutions throughout Western Europe. But these did not occur, and the Socialist movements of the West continued to be divided between increasingly hostile Socialist and Communist parties. The Communists eventually came under the domination of the Soviet Union, in part because of the prestige it enjoyed and in part because it provided financial aid upon which the western Communist parties depended. In the 1920's and 1930's, the Soviet Union successfully weathered a series of crises to qualify after World War II as one of the world's leading industrial and military powers.

European fascism, which reached its zenith in German National Socialism, is the second movement fashioned from the strains produced by World War I; but again, its origins are to be found in the nineteenth century. Conservatism in Europe had been a reaction against both liberalism and industrialization. By the end of the nineteenth century, however, conservative parties in many countries were suffering a serious malaise. Based upon a landowning aristocracy, they were identified with a hierarchical society, monarchy, and the church. As land became a less important source of wealth, as the tenets of aristocratic authority were weakened by the challenge of democratic ideologies, and as the participation of the mass of the people in political life increased, the power of the European aristocracy faded. In addition, the old attachments to both monarchy and the church were slowly being undermined.

In England and certain other countries, conservative parties adapted to the new epoch, established a mass political base, and continued to flourish. But for many reasons, conservative parties in some nations could not successfully adjust to the new conditions. Their decline did not necessarily mean, however, that hostility to industrial society had disappeared on the "ideological" right and among substantial segments of the peasantry and working class. On the contrary: this hostility gave rise to fascism. While fascism appealed to the masses, claimed to speak for them, and used "pseudo-democratic" slogans, it was a movement that nevertheless represented a reaction against modernity; its aim was to restore the values of a vanishing, traditional society. Paradoxically, fascism based its attack on modernity on some of the slogans of modernity. A belief in the rule of the people's will—or in a ruling, racial elite issuing from and speaking for the people— was combined with an attack upon industrial society and its ramifications. Fascists thus rejected liberal capitalism because of the heartlessness and philistinism of bourgeois society, and they rejected Marxist socialism because, like liberalism, it denied traditional values and the concept of a heroic, disciplined social

order. Fascists were at one with conservatives in calling for a society in which the community regulated economic activities for the common good, but they discarded a hereditary class elite in favor of a racial elite; and Fascists, particularly German Fascists, maintained that a particular race of people was superior to all other peoples.

Curiously enough, although the Fascists sought to restore traditional values and disciplined authority, fascism was the child of bohemianism and nihilism, the offspring of those who "thought with their blood" and seemingly rejected rational order as well as traditional values. The contradiction is only superficial: the swift breakdown of traditional values in many cases seemed particularly threatening to those who lacked the capacity for self-control in an increasingly pluralistic environment. In essence, these people feared the destructive impulses that they had discovered in themselves. Their salvation seemed to lie in the necessity for more rigorous discipline, lest their own impulses overwhelm them. It is not an uncommon phenomenon that insistence on the need for external discipline is characteristic of persons who doubt their ability to control themselves.

For different reasons, then, fascism appealed to different types of people: those who deplored the "heartlessness" of urban, industrial society; those who feared the destruction of traditional values; those who applauded the collapse of traditional society; and finally, those who felt personally threatened by the loosening of long-established controls.

With some exceptions, European Fascist movements were also anti-Semitic. The Jews served as a convenient focus of aggression for several reasons. A traditional Christian hostility emanating from religious differences was heightened by the fact that Jews conspicuously retained their identity as a separate ethnic group within the larger society at a time of nationalistic fervor. At least as important was the social position of the Jew in nineteenth-century European society. Denied land and barred from many traditional occupations throughout European history, Jews were mostly an urban people. With their release from the ghetto, they moved into such professions as law, medicine, and the arts, and into trade and commerce as well as finance. Many of these occupations—retail trade, for example—were highly unstable and competitive. In a depression or inflationary period, the self-employed store owner, functioning as "middleman," is a much more obvious target for hostility than the industrial capitalist. In addition, most of these occupations and professions were identified with the new industrial, urban culture and with the breakdown of both traditional society and traditional patterns of morality. Besides, Jews were identified with cities; in Europe, where the gap between city and countryside was far wider than in the United States, the city was regarded by the tradition-minded peasant as a cesspool of iniquity. After leaving the ghetto, Jews tended to support Liberal, Socialist, or Communist parties, because these parties insisted upon equal rights for all citizens and denied the relevance of religious considerations or ethnic origins.

The Jewish citizen thus garnered the animosity of persons who believed that the old values of the society were being threatened, as well as of those who, rebelling against traditional values, feared their own impulses and projected them upon the Jew. Jews also served as a convenient scapegoat for bohemian intellectuals who rejected all repression and wished to establish values based upon a free expression of the heroic passions. In Germany, especially, these groups identified repression with Christianity and traced the sources of Christian submissiveness to its Jewish origins.

Since Socialist movements derived their own support in part from elements that were reacting against the values of an industrial society, it is not surprising that some Socialist groups were openly anti-Semitic. And it is no accident that the leadership of the German National Socialist Party included more than a sprinkling of homosexuals, pornographers,

and drug addicts who, at the same time, violently attacked Jews as "sexual perverts."

The fear of Jews by many anti-Semites, a fear of their own impulses, was a genuine fear. When Captain Dreyfus, a French officer of Jewish descent, was convicted in 1894 of treason (a conviction based on the flimsiest evidence and later rescinded) and sent to Devil's Island, a French penal colony off the coast of French Guiana, French military officials ordered an immediate strengthening of the island's defenses, fearing an attempt to liberate him by the "international Jewish navy." The same fear of Jews runs through Hitler's *Mein Kampf,* the bible of the Nazi movement, and explains the widespread credence given to the spurious *Protocols of the Elders of Zion,* a document which, it was claimed, was the Jews' secret plan for the destruction of Christian civilization.

These were the strains that produced fascism, strains which were exacerbated by World War I and which might never have been significant if the war had not worked such chaos on Europe. That fascism came to power in Germany in its most virulent form was due to certain additional problems with which the country was faced, but German developments cannot be understood except in terms of the overall European pattern.

Fascist movements reached their peak in the 1920's and 1930's, drawing their support primarily from the peasantry, small businessmen, and elements of the working classes, who, in many cases, deserted the liberal, anti-aristocratic parties they had supported earlier. Their switch in allegiance is understandable if one recognizes that fascism was a postdemocratic movement that contained genuine populist overtones. It is important to distinguish fascism from traditional conservatism or even from traditional dictatorships like that of Franco's Spain which, despite some Fascist elements, has lacked the populist and totalitarian character of Nazi Germany and, to a lesser extent, of Fascist Italy.

Fascism led to World War II—and an-

other turning point in European development. Again, some of the changes that have
occurred since 1945 are merely a continuation of earlier trends. In some cases the
changes were accelerated by the war itself,
while others represent new directions.

Europe has by and large completed the
transition to a modern society. The technological impetus provided by the war, and the
increasing rate of technological development
since 1940, have contributed to rapid social
change. Europe is now entering an age of
affluence—an era of television sets, washing
machines, and automobiles, an era that is
closing the material gap between rural and
urban existence. It is also an age in which
regional variations are declining and in which
some of the superficial indications of class
differences—language, dress, luxuries—are
vanishing. One sign of the times has been
the disappearance of that traditional emblem
of middle- or upper-class status, the domestic
servant.

In all European countries there are still
substantial pockets of poverty, especially in
the rural areas and among the elderly; and
housing conditions in England, France, and
Germany are still painfully inadequate. Further, the distribution of income has not become noticeably more equal. Yet compared
with prewar Europe, it is the affluence, geographic mobility, and greater homogeneity of

the population that are most striking, just as
the destruction of old landmarks and the
building of new highways and supermarkets
are visible everywhere. It is quite clear that
Western Europe, with the possible exception
of Spain and Portugal, has accepted modernity. The restoration of traditional institutions
no longer seems even remotely possible.

Given these facts and the emergence and
widespread acceptance of the "welfare state,"
intellectuals in the West are speaking more
frequently of European society as entering a
"postcapitalist" epoch, and the old ideological
controversies seem less meaningful. Liberal
and conservative parties (the terms are no
longer completely descriptive) accept democracy and social-welfare policies. Socialist
parties, too, are committed to parliamentary
regimes: in fact, they have tended to become parties of reform accepting the framework of a mixed economy with, however, an
ever expanding public sector. In France and
Italy, strong Communist parties remain, but
the size of their "militant" following has declined and, since the death of Stalin, both
revolutionary élan and Leninist dogma have
also waned. There are, however, new sources
of strain and conflict developing in Western
countries. These sources have to do with desires for greater equality and greater political
participation. But just as importantly, they
represent a demand for more emphasis upon

TABLE 1.3.   THE AFFLUENT SOCIETY IN EUROPE
AND THE UNITED STATES

Number per 1,000 inhabitants

	Motor vehicles in use, 1966	Physicians, 1965	Television sets, 1966
United Kingdom	212.5	0.86	254
France	262.5	1.11	151
West Germany	189.3	1.54	213
United States	471.5	1.48	376
U.S.S.R.	—	2.10	82

Source: U.S. Bureau of the Census, *Statistical Abstract of the United States:
1968*, 89th edition (Washington, D.C.: 1968), pp. 835–837, 862–865; and
U.N. Statistical Yearbook, 1968, pp. 78–86.

community goals as opposed to private affluence. As such, they are an assault, once again, upon the "bourgeois" mentality. Thus far, however, the renewal of ideological fervor has failed to ignite any but relatively small bands of students and, in France, some labor unions. The implications of these developments in the late 1960's will be discussed in later chapters and in the concluding chapter of this study.

World War II marked another turning point for Europe—the sudden decline of its empires and the power of its individual nations. The disintegration of empires was, basically and somewhat ironically, the consequence of two factors: the general acceptance of Europe's own ideas of independence and self-determination and the far-reaching technological revolution induced by Europe's example. The power aggregated by Europe as a whole, and by the individual nations of Europe, was a temporary phenomenon based upon early industrialization. The loss of this advantage abetted the decline of Western European nations to second-rank powers.

The forfeiture of empire and power involved severe dislocations, and necessitated a readjustment of conceptions of national self-identity. These strains have been sharper in France than in England, but they have affected the politics of both countries. While they have adjusted to the loss of their empires, Europeans have become increasingly self-conscious regarding their identification as Europeans. Since 1945, organizations of a supranational type have been formed to promote economic and perhaps political unification among the nations of Western Europe. Here the ambivalence of England and, after 1958, the intransigence of Charles de Gaulle have raised critical problems. Even so, the future will probably see the increasing integration of Western Europe.

7. THE EUROPEAN NATION STATE

In the introduction to this volume, the term "political system" was explained as that set of institutions which a society establishes both to define and to reach its goals. At a minimum, such goals include survival against the natural environment and other political systems. But in all historical societies beyond the most primitive, the choosing of goals has also involved the determination of the style of political and social life. This has been true even when, as in the United States for many years, it was thought that the state should restrict itself to keeping order and should permit interest groups as much latitude as possible in attaining their own ends. Any political system, therefore, takes a major responsibility for determining the distribution of values within the society as a whole. The pattern of social stratification in a community, for example, including rights to personal or other property, is the result of essentially political decisions.

A functioning society must be characterized by a reasonable amount of order. A working political system must maintain a monopoly upon the legitimate use of force within the system itself and in relation to other political systems. Further, if it is to survive for any length of time, it must create mechanisms that allow for the recruitment and replacement of political elites, and it also must develop sufficient flexibility and resources to adapt effectively to new problems—whether they arise as demands from within the society, changes in the natural environment, or contact with other societies.

Goal attainment, then, is a very broad concept and the functions of the political system are far more pervasive than they may appear to be at first glance. The organization of the economy, the system of education, the leeway allowed special-interest groups—all these are political decisions. It is, accordingly, the political order with which the citizen most often identifies in modern communities because, for him, it symbolizes the whole spectrum of social, cultural, and economic institutions of his society. Aristotle put the point well in his *Politics* when he argued that the *polis,* or political system, was higher and logically prior to all others, including the family, because the existence of all other associations—or institutions or structures—was contingent upon the creation of some form of political order.

The use of the term "political system" rather than of more conventional terms like "state" or "government" is comparatively new in political science, and is a reflection of the discipline's growing sophistication. The impetus to change the terminology first came from the cultural anthropologists studying primitive societies. It became apparent that while these societies were governed, it was often extremely difficult to identify a particular set of institutions which could be called governments.[5] Certainly, in tribal societies or religio-political empires like the Muslim, one cannot meaningfully speak of the government or the state. The fact of the matter is that the territorial nation state is a rather recent invention in the history of mankind—a European invention which is now spreading around the world, although it is very possible that as it does so it is in the process of becoming obsolete.

Discussing the political system rather than talking about the "state" thus enables us to compare European societies with those of other areas, and contemporary societies with those of the past. It also enables us to escape those interminable arguments as to the relationship between the "state" and "society," arguments which historically have reflected the fact that the nation state as a political system emerged out of an earlier pattern—namely, European feudalism—in which social and political authority were fused in the same men or institutions.

THE RISE OF THE NATION STATE: S. N. Eisenstadt[6] has listed seven basic types of political systems: (1) primitive, such as

those existing among tribes; (2) patrimonial empires, including the Carolingian, Ahmenid, and Parthian; (3) nomad or conquest empires—the Mongols and the Arab kingdoms under the first caliphs; (4) city states, such as ancient Athens and republican Rome; (5) feudal, such as those which flourished in medieval Europe and Japan; (6) centralized historical bureaucratic empires, like the Chinese and the Byzantine; and (7) modern nation states—democratic, autocratic, or totalitarian.[7]

These can be placed rather roughly along an evolutionary scale. On the whole, modern societies are much more highly differentiated; they have developed specialized institutions, including bureaucracies, which enable them to adapt to their environment more readily and to mobilize their resources more effectively. Moreover, the inclination of modern societies has been to replace hereditary authority with authority based on special competence. Finally, modern political systems usually involve the population in the political process, even if only symbolically.

The origin of modern European nation states is to be found in feudal societies which, by the seventeenth century, had been transformed into more or less centralized, secular, bureaucratic empires. The transformation occurred first in the West, partly because secular and religious authority could be differentiated far more easily in Christian societies than in others, for reasons indicated earlier in this chapter. The period from the seventeenth century to the twentieth was marked by the gradual application of constitutional limitations upon the monarch and the eventual development of representative institutions. Loyalty shifted from the king, whose realm had been his patrimony, to the nation state as a legal entity, which belonged to the growing number of people who were acquiring full citizenship.

Loyalty also shifted from a particular ter-

[5] Government may be defined as that institution, or set of institutions, that has the power to make binding decisions for the society as a whole and enjoys at least a quasi-monopoly of force.
[6] In *The Political Systems of Empires* (Glencoe, Ill.: The Free Press, 1963).

[7] I use a slightly different classification for modern states, which will be discussed on p. 88.

ritory or from a supernational religious organization, and sometimes both, to the nation state itself. The French Revolution was perhaps symbolic of this momentous change, even though the conversion of allegiances had already taken place, albeit gradually, in England. To a considerable extent, ethnic (or tribal) and cultural self-identification went hand in hand in Europe. This was not always the case, of course, for in a number of instances the creation of the state helped produce a common culture and a sense of common identity. The United States is a prime example of this process, but there are others as well, and the pattern is being repeated now or at least attempted in the newer African and Asian states whose boundaries cross ethnic lines.

It can be argued that the democratic nation state in Western Europe and the United States represents a more "modern" form of organization than that of the Soviet or Chinese one-party state. In the two Communist countries, structural differentiation is less advanced and key decisions are made by a small elite that has refused to institutionalize restraints upon its exercise of power. It should be noted, even so, that in recent years interest groups in the U.S.S.R. have begun to demonstrate a degree of autonomy.

THE EMERGENCE OF CONSTITUTIONAL GOVERNMENT IN EUROPE: Political systems with written constitutions—which theoretically outline the basic structure of the political system, establish curbs upon government actions, and stand, in some way, above ordinary law and custom, are a rather recent innovation. Aristotle spoke of and collected the "constitutions" of various Greek city states. But to him, as to other Greeks, a "constitution" simply referred to the city's total pattern of social and political institutions; it was not regarded as a basic framework of *political* institutions to which ordinary law *should* conform.

The idea of a written constitution seems to have originated with the more radical English

Calvinist sects, and to have derived from their conception of the church as a convenant among the faithful, although one can discover antecedents in medieval and even Stoic conceptions of natural law. From there it entered into the social-contract theory of modern liberal thought as expressed by John Locke. The idea of a constitution as the "basic" law of the community, subject to final interpretation of judges, reached its fullest manifestation in the United States, where judicial review by a constitutional court has always carried far more weight than it has in any other nation. Traditionally, other European nations that adopted constitutions assigned to legislative bodies the task of determining their meaning. Since World War II a number of countries—some of them, like Germany and Japan, under the influence of American occupation—have created constitutional courts. None, however, has acquired the power or influence of the United States Supreme Court.

The American experience must, then, be regarded as unique. Certainly the fact that the United States was formed as a federal republic contributed to the evolution of the Supreme Court as a powerful instrument, although such an eventuality does not always occur in a federal system (it did not occur either under the German Empire or during the Weimar Republic, despite the fact that Germany was a federal state). That Americans and Englishmen have been prone to regard law (and judges) as a force for progress—a view not shared by most Continentals—has also been a factor aiding the establishment of a powerful court.[8] Yet the "covenant" theory, evoked by Calvinism and transformed by liberalism into the idea of a "social compact," was probably the crucial variable in determining that Americans should come to regard their constitution as a form of higher law limiting even the free expression of the popular will.

Nevertheless, the American Constitution

[8] See the discussion of legal systems in Chapter 23.

and the Supreme Court as an institution have survived, to a large degree, because of the flexibility of both the document and the court. It is also true that compared with most European nations, which have drafted one constitution after another, the stability of the American document has depended upon the relative lack of ideological conflicts within the United States. The reason for this should become more apparent as we examine the Continental experience.

Certain common themes run through the framing of constitutions in Europe. The period of absolute monarchy was followed by institutional changes that first limited the authority of the king and later transferred power to legislative bodies. In almost every case, these legislatures consisted initially of two chambers, one representing the hereditary aristocracy, the other representing, first, the middle classes, and then, as property qualifications for voting were lowered, the entire adult population. In almost every case, too, the balance of power shifted by degrees from the upper house to the lower, popularly elected chamber. On the Continent these changes were often the result of revolutionary action and the writing of new constitutions; in England they were gradual and organic. The end results, however, were similar: by the twentieth century, the upper houses of Continental countries, while designed to represent more conservative constituencies, were no longer hereditary chambers of the aristocracy. England, paradoxically enough, was the only nation with which we are concerned to retain a hereditary House of Lords. It is perhaps because the Lords has remained largely hereditary that its power has continued to decline, while there are signs that second chambers on the Continent, now that they are elective, are regaining strength.

Both the Soviet Union and the United States represent exceptions to this general trend. In Russia, the parliamentary pattern characteristic of the rest of Europe had begun to show itself in the first part of the twentieth century with the creation of a na-

tional legislative body, the Duma. However, the Bolshevik Revolution brought to an abrupt halt the further development of parliamentary government of the European type, and, despite a series of constitutions along European lines, the Revolution placed authority—that is, legitimate power—essentially in the hands of a political party.

In the United States, the constitution adopted in 1789 has retained its essential features. Modeled on the British pattern, it provided for an indirectly elected upper house (in deference to the conservative as well as the federal element); a popularly elected lower chamber; and a president, indirectly elected, whose powers, like those of the English king and various Continental monarchs, were independent of the legislature. In Europe, as a result of explicit or implicit constitutional changes, power eventually fell to a single chamber with an executive dependent upon it; but the American system has remained unchanged, at least in form. Those who wrote the American Constitution had created a political rather than a social balance. The lack of a feudal heritage and the swift transformation of the United States into a democratic society made it comparatively easy for later reformers to remake both the senate and the presidency into democratic institutions. Thus, they felt little or no need to abolish them, as Continental reformers did with hereditary upper chambers and monarchs, or to reduce their power even as the institutions were retained in their "dignified" aspects, as in England.

In one sense, therefore, the United States, despite the fact that it became the first "modern" nation, has retained eighteenth- and even seventeenth-century institutions, or so some critics have charged. Yet it is interesting to note that some Europeans, now that the traditional social question—the aristocratic principle versus the democratic principle—has been settled, are reconsidering the function and desirability of two-house legislative chambers as well as strong, independently elected executives. In the French Fifth Republic and the Federal Republic of Germany, the upper chambers are now stronger than they were under previous constitutional arrangements. Of course, the Fifth Republic also boasts a popularly elected president, although it is too early to say for certain whether the institution, even in modified form, will long survive Charles de Gaulle.

Europe's role in introducing "modernity" to the world, then, is to be explained in terms of a peculiar combination of social and cultural elements, including its Christian heritage and, particularly, Calvinist Protestantism. It is important to re-emphasize, however, that the religious influence was but one of the factors contributing to modernization, which, as a process, can take different lines under different auspices at different times. Indeed, as we shall see, the English example induced the beginnings of modernization in France where professional classes, moved by revolutionary ideology, were instrumental in altering the course of French history. The French example as well as the English spurred modernization in Germany, where nationalism was an essential factor. And, finally, the Western European example as a whole provided the impetus for Russian attempts at modernization, first under despotic rulers, later under a revolutionary elite.

The next two chapters will explain why the four countries with which we are primarily concerned took the particular path they did toward modernization. In each nation, the significance of religious institutions, the problems of nation building, and the social and ideological conflicts kindled by industrialization will be examined.

2

England,

France, and Germany

1. THE PATTERN OF ENGLISH DEVELOPMENT

INTRODUCTION: Great Britain is a group of islands just off the Eurasian mainland, about the size of the state of Oregon.[1] It enjoys the cool summers and relatively warm winters of the western coast of Europe; over most of the island the temperature rarely falls below freezing. Precipitation is heavier than on the Continent, averaging some three hundred days of rain or fog a year.

English soil is only moderately good, suited primarily to cereals, potatoes, and grazing; with two exceptions—coal and iron —the country is not well endowed with mineral resources. The best coal fields have long since been worked out. But iron and coal were once plentiful enough, and conveniently found in the same general area near the ocean, to provide England with an economic windfall when Europe was creating a

technology based on both. Today Britain continues, as it has always done in the past, to import most of the other raw materials needed to sustain modern industry. (See Maps 2.2 and 2.3.)

Despite its small size, for more than a century England was among the dominant powers of the world, ruler of the modern world's largest empire and center of its industrial and financial life. Today more people speak English than any other language, except possibly Chinese.

England's world position stems from the fact that it was this small island that introduced the world to modernity through its own commercial and industrial revolutions. England's power has declined markedly in the past few decades—partly because the revolutions it nurtured in industry and commerce now encompass the globe.

It was in England, too, that modern liberalism and liberal capitalism first developed. The British Parliament is among the oldest legislative assemblies in the world, and in form it has been the most widely copied. Francis Bacon, Thomas Hobbes, and John

[1] The terms "England," "the United Kingdom," and "Great Britain" will be used interchangeably to refer to the United Kingdom of Great Britain and Northern Ireland. Technically, England consists only of the island of Great Britain, without Scotland and Wales.

Locke were the source of most of the ideas that provide the framework of contemporary political discourse.

Even though England was the first nation to bring modernity to the world, it remains one of the few countries that has made a comparatively peaceful transition from a traditional agricultural society to a modern industrial society. The ideological conflicts that convulsed every other European nation echoed in England, but they never rent the social fabric. This is all the more surprising when one realizes that Englishmen today are as class-conscious as Frenchmen or Germans and that England retains more of its traditional past than does France or Germany, neither of which has a monarchy, for instance, or a largely hereditary House of Lords.

The British achievement has been explained in a multitude of ways. The early genesis of stable representative institutions has been credited to England's insular position which, it is argued, offers protection against invasion and obviates the need for a large standing army. The "phlegmatic" quality of English politics has been attributed to the climate and the nation's industrial development to its resources. But while insularity, climate, and resources were significant, any or all of them are insufficient to explain the English experience. Japan and Java are also islands, but they evolved quite differently; as already suggested, there is little reason to draw a connection between climate and civilization, except at the extremes—or, for that matter, between climate and national character. While England's resources have directly affected its industrial growth, the early phase of industrialization depended on the importation of Swedish ores: Birmingham, the early center of English iron and steel, became a large industrial community before local resources were extensively exploited.

Why England modernized first, and why it was able to do so relatively peacefully, can be understood only by examining English developments within a general European framework. Within that framework three factors appear to be crucial in explaining England's uniqueness: the time and manner in which England attained unity as a nation, the role of the English Protestant sects, and the pattern of English industrialization.

THE ACHIEVEMENT OF NATIONAL UNITY: In 1066 England was invaded successfully by William the Conqueror, duke of Normandy, who brought with him the feudal characteristics of his duchy; under William and his successors English feudalism reached its full maturity. Paradoxically, the Plantagenets contrived to modify English feudalism to strengthen the central authority, in part by their effective use of force. The English barony—the Norman followers of William—had obtained their fiefs, the great earldoms, directly from him, so that he and his successors had the fealty of more great vassals than did any other European feudal monarch; far more quickly and completely than their French or German counterparts, English barons developed a sense of being part of a single realm to which they owed a common allegiance. English insularity also contributed to the growth of monarchial power. Separated by the English Channel and the North Sea from most of the costly territorial conflicts of the Continent, English sovereigns found it far easier than did Continental kings to assert and maintain the prerogatives of the monarchy.

The process was a slow one, but, far more easily than France or Germany, England was transformed from a collection of feudalities to a unified nation bound by a "common law," subject to a sovereign monarchy, and infused with a sense of national identification. Thus, in England the creation of a national state proceeded almost naturally, whereas in France the destruction of feudal suzerainties required political absolutism. Further, the evolution of a national consciousness coincided with the realization of national unity; unlike the Germans, whose late political unification partly accounts for their manifesting an exaggerated sense of national exclusiveness, Englishmen were able to take their nationality for granted.

THE ENGLISH REFORMATION: England's early emergence as a national state and its insular position are closely related to its religious experience. The final break with the Roman Catholic Church in 1534 was accomplished by a strong and secure monarch, Henry VIII. Compared to the violent religious wars of the Continent, the English revolt against Catholicism was peaceful: Henry was not faced with the opposition of powerful baronial factions as was Henry IV of France, whose nobility chose allegiance to the church out of their opposition to royal abridgment of their privileges and authority. So long as the changes in doctrine and services were not too radical, Englishmen were willing to accept the idea of a national church. They regarded the Catholic Church as foreign, and Henry only had to imply that the church was denying him an heir to turn the national feelings of the English against the papacy.

The Anglican Communion was originally Catholic in all but name. Yet soon after the break with Rome many Protestant sects appeared in England, including that radical Calvinism which was to be closely related to the founding of liberal capitalism. In the seventeenth century, it seemed as if the radical Puritan sects would sweep all before them. But after the fall of Cromwell's Puritan Commonwealth in 1660, Calvinism was integrated as one strand in the fabric of English tradition; it became a part of, rather than the dominant factor in, English social history. Here the English experience contrasts with the American, in which the Calvinist ethos was to have such a determining influence on America's future.

INDUSTRIALIZATION: The third factor, the manner of England's industrialization and the social and ideological changes associated with

it, is closely related to the first two. Clearly, the secularized Protestant ethic was particularly important here. The fact that industrialization had established itself in England meant that the values and orientations necessary for its development were indigenous, and hence the disruption of previous patterns of life and ideas was not nearly so distinct as it was to be in other European nations. Also, the existence of a modern national state and a national system of law in England helped pave the way for industrialization.

There was in England, therefore, little support for the kind of royal absolutism that the commercial strata in other nations, notably France, were willing to endorse in order to create a national community. England entered the modern era as a society in which the power of the monarchy was limited by customary or constitutional rules and usages —rules which evolved from the tradition of reciprocal obligations that was feudalism. In England the central authority had grown stronger at the expense of local and class interests only by conceding specific rights to them, rights that became so well established by law as to limit the central authority itself. These rights could be granted without leading to political fragmentation because the barony implicitly accepted the notion that loyalty to the national community transcended local, parochial ties. It was for this reason that Magna Carta (1215), the feudal document designed to preserve the prerogatives of the nobility from encroachments and abuses by King John, could become in the seventeenth century the symbol of English liberties. The fact that the prerogatives of the gentry and local interests could be dovetailed—and dovetailed easily—with the other requirements for creating a national state meant that these specific rights did not have to be destroyed as they were in France during the age of absolutism.

By the mid-eighteenth century, at the onset of industrialization, England was a constitutional monarchy whose "constitution" maintained a balance between localism and centralism, between king and aristocracy (or gentry), and, in general, between the various estates or classes of the population. English traditional institutions were adapted to meet the requirements of a new society. While in France the monarchy largely succeeded in destroying an entrenched aristocracy and in completely depriving them of their real power and their customary authority, in England this never occurred. A national state developed by modifying earlier feudal patterns of privilege and responsibility. From the local, customary law of the middle ages evolved a nationwide common law, applied to all by royal courts and administered by the gentry. The upper classes no longer maintained private armies, but their voices were heard in Parliament in both the House of Lords and the House of Commons. The lord of the manor was no longer solely responsible for the welfare of his tenants and workers; instead, under the supervision of the state, the gentry contributed to "poor rates" which provided basic subsistence for the poor. Though a national state had replaced the earlier congeries of feudal authorities, the English community retained much of the sense of class rights, duties, and mutual responsibility characteristic of the earlier period.

THE CONSEQUENCES OF INDUSTRIALIZATION: The changes in the distribution of wealth and population, and in occupations, levels, and styles of living, that industrialization entailed were accompanied by increasingly vociferous attacks upon what was left of the old social order. In the last half of the eighteenth century and first half of the nineteenth, Parliament, under the influence of laissez-faire doctrines, repealed (or allowed to die) many of the old codes which had regulated apprenticeship, wages, and conditions of work because these contradicted liberal notions of the proper relationship between employers and employees.

Liberals also sought to reform the poor laws. Since the seventeenth century the very poor had been required to stay in their own parishes if they were to receive relief, and under the Speenhamland Law of 1795, all persons became entitled to supplementary payments if their incomes fell below a certain level. The payments were not large, but the reformers came to feel that the system not only reduced the mobility of workers but that it was encouraging sloth. As a result, Parliament in 1834 passed a new poor law which required that all able-bodied poor enter workhouses in return for subsistence if they could not secure private employment. The law represented a conscious effort to encourage the able-bodied poor to seek work.

At the same time, liberals fought for a more representative and democratic parliament; they tried to reduce the powers of the House of Lords and of the monarchy, to reorganize scientifically the public services in the growing cities, and to end the slave trade. All these goals were pursued in the name of an ideology that saw laissez-faire and democratic institutions as the mark and source of progress.

But if the liberal campaign in England was sometimes radical, it was not nearly so radical as that of Continental liberals. British reformers settled for piecemeal change and were not, on the whole, interested in destroying all traditional institutions. They believed, also, that persuasion and rhetoric would serve to bring about needed reforms. Further, they did not share the anticlericalism of Continental liberals.

If the temperament of British liberalism was moderate, it was because the traditional institutions of England did not prevent effective change. If British conservatives—Burke or Disraeli, for instance—were somewhat restrained in their responses, it was because they were not unalterably opposed to change and because their opponents were also moderate men. In a sense, the broad feeling of community that underlay British life served to blur divisions and to take the edge off social conflict.

Nonetheless, liberal ideology in nineteenth-century England did not triumph absolutely as it did in the United States. Rather, as liberalism transformed British society, so it was transformed by the society out of which it sprang. In this respect both England and the United States stand in contrast to France, where the radicalism of both liberals and conservatives produced a protracted period of violent conflict.

The triumph of the liberal idea in England is easy to follow. The Reform Bill of 1832 provided a rational system for comparatively equal parliamentary representation. The repeal of the poor laws, the repeal of the corn laws, the formulation of a policy of free trade, and other electoral reforms that culminated in universal manhood suffrage in 1918 were all justified in terms of liberal political and economic values and assumptions. The constitutional shift in the control of political power from a balance among king, Lords, and Commons to the House of Commons alone was accepted on the same grounds.

So completely had liberal assumptions permeated English political life by the last quarter of the nineteenth century that a Conservative prime minister, Disraeli, could be instrumental in securing passage of the Reform Bill of 1867, which extended the suffrage to the skilled workers of the cities. Of course, Disraeli was moved by the necessity of adjusting to "irresistible" pressures and by hope for political gain. But rational self-interest alone does not explain his actions. Conservatives in other countries, faced with the same pressures, preferred to fight to the last ditch against reform. In short, the willingness of the Conservative Party to extend electoral reform must be seen as evidence of its willingness to accept the legitimacy of a society in which the masses were granted the full rights of citizenship.

On the other hand, the continued impact of traditional conceptions of community and mutual class responsibilities on liberals themselves is indicated by their willingness to support social-reform measures which violated their ideological position that the state should not interfere in the free workings of the

market. Thus, the parliament that enacted the new poor law also passed a law (in 1833) prohibiting the employment of children under nine in textile mills and limiting the work of children under 13 to 48 hours a week. This legislation was partially the handiwork of Conservative landowners who wanted to strike back at the commercial interests for supporting measures that weakened their traditional authority, and who, though autocrats, believed in community responsibility. Many liberals opposed it, quoting the laissez-faire economists in arguing that the measure would pauperize England and in the long run serve all her people ill. It was, however, supported by many reformers who, despite their belief in the liberal economists in theory, thought that in practice the more fortunate members of the community had a responsibility for the less fortunate.

Through the latter half of the nineteenth century, the pace of reform accelerated until in 1911 a Liberal government could sponsor legislation, The National Insurance Act, providing for universal unemployment insurance and extensive medical care for individuals in the lower income brackets. By the turn of the century, English liberals had so much accepted the state's responsibility for social welfare that even in the United States of the early 1960's their views would have been considered somewhat radical. In the United States, of course, the liberal idea represented the only tradition. The concept of a fully free economy, consequently, lasted much longer, and even though various social-welfare measures are generally accepted, many Americans still prefer to pretend that they have an absolutely "free" economy.

These nineteenth-century conflicts of conservative and liberal ideologies were accompanied by a headlong growth in industry. In 1851, for example, agriculture accounted for 25 per cent of the British labor force; by 1911 the percentage had dropped to 11. As the aristocracy's economic base—land—declined in value, so its power diminished as that of the commercial and industrial middle class rose. And as the peasantry swarmed to the cities, it was transformed as a class into an industrial proletariat increasingly attracted by radical—eventually Socialist—ideas.

But again in contrast with circumstances on the Continent, socialism in Britain took on a peculiarly British cast. It was usually moderate and reformist; both Socialist intellectuals and workers were convinced that reform could come through educating the community, and they never engaged in a full-scale assault on the traditional institutions of British society. The comparative moderateness of British workers was the result of the easier transition to an industrial society in Britain than in France; but it also stemmed from the fact that the British working class never felt completely alienated from the community. Almost from the beginning British workers were part of a society whose leaders accepted some responsibility for the workers' welfare and provided for it by enacting social legislation and accepting the formation of trade unions.

The possibilities of social upheaval were further reduced by the renewed vigor of the Puritan temperament, as it expressed itself in the spread of Methodism during the first half of the nineteenth century. Like the original Calvinism out of which it sprang, Methodism emphasized hard work and self-discipline as a religious duty; at the same time it provided emotional release at revivalist meetings. In these ways it helped to mitigate working-class discontent and violence. But if the Puritan ethic served to maintain social moderation in England, so, too, did traditional values. Because the British middle classes adopted many of the attitudes of the gentry, the British working class became more class-conscious than did the American. Bourgeois class consciousness was associated with a sense of noblesse oblige, however, which goes a long way toward explaining the acceptance by the English working class of the rule of its "betters."

The transition from rural to urban life and from a traditional to an industrial society quite naturally was an enormously traumatic experience for millions, especially for workers crowded into the spawning urban slums. For some former artisans, it meant lower living standards during the first half of the nineteenth century. Moreover, the limits of knowledge as well as of liberal ideology allowed the society as a whole to learn only slowly how best to deal with the problems of the new age. By modern standards, the attempts made to ameliorate the tremendously disruptive conditions were feeble indeed, and the possibility of large-scale violence was, obviously, never completely absent. Yet in comparison with parallel events in France, it is still the docility of the British working class, and the sense of responsibility of other social classes, that are so striking.

Other factors contributed to the comparative tranquillity of British political life. Because England was the first nation to industrialize, it enjoyed a commercial supremacy which, during most of the nineteenth century, yielded a slow but continuing rise in the standard of living for most of its burgeoning population. There were no models of advanced societies, as there are today, to make the gap between aspirations and accomplishments painfully apparent. Nor had literacy been so far extended or the media so widely disseminated that workers could become more aware of possibilities for changing their lot. Finally, the British Empire offered an outlet for service, prestige, and power to the sons of an aristocracy whose social primacy was gradually being usurped by other classes; and large-scale emigration to North America, Australia, and later to South Africa gave England a means of providing the more "restless" members of the working class with an equivalent of the American frontier.

CONTEMPORARY BRITAIN: Many of these props to a stable social order began to fall away after World War I. By the 1920's England had plainly lost its commercial supremacy, partly because of the war itself and partly because of trends that had set in even before the war. Other nations, some non-European, were industrializing at full tilt, and as late entrants in the industrial race they were able to make effective use of modern plants and techniques. Moreover, having broken more abruptly with their historical values, these newly industrialized states nurtured economies that were in many cases more dynamic; their business classes were also less "gentlemanly" and more aggressive than those of England. Moreover, the coal and iron that had supported England's early industrial achievement no longer offered the advantages they once had; they were also becoming far less easy to exploit as the more readily available sources of ore were exhausted.

The loss of commercial supremacy had profound repercussions on British social and economic life. England in the 1920's was already a fully industrialized nation whose prosperity depended upon the ability to sell manufactured goods to other nations and to purchase needed raw materials. During the interwar years, the effects of England's failure to sustain its worldwide commercial advantage were cushioned somewhat by the markets and raw materials of British colonies and by the continuing returns to Britain from earlier investments in its empire. Even so, Britain was plagued from 1920 to the late 1930's by a high rate of unemployment. Some ten per cent of the labor force was receiving relief payments ("the dole") during all of the 1920's, and during the Great Depression this figure rose to more than twenty per cent; many English workers spent their entire adult lives on the dole.

Britain's loss of military dominance, which also was associated with the emergence of other powerful industrial states, had equally profound effects. England could no longer take "bold" steps in foreign policy; it was forced to temporize and retreat. These two changes in England's world position, in combination with other factors, caused the British in the interwar decades to abandon the remnants of economic liberalism that had survived from the nineteenth century. Free trade went out the window in favor of imperial preference, and the state began to intervene more and more frequently in all aspects of the nation's economic and social life.

Much of the increase in state involvement in social problems was brought about by the Conservative Party, Britain's governing party during most of the period of the two world wars. With the erosion of the liberal idea, the Liberal Party, which had reached the peak of its strength in the late nineteenth century, quickly deteriorated. By the 1930's the political scene was dominated by a Conservative Party committed to preserving tradition and the rule of the "better" element—within a social-welfare framework—and a Socialist party, the Labor Party, committed to a Socialist community.

These changes were accelerated by World War II and have continued into the postwar era. Since the war, the British Empire has gradually been liquidated and England reduced to the status of a second-rank power. Britain has also lost whatever advantages of natural resources it once possessed. The British now find that other European countries, not to mention the United States, the Soviet Union, and Japan, are cutting more deeply into their share of the world's markets. In fact, since 1945 the British growth rate has been slow compared with that of other European nations (see Table 2.1), and the British have experienced several acute financial crises. The decline in England's ability to compete on the world market has forced the British to relinquish its insular position and to join other European nations in supranational economic arrangements—moves that obviously herald the end of the once formidable British Commonwealth and England's stance as a European nation not quite part of Europe. The postwar position of England has not, of course, been entirely desperate. In absolute terms, the British standard of living has continued to rise, and England led the Continent in making the breakthrough to "the consumer society."

TABLE 2.1.   GROWTH OF THE EUROPEAN AND UNITED STATES ECONOMY

Movement in total volume of output (1913 = 100)

	France	Germany (F.R.)[1]	United Kingdom	United States
1870	51.1	30.0	39.1	16.9[2]
1880	57.5	38.7	45.1	
1890	72.2	51.3	69.1	41.5
1900	87.9	68.4	85.8	60.4
1901	—	73.0	85.5	67.2
1902	—	76.1	86.6	67.9
1903	—	78.9	84.2	71.2
1904	—	81.1	84.7	70.3
1905	—	80.3	88.0	75.5
1906	—	81.8	91.7	84.2
1907	—	82.0	93.1	85.5
1908	—	89.9	89.5	78.5
1909	—	91.6	91.3	88.1
1910	—	95.1	93.7	89.0
1911	—	96.0	95.7	91.9
1912	—	92.2	99.3	96.2
1913	100.0	100.0	100.0	100.0
1920	77.6	—	—	114.5
1921	71.8	—	—	112.0
1922	88.2	—	—	118.3
1923	95.3	—	—	133.8
1924	110.6	—	112.1	138.0
1925	110.6	90.3	113.4	141.3
1926	116.5	92.9	114.4	150.6
1927	111.8	102.1	124.5	152.2
1928	118.8	106.7	126.5	154.0
1929	130.6	106.2	128.7	163.4
1930	129.4	104.9	128.6	149.1
1931	123.5	96.7	130.0	140.8
1932	115.3	89.5	131.3	120.9
1933	115.3	94.9	139.3	117.7
1934	112.9	103.4	144.0	128.0
1935	108.2	112.8	149.3	144.7
1936	107.1	122.5	155.2	159.7
1937	110.6	136.4	155.8	172.6
1938	109.4	149.9	158.3	163.3
1948	107.7	110.9	177.3	269.6
1949	120.9	128.9	182.8	269.3
1950	130.3	157.3	189.7	293.0
1951	138.2	173.8	196.3	312.7
1952	141.7	188.3	195.8	325.9
1953	146.0	202.4	204.0	339.4
1954	153.1	217.5	212.0	334.0
1955	162.0	242.5	218.8	360.9

[1] Figures adjusted to eliminate the effect of territorial change.
[2] Figures for 1871.

Adapted from Angus Maddison, *Economic Growth in the West* (New York: Twentieth Century Fund, 1964), pp. 201, 202 (reprinted by permission of the publisher); and *U.N. Statistical Yearbook, 1968*, pp. 217–227.

TABLE 2.1—*Cont.*

Movement in total volume of output (1913 = 100)

	France	Germany (F.R.)[1]	United Kingdom	United States
1956	170.1	259.2	224.6	367.6
1957	180.3	273.2	228.0	375.0
1958	183.4	282.1	227.3	369.2
1959	187.8	301.0	234.3	394.0
1960	199.8	327.4	244.3	403.1
1961	208.8	344.5	248.8	410.9
1962	223.5	358.1	251.0	442.6
1963	234.4	375.7	259.7	467.2
1964	250.8	408.6	279.3	495.3
1965	256.2	430.5	288.0	537.5
1966	272.6	438.7	290.2	586.6

Also, government policies managed to insure full employment for most of the postwar years.

This breakthrough toward a consumer society has exerted a deep influence on English social life. So, too, has government directed by a Socialist party. The Labor Party, between 1945 and 1951, nationalized about twenty per cent of the British economy during the immediate postwar years; it also considerably expanded welfare services and devised a tax program to reduce income inequalities. The Conservative Party, which came back to power in 1951, continued most of the Labor Party's program, and by the early 1960's the Conservatives had even begun reluctantly to admit the need for some form of national planning to enable England to modernize her economy. Although the Conservatives moved slightly toward a "freer" economy, the welfare state and a mixed economy are now broadly accepted as the pattern for England's future. The Labor Party, which returned to power in 1964, has moved still further in the direction of revamping and modernizing the economy even as it has attempted to increase and further rationalize social-welfare benefits. However, the Labor government's ability to carry out its program has been hampered by the economic difficulties that face the country.

Meanwhile, class differences in dress, language, and culture are disappearing, together with the traditional class attitudes of deference and responsibility. It is not so much that the working class has adopted middle-class values, but rather that England is moving in the direction of a more homogeneous mass culture that, in its most important aspects, resembles that of the United States.

The changes have had political ramifications. The Labor Party, in the past ten years, has de-emphasized many of its old-time slogans. It continues to press for social equality and social reform, for national planning and for some further nationalization, but its approach is self-consciously pragmatic. Further, it has tried to change its image from that of a nineteenth-century working-class party to one that stresses its ability to modernize and reform an "archaic" social and political structure. Even the left within the party, while more ideological in its approach, now thinks of itself less as the vanguard of the working class and more as a group dedicated to restructuring English social life in ways that take into account the needs of a "post-industrial" society.

The Conservatives, too, have responded to the appeal of modernization. They no longer woo the electorate as the party of the "better elements" in British society whose mission it is to govern in the interest of all. Instead, they have come more and more to emphasize

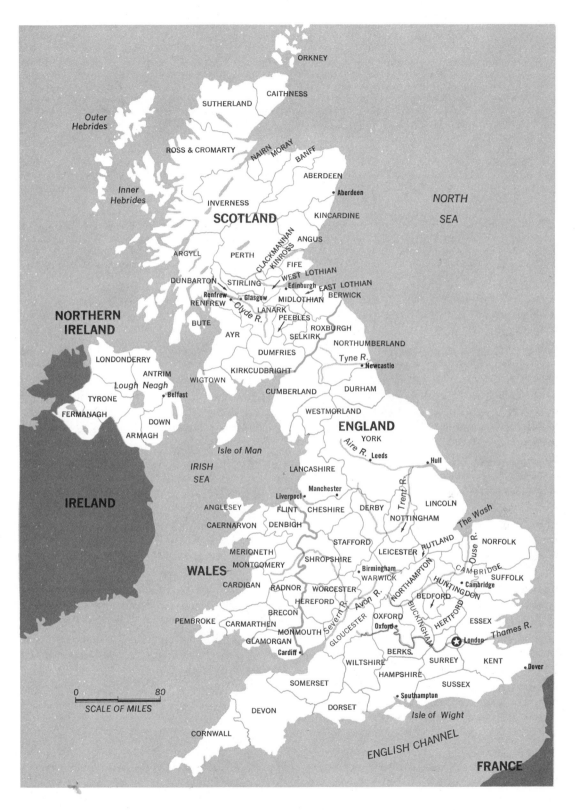

MAP 2.1. THE UNITED KINGDOM

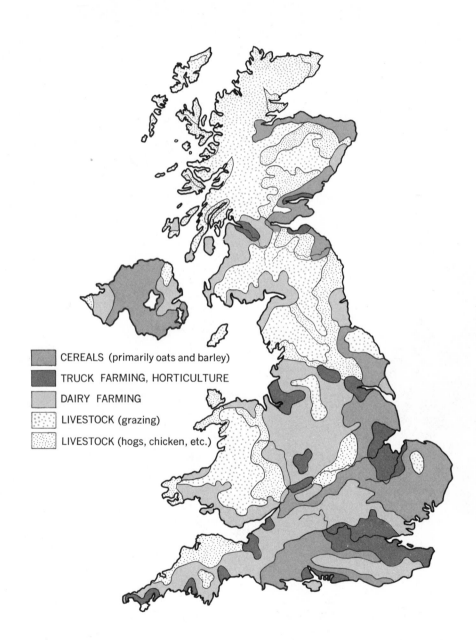

CEREALS (primarily oats and barley)

TRUCK FARMING, HORTICULTURE

DAIRY FARMING

LIVESTOCK (grazing)

LIVESTOCK (hogs, chicken, etc.)

MAP 2.2. ENGLISH AGRICULTURAL RESOURCES

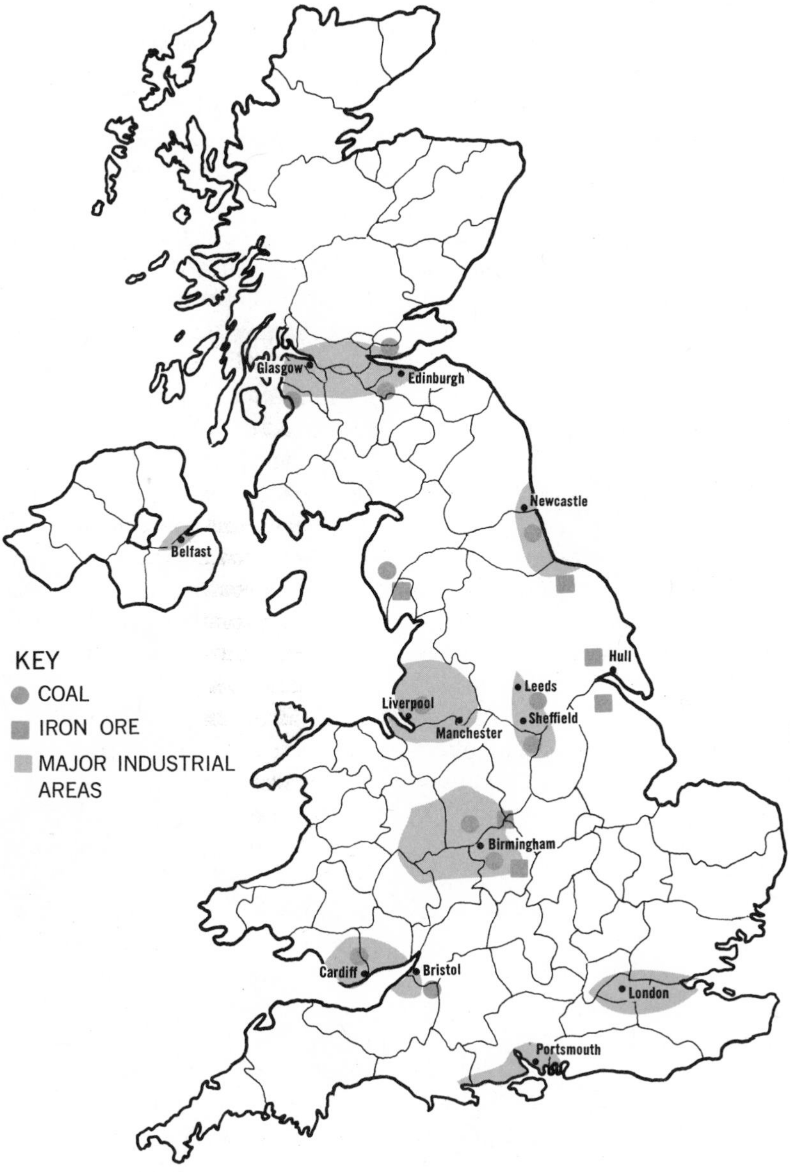

MAP 2.3. ENGLISH INDUSTRIAL RESOURCES

their party's democratic organization and its promise to give the electorate what the electorate wants. At the same time they have accepted the need to "get Britain moving" by calling for technological innovation and professional expertise. Elements representing an older orientation are still influential within the party, but they are very much on the defensive.

Class tensions and differences have certainly not disappeared; in fact, nothing is more infuriating than the vestiges of an old order that is no longer dominant. Thus, such institutions as the public school and the gentlemen's club are assailed by the younger British intellectuals as galling reminders of an outworn, aristocratic style of life. Indeed, the decline in British power has led more and more intellectuals to raise doubts about other English institutions—including even the structure of Parliament.

Other problems are surfacing as well. All forms of traditional authority are under attack, as are traditional taboos and standards in the area of sexual relations, styles of dress, and attitudes toward work and leisure. Population growth, although slow in comparison with that of other nations, is creating immense problems for urban living. To the natural growth of population has been added the greater mobility provided by private automobiles; together they pose serious transportation problems for London and other cities. And ahead for Britain, as for all advanced countries, lies the revolution in automation that raises issues of a new kind, issues that are likely to be as significant for British society as were the great changes England pioneered in the nineteenth century.

THE ENGLISH CONSTITUTION: England today is officially a constitutional monarchy. It is also a parliamentary regime in that sovereignty resides in a popularly elected House of Commons, from which the prime minister and the cabinet are drawn and to which they are both responsible.

Although British practice and ideas have been among the more important sources of modern constitutionalism, England is the only nation of those we are studying that lacks a formal constitution.[2] The reasons for this lie in the nature of the English community. Except for a short republican interregnum, the English have never believed it necessary to transform radically the institutions of the society according to an abstract model, or even to think systematically about the assumptions on which those institutions rest. Moreover, national unity was achieved before the idea of constitution-making had become part of modern thought. The English constitution, therefore, consists of a series of historical documents and legislative decrees, and, most important, a sense of what constitutional practice really is, for many statutes and customs that once gave legal sanction to a certain structure of political power are no longer operative simply because no one believes that they are.

By law, the government of the day is Her Majesty's Government. By law, the monarch summons the parliament, reads her program for the session from the throne, and may dismiss Parliament at will. She must give her assent to all legislation; she declares war, makes treaties of peace, and appoints all her ministers. This is all part of the traditional prerogative of the crown. In actuality, of course, the monarch does none of these things. All power resides in the cabinet and Parliament.

Many other examples could be cited. There is in England no constitutional right to free speech; nor are there any constitutional guarantees to freedom of travel. Theoretically, the government can prohibit both whenever it so desires, but this is rarely if ever done, and English citizens enjoy political freedoms that are perhaps unparalleled anywhere in the world, not excepting the United States. It used to be said that Parliament could do anything except make a man

---

[2] The appointment in 1968 of a constitutional commission to examine the political relationship between England and Wales and Scotland may change this.

into a woman or a woman into a man; it has, in fact, accomplished even this, through legislation dealing with transvestites.

The history of the English constitution, therefore, is essentially the history of British political culture. And yet key documents and legislative enactments do stand out, which in some ways help define its character. The first is Magna Carta. Historical interpretation has transformed the charter from what it actually was—an attempt by a feudal barony to retain some of its rights—into one of the founts of English liberty. Thus, the charter's primary function is symbolic, and as a symbol it illustrates the essential continuity of English institutions. It did, nevertheless, contain a number of points that enabled it to serve a symbolic function. Among these was the famous provision in Article 39 that no free man might be arrested, imprisoned, dispossessed, outlawed, or exiled, or harassed in any other way save by the lawful judgment of his peers or the law of the land.

Other documents include the Petition of Right, drawn up in 1628 to "reassert" the "traditional" rights of Englishmen against Charles I, and the Bill of Rights of 1689, which guaranteed the legislative supremacy of Parliament, particularly in the matter of levying taxes. The Act of Settlement in 1701 established the authority of the parliament beyond all question by changing the order of succession to the throne, and requiring that all future monarchs belong to the Church of England. To these must be added the Reform Bill of 1832, and later acts which gradually extended the suffrage, as well as the Parliament Act of 1911, which curtailed the powers of the House of Lords.

In the last analysis, however, the conventions of the constitution are still the most significant elements of its character. It is difficult to summarize these because they are constantly changing, as new legislation is passed and as new practices become accepted. But among the more important are the following:

1. Where Parliament has not legislated,

the common law as interpreted by the judiciary is supreme, and the individual Englishman is free to do anything not prohibited by law.

2. In matters of legislation, Parliament is absolutely sovereign; no authority, not even the courts, can override it. It can legislate on any matter it chooses.

3. The executive, in the form of the cabinet, is chosen from Parliament and is responsible to it. This means that if it loses majority support in Parliament on issues of major importance, it must resign to allow the opposition to form a government or call for a new election.

4. Parliament itself must meet at least once a year.

5. Finally, England is a unitary state. Local authorities may be altered, disbanded, or changed by act of Parliament.

The foregoing represents only the barest outline of what the British constitution is. In some sense, any attempt at a brief summary of its elements is a distortion. Our description of it will be reasonably complete only when we have concluded an examination of the complex interrelationship of British political institutions.

2. THE PATTERN OF FRENCH DEVELOPMENT

Although it is smaller than Texas, France is the largest country in Western Europe. Its extent and location give it a variety of climates. The north and west share England's mists; in Alsace, winters are colder and summers warmer; and in the south the nation is warmed by the Mediterranean. France's temperate climate and rich soil have been conducive to the development of a highly diverse agriculture ranging from the production of wheat and oats to grapes. The nation does not possess a river system that penetrates the interior as the Rhine does in Germany, but even so the lack of mountain barriers could have permitted far more effective railway and canal systems had the French applied their resources to this end. France has less coal than England or Germany, but it has extensive reserves of iron ore and the world's largest deposits of bauxite, from which aluminum is made. (See Maps 2.5 and 2.6.)

France's wealth in natural resources, in other words, compares favorably with that of the other major West European countries. Yet French economic growth in the nineteenth century and the first half of the twentieth lagged far behind that of England and, later, Germany; consequently, the dominance that France had once held on the Continent declined steadily after Waterloo. French population stabilized, and in certain periods even declined, which further weakened the nation's industrial and military potential. And over a long interval, political instability continually stymied efforts by the community to solve common problems. In 1958, when the Fifth Republic was established and Frenchmen adopted their twelfth constitution since 1789, the event prompted a good many anecdotes; one told of the man who, in trying to buy a copy of the new constitution, was informed by his bookseller that he did not carry periodical literature.

The Fifth Republic, however, has provided a fairly effective government, even though under Charles de Gaulle it was also fairly authoritarian. At the same time, the French economy has moved forward steadily and at a pace that has astonished economic analysts, despite some recent difficulties. (See Table 2.1, p. 47.)

The history of France's industrial backwardness and political instability has long been examined and argued by students of French life. The causes have been said to lie in certain basic traits of French national character—in the extreme individualism of the French, for example—or in the unresolved tensions generated by the French Revolution that irreconcilably divided the French public. Political scientists have sought the sources of political instability in France's inability to develop a strong and stable executive under the Third and Fourth Republics,

and they have blamed the weakness of the French executive at least partially on the particular constitutional arrangements adopted by the country. None of these explanations is completely satisfactory, although all contain elements of truth. Rather, the social and political patterns of contemporary France can best be understood as part of a general European pattern; within that pattern, it was such crucial factors in French history as the nature of its feudal inheritance, the manner in which national unity was consummated, and the character of religious and industrial development that set the conditions under which France became a modern state—and also created its seemingly intractable social and political difficulties.

THE CREATION OF THE FRENCH STATE: The final destruction of the French nobility's power and the creation of a relatively modern state was the work of Louis XIV. The last attempt by the aristocracy to assert its prerogatives culminated in the rebellion of 1650–1652, when the king was only in his early teens. It was crushed by Cardinal Mazarin, the boy king's chief minister, who followed his victory with policies fashioned to make sure that this kind of challenge to the throne could never occur again. Louis himself continued those policies, stripping the aristocracy of the remainder of its traditional authority and establishing his absolute political control over France in theory if not in practice.

The process of nation building had begun much earlier, in the tenth century under the Capetian kings, who gradually extended their authority from Paris and its environs until it encompassed all of France. Their efforts, and those of the Valois kings who succeeded them in the fourteenth century, to transform France into a nation, had been effectively hindered both by the complex territorial and dynastic struggles that Europe experienced during these centuries and by the religious wars that exploded after the Protestant Reformation. In contrast with England, political unity was imposed on France by a monarchy which was forced to rely upon its own centralized bureaucracy to create the framework of a modern state.

The French nobility lost its authority but not its privileges. It became a class largely composed of absentee landlords who spent their time at court and insisted resolutely upon their class prerogatives when the substance of their power was gone. While the British aristocracy was sufficiently self-confident to permit a blurring of the lines between itself and the newer commercial strata of society, the French aristocracy accentuated traditional distinctions. The result was that the French monarchy was unable to carry its centralizing policies to a logical conclusion. In England a gentry that identified itself with the nation provided administrative personnel who engendered social and economic as well as political unity. But France remained in some sense a confederation of cities and provinces, each maintaining its own customs and, to a considerable extent, its own laws. In fact, France was not even a free-trade area within its own borders until the Revolution of 1789.

THE REFORMATION IN FRANCE: France differed from England in her religious experience as well. Calvinism gained a substantial foothold in France, but Protestants, mostly Huguenots, remained a minority. After a series of bitter religious wars, a compromise was effected in the Edict of Nantes (1598), which temporarily stabilized the religious situation; it granted the Protestant minority political rights equal to those of Catholics, and permission to retain fortified towns. Under Louis XIII and Louis XIV, however, the rights of the Protestant minority were gradually curbed, and finally, by revoking the Edict of Nantes in 1685, Louis XIV tried to force their conversion to the Roman confession. Thousands of French Protestants chose instead to emigrate.

France thus continued to be a Catholic nation. The intellectuals of the Enlightenment, drawing philosophical inspiration from observing the English scene, confronted in France a society still operating on the basis of highly traditional mores. The rigidity of French society was such that many reformers opted for a root change in its institutions and reacted against the existing regimes with millenarian fervor. And because liberals believed that the most backward aspects of French culture were derived from the Catholic tradition and maintained by the Catholic Church, liberalism in France was strongly anticlerical.

POLITICAL REVOLUTION: The revolutionaries of 1789 had a multitude of aims. The peasants, for the most part, simply wanted land or the redress of certain grievances under the old law. The intellectuals, who drove and directed the Revolution, wanted to establish a representative republic of free men with a rational political and legal structure. They were supported by the commercial classes, who regarded the ancient privileges and the feudal, local rights and restrictions as inhibiting the development of the good society.

The Revolution of 1789, which centered in Paris, achieved only some of these goals—and a rift in French society that still influences French politics. As authority disintegrated, the Revolution quickly slipped under the control of its most radical elements. The extreme radicals were abetted unwittingly by both the resistance of conservative elements in French society and the hostility of Europe. The increasing antipathy of the church and segments of both the aristocracy and bourgeoisie, plus the threat of invasion by other monarchs who denounced the Revolution, served only to create a climate in which the radicals could gain support for ever more extreme policies. Further, the breakdown of authority and the ferment of ideas produced a hypertrophy of political organizations, each dedicated to its own ideological vision.

The radicals could not remake France completely, despite—and partly because of—

the bloodbath they started. They did not have the power to gain full control, and the great majority of the people were not sympathetic to the revolutionary changes they envisioned. The more conservative forces—the church, the aristocracy, large elements of the peasantry, and some elements of the middle classes —were unable, of course, to turn the clock back. Out of the resulting chaos emerged France's first "democratic despot": Napoleon. Promising to preserve the best of the Revolution and to restore order, Napoleon also sought to reunify Europe under France, all in the name of the principles of the Enlightenment. His rule was based on both force and demagogic appeal.

The dynamism of Napoleon's dictatorship eventually led to its downfall, and the Bourbon monarchy was restored by France's enemies. Many of the emigrés, nobles who had fled France, especially during the Terror, returned hoping to restore the old regime. This was impossible, and Louis XVIII, having learned from his English exile, did not even wish to do so. Those on the radical right did, however, institute their own reign of terror in the countryside against the remnants of the Jacobins, the extreme left wing of the revolutionary parties, and they did restore most of the prerogatives of the Catholic Church.

Nevertheless, a return to the times before the Bastille was impossible; the Revolution and Napoleon had made momentous, permanent changes in French life. For one thing, French administration had been unified and centralized. Reacting decisively against localism and diversity, provinces had been replaced, administratively, with a set of 83 departments (which, by design, lacked any geographic or historical unity) responsible directly to the central government in Paris. For another, the traditional and confusing conglomeration of three hundred local legal systems of the old regime had been superseded by a civil code that drew upon Roman law and codified these local customs. The judicial reforms of Napoleon provided France with an integrated legal system based as nearly as possible upon a minimum set of general assumptions. The Napoleonic Code eliminated feudal privileges and modernized the law of property, satisfying those who wanted a legal system conducive to trade and commerce. These issues of law and administration were settled by the Revolution. What had not been settled was who should rule and for what ends. By the end of the Revolution one can already distinguish at least five ideological groupings in French politics, each with a different answer to these two questions.

The first to appear was that of the "ultras," who wished to restore the old regime as nearly as possible. Composed of the emigré aristocracy, segments of the peasantry, and some elements of the middle class, this group heaped anathemas on the Revolution and all its works. The ultras believed that any concession to liberalism or secularism could lead only to chaos; they were strongly supported, consequently, by the dominant elements among the Catholic clergy and the more religious citizens. The Revolution, they argued, had attempted to destroy the Catholic Church; the church therefore would remain hostile to all ideas associated with the Revolution. Many of the ultras, including a good part of the clergy, had originally sympathized with the idea of reform, but the radical outcome of the Revolution froze them in a conservative mold that was not to be broken for almost a century. The church's antipathy to reform carried over into Italy, Spain, and other predominantly Catholic countries in which liberals mounted violent attacks against "clericalism"—which helps explain the conservative cast of European Catholic thought throughout the nineteenth century.

The other extreme was represented by Jacobin remnants who, after the Bourbon restoration, still believed that the Great Revolution had yet to be consummated and who continued to hope and fight for an egalitarian, democratic, and secular republic. Because the attitude of the clergy remained conservative, this group was consistently anticlerical.

On the left wing of the Jacobins there developed a third group, quite small, that carried Jacobinism to its ultimate egalitarian conclusions: it called for a Socialist republic and the communalization of property.

A variety of more "moderate" groups occupied intermediate positions between the ultra right and the Jacobin left. The two most important were the Doctrinaires and the Bonapartists. The Doctrinaires accepted some of the fruits of the Revolution and wished to see a constitutional monarchy established on the English model. They were primarily associated with the House of Orléans, which claimed, after the House of Bourbon, the right of succession to the throne. The Bonapartists, too, accepted a compromise between the Revolution and traditional institutions, but they rallied around the Napoleonic legend and extolled the greatness that Napoleon had brought to France.

Between 1815 and 1870, France went through three revolutions and one coup d'etat. Frenchmen were governed successively by a semi-absolutist monarchy, a constitutional monarchy, a radical democratic republic, a presidential regime, an empire, and finally, in 1871, by a conservative and "temporary" republic—the Third Republic —that lasted until 1940. None of the political ideologies described above was strong enough to dominate the others, and because they were violently hostile to one another, no enduring compromise was possible. Advocates of various policies became more intransigent with the years, and attempts at compromise only resulted in new, divisive political tendencies. Thus, Frenchmen slaughtered Frenchmen in endless civil violence.

INDUSTRIAL CHANGE: In addition to political difficulties, France suffered the dilemmas concomitant with industrialization. In the cities there appeared an urban proletariat, largely alienated from the rest of the community and attracted sporadically to sundry revolutionary movements. Working-class alienation was the result of most of the same factors that had already fragmented French society. The aristocracy had lost its authority and sense of responsibility under the Bourbons, and the Revolution had convinced it that it had to resist any demands of the masses. France, then, lacked a governing class that could stand as an exemplar of civic responsibility to be emulated by the bourgeoisie, as had been the case in England. Further, large segments of the bourgeoisie had become frightened by the mobs that seemed to spring up in the wake of reform movements. Many felt that concessions to workers' demands would open the way for another revolution—and the loss of their property. The radicalism of the French working class only confirmed and strengthened these suspicions, and the uncompromising attitude of the middle classes, in turn, aggravated working-class alienation.

In France industrialization proceeded far more slowly than it did in England, partly because of a less fortuitous combination of crucial resources. Yet of greater importance were the traditional patterns of thought and action and the mutual hostility and suspicion of French social life. The French bourgeois lacked the confidence of his American, English, or German counterparts. He hoarded cash or invested his money overseas, hampering the growth of capital resources necessary to industry. The Revolution had divided agricultural estates into small peasant holdings that by French law descended equally to all children, not to the oldest son as in England; property was consequently divided into ever smaller parcels (see Table 2.2), inhibiting the modernization of agriculture. These property laws encouraged the peasant to limit the size of his family, and France's declining rate of population growth in turn delayed the creation of a large domestic market. Finally, to complete the circle, the French political stalemate inhibited formulation of sound policies that might have contributed to economic growth.

During the nineteenth century, therefore, despite periods of dramatic growth, France

TABLE 2.2. LANDHOLDING IN FRANCE, 1862–1908

Size of holding, in acres	Number of holdings			
	1862	1882	1892	1908
Very small: less than 2½	—	2,167,667	2,235,405	2,087,851
Small: 2½–25	2,435,401	2,635,030	2,617,558	2,523,713
Medium: 25–100	636,309	727,222	711,118	745,862
Large: 100–250	154,167	142,088	105,391	118,497
Very large: over 250	—	—	33,280	29,541

Adapted from Shepherd B. Clough, *The Economic Development of Western Civilization* (New York: McGraw-Hill Co., 1959), p. 300. Reprinted by permission of the publisher.

slipped behind other European nations. Its population increased by only five million between 1850 and 1940, while England's rose by 19 million and Germany's by 35 million. In 1814 one out of every seven Europeans west of Russia was French; by 1914 the proportion was one in ten.[3] As other European countries industrialized, France's economic importance also waned. In fact, the French population until after World War I was predominantly small-town and rural. As late as 1930, some thirty per cent of the labor force worked in agriculture, and most industrial workers were employed by small establishments.

THE THIRD AND FOURTH REPUBLICS: The year after France's defeat in the Franco-Prussian War of 1870, a National Assembly was elected, and it convened to draft a new constitution. Monarchists dominated the assembly, although there was also a strong Bonapartist minority consisting of about two hundred of the more than six hundred deputies. But the monarchists were hopelessly divided into Bourbons and Orléanists, and the only thing their leaders could agree on was to establish temporarily a "conservative" republic with a strong president who would later be replaced by a king. The monarchists never reached any larger agreement, pri-

[3] C. Gordon Wright, *France in Modern Times* (Chicago: Rand McNally and Company, 1960), p. 226.

marily because the count of Chambord, of the House of Bourbon, insisted upon the Bourbon flag and would not accept the tricolor. It is not without reason that Adolphe Thiers, one of the architects of the Third Republic, ironically called the count "The George Washington of France."

The Third Republic was thus established *faute de mieux*. It maintained itself, nevertheless, against both the right and the left, gaining support as it grew older and more familiar. It survived also because it did very little to resolve the tensions inherent in French life. The divisions in the nation were so serious that systematic politics were difficult to implement. Even so, the achievements of the period from 1871 to 1914 should not be ignored. True, the French did fall further and further behind the English and the Germans, but the last quarter of the nineteenth century witnessed the creation of a modern banking system; substantial rail and road construction; the beginnings of a system of free, secular education; and, from 1880 to 1910, reasonably healthy economic growth. Indeed, by 1914 it seemed as if France might achieve political stability and social reconciliation. The Catholic Church had been disestablished and the important segments of the Catholic hierarchy had come to accept the legitimacy of the republican regime. The idea of restoring the monarchy had all but disappeared; even conservatives had come to accept the republic. And within the working class, despite the lack of social measures, reformism was replacing revolutionary tendencies.

World War I and its aftermath, however, caused new disruptions, new problems, new tensions. France suffered more than any other Western European participant in the war. To the destruction of farms, homes, and factories and the loss of manpower was added the moral ferment of the twenties, the Depression of the 1930's, and the emergence of a powerful and highly expansionist National Socialist regime in Germany. The Depression brought with it an intensification of radicalism on both the right and the left; semi-Fascist organizations dedicated to aping Italy or Germany grew in strength, and so did the Communist Party. The role of the Roman church in the Spanish Civil War once again brought to the surface the latent antagonism between French Catholics and anticlericals.

The polarization and fragmentation of French politics did not bring down the republic, but they weakened the regime, and they help explain why France collapsed so quickly in 1940. During the German occupation and the Vichy government, conservative elements dominated politics in France, and while neither Marshal Pétain nor Pierre Laval were Fascists, the government they established substituted authority for liberty and sought to strengthen traditional institutions, including the Catholic Church.[4] The support that many elements of the business community, alarmed by the Communist Party's growth in the interwar years, gave to Pétain, and their collaboration with the Germans, compromised them seriously with other groups in France.

With the end of World War II, therefore,

the ideological right was largely discredited. In the first postwar elections, left-wing parties—the Communists, the Socialists, and the Popular Republican Movement (*Mouvement républicain populaire*—M.R.P.)— dominated the political scene. The M.R.P. was something new to French politics, though it had long antecedents—a lay Catholic party committed to democratic institutions. At first the Communists behaved with moderation and the three parties cooperated to draft a new constitution, a circumstance singular enough to cause a wave of optimism to sweep through France. At last a "left democratic" republic had been established. At last France was starting, under the Fourth Republic, with a clean slate.

The optimism did not last long. The three parties first collided with General Charles de Gaulle, then the temporary president, over the new constitution. De Gaulle wanted a strong executive, modeled after the American presidency. The left, on the other hand, associated a strong presidency with conservatism in general, and, in particular, with the personal dictatorship of Napoleon III.

After defeating de Gaulle on the constitutional issue, the parties fell to quarreling among themselves. The Communists were in theory dedicated to revolution and to the establishment of a Marxist utopia, and in practice they were dominated by Moscow. As the cold war between East and West grew more intense, the Communists became more intransigent. The Socialists and the M.R.P. were divided by the clerical and other issues, though they joined in opposing the Communists.

By 1947 the left coalition had disintegrated and the Communists had been forced from participation in the government, taking with them more than 25 per cent of the electorate and the support of more than 30 per cent of the deputies in Parliament. At the same time, de Gaulle and his followers had created the Rally of the French People (*Rassemblement du peuple français*—R.P.F.)

---

[4] Pétain was given credit for stopping the Germans at Verdun in the First World War and later became chief of the French armies. A national hero, he was called upon to form a government at Vichy when France surrendered to the Germans in 1940. Laval, twice premier of France in the 1930's, took over Pétain's Vichy government in 1942. He was tried and executed for treason after the war. Pétain was also convicted of treason; his sentence was commuted to life imprisonment and he died in 1951.

dedicated to a new constitution that would provide France with effective government, a strong president, and the return of greatness. Initially, the R.P.F. received substantial support from the people and within Parliament; however, both the Socialists and the M.R.P. were suspicious of the party and de Gaulle, believing them to have as their ultimate, and devious, purpose the restoration of an authoritarian regime.

In the 1951 elections, the R.P.F. and the Communists together received approximately 45 per cent of the popular vote and therefore, by law, almost that proportion of seats in the assembly. As a result, the center and center-left parties were thrown together in a coalition mortised only by the desire to preserve the institutions of the Fourth Republic. The situation grew more complicated as the hitherto quiescent French right revived and, in old and new conservative groupings, won ever larger percentages of the popular vote. Also, the very multiplicity of parties and the weakness of the broadly based coalition governments encouraged the formation of additional parties and policies.

The result—so familiar to Frenchmen—was political stagnation and instability. Under the Fourth Republic as under the Third, the prime minister and the cabinet were responsible to the parliament; that is, they could govern only if they had the support of a majority in the national legislature. The coalition majorities that could be arranged in the assembly were always minimal majorities, so that no particular government lasted very long; and because opinions within any government were as diverse as the parties making up the coalition to support it, no government could act decisively. Even after de Gaulle dissolved the R.P.F. and retired from politics in 1953, the situation did not substantially improve.

A NEW FRANCE? Important changes were, nevertheless, taking place in France. France's birth rate, which had remained fixed for one hundred years, began to rise, and suddenly the nation was becoming one of the youngest in Western Europe. In 1946 responsibility for overhauling large segments of the French economy had been entrusted to a group of dedicated civil servants led by Jean Monnet, and despite recurring financial crises, Monnet's work was beginning to pay off: the French economy entered upon a period of rapid expansion, increasing as fast as that of any other country in Europe.

By the 1950's, this economic rejuvenation was yielding higher living standards for the French people. For the first time since 1913, the economic position of the working class improved materially; and consumer goods, such as automobiles and television sets, began to flood the market at prices the worker could afford. The nation's growth rate was aided by greater commercial cooperation between France and her neighbors. For example, the European Coal and Steel Community, consisting of France, Germany, the Benelux countries (Belgium, the Netherlands, and Luxembourg), and Italy, created a common market in iron and coal that benefited all six countries.

Among younger businessmen a new optimism was manifesting itself—an optimism that encouraged investigation of and investment in the techniques of mass production. Part of it was based on the fact that the French working class was becoming politically apathetic, but the apathy was born of contentment rather than defeat. French workers might still vote out of historical and institutional loyalty for Communist candidates, but the circulation of the party's newspaper and its dues-paying membership had dropped precipitously.

The sons of peasants were leaving the land in ever greater numbers, and even those who remained in rural occupations found their vistas broadened by automobiles, which enabled them to get to the city frequently; by television sets; by vacationing urbanites; and by the variety of new products widely available. The impact of some of these changes on Roussillon, a small commune in the south of

France, is described by one American who had lived there on and off for brief periods after World War II.

Fifteen years ago several farms in . . . Roussillon did not have electricity; today there is not a single farm without it. It is usual for farms to have an electric pump; thus, with a bottled gas heater, hot running water is available. Electric refrigerators are not uncommon. When I called on some of my wine growing friends on a hot July day in 1961, they did not need to go to the cool wine cellar; there were bottles of rosé in the refrigerator.[5]

In the 1950's only one thing seemed to be keeping France from a real breakthrough in material prosperity: the colonial wars it was continually fighting to preserve the remnants of an empire. After the liquidation of the war in Indochina in 1954, French North Africa erupted in rebellion to renew the drain on French manpower and financial resources, though American aid alleviated this considerably. The Algerian situation constituted an especially difficult problem. The population of Algeria included some one million Europeans, many of them descendants of workers who had been exiled after the failure of revolutionary upheavals in the nineteenth century. Ties of sentiment, the influence of the European settler (the *colon*) in Algeria, and the possibility, after the discovery of huge oil reserves in the Sahara, of reducing French dependence upon Middle East oil supplies—all combined with a misplaced pride to prevent a settlement of the explosive Algerian issue. To these troubles were added a genuine and legitimate fear for the safety of Europeans in an Arab-dominated state and the stiff-necked attitude of professional soldiers who were angered by losing a series of small wars in which, they

believed, they had not received adequate moral and material support from the politicians. Tired of the government's vacillation and inability to make or implement effective decisions, and adamant in its insistence that Algeria was French, the army brought about the downfall of the Fourth Republic by supporting a rebellion by the Algerian colons in 1958. It was a rebellion that ushered in the return to power of Charles de Gaulle.

Basing his authority upon a referendum which gave him overwhelming popular support, de Gaulle established the Fifth French Republic, a republic led by a president with the strong powers he had always advocated. He instituted a series of dramatic new policies, the most important of which were the liquidation of the French African empire and an international role for France independent of the North Atlantic Treaty Organization (NATO). Domestically, the Fifth Republic has been associated with many significant reforms, but its major contribution has been to provide France with a stable government, one capable of carrying through consistent policies.

By 1965 the euphoria that had marked the early years of the de Gaulle regime was beginning to wear off. A variety of groups had been alienated by one policy or another and, after a period of domestic tranquillity, more and more Frenchmen were becoming restive under what they considered the growing authoritarianism of the regime. More importantly, perhaps, the end of the Algerian crisis and a prolonged period of stability encouraged the re-emergence of traditional political allegiances. De Gaulle won the presidential election of 1965 with a mere 55 per cent of the vote, after failing to obtain a majority on the first ballot—a considerable drop in his support from earlier "yes" votes ranging from 62 to more than ninety per cent on de Gaulle–sponsored referendums. Left-wing parties, electorally united in opposition to de Gaulle for the first time in 20 years, made significant gains in the parliamentary elections of 1967.

[5] Lawrence Wylie, "Social Change at the Grass Roots," in Stanley Hoffmann et al., *In Search of France* (Cambridge: Harvard University Press, 1963), pp. 168–169.

By the beginning of 1968, the regime's power was on the wane and traditional French political allegiances were reasserting themselves. Many commentators speculating on a post–de Gaulle political scene believed that, despite a number of thorny problems, French politics would have considerably greater stability even without the General than it had in the years before the Fifth Republic. The French Communist Party, though it had recouped some of its losses, had become more respectable and, having moved since the death of Stalin in the direction of greater autonomy, seemed likely to come eventually to accept the rules of the parliamentary game. The French working class, while still voting Communist in large numbers, was clearly no longer a revolutionary force, and the French business community had become increasingly oriented to creating a modern planned economy. For the immediate future, then, the issues that confronted the French seemed to lack the divisive force they once had. The gains made by the left in the 1967 election stemmed primarily from its ability to agree upon a candidate in the runoff elections. The left as a whole had never recovered from the debacle of 1958; indeed, it had been slowly declining in terms of popular vote since the beginning of the Fourth Republic, and there were indications that this decline would continue.

Certain elements of traditional French cultural and political style were changing only by degrees. Sustained group activity based on informal relationships was still far less frequent in France than in the United States; Frenchmen appeared to feel the need for external authority, even as they rebelled against it, much more than did Englishmen or Americans. Nor had de Gaulle's quasi-authoritarian regime encouraged the development of civic responsibility. Nevertheless, those changes which had occurred since World War II seemed likely to prove far more important in terms of future French development, or so it appeared to most students of French politics.

Then, in the spring of 1968, French students, hitherto relatively quiescent in comparison with their German and American counterparts, exploded into a mass confrontation with the government. This was closely followed by a massive general strike by French workers, who argued that their living standards had lagged behind growth in productivity. For a short time the government seemed on the verge of collapse. However, after making economic concessions to the workers and promising educational reform, de Gaulle called for new legislative elections, warning the populace that failure to support him would result in anarchy or worse. The result: the Gaullists won a massive electoral victory and all the major left-wing parties, despite Communist attacks on student militancy, suffered serious losses. Indeed, French workers, while desirous of wage increases, were not about to support an effort to overthrow the regime.

Yet despite de Gaulle's triumph in 1968, the strikes and his concessions to the workers produced a monetary and balance-of-payments crisis requiring measures of austerity and leaving the nation with a sense of malaise and drift. In addition, sporadic student violence continued at major universities.

De Gaulle's 1968 victory was a reaction to fears of chaos rather than the result of massive support for maintaining him in power. This was confirmed in the spring of 1969 when, staking his regime on the results of a national referendum on replacing the Senate with a new body based on regional representation, he was decisively defeated. The presidential election that followed found the left in disarray and brought to power Georges Pompidou, one of de Gaulle's former premiers. Creating a government that combined Gaullists with members of center and conservative groupings, Pompidou indicated that he would continue the broad outlines of de Gaulle's policies, but with a rather less authoritarian hand.

Thus, France is once again entering a new political phase, the fixed contours of which it is difficult to discern. What is clear is that many of the problems involved in France's transition from a traditional to a modern society have become less pressing. Even so, in France, as in other European nations, the politics of "postindustrial" society has yet to take shape.

FRENCH POLITICAL INSTITUTIONS: France's first written constitution was drawn up by the Constituent Assembly which sat from 1789 to 1791; it was signed by the king on September 2, 1791. Since that time, the French have been governed under at least 14 different constitutions and two provisional governments. The French experience is not unique. Rather, it accords with that of a large number of societies which have been so rent by fundamental social and group conflicts that they have been unable to reach lasting agreement even on the rules of the game.

Before the advent of the Third Republic, the constitutional form that lasted longest, although with substantial modifications along the way, was the Charter of 1814. The charter, which restored the monarchy, more or less followed the British constitutional model: the king was given wide executive authority in the field of foreign affairs; a legislature consisting of two houses, roughly equivalent to the House of Commons and the House of Lords, was formed; the king appointed his own cabinet from either chamber, and it was responsible to him. The king could also dissolve the parliament whenever he wished, and his assent was required before any proposal became law.

The charter was modified by the July Revolution of 1830 which brought Louis Philippe, of the House of Orléans, to the throne; it was destroyed by the February Revolution of 1848 and replaced by a republic. The constitution of the Second Republic, which lasted from 1848 to 1852, provided for a unicameral legislature and a popularly elected president. The republic was overthrown by Napoleon III, who established the Second Empire; that lasted until France's defeat by the Prussians.

The Third French Republic, which came into existence in 1871, lacked a formal constitution. If the word can be used at all, it can be done so only to designate a series of "temporary" organic laws. The Constituent Assembly had been dominated by monarchists and Bonapartists, and the only thing preventing the re-establishment of a monarchy was a split between those who favored the House of Orléans and those favoring the House of Bourbon; by the time that difference was resolved, the provisional government had become institutionalized—and dominated by republicans.

The organic laws established a two-house legislature: a chamber of deputies and a senate. The chamber was to be elected by universal manhood suffrage and the senate elected indirectly by local notables. The terms of office for senators were longer than those of deputies and their age requirements higher. In general, it was expected that the senate would act as a conservative counterweight to the chamber.

Executive authority was divided between a president and a council of ministers headed by a vice-president (premier). The president appointed all members of the council, or cabinet—including the vice-president—but they were collectively responsible to the legislature. The president was elected at a joint meeting of the two chambers for a period of seven years, and he was given the authority to dissolve the legislature when he wished— part of the traditional prerogative of the monarchy.

Within a fairly short time the power of the president almost disappeared, and real authority became vested in the legislature and in the council of ministers and its vice-president. Unlike the British system, however, both the cabinet and the premier remained extremely weak and the legislature made and remade governments at will. Between 1871 and 1898, France was governed by 39 cabinets, with an average life of eight months; between 1924 and 1940, by 37, with an average life of five months. Thus, an institutional pattern which resembled England's, at least on the surface, took on quite different characteristics; and the reasons for the differences lay in the fundamental fragmentation of French society and in the party system it produced. During the 1920's and 1930's, the French found it impossible to develop a coherent set of national policies with the institutions they had at their disposal. The differences in practice between the British and French systems can be epitomized in what became of the power of dissolution. In both England and France the power to dissolve the legislature and call for new elections was originally the privilege of the monarchy. In England it passed to the prime minister, who could and did use it. In France, it was explicitly placed in the hands of the president; but very soon it became accepted doctrine that this authority would not be used by either the president or the premier, for reasons which will become clear in later chapters.

At the end of World War II, therefore, most Frenchmen had no wish to return to the prewar paralysis of the Third Republic. A Constituent Assembly was elected to correct the faults in the governmental structure, which had plagued France for so many decades, by creating what was eventually to become the constitution of the Fourth Republic. In the debates over the new constitution, Charles de Gaulle, the first head of the provisional government, called for a strong executive in the form of a president. This option, however, was rejected by the political parties in control of the assembly, and the first constitution that was adopted placed government authority almost entirely in the hands of a popularly elected National Assembly. The constitution, however, was submitted to a referendum and defeated. In 1946 a second Constituent Assembly was elected to try again, and the new document strengthened somewhat the executive power of the premier and added a second, albeit very weak, chamber: the Council of the Republic. The constitution also provided for a president, but he

was to be only a figurehead, not unlike the president of the Third Republic after 1875. Although almost one-third of the eligible voters abstained, the new constitution was approved in a referendum in October 1946.

The efforts of those who sought to give France a more stable executive—partly by specifically providing the premier with authority to dissolve the legislature under certain, if limited, circumstances—proved fruitless. The Fourth Republic came very quickly to resemble the Third. Between 1947 and 1958, 21 cabinets came and went, only six of which lasted longer than eight months. The power of dissolution was used only once. The result, again, was immobility coupled with instability.

In June 1958, when the Fourth Republic collapsed and de Gaulle returned to power, he was granted authority to draw up a new constitution, which was submitted to the people in September. It was approved by 79 per cent of those voting.

The constitution of the Fifth Republic was essentially an attempt to fuse presidential and parliamentary government, and at the same time to transform parliamentary government into cabinet government. It also created a second chamber with more power than had been assigned to the Fourth Republic's Council of the Republic, but less than the amount delegated to the Third Republic's senate, whose name it adopted. For the first time in French history, a Constitutional Council was established for the purpose, among others, of passing on the constitutionality of both legislation and any standing orders governing its operation that the legislature might adopt. Hitherto, the assembly itself had been regarded as the arbiter of the constitutionality of its legislation and standing orders.

The French constitution can be amended easily; therefore, the powers of the Constitutional Council cannot be equated with those of the United States Supreme Court. A constitutional amendment may be enacted either by a simple majority of both chambers plus confirmation by a national referendum,

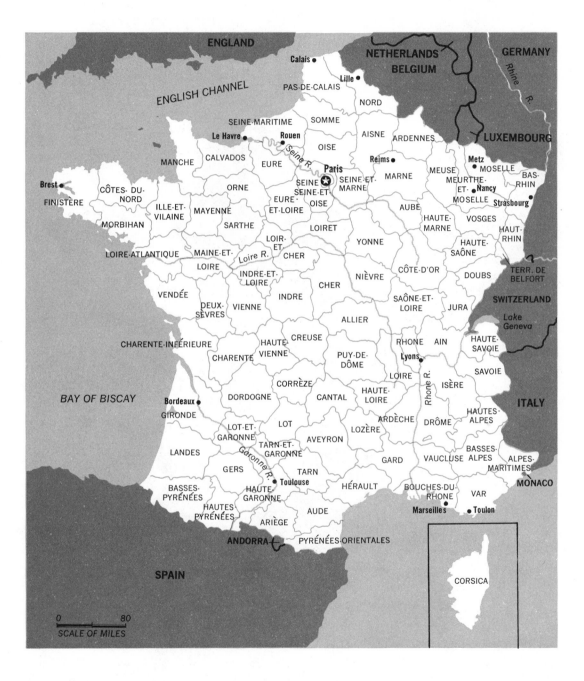

ENGLAND

ENGLISH CHANNEL

Calais

Lille

PAS-DE-CALAIS

NORD

NETHERLANDS
BELGIUM

GERMANY

Rhine R.

SEINE-MARITIME

SOMME

AISNE

ARDENNES

LUXEMBOURG

Le Havre

Rouen

Seine R.

OISE

MANCHE

CALVADOS

EURE

SEINE
SEINE-ET-
OISE

Paris

Reims

MARNE

MEUSE

Metz
MOSELLE

BAS-
RHIN

Brest

CÔTES- DU-
NORD

ORNE

EURE-
ET-LOIRE

SEINE-ET-
MARNE

MEURTHE-
ET-
MOSELLE

Nancy

FINISTÈRE

ILLE-ET-
VILAINE

MAYENNE

SARTHE

LOIRET

AUBE

HAUTE-
MARNE

VOSGES

Strasbourg

HAUT-
RHIN

MORBIHAN

LOIRE-ATLANTIQUE

MAINE-ET-
LOIRE

Loire R.

LOIR-
ET-
CHER

YONNE

HAUTE-
SAÔNE

TERR. DE
BELFORT

INDRE-ET-
LOIRE

CÔTE-D'OR

DOUBS

VENDÉE

DEUX-
SÈVRES

VIENNE

INDRE

CHER

NIÈVRE

SAÔNE-ET-
LOIRE

JURA

SWITZERLAND

Lake
Geneva

CHARENTE-INFÉRIEURE

CHARENTE

HAUTE-
VIENNE

CREUSE

ALLIER

RHONE

AIN

HAUTE-
SAVOIE

PUY-DE-
DÔME

Lyons

SAVOIE

BAY OF BISCAY

Bordeaux

GIRONDE

DORDOGNE

CORRÈZE

CANTAL

HAUTE-
LOIRE

LOIRE

Rhone R.

ISÈRE

HAUTES-
ALPES

ITALY

LOT-ET-
GARONNE

LOT

AVEYRON

LOZÈRE

ARDÈCHE

DRÔME

LANDES

TARN-ET-
GARONNE

Garonne R.

GARD

VAUCLUSE

BASSES-
ALPES

ALPES-
MARITIMES

GERS

Toulouse

TARN

HÉRAULT

BOUCHES-DU-
RHONE

VAR

MONACO

BASSES-
PYRÉNÉES

HAUTE-
GARONNE

AUDE

Marseilles

Toulon

HAUTES
PYRÉNÉES

ARIÈGE

ANDORRA

PYRÉNÉES-ORIENTALES

SPAIN

CORSICA

0   80
SCALE OF MILES

MAP 2.4. FRANCE

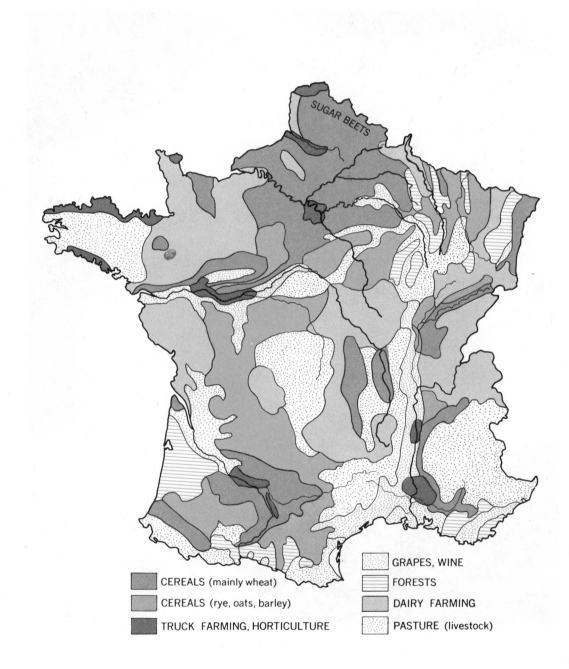

SUGAR BEETS

	CEREALS (mainly wheat)
	CEREALS (rye, oats, barley)
	TRUCK FARMING, HORTICULTURE

	GRAPES, WINE
	FORESTS
	DAIRY FARMING
	PASTURE (livestock)

MAP 2.5. FRENCH AGRICULTURAL RESOURCES

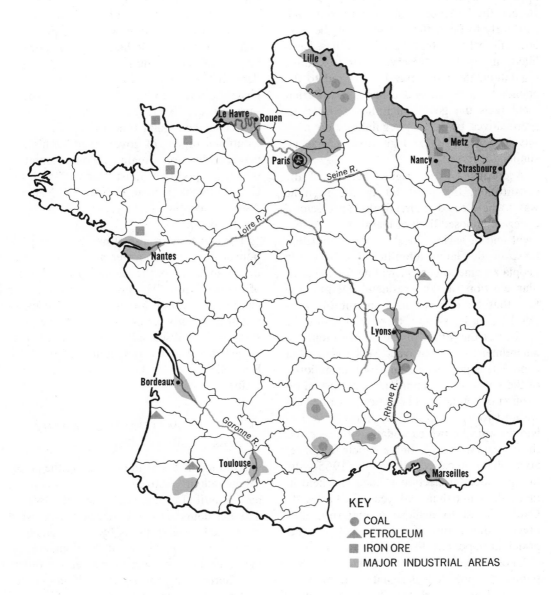

KEY

● COAL
▲ PETROLEUM
■ IRON ORE
■ MAJOR INDUSTRIAL AREAS

MAP 2.6. FRENCH INDUSTRIAL RESOURCES

or by three-fifths vote of the two chambers sitting jointly. The council, moreover, can rule on the constitutionality of a law only if its opinion is sought by the president, the prime minister, or the president of either house of the legislature. The citizen cannot appeal to it; neither can any courts of law. In fact, the jurisdiction of the council is such as clearly to favor the executive: if the government believes that Parliament has legislated in a field reserved for executive regulation, the issue may be referred to the council for a definitive decision. But if Parliament feels the government has usurped its prerogatives by issuing regulations on matters it believes to be legislative, it has no similar recourse.

According to the original version of the constitution, the president of the republic was to be elected indirectly by an electoral college composed both of members of Parliament and of various local notables. In 1962, however, de Gaulle submitted directly to the people an amendment providing for the popular election of the president. Despite the fact that he did not first submit his proposal to the legislature, thereby violating the spirit, not the letter, of the constitution, the amendment was approved. To be elected, a candidate must receive an absolute majority of the votes. If no candidate is successful on the first ballot, a second election must be held within two weeks, in which, unless there is a withdrawal, the two candidates who received the largest number of votes compete for office. Somewhat ironically, in December 1965—the first presidential election France had held in more than one hundred years—Charles de Gaulle failed to achieve a majority, thus precipitating a run-off between him and his principal opponent, François Mitterrand.

Under the constitution of the Fifth Republic, the president designates the premier, as he did under both the Third and Fourth Republics. However, this choice is now more than a mere formality, as the president once again can dissolve the legislature and call for new elections at any time and under any

conditions. The only limitations upon this power are the requirement that he consult with the premier and the presidents of both chambers, and that he cannot dissolve the legislature twice in the same year. In essence, this means that a refusal by the assembly to accept the premier designated by the popularly elected president could result in dissolution and a new election. While the president of the Third Republic had the same powers, he was elected by the legislature and dependent upon it. The president has also been given the power to take any measures necessary to preserve France's territorial integrity as well as the regular functioning of its "constitutional organs of government." This is a personal decision. Again, the only limitation is that the president must "consult" with the Constitutional Council. Further, the National Assembly continues to meet by right and cannot be dissolved.

The constitution also strengthens the position of the prime minister at the expense of the cabinet, and of the cabinet at the expense of the legislature. The premier's control over legislation has been broadened and the length of parliamentary terms reduced. These measures will be discussed in detail in Chapter 16, when the actual functioning of the Fifth Republic under de Gaulle will also be described.

3. THE PATTERN OF GERMAN DEVELOPMENT

Although France did not acquire the political and administrative structures of a modern nation until after the Revolution of 1789, its national boundaries had reached what were to be their modern limits by the seventeenth century. German historical development, on the other hand, has been considerably different. Germany's geographic position—its location in the heart of Europe and its lack of easily defended natural boundaries—complicated the problem of nation building. Germans, Slavs, and other ethnic and linguistic groups competed for the same territories in the middle ages, even as the German states competed for control of the entire German realm. The ethnic issue, in fact, was an important part of German foreign policy until after World War II. At least some of Hitler's territorial claims during the interwar years, including the Saar and parts of Poland and Czechoslovakia (some of which had been taken from Germany after World War I), were based on the existence of large German populations in those areas. At the end of World War II the Germans were expelled from Poland and Czechoslovakia, and although there are still persons in Germany who talk about incorporating some of the "Germanic" areas into the homeland again, no regime in the foreseeable future is likely to try to do so.

Today, East and West Germany together are smaller than Montana; West Germany alone is about the size of Oregon. The German Empire before World War I was somewhat larger than the two states combined. Imperial Germany was traversed by five large rivers, the Rhine, the Weser, the Elbe, the Oder, and the Vistula; all were made navigable for long distances by dredging and the large-scale program of canal building that was initiated in the late nineteenth century. A variety of soils and temperate climatic conditions permits considerable agricultural diversity. The country also contains substantial deposits of high-grade coal, the most important of which, in the Ruhr valley, is located very close to river transportation. German reserves of iron ore have never been large except between 1870 and 1914, when the French province of Alsace-Lorraine was incorporated into the German Reich. Then as before, however, the Germans relied heavily upon Swedish ores for the production of iron and steel. Aside from potash, Germany possesses no other mineral resources of note. (See Maps 2.8 and 2.9.)

In the dismemberment and partition of Germany after World War II, the nation lost the Oder River, which now forms the border between East Germany and Poland, as well as the croplands of Prussia. These territories contained some of the poorer German soils, however, and the production of certain important crops, such as wheat, in West Germany alone now equals or surpasses the prewar production of all of Germany. Further, the major coal resources of Germany and the center of its industrial production have always been located in the west.

Ever since the Nazi regime, studies of German history and politics have concentrated on attempts to understand the nation's historical bases and to answer the question of Germany's future commitment to democratic institutions. Both issues are best approached by examining German history within a general European framework.

RELIGION AND THE FORMATION OF THE GERMAN STATE: In the middle ages, Germany, like France, was divided into many principalities, baronies (both religious and secular), and free cities, all of which asserted their independence. Theoretically, the Germans were ruled by the emperor of the Holy Roman Empire, a traditional fiction originating in the Carolingian empire of Charlemagne and revived in the tenth century by Otto I, whose territories included what was to become the western part of Germany, Austria, and half of Italy. In theory, the empire was the successor of the Christian Roman Empire, and the emperor, who received his authority directly from God, was the supreme suzerain of Christian Europe even as the pope was its spiritual lord. Like Charlemagne before him, Otto was crowned emperor by the pope, whom he had nominated for the office.

Because the German monarchs were continually in conflict with the papacy and had to fight dynastic wars involving almost the entire continent, the myth of the Holy Roman Empire hindered the building of a German state. In the end the empire collapsed, but the attempt by Otto and his successors to achieve universal sway for it only thwarted the achievement of more modest goals.

The development of a national state in Germany was further delayed by the religious wars of the sixteenth and seventeenth centuries, wars which ravaged the countryside, left Germany divided into Protestant and Catholic states, and created a residue of bitterness that lasted well into the twentieth century. German Protestantism, the work of Martin Luther, shared with Calvinism an emphasis on order and a rigid puritanism. In other areas, however, including its insistence on respect for hierarchical authority, it was far more traditional.

Until the nineteenth century, the German realm was divided into 314 states and 1,475 estates—a total of 1,789 sovereignties. The two most powerful of these were the Protestant kingdom of Brandenburg-Prussia and the Catholic Austro-Hungarian Empire. Prussia had emerged as a state in the seventeenth century under the leadership of strong kings and a military aristocracy that had gradually expanded its borders. Its resources were limited and its ability to survive and enlarge, especially at the expense of the Slavs, was based on the disciplined military prowess of its landowning aristocracy, the Junkers. Long after the British and French aristocracies had abandoned private warfare for the world of culture or the life style of the gentleman farmer, the Junker remained a warrior. It was said of Prussia that the state was built around the army, not the army around the state.

The unity of Prussia had been achieved by the Hohenzollern dynasty, Frederick William of Brandenburg, The Great Elector, and his grandson and great-grandson, Frederick William I and Frederick II, "The Great," who died in 1786. Together they welded Prussia into an important force in Europe. They broke the power of the barony, but, unlike the Bourbons, brought the aristocracy into the service of the state somewhat on the English model.

The northern German princes had supported Luther against the papacy, and Lutheranism became the established state religion of Prussia. The Prussian temperament and Luther's emphasis upon self-discipline and submission to secular authority combined to create a religious ethos that reinforced the authoritarian character of German society. The Prussian state was to unify Germany and impress its personality upon all of Germany. Whereas in England national unity had been achieved before the development of liberal ideologies, and in France the Jacobin liberals were nationalists responsible for the final centralized political order, national unity was achieved in Germany in part as a reaction against liberalism. In England liberalism was indigenous; although imported to France, it was adopted by a native intelligentsia. In Germany, it came with a foreign invader and was always tainted as being fundamentally anti-German.

The foreign invader was Napoleon. During France's seven-year domination of Germany, which began in 1806, the number of petty German principalities was sharply reduced. Also, the administrative and legal systems of many German states were overhauled. Local lords lost jurisdiction over their peasants, who became subjects of the state legally free to move, migrate, or marry, and entitled to bring suits in courts of law. Jews, too, were granted full citizenship rights and permitted to leave the ghetto. By and large, then, the principles of the Enlightenment were applied to the reordering of social life.

Initially, many German intellectuals, including Immanuel Kant and the young Georg Wilhelm Friedrich Hegel, welcomed the French Revolution as the birth of a new freedom. In the aftermath of the Napoleonic Wars, however, the nationalism Napoleon had awakened became anti-French and anti-liberal. Many Germans thought their defeat was the result of weakness produced by disunity, and many thought the ideals of the French Revolution were foreign ideals, inferior to traditional German values. To be a liberal was to be anti-German, and therefore anti-national. Consequently, German liberalism during the nineteenth century was fairly ineffective, and liberals tended to share the nationalism embraced by other segments of the population.

While the Prussians, especially, rejected many of the values of liberalism, they did not reject its techniques. Napoleon's victories resulted from the use of a mass army, the fruits of science, and the rational administration of a national community. The Prussians, led by their great reformers of the nineteenth century, imitated Napoleon's accomplishments of statecraft within the framework of their highly authoritarian society. In fact, many of the moves toward liberalization initiated during the Napoleonic period were aborted. For example, the relationship between peasant and Junker in Prussia retained distinctly feudal overtones until much later in the century. In many respects, the Prussian adoption of modern statecraft was like that of Japan, which also copied the technical aspects of modernity while retaining traditional institutions, although unlike the Japanese, the Prussians could draw upon a highly developed system of bureaucratic organization.

When Bismarck finally united Germany in 1871, Austria was excluded—one reason being to insure Prussian predominance and another to insure that the new German state contained a Protestant majority. Prussia, which was responsible for the unification, was a hierarchical state dominated by traditional values. Only once, in 1848, had there seemed

any chance that the Prussian monarchy would adopt a liberal outlook, but German liberalism was so fragile that the attempt to achieve reforms was completely squelched. That a conservative Prussia had brought about unification heightened the prestige of Prussian values, and they became the dominant German ones.

INDUSTRIALIZATION AND ITS CONSEQUENCES: German national unity was followed by a tremendous upsurge in industrial growth. National unification and the goal of national greatness served the same function in Germany that the Calvinist ethic had in England, though of course, the disciplined respect for authority of the Germans was an important factor as well. Industrial progress was so rapid that by 1914 Germany was challenging England's leadership (see Tables 2.3 and 2.4). The nation had been transformed from a rural society to a predominantly urban one. The percentage of the population in urban areas jumped from forty to sixty between 1871 and 1910; the population of Berlin alone increased from 750,000 to more than two million in the same period.

Industrialization in Germany, however, did not bring with it the ideology of laissez faire. The government was an active participant in the economy—subsidizing industries, imposing tariffs, and creating a state-owned transportation network and a state-controlled banking system. At the same time the Ger-

TABLE 2.3. COAL OUTPUT IN SELECTED
EUROPEAN COUNTRIES, 1871–1913

In millions of metric tons

	1871	1880	1890	1900	1910	1913
England	118.0	149.0	184.5	228.8	268.7	292.0
France	13.3	19.4	26.1	33.4	38.4	40.8
Germany	37.9	59.1	89.3	149.8	222.3	279.0
Belgium	13.7	16.9	20.4	23.5	23.9	22.8

Adapted from J. H. Clapham, *The Economic Development of France and Germany*, 4th ed. (Cambridge: Cambridge University Press, 1936), p. 281. Reprinted by permission of the publisher.

TABLE 2.4. IRON AND STEEL PRODUCTION IN SELECTED
EUROPEAN COUNTRIES, 1871–1910

Output in thousands of metric tons

	1880		1890		1900		1910	
	Pig iron	Steel	Pig iron	Steel	Pig iron	Steel	Pig iron	Steel
United Kingdom	7,873	3,730	8,031	5,301	9,103	5,981	10,172	7,613
Germany (with Luxembourg)	2,729	1,548	4,658	3,164	8,521	7,372	14,794	13,149
France	1,725	1,354	1,962	1,407	2,714	1,935	4,038	2,850
Belgium	608	596	788	716	1,019	927	1,852	1,857

Adapted from Clapham, *Economic Development*, p. 285. Reprinted by permission.

man state developed the earliest and broadest measures for social welfare of any of the industrial powers. Whatever reasons of practical politics led the German elite groups to pioneer state programs of social welfare, the traditional paternalistic attitudes that continued to characterize German society were also significant. In essence, German industrialization was sponsored by segments of the traditional elite which held on to the reins of power even though its economic power, based on land, receded. At least initially, the bourgeoisie did not mount a challenge to this elite. Instead, it adopted elite values and tried to emulate the aristocracy—thus rejecting, for the most part, the liberal ideology which in England had been so closely associated with the emergence of a commercial and industrial middle class.

Germany, then, seemed to have become a modern industrial state, even while it retained much of its traditional culture and social structure. This appearance, however, was somewhat deceptive, for industrialization and urbanization were producing new subcultures and undermining the foundations of the old social values. The clash between the old and the new was far more serious in Germany than in England or France, although before World War I the tensions were masked both by increasing prosperity and by the growth of national power. These tensions stemmed from the rapidity with which Germany industrialized and the widening gap between urban and peasant culture, as well as from the repressiveness of traditional German society and the rigidity with which Germans demanded their lives be organized. To many Germans, social restraints had to be enforced, otherwise powerful, violent, and evil forces would be released. Thus, even moderate reform was considered a major threat to public order and tranquillity. Finally, while in both England and France rebellion against traditional institutions could be directed into liberal or radical channels, these alternatives were not as easily available in Germany. Rebellion against traditional values often took the direction of nihilism—the rejection of all values.

The virulent racism often associated with these nihilistic movements was the consequence of several factors. One was a sense of national inferiority—the other aspect of continually frustrated national ambitions. Another was the exposed position of the German Jew: because of the unique features of German development, the Jewish citizen's liberalism and his association with urban culture made him seem much more of an alien in Germany than he did in other Western countries, and racism was a convenient rationalization which assuaged feelings of inferiority not only for members of the German

Catholic minority but also for the German Protestant peasant and small businessman. Since they could not use liberal slogans to challenge the authority of the Junker class, they tried to establish their equality with the Junkers by emphasizing the racial equality of the German people and their superiority over other peoples.

These radical and racist tendencies remained on the periphery of German life until the end of World War I. Then, however, a succession of national catastrophes spread, enlarged, and strengthened racism to the point where the Nazi Party could obtain control of the German state. The first national catastrophe was defeat in World War I and the Treaty of Versailles; the second, the elimination of the monarchy and the establishment of a democratic republic with institutions for which many Germans were not ready; the third, the inflation of the 1920's and the Great Depression that began in 1929, which ruined thousands of peasants, small businessmen, and white-collar workers. All these national ills, plus the general ferment of the 1920's, produced a moral and intellectual chaos that seemed about to destroy all traditional standards.

Beset on the ideological right by groups hostile to a democratic state and on the left by a growing Communist movement, the Weimar Republic was incapable of action. It could not even control the violent street fighting that became typical of German civic politics. Nor could it make effective policy decisions. Governments rose and fell, and new elections were held without any issues having been decided; democracy became a beer-hall joke.

THE NAZI REGIME: Adolf Hitler came to power in Germany in part because some Germans hoped he would restore traditional institutions, including the monarchy; in part because many saw him as the only alternative to communism or chaos; and in part because many simply longed for a more stable political order.

The secret of Hitler's great appeal, however, can be understood only if one recognizes that he reflected the contradictions in German society. His fears were the fears of many Germans. His aspirations were their aspirations. His madness was their madness. In his own person he synthesized their rejection of old values and their fear of rejecting them. In himself he reflected their loss of bearings in the modern world.

Explaining Hitler's speaking ability, one of his early supporters, who later split with him, noted:

I've been asked many times what is the secret of Hitler's extraordinary power as a speaker. I can only attribute it to his uncanny intuition, which infallibly diagnoses the ills from which his audience is suffering. If he tries to bolster his arguments with theories from books . . . he scarcely rises above a very poor mediocrity . . . but let him throw away his crutches and step out boldly, speaking as the spirit moves him, and he is promptly transformed into one of the greatest speakers of the century. . . .

His words go like an arrow to their target; he touches each private wound on the raw, liberating the mass unconscious, expressing its innermost aspirations, telling it what it most wants to hear.[6]

Hitler was an ex-Catholic, as were many of his early followers, and the Nazi movement began in Catholic Bavaria. Later his support came predominantly, as voting studies have shown, from Protestant peasants in the north and from small shopkeepers and white-collar workers. Many of these same people had voted for the liberal German Democratic Party in the first election of the Weimar Republic; that party dropped from some 18 per cent of the popular vote to less than one per cent between 1920 and 1932. Its erstwhile supporters could not turn to the

[6] Otto Strasser, *Hitler and I*, trans. from the French by G. David and E. Mosbacher (London: Jonathan Cape, Ltd., 1940), pp. 76–77.

Nationalist Party, the party of big business and the Junker aristocracy, because they no longer accepted the authority of these groups. They would not vote for radical parties like the Socialist or Communist parties because they regarded them as un-German, as associated with the evils of urban society, and as instruments to reduce them to the status of industrial workers.

Catholics of all classes, and both Protestant and Catholic industrial workers, did not support Hitler in such substantial proportions as did other segments of the society. Both groups belonged to parties—the Catholics to the specifically Catholic Center Party—that gave them a sense of personal value and social purpose. Big business and the army did not, on the whole, turn to Hitler until the very end. At first they regarded him as an upstart, and slightly paranoid; by 1932, however, influential elements of the military and business communities had become convinced that he was the only alternative to possible anarchy. Besides, they thought they could control Hitler.

Hitler's aim was to create a new, heroic Germany, ruled by a heroic, disciplined, responsible racial elite—a racial community united by love and thriving in unity and harmony. In working toward this end he believed that he represented the real will of the German people, even if the people themselves were not actually aware of their true goals. He attacked the philistinism and egoistic individualism of capitalist civilization. His intention was to combine modern technological society with the best of the German past, although his view of that past was considerably distorted. Thus, the regime implemented programs designed to recapture the world of the past, to re-educate the German people, to purify Germany, and, finally, to make Germany great. These programs required a political system that had control over the entire life of the nation—in other words, a totalitarian political order. What these programs resulted in, of course, was World War II and the destruction of Nazi Germany.

Hitler sought, under the Third Reich, to create a corporate society. He emphasized protecting the peasantry, who represented to him the purest German racial type. A limited program of land redistribution was begun and decrees were issued providing peasants with a cushion from economic fluctuations, but most proposals to assist the peasants failed to achieve their purpose. The Hitler regime also developed substantial public-works programs, including the construction of public buildings and housing. Family allowances were given married couples with children; free holidays were provided for lower-paid workers at state-owned resorts, and special arrangements were made for them to attend the theater and concerts.

The state also stepped up its inspection of factories to insure that working conditions were adequate. Both workers and employers were organized in a National Labor Front directed by the Nazi Party. All professional people were required to join guildlike organizations under the direction of the party and to form professional courts to insure competence and fair charges for services. The great bulk of industrial capital remained in private hands and large profits were permitted, but the state came more and more to regulate the direction of production as well as working conditions and wages.

To re-educate the German people, the Nazis extended control over universities and centralized education in the lower grades. Youth organizations were formed which placed great stress on physical fitness. Every association, from churches to birdwatching groups, came under the supervision of the party and the state to make certain that the proper attitudes and orientations were spread among the population. To guarantee Germany's racial purity, "undesirable" individuals were sterilized or killed; these included the feebleminded, the elderly and infirm, the incurably ill, defective infants, and homosexuals. The purity program finally came to include genocide; all Jews and gypsies were slaughtered, as well as large numbers of Poles and Russians. Hitler also tried to develop a racially pure leadership for the future. The so-called SS (*Schutzstaffel*), which had begun as a personal bodyguard for Hitler, was expanded with the hope of achieving a racially pure elite class. Membership in the SS was limited to certain physical types and to those who were racially pure; members could marry only racially pure women.

This elite would, Hitler felt, guarantee a thousand-year empire, greater than the Holy Roman Empire—which had been the First Reich. But Germany also needed living space (*Lebensraum*), Hitler claimed, and he sought to obtain it primarily at the expense of the "racially inferior" peoples to the east. This ambition eventually led him to invade the Soviet Union, and because of his racial ideas he failed to make effective use of the substantial support the Germans initially received from Ukrainian peasants who, until they experienced the reality of Nazi rule, had regarded the Germans almost as liberators.

CONTEMPORARY GERMANY:[7] At the conclusion of World War II, Germany was in ruins. The alliance that had defeated Hitler prepared to prevent the German people from ever again becoming a "threat" to world peace. Numerous plans were made for trying war criminals, for lengthy occupation, and even for permanently splitting Germany into a number of fragments or at least limiting her industrial capacity. The first major discussions of Germany's future had taken place during the war, at Tehran in 1943. Roosevelt, Stalin, and Churchill, especially the first two, seemed to agree then that Germany should be permanently partitioned once the war ended; but they reached no formal agreement. Rather, a three-power European Advisory Commission was established to make recommendations on what to do with a defeated Germany. The commission made a detailed plan for

[7] For reasons of space, the discussions of postwar Germany will deal only with the Federal Republic of Germany. Unless otherwise specified, the word "Germany" will usually refer to West Germany.

postwar zones of occupation and presented its proposals two years later to the Big Three at Yalta. The plan was accepted with some modifications, the most important of which involved carving an occupation zone for France out of the British and American zones. A number of additional issues were discussed at Yalta, including reparations and German boundaries. On reparations, a compromise was reached after the Russians scaled down demands which the Western allies considered excessive. On the issue of borders, however, the boundary between Poland and Germany remained at issue. The Soviet Union was awarded former Polish territory up to the so-called Curzon Line, and it was decided to compensate Poland with territory that had formerly been German. Churchill had argued that Germany be granted land west to the Oder and Eastern Neisse rivers. Stalin, however, urged that the Polish boundary be extended to the Western Neisse. The difference was considerable. For one thing, while the boundary Churchill proposed included areas that contained a substantial Polish population, the area between the Eastern Neisse and the Western Neisse was, ethnically at least, clearly German.

Yalta marked the high point of Allied unity. When the Potsdam Conference met later in 1945—with Truman replacing Roosevelt and Clement Attlee taking over from Churchill—relations were still cordial, but increasing disagreement foreshadowed the conflict that was to come. Truman came to Potsdam thinking that permanently dividing Germany was still a possible policy. Stalin completely lacked interest in it, and Truman dropped the idea. At Potsdam, too, the Russians presented the West with a fait accompli: they had transferred all territory east of the Oder and Western Neisse rivers to the Poles, who were already expelling the German population from these areas. The Western Allies refused to accept this decision as permanent, and a compromise was reached whereby the final determination of Germany's new boundaries was to be left to the peace conference. Meanwhile, the Polish-occupied areas were to be administered by Poland.

The Potsdam Conference also completed the agreements on the occupation of Germany, providing for an Allied Control Council with ultimate authority. Berlin was to remain an enclave in the Soviet zone, governed jointly by the Allies and split into four sectors. Theoretically, the control council was to establish common policies for all of Germany, especially in the economic sphere; theoretically, too, central administrative agencies were to be established for finance, transport, and communication. The agencies were never established. More important, the Soviet Union and the Western Allies found it more and more difficult, after Potsdam, to reach any kind of agreement on common policies. Within a short time, this friction became part and parcel of the cold war. Divergent programs were instituted in the different zones of occupation, the Soviets deciding the fate of the East German Democratic Republic, while France, England, and the United States eventually worked out common policies for the western zones.

The upshot of the East-West split was first the merger of the three western zones, and, in 1949, the formation of the German Federal Republic. In the meantime, western Germany had been brought into the Organization for European Economic Cooperation and more authority was given to German civil officials, including control over "de-Nazification." The political structure of the German Federal Republic was determined by a "Basic Law" largely developed by the Germans themselves, in a Constituent Assembly that met during 1948 and 1949, although the Western Allies did exercise a significant influence over the deliberations at several points. The Germans wanted to include West Berlin in the Federal Republic, but this was opposed by the Allies, who felt that it would jeopardize their rights in the city. As a result, West Berlin, while it is now tied more closely to German civil authority, retains a separate existence.

The Basic Law was ratified in 1949, and shortly thereafter the first general elections were held. The creation of the Federal Republic did not mean that Germany had been granted full sovereignty. The Allied High Commissioners kept the reins in many areas, and retained the right to withdraw all privileges in case of emergency. But because of the intensification of the cold war and the desire to enlist the cooperation of West Germany in the defense of Europe, the re-entry of Germany into the family of nations proceeded apace. In 1955 Germany was admitted to the North Atlantic Treaty Organization and granted full sovereignty. Two years later, the Saar, which had been placed under the administration of the French, was reintegrated into the German state, and shortly thereafter Germany joined with other Western European powers in the formation of the European Common Market.

From 1949 to 1963, Germany was led by Chancellor Konrad Adenauer of the Christian Democratic Party, whose shrewdness, toughness, and ability—particularly in the use of power—enabled him to dominate the political scene. In foreign affairs, Adenauer followed a policy of aligning Germany with the West, especially with France, in an effort to end once and for all the antagonisms that had existed between Germany and its neighbors and to ease the way for the establishment of a unified Western Europe. In domestic affairs, Adenauer's government, accepting the direction of its Minister of Economic Affairs, Ludwig Erhard, adopted what came to be known as a "social market" policy. In effect, this meant some reduction in direct government control of the economy; but it also meant the continuation and, in some areas, even the expansion of the government's social-welfare role.

On the whole, Erhard's policies were successful, and Germany recovered from the war with remarkable speed. By 1955 the gross national product of the Bonn Republic already exceeded the 1936 GNP of all Germany. By 1960 Germany was producing more automobiles than England. In 1950 there had been 11.1 motor vehicles for every thousand inhabitants; by 1963 this figure was 133 per thousand. In 1954, 125,000 television sets were in use in France, as compared with fewer than 22,000 in Germany; by 1962 more than seven million television sets were in use in Germany, more than twice the total in France.

By 1965, however, there began to be signs that all was not well. Erhard, Adenauer's successor as chancellor, was having difficulty in maintaining unity within his own party, and in 1966 he was finally forced to resign. He was replaced by a coalition of the Christian Democratic and Social Democratic parties under the chancellorship of Kurt Kiesinger, a Christian Democrat. At about the same time a neonationalist political organization, the National Democratic Party (N.P.D.) began to score significant electoral victories in local elections, capturing from ten to 15 per cent of the popular vote in some cases. While it carefully eschewed anti-Semitism in its public utterances, and denied vigorously that it was neo-Nazi, the party was clearly drawing upon elements in German society that were highly authoritarian.

The emergence of the N.P.D. was related to the mild economic recession that began in 1966. In larger measure, however, it was a reaction to the frustration felt by many Germans over their country's international position during the 1960's. Although once again among the most powerful nations in Europe in terms of economic development, politically Germany was still a midget. Such was the burden of the Nazi past that almost any independent moves made by the Germans were regarded with extreme suspicion. Moreover, Communist East Germany, now the German Democratic Republic, had stabilized its economic and political organization after managing to cut off the flow of refugees to the West by construction of the Berlin Wall in 1961. The prospects of reunifying Germany seemed further off than ever, and even the status of West Berlin appeared to be more and more uncertain.

In the past many Germans, following Adenauer's lead, had been willing to forego the prospect of immediate unity in the hope that East Germany would eventually wither on the vine. Also, they were drawn to the possibility of becoming part of a unified Western Europe, as symbolized by the Common Market and other supranational institutions. By the mid-1960's, however, the prospect of European unity was receding into the distance, and the efforts of England, France, and the United States to seek greater accommodation with Russia on the basis of the status quo in Europe appeared to imply that Germany would be left in the lurch.

The re-emergence of the German right was paralleled by agitation on the left. Drawing upon events in the United States, a vocal segment of German university students campaigned, through both passive and active civil disobedience, against what they considered to be the surviving elements of authoritarianism remaining in German life. Many identified themselves with revolutionary regimes in the underdeveloped countries. Once again, German political life seemed to be polarizing.

There is not much question, of course, about German society still containing authoritarian elements, or about Germany's political strains a generation after Hitler. Yet it is also true that Germany at the end of the 1960's is a far different place from Germany during the 1920's. Germany in the twenties was a nation of anguishing contradictions, facing forward, looking backward, fragmented, bitter, desperate; and out of all these conflicting forces arose National Socialism. The Nazi regime was in one sense an attempt to restore traditional society, at least a warped version of it; at the same time, nazism contained elements of socialism mixed with a strongly populist appeal.

The attempt to restore the traditional was, to be sure, a horrifying failure, and, indeed, the Nazi experience went a long way toward weakening still further Germany's social customs. Youth camps created by the regime brought young people of all social strata together for common purposes. The network of autobahns—military highways built by the regime—reduced not only geographic distance but social distance among Germany's regions. The imperatives of preparing for war further urbanized German society. The war itself contributed greatly to social change. The officer corps, still dominated by the Junker aristocracy despite the emergence of Nazi officers in the 1930's, was decimated by the Russian campaign; many more officers died after supporting the unsuccessful attempt on Hitler's life in 1944. Finally, the occupation and division of Germany and the destruction of the old Junker estates completely undermined the economic base of the aristocracy.

Postwar developments continued the process of weakening traditional values. Many German Protestants who fled from the east into West Germany settled in predominantly Catholic areas, reducing religious separateness. The economic revolution common to all European nations after the war (see Table 2.5) produced still further changes. Mass production of consumer goods has reduced their value as status symbols; the universal automobile has greatly enhanced geographic mobility; inexpensive television sets have helped to create an ever more homogeneous culture, drawing Germans closer together even as they introduce ideas and

values typical of other European nations. And the continued rise in power of non-European countries not only has added to the Germans' feeling that they are an integral part of Europe, but has led most of them to accept the fact that Germany is only a "small country" that cannot hope to be more than a second-rank power. German society is still more highly stratified than most others in Europe, and certain kinds of traditional attitudes remain important. A series of economic and political shocks could conceivably pose a threat to German democracy. But whatever Germany's future, the peculiar combination of forces that brought the triumph of National Socialism is no longer present.

The 1969 parliamentary elections confirmed the importance of these social changes to German political life. The N.P.D. failed to win a single Bundestag seat. The Social Democrats, on the other hand, increased their percentage of the total vote and formed a new government in alliance with the small Free Democratic Party. Assuming that the coalition holds together, the next few years should witness the further democratization of German society.

GERMAN POLITICAL INSTITUTIONS: The French Revolution and the occupation of

TABLE 2.5. GROWTH RATES OF GROSS NATIONAL PRODUCT: EUROPE AND THE UNITED STATES[1]

Selected Periods, 1913-1966

	United States		France		West Germany[2]		United Kingdom	
	total	per capita	total	per capita	total	per capita	total	per capita
1913–1929	3.1%	1.7%	1.7%	1.8%	0.4%	—	0.8%	0.3%
1929–1950	2.9	1.7	—	—	1.9	0.7%	1.6	1.2
1950–1960	3.2	1.5	4.6	3.7	8.5	6.9	2.7	2.3
1960–1966	5.0	3.5	5.3	3.9	4.5	3.2	3.1	2.4

[1] Rates represent annual compounded changes in real output.
[2] Beginning in 1960, includes Saar and West Berlin.

Adapted from *Statistical Abstract of the United States, 1969,* p. 313.

large portions of Germany by French forces in the early nineteenth century had not been without its positive results. After 1820, at least four of the most important South German states adopted constitutions limiting the power of the monarchy. In most of these states, parliaments were created consisting of two houses, an aristocratic upper house and a lower house elected on the basis of secret, direct—and in some cases universal —male suffrage. In 1848 it seemed for a brief moment that even Prussia itself would adopt a liberal constitution.

After the 1848 revolution had failed, the king did approve a constitution that transformed Prussia into a constitutional monarchy, albeit an extremely conservative one. It established an upper house (*Herrenhaus*) as a chamber of peers, and a lower house ostensibly based upon popular representation. Voters for the lower chamber were divided into three classes according to their tax assessments, therefore permitting fairly complete control of the legislature by wealthy landowners. The prime minister continued to be responsible to the king, who retained his authority to rule by decree in emergencies. Despite some efforts by the diet to liberalize the constitution after the 1862 elections, it determined, for all intents and purposes, the structure of the empire that officially came into existence in 1871. Under it, the essentially authoritarian nature of German government continued unchanged until World War I.

The German Empire was a federal state comprising Prussia; the seven smaller states of Baden, Bavaria, Württemberg, Saxony, Hesse, Mecklenburg-Schwerin, and Oldenburg; fifteen tiny states; and three free and imperial cities. Alsace-Lorraine was given the status of an imperial territory.

Under the imperial constitution the federal government of the empire consisted of an emperor, who was the king of Prussia; an imperial chancellor; a Federal Council (*Bundesrat*); and an assembly elected by universal manhood suffrage (*Reichstag*). The new national government received certain expressly enumerated powers that took precedence over those of the German states. It was given control of foreign affairs, military and naval matters, imperial finances, foreign commerce, posts and telegraphs (except in Bavaria and Württemberg), and matters relating to the use of railways for national defense. Laws of the national government— including citizenship, the regulation of banking, social insurance, and labor regulation —also took precedence in other areas. The rights of the states were both enumerated and residual, extending to interior, police, fiscal, and cultural administration. Some of the states controlled their own military establishments and even maintained diplomatic missions in certain countries.

As the dominant power in the empire, Prussia enjoyed a privileged position. Not only did the Prussian king have a special role, but Prussians held the presidency and chairmanships of all standing committees in the Federal Council, where, in effect, the sovereignty in the empire was vested. Composed of representatives of the state governments, the council shared with the emperor and the chancellor the tasks of making treaties, authorizing appointments, and declaring war. It also determined what bills were to be brought before the Reichstag and, as the Supreme Constitutional and Administrative Court of the empire, rendered decisions in disputes among the different states. Within this body, the Prussians had sufficient votes to defeat any constitutional amendment, as well as a veto on all proposed changes affecting the army, the navy, and finances. Prussia was also given the right to combine the offices of Prussian chancellor and imperial chancellor.

Executive authority was placed with the emperor, who was supreme commander of the army and navy and exercised almost complete control over foreign affairs. He had the right to convoke and dismiss both the Federal Council and the Reichstag, and the chancellor as well as other officials were directly responsible to him.

The Reichstag's powers were extremely circumscribed, although it did function as a national sounding board. Its requests for so much as information could be, and often were, ignored with impunity, and the emperor dissolved it frequently if he found it becoming too obstreperous—even though the election districts were so drawn that rural, more conservative areas were overrepresented.

On the whole, the governments of the German states were no less authoritarian. The threefold system of representation that existed in most of them, and the lack of executive responsibility to the legislature, assured control by conservative elements. Nevertheless, the empire was a *Rechtstaat*—a state ruled by law—and, except for certain periods, the civil rights of its citizens were protected, including the right to criticize the government both orally and in print.

After the defeat of Germany in World War I, and the crushing of a "radical" Socialist move to create a Socialist state, a National Constituent Assembly was elected to write a new constitution. Following extensive discussions and revisions, the constitution was promulgated on August 11, 1919. A long, complicated document, it contained an elaborate bill of rights and other democratic provisions.

Government authority was now placed in a popularly elected Reichstag, to which the chancellor and his cabinet were responsible. Elections to the Reichstag were by proportional representation[8] to insure the full expression of every possible ideological viewpoint. The chancellor shared executive authority with a popularly elected president, and the Reichstag shared its authority with a Federal Council (*Reichsrat*), which superseded the old upper house as representative of the states, but with greatly reduced power.

At first the Constituent Assembly had

wanted to set up a strong central government, and there were also plans to divide Prussia into a number of smaller states in order to prevent it from dominating national affairs. These proposals, however, never came to fruition, and the republic remained a federal state, but with considerably more powers than those allocated the Reichstag under the empire. The constitution, incidentally, provided that each state (*Land*) should have a cabinet responsible to a parliament elected by universal suffrage and proportional representation.

On the national level, legislation was to be introduced by the cabinet, the Reichsrat, or individual members of the Reichstag working through state ministers. Legislation could also be introduced by popular initiative, through petitions signed by one-tenth of the voters, and a petition of one-twentieth of the voters could demand a referendum on any law. Otherwise, the Reichstag had the final word. It could also overrule the Reichsrat by a two-thirds vote if the two houses disagreed on a piece of legislation.

The chancellor had the power to legislate by decree—provided that an enabling act allowing him to do so was passed by a two-thirds vote of the Reichstag. The limits of his decree authority were set by the act itself. More important, the president was given the authority, under Article 48 of the constitution, to take all necessary measures to protect the republic in case of national emergency, although such measures had to be within the constitution's framework.

The Weimar constitution came under heavy criticism after the fall of the republic. Both Article 48, which was used under circumstances that amounted to presidential dictatorship, and the provision for enabling acts, which allowed Hitler to obtain almost unlimited authority, were blamed for the collapse of the Weimar Republic. So, too, was the system of proportional representation; this, critics argued, encouraged a multiplicity of parties and prevented effective policy decisions. The malaise that destroyed the

[8] For a full discussion of proportional representation, see Chapter 9.

republic, however, was social rather than political; the same instruments, under other circumstances, would not have been used in the same way.[9]

On March 23, 1933, the Reichstag presented Adolf Hitler with an enabling act that virtually gave him carte blanche to transform the Weimar Republic into a totalitarian state. All power of the state, which would now be dominated by the Nazi Party, was handed over to Hitler, who then proceeded to combine the roles of party leader, chancellor, and, after 1934, president. The Weimar constitution was never formally repealed, but that was scarcely necessary; organic laws issued by Hitler and his subordinates thoroughly reorganized the administration of the German nation. The states were subordinated completely to the national government, which took control over every aspect of national life. In effect, the Nazi Party and the state were so merged that governmental decisions emanated from both, a practice resembling other one-party states such as the Soviet Union.

Immediately after the conclusion of hostilities in 1945, the Western occupying powers gradually revived local political institutions in Germany. Wherever possible, they took steps to place a degree of authority in the hands of local officials. As the cold war developed, France, England, and the United States moved further along these lines, first integrating their zones economically, and then encouraging the Germans to create a new set of national institutions. The machinery for drafting such a constitution was put in motion by the Western military governors in the spring of 1948, and that summer the minister presidents of the German states (*Länder*) commissioned a group of constitutional and political experts to prepare a draft Basic Law for what was to become the Federal Republic of Germany. By fall, a Parliamentary Council elected by the Länder

was meeting in Bonn to consider just what form the Basic Law should take. After lengthy negotiations among the political parties (the council consisted of 27 representatives from both the Christian Democratic Party and the Socialist Party, five from the Free Democratic Party, and five from all other parties) and between the council and the military governors, the Basic Law won final approval from the Parliamentary Council on May 8, 1949 and from the military governors on May 12. After consideration by the state legislatures, the Basic Law was officially promulgated on May 23, and the first general election under the new law was held three months later. At a special ceremony held at the Allied headquarters on September 21, the Federal Republic of Germany came formally into existence.

The Basic Law was and is considered to be a temporary expedient, to be replaced when a formal peace treaty is signed. It is specifically a transitional document. Despite this, it presumes to represent not only West Germans but those Germans "to whom participation was denied," namely, those living in East Germany and, at that time, the Saar. The Federal Republic is defined as a "democratic and social federal state" in which authority emanates from the people. The constitution establishes three branches of government with certain checks and balances between them, and it specifies the governmental form as parliamentary; the executive, or chancellor, is fully responsible to the parliament. The executive was deprived of the authority granted under Article 48 of the Weimar constitution to suspend any of the long list of fundamental rights now guaranteed in a rather comprehensive bill of rights; however, in 1968, after years of acrimonious debate, the Bundestag did give the government extended powers in case of national emergency. Even so, plagued by memories of the use of Article 48 during the Weimar Republic, it was extremely careful to limit the use of such powers and provided for continuous legislative supervision should

---

[9] The problems involved here will be discussed again in Chapters 9, 12, and 17.

they be exercised. In general, the powers conferred are far less extensive than those available to most other European executives.

As part of its protection of rights, the constitution's first article proclaims that the dignity of man must be respected. This has been interpreted very broadly in the courts, which have held that it also protects prisoners against corporal punishment and the use of "truth drugs" and lie detectors. Other rights include full equality before the law regardless of sex, race, or language; freedom of religion; the right to refuse to serve in the military on grounds of conscience; freedom of expression and freedom of the press; and full equality for illegitimate children.

These rights are protected by articles specifying that the constitution cannot be amended except by a two-thirds vote of the Bundestag and Bundesrat, and by the establishment, at the urging of the Americans, of a Federal Constitutional Court with power to rule on the constitutionality of actions by the government and the Länder. The court also has authority to decide when to apply the provisions of Article 18, which states that whoever denies the basic rights of others forfeits his own. The article has been invoked to outlaw the Communist Party and neo-Nazi groups.

The constitution restores to the various component units of Germany some of the powers that had been stripped from them by the National Socialists. In so doing, it reestablishes to a certain extent the nation's initial federal character. However, unlike both the empire and Weimar periods, the differences between the Länder in terms of size, population, and wealth are no longer very great.

The powers of the federal government are enumerated powers, and, as in the United States, those not assigned to the federal government are restricted to the states. The constitution lists those powers that are peculiarly a federal concern: these include foreign affairs, defense, citizenship, freedom of movement and internal trade, currency, rail-roads, mails, telecommunications, and the legal position of federal employees. Both federal and state governments may pass laws pertaining to such matters as the economy, labor, nationalization, agriculture, health, and shipping. In these areas, federal law takes precedence, although the federal government may legislate only when the situation is such as to require national action. Finally, the federal government is responsible for guaranteeing the constitutional order of Länder. The states are solely responsible for education, cultural and religious affairs (including relations between church and state), and their own internal administrative organization. This is a very limited list, so limited that the federal government's authority obviously extends to nearly every sphere of German life. In that sense, some have argued that Germany is not truly a federal republic after all.

Unlike the United States pattern, the Länder are responsible, as under the empire and Weimar, for the administration of all federal laws unless the government makes its own administrative provisions. The federal government may also issue general administrative instructions and supervise the legality of the execution of its laws by state authorities. The government may give specific instructions to Land officials if it has reason to believe a federal law is not being carried out effectively—provided authority to do so is granted by both the Bundestag and the Bundesrat. Thus, recalcitrant Länder can be forced into line, if most of the other Länder, through their Bundesrat representation, offer the national government their support.

The Weimar experience—with its potentially all-powerful, popularly elected president—aroused strong suspiciousness in postwar Germany concerning presidential government. Yet even in clearly parliamentary regimes, such as the French Fourth Republic, the need had been felt for a figure who would serve as an expression of the continuity of the state—perhaps an elected mon-

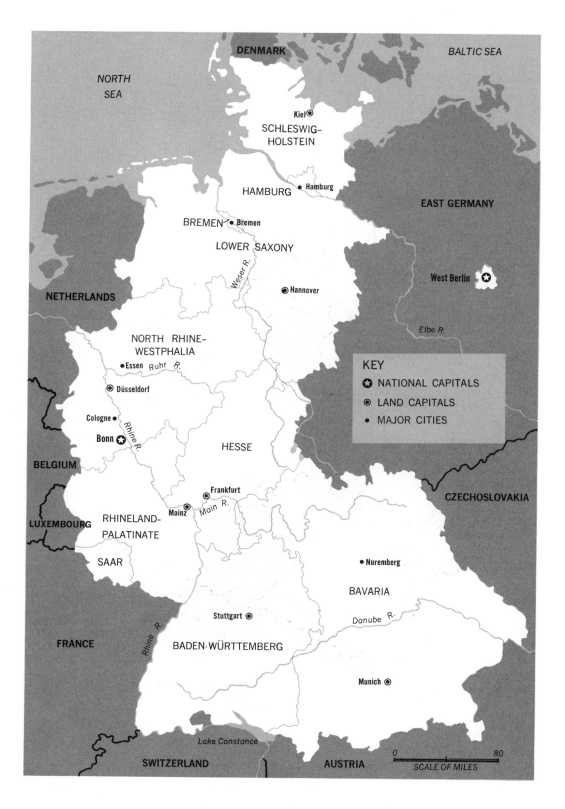

MAP 2.7. THE FEDERAL REPUBLIC OF GERMANY

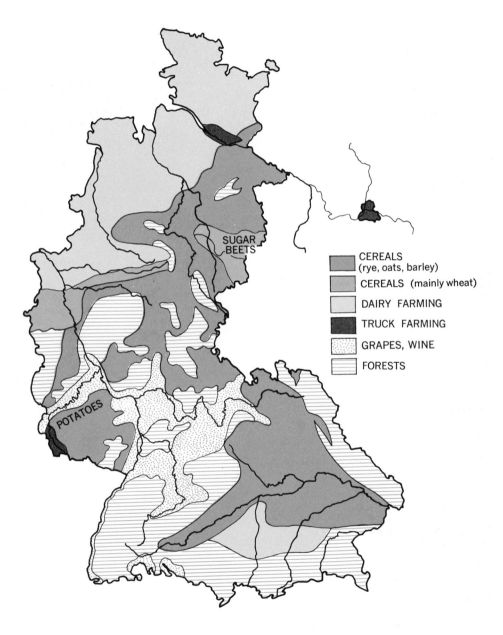

SUGAR
BEETS

POTATOES

CEREALS
(rye, oats, barley)

CEREALS (mainly wheat)

DAIRY FARMING

TRUCK FARMING

GRAPES, WINE

FORESTS

MAP 2.8. GERMAN AGRICULTURAL RESOURCES

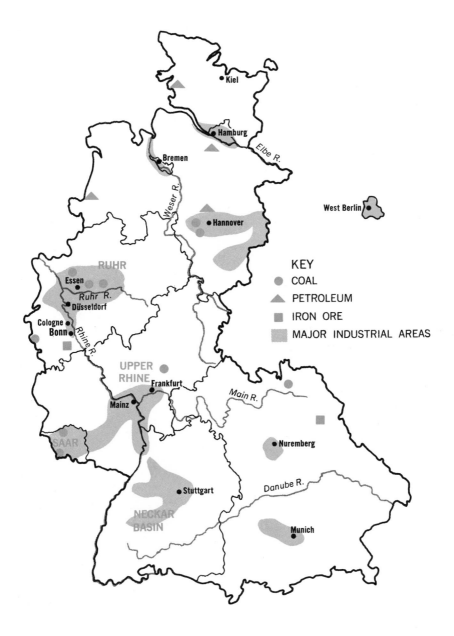

KEY

● COAL

▲ PETROLEUM

■ IRON ORE

▨ MAJOR INDUSTRIAL AREAS

Kiel

Hamburg

Bremen

West Berlin

Hannover

Weser R.

Elbe R.

RUHR

Essen

Ruhr R.

Düsseldorf

Cologne

Bonn

Rhine R.

UPPER RHINE

Frankfurt

Main R.

Mainz

SAAR

Nuremberg

NECKAR BASIN

Stuttgart

Danube R.

Munich

MAP 2.9. GERMAN INDUSTRIAL RESOURCES

arch, albeit a constitutional one, without power.

Essentially, the office of the president in the Bonn Republic is just that. The constitution says that he will be elected at a federal convention—a special meeting of Bundestag members and an equal number of members elected, according to proportional representation, by the state assemblies. The president, whose term of office is five years, is responsible for such routine tasks as receiving ambassadors and issuing letters of appointment to officials—countersigned by a cabinet minister. He also proposes to the Bundestag candidates for chancellor, appoints ministers on the chancellor's recommendation, and can dissolve the Bundestag in certain special situations. Under all but the most extreme circumstances, he has no real power.

In the first election in 1949, the presidency went to Theodor Heuss, a leader of the Free Democratic Party, who institutionalized the office by playing the role of wise, nonpartisan elder statesman. Such was the affection he engendered that he was re-elected unanimously in 1954. When the question of Heuss's successor came up in 1959 (the president can be re-elected only once), Chancellor Adenauer, under increasing pressure to step aside and let a younger man take over the chancellorship, considered running himself. Adenauer let it be known that he considered the office one that could influence policy, especially in the area of foreign affairs. However, contingent upon his seeking the presidency was Adenauer's insistence that the Christian Democratic Party allow him to choose his successor as chancellor. When his party refused to do this, Adenauer decided to remain as chancellor, and, at the last minute, the Christian Democratic Party found another candidate in Heinrich Luebke, the minister of agriculture. Despite early indications that Luebke might take a more partisan stance—particularly just before and during Erhard's term as chancellor—he basically continued the nonpartisanship of his predecessor. Under Luebke's 1969 successor,

Social Democrat Gustav Heinemann, the minister of justice in the coalition government, it seems likely that the presidency will remain the symbolic office it was intended to be.

In drafting the constitution, the Parliamentary Council was anxious to provide for the stability that was lacking during the Weimar period. Council delegates had become convinced that it was necessary to establish a constitutional system that would permit the government to act in terms of a relatively consistent set of programs. They also concluded that German government should no longer be subject to overthrow by extremists who could agree on little else except their opposition to the existing regime. Assuming the continuation of a multiparty system, they believed that most governments would be coalitions, and that it would be impossible to develop the kind of strong cabinet so typical of British politics. They therefore concentrated their efforts on strengthening the position of the chancellor; it was their purpose to provide his office with sufficient power to guarantee effective governance.

The chancellor, who is personally responsible for general government policy, is elected every four years at the beginning of a new Bundestag. The Bundestag votes on the president's nominee for chancellor without prior debate. If the nominee is not elected by a majority—an absolute majority—of the total membership, the Bundestag must vote on another nominee. Only after a two-week deadlock may the Bundestag, with the approval of the president, elect a chancellor by a majority of those present and voting—a plurality.

Once elected, the chancellor is not required to ask for a vote of confidence for his government's program or for approval of the list of ministers whom he appoints. He can only be removed by a motion of no confidence, at which time the Bundestag must elect his successor by an absolute majority. The chancellor can ask for a vote of confidence at any time if he so chooses, and if defeated request that the Bundestag be dissolved by the president and new elections held.

Nor is this the end of his authority. If the Bundestag refuses to pass legislation which the chancellor declares to be urgent, the president—with the consent of the Bundesrat—may declare a state of legislative emergency. The legislation is then resubmitted to the Bundestag. If it is again not passed, or passed in a form not satisfactory to the government, the bill becomes law upon passage by the Bundesrat.

The German legal system from Bismarck to Hitler had provided for courts whose function it was to settle disputes arising among the states and between state and federal laws. While the High Court of the Weimar era had more power than the National Supreme Court of the German Empire, it never really took on the function of judging the constitutionality of federal or state enactments. Conservatives and radicals both opposed such a procedure, and the Socialists and Communists considered the courts to be reactionary instruments standing in the way of the people's will and necessary reform. Also, to conservatives in Germany as elsewhere, the idea of a constitution as a basic document standing above the state was unacceptable.

This attitude had changed when the time came to write the Basic Law of the Bonn constitution. Partly under the influence of the Americans, partly because of the Nazi experience, and partly because the extreme wings of the German political spectrum had been eliminated, those drawing up the instrument found themselves largely in agreement on the necessity of creating some form of court that would serve to place limits both upon the federal government and the Länder, especially if their actions seemed to violate the basic rights of citizens as guaranteed by the constitution.

The result was the creation of a Federal Constitutional Court which today is divided into two sections of ten judges each. The court president sits in the first section; his deputy is chairman of the second. Judges must be at least forty years old and hold a law degree; they are not permitted to be members of any political body. Half of the court membership is elected by the Bundestag, the other by the Bundesrat. In each section of the court, three of the judges must be chosen from the higher federal courts; these are elected for life. The other 14 judges are appointed for only eight years, although unlimited re-election is permitted and most of the judges have been re-elected.

The constitutional court has jurisdiction, as it did under previous regimes, over the compatibility of federal and Länder legislation. Now, however, the court possesses specific authority to rule on the constitutionality of their legislation. It may take cases that have been adjudicated in lower courts upon the request of any organ of federal or state government or of any person who believes his constitutional rights have been violated.

Since 1956 the court has decided a number of cases which the U.S. Supreme Court would have dismissed as essentially political matters. Some commentators are concerned lest such decisions lead to too many judicial resolutions of political questions. The constitutional court has also been deluged with requests to protect personal liberties, since the submission of such requests by an ordinary citizen requires neither the payment of court costs nor the participation of legal counsel. Such cases became so numerous that the court was forced to set up smaller committees of judges empowered, by unanimous vote, to dismiss complaints unless a court decision would either help clarify a constitutional issue or prevent those appealing from suffering serious damage.

4. SOME PRELIMINARY CONCLUSIONS

During the past several hundred years, England, France, and Germany have confronted essentially the same problems, problems generated by the changes that have taken place in European society. Each has been involved in a process of national integration as the nation state became the predominant form of European social organization, and within that framework each has been concerned with the problem of the relationship between secular and religious authority. All three societies have also had to cope with the problems engendered by the Industrial Revolution and the erosion of traditional forms of behavior and political authority.

The manner in which the three nations met these problems depended upon any number of factors, principally the religious and class structures of their traditional societies, their geographic position, and the time sequence in which the problems themselves arose. The political patterns and political institutions that have come to characterize these societies, while clearly European, reflect the unique historical development of each, as we shall see in more detail in succeeding chapters.

Of the three, England was the most successful in dealing with its problems relatively peacefully. The British had created a national state and an adaptable national community based on mutual class rights and responsibilities before the onset of industrialization. The forces that led to industrialization were indigenous and could be incorporated into traditional structures even as they modified them. The result was a unique fusion of traditional feudal and modern institutions.

All three Western European countries are conventionally labeled constitutional democracies. While the appellation is not incorrect, it is less than fully useful as a description of the political process in any of them. They are more accurately described in Robert Dahl's terms, as "polyarchies," in that political decisions result from competition among a plurality of elites of varying power and influence that freely vie for the support of the larger public.[10] They can also be described as pluralistic, reconciliation regimes in that politics in

all of them is conceived as a process whereby various interests in the community freely compete for a large share of the community's values according to certain rules, and the political system is conceived as a mechanism by which the goals sought by these interests can somehow be integrated into overall policies that will command the assent of most of the people. The usefulness of such a term as "polyarchy" will become more apparent as we compare the political processes of these nations with that of the Soviet Union, for in such comparisons, traditional terminology is less than completely satisfactory.

All three nations are now modern as the term is generally used, and developments during the past twenty years have considerably reduced, if not completely eliminated, differences among them. As the European student movement indicates, events in any one of them have an almost instantaneous impact upon the others, and the problems now faced by all of them, as Europe moves toward a postindustrial age, are of much the same order.

Following the framework elaborated by Gabriel Almond, we may summarize the analysis in a somewhat different way.[11] Almond lists four problems confronted by political systems as they develop—state building, nation building, participation, and distribution. "State building" pertains to the creation of institutions that enable the political system to regulate behavior and extract a larger volume of resources from the community. Nation building is the process of evolving allegiance to the larger community at the expense of parochial attachments to tribes, villages, or regions. Problems of participation and distribution arise as more and more members of the community demand a voice in the decisions that affect them and what

[10] See Robert A. Dahl and Charles E. Lindblom, *Politics, Economics and Welfare* (New York: Harper and Row, 1953).

[11] Gabriel Almond and G. Bingham Powell, Jr., *Comparative Politics: A Developmental Approach* (Boston: Little, Brown and Company, 1966), pp. 34–37 and 314–322.

they consider to be a more equitable division of the society's values.

These problems, for reasons which have been outlined, were solved more easily in England than in France or Germany, and the British faced them, for the most part, one at a time. A viable, dynamic national state had been created in England before, or at least together with, the emergence of national identity, and demands for participation were satisfied before demands for greater equality became too intense. In both France and Germany some of the earlier problems had not been solved before new ones appeared, producing fragmentation and violent conflict.

None of the problems cited by Almond are ever solved for all time. In the second half of the twentieth century, all three societies may be about to face some of them once again, albeit in different ways.

3

Russia

and the Soviet Union

1. INTRODUCTION

The Soviet Union is the largest political unit in the world; its total area (7,877,595 square miles) is twice that of the United States. When it is 6:00 A.M. in Kaliningrad in the west, it is already 9:00 A.M. in the Ural Mountains, and 5:00 in the afternoon at Cape Dezhnev, on the Pacific. This huge land mass is very unevenly settled. Moreover, the "Great Russians," who provide the ethnic base for the Russian state, constitute only a bare majority of the total population, which also includes large numbers of Asian peoples—among them Tartars, Uzbeks, and Kazakhs.

The vast distances between population centers and resources, as well as the country's topology and climate, have hindered Russia's industrial and agricultural development. These factors still create tremendous problems. A good deal of territory is permanently frozen. The country lacks an adequate river network and has only limited access to the ocean, since most of its important rivers flow north and south—into the Arctic Ocean, in-

land seas, or seas controlled by other nations. Further, Russia's climate is characterized by long cold winters and short hot summers. The only exceptions are the extreme eastern tip of Siberia, the southern Crimea, and those parts of Transcaucasia where high mountains serve as barriers against cold air from the north. Precipitation drops sharply from north to south, so that areas which might be suitable for cultivation in terms of climate lack sufficient water. The combination of adequate soil and conducive climate exists only in a great triangle bounded by the cities of Leningrad, Irkutsk, and Odessa. Within this triangle, which makes up only 25 per cent of the total area of the country, live almost eighty per cent of the population of the Soviet Union. Thus, despite its size, the Soviet Union does not have as much good cropland as the United States. (See Map 3.2.)

Soviet mineral resources, on the other hand, are at least comparable to those of the United States, and probably somewhat superior. However, these resources are located in areas that have always been poor in food and population; thus transportation difficulties have placed great limitations on their exploitation. One major and continuing effort of the present regime is to open these areas to colonization so that their resources may be adequately exploited. (See Map 3.3.)

Since 1917 Russia has been dominated by an elite whose professed aim has been to bring about a Socialist, or rather a Communist, society and whose ideology has been profoundly shaped by Western European socialism—primarily by the thought of Karl Marx. Soviet intellectuals explain the development of both old Russia and modern Russia in terms of Marxist categories, as modified by Lenin and others. Non-Marxist European scholars have developed a host of alternative analyses. To some the Russian Revolution and its aftermath are to be explained in purely ideological terms: the attempt to create a utopian society of a certain kind by a small group of men dedicated to that end. Others have seen modern Russian history primarily as an effort by a backward society to mobilize its resources for rapid modernization, and still others have analyzed Soviet politics in terms of the elite groups whose aim was to seize and maintain power. Many scholars have seen the present regime as peculiarly Russian, brought to power by specific Russian conditions and following policies derived from the heritage of the nation.

In attempting to understand the current regime, scholars have used various models, depending upon their particular analysis of its sources and nature. Some have continued to stress the regime's Russian characteristics; others, its resemblance to other industrial societies. For a time, during the 1950's, many American scholars emphasized its totalitarianism, contending that, for purposes of analysis, it was best compared with other totalitarian regimes such as that of Nazi Germany.

While each of these approaches has some merit, no single one seems quite satisfactory. The "totalitarian" analysis has declined in popularity since the death of Stalin, as have

analyses couched purely in terms of power. An approach which emphasizes fairly static cultural variables cannot deal effectively with the widespread changes that have occurred since 1917, and a purely ideological approach is incapable of explaining many aspects of Soviet policy. On the other hand, a model that deals with the Soviet Union simply as a modernizing (or, more recently, "modern bureaucratic") society fails to enlighten us as to the reasons for its differences from other industrial societies. It seems clear, therefore, that the pattern of Soviet social and political life today has been the result of a long and complex interplay among all these variables, and that both the nature and the relative importance of each have changed in given historical periods.

The reasons for the success of the Revolution, and even some of the regime's policies, cannot be understood without an examination of traditional Russian society: the conditions under which the Russian state was created; its cultural heritage, especially the religious dimension; and the manner in which it industrialized. Nor can the Revolution itself be understood without an examination of its leaders' ideology, and the analysis of subsequent events must relate this ideology to the tradition out of which that leadership sprang, as well as to the problems faced by all industrializing societies. Finally, the political structure created by the regime has had a continuing impact upon Soviet politics.

In the remainder of this chapter, and throughout our discussion of Soviet politics, an attempt will be made to relate all these variables to each other in order to construct a reasonably coherent analysis of Soviet social and political life. Because the Soviet elite continues to stress the Marxist heritage of the regime, it seems logical that our discussion begin with a detailed analysis of classical Marxism.

2. CLASSICAL MARXISM

MARX'S CONCEPTION OF MAN: To Marx, man differs only in degree from creatures lower on the evolutionary scale. An opposable thumb and a more complex brain have given him, unlike other animals, the power to create tools and mold nature to his ends. The creation of such tools requires social cooperation—hence the development of language and of some form of social order. Thus man's capacities and needs lead to the emergence of civilization and, in fact, we can begin to speak of man only as part of a social order.

The interaction among society, work, and human development is exceedingly complicated. As man impresses himself upon nature through work and in cooperation with other men, he develops self-consciousness, an awareness of the self as separate from the rest of nature; as his technical competence and understanding advance, he develops a more rational understanding of the universe in which he lives. Ultimately, he will achieve relatively complete control over nature and attain fantastically high levels of civilized existence.

Barring accident, the ultimate end is inevitable, but the route is long and circuitous. During all of history to date, men have been the victims of superstition and ignorance, and have battled like the lower animals over scarce resources. Eventually, however, all this will change. Man's complete control over nature will mark both the end of superstition and the solution to the economic problem. Once the latter has been solved, human conflicts will disappear. Men will realize that their own evolution requires relating "creatively" to other men. They will realize that no individual can achieve full self-realization unless all other men do so.

This end, however, can only be reached through a Communist organization of society. As Engels put it:

With the seizing of the means of production by society. . . . The struggle for individual existence disappears. Then for the first time man, in a certain sense, is finally marked off from the rest of the animal kingdom, and emerges from mere animal conditions of existence into really human ones. The whole sphere of the conditions of life which environ man and which have hitherto ruled man, now comes under the dominion and control of man. . . . The extraneous objective forces that have hitherto governed history pass under the control of man himself. Only from that time will man himself . . . make his own history—only from that time will the social causes set in movement by him have . . . the results intended by him. It is the ascent of man from the kingdom of necessity to the kingdom of freedom.[1]

This transition, however, cannot occur until the economic and technological conditions are ripe; it cannot be brought about through a free act of will or through education. Instead, at a particular time, the "real" forces of history will make a revolutionary transformation inevitable. To understand why Marx believed this to be so, we must understand the nature of these "real" historical forces and their relation to human action.

The factors which have determined human development thus far have been economic ones; to put it more precisely, the course of human progress has been prescribed by a constantly renewing tension between the "forces of production" and the "mode of production." The forces of production consist of the natural, technological, and human resources of the world. In order to make use of these forces, men enter into economic relationships ("relations of production"), the structure of which, within a particular society at a particular time, constitutes that society's mode of production. Capitalism and feudalism and communism, for example, are particular modes of production. Tensions between the forces and mode of production develop, because as men devise a set of economic rela-

1 Karl Marx and Friedrich Engels, *Selected Works* (Moscow: Foreign Languages Publishing House, 1951), II, 140–141.

tions to manage existing productive forces, they invariably create new forces of production which cannot be effectively exploited by the current economic system.

Because of the strength of constantly expanding human wants, the old system of economic relations is eventually overthrown. Yet the mode of production which emerges does not completely discard the old forms; rather it assimilates them. Hence the pattern of human development, in Marx's term, is "dialectical."

In a world of scarcity, the great bulk of human energy so far has been directed toward satisfying basic physical needs, and man's primary experience has been that of work. It is little wonder, then, that the social and political structures of all societies, as well as their culture, have been largely shaped by their mode of production. Marx regarded the economic structure of any society as its "base," and its political, social, and cultural life as merely its "superstructure." Changes in the mode of production of any society, therefore, were the primary source of changes in every other area of the community's life.

Marx also argued that conflicts between the forces of production and the mode of production were the motor of social change; this, for him, was a shorthand method of describing a much more intricate process. In all historical societies, except for the most primitive, the mode of production established has involved the creation of a system of social classes in which the economic pie and political power have been divided unequally between those who control the instruments of production (the "exploiting" class) and those who do not. The division has been inevitable because of human inequality, the need for coordinating the efforts of large numbers of men, and, most importantly, the existence of scarcity, which makes men seek to exploit others. It is scarcity, in fact, which has made both exploitation and the class system serve as engines of progress. The development of civilization requires the existence of a rela-

tively leisured class. In the past, an attempt to divide the resources of the community equally would have resulted only in universal poverty.

Historically, the beliefs and values of members of a society have been determined by their position in the class system, that is, by their relation to the established mode of production. A society, then, can change in fundamental ways only when a new class emerges or when the position of the exploited social class produces among its members a new set of values and beliefs with which to challenge the existing social order.

The changes which take place under these circumstances are inevitably accompanied by violence. This is not because the predominant elite is particularly evil or self-interested; indeed, an awareness of their true self-interest might lead them to accept the changes from which, ideally, all would benefit, or at least to reform the system they dominate in order to stave off revolution. It is true that the dominant class does derive some benefits from the existing system, but the major source of its resistance to change stems from a belief that the system is both natural and right. The dominating class, therefore, is the victim of a partial or "false" consciousness.

Marx did not believe that economic forces were the only ones which affected social developments. National differences—produced by geographic, individual, or accidental factors—affected the pace of change and even, to some extent, influenced social and economic patterns. However, these variations were comparatively unimportant. Nineteenth-century English society was a parliamentary monarchy based upon a common law, while France had experienced a variety of regimes and produced a legal system characterized by a written code; but both were essentially bourgeois capitalist societies moving in the same general direction. England and France, retaining their differences, would pass from bourgeois to Communist societies.

The similarities between the two Communist societies would be far more important than any differences, just as the difference between Communist society and capitalist society was far more important than variations among individual societies within either broad pattern.

As Marx understood it, men have moved through four stages of production: primitive communism, the Asian mode of production, feudalism, and capitalism.[2] Each of the last three involved an advance over the earlier stage because each, given man's nature, involved increasing mastery over the world. The final stage—communism—will make this mastery complete; again, given man's nature, it is inevitable. Our understanding of Marx's analysis may be clarified if we examine Marx's discussion of the transition from feudalism to capitalism, the nature of capitalism, the reasons it must inevitably lead to a Communist revolution, and the nature of that revolution. Finally, we shall also examine the role of the Communist Party as Marx conceived that role.

FEUDALISM, CAPITALISM, COMMUNISM: Feudalism was essentially a system of economic relationships between armed barons and impoverished peasants. The level of technology was fairly primitive and, for the great mass of people, only the most basic needs could be satisfied. This economic system colored the whole structure of the society. As its organization was collective, so its religion was collective—that is, Catholic—in orientation; as the society was hierarchical, so the religion was hierarchically ordered. What is more, the nature of the relations of production fixed the particular pattern of political and legal organization: both were hierarchical, with differential rights and obligations attached to particular classes, and both legitimized a set of relationships which emphasized collective

responsibility. Even the pattern of culture can be understood in these terms. For example, for the exploiting classes at least, it was a military culture accentuating military virtues.

But the system contained within it the seeds of its own transformation. The military classes needed more and more weapons to meet the requirements of a changing military technology. A leisured class desired material comforts: spices, rich cloths, and other goods. A merchant class (the bourgeoisie) and urban centers sprang up to satisfy these needs, certain forms of technology were encouraged, and new productive techniques were devised.

The emergence of a commercial class technology accelerated the advance of a system of factories; and a more functional division of labor developed in order to satisfy the capitalist desires for profits and increased production. As the outlook of this middle class was predicated on its relation to the competitive production of goods, so its attitudes toward religion, politics, and even art came to differ sharply from those of the aristocratic culture which nourished it. Its religion was and is individualistic—that is, Protestant. Its culture is antimilitary and its politics is liberal—the free competition of ideas, a rational legal system, representative forms of government.

These differing values eventually brought the middle class into conflict with the aristocracy and aristocratic regimes. In part, the clash mirrored divergent interests: the bourgeoisie wanted, for example, a free labor force and an end to feudal economic restrictions. However, the conflict was much broader, and based essentially upon differing ideologies. The bourgeois desired to change the economic system, not only because they believed they would benefit, but also because they believed that the policies they espoused were superior to traditional economic relations and would maximize the general welfare. Both bourgeois and aristocrat, therefore, were motivated by differing conceptions of the

[2] Marx's discussion of the Asian mode of production was an addendum formulated after he had worked out his overall scheme of economic development, and does not really fit very well into his general theory.

good, although the underlying mechanisms of the conflict were fundamentally economic. The old regime was overthrown and the bourgeois capitalist states of Europe emerged.

Capitalist society, Marx argued, is far superior to the one which it replaced. Under capitalism, productivity has increased by leaps and bounds, for the system constantly calls forth new technical and scientific advances. A related advantage is that increasing control over nature destroys old myths and superstitions. For precisely these reasons, capitalism paves the way for the leap into freedom. For the first time in human history, the veils (such as religious justification) which have concealed the domination of particular ruling classes are ripped asunder, and man possesses the means by which nature may be fully subdued and turned to his own use. But capitalism cannot survive: it has brought into existence new productive forces which, because the system is chaotic and unplanned and because capitalists are victims of a "false consciousness," are beyond its control.

In fact, while capitalism in one sense is a tremendous advance over the feudal system which it replaces, in another sense it is retrograde. It replaces the aristocracy and the peasantry with two new classes, the bourgeoisie and the proletariat. The latter are herded into sprawling ugly urban centers in which they live under unbearable conditions. Completely deprived of any ownership of the tools of production, the worker has only his labor to sell. Even worse, he becomes a slave to the machine; his work becomes ever more routinized and specialized, and comes to lack creative meaning. As Marx put it, speaking of the worker:

He works in order to live. He does not even reckon labor as part of his life, it is rather a sacrifice of his life. . . . The product of his activity is not the object of his activity. What he produces for himself is not the silk that he weaves, not the gold that he draws from the mine. . . . What he produces for himself are

wages. . . . Does he consider this twelve hours' weaving, spinning, drilling, turning . . . as an expression of his life, as life? On the contrary, life begins for him where this activity ceases.[3]

And his condition grows progressively worse. Because the proletariat is part of an industrial reserve army of employed and unemployed, his wages can never rise above the subsistence level, and economic crises of ever greater intensity and duration deepen the poverty of the great mass of workers for whom no employment is available. This situation is not the result of the perfidy of capitalists as a class; it is inherent in the system itself.

To the capitalist who is intent upon expanding production, the worker is a commodity like any other, to be bought as cheaply as possible and used as effectively as possible. In fact, since the worker is almost the only commodity which can return more than cost, it is through exploitation of labor that the capitalist makes the profits (or "surplus value") which enable him to expand his enterprise. And such expansion is necessary —not only as an ideal goal, but also because the capitalist is constantly faced with competition from others and will face ruin if he does not expand. Accordingly, he must seek to increase his profits by further exploiting his workers, and to lower unit costs by expanding his production through the stepped-up use of machinery. Those who fail in the competitive race are weeded out and sink to the ranks of the proletariat. Thus, the competitive race ultimately produces an economy run by a small number of gigantic enterprises in which the few own everything and the great mass of people is "disinherited." And the economic consequences increase in severity. The capitalist, therefore, is caught on a treadmill: the machines he uses, since they do not represent "living" labor power, cannot produce surplus value; yet given his lower rate of profit, he must produce all the more in order to achieve

3 Karl Marx, *Selected Works,* ed. V. Adoratsky (London: Lawrence & Wishart, Limited, 1942), I, 256.

any return. As a result, the market periodically becomes cluttered with goods that the mass of the population cannot afford. Hence the crises noted earlier.

As the situation of the great mass of workers, the proletariat, becomes worse and worse, they begin to develop self-consciousness. Thrust together in the city and in the factory, they can communicate with each other. Educated by the bourgeoisie to the idea of equality, they can criticize the injustice of the existing situation. Recognizing the power of machines, they refuse to accept the need for these to remain idle while people starve. Aware of the collective nature of the productive process, they begin to reject the individualistic conception of property ownership and distribution. Eventually they revolt and overturn the existing system; for a short time they establish a "dictatorship of the proletariat" over the capitalists who might wish to restore the old system. In the very process of revolution their collective consciousness has been expanded, and they have come to realize that the fates of all men are bound together. At this point, they move fairly quickly toward a Socialist society and then beyond that to a Communist society which takes "from each according to his capacities" and gives "to each according to his needs." In such a society, man will at last have solved the economic problem, and he will have mastered his environment. Men will live together without compulsion, accepting rational authority freely because they recognize the requirements of the common good. The state will then "wither away," and the government of people will be replaced by the administration of things. At the same time, hours of work will be reduced to a bare minimum, and men will use their leisure time to achieve new heights of culture and self-development.

It is important to understand precisely what Marx meant by the state's withering away. As he defined it, the state was an instrument of the ruling class. Its major function was the use of force to obtain the compliance of the exploited classes. In a Socialist society, authority would continue to be exerted; but it would be "rational" authority, freely accepted because men would realize that it was in their interest to do so, as a ship's crew accepts its captain's orders, understanding that those orders are based on the captain's expert knowledge and that someone must coordinate the efforts of a large group of individuals.

No matter how hard capitalists try, Marx vouched, they cannot change the logic of the system. This end must inevitably come about. Yet it cannot come until the conditions are ripe. Capitalism must first have developed the productive tools of the society to a point where mastery of the environment is really possible, and the experience of capitalism must have first produced among the workers the consciousness of class and mutual interdependence which are requisites for the emergence of the new Socialist man. Under such circumstances, the role of those middle-class intellectuals, like Marx, who see the future with some clarity must of necessity be limited. The convinced Communist can serve only as a "midwife," speeding up the tempo of the process just a bit, heightening self-consciousness through education, and helping to time revolutionary outbreaks. In the last analysis, however, his influence is relatively marginal.

In the last years of his life, Marx shifted his argument in certain respects. In some late speeches and letters he noted that it might be possible for socialism to be achieved peacefully in some countries and, further, that it might be possible for Russia to move directly from the peasant commune to socialism without passing through a capitalist phase. However, these remarks stand in direct contradiction to the whole framework of earlier Marxist thought. Marx never undertook a fundamental revision of his analysis; and his system, which requires a particular set of developmental stages, remains both revolutionary and apocalyptic.

3. THE OLD REGIME

Those who came to power in Russia on the basis of Marx's slogans revised significant portions of his theoretical framework; since the Revolution, additional revisions have been made. To understand these, however, as well as the interplay between Marxist ideology and other factors, we must turn to an analysis of Russian and Soviet history.

RELIGION AND THE FORGING OF THE RUSSIAN STATE: It has been said that Russia straddles Asia and Europe culturally as it does geographically. Despite the fact that Christianity was adopted by the Kievan kingdom in the tenth century, Russia shared none of the great cultural movements which created the modern West: the Renaissance, the Reformation, and, more importantly, the rationalistic attitudes which were instrumental in developing modern science—all these were unknown in Russia.

The reasons for this lack of participation are varied. Undoubtedly geography was a factor. The Slavs, who have dominated Russia, are a European people, ethnically akin to the Germanic tribes immediately to the west. But Russia's physical distance from the centers of Western culture was sufficiently great that it had no direct contact with Roman civilization; this isolation was further accentuated by the Tartar conquests of the thirteenth century, which destroyed Kievan Russia and completely cut off the eastern Slavs from the West for several centuries.

The geographic factor was also partially responsible for the fact that Russian Christianity came from Byzantium rather than from Rome. Although the roots of Orthodoxy lay in Hellenic civilization, it was characterized by an emphasis on mysticism and passivity which was quite alien to Western Christianity. And, as the Byzantine Empire grew weaker, the Russian church was deprived of even those elements of Byzantine culture which reflected a more rationalistic tradition. Thus,

as a crucial component of Russian culture, the Orthodox Church—passive toward nature, submissive to political authority, mystical in its views of God and man—hardly served as an energizing factor. Indeed, it was these very elements, including Orthodoxy's refusal to explain God's way to man in rational terms, that Russian Slavophiles, seeking to prove the superiority of Russia over Western Europe, emphasized in later centuries. Western scholasticism, they argued, was the source of rationalism and Protestantism— forces which were combining to destroy religion in the West.

For all these reasons, the course of Russian development was quite different from that of Western Europe. As European feudalism was breaking down, the remnants of a free peasantry in Russia were being reduced to the level of serfs. And, later, as absolutism in the West was being eroded by the beginnings of parliamentarianism, the Russian czars were just completing their destruction of a quasi-independent nobility and establishing an absolutist regime.

Yet, despite the differences between Russia and Western Europe, Russian "high" culture at least was essentially European; it is no accident that, once the barriers to communication with the rest of Europe were reduced with the decline of the Tartar Empire in the fifteenth century, the Russian elite turned to the West as a model. Even when Russian intellectuals stressed the superiority of their traditional institutions, they did so in dialogue with the West and used essentially Western categories. In the seventeenth and eighteenth centuries, Peter the Great tried to rationalize the bureaucratic apparatus of the Russian state and hired technicians and artists from Western European countries. Catherine II invited Western philosophers to her court to disseminate European ideas; she also encouraged the settlement of German peasants (the Volga Germans) who, she hoped, would serve as models for the backward Russian peasantry.

The results of all these efforts were minimal. Russia entered the nineteenth century a highly traditional society. The little industrialization that had begun was chiefly government-sponsored and oriented to military requirements. Most of the peasants, who constituted some three-fourths of the population, lived under personal bondage—either to the state, which employed them in mines and metallurgical plants, or to one of the 250,000 or so serf-owning members of the nobility. The rights of the lord over his serfs were extensive. He determined the distribution of their land and the time they would spend working his demesne. He could contract serfs to work for others, or prohibit their movement. And, until well into the nineteenth century, he could punish a serf by flogging or by exile to Siberia, without having to account for his actions.

As in other manorial systems, the serf cultivated some land for his own use. In Russia, far more than in the West, the use of the land was governed through a common social organization, the village commune (*mir,* or *obshchina*), under the leadership of village elders. The commune was responsible for paying the peasants' poll taxes, issuing the passports that were needed to leave the village, and, of greater importance, deciding what crops would be grown. In the "repartitional" communes, the community as a whole redistributed land from time to time to maintain a rough equality, or at least to make sure that individual families possessed sufficient land to meet their needs.

Politically, the regime was an absolute monarchy. The czar functioned through a state bureaucracy, composed largely of minor nobility, which was completely dependent upon his authority. He was assisted, too, by a personal chancellery consisting of a secretariat, a bureau for the codification of the law, and the so-called "third section," created in 1826, which was concerned with crimes against the state. The secret police of the third section had the authority to place offenders under administrative arrest and, during most of the nineteenth century, to sentence them without benefit of trial.

In theory, then, the regime was centralized and absolute, but it was not so in practice. The Russian czars had consolidated their power, even as Muscovy had enlarged its empire, by destroying the political authority of the Russian aristocracy. As in France, the aristocracy's loss of authority was offset by the increase in local prerogative; and, also as in France, the central bureaucracy had insufficient tools at its disposal to forge an integrated national state. The Russian situation, however, was even more complicated than the French. The vast expanse of Russia and the difficulties of communication, especially in winter, effectively inhibited the implementation of national policies; moreover, the absence of cultural patterns which emphasized the rational organization of work meant that Russian absolutism was tempered by considerable inefficiency. The various organs of the government, by and large, went their own ways without any overall purpose, aside from that of either continuing the status quo or trying to increase the prerogatives and rewards of office.

During the nineteenth century the system came under mounting criticism—first, from members of the aristocracy who had visited or read of Western Europe, and later from other segments of the population as well. Many of the growing intelligentsia found Russian life stifling and longed to have Russia follow the Western example, developing a constitutional government and a scientific "modern society." Some went further and hoped to skip a stage in Western development by moving directly from a traditional society to socialism, thus taking the best from Western Europe, yet avoiding the extreme anarchic individualism that, so they argued, had created an alienated urban proletariat. In the last analysis, Marxism, at least as it initially developed in Russia, was part of this Westernizing strand.

To others among the intelligentsia, however—the so-called Slavophiles—the West taught only that such developments should be avoided. Western rationalism and liberalism were disintegrating forces, and the individualism of Western bourgeois society was cold and philistine as contrasted with the Russian feeling of community. In fact, Russia had a mission: to bring to the West its own unique set of values. Slavophilism was, of course, encouraged by the state, for its fundamental elements were conservative. But not all Slavophiles supported the status quo; some, the forerunners of populism, saw the future of Russia in an agrarian Socialist society based on the Russian commune.

Whichever strand they belonged to, the intelligentsia of Russia could accomplish very little of practical value. They were far removed from the Russian peasant; their own culture may have been of the nineteenth century, but that of the great mass of the population was, in Western terms, of the thirteenth. Even had this not been so, the absolutism of the regime would still have inhibited all action. Attempts at reform always came up against the prejudices of tradition and the power of the police. It is little wonder, then, that the intelligentsia retreated to that hothouse of lengthy but essentially meaningless utopian speculation and argumentation immortalized by Turgenev and other Russian authors.

REFORM AND REACTION: In the second half of the nineteenth century, however, it began to appear that Russia might indeed take the road followed by Western Europe. In 1855, Alexander II became Czar of all the Russians. Despite his conservative training, he was convinced that the increasing interaction between Russia and the West demanded the modernizing of Russian society. If the Crimean War (1853–1856) had done anything, it had revealed that a society without a technological base could not compete with a technologically powerful one. To Alexander, Russia's backwardness could be corrected only by modifying key elements of its social structure. In 1861, therefore, he issued a *ukaz*

(ordinance) abolishing serfdom (although with substantial compensation to the landlords); in 1864 he initiated a system of local self-government, under the aegis of assemblies (*zemstvos*) in the provinces and municipal councils in the cities. While the powers of the zemstvos were limited and suffrage was restricted, this was, at least, a beginning.

Also in 1864, Alexander inaugurated substantial judicial reforms, designed to develop an independent judiciary, an independent legal profession, and trial by jury even in cases which involved crimes against the state. He also extended the freedom of the press and expanded the intellectual autonomy and freedom of universities.

These reforms were, in part, a response to active discontent. As such they failed. The zemstvos, the press, and the universities became sounding boards against the monarchy. Groups which had concluded that peaceful social reform was impossible stepped up their terrorist activities. Faced with these circumstances on the one hand and the nobility's opposition to his reforms on the other, and convinced by now that further concessions would lead to the regime's destruction, Alexander retreated. Administrative arrest was restored, censorship of the press and universities reinstituted, and the power of the zemstvos curtailed. The response was mounting terrorist activity. In 1881 Alexander was assassinated; the terrorist groups responsible for this act informed his son and successor that such was the fate of tyrants and counseled a more liberal policy.

Alexander III, however, drew a different moral from his father's fate: stricter control, rather than reform, would preserve the regime. Accordingly, by 1894, when Alexander III died (in bed), the regime he left to his son was in some ways almost as oppressive as the one his father had inherited. Nicholas II made little effort to change this framework, at least until the war with Japan in 1904 which set off new revolutionary upheavals and a further round of reform and reaction. The discontent of the next dozen years culminated in the great Revolution of 1917.

THE BEGINNINGS OF INDUSTRIALIZATION: Between the emancipation of the serfs and the start of World War I, Russia began to undergo an economic revolution involving both a dramatic shift in the position of the peasantry and the first stages of industrialization. For a time, it seemed likely that these economic changes would eventually lead to the development of a full-fledged capitalist industrial society.

The freeing of the serfs had not alleviated the agricultural problem; in some ways it had even aggravated the situation. In general, the peasants had been given the worst lands, and a large part of the burden of compensating their former owners had been placed upon them. Also, the village commune system, a system which, despite its admirable features, was wholly inefficient from a practical point of view, had been retained. The continued reapportioning of holdings encouraged strip farming and discouraged individual initiative. With a highly regressive tax system and a growing population, it is not surprising that economic improvement did not follow upon formal freedom. In fact, it is probable that living standards among the peasants declined between 1865 and 1900; certainly the famine of 1891–1892 was among the worst the Russians had experienced in some time.

The government responded to these circumstances in two ways. A land bank was set up to lend money to peasants at very low interest. The regressive poll tax was eliminated, and land payments were reduced and even repeatedly postponed. Yet at the same time the government stepped up its repressive measures. Agriculture was centralized in the Ministry of the Interior, which also controlled the police, and provincial detachments of troops were strengthened.

After the Revolution of 1905, however, the government recognized the need for more radical measures; it sponsored a new series of reforms to break up the peasant communes

and to encourage private ownership of the land. The program, initiated by Pëtr A. Stolypin, minister of the interior, permitted and even encouraged certain groups of peasants to break with the mir. Between 1907 and 1915, approximately two and half million peasants in European Russia (about 24 per cent of the total) were given title to their own farms. At the same time about three million peasants, attracted by government subsidies, moved from European to Asian Russia, where they could obtain land of their own. Productivity began to increase; it might conceivably have done so significantly if the war had not intervened.

In the meantime, the industrial picture was also changing. In the eighteenth and nineteenth centuries, the economy's industrial sector, which had originated with Peter the Great, grew steadily, although the great outburst of productive energy in the West was such that Russia fell further and further behind. The entrepreneurial class remained small, however, and was drawn largely from elite groups, in contrast with England or France where substantial elements of the new industrial bourgeoisie emerged out of the class of skilled craftsmen.

The pace of industrialization quickened after 1860. Large amounts of foreign capital were invested in the country; new exploitable resources were discovered, bringing about the creation of new enterprises. Between 1890 and 1900, the rate of industrial growth in Russia was greater than in many of the industrial countries of the West, averaging some eight per cent a year. A period of stagnation followed, but between 1905 and 1914 the rate again rose to an average of six per cent a year. Russia seemed on the verge of sustained economic growth.[4]

Because most Russian enterprises were relatively large and concentrated around a few

4 Data from Alexander Gerschenkron, "Problems and Patterns of Russian Economic Development," in Cyril E. Black, ed., *The Transformation of Russian Society* (Cambridge, Mass.: Harvard University Press, 1960), pp. 42–72.

TABLE 3.1. THE GROWTH OF RUSSIAN CITIES

Population in thousands

	1800	1850	1900	1910	1939	1959	1967
Moscow	250	365	989	1506	4,137	5,032	6,422
Leningrad	220	485	1,133	1911	3,191	2,888	3,296
Kharkov	—	45	175	224	833	934	1,125
Kiev	—	61	247	446	846	1,104	1,413
Gorki	—	—	—	106	644	942	1,120
Odessa	6	90	405	498	604	667	776
Baku	—	—	112	218	809	636	772
Tashkent	—	—	156	165	585	911	1,239

Source: For data to 1910, W. S. Woytinsky and E. S. Woytinsky, *World Population and Production* (New York: The Twentieth Century Fund, 1953), p. 121; reprinted by permission of the publisher. For data from 1910, United Nations, *Demographic Yearbook 1960*, Table 6 (pp. 344–348), 1967, Table 7 (pp. 229–230).

cities, a self-conscious urban proletariat formed there much more rapidly than in either England or France.[5] The transition of these workers from rural to urban living conditions brought with it the same violent reactions to the stresses of industrialization experienced by both English and French workers. To this violence, and to the efforts of the workers to create trade unions, the government responded in a number of ways. In 1897, an 11½-hour day was established as the maximum for all workers, with a limit of 10½ hours for night work, and the Ministry of the Interior encouraged the formation of mutual-aid societies. These societies were heavily infiltrated, or even led, by police agents. Often, however, this effort at central control of workers' organizations backfired, with the agents playing a double role and ultimately identifying with the workers they led. Finally, the government relied upon repression: detachments of cossacks were used to crush strikes, and police representatives were placed in some of the larger factories. Given the extent of repression and of the fact that the working force, even though highly

concentrated, was rather small, organized trade unionism made very little progress until the Revolution. Working-class unrest and alienation continued to grow and was an important factor in the downfall of the czarist regime.

4. THE ORIGINS AND DEVELOPMENT OF RUSSIAN MARXISM

RUSSIAN POPULISM: During the entire nineteenth century, the difficulty of securing reforms and the lack of institutional channels for seeking a redress of grievances encouraged the proliferation of a revolutionary and quasi-revolutionary underground. The radicalism of many of these groups was the direct result of the tremendous frustration experienced by Russian intellectuals who, comparing Russia with the advanced countries of the West, noted the ever-widening gap between the two. Such groups grew in number as the nineteenth century wore on. Many of the most important of these started as populist groups, which hoped to find a uniquely Russian way toward a more "advanced" society and to avoid the evils of the West.

The populist movement drew much of its inspiration from Nikolai G. Chernyshevsky, the author of the famous novel *What Is to Be Done?* (Lenin later used this title for an

[5] In 1913, 44 per cent of all workers were concentrated in plants employing more than one thousand people. See Jerzy G. Gliksman, "The Russian Urban Worker from Serf to Proletarian," in Black, *Transformation*, p. 315.

equally famous essay on the organization of the Russian Social Democratic Party.) Chernyshevsky came from a provincial ecclesiastical family, and spent nineteen years in Siberian exile for his political agitation. Other forebears of populism included Dimitry I. Pisarev, Mikhail A. Bakunin, Pëtr N. Tkachev, and Pëtr L. Lavrov. All these men were utopians who, although they "loved" Russia's peasant masses, despised the stupidity of those masses and believed that the millennium could be achieved only through the efforts of a disciplined group of revolutionary intellectuals, that is, an elite. In fact, from the very beginning Russian populists were torn between a "love" of the peasants who had to be educated to the new society and the feeling that, given the backwardness of the masses, the peasants must "be forced to be free."

In 1869 a group of young revolutionaries in Saint Petersburg formed a group whose program called for the use of the mir as the basis of a future free and Socialist society. To accomplish this end required the education of peasant leaders, and in the early 1870's literally thousands of students, as part of the so-called *Narodnik* (populist) movement, went to the countryside to preach the gospel. But the peasants proved uninterested and even suspicious; the chief result of the movement was that the jails were filled with idealistic young intellectuals, reported to the police by those they were attempting to save.

It is little wonder, then, that many intellectuals abandoned these efforts, turning either to political assassination and terror—in the hope that a revolutionary elite might achieve what the people would not—or else to a vision of Russia's future based not on the backward peasant but on a new class which would emerge as Russia recapitulated developments in Western Europe. The impact of continued terror upon Russian society was minimal; if anything, it served only to freeze existing patterns as the government expanded its penetration of terrorist organizations. Periodically these groups were decimated and their mem-

bers exiled or executed. An especially rigorous and effective campaign was instituted in the 1880's, the decade following the assassination of Alexander II. One of those executed, for complicity in a plot to assassinate Alexander III, was a young university student by the name of Alexander Ulyanov—the older brother of Vladimir Ilich Ulyanov, who was later to take the revolutionary pseudonym of Lenin.

The other course, that of turning to new theories, resulted in the formation in 1883 of a Russian Socialist Party which based its analyses on the work of Marx. The founder of the party was Georgi V. Plekhanov, an exiled intellectual who had given up his previous populist hopes and was now convinced that Russia would, in fact, develop along the same lines as the West—that this was its promise and its hope. In 1883 he founded the Liberation of Labor Group which, in 1898, joined with a number of other organizations to form the Social Democratic Labor Party. But Russian Marxists were little more successful than the populists had been in spreading their tenets and organizing political action within Russia. They were infiltrated by police spies, their meetings were broken up, and their leaders were imprisoned. Actually, most of the meetings of the organization were held outside Russia.

MARXISM AND LENINISM: Vladimir Ulyanov turned to Marxism in 1893, after having become disillusioned with the populism that initially attracted him. The son of a minor civil servant, he had planned upon a legal career and had received a law degree. He was arrested for Socialist agitation in 1895 and, after completing a year in prison, was exiled to Siberia for three more years. Upon his release, he emigrated to Western Europe.

By this time he had published a book called *The Development of Capitalism in Russia,* and was counted among the emigré leaders of Russian socialism. More and more, he found himself in disagreement with Plekhanov and other leaders within the organization—those who conceived of Russian Social Democracy as developing along the same lines as comparable parties in the West, and who saw their primary function as that of educating the working class through a mass party which would agitate for socialism. Lenin countered with a number of essays—most notably, perhaps, *What Is to Be Done?* (published in 1902)—which offered instead a conception of the party as a revolutionary elite; the function of this elite was, indeed, to educate the workers, but it was also to take an active part in determining strategy and was to be effectively organized for revolutionary action. Thus, while the party could and should freely discuss issues, once these were resolved, the decision must be accepted and debate must cease.

In one sense, the differences between Lenin and those who opposed him were marginal. Although he disagreed with his opponents in certain respects, arguing, for instance, that the working class by itself would not develop adequate Socialist theory but might remain content with "trade-union consciousness," he did not (at least initially) deny that, in the last analysis, the revolution could be achieved only when the working class had been educated and the proper social and economic conditions were present. Nonetheless, his elitist emphasis and the elements of "voluntarism" in his thinking did involve a qualitative break with Marxist analysis.

The issues which divided Lenin from many in the party came to a head at the second meeting of the Russian Social Democratic Party, held in 1903, first in Brussels and then, because of police intervention, in London. Taking advantage of a temporary majority, Lenin captured control of the executive organization of the party. The faction he represented became known as Bolsheviks ("majority"), while his opponents became known as Mensheviks ("minority"). Even though attempts were made to reconcile differences, Russian Social Democracy split and resplit between 1903 and 1917, but Lenin stuck to his own image of the future over all

opposition. To this image he was to add one further notion, suggested to him by perhaps the second most important figure in the Russian Revolution—Leon Trotsky. Trotsky was of Jewish background, as were a good number of the early Social Democratic leaders, including many who later became prominent Bolsheviks, among them Grigori E. Zinoviev, Lev Kamenev, Grigori Sokolnikov, and Karl Radek.

The Trotsky-suggested addendum, the concept of "permanent revolution," was based on the "law of combined development." The Socialist revolution did not first have to occur, as had been customarily thought, in the advanced capitalist nations which had already passed through the bourgeois-democratic stage and were theoretically ready to move on to socialism. Rather, it could develop in Russia immediately out of the bourgeois revolution, provided that Russia served as a spark for the more advanced Western European nations, which would then come to the aid of the fledgling and backward Socialist state. Revolution had not occurred first in the advanced states, Lenin explained, because nations such as England and France had bought off their proletariat by imperialist ventures at the expense of the exploited peoples. In the twentieth century, then, the world could be divided into bourgeois and proletarian states, and world capitalism could be treated as a worldwide phenomenon, with revolution occurring at the weakest link: Russia.

Lenin did not come to this last conclusion until the Russian Revolution had actually begun. In 1917, in fact, only a few weeks before leaving Switzerland for Russia, he still expected that the revolution could only be an advanced type of "bourgeois" democratic revolution. His theory, then, came after the fact—action had assumed primacy. With this statement Lenin would agree. He had always argued that Marxism was not a closed system, but a method, which he was attempting to apply to a situation which Marx could not foresee; he argued, too, that he was closer in spirit to Marx than were those "reformists" who, waiting for the people to become fully aware of what they should do, had, in reality, moved far away from the spirit of Marx.

Although Lenin had altered some very important Marxian concepts, he was justified in claiming that his alterations were no more fundamental than those made by Marxists who opposed him. The fact of the matter is that pure Marxism was inapplicable to the European environment. Marx had expected a spontaneous rising of the masses in capitalist countries, but an increasing affluence, combined with modifications in European capitalism, made this less and less likely. Two courses, then, were open. One could begin to revise classical Marxism, accepting the possibility of a peaceful parliamentary evolution to socialism and eventually rejecting Marx's apocalyptic vision, a course followed by many Western Socialists, or else one could retain the vision but reject the democratic elements of Marxist thought. It was the second course that Lenin chose.

Some students of the Soviet Union, regarding Leninism as a fusion of Marxism and the elitist elements of populism, believe that bolshevism is the "russification" of Marx. As evidence they cite Lenin's key essay, *What Is to Be Done?,* as well as the words of praise he had for Chernyshevsky and other populists. We shall return to this question later, but it should be pointed out that Lenin's 1902 writings on the role of the intelligentsia could just as easily have been derived from the noted German Marxist Karl Kautsky, for whom he had considerable respect at that time. It also should be noted that in 1902 Lenin's recommendations for a revolutionary party were limited to Russia and were justified almost entirely in terms of the repressive nature of the regime; he argued that in Western countries, including Germany, a mass, democratically organized party was feasible. Of course, after the Revolution he changed his mind and encouraged the development of tightly organized Communist parties in Western European countries; but by this time the

need for immediate revolution in the West completely dominated his thinking.

And Lenin did retain the central element of Marx's vision: the belief that a change in the socioeconomic structure of the society would in fact lead to a new world—a humane world in which all men were brothers. It was this faith which drove him on, and which, in his eyes, justified violence as the necessary midwife of revolution. It was this belief, too, which came to justify widespread acts of repression on the grounds that they would bring about the ends he and the party sought. Hatred of the enemy was legitimate and necessary if men were to be moved to act, and repression was necessary to make sure that the right road was chosen. For those Mensheviks and even Bolsheviks who feared that elimination of democratic practices might have far-reaching consequences, he had a ready reply: political institutions were reflections of the existing socioeconomic order. Once the new Communist order was created, true democracy would automatically emerge.

The nature of Lenin's faith and that of those who followed him is, perhaps, best illustrated by a quotation from Trotsky, who, in addition to his other talents, was perhaps the most brilliant polemicist of the Communist movement. In an essay written early in 1901, Trotsky engages in an imaginary conversation with a cynical pessimist.

Dum spiro spero! . . . *If I were one of the celestial bodies, I would look with complete detachment upon this miserable ball of dust and dirt. . . . I would shine upon the good and evil alike. . . . But I am a* man. . . . *As long as I breathe, I shall fight for the future, that radiant future in which man, strong and beautiful, will become master of the drifting stream of his history and will direct it towards the boundless horizon of beauty, joy and happiness! . . .*

The nineteenth century has in many ways satisfied and has in even more ways deceived the hopes of the optimist. . . . It has compelled him to transfer most of his hopes to the twentieth century. Whenever the optimist was confronted by an atrocious fact, he exclaimed: What, and this can happen on the threshold of the twentieth century!

And now that century has come! What has it brought with it at the outset?

. . . Hatred and murder, famine and blood.

. . .

It seems as if the new century, this gigantic newcomer, were bent at the very moment of its appearance to drive the optimist into absolute pessimism and civic nirvana.

—Death to Utopia! Death to faith! Death to love! Death to hope! thunders the twentieth century in salvoes of fire and in the rumbling of guns.

—Surrender, you pathetic dreamer. Here I am, your long awaited twentieth century, your "future."

—No, replies the unhumbled optimist: You—you are only the present.[6]

5. THE FALL OF IMPERIAL RUSSIA

The Bolsheviks did not play a major role in Russian history until 1917. Lenin remained in exile most of the time; he was caught by surprise by the Revolution of 1905, which resulted from the disruption and difficulties caused by the disastrous Russian war with Japan. A strike in Saint Petersburg (renamed Petrograd in 1914 and Leningrad in 1924) was followed by widespread peasant upheavals and a call by moderate groups for constitutional reforms. The regime responded by relaxing censorship and creating two representative institutions of limited power—a state Duma and a State Council.

But these, for the most part, turned out to be only temporary concessions. When the Duma proved recalcitrant, Czar Nicholas II dissolved it and called for new elections; then, after a second election had produced an equally inflexible body, he packed it. And when, as in the late nineteenth century, the

freedoms accorded to the universities and the press resulted in criticism of the regime, censorship was restored; as before, limited reforms had prompted demands for greater freedom and had convinced the czar and those who advised him that only repression could produce stability. Thus the vicious circle so characteristic of Russian politics closed once again. By 1914 many observers were predicting the eventual collapse of a regime which seemed increasingly anachronistic. The impetus for that collapse was provided by World War I.

Russia rose to the conflict with an upsurge of patriotism, but it was in no position to fight a war against an industrialized nation. It lacked the capacity to produce and use modern weapons; it lacked facilities for adequate transport of troops. It did not take long, therefore, for its position to deteriorate. In 1916 alone, more than two million Russian soldiers were killed or wounded and another 350,000 were prisoners of the Germans. The economy was cracking, and living conditions within Russia were becoming more and more arduous.

The spark that set off the Revolution was a series of strikes in Petrograd which quickly spread and infected the troops supposedly called in to repress them. The eventual upshot was the abdication of the czar on March 15, 1917, and the formation of a provisional government dominated by liberals, and later moderate Socialists. The government promised to organize a constitutional assembly and to hold free elections. In the meantime it pledged itself to continuation of the war. The Bolsheviks were hostile to the government, but, initially at least, they seemed unwilling to move further. However, on April 16 Lenin arrived at the Finland Station in Petrograd and urged more radical steps, including transfer of authority from the provisional government to the soviets—the ad hoc committees of workers and soldiers dating back to the 1905 Revolution—which had formed in the major cities. He also urged the immediate signing of a separate peace with the Central

---

[6] Quoted in Isaac Deutscher, *The Prophet Armed* (New York: Oxford University Press, 1954), pp. 54–55.

Powers and the immediate seizure of land by the peasants.

Attacked from both the right and the left, the provisional government grew increasingly weaker. Discipline in the army had broken down, the economy had crumbled, and with the collapse of effective authority the country was gripped by chaos. Despite splits in their ranks, the Bolsheviks benefited from all this as they did from the fact that in an increasingly polarized situation the Mensheviks and Socialist Revolutionaries were forced to support them as the less evil of what seemed to be two radically opposed alternatives: Socialist revolution or the return of the old regime.[7] While many Mensheviks disliked the repressive means of the Bolsheviks, they shared their ends and retained the hope that Lenin would modify some of his more authoritarian views. Indeed, time and time again, conversations with Lenin would convince them that he was not as rigid as he sometimes appeared to be and that he would respond to reasonable arguments. On November 6, 1917, then, the Bolsheviks in Petrograd seized the government offices, arrested the members of the provisional government, and assumed control of the Russian state. Nearly four years of bloody civil war and limited conflicts with neighbors were to follow (in which the Allied powers—France, Great Britain, and the United States—participated sporadically), but Russia had reached a turning point in her history.

A variety of complex reasons made it possible for the Bolsheviks to win and maintain power. The radicalism of their program appealed to masses for whom the breakdown of authority meant the settling of old scores and the achievement of long-desired goals, specifically the seizure of the land. The Bolsheviks' appeal was further broadened by their willingness to end the war—a program which no other party would accept, and on which even they themselves were split. The

Bolsheviks won support of the many minority groups that made up the Russian state by means of liberal promises; they controlled the major cities and had the advantage of interior lines of communication in the civil war which followed the seizure of power. And finally, the party was led by a group of dedicated and brilliant men whose talents lay not only in general organization and self-discipline but also in military activity of the highest order.

The Bolsheviks exhibited a ruthlessness and tactical flexibility with which the more moderate parties could not cope; yet they were no more ruthless than their right-wing opponents. Their victory was certainly not inevitable. But in a political culture in which democratic values and orientations were largely lacking, the choice which probably faced Russia in 1917 was between a reactionary quasi-Fascist regime of the type that dominated most eastern European countries in the years between the war, and an authoritarian regime of the left.

6. THE CONSOLIDATION OF SOVIET POWER

The aim of the Bolsheviks was to establish a democratic, humane society characterized by equality and brotherhood. They recognized that some ultimate goals might have to be indefinitely postponed, and that until internal and external enemies had been destroyed, the party must consider itself an army and enforce military discipline. Nevertheless, in the first flush of revolutionary enthusiasm, the party attempted to reach some of the goals to which its members aspired.

The Bolsheviks planned eventually to place political authority in the hands of the soviets, which they conceived of as freely elected bodies whose members could be removed at the will of the people—bodies in which the separation of powers, so common in bourgeois regimes as a mechanism for blocking the will of the people, would be eliminated. They democratized the organization of factories, and for a while many plants

---

[7] The Socialist Revolutionary Party was formed in 1902 and represented the old populist revolutionary tradition.

were run by committees of workers or trade-union delegates. They significantly reduced authority in the army, effectively eliminating rank and giving the common soldier a voice in decision-making. They eliminated formal requirements for marriage and divorce; marriage was to be a free association of those in love. They recognized the equality of women and legalized abortion. They established equality of compensation at most levels of the bureaucracy. They recognized the principle of self-determination for minority groups, accepting, for example, the independence of Finland on December 31, 1918.

However, most of these policies were soon to be reversed. In many cases, full implementation of the reforms was postponed to that ever-receding day when communism would finally be achieved; in others, attitudes originally considered to be implied by Marxism were later discovered to be incompatible with a correct analysis of Marxist theory. Thus, discipline and rank were gradually reestablished in the army; discipline and pay differentials returned to the factory. Thus, too, divorce became increasingly difficult, and limitations were placed on educational opportunity.[8] The reasons for what one writer has called "the Great Retreat" are innumerable, but one of them is that the original policies were—as the Bolsheviks discovered but had yet to admit in theory—incompatible with a stable social order. Some policies were reversed simply because they proved incompatible with other goals—the industrialization of a fundamentally traditionalist and "underdeveloped" country or the maintenance of the traditional Russian patrimony. For example, while Lenin and those around him wished to permit various minority groups self-determination, they expected that, given a free choice, those groups would wish to retain their adherence to the Soviet Union; when such minorities as Ukrainians, Georgians, and others

[8] Educational opportunities have been widened again as resources have become available, and it is easier to obtain a divorce, although the regime has not returned to the radicalism of the 1920's.

refused to respond to this freedom with the "correct" decisions, the Bolsheviks were faced with the possibility that peoples who might otherwise be incorporated into a Communist society would continue under bourgeois domination, and also, with the possibility of great losses of territory and even the destruction of the Soviet regime itself. The decision to engage in the alternative—a policy of suppression of nationalist aspirations—came easily; Soviet leaders were convinced that their programs and doctrines represented the "truth." If Ukrainians, then, seemed to wish for an independent state, it was only because they were deceived or as yet unable to realize where their own interests lay.

The same second thoughts were applied to internal democratic processes. Truth lay with the Communist Party, and most particularly with Lenin and those immediately around him. The party or Lenin might make mistakes, but in the long run they represented the hope of mankind. To allow power to be snatched from them by groups which did not or would not understand was tantamount to falling once again into the hands of the counterrevolutionaries, for only two alternatives existed. Accordingly, groups and institutions that blocked the way to the achievement of communism had to be repressed; and, because of the existence of both internal and external enemies (which the party itself continued to create because of the militancy and intransigence of its own utopian goals), discipline and order were of prime necessity.

When elections to the Constituent Assembly returned a Socialist but non-Bolshevik majority, therefore, the Bolsheviks dissolved the assembly by force, even though they had originally been among those who called for the formation of such an institution. Lenin had a ready, and probably quite sincere, answer for those in the Communist Party who felt that his decision had not been a democratic one. The Constituent Assembly was fundamentally a reactionary institution, he argued, for it overrepresented reactionary elements in the population. The soviets of the cities, which were coming increasingly under Bolshevik control, represented the advanced segments of the people and hence, by definition, were far more democratic bodies:

Those who remind us of the time when we also stood for the Constituent Assembly and rebuke us for now "dispersing" it don't have a grain of sense in their minds, only pompous and empty phrases. For as compared with Tsarism and the Kerensky Republic, the Constituent Assembly at one time seemed to us better than their notorious organs of power; but with their establishment the soviets, being revolutionary organizations of all the people, naturally became immeasurably superior to any parliament in the world. . . . All power to the soviets! And we shall crush the saboteurs.[9]

Similar arguments justified the harassment and ultimate repression of all parties except the Bolshevik. Reactionary and bourgeois parties could not, of course, be permitted to exist once the Revolution had occurred, but at the outset the Bolsheviks seemed willing to tolerate such Socialist groupings as the Socialist Revolutionaries and the Mensheviks. This toleration, however, presupposed those parties' acceptance of Bolshevik leadership, and their willingness to forego criticism of Bolshevik decisions. After all, open criticism of the activities of the Bolsheviks was tantamount to objective encouragement of counterrevolutionary forces. Deprived of the possibility of legitimate criticism, many among the Mensheviks and Socialist Revolutionaries turned to clandestine activities directed against Bolshevik policies and the Communist Party, thus convincing Lenin and others of what they had suspected all along: that all parties other than the Bolsheviks were willy-nilly supporters of counterrevolution. By 1922 the Communist Party of the Soviet Union (the Bolsheviks) was the only political organization permitted to function legally within the Soviet Union.

In the meantime, the character of the Communist Party itself was changing. Before the Revolution, Lenin's conception of "democratic centralism" had involved full discussion before decisions were made and permission to express disagreement afterward, provided this did not impair the position of the party; and discipline among the Bolsheviks was actually somewhat looser than even this. Lenin, for instance, had disagreed a number of times with party decisions and had continued to work for his own program. And both Kamenev and Zinoviev had opposed Lenin's plans for an insurrection and went so far as to publicize their disagreement in the press, thereby providing the government with ample warning of the Bolsheviks' plans. Yet despite Lenin's initial fury, their action was not counted seriously against them.

After the Revolution this relatively democratic policy went by the board. First the party was faced with several years of civil war, and, even after it had consolidated its authority, the threat of counterrevolution could not be discounted. Moreover, inasmuch as the expected Communist revolutions in the advanced countries of the West had not occurred, the Bolsheviks were convinced that they were operating on the verge of attack from the capitalist regimes. There were as well the problems of rebuilding the economy and proceeding, insofar as possible, toward the goals of a Socialist economic system. Faced with innumerable tasks which required organization, the party took on more and more responsibilities, and authority within the party was increasingly delegated to the small group of men who composed the party's political bureau (*Politburo*).

For all of these reasons, the Bolshevik leadership became intolerant of even internal opposition and disagreement. Differences over policy, Lenin came to believe, were a menace to the future of the Revolution. Freedom of discussion within the party itself had to be foreclosed.

[9] Quoted in Merle Fainsod, *How Russia Is Ruled,* 2nd ed. (Cambridge, Mass.: Harvard University Press, 1963), p. 134.

The trend became clear at the Tenth Party Congress in March 1921. During the congress, the sailors at Kronstadt, a naval base in the Gulf of Finland, rose up and imprisoned the Bolshevik commissars at the base. The sailors had supported the Bolshevik Revolution in 1917; while they claimed to be loyal Bolsheviks, they attacked Lenin's economic and political policies, demanding a new deal for the peasants and truly free elections. They made no attempt to engage in aggressive action; but despite the pleas of Trotsky, who had been dispatched to deal with the situation, they refused to surrender the fortress. In the end, government troops attacked and, after a fierce battle, the defenders of the fortress were destroyed. Trotsky silenced his own doubts about the wisdom or humanity of this action by justifying it in terms of the revolutionary necessity of maintaining discipline.

At the congress itself, Lenin attacked prolonged discussion and the formation of intraparty factions such as the so-called Workers' Opposition. At the end of a particularly long and, to him, fruitless session of wrangling, he noted:

Probably there are not many among you who do not regard this discussion as having been an excessive luxury. . . . I cannot but add that in my opinion this luxury was . . . absolutely impermissible. . . . We wallowed in luxury and failed to see to what an extent we were distracting attention from the urgent and menacing question of this very crisis that confronted us so closely.[10]

Later he added:

We have spent a great deal of time in discussion, and I must say that now it is a great deal better to "discuss with rifles." . . . We need no opposition now, comrades, it is not the time! Either on this side, or on that. . . . And

I think that the Party Congress will have to draw that conclusion too . . . that the time has come to put an end to the opposition, to put a lid on it; we have had enough of opposition now![11]

The congress eventually adopted a resolution on party unity which, in effect, prohibited "factionalism" within the party and gave the Central Committee the power even to expel factionalists from the party. The resolution reduced the effectiveness of the last possible check upon the power of the leadership, for no independent source of political authority now remained outside the party. Further, as the party grew larger, it became better able to dominate the society as a whole, and, as the bureaucratic apparatus of the party grew in size, a mechanism was created whereby that man who controlled the apparatus could isolate and destroy any individuals or groups who sought to oppose him. The party had created the dictatorship of the party, and even the dictatorship of the Central Committee and the Politburo. It had paved the way for the dictatorship of the individual. The consequences of its actions were to become apparent during the next several years. In the struggle for succession following the death of Lenin, Joseph Stalin, using the administrative instruments which had been created, destroyed his opposition, seized control over the party, and then used the power at his disposal to create a totalitarian state.

7. STALIN'S RUSSIA

Lenin fell ill in 1922, and his condition slowly deteriorated until his death in 1924. As his illness became more serious, a partly ideological and partly personal power struggle developed among his associates; that struggle was to last until 1929. The victor was Joseph Stalin, who had played a relatively minor role in the Revolution itself but

---

10 Quoted in Barrington Moore, Jr., *Soviet Politics: The Dilemma of Power* (Cambridge, Mass.: Harvard University Press, 1950), p. 145.

11 Quoted in Fainsod, *How Russia Is Ruled*, p. 144.

who had become increasingly important in the years immediately following. Although originally cast as a moderate, Stalin had, during Lenin's last years, alienated his chief for what Lenin considered his tendencies to accumulate personal power, his ruthlessness, and his "Great Russian chauvinism." (Actually, Stalin was a Georgian by birth.) Fortunately for Stalin, Lenin's "testament," in which many of these opinions were aired, was repressed, though it is difficult to argue that its publication would have significantly changed the major directions of Soviet policy.

THE STRUGGLE FOR POWER: The origin and context of conflict among Lenin's former associates are to be found in Soviet internal developments and foreign relations during the 1920's. This was the period of the New Economic Policy (N.E.P.), established by the party in 1921, and involving the continuation of a mixed economy—most importantly, of a free peasantry selling their produce in an open market. The 1920's witnessed also the ebb of the revolutionary tide in Europe and the necessity of Russian adjustment to that fact. In the opening stages of the Soviet Revolution, Lenin and his associates had predicated their success on the expectation that the new regime would inspire revolutions in some of the advanced countries. Wherever possible, then, they encouraged, or contributed to, the upheavals which were taking place in France, Germany, and various countries of Eastern Europe. When all these attempts failed, the regime was left with the necessity of adjusting its perspective to a situation that Lenin had regarded as impossible.

Finally, in the mid-twenties, at least, there was a temporary relaxation of external pressures against the Soviet regime. The Cordon Sanitaire came to an end, and the regime was recognized by most European countries, although England broke off diplomatic relations again in 1927 and did not resume them until 1929. The Communists continued to expect attacks from other nations, but they

seemed to have been granted some breathing space.

On the ideological level, the struggle for power represented a conflict among several alternative possible courses. Identified primarily with Trotsky (even though he did not always subscribe to all its tenets) was a left-wing position which urged a continued policy of militant action directed toward the encouragement of revolution in other countries and immediate industrialization at home. Such a policy, the left argued, required the elimination of both small peasant holdings and the free market. The current system of agriculture was inefficient; collectivization of agriculture would increase production and it would do so with less manpower, thereby providing workers for industrialization. Collectivization would also eliminate a class which was fundamentally hostile to the regime—the well-to-do peasants or, as they came to be called, kulaks. In sum, the viability of the regime depended on the renewal of a radical Socialist program. It should be noted that this new left program did not involve a call for internal party democracy as the original left opposition to Lenin had. Although Trotsky was later to attack Stalin for his authoritarian policies, he was as fully committed to the need for authority and discipline as were his opponents during this period. The right-wing position, associated with the names of Nikolai Bukharin, Aleksei I. Rykov, and Mikhail P. Tomski, argued not only that socialism could be built in one country, but that such building could and should be accomplished under a policy which continued to make concessions to the Russian peasantry; any attempt at a rapid change, they believed, would involve the country in a bloodbath in which the Communist Party itself might be the ultimate loser.

Stalin, Kamenev, and Zinoviev vacillated between the two positions. Initially, at least, Stalin had accepted Trotsky's dictum that the Soviet state must continue to strive for revolutionary upheavals. Yet he, Kamenev, and

Zinoviev all regarded Trotsky as the most likely person to succeed Lenin and, hence, the one to be defeated. Thus, seeking to outmaneuver his rival, Stalin quickly shifted his position; in fact, it was he who coined the phrase "Socialism in one country." Once Kamenev and Zinoviev realized that Stalin was the man to be most feared, they joined with Trotsky in opposing him. During the early twenties, Stalin played the role of a moderate, whatever his true feelings; he refused to take extreme steps against Trotsky, arguing that once one began to cut off heads one never knew where the process would stop.

By 1924 Trotsky had been decisively defeated, although, along with Kamenev and Zinoviev, he continued his unsuccessful battle against Stalin until he was expelled from the party in 1927. Shortly afterward, Stalin turned on the right-wing group which had supported him, and easily defeated them; he inaugurated the policy of rapid industrialization and collectivization which was to lead to the second Russian revolution—an even more radical transformation of Soviet society than had been produced by the first. It was also to lead to the totalitarian society.

Stalin's victory was based on a number of factors. For one thing, his willingness to engage in detailed administrative work had given him control of the newly developing cadres of bureaucratic officials who were coming to control the Communist Party and hence to dominate party congresses. His posts as general secretary of the party's Central Committee and as head of the Commissariat of Workers' and Peasants' Inspection also stood him in good stead. Another reason for Stalin's triumph was that his opponents—Kamenev, Zinoviev, Trotsky, and Bukharin, among others—underestimated him and exhausted themselves fighting each other, until, too late, they recognized their error.

These factors were important, but they were not the only ones. At first, the party had been dominated by highly cosmopolitan in-

tellectuals and self-educated, relatively self-conscious skilled workers. With the success of the Revolution, the party was flooded by masses of quasi-literate workers and peasants with little understanding of Marxism and scant concern for internationalism or for the intellectual interests of a previous generation. These new cadres had even less experience or patience with discussion and debate than Lenin or Trotsky had shown. Furthermore, they distrusted intellectuals and preferred someone of their own type, even if he were a Georgian rather than a Great Russian. Trotsky and a good portion of his entourage were Jewish and hence victims of the widespread anti-Semitism prevalent among the Russian working class and peasantry. While there is little evidence that Stalin used anti-Semitism as a weapon against Trotsky, he hardly needed to: the facts had been widely publicized at the time of the conflicts between the Bolsheviks and the White armies, and during the struggle between Stalin and Trotsky it was widely rumored in the countryside that the Jews were about to take over and massacre large numbers of Christians. In one important sense, then, Stalin's victory was the victory of the Russian common man.

Finally, the ideology of the Trotsky opposition worked to its own detriment. Once that opposition had been defeated within the party, efforts to organize against party policy might destroy the Revolution; whatever its limitations, the party must not be weakened, for it was the only available instrument for achieving communism. As Trotsky himself said to his party comrades after his 1924 defeat:

The party in the last analysis is always right, because the party is the single historic instrument given to the proletariat for the solution of its fundamental problems. I have already said that in front of one's own party nothing could be easier . . . than to say: all my criticisms, my statements, my warnings, my protests—the whole thing was a mere mistake. I, however, comrades, cannot say that, because I do not think it. I know that one must not be right against the party. One can be right only with the party, and through the party, for history has created no other road for the realization of what is right. . . .[12]

∽ THE SECOND RUSSIAN REVOLUTION: In 1927 the Fifteenth Congress of the Communist Party had ordered the preparation of a Five Year Plan designed to bring about substantial growth in all segments of the economy. Although Stalin criticized those in the party who still desired rapid and total collectivization, he did express agreement with the plan's proposals for the development of state and collective farms as a means of creating a more efficient agriculture. But by 1929, he had radically shifted his position.[13] Fears of foreign attack had strengthened his belief that Russia must become a strong industrial power soon, or risk destruction.

Moreover, Stalin had become convinced that the "rich" peasants were attempting to blackmail the regime and that this group alone was blocking voluntary collectivization. These peasants, who had been getting low prices for agricultural products, were withholding grain from the market, and grain deliveries had dropped to a new low. Thus Stalin initiated a program of quasi-compulsory collectivization. The drive soon got out of hand. In the countryside, militant party cadres, many of them drawn from the youth organization, moved quickly to bring about the millennium—and settle old scores. The ruthlessness of the process only encouraged thousands to burn their crops or destroy their livestock. This resistance, in turn, brought forth more vigorous action against those who

had now confirmed the expectations of party militants by revealing their hostility to the Soviet state. And so the crescendo of attempted collectivization, resistance, deportation, and killing mounted to a fury.

In the midst of the chaos, Stalin called a halt. In an article, "Dizzy with Success," he upbraided comrades for excessive zeal and suggested that persuasion be substituted for coercion. But when the subsequent pause resulted in a rapid drop in the number of peasants on collective farms, a coercive pattern was established again. By the end of the first Five Year Plan, some sixty per cent of peasant holdings had been collectivized; by 1940 private peasant holdings had, for all practical purposes, ceased to exist, except for small individual plots on collective farms. In fact, Stalin had been caught in a bind. Once the program of collectivization had been started, all the pressures upon him required him either to back down entirely, or to smash through to ultimate resolution of the problem. Both his theoretical assumptions and his personality caused him to choose the latter course, although at a terrible cost in life and in agricultural productivity. Famine stalked Russia through the winter of 1931–1932; an estimated five to ten million people either were killed or starved to death. However, it should be noted that grain deliveries to the cities actually rose in 1931–1932. Thus, in a sense, Stalin's gamble had been successful.

At the same time, the regime moved ahead with a crash program of industrialization which led more and more to the use of force and the extension of controls. These violent changes were, naturally enough, met with opposition. Facing this opposition, and the failures which were the result of poor management as much as anything else, the party's typical response was more vigilance and tighter control: if the human material proved recalcitrant, it was only because of bourgeois hangovers or sabotage. One more effort, the cutting off of a few more heads, would bring into being the new utopia. And given the expectation of internal and external enemies,

[12] Quoted in Isaac Deutscher, *Stalin: A Political Biography* (New York: Oxford University Press, 1949), p. 278.

[13] Some students of Soviet history believe that his decision had been made much earlier and he was simply waiting for the full consolidation of his power before acting. I regard this interpretation as based on a view of Stalin as a completely rational Machiavellian, and do not think that it fits the facts.

mistakes in judgment were very often confused with sabotage. It was, of course, never considered that the overall program of the party might be at fault.

The situation was compounded both by the primitiveness of party cadres, who operated in terms of extremes, and by the fact that the nature of the intra-party struggles encouraged the rise of ruthless, hard men—the only kind who could succeed in a situation in which failure might mean imprisonment or even death. Thus, just as the very nature of the tasks to which the party had committed itself encouraged the emergence of a new Soviet man, one in whom all personal qualms were subordinated to achieving power within the party by carrying out and surpassing party goals, so the presence of such men in the party encouraged the development of ruthless programs.

Trade unions were completely stripped of their power and subordinated to the party. Wage differentials among various groups of workers widened as the party attempted to add the carrot to the stick. Increasingly tight controls were instituted to prevent workers from moving from one job to another; severe punishments were put into effect for the infraction of labor discipline, and large numbers of individuals were imprisoned in "labor" camps. All these measures, especially those that involved retreats from the Marxist goals, were justified as temporary expedients necessary for the transition from a feudal to a truly Socialist and, finally, Communist society.

But the regime did not stop at that; its controls extended to every area of Soviet life. The arts, literature, education, and historiography came under the control of the party and the state; all were molded to meet the people's needs, as those needs were understood by the party. Hence the creation of an official literary and artistic style, "Socialist realism": a purely representational art whose themes were such as to encourage not only dedication to Soviet goals, but also belief in the certainty of victory. Soviet literature, in addition to its unfailing optimism, took on a puritanical quality characterized by total commitment to hard work and the absence of references to sex. In music, simple rhythms and traditional melody, largely romantic in character, constituted the officially approved style.

These standards were derived from the theoretical assumption that the dark recesses of the soul existed only in bourgeois society and were indicative of the decadence of that society. But there were practical considerations as well. Themes which emphasized self-doubt, among a people already given to such a tendency, obviously would not encourage the kinds of activity that would enable the party to achieve its goals. Finally, the canons of Socialist realism reflected the nature of the party cadres themselves. Stalin and other party leaders, influenced by the popular culture which was their inheritance, thought this was the kind of literature and art that was healthy and human.

Similarly, there was a renewed emphasis on Russian nationality and Russian history, glorifying national achievements. Stalin was increasingly deified; his universal brilliance and his great humanity were praised on all possible occasions, and his portrait or statue appeared everywhere. Such sycophancy reflected the continuing tradition-mindedness of the Russian people, to whom this kind of image of a ruler made far more sense than dedication to abstract theory; it also reflected Stalin's tendency to megalomania, always latent but exacerbated by the absolute power which he had grasped.

That megalomania also helps to explain the great purge of the 1930's, in which millions lost their lives and other millions were imprisoned for antistate activities. To a certain extent, this represented the natural climax of Stalinist rule. The purge of party cadres and army officers and the arrest of thousands of ordinary Soviet citizens began in 1934 shortly after the assassination of Sergei Kirov, a Bolshevik widely regarded as among Stalin's likely successors. It reached its peak in 1937 and 1938, and gradually burnt itself out the following year. We now know that Soviet citizens lived during this period under a reign of terror, afraid to confide even in members of their family and expecting at any moment to be seized by the secret police for deportation or worse. The purge and terror decimated the highest ranks of the party, killing off most of the old Bolsheviks, who had been living in relative obscurity since their defeat by Stalin; thus Kamenev, Bukharin, and Zinoviev were executed after a series of show trials.

But the purge went far beyond the ranks of party leadership. Three of the five army marshals of the Soviet Union were executed, as were thirteen of the fifteen army commanders. Nor did the secret police responsible for conducting the purge escape its effects. Genrikh Yagoda, who had headed the N.K.V.D. (People's Commissariat of Internal Affairs) when the purge began, was executed in the middle of it, and Nikolai Yezhov, his replacement, disappeared as it was burning itself out.

In a now famous speech delivered at the time of the Twentieth Congress of the Soviet Communist Party in 1956, Nikita Khrushchev, by then first secretary of the party, blamed the extent of the purge on Stalin's madness in his later years. If we take Khrushchev at his word, we can inquire into the sources of this madness. In the eighth book of the *Republic,* Plato describes the career of the tyrant. He rules by force rather than legitimate authority; his consequent isolation from the society around him causes him to become suspicious of everyone, convinced that he is surrounded by those who plot his destruction. A reign of terror is the natural consequence of his fear.

Yet this cannot be the full story. For one thing, we know that Stalin himself was shocked at the excesses of the purge and attempted to bring it under control. Furthermore, the very magnitude of the purge precludes analyzing it in terms of the decisions of a single man. The evidence suggests that other factors were at work. Because of its radical new policies, the regime was faced with opposition, mostly passive, and with a constant series of failures. In addition, the threat of an attack by Germany appeared ever more likely, as the Nazi regime consolidated its power. Given the ideological presuppositions of the Soviet leadership and the tensions within the nation, it was easy to imagine that internal enemies abounded. Once the purge began it built on itself: people "confessed" and accused others to escape severe penalties or to settle private grievances. As the circle of those charged with crimes against the state grew, some accused others out of fear that if they did not do so they themselves would be accused. As fear grew, Soviet society took on a paranoid quality. Thought and action were regarded as the same thing. Anyone who made a hostile remark or even expressed doubt about the regime must be intending to overthrow it; anyone who associated with someone who was suspect must himself be suspect, or else why the association? The Smolensk archives are full of cases of persons accused on grounds as flimsy as these.[14] Men and women were arrested for having once associated with someone who had been arrested for making some chance remark. Ignored was the fact that associating with, or being related to, a person who might have doubts about the regime did not automatically mean sharing those doubts—or even being aware of them.

Of course, the mood provided a field day for the mentally disturbed who exist on the margins of all societies. Seeing enemies everywhere, such types interpret every gesture so as to confirm their beliefs and read plots into casual remarks. In times of tension and fear, they come into their own; the logic

[14] The Archives of the Smolensk Party Organization were captured by the Germans in 1941 and by the Americans after the war. They served as the basis for an excellent study by Merle Fainsod, *Smolensk Under Soviet Rule* (Cambridge, Mass.: Harvard University Press, 1958). See also Eugenia S. Ginzburg, *Journey into the Whirlwind* (New York: Harcourt, Brace and World, 1967).

of their argument seems inescapable. The Smolensk archives offer many examples of this behavior, but we can turn to the experience of the United States at the time of the Salem witch trials or in the early 1950's for similar manifestations.

Yet during the heyday of Senator Joseph McCarthy, the strains were not nearly so severe as in the Soviet Union during the 1930's; furthermore, a respect for law and other elements of constitutional procedure provided institutional safeguards for those accused in the United States. In the Soviet Union, these were absent. The party had created a massive, almost autonomous police organization whose function it was to root out enemies; as with all such organizations, professional commitment often resulted in excessive zeal.

The atmosphere of the period is very neatly summed up in an exchange between Karl Radek, the old Bolshevik, and Andrei Vyshinski, the chief state prosecutor, during one of the show trials of the period:

Vishinsky: Were you in favor of defeat [that is, the collapse of the Soviet regime] *in 1934?*

Radek: In 1934, I considered defeat inevitable.

Vishinsky: Were you in favor of defeat in 1934?

Radek: If I could avert defeat, I would be against defeat.

Vishinsky: You consider that you could not have averted it?

Radek: I considered it an inevitable fact.

Vishinsky: You are answering my question incorrectly. Did you accept the whole of Trotsky's line given to you in 1934?

Radek: I accepted the whole of Trotsky's line in 1934.

Vishinsky: Was defeat part of it?

Radek: Yes, it was a line of defeat.

Vishinsky: Trotsky's line included defeat?

Radek: Yes.

Vishinsky: Did you accept it?

Radek: I did.

Vishinsky: Hence, since you accepted it you were in favor of defeat?

Radek: From the standpoint . . .

Vishinsky: You headed for defeat?

Radek: Yes, of course.

Vishinsky: That is, you were in favor of defeat?

Radek: Of course, if I say yes, that means we headed for it.

Vishinsky: Which of us, then, is putting the question rightly?

Radek: All the same, I think that you are not putting the question rightly.

Vishinsky: In 1934 you were not against defeat, but in favor of defeat?

Radek: Yes, I have said so.[15]

All the old Bolsheviks who had opposed Stalin were executed; in 1940 Leon Trotsky was murdered in Mexico by a Soviet agent. The Revolution had destroyed most of those who had taken a leading part in bringing it about. The final irony is that in an important sense the old Bolsheviks were their own murderers: they had been responsible for the regime which served as their executioner, however far that regime may have been from their initial aspirations.

Many students of Soviet politics argue that the real source of the Stalinist regime lay in Lenin's authoritarian personality or the elitist tradition of Russian populism. But authoritarian personalities abound in positions of leadership; whether such individuals create or prepare the way for absolutist regimes depends upon what goals they regard as legitimate. Moreover, the quick adoption of authoritarian patterns by Communist parties and regimes in other parts of the world indicates that the phenomenon is not merely a Russian one. In the last analysis, the authoritarianism of the Soviet regime was a natural result of the impatience of those who wanted to produce a sudden, radical social change in a situation in which the masses of people were

---

[15] Quoted in Carl J. Friedrich and Zbigniew Brzezinski, *Totalitarian Dictatorship and Autocracy* (Cambridge, Mass.: Harvard University Press, 1956), p. 159.

unwilling or unable to act in the required manner. The utopian elements in Marxism only added to the pressures for total control, since the gap between the reality and the goals was too wide to be bridged.

8. KHRUSHCHEV AND BEYOND

The essential features of the Soviet regime did not change so long as Stalin remained in power. During the war there was some loosening of control, along with a heightened emphasis on nationalism. But afterward, the party again tightened its restrictions and, although no reign of terror recurred comparable to the purges of the 1930's, the regime relied heavily on repression and periodic purges, with accompanying deportation to labor camps or execution. The labor camps, in fact, continued to contain a very large number of prisoners living and working under the most difficult conditions.

In the very last years of Stalin's life there were signs of relaxation in various areas. A few timid voices were raised against Socialist realism, labor discipline was eased slightly, and a few legal restraints were placed upon the secret police. However, the changes were too few and too minor to be called a trend, and the movement toward liberalism was counterpointed by a continuation of irrational brutality. Suddenly, on March 5, 1953, Stalin died, precipitating a second struggle for succession.

It had been widely forecast in the West that the Soviet Union would be unable to handle the problem of the transfer of power when Stalin died, but events immediately after his death belied these expectations. A triumvirate was established in Stalin's place, consisting of Georgi M. Malenkov as chairman of the Council of Ministers (premier), Lavrenty Beria as head of the secret police, and Vyacheslav M. Molotov (who had been one of Stalin's closest collaborators) as foreign secretary. Shortly after assuming the post of premier, however, Malenkov was relieved of his duties as "senior" secretary

within the Communist Party; that post was given to Nikita Khrushchev. On September 12, 1953, Khrushchev was officially designated first secretary of the party; it became obvious that his position was effectively a very powerful one, and that he had joined the inner core of rulers. In the meantime, in fact, this inner core had been reduced by one. On the basis of his police apparatus, Lavrenty Beria had made a bid for total power; defeated by the party in conjunction with the armed forces, he was arrested and executed, along with many of his followers.

Malenkov remained, or seemed to remain, in power for almost two years. Then, on February 8, 1955, he confessed that his policies had failed, and he resigned; at the recommendation of Khrushchev, he was replaced by Nikolai A. Bulganin. By this time it had become clear that the person to watch was indeed Khrushchev, and further evidence was provided when, at the Twentieth Congress of the Communist Party, he delivered a then secret speech (February 24, 1956), denouncing the "crimes" of the Stalin period and the deification of Stalin, and called for "collective" as opposed to personal leadership.

In the year following, Khrushchev further consolidated his power. In the meantime, he had placed more and more of his supporters in prominent positions, both in the party and in the state apparatus. In June 1957, a coalition of his opponents attempted to drive him from power. The effort failed, and those responsible were removed from the party Presidium and Central Committee. It should be noted, however, that under Khrushchev, retribution came in the form of demotion within the government, not execution or imprisonment.

Shortly thereafter, Khrushchev took over the position of chairman of the Council of Ministers. Thus, as Stalin had done before him, he combined in one man the leadership in both the state and the party apparatus.

However, both his style and the control he exercised were different in kind from that of his predecessor. He made relatively little effort to demand the sycophancy in which Stalin had gloried; although he tended to insist upon the initiation of certain crash programs which appealed to him, he relied increasingly upon the policy advice of technical experts and other party leaders. Further, it was obvious that he was unable or at least unwilling to press for the adoption of some policies which other strategic elites were unwilling to accept.

Some of the differences between Stalin's style of leadership and that of Khrushchev stemmed from their dissimilar personalities. More importantly, however, since the end of World War II the pace of change had been accelerating rapidly in the Soviet Union. By the early 1960's, Russia had developed into a reasonably modern industrial society, boasting a disciplined and skilled working class, an almost completely literate population, and a large, educated middle class of bureaucrats, technicians, and professional people whose expectations were greater than those of previous generations, and whose attitudes and characteristics had become much closer to those of urban populations in other industrial societies. (See Table 3.2.) The growth of the Soviet economy provided such people with the fruits of an advanced industrial society, as automobiles, washing machines, and

other consumer products became increasingly available. In this sense, then, the revolution wrought by Stalin was successful, despite the costs it entailed.

These social changes resulted in a restructuring of the context of social and political action. The development of a relatively skilled labor force reduced the need for certain kinds of compulsion: the harsher forms of state-imposed labor discipline, for example, were gradually eliminated. The pressure for immediate results eased when the Soviet Union's economic growth began to accelerate. The professionalization of party cadres, industrial managers, and technicians encouraged a more realistic assessment of what was possible, and the emergence of a postrevolutionary elite eliminated much of the suspiciousness with which the party regarded those whose antecedents lay in the old regime. All these changes helped to set more rational standards for success and failure in the area of industrial production; they certainly contributed to the party's increased tolerance of free experimentation in the realm of the sciences and some of the social sciences, as well as the freeing of disciplines such as physics and biology and certain aspects of economics, psychology, and sociology from tight doctrinal control.

The changing structure of Soviet society

TABLE 3.2. POPULATION OF THE U.S.S.R. WITH HIGHER AND
SECONDARY EDUCATION

	Percentage of all inhabitants				Percentage of working inhabitants			
	1939	1959	1964	1965	1939	1959	1964	1965
Complete higher education	.6	1.8	2.4	2.5	1.3	3.3	4.3	4.5
Incomplete higher, complete and incomplete secondary	7.7	26.3	29.6	30.8	11.0	40.0	45.8	47.7

Source: Joint Economic Committee, Congress of the United States, *New Directions in the Soviet Economy*, Part III: Human Resources (Washington: U.S. Government Printing Office, 1966), p. 842.

was undoubtedly responsible, too, for the decline in the authority of the secret police and a more permissive attitude in the arts. All in all, then, there seems to be some relationship between the development of an increasingly modern society and the greater flexibility that came to characterize Soviet life in the late 1950's and early 1960's.

These and other changes had a profound effect upon the relationship of the Soviet Union to other nations. Although Khrushchev first took a somewhat hard line in foreign policy, he in time became identified with a relatively softer position, which emphasized the horrors of hydrogen war and declared that peaceful coexistence between capitalist and Socialist countries—as well as the peaceful victory of communism—was possible. This was one factor in the developing conflict between the Soviet Union and the other major country of the Communist bloc, the People's Republic of China, whose leadership continued to insist that a militant international policy and a more radical domestic policy were required if communism was to be achieved. The tension between the two nations all but split the Communist camp and had a profound effect on the relations between various national Communist parties.

During the Stalin period the Soviet regime exercised a fairly tight control over most of the Communist parties in non-Communist countries, and those countries in Eastern Europe in which Communist regimes had been created by the Soviet Union. But such control never existed in China, especially after the Communists came to power. With Stalin's death and denunciation, the Soviet regime relaxed its hold somewhat on the satellite countries of Eastern Europe, although the suppression of the Hungarian rebellion in 1956 indicated quite clearly that there were fairly rigid limits to the regime's tolerance of deviation. In the meantime Communist parties in various non-Communist states, shaken by the denunciation of Stalin's crimes, began to act in a somewhat more independent manner. Partly because the Soviets

were in the position of having to bargain for the loyalty of national Communist parties in competition with the Chinese, the conflict accelerated the drive of such parties for more independence.

In 1964 Khrushchev was retired from office by his colleagues in the Presidium of the party, with the support of the party's Central Committee. Perhaps the most important among the factors which precipitated his fall from power was his political style. Still close in temperament to the peasant roots from which he sprang, Khrushchev was a free-wheeling, impatient, mercurial politician who, to many of the new middle class of technocrats, was uncultured and unable to deal with the increasingly complex problems of Soviet economic life. The rapid series of innovations he introduced unsettled the bureaucracy; some of those innovations, perhaps most significantly in the field of agriculture, had failed dismally.

His decision to send atomic missiles to Cuba in 1962 was regarded by some in the party as mere adventurism, and withdrawal of the missiles under pressure from the United States was regarded as seriously injurious to Soviet prestige. To many in the party, the sharp deterioration in Sino-Soviet relations was thought to be in part the result of Khrushchev's lack of tact. The changes initiated by Khrushchev, of course, were far less significant than those proclaimed by Stalin, and he changed direction far less frequently than had his predecessor. The opposition he aroused, then, was less a function of his policies than of the changing nature of Soviet politics.

Khrushchev's fall from power was accomplished with a minimum of purging, partly because most of the second echelon of leadership agreed that his removal was necessary. In the years since he left office, no single figure has emerged to take his place. Although Leonid Brezhnev, the general secretary of the party, is probably *primus inter pares,* he shares power with Aleksei Kosygin, the chairman of the Council of Ministers. In fact, it is apparent that the combined authority of these two men is rather less than that of Khrushchev and that, even more than he, they are bound by the decisions of the new technical and party elites.

Indeed, Brezhnev and Kosygin represent these new cadres. Both rose slowly in the party, advancing primarily because of bureaucratic competence; both manifest the cautious and conservative style that seems to typify bureaucrats in most societies. Thus, aside from the dumping of a number of Khrushchev's administrative reforms, the Soviet Union has experienced a relative lack of innovation since 1964. Even the economic reforms begun in 1965 and 1966 represented a carrying out of policies to which Khrushchev himself had been lending a sympathetic ear.

The new leaders' caution has been just as marked in the area of foreign policy. On the major issue of Soviet relations with China, they discovered rather early that the sources of the conflict were far more complicated than they had imagined, and the gap between the two nations has, if anything, widened. The decision to invade Czechoslovakia in 1968 was essentially a defensive move, produced by fears that the Communist Party in Prague was losing control and that the Czechoslovakian example might have repercussions not only in other Eastern European nations but in the Soviet Union as well. It also indicated that traditional policy assumptions were still in force; the Soviets remain convinced that, on their borders at least, only a Communist regime, as defined in their terms, can be counted on to be reliable.

During the past four years the trends which had become noticeable in the early 1960's have continued. Domestically, this has meant a rise in Soviet living standards and the beginnings of a consumer society. It has also meant the emergence of a generation somewhat bolder in its dealings with authority than the one that preceded it. The consequence of this has been an increasing ferment in the Soviet Union as, for the first time since the 1920's, some of the policies of the regime come under direct challenge.

Khrushchev followed a somewhat vacillating course on the question of artistic and, more broadly, intellectual freedom. Periods of liberalization associated with criticisms of the Stalin period were followed by a clamping down, when the authority of the regime came under what Khrushchev thought was too sharp a challenge or when artists began to experiment with styles that he considered "decadent." On the whole, the current leadership has been somewhat more conservative in this area from the very beginning. The number of people arrested and held without trial, or tried in secret, has increased, and the Soviet secret police have become more active than they were in the early 1960's. Repression was stepped up in 1967 and 1968 in response to the protests over the arrest of some Soviet writers and over the Czechoslovakian invasion. Increasing numbers of people were incarcerated, and attempts by a few dissenters to distribute handbills objecting to government policies were met with considerable brutality. To some, the Soviet Union seemed to be regressing to an earlier period in its recent history. However, the fact that information describing protests is now regularly smuggled out of the Soviet Union, that texts banned in Russia now somehow make their way to other countries, and that a small number of intellectuals are no longer afraid to speak out, indicates that the social changes described earlier may have a momentum of their own.

The possibility of the regime's regression to the greater use of compulsion at some future time cannot be denied. Even so, among some groups in Soviet society a new mood has developed, a mood which was well expressed some years back by the poet Yevgeny Yevtushenko:

Long live travel, and scorching heat
And greed, triumphant greed!
Frontiers hamper me . . . I find it awkward

Not to know Buenos Aires, New York,
I want to roam to my heart's content around
* London,*
To talk to everyone, even if it be in broken
* speech!*

. . . . . .

I want art—as varied as I![16]

RUSSIAN AND SOVIET POLITICAL INSTITU-
TIONS: The main outlines of the Russian state
had been fixed by the late sixteenth century,
and the pattern remained remarkably stable
until the late nineteenth. The czar was both
secular and religious ruler, and theoretically
possessed total power in both realms. Yet
such was the inefficiency of the Russian
autocracy and the vastness of the Russian
domain that considerable de facto power was
retained by provincial and communal authorities. Even on the highest level, the czar's
ministries often worked independently of
him, and at cross purposes.

In the middle of the nineteenth century,
some slight modifications to this pattern began to appear. The local zemstvos created
under Alexander II allowed for more self-
government on the local level. Despite their
domination by the rural gentry, and the handicap of limited budgets, the zemstvos did provide something of a break with the centuries
of absolutism.

The major polity shift, however, occurred
after the Revolution of 1905. Czar Nicholas
II then proclaimed a set of "Fundamental
Laws"—he did not wish to use the word "constitution"—establishing a national parliament
of two houses with power to share in the lawmaking process. Members of the lower house,
or Duma, were to be popularly elected under
a limited franchise. The upper house became
an expanded version of the State Council, a
body created by Alexander I in 1810 in an
effort to introduce some coordination among
the state ministries. In its expanded form as
the upper house, half the members of the
State Council were to be appointed by the
czar himself, while the remaining members
were chosen indirectly by representatives of
the Russian Orthodox Church, the nobility,
the universities, and provincial councils.

The new parliament was authorized to initiate and adopt legislation and to exercise
control over the budget; but most bills were
actually drawn up and introduced by the
government, and the Duma was considerably
hamstrung in its power to consider budgetary
matters. The Council of Ministers remained
responsible to the czar, who was also empowered to dissolve parliament at his pleasure so long as he summoned it at least once
a year. The Fundamental Laws also allowed
the czar to declare a state of emergency during which he could govern by decree, and
although the Duma was expected to remain
in session during these periods—and thus
have the opportunity to debate the emergency
measures taken—frequent dissolution effectively nullified this right.

For a year or so, it seemed as if the czar,
or at least some of his more progressive ministers, might be willing to cooperate. However, the liberals who dominated the Duma
made demands that far exceeded anything the
government was willing to accept, and Nicholas turned more and more frequently for
advice to the more conservative elements of
his entourage. The electoral system was then
changed so as to weight representation more
heavily in favor of the conservative nobility,
and some elements of repression and censorship were introduced. Nevertheless, it is possible that Russia would have evolved into
a true parliamentary government if World
War I had not occurred and, with it, the collapse of the Romanov regime.[17]

Marx never spelled out in any detail the
structure that the future Communist state

[16] From "The Promise," in Max Hayward and Edward L. Crowley, *Soviet Literature in the Sixties* (New
York: Frederick A. Praeger, 1964), p. 28.

[17] This is the thesis of Jacob Walkin, *The Rise of
Democracy in Pre-Revolutionary Russia* (New York:
Frederick A. Praeger, 1962).

would take. In an address entitled "The Civil War in France," which dealt with the Paris Commune of 1871, he spoke of representative assemblies elected for short terms, the possibility of recall of any and all deputies as well as judges, and district and national assemblies elected by local bodies. This structure he described as the model of the state during the relatively short period of the "dictatorship of the proletariat."

During the 1905 Revolution, soviets of "workers' and soldiers' deputies" sprang up in a number of Russian cities—ad hoc groups that served to coordinate the activities of various strike committees. In 1917 such soviets formed again, and Lenin began to speak of them as the nucleus of the future Soviet Socialist state. By June 1917 the soviets had become national in scope, and a first meeting of the All-Russian Congress of Soviets established an inner executive and administrative body—the Central Committee—to manage business until the next Congress.

In the meantime, the provisional government of Kerensky had arranged for the election of a Constituent Assembly to draft a new constitution. Since the Bolsheviks had pushed for just such a move, Lenin felt compelled to go through with the election even after his party had seized power. The Bolsheviks, however, received only 25 per cent of the vote. Thus, the Constituent Assembly held only one meeting, that of January 18, 1918. When the Bolsheviks found they could not control the assembly, the Central Committee of the soviets, which was dominated by the party, voted its dissolution and the delegates were dispersed by force.

Late in January 1918, the Congress of Soviets resolved to establish a Russian Soviet Socialist Republic. The supreme organ of the republic was to be the All-Russian Congress of Soviets. The congress was to choose a Central Executive Committee, which was to be vested with supreme power between sessions of the congress. Administrative duties were to be exercised by a Council of People's Commissars controlled by the congress or its

executive committee, and the committee was charged with the task of drafting a constitution for submission to the next congress.

The constitution of the Russian Soviet Federal Socialist Republic, as finally approved by the Fifth All-Russian Congress of Soviets on July 10, 1918, codified the existing structure. Supreme authority was vested in the All-Russian Congress of Soviets, which was to be composed of representatives of urban soviets, on the basis of one deputy per 25,000 voters, and representatives of provincial congresses of soviets, on the basis of one deputy for every 125,000 inhabitants. In the intervals between congressional sessions, supreme power would be held by a Central Executive Committee consisting of not more than two hundred members chosen by the congress. The committee was authorized to appoint a Council of People's Commissars to direct the different branches of government and administration. The constitution also contained an elaborate bill of rights guaranteeing freedom of speech, press, and association to the working class, but disenfranchising members of the "exploiting" classes. The Communist Party was not mentioned in the document.

With the reconquest of the borderlands of the empire and the end of the civil war, the Bolsheviks turned to the writing of a new constitution. The document was approved by the Central Executive Committee of the All-Russian Congress of Soviets in 1923 and ratified by the second All-Union Congress of Soviets on January 31, 1924. The new state was described as a "union" of Soviet Socialist Republics—federal in form and Socialist in content. The Soviet state was to consist of a number of union republics, as well as autonomous republics, provinces, and regions based, insofar as possible, on ethnic divisions. Following the pattern of the 1918 constitution, the Congress of Soviets was again established as the organ of supreme authority, with representation weighted, as before, in favor of the urban workers. Again, the Congress of Soviets selected a Central Executive Committee—now, however, divided into two chambers: a Council of the Union, with members selected on the basis of population, and a Council of Nationalities, made up of five delegates from each union and autonomous republic and one delegate from each autonomous province. The concurrence of both chambers of the executive committee, which also served between sessions of the congress, was required for all decrees and regulations. Between sessions of the committee, its Presidium, consisting of representatives of both chambers, acted for it.

While the new state was theoretically a federal republic, it was clear, even from the constitution itself, that the reins of power in major areas, such as foreign affairs, foreign trade, and the national economy, were in the hands of the national organs. The jurisdiction of the union republics and other areas was stated in residual form. Again, no mention was made of the Communist Party, which had now become a highly centralized, national organization that, in the final analysis, would be responsible for most of the major policy decisions.

On the administrative level, the constitution provided for three categories of people's commissariats. There were to be all-union commissariats on the national level only; union-republic or unified commissariats both on the national level and in the union republics, with the latter responsible for carrying out the decisions of the former; and republic commissariats which had no national counterparts and which dealt with such matters as internal affairs, justice, and education. The national government, however, retained the authority to issue the primary regulations on all these subjects, and, in fact, while administration of some of the programs was somewhat decentralized, the content of Soviet law, education, and cultural activity was largely determined on the national level.

The 1924 constitution contained other innovations, too. It provided for a Federal Supreme Court and a procurator attached to the Central Committee. The Supreme Court's jurisdiction included giving opinions on questions of union legislation to the supreme courts of the union republics, rendering decisions on the constitutionality of laws passed by individual union republics, and settling disputes among them. The procurator's office had authority to check on the legality of all actions of subordinate bodies—including the Supreme Court; it was responsible only to the Central Committee of the Supreme Soviet.

The constitution of 1924 lasted 12 years. In 1935 a Constitutional Commission headed by Stalin was assigned the task of drafting a new constitution to bring Russia's political institutions into conformity with "the present correlation of class forces in the U.S.S.R." On June 1, 1936, the draft of the new constitution was submitted to a plenum of the Central Committee of the Communist Party, which ordered the convocation of an Extraordinary All-Union Congress of Soviets to ratify it. In the meantime, the draft was published for purposes of "public" discussion. The final text was adopted by the congress on December 6. It is still in force today, although it has been amended on many occasions.

The ostensible reason for the new constitution was that, having liquidated the kulaks as a class and nationalized industry, the Soviet Union had now entered a Socialist phase in which the state represented the people as a whole and not just workers. It was felt that a new constitution should reflect these changes; it did, in fact, end formal discrimination in favor of urban workers in its voting provisions. It also, for the first time, officially mentioned the Communist Party as representing the "leading core of all organizations of the working people, both public and state." In effect, however, despite a number of changes in the organization of the state, the 1936 constitution has had, as one might expect, little effect upon the realities of Soviet decision-making.

The highest organ of state authority is declared to be the Supreme Soviet of the U.S.S.R., which is now divided into two chambers: the Council of the Union, directly elected on the basis of one deputy for every three hundred thousand inhabitants, and the Council of Nationalities, directly elected on the basis of 25 deputies from each union republic, eleven from each autonomous republic, five from each autonomous region, and one deputy from each national district. Both chambers serve for a term of four years, have equal rights in initiating and enacting legislation, and elect a Presidium which serves between meetings of the Supreme Soviet.

Executive and administrative authority was vested in a Council of People's Commissars. However, in 1946 the name was changed to the Council of Ministers, thus returning to traditional czarist and Western European terminology. The council is responsible to the Supreme Soviet and its Presidium. In practice, as we shall see later in more detail, members are chosen and removed by the Communist Party leadership.

The 1936 constitution retained three types of ministries: all-union, union-republic, and republic, paralleling the earlier commissariats in structure and function. Their character has undergone many changes since 1936, and on a number of occasions the constitution has had to be amended. Perhaps the most important shake-up occurred in 1957, when Khrushchev, in an effort to decentralize the control and planning of Soviet economic activity, pushed through the creation of regional councils of the economy (*sovnarkhozes*) and eliminated many ministries. Yet even before Khrushchev's fall from power, it had become apparent that the attempt had failed; ministries were beginning to reappear on all levels, either as ministries or "state committees." This process of administrative recentralization has continued under Brezhnev and Kosygin, although other forms of decentralization, such as the greater flexibility allowed to individual industrial managers, have been developed.

Written into the 1936 constitution is an extensive bill of rights, limited, of course, by the fact that these rights can serve only the interest of the "working class." In fact, the years

immediately following the adoption of the constitution were the height of the great purge in which literally millions of people were imprisoned or executed in violation of these rights.

The pattern of organization on the national level was followed, with some variation, in the union republics and the autonomous republics, as well as on the local level. For example, the legislatures of the union republics are unicameral, and on the local level the presidium is replaced by an executive committee. It has always been clear that the real authority in the U.S.S.R. lies with the Communist Party. On both the national and union-republic levels, meetings of the Supreme Soviet are largely perfunctory and primarily dedicated to ratifying party decisions. The local soviets exercise somewhat more authority, although here again the party plays a dominant role.

In 1962 Khrushchev spoke of the need for a complete revision of the constitution, and a constitutional commission was created with Khrushchev as chairman. It has remained in existence, despite his departure from the scene, but there seems to be no hurry to fashion a new document. Soviet leaders have also hinted that the people might, at some future date, be given the opportunity to choose among several candidates in some elections, and there have been suggestions that legislative bodies might begin to serve functions other than the mere rubber-stamping of decisions taken by the party leadership. Whether the Soviet Union will move in a direction that takes the formal provisions of the present constitution more seriously and allows for more genuine freedom of choice, and what effect such an eventuality would have upon the party itself, remains to be seen.

Soviet politics today can only be understood as the result of a complex interplay of factors operating with different force at different times in the nation's history. Until 1917, the Russian state seemed to be moving into the mainstream of European development as the problems that had inhibited

MAP 3.1. UNION OF SOVIET SOCIALIST REPUBLICS

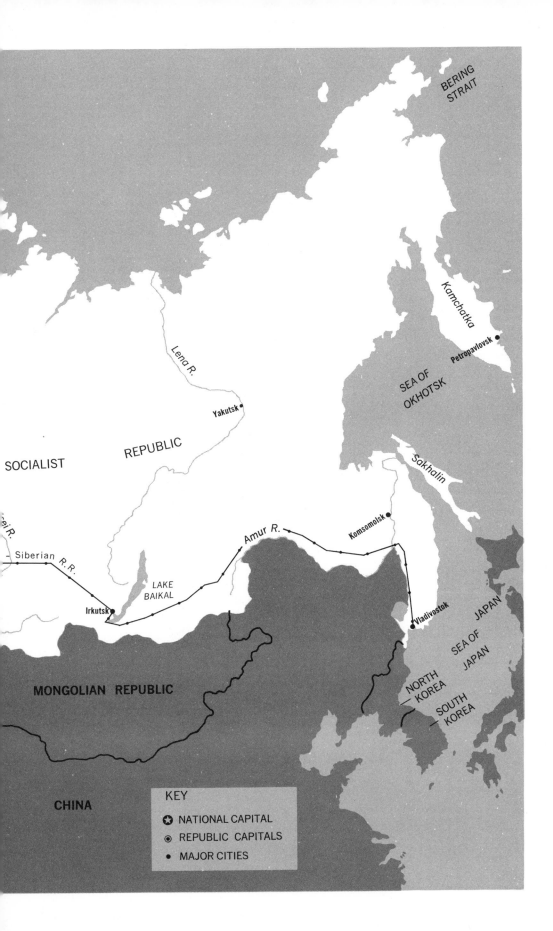

BERING
STRAIT

Kamchatka

Petropavlovsk •

SEA OF
OKHOTSK

Lena R.

Yakutsk •

REPUBLIC

Sakhalin

SOCIALIST

Komsomolsk •

Amur R.

ei R.

Siberian R. R.

LAKE
BAIKAL

Irkutsk •

JAPAN

Vladivostok •

SEA OF
JAPAN

MONGOLIAN REPUBLIC

NORTH
KOREA

SOUTH
KOREA

CHINA

KEY

★ NATIONAL CAPITAL

◉ REPUBLIC CAPITALS

• MAJOR CITIES

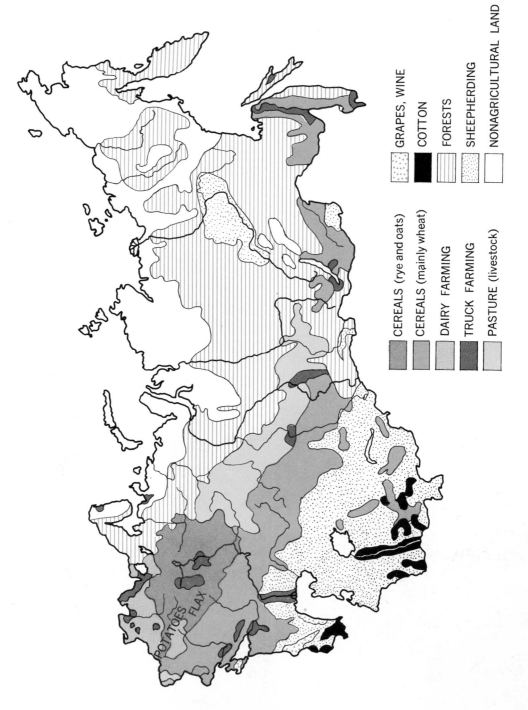

MAP 3.2. AGRICULTURAL RESOURCES OF THE U.S.S.R.

GRAPES, WINE
COTTON
FORESTS
SHEEPHERDING
NONAGRICULTURAL LAND

CEREALS (rye and oats)
CEREALS (mainly wheat)
DAIRY FARMING
TRUCK FARMING
PASTURE (livestock)

POTATOES
FLAX

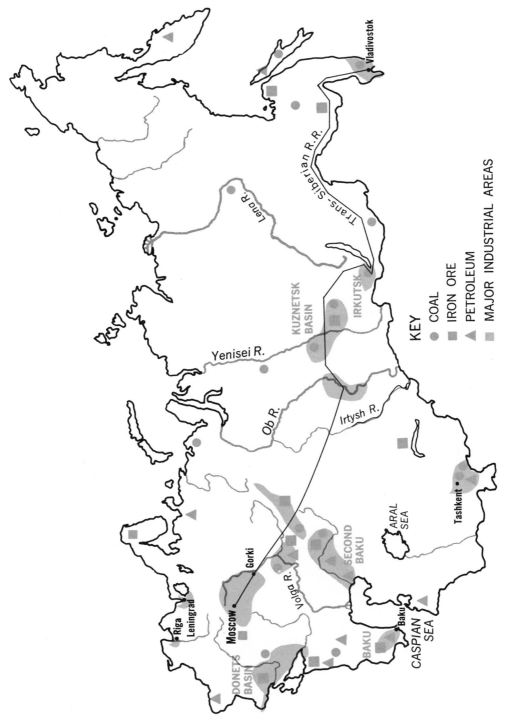

KEY

● COAL
■ IRON ORE
▲ PETROLEUM
■ MAJOR INDUSTRIAL AREAS

MAP 3.3. INDUSTRIAL RESOURCES OF THE U.S.S.R.

Vladivostok

Trans-Siberian R.R.

Lena R.

KUZNETSK BASIN

IRKUTSK

Yenisei R.

Ob R.

Irtysh R.

ARAL SEA

Tashkent

Gorki

SECOND BAKU

Volga R.

Riga

Leningrad

Moscow

DONETS BASIN

BAKU

Baku

CASPIAN SEA

modernization were overcome. The Revolution, however, resulted in a break with the Russian past of far greater magnitude than that ever experienced by any other European state in a comparable period of time.

Seizing power in a highly chaotic situation, the Soviet elite created a new and more effective state structure, welded the Soviet people into a nation, restructured the whole system of property relationships, established new bases of authority, and embarked upon a massive program of forced industrialization that, within a half century, transformed Russia into a relatively advanced industrial nation.

The members of the intellectual elite who seized power were, for the most part, modernizers. But to regard them simply as such is a serious error. The nature of their ideology was crucial in determining the manner in which the Soviet Union would industrialize and the kind of industrial state it would become. Yet despite the abruptness of the break produced by the Revolution, the Russian heritage was not simply discarded. Indeed, the leadership of the Communist Party drew upon traditional institutions and attitudes even as it continued to be shaped by them, and this occurred with greater frequency after the defeat of the cosmopolitan intellectuals, represented by Trotsky, and the victory of Stalin.

The Soviets, from the beginning, were also forced to modify portions of their ideology as they dealt with Russia's problems, and, indeed, the imperatives of managing an advanced industrial society have led to still further shifts in attitude and orientation. Marxism-Leninism as an ideology has not

been tossed away, but it has been significantly modified.

In short, what Soviet leaders created was a one-party, mobilization regime. The goal of the party was not to represent and reconcile the free expression of group interests, but to change the very nature of these interests. In its current phase, the Soviet regime can be called "neo-mercantilist." As we shall see, policy formation is more and more the result of elite competition and compromise, with the different professional groups haggling over policy alternatives. Aside from the fact that it is a Socialist regime, it differs from those of Western Europe primarily because its elite groups do not try to augment their power by turning to a larger public constituency; basic decisions are still made *in camera* and within the framework of an ideology which continues to assume that, because of its special knowledge and capacity, the Communist Party is the ultimate source of legitimacy.[18]

In this connection alone one major problem has yet to be solved by the regime. Coming to power after centuries of authoritarian rule, the Communist Party merely substituted another form of authoritarianism for the one it had destroyed. In a very important sense, therefore, the great mass of the Soviet people remain, as under the old regime, subjects rather than active citizens, despite party efforts to encourage guided participation. What this may mean for the future of Soviet politics will be discussed later.

---

[18] All these points will be discussed in later chapters. The term "neo-mercantilist" is derived from David Apter, *The Politics of Modernization* (Chicago: The University of Chicago Press, 1965).

4

Introduction

1. POLITICS, CULTURE, AND SOCIAL STRUCTURE

To Marxists, the political system of any society is part of its superstructure; while political decisions are not without importance they are, for the most part, dependent upon more basic economic factors. The analysis of any society's politics, however, is necessarily more complex if one rejects a purely Marxist interpretation or other monistic theories. The structure of political institutions, the emergence of a charismatic political figure, even ill-chosen public policies—all can have a significant impact upon the society and affect its future development. Theorizing becomes even more complicated if one is willing to entertain the possibility that such factors as the environment of the society and the cultural values of its population must all be taken into account in attempting to understand the problems which it faces and the structure of its politics. It is the argument of this volume that such is the case—that to understand the politics of any society, one must examine the interrelationships of these and other variables.

Certainly the manner in which societies have organized their system of productive relationships has greatly influenced their social and political life; broadly conceived, the economic system is one of the more important determinants of social and political consciousness. An individual's relation to a given mode of production does influence his life style: the peasant's frame of reference is quite different from that of the industrial worker, and that of both differs from the frame of reference of the lord of the manor or the capitalist entrepreneur. Structurally, then, the transition from various primitive or peasant societies to modern industrial ones has been the most significant social change of the past two hundred years.

Historically, too, the question of how to distribute material goods, power, and prestige among various strata of the society has been among the most important sources of social conflict. The next section of this chapter will offer a brief summary of how the evolution of an industrial society had its impact upon all facets of European life; Chapter 5 will deal primarily with the class structure of various European countries as it has influenced political attitudes and actions.

The economic system of any social order, however, does not emerge naturally as the result of an inner dialectical movement, as Marx thought. Rather, the manner in which a society—be it "traditional" or "modern"— mobilizes and distributes its resources is determined by its cultural heritage together with a number of other factors. Section 3 of this chapter will describe how some of the elements in the inheritance of each of the countries under study contribute to differences among them. The emphasis will be on political values and beliefs—that is, the political culture—of each country, as well as those aspects of the general culture which are relevant to politics. The section consists of a brief systematic summary of material already covered in the historical sections; other aspects of the value orientation of each country will be discussed in later chapters. It must be remembered, however, that the values and attitudes summarized are not universally shared, although they are held by large groups in the society. The particular constellation of values and beliefs that characterizes particular segments of the population will be spelled out later.

Other inter-group tensions have, at times, been at least as significant as class conflict; notably, religious and ethnic antagonisms. There is much to be said for the view that the religious variable has, in the past, been of key importance in determining the general cultural pattern of most societies. Religious and ethnic factors will be discussed in Chapter 6.

All societies must develop mechanisms by which their members are motivated to accept the more important norms of the society and to perform those tasks which the society defines as productive. They must also acquire necessary skills. The family is still important in this respect, although both the mass media and education have brought the influence of the larger community to bear as well. How

the process of socialization is organized depends upon a variety of factors, including the society's economic structure and general culture. But the structure of the family itself, the system of formal education which has been developed, and the organization of the media of communication may also serve as agents of social change—or, equally, may inhibit social change. Educational systems also determine what kind of training will be received by social and political elites. All of these institutions are treated in Chapter 8; their impact on generational conflicts is discussed in Chapter 9.

The discussion of these topics will, it is hoped, not only help us understand the political conflicts within various European political systems, insofar as these are reflections of group antagonisms, it will also clarify the values and beliefs which help to determine what goals each of the societies deems most important, and the means by which each tries to attain them. But the relationship is by no means unilateral: political decisions made in the past have significantly affected the political culture and group structures of the societies with which we are concerned; they have also affected the institutions within them which are responsible for socialization or the communication of information. The Soviet manager is not a Western European entrepreneur, whatever resemblances one may find, and the role of education in European societies cannot be understood apart from public policy decisions in the field of education. The sectional divisions of this volume, then, are in a sense arbitrary. Every social system consists of an intricate web of relationships; it would be foolish to insist upon too sharp a differentiation between what is properly considered political and other aspects of the life of the society.

2. INDUSTRIAL SOCIETY

England, France, Germany—and, to a lesser extent, the Soviet Union—are highly developed industrial societies experiencing rather rapid technological and social change. Thus they have come increasingly to resemble each other in some very important ways. In every case, industrialization has involved a more or less radical break with traditional social and cultural patterns, although these patterns have not entirely disappeared.

The three Western European countries are highly urbanized, and the Soviet Union is becoming so. In all four countries, the population is almost entirely literate, and both social and geographic mobility are relatively high as compared with earlier periods. In all four countries, too, the structure of social life has become highly differentiated, and the world and products of the machine have replaced the natural environment.

In the case of other far-reaching changes associated with industrialization, it is not always easy to determine causal relationships. Increased mobility and literacy have generally involved wider contacts with the world and have tended both to broaden perspectives and, more importantly, to weaken the hold of traditional authority. The extended family, with its complex net of kinship relations, has tended to break down in favor of the conjugal family (husband, wife, and children); at the same time, the authority of the husband over the wife and that of the parents over their children have been reduced. All of this, coupled with the instrumental view of the world fostered by modern science and technology, has resulted in a decline of religious sensibility and an emphasis on the satisfaction of personal, and for the most part material, needs.

Further, the emphasis on production and on the skills required in both science and industry has raised the status of the professional, including the scientist and the manager; these groups have increasingly come to serve as models for legitimate authority, with skill rather than birth providing the criterion for differential rewards. Greater specialization has led to the multiplication of impersonal, functionally specific relationships, while urban life has produced a breakdown

in the communal patterns associated with the village or even the small city. All these changes, leading to the replacement of traditional authority by functionally based authority, have had immense implications for the political process in every country with which we are concerned.

In general, the class patterns of each of these societies have grown more complex; a plurality of "strategic elites" within a given society has replaced the relatively simple class divisions which seemed to characterize Europe, at least during an earlier period. This means that it is far more difficult to determine with any precision where power really lies and how political decisions are actually made. Finally, the capacity of a nation's political system to produce fundamental changes in the social order has increased tremendously, whether or not those in authority actually use that capacity. The changes produced by the Soviet regime in the twentieth century, as in many of the developing nations, would not have been possible in the nineteenth.

But some caveats are required here. The social patterns we have come to associate with highly industrialized societies are by no means immutable. Both the high level of specialization and the emphasis on production which characterize modern Europe may change in the future, and some of the values associated with "modernity" have begun to be attacked in the past few years. Further, not all of the patterns outlined hold for all areas of the world. The organization of industrial relations in Japan, for example, is still different from the standard European pattern in important ways, even as the European countries differ from each other. Finally, it is certainly not true that all societies will take the European path in modernizing; African countries, for example, are unlikely to pass through a stage comparable with that of nineteenth-century Europe, and, insofar as the consequences of the nineteenth century still have a profound impact upon the social life and politics of the twentieth, many features of European life will almost certainly remain unique for some time to come.

3. VARIATIONS ON THE EUROPEAN EXPERIENCE

Whether or not the Western European industrial and scientific breakthrough could have developed under other auspices, the fact remains that it was associated with both liberalism and capitalism. This has had certain important consequences.

The emphasis on individualism and private property contributed to the development of an entrepreneurial class which acquired considerable economic and political power, even in those countries which retained important elements of an older tradition. At the same time, however, the existence of that older tradition, combined with the revolution of ideas sparked by liberalism, opened the way for increasing restrictions on the free economic activity of entrepreneurs and a sharp curtailment of their political influence.

Today, for example, no European country approximates the classical laissez-faire model. Whether one calls Germany, France, and England "neocapitalist economies" or "welfare states," all of them, much as they may still differ, are committed to fairly widespread systems of social insurance as well as to substantial governmental economic intervention, through both fiscal controls and economic planning.[1] To be sure, all three are still "market" economies, as opposed to a largely "command" economy like the Soviet Union, and in all three the private sector predominates. Yet traditional economic liberalism is dead.

Further, the real wages of industrial workers in most European countries have more than doubled since the war, and while large segments of the working class (or the peasantry, for that matter) are by no means affluent, there can be no gainsaying the general trend. Social mobility, too, is on the increase, although within all European countries those composing the elite still tend to be from middle-class backgrounds. A recent study of social mobility in France, for example, revealed that some 81 per cent of those occupying elite positions were drawn from fifteen per cent of the population.

In general, positions at the top are being opened to children of middle- and lower-middle-class backgrounds who are taking advantage of expanded educational opportunities; at the same time, the size of the elite stratum itself is growing rapidly in proportion with the continued growth of professional services. Even within industry, "managers" are replacing "entrepreneurs," and control is being separated from ownership. Then, too, the complexion of the work force is changing: the number of white-collar jobs is rising much more rapidly than the demand for industrial workers. The extent and the pace of these developments vary from country to country, but the social impact of the trend cannot be denied.

Finally, the newly developed self-consciousness of the lower classes and their more active participation in social and political life have significantly changed the whole power structure of these societies. As late as 1913 no more than 25 per cent of the population of many European countries was eligible to vote; today the norm in Western Europe is universal suffrage. Seventy-five years ago trade unions were still operating on the border of illegality; today, with the possible exception of France, they command considerable economic and political power. Wealth and power are still unevenly distributed in all European countries (see Tables 4.1, 4.2, and 4.3), but a new Europe is emerging—a Europe whose social structure is radically different even from that of the period immediately preceding the Second World War.

THE ENGLISH PATTERN: The outstanding fact of English social life has been that continued intermingling of old and new which

---

[1] A more detailed discussion of the role of the state in the economic life of Western Europe will be found in Chapter 24.

TABLE 4.1. PORTION OF TOTAL INCOME RECEIVED BY
TOP TEN PER CENT OF FAMILIES BEFORE TAXES

	1938	1954[2]	1964
United Kingdom	38.0%	30.4%	29.3%
France	—	34.1	36.8[3]
West Germany	39.0[1]	44.0	41.4
United States	36.0	30.0	28.0

[1] Data for all Germany in 1936.
[2] French data for 1956; German, for 1955.
[3] Data for 1962.

Sources: United Nations, Department of Economic
and Social Affairs, *Economic Survey of Europe in
1956* (Geneva: United Nations Publication, 1957),
chap. 9, p. 6; United Nations, *Incomes in Postwar
Europe* (Geneva: United Nations Publication, 1967),
chap. 6, p. 15; *Statistical Abstract of the United
States, 1939*, p. 313; *Statistical Abstract, 1968*, p. 323.

TABLE 4.2. AVERAGE INCOME PER PERSON

In U.S. dollars of 1957–1959 purchasing power

	1949	1961
United Kingdom	773	1,149
France	482	1,034
West Germany	320	1,072
United States	1,453	2,308

Adapted from Charles P. Kindleberger, *Economic
Development*, 2nd ed. (New York: McGraw-Hill,
1965), pp. 12–13. Reprinted by permission of the
publisher.

TABLE 4.3. INEQUALITY OF TAXABLE INCOME IN VARIOUS COUNTRIES

*Based on a range from .000 (complete equality of
income distribution) to 1.000[1]*

	Index of Inequality	Year
West Germany	.432	1950
United States	.373	1956
United Kingdom	.318	1955

[1] The index is highly stable over time, reflecting the
constancy of income distribution within a country.

Source: Bruce M. Russett et al., *World Hand-
book of Political and Social Indicators* (New
Haven: Yale University Press, 1964), p. 247.
Reprinted by permission of the publisher.

has permitted traditional forms to be retained even as the content of institutions has been changed. The sense of being part of an evolving organic community has served to moderate social conflict and has encouraged the maintenance of a class system, associated on the positive side with a sense of noblesse oblige and community service and on the negative with both snobbery and deference.

These values still permeate British life. They are tied in with the whole apparatus of the monarchy and the court, with the public schools, with Oxford and Cambridge, and with the "old boy" network that enables a British elite—by American standards comparatively small—to communicate freely and easily with each other, whether they are businessmen, civil servants, or top-level professionals. The values are also reflected in the attitudes of those workers who still vote for Tory candidates because they prefer to be governed by their "betters"; they are seen, too, in the ideal of the "amateur" whose broad interest in the classics, general deportment, and competence in socially approved sports supposedly fit him for an elite position in business, politics, or the professions. These values have also contributed to a trust in the good intentions of the state and its officials, as well as to a sense of moderation which prevents any group from pushing its claims too far against what is considered to be the "objective" interest of the community as a whole.

The deference of members of the working class toward their "betters" stems from the patterns of a traditional class society, but intense class consciousness and pride in class come out of later developments; both sets of attitudes may be present in the same worker. The assumption by any government that organized groups representing all major interests should be consulted before new policies are initiated reflects a tendency to regard the realm as composed of different estates— an attitude which can be traced back to its feudal origins. On the other hand, the individualism of Englishmen—revealed, for example, in their reluctance to create a centralized police force, or preference for individual houses rather than apartments—can be traced to another period of English history.

Perhaps nothing indicates the differences between Englishmen and Americans better than their contrasting attitudes toward social welfare and public education. Far before the United States, the British accepted the idea that the community as a whole was responsible for social-welfare measures; although the Socialists helped to advance this belief, its origins lie in an earlier tradition. Yet the British have maintained until very recently a highly elite educational system, whereas, from a very early period, Americans poured money into a relatively democratic system of mass education designed to provide for equality of opportunity.

Yet the signs of change are equally omnipresent. Newly trained technical personnel are beginning to challenge some of the older values; another generation of intellectuals, stifled by the insularity of British culture, is making repeated attacks on traditional values; the inviolability of the police has been attacked and there has been an abrupt increase of crime, particularly crimes of violence. All these facts indicate that traditional patterns are crumbling. There are other signs too: the victory of architectural functionalism and modernism over those who wish to retain traditional landmarks in cities like London, the easing of sexual mores, the changing ideals of British women as to what constitutes personal attractiveness, and the gradual erosion of both class and regional accents.

Some of these and other changes are the result simply of technical imperatives, as for example the decision finally to shift to a metric system of weights and measures and a decimal system of money. Others arise from greater contact with other cultural patterns, including American television, and the increasing opportunities of the middle and lower classes to travel to the Continent. The loss of empire and the reduction of England to a second-class power have also had their effect by removing the halo from institutions which somehow seemed associated with the claim that the sun never set on the British Empire.

And all sides seem dedicated to change: the Tory businessman, who wishes to join the Common Market so as to have the opportunity to make the operation of his firm more rational by developing a lever against "excessive" trade-union demands; the left-wing intellectual, who rails against the continued cant of an Establishment that refuses to adjust to the imperatives of modernity. Tradition, then, finds fewer and fewer champions; there are still those who lament the advent of the "mass society" and "mass culture," but they are less and less part of the national dialogue. And there are still many, of course, who attack "mass society," but they come almost entirely from the left; whatever their goals, they certainly do not include the restoration of a community characterized by sharp class and status lines.

THE FRENCH PATTERN: Perhaps the outstanding feature of France during the 150 years since the Great Revolution has been the nation's social and political fragmentation —a fragmentation which has been woven into the whole tapestry of French history, but which is most specifically a product of the trauma of modernization and the Revolution, upon which French scholars still focus so much attention.

Like comparable events in many other European Catholic countries, the French Revolution produced a schism which has divided French society until the present time into two hostile subcultures: the one traditional and Catholic; the other, at least on the surface, dedicated to such ideals as liberty, the Enlightenment, secularization, and science. Yet actually the two cultures were, in some senses, caricatures. In their hostility, each developed a rigid outlook which only heightened mutual antagonism and inhibited compromise. For all practical purposes, the

conflict was a religious one, for the Jacobin mentality's insistence upon the culture of scientific rationality had as much air of conviction and dogmatic belief as the Catholic position.

This fault throws light on a number of the paradoxes that characterized French social and political life well into the twentieth century: the development of a legal system representing the height of rational creativity, in a country where the bulk of the population retained a traditional peasant outlook; the existence of a subculture that stressed training in the sciences and technical proficiency, side by side with one that emphasized classical culture; individual entrepreneurs' experimentation with highly advanced industrial techniques, in a country dominated by small, tradition-minded family firms.

The Revolution had other consequences of equal significance. The subsequent social and cultural polarization, and the inability of the French to develop common conceptions of national purpose or authority, led to a proliferation of ideological positions, each of which offered some new panacea. But this proliferation only contributed to a social and political stalemate, as well as to the recurring emergence of charismatic leaders—Napoleon I, Napoleon III, and Charles de Gaulle, for example—who promised to resolve France's problems in their own person. For the most part, however, all such efforts failed, and the movements sparked by these figures became but one more ideological current. Under such circumstances literally anything was possible—except compromise.

On the positive side, it can be said that the tensions were the source of a remarkable creativity. But the negative side was a resultant stasis which inhibited France's ability to deal effectively with new problems except in terms of traditional slogans, and a narrow conception of self-interest which reduced the possibilities of effective community action, and even effective action by various interest groups within the community. The Frenchman believed that, except for his immediate family or perhaps some limited group, he was surrounded by *les autres,* who sought to exploit his weaknesses for their own benefit.

Thus, while it is possible to speak of a business or agricultural interest in the United States or England and make at least cautious generalizations about the political behavior of such groups, this has, historically, been far more difficult in France. Economic diversity in France has been augmented by regional variations based upon frozen historical stances, and beyond this by the sheer unwillingness of individuals to subordinate their conceptions of self-interest to any larger group.

It is only in the past 15 years that these patterns have begun to dissolve in a period of rapid economic and technical growth that has far outstripped the efforts of the British since the end of World War II. The sources of these changes, while in most cases the same as those which have affected all Europe, stem in part from the experience of the war and the Vichy regime. The French political right was discredited by its alliance with Vichy, and many firms, charged with collaboration, were nationalized. In the nationalized sector of the economy, traditional management was replaced by younger men committed to technological progress. In the private business world, control passed to a new generation whose orientation, shaped by the war and the experience of the 1930's, involved a complete break with the past. Thus, what many argued in the period immediately following the liberation of France is true: the war did provide some of the bases for France's regeneration. However, as in all European societies, the social changes associated with this regeneration have created new problems and new social tensions.

THE GERMAN PATTERN: German society in the late nineteenth century was dominated by an aristocracy which, far more than its French or English counterparts, emphasized the values of status, discipline, and "manliness"; these virtues were defined largely in

military terms. The road to social improvement for the petty-bourgeois young man was to attend a business college, join a dueling fraternity and acquire a scar, and then enter into those circles which might enable him to marry the daughter of his employer.

The emphasis upon self-control and status was related to a need for an ordered environment and strong sources of authority. The whole structure of German society was authoritarian, orderly, and disciplined; in mirroring these values, it also perpetuated them. Crime rates were relatively low; business, scientific, and military life were characterized by a passion for order which undoubtedly played a role in the industrial and scientific success the empire achieved so quickly.

The "responsible" German would do his public duty by voting and by obeying the law, but he left political affairs in the hands of those whose superior authority gave them the right to make such decisions. He tended to regard those who rejected traditional values, especially when such a rejection threatened to produce disorder, merely as wicked men who should be punished by "right-thinking" people. By contrast, the American pattern has much more often regarded group deviation as a function of faults in the system which must be adjusted in order to re-establish a consensus.

These patterns have not completely disappeared from German life. Studies demonstrate that German students still tend to emphasize individual mastery and the respect for age and legitimate authority more than their American or English counterparts. Yet their attitudes are ambivalent: in concrete situations they are less likely to admit responsibility to authority for acts they know to be wrong.

Such attitudes are far less pronounced, however, than in the Weimar period. The general European pattern seems again to hold in Germany. The gap between the attitudes of the urban and rural populations is disappearing; formal status is less and less important among social strata; skill is replacing birth as the basis for social advancement; and leisure is increasingly valued—perhaps somewhat frenetically—for its own sake. So, too, the structure of the family is far less authoritarian, in both husband-wife and parent-child relationships. It is these changes, far more than verbal commitments to democracy, that are shaping the emergent pattern of German society.

In the early postwar period, one group did seem significantly alienated, for a time. At the end of World War II West Germany was inundated with a flood of refugees. More than eight million Germans, fleeing from East Germany, expelled from the Czech Sudetenland or from prewar Poland, were added to those expelled from the parts of Germany placed under "temporary" Polish administration. For many of these people, the expulsion put an end to reasonably comfortable middle- and upper-class existence; for all, it involved a profound uprooting. At first the situation seemed fairly dangerous, as the refugees talked about returning to and reintegrating their former homelands. Such conversation continues, but less insistently, as the older generation dies and the younger generation becomes more fully integrated into German life.

The appearance of the National Democratic Party demonstrates the continued existence of authoritarian trends in a segment of the German population—a segment that could conceivably grow if the political situation became polarized. The difference between the Weimar period and the present, however, is indicated quite dramatically by the German student movement. In the late 1920's, the most active and vociferous student groups were invariably dominated by the right, if not by the Nazi Party. Today, however, in line with other Western European countries, the student movement leans toward the left. The goal of the activists is not the restoration of traditional values, but rather the reform or reconstruction of German society.

THE RUSSIAN AND SOVIET PATTERN: By the early twentieth century, the Russian Empire included so many diverse ethnic groups that it is difficult to generalize about either its culture or the "national character" of its peoples. The typical stereotype of the Great Russian—and, like all typical stereotypes, it contains kernels of truth among the grains of salt—is that of an essentially passive and fatalistic man given to periodic emotional outbursts, usually associated with wild bouts of drinking. His attitude toward authority vacillated between a fascination with anarchy and a conviction that without very rigid controls civic order would collapse. In everyday affairs, he accepted a strict hierarchy of authority; nevertheless, it was considered legitimate to deceive those in authority in any way possible. It was this peculiar volatility of Russian character, as well as a general incapacity for sustained, self-disciplined work, which, in the eyes of many Western observers, explained the combination of excessive legalism and constant disorder in Russian governmental and industrial bureaucracies. Formal written rules seem to inspire widespread violations. Some of the modernizing rulers of Russia shared these Western views of their subjects, and this is one of the reasons why Catherine the Great encouraged the settlement in Russia of German peasants. It was her hope that the Germans would, by their example, cause a change in the attitudes of the Russian peasantry.

The Bolsheviks, in theory at least, regarded so-called national characteristics as unimportant, if not entirely mythical. To them, although Lenin often railed against the slovenliness of the Russians, the explanation of the behavior of all peoples was to be found in their stage of economic development. Of course, by the time the Bolsheviks had come to power in the Soviet Union, they had made several important changes in classical Marxism. They had added an element of voluntarism, as implied by the idea that revolutionary consciousness would be brought to the worker from the outside; a conception of a tight party organization (democratic centralism); and a theory, called "the law of combined development," which explained why the Revolution had occurred in Russia first and under what conditions it would succeed. The success of the Russian Revolution, in fact, required that it set off revolutions in Western Europe.

The hope that it would do so, the expectation that full communism would arrive very shortly, had all but disappeared by the time Lenin died. It was in this context that Stalin developed the theory of socialism in one country; in this context, too, he justified the key role of the Communist Party as implementing the "dictatorship of the proletariat," increased the power of the party and state apparatus, and made the other retreats from initial Bolshevik goals that marked the 1930's and 1940's. And this was also the context of the second Soviet revolution—the revolution of collectivization and industrialization. So long as the Soviet Union remained backward and surrounded by hostile and powerful enemies, Stalin argued, it was imperative that the Soviet state continue to exist; so long as both internal and external enemies continued to attack the regime (that is, so long as major centers of anti-Communist power remained), terror and coercion were necessary.

In part, the policies of the regime during the Stalin period were motivated simply by a desire to maintain or enhance personal power; in part, they reflected both Stalin's personality and the traditional Russian culture inherited by the Soviet elite; in part, they represented pragmatic responses to emerging problems. However, the general direction of policy was determined by a Marxist framework which, however modified in practice, the party leadership endorsed.

In the post-Stalin era, ideological commitment to the goals of a Communist society has continued to serve as the broad standard by which policy is to be judged, and the tensions between the regime's commitment to this ultimate standard and the facts of social and economic life in an advanced industrial so-

ciety help explain many of the apparent eccentricities in Soviet policy since Stalin's death. As before, of course, practical problems, power conflicts, and international events also exert their influence; it is obvious that some elements of the Marxist vision have eroded or been transformed. But to see the regime *merely* as a bureaucratic organization whose leaders desire only power, or to regard the Soviet system simply as an "administered" society, is to miss a principal element in its dynamics.

For example, the discussions which preceded the adoption of the program at the Twenty-Second Party Congress in 1962, and that program itself, represented more than the mechanical repetition of pious platitudes. So, too, it is necessary to interpret the wage reforms and school reforms, the moderate democratization of the party, and even the creation of comrades' courts and a "people's militia," as at least partially the consequence of a particular ideological commitment.[2]

There can be no precise measurement of the importance of ideology in all of these policy decisions, or of the extent of the ideological commitment of the party elite or the population as a whole. It is unquestionably true that at least a small portion of the Soviet population is quite nonideological, or even hostile to the regime, although a very comprehensive study of Russians who defected to the West after World War II indicates that the views of even the most disaffected were heavily influenced by Marxist assumptions.[3] For the great majority of the population, Marxism-Leninism undoubtedly plays a role comparable to the basic puritanical and liberal values and beliefs which still permeate American culture. Finally, there remains a group, probably including a substantial portion of the membership of the Communist Party, which is more or less highly dedicated

[2] See Chapters 21 and 23.
[3] See Alex Inkeles and Raymond A. Bauer, *The Soviet Citizen* (Cambridge, Mass.: Harvard University Press, 1959), pp. 233–255.

in principle to the expressed goals of the regime, however much they may deviate from these goals in making policy decisions—and then rationalize their deviation.

If it is difficult to measure the influence of ideology in Russia today, it is even more difficult to predict the future character of its influence and development. Some of its important tenets have, at least temporarily, disappeared. The party almost never talks of completely eliminating money as a mechanism of exchange; and, in the natural sciences and some of the social sciences, doctrines which were felt to be, and in some cases are, incompatible with Marxism are now accepted—or they are somehow incorporated into the framework of Marxist thought. There is also no more talk of the dissolution of the family; Khrushchev's expressed hope in the late 1950's that boarding schools would provide for the care of *all* children has been toned down. In the new party platform, the withering of the state is mentioned only once. In fact, the document emphasizes the state's continuing role in Soviet society, along with that of the party. Also, the elimination of the incentive of personal economic gain is placed far in the future; during the past four years, the re-

gime has begun to make more use of the profit motive to encourage production.

Whether trends in this direction will continue, and how far they will go, depend on many factors. But there is little reason to expect that Communist ideology will cease to be an important element in Soviet social life in the near future.

In the meantime, the Soviet Union has become an advanced industrial society; as in the West, this transformation has created professional technical elites whose expertise has made them increasingly influential. It has also created a system of stratification in which advancement is dependent upon education. But it must be pointed out that while social mobility has increased in the Soviet Union, social classes (unless one uses a Marxist definition) have not disappeared. Our data is limited, and most of it gives us a picture only of the late 1930's; what evidence we have indicates that upward mobility from peasant or worker to white-collar status is about the same as in the Western European countries. In the United States and France approximately 35 per cent of the sons of workers move into white-collar positions; in the Soviet Union the percentage seems to be about 39 (see Table 4.4). It is

TABLE 4.4. SOCIAL MOBILITY IN THE SOVIET UNION, 1940

Occupation	Father's occupation					
	Professional administrative	Semiprofessional	White collar	Skilled worker	Ordinary worker	Peasant
Professional-administrative	65%	47%	40%	26%	9%	8%
Semiprofessional	8	27	14	17	6	6
White collar	9	17	30	9	11	10
Skilled worker	7	0	4	25	16	15
Ordinary worker	7	9	10	23	55	29
Collective farmer	4	0	2	0	3	32

Source: Alex Inkeles and Raymond A. Bauer, *The Soviet Citizen* (Cambridge, Mass.: Harvard University Press, 1959), p. 81. Reprinted by permission of the publisher.

also true that in the Soviet Union as in other countries young men and women tend to marry people whose class position is roughly similar to that of their own.[4]

And the values associated with social class have changed. It is no longer the vogue in Russia to be a roughhewn worker. Greater emphasis is being placed on middle-class deportment, including standards of politeness and of formal address which do not differ appreciably from those found in Western Europe. In fact, one of the major criticisms leveled against Khrushchev by many of the younger members of the Soviet elite was that he was "uncultured."

In general, the regime strives to inculcate values which, except for their greater emphasis upon collective responsibility, are not unlike those of Western countries. The importance of responsibility for personal actions is emphasized; hard work is regarded as a positive good, and those who idle away their time are subject to a prolonged stay in a labor camp.

Both the efforts of the regime and the structural changes produced by industrialization, then, have yielded some changes in traditional Russian behavior. Studies indicate that parents now stress personal values such as the achievement of success and individual satisfaction in the training of their children, rather than more traditional familial or religious values. The authority of the family appears to be breaking down somewhat, and the Soviet Union is more and more frequently faced with juvenile-delinquency problems which resemble those in other European cultures. Jazz and other components of the youth culture in Western Europe are more and more attractive to Soviet youngsters and,

finally, the position of women in Soviet society has also changed considerably; women, in fact, constitute a larger proportion of the professional work force than in the United States.

On the other hand, many traditional elements of Russian culture still remain. The sexual puritanism emphasized by the regime under Stalin was partly a reflection of Russian behavior patterns. Other elements, usually considered to be characteristic of Russians, are still present; their expansiveness, volatility, impulsiveness, and the general emotional warmth which observers have always noticed. Drunkenness is a major problem for the regime, especially in rural areas; most crimes in the Soviet Union are still crimes of passion, committed under the influence of liquor or as the result of a heated argument, and followed by intense remorse. Like all societies, the Soviet Union remains, to some extent, the product of its social and cultural heritage. Nor—judging from the regime's incentives—is there any indication that the Soviets have succeeded in eliminating general acquisitiveness; the use of monetary incentives and the impulse to personal gain seem as strong as ever. In 1966, for example, when catskin coats had become very popular, collective-farm and cooperative shops in many provincial towns raised the price paid for the hides. There was a mass advertising campaign; subsequently thousands of cats—including large numbers registered as belonging to members of the community—were shot in the streets and finished off with pikes. As *Izvestia* noted:

We write in such detail about the goings-on in Kerch where thousands of registered and taxed cats and dogs were shot, because we see this and similar actions as a possible cause of the meaningless cruelty rampant among teen-agers today.[5]

---

[4] For all this data see Inkeles, *Soviet Citizen*, pp. 82, 86, 138, 196, 226. At least 75 per cent of those with a college education ended up in ranks of the professional strata; only five per cent of those with five to seven years of education achieved this status.

[5] Quoted in *Atlas*, XI, 6 (June 1966), p. 367.

5

Social Class

and Politics

1. GENTRY, PEASANTS, AND FARMERS

Western European feudalism involved a reciprocal relationship between a feudal aristocracy and a dependent peasantry. The role played by both social classes during the transition from traditional to modern society varied widely in the four countries with which we are concerned. In England, a progressive gentry generated an agricultural revolution that helped facilitate industrial development, and, in fact, contributed directly to that development; at the same time, the gentry continued to serve as a responsible political elite. The English peasantry disappeared as an important social force by the end of the eighteenth century.

In France, the aristocracy helped to start the Revolution which was to bring down the monarchy, but, once the Revolution actually got under way, that class was itself the object of attack; during most of the nineteenth century, it had an extremely conservative influence on French politics. The peasantry, on the other hand, benefited from the Revolution and the resultant land reforms; during a good

part of the nineteenth and twentieth centuries, it was the backbone of movements which were at once radical and conservative —radical in that they tended to support republican institutions, and conservative in that they remained hostile to the new industrial society.

In Germany, the Junker aristocracy served as a political elite which modernized German society from above. The peasantry was generally conservative, although segments of it did develop a quasi-Jacobin outlook; the problems peasants faced in the post–World War I period, and their antipathy toward urban society, led many of them to support the Nazi revolution.

The Russian peasantry continued to be essentially conservative and passive, except for sporadic outbreaks, until 1917, when it contributed directly to the destruction of the old regime. It is ironic that its major desire had been to obtain land, for the Revolution which it supported resulted ultimately in collectivization.

Today, the European landed aristocracy has all but disappeared; the peasant is being

145

replaced by the farmer, and the proportion of those who till the soil is rapidly declining. In none of the four Western European nations we are discussing do those who till the soil make up more than 18 per cent of the working force, and in Russia the proportion has dropped from more than fifty per cent in 1949 to about 35 per cent in 1968 (see Table 5.1). In all these countries the "peasant mentality" is becoming part of the past, although in some parts of France and Germany, and especially in the Soviet Union, traditional attitudes are still fairly strong.

Yet not all the traditional problems have been solved, and new ones are appearing. These take different forms in Western Europe and the Soviet Union. In France and Germany, many farm holdings are too small to provide an adequate standard of living for their owners; farm incomes have risen since the war, but they have lagged behind those in other sectors of the economy. In France, especially, this problem is complicated by the fact that more is being produced than can be consumed in the home market or sold at a profit abroad. Both governments have attempted to deal with this problem by actively supporting the consolidation of holdings and encouraging marginal farmers to leave the land; these efforts have met with resistance. In the Soviet Union, the major problem is still one of increasing productivity, for agriculture remains among the most inefficient and backward sectors of the Soviet economy.

THE ENGLISH PATTERN: By the end of the eighteenth century, independent peasants were no longer a significant social force in England. The enclosure movement, which began in the later middle ages, had resulted in the concentration of land in the hands of a comparatively small number of families, and the large-scale commercial agriculture of the eighteenth century completed the process. By English law, ownership descended to the eldest son, insuring that land holdings would be passed on intact. By 1800, then, about 75 per cent of the cultivated land was owned by nineteen thousand families; by 1870, seven thousand families owned four-fifths of it.[1]

Whatever their disruptive effects, the enclosures of the seventeenth and eighteenth centuries had two very beneficial consequences. First, the absence of a highly tra-

[1] David Mingay, *English Landed Society in the Eighteenth Century* (London: Routledge and Kegan Paul, 1963), p. 26; and F. M. L. Thompson, *English Landed Society in the Nineteenth Century* (London: Routledge and Kegan Paul, 1963), p. 27.

TABLE 5.1. THE DECLINE OF FARMING AS AN OCCUPATION

Percentage of work force engaged in agriculture

	1850–60	*1900*	*1930*	*1950*	*1960*	*1967[2]*
Great Britain	18	8	8	6	6	6
France	60–65	42	34	28	21	18
Germany[1]	—	40	30	22	11	9
U.S.S.R.	—	75	—	45	40	35
United States	59	36	19	11	7	5

[1]Post–World War II percentages apply only to West Germany.
[2]Estimates.

Sources: European data from Folke Dovring, *Land and Labor in Europe* (The Hague: Martinus Nijhoff, 1965); Michael Tracy, *Agriculture in Western Europe* (New York: Frederick A. Praeger, 1964), pp. 50, 80, 85. Reprinted by permission of Frederick A. Praeger, Jonathan Cape, Ltd., and the author. United States data to 1900 from *Statistical Abstract of the United States, 1937*, sec. 23; from 1930, *National Income and Product Accounts of the U.S., 1965*, pp. 90–94.

TABLE 5.2.   AGRICULTURAL DEVELOPMENT, 1955

	Acres per tractor	Farmers per extension agent
France	156.2	6,000
West Germany	59.5	420
United Kingdom	69.4	800
United States	276.0	—

Adapted from J. Frederick Dewhurst, John O. Coppock, P. Lamartine Yates, and associates, *Europe's Needs and Resources* (New York: Twentieth Century Fund, 1961), pp. 496, 497, 504; reprinted by permission of the publisher. U.S. data from *Statistical Abstract of the United States, 1968*, p. 609.

ditional landowning peasantry enabled the British to avoid some of the tension between urban and rural life that was present in both France and Germany. Second, the enclosures coincided with and contributed to the development of relatively efficient commercial farming at a fairly early period, compared with the Continent. This agricultural revolution, in turn, helped to precipitate the subsequent industrial revolution which, in conjunction with free trade (as symbolized by the repeal of duties on the import of corn in 1846), resulted in the abrupt decline of agriculture as the major source of national wealth, and, for all but a few, as a way of life. By 1900, then, less than nine per cent of the English working force was employed in agriculture as against forty to 45 per cent for other European countries.

In the meantime, the nature of the landed interest itself was undergoing a change. Aristocrats who had invested their wealth in industry, or married into families whose wealth was based on industry, increasingly left their land to the management of professional land stewards and agents. That they retained title to it at all was primarily a question of prestige; similarly, industrialists bought estates in the hope of obtaining a title. Both groups gradually divested themselves of substantial portions of their holdings, preserving only that which was essential to maintaining their life-styles.

Thus emerged a new class of farmers, the former tenants or land stewards of estates, who bought portions of these estates as purely commercial enterprises. The movement in this direction accelerated in the years between the two world wars when, by some estimates, at least one-fourth of English land holdings changed hands. Today, the great bulk of English agricultural land is owned by commercial farmers, a circumstance abetted by the Agricultural Act of 1947, which allowed for public seizure of land on which owners did not comply with the "rules of good husbandry" and the "rules of good estate management."

The landed gentry of nineteenth-century England were not highly motivated to develop associations for promoting their common interests. In the early part of the century, their influence was sufficiently great for this to be unnecessary; even when their political power declined, their traditional attitudes toward politics and unwillingness to sully their hands with formal "politicking" inhibited organization.

It took the new ownership patterns to bring about effective farmers' associations; after a number of unsuccessful attempts at organization, the National Farmer's Union (N.F.U.), representing both farmers (owner-occupiers) and farm tenants, came into existence in 1908. Since that year it has grown until today its membership includes the great bulk of the full-time farmers in England and Wales.

Despite the small size of the agricultural population, the N.F.U. has been fairly successful in obtaining government policies that it considers favorable to its interests. Its ability to do so stems both from a continuing British idealization of rural life (shared by America, Germany, and France) and the desire of every British government to make sure the country can produce a reasonable portion of its food supply. Of course, the fact that farmers are concentrated in a number of marginal election districts also helps.

In the 1930's the N.F.U. was more or less associated with the Conservative Party, although its politics were officially neutral. They remain so in the postwar period; but aside from talk by the Labor Party's left wing about nationalizing all the land, the union has found the program of Labor somewhat more to its taste.

The amount of agricultural land owned by absentee landlords is still quite large. This interest is represented by the Country Land Association, an organization which began as a small group of influential gentlemen, but in recent years has sought to broaden its membership by appealing to farmers, who now constitute some 75 per cent of its membership. Farmers still tend to rely upon the N.F.U. to support their political interests, but look to the association for the technical services it provides.

The landless agricultural workers manning larger estates and farms have continued to be among the most tradition-bound and deferential groups in England; a very large portion of them still regularly vote Conservative. Efforts to organize them, prompted by the trade-union movement, resulted in the National Union of Agricultural Workers; as of now, however, it boasts a membership of only about 112,000, somewhat less than thirty per cent of the agricultural labor force.

THE FRENCH PATTERN: By the time of the Revolution, France already possessed a substantial "free" peasant population; this was augmented by the redistribution of Catholic Church and aristocratic property which increased the number of small peasant holdings and permitted many of the more ambitious and well-to-do peasants to acquire more land. It also helped to make a sizable number of peasants loyal to the Revolution, and alienate them from the church.

The common (although not universal) practice in bequeathing land in France had differed from the English pattern in that land was divided equally among all sons. Napoleon's Civil Code formalized this practice, insuring the continued fragmentation of peasant holdings and inhibiting the introduction of more rational agricultural methods. It did, however, provide France with a social stability that was impervious to the frequency of political shifts.

Little wonder, then, that the French peasant retained his traditional outlook more than did the peasantry of surrounding countries, who, by the middle of the nineteenth century, were increasingly producing for commercial markets and being transformed into farmers. Some large-scale commercial farming did develop in the north of France and in certain areas dedicated primarily to winemaking. These were the exceptions, however; with the richest soil in Western Europe, France never came close to producing its capacity.

The relatively small size of French farms, however, was by no means the only factor of importance here. Mechanization and the application of scientific techniques to agriculture had gone much further in countries such as West Germany, the Netherlands, and Denmark, in which the average size of farms was comparable or even smaller.

A full explanation of French peasant attitudes, then, must take into account not only the small size of French farms and the relative absence of modern scientific methods, but also the traditional Catholic culture of rural France, even in "de-Christianized" areas, and the suspicion and hostility which characterized so much of French life. In Denmark and even Germany, for example, agricultural cooperatives enabled small holders to obtain some of the benefits of a larger-scale operation; in France, this was not the case, for reasons evident in one author's description of a fairly typical French village:

As we came to know . . . families . . . it seemed to us . . . that all . . . were suspicious of each other. "Of course you can trust me and my family and few other people . . . mais les autres. . . ."[2]

Likewise, after studying another community, a prominent French rural sociologist concluded that, with some exceptions among young people, the inhabitants had neighbors but no friends.[3]

Such suspicion and individual isolation long characterized much of French social life. To the peasant, the state was traditionally an instrument which one manipulated, if possible, to secure special privileges such as subsidies; but it was not to be trusted, especially if it were in the hands of "les autres"—a generalized and hostile *them*. And, therefore, if the state attempted to implement policies which seemed to run counter to immediate interests, it was quite legitimate to use any technique, including violence, to defeat its efforts. The history of France is replete with minor and major peasant upheavals which ranged from the tarring and feathering of tax collectors to the destruction of competitors' crops.

Generally, though, the peasant was still a passive force in French politics during most of the nineteenth century, reacting to rather than participating in the formulation of agricultural policy. Provided he was left alone, and conditions did not deteriorate too far, his interest in Paris and in politics remained minimal. The same was true of the growing number of workers on the larger commercial farms. The one exception to this passivity was the specialized groups representing commercial or semi-commercial agriculture which succeeded time and time again in obtaining protective tariffs or special subsidies.

Like all Frenchmen, the peasants were sharply divided ideologically; these divisions were, and are, related in a complex way to religious practice, size of holdings, and type of crops. During a substantial part of the nineteenth century, peasants in those areas where the church was strong tended to be anti-republican; anticlerical areas tended toward a politically radical but in some ways socially conservative type of Jacobinism, distrusting not only the church, but also business, the city, and radical social ideas. The votes of these latter peasants went to the Radical Socialist Party which, during most of the Third Republic, was divided through an attempt to reconcile its peasant base with the revolutionary catchwords that gained the vote of the urban working class, when these two groups had in common only Jacobin slogans and hostility to the church. In fact, it is not surprising that, as in Germany, the same peasants who usually voted for Radical Socialist deputies sometimes supported Fascist or quasi-Fascist movements, including that of Pierre Poujade, during the last years of the Fourth Republic.

In line with its corporatist, traditionalist ideology, the Vichy regime of World War II sponsored moves back to the land and tried to strengthen individual peasant holdings. Although it initiated some significant programs, it did not and could not deal with the basic problems, and agricultural production dropped markedly during the period of the German occupation.

Both a change in peasant attitudes and a massive effort by the state were necessary if the peasants' condition was to improve. Modernization programs were initiated by the Fourth Republic and continued under the Fifth. Combined with important shifts in peasant attitudes, they are changing the contours of rural life. The state has been attempting to facilitate the consolidation of scattered

2 Lawrence Wylie, *Village in the Vaucluse* (Cambridge, Mass.: Harvard University Press, 1957), p. 194.
3 Henri Mendras, *Etudes de Sociologie Rurale* (Paris: Armand Colin, 1953), p. 75.

holdings and to remove marginal farms from production; consequently the number of small holdings has declined and the size of the average holding has increased. An intensive effort has also been made to provide peasants with modern agricultural tools—the number of farm tractors in France tripled between 1955 and 1964—and to break traditional peasant attitudes toward the use of machinery. The younger generation is increasingly enthusiastic about technical training, once universally regarded as useless. In Catholic areas, a Catholic Agricultural Youth movement (*Jeunesse agricole chrétienne*—J.A.C.) sprang up and is working actively and effectively to encourage consolidation and modernization. And, in every part of France, peasants have begun to join cooperatives of various kinds.

Yet problems persist. The older generation continues to resist change; given the problems of overproduction, increased efficiency has been a mixed blessing. Modernization has generally tended to benefit the larger commercial farms in the northwest and around Paris, whereas tradition, distance from commercial centers, and the quality of the soil have held back many of the smaller farmers of the south and in Brittany. Often the policies of the de Gaulle regime seemed oriented toward preserving the more efficient agricultural enterprises and driving the marginal farmers from the land. Certainly, the gap between the income of the latter group and that of the rest of the country has widened, with the consequence that the government has been plagued by farm strikes and outbreaks of violence.

Hampered by the French peasant's traditionalism, suspiciousness, and ideological conflict, then, groups to articulate the interests of agriculture developed slowly. The first to achieve any real success in terms of staying power were those representing specialized commercial farmers such as the winegrowers, who came together to form the *Fédération des associations viticoles*. Since

its formation in 1913, the "alcohol" lobby has been quite effective as an organized interest group.

In the period between the wars, the government was responsible for organizing semiofficial chambers of agriculture elected by the peasants of each department. At the same time, unsuccessful efforts were made by various groups to establish all-inclusive agricultural associations. The peasants' traditional unwillingness to organize was compounded by an ideological fragmentation which effectively blocked common action. Fascists, Communists, Socialists, and Catholics all developed their own organizations, each of which regarded the others with undisguised hostility. The only groups that lasted were those that catered to specialized interests such as beet farmers or wheat growers.

Immediately after the liberation of France, new attempts were made to develop broadly based peasant organizations. The first effort was a Socialist-sponsored General Confederation of Agriculture (*Confédération générale de l'agriculture*—C.G.A.), originally organized in 1943 as a clandestine group. The Communists had begun by forming their own group, but then decided to work within (and, if possible, take over) the C.G.A. Thus in 1945 the size and strength of the C.G.A. made it seem ready to emerge as the preeminent national agricultural organization. At its first postwar organizational meeting, it was reorganized into a holding company including a number of semiautonomous specialized organizations, the most important of which—the National Federation of Farmers' Unions (*Fédération nationale des syndicats d'exploitants agricoles*—F.N.S.E.A.)—was to concentrate on trade union and political activities.

However, in a short time traditional antagonisms emerged once again. The organizations were rent by ideological and local conflicts. The F.N.S.E.A. gradually came under the control of the larger, and somewhat more conservative, commercial farmers, and increasingly asserted its independence of the

C.G.A., which was still dominated by left-wing groups. The latter dwindled rapidly in size, at least in part because of its own internal conflicts, and was eventually reduced to relative insignificance. The independent efforts on the part of the Communists to organize farm workers were at first successful, but, in the end, met with the same failure.

The most broadly based agricultural organization today is still the F.N.S.E.A., although its membership includes only a small percentage of farmers, and it continues to be dominated by moderately conservative groups. In recent years it has been challenged organizationally by the departmental chambers of agriculture, which were revived in 1949 after their suppression by the Vichy government. The two organizations, however, more or less share the same point of view and often the same personnel.

Another, and perhaps more important, challenge has come from the J.A.C., which has dropped its specifically Catholic outlook to concentrate on appealing to a wider segment of the population. Spurred primarily by younger farmers with an increasingly technical and modern outlook, the J.A.C.'s influence has broadened. In 1956 it gained control of the practically moribund youth section of the F.N.S.E.A., the National Society of Young Farmers (*Cercle national des jeunes agriculteurs*—C.N.J.A.), and has obtained more and more power within the parent organization. In fact, it seems only a matter of time before those who lead the group come to dominate the larger organization. The program of the C.N.J.A. group involves not only modernization but an emphasis on "group agriculture," including cooperative cultivation and cooperative ownership of machinery. Both of these derive to a considerable extent from a reworking of traditional Catholic corporatist ideas, within the framework of a modern democratic society.

Finally, beginning in 1964, a new radical farm group, organized by the Communist Party and appealing specifically to small mar-ginal farmers, came into existence. The Movement for the Defense of Family Farms (*Mouvement de défense de l'exploitation familiale*—M.O.D.E.F.) is dedicated to preserving the family farm through government subsidies and other measures, and has obtained considerable support in the south and in Brittany. However, as the 1967 and 1968 elections indicated, the overall political views of even the marginal farmers remain quite conservative.

THE GERMAN PATTERN: Regional variations in German agriculture were at least as great as those in France. In the west and south, feudal patterns gradually gave way to individual peasant holdings, and although some reasonably large-scale commercial farming developed, the standard was the independent peasant proprietor who worked his farm with the aid of his family and a few farm workers. On the whole, status differences between owner and worker were not important; the farm worker was looked upon as a potential owner himself.

The size of even smaller holdings varied considerably depending upon the nature of the terrain and the local inheritance laws. In some areas, property descended to the oldest son, while in other areas, an open inheritance system was the rule, especially in those areas which had once been part of the Napoleonic system.

The efficiency with which agricultural holdings were worked also varied. In general, the Protestant farmers of the north were likely to be somewhat more attuned to both cooperation and technical innovation, while the south was more traditionally oriented. For all, however, the soil was primarily a way of life rather than merely a vocation.

In the east, the pattern differed considerably. Here the Prussian aristocracy had acquired its estates by the conquest of Slavic peoples, and aristocratic domination continued long after feudal patterns had broken down in the west. In fact, the end of feudalism was associated with large-scale enclosures which produced a sharp two-class division between aristocrat and landless agricultural workers; a handful of Junkers owned more than forty per cent of the available agricultural land. (See Table 5.3.) Until after World War II, agricultural workers remained highly dependent upon their employers, who often combined a benevolent paternalism with authoritarian control of their workers' activities.

The agricultural policies of the Second Empire reflected for the most part the interests of the aristocracy, whose demands for tariffs and subsidies were almost always met. During the years of the Weimar Republic, some effort was made to improve the status of the farm worker as well as of the peasant, both of whom suffered heavily from the inflation and Depression of the 1920's. But the development of an effective agricultural program was inhibited by the regime's inability to act effectively and by the relative lack of understanding of peasant problems by liberal and Socialist politicians.

In the meantime, the peasants' natural hostility to a central government and social atmosphere which seemed to be destroying traditional patterns brought more and more of them into, or at least into sympathy with, the Nazi Party. With its emphasis on the glory of the soil, its assertion of the racial equality of all Germans, its half-concealed anti-Junkerism, and its anti-Semitism, the party appealed to the peasant's resentment of aristocratic

authority even as it promised concrete measures to alleviate his economic distress. In the end, many villages voted unanimously for the Nazis.

In fact, the Nazi regime's policies did represent a self-conscious effort to turn the clock back to a caricature of the past. All agricultural organizations were incorporated into the state and party structure. Farms were regarded as the property of blood-related families; the peasant, as trustee of the land, was prohibited from subdividing, permanently leasing, or selling the farm without the sanction of special courts. The owner of a hereditary farm was given the title of *Bauer* (peasant), which was superior to that of farmer; this honorific title could be conferred only upon those who could prove that there had been no Jewish or Negro blood in the family since 1800.

Inheritance was fixed by laws on the basis of blood ties, with discrimination against female heirs. The peasant was bound to the soil; his standard of "honor" was supervised by special courts, and he could be deprived of his land by the courts if convicted of excessive drunkenness, failure to pay debts, and so forth.

Attempts were also made to convert landless agricultural workers into peasants by buying up and redistributing a few large estates. There was a more radical group within the Nazi Party which fought unsuccessfully for a more aggressive policy along these lines;

TABLE 5.3. AGRICULTURAL HOLDINGS IN GERMANY, 1865

Size	Percentage of total holdings		Percentage of land area	
(in acres)	Prussia[1]	Rest of Germany	Prussia[1]	Rest of Germany
0–5	58	58	3	7
5–50	34	37	25	50
50–250	7	4.5	29	32
Over 250	1	0.5	43	11

[1]Six eastern provinces.

Adapted from Tracy, *Agriculture in Western Europe*, p. 85. Reprinted by permission of the publisher.

but on the whole, the larger estates were left intact both because of the continued power of the Junkers and because economic efficiency seemed to require large-scale farming. In fact, the efforts of the regime to increase agricultural production contributed significantly to the modernization of German rural life.

After World War II, of course, the bifurcation of Germany and the Soviet domination of most of what was formerly Prussia brought an end to the aristocracy. Since the truncated Federal Republic incorporated only areas in which smaller holdings predominated, the nature of Germany's agricultural problem changed.

To begin with, in the German Federal Republic no more than ten per cent of the total work force is employed in agriculture, and, given the relatively small size of holdings, farm workers have practically disappeared as a group. The Federal Republic is now actively encouraging the consolidation of holdings and the development of cooperatives, so as to make the most effective use of modern technology.

Further, the peasant is no longer isolated from urban life. What evidence we have indicates that the peasant is still more authoritarian than the urban dweller, but the cultural differences between city and country are rapidly disappearing.

Young people who remain in agriculture are farmers rather than peasants. Primarily because it offers independence, agriculture is regarded as a rewarding life and young farmers are increasingly interested in vocational training and easy access to the city. The fact that many German villages today contain a substantial number of persons of urban background who commute to work in the city has greatly contributed to the erosion of traditional values.

The first national agricultural interest group in Germany was the Junker-dominated Farmers' League, which was founded in 1897 to press for higher tariffs; except in southern Germany, it had no rivals. After World War I the organization reformed as the *Landbund* and took an extremely conservative line, associating itself closely with the Nationalist Party.

Among the other groups formed during the 1920's, each claimed to speak directly for the independent peasant, but their religious, ideological, and local differences kept them from achieving any national significance until the few years immediately preceding the rise of Hitler. At that time peasant unrest increased, and regional peasant organizations, most of which took a strongly anti-urban line, expanded quickly. But ultimately the peasant expressed his discontent by voting for the Nazi Party.

In 1949, various farm organizations joined on the national level, this time to form the German Farmers' League (*Deutscher Bauernverband*) which now comprises more than 75 per cent of all independent farmers. The relative homogeneity of the farm population has enabled farmers to speak with a common voice, and the changing nature of peasant attitudes has led the organization to take a moderate line. In some cases, it has worked with the trade unions to achieve common ends, and it has been extremely effective in securing subsidies and other forms of state assistance. Landless farm workers, on the other hand, are still usually apathetic and, as yet, have been unable to organize effectively.

Germany, unlike most other Western countries, still has a sizable group of independent artisans who retain pre-industrial attitudes toward their craft. Although there are fewer and fewer of them, they remain a highly self-conscious and conservative group. Almost all of them belong to the League of German Artisans, but the influence of this organization is quite limited.

THE RUSSIAN AND SOVIET PATTERN: The Bolshevik solution to Russia's agricultural problem called for the development of large-scale mechanized farming, and the fusion of city and country; thus, it was believed, the peasant would be transformed into a worker. But knowing that such a program would have little or no appeal, the party was content, in the initial stages of the Revolution, merely to nationalize the land the peasants had seized, leaving them in control of it, and establishing only a few rural communes. During the period of the civil war, the party went somewhat further, prompted by millennial expectations as well as immediate needs; a policy of forced grain and livestock requisition was initiated.

The peasantry resisted by burning crops and cutting back production; as the civil war drew to a close the regime retreated. The New Economic Policy established a free market in agriculture, and, while ownership of land theoretically remained in the hands of the state, peasants were permitted to lease new land and employ hired labor. The result was the emergence of a new class of rather well-to-do peasants (*kulaks*)—a class which was liquidated during the period of collectivization.

During the 1930's, most of the agricultural working force was grouped into collective farms (*kolkhozes*), cooperatives of peasants working public land but collectively owning farm machinery and houses. At the same time the government began to expand its system of state farms (*sovkhozes*), organizing them like any state enterprise, providing their investment capital and underwriting subsidies from tax-based sources.

Until the early 1950's, the kolkhozes completely dominated Soviet agriculture, despite Stalin's assertion that the sovkhoz was a superior—that is, more Socialist—form of organization. As late as 1952, sovkhoz land sown to grain represented no more than 10.5 per cent of the total. However, during the period of Khrushchev's dominance, the number of sovkhozes increased rapidly, notably in the virgin-lands experiment. In other areas, moreover, many kolkhozes were combined into large state farms, and the party urged the amalgamation of the remainder. Between 1950 and 1964 the number of collective farms declined from 250,000 to a little more

than 38,000, while the number of state farms increased from about five thousand to 9,176. In 1950 the average collective farm had a sown area of a little less than 2,400 acres; by 1963 the average had jumped to 7,156 acres. The increase in the size of state farms was even greater.[4] With Khrushchev's fall, however, the policy was changed, and the new leadership argued that, for the time at least, efforts would be directed to improving the output of all farms rather than to changing their structure. Indeed, the proposed new kolkhoz charter published by the government in 1969 strongly implied that kolkhozes would continue as part of the Soviet agricultural picture for a long time to come.

Today, the kolkhoz is still run as a cooperative, thus, in theory, setting its own rules and electing its own officers. Collectives are ineligible for subsidies and must finance their development out of funds obtained through the sale of goods to state organizations in semi-free kolkhoz markets.

Kolkhoz policy is supposedly set by all working members over sixteen years of age, who meet to elect a chairman, a board of managers, and an auditing committee. In actuality, however, the chairman is usually an outsider designated by the party. The members of the management committee, too, are generally recruited from outside the kolkhoz; more and more, both chairman and managers are professionally trained.

The role of the general meeting in determining overall policy is minimal. However, the chairman is supervised by local and district party organizations, as well as by various state officials, and complaints by members of the collective reach their ears one way or another. Note the following incident, which took place in the 1930's, as reported by a Soviet emigré:

The peasants' chance came up at the general meetings when deliveries and the division of the crop were discussed. A kolkhoznik in

[4] Jerzy F. Karcz, ed., *Soviet and East European Agriculture* (Berkeley: University of California Press, 1967), p. 16.

a corner might say something to someone sitting next to him, which was hostile to the chairman. They would never address the chair. Then this man would say something to the person next to him and very soon there would be a good deal of noise in the room, and what they were saying would be heard on the speaker's platform, although it would not be quite certain who was saying it. Then the man conducting the meeting, usually a political leader from outside the kolkhoz, would say: "Well, I hear the kolkhozniks are complaining. . . . Will the comrade chairman kindly explain?" Then, while he is explaining, there is even more noise. Then, finally, someone stands up and makes a non-anonymous complaint. Such a person is almost always an older woman who is not afraid.[5]

In fact, the lot of the chairman during the 1930's was not an easy one; he was caught between the unrealistic demands of the party and the general hostility and backwardness of the peasants he supervised. Many chairmen were sentenced during the great purges, accused of sabotage for failures which were not their fault.

The situation is somewhat improved today; but agriculture is still an area of considerable tension, and Soviet press reports indicate the job of chairman still lacks security. It is for this reason, probably, as well as the relative primitiveness, discomfort, and isolation of kolkhoz life, that the regime finds it difficult to secure adequate managerial personnel.

In general, the average kolkhoznik is still rather unreliable, often working as little as possible for the collective and spending the rest of the time on the small private plots—in 1967 estimated at almost one-third of total agricultural production[6]—which are still per-

mitted on both kolkhoz and sovkhoz as a concession to the remnants of "petty-bourgeois" mentality. While urban Russia is rapidly modernizing, the peasants themselves, especially the older generation, are still traditional in outlook. They are careless with machinery and refuse to adjust to the tempo demanded by the party. Holidays are likely to lead to long bouts of drunkenness and subsequent absenteeism, and attempts at modernization tend to be resisted.

Among the various methods of payment for peasants on the kolkhoz, the most usual has been the *trudoden*, or workday unit. The different jobs on the collective were classified in terms of this standard, with additional rewards provided for individuals who exceeded standard norms. Thus, certain unskilled jobs may be graded as worth only one workday unit per day, while others may be evaluated at two units for every day worked.

In the 1930's, the party tried to group workers into small teams, each of which would concentrate on one small plot from sowing through harvesting. It was believed that this method would make it easier to evaluate the work of individuals, and would maximize personal incentive. After the war, the general trend shifted to larger groups, as a more effective way to make better use of tractors and other mechanical devices. But just before Khrushchev's downfall, there were signs of another reversal. Attempting to reduce the necessity for bureaucratic control, Khrushchev suggested a return to small brigades, each responsible for a given piece of land. He also urged that the system be extended to the state farms, and that each brigade's payment should, in some way, be proportional to the productivity of its own particular plot.[7]

This suggestion has not been followed by Khrushchev's successors, but they have implemented a number of other reforms. Price and procurement policies have been altered

[5] Quoted in Herbert S. Dinerstein and Leon Goure, *Two Studies in Soviet Controls, Communism and the Russian Peasant and Moscow in Crisis* (Glencoe: The Free Press, 1955), pp. 67–68.

[6] Karl-Eugen Wadekin, "Private Production in Soviet Agriculture," *Problems of Communism*, XVII (January–February 1968), p. 23.

[7] *Pravda*, August 5, 1964. Condensed and translated in *Current Digest of the Soviet Press*, XVI, 32 (September 2, 1964), p. 5.

to allow for increased returns to collective farmers, who have now been guaranteed a minimum wage. Further, instead of the previous requirement that pension funds for members of the collective be derived from their own earnings, kolkhozniks have now been brought into the state pension scheme. Changes have been made in methods of payment for state farms, too: the managers of sovkhozes have been given rather more authority over the use of their funds, with the option of granting bonuses to exceptional workers.

Beyond all this, the regime is expanding educational facilities and extending communications and transport networks in an effort to bring even distant kolkhozes into contact with modern society. Yet despite the regime's efforts to improve conditions on the kolkhozes, and despite its control over the movement of its population, young people are leaving the land as fast as they can. This exodus is creating a serious problem, for agriculture is still the weakest link in the Soviet economy, and the government has hopes that young people of a more "modern" outlook will increase the efficiency of the agricultural sector. It will, even so, be at least another generation before the Russian peasant begins to take on the modern life-style of his Western European counterparts.[8]

2. ENTREPRENEURS AND MANAGERS

The Industrial Revolution in England was instigated by an entrepreneurial elite drawn from very diverse backgrounds. Some were gentry who had either invested in industry capital derived from their land or else had used their political position to take advantage of economic opportunities; but most of the innovators came from varying segments of a constantly expanding urban middle class. In France, although the pattern was less

marked, it resembled that of England; so, too, in Germany, except that an extremely important role in industrialization was played by the state, which remained under the control of the Prussian aristocracy. This was not the case in the Soviet Union; an entrepreneurial elite did begin to emerge in the last years of the empire, but the major breakthrough was accomplished by the revolutionary intellectuals.

In all Western European countries, the recent evolution of the entrepreneurial role reveals certain common trends: the increasing separation of ownership and management; the development of a new managerial class, recruited more and more from the universities; and the decline of the economic power of the business community in general because of the state's greater participation in economic activity and the emergence of other powerful interests within the community. In the Soviet Union, on the other hand, as management has become professionalized, it seems to have become more powerful. In both Western Europe and the Soviet Union, the firm has become increasingly bureaucratized, and the ratio of administrative to production personnel has grown. One of the major influences on the changing pattern of European business has been the example set by America. Since the mid-fifties, Europeans have come to realize more frequently that American research techniques and innovations have far outpaced their own; consequently, certain segments of the European market have been dominated by American products, and American subsidiaries have played a larger and larger role in Europe. Some Europeans, especially in France, fear that what has come to be called the "technology gap" will continue to widen in the future, unless fairly drastic steps are taken.[9]

THE BRITISH PATTERN: The influence of the commercial and industrial strata of En-

8 For an excellent analysis of the life of Soviet peasants, based largely on newer Soviet anthropological studies, see Stephen P. Dunn and Ethel Dunn, *The Peasants of Central Russia* (New York: Holt, Rinehart and Winston, 1967).

9 See J. J. Servan-Schreiber, *The American Challenge*, Ronald Steel, trans. (New York: Atheneum, 1968).

glish society had made itself felt, in London and elsewhere, since the sixteenth century; by the middle of the eighteenth, that group could exercise substantial power.

An unusually large portion of those responsible for industrial growth were from Calvinist lower-middle-class or artisan backgrounds, men who managed to amass fortunes through a combination of luck, shrewdness, and hard work. The newly prosperous tended to be less concerned than were entrepreneurs from the gentry about the welfare of those they employed, believing that the nation's prosperity depended upon a policy of laissez faire and that worldly success should be the result of rational self-help.

Nonetheless, their Protestant and utilitarian values, so beautifully caricatured by Dickens, never dominated English society as they did American; in fact, they were quickly fused with an older tradition which maintained that social success, that is, acceptance as a gentleman, depended on certain behavior patterns. Even if the newly rich businessman did not harbor these ambitions, certainly his sons did, especially after having attended the "right" schools.

The resultant pattern of business behavior emphasized a sense of civic responsibility, a reasonably high code of business ethics, and, as with other elite groups, the notion that the ideal man of business was a gentleman of broad humanist background, not a trained technician. In fact, by the end of the nineteenth century observers were already remarking that English business, whether the new impersonal corporation or the older family firm, had already lost much of its early aggressiveness.

This was not very detrimental while British industry and the British Empire were still major world forces, but since World War II there has been a greater awareness of the shortcomings in British entrepreneurship. More and more managers are being recruited from the universities, but, until very recently, the emphasis has still been upon a broad background of culture rather than upon tech-

nical competence, and on the whole the British have not made as imaginative use of newer techniques as the Germans or even those Frenchmen who have had technical training.

Yet today, an education in engineering and economics is more readily accepted as useful background for business activity, and British computer technology has advanced further than that of any country in Western Europe. The tradition of the amateur and the gentleman, nonetheless, continues to bear some responsibility for the relative stagnation of the British economy in recent years.

Compared with their French and German counterparts, British businessmen as a political group accepted democratic institutions, the organizaton of trade unions by workers, and the social-service state with very good grace. They also developed some fairly cohesive organizations for dealing with economic and political problems. The most important of these was the Federation of British Industries (F.B.I.), which, in 1964, had a membership of some eight thousand firms and three hundred trade associations.

The larger industries generally determined the political line of the F.B.I., and small businessmen invariably followed their lead. However, as a whole, business leadership moved very cautiously in the political arena, preferring to avoid taking a stand when it could not achieve something like a consensus among its members. In the period between the two world wars, the F.B.I. was closely, if informally, associated with the Conservative Party, although there is little evidence that it systematically attempted to exert pressure on the government; indeed, its leadership seems always to have deferred to government officials.

Its caution increased, if anything, after World War II. The leadership preferred to heighten the image of business by presenting "reasonable" arguments, rather than by using pressure, and concentrated on demonstrating how cooperative it would be if the programs of either party were "reasonable." In recent years British business has made one sharp break with traditional attitudes, relying increasingly upon public relations firms to create a favorable image. On the whole, however, its approach remains conservative, despite the occasional use of more flamboyant techniques on the issue of nationalization.

As successive British governments moved in the direction of national planning in the 1960's, the relations of industry to government grew closer, under both the Conservatives and Labor. In 1965, the F.B.I. combined with two other major business associations to form the Confederation of British Industries. Over the opposition of some members, the nationalized industries were given representation.

THE FRENCH PATTERN: It is far more difficult to generalize about the French business community than those of Britain or America, where the attitudes of entrepreneurs and managers toward business and politics are related to the size and nature of the business enterprise, the section of the country, and so forth. In France, the diversity of types of enterprise is much greater, ranging from the large, highly rationalized firm which makes effective use of technological innovation (such as the gas industry, oil, electricity, and some automobile firms) to thousands of traditional family firms which refuse even to use decent methods of accounting, the better to evade the tax collector. Similarly, the French business community contains some who have welcomed unions and collective bargaining and who have developed progressive systems of labor-management relations while at the same time others in the business community still feel that any trade-union activity is an attack upon their sacred prerogatives and who, in the 1930's, preferred a Fascist regime to the mildly Socialist government of Léon Blum.

Still, it can be said that until recently the French businessman lacked both the dynamism of the American and the civic sense of the Englishman. He usually preferred security and small profits to risk. His aim was simply

to make enough to enjoy a life of culture and to pass the family firm, his patrimony, on to his heirs. He was wary of the corporate form, uninterested in expanding markets, and dubious of his more aggressive competitors. His distrust of his fellow businessmen went so far that even efforts to develop trade associations limited to matters of technical cooperation invariably failed. He also distrusted the state; while it was of use in obtaining subsidies, it was also to be held at arm's length and fooled whenever possible. He even distrusted his sons, permitting them to learn little or nothing about the business until it was time for them to replace him.

During part of the nineteenth century, there were liberal and anticlerical elements within the French bourgeoisie, but by the 1870's they had become conservative and had returned to the fold of the church, at least in part because they associated religious skepticism with radical democracy, mob rule, and socialism. Under the Third and Fourth Republics, businessmen protected themselves from the controls which might be exercised through Parliament by using contacts with the upper echelons of the bureaucracy—men of a similar class background, often hoping to move to the business community at some time in their lives.

Finally, French entrepreneurs in the past have been violently opposed to workers' efforts to organize for the purpose of winning economic concessions; throughout the nineteenth century, the forceful intervention of the state was used to repress attempts at such organization. The businessman considered his relationship to the worker to be that of father to child. Workers were thought to be stupid and rather primitive, easily stirred to violence by agitators but just as easily controlled if one stood firm. Any concessions would only spoil them and lead to even greater demands. Unfortunately, these attitudes were only rarely associated with the sense of noblesse oblige that characterized businessmen in England and Germany.

The beliefs and values of the French bourgeoisie reflected the society of which it was a part. The highly traditional business attitude —more mercantilist than feudal—became frozen in France, partly because liberalism *did* seem to have radical consequences there, and the French working class *was* hostile and given to violence. The slow rate of population growth and the lack of an expanding market made the Malthusian outlook of the French businessman even more understandable. The criticisms of the French bourgeoisie voiced by generations of French intellectuals are in large measure true, but they usually fail to go to the root of the problem: the bourgeoisie has always been as much victim as victimizer.

The result, of course, was a slackness in economic development and a plethora of small, marginal, family-owned firms, employing only thirty to forty workers, catering to specialized demands, and resisting expansion. It is significant that the small segment of the Protestant and Jewish population furnished an extraordinarily substantial portion of the more progressive elements in the business and financial community.

This was the case as late as the 1930's, but things began to change after the war. Now,

although much of French business remains highly traditional, the more dynamic elements have taken the lead and are increasingly setting the tone for French industry. Many of these industries are staffed at the higher levels by graduates of one of the several engineering *Grandes Écoles* (such as Polytechnique, École Nationale Supérieure des Mines, or Centrale); these men are still humanists, but they are also technocrats of considerable competence. (See Table 5.4.) Many came to business after a career in the state service. These facts, plus the population boom, reasonably effective planning, and the opening, finally, of a mass market, are altering the whole structure of French enterprise.

Despite the myths created by leftist critics, French business was poorly organized before World War II. A national business organization, the *Confédération générale de la production française* (C.G.P.F.), was formed in 1920, but, like an earlier attempt, the association spoke for only a small segment of French industry. Certain groups speaking for a particular region or industry exhibited slightly more cohesion, but the total picture stands in clear contrast to that of England or Germany.

TABLE 5.4. EDUCATIONAL BACKGROUND OF FRENCH BUSINESSMEN

Representative sample of 2,500 chairmen and chief executives of large companies who received university degrees

Type of institution	Percentage of sample attending
École Polytechnique	21.4
Other engineering schools	34.5
Science faculties	3.8
Arts faculties	3.8
Law faculties	8.8
Political science	9.6
Commercial schools	1.7
Military schools	2.6
Other schools	10.1
No answer	3.7

Source: F. F. Ridley, "French Technocracy and Comparative Government," *Political Studies*, XIV (February 1966), p. 49. Reprinted by permission of the publisher.

In part, these differences stem from the reluctance of a business community with aristocratic tastes to sully its hands with interest-group activity; in part, from the general French hostility to large business; and also, in large measure, from the refusal to subordinate the interest of a particular firm to a larger group, even a group which represented that very interest. One other factor is relevant: given the inability of the left to organize for effective action during the Third Republic, it was always possible for a businessman to achieve his objective through personal contact with individual members of the bureaucracy or strategically placed political figures, thus making concerted political action unnecessary.

The growth of the Communist Party and labor militancy during the 1930's precipitated an effort to develop a more cohesive organization; at the same time it convinced large numbers of businessmen that the Vichy regime was a good thing. It also served, in the immediate postwar years, to place business, especially large business, very much on the defensive.

With the liberation, the C.G.P.F. was reorganized as the National Council of French Employers (*Conseil national du patronat français*—C.N.P.F.). Again its structure was federal, with membership open to regional and industrial federations. As it had during the Third Republic, it relied on informal contacts rather than formal pressures. Its influence increased during the last years of the Fourth Republic, as the prestige of large business began to grow; in the Fifth Republic it has increased still further. Both the relatively pro-business attitude of de Gaulle and his associates and the parliament's limited power as compared with that of the bureaucracy were important factors here.

In recent years, the C.N.P.F. has taken a more progressive stand, at least on issues relating to the French economy. It has certainly been far more forward-looking than Léon Gingembre's General Confederation of Small and Medium Enterprises (*Confédéra-*tion générale des petites et moyennes entreprises*—C.G.P.M.E.), which is affiliated with the C.N.P.F. but has followed an independent line, emphasizing the cult of the little man and simultaneously opposing modernization, labor unions, taxes, trusts, European cooperation, and the "malefactors" of wealth. For a short time, the C.G.P.M.E. was almost outflanked on the Jacobin right by Pierre Poujade's *Union de commerçants et artisans,* later the Union and French Fraternity (*Union et fraternité française*—U.F.F.), which started among small shopkeepers and peasants who opposed the government's attempts to develop more effective tax-collecting methods. Its program, which combined hostility to large business with anti-Semitism and strong-arm tactics, again revealed the latent authoritarianism that was part of the Jacobin tradition. But the group represented the last gasp of a dying subculture; it died quickly, and its efforts were more pathetic than significant.

THE GERMAN PATTERN. Although a large commercial bourgeoisie developed in some of Germany's free cities in the late middle ages, the society remained a primarily agricultural one; only in the late nineteenth century, under the encouragement of a state bureaucracy, did the nation enter upon a period of industrialization. The state subsidized and protected industry; it also initiated programs in transportation and other fields which facilitated economic development, and encouraged rational reorganization and combination (cartels) as a means for ordering the market. From the very beginning, then, German industry was highly concentrated.

German businessmen tended to be orderly, disciplined, and technologically efficient. More than other European countries, the managerial elite had received the equivalent of a college education. Degrees in engineering were almost always considered a good training for a business profession, with legal training a close second, and more recently, business administration and economics. A comprehensive study estimates that some 31 per cent of the top level of German management, as opposed to 19 per cent in America, has received advanced degrees.[10] The figures are somewhat misleading because German graduate work begins at an earlier age; on the other hand, a much larger portion of the American population has graduated from college.

In their employee relations, German businessmen emulated the aristocracy whose values they had made their own; their authoritarian paternalism outdid even that of the British. Individual plants established insurance programs before the state did, and, in contrast with France, every effort was made to provide satisfactory working conditions. Partly as a consequence of this paternalism, the German businessman believed that the trade unions' attempts to assert independent bargaining power were an unwarranted challenge to his authority, and he vigorously resisted them.

During the 1920's, most of the important industrial leaders were hostile to the Weimar Republic, although few supported the Nazi Party until 1932 when, seeing support slip from the nationalist parties and fearing a Communist revolution, some of them turned to Hitler. Even then they expected to be able to control him by surrounding him with more "responsible" figures; but in the end, of course, Hitler completely dominated them. Although, in general, profits were untouched by the regime, German business found itself forced to organize its economic activities within the framework set by the political leadership. Like most other groups within German society, businessmen may have felt general distaste for some of the more extremist policies of the regime, but only a few opposed it actively.

At the end of World War II, the condition of German business was, of course, chaotic. The Allies held many business leaders responsible for the Nazi regime, and believed that the high degree of cartelization had contributed to the rise of National Socialism. Some German businessmen were tried for complicity in Nazi war crimes, and a good many industrial empires were required to relinquish some of their holdings. This took place largely under the impetus of the Americans; the British, like the Continentals, have never looked with such dread upon business combination, and even European Socialists have thought that industrial concentration was a natural step along the road to future nationalization.

The industrial leaders released from prison a few years after the war lost no time in regaining and integrating their holdings. The tendency toward greater concentration—a tendency shared by the United States despite continuing lip service to competition—had returned, but other German attitudes were new. In reaction to the tight controls of the Nazi period, businessmen turned with alacrity to the "free market" policies of the Christian Democratic Union (C.D.U.), even cautiously accepting Germany's first antitrust law, which placed rather mild limits upon price-fixing agreements. German business has also demonstrated more willingness to share its power with trade unions; copying American models, it has increasingly emphasized the need for more "democratic" employer-employee relations. The traditional authoritarian attitudes are still in evidence, but such changes indubitably reflect a decrease in the importance of status in German life.

Even so, other traditional patterns are still significant: more than in almost any other Western country, for example, the family firm remains important in Germany, and the German businessman still feels that his position is a "calling" and that he is part of a talented elite which should exercise more authority than the masses.

The first German business association, the Central Association of German Industrialists, founded in 1876, was concerned pri-

---

10 From Heinz Hartmann, *Authority and Organization in German Industry* (Princeton: Princeton University Press, 1959), p. 165.

marily with political influence. It represented largely textile and steel interests; in 1895 it was joined by the League of Industrialists, representing the chemical and processing industries. The two organizations were rivals until World War I; after the war, they were merged in the National Association of German Industry (*Reichsverband der Deutschen Industrie*—R.D.I.). Unlike comparable French efforts, but even more than the British, the organization became highly centralized and was dominated by large businesses. It offered various conservative political parties financial aid in return for the promise of favorable policies and achieved considerable influence within the upper levels of the bureaucracy. Association officials, and businessmen in general (although very few among the top leadership), also ran for political office, where they spoke directly for business interests. In the 1928 Reichstag, for example, 76 of the 490 deputies were businessmen.[11]

With the coming of the Nazi regime, business and trade associations were incorporated into the state structure and brought under the control of both the state and the Nazi Party; they were not recreated until some years after the war. The successor to the R.D.I. is the Federation of German Industry (*Bundesverband der Deutschen Industrie*—B.D.I.), an organization whose membership is limited to federally structured associations representing various branches of industry. Approximately 94,000 employers—about 98 per cent of those eligible—are members of the organization through their associations; this figure can be compared with six per cent for the American equivalent, the National Association of Manufacturers, although that six per cent is responsible for 75 per cent of total U.S. manufacturing output.

The B.D.I. has twelve regional offices which coordinate association work at the state (*Land*) level. Policies are theoretically set by an assembly, at which the voting

strength of the member associations is roughly proportional to the number of employees of each firm. In actuality, power is heavily, although not completely, centralized in the executive committees and a very large professional staff. Large business invariably takes the lead in determining policy; smaller enterprises may lodge occasional complaints but, as in England, they are usually willing to accept this arrangement.

The B.D.I. and other business groups continue to maintain direct contacts with deputies and the government. They contribute to all non-Socialist parties, especially the Christian Democratic Union; these contributions, usually made through "civic associations," are largely tax-deductible, although portions of a 1954 law making all such contributions tax-deductible were declared unconstitutional in 1958. The industrial federation has been dominated by a pro-C.D.U. faction and has generally supported European economic integration. However, a small vociferous group has continually called for a more "nationalistic" economic policy.

Two other national business associations are of some importance on the German political scene. The first, the German Chamber of Commerce and Industry (*Deutscher Industrie und Handelstag*—D.I.H.T.), closely resembles the United States Chamber of Commerce. Membership in the D.I.H.T. is now compulsory for all enterprises, thus giving it a quasi-official status. It is primarily concerned with analyzing economic developments and serving as a liaison between the government and the business community; but it also engages in lobbying activities and is considered to be somewhat more liberal than the B.D.I.

The second group, the Federation of German Employers Associations (*Bundesvereinigung der Deutschen Arbeitgeberverbände*—B.D.A.), serves primarily as a coordinating and advisory center to employers in matters relating to labor and social policies. It recommends basic wage policies to its members and participates with the

[11] Gerard Braunthal, *The Federation of German Industry in Politics* (Ithaca: Cornell University Press, 1965), p. 11.

government in certain aspects of social security and the labor market. The attitude of its leadership resembles that of the B.D.I.

German industrialists have adopted the public-relations techniques of American business with a vengeance. The Institute of German Industry sponsors a wide variety of publications that represent the viewpoint of the business community, and the League for the Promotion of the Social Market Economy specializes in paid newspaper advertisements that often indirectly support the Christian Democrats.

THE RUSSIAN AND SOVIET PATTERN:[12] By the time of the Russian Revolution, a small entrepreneurial class had developed in Russia; but the cultural patterns of Russian society, the lack of an artisan class, the inheritance of serfdom, and the policies of the government all kept entrepreneurial influence to a minimum. As the Revolution approached, a good deal of Soviet industrial activity was financed and controlled by foreign investors; a substantial portion of the rest was heavily dependent upon the state.

In the early days of the Revolution, Lenin tried to encourage at least a few bourgeois entrepreneurs to remain at their posts. But many fled the country, forcing the new regime to nationalize some enterprises more quickly than it had intended. During the period of the New Economic Policy, a certain amount of small-scale industry remained in private hands, although there was less and less private ownership as the decade wore on. In 1925 and 1926, private industry accounted for some 19.9 per cent of all industrial production. This had fallen to 5.6 per cent by 1930, and to 0.5 per cent in 1932.[13]

Lenin believed at first that management was a simple task which could be performed by almost any worker, but it was not very long before he learned otherwise. Through-

out the 1920's and early 1930's the government made effective use of whatever entrepreneurial talent remained within the country, although always under the close supervision of the party. At the same time, every effort was made to train new cadres. The more talented workers were taken from the bench and sent to school for training; as educational opportunities expanded, young men were recruited for managerial positions from the universities. In general, the regime felt that the combination of engineering training and practical experience was the appropriate preparation for managerial posts—an emphasis which has continued to the present. Today, in fact, it is almost impossible to obtain a managerial position without a university degree or its equivalent.

During the 1930's, especially, the career of the Soviet manager was both difficult and dangerous. The government remained highly suspicious—justly so, to some extent—of carry-overs from the old regime and children of middle-class background. It was this group which suffered most heavily in the great purges of 1936 to 1938; they were eventually replaced by younger and thoroughly Bolshevik cadres.

Even the newer managers did not have an easy time of it, especially in the late 1930's, when failure to meet the unrealistically high quotas could mean imprisonment or worse. Given the constant shortage of supplies, and the massive and inefficient bureaucratic organization, managers almost had to use procedures which violated the canons of economic rationality: they were forced into excessive stockpiling of supplies, using influence (*blat*) and influence peddlers (*tolkachi*), and violating the planned assortment of goods by producing items which were easy to manufacture in quantity. They also falsified reports and produced defective goods —when they could get away with it.

In the period since Stalin's death, especially, the regime has tried to reduce the topheaviness of the bureaucracy and to allow for more initiative on the part of plant

---

[12] Some of the points discussed only briefly in this section will be dealt with more fully in the chapters on bureaucracy and public policy.

[13] Harry Schwartz, *Russia's Soviet Economy*, 2nd ed. (New York: Prentice-Hall, 1954), p. 109.

managers. Beginning in 1962, a number of economists urged that the system be reorganized to attain these ends, and by 1969 several reforms had taken place in the structure of the Soviet economy, all of which were designed to emphasize profitability rather than plan fulfillment or overfulfillment and to provide for greater managerial autonomy. However, as we shall see in Chapter 24, the reforms have had, as yet, only a marginal effect upon the manager's position.

Furthermore, the placement of professionally trained people in government posts has meant that production quotas have been scaled down to reasonable dimensions, and failure is less likely to be equated with sabotage. As late as 1956, annual turnover rates in some sectors of the economy were as high as forty to fifty per cent. In recent years, however, a system of bureaucratic seniority has begun to be instituted, entailing a considerable degree of job security.

In addition to being under the control of the state apparatus, the plant manager has always shared his authority with trade unions and local party secretaries. Actually, trade-union power dropped during the 1930's and has only recently been on the rise again. The relationship between the manager and the party, however, has swung back and forth erratically. Local party organizations have always been supposed to cooperate with the manager to insure the most effective possible operation of the plant, but the regime has never been certain as to what the exact relationship between the two should be. In the 1930's, party supervision of managerial authority and the bureaucracy was very important, but in the late 1940's and early 1950's, the party's role seemed to have diminished. Khrushchev's industrial reorganization appears to have made it newly significant, although this is difficult to measure exactly; nonetheless, his successors have indicated that the supervisory function of the party in management will henceforth be somewhat smaller than during the last few years.

If, in the 1930's, the managers were in a risky position, they were also substantially rewarded for successful initiative within the overall framework of the plan. The gap between the salaries of managers and those of wage earners had broadened so that top executives could afford luxuries like country houses and automobiles, or at least the use of a company car.

Since the war, the gap between managerial and working-class earnings has narrowed somewhat, although it is still considerable, both in terms of salary, bonuses, and other benefits. Also, the fact that savings and personal property can now be passed on freely to one's children offers the managerial class advantages which are not enjoyed by those in other social strata. The U.S.S.R. does not have the extremes of wealth which still exist in most non-Socialist countries; these extremes stem from ownership of income-producing property, a type of income which does not exist there. However, the average salaried Russian manager's position as compared with an industrial worker is probably similar to the American counterpart, except that the Russian manager's economic power has less chance of being translated into political power.[14]

In recent years, American students of the Soviet Union have spoken of one or another political leader as representing the bureaucracy instead of the party. It may be true that managers and the upper-level state bureaucrats may share certain views somewhat different from those of the party bureaucracy, but there is little evidence to suggest that this fact has led to any organized action. It now seems likely that Khrushchev's ouster was partially the result of the hostility of the more professionally oriented cadres of both party and state bureaucracy to his free-wheel-

[14] Accurate data on income distribution in the Soviet Union is difficult to come by. For an estimate, based on fragmentary data and placed in a comparative context, see Simon Kuznetz, "Quantitative Aspects of the Economic Growth of Nations," *Economic Development and Cultural Change*, XI (January 1963), 1–79. See also Arvid Brodersen, *The Soviet Worker* (New York: Random House, 1966), pp. 171–193.

ing methods, rather than the victory of any self-consciously organized faction representing one group or the other.

3. THE INDUSTRIAL WORKER

The European Industrial Revolution of the eighteenth and nineteenth centuries transformed both peasant and artisan into an industrial working class tied to the rhythm of the machine in an urban factory system. It is undoubtedly true that much of the inspiration for early anarchist and Socialist movements came as a reaction to the change in life-style demanded by industrialization. Yet the machine promised to improve the material conditions of life and reduce the effort required for achieving a satisfactory level of existence. This promise has slowly been fulfilled. In every European country, hours of work have gradually been reduced (see Table 5.5).

At least as important, the standard of living of the average worker has risen rapidly since World War II. In some cases, his style of life is no longer qualitatively different from that of other social groups; moreover, the expansion of state and social services has more and more provided him with protection against unemployment (see Table 5.6) and illness, and with the opportunity to obtain the skills necessary for moving a step or two up in the class system.

Working conditions, too, have improved. Although the average factory worker still performs rather simple, relatively meaningless tasks, industrial plants often provide reasonably congenial surroundings; also, in recent years, more attention has been paid to creating patterns of social relations in the plant which reduce the tedium of the work situation. There is evidence, too, that opportunities for in-plant promotion have expanded.

Finally, the worker is no longer someone who is merely acted upon. Despite the books which have been written about "mass society" and "power elites," the working class, as a group, plays a much more active role in making social policy than it did one hundred or even fifty years ago. In every Western country, trade unions are now a legitimate part of the power structure, however much their strength and role may vary. In every Western country, too, the worker is fully enfranchised, and has access to information which enables him to participate to at least some extent in political life.

All these changes are the result of an increasing affluence, of the transformation of social attitudes over the past hundred years, and of workers' having developed mechanisms for protecting and advancing their own interests. Primary among these mechanisms are the trade unions, in part the direct descendants of the old artisan guilds and in part new creations.

It is little wonder, then, that the class consciousness which has traditionally characterized industrial workers' thinking has eroded,

TABLE 5.5. WEEKLY WORKING HOURS, SELECTED COUNTRIES

	1870	1913	1929	1938	1950	1960	1967
United Kingdom	63.0	53.8	46.9	46.5	45.9	46.1	43.3
France	63.0	53.8	48.0	38.7	45.0	45.9	46.1
Germany (F.R.)	63.0	53.8	46.0	48.5	48.2	45.6	42.3
United States	63.0	53.8	44.2	35.6	40.5	39.7	40.0

Adapted from Angus Maddison, *Economic Growth in the West* (New York: Twentieth Century Fund, 1964), p. 228, and International Labour Office, *Yearbook of Labour Statistics 1956–1967* (Paris, 1969), p. 163. Reprinted by permission of the publishers.

TABLE 5.6.   UNEMPLOYMENT IN WESTERN EUROPE AND
THE UNITED STATES, 1968

	Percentage of civilian labor force
United States	3.6
France[1]	3.5
West Germany[1]	0.7
Great Britain[1]	3.1

[1] Preliminary estimates.

Source: *Statistical Abstract of the United States, 1969*, p. 835.

as have some of the distinctive qualities of working-class culture. There is, for example, less tendency among the younger generation workers to think of their employers as constituting a hostile—and exploiting—"them." As early as 1956, for example, a French study indicated that some 53 per cent of the workers interviewed thought that there was "trust" in relations between employers and employees, and only 27 per cent thought that there was distrust.[15] And in all the countries under consideration, fewer workers, for the moment at least, support Socialist programs such as nationalization, even when, as in France, they continue to vote for the Communist Party.

Certain related changes have taken place in the worker's attitude. Rather than seeking male companionship in a pub or tavern, he expects to spend his evenings at home with his family watching television, or make more money by taking on an additional job. Both he and his family are beginning to join various clubs and associations (aside from trade unions) in larger numbers, and to take a more active role in them. The worker who thought primarily of rising with his "class" is being replaced to a certain extent by the worker whose major concern is to make more money as an individual. The skilled or semiskilled worker who felt both deferential and hostile vis-à-vis even the lower-middle-class

white-collar employee no longer regards the differences between them as cause for such envy or hostility; his earnings are comparable, the fringe benefits are equal, and his own wife is often supplementing family income as a white-collar worker.

Class and status differences have certainly not disappeared, nor have differences in lifestyles. Yet it is quite obvious that the outlook and orientation of the working class are closer to those of other strata today than twenty years ago, if only because almost all segments of the population have come to share elements of a common mass culture.[16] It is for these reasons that the new left in both Europe and the United States has all but despaired of developing a "revolutionary mentality" among the working class and has placed its hopes upon alienated middle-class students.

However, changes that offer both a promise and a threat are just over the horizon. The advent of universal television in Europe in the late 1960's, with its portrayal of middle-class affluence both at home and in other countries, could yield an increase in class conflict—in much the same way that

[15] *Réalités*, 65 (April 1956), 8–18.

[16] The evidence for these changes is mixed, and a good many on the left argue that the situation of the working class is not fundamentally different from that of twenty years ago. For a discussion which supports the view taken here, but summarizes the alternative views, see M. M. Postan, *An Economic History of Western Europe, 1945–1964* (London: Methuen and Co., Ltd., 1967), pp. 302–344; see also the bibliography.

television helped make American Negroes even more aware of their poverty.

Just as importantly, the rapid progress of technology and the automation of the simpler industrial operations is reducing the demand for industrial workers, even as the need for skilled technicians and white-collar workers in various service industries continues to rise. There is some question whether a market-oriented economy can handle the problems created by this situation; but if it can, such developments promise still greater leisure, and also the possibility of more imagination and thought being channeled into the work which has to be done.

On the other hand, Western countries seem finally to be approaching a time when the need to work is no longer among the most significant factors in human life. It almost seems as if certain aspects of Marx's utopia may become reality within the next fifty to one hundred years. In any case, Western Europe and the United States are unquestionably on the verge of another revolution that is likely to have profound social and political effects.

THE BRITISH PATTERN: By the first quarter of the nineteenth century, a substantial modern working class had developed in England. Although it included those in traditional crafts such as the building trades, it was increasingly augmented by unskilled ex-farmers working at jobs created by the machine—jobs which involved simple operations within the framework of a factory system.

Actually, the old artisan class, which found its status threatened by the new machines, was the first to respond with any militancy to the new patterns of industrial life. In some cases, artisans attempted to fight the machines by destroying them, but the amount of violence directed against persons was surprisingly small; in many cases, artisans simply sank into the proletariat. But in trades not eliminated by the machine, modern trade unions were created, or evolved out of the old guilds; by the middle of the nineteenth century a number of very strong craft unions had been established.

Their success reflected not only the workers' sense of class solidarity and discipline, but the relative willingness of English elite groups—as against, for example, the French middle class—to accept the legitimacy of working-class organization. The Combination Acts, which had prohibited organizations of either working men or employers, were repealed in 1825, and although unions were inhibited by various restrictions until 1867 (and to a certain extent even until the Trades Disputes Act of 1906), their legality and that of peacefully conducted strikes were acknowledged. A very large number of employers opposed trade unions until much later; but compared with other countries, the British middle class was disposed to accept the legitimacy of their existence.

These developments, of course, made little or no impression on the great mass of unskilled workers; led by middle-class intellectuals, they made some abortive attempts to

TABLE 5.7.   GROWTH RATES OF OUTPUT PER EMPLOYEE

Selected periods, 1913 to 1966

	England	*France*	*Germany (F.R.)*[1]	*United States*
1913–1929	0.4	2.0	—0.2	1.5
1929–1950	1.1	0.3	1.2	1.7
1950–1960	2.0	4.6	5.9	2.1
1960–1966	2.3	4.5	4.1	3.2

Adapted from *Statistical Abstract of the United States, 1969,* p. 841.

form one giant industrial union in the 1830's but then sank back into relative passivity. Still, there were attempts to ameliorate their condition. Beginning in the early nineteenth century, a series of laws placed limits upon exploitation, provided for benefits in case of industrial accidents, and extended the opportunities for education and for participation in politics.

By the end of the nineteenth century, the unskilled and semiskilled were moving quickly into trade-union organizations. In 1894 the total number of English workers in trade unions was about 1,530,000. By 1914 the figure had risen to more than four million, or well over one-third of the working force.[17] Except for short periods, this percentage has never been equaled in France. It was not achieved until the 1930's in the United States, where the percentage of workers in trade unions has now dropped back to about thirty. A lack of class consciousness in America and the acceptance of economic individualism by the workers themselves hampered the development of an effective trade-union organization. In France, the sharp cleavages which ran through the working class, the violent hostility of the peasantry and the business elites, and the rather slow pace of industrialization inhibited the growth of trade unions. In England, on the other hand, the National Insurance Act of 1911, which provided medical and other benefits for workers, included a provision that such funds be administered in part by the trade unions. Thus, in effect, the state was encouraging workers to join trade unions, and within two years after passage of the bill union membership rose by more than a million.

England also differed from France in that the development of working-class self-consciousness did not result in an upsurge of violence—partly because of the influence of Methodism upon the working-class elite (a

good many trade-union organizers began as Methodist lay preachers), but also partly because the British working class did not feel as alienated as the French in a society in which important elites had demonstrated a sense of social responsibility.

Violence did threaten to flare up between 1900 and 1914 as the unions of the unskilled developed, and a newly self-conscious generation of trade-union organizers found themselves attracted to Marxist and syndicalist doctrines. However, the very success of the trade-union movement served to weaken such impulses. The trade unions provided a career for the ambitious and transformed young radicals into "responsible leaders" who had large union treasuries to worry about. Moreover, trade-union leaders who negotiated as equals with businessmen found it increasingly difficult to think of the business community as an undifferentiated, totally wicked "them"; with powerful unions to protect them and advance their interests, workers felt that they now had a stake in the existing system. In the next generation, in fact, the early militants were to be replaced by men who had worked up slowly in the union hierarchy, and were emotionally more attuned to the boardroom than to the picket line. There were exceptions to this mode of accommodation on the part of union leaders in industries with a long record of bad labor-management relations, such as mining. But in general, the very success of British trade unionism encouraged moderation.

In 1868, the major British trade unions joined to form the Trades Union Congress, whose function it was not only to shape common policy but also to enable the unions to bring their total strength to bear in lobbying for desired legislation. Over the years, the authority of the T.U.C. has slowly grown. Individual unions still retain a good deal of independence, but compared with the United States, where trade unions achieved only a precarious and short-lived unity on the national level after World War II, and with

17 B. C. Roberts, *Trade Union Government and Administration in Great Britain* (Cambridge, Mass.: Harvard University Press, 1956), pp. 472, 474.

France, where such unity has never been achieved, British ability to subordinate the interests of individual unions to a larger whole is rather impressive. Here again, the class consciousness of British workers had considerable significance, but so did action by the state. It has long been considered quite proper in England for any government to discuss matters of public policy with the major interests involved, and it was thought that such discussions would be much easier to conduct if one representative group spoke for each. This whole attitude, of course, is a carry-over from a more traditional period of British history, in which the kingdom was thought to be made up of estates rather than merely of individuals.

The British trade-union movement also differed from the French and American ones in that it was instrumental in founding a Socialist party, the Labor Party, to which it is still closely tied. The ideology of British trade-union leaders has usually been far more pragmatic and conservative than that of the middle-class intellectuals who provided it with militants, and the Labor Party would be a very different kind of organization without trade-union affiliation and support.

While British trade unions may exercise slightly more influence when a Labor government is in office, no government could initiate a policy that unions considered an attack on their most basic interests. In fact, their power

is large enough to limit their flexibility, for almost any strike threatens to take on national importance and to have a serious effect upon the economy as a whole.

Membership in unions today is well over ten million, almost 43 per cent of the total labor force, but it varies widely from industry to industry. Something like ninety per cent of those who work in coal mines are union members, compared with some 15 per cent in distributive trades. The movement is dominated by a few large "general" and industrial unions, such as the Transport and General Workers Union (T.& G.W.U.); the eight largest unions contain almost fifty per cent of the total membership. The T.& G.W.U. alone has a membership of almost one and one-half million. (See Table 5.8.)

Originally, British unions were organized on the basis of individual crafts; as with so many other aspects of British life, the traditional pattern has continued to exert a good deal of influence. Thus, even the so-called general or industrial unions like the T. & G.-W.U. are basically amalgamations of various craft groups (truckers, dock workers, quarrymen, bus drivers) organized on a national level. This pattern of organization has led to any number of difficulties. For one thing, despite a trend toward consolidation, many craft unions remain in existence even though their numbers have dropped to practically zero: the Wool Shear Workers Union, for

TABLE 5.8. THE SIZE OF BRITISH TRADE UNIONS, 1966

Number of members in unions	Percentage of total number of unions	Percentage of total union membership
Under 1,000	53.0	0.8
1,000–5,000	25.6	3.5
5,000–15,000	8.4	4.4
15,000–50,000	6.5	9.8
50,000–100,000	3.3	12.8
100,000–250,000	3.2	68.7

Adapted from Central Statistics Office, *Annual Abstract of Statistics* (London: HMSO, 1968), p. 133.

example, had a membership of 56 in 1964 and the Spring Trapmakers a membership of ninety. More importantly, the fact that union management negotiations are conducted by craft or job on a national level leaves unions unequipped to handle problems in any given plant; such matters are left in the hands of the shop stewards of the various unions represented there, and coordination with the national union organization is often difficult. Finally, most unions tend to have something of a "craft" mentality, and are greatly concerned with preserving the particular jobs, however unskilled, of their members. Unions have usually been quite conservative about automation; and their strength is such that this conservatism has inhibited the modernization of British industry in recent years.

The power of the trade-union movement has given rise to another problem. Many important industries today operate on the basis of a union shop. Thus, in effect, a worker's opportunity to use his skills is dependent upon his union membership, and many unions have failed to recognize the need to set up mechanisms by which the individual worker can be protected from the improper use of power by the union bureaucracy.

And new problems are emerging. The labor force is increasingly made up of white-collar workers. The record of British trade unions here has been better than the American; still, in the last few years, union membership has not even kept pace with the growth of the labor force.

There are those among the top leadership of the T.U.C. who feel that trade unions may face a period of decline unless the unions break with their past tradition and abandon certain conceptions, held especially by older leaders, of what the function of the trade union is. Unlike their American counterparts, for example, British trade unions pay their professional staffs relatively low salaries, and, on the whole, refuse to invest their funds in private industry where returns would be much greater. There is, however, evidence that the next generation of trade-union leaders will be a different breed.

There are also more and more signs of apathy among rank-and-file members, who now think of their union as an instrument for improving their bargaining position rather than as purely an instrument of class warfare. Attendance at union meetings has dropped off, and some of the old fervor has died away. In fact, a surprising number of working-class people believe that British unions are too powerful today—that they have injured the nation's economy by unwarranted strikes and that their leadership has become too arrogant.

Some of the problems faced by the trade-union movement in relation to the individual and overall economic policy gave rise to the creation of a Royal Commission on Trade Unions and Employers Associations in 1965. Of special concern was the growth of "unofficial" strikes—those led by shop stewards in individual plants—which accounted for about 95 per cent of total strikes in the period between 1964 and 1966. While time lost due to strikes per worker in England remained far smaller than in the United States or France (see Table 5.9), the effects of such strikes, given England's economic position, had been regarded as extremely serious. Figures on time lost per thousand workers do not tell the full story. A large number of short, flash strikes of the kind that England has experienced can be more disruptive from the point of view of productivity than a smaller number of lengthy strikes which come at the end of a long period of negotiation and for which everyone is prepared, as is frequently the case in the United States.

The commission's report in 1968 pointed out that while, in theory, negotiations on wages and hours were conducted on an industry-wide basis, the fact of the matter was that workers were dealing with individual corporations through unofficial strikes. It recommended that this fact be recognized and that relations be formalized on the plant level.

TABLE 5.9. WORK STOPPAGES DUE TO INDUSTRIAL DISPUTES IN MINING,
MANUFACTURING, CONSTRUCTION, AND TRANSPORT

Annual averages

	Number of stoppages per 100,000 employees[1]	Average number of persons involved per stoppage	Average duration of each stoppage in working days	Number of working days lost per 1,000 employees
Great Britain	16.8	340	3.4	184
France	21.8	1,090	0.8	347
West Germany	—	—	3.6	34[2]
United States[3]	13.2	470	14.2	934

[1] First three columns for 1963–66; fourth column for 1963–67.
[2] Average for 1963–66 only; figures for 1967 not available.
[3] Includes electricity, gas, water, sanitary services.

Adapted from Conservative Research Department, *Notes on Current Politics* (March 24, 1969), p. 99.

Other proposals included safeguards for workers who thought they had been unjustifiably refused admission to or expelled from a union and the need to improve arbitration methods for settling disputes.

In 1969, the government announced its intention to introduce legislation implementing some of the recommendations of the Royal Commission, including the establishment of a Commission on Industrial Relations to investigate ways of improving procedural agreements and disciplinary practices. The legislation also would have provided for a 28-day "conciliation pause" on the initiative of the government when a strike was threatened. Despite what seemed to be widespread public support, however, the Wilson administration was forced to drop its plans for the legislation in the face of strong opposition from the Trades Union Council and the left wing of the Labor Party. On its side, the T.U.C. promised to make greater efforts to prevent wildcat strikes; these "efforts" have not, thus far, been notably successful.

THE FRENCH PATTERN: Until 1884, to be a French worker was, in effect, to live in a police state. Trade unions were still illegal (although partly tolerated); workers were forced to carry a passbook (*livret*) which they presented to the local police authorities upon assuming a new job. They could not change jobs unless their previous employer signified that they had fulfilled all their legal obligations to him.

Both the livret and the restrictions upon associations of workers had their origins in the Revolution and its aftermath. The legal prohibition of trade unions was partly based on the belief that no organization should interfere with the free contractual relationship between employer and employee; but bourgeois antagonism to working-class combination, sustained by the class antagonism which permeated French life, was also relevant.

Trade unions were finally legalized in 1884. Their growth, however, was inhibited by the same factors as before: the slowness of French industrialization, the small size of the French firm, and the French businessman's violent hostility to unions. But there were internal causes as well: the fragmentation of the trade-union movement into ideological factions (anarchist, syndicalist, Catholic) and the workers' unwillingness to maintain a disciplined cohesive organization or even to pay union dues.

The alienation of the French worker helps explain why he was drawn to trade unions advocating total and violent change, and why French workers, unlike the English, refused to cooperate with Socialist parties. Instead, they adhered to a syndicalist ideology which emphasized that bourgeois politicians, whatever their party, could not be trusted and that change must come from the working class itself, through its own organizations.

Thus, in the period before World War I, French industrial relations were characterized by violent strikes, often just as violently repressed, and by the failure of French workers to establish a mass trade-union organization. In the period just before the war, things seemed capable of change. Many trade unions combined to form the General Confederation of Labor (Confédération générale du travail—C.G.T.) in which "reformist" voices seemed to predominate. But the C.G.T. split in the 1920's and the radicals, who had become closely tied to the Communist Party, formed their own national organization, the Confédération générale du travail unifié (C.G.T.U.). Trade-union membership, which had jumped into the millions at the end of the war as the result of expectations that the revolution was at hand, declined precipitously.

The pattern recurred again and again. In 1936, after the election of the Popular Front government, trade-union membership grew quickly, and the C.G.T. and C.G.T.U. merged; as before, the decline was just as swift, and the Communists were forced out of the C.G.T. The end of World War II brought yet another influx of workers, and trade-union membership rose to more than six million; again, Communist and reformist trade unions merged, and again the organization split shortly thereafter. By 1952 total trade-union membership was well below three million.

The Communists retained control over the C.G.T., and reformist elements were forced to build their own organization, the General Confederation of Labor, Workers' Force

(Confédération générale du travail/Force ouvrière—C.G.T./F.O.). The C.G.T. has remained the most important national trade-union organization in the postwar period, despite the fact that its membership is probably not much greater than one and one-half million workers.[18] After serving for many years simply as the trade-union wing of the Communist Party, it has begun to emphasize trade-union functions, including the attainment of immediate concessions from management. On the other hand, the Force Ouvrière has stagnated; except for a few areas, it consists very largely of white-collar workers, and its leadership still adheres to traditional syndicalist views which are no longer applicable.

Actually, the strongest of the "reformist" national union organizations today is the former French Confederation of Christian Workers (Confédération française des travailleurs chrétiens—C.F.T.C.). Founded as a specifically Catholic trade union which hoped to bring workers back to the Catholic Church, it originally attracted white-collar employees and was relatively conservative; in the early 1920's, for example, it contributed to the failure of an attempted general strike by refusing to collaborate with the C.G.T. In recent years, however, its leadership has become more militant, and the C.F.T.C. has gradually picked up industrial strength; it now has about six hundred thousand members. While it worked actively with the Popular Republican Movement, serving as a liberalizing influence, it also made less and less of its religious origins and, in 1964, changed its name to the Democratic Confederation of Labor (Confédération française et démocratique du travail—C.F.D.T.). A few of the more conservative unions have since split with the new organization in order to retain their traditional Christian orientation, causing the C.F.D.T. to become even more militant. In 1968 it was the only major trade

[18] Characteristically, it is difficult to obtain accurate figures on trade-union membership in France. Unions regularly offer inflated estimates.

union that unabashedly supported the student upheaval.

Thus the French trade-union movement is still highly fragmented; anarchist unions and a substantial number of unaffiliated unions continue to exist. Furthermore, more than 75 per cent of French workers do not belong to any trade-union organization whatever. Their apathy, of course, builds on itself; insofar as French trade unions remain small, poor, and ineffective, they are unlikely to attract workers to them.

Working-class advances since World War II have owed little, in fact, to collective bargaining. Rather, they have stemmed from a fairly tight labor market, political decisions establishing minimum wages and social benefits, and unilateral acts by enlightened employers.

The de Gaulle regime tried to apply to the labor field some of the "corporatist" ideals that were integral to the general's conception of a new France. Extending a program initiated under the Fourth Republic, the government offered tax concessions to firms which instituted profit-sharing schemes.

Nevertheless, until 1968, the economic condition of the French worker had improved far less than that of his English counterpart. Skilled workers, especially, were beginning to share in the consumer revolution, but many of the less skilled were earning wages not much higher than in the 1920's. While the distribution of income among various strata of the English and German population had become more equal, the opposite was true in France.[19] Housing conditions were especially difficult. In fact, de Gaulle preferred to concentrate on economic growth and on "grandeur" in the form of nuclear weapons, rather than on social-welfare measures. Finally, the limited evidence we have indicates that the social gap between the middle and the working class remained substantially wider in France than in England.

[19] United Nations, Secretariat of the Economic Commission for Europe, *Incomes in Post War Europe* (Geneva, 1967), Chap. 6, p. 21.

The French worker's impatience with his economic situation reached a climax in the late spring of 1968, when massive spontaneous strikes all but paralyzed the country. These were settled only after the government had promised sizable, across-the-board wage increases, the expansion of profit-sharing schemes, and plans for worker participation in the management of industry. The seizure of many French universities by students had served as the spark which set off the strikes. Interestingly enough, however, the demands of the workers remained relatively moderate. The strikers made it clear that their efforts were not political. In fact, in the elections which followed, many deserted the Communist Party to vote for the Gaullists in response to the president's appeal for a strong mandate to insure the maintenance of public order. It was quite clear that, for the time being at least, most French workers were less interested in overturning the system than in sharing in its benefits. By late 1969, however, continuing inflation and other economic difficulties, prompted partly by the strikes themselves, had eaten away more of the gains achieved by the workers, and the new Pompidou government was faced with the possibility of renewed unrest.

THE GERMAN PATTERN: As in England, German workers began to organize early in the process of industrialization. In fact, given Germany's late start and the anti-Socialist (and anti–trade-union) laws which were in effect from 1878 to 1890, trade unions grew at a remarkable pace; by 1913 about three million workers were union members. (See Table 5.10.)

The major impetus to trade-union organization in Germany had come from Socialist intellectuals. Although a few unions were avowedly nonpolitical and nonideological, most were closely tied to the German Social Democratic Party and, from the beginning, had accepted as their ultimate aim the creation of a Socialist society. The Socialist, or "free," unions quickly developed a national

TABLE 5.10.   MEMBERSHIP IN GERMAN TRADE UNIONS, 1891–1931

(*In thousands*)

	"Free" trade unions	*Hirsch-Duncker unions*	*Christian trade unions*
1891	278	66	—
1896	329	72	8
1900	680	92	79
1905	1,345	117	188
1910	2,017	123	295
1913	2,574	107	343
1919	5,479	190	858
1921	7,568	225	986
1923	7,138	185	938
1925	-4,156	158	588
1927	4,150	168	606
1929	4,906	169	673
1931	4,418	181	578

Adapted from Kopel S. Pinson, *Modern Germany* (New York: Macmillan, 1964), p. 247, and W. Galenson, *Comparative Labor Movements* (New York: Macmillan, 1952), p. 290. Reprinted by permission of the publishers.

organization, the General Commission of Trade Unions, which, after World War I, became the General German Federation of Labor (*Allgemeine Deutsche Gewerkschaftsbund*).

The relation between the Social Democratic Party and the trade unions was complex and shifting. At first, the unions were regarded almost as an arm of the party. As they grew, they began to assert their independence, separating industrial from political activity; but they continued to collaborate closely with the party. Even without any formal affiliation the most active trade-union members were also party activists. Trade-union leaders and party officials met to discuss common policy, and trade-union officials ran for office as party candidates; trade unions also contributed heavily to party coffers.

Both the ideological orientation and the effective organization of German trade unions are to be explained partly by the same variables that affected almost every European country. To these, however, must be added the rapidity with which Germany industrial-ized and the high concentration of German industry, as well as the characteristically German capacity for organization and discipline.

Like their British counterparts, the leaders of the German trade-union movement became more moderate as trade unions grew in size, and—despite a temporary upsurge of Communist strength in the period just after World War I—the movement became essentially reformist even as it retained revolutionary slogans. It may be that the unions' deference to both tradition and constituted authority served to reduce their economic and political effectiveness; but it should be remembered that the Socialist trade unions were among the few important groups that were fully committed to democracy during the Weimar period.

Two other national trade-union associations played some role during this period. The first was the German Trades Association, an organization of liberal trade unions which in 1920 combined with several white-collar trade unions—more popularly known as the Hirsch-Duncker unions, after the names of their original founders—to form the Federation of Unions of German Workers, Employees, and Civil Servants. It remained quite small, however, and never exercised much influence. More important was the *Deutscher Gewerkschaftsbund*, primarily a church-sponsored organization. Partly inspired by the encyclical *Rerum Novarum*, and partly to combat the influence of the Socialist unions, the Catholic Church had begun to encourage the organization of trade unions at the turn of the century. Some Protestant leaders had initiated similar efforts, and, after a good deal of negotiation, they combined their forces in 1920, despite strong opposition from those among the Catholic clergy who were hostile to such interdenominational collaboration. Although membership in the organization reached a million in the middle 1920's, it began to decline soon after. The Protestant unions appealed primarily to white-collar workers, and the more heavily Catholic areas were, on the whole, less industrialized. Further, workers who were practicing Catholics were not very likely to join trade unions of any kind. With the advent of Hitler, all trade unions were dissolved; their leaders, if they escaped imprisonment, either migrated or went underground. German workers were enrolled in the German Labor Front, a section of the Nazi Party.

Immediately after Germany's defeat, the trade-union movement began to reorganize with the strong encouragement of the Allies, who regarded trade-union leaders as among the most responsible democratic elements within the country. At first there was some impetus to readopt a traditional Socialist program, but the cold war, the success of the Christian Democrats' "free market policy," and the general erosion of ideological divisions dictated other policies. Most trade-union leaders saw their primary task to be the creation of a fully unified trade-union movement, even at the price of cutting at least some of their ties with the Social Democrats and abandoning their traditional anticlerical-

ism. Thus the German Federation of Trade Unions (*Deutscher Gewerkschaftsbund—D.G.B.*), created in 1949, specifically disassociated itself from any political tendency; as a result it was able to attract Christian unions, and most of the others which had once refused to affiliate for ideological reasons, into the organization.

The D.G.B. today has a membership of some 6.5 million—about 30 per cent of the total working force. As in England, the rate of its growth has declined in recent years; even the ratio of union members to the total working force has dropped. The organization's federal structure is probably somewhat stronger than its British counterpart, but the individual unions which compose it still possess considerable freedom.

Traditionally, German unions organized according to craft or occupation, with white-collar workers, manual workers, and civil servants all belonging to separate unions; the sharpness of status differences in Germany intensified these divisions. At the end of the war, however, the number of unions was deliberately reduced and they were regrouped along industrial lines. Thus, today, the D.G.B. consists of 16 vertical unions, of which the metal workers, miners, and public-service unions are the most important.

On the whole, the D.G.B. has formally maintained political neutrality; but its sympathies are clearly with the Social Democrats, and it still works closely with them. Some of the unions—the Metal Workers, for example—are even more closely connected to the party. On the whole, too, the D.G.B. has moved increasingly away from specific ideological commitments, although a number of its constituent unions continue to emphasize Socialist goals. Conflict over political leanings did lead to one split within the D.G.B. in 1953, when many Catholic unionists left the parent organization in protest over an election manifesto which they regarded as too pro-Socialist. With the strong support of some members of the Catholic clergy and some encouragement from Chancellor Adenauer, they organized a German Christian Trade Union Movement; but its total membership has never exceeded two hundred thousand.

Some 12 per cent of white-collar workers and 41 per cent of civil servants, mainly railroad and postal employees, are members of D.G.B.-affiliated unions. About eight per cent of white-collar workers (450,000 in 1961) are members of the independent German Trade Union for White-Collar Employees, and about 43 per cent of civil servants belong to the German Federation of Civil Servants; both groups attempt to cater to the distinct economic and professional interests of their members.

German trade unions have no formal status at the plant level. Instead, workers at each plant are represented by an elected "works council," which has certain rights to "co-determination" and consultation on various matters affecting working conditions and personnel policy. These work councils were first conceived during the Weimar period by moderate Socialists who hoped thus to insure workers' participation in plant management; but by and large, they have weakened the position of the trade unions, even though the latter make every effort to secure the election of personnel who represent their point of view. The unions' position at the plant level is also weakened by the absence of closed- or even union-shop agreements, and by the government's authority to extend collective agreements to non-unionized plants once fifty per cent of the workers in any industry are covered.

Immediately after World War II, German trade unions pressed extremely hard for the principle of "co-determination." In one form or another, this principle has been extended by federal law to most large German corporations. In effect, it guarantees worker participation in managerial decisions on questions such as changes in the nature of the enterprise, mergers, and shutdowns. It was hoped that such participation would help to democratize the economic system. But although labor representatives have had some beneficial influence, they have not been able to wield much strength in managerial decision-making—partly because the German worker is still deferential to authority, but also because he is more concerned with wages and fringe benefits than with participation in policy-making.

In Germany, as elsewhere, the decline in salary differentials between white-collar workers (at least in the lower echelons) and industrial workers has reduced status differences; the gaps between strata have, in fact, declined. Moreover, the educational opportunities for working-class children are slowly expanding; class attitudes and class militancy are both being eroded. Some 72 per cent of German workers questioned in one sample responded that the chances of a competent person improving his class position were good. (The corresponding figure for England was 82 per cent.) In another survey only six out of six hundred workers questioned subscribed to a "class war" ideology and only twelve to a "radical-reformist" view.[20]

THE RUSSIAN AND SOVIET PATTERN: Until the middle of the nineteenth century, serfs composed a large part of the Russian industrial work force. Free labor remained in short supply until emancipation left many peasants landless or with plots insufficient to support them, thus creating a large reservoir of manpower. It was only very slowly that these peasants were transformed into an industrial work force in the modern sense. For one thing, because of the lack of a Russian artisan tradition, there was no base of skilled workers. Furthermore, the peasant-turned-worker remained legally tied to the village commune, which retained responsibility for his taxes and through which he had to obtain regular renewals of his passport. Many peasants who came to the cities under the stress of poverty left behind them families to whom they sent money, and they periodically re-

[20] Stephen R. Graubard, ed., *A New Europe?* (Boston: Houghton-Mifflin, 1964), p. 350.

turned to the land to help with the harvest. At the time of the Revolution, therefore, the great bulk of Russian workers were still half-proletarian and half-peasant.

Workers began to form trade unions at the turn of the century. At first these were under Menshevik leadership, but during the Revolution they passed into the hands of Bolshevik cadres, and they were instrumental in securing their victory. Once victorious, the Bolsheviks were faced with the necessity of reorganizing the economy; this circumstance confronted them with a series of dilemmas. To both Marx and Lenin, the inequalities of capitalist society sprang ultimately from the division of labor itself. In a fully Communist society, the division of labor would disappear, as would social classes; after a short period of transition, society's standard would be: "From each according to his ability, to each according to his needs." With this expectation, both Marx and Engels had left unclear the organizational pattern of the new Socialist society. For example, what form would authority take in the factory: what role, if any, would trade unions play in the period of transition?

During the early stages of the Revolution, the party encouraged the formation of workers' factory committees, which were to share responsibility for management with the remaining members of the bourgeoisie; but since most of the traditional managerial elite fled the country or were imprisoned by the regime, the workers soon found themselves in complete charge, with chaotic results. In an effort to rationalize the organization of the economy, the Bolsheviks called upon the trade unions to discipline the factory committees; a compromise was effected whereby the committees gradually relinquished their authority to the trade unions in return for the promise that unions would be reorganized in such a way that the committees formed their basic units.

At the time of the civil war, the trade unions were an integral part of the state machinery. Through them, the government mobil-ized manpower and regulated wages and conditions of employment; in the factory, they shared responsibility with managerial personnel. But by 1920, their power was waning. Even though the party still tried to discover and train competent workers for managerial positions, it was also beginning to stress the need for a single source of authority within the factory, and, perhaps more important, the need to subordinate trade unions to both the party and the state apparatus. In 1921, the Tenth Party Congress brought the issue to a head. During a furious debate as to the future function of trade unions in the society, three positions emerged. The first was that of the Workers' Opposition, voiced by many delegates who were disturbed by what they considered to be the increasing centralization of authority in the hands of the party. A Communist state, they argued, should be run by the free organizations of the workers—that is, by the trade unions. They went on to demand a return to the principle of full equality of wages.

On the other hand, Leon Trotsky and a number of others argued that the workers' opposition misunderstood the implications of Marxism. Trotsky maintained that the trade unions had no independent function in a workers' state, but instead should aid the party to achieve those ends from which all would benefit. To allow trade-union representatives to dictate policy would be to cater to the worker's immediate conception of his self-interest, rather than to work for his long-range, true interest. As he put it:

The Workers' Opposition has come out with dangerous slogans, making a fetish of democratic principles. They place the workers' right to elect their representatives— above the party, as it were, as if the party were not entitled to assert its dictatorship even if that dictatorship temporarily clashed with the passing moods of the workers' democracy.

It is necessary to create among us the awareness of the revolutionary historical birthright of the party, which is obliged to maintain its dictatorship, regardless of temporary wavering in the spontaneous moods of the masses, regardless of the temporary waverings even in the working classes. This awareness is for us the indispensable unifying element. The dictatorship does not base itself at every given moment on the formal principle of workers' democracy, although the workers' democracy is, of course, the only method by which the masses can be drawn more and more into political life.[21]

Although Trotsky did call for a leveling-out of wage differentials, he differed from the workers' opposition by rejecting the notion of complete equality in the immediate future.

The third position, which was taken by Lenin and most of the party leadership ("The Platform of the Ten"), represented an attempt to find a middle ground. Complete equality of wages, Lenin claimed, was impossible during the period of the transition to communism. While he rejected the argument that the state apparatus should be directed by the trade unions, he also criticized Trotsky's position, contending that trade unions in a workers' state did have two unique functions: that of mobilizing the workers to achieve the ends determined by the party and that of representing working-class interests and needs. Whatever might be true in the future, such representation was important during the time of transition. Thus the unions would serve as quasi-independent organs, subordinate to both party and state but working closely with them.

This was the position finally adopted by the party congress. In a sense, party leaders have tried to adhere to it; but in actuality, the dynamics of Soviet society were such that the role of trade unions quickly came to resemble that envisaged by Trotsky and it has continued so.

In 1922, for example, the Eleventh Party

Congress, while recognizing the right of trade unions to conduct strikes in the private sector (although this was discouraged), positively prohibited them in the public sector, and imposed still further limitations upon trade-union interference in management. The party continued, of course, to make every effort to draw managerial personnel from the ranks of the working class; but their ideological presuppositions kept them from recognizing that this effort alone could not eliminate conflicts of interest between workers and managers. When such conflicts continued to develop, they were blamed on inadequate education and indoctrination; the solution was to bring trade unions under even tighter party control. Thus, at the eleventh Congress, it was decreed that while trade-union secretaries and chairmen of trade-union central committees were to be elected by the membership, they were also to be party members—in effect, by the 1930's, trade-union leaders were appointed by the party.

Despite increasing party control, trade unions had retained some independence through the 1920's, and wage differentials had remained relatively small. But the status of both the worker and the trade union began to change with the first Five Year Plan. One of the requirements of rapid industrialization is a relatively mobile and disciplined labor force. In a market economy, this is theoretically provided by the price mechanism; workers go where there are jobs, and the promise of material rewards induces them to develop the necessary skills. In practice this mechanism works imperfectly, at best. However, in advanced industrial societies, necessary skills are widely dispersed; with some exceptions, they are available or become so within a reasonable time.

No such disciplined and skilled working force existed in the Soviet Union; it had to be created. Thus the trade unions were instructed to work out measures that would insure an adequate supply of workers, and the state arranged for a quasi-compulsory influx of "redundant" workers from the collective

[21] Quoted in *Soviet Trade Unions*, by Isaac Deutscher, p. 55. Published by Oxford University Press for the Royal Institute of International Affairs, 1950.

farms to the city. At first this influx was arranged by means of "voluntary" contracts, but in 1939, just before the outbreak of World War II, this procedure was replaced by the formation of an organized labor reserve to be supplied on demand by the collective farm.

However, the flood of manpower thus provided did not put an end to the party's problems. The newly recruited peasants were not attuned to the tempo and conditions of industrial life; moreover, they faced extremely poor housing conditions in most Soviet cities, and poor working conditions in both factories and mines. The results were fantastically high levels of absenteeism, as well as extensive drifting from one job to another, caused in part by individual factory managers' cutthroat competition to secure labor. Early in 1933, a joint resolution by the party and the government noted:

. . . according to the information of the statistical officers, 423,000 workers and employees left the mines in 1932. During the same period 458,000 workers and employees entered employment. . . . This means that a considerable part of workers and employees, if not the majority, drifts restlessly from mine to mine, from the mines into the countryside, and from the countryside into the mines rather than work. . . . It goes without saying that in view of such fluidity it is impossible to assimilate, if only in a half-satisfactory manner, the new technique and to master the new machines. Yet the mastery of the new technique is the key to the rise of the entire coal industry of the Donbas [Donets Basin].[22]

The government responded to this problem and others by the use of both coercion and incentives. Workers who deserted their jobs could not be re-employed for six months, and would lose many benefits such as holidays. These initial steps, however, were not too successful, for the badly pressed managers ignored the letter of the law. Therefore, controls were gradually tightened. Workers were supplied with identity cards, which enabled trade unions to keep track of them. They were not entitled to a holiday or to housing until they had been on a job for a certain length of time. Notorious "loiterers" or habitual latecomers could be dismissed from their jobs and even prosecuted.

On the other hand, an increasingly differentiated scale of rewards went into effect. In 1929 the party launched a program of "Socialist emulation" and instructed trade unions to give public accolades to the best workers. When this moral suasion proved insufficient, certain material rewards, such as better housing, began to be offered to workers who periodically overfulfilled quotas. By the mid-thirties, the whole Soviet wage structure had changed significantly. Industries that employed skilled labor or called for particularly difficult work could pay higher wages; within individual plants, wage differentiations among various skills increased. This was compounded by the extension of piecework methods, culminating in "progressive" piecework: payments per unit of work were fixed in terms of certain norms, which workers were encouraged to break; when they succeeded, new and higher norms were created. In fact, "rate busting" became institutionalized in the form of "Stakhanovism," named after a worker who supposedly initiated the whole program: special shock workers were brought in to break norms (often by being given special assistants) and provide a stimulus to other workers. All the practices introduced at this time were those which trade unions in the West, after one hundred years, had finally begun to eliminate.

As might be imagined, working-class resistance to Stakhanovism was often violent. There is evidence that in the middle 1930's some Stakhanovites were killed by irate fellow workers and that some sabotage occurred—which only contributed to the party leadership's conviction that saboteurs were everywhere.

22 Ibid., p. 90.

After World War II, there was a gradual reduction of both labor discipline and wage differentials, a trend accelerated by the death of Stalin. In 1951, a decree reduced criminal penalties for absenteeism—in general, they had been enforced only sporadically since the end of the war—and another in 1956 abolished such penalties altogether. Another decree (1955) abolished the forced draft of youth into trade and railroad schools; another (1960) permitted workers who changed jobs to retain disability benefits and other seniority rights, provided they began work at a new job within a month of leaving the old.

The use of draft procedures for recruiting workers to new industries has diminished considerably. Progressive piecework, along with Stakhanovism, seems to have all but disappeared; piecework itself, in fact, is being replaced by time rates.

Between 1955 and 1967, the proportion of workers paid by piecework had fallen from about 75 to 55 per cent of the industrial labor force, and is scheduled to fall to between 45 and fifty per cent by 1970.[23] At the same time, the regime has moved toward reducing wage differentials, largely by raising the bottom levels of the wage scale. General social benefits have also been expanded, and the number of work-hours per week has declined. As of now the official standard is 41 hours and a five-day week, although many Soviet employees work overtime.

Changes in the status of the working class reflect the same general forces that led to other areas of de-Stalinization. The Soviet Union now possesses a fairly mature industrial working class, and the nation has reached levels of productivity and self-confidence which have permitted it some increase in rewards and reduction of controls. Other forces are at work, too. Well over one-third of Soviet workers have had at least a secondary education, and, as in the West,

the increasing availability of skilled workers has resulted in a narrowing of the wage differentiations between the skilled and the unskilled.

Controls have by no means disappeared. A worker must give two weeks' notice before he leaves a firm and, in doing so, loses housing rights and garden plots. There is still no system of unemployment benefits, but there is comparatively little long-term unemployment. The worker must still carry both a work book and an internal passport. If the former contains a record of too many job shifts he may find himself in some difficulty.

Then, too, while compulsory drafts seem to be relied on less and less, considerable pressure is still exerted upon workers to move where they are needed. Various disciplinary techniques, too, remain in force; workers can be penalized for tardiness or carelessness. Since 1959, the so-called comrades' courts, set up in most larger enterprises, handle such offenses; these courts are theoretically elected by the workers themselves, but are sometimes "packed" by supervisory personnel. They may impose fairly heavy fines, or even remand the offender to the regular court system for further action. It is possible for a worker to appeal a decision of a comrades' court, although it is difficult to know how effective a check this really is. Some commentators regard the courts merely as shock absorbers which further the aims of management; but it seems more realistic to accept them at face value, as a mechanism by which the workers, under party guidance, take some responsibility for on-the-job problems. In addition to the comrades' courts, anti-parasite laws, introduced in 1961, permit sentences of exile and compulsory labor for people who consistently fail to take a correct attitude toward productive work.[24]

That certain kinds of disciplinary procedures have been retained and, since 1961, extended indicates that the Soviet Union still

23 Robert Conquest, ed., *Industrial Workers in the U.S.S.R.* (New York: Frederick A. Praeger, 1967), p. 55.

24 Both the comrades' courts and the anti-parasite laws will be discussed in more detail later (see Chapter 21).

has labor problems. In the past several years, the rate of increase of labor productivity has slowed down, labor turnover and drift have increased, and on a number of occasions unofficial and violent strikes have occurred. Within the party there has been disagreement about how best to deal with these problems. At least a few high-level officials have argued for a return to even stricter discipline, as well as a new increase in wage differentials based upon performance.

Meanwhile, the role of Soviet trade unions has also been changing. By 1930 they were no longer independent bargaining agents and they had come under the complete control of the party. Yet even during the Stalin period they served as checks upon managerial violations of production norms. To a lesser extent, they also protected the worker against serious deterioration in working conditions caused by the managers' desire to fulfill or surpass quotas, and they served as a means of spurring workers to greater efforts.

Trade unions still continue to be under the control of the party—and they still fail to fulfill many of the more important functions that they exercise in Western European nations, such as the negotiation of wage rates. However, they do have at least a consultative role on national decision-making bodies, and, on the local level, they seem to be taking a more active part in the individual plant. They are supposed to participate in working out the production and financial plans of enterprises and to express their opinions on candidates for managerial posts. They also represent the workers with regard to grievances; most disputes which cannot be settled are referred to a commission representing both trade union and management, and decisions of this body may be appealed to the courts.

Soviet trade unions also serve as service organizations, administering social-insurance funds, sanatoriums, and rest homes, and organizing recreational facilities. They are responsible, too, for the assignment of auxiliary housing and farm and garden enterprises attached to factories.

The Revolution of 1917 was carried out in the name of the Soviet working class. The aim of the Bolsheviks was to create a classless society in which the workers would own the means of production and in which the alienation which was their lot in capitalist society

"From now on the practice of ordering people around is strictly forbidden! Dis—missed!"—*From Krokodil (Moscow), June 30, 1965.*

would come to an end. Needless to say, the results so far have not lived up to expectations. The Soviet working class is part of a society in which income differentials remain substantial; social mobility is high, but apparently no higher than in most advanced industrial societies. The worker's power over decision-making in industrial enterprises or over the wages he receives is, on the whole, rather less than that of workers in England or the United States. He has not become the "new man" of Soviet rhetoric; indeed, recent studies by Soviet sociologists indicate that the attitudes of the Soviet worker toward his job do not differ very much from those of his Western counterpart. Also, the job preferences of Soviet youth closely resemble those of youth in other industrial societies.[25]

Some Western radicals who reject the Soviet model have argued that the failure of the regime to achieve its ideal goals is a result of the "betrayal" of the Revolution, and the creation of a bureaucratized form of state capitalism. It is hard to accept the validity of this analysis. It seems more plausible to argue that the similarities between the position of the worker in Communist and capitalist societies has more to do with the objective requirements of running a modern industrial economy. The authoritarian character of industrial relations in the Soviet Union under Stalin—and to a certain extent today—would appear to be less a betrayal of the Revolution than a natural consequence of the attempt to achieve the goals which its leaders set for Russian society and Russian culture.

As both the capitalist nations of Western Europe and the Soviet Union move toward a postindustrial society, one suspects that the relations of the worker to other strata in the society will continue to move in the direction of greater equality and greater participation

by workers in decision-making, but this is a topic to which we will return in the concluding chapter of the text.

4. WHITE-COLLAR WORKERS, PROFESSIONALS, AND INTELLECTUALS

Among the most important developments in all European societies during the past fifty years has been the growth of two separate but related groups: white-collar workers and professional people. The professions, of course, have a long history, and in many traditional societies professional groups such as priests or the military cadres exercised considerable authority. The technical advances of recent decades have made social life more complex; this, in turn, has meant that the professions have proliferated and that a greater proportion of the population is engaged in occupations which call for a lengthy period of technical training.

WHITE-COLLAR WORKERS: The emergence of a stratum of white-collar workers was a result of the increasing size and differentiation of economic enterprises and the consequent devolution and bureaucratization of managerial authority. The first white-collar workers were bookkeepers and plant foremen, although the latter are, strictly speaking, blue-collar workers. The growth of the government bureaucracy, and the increasing number of service industries in societies whose economic development has passed beyond a certain point, have also contributed to the proliferation of white-collar positions. In France, salaried employees constituted about 2.3 per cent of the nonagricultural work force in 1851, 18.2 per cent in 1921, 23.3 per cent in 1946, and more than 29 per cent today, including government employees. The present figure for Germany and England is more than thirty per cent. White-collar workers, of course, are a very dissimilar group, and range from high-level engineers to professional bank clerks: their life-styles and political behavior reflect this heterogeneity.

On the lower echelons, the difference be-

25 See George Fischer, ed., *Science and Ideology in Soviet Society* (New York: Atherton, 1967), p. 27, and Paul Hollander, "The Dilemmas of Soviet Sociology," *Problems of Communism*, XIV (November-December 1965), 41–42.

FIGURE 5.1. INCOME BY OCCUPATIONAL LEVEL AND AGE IN FRANCE, 1969

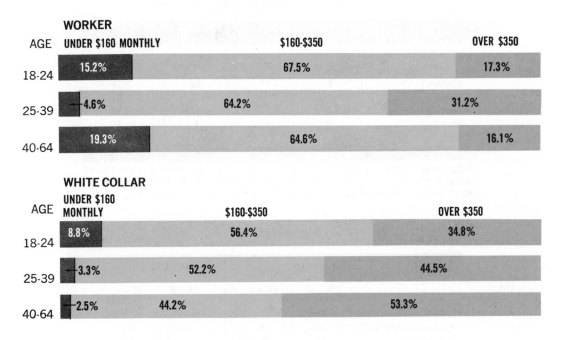

Source: Institut français d'Opinion publique, March
1969. Reprinted by permission. Data supplied by the
Roper Public Opinion Research Center.

tween their incomes and those of the skilled working class has probably declined in all European countries; but the earnings of white-collar employees still tend to rise with age while those of most industrial workers reach a stable level fairly early and then begin to fall. (See Figure 5.1.) Further, white-collar workers still feel more secure in, and satisfied with, their jobs. On the whole, too, both their self-images and their life-styles differ from those of industrial workers: they feel their chances of upward mobility are greater, and they are more likely to identify themselves as middle class. They read more books and newspapers, as surveys in France prove (see Table 5.11), and they are far more concerned with education than are blue-collar workers; even when wages are roughly comparable, a great percentage of their income goes into savings, and their interest in the outward manifestations of status is reflected in their desire to possess various consumer durables. (See Tables 5.12 and 5.13.)

Again, the situation varies from country to country. The relative position of the blue-collar worker in both Germany and England is superior to that of the blue-collar worker in France. In 1900 a high official in the public service in Germany probably earned ten times as much as an unskilled worker.[26] Today he earns no more than three times as much, and skilled workers, certainly, earn more than many lower-echelon white-collar workers or even professional people. In England there would seem to be even less difference between the average earnings of white- and blue-collar workers as a whole (see Table 5.14) and the difference in hours worked has all but vanished.[27]

[26] Helmut Arntz, *Facts About Germany* (Press and Information Office: Federal Government of Germany, 1968), p. 216.

[27] "Social Changes in Britain," quoted in *New Society* (December 27, 1962), p. 27.

TABLE 5.11. NEWSPAPER READING IN FRANCE, 1955

Occupational level and newspaper reading (in per cent)

	Unskilled	Skilled	White collar	Executive
Reads daily	60	69	73	78
Reads regularly:				
National news	53	55	66	79
Foreign news	29	34	54	64
Human-interest	78	72	58	59
Sports	60	66	56	51
Local news	88	82	72	69

Adapted from Richard Hamilton, *Affluence and the French Worker in the Fourth Republic* (Princeton: Princeton University Press, 1967), p. 95. Copyright © 1967 by Princeton University Press. Reprinted by permission of the publisher.

TABLE 5.12. THE OWNERSHIP OF CONSUMER DURABLES BY WHITE- AND BLUE-COLLAR WORKERS IN ENGLAND, 1958–1959, 1968–1969

	Middle class		Working class	
	58–59	68–69	58–59	68–69
Television set	65%	96%	61%	95%
Washing machine	40	79	24	69
Automobile	45	78	15	51
Refrigerator	28	79	47	58

Adapted from *Market Research*, December 1968, no. 2, p. 19; vol. 9, no. 1 (January 1969), p. 32; no. 2 (February 1969), p. 6; no. 5 (May 1969), p. 45. Reprinted by permission of European Research Consultants Ltd.

TABLE 5.13. THE OWNERSHIP OF CONSUMER DURABLES BY WHITE- AND BLUE-COLLAR WORKERS IN FRANCE, 1966

	White collar[1]	Workers
Washing machine	48%	48%
Refrigerator	78	64
Television set	55	53
Automobile	66	49

[1]Estimates.

Source: *Annuaire Statistique de la France, 1967* (Paris: Institut Nationale de la Statistique et des Etudes Economiques, 1967), p. 706.

The increase in the number of white-collar workers, and the decline in status differentiation between white- and blue-collar workers, have undoubtedly helped to depolarize politics in all three countries. White-collar workers have never been quite so attached to the status quo as was the old "independent" middle class, and have usually tended to support, or at least accept, political action regulating private property. The reasons for this are fairly clear. In smaller, more traditional factories, white-collar workers can

TABLE 5.14. INCOME AND EMPLOYMENT BY OCCUPATIONAL LEVEL,
GREAT BRITAIN, 1967

Yearly income	Manual workers	Shop assistants	Clerks	Professionals, administrators, and teachers
Under $1,248	9%	66%	17%	3%
$1,248–2,496	50	31	59	25
$2,496–3,744	35	2	20	36
$3,744–4,992	5	1	3	19
Over $4,992	1	0	1	17

Source: *Family Expenditure Survey, Report for 1967* (London: HMSO, 1968), pp. 96–97.

identify with management. They are salaried while blue-collar workers are not, and their relationships with employers are likely to be informal. In larger enterprises this is not the case. And this is more and more true as their work becomes routinized and impersonal— that is, increasingly resembles that of industrial workers. German studies, for example, have shown that white-collar workers in large modern factories are more inclined to express dissatisfaction with their jobs and to vote Socialist than their counterparts in smaller, more traditional business enterprises.[28]

On the other hand, studies of English white-collar workers indicate that they are still committed to the image of individual initiative leading to social advancement (see Table 5.15). Their situation, in fact, encourages this view. The chances for in-plant promotion may be smaller than before, but advancement to professional positions is more probable in societies where the technical professions are becoming more influential. Indeed, so far, it is the white-collar groups that have benefited most from the educational revolution which has been taking place in France and England since the war. The sons and daughters of white-collar workers are moving into the professions, even as more and more working-class children achieve white-collar status. (See Figure 5.2.)

Of course, the pattern still varies from England to France to Germany, as do the attitudes of white-collar workers as a stratum within the society. In Germany, status is probably still more important than in the other two Western countries, and a larger portion of white-collar workers range over the entire political spectrum, although they are most concentrated around the center left. Government employees tend to the left of those in private industry and teachers, too, are generally leftist. In all three countries, white-collar workers are less attracted to trade unions than are industrial workers; they usually form their own unions, and are less likely to affiliate with national organizations dominated by unions of blue-collar workers.

Unfortunately, there is little data dealing with the Soviet Union in this respect. The 1961 Soviet census lists "mental workers" as constituting some 20.7 per cent of the population. Evidence from the 1930's indicates that white-collar workers enjoy significant income advantages, that they usually marry and associate with members of their own stratum, and that they have tremendous educational advantages. Statistics on party membership and especially on membership in the party elite give us some indication that the situation does not differ substantially today, even though standards of living and opportunities have increased tremendously for the entire population. In 1966, nonmanual workers made up about 46 per cent of party members,

28 Juan Linz, *The Social Basis of German Politics* (unpublished doctoral dissertation, Columbia University, 1958), p. 538.

TABLE 5.15. WORKING-CLASS AND MIDDLE-CLASS ATTITUDES
IN GREAT BRITAIN

	Working-class perspective	*Middle-class perspective*
General beliefs	The social order is divided into "us" and "them": those who do not have authority and those who do.	The social order is a hierarchy of differentially rewarded positions; a ladder containing many rungs.
	The division between "us" and "them" is virtually fixed, at least from the point of view of one man's life chances.	It is possible for individuals to move from one level of the hierarchy to another.
	What happens to you depends a lot on luck; otherwise you have to learn to put up with things.	Those who have ability and initiative can overcome obstacles and create their own opportunities. Where a man ends up depends on what he makes of himself.
	"We" ought to stick together and get what we can as a group.	Every man ought to make the most of his own capabilities and be responsible for his own welfare.
General values	You may as well enjoy yourself while you can instead of trying to make yourself "a cut above the rest."	You cannot expect to get anywhere in the world if you squander your time and money. "Getting on" means making sacrifices.
Attitudes on more specific issues:		
On the best job for a son	"A trade in his hands."—"A good steady job."	"As good a start as you can give him."—"A job that leads somewhere."
Toward people needing social assistance	"They have been unlucky."—"They never had a chance."—"It could happen to any of us."	"Many of them have had the same opportunities as others who have managed well enough."—"They are a burden on those who are trying to help themselves."
On trade unions	"Trade unions are the only means workers have of protecting themselves and of improving their standard of living."	"Trade unions have too much power in the country."—"The unions put the interests of a section before the interests of the nation as a whole."

Source: Goldthorpe and Lockwood, "Affluence and the British Class Structure," *The Sociological Review*, XII, 2 (July 1963), p. 147. Reprinted by permission of the publisher.

FIGURE 5.2. SOCIAL MOBILITY AMONG
NONMANUAL WORKERS IN FRANCE, 1959

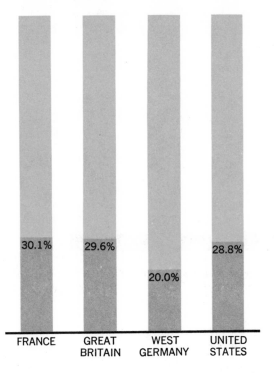

Adapted from "Comparative Social Mobility," *Current Sociology*, IX, 1 (1960), p. 30. Reprinted by permission of the publisher.

65.7 per cent of the members of the 1966 Party Congress, and 96 per cent of the party Central Committee. Many members of the elite, of course, had moved up in the ranks from jobs as manual workers, and others were the sons and daughters of workers and peasants; nevertheless, important differentiations clearly remain.

THE PROFESSIONS: In almost every European country today, the professions constitute between eight and ten per cent of the population. Some, like medicine and law, have a long tradition; but there are also many newer specializations, such as engineering, economics, and architecture. Most of the professions have become more and more

differentiated and require increasingly technical training. The social role of a number of professional elites will be discussed in other contexts;[29] at this point only a few general remarks are in order.

By the late middle ages, those who wished to enter the legal, medical, or academic professions usually had to obtain a university degree and, since the universities were under the control of the Catholic Church, those attending had to take at least minor religious orders. In the sixteenth and seventeenth centuries, as these professions began to be secularized, the religious requirement was gradually eliminated.

At about the same time, other professional groups began to appear. The early development of commerce in Renaissance Italy sparked the formation of colleges of accountants to which only those who could provide satisfactory evidence of training were admitted. Architecture, and then dentistry, acquired professional status shortly thereafter. With the Industrial Revolution, the list grew, and came to include engineers, physicists, chemists, actuaries, and surveyors. The list of professions has constantly expanded ever since, and particularly as science and technology have achieved new levels of sophistication. Moreover, the social sciences —psychology, economics, sociology, and political science—have now come to be professional disciplines.

The demand for professional services, and the long training they require, placed a premium upon those with requisite skills; both industry and government compete for their services. In Germany, France, and postrevolutionary Russia, professional training in the sciences has become one important means of achieving high-level administrative and even political positions. The Soviet Union has, perhaps, gone farthest in this direction; engineering training seems to be almost a requisite for important managerial and party posts.

[29] See, for example, the chapters on law, the military, and education.

TABLE 5.16. OCCUPATIONAL COMPOSITION OF THE C.P.S.U., 1967

Field of employment	Number	Percentage
Bureaucracy:		
government, economic, party, etc.	936,000	7.4
Science, education, health, culture	1,740,000	13.7
Trade and materials–handling	463,000	3.7
Housing, civic and personal services	136,000	1.1
Communications	109,000	0.9
Transport	838,000	6.6
Industry	3,196,000	25.2
Construction	666,000	5.2
Kolkhozes	1,330,000	10.5
State farms	838,000	6.6
Miscellaneous agriculture and		
related branches	166,000	1.3
Other branches of economy	116,000	0.9
Armed forces (including border guards)	890,000	7.0
Pensioners	760,000	6.0
Students	200,000	1.6
Housewives and miscellaneous	300,000	2.3
Total	12,684,000	100.0

Source: Thomas H. Rigby, *Communist Party Membership in the U.S.S.R., 1917–1967* (Princeton: Princeton University Press, 1968), p. 348. Reprinted by permission of the publisher.

TABLE 5.17. "SOCIAL POSITION" OF C.P.S.U. MEMBERSHIP:
1924–1932 AND 1956–1967

Per cent of all members and candidates

	1924	1930	1932	1956	1961	1964	1966	1967
Workers	44.0	65.3	65.2	32.0	34.5	37.3	37.8	38.1
Peasants	28.8	20.2	26.9	17.1	17.5	16.5	16.2	16.0
White-collar workers and others	27.2	14.5	7.9	50.9	48.0	46.2	46.0	45.9

Source: Rigby, *Communist Party Membership*, p. 325. Reprinted by permission.

As the role of the professions has grown, political decisions have come to be influenced by professional thinking, professional styles, and professional standards. The greater participation of government in every aspect of community life has also contributed to this process. The higher level of the bureaucracy in every country relies upon economists for advice, and increasingly turns to academically trained sociologists and political scientists for "objective" analyses of social problems.

Again, the trend is especially marked in the Soviet Union, where every social problem is a political problem as well; it is here, perhaps, that the impact of professionalization upon political action, and even upon changes in political ideology, can be most readily seen. Relativity theory, for example—long regarded as a product of "idealistic," "reactionary" bourgeois science—began to be accepted even before the death of Stalin, through the efforts of Soviet scientists. Similarly, the party had rejected classical genetics in favor of the approved position that important genetic changes could be induced through manipulation of the environment; biologists who opposed this position had, in some cases, been executed. But by the time of Khrushchev's removal from office, the environmentalist theory had fallen into disrepute under the pressure of continued professional attacks. The same swaying of party position by professionals—who are partly influenced by Western theories and techniques—can also be seen in the fields of economics and sociology.

This is not to argue that professional ways of looking at particular problems will necessarily lead to an undermining of basic Marxist assumptions. The capacity of human beings to rationalize is very considerable. For example, following Marx, Soviet economists have always argued that the value of a commodity equals only the amount of socially useful labor time expended on it; in recent years, however, professionals have come to the conclusion that such items as depreciation of capital equipment should be taken into account in estimating costs, and they have evolved economic indicators that look suspiciously bourgeois. Such changes might seem to contradict a Marxist analysis, but as a leading Soviet economist noted, in response to an attack on his position as non-Marxist by more traditional ideologues:

The basic accusation . . . consists of the question: Do the objective evaluators constitute value?

This is scholasticism. Value and the objectively determined evaluators are completely different. . . . Value is a category of political economy, and the objective evaluators constitute an algorithmic formula for the calculation of equilibrium prices in an optimum plan.[30]

The growth of professionalism in advanced societies has had a far more general impact upon the politics of these societies than in the narrow application of technical expertise. In general, professionals are somewhat to the left of comparable income groups, especially salaried intellectuals, for they have a smaller commitment than the traditional middle class to the structure of property relations in capitalist society.[31] Just as significantly, the learned professions and the academic community have always been an important part of the European political elite as both the creators and consumers of political ideologies. It is extremely difficult to generalize about their role, because good empirical studies are lacking, but a few remarks can be made.

In pre-modern Europe, intellectuals were part of the social and political establishment, whether clerical or secular, and they came predominantly from the upper classes. Indeed, it is hard to regard them as a distinctive group until the eighteenth century and the French Enlightenment. Associated at first with democratic capitalist revolutions, a significant number of intellectuals, especially those concerned with art and literature, became increasingly alienated from bourgeois society. In fact, attacks upon that society came from both the right and the left, as critics pointed out the contrast between a philistine world ruled by men interested in the rational accumulation of wealth and a world of the past in which esthetic and other values were more important, or of the future in which these would again become more important. On the Continent the alienation of intellectuals in the nineteenth century was accentuated by a university structure which turned out more of them than the society could find employment for—a factor which contributed to many of them assuming an important part in the leadership of revolutionary movements.[32]

The role of intellectuals varied from coun-

---

30 Quoted in George Fischer, ed., *Science and Ideology in the Soviet Union* (New York: Atherton, 1967), pp. 131–132.

31 See S. M. Lipset and M. A. Schwartz, "The Politics of Professionals," in H. M. Vollmer and Donald L. Mills, *Professionalization* (Englewood Cliffs: Prentice-Hall, 1966), pp. 299–309.

32 See Chapter 7 for a fuller discussion of this point.

try to country. In England they tended to be drawn from the upper class and to form a small elite. Reflecting the basic cohesion of English society, they never formed an alienated class, and were politically moderate. In France such a class did exist, and while one finds a substantial segment of intellectuals who continued to long for the ancien régime, the center of gravity was to the left. In a sense intellectuals merely reflected and articulated the tensions of French society, even as they provided the leadership for radical political movements.

A left-wing intelligentsia manifested itself in Germany as well, but there—again reflecting and articulating underlying social tensions —a larger portion of the intellectual community was conservative and nationalist. In both France and Germany, during the early part of the twentieth century, bohemian intellectuals —rejecting the "philistinism," "repression," and "injustices" of bourgeois society—provided some of the initial guidance for both Communist and Fascist movements.

In the decades following the end of World War II, the extreme right has been completely discredited in both countries. In Germany, the academic community and the educated remain, on the whole, fairly conservative, but the activists that do exist are primarily on the left. In France, radical orientations are quite clearly predominant, but a new split has developed between those who represent the social sciences—and therefore tend to be concerned with the effective organization of society—and those who, drawn primarily from the humanities, continue to see Western bourgeois society, as well as that of the Soviet Union, as highly repressive—as communities in which men are inevitably alienated. Another significant development has occurred in France and other countries as higher education has expanded: the democratization of the intellectual class. So many voices are now raised at once, and ideas communicated so rapidly, that men of genius, leaders of a generation—philosophers such as Hegel or Marx—have all but disappeared. Jean-Paul

Sartre, in France, may be the last of his type. Finally, for the time being, intellectuals have lost their old constituency. Their shock troops are found less among the workers than among the middle class, especially university students. In England, these changes have been less pronounced. While there are some signs of a growing intellectual class in the European sense, there are fewer signs of its alienation.

In Russia, large segments of the intelligentsia were completely alienated from the old regime by the end of the nineteenth century, and provided the ideas and some of the leadership for the Bolshevik Revolution. Once the Communist Party came to power, they lost control to more bureaucratic types, and, after a short period of fermentation in the 1920's, intellectual freedom all but disappeared. Intellectuals were placed under rigid political controls, and dissidents permanently silenced. After the death of Stalin, controls were relaxed, within limits, and the party leadership has passed through a number of phases in which a measure of freedom has been followed by a measure of repression.

5. SOME AMERICAN COMPARISONS

Because it was first settled by lower-middle-class Calvinists and stamped with their values, the United States developed neither a gentry nor a peasantry in the European sense. For a considerable portion of American history, much of the agricultural community was not part of a market economy, but the attachment to tradition and consciousness of estate which characterized the European peasant were never present in America. As a market system developed, agriculture was quickly transformed from a calling to a business. Consequently, although there have been tensions between the rural and urban populations (for example, the anti-urbanism of the populist movement), such currents have been minor as compared with those of the German or French scene.

It is not simply that the frontier produced

a "democratic" or "individualistic" mentality; what role the frontier played existed only within the broader framework of Calvinist values. Russia and Argentina also possessed frontiers, but the results of westward or eastward migration in each country were quite different; so, too, the French Canadians, whose thinking was until recently closer to old-regime France than to modern France.

Just as the United States lacked a peasantry like that of Europe, so, too, both American business and the American working class responded quite differently to the process of industrialization than did their European counterparts. Most American businessmen totally accepted the tenets of liberalism: equality of opportunity, laissez faire, democracy, and the minimum state. Entrepreneurs did not aspire to titles and eventual retirement to the life of a gentleman; for them, the goal of building a business was to build a business.

By and large, the aim of the working class in the United States has been only to secure a larger piece of the economic pie; thus, the American businessman has rarely found it necessary to keep that class in its place by supporting authoritarian movements. Self-interest may have led him to oppose trade unions; but he accepted, and in many cases supported, anti-trust legislation to control what he felt to be violations of the free market. By contrast, European businessmen did not consider such legislation to be of any importance until after World War II. Nor, for that matter, did their sharpest critics: Socialists, for example, always felt that concentration, while an inevitable result of capitalism, would help pave the way for the Socialist millennium.

In the twentieth century, business organization and the attitudes of businessmen in the United States have undergone a change. Individualism has given way to "cooperation" with other groups in limiting the effects of "unbridled" competition. In fact, the American economy is no longer a free economy in the classical liberal sense, even though some of the traditional rhetoric is still used to justify opposition to government intervention. Moreover, the development of the large bureaucratic corporation has produced a new breed of manager who is more a professional than an entrepreneur, and whose values embrace both work and—although not in the aristocratic sense—culture.

The working class, too, has generally accepted the "liberal" society. Whatever the realities of social mobility in the United States—and there has been greater mobility than in Europe—a member of the working class has always felt it possible that either he or his son could rise within the system. His lack of class consciousness, and therefore of both deference and hostility, has been remarked upon time and time again by European observers, who have also noted the *relative* similarity of life styles and the *relative* ease of relationships among various social strata. This lack of class consciousness hampered the development of a trade-union movement; when the movement did develop, it took the road of "business" trade unionism, within the general framework of the economic system. In some ways, of course, the competitive and individualistic values that dominated American life for so long have placed a greater burden upon the worker than had to be borne by workers in Europe. Failure to climb the ladder could not be as easily interpreted as the result of the system. One could only blame oneself.

In the United States, as in Europe, automation and professionalization are having their effect upon society; so, too, is America's racial problem. Formal education is now so necessary for climbing the social ladder that the gap between those who succeed and those who fail seems to be widening—despite new educational opportunities for vast segments of the population. Some observers see a danger of the United States becoming a society with a very affluent middle and quasi–middle class, but with a permanently depressed group which, for one reason or another, cannot secure the minimal educational requisites.

As a result of their history in the United States, Negroes have generally constituted an inordinately large portion of this latter group, and the civil-rights movement was ignited, at least in part, by an awareness of this problem.

But at this time it does not seem as if such tensions have resulted in a class cleavage or in ideological politics of the European kind. While a portion of the leadership of the black community has taken a radical political stance, the emphasis on "black power" effectively limits the movement to that community. In fact, there are signs that a part of the white working class has been pushed to the right by Negro militancy.

As in Europe, American professionals in general and intellectuals in particular have usually been somewhat to the left of other social strata with comparable incomes. Until the twentieth century, however, radical intellectual critics of American society, speaking either from the right or from the left, were few in number, and without real influence. On the whole, then, the American intellectual spectrum was far narrower than the European. Searching for a native American radicalism, Communist intellectuals of the 1930's, and today's "new left" as well, have usually been forced to pick as heroes men who were essentially liberal in outlook, albeit populist or Jacobin in their orientation.

Even during the first half of the twentieth century, the number of radical intellectuals in America remained relatively small, and their influence was extremely limited. By and large, both they and their constituency consisted of members of immigrant groups from European countries which had, in the nineteenth century, developed a strong Socialist tradition, such as the Scandinavian countries, or, to a more limited extent, Germany and Italy. Even here, the second generation tended to move in a more conservative direction. The largest number of radical intellectuals were the Jewish immigrants from Eastern Europe—a group whose

radicalism in Europe had been a response to the marginal position its members held in Christian societies; they continued the tradition in the United States.[33]

In fact, because of their concentration in New York, and their participation in the "highbrow" intellectual media and the universities, intellectuals of Jewish background continue to have a vital part in radical politics. During the 1930's, their influence on the larger society remained very limited, but during the 1960's it has grown considerably.[34] This has been the result, in part, of the civil-rights revolution, and in part of the emergence of a large well-educated professional middle class.

However, other factors have been extremely important. Relatively isolated from Europe and the rest of the world until World War II, Americans had a tendency to regard themselves as having created a "new world" whose destiny was very different from that of the old. American involvement in world politics since the war, and the development of almost instantaneous international communications, made at least the well-educated American more aware of the world as a whole. With that, the sense of American exceptionalism has subsided, and Americans have come to realize that their own tradition is but one part of a much larger one.

Also, the growth of the professions has been much faster in the United States than in Europe, and, as in Europe, many members of the professional class lack a vested interest in capitalist institutions. Finally, in a highly affluent society, the traditional busi-

[33] Robert Michels, *Political Parties* (New York: Crowell-Collier, 1962), pp. 238–253; Richard V. Burks, *The Dynamics of Communism in Eastern Europe* (Princeton: Princeton University Press, 1961); Nathan Glazer, *The Social Bases of American Communism* (New York: Harcourt, Brace and World, 1961).

[34] Norman Podhoretz, *Making It* (New York: Random House, 1967); Victor R. Navasky, "Notes on a Cult, or, How to Join the Intellectual Establishment," *New York Times Magazine Section*, March 27, 1966, pp. 28ff.

ness ethic is beginning to erode among middle-class youth, who look increasingly to public-service activities to satisfy their desires for status and achievement. This, too, has begun to diminish the hold of traditional ideology.

Thus, aside from the Negroes, contemporary radicalism in the United States bears little or no relation to a sense of class consciousness or class oppression. It is largely a middle-class, or even an upper-middle-class, phenomenon.

6

Religious

and Ethnic

Groups

1. INTRODUCTION

Religion may be defined as "a set of symbolic forms and acts which relate man to the ultimate conditions of his existence."[1] As such, it seems to be as old as human self-consciousness. In all traditional societies we know of, religion has helped to define the major ingredients of culture and social structure and in maintaining societal cohesion.

The major trend of religious evolution has involved both the differentiation of religious institutions from other kinds and the "demythologization" of the natural world. In the most primitive societies, there was no clear distinction between the sacred and the profane: almost every act contained elements of religious significance. The religious and the secular life of the community were part and parcel of the same set of experiences, and the line between priesthood and laity was vague or nonexistent.

When communities grew more complex that line became more clearly drawn, and a

religious elite did emerge. Almost all major civilizations have experienced at least the beginnings of a distinction between those objects and acts directly associated with religious experience and those which were not. Most of these civilizations were founded on a conception of the profane world, that of the flesh, as representing a lower order of existence than the world of spirit. In its more extreme manifestations, as in some Eastern religions, this devaluation of the natural world approached complete rejection.

The distinction between Christianity and Eastern religions lay not in the differentiaton between religious and profane experience, but rather in the fact that the Christian Church counseled secular action as the road to salvation, and assumed that both sacred and profane experience could be understood through the application of human reason. Moreover, Western Christianity especially distinguished more sharply between religious institutions and political ones, and placed more emphasis upon the individual's personal relation to a transcendent God. The Protestant variant stressed the individual-

[1] Robert N. Bellah, "Religious Evolution," *American Sociological Review,* XXIV (June 1964), 359.

istic component still further, and eventually drew an even more clear-cut distinction between the natural, which was subject to the laws of science, and the sacred, which became an object of faith alone.

Even in those traditional societies in which religious and political institutions were more or less differentiated, the former served as an underpinning and basis of coherence for the latter. Religious institutions had other roles as well: they supported activities which required the inhibition of individual desires in the interest of the larger community, and they sanctified existing authority relations and the system of social stratification. For the individual, religion offered a sense of identity as well as solace for suffering. Thus, religious institutions were vital in insuring that members were socialized into the community—that they were provided with those standards and beliefs necessary for performing the tasks which would enable the society to adapt effectively to its environment.

The influence of Marxist thinking and science's attack on religion have created the impression that religious institutions are inherently conservative. In a world in which scientific advance has been the most dynamic factor in producing social changes (as in Europe since the sixteenth century and the rest of the world since the end of the nineteenth), this would appear to be the case; yet it should again be emphasized that the advance from pre-civilization to civilization occurred under the aegis of "new religions," and that the creation of the scientific world view was intimately related to the emergence of both Catholic and Protestant Christianity.

The secularization of political authority, which occurred first in the West, produced a tension between the religious and the secular which has continued until our time and has resulted, in Western Europe and increasingly all over the world, in the reduction of religious institutions to the status of voluntary associations within the larger framework of the nation state. The simultaneous existence of a number of religious communities in many societies, and the emergence for the first time in the twentieth century of political communities whose avowed intention has been the elimination of religion, have also created new conflicts and problems.

In the European countries we are discussing, religious groups are in practice merely associations of believers, although the role of religion varies in each country. This is not to say that religious institutions are without functional significance: in all Western countries they are important in the socialization process, and even contemporary Russian society cannot be understood aside from the religious heritage which in the past was so integral a part of its culture.

2. THE CATHOLIC CHURCH IN WESTERN EUROPE

By the thirteenth century, the Roman Catholic Church in the West had been transformed from a loosely organized sect of "religious enthusiasts" into a highly institutionalized bureaucratic structure of authority, a complex hierarchy of religious officials whose apex was the pope. The authority of the papacy, by no means absolute, continued to be challenged by those who claimed that ultimate legitimacy lay with general councils of church bishops; yet it was clear, even by that time, that the logic of the structure favored centralization.

By that time, too, the church possessed the highly structured body of religious thought which it has retained, with relatively minor modification, to the present. The practice and thinking of the ordinary communicant may very often have differed considerably from the theological and philosophic pattern of this thought, but it continued to exercise a decisive influence on him.

To the medieval church the universe was the creation of God. Both its structure and its ultimate purpose were determined by His will, and only by accepting the fact of this

TABLE 6.1. RELIGIOUS BELIEF: A THREE-NATION SURVEY

	Per cent of respondents believing in God	Per cent of respondents believing in immortality of the soul
Great Britain	71	53
France	73	36
United States	98	73

Sources: Social Survey (Gallup Poll) Ltd., March 1963; Institut français d'Opinion publique, May 1968; American Institute of Public Opinion, August 1967, June 1968. Reprinted by permission. Data supplied by the Roper Public Opinion Research Center.

determination could one understand the world. Life itself was considered both a testing and a preparation for salvation, which could be achieved only through the Catholic Church (or, at least, was very unlikely to be achieved outside this church). A few men could come to God through knowledge, but for the vast majority the truths of the Catholic Church had to be conveyed through allegory and a symbolism which appealed to the soul; thus the church's role was that of a teacher. Its goal was to control education in the widest sense, including the prohibition of books and other materials that might be harmful to faith.

To the church, the individual, in this life, was to follow his calling—to take his natural place in a community governed by secular leaders whose authority was ultimately derived from God and was justified only if they fulfilled their proper function: the organization of the community so as to achieve the general welfare, and full cooperation with the church to insure a Christian (that is, Catholic) community.

In the sight of God, all men were equal—in fact, a poor man might have an edge on salvation; still, the church taught that inequality in this world was natural and justified, a reflection of man's fall from grace. This justification entailed support of private property, but it did not follow that such property could be used willfully and irresponsibly; the rich were responsible for the poor, and their wealth had to be used in accordance with certain ethical precepts. Thus, employers were required to provide a just wage, and money was not to be lent at interest; the community, in fact, had the right to regulate economic activities in close detail so as to insure that they contributed to its overall welfare.

Within the community, man's natural state was monogamous marriage (except for those who remained celibate in response to a higher calling). Because the institution of marriage was sanctified, neither divorce nor extramarital sexual activity was permitted. The purpose of marriage was procreation; it followed that the artificial limiting of the family violated both divine and natural law.

From the sixteenth century onward, the Catholic Church suffered a series of upheavals. Its secular power as well as its religious authority were weakened by the consolidation of the national state and the Protestant Reformation. Both developments contributed to the emergence in many countries of what were effectively national Catholic churches, dependent upon the monarchy and, consequently, somewhat more socially and politically conservative. Then, in the seventeenth, eighteenth, and nineteenth centuries, an increasingly scientific and secular culture evolved and began to weaken the hold of many traditional religious beliefs by demonstrating their incorrectness (the motion of the sun, the shape of the earth) and by promoting a more rational and a more worldly outlook.

Simultaneously, the growth of liberalism and the development of an industrial society —with its emphasis on free thought, free economic activity, and generally acquisitive economic values—represented an even more devastating attack on basic Catholic assumptions. Nor was this attack limited to the economic and political spheres: the newer concern with the satisfaction of individual wants and needs had its effect upon marriage, divorce, and general sexual morality.

On the whole the Protestant sects managed to adjust to these patterns with reasonable ease. Radical Calvinism had, in fact, been partially responsible for the emergence of the newer outlook, and the radical separation of faith and science which fairly early came to characterize the outlook of many Protestants permitted the ready acceptance of scientific doctrines; discoveries concerning the causal patterns of the natural world could not undermine their faith. Moreover, the lack of a centrally organized authoritarian pattern of control and the frequent fragmentation of Protestantism permitted, and even encouraged, prompt adjustment to newer trends in opinion. The same fragmentation contributed, as well, to an insistence on toleration within Protestant communities and the quick acceptance of, or even pressure for, a separation of secular and religious authority. All these circumstances, of course, were far less true of Lutheran Germany, for reasons which will be dealt with later.

The slower adjustment of the Catholic Church stemmed from reasons which were precisely the obverse. On the whole, it clung to traditional doctrine and the traditional social order. This traditionalism caused liberals in Catholic countries (as opposed, for example, to England and the United States) to be strongly anticlerical, and to identify the Catholic Church with the medieval social order and the encouragement of fantastic superstition. It was, they believed, one of the major obstacles to the true human happiness which could be achieved through science, free trade, and a constitutionally tolerant political order.

The violent anticlericalism of the French Revolution was the result of all these factors and did not, as is often proposed, merely represent resentment of the large landholdings the church possessed; a similar anticlericalism spread, with the ideas of the Revolution, to other Catholic European countries.

The Catholic Church's reaction was to pronounce anathema on liberalism and all that was associated with it. Traditional Catholic thought had regarded democratic institutions as less satisfactory than a mixed constitution that provided for some representation from all social orders and combined monarchical, aristocratic, and democratic principles. Republican governments, however, were considered legitimate provided they respected the rights of the church; hence the ready recognition of the new American republic in the eighteenth century. Still, it remains true that through most of the nineteenth century the Catholic Church identified liberal democracy with "license" and militant atheism, and in almost every European country ranged itself with traditionalist elements. The mutual antagonism between liberal reformers and the church maintained itself, as each group's action confirmed the suspicions of the other; even popes who began as reformers, like Pius IX, ended their careers by reiterating the church's opposition to liberal doctrine. The most famous statement of the church's position in this regard was the encyclical *Quanta Cura* and its attached Syllabus of Errors (1864), which leveled a violent attack upon popular sovereignty, toleration, and the whole liberal conception of freedom of thought.

The church's reaction to liberalism even caused it to forget some traditional doctrine. During the nineteenth century, for example, it condemned trade unionism and social reform almost indiscriminately, associating these movements with anticlericalism and with ideas hostile to Catholicism. In most countries the only groups actively upholding the prerogatives of the Catholic Church were the more privileged strata of the society, for whom it served as a source of support against threats to their status. In such attitudes, of course, the church was rejecting its own traditional social message, or burying the more positive aspects of that message in a barrage of negative and purely defensive criticism.

Leo XIII, whose pontificate followed that of Pius IX in 1878, permitted some adjustments in church doctrine, even as he condemned "modernist" tendencies within the church. He was also prepared to accept democracy as a legitimate form of government under certain circumstances; moreover, he condoned religious toleration under conditions in which its denial would result in significant social evils.

Leo's policies coincided with the beginnings of a decline in anticlericalism among European liberals. In most cases, church and state had become separated, and the real political power of the church effectively reduced; therefore, newer generations of liberals found themselves less and less antagonistic to the Catholic Church, and identified anticlericalism with socialism and later with communism. Then, too, the early liberal faith in science had gradually eroded, and although the result was not necessarily a return to religion, "scientific secularism" lost a good deal of its militancy.

This pattern continued and developed through the first part of the twentieth century, abetted by an increasingly social outlook in the church, as manifested in the encyclicals *Rerum novarum* (1891), *Quadragesimo anno* (1931), and *Mater et Magistra* (1961). In each of these the church lent its support to the legitimacy of working-class organization and pressed for social reform legislation of varying kinds.

During the 1920's and 1930's, the Catholic Church flirted with Fascist and quasi-Fascist movements in several countries, hoping to reach a modus vivendi with them as a defense against communism. This was notably the case in Italy, Germany, and Spain; but in both Italy and Germany the church's fingers were severely burned. Since the war,

the papacy has tended increasingly to identify legitimate government with representative government, although it has refrained from criticizing church leadership in those countries where the church has continued to support authoritarian regimes.

In the meantime pressure had mounted within the Catholic Church for a formal restatement of its attitude toward liberty and toleration, and a fuller acceptance of these values as good in themselves. This pressure came primarily from clergy and laity in France, Germany, England, and the United States, and in parts of Latin America; the Italian and Spanish clergy have retained a more conservative stance. At the same time, as the postwar ecumenical movement grew, Christians became much more aware of the fact that what they had in common was at least as important as the differences among them.

The ferment within the church came to the surface during the short pontificate of John XXIII and has continued under his successor Paul VI. The calling of a second Vatican Council (1962–1965) not only revealed the power of more modern currents of thought and brought about pronouncements liberalizing the views of the church and increasing the power of the bishops, priests, and laity, it also provided psychological support for those within the church who held even more radical views. The Catholic Church today is undergoing a series of rapid changes which seem likely to cause important alterations in its structure and doctrine. It has fully accepted religious freedom; it is accepting, if not encouraging, a more active and questioning role of the laity. Further, it has become open to varieties of modern biblical criticism which accept the method and findings of science and see much of traditional religious doctrine as metaphorically, not literally, true. Indeed, the council implicitly accepted a very non-Thomist view of theology, one which held that religious truth, rather than being fixed, might well evolve as mankind itself evolved. And finally, the church is attempting to identify itself with reform programs for the reduction of economic inequality and the promotion of social welfare.

Strong conservative elements remain within the church, however, as indicated by Paul VI's 1968 encyclical on birth control, which, to the disappointment of many, reaffirmed in even stronger terms the traditional Catholic stand on that issue. Aside from purely doctrinal considerations, the Vatican obviously was becoming more and more concerned with what it considered the precipitous decline of papal authority, as manifested in the formation of "underground" churches in many countries and increasing attacks upon the authority of the bishops and doctrines of clerical celibacy. If, indeed, the encyclical was designed to dampen desires for change, it failed dismally. Negative reactions among both the laity and the clergy were expressed with a stridency scarcely conceivable twenty years earlier. In the long run the pope's attempt to maintain the church's traditional bans on contraception can only reduce his moral authority. Under attack themselves, many bishops, now openly criticizing the Curia for what they consider its refusal to permit free discussion of basic issues in the church, are now demanding a larger voice in its government.

THE FRENCH PATTERN: For some time before the French Revolution, the Catholic Church in France had been in disrepute. Widespread skepticism had appeared among the aristocracy and the *haute bourgeoisie,* and in the minds of reformers the church had become identified with the worst aspects of the old regime—and it did indeed enjoy a privileged position. Its substantial landholdings were free from taxation, its clergy was not subject to regular courts of law, and its drive against heretical doctrines was strongly supported by the state. Yet these close ties worked in both directions. The French monarchy, in turn, exercised considerable authority in determining who would fill various ecclesiastical offices, and significantly influ-

enced church policy in many areas. This mutually advantageous association helps explain why the hostility toward the monarchy on the part of those who led the French Revolution was extended to the church.

Many of the lower clergy were originally sympathetic to the Revolution's aims. But as it took more of an anticlerical turn, their support melted away; on March 10, 1791, the pope condemned the Revolution and all its works. That antagonism hardened and maintained itself throughout the nineteenth century. The church became identified with the more conservative elements in the society, and Jacobin liberals, as well as other radicals, maintained a violent anticlericalism.

Within the church there were always those who urged a reconsideration of its position and the end of its identification with the old regime. The effectiveness of such counsel, however, was limited by the status of the church's supporters, certain aspects of its doctrine, and the nature of its opponents.

In general, the Catholic Church in France was initially hostile to the Third Republic, fearing that it would induce the establishment of a Jacobin state. But the republic's generally conservative stance permitted a modus vivendi between the church and republican principles. The movement of many of the French clergy toward support of the republic was encouraged by Leo XIII, whose encyclical letter *Au Milieu des Sollicitudes* for the first time accepted democratic regimes as legitimate political systems—or, at least, broke with the church's previous preference for monarchy, arguing that the church was neutral with respect to forms of government, provided its own rights were protected.

Unfortunately, shortly after the issuance of the letter, in 1892, the Dreyfus affair polarized the French community; again the church identified itself with anti-republican France over an issue which would never have arisen had it not been for the sheer stupidity of the military elite and the demagoguery of both the extreme right and the Jacobin left.

The aftermath of the Dreyfus affair was

the full separation of church and state, and the end of state support for any church activities whatever. The decrees effecting this separation confiscated substantial amounts of church property, but this impoverishment was counteracted by the fact that the church now became a private organization, with no further governmental regulation of its activities.

In the long run, it can be argued, the separation of church and state in France was a significant step in healing ancient wounds. Since 1905 the religious issue has become less and less important, and the church is less and less associated with the forces of economic and political conservatism.

The church's acceptance of the separation served gradually to diminish anticlerical feeling among democrats, and the unity forged by World War I contributed to increased understanding on both sides. Between the wars, more and more French Catholics found themselves taking rather advanced economic and political positions and asserting that Catholicism was not only compatible with democracy, but demanded it.

The Popular Front and the Spanish Civil War threatened once more to raise the issue of religion versus democracy, but many Catholic intellectuals supported the Loyalist regime in Spain, arguing that the church had brought persecution on itself by its failure to accept reform. Later, the disenchantment of the Catholic Church with fascism tended to unite Frenchmen against dictatorship in general.

The postwar formation of the Popular Republican Movement (*Mouvement républicain populaire*—M.R.P.) as a lay Catholic party of the moderate left, at least initially, and the increasingly liberal and reformist attitudes taken by prominent French Catholics, have resulted in a very significant shift in Catholic orientation. It is still true that there are certain associations of Catholicism with conservatism, and certain tensions between the church and more secular-minded Frenchmen, notably in the area of education,[2] but these areas are becoming more and more marginal. Even as most religiously oriented Catholics have come to accept many aspects of modernity, so the more secular-minded among Frenchmen have lost their sense of hostility toward the church. (See Table 6.2.)

The church, on the other hand, tends to regard France as displaying many characteristics of a missionary country; it continually tries to revitalize French religious life—as, indeed, it does in most other countries with a substantial Catholic population. Thus, it supports organizations which aim to maintain and spread the faith, as well as a wide variety of periodicals whose viewpoint is primarily Catholic. These organizations are more and more often nonpolitical, except for those that are specifically concerned with an issue of

[2] See Chapter 7.

TABLE 6.2. ATTITUDES OF FRENCH CATHOLICS AND
NONBELIEVERS TOWARD EACH OTHER

Percentage of respondents manifesting attitude

	Attitudes of Catholics toward nonbelievers	Attitudes of nonbelievers toward Catholics
Tolerant	30.5%	47.5%
Favorable	32.5	14.3
Hostile	17.4	28.3
Other responses	19.6	9.6

Adapted from *Sondages*, no. 3, 1959, pp. 33, 35. Reprinted by permission of the publisher.

FIGURE 6.1. ATTITUDES TOWARD RELIGION AMONG FRENCH YOUTH, 1959

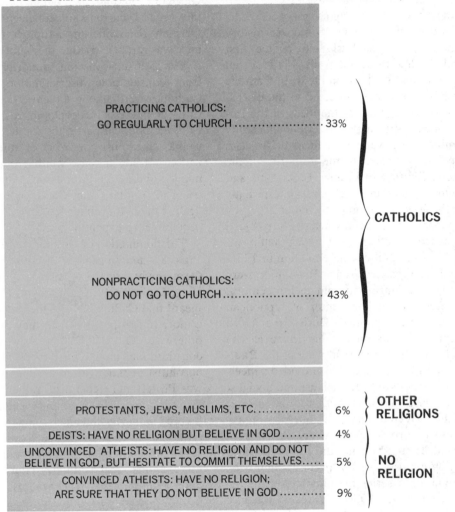

PRACTICING CATHOLICS:
GO REGULARLY TO CHURCH 33%

NONPRACTICING CATHOLICS:
DO NOT GO TO CHURCH 43%

CATHOLICS

PROTESTANTS, JEWS, MUSLIMS, ETC. .... 6%   OTHER RELIGIONS

DEISTS: HAVE NO RELIGION BUT BELIEVE IN GOD 4%

UNCONVINCED ATHEISTS: HAVE NO RELIGION AND DO NOT
BELIEVE IN GOD, BUT HESITATE TO COMMIT THEMSELVES ...... 5%   NO RELIGION

CONVINCED ATHEISTS: HAVE NO RELIGION;
ARE SURE THAT THEY DO NOT BELIEVE IN GOD 9%

Adapted from *Sondages,* no. 3, 1959, p. 65.
Reprinted by permission of the publisher.

crucial importance to the church, such as education.

In the late 1940's and early 1950's there developed a "worker-priest" movement, in which members of the clergy worked side by side with factory workers and lived in working-class areas; the goal was to bring the message of the Catholic Church to the working class. Despite some success, the movement was soon criticized by both the French hierarchy and Rome, primarily because a number of priests had so fully identified with working-class radicalism that they were participating in Communist-organized political demonstrations and in strikes. The movement was never formally disbanded, but it did become moribund under the church's disapproval; its revival with restrictions in late 1965 was an indication of how far the church had traveled in but ten years.

A discussion of the role of the French Catholic Church would not be complete without a brief note on the history of French Freemasonry, whose origins go back to the medieval guilds, although its modern history began with the establishment of the first Grand Lodge in London in 1717. From there it spread to the Continent; in Catholic countries, it became dedicated to the discussion and propagation of the ideas of the Enlightenment. Its members were generally committed to a vaguely defined deism, and tended to be hostile to the authority of the Catholic Church. In France, Protestants and Jansenists joined in large numbers, especially after the condemnation of the latter group by the papacy. The secrecy which surrounded Freemason meetings and membership inspired a papal bull of condemnation in 1738. Many leaders of the French Revolution were Masons, and, during the nineteenth century, the order became the center of republican and anticlerical politics. During the Third Republic, Freemasonry came to be closely linked with the anticlerical wing of the Radical Socialist Party, and later provided a meeting ground for Radical Socialist and Socialist intellectuals. The Communist Party, at first regarding Freemasonry as a bourgeois organization and forbidding party members to join, reversed its stand during the Fourth Republic; Communists joined in large numbers, precipitating a series of splits within the organization. By the 1950's, however, Masonry had shed much of its political and anti-Catholic overtones, and was on the way to becoming the purely fraternal organization which it has been in both England and the United States for the past 150 years.

THE GERMAN PATTERN: German Catholicism developed along lines conditioned both by the general features of German culture and by the fact that until World War II Catholics were a distinct, though sizable, minority in a country dominated by a fairly conservative Protestant establishment.

German Catholics were subject to many of the same philosophic and social influences as German Protestants: the Catholic Church in Germany could not help but be influenced by the general currents of nineteenth-century German Romanticism, although this influence was rarely carried to the point of heresy.

Yet as a self-conscious minority suffering from considerable discrimination, German Catholics were among the earliest to protect Catholic interests by developing a specifically Catholic political party, the Center Party, as well as an extensive network of other organizations—trade unions, youth groups, newspapers, and agricultural associations—which tried to insulate the Catholic community against the blandishments of Protestants and, if possible, to expand its influence.

The domination of Germany by Protestant Prussia—and, in general, of both Prussia and Germany by orientations which were centralizing, Lutheran Protestant, and autocratic—meant that Catholics found themselves taking a more liberal position than they might have otherwise. On the whole, they supported constitutional monarchy rather than a more absolutist regime (after all, the monarchy was Protestant), federalism rather than centralism (a federal regime and local autonomy favored minority interests), and freedom of group activity rather than state-imposed restrictions (freedom for all groups meant, for example, that Catholics could establish and maintain their own schools). German Catholics also were much more aware than Protestants of the necessity for social reform, since they tended to come from the less advantaged portion of the population.

Except for certain groups in Bavaria, most Catholics supported the Weimar Republic, in which the Center Party figured so prominently. With some notable exceptions, both the Catholic Church and the party were hostile to nazism—even though Hitler was a nominal Catholic—believing that its racism and totalitarianism marked it as an essentially anti-Catholic force. Yet the Catholic Church quickly (some say too quickly) accepted the Nazi regime, and attempted to reach an accommodation with it: a concordat with the Vatican promised Catholic acquiescence,

FIGURE 6.2. ROMAN CATHOLIC POPULATION OF WEST GERMANY

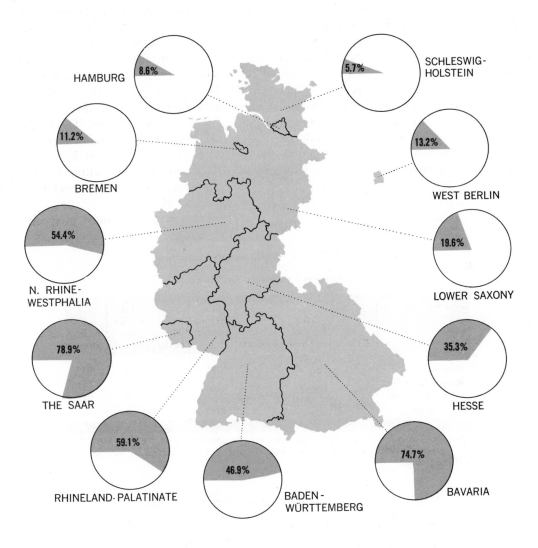

Adapted from *The German Tribune,* April 29, 1967,
p. 4. Reprinted by permission of the publisher.

provided that the church was permitted to continue its own activities. Many in the church, going further, became active partisans of the regime. But after Nazi power was fully consolidated, the government became increasingly oppressive, pushing racist doctrines and interfering with what the church considered to be its prerogatives. Although

German bishops either supported the war or remained silent, the Nazi state and the Catholic Church had become fully estranged by 1939.

After the war, the German religious picture was fundamentally changed. The Nazi regime's repression of Catholics and Protestants alike had brought the two groups closer together, and the growing secularization of postwar German society, as well as changes in the outlook of both Catholics and Protestants, served to reduce their militancy and their mutual suspiciousness. Further, while Catholics had constituted only about one-third of the population of prewar Germany, they made up approximately 49 per cent of the population of the German Federal Republic. In fact, they actually constitute a majority of those who attend church. It should be added, however, that social mobility is still somewhat lower among Catholics than among Protestants, so that the latter make up a larger segment of the urban elite. (See Tables 6.3 and 6.4.)

Perhaps the most significant sign of the increasing accommodation between Catholics and Protestants was the replacement of the old Catholic Center Party by the Christian Democratic Union and its Bavarian affiliate, the Christian Social Union (*Christlich Demokratische Union/Christlich Soziale Union*— C.D.U./C.S.U.), whose specific aim is to transcend denominational lines and unite Christians of all persuasions. The C.D.U. is now the leading German political party, and while the bulk of its support is Catholic, it still draws upon elements within the Protestant community, to which it is careful to allot leadership positions.

There still remains interest in specifically

TABLE 6.3.   RELIGIOUS AFFILIATION OF GERMAN ELITES

Figures in rounded-out percentages

	Politics	Public administration	Business	Non-business associations	Mass media	University professors	All elites
Protestant	45	47	58	33	60	68	50
Roman Catholic	42	27	19	30	21	14	28
Other and none	6	0	14	23	9	14	10
No answer	8	27	8	15	10	5	13

Source: Lewis J. Edinger, *Politics in Germany* (Boston: Little, Brown, 1968), p. 181. Copyright © 1968 by Little, Brown and Company, Inc. Adapted by permission of the publisher.

TABLE 6.4.   RELIGION AND YOUTH: GERMANY

Students in the Federal Republic for school year 1957–1958, classified according to religion

	Catholic	Protestant	Other
General education schools	45.6%	52.8%	1.6%
Primary schools	48.6	50.4	1.4
Schools for backward children	45.1	53.4	1.5
Mittelschule (intermediate schools)	33.1	64.8	2.1
Grammar schools	39.8	58.0	2.2
Vocational training schools	46.7	51.8	1.5
Teacher training colleges	45.7	52.7	1.6
Universities (nonpedagogical only)	37.3	58.7	4.0

Adapted from F. Groner, "The Social Standing of Catholics in the Federal Republic of Germany," *Social Compass*, IX, 5, 6 (1962), p. 547. Reprinted by permission of the publisher and the author.

Catholic organizations in Germany: church-supported newspapers, periodicals, and youth and working-class groups all attempt to preserve and enhance the Catholic faith. The church has also continued to press for state-supported denominational schools, which segregated Catholic and Protestant children; but Catholics themselves are divided on this issue, with at least one-half preferring mixed schools with separate classes for religious instruction. Whatever the intent in specifically Catholic organizations, there are also signs that church attendance and religious belief are dropping off at an alarming rate among the young, especially those living in urban areas and those who are better educated.

In the early years of the new republic, the church actively supported the C.D.U., and bishops urged Catholics to vote for Christian candidates, instead of the materialistic atheistic Socialists; even so, some 26 per cent of Catholic voters (usually the less religious) supported the Social Democratic Party (*Sozialdemokratische Partei Deutschlands*— S.P.D.). Since 1955, however, the political partisanship of the Catholic Church has considerably declined, partly because of the changes within the S.P.D. itself. In an attempt to attract more "left-wing" Catholics, the party has substituted for its Marxist ideology a broad philosophy of social reform which can cite John XXIII's *Mater et Magistra* in support of its position; it has also retreated from its insistence upon secular or interdenominational schools, and now accepts the existence of communal schools where the parents desire them. At the same time, the German Catholic establishment has moved haltingly in the direction of greater liberalism, even in Bavaria.

THE ENGLISH PATTERN: By the end of the seventeenth century, Catholics in England were a small minority subject to laws which, in effect, made them second-class citizens. Such legal disabilities were not fully eliminated until the nineteenth century, although the laws were rarely enforced with any vigor.

Until the mid-nineteenth century, the Catholic Church in England remained very small. Most Catholics were from old aristocratic families that had retained the faith, although there was a steady but small stream of converts. The great Irish migration changed all this; although many Irish lost their faith within a short time after their arrival, enough of them retained it to swell the Catholic population. Separated by both ethnic and religious differences, Irish Catholics in England formed tightly knit working-class communities; as in other Protestant countries, they tended to insulate themselves against the dangers of Protestantism by developing a wide variety of social groups and specifically Catholic channels of communication. But whether because their numbers remain small—only ten per cent of the population—or because of the peculiarities of the English environment, these groups have never proliferated as they did in Germany.

Catholic voting behavior in England has usually followed class lines rather than religious ones, although the workers of Irish background both support the Labor Party in relatively larger numbers than Protestant workers and are rather more conservative and authoritarian than Protestants of a comparable socioeconomic background. Nor has the Catholic Church in England ever become identified with a particular political outlook, although it has always pressed for acceptance of its views on education, birth control, and divorce. English Catholic intellectuals have developed a reputation for representing a more uniformly "liberal" attitude within the church than their counterparts in almost any other country; during a good part of the nineteenth and twentieth centuries, in fact, their main function seemed to be that of explaining to other Englishmen that the papacy was not nearly so conservative as it appeared to be.

3. PROTESTANTISM IN WESTERN EUROPE

The Protestant Reformation in Europe took many forms, depending upon accidental factors as well as the national tradition within which it developed. In Prussia and other German principalities, Lutheranism emerged as the dominant religion and became a state church, exalting established hierarchical authority. Its authoritarian characteristics were as much German as Lutheran, as its development in the Scandinavian countries indicates. In France, where Protestants were reduced to a small minority, Calvinism predominated. In England, the Anglican Church became the state church—a peculiarly English institution which after some evolution represented an uneasy compromise between a national Catholicism and the more radical Protestant churches. Among the latter, the Calvinist orientation quickly became uppermost, although it rapidly fragmented into such sects as the Presbyterian, Congregationalist, Baptist, and Quaker.

The more radical Protestant groups emphasized the personal relationship between the individual and God, which considerably curtailed clerical mediation; personal asceticism; the rational organization of one's workaday life; and the dichotomy between faith and reason. The absence of central authority meant, of course, that each Protestant church adapted itself more readily to the general culture of its society.

All these factors accelerated the secularization of Protestantism and allowed it to adjust more readily than did Catholicism to changing social conditions. On the whole, Protestants were far more receptive to—and, in fact, were partially responsible for—the new orientations produced by a technical scientific culture. With some exceptions, the concern of Protestants with specific theological dogma and ritual faded more quickly than that of Catholics, as comparative figures on church attendance verify.

Within Protestantism, too, searching analyses and criticisms of the Bible, and of revealed religion in general, proceeded apace. By the mid-twentieth century, traditional Protestant positions, including the belief in a personal God standing apart from nature,

were giving way to a conception of religion as one among many ways by which man tries to answer the ultimate personal and moral questions about his existence. The line between Protestantism and secular humanism is becoming increasingly blurred.[3]

THE ENGLISH PATTERN: The seed of Anglican tradition in English Protestantism was sown in a political conflict between the English monarchy and the papacy. From a theological point of view, therefore, the initial phases of the Reformation in England were relatively unimportant. Henry VIII became "the only supreme head on Earth of the Church of England," but the essentials of the medieval synthesis remained untouched. Events after Henry's death gave the church a somewhat more "Protestant" cast—a cast confirmed in the religious settlement developed by Elizabeth I. Elizabeth's aim, in which she largely succeeded, was to establish a broadly based Protestant church which stressed common ritual but permitted considerable theological flexibility. Despite shifts in emphasis, this has remained the general tone of the Church of England up to the present.

Simultaneously, Continental Protestantism began to have an impact upon the English scene, first in its Lutheran and then, more importantly, in its Calvinist formulation. The rise of the "radicals"—Protestant sects such as Presbyterians, Congregationalists, and Baptists—and the attempt by the Stuarts to restrain their influence were important factors leading to the English Civil War and the temporary ascendancy of a radical Protestant establishment.

The Calvinist Revolution, however, failed to consolidate its gains. After a period of repression during the Restoration, the "Glorious Revolution" of 1689 ushered in a settle-

[3] For a discussion of some current trends in Protestant theology see William Hordern, *New Directions in Theology Today* (Philadelphia: Westminster, 1968). For an argument that these trends presage new forms of religious sensibility, see Robert N. Bellah, "Religious Evolution," *American Sociological Review,* 29 (June 1964), pp. 358–374.

ment paving the way for a religiously plural-istic society marked by relative toleration and confessional neutrality on the part of the state. Legally, the Church of England was still the national church; in actuality, it was little more than the largest. It would continue for a long time to possess privileges, but it had as competitors other legal, self-governing, self-maintained free churches. By the 1820's, most legal restrictions upon even the dis-senters had been removed. The more radical Protestant groups had a decisive influence upon the development of both democracy and capitalism in England. Methodism, particu-larly, contributed to social stability during the nineteenth century. Although at first Method-ism tended to turn the working-class elite from political to religious activity, by the end of the nineteenth century it was providing a significant impetus for social reform; many of its adherents became leaders of the trade unions, and of the Labor party as well. The evangelical quality of British socialism can be understood only by recognizing that many of its early leaders began their careers as Methodist lay preachers.[4]

The Church of England is still officially the established church; the monarch is its head, and its representatives sit in the House of Lords. The highest members of the clergy are nominated by the queen, acting on the

[4] See Robert F. Wearmouth, *The Social and Political Influence of Methodism in the Twentieth Century* (Lon-don: The Epworth Press, 1957).

advice of her prime minister, and the creed of the Church of England is established by, and can only be changed by, Parliament. Except in the field of education, where other relig-ious groups also receive assistance, the church is not subsidized by the state, and it is largely self-governing—despite Parlia-ment's prerogatives on creed. Here, in fact, attempts by the church to secure changes in the prayer book have been defeated, with the aid of votes of Nonconformists.

As might be expected, members of the Church of England are, today, more likely to vote Conservative than are members of the Noncomformist groups, although these voting patterns largely reflect class differences. (See Table 6.5.) The nonreligious, however, whatever their class background, usually vote for the Labor Party.

Since the turn of the century, church mem-bership and church attendance in England for all Protestant denominations have steadily declined. Only 53 of every hundred English-men baptized their children in the Church of England in 1962, compared with 69 per cent in 1910. A 1950 survey showed that 51 per cent of the population regarded them-selves as members of the Church of England, while 23 per cent considered themselves Nonconformists; but the percentage of Easter Day communicants in the Anglican Church had dropped from 9.3 per cent of the popula-tion in 1900 to six per cent in 1962. More important, while thirty per cent of the chil-

TABLE 6.5. WORKING-CLASS VOTING BY RELIGION: ENGLAND

	Total adherents	Conservative	Labor	Other
Church of England	64%	32%	55%	13%
Church of Scotland	7	29	64	7
Nonconformist	10	29	49	22
Roman Catholic	10	17	73	10
Other	4	30	46	24
None	5	24	49	27

Adapted from Richard Rose, "Class and Party Divisions: Britain as a Test Case," *Sociology*, 2 (May 1968), p. 140. Reprinted by permission of the publisher and the author.

dren attended Anglican Sunday schools in 1900, less than 14 per cent did so in 1960. Parallel with these trends, the number of ordained ministers in the Church of England fell from 23,670 in 1905 (when they were serving a population of 34 million) to about 19,000 in 1961 (serving a population of about 44 million).[5]

How does the Englishman compare with his American counterpart in terms of church attendance and religious belief? Between ten and 15 per cent of the English population attends church at least once a week; the figure in the United States is about 45 per cent. Seventy-one per cent of Englishmen believe in God, far less than the American percentage of 98; only 53 per cent of the English, as compared with about 73 per cent of those Americans polled, believe in an afterlife.[6] Concern with these developments has prompted the Protestant denominations to seek some basis for greater cooperation; in England this has been especially true among Anglicans and Methodists. A proposal to take the first step toward merging the two churches was narrowly defeated in the Anglican Church in 1969, after winning approval from the Methodists. Even so, the trend is certainly toward greater collaboration.

At the same time, all Protestant denominations are attempting not only to bring the laity more fully into church activities, but to grapple more realistically with the everyday problems of the modern world. This has meant that more members of the clergy are involved in liberal social movements and that some traditional church practices are being dropped. And this, in turn, has meant that

[5] Data from Bryan R. Wilson, *Religion in a Secular Society* (London: C. A. Watts & Co., 1966), pp. 1–18, 77; David Martin, *A Sociological Yearbook of Religion in Britain* (London: SCM Press Ltd., 1968), pp. 146–197; Charles Y. Glock and Rodney Stark, *Christian Beliefs and Anti-Semitism* (New York: Harper & Row, 1966), pp. 5, 12.

[6] See Michael Argyle, *Religious Behavior* (London: Routledge and Kegan Paul, 1958), p. 35, and Wilson, *Religion in a Secular Society*, pp. 2, 87.

the churches, particularly the Anglican Church, are caught in a dilemma. For most of their remaining constituency, it is the tradition of the church and individual salvation that are the most important sources of loyalty; a church that becomes too modern and too activist can only face the fact that it is bound to lose some of its support. All in all, it seems unlikely that the decline of religion in England will be reversed in the immediate future.

THE FRENCH PATTERN: The revocation of the Edict of Nantes in 1685 was a devastating blow to the French Protestant community: in its immediate aftermath, thousands of Protestants either abjured the faith or fled from the country. It is estimated that during the reign of Louis XIV, 250,000 Protestants (Huguenots) left France, primarily for Holland, Germany, and England. While French Calvinism had obtained considerable support among the rural population, it had also drawn to it a significant proportion of the urban aristocracy and bourgeoisie. It was this group that suffered most and emigrated in the largest numbers, depriving France of many individuals who had contributed to its economic growth and scientific achievement.

By the time persecution eased, the face of Protestant France had radically altered. Except for Alsace, where relations between France and Prussia permitted the Lutheran community to escape the brunt of the repression, the remnants of the French Protestant community consisted largely of peasants and the rural petite bourgeoisie. This erosion of Protestant ranks reached its culmination during the French Revolution and its aftermath: increasing numbers of the remaining aristocratic Huguenot families, reacting to the excesses of the Revolution, returned to the Catholic faith. In fact, by the time of the Revolution of 1848 the old Protestant nobility had all but disappeared.

Throughout the nineteenth century, legal discrimination against Protestants gradually diminished, and by 1905, when church and

MAP 6.1. PROTESTANT STRONGHOLDS IN FRANCE, 1965

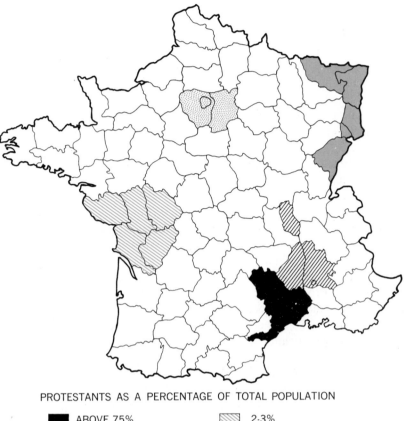

PROTESTANTS AS A PERCENTAGE OF TOTAL POPULATION

■ ABOVE 75%		⊠ 2-3%	
⧄ 35-40%		⊡ 0.1-1%	
▨ 10-12%		☐ LESS THAN 0.1%	

Adapted from A. Coutrot and F. Dreyfus, *Les Forces religieuses dans la société française* (Paris: Armand Colin, 1965), p. 112. Reprinted by permission of the publisher.

state were separated, French Protestants were free to worship as they chose. In the meantime, Protestants began to leave the countryside with greater frequency to enter industry, the professions, and politics; in all three fields, they came to exercise an influence beyond their numbers. Today Protestants are scattered throughout the country, although they tend to be concentrated in specific areas. (See Map 6.1.) Of the approximately eight hundred thousand Protes-

tants—1.6 per cent of the French population —more than five hundred thousand are urban dwellers. In rural areas, their class position does not differ markedly from that of their neighbors; in urban areas, however, their status is mostly middle class.[7]

Throughout most of the nineteenth century, Protestants as a whole identified with

[7] See A. Coutrot and F. Dreyfus, *Les Forces religieuses dans la société française* (Paris: Librairie Armand Colin, 1965), p. 114.

the left, partly because they believed that a "laic" republic would be more inclined to protect their interests than one dominated or supported by the Catholic Church. This pattern has continued to the present (see Table 6.6), with Protestants giving a larger portion of their votes to the Socialist and Communist parties than do practicing Catholics of similar economic and class background. The exceptions are the Lutherans of Alsace, who have remained more conservative.

THE GERMAN PATTERN: The religious wars of the seventeenth century not only inhibited the forging of German unity, they virtually halved the population, which dropped from 20 million to 12 million, of the lands which were later to make up the German nation. The effect of the wars, together with the establishment of Lutheranism as a state religion, gave to German Protestantism a conservative political character which continued into the twentieth century. To the orthodox, the existence of original sin meant that while it might be possible for the individual, through grace, to live according to the ethics of love, the world would continue to be ruled by force. It was impossible to establish the kingdom of God in this world, and order—constantly threatened by chaos and anarchy—could be imposed only by a strong government. Consequently, obedience to established

authority must be enjoined even if the government should abuse its power and become a tyranny. Further, since life on earth had little significance, the true Christian concerned himself with spiritual rather than worldly matters.

The support these views gave to a traditionalist authoritarian regime is obvious. The clearest evidence of this was found in Brandenburg-Prussia, where the church became a cog in the state bureaucracy. By the end of the eighteenth century, Lutheran ministers had been made responsible for vital statistics, schools, and poor relief, and the pulpit was used by the state for all announcements concerning taxes, public health, and roads. All ecclesiastical—and, incidentally, academic—appointments were closely regulated by state authorities. It is little wonder, then, that when political liberalism emerged in Germany, it grew out of the rationalism of the French Enlightenment and tended to be quite anticlerical, despite the development of some liberal currents within the Lutheran Church itself.

The political unification of Germany after 1870 did not result in ecclesiastical consolidation. The territorial churches in the several states retained their separate administrations, although Prussia dominated the structure of both the church and the empire. During the period of the empire, the Lutheran churches

TABLE 6.6. PROTESTANT AND CATHOLIC VOTING IN FRANCE, 1967

	Catholics			Protestants and other	No religion
	Practicing	Occasional	Non-practicing		
Communist	1%	7%	23%	8%	32%
Socialist	7	13	19	13	22
Radical	1	6	6	5	5
M.R.P.	13	6	4	6	2
U.N.R.–U.D.T.	35	25	19	25	9
Independent-Giscard	10	9	6	12	3
Independent-Pinay	10	9	4	12	2
No response	23	25	19	19	25

Source: *Sondages*, no. 2, 1967, p. 25. Reprinted by permission.

began to grapple with the social questions brought on by industrialization and developed a highly advanced philanthropic and social-welfare program. Basically, however, empire and church remained committed to a conservative social ethic. At the same time, German Protestants made some of the most significant contributions to theological speculation in general, and biblical criticism in particular; German theological faculties drew students from all over the world.

Under the Weimar Republic, the church was partially disestablished. Full religious freedom was declared, and the state was deprived of the right to name ecclesiastical officers. No teacher was henceforth required to give instruction in religion, and no student compelled to submit to it. Yet except in secular schools, religious instruction continued. The theological faculties of the universities were maintained by state aid, and the tax for support of the church was continued —although any individual could declare himself unwilling to pay it.

The Weimar period was marked by increased liberal ferment within the Lutheran Church; even so, most of the clergy remained hostile to the republic and many supported the Nazi movement, a position that helped account for the growing alienation of both the working and the professional classes—as well as the youth—from traditional religious institutions.

Shortly before the Nazis came to power, they organized a "German Christian" group within the Lutheran (Evangelical) Church, designed to "purify" Christianity of its Judaic influences and dedicate it to recapturing the essential elements of the "German soul" by stressing heroic instead of humble virtues. These purposes were relentlessly pursued during the whole period of Nazi rule, and thousands of clerics were deprived of their congregations or dismissed in the policy conflicts that ensued. Nevertheless, the effort came to naught even though the great bulk of Protestant ministers either remained silent or supported the regime, especially during the war years.

After the surrender of Nazi Germany in 1945, leading Protestant dignitaries met at Treysa in Hesse and embarked upon a soul-searching evaluation of the church's role both before and during the Nazi regime. The conference, dominated by the men who had most actively resisted National Socialism, concluded that the church had erred fundamentally in believing that the only duty owed the state was obedience. In the future, the churches must foster among the faithful a sense of civic responsibility and an awareness of the realities of political and social life. The conference re-established the loose federal church structure which had been destroyed by the Nazi regime.[8] It also changed the church's name from the Evangelical German Church to the Evangelical Church in Germany—thus emphasizing not its uniquely German quality but its relation to world Protestantism as a whole.

In an effort to fulfill civic responsibilities, the church set up a series of "evangelical academies" to deal with social problems. A lay movement, known as the *Kirchentag,* also was initiated to encourage a more active role by the laity in church affairs. Neither program has been as effective as was originally hoped, but both indicate a fundamental reorientation in church thinking, and the academics have been a liberalizing force within the church.

There is no sign, either, of a mass return to the church by those who have left. The trend toward secularization is continuing. Despite the fact that there is a slightly greater number of Protestants than Catholics in West Germany, about eleven million Catholics attend church on Sunday as compared with about two million Protestants. No more than ten per cent of the Protestants in urban areas attend church "regularly," according to public-opinion polls.

8 Under the German Federal Republic, the policy of "partial disestablishment" set by the Weimar regime was reinstituted. There are, incidentally, other Protestant denominations besides the Evangelical in Germany, but these represent no more than one per cent of the population.

In 1945, the majority of leading Protestant theologians opposed the formation of a specifically "Christian" political party; however, the Treysa Conference left the question open, and a number of prominent Protestant clergymen supported the creation of the Christian Democratic Union. Others have been active in the Social Democratic Party and the Free Democratic Party. The C.D.U. has had an appeal for middle-class German Protestants, both because of their general conservatism and because they regard it, to a greater extent than the clergy, as a party of "Christian reconciliation."

Most Protestant clergymen are fairly conservative in social matters, partly because they espouse an ideology that still tends to counsel noninterference in political matters and partly because Protestantism lacks a strongly articulated central hierarchy; both factors, of course, work against their taking stands on most public issues. Their caution on matters of foreign policy is heightened by a desire to maintain contacts with the church in East Germany, which has been under considerable pressure from the Communists. The few stands taken by the church as a group on foreign policy have commanded wide attention in Germany. In March 1966, for example, the governing church synod endorsed a policy of more flexibility in dealing with East European Communist countries. Its action undoubtedly contributed to making such a position more respectable and was partly responsible for movements toward accommodation with East European regimes by the Bonn government. This move notwithstanding, the East German regime in 1969 effectively cut off the last formal institutional contacts between East and West German Protestants.

4. THE ORTHODOX CHURCH IN RUSSIA AND THE SOVIET UNION

The Russian Empire before World War I contained within it almost as many religious groups as ethnic, and religion and ethnicity were closely associated. The Great Russians, the Ukrainians, and the Byelorussians were primarily Orthodox in faith, although the Ukraine and Byelorussia also had many Uniates[9] and Roman Catholics. The Lithuanians were predominantly Catholic, although a sizable minority were Lutherans or Calvinists. Various Muslim sects were represented by Uzbeks, Kazakhs, and Turks, and both Confucianism and Buddhism prevailed in areas of Asian Russia. The present discussion deals primarily with the Russian Orthodox Church; attention is given other religious groups in the section on ethnic and race relations.

In A.D. 990 Vladimir, the ruler of Kievan Rus, returned to Kiev with his bride, the sister of the Byzantine emperor, and ordered the mass conversion of his subjects to the Orthodox faith. Bishoprics were established shortly thereafter in all the major centers of Rus, and in 1037 the first metropolitan[10] arrived from Constantinople to head the new Russian branch of the Greek Orthodox Church.

If the influence of Christianity in medieval Russia on the mass of the population is open to question, there is none about its impact on "high culture." Russian architecture was profoundly affected by Byzantine models, canon law provided an early channel for the penetration of Roman legal concepts, and education was dominated by the church. Unlike the ecclesiastical situation in the West, the church was completely controlled by secular authority, of which it was an arm—thereby initiating a caesaropapism unknown in Western Europe. Yet the church, and Kievan Russia in general, did not share Byzantium's hostility toward Roman Catholicism, and until the Tartar conquest considerable economic and cultural exchange between

[9] Communions that, although originally deriving from Eastern Orthodox churches and still retaining the Byzantine rite and usages, accepted the supremacy of the papacy and most of the doctrines of the Catholic Church.

[10] Roughly equivalent to an archbishop in the Catholic Church.

Orthodox Russia and the Catholic West was maintained.

Important cultural differences did emerge, nevertheless. Kievan Russia knew no chivalry, no crusades, and, most important, little philosophic or scientific inquiry. From the beginning, the Russian church was extremely weak in theological and philosophic creativeness.

The Tartar hordes that held sway over the Russian steppes for almost two centuries were predominantly Muslim; despite their considerable tolerance of Christianity, the liberation of Russia from their yoke took on the qualities of a religious war. Constant conflict with Polish and Lithuanian Catholics in the West also served to develop a sense of national religious identity, a process completed by the fall of Constantinople in 1453. Thereafter, the metropolitan of the church would be a Russian. The church, moreover, retained its traditional sense of having a universal mission: to many of the Orthodox, Russia became the "third Rome," destined to save the world; Rome had fallen to the barbarians and Byzantium to the Muslims, but Moscow, it was believed, would remain the eternal repository of Christian truths.

The rise of the Muscovite princes and the "nationalization" of the church completed—not without some resistance—the subordination of religious to secular authority. Ivan the Great deprived many monasteries of their lands, and other czars followed his policy; by 1764, all church lands had been secularized and brought under state control. Henceforth, the state would keep most of the revenues from these lands and dole out the residue to the clergy. In effect, the church had become a department of the state by the eighteenth century.

In the meantime, a schism had developed within Orthodoxy between the religious establishment and the "Old Believers." Patriarch Nikon had attempted to reform church liturgy in the seventeenth century by returning to traditional Byzantine and Greek practices. Although he was deposed at the behest of the czar by an ecumenical council meeting in 1667, because of his claims of the superiority of religious authority over secular, the council and the government endorsed and enforced his reforms. The changes alienated large portions of the Orthodox community and gave rise to various sects that came to regard all state power as evil; many associated the reforms with the coming of the "Antichrist." The messianic nihilism with which these Old Believers identified is thought, by many scholars, to have had a significant effect upon the social and political viewpoint of the nineteenth-century revolutionaries. Considerable repression notwithstanding, the sects continued to exist—often underground—and by the time of the Russian Revolution of 1917 they claimed the allegiance of twenty to 25 million Russians.

The church's subordination to state authority and its association with reactionary forces meant that reform and anticlericalism went hand in hand—as they did in Catholic countries of the European West. And although currents of reform appeared during the last years of the Romanov regime, they failed to achieve anything: the collapse of the dynasty brought down the church as well.

The policy of Kerensky's provisional government toward religion fell into line with the liberal and constitutional ideology which it accepted—namely, the separation of church and state. In July 1917, full religious liberty was granted for the first time in Russia; the government also encouraged and financed the convocation of a council (*sobor*) to allow the church to reorganize itself. The sobor, however, was controlled by the more conservative elements of the church; while they accepted the need for some changes, they balked at the proposals of the regime, deeming them too radical. In fact, many hoped for a counterrevolution and the restoration of the monarchy. Nevertheless, reforms were instituted which, had the provisional government survived, might have led to a democratization of the church's structure and the full separation of church and state. But changes within the church came to naught, and even as the council was meeting the provisional government was overthrown by the Bolsheviks.

To Marx, religious faith was an opiate which had the allegiance of the masses because of the wretchedness of their condition; with the coming of communism, religion would automatically lose its appeal and disappear. This view was shared by most of the new Soviet elite. Logically, then, Soviet policy, while engaging in anti-religious propaganda, could have removed certain restrictions upon religious activity and permitted the relatively free exercise of religion as a private institution. Indeed, at least some statements of Lenin indicate that this was partially his view. Such a policy would indeed have involved serious conflicts with the faithful, as well as some repression, but it might have permitted a modus vivendi with the church in a reasonable time.

But within the Communist Party there existed an emotional antagonism to the church and a desire to create the political millennium immediately. This attitude, strongest among the militants and many of the Communist leaders, led to radical policies that accentuated the division between party and church. As repressive actions convinced the faithful that the party represented the "Antichrist," so resistance mounted; and as resistance mounted, so the militants became more determined that the church must be destroyed if communism was to be achieved. The first years of the Bolshevik regime, therefore, were marked by repression, violence, and bloodshed.

In January 1918 the regime nationalized all land, including that of the church, and established civil marriage. Religious instruction was forbidden in private as well as secular schools. (In 1922 it became a crime to teach religion to minors.) At the same time, all state salaries were withdrawn from the clergy, the church was given one month to organize a system of voluntary financing, and

all church buildings were confiscated. These buildings might still be used by the church, but permission to do so became increasingly difficult to obtain. Meanwhile, church buildings were desecrated by militants, and hundreds of priests were arrested or killed. Tikhon, the newly elected patriarch of the church,[11] denounced the Revolution and its consequences as "satanic." Placed immediately under house arrest, he issued statements denouncing the signing of the Treaty of Brest-Litovsk and the assassination of the royal family. The government responded by closing more and more churches.

By the end of 1919, it was obvious that the Bolshevik regime was consolidating its power. Tikhon and other church leaders slowly came to the view that the church should withdraw completely from politics and accept the new regime as a fait accompli in the hope of winning concessions. To that end he refused to give any support, verbal or otherwise, to the opponents of the government. Many leading prelates, however, went into exile and continued their attacks upon the regime—attacks from which Tikhon disassociated himself.

Despite Tikhon's efforts at conciliation, tension between the church and the party persisted. During the 1921 famine, for example, the government seized church valuables. Although the regime attempted to distinguish between "consecrated" and "nonconsecrated" objects, Tikhon attacked these policies and widespread riots by the faithful occurred. Again thousands were arrested and executed, and the party began to encourage a "progressive" religious group which would support its goals. Finally, in 1923, a compromise was achieved. The party, partly because of the progressives' lack of success, was anxious to reduce tensions, and Tikhon, still under house arrest, was willing to accept the authority of the regime. The government dropped its support of the progressives and

---

11 The patriarchate had been abolished by Peter the Great in 1721, but the provisional government had permitted its re-establishment.

released Tikhon, who gave his unconditional support to the Communists and "confessed" his previous sins:

Having been nurtured in a monarchist society, and until my arrest having been under the influence of anti-Soviet individuals, I was filled with hostility against the Soviet authorities.

. . . Acknowledging the correctness of the accusations of the Supreme Court and its sentence as conforming to the clauses of the criminal code, I repent of all my actions directed against the government and petition the Supreme Court to change its sentence and to set me free.

I declare hereby to the Soviet authorities that henceforth I am no more an enemy to the Soviet Government and that I have completely and resolutely severed all connections with the foreign and domestic monarchists and the counter-revolutionary activity of the White Guards.[12]

Tikhon's successor in 1925, the metropolitan Sergius Starogorodsky, proved even more tractable, urging those who had gone abroad to cease their attacks upon the regime. Thus, despite sporadic acts of violence and an expansion of anti-religious propaganda, the period from 1923 to 1928 was one in which an uneasy truce existed between the church and the Soviet state. However, as the N.E.P. period ended and collectivization began, a new wave of militancy swept the country and attacks were renewed upon all religious institutions.

In 1928, the constitution of the Russian Soviet Federal Republic was changed; while freedom of religious confession was granted to believers, freedom of religious propaganda was granted only to anti-religious organizations and citizens. Religious teaching was thus restricted to purely liturgical activities. As the pace of collectivization increased, so, too, did the regime's attacks upon priests; thousands were imprisoned or executed and, as "nonworkers," could not obtain food cards during the famine. Systematic anti-religious education was introduced in the schools, and the League of Militant Atheists broadened its activities. In 1929, league membership stood at 465,000, according to official Soviet figures; by 1932 it numbered more than five million, and three years later its chairman, Yemelyan Yaroslavski, announced that the anti-religious campaign had been so successful that, in fact, religion was dead in the Soviet Union.

Yaroslavski was not only guilty of hyperbole, he was out of step with the times: the campaign against religion had begun to subside. The change in official policy stemmed, in part, from the same forces which were leading to the renewal of traditional symbols in Soviet life. Although there was a flurry of arrests during the great purge trials, in the next few years the Communist regime moved toward accommodation with the church. Sunday was restored as a day of rest, many anti-religious museums were closed down, and, in 1941, anti-religious publications were shut down because of the "paper shortage."

Accommodation reached its highest level during and immediately after World War II. An open Easter celebration was held in Moscow in 1943; a national sobor was permitted to meet to consider questions of doctrine and organization, and a government department, attached to the Council of Ministers, was created to deal with church affairs. In return, the church contributed to the war effort by raising money, bestowing its blessing on the regime, and arguing, in external propaganda, that full freedom of religion existed in the Soviet Union. During the postwar period this pattern continued. Anti-religious propaganda became less blatant, and the church was authorized to open new schools for the training of clergy. It also continued to support the regime and used its influence upon Orthodox churches outside Russia to create more favorable attitudes toward the homeland.

---

12 Quoted by Matthew Spinka in *The Church in Soviet Russia* (New York: Oxford University Press, 1956), p. 38.

In the mid-1950's, Western observers in the Soviet Union reported that a religious revival was taking place—at least more young people were attending church and baptizing their children. The party and state indirectly confirmed this view in 1954 with a new series of anti-religious campaigns that have continued, with some shifts, until the present. The party claimed it was concerned with "waverers" who did not correctly perceive the incompatibility of science and religion. Since 1958 many churches and seminaries have beeen closed. Young people have been actively discouraged from entering the clergy, and many priests have been arrested and sent to labor camps or mental institutions without benefit of trial. In 1961, under pressure from the regime, the Synod of the Orthodox Church agreed to place control over parish affairs in the hands of local religious associations of laymen. Finally, in 1966 the criminal code of the Russian Soviet Federal Republic, and later of other Soviet republics, was reworded to limit religious activity more stringently, including prohibitions on the religious education of minors and the mass distribution of religious literature. Further, the state asserted its right to punish persons conducting religious meetings that "disturb the public order." On the other hand, the code does provide, almost ironically, for the criminal prosecution of those who discriminate against citizens because of their religious beliefs. Moreover, the Soviet press has recently been urging militants to avoid the use of "vulgar language" in discussing religion, and to try to convince believers of their errors rather than browbeat them.

The tightening of controls over religion in the early 1960's has reflected party uneasiness stemming from a moderate religious revival. The churches, of course, have aggravated this uneasiness by not remaining completely passive in the face of threats to their domain. Individual members of the Orthodox clergy have lodged public protests, and the small but growing Baptist community in the Soviet Union has been particularly vociferous in criticizing some of the new policies.[13]

One suspects that the party's campaign against religion will continue for some time, although it is unlikely to reach the vituperative pitch of the early years of communism. And despite continued indications of the regime's growing concern with religious symbols employed by contemporary Soviet writers, one also suspects that in the Soviet Union, as in other industrial societies, organized religion will become increasingly weaker in what is fundamentally a postreligious epoch.

5. ETHNIC GROUPS AND POLITICS

Ethnic and racial contact, conflict, and amalgamation have been among the basic themes of human history. Western Europe itself is a fusion of many ethnic groups: Celts, Normans, Picts, Goths, Saxons, Vandals, whose identity was gradually submerged in the larger territorial units that became nation states. In general, the history of civilization is the development of ever larger social units, the members of which share a common identity and purpose.

Historically, cultural as well as physical differences among population groups have been the result of particular adaptations to diverse environments. These differences begin to erode as various people form a community. The pace of erosion is now growing because technology is producing a world culture—a culture sharing more and more common features imparted through the tremendous growth of communications and transportation networks, and through the imperatives of creating and maintaining an industrial society.

Initial contacts between ethnic groups have been marked by considerable violence; the history of the world is a record of mass enslavement and murder. People—especially

[13] For a discussion of the recent role of the Baptists see M. Bordeaux and P. Reddaway, "Soviet Baptists Today," *Survey*, 66 (January 1968), pp. 48–66.

the militarily more efficient—competing for scarce resources have always found it psychologically easier to kill, exploit, or enslave those whose language and culture differed from their own. Even when groups have finally become part of a common community, tensions have persisted; on occasion, they have been exacerbated by the very processes of change directed toward amalgamation. In highly traditional multi-ethnic societies, different groups could exist in relatively close proximity without even being aware of each other. But as economic and political development, growing economic interdependence, and competition broaden contact, recognition of ethnic differences begins to appear.

The problem of ethnic tension would be far simpler if, indeed, its sources were only economic; unfortunately, its roots lie much deeper. Every major society has been built on the repression of sexual and other instinctual drives. The success of repressive mechanisms has required that particular styles of life be reinforced with strong moral sanctions. There is no greater threat to an individual's equanimity than the discovery that those things which he holds sacred—and which involve repression—are not accepted by others. His own equilibrium requires that sexual and other mores different from his own be condemned, and that those adhering to other standards be labeled savages, or barbarians. It is a short step from this attitude to the justification of exploitation or carnage. Thus, Europeans slaughtered Africans and Indians without serious qualms; Christians slaughtered Muslims, Jews, and even fellow Christians. Jews, when they had the power, killed other peoples and seized their lands; Arabs enslaved or killed black Africans and Hindus; and Chinese slaughtered all "barbarians." In southern Africa, the Bushmen were hunted down first by the Hottentots and then by the Boers.

In twentieth-century Western Europe, the problem of inter-ethnic conflict within the nation state has ceased to be an important political factor, with some notable exceptions. The problem of German-speaking peoples in areas adjacent to Germany helped set off World War II, and, of course, the Jews posed a disturbing question for a number of European countries. In England, the role of the Irish was not without moment. But in none of these countries today are ethnic relations as important as in the Soviet Union; consequently, it is the Soviet Union which will command most of our attention. A few comments will be made about the problem in the United States and England, and about the migration of workers from Southern Europe, Turkey, and Algeria to France and Germany.

THE RUSSIAN AND SOVIET PATTERN—A GENERAL ANALYSIS: The Soviet Union today consists of approximately 109 different ethnic groups, although only about 12 are important in size. The dominant group, of course, is that of the so-called "Great Russians," a Slavic people who make up 54 per cent of the Soviet Union's population. Two other major nationalities are the Ukrainians, or "Little Russians" (37 million), and the Byelorussians (eight million). Although they are of similar ethnic origins, both groups developed differently from the Great Russians because of closer contact with Western European influences.

Other important groups include six million Turkish-speaking Uzbeks, descendants of the "Golden Horde" located primarily in Central Asia, and five million Tartars (Turkic-speaking Muslims) scattered throughout the Soviet Union. Another large Turkic-speaking Muslim group is the Kazakhs, 3.6 million of whom are concentrated in the Union Republic of Kazakhstan. More than two million Jews remain in the Soviet Union; approximately 2.5 million Russian Jews were slaughtered in the Second World War by the Germans during their occupation of western Russia.

The diversity of the Soviet ethnic pattern is the result of four centuries of expansion by the Great Russians from the Moscow area.

Shortly after its founding, the new Russian state brought non-Slavic people under its domination with the conquest of Kazan and Astrakhan. In the seventeenth century, the czars added Siberia and the left bank of the Dnieper, which later became part of the Ukraine. Expansion continued until well into the nineteenth century, when the borders of the empire included most of the areas that now make up the Union of Soviet Socialist Republics.

On the whole, the empire was treated as a single administrative unit, with few concessions made to ethnic diversity. However, the limitations of the regime were such that, despite occasional attempts at russification, traditional ethnic institutions were not destroyed and provincial governors, especially in outlying areas, were permitted considerable freedom. This began to change during the reign of Alexander III, and after 1881 the Russian government embarked upon a program of minority repression to counter unrest in European Russia. Great Russian national sentiments were proclaimed and restrictions placed upon the cultural activity of minority groups, the compulsory learning of Russian was pressed, and violent massacres of Jews (pogroms) were tolerated if not encouraged. Even the Duchy of Finland, which had occupied a unique place in the empire and enjoyed considerable internal autonomy, found its freedom abrogated. In general, these policies continued until the fall of the Romanov dynasty.

To Marx, and later to Lenin and Stalin, the nation state was the product of a particular historical epoch and a particular socio-economic structure, that of capitalism; with the flowering of the Communist Revolution, national and ethnic self-identification would disappear, to be replaced by the worldwide unity of all working people. During the transition from capitalism to the new society, however, both Lenin and Stalin faced the problem of defining Bolshevik Party policies

regarding minorities. Under Lenin's tutelage, Stalin defined official policy in this area.[14] The Communist Party, he argued, should plan to create a federal republic in the new Communist state which would guarantee complete equality for all nationalities. Minority groups would speak their own language, control their own schools, and have the right to secede from the republic if they so desired.

The liberalism of Bolshevik policy did not arise from a positive belief in the virtues of pluralism, or of a multi-national state. Rather, the party's utopian goal was a common humanity sharing a common Socialist culture. However, given the need to end the suspicions with which minorities viewed the Great Russians, a pluralistic policy seemed the most appropriate. To offer minority groups the legal right to secede from the union was to make sure that they would not want to do so. As Lenin put it:

To accuse the supporters of freedom of self-determination, i.e., freedom to secede, of encouraging separatism, is as foolish and as hypocritical as accusing the advocates of freedom of divorce as encouraging the destruction of family ties.

. . .

The mass of the population knows perfectly well from daily experience the value of geographical and economic ties and the advantages of a big market and of a big state. They will, therefore, resort to secession only when national oppression and national friction make joint life absolutely intolerable.[15]

In advocating this policy, Lenin found himself opposed by most other Socialist groups, which argued that the right of secession should always be subordinated to the "objective" interest of any nation's working

[14] His essays are reprinted in a volume entitled *Marxism and the National Question* (New York: International Publishers, 1942).

[15] V. I. Lenin, *Selected Works*, I, 2 (Moscow: Foreign Languages Publishing House, 1950), 349.

class. In the last analysis, this was Lenin's position, too, and the more extreme libertarian stance was primarily a tactic. As Stalin pointed out in 1913:

The Transcaucasian Tartars may assemble . . . in their Diet and, succumbing to the influence of their beys and mullahs, decide to restore the old order of things and secede from the state. According to the meaning of the clause of self-determination, they are fully entitled to do so. But will this be in the interest of the toiling strata of the Tartar nation? Can Social Democrats remain indifferent when the beys and mullahs take the lead of the masses in the solution of the national problem? Should not Social Democrats interfere in the matter and influence the will of the nation in a definite way?[16]

In fact, this is just what the Bolsheviks did. In 1918, as the borderlands, usually under the control of anti-Bolshevik (but sometimes Social Democratic) groups, began to break off from the new Soviet state, the Bolsheviks responded with armed persuasion. Stalin justified the "interference" as follows:

All this points to the necessity of interpreting the principle of self-determination as a right not of the bourgeoisie but of the working masses of the given nation. The principle of self-determination must be an instrument in the struggle for socialism and must be subordinated to the principles of socialism.[17]

By definition, Mensheviks were "objectively" supporters of bourgeois reaction, and their desire for secession only proved the point. Of course, the Bolsheviks—especially Stalin—went even further than this, for eventually the mere fact of a desire for "excessive" autonomy was enough to brand a

man as "objectively" a member of the bourgeois reaction even if, in all other respects including party membership, he considered himself a loyal Bolshevik. This was certainly Stalin's reaction to events in Georgia in the early 1920's, when he treated many Bolsheviks who were advocating greater autonomy as though they were class enemies. In fairness, it must be recognized that Lenin was shocked by the violence of Stalin's actions; yet, committed to a politically centralized state, he could not accept the Georgians' demands.

By 1922, then, the Soviet state had been consolidated and most of the secession-minded national minorities brought back into the fold. Even so, the new Soviet state was considerably smaller than the old Russian Empire. In the West, intervention of outside forces had limited the state's ability to maintain its traditional borders. In 1917, the Communists had recognized the independence of Finland. However, they encouraged an abortive attempt by Finnish Bolsheviks to seize power. The same was true for Latvia, Estonia, Lithuania, and Poland. The new Polish state, in fact, encompassed a substantial area populated by White Russians and Ukrainians. The Russians also lost Bessarabia to Rumania.

With the end of the civil war, the Communist Party turned to the question of developing a formal state structure. On the issue of centralism versus federalism, two factions emerged within the party. The "internationalists," believing that ethnic loyalties were outdated, aimed at developing a fully unified Soviet Socialist state that could thus more readily attain its goals. While some of the members of this group were genuinely what they claimed to be, for others the rhetoric was merely a cover for Great Russian nationalism.

Opposing the "internationalists" were those, most of them members of minority ethnic groups, who urged a confederal rather than a centralized state and party structure.

16 Quoted in Merle Fainsod, *How Russia Is Ruled*, rev. ed. (Cambridge, Mass.: Harvard University Press, 1963), p. 58.
17 *Ibid.*

In the federalist vanguard were the Ukrainian Bolsheviks, under the leadership of Mikola Skrypnik, although the Georgians also actively supported decentralization.

In theory both Lenin and Stalin represented an intermediate position; in reality, of course, they believed in the centralization of power. The Ukrainians argued for a two-chamber Supreme Soviet, each chamber with its own Presidium; they also urged that no constituent republic in the Soviet of Nationalities be permitted more than two-fifths of the representatives. Further, they wanted foreign trade and, indeed, foreign policy, to remain in the hands of the republics. Lenin rejected these demands as unrealistic, and the constitution finally adopted was far more centralized. The party did, however, continue to profess that individual republics would be granted ample autonomy regarding their own courts, administrative agencies, and economic bodies. They would also be permitted to use their own language in the schools and to develop their individual culture. The aim, in Stalin's words, was to be a society whose culture was "proletarian in content and national in form."[18]

Until 1929, a genuine attempt was made not only to put this policy into effect but also to assist the more backward areas with their problems of economic growth. Languages of minority groups—even relatively small ones, such as the Crimean Tartars—were placed on an equal footing with Russian. In some cases the state encouraged the development of a written language by helping more "primitive" groups to master an alphabet—a Latin alphabet at that. Efforts also were extended to insure that the leadership of the local party and state apparatus was indigenous. Thus, in 1926, the Ukrainian Soviet Socialist Republic, with Moscow's permission, refused to employ anyone in a position of governmental responsibility who could not speak Ukrainian. Along with this, many Great Russians and Jews, who invariably controlled the local

governmental and party apparatus, were replaced by native Ukrainians.

All these efforts, however, did not last long. The beginnings of the second Soviet revolution and the drive toward industrialization led to quite restrictive policies. Yet the reasons for instituting tighter central control, as the twists and turns of official policy during the 1920's show, had existed earlier.

The real problem from the beginning was this: cultural autonomy, even of a limited nature, produced unexpected results for the Soviet leadership. In such advanced cultures as the Ukraine, any degree of autonomy highlighted ethnic self-awareness and led to demands for still further autonomy. And in both advanced and backward areas, cultural autonomy nurtured traits which ran counter to Soviet policy. The encouragement of traditional culture patterns among nomadic peoples, for example, hampered the creation of "positive" attitudes toward socialism.

During the 1920's, then, Soviet policy on nationality was, in many ways, erratic. National autonomy and cultural freedom would be supported until suddenly it was discovered that this policy was causing socially undesirable attitudes. The party leadership could not blame these attitudes on theoretical flaws in their policies—that would cast serious doubt upon its basic assumptions. The deviations, therefore, were always blamed on "saboteurs" or "wreckers" or "spies," or else were considered to be the consequence of bourgeois hangovers. The corrective solution was usually a purge and a period of repression, followed by another cycle of relaxed controls, increased freedom, repression, and purge.

The cycle sputtered out in the 1930's as the newer generation of Soviet leadership became less internationalist and more Great Russian in its assumptions, and as the imperatives of industrialization demanded centralization and rigid control. This is not to imply that the Soviets ever completely abandoned their original nationality policy; the ideological commitment was too deep. Con-

18 For a fuller discussion of the genesis of the Soviet constitution, see pp. 120–123.

tinued efforts have been made to promote a certain degree of cultural autonomy within the centralized framework, which by its very nature, of course, is Great Russian. Thus, in many areas the native tongue as the "first" language is permitted, although Russian is a required subject from grade school on. Today, 67 per cent of all newspapers, eighty per cent of all books, and nearly ninety per cent of all magazines are published in Russian. As the new party program states: ". . . the Russian language . . . has become the common medium of intercourse and cooperation between all peoples of the U.S.S.R." Ethnic cultural manifestations, whenever permitted, are closely watched for evidence of either bourgeois or anti-Soviet colorations.

During the period of industrialization, many of the non–Great Russian areas received preferential economic treatment as the regime sought also to extend the development of agriculture. But it was these areas that suffered far more than the Great Russians from the purges of the 1930's—partly because they offered greater resistance to collectivization. The Ukrainians, with their long tradition of individual peasant farming, felt intensely the effects of the purges, and the Kazakhs suffered fantastic hardships because of their unwillingness to substitute Soviet

versions of the good life for a traditional nomadic existence. During World War II, Stalin ordered the mass deportation to Siberia of such groups as the Volga Germans, who had continued to speak German, and the Crimean Tartars, because of fears they might assist the invaders; since Stalin's death, the remnants of these groups have gradually been rehabilitated. Latvia, Lithuania, and other areas incorporated into the Soviet Union in 1940 during the period of the Nazi-Soviet Pact suffered at least as much; a substantial proportion of their intelligentsia was killed or imprisoned, including leading non-Communist Socialists.

In recent years, tensions between the Great Russians and other groups within the Soviet Union have receded, with the exception of such areas as Latvia and Lithuania. Among the main factors easing antagonisms has been the homogenization of Soviet life through both the Kremlin's policies and industrialization itself. The massive dispersion of some national minority groups throughout the Soviet Union and the settlement of Great Russians in crucial areas has also been significant. In any event, it has become more and more possible to maintain a policy of limited cultural autonomy within the framework of wider loyalties. As Table 6.7 indicates, Great

TABLE 6.7. ETHNIC COMPOSITION OF THE SOVIET POLITICAL ELITE

Nationality	Percentage of population 1959	Membership in Central Committee 1961	Membership in Central Committee 1966	Membership in Presidium 1961	Membership in Presidium 1966	Membership on Council of Ministers 1962	Membership on Council of Ministers 1966
Great Russians	54.65	58.29%	57.95%	61.90%	58.33%	66.07%	72.46%
Ukrainians	17.84	20.00	18.46	14.29	16.67	17.86	20.29
Byelorussians	3.79	3.43	5.13	4.76	8.33	0	1.45
Armenians	1.33	1.71	1.54	4.76	0	1.79	1.45
Jews	1.09	0.57	0.51	0	0	1.79	1.45
Tartars	2.38	0.57	0.51	0	0	0	1.45
Komis	0.21	0	0	0	0	1.79	1.45
Others	18.71	15.43	15.90	14.29	16.67	10.70	0

Adapted from Yaroslav Bilinsky, "The Rulers and the Ruled," *Problems of Communism* (September–October 1967), pp. 23, 25.

Russians still dominate the political scene in numbers much larger than their proportion of the total population of the Soviet Union would seem to warrant.

TWO CASE STUDIES—THE MUSLIMS AND THE UKRAINIANS: There are, today, about twenty million Muslims in the U.S.S.R. Most of them are descendants of the Turkic tribes that settled on the eastern and southern borders of old Russia. Muslim peoples are concentrated primarily in three areas: the Volga-Ural region, the Caucasus, and Central Asia.

From the late seventeenth century to the first part of the twentieth, the Muslim groups were permitted considerable cultural and administrative independence; under the Romanovs, however, Muslim privileges were rescinded. New pressures for russification and, after 1905, a large, government-sponsored migration of Ukrainian and Great Russian peasants to Central Asia in search of new land brought an end to the old policy on Muslims, who soon found themselves subjects of the new colonists. With the coming of the Bolshevik Revolution and its promises of autonomy, a number of prominent Muslim intellectuals were won over, the most important of whom was Sultan Galiev. The Muslim masses, however, remained hostile, and Central Asia was brought under Bolshevik domination only through the efforts of the transplanted Great Russians who, whatever their ideological orientation, preferred rule by other Russians to Muslim domination.

Once the Communist regime was stabilized, Muslims were again granted relative cultural autonomy. A number of union and autonomous republics were created on an ethnic basis—including Kazakhstan, Uzbekistan, and Turkmenistan.[19] Despite these concessions, guerrilla resistance continued until the late 1920's. While some Muslim groups proved tractable, most were prey to Communist repression. Sultan Galiev himself was jailed in 1923 for "bourgeois nationalist tendencies," was released and then rearrested in 1929, and probably died in a concentration camp.

With collectivization and the second Russian Revolution, both control from Moscow and repression intensified. The Kazakhs' sharp resistance to collectivization brought wholesale imprisonment.[20] Arabic script was banned, a full-scale attack upon the Muslim religion was initiated, and such "backward" customs as the veiling of women and arranged marriages were prohibited. However, women who removed their veils were, in many cases, killed by outraged husbands or treated as common prostitutes; on this issue, the regime was forced to backtrack temporarily.

The hostility of Muslims toward the Soviet regime explains Stalin's suspicion of them during World War II. Since the war, ethnic tensions have subsided somewhat, and, with the aid of Soviet technicians, Muslim areas in the Soviet Union have moved ahead economically. The Great Russians still dominate the party and the state apparatus in many Muslim areas, but this will undoubtedly change as more and more Muslims acquire technical skills. Some commentators believe that a latent Muslim nationalism will materialize with the loosening of political controls. Whether it does or not, it is certainly true that Muslims are still culturally more distinct, and more aware of their differences from the Russians, than are the Ukrainians.

The Ukraine represents a different pattern. Ukrainian culture and Great Russian culture are not dissimilar, although the Ukrainians, because of their closer ties with Western Europe, have always regarded themselves as

---

[19] The structure and place of both union and autonomous republics within the Soviet Union is discussed on pp. 596–597.

[20] According to official Soviet figures, the number of Kazakhs declined from four million in 1926 to 3.1 million in 1939. Correcting for natural population growth, it can be assumed that well over a million were killed by the regime.

somewhat superior to the Great Russians. The western Ukraine contained a very large number of Catholics and Uniates.[21]

The cultural split between the two groups grew out of the Mongol conquest of the east, and it was not until 1654, after a period of being part of Poland and then a period of independence, that the Ukrainians voluntarily incorporated themselves into the Russian Empire. Separatist tendencies continued to exist, however, and reached their peak during the Russian Revolution, when an independent Ukrainian nation seemed a real possibility.

With the end of the civil war, the Ukrainians were allowed to exercise a good measure of freedom. The Ukrainian language was put on a par with the Russian, the Ukrainians were given every opportunity to glorify their culture and history, and efforts were made toward the "ukrainization" of the Communist Party. The consequences of relative autonomy were as might have been expected: a group of Ukrainian Communist intellectuals —the *Borotbists*—stressed the uniqueness and separateness of the Ukraine to a point far beyond Moscow's capacity for tolerance. Loksandr Shumsky, commissar of education, pointing to the Western element in Ukrainian literature, urged his fellow intellectuals to look to the West for inspiration. He also advocated that the Ukrainian Communist Party no longer be subordinate to, but be equal with, the Communist Party of the Soviet Union.

The crisis that resulted from the dispersion of these ideas came to a climax in 1926. Moscow sent one of its leading trouble shooters, Lazar Kaganovich, to the Ukraine as party secretary, and those responsible for the deviations were expelled from the party and, in some cases, imprisoned or executed. After this "purification," controls were once again relaxed and ukrainization permitted. It was only a temporary respite. During the

remainder of the 1920's, the inexorable cycle recurred: encouragement of local autonomy, discovery of tendencies toward deviation, and then repression.

As in all other areas of the Soviet Union, Moscow's control of the Ukraine tightened during collectivization. The Ukrainians resisted collectivization more vigorously than the Great Russian peasants, and the consequent repression was even harsher. By the late 1930's, the Ukrainian Communist Party had been decimated, most of its former leaders either put in jail or shot. Moscow's chief troubleshooter during this period of unrest, and the person responsible for disposing of the deviationists, was Kaganovich's protégé, Nikita Khrushchev.

Not surprisingly, many Ukrainians (particularly those in the western Ukraine) welcomed the Germans as liberators in 1941; even more of them would have cooperated with the Germans had not Hitler's conception of their racial inferiority and his consequent atrocities prevented them. As it was, many Ukrainians did assist the Nazis in fighting the Stalin regime, and thousands more fled the country. At the end of the war, a large percentage of the exiles were forced to return under terms of the Allied agreement. Many of them committed suicide, and others joined guerrilla groups which continued fighting the regime until 1950. Needless to say, their cause was hopeless; hundreds of thousands of young men were killed as Soviet authorities moved ruthlessly to stamp out the insurgents. Those who escaped death were scattered throughout the Soviet Union.

The situation in the Ukraine since 1950 has gradually altered. The proportion of Great Russians living in the area has increased, and the same factors operating in other areas—such as intermarriage and the greater interdependence of a technological society—have reduced ethnic differences. While Ukrainian is still spoken in the Union Republic, ambitious young men find it wise to know Russian and to become a part of the new middle-class culture. In general, Ukrain-

---

[21] In 1946 the Uniates were reincorporated into the Orthodox Church by the Soviet government.

ian nationalism is being deprived of its potential leadership, and it is most probable that the Ukrainians will be increasingly integrated into Soviet society.

SOME NOTES ON CONTEMPORARY EUROPE: Since the end of World War II, more than eight million migrants have arrived in France, Germany, and England in search of employment opportunities. In England, in addition to the traditional Irish influx, substantial numbers have come from India, Pakistan, and the West Indies. Many Algerians entered France in the 1940's and remained even after Algerian independence. Also, both France and Germany have received an influx of workers from Italy, Spain, Portugal, Turkey, Yugoslavia, and Greece.

The immigration has had certain common features. All three countries have had a demand for unskilled workers, and it is these jobs that the immigrants have filled. Most migrants have been young men, arriving either unmarried or without their families. Although most of them probably planned to return home, many have settled permanently in the host nation.

Perhaps the most serious problem of interethnic adjustment has occurred in England, where the number of immigrants classified as "colored" has risen to nearly one million and, if present trends continue, may rise as high as three per cent of the population by 1970. With their higher birth rate, the migrants may constitute ten per cent of the population in some of the larger cities where they have concentrated.

To Englishmen, the term "colored" includes Pakistanis, Indians, and Jamaicans, and their attitudes toward them are a consequence of a general hostility toward "foreigners," compounded by the color question and cultural differences. Despite some discrimination in employment opportunities, economic competition—with the newcomers taking unskilled jobs—has not been as touchy an issue as housing. As for the migrant groups themselves, although they all face some of the same barriers, each reacts differently to the English scene. The Jamaicans, for example, know English and are far more anxious to integrate into the community than the Pakistanis, who, with their language handicap, have a stronger sense of ethnic identification.

England's migrant problems are minimal compared with those of the United States in the relocation of Negroes from the South to the North. Unlike Negroes moving into Harlem ghettos from the Black Belt, the "colored" immigrants of England are not coming from a background in which they were treated as less than men. Crime rates among England's newcomers are comparatively low, although crimes of violence are higher than average; the family structure is more stable than that of the American Negro; and the social disorganization that has turned portions of the American black ghetto into a human jungle does not exist.

Moreover, the British government has continued to take measures to prevent, or at least inhibit, the formation of ghettos. In 1965, Parliament prohibited discrimination in the rental or sale of apartments or housing, and three years later, the prohibition was extended to such areas as employment and trade-union membership.

Nevertheless, conflicts—including race riots—have erupted. The Conservative government, in response to public pressure, finally sponsored restrictive legislation, the Commonwealth Immigration Act of 1962, which clearly discriminated against "colored" immigrants even though the bill made no mention of race or color. The Labor government continued these restrictions and, in 1965, reduced from twenty thousand to 8,500 a year the number of West Indians and Asians permitted to enter the country. Immigration permits were restricted to those who had either specialized skills or jobs awaiting them in England. In 1968, faced with the fairly substantial immigration of Indians and Pakistanis from Kenya, the Labor government introduced, and Parliament quickly passed, legislation to exclude most of them. The public debates made it obvious that color was the principal factor involved.

Of course, Great Britain itself, despite the domination of England, has always been a conglomeration of nationalities. In Northern Ireland, many Catholics have long yearned for unity with the south, resenting Protestant political and economic domination, and the bitter religious riots of 1969 made this feeling stronger than ever. In the past several years nationalist movements have gained strength in Scotland and Wales, both of which boast cultural traditions of their own. In fact, in May 1968, Nationalist candidates in Scotland polled about one-third of the vote in local elections, mainly at the expense of the Labor Party. In both Scotland and Wales, the demand of the nationalists is for greater regional authority. It seems quite unlikely, however, that regional nationalism will become of prime importance in British politics; the overall trend is in the direction of greater homogeneity. Nevertheless, in an effort to appease the Scots and Welsh, the Labor Party has created a Commission on the Constitution to examine the relation of their areas and that of Northern Ireland to the central government.

The 1950's witnessed the beginnings of a vast migration into France and Germany from Italy, Portugal, Spain, Turkey, and Algeria. How these millions have adjusted has depended on a number of circumstances. The French have done relatively little for the migrants. Algerian immigrants, for example, are concentrated in the worst slums in France and subject to the same prejudices experienced by the American Negro. Italians and Portuguese have fared somewhat better, although the French tend to regard the Italians as lacking sexual self-control. In almost all cases, however, the assimilation by aliens of French cultural patterns has brought almost full acceptance by the larger society, and many have married French women.

The Germans, on the other hand, have done their utmost to accommodate the migrants, who are officially termed "guest workers" rather than "foreign workers." Many factories employing Muslims have built mosques and organized special canteens to cater to religious requisites; Spanish priests have been brought in to help with the needs of Spanish Catholic workers. Germany has also built special cultural centers, and housing conditions for the immigrant workers are generally good. Many German manufacturers no longer recruit directly in those countries from which the guest workers come, but "pirate" them from France and Belgium after the immigrants have mastered necessary industrial skills. Germany's reputation for treating its "guests" well made pirating easy, at least for a time.

However, very few of the guest workers were absorbed into the larger German community, and with the mild recession of 1965–1966, more and more demands began to be heard for their deportation. The Germans are still more "tribal" in their attitudes than the French.

6. RELIGIOUS AND ETHNIC MINORITIES IN THE UNITED STATES

The United States is the product of the English Calvinist tradition. It also became, later in its history, the refuge of people from almost every European ethnic group, and the home of a large number of Africans originally brought to the country as slaves. That its culture has remained primarily English Calvinist in inspiration testifies to the importance of its formative years and the myths associated with those years.

The fact that the English Calvinists were opening a new continent—one that was thinly populated by people who, in their minds, did not really count in the scheme of things—meant that the inherent characteristics of Calvinism unfolded in their purest form: the continuous splitting into a multiplicity of sects; the rapid development of a liberal democratic ideology; the separation of church and state; and the evolution of a secular, although Protestant, political order.

Since liberal Protestantism represented *the* American tradition, rather than only one portion of a broader culture as in England,

Americans more than other peoples identified it with the natural and the good. Thus, their attitudes toward Catholics who flooded the country after 1830 were mixed; many feared and detested Catholicism for what they considered its primitive, authoritarian, and harmfully superstitious qualities. They also regarded with distaste those immigrant peasants who fought and drank and failed to exhibit the self-restraint all men should possess. On the other hand, a general belief in toleration prevented the enactment of laws that would have made the immigrants second-class citizens.

The aim of American Protestants, of course, although they may not have been fully aware of it, was to Protestantize the Catholic immigrant, and they probably would have succeeded had it not been for the sheer size of the immigration. As it was, hundreds of thousands of Catholics were lost to the church during the early years of the nineteenth century.

The Catholic and Protestant peasants of Europe were quickly transformed into "modern" Americans—each new wave of immigrants taking, on the average, no more than two or three generations to adopt as their own the values of a liberal industrial society.[22] In the case of American Catholics, this took on the guise of a collective amnesia; most refused to believe that traditional Catholic doctrine differed in any way from "Americanism." The election of 1960 marked, in effect, the end of the American white Protestant "establishment," although Protestants continue to dominate large segments of American political and economic life.

America, too, was the only country in

which the European Jew found a real haven. In Europe, Jews were a "pariah" people living in isolated groups within the larger society. Throughout most of European history, they were subject to periodic pogroms by populations that considered them the assassins of the son of God and the persistent murderers of Christians. In a sense, Christians' hostility toward Jews was greater than that toward other non-Christian peoples because, in their eyes, the Jews had rejected the Messiah. The antagonism was made more acute by the fact that Jews were at once both a religious and an ethnic group, and to most Europeans, citizenship was, until recently, a tribal affair. One was a Frenchman or a German because one's ancestors were descendants of Gauls or Franks; a Jew, therefore, was not really part of the French nation—even though the French have been far less tribal in this sense than the Germans or the English.

America, on the other hand, was different; here all peoples were immigrants. The land belonged to no one in particular, and citizenship was defined in terms of accepting a set of common values. The Jew arriving in the United States had the same status as the Irish Catholic or even, in the end, the Yankee Protestant. What is more, given the early development of a secular state and toleration, the Jew could feel far safer in the American environment than elsewhere. In fact, many Calvinists possessed a highly philo-Semitic attitude—Jews after all were people of the Book.

After the diaspora, Jews became an urban people, and they shared Protestant attitudes toward work and respect for practical knowledge that enabled them to adjust easily to the American milieu. Finally, except for tendencies which attracted only fringe elements, there never developed in the United States a major "traditionalist" reaction identifying the Jews with the "liberal capitalism" that was destroying traditional society, for the American tradition itself was liberal.

This is not to deny that the Jew in the

22 In recent years American sociologists have attacked the "melting pot" hypothesis and have emphasized the continued retention by immigrants of traditional ethnic traits. Nevertheless, in *comparative* perspective, it is the relatively rapid assimilation of these groups that is significant. It is well to point out, however, that while most of the immigrants have adopted American cultural norms, they have retained a sense of group identity—even though this, too, is beginning to disappear.

United States encountered difficulties, but compared with his status in Europe, America represented utopia. By the mid-1950's, Jews boasted a larger portion of college graduates and a higher per capita income than any other ethnic group in the United States. They had also become an important part of American academic life and the amusement and mass-media industries.

The major ethnic group, aside from the American Indians, that has not been easily incorporated into American society is the Negro. To Europeans, African society was highly primitive, and Africans were, therefore, in some sense less than human. The more expressive culture of Africans, as well as their color, led European Protestants to project upon them the sexual and aggressive impulses that they so feared in themselves.

The impact of these variables upon the later history of race relations in the United States can be demonstrated by a comparison with Brazil, where racial tensions have always been less severe. In Brazil, the color differences between Portuguese settlers and their African slaves were not nearly so pronounced —nor was the expressive culture of the African nearly so significant a threat. Moreover, the Portuguese and Spanish empires in the New World recreated the old feudal institutions. To the Iberian settler, society consisted of a myriad of classes and statuses. To free a slave did not mean that one had to accept him as an equal until he became fully acculturated; there were, after all, many gradations between slavery and full equality. Thus, although the number of blacks reaching the highest social positions was always small, the African who took on the behavior patterns of the European did not find that his color completely blocked social acceptance.

To the American accepting the liberal faith, however, all men were created equal and entitled to all the rights of citizens. To accept the fact that the African was a man would, of necessity, mean treating him as a peer. If the North Americans were to keep the black man from participating as their equal, therefore, they were forced to deny him *all* human attributes.[23]

The results of this difference in outlook are to be seen in the resolution of the issue of slavery. In Brazil, abolition came naturally and without great conflict. Most Portuguese continued to regard Brazilians of African descent as their cultural inferiors, but, in a society characterized by rigid class lines, they were at least allowed to attain the lowest rung of citizenship. In the United States the issue was drawn more fiercely between those who denied the Negro any humanity and those who denied that there were any differences— even cultural differences—between Americans of African and of European descent.

The consequence today of America's deeply conflicting attitudes has been, of course, the emergence of racial tension and violence, the outcome of which is difficult to predict. It may well be that racial strife will in the end prove far more disruptive to American society than class conflict has to European society.

23 Much of the above analysis is derived from Louis Hartz, ed., *The Founding of New Societies* (New York: Harcourt, Brace and World, 1965), and Gilberto Freyre, *The Masters and the Slaves* (New York: Alfred A. Knopf, 1946).

7

Political Socialization:
Family, Education,
and Mass Media

1. INTRODUCTION

Whatever instincts man possesses, most of his reactions to his external environment are learned. It is the infant's plasticity and helplessness that necessitate a long period of care and teaching before he can deal effectively with the world around him. During this period he begins to learn forms of behavior that are appropriate to the society of which he is part—and the skills required for a useful place in that society.

In most traditional societies, behavioral patterns and skills are transmitted largely through the family, whatever the family structure may be. In advanced and constantly changing societies, the role of the family, although still crucial, has gradually declined, and specialized institutions—for instance, schools—have become more and more vital in the socialization process.

Socialization, of course, does not end with adulthood. In contemporary societies, the mass media have an important effect in the progressive restructuring of attitudes and beliefs; they also provide a continuing source of knowledge. Since most twentieth-century societies are highly differentiated, individuals develop separate perceptions of reality, depending upon their function and associates in society. Almost every activity in which the individual participates, even vicariously, affects his insight, values, and motivations. Even an election campaign is part of the general process of socialization.

Every society emphasizes certain values and perceptions, and de-emphasizes others. As a society defines its requirements, individuals must be motivated to meet them in order for the society to be maintained. And every generation develops a vested interest in passing to the next those values it considers important. Given the necessity of fulfilling certain tasks, and given the requirement for some structure of roles by which human beings can relate to one another, no individual is completely free to choose or create his own values. Taboos manifest themselves with respect to behavior and are invariably reinforced with sanctions. Both are most stringent when modes of behavior are contrary to those which the culture has defined as central.

In general, and with one major exception, the individual's freedom in modern societies is far greater than in most traditional ones. Not only have men become increasingly aware of cultural patterns influencing their own behavior, but the stress placed upon innovation and knowledge has yielded that continuing change of culture and social structure which we label progress. The very heterogeneity of most modern societies provides far more alternatives than in those communities in which the division of labor was minimal, and in which far greater stress was placed on the sanctity of traditional mores. This generalization remains true despite the fact that the mass media are contributing to cultural homogenization in all European countries. The major burden of modern pluralistic societies is in the very freedom which they grant—and in the difficulty so many have in coping with this freedom. It is no accident that one perpetual theme of utopian thought in the West has been the need to reestablish the close-knit, individual-community relationship characteristic of traditional societies.

The major exception, of course, is to be found in modern authoritarian societies. The continued attraction that authoritarian regimes have for large numbers of people may lie in the fact that they promise to reduce the burdens imposed by freedom.

This chapter will concentrate on three institutions important to the socialization process—the family, the schools, and the mass media—underscoring aspects most directly related to the formation and change of political attitudes. As already noted, the formation of such attitudes cannot be considered in a vacuum; the values and perceptions that people hold regarding political matters are closely related to a broad range of variables. For example, the type of family structure that distinguishes a society may have a decided impact on the personality of its members, and their general orientation to interpersonal relations may be reflected in their approach to politics.

Again, the institutions cited are not the only ones involved in the socialization process. Indeed, most of the institutions of the community take part in the socialization of the citizen. Most of those considered in this chapter have functions in addition to that of socialization. Educational institutions, for instance, provide societies with the skills necessary to adapt to their environments. The mass media not only offer information but serve a purely expressive function as providers of entertainment. While the socialization role of these institutions will be stressed, some of their other functions will also be treated.

2. THE FAMILY

For the past thousand years, Western family systems have differed considerably from those in the Far and Middle East and Africa. The West lacked the clan systems of the Middle and Far East, and individuals rather than families have borne responsibility for crimes. Until the late nineteenth century, arranged marriages were common; but even so, the young people in the West always had more to say about whom they would—or would not—marry than did those in the rest of the world. Polygamy and regularized concubinage have not been an integral part of Western culture.

In all Western countries, the father dominated the family and the rights of mother and child were minimal. The force largely responsible for upsetting this pattern was Calvinism. The Puritans emphasized, far more than in countries where Calvinism was not an important factor, that the relation of husband and wife should be that of loving companions rather than links in a family network.

Insofar as the transition from the extended to the conjugal family increased the possibilities of geographic mobility, it may have been an additional factor that contributed to early industrialization in England. And the domination of the United States by a Calvinist ethic was probably a major factor in the more rapid democratization of the American family as compared with the European. Differences between American and European family structures continue, despite the fact that industrialization and modernization are bringing about a convergence of attitudes and practices. For instance, a substantially higher portion of Americans remember having had the opportunity to participate in family decisions as children than is true of Germans (see Table 7.1). Far more than Europeans, Americans tend to regard husbands and wives as more or less equal companions in marriage; they are also far less strict than Europeans in disciplining their children. The British have moved more quickly toward a "democratic" and "permissive" family structure than have the French, and the French faster than the Germans, although in the case of France and Germany the differences are marginal.

The relationship between family structures and the patterns of socialization is difficult to measure with any precision. During the 1930's and 1940's, many authors argued that there was an obvious parallel between the authoritarian nature of the German family and the growth of National Socialism.[1] Some evidence does indeed exist which indicates that youngsters who grow up within a family

___

[1] See, for example, Bertram Schaffner, *Fatherland: A Study of Authoritarianism in the German Family* (New York: Columbia University Press, 1948) and David Rodnick, *Post-War Germans* (New Haven: Yale University Press, 1958).

framework of rigid discipline feel less competent to participate in political activity. Other studies indicate that an authoritarian family structure is correlated with a strict insistence upon the rightness of traditional norms and a lack of flexibility toward or empathy with those who hold to different values.

There is also a good deal of evidence to show that young people reared in an authoritarian manner tend to expect hostility from those outside the immediate family—and are less likely to take on personal responsibility for actions in which they transgress authority. In fact, they have a general inclination to appear to be accepting the rules of society while at the same time developing cliques whose principal objective is to disobey them. German and French youth are less likely to admit their transgressions of societal norms than Americans; English youngsters stand somewhere in between. When asked to complete a story in which fifty cents had disappeared from a teacher's desk, 55 per cent of the students in Karlsruhe, Germany, assumed that it had been stolen. The percentage of youngsters in Knoxville, Tennessee, and Birmingham, England, who made the same assumption was 33.5 per cent and 36 per cent, respectively. Another question required completion of a story in which children had accidentally broken a window in a house while playing ball. More than 70 per cent of the American children completed it by having the youngsters communicate with the

TABLE 7.1. PARTICIPATION BY YOUTH IN FAMILY
DECISION-MAKING: SELECTED COUNTRIES

Extent of remembered participation	United States	United Kingdom	Germany
Had some influence	73%	69%	54%
Had no influence	22	26	37
Don't know	5	5	9

Adapted from Gabriel A. Almond and Sidney Verba, *The Civic Culture* (Princeton: Princeton University Press, 1963), p. 331. Reprinted by permission of the publisher.

owner. Such a gesture occurred to only 26.4 per cent of the schoolchildren in Karlsruhe and 50.4 per cent in Birmingham.[2]

The pattern of internal family organization, then, and the manner in which children are raised would seem to be related in some way to the type of political action which characterizes a society. Children who grow up in an authoritarian family atmosphere are probably less well equipped to participate in and maintain a free society. Yet the relationship is by no means a simple or incontrovertible one; a number of societies in which fairly authoritarian families are the general rule are also noted for their democratic institutions. Nor can this factor alone explain the rise of National Socialism in twentieth-century Germany, for family patterns throughout Europe were far more authoritarian in the eighteenth and nineteenth centuries. Then, too, the relationship is by no means a one-way affair: just as the nature of the family may influence the operation of the political system, so the political system itself may influence the structure of the family.

Interestingly enough, the Nazi regime contributed to the breakdown of the traditional nature of the German family. The regime's attitude toward the family was ambivalent: National Socialist ideology insisted that women concentrate on children and church, and even frowned on the use of such bourgeois devices as lipstick; at the same time it encouraged and rewarded illegitimacy in order to "breed" Germans of "pure" Aryan stock. Most important, the regime's efforts to win over young people, which included the glorification of spying on their parents, and

the wartime mobilization of women weakened the ties between parents and children and between husband and wife.

In any event, analyses in terms of differential family structure are less and less pertinent to Western Europe. In every country, the authority of the husband is diminishing, although the wife's status is likely to remain a subordinate one for a long time to come. In all countries, too, kinship networks and ties no longer have the significance they once did, and child-rearing practices are becoming more permissive. Women are participating more actively in politics and on the job market, and for young people the norms of their "peer culture" increasingly compete with those set by their families. There are those who argue that the pendulum has now swung too far in the direction of license. In the United States, especially, some psychologists maintain that the unwillingness of parents to impose values upon their children has caused a growing sense of "normlessness," and that the emphasis upon gratifying the child's every wish has resulted in a situation in which adolescents are unable to accept any restraints or frustrations.

THE FAMILY IN THE U.S.S.R.: The Great Russian family remained strongly patriarchal, until the Revolution. As in Western Europe, social status had much to do with family behavior. Wife-beating was common among the peasantry, for example, but not usually practiced by the upper classes. Also, as in Western Europe, daughters of professional people were beginning to attend universities by the end of the nineteenth century. Of course, family patterns differed widely among non-Russian ethnic groups: Muslim peoples in Russia, for instance, practiced polygamy.

To both Engels and Marx, legal marriage was essentially a bourgeois institution that would disappear with the end of capitalism. To them, marriage would be based on companionship, with each partner free to leave when he or she wished. In a Communist soci-

---

2 See Harold H. Anderson and Gladys L. Anderson, "A Cross-National Study of Children: A Study of Creativity and Mental Health," a paper presented at the Sixth International Congress on Mental Health, Paris, 1961 (mimeographed). In all these studies, social class was held constant. For material on France, refer to Jesse R. Pitts, "Continuity and Change in Bourgeois France," in Stanley Hoffmann et al., *In Search of France* (Cambridge, Mass.: Harvard University Press, 1963), pp. 235–304. See also Michel Crozier, *The Bureaucratic Phenomenon* (Chicago: University of Chicago Press, 1964).

ety women would be treated equally by being assured of the opportunity to use their talents productively; they would have time to do so because the community would provide care for all children, whether or not they were legitimate.

When the Bolsheviks seized power they began to implement these theories. Their chief spokesman was Madame Alexandra Kollontai, a member of the Central Committee and head of its women's department; it was she who was the intellectual and practical leader of the "free love" movement. While Lenin himself held somewhat more conservative views, he went along with the tide, and in 1918 the government issued a decree declaring birth to be the basis of the family. There was to be no difference between children born in wedlock and out. Parents remained responsible for their children as minors, and neither parent nor child had rights to the other's property. Later decrees continued the same pattern. The 1926 code provided that cohabitation was to be regarded as evidence of marriage and that each partner was free to dissolve it at any time. The regime recommended that individuals wishing to marry or divorce register the fact, but there was no requirement that this be done. Abortion was also permitted under any circumstances, and legal penalties for bigamy, incest, adultery, and homosexuality were eliminated. Only Muslim areas, where the regime was attempting to stamp out polygamy, were exempt from the decrees.

By the early 1930's, a reaction against these practices had set in. Stalin was undoubtedly more conservative, or had become more conservative, than official Bolshevik doctrine. Just as important, while most rural families were unaffected by the decrees, enough adults were reneging on their responsibilities that Russian cities began to be filled with "parentless" gangs; the regime did not, at the time, have the facilities for taking care of them. And with complete freedom of abortion, as well as a serious lack of housing facilities, the birth rate was dropping alarmingly. There

seemed to be some feeling that "free love" and "promiscuity" were not conducive to either social stability or building a powerful Soviet state. No doubt these feelings were reinforced by the prudery of the more conservative cadres that rose to influential positions with Stalin's consolidation of power.

In any event, in the mid-1930's laws were passed holding parents responsible for their children's behavior and imposing stiff fines for failure to meet their responsibilities. Formal marriage and divorce were now required, divorce was made more difficult and more expensive, and punishments were decreed for both homosexuality and abortion. Coupled with this reaction was the emergence of "Socialist realism" in literature and a campaign to foster not only family responsibility but a puritanical attitude toward sex. As *Pravda* commented in 1936:

So-called free love and loose sexual life are altogether bourgeois and have nothing in common either with Socialist principles and ethics or with the rules of behavior of a Soviet citizen. Marriage is the most serious affair in life. . . . Fatherhood and motherhood become virtues in the Soviet land.[3]

The swing toward conservative family attitudes continued during World War II. In 1944, only marriages recorded with the civil registry were considered legal. While legitimate children were now entitled to inherit their father's property, illegitimate children had no such rights, nor could they claim their father's name. Thus, although no formal stigma was supposed to be attached to illegitimacy, the fact became part of the public record. Attempts were also made to solemnize marriage ceremonies: marriage "palaces" were created, and civil ceremonies took on more style. In divorce cases, judges were instructed to make every effort toward recon-

[3] Quoted in Vladimir Gsovski and K. Grzybowski, *Government, Law and the Courts in the Soviet Union and Eastern Europe,* II (New York: Frederick A. Praeger, 1959), 1,158.

ciliation and to deny divorces that were considered inappropriate. Family ties were further tightened by revision of the inheritance laws.

With the end of the Stalin era, a move toward more liberal policies took place. Most restrictions upon inheriting personal property, including bank deposits, were lifted. Abortions were once again permitted provided they were performed in hospitals, divorce was gradually made somewhat easier, and, in 1968, a new Family Code permitted unwed mothers to make up a father's name to put on the child's birth certificate and other documents. The same code also dealt with the problem of Russia's rising divorce rate: it prohibited divorces if the wife was pregnant and until her child reached his first birthday, and it lengthened the waiting period for marriages in order to discourage hasty unions. There are those within the party who still talk of abolishing the family as an institution, though a return to the practices advocated by Madame Kollontai appears rather distant.

Even so, the Soviet family has changed drastically in recent years, particularly in urban areas, and these changes promise to continue. In many ways, the changes have paralleled those in the West, although in others they have gone further. The extended family with its intergenerational attachments is deteriorating, despite severe housing shortages which have slowed the process. Also, the relationship between husband and wife is far more egalitarian than it ever has been. Today, most Soviet women work, and they enjoy, at least theoretically, full equality with men in terms of educational and employment opportunities. The regime is bending every effort to provide nursery and day-school care for the children of working mothers, although, in contrast with the late 1920's, sending children to these care centers is completely voluntary.

Reality, of course, does not quite match ideology. Despite the efforts of the regime, space available in nurseries does not approach demand; most working mothers have had to rely upon grandparents to take care of children. Also, women are, on the whole, concentrated in menial or heavy-labor occupations (almost all hod carriers are women). There are comparatively few women among the higher party bureaucracy, in leadership positions in management, or in the technical professions. There are two exceptions to this: about 85 per cent of Soviet doctors are women (although most specialists are men), and the vast majority of primary and secondary school teachers are women. Schoolteaching is a traditional woman's occupation, but the number of woman doctors reflects the status of medicine in Soviet society: it is not the prestige occupation it is in the West, training requirements are less rigid, and medical salaries are much lower than in other professions. While many women welcome the opportunity to work, others do so only because of economic necessity. Soviet husbands are still reluctant to help their wives with household chores, and most working wives have to take care of these after a full day on the job. Officially, Communist doctrine emphasizes the complete equality of the sexes. But it is still a man's world in the Soviet Union—and it promises to be so for some time.

This circumstance, however, may account for what appears to be a growing crisis in family relations. With the breakdown of the extended family, working mothers are less and less able to rely upon grandparents for child and household care. Given the still primitive state of Soviet service industries, more and more women are caught between the demands of their jobs and norms that call for them to also be mothers, housewives, and companions. The result has been a sharp rise in the divorce rate, a matter that has been given considerable attention in the Soviet press.

The Communist regime has also wrought a profound transformation in the relationship between parents and children; again, the change coincided with that taking place in the West, and, again, it went somewhat further in weakening parental authority. The government took a special interest in youth, developing a variety of groups to counter the influence of the older generation's more conservative attitudes. In fact, the regime emphasized the important role of youth in re-educating parents toward party goals. During the 1930's, it launched an intensive propaganda campaign to make a hero of the boy Pavlik Morozov, who was murdered by his uncle for having denounced his father to the Soviet secret police. Morozov is still an official hero for Soviet youth.

The 1930's and 1940's, then, were extremely tense decades in terms of parent-child relations. With a new generation of Soviet parents, the gap has closed somewhat. Parental authority has continued to decline as the community assumes an ever larger number of family functions, and there now is a more democratic relationship between parents and children than existed during the empire. However, political loyalty is no longer a serious source of antagonism between parents and youth, although generational conflicts of another type are coming to the fore.

All these basic changes notwithstanding, the regime still emphasizes, as it has since the 1930's, the importance of youths' respect for parents. It has also made clear to parents their responsibilities in disciplining children. The press is constantly blaming juvenile delinquency on excessive permissiveness and "spoiling" by Soviet parents. In this respect, official Soviet attitudes on parent-child behavior are far more conservative than those now accepted by middle-class parents in the United States.

The position of the Communist Party with regard to the family as a unit continues to be highly equivocal. There are some party members, mostly women, who still see the family as a formidable impediment to developing a Communist society. To them, the dissolution of the family is mandatory. They point out that family life perpetuates the subordinate role of women, that it results in unequal opportunities for children, that it continues to foster an individualistic attitude, and that many parents still attempt to inculcate their children with religious and other ideas that are counter to official policy.

The ascendant groups within the party, however, now view the family as an institution which will last for a considerable time, perhaps indefinitely. As Khrushchev put it in 1961:

Those who maintain that the family will become less important in the transition to Communism and that with time it will disappear are entirely wrong. Actually the family will grow stronger under Communism; family relations will be finally cleansed of material considerations and will attain great purity and stability.[4]

This majority appraisal is the result of several factors, not the least of which are the durability of traditional Russian culture and the opinion that both "morality" and the birth rate will suffer if family ties disappear. Evidence that the party has become committed to the family as an institution is provided by the fact that the regime is no longer talking about full-time boarding schools for all children and that, moreover, some of these schools are being converted to day-care centers.[5] Nevertheless, the party does embrace a policy of establishing institutions that are bound to reduce family functions and to relate the family to other social structures, as the existence of day-care centers and youth groups testify. In addition, the comrades' courts found in apartment houses are being used not only to make sure that the family

[4] *Pravda*, October 20, 1961. Quoted in Peter Juviler, "Family Reforms on the Road to Communism," in Peter H. Juviler and Henry W. Morton, eds., *Soviet Policy Making* (New York: Frederick A. Praeger, 1967), pp. 48–49.

[5] One reason for the policy reversal may stem from empirical evidence cited by Soviet psychologists to the effect that children who grow up in public institutions have far more emotional problems, on the average, than those who have a normal family life. However, such schools can provide a superior environment for some children.

instills in children the "right kind" of social morality, but also to settle disputes between husbands and wives. And parents whose children do badly in school are likely to be upbraided at their place of employment for being remiss. These family controls are facilitated by the growing preference of the regime for cooperative apartment houses instead of private homes in urban areas.

In general, then, the Soviet family, like those in Western Europe, has passed from a predominantly patriarchal type, in which it was part of an extended network of kin, to the conjugal type consisting of husband and wife and a small number of children. In all of these countries, the relationship between the sexes and between parents and children has become more egalitarian. In some ways the Soviet Union has gone further in this direction than other European countries; in some ways it has not gone as far. But in none does the family show any sign of disappearing in the near future; it will remain a basic social institution in most societies for a long time to come.

3. EDUCATION

Traditionally, the most significant functions of early socialization have been performed by the family. It has been the family that has provided the child with the values and norms of the society and, until quite recent times, taught him the skills which enabled him to function within that society. Even in fairly primitive societies, however, the community has always reserved for itself part of the responsibility for the socialization of some of its members—if only to provide means by which they can acquire the military skills and attitudes necessary for the society's survival.

As societies become more highly differentiated and complex, socializing agencies other than the family become more important. Skills must be taught which require specialized instruction. With the development of a written language and "high culture,"

formal schooling becomes imperative for those destined to become the guardians of the society's heritage and members of its bureaucracy. Even the priesthood must now be schooled in the ever more intricate systems of religious belief.

In most traditional societies, formal education was reserved for the few. But today, if a society is to mobilize its resources to the fullest and create an industrial culture, education must be extended to the many. Not only is widespread literacy essential, but the number of required specialized skills that cannot be taught in the home or through apprenticeship is increasing geometrically. Technological growth has reached the point where only those who are professionally dedicated to mastering fairly limited aspects of the new sciences can provide the requisite training for a new generation. And as competence in technical fields becomes necessary to the society, education becomes a prime source of social mobility.

In advanced societies, the field of education also takes on additional functions. In traditional societies it served as the transmitter of a slowly developing culture, a mechanism for training personnel to fulfill key functions, and a means by which the select few acquired that knowledge and understanding of their culture and the world about them that enabled them to become "excellent" human beings. Today universities, especially, have undertaken the duty of augmenting the total sum of human knowledge, and it is through them, as "knowledge industries," that the society is better able to understand both itself and the outside world. Universities are, therefore, abetting the creation of new beliefs, values, and norms, and usurping the functions that, at an earlier stage, were the province of a "free" intelligentsia or priesthood.

THE DEVELOPMENT OF EDUCATION IN WESTERN EUROPE: With the collapse of the Roman Empire, the Catholic Church took over most of the schools that survived and used them primarily for the propagation of Christian doctrine. Church schools were, in fact, about the only ones to outlast the triumph of the "barbarians" in the West. Education was directed to preparing young men for the priesthood; it was primarily moral and disciplinary rather than intellectual.

Not until the eleventh and twelfth centuries did education, in the classical sense, begin once again to take form. The first universities were founded in Bologna in 1158 and in Paris in 1180. By 1600, Western Europe boasted 108 universities. Most of these obtained special privileges from existing regimes because of their close association with the church, and consequently they acquired considerable freedom and influence.

At about the same time, various guilds opened "professional" schools, and private, secular institutions were established for more general educational purposes. Education to equip the lower classes with basic skills was also begun. Unlike the German *Gymnasium* or the English grammar school, both of which prepared future members of the elite for university training, all these schools were regarded as terminal.

During the Renaissance, religious authorities lost some of their control over education. The trend was reversed during the Reformation and the Counter-Reformation, as rival religious groups fought for control of the schools. In countries dominated by radical Calvinist sects the reversal was very temporary, for these groups moved rather quickly to a position of toleration which led, finally, to the development of secular school systems. The United States is the most obvious example of the Calvinist view. It established a public, secular—though vaguely Protestant—school system at a far earlier period than any European nation. Calvinist Protestantism had other consequences, too, in terms of the proportion of the community's resources which would be devoted to education. The affirmation of the individual's personal relation to God and the importance of reading the Bible caused Calvinists to emphasize elementary education for all children. As early as 1647 the General Court of Massachusetts required all towns of a certain size to establish and maintain reading schools. By the time of the American Revolution, it is estimated, 90 to 95 per cent of the white inhabitants of the New England colonies were at least literate, a level which was not achieved by any area in Europe, with the exception of Scotland, until the late nineteenth century.

Even in Catholic and Lutheran countries, events in Europe were forcing states to take on more of the responsibility for educating the community. The connection between literacy and national power had become more and more obvious as technology advanced, and national states moved to centralize the control of education in their hands. In Prussia, education at all levels was placed under state jurisdiction, although the church supplied teachers and its contribution to "moral" education was recognized. In France, Napoleon wrested education from the church and established a national system. The dispersion of democratic ideologies in the nineteenth century fostered the widespread growth of educational opportunity. By the end of the century, most countries in Western Europe were providing compulsory schooling for all children between the ages of six or seven and 13 or 14. The United States was still far ahead in this field, having by then established the first system of mass education in the world, including the huge expansion of schools of higher learning.

In Germany, Prussia's hegemony over education and the development of a national educational system were the result of a conscious desire to enhance state power. In France, reformers helped achieve the same result through their desire for centralization and their antagonism toward a church whose educational system they considered both stifling and defective. In England, however, where local church and philanthropic efforts had provided a network of schools and localism was not considered a threat to the nation's welfare, a state school system was not established until the end of the nineteenth century.

In all three countries, intense conflicts, which continued into the twentieth century, occurred between those who believed in religious education and those who maintained that education should remain under the control of secular authorities. The dispute was most bitter in Catholic countries because of Catholic protective attitudes toward the educational process. To the radical Calvinist, religion was a matter of faith pure and simple: science and religious belief were two separate compartments. To the Calvinist, the secular school could do his children little harm, provided, of course, it was not actively anti-religious; he became quite willing, then, to leave religious instruction to the Sunday school. Catholics, however, believed otherwise: the primary purpose of education was to produce the good Christian, and all other purposes were secondary. To the Catholic, science could not so easily be separated from religion because Catholicism was a comprehensive and rationalistic ideology. As Pius XI declared in his encyclical *On the Christian Education of Youth,* issued in 1929:

. . . the mere fact that a school gives some religious instruction . . . does not bring it in accord with the rights of the Church and of the Christian family, or make it a fit place for Catholic students. To be this, it is necessary that all the teaching and the whole organiza-tion of the school, and its teachers, syllabus and textbooks in every branch, be regulated by the Christian spirit, under the direction and maternal supervision of the Church; so that religion may be in very truth the foundation and crown of the youth's entire training.[6]

Until the mid-twentieth century, education in most European countries remained segregated by social class. The mass of the population received an elementary education and then some vocational training until they were fifteen or sixteen. Relatively few went from special elementary schools to public or grammar schools in England, to gymnasia in Germany, or lycées in France; a still smaller number continued on to the university or its equivalent. As late as 1966, as Table 7.2 shows, only seven per cent of the relevant age group were enrolled in institutions of higher learning in England. The comparable figure for France was 16 per cent. Even the U.S.S.R., which had made tremendous strides in education since the Revolution, had admitted only 24 per cent.[7]

Opportunities have broadened in Europe, however, since World War II. More and more youth are entering college-preparatory programs as the movement toward the comprehensive school so characteristic of both the

[6] Quoted in Joseph Husslein, ed., *Social Wellsprings,* Vol. II: *Eighteen Encyclicals of Social Reconstruction* (Milwaukee: Bruce Publishing Co., 1942), 114.

[7] See J.-J. Servan-Schreiber, *The American Challenge,* p. 73.

TABLE 7.2. HIGHER EDUCATION

	Number of students in 1966	As percentage of population between 20 and 24
Britain	165,000	7.0
France	500,000	16.0
Germany	280,000	7.5
U.S.S.R.	4,200,000	24.0
United States	5,526,000	43.0

Adapted from Dimitri Chorafas, *The Knowledge Revolution* (London: George Allen and Unwin, Ltd., 1969, New York: McGraw-Hill, 1970). Reprinted by permission of the publishers and the author.

United States and the Soviet Union gains ground. Educators are also de-emphasizing the classics and changing from a highly authoritarian teaching pattern to one which stresses a more democratic and active relationship between faculty and students. Nonetheless, all European systems still retain a larger element of tradition than the American. The number of hours spent in school is much greater, discipline is more rigid, the amount of homework required is more taxing, and sheer memorization is allotted far greater importance.[8]

European universities were created originally to educate scholars, gentlemen, and clerics, or to prepare individuals for the traditional professions. With the possible exception of those in Germany, they responded slowly to the enormous changes that took place in the European economy in the seventeenth, eighteenth, and nineteenth centuries.[9] Well into the twentieth century, most universities were still emphasizing the humanities or law and ignoring technical training in such fields as engineering, agriculture, and business administration. A vicious circle resulted. Lower-middle-class students who chose higher education as the main avenue of social advancement could use their training only in the civil service, teaching, or legal practice. They did not, therefore, enter occupations that would have contributed to economic growth. And, of course, the number of places available for those trained in traditional professions depended very much upon the creation of an advanced economy. Consequently, in France and Russia particularly, university graduates became part of an unemployed intellectual proletariat of the large cities in which they clustered, and provided leadership for radical political movements of both the right and the left.

The problem was far less acute in England. For one thing, a large and articulate middle class had formed before the rise of the modern university in the nineteenth century. England's middle class not only had a high standard of living, it had a tradition of education and culture capable of competing with academic-professional culture. Education at Oxford or Cambridge was a confirmation of status rather than a way of attaining it; higher education never became the only channel of social mobility, or even the principal one. Many lower-middle-class students attended nonacademic technical schools or learned a useful profession by attending provincial universities.

While there were fewer students attending British universities than on the Continent, the proportion enrolled from the lower classes was greater. In this sense, England has always been a less stratified society than either Germany or France. In the 1940's, for example, 23 per cent of British university students were sons and daughters of manual workers, as compared with about four per cent in Germany and France.[10]

In the United States, the evolution of the university was considerably different. Until the 1860's, universities adhered closely to the upper-class values of British institutions and were attended only by a small elite. But with the establishment of the land-grant colleges, which introduced scientific and technical training, universities became extremely popular. By the middle 1950's, forty per cent of those graduating from college were from working-class or farm backgrounds. At about the same time, according to official Soviet figures (which must be taken with a little caution), between thirty and forty per cent of those graduating from Soviet universities were of working-class or peasant background.

---

8 See the comparative study conducted by the Gallup Institute as reported in the *Saturday Evening Post*, December 24, 1960, pp. 60–76. See also the more detailed summary in *Sondages*, no. 4, 1961.

9 The following paragraphs are based upon Joseph Ben-David, "Professions in the Class System of Present Day Societies," *Current Sociology*, XII, 3 (1963–1964), 297–298.

10 *Ibid.*, pp. 285–286.

Eighty-three per cent of the Soviet population in 1958 were classified as workers or peasants; the comparable figure for the United States was fifty five per cent. Thus, the chances of a Soviet working-class child obtaining a higher education compared with a youngster of "white-collar" background are considerably less than in the United States.[11]

With the end of World War II, European universities began to expand quickly and to give more attention to newer disciplines. If present trends continue, more than twenty per cent of the college-age group will be entering French and English institutions of higher learning by the 1970's. Expectations for Germany are somewhat lower, although pressures for a larger enrollment are growing.

THE ENGLISH PATTERN: Until 1833 the English state had hardly anything to do with the educational process. What education the poor received was provided by church schools, the charity of philanthropists, or apprenticeship. The rich were educated by tutors or at exclusive private or church schools. Many middle-class children attended the new academies established by the several Nonconformist groups.

In 1833, however, Parliament authorized that money be used "in aid of private subscriptions for the education of the poorer classes," and in 1880 it made elementary education compulsory. It is estimated that in 1816, 875,000 children out of a possible 1,500,000 attended school. By 1835 the figure was 1,450,000 out of 1,700,000, and by 1861 2,500,000 out of a possible 2,750,000. The amount of schooling also increased: the average duration of school attendance in 1835 was one year, and by 1851 it had risen to two years. In 1893, 11 was fixed as the

terminal age for education; in 1918 it was raised to 14.[12] Although school facilities continued to expand and the number of students attending school until the age of 17 or 18 continued to grow, the next major piece of educational legislation was not enacted until 1944.

In 1944, Parliament divided the educational system into elementary and secondary schools; examinations would be given to 11-year-olds to determine which type of secondary schools they could attend. Parliament also created scholarships to help students enter some of the better private schools and universities. Under the new law, three categories of secondary schools were established: "grammar schools" to provide primarily academic training for university attendance; "modern" schools to furnish both general and vocational training—and a limited opportunity for advancing to an institution of higher learning; and "technical" schools to offer students the skills needed to move directly into industry. As late as 1963 close to sixty per cent of the school children between 12 and 15 who were attending schools were attending secondary "modern" schools. And, of these, the great bulk were still leaving school at 15.

English education, despite the state's intercession regarding its structure, continues to be largely under local control. The British never believed in the need for that complete reorganization of the school system which occurred in France after the Revolution. And, unlike the German pattern, a substantial portion of British schools remain private, even though most of them now receive extensive public support and are subject to public regulation. In numbers, the most important of these schools are those which are church-related, primarily Anglican or Catholic. After a long period of wrangling, Parliament approved the Education Act of 1944 under which a compulsory (nondenominational)

11 *Ibid.*, p. 286. Using 1950 data, the Japanese Ministry of Education concluded that the chances of an upper-class child graduating from an institution of higher learning exceeded that of a lower-class child by 3.0 in the United States; 3.5 in England; 4.0 in the Soviet Union; and 22.0 in France. *The American Behavioral Scientist*, IX, 1 (January 1965), 31.

12 Raymond Williams, *The Long Revolution* (New York: Columbia University Press, 1961), pp. 136–137.

religion course would be given in all state schools and substantial aid extended to church-related schools. Approximately ninety per cent of the maintenance costs in these schools are met by the government, which also pays eighty per cent of replacement and expansion costs. As in the United States, those calling most aggressively for a fully secularized state education system with no direct aid allowed religious schools are the Nonconformist sects. Unlike the United States, however, they have never been able to muster enough strength to achieve their goal, even though England today is a more secularized society than the United States.

The most important private schools in terms of their impact on British social and political life are undoubtedly the public schools. Like the state-supported lycées in France and the German gymnasia, public schools have been the traditional training ground for the country's elite—those who would go on to the most prestigious universities and become the nation's rulers.

The public school, developed in the nineteenth century, derives its name from the fact that it is directed by a board of governors, who, unlike those managing many other private schools, have no financial stake in the institution. Many of the public schools originated in Tudor times or the late middle ages, when the oldest of them, Winchester (1382) and Eton (1440), were founded. At the time they were called grammar schools, because they concentrated on Latin grammar.

By the middle of the nineteenth century, their prestige had fallen below that of the newly created Nonconformist academies. Under the leadership of Thomas Arnold, the public schools underwent a renaissance and became highly attractive, particularly to the nouveaux riches of the Victorian middle class who wished their children to have a "proper" education. Those institutions which remained "day" schools continued to be called "grammar" schools, a name applied now to all nonboarding schools which offer a primarily

academic education. Others were transformed into boarding schools, drawing their pupils from a national constituency. These became the modern English public schools, at which students were expected to learn how to give and take orders (younger students were placed under the authority of older ones) and to acquire a sense of fair play, group loyalty, and dedication to public service.

The ideal public-school graduate was trained to be a gentleman who combined the best features of aristocratic bearing and Victorian taste. He would have a smattering of the classics, and be sexually and emotionally restrained, fairly good at sports, and not too materialistic. He would be an individual of broad general culture, knowing some, but not too much, Latin and Greek. The aim of the public school, then, was to turn out young men of good character who could adapt themselves to any situation. Of course, schools differed considerably from each other in their approach to this end. Winchester, for example, was and still is more scholarly than Eton or Harrow, although all have produced a number of graduates who later became first-rank scholars.

The graduates of England's public schools went on to dominate the university life at Oxford and Cambridge—and later the political and social life of the country as well. Although the public schools educated a mere fraction of the population, their graduates made up 56 per cent of the members of Commons and filled the great bulk of positions in the upper levels of government, especially the foreign service, during the 1920's and 1930's. Foreign-service personnel are still predominantly public-school graduates. Harold Wilson is the first twentieth-century prime minister who is not a public-school alumnus.

Even in the late nineteenth century, the public schools and grammar schools offered extensive scholarship aid which opened their doors to some children of lower-middle- and working-class background. English working-class youth had more opportunities to attend an academic secondary school than French or German youngsters of comparable background,[13] even though German and French elite schools were run by the state.

With the Education Act of 1944 and the expansion of educational opportunities after World War II, more and more students are receiving "grammar" school training. In return for government aid, these schools have opened their doors to more scholarship students. It was, in fact, expected that with the expansion of state-sponsored "grammar" schools the private grammar schools and public schools would gradually lose their appeal.

It is true that public schools no longer supply as large a proportion of Oxford and Cambridge students as they once did, and that the "establishment" is taking on a more varied character, partly because of its greater size and diffusion.[14] Nevertheless, public schools have shown little sign of dying out. If anything, their assets—and the demand for enrollment—are increasing. In the past several years, tax subventions by the government and financial support from industry have improved their financial position.

Englishmen, then, go on sending their children to public schools when they can, not only because classes are smaller and teachers better, but also because of class snobbery and a genuine respect for the values institutionalized by these schools. Yet both public and private grammar schools are the target of mounting criticism. The basic charge is that they continue to cultivate elitist attitudes in their students, even as the public persists in exhibiting what critics would describe as an unhealthy deference to the public-school product. Added to this judgment is the argument that the kind of training offered—as at Oxford and Cambridge—is out of tune with modern trends, that it encourages the

cult of the amateur which is responsible for England's remaining a "fuddy-duddy" society, while America and even France and Germany place more emphasis on the natural and social sciences. The most bitter attacks have been leveled by ex-students: young men who emerged from the working class on the basis of scholarships, discovered the social climate of public schools to be almost intolerable, and later found themselves torn between two worlds, yet belonging to neither.

When it came to power in 1964, the Labor Party was tacitly committed to eliminating public schools in their traditional form, or at least fully incorporating them into the state system. A commission appointed to investigate the problem, however, ruled out both alternatives, and, with some dissent, urged that the public schools be required to admit still larger numbers of state-supported students and that they eliminate some of their more archaic practices.

The system of examinations taken by students at the age of 11 for purposes of streaming has also been subject to increasing attack.[15] It has been argued that the examinations do not catch "late bloomers" in the working class, and that streaming itself contributes to snobbery. Polls of students in grammar schools reveal that some students there regard the rest of the population as a "moronic" mass. Studies also reveal that once students are assigned to secondary modern schools, they get the notion they have no further to go and may as well quit trying.

These studies and criticisms have resulted not only in the gradual discontinuance of the 11-plus examination but in experimentation with one or another variety of comprehensive school on the American order. In 1965, the government requested all school systems to develop plans for a comprehensive school. Between 1962 and 1967 the number of students of secondary-school age attending comprehensive schools rose from two per cent to

---

13 Ben-David, "Professions in the Class System," pp. 289–295.

14 The term "establishment" is generally used to refer to the British "ruling class" in the social and economic as well as the political sense.

15 "Streaming" refers to the practice of segregating students, theoretically by ability, and placing them on separate educational tracks.

14 per cent. In order to speed up the process of switching over to comprehensive schools, the Labor government said in 1969 that it would seek laws making the submission of "satisfactory" plans compulsory.

The government has also extended the period of compulsory education to age 16, beginning in 1970. Further, more and more children of working-class background are receiving special study assistance in order to help them make full use of their capabilities. As in the United States, investigators have concluded that the home environment of working-class children tends to inhibit their ability to learn in the absence of such assistance.

The changes that have swept through England's elementary and secondary schools have also brushed universities. The English university system still revolves about Oxford and Cambridge (Oxbridge).[16] Until the mid-nineteenth century, these two universities educated primarily the sons of the nobility, gentry, and clergy. Their scholarly standards were low, but scholarship was irrelevant for most professions. The few students who subsequently became physicians or lawyers could comfortably acquire the necessary skills as guild apprentices; a university degree to practice law or medicine was not required.

Beginning in 1836 with the University of London, urban and provincial universities were founded to meet the more utilitarian needs of a new age, and, of equal importance, to provide higher educational opportunities for lower-middle-class and even working-class students. The "redbricks," as these universities came to be called, placed greater emphasis on the social and applied sciences. Most of the redbrick universities were established in small towns; their growth remained sluggish until after the turn of the century, and few of them established graduate schools

on the order of those founded in Germany and the United States. For most provincial universities, however, Oxbridge remained the model; they have invariably suffered from a sense of inferiority that has led their staffs to regard an appointment at Oxbridge as the culminating experience of their lives.

In the meantime Oxford and Cambridge were themselves making adjustments to the changing environment. Degrees validating serious intellectual study in the arts and sciences were established, and some first-rate research laboratories were installed. As with so many other English institutions, the flexibility of Oxbridge enabled it to retain its hold on British intellectual life and to remain the training ground for the British governing class. Between 1870 and 1960, for example, Oxford and Cambridge provided 87 per cent of the permanent secretaries of the British Civil Service, and 72 per cent of the members of British cabinets. Indeed, as late as 1959 they provided all but one of the successful candidates for the senior civil service and foreign service.

The postwar explosion in university admissions and new developments in the social sciences and technology have led to the creation of a substantial number of "plate glass" universities. Self-consciously contemporary in their outlook, some of them have established reputations in specific fields superior to those of more traditional institutions. They are also offering Oxbridge a taste of real competition—even as the latter attempts to adapt itself to the demands of the 1960's and 1970's.[17]

As with other European countries, England is also facing a serious dilemma in higher education as the demand for places in universities rises faster than society is able to satisfy it. Most other nations in Europe have partially solved the problem by increasing admissions, with the expectation of a sub-

---

[16] Much of the following several paragraphs is based on Joseph Ben-David and Awraham Zloczower, "University and Academic Systems in Modern Societies," *European Journal of Sociology*, III (1962), 45–85.

[17] A discussion and analysis of some recent trends and problems will be found in Sir Eric Ashby, "The Future of the Nineteenth Century Idea of a University," *Minerva*, VI (Autumn 1967), 3–17.

stantial dropout rate. Thus far, the British have, on the whole, resisted this alternative. Students admitted to British universities are carefully selected and the vast majority of them can expect to graduate. The British have not allowed university facilities to become as overcrowded as in France and Germany, which may help explain the relative mildness of the British student revolt.

What is also true of the British university, and of the European, is that it is being transformed from an "elite" institution, in which academic authority mirrored the hierarchical character of the society, into an "expert" institution, in which academic authority is based on the knowledge of those who teach there. And as in all European nations, the transition in England is meeting with resistance, and the problem of transition is further complicated by student upheavals which demand the ultimate democratization of university authority.[18]

THE FRENCH PATTERN: At the time of the French Revolution, three quarters of the women and more than half of the men in France were illiterate. Despite some meager attempts by the state to enlarge educational facilities in the seventeenth and eighteenth centuries, most of them had remained under the aegis of the Catholic Church and were primarily for the well-to-do or those in religious orders. Nor did there develop in France that tradition of philanthropy or concern with the education of the poor that was an earmark of England. Even institutions like the University of Paris that had achieved international reputations during the middle ages had, for the most part, declined. The whole movement of the Enlightenment developed outside the university, not within; in fact, the universities, having become politi-

cized, were highly conservative institutions bent on maintaining the intellectual status quo.

During the Revolution, church schools were confiscated and plans were drawn up to organize a centralized national system of education. The universities were abolished on the ground that they were reactionary, the idea being that they would be replaced by specialized institutes for training people in those technical areas in which the nation was weak. Thus were created the *Grandes Écoles* that were to figure so significantly in both research and professional education in France.

Aside from these acts and a considerable amount of theorizing, the revolutionaries accomplished little in the way of positive educational reform. It was left to Napoleon to carry their ideas to fruition and to set the pattern of French education. The entire educational system was centralized as the University of France and placed under a grand master whose authority extended to every aspect of educational activity. One of the major devices used to secure uniformity of curriculum and standards was the creation of that system of stiff national examinations which is still a part of French education. The concept of special, autonomous faculties as corporate bodies was retained rather than the concept of the corporate university.

The faculties concentrated on training students for traditional professional careers, while the Grandes Écoles became centers of training for specific technical professions such as engineering. The university's function was generally regarded solely as educational; scientific research was, and still is, reserved for special schools like the Institut de France.

While the universities were eventually reorganized to contain at least a faculty of science and a faculty of letters, these were not linked to form a university in the traditional sense until late in the nineteenth century. Even so, the structure of the French university is still fairly different from its English or German counterpart.

[18] For a discussion of the differences between "elite" and "expert" universities, which takes the American and Soviet patterns as examples of the latter, see Joseph Ben-David and Randall Collins, "A Comparative Study of Academic Freedom and Student Politics," in Reinhard Bendix, ed., *State and Society* (Boston: Little, Brown and Company, 1968), pp. 402–423.

Under the First Empire, a beginning was also made in establishing a system of public primary schools to provide terminal education for the masses, although facilities were greatly limited. In addition, Napoleon I set up a system of public secondary schools (*lycées*) supported and controlled by the national government. These were typical boarding schools charging fees and offering a classical curriculum. The great majority had their own primary schools from which they drew most of their students. Other nonboarding schools (*collèges*), offering the same type of curriculum, were founded by local communities, but kept under strict national jurisdiction.

The system of public primary schools grew slowly, and it was not until late in the nineteenth century, under the Third Republic, that the goal of primary education for all was implemented. In 1881, compulsory schooling for children from the ages of 6 to 13 became law, and it was a consequence of this action that the illiteracy rate, which had been twenty per cent in 1872, fell to 4.2 per cent in 1910. Until the end of World War II, however, the basic elements of the two-track system were relatively unchanged. For the few, special primary schools led to a highly academic secondary education and, in some cases, eventual admission to a university faculty. For most students, primary education was terminal, although vocational schools, some of which dated back to the turn of the century, were available for special training.

Despite the fact that the lycées were public rather than private institutions, the proportion of children of working-class or peasant background that attended them was lower than the proportion of working-class students in English public or grammar schools. French education was, however, more democratic in this regard than German, and in terms of numbers, more students gained admission to academic secondary schools in France than in England.

From the time of the Revolution, the re-lationship between church and state in the field of education fluctuated widely, depending on the regime in power. After a long period in the nineteenth century during which the Catholic Church was given considerable leeway in the field of education, the Third Republic moved toward a secular school system with restrictions upon private church schools. The conflict between the local curé and the public schoolteacher during this period, especially in rural France, has been immortalized in French literature. It came to a head after the Dreyfus affair, when all teaching by religious orders was prohibited and church and state were formally separated.

Although the law forced the closing of a large number of private schools, its provisions were never totally enforced and many schools managed to continue functioning. During the interwar period, Catholic school enrollment grew from a low of 92,000 in 1920–1921 to 240,000 in 1938–1939. The Vichy regime assisted religious schools, but the practice was eliminated again with the creation of the Fourth Republic.

The partisans of aid to private schools and those who opposed all subventions engaged in acrimonious debate throughout the early years of the Fourth Republic. Each side organized monster rallies and petitions, and some of the clergy counseled their parishioners to refuse to pay taxes unless aid was forthcoming. It was a major election issue in 1951 and, shortly afterward, the Loi Barangé, providing for some aid to Catholic schools, was passed by the National Assembly. The result was a split between the Socialists and the Popular Republican Movement; united, they had formed part of the center-left coalition of which most French governments had been composed after 1947.

The financial aid, however, was minimal, and the proportion of students in Catholic schools began to decline once again as the quality and number of public schools rose. Between 1951 and 1959 the percentage of students attending Catholic secondary schools, for example, dropped from 35.2 to 28.4.

French universities, in the meantime, had more or less retained the structure and organization bequeathed by Napoleon. The university faculties remained separated professional schools that trained students for specific careers as, indeed, did the Grandes Écoles. The Grandes Écoles have become increasingly prominent, their entry examinations increasingly difficult, and the social class from which students are recruited increasingly narrow. Many of them are still the best passports to high-level posts in industry and government, and they continue to turn out young men of great technical competence. In fact, graduates of the Grandes Écoles have been largely responsible for the post–World War II remodeling of France.

In 1896 a reform of the universities had brought the faculties together under a single administrative structure. Universities still lacked the curricular diversity of American or British institutions, however, and the different faculties retained a good deal of autonomy. The typical French university, then, remained a scattered conglomeration of buildings without a central focus. Students lived at home or found private lodgings, and attendance at courses was not required. Not until after 1920 did French universities begin to offer a wider choice of course work; this was partially accomplished by permitting specialized

research institutes, which engaged in some teaching, to attach themselves to universities. Equally important, as higher education has become more and more democratized, efforts have been made to provide a common "general education" curriculum for at least the first year of university attendance. Other changes include the building of dormitories and some compulsory attendance at courses. Most French students, however, especially in Paris, are still left on their own: they may attend lectures if they wish and live where they want to; they may take and retake the qualifying examinations and are free to prepare for them in whatever manner they choose. Despite the latitude granted students in these areas, the restrictive, traditional nature of the curriculum has met with mounting criticism. This, as well as overcentralization and overcrowding, the lack of communication between faculty and students —and, indeed, the lack of faculty interest in teaching—was among the sources of student revolt in 1968. The de Gaulle regime responded with moves that would permit decentralization of the university structure and greater participation in the decision-making process by faculty and students. The implementation of plans for university expansion, which had been on the boards before the 1968 riots, should help relieve the overcrowding. If the plans are carried through, moreover, the proportion of students enrolled in

TABLE 7.3. HIGHER EDUCATION ENROLLMENTS IN FRANCE

Selected years, 1937–1966

	Law	Science	Letters	Medicine	Pharmacy	Total
1937–1938	20,400	10,173	16,750	17,930	6,022	71,275
1949–1950	39,056	25,306	35,279	29,491	7,256	136,388
1960–1961	33,980	77,250	59,550	40,305[1]		211,085
1962–1963	45,468	88,595	88,734	37,822	10,169	270,788
1965–1966	77,114	121,539	133,216	48,014	13,776	393,659

[1] Data include pharmacy.

Source: George A. Male, *Education in France* (Washington: U.S. Department of Health, Education, and Welfare, 1963), p. 163; *Annuaire Statistique de la France, 1967* (Paris: Institut Nationale de la Statistique et des Etudes Economiques, 1967), p. 136.

institutions of higher learning will be considerably greater than in England by 1970. And, as in England, a shift from the customary humanistic courses to the newer sciences and social sciences is accelerating.

The democratization and expansion of higher education has coincided with similar developments at the secondary-school level. The proportion of eligible students receiving a diploma from a secondary school jumped from 5.0 per cent in 1950 to 11.5 per cent in 1960; it is expected to reach 23.5 per cent in 1970. The de Gaulle government further manifested its commitment to educational expansion and reform by raising the terminal school age from 14 to 16. And perhaps most important of all, the fate of students is no longer determined by an examination taken at the age of 11. Rather, under the reforms now being put into effect, students will remain in comprehensive schools until age 15, when, on the basis of their overall records, they will proceed to either a technical school or the lycée. Quite

understandably, a reform of secondary-school education of this dimension is being fought tenaciously—in France as it is in England—by the conservative educationists. Programs for building new secondary schools, as well as enlarging university facilities, are being pushed, although the nation still suffers from serious shortages of both buildings and teachers.

The de Gaulle government also sponsored legislation to assist the parochial schools. Again the proposals sparked a serious political conflict. Public opinion polls showed most Frenchmen opposed to the legislation, but such was de Gaulle's influence over the General Assembly that the bill passed. In essence, it allowed private schools to enter into one of four types of contract with the government, each involving more financial assistance—and more extensive government regulation.

The slight increase in aid notwithstanding, the proportion of students educated in private schools has continued to drop (see Table

TABLE 7.4.   ENROLLMENT IN SELECTED FRENCH UNIVERSITIES
BY FIELDS OF CONCENTRATION, 1965–1966

University	Total students 1965–1966	Fields of concentration				
		Law	Sciences	Letters	Medicine	Pharmacy
Paris	127,883	30,660	33,886	38,135	13,582	3,497
Aix	27,397	3,638	8,780	8,525	2,962	1,109
Besançon	5,648	712	1,879	2,511	182	132
Bordeaux	23,307	4,330	8,150	7,931	3,646	877
Caen	9,538	1,882	3,060	3,941	362	170
Clermont	9,142	1,445	3,107	3,316	588	439
Dijon	8,179	2,055	2,384	2,980	231	164
Grenoble	17,518	2,259	6,540	6,058	513	348
Lille	20,404	3,378	6,561	6,060	2,254	815
Lyon	27,475	4,166	8,484	7,605	3,885	1,062
Montpellier	20,565	3,220	4,862	6,946	3,285	1,327
Nancy	14,301	2,048	3,722	4,386	2,062	572
Poitiers	8,906	1,834	2,423	4,109	210	96
Rennes	15,445	2,563	5,076	6,018	892	344
Strasbourg	17,490	3,365	4,550	5,310	1,904	594
Toulouse	25,956	3,078	9,731	7,759	2,266	841

Source: *Annuaire Statistique, 1967,* p. 136.

7.5). Catholic secondary schools, especially, have always had the reputation of being inferior to public schools, and they tend to cater to young women being prepared for marriage or young men who have failed public-school examinations. Whether the additional government aid will enable Catholic schools to improve their educational standing is uncertain. They are being forced to hire, as are Catholic schools in the United States, an ever larger number of lay teachers, and both their curriculum and their outlook have come to resemble those of the public-school system. Nevertheless, the issue of aid to religious schools is still a touchy one in France. It was one of the factors which prevented Gaston Defferre, the Socialist mayor of Marseilles, from forming a Socialist-M.R.P. coalition to back him against Charles

de Gaulle in the 1965 presidential elections.

French education is still marked by authoritarian discipline in the classroom, and by memorization and long hard hours of work, far more so than American or even English schools (except for the British public schools). It also is still far more examination-oriented. In addition to examinations to determine whether a student can or cannot enter an academic secondary school, uniform state examinations, which more than one-third fail, are required for a school degree. At the university, which a student can attend only if he has passed his secondary-school examination, another examination must be taken at the end of the first year. It is estimated that 65 per cent of the students who enter French universities fail to graduate.

For many a bourgeois family, failure by a

TABLE 7.5. FRENCH PUBLIC- AND PRIVATE-SCHOOL ENROLLMENT, 1951-1966

In thousands of students

	1951–1952		1957–1958		1961–1962		1965–1966	
	Public	*Private*	*Public*	*Private*	*Public*	*Private*	*Public*	*Private*
Nursery schools and kinder-gartens	1,000	221	1,097	210	1,200	176	1,508	271
Elementary schools[1]	3,336	801	4,655	976	4,882	946	4,825	823
Lower secondary (*cours complémentaires*)	218	60	351	93	630	146	753	186
Apprentice-ship centers	143	70	159	90	222	130	322	196
Academic secondary	353	186	569	242	822	320	1,196	422
Vocational secondary[2]	124	35	142	44	205	59	210	0
Teacher training schools	15	0	19	0	25	0	32	0
Universities	137	2	176	2	235	2	345	0
Total	5,326	1,375	7,167	1,657	8,221	1,779	9,191	1,895

[1] Including those in elementary classes attached to academic secondary schools.
[2] Including those in vocational sections in academic secondary schools.

Adapted from Male, *Education in France*, p. 4; *Annuaire Statistique, 1967*, p. 114.

son to obtain a secondary-school diploma is a major tragedy. Because of the centralization and uniformity of the educational system, requirements for university admission are the same everywhere in France. The son who does not succeed at the secondary-school level is blocked from any further academic schooling. Also, unlike the system in the United States, secondary and university education in France have trained students only for elite positions; the French have made scant effort to cater to the multiplicity of student tastes, requirements, or aptitude. In the United States, students can major in home economics, agriculture, or business administration, and aptitude tests are used to channel them into courses suited to their capacities or needs. In France, until recently, the alternatives have been much more limited—a circumstance that not only has reduced the number of individuals in second-echelon positions who could obtain further formal training, but has also created a society that draws a more cutting distinction between the highly trained elite and the "unintelligent masses." This pattern is changing in France —as it is elsewhere in Europe—and the evolution of a broader educational system is contributing to the democratization of French society.

THE GERMAN PATTERN: Prussia was the first major European power to enunciate the idea of universal elementary education. Again, the system which developed consisted of two basic tracks. As late as 1911, more than ninety per cent of the students attended an elementary school (*Volksschule*) until age 14, after which they found employment or entered an apprenticeship. Some states of the empire, including Prussia, provided for a minimum of 240 hours of continuation school (*Fortbildungsschule*) for those from 14 through 17, and courses for specific trades such as forestry, gardening, and cabinetmaking.

A few students, drawn almost entirely from the middle classes and the aristocracy,

entered a three-year preparatory school at age six and then continued their education for nine years at a Gymnasium. Originally these institutions provided only a rigidly defined classical education, but by the middle of the nineteenth century two new types of gymnasia had emerged, the so-called *Realschulen* and *Oberrealschulen*. The latter reduced classical language requirements and stressed modern languages, mathematics, and science. Graduation from a Gymnasium and the passage of an entrance examination were required for admission to a university.

During the nineteenth century and the first part of the twentieth, German universities were held in high esteem throughout Europe. They were regarded as places for research, in which professors were entitled to teach more or less what they wished, and academic reputations were based upon contributions to scholarly research. Contacts between professors and students were infrequent, the professors being interested only in students who could further their own work. And this work, on the whole, was of a very high standard. Of the 69 Nobel Prizes awarded in physics, chemistry, medicine, and literature between 1901 and 1918, 21 went to Germans. Even today, German academics enjoy a prestige and deference unmatched in any other Western country. Their academic freedom, however, has not been without its limitations.

While a professor was free to expound his views within the university, it was expected that he would refrain from partisan political activity outside its walls. The large majority of academics, in part because of discrimination against Socialists in appointments, but mostly because they were fairly conservative, adhered to this line. And although German scholars boasted of their academic freedom, it is doubtful that it would have been maintained had many of them expressed views which the state considered subversive.

Students, too, enjoyed a freedom unparalleled in other countries. They were permitted to attend lectures as they wished, and they could even move from one university to another seeking professors who they felt had the most to offer. Except in some science courses, the only limitations on a student's freedom were those imposed by the necessity of passing certain examinations. It must be remembered, of course, that university students were theoretically obtaining professional training; they had completed their general education in a highly disciplined Gymnasium whose curriculum and requirements were far more rigid than in secondary schools in the United States and England. For many German students, a university was also a place where "education" was subsidiary to companionship, drinking bouts, and dueling fraternities. The degree itself, family connections, and the dueling scar secured their place in society. It should also be remembered that, partly because of the system of national examinations for civil-service positions, the basic curricula of all German universities were very similar.

The administration of education at all levels was largely left in the hands of the empire's various states, most of them following the Prussian model more or less closely even on the secondary- and primary-school levels. Private schools continued to exist, but these were few and never comparable with the English public school. The Prussian state had handled the problem of religious teaching by permitting religious authorities to exert influence on the curriculum and by providing for compulsory courses in religion. With the formation of the empire, the tendency was to continue this system; Protestant and Catholic parents could send their children to schools in which classes were taught by members of their own faith. In a number of areas, however, *Simultanschulen* were created to teach both Catholic and Protestant children, with separate religious classes for each. In states of mixed religious composition, Catholics usually supported denominational schools (*Bekenntnisschulen*), which were the most numerous, and non-Socialist Protestants favored the Simultanschulen. The Socialists opposed any religious instruction, although their position did not receive much popular support.

The Weimar Republic maintained the policy of allowing the states to keep control of education. The national government had been expected to move toward centralization, but plans in this direction never materialized. Some changes were made in the general pattern of education, such as the elimination of special preparatory schools and the establishment of a common elementary education for all children in the *Grundschule*. Also, middle schools (*Mittelschulen*), charging tuition, were organized; these enabled lower-middle-class children to obtain a more comprehensive training in order to fit them for better jobs. Further, subject matter requirements for admission to universities were liberalized, and educational opportunities for girls were expanded. But none of these innovations involved a transfer of authority from the states to Berlin, and even fewer changes were made at the university level. The academic profession remained the preserve of the upper middle classes, as did university education itself. In general, the academic profession was hostile to the republic, and, in the late 1920's, the more liberal professors found themselves aggressively censured not only by the state and their colleagues, but by right-wing student movements, including those created by the Nazis.

With the triumph of National Socialism, German education underwent a number of drastic changes. Control over education became the exclusive prerogative of the central government, and all teachers suspected of subversive leanings were dismissed. To the Nazis, the traditional gymnasia were an anachronism; the regime eliminated a good many of them, insisting instead upon a common secondary schooling for those permitted to advance further with their education. The Hitler regime also restricted educational opportunities for girls and created special boarding schools to generate a new Nazi elite. Its aim in all cases was to replace an emphasis on traditional culture by "education for life." As Reich minister of education August Heissmeyer described it:

> ... All true education is education for real life in its full extent; it is political education. ... It is formative education, education designed to mould a type, and such education is achieved ... through community and team education ... which embraces, as far as possible, all human powers.[19]

Confessional and private schools were gradually done away with and all schools made interdenominational. While religion continued as part of the curriculum, the time allotted to it was shortened considerably. The Nazis also curtailed the number of students entering universities and prohibited any form of academic self-government on campus. They did, however, increase the number of scholarships, and made an effort to "democratize" universities by allowing persons between 25 and forty to enter without a secondary-school degree—if they passed special "maturity" examinations designed to reveal unexpected talents.

With the end of the war, the Western allies dispatched the Nazi teachers and concentrated on what they termed "re-education for democracy." In the end, however, the structural alterations that were made in the occupied zones, with the exception of the Russian, had little lasting effect, and the Federal Republic reverted to the Weimar format of organization. The Länder[20] once again control educational policy, despite the fact that the West German government now coordinates these policies and is assuming an increasing portion of the financial burden. The religious organization of schools also has reverted to the pre-Nazi pattern, with Länder free to choose denominational or nondenomi-

national schools. The religious issue is important only on the elementary level; all gymnasia are now nondenominational.

Today about 55 per cent of the West German students attend denominational schools, 39.5 per cent of them Catholic and 15.5 per cent Protestant. In Länder where Protestants have been in a majority, nondenominational schools have been favored—even by the Catholics themselves in these states. Denominational schools are still an integral part of the educational system, but only because the clergy has insisted that Catholic youngsters attend them.

In general, the two- (or rather three-) track system of German education is still in operation. All German children attend a common Volksschule for their first eight or nine years of education; afterwards, approximately 25 per cent move on to some form of secondary education, while the remainder move directly into the labor market, although all are required, as part of apprenticeship training, to attend classes part time until they are 18. Only about ten per cent of German students now enter an academic secondary school (one of the three types of gymnasia), which they attend until age 19. Assuming they then pass their Abitur, they can be admitted to a university. However, movements to establish a system of comprehensive schools are gaining ground in some Länder.

Enrollment in German universities has grown, but as yet attendance has failed to match that in England and France. It jumped from approximately 110,800 in 1950–1951 to 280,000 in 1966, but the enrollment gap between Germany and her two neighbors will increase substantially unless plans materialize for a vast expansion of educational facilities. Until very recently, no such expansion was in the offing. Germans as a whole still regard university education as something for a small elite, and despite the elimination of Gymnasium fees, youth in Germany have been far less anxious to pursue an advanced academic career than in France or England.

---

[19] Quoted in R. H. Samuel and R. Hinton Thomas, *Education and Society in Modern Germany* (London: Routledge and Kegan Paul, Ltd., 1949), p. 52.

[20] German Länder are roughly equivalent to American states.

Thus, little pressure has been exerted on the government to review its attitude on university education. There are now signs, however, not only of greater demands by youngsters for educational opportunities, but of concern on the part of political authorities regarding Germany's future reserves of trained manpower.

German university education has, by and large, continued its traditional pattern, having thrown off the shackles of the Nazi experience. Students are still free to move from university to university, the only requirement being passage of a final examination. Yet partly as a result of this leeway on attendance, the student dropout rate is extremely high, despite the Abitur required for admission. The best estimates indicate that some fifty per cent of students who begin a university education never complete it. Critics of the university system argue that students should receive more careful help in planning their programs, and, indeed, some universities have established counseling services, particularly in the natural sciences. It has also been urged that courses in the liberal arts conform to a specific content and that some compulsory attendance be instituted.

At all levels, German education has become less authoritarian as the distance between students and teachers has been bridged. In addition, educational opportunities have widened. Even so, as late as 1965 Germany still had not fully adapted itself to the educational requirements of the second half of the twentieth century. Curricula at universities were still more traditional than in either France or England, and professors continued to insist adamantly upon their old prerogatives. Some of the steam behind the student rebellions that began in 1966 is to be explained in these terms, and the pressure exerted by students has resulted in a re-examination of the educational system, especially the university structure. Without much question, in Germany as throughout Europe, the trend in higher education is toward greater student participation on decision-making bodies. Current movements toward reform are designed both to reduce the authority of the small number of professors who hold chairs and increase that of the younger faculty members, and to organize universities around departments instead of faculties. The tradition of universities being run by chancellors chosen every few years by the senior faculty is being replaced; the trend is now in the direction of appointing full-time presidents. One promising reform of the mid-1960's, that university students who do not receive their degrees by age 26 or 27 be asked to leave, has not, however, been carried out—blocked, for the time being at least, by the weight of tradition and violent student opposition.

THE RUSSIAN AND SOVIET PATTERN: Very little provision for formal education seems to have existed in Russia until the time of Peter the Great, despite some evidence to the contrary for the Kievan period. The monasteries did make attempts toward educating a few, but the population as a whole was left to its illiterate ways. Those among the aristocracy who wanted to educate their children sent them abroad, or else employed private tutors, often foreigners. Even under Peter, progress was slow, and the first Russian university, the University of Moscow, did not open its doors until 1755. Catherine the Great furthered the educational program in urban areas, although many of her efforts were reversed by her successor.

Both public and private schools were established during the nineteenth century in urban areas, several universities were founded, and, after the 1850's, educational opportunity was broadened at the primary and secondary level. The educational program established for European Russia followed that of the West: a two-track model with the equivalent of the Gymnasium or lycée serving as the route to university education. Between 1895 and 1915, the number of students admitted to secondary schools trebled. In 1908, the Duma made primary-school attendance compulsory between the ages of eight and 11 (the law was to take full effect in 1922); in 1912, it created a system of higher elementary education.

According to the census of 1911, only 21 per cent of the population in the empire was literate, although the figure for towns and cities was 45 per cent. Five years later, 91 per cent of the children were attending schools and the literacy rate had risen to more than 50 per cent. It seems possible, therefore, that basic literacy would have been achieved quickly for the great bulk of the population, even under the empire, had not the war and the Revolution intervened.

Simultaneously, university education was extended, and a number of institutions attained a relatively high level of competence. The Romanovs, however, vacillated in their attitude toward universities; Alexander II granted them considerable independence, but as they became hotbeds of revolutionary activity, controls and censorship were restored. Alexander's murder led to even tighter controls: student rights were revoked, the police were given wide latitude to root out subversives, and faculty appointments were placed under the control of the Ministry of Education. Some concessions to both students and faculty were made after the Revolution of 1905, but these were not extensive, and until the end of the empire, universities went right on being centers of unrest.

One of the first acts of the Kerensky government was the secularization of all church schools. The Communists later endorsed this policy, and while local schools came under the control of the Soviets, overall direction was determined by the Commissariat of Education. The Bolsheviks had two major educational aims: to eliminate illiteracy as quickly as possible and to develop a new and "democratic" style of teaching consonant with their ideology. Bolshevik education would not only provide the population with the necessary skills to establish an advanced industrial society, it would also contribute to the emergence of the ideal Communist man—a man whose moral fulfillment would lie in creating a society in which individual self-fulfillment was inextricably interwoven with the personal fulfillment of all.

To accomplish this end, Soviet leadership decided to end the two-track system. Education for all students would be the same, and it would be accessible at all levels to everybody. Examinations and diplomas would be eliminated even at the university level, and a university education would become available to all who wanted it. Within the school, students would learn by doing—intellectual life would be combined with practical work experiences. Memorization of historical dates and other minutiae would be cut to a minimum. Students would be responsible for their own behavior, and, especially in universities, they and their teachers would together establish disciplinary standards. Of course, those teachers whose political opinions were not in accord with the regime were to be ejected and replaced by educators dedicated to the Marxist-Leninist view.

A program to reduce adult illiteracy was also instituted. In 1920 the All-Russian Extraordinary Commission for the Liquidation of Illiteracy was created for this purpose, and a massive campaign was undertaken which combined education in the fundamentals of reading with intensive propaganda.

In the first few years of the Communist regime, little of a positive nature was accomplished. The destruction of school buildings and the loss of teachers seriously hampered the development of effective programs. By the late 1920's, however, the Soviet educational system seemed to be making headway; certainly, some American visitors to the Soviet Union were impressed. John Dewey, for example (from whom the Soviets had borrowed heavily), while somewhat concerned at the excessive political indoctrination in Soviet schools, found that Russian school children were "much more democratically organized than our own," and much more adequately trained "for later active participation in the self-direction of both local communities and industries."[21]

The Russians, however, were not nearly so convinced, and by the early 1930's the tide had begun to turn in the other direction. Detractors complained that children were not learning anything, that teachers had no control, and that "hooligans" were taking over the classroom. Thus, the prerogatives of the teacher were slowly restored to a degree comparable with Western Europe, and permissive practices were abandoned. Examinations were reinstituted, memorization was again emphasized, and new textbooks underlined the importance of practical, systematic knowledge over theory. The methods of Dewey, which had for so long been praised, were considered anathema. The 1952 edition of the *Bolshaia Sovetskaia Entsiklopediia* declared:

> *The philosophy of Dewey is a philosophy of war and Fascism. Dewey is a proclaimer of contemporary American reaction, an ideologist of American imperialism [and] a violent enemy of the U.S.S.R.*[22]

Whatever the merits of Dewey's "progressive" education, the Soviet leaders found his approach unsatisfactory in terms of their principal goal—the creation of a technologically advanced society. This social resolve, coupled with the more "traditional" orientation of the new leadership, helps explain Communist Russia's "great retreat" in the field of education.

The lack of funds also contributed to further changes in Soviet education during the 1930's and 1940's. Fees were charged for secondary school as well as for higher education. Long before, the practice of admitting

almost anyone to a university had been dropped and more rigorous standards were adopted. The growing disparity between the proportion of middle-class and working-class children who entered the university did lead to attempts at "proletarianization" in the 1930's. But this failed, and after 1938 the government ceased to release information on the class origin of students.

With the end of World War II, and especially after the death of Stalin, new trends appeared in Soviet educational policy. Tuition fees were eliminated, coeducation restored (it had been abolished in 1943), and educational facilities extended. By the 1950's Soviet schools were coming to resemble those of Western Europe in very important ways. Universities were expanding and Soviet provisions for continuing higher education were more advanced than those in many other countries. The old dream of polytechnical training that would combine learning with practical activity on all levels had been largely discarded. The favored few—usually from middle-class backgrounds—moved from secondary school directly to the university, while the great bulk of students entered the job market.

In a move to reverse this trend, as well as to obtain needed manpower, Khrushchev initiated a series of reforms in 1958, the central feature of which was to combine work in industry with schooling. Most students who wished to enter the university were required to work in industry for two years. The reforms were dropped shortly after Khrushchev's ouster. Teachers had complained that students were being "overloaded" with the combination of work and education, and that much of the employment was of the make-work variety, anyway. The Brezhnev-Kosygin regime has been responsive to more modern educational techniques and has also provided special assistance for "disadvantaged" children. Indeed, for the first time, in the 1960's, Soviet educators began to point up the great disparity in the educational at-

---

21 He wrote this in a series of articles in *The New Republic* in 1928. His opinions are quoted in George Z. F. Bereday *et al.*, eds., *The Changing Soviet School* (Cambridge: The Riverside Press, 1960), p. 66.

22 *Ibid.*, pp. 67–68.

TABLE 7.6. EDUCATIONAL ATTAINMENT AND SOCIAL CLASS IN THE
SOVIET UNION: THE 1930'S

*Data based on interviews of émigrés from the Soviet Union during and after
World War II*

Educational level attained	Intelligentsia	White-collar employees	Skilled workers	Ordinary workers	Collective-farm peasants
0–4 years	—[1]	7%	30%	56%	69%
5–7 years	7%	26	43	33	22
8–10 years	22	40	24	11	9
Some college	28	12	3	—[1]	—[1]
College graduate	43	15	—[1]	—[1]	0
Total number of respondents	557	553	225	382	267

[1] Less than one per cent.

Adapted from Alex Inkeles and Raymond A. Bauer, *The Soviet Citizen* (Cambridge, Mass.: Harvard University Press, 1959), p. 138. Reprinted by permission of the publisher.

tainment of various social classes, noting that as many as 82 per cent of the children of white-collar workers enter universities, as compared with only ten per cent of peasant children.[23]

Soviet education today is strongly centralized. With some variation allowed for language and ethnic differences, all Soviet students wear the same uniforms, follow the same syllabi, and have more or less the same classroom experience.

Compared with American or English schools, the Russian are far more traditional, relying to a much greater extent upon tests, lectures, and recitations. The school day and year are much longer and the amount of assigned homework considerably heavier. Soviet intentions, right from the beginning, are to cram youngsters with knowledge useful to a Socialist society and to provide them with those moral characteristics which will make

for the new Soviet man. Students are given large doses of Communist ideology and taught personal values not very different from those characteristic of American middle-class life: punctuality, neatness, politeness, and responsibility. Among the twenty standard rules that every student must memorize are the following:

2. To study diligently, to be punctual in attendance, and not arrive late for classes.

3. To obey the instructions of the school director and teachers without question. . . .

8. To sit upright during the lesson, not leaning on his elbows or slouching. . . .

9. To rise when the teacher or director enters or leaves the room. . . .

14. Not to use coarse expressions, not to smoke, not to gamble for money or other objects.

17. To obey his parents, to help them take care of his small brothers and sisters.[24]

These efforts are all part of the desire to create a new individual utterly different from

[23] For a review of the still fairly sparse Soviet literature on this subject, see Murray Yanowitch and Norton Dodge, "Social Class and Education: Soviet Findings and Reactions," *Comparative Education Review,* XII (October 1968), 248–267.

[24] Quoted in Nigel Grant, *Soviet Education* (Baltimore: Penguin Books, Inc., 1964), pp. 48–49.

the traditional Russian character—and to eliminate that "spontaneity" and disorder which the Soviets view as among the curses of old Russia. One widely read book on child-rearing practices says:

The old intellectual "Russian" impetuousness was able to combine, it would seem, two incompatible things. On the one hand, thinking intellectuals could always come out with the most radical and rational ideas often exceeding the bounds of plain reality, while at the same time they always exhibited a passionate love of slovenliness and disorder . . . the fact is that in this slipshod "leftish" way of living there is nothing except historical poverty and nakedness. Some people even today, at the bottom of their hearts, still despise punctuality and orderly movement. . . .

A slovenly attitude toward life cannot fit with the style of Soviet life. With all the means at our disposal we should exorcise that belated Bohemian spirit which only by a great misunderstanding is considered . . . a token of poetic taste.[25]

The de-emphasis on individual spontaneity aside, the other major difference between Soviet education and more "enlightened" Western practices lies in the insistence of the former upon collective action and its minimizing of personal achievement. This difference, of course, can be exaggerated—given the rather stiff competition for places in special schools and higher education.

Discipline is enforced in several ways. By law and by custom, Soviet teachers are prohibited from striking children; other than assigning special tasks or ordering a student to stay after classes end, the teacher relies upon the persuasive powers of shame. The teacher can also make use of youth organizations that work closely with the school administration and exercise a rather energetic

influence over students to make them conform to group norms. Parents, too, are held responsible for their childrens' actions, and may find themselves criticized at meetings in their apartment house or place of employment.

Theoretically, the Soviets believe in a comprehensive school system in which there is no differentiation within classes between "brighter" and "duller" students. Until recently, intelligence tests were unacceptable in theory, and while individual differences are recognized, they are—officially—not regarded as important. If some students are "backward," their classmates are encouraged to help them; if they fail, they repeat the course. It is estimated that some twenty per cent of all students are regular repeaters. The high percentage of failures and the growing number of special schools for the talented have tended to add elements of streaming to the educational process.

There are other more significant signs of change in the Soviet system. More teachers are calling for new classroom methods, criticizing the accent on lectures and formal recitations. Others are asking for the explicit recognition of individual student differences and the employment of techniques to take them into account. As in so many other areas of Soviet life, education is in a state of considerable ferment.

Since the Revolution, higher education in the Soviet Union has grown rapidly—but not fast enough to meet the demand of all those who want it. As in France, the facilities of higher learning (*vuz*) are divided into universities and institutes. The universities provide training in the pure sciences and humanities, although the range of available subjects varies with the institution. While theoretically the standing of all universities is equal, the Universities of Moscow and Leningrad are among the elite institutions. Specialized institutes include the following: (1) polytechnical, which offer a diversity of courses including metallurgy and chemical

25 A. S. Makarenko, *A Book for Parents* (Moscow: Foreign Language Publishing House, n.d.), p. 302. Quoted in Edmund J. King, ed., *Communist Education* (Indianapolis: Bobbs-Merrill, 1963), p. 91.

technology; (2) branch technical, which are normally restricted to a particular industry such as the Mining Institute at Dnepropetrovsk; (3) agricultural; (4) medical, for the training not only of doctors but also of specialists in such fields as sanitation; (5) pedagogical; (6) economics; (7) law; (8) art; and (9) physical culture. Competition to enter either a university or an institute is intense; examinations are used to screen applicants, but recommendations from Komsomol or Communist Party groups can be decisive. Only slightly more than half the students attending universities are full-time; the rest are part-time and correspondence students.

Russian universities do not charge tuition, and most students who do reasonably well are awarded a basic stipend to meet living costs. The stipend is minimal, however, and must be supplemented by either work or family assistance. Right from his first year at the university, the student's program is highly specialized, and is regarded as training for professional employment. There is little room for the dilettante: the student's time under instruction is roughly twice that in most Western countries, and attendance at lectures and seminars is compulsory, although cutting is not unknown. Recently, academic voices have been raised against the "passive" quality of the educational experience, particularly its emphasis on memorization.

All Soviet students must take and pass courses in Marxist-Leninist political theory. For those working in the humanities, these courses absorb about six hundred hours over a five-year period; in the technical fields, the number of hours is closer to three hundred. The testimony of defectors and observers seems to be that most students find these courses a "drag" and give them only slight attention.

Essays, laboratory work, homework assignments, tests—these are the means by which students are assessed. The final test is the diploma thesis or project, during which the student must defend a specific piece of

work before a board consisting of professors and representatives of the relevant ministry. The state can assign graduates to any job in any part of the Soviet Union for two or three years; after that, they are free to seek employment wherever they wish. There are, of course, many ways of avoiding the government assignment, as shown by the number of complaints about parents using influence to keep their children from being sent to areas far from the amenities of urban life.

All members of the academic community are expected to engage in research, and prestige quite naturally is engendered by those whose work is more extensive or significant. Most research is organized under government auspices and is conducted in connection with industry. The All-Union Academy of Sciences and the State Research Coordination Committee are the most important agencies in this regard, although other sponsoring institutes have been created. There has always been some tension between scientists who wish to pursue their own theoretical interests and the demand of the government and the party that research be "practical." For the most part, the government has had its way—most recent Soviet scientific contributions in fields such as physics have been of a technical variety. A listing of the discoveries in pure physics since World War II by Eugene P. Wigner gives credit for 18 to the United States, eight to Western Europe, and only six to the Soviet Union. In the field of applied technology, however, the Soviet Union has done much better. As Soviet scientists and social scientists achieve more freedom, this picture may change.[26]

Many educators have been attacking the well-defined separation between the institutes, which concentrate on research, and the universities, which do not. They argue that a closer connection between the two would be far more beneficial to the student, the school, and the nation. In this respect, the Russians, and other continental Europeans, seem to be

[26] *Survey*, July 1964, pp. 22–23.

moving closer to the American university practice of combining both research and teaching activities. Ironically, many American educators are now recommending the traditional French and Soviet patterns, contending that when teaching and research are joined in a single institution, teaching suffers.

Throughout the early 1920's, Soviet academics were reasonably free to explore varying points of view in nonpolitical disciplines which skirted political questions. During most of Stalin's rule, however, even the natural sciences came under the close scrutiny of the Communist Party. For a short time, the theory of relativity was taboo because of what the Soviets considered to be its "idealistic" reactionary implications. But by the early 1950's physicists had begun to regain their freedom, and the party now no longer intervenes in this area of natural science. The biological sciences proved somewhat stickier. Stalin supported Lysenko's view that inheritable changes could be brought about by environmental influences; Mendelian genetics was proscribed as reactionary, and many Soviet biologists sympathetic to the genetic theory were imprisoned or executed. Here, too, control has loosened, as it has even in economics, where Soviet scholars have been borrowing some of the techniques used in "bourgeois" countries. There is also some easing of party restrictions on the teaching of sociology, and they have been tentatively slackened for such courses as psychology and history. The Soviet Union still has a long way to go, however, before the academic freedom enjoyed by almost all European nations becomes a reality for it, too.

4. THE IMPACT OF THE MASS MEDIA

The existence of a written language is one of the most important factors that differentiate civilizations from primitive societies. While some societies have developed fairly complex social systems without this tool, they are few in number. The reasons are obvious. The invention of writing enabled men to record new discoveries and ideas; the written language, then, provided a basis for storing and increasing the total amount of knowledge available. It also enabled men to develop a sense of time—to distinguish between present and past with some precision.

The development of a written language was also, as Rousseau noted, among the major causes of inequality among men: it permitted the creation of a "high culture" known only to the few. Nevertheless, the relative simplicity of European languages—as contrasted with, say, Chinese—caused mass literacy to be more easily achieved and contributed to the comparatively early formation of democratic institutions in the West.

For a long time, communications technology in Europe was dormant. With the invention of the printing press in the sixteenth century, it began to grow at a spectacular rate. The result was not only the mass output of books, but the evolution of media specializing in providing "news" to a widening audience. The printing press as a technological development permitted the expansion of cultural horizons and the amalgamation of peoples into ever larger units.

Radio, the telephone and telegraph, and especially television have produced another revolution in communications, not only in the advanced countries but also in those "developing areas" which find that national consciousness can be created without universal literacy. As a result of this revolution, a vast proportion of the population in all modern states obtains much of its picture of political events from television broadcasts. The impact of television can be overstated, of course. Research indicates that newspapers, and, more significantly, face-to-face discussions are still extremely important in structuring social and political attitudes. Nevertheless, television is contributing to a broadening of man's outlook—even as it contributes to his cultural homogenization in all European countries.

Television has also become a major instrument of social mobilization. Events which might have had only local significance thirty years ago now take on national, and sometimes international, dimensions. The momentous growth of the civil-rights movement in the United States was, in part, caused by television, as was the spread of student "confrontations" from America to Europe. Unquestionably, the publicity attending demonstrations in one nation has given students in others a feeling of power—a sense of being part of a worldwide movement. This is obvious not only from the spread of student riots, but from the fact, for instance, that European students quite self-consciously borrowed American techniques. Finally, it seems quite clear that students in all European countries, partly through the impact of television, are acquiring a sense of participation in a common European culture. Thus, American involvement in Vietnam is regarded as a general European involvement and opposition to American policies is easily transmuted into opposition to one's own society.

The long revolution in communications technology has had many effects upon the political order. Insofar as it has increased the ability of any community to acquire, store, and transmit information, it has augmented the community's capacity to adapt more effectively to environmental changes. It has become possible to create larger and more complex organizations and to coordinate their activities more efficiently. It has also become possible to discern more easily the consequences of public policies. Finally, it has become easier to mobilize the community for the achievement of common goals. Some social analysts have been so impressed by the central role played by the mass media that they see contemporary societies as giant communications grids and examine political systems in these terms.

However, the revolution has not been an unmixed blessing. The opportunities for greater public participation in the life of the community and the growing facility with which many people can be mobilized create

new problems for political leaders. The mass media can help escalate group demands, with attendant disorder a possibility, far more quickly than was true in the past, and they can reveal to different groups more sharply than ever where and how their interests actually conflict. As for political leaders, their constant exposure to a mass audience places them under tremendous strains. This, in turn, inhibits the execution of policies whose long-range results may be beneficial but which, if exposed to the premature glare of publicity, can be undermined by a suddenly aroused opposition. In short, the mass media are among the principal factors in the crisis of authority that is now facing all Western European nations.

5. THE MASS MEDIA IN WESTERN EUROPE

The origins of the European mass media can be traced back to the Roman Empire, where their primary function was dissemination of information by the government to officials and to the population. The *Acta diurna* of the Empire was an official publication in bulletin-board form; in addition to communicating official government decrees, it served many other functions which characterize mass media today, reporting, for example, news of crime, sports, and "sensational" events.

When the empire died, institutions bearing any resemblance to the modern mass media disappeared from the West until about the fifteenth century. It was the printers of the 1400's who were among the first creators of modern newspapers—single sheets of "sensational" news that sold for a small price and brought in a fairly tidy profit. Although there were periods of freedom for their publication, especially in German cities, most newspapers and periodicals quickly came under preventive censorship, and the establishment of journals usually required a charter granted only by those in authority. Until well into the eighteenth century, European monarchs in every country regarded the press, aside from its entertainment or news value, primarily as a mechanism for communicating edicts and obtaining public support for the regime's policies.

The idea that the press might serve other functions—provide a source of news and opinion free from government censorship, and hence act both as a check upon government and as a means by which the community could refine its attitudes on public policy—began to appear only with the development of liberalism and the democratic state. It is not surprising, then, that the concept of a "free press" was first propounded in England and first realized in the United States; nor any accident that a mass-circulation press appeared first in the United States and then in England. The latter phenomenon was accompanied by mass literacy, which, of course, it required in order to prosper. The success of the mass-circulation press was also contingent upon technological innovations that permitted the printing of large numbers of newspapers quickly and cheaply, and the speedy transmission of news from all parts of the world.

Most forms of censorship were eliminated in England after the Glorious Revolution of 1688. But a stamp tax upon newspapers, designed to hamper the publication of a press that might cater to the "masses," was not repealed until 1855. In France, censorship and government control were initially eliminated by those who made the Revolution, but were restored during the period of Jacobin rule and tightened even further by Napoleon. From then until the Third Republic, repression alternated with periods of relative freedom. The law of 1881 finally established complete freedom of the press and remained the fundamental charter of the French press until the Vichy regime. Press freedom was restored after World War II, although limitations upon the press are still greater in France than in England or the United States.

In Germany, censorship depended upon the individual rulers and individual states. Again, periods of liberalism alternated with periods of repression. In 1874, shortly after the unification of Germany, Bismarck established a comparatively liberal press law, although during the time of the Kulturkampf and later, when he was campaigning against the Socialists, many newspaper editors were intimidated and newspapers repressed. In fact, from 1878 until 1890, only two out of 47 existing Social Democratic newspapers were permitted to continue functioning. The Weimar Republic retained the German Press Law of 1874, but administered it in conjunction with the elaborate Bill of Rights of the 1919 Constitution, which permitted almost complete freedom of the press. During a good part of the nineteenth century, however, both the German and the French governments sponsored their own newspapers, and even today both governments have special funds for subsidizing friendly periodicals.

With the turn of the century, the circulation of the press increased in all Western countries. Again, the United States led the way. By 1910 some 24 million newspapers were being published daily, and by 1930 the number had climbed to more than 42 million. In England, roughly two million papers were being printed daily by 1910, and this figure had jumped to five million by 1920; the Sunday press had reached 13 million copies. In both countries, the press had become primarily a commercial venture with most of the revenue coming from advertising. Whatever their political leanings, publishers regarded their papers as money-making propositions. Even so, the better papers attempted to separate news reporting from editorializing. There were exceptions: in the United States, the Catholic Church established diocesan newspapers, and in England the Labor Party established its own newspaper, the *Daily Herald,* to serve as its mouthpiece. Almost from its inception, however, the paper was forced to take commercial factors into account.

In both France and Germany the growth of the press took a quite different form. Aside from the fact that newspapers regarded themselves as quasi-literary journals, many of them were sponsored during the late nineteenth and early twentieth centuries by religious and political groups. Both the Catholic Church and political parties, especially the mass parties of the left and the right, looked upon newspapers as a crucial part of their effort to create a total environment for their constituents—either to protect them from a hostile (secular or radical) world in the case of Catholics, or, in the case of Socialists, Communists, or National Socialists, to prepare them for tomorrow's new world.

In the aftermath of World War I, popular, "commercial" newspapers in France and Germany began to replace the party or church press, at least in terms of circulation. As late as 1930, however, German newspapers included 444 published by the various nationalist parties, 312 published by the Catholic Center Party and the church, 169 published by the Socialists, and eight published by the National Socialist Party. The end of the Second World War did nothing to change the general pattern: the commercial press increased in circulation, the special press declined. In 1946, for example, the daily organ of the French Communist Party, *L'Humanité,* had a total circulation of five hundred thousand; by 1950 its circulation had dropped to fewer than two hundred thousand, where it has since remained. The same has been true of the press of other political parties. In England, the Labor Party and Trades Union Congress sold the *Daily Herald,* which finally ceased publication in 1964. In Germany, even where a party press has continued to exist, its orientation has become more and more commercial. In 1930, about half the German newspapers represented some political party; today the figure is less than twenty per cent, and in terms of circulation, no more than four or five per cent.

The growth of the press as a commercial venture requiring large outlays of capital and heavy reliance upon advertising revenue has had a significant effect on the number of

papers published. As both competition and operating costs increased, the number has been declining even as overall circulation has risen. In several countries, most particularly England, which early developed a tradition of a national press centered in London, press ownership has fallen into fewer and fewer hands. By the 1960's, over 65 per cent of the circulation of the English press was controlled by three organizations.

Most European newspapers—with the exception of the big-city press—have come to rely almost entirely upon a small number of news agencies for national and foreign news. The earliest of these was Agence Havas, formed by Charles Havas in France in 1835. After World War II, it was reconstituted as Agence France Presse, but it had to turn to the government for financial aid. Not until 1957 did it obtain an autonomous board of directors controlled by newspaper editors. For a long time, the most famous of the international news services was England's Reuters, formed in 1851. It, too, is a privately owned, nonprofit corporation with about 2,000 fulltime employees scattered throughout the world. The United States boasted three press agencies for many years: the Associated Press, the United Press, and the International News Service; the latter two merged in 1958. Most of these agencies have reciprocal relationships with each other and with newspapers for the exchange of news.

Not only have newspapers fought each other for survival, but the end of the two world wars brought competition from other media—first radio, then television. In the United States, both media remained in private hands, although the limited number of channels available, among other considerations, quickly led to some government regulations. In England, radio and television broadcasting came under the control of a public corporation, the British Broadcasting Corporation (BBC). During the period of its monopoly, the BBC maintained a reputation for studied impartiality in dealing with political news, and remained free from government control. In 1955, another network, the Independent Television Authority, was created as a commercial organization; it operates, however, under fairly tight regulation. In Third Republic France, private, regulated networks were allowed to broadcast along with an official government station. Under the Fourth Republic, both radio and television were brought completely under government control, and while they were supposedly given quasi-independent status, they were used as a propaganda device, especially at times of crisis. The de Gaulle regime exercised even closer supervision over television, discriminating openly against opposition and using the media to arouse support for de Gaulle's policies.

In Weimar Germany, radio was organized under an independent public corporation, and it was conducted with commendable impartiality. The National Socialist regime, of course, usurped all broadcasting rights, and radio became a major instrument for state propaganda. Since 1945, control of radio and television has been decentralized among the Länder.

THE BRITISH PATTERN: England was one of the first European nations to eliminate censorship—an action that followed widespread pressures on newspapers and periodicals in the eighteenth and nineteenth centuries. The greatest impediment to the development of a really popular press was the stamp tax, but bribery and government prosecution under rigid libel and security laws were also significant. Lord Clarendon as lord lieutenant of Ireland in 1850 thought it important to have a newspaper putting forth the Whig unionist case, and provided the editor of the *World* with £1,000. The violent attacks by the press on the first Derby-Disraeli ministry in 1852 prompted Disraeli to start a new weekly, which he published until 1858. But such practices were becoming rare; the press was beginning to rely more and more on advertising for its income, and outright bribery was no longer generally considered to be a legitimate mechanism by which politicians might influence public opinion.

Until the repeal of the stamp tax, the *Times* was probably the most influential paper in England; it certainly had the largest circulation, and was widely read and respected among the small elite that constituted the British governing class. Under the editorship of John T. Delane, the *Times* influenced the making—and unmaking—of British governments and managed quite easily to obtain and publish confidential cabinet decisions and state documents; nineteenth-century British cabinets were not cohesive party bodies whose members were bound to secrecy, but rather loose coalitions of party politicians who thought it natural to advance their particular interests in any way that seemed reasonable. Reporting of parliamentary activities had become routine by this time, incidentally, even though, characteristically, Parliament has never repealed these laws which prohibit such reporting, and members of the press are theoretically subject to fines.

With the stamp tax dead and new press techniques being developed, newspaper circulation grew very quickly. The first of the modern press lords was Alfred Harmsworth, later Lord Northcliffe, who, in 1896, began publication of the *Daily Mail* as a halfpenny newspaper. By 1900 its circulation had reached one million. He was followed by a number of other press lords, including the future Lord Rothemere and, later, Lord Beaverbrook, who took control of the *Daily Express* in 1924. By the 1920's and 1930's, newspaper circulation had reached more than two million, and most of the papers were fighting cutthroat circulation wars.

There also developed that dichotomy between the "quality" press and the "popular" press that persists even today and is far sharper than in the United States. The "quality" papers, limited to the *Times,* the *Guard-*

ian, the *Observer* (published on Sundays only), and, to a certain extent, the *Daily Telegraph,* concentrate on the presentation of serious news; the "popular" press emphasizes "entertainment" and life's gaudier aspects to an extent that even Americans brought up on the *Daily News* or the Hearst press might find rather shocking. Augmenting the field of serious newspapers are several high-quality weeklies such as the *New Statesman,* the *Spectator,* and the *Economist,* whose combined circulation is about 202,000. (See Table 7.7.)

The end of World War II and the advent of television brought with them vast changes in the newspaper world. Newspapers found themselves not only in deadly competition with each other but fighting desperately against television's encroachment on the public's attention. Many newspapers, particularly the smaller ones, either merged or went out of business. Between 1949 and 1962, 17 daily and Sunday newspapers ceased publication, often despite substantial circulations. In 1964, for example, the pro-Labor *Daily Herald,* which had effectively severed its

TABLE 7.7. CIRCULATION AND OWNERSHIP OF BRITISH NEWSPAPERS, 1968

Title and date founded	General political tendency	Ownership	Circulation average, Jan.–June (incl.) 1968
Dailies			
The Times (1785)	Independent	The Thomson Organisation Ltd.	401,315
The Daily Telegraph (1855)	Conservative	Daily Telegraph Ltd.	1,407,328
The Guardian (1821)	Independent	Manchester Guardian and Evening News Ltd.	280,877
Daily Express (1900)	Independent	Beaverbrook Newspapers Ltd.	3,852,613
Daily Mail (1896)	Independent	Associated Newspapers Ltd.	2,095,474
The Sun (1964)	Left of center	International Publishing Corporation Ltd.	1,065,972
Morning Star (1966)	Communist	People's Press Printing Society Ltd.	55,554
Daily Mirror (1903)	Left of center	International Publishing Corporation Ltd.	5,034,236
Daily Sketch (1909)	Conservative	Associated Newspapers Ltd.	914,946
Financial Times (1888)	Independent	Financial Times Ltd.	156,150
London evenings			
Evening News (1881)	Independent	Associated Newspapers Ltd.	1,181,824
Evening Standard (1827)	Independent	Beaverbrook Newspapers Ltd.	657,050
Sundays			
The Observer (1791)	Independent	The Observer Trust	902,647
The Sunday Times (1822)	Independent	The Thomson Organisation Ltd.	1,460,994
The Sunday Telegraph (1961)	Conservative	Daily Telegraph Ltd.	712,658
News of the World (1843)	Independent	News of the World Organisation Ltd.	6,191,142
The People (1881)	Independent	International Publishing Corporation Ltd.	5,532,959
Sunday Express (1918)	Independent	Beaverbrook Newspapers Ltd.	4,327,545
Sunday Mirror (1963)	Left of center	International Publishing Corporation Ltd.	5,137,531

Source: Central Office of Information, *Britain: An Official Handbook* (London: HMSO, 1969), p. 439.

direct editorial connections with the Labor Party in 1960, ended publication with a circulation of more than one million; it simply could not compete for advertising with such giants as the *Daily Mirror* (4,951,448), the *Daily Express* (4,275,643), or the *Daily Mail* (2,423,424).[27]

Both consolidation and the growth of newspaper chains placed the ownership of newspapers in fewer and fewer hands, and some of these powerful chains extended their influence to television. For example, Cecil King, a nephew of Lord Northcliffe and chairman of the *Daily Mirror* group, not only acquired ownership in 1961 of Odhams Press, thus gaining control over newspapers with 38 per cent of the daily and more than forty per cent of the Sunday circulation, he also purchased a share of a television station. Consolidation continued throughout the 1960's as more and more newspapers faced financial difficulties. Thus, in 1966, the stately *London Times* merged with the *Sunday Times* and became part of the newspaper empire of Lord Roy Thomson. Popular identification of these empires with a single man is not, however, always accurate, as indeed Cecil King was to learn in 1968 when he was ousted by stockholders for what many of his colleagues considered excessively vitriolic attacks upon the Wilson Labor government.

The one bright spot in the newspaper picture has been the gradual rise in the circulation of the quality press—a trend that is counter to the general drop in total newspaper circulation. However, even the quality papers are facing critical financial problems, despite the introduction of new techniques of printing and distribution.

It was concern with the trend toward consolidation and the increasing incidence of what some considered irresponsible journalism that led to the formation of two Royal Commissions on the Press (1947–1949 and 1961–1962). Both commissions deplored the

"sensationalism" of some of the popular press and expressed concern over trends toward newspaper empires; both also argued that the press did present a wide spectrum of political views, and that there was little evidence that pressures from advertisers or other groups had resulted in conscious distortion of the news.

Neither commission recommended any fundamental changes in British newspapers. Calling for a greater sense of public responsibility, they urged the formation of a voluntary press council for purposes of self-regulation. The council was formed, but there is little evidence that it has exercised any real authority. In an effort to deal with trends toward continuing consolidation, a law was passed in 1965 requiring that proposed mergers be approved by a monopolies commission; thus far, however, the commission has exercised very little influence.

It is difficult to measure the influence of the British press upon voting behavior, and even more difficult to judge its impact upon those basic social attitudes that affect the community's goals. Some critics argue that commercialization has caused a situation in which the press has failed to deal adequately with the main issues before the community and that it has, moreover, lowered—or at least not raised—the level of political discourse. These critics also argue that radical reforms such as the creation of publicly supported newspapers are required if the trend is to be reversed. The impact of the press on actual voting behavior, however, would seem to be rather limited, at least in the short run.

It is just as difficult to measure the effects of the press and its actions upon the policies developed by politicians.[28] Certainly reporters in England find it more difficult to get at political news today than do their counterparts in the United States. Even when they

---

27 See Table 7.7 for their 1968 circulation figures.

28 The following section is based on James B. Christoph, "The Press and Politics in Britain and America," *Political Quarterly*, XXXIV, 2 (April 1963), 137–150.

are given access to it, they are much more constrained about publication. For example, the British political journalist, unlike his American colleague, must wait fifty years for cabinet papers to become available, and the ministerial oath to observe the Official Secrets Act, plus the realities of cabinet politics in England, often prevent politicians from giving out information until long after the event.

One of the basic differences between the two countries is that despite the changes which have occurred since the war, the English population and the press itself still tend to defer to authority. Further, the status of newspapermen, in terms of both public esteem and educational background, is much higher in the United States than in England. Most newspapermen in England are not college graduates; today most American journalists are. It is no accident that most of the newspapermen who sit in Parliament are members of the Labor Party.

There are two other important points of difference. While both the United States and England have libel laws, those laws are more severe and more strictly enforced in England. American practice, of course, differs from state to state, but on the whole juries are much more likely to be sympathetic to "fair comment" in the United States than in England. Secondly, the dissimilarity in party and parliamentary structure has its effect upon news coverage. In England, party loyalty is still extremely strong and party discipline tight, even within the cabinet. To rise in the party, one must exhibit loyalty to it, and the cabinet works together as a party team. If trial balloons are to be flown, they are discussed in the party, or, because of its prestige, in Parliament. In America, not only the president, but cabinet officials and even individual members of Congress are far more independent in their political behavior. Thus the political leak and the inside story are a far more common phenomenon. The differences become obvious if one compares the Suez

crisis in England with the Cuban Bay of Pigs fiasco in the United States. In England, there was almost a complete news blackout, and the full story of Suez has yet to be told. In America, many reporters knew from the start almost as much about the Cuban invasion attempt as did the president. The same has been true during the entire Vietnam campaign, despite the complaints of American journalists. In comparative terms, American newspapermen have more freedom and are far better informed than their colleagues in England (or France), and are far more likely to be able to print what they wish.

Given the new opportunities provided by television today, it is clear that the British politician has less concern with the attitudes of the press than he once did. One must not exaggerate, of course, for the elaborate briefings that the press receives from political parties indicate they still believe British newspapers are a power to be reckoned with.

The British Broadcasting Company (BBC) was licensed in 1923 as a private corporation, and the major stockholders were six radio manufacturing companies. At first the government showed little interest in the new medium, although broadcast material had to satisfy the postmaster general. Sir John Reith, the first general manager of the corporation, quickly developed strong convictions about the proper role of broadcasting as a public service, and he proceeded to put them into effect without hindrance from either station managers or the government. The implementation of Reith's policies was followed by a government commission of inquiry which concluded that the BBC should not permit advertising and that radio broadcasting should be financed by a license fee for each radio set—a method that still provides BBC radio and television with its only significant source of income.

In 1926 the BBC was converted into a public corporation, independent in matters of day-to-day administration, but ultimately answerable to the cabinet and to Parliament on general policy. It was given a ten-year charter that was renewed in 1936. The postwar Labor government renewed the charter for five years in 1946, and commissioned a full-scale investigation of the service in 1949 by a committee headed by Lord Beveridge. The investigation was prompted by criticisms of the service and concern with the developing medium of television, but concluded that the BBC monopoly should be continued provided certain changes were made in its structure.

Action on the report was forestalled by the return to power of a Conservative government, and, in 1954, after a rather nasty fight, Parliament passed a television act that permitted the creation of a second television service. A new corporation, the Independent Television Authority (ITA), was created with the responsibility for appointing commercial broadcasting companies in more than a dozen regions and for supervising their performance. These companies were to sell time spots of controlled length and frequency to advertisers who would have no say in program content. The BBC retained control of all broadcasting facilities.

The first official assessment of the new system was made by a Royal Commission in 1962 (the Pilkington Report), which condemned the incidence of violence and "triviality" in the commercial service. The result was a strengthening of ITA's power to intervene in programming decisions. Commission endorsement of the BBC's record also led to the opening of a second BBC television channel in 1964. The new channel, on ultra-high frequency to which all television would eventually convert, has emphasized more serious intellectual and cultural fare than the other channels, directing its programs rather self-consciously to those who have been dissatisfied with the content of television.

British television has gone through a number of phases since the inception of ITA, and they can be understood only in terms of

its history. Lord Reith regarded radio as a medium designed to raise the intellectual and moral level of the population, and at first British radio concentrated on broadcasting Reith's version of "high culture." As a concession to popular preferences, diversification was gradually introduced until, by World War II, British audiences could choose among three stations, one of which, the so-called "third program," catered to highbrow tastes, even though it had limited appeal. In its political broadcasting, the BBC was scrupulously, even antiseptically, fair, emphasizing neutral commentary and carefully presenting as many possible sides of a given issue as it could.

Initially, BBC television followed the same pattern. It divided the time on the single available channel so as to insure the presentation of material with serious cultural and intellectual content at peak viewing hours. By the middle 1950's, however, BBC policies were caught in a crossfire of criticism. There were those, especially on the left, who, while committed to "raising the level of the masses," conceived high culture to be something different from what Lord Reith had in mind. They resented the timidity and "puritanism" that weighted Sundays with religious broadcasts and limited the opportunity for franker discussions of sacred British tradition. They urged a freer, more creative use of the medium.

Within the Conservative Party, on the other hand, a younger generation of M.P.'s thought that television, rather than giving audiences what Reith or anyone else believed they should have, should give them what they wanted. Both sides believed a dash of competition would benefit the medium. Some radio competition did, in fact, exist, for many British listeners could and did turn to Radio Luxembourg and other commercial outlets that catered to mass tastes.

The first result of competition from ITA was an abrupt drop in the BBC's audience, followed by an attempt to imitate its competitor—hence, the criticisms leveled by the Pilkington Report. By the middle 1960's, however, younger men in charge of BBC television programming were employing new techniques, and while catering somewhat to popular standards, they were also experimenting rather freely and interestingly. By 1966 and 1967, BBC television had begun to exhibit a social boldness which went beyond anything on American or Continental television. Programs were produced exploring religious and sexual themes in ways that shocked and angered a good many Britons— even as it made them watch the channel. Something of a reaction had set in by 1968, but despite active lobbying by a number of groups, the BBC has not pulled in its horns.

Political broadcasting followed a similar pattern. At first television retained the "balanced" quality of BBC radio; even its non-election political broadcasts were comprehensively dull. By the 1960's, however, political commentary became slightly acerb; political figures appearing on television were giving and receiving some fairly cutting barbs—and arousing the hostility of some political leaders. The BBC, however, has yet to develop a pattern of political commentary on television comparable to that of the United States. Concern with objectivity—whatever its virtues—has all too frequently had an inhibiting effect upon the lively presentation of news.

THE FRENCH PATTERN: All through the Third Republic, the French press was far more "political" than the English. Every major and some minor parties published their own newspaper. In all of them, articles were highly personal, usually signed by their author, and primarily expressions of opinion rather than attempts to relate the news.

By the end of World War I, however, a new type of journal had appeared, seeking a mass audience and, theoretically at least, attempting to be impartial on political matters. The new papers included *Le Petit Parisien,*

with probably the largest circulation in France, *L'Echo de Paris, Le Journal,* and *Paris Soir.* By the 1920's, the five largest of the new journals represented seventy to eighty per cent of newspaper sales. Perhaps the most influential paper during the 1930's, from a political point of view, was *Le Temps,* which was widely regarded as a spokesman for the government—when the government was conservative. However, not even the so-called *journaux d'information* were noted for accuracy in news reporting. Many received subsidies from special interest groups, including foreign interests, and *Le Temps* received secret financial assistance from the Ministries of Foreign Affairs and Interior. The result, for most French papers, was a continued succession of news stories of dubious accuracy in which fact and fancy were mixed, or even from which fact was conspicuously absent, capped by headlines designed to secure attention rather than to convey an accurate account of content. Moreover, the libel law in France has always made it difficult, if not impossible, for individuals to secure redress for fairly scurrilous personal attacks. The government, of course, did seek its own form of redress quickly: despite formal guarantees of press freedom, it was not loath to seize issues of newspapers that it deemed a threat to public order.

Since World War II, many of the older papers, including *Le Temps,* have gone out of existence as the result of collaboration with the Nazis. Following the publication of a spate of political journals immediately after the war, the trend toward a commercial press has continued and the number of political papers has declined. Those remaining in existence, such as *L'Humanité* and the Socialist Party's *Le Populaire,* do so only with heavy party subsidization. Thirty years ago there were 34 daily newspapers in Paris, 15 of them the organs of political groups. Today there are only 14, and most of them lack party affiliation.

The provincial press, on the other hand,

has grown enormously in importance, reflecting, in part, Paris's decline as the omnipotent center of French culture. Such papers as *La Dépêche de Toulouse* have sound reputations, and today the press in the provinces accounts for more than two-thirds of newspaper circulation—almost exactly the reverse of the prewar situation.

French weeklies, both serious and popular, have also gained wide acceptance since the war. They range from the ultrapolitical, left-wing *L'Express* through the brilliantly satirical and political *Le Canard Enchainé* to the entertainment-orientated, anti-American *Paris Match,* which has a circulation of 1,200,000.

On the whole, French newspapers are better written and more accurate in their reporting than before the war. Even the most influential papers among intellectuals, however, particularly the daily *Le Monde* and the weekly *L'Express,* are not without faults. Both are independent and honest according to their own lights, and, in contrast with American newspapers, they offer far more in-depth reporting. But both have also been irresponsible on occasion for printing and headlining as fact articles that, to say the least, are of dubious accuracy. *Le Monde,* for example, which is moderately left and neutralist, reported as fact that the *colon* riots in Algiers and their support by the French army were an American plot. Somewhat later *L'Express* ran a series of articles on the assassination of President Kennedy which were so full of simple factual errors that even the least respectable British newspaper would have hesitated to consider them. In 1965, the French press, itself on the whole critical of de Gaulle, decided that attacks on his foreign policy by American newspapers were a consequence of pressure from the Johnson administration. Again *Le Monde* offered this analysis to its readers as fact, revealing a complete lack of understanding of the American scene.

Government subsidies of the press are still used from time to time to cull effective support, though much less so than during the Fourth Republic, and individual reporters are regularly subject to police violence when covering riots. The government also continues to seize individual issues of newspapers containing stories it regards as a "threat to national security." Between 1955 and 1962, for example, 269 issues were confiscated, most of them for their reporting of the Algerian war. In many cases, the seizures were illegal, but even so, it was almost impossible for the newspapers to obtain compensation. In some instances, of course, the papers seized were irresponsible in their reporting and guilty of printing confidential information leaked to them by their partisans in the government. This was principally true during the Fourth Republic, when both Gaullist and Communist supporters regularly supplied "secret" military plans to their respective political mouthpieces.

As in other European countries, competition from television has contributed to a decline in newspaper reading. Here the French are faced with problems that the British do not share. There is less faith in the accuracy of the press in France than in England, and this circumstance is not unrelated to the comparatively small circulation of most French newspapers—a factor that keeps the size of their editorial staff and their technical capacity relatively low. French television also lacks the firm confidence of the public. It was only in the late 1960's that ownership of television sets became widespread in France, and even today the controls exercised by the government over the media yield a bias in the presentation—or nonpresentation —of political events.

Until 1964 television broadcasting was directly under the control of the Ministry of Information. The governments of the Fourth Republic used it to further their propaganda, and only the fact that most of them were short-lived coalitions usually outlasted by the medium's personnel permitted any development and diversity. In its first years, the de Gaulle regime was even more efficient in using television for its own ends. Thus, legislation that theoretically transferred the control of television to a quasi-independent body —the Office de Radiodiffusion Télévision Française (ORTF), modeled after the BBC —made little difference; the leading personnel remained Gaullist.

After 1964, the regime loosened its restrictions to permit the presentation of the opposition's viewpoints; it even allowed opposition candidates to appear on television during election campaigns. This freedom, however, was considerably circumscribed, as one of the effects of the student upheavals of 1968 proved. When television personnel responded to Gaullist moves to manage the news by going on strike and demanding greater independence, de Gaulle's response was to "reduce" the size of the television staff by firing strike leaders. The Pompidou government has promised to grant more autonomy to the ORTF.

In the meantime, French television had been facing other difficulties. While cultural standards were originally rather high (along the lines of Reith's "high culture"), there was little on French television to appeal to working-class audiences. In northeastern France, French viewers were turning to telecasts from Luxembourg and the Saar. Moreover, the financing of television by fees was not producing needed funds. The de Gaulle government responded by catering somewhat more to popular tastes, and, in 1968, it authorized the limited use of commercials.

THE GERMAN PATTERN: The German press before the Nazis took it over resembled the French in many ways. Political party organs, newspapers directly affiliated with the Catholic Church, and government-sponsored newspapers—all of them competed with a commercial press bent on making as much money as possible. However, the political and politically controlled press were even more significant in Germany than they were in France. So, too, were the "official" newspapers, of which the *Deutscher Reichsanzeiger und Preussischer Staatsanzeiger* was a classic example. Owned by the government, it was devoted to publication of state documents. In addition to government newspapers, there was the commercial press, founded by private interests but open to generous government subsidies and easily susceptible to government pressures.

The relationship between the party press and the political parties varied widely. Communist newspapers operated under strict party control, as did those of the National Socialist Party, whose central organ was the *Völkischer Beobachter*. The Social Democrats permitted their papers to have some freedom, and the most prominent Catholic papers were not formally under Center Party domination at all.

The commercial press, as indicated, was not above political tampering, a circumstance somewhat understandable in view of the economic problems it faced during most of the Weimar period. The weakness of commercial papers encouraged industrial interests, especially banks and heavy industry, to acquire stock in them for the purpose of expressing their political views.

Yet Germany was not without its independent and responsible press. Such papers as the *Frankfurter Zeitung* and the *Berliner Tageblatt,* while perhaps not comparable with the better British and American newspapers in the objectivity of their reporting, provided full, detailed, and reasonably fair coverage of the news, as well as considerable cultural material, and earned national and international reputations.

In the early years of the Weimar Republic, freedom of the press was strongly safeguarded, although vitriolic attacks upon certain political figures, in some cases virtually urging assassination, did lead to some government regulations. As the political situation grew more and more turbulent in the late 1920's and early 1930's, newspaper repression intensified. During the chancellorship of Heinrich Brüning (1930–1932), 284 newspaper issues were suspended, primarily those of the Communist and National Socialist press. For much of this period, no valid modus operandi existed between newsmen and political leaders. An authoritarian tradition kept the government from providing reporters with complete information. But the fact that most German regimes were coalitions, plus the strong political attachments of many bureaucrats, caused a constant series of disclosures to political newspapers. For example, between 1930 and 1932, important government decrees designed to alleviate the economic depression were regularly leaked to Nazi newspapers by civil servants who were party members; their intention, of course, was to undermine the Brüning government.

Under the Nazis, freedom of the press was abolished. In September 1933, publishers were stripped of their authority and made merely the nominal heads of their newspapers. Journalists and editors continued to be paid by publishers, but staff hiring and firing was centralized in the state. The government controlled the press through the Ministry of Propaganda, the undersecretary of which was both party press chief and government press chief. Radio broadcasting was also centralized in the Ministry of Propaganda, and personnel of both media were closely supervised by party-controlled organizations; "unreliable" persons were dismissed from their posts.

One day after the May 8, 1945 armistice, a decree issued by the military government required that every newspaper published in Germany must first be licensed by one of the four Allied authorities. In the Western zones, the first papers to establish considerable circulation were *Die Neue Zeitung* in the American zone and *Die Welt* in the British. The most important criterion in determining who was to be granted a publishing license was

political. In the American zone, anyone connected in any way whatsoever with the Nazi Party was prohibited from obtaining a license. Both the British and the French were somewhat more lenient; their refusal was extended only to those who had been prominent Nazis. Allied licensing came to an end in 1949. Many of the licensed papers continued to operate successfully.

Press developments in Germany in the next several years were markedly parallel to those in other Western countries, although some differences persist. The most important trend has been the decline of party and religious newspapers. The papers sponsored by the Social Democratic and Christian Democratic parties are still important, of course, and in both cases, but especially in the former, control is far looser and more flexible than it was before the Nazi regime.

The second general trend has been the emergence of the mass-circulation press emphasizing sex and violence and having little political content. Although this development has not matched British proportions, *Bild Zeitung,* which is perhaps the best example, had reached a circulation of nearly four million by the end of 1964. The paper is one of many dominated directly or indirectly by Axel Springer, Germany's closest approximation of a press lord. Springer's share of German newspaper circulation is about 37 per cent.

The third trend, which has also been experienced in France and England, has been the drop in the number of newspapers; most of them went out of business, but some have merged. Roughly 470 daily newspapers are published in Germany, with a total circulation of about 17 million, as compared with 4,700 newspapers during the period of the Weimar Republic. Between 1959 and 1964 almost fifty newspapers closed down. The concentration of newspapers in the nation's capital, however, has not been nearly so great as in England. The divorce of Berlin from Western Germany and the emphasis on a federal governmental structure have enhanced the importance of the local and regional press, far more than during the Weimar years.

The quality of German newspapers since World War II is generally better than it was before the Nazi regime. There are now several journalism schools, journalists are getting better training on the job, and while there is still more subjective reporting than in England or the United States, the good papers make strenuous attempts at objective news coverage. No German paper has quite the international status that a few attained during the Weimar period, but *Die Zeit* and *Die Welt,* both of Hamburg, and the *Frankfurter Allgemeine* and *Frankfurter Rundschau* are on a par with the best of today's European newspapers. Of these, *Die Welt* (263,-400) and *Frankfurter Allgemeine* (243,800) have the largest circulation.

German newspapers do not carry columnists of national reputation comparable with those syndicated in the American press, and there are no journals equivalent to England's *Economist* or *New Statesman,* publications influential in shaping the elite's opinion. Also lacking are satirical journals like England's *Punch* or France's *Canard Enchainé; Simplicissimus,* an attempt in this direction, was generally trivial and was forced to close down in 1967. In *Der Spiegel,* whose circulation has risen rapidly to 800,000, Germany has a weekly news magazine patterned after *Time. Der Spiegel's* publisher, Rudolf Augstein, has encouraged the writing of long, unsigned articles, casual in style but slanted in viewpoint, and they have sometimes been irresponsible. However, the journal is exceptionally well informed and has refused to knuckle under to government authority.

For many years *Der Spiegel* engaged in a bitter feud with Franz Joseph Strauss, a leading C.D.U. politician and at one time minister of defense. In 1962, as the result of *Der Spiegel's* publication of certain hitherto classified information on the German army, its publisher was arrested and its offices sealed. The government's action, carried out in the clumsiest authoritarian fashion, resulted in the reshuffling of the Adenauer cabinet and the dismissal of Strauss from his post. *Der Spiegel* was soon publishing again, and charges against all those arrested were either dropped or dismissed. On the other hand, the West German Constitutional Court refused to declare the seizures unconstitutional; half the judges argued that the state had not been unreasonable in assuming that *Der Spiegel* unlawfully possessed secret military documents.

In general, German newspapers, including those that are pro-government, have been quite willing to criticize the nation's leaders. Many newspapers have also consistently fought and exposed neo-Nazi elements, and if the press is relatively moderate politically, this may be counted a gain when compared with the Weimar period. The government still has funds available to aid its public relations, and German industry still tries to support those papers that are most friendly to it. Nevertheless, German newspapers are far more independent today than they have ever been in the past.

There is no special press law in the Federal Republic. The basic rights of the press are laid down in the constitution, which guarantees freedom of the press. The only limits upon this freedom are those which prohibit publication of items that might corrupt young people or violate a man's honor. Article 80 also provides that whoever abuses the freedom of expression to attack free democratic institutions forfeits his basic rights. The Länder do have specific laws governing the press; although a few states still retain provisions adopted during the empire, more and more of them now have laws to protect the sources of a reporter's information and to guarantee him the right of access to material of public interest.

The issues of consolidation and the role of the press in German life came to a head in 1967–1968 with the mounting of verbal and physical assaults upon the Springer organization by left-wing students. The large circulation of his newspapers, they argued, was part of and part cause of Germany's continued authoritarianism. They were joined in their attack by many intellectuals and magazine and newspaper editors. A committee set up by Parliament to investigate the matter actually suggested that no one organization should be permitted to control more than thirty per cent of daily newspaper circulation. The proposal, however, seems unlikely to become law; the only immediately tangible result of the student demonstrations was Springer's decision to liquidate some of his magazine holdings in order to concentrate on his newspaper empire.

The attacks against Springer stemmed less from the size of his newspapers' circulation than from his political opinions, which are very bourgeois, rather conservative, and fairly nationalistic, although by no means right-wing. This point seems to be confirmed by the fact that no attacks have been leveled against Augstein's *Der Spiegel,* which now dominates the weekly newsmagazine field, at least so far as political commentary is concerned. Augstein himself, somewhat ironically, was one of the leading critics of Springer.

Vestiges of the old authoritarian attitude toward journalists still exist in Germany, based, as in England, on class distinctions. They were particularly obvious during the Adenauer administration. But on the whole, a fairly sound relationship, partly caused by a growing mutual respect, has developed in more recent years between the press and the government. This circumstance is true in all European countries, and from it the public can hope to benefit.

If the German press has changed since the Weimar period, German television has added an entirely new dimension to political life. Under the Nazis, radio was a prime instrument of propaganda and broadcasting was completely centralized. The Bonn republic,

however, has shifted control over broadcasting facilities to the Länder. Each Land maintains its own television company, and national law requires that all the companies be administered by a television council and a director responsible for programming. The companies are permitted to broadcast specific forms of advertising up to twenty minutes a day. Representatives of the ten regional television companies meet regularly to discuss mutual problems.

The largest proportion of television programs is produced in Hamburg (*Norddeutsche*) and Cologne (*Westdeutsche*); together they account for almost half of the national programs. Some programs are obtained from abroad. Norddeutsche has taken a more independent political line and has produced program after program reminding Germans of the Nazi era and the horror of the living corpses at Dachau. Using authors and newspaper editors as interrogators, it has established the equivalent of a "Meet the Press" program called "In Person" (*"Zur Person"*), in which German political figures are handled rather roughly.

For some years, various commercial interests in Germany, including the press, had been calling for a second television network, to be operated under loose public control but with the stations financed by advertising and owned by private interests. In 1960, Chancellor Adenauer established the privately incorporated German Television Authority by administrative edict; the authority was granted the power to issue licenses to "responsible" private organizations capable of producing television programs.

The Länder responded by bringing suit in the Constitutional Court, and the chancellor's action was declared unconstitutional. A second German television network was organized on the same basis as the first, although under different directorship. German television does accept advertising, but advertisers have no say whatsoever about program content.

6. MASS MEDIA IN THE SOVIET UNION

The origin of Russian newspapers, like those in Western Europe, is to be found in handwritten "news letters" that provided information about such matters as the reception of ambassadors, battles, treaties, and the arrival of merchant ships. The first printed newspaper was established by the government under Peter I, and the first issue of his magazine *Vedomosti* (Gazette) appeared in 1703. With a circulation that ranged from about 150 copies to four thousand, *Vedomosti* was discontinued two years after his death in 1725. In the meantime, other government journals, mostly of a scientific or literary nature, had begun to circulate, sponsored by such organizations as the Academy of Sciences. These periodicals expanded in number and size during the eighteenth and nineteenth centuries. Simultaneously, private interests started the regular publication of other periodicals whose principal function was the dissemination of news. Some of them, however, also contained criticism implicitly directed against the regime. By the beginning of the nineteenth century, the criticism, plus the recognition that these periodicals were growing in importance, led to censorship which continued, alternating with periods of some freedom, down to the Revolution of 1917. It should be noted, however, that from 1905 until 1917 the Russian press enjoyed more freedom than it has since the Revolution.

In 1912 there were 1,131 newspapers and 1,656 magazines published in Russia, including 678 foreign-language publications. The one commercial newspaper which achieved something like a mass circulation was the *Kopeika* of Saint Petersburg, which claimed five hundred thousand readers in 1916. Most of the press at this time emphasized editorial comment and features rather than straight news reporting, and most were closely identified with a particular political position. The first newspaper of the Bolshevik faction of the Russian Socialist Party was *Iskra* (The Spark). In 1912 it was replaced by *Pravda* (Truth), which has continued to be the chief organ of the Communist Party, and which has been published continuously since then except for the period between 1914–1917, when it was suppressed by the government because of its "defeatist" policy.

Once the Bolsheviks seized power, an official government paper was established, *Izvestia* (News), and all papers not directly controlled by the Communist Party were eliminated. There was some opposition to such action within the party itself, but it was quickly squelched. To both Lenin and Trotsky, the idea of an "opposition" press, or even an "objective" press, in the Western sense of the term, was meaningless. As early as "What Is to Be Done?" Lenin had pointed out what the real role of the press must be:

A newspaper is not only a collective propagandist and collective agitator, but also a collective organizer. In this respect it can be compared to the scaffolding *erected around a building under construction; it marks the contours of the structure and facilitates communication between builders, permitting them to distribute the work and to view the common results achieved by their organized labour.*[29]

Given this view, the party established control over the entire structure and organization of the press. From the very beginning, it issued directives not only on what kind of newspapers were to be published and how they were to be distributed, but also on the precise format and layout to be followed. Communist Party conferences and Politburo meetings continually discussed and issued detailed orders on these matters—invariably reiterating the functions that the press was to serve. The *Large Soviet Encyclopedia* (1952

[29] Quoted in Anthony Buzek, *How the Communist Press Works* (London: Pall Mall Press, 1964), p. 438.

edition) listed some of the functions as follows:

To propagate the ideas of Marxism-Leninism;

To agitate for the principles of the Party;

To organize the workers in the fight for the application of these principles to everyday life;

To forge a lasting link with the popular masses;

To educate them in a spirit of Communism;

To explain the policy of the Party and government;

To foster vigorously a habit of criticism and self-criticism.

The party, to insure that these policies were carried out, created administrative groups to supervise and direct the activities of the press. On every level of party organization, a propaganda and agitation department (*Agitprop*) was set up with the ultimate authority resting in the national party organization. On the national level, Agitprop has developed into a highly complex organization with special sections for party propaganda, mass propaganda, culture, central press, local press, radio, and television. At all organizational levels, the duty of Agitprop has been to facilitate the implementation of party directives.

Paralleling Agitprop were other governmental units responsible for the administration of all activities having to do with communication. Among the most important has been *Glavlit* (The Chief Administration for Literary and Publishing Affairs), created in 1932 for the purpose of making sure that only material reflecting party and government policy reaches the masses. However, since the death of Stalin, Glavlit's major functions have been limited to keeping security information out of the press and censoring materials sent out of the Soviet Union by foreign correspondents. Pre-dispatch censorship has

become far less stringent, although foreign correspondents are still subject to expulsion, particularly if they transmit "incorrect" reports. For example, Peter Johnson of Reuters was forced to leave the Soviet Union in 1964 because of his reporting of demonstrations by African students; in 1968 foreign correspondents were warned that attempts to interview the families of dissident literary figures who had been imprisoned would have serious repercussions.

During the 1920's, the very disorganization of Soviet society, as well as the lack of unanimity among Soviet leaders, permitted a certain amount of leeway for discussion and argument of basic policies in the press. For example, during the period when Nikolai Bukharin edited *Pravda* (1918–1928), editorials were lively and the articles contained an element of controversy. After Stalin consolidated his power, all this changed, and the Soviet press became overwhelmingly dull. Both government and party newspapers, together with the growing glut of special-interest journals, used a great deal of space in simply printing government pronouncements and other material faithfully reflecting the party line. Journalists who refused to do so were purged, and, in many cases, executed.

The iron-handed control of the press and the Russian citizens' lack of information from other sources proved, in many ways, to be self-defeating. The effectiveness of the press was so reduced that many citizens relied upon word of mouth for their information, and, as the government itself recognized, official statements in the press were not sufficient to prevent the widespread dissemination of the wildest rumors. Further, party insistence that loyalty was more important than journalistic expertise yielded a lower standard of competence in the writing and organizing of newspapers. Soviet citizens seemed to agree that there was "no news in *Izvestia* and no truth in *Pravda*."

In the Stalin era, then, the major function of the press was to serve as a means of enabling the regime to achieve its goals. It cajoled, propagandized, exhorted, and demanded that the population assume its responsibilities in the new society. It also served as a mechanism for a type of "self-criticism," and here some flexibility was allowed. Letters to the editor, for example, became an instrument through which the regime could discover and act upon instances of venality in office by professional party cadres or managers, and, from time to time, enterprising journalists could enhance their reputations by discovering evidence of this on their own. Also, *Krokodil,* the official Soviet humor magazine, especially encouraged its readers to send in complaints. But even these critical exercises were carefully circumscribed; the regime was never willing to permit the presentation of too unflattering a view of Soviet life.

During the 1920's and 1930's, the press and radio were only two of the means through which the regime promoted its campaign for the new Soviet man. Far more important were factory newspapers and bulletin boards, and the face-to-face encounters with doctrinaire "agitators" whose duty it was to explain Communist policy and goad the citizens. Here, of course, party members were influential in organizing meetings in factories, collectives, and apartment houses. These confrontations are still significant in the formation and control of public opinion, although since Stalin's death wider newspaper circulation and the growth in ownership of radio and television sets have increased the importance of the mass media.

There have been other changes since Stalin's death in the Soviet communication media, changes which represent a shift of emphasis. They began under Khrushchev, and, despite some backing and filling, have continued thus far under his successors. The primary change has involved an attempt to liven up the newspapers and improve both content and format. The goal is not a "free" press in the Western style, for as Khrushchev

and his successors have stated on many occasions, the fundamental job of the Soviet media is to consolidate and advance the Revolution. Rather, the intention has been to diversify the press and to make it more readable. Under Stalin, for example, regional and local newspapers were almost exact copies of *Pravda* and *Izvestia*—and just as dismal. As one Soviet writer described it:

Before me lie several issues of province and territory newspapers published on the same day. Above all, one is arrested by the papers' striking similarity. Like twins, they can hardly be distinguished from one another. If it were not for the masthead . . . any one of the newspapers could be substituted for another, and neither the reader nor the staff itself would notice.[30]

The year 1959 was a fairly revolutionary one for the Soviet press—it was the year Alexei Adzhubei, Khrushchev's son-in-law, became editor of *Izvestia.* Not yet quite 35, Adzhubei had been educated by the journalism faculty of Moscow University and had served his apprenticeship on *Komsomolskaya Pravda* instead of in the party apparatus. In this earlier post, he had been responsible for changing the format of the paper and for featuring eye-catching photographs and human-interest articles. He carried this approach with him to *Izvestia.* Headlines grew large and articles grew shorter, a family page was instituted and pictures multiplied. In five years, Adzhubei more than tripled the paper's circulation until it reached six million, only a few hundred thousand less than the theoretically more important *Pravda.* In fact, during Adzhubei's tenure there were a number of occasions when the policy orientations of the two papers revealed what for

30 M. Strepukhov in *Kommunist,* organ of the C.P.S.U. Central Committee, No. 6 (April 1955). Quoted by Leo Gruliow, "The Soviet Press and Censorship," *Problems of Communism,* V, 2 (March-April 1956), 5.

Soviet periodicals were substantial differences in outlook. Adzhubei's innovations did not go unnoticed by *Pravda*'s editor Pavel Satyukov. *Pravda* soon began to take on a fresher look, and a note of competition was introduced which had never been present before.

None of these modifications, of course, involved any fundamental change in the nature of reporting. Newspaper headlines and stories remained didactic and exhortative. For example, during the Cuban missile crisis, *Pravda* headlined its stories: "Frustrate the Criminal Intentions of the Enemies of Peace!" "The Peoples of the World Angrily Denounce American Adventurers," and "Bridle the Aggressors." Nor did the press ever veer from the policy of printing only that news which it was "correct" for the Soviet people to know. As far as Soviet readers were concerned, no one except a handful of criminals fled from East to West Germany, and no wall was being constructed in Berlin. In fact, it was only a month after the wall had been erected that *Izvestia* made brief mention of a barrier of barbed wire, bricks, and cement. The Soviet invasion of Czechoslovakia was initially reported as being more or less at the invitation of the Czechoslovak Communist Party and the people; no official information was presented on the outrage felt by the Czechoslovaks or on the extraordinary criticisms of the Soviet action by some West European Communist parties.

After Khrushchev's fall, Adzhubei was dismissed from his post and Satyukov from his. However, there is little indication of a fundamental change in editorial policy; in line with the new emphasis on collective leadership, personal statements by party leaders are played down and news of party dignitaries attending party functions, formerly given front-page coverage, is now placed on inside pages or omitted altogether. Newspapers also continue to encourage readers to submit their views, especially those pointing out improbity

in office, and suggestions are sought for more interesting features.

Changes in the Soviet press have been paralleled by those in radio and television. Soviet radio broadcasting began in the 1920's, but it was not until the 1930's that it had developed to a point where it could reach a mass audience. Throughout Stalin's rule, most outlets were wired speakers in homes, factories or various other public places. This method of broadcasting was less expensive and, of course, reduced the possibility that the owners of radio sets could receive foreign stations.

The content of early radio programs was primarily serious music and propaganda. During the late 1930's and 1940's, works of literature and special programs for children began to make their appearance. Most programs, aside from music, were oriented toward "teaching" the public, and the works performed, if modern, were designed to enhance the values desired by the regime.

By the late 1950's, new trends in the radio and television media were discernible. The number of privately owned radio sets had, of course, increased enormously, and television sets were entirely wireless. Didactic programs continued to take up by far the largest portion of nonmusical broadcast time, but Russian authorities had become more attuned to Western programs. New programs were introduced, including quiz shows, that were purely entertaining.

Of more importance, greater ownership of individual radio sets opened the possibility of Soviet citizens receiving *news* from Western Europe. The natural consequence of this was the extensive development of jamming mechanisms. By the early 1960's, however, jamming was becoming more and more expensive and despite the best efforts of the regime, many Soviet citizens could still get broadcasting from the West. These factors, plus the general loosening of Soviet controls, prompted the regime, in 1963, to end its efforts at blocking Western broadcasts and to try to counter them wherever necessary. Thus, in 1965 the Soviet Union was finally forced to discuss the defection of two Soviet jazz musicians because foreign radio broadcasts had made their defections common knowledge. Taking up this theme, *Kommunist,* the chief theoretical journal of the Soviet Communist Party, argued that the Soviet press must be prepared to counter Western propaganda by better and fuller reporting of events of this type. It was an argument that was certainly dismissed in the aftermath of the 1968 invasion of Czechoslovakia, when selective jamming of Western broadcasts was resumed.

8

Political Socialization:

Youth and Politics

1. INTRODUCTION

Every society about which we have any knowledge has established a system assigning responsibility and authority in some measure according to age. In primitive, nomadic societies, in which military prowess was of prime importance, young manhood was often an age of considerable authority. In most societies, however, youth has played a secondary role in decision-making. In most societies, too, special rites have marked the transitions from childhood to puberty and from youth to manhood—transitions which have always involved some difficulty. Adolescence and young manhood, marked as they are as rich, inquisitive years, are at the same time trying periods associated with violent emotions and considerable physical aggressiveness.

These early discontinuities are more pronounced with the creation of institutional structures which reduce the family's role in the socialization process and strengthen that sense of group identity common to all of a particular age. It is in modern industrial so-

cieties that this process has gone furthest. The state's extension of education creates an environment for young people in which they are partially divorced from parental control and yet largely free of adult responsibilities. In technologically advanced societies, requirements for education are constantly increasing. At the same time there exists the propensity to prolong the years of youth, that time during which, theoretically, a person can enjoy life because he *is* free of responsibility. This is particularly true in the United States and it is becoming more so in other countries.

Thus has been created in the West, and elsewhere, a "youth culture" unknown to most traditional societies, with its own special characteristics and problems. The tensions associated with adolescence can be exaggerated, as can the rebelliousness of young people. Most studies indicate that the great majority of youth make the transition without undue shock and without seriously questioning the values inculcated by their family, social class, and ethnic group.

Nevertheless, adolescence for some is a

time of intense self-exploration and doubt, as well as rebellion. Having passed beyond childhood but not yet having committed themselves to an adult role, adolescents are seeking a meaningful self-identity. In some cases this search requires that they prove their superiority to their parents. They may, for example, stress cultural ideals to which most adults pay only lip service; in this way, they can lift themselves through a spirit of self-denial above the corrupt adult world. Since the Enlightenment, this rebelliousness has often involved the adoption by youth of radical ideologies designed *really* to achieve goals their parents merely talk about. On the other hand, they may totally reject parental and societal values and become "bohemians" or "beats," claiming that punctuality, sublimation, and commitment to work, for instance, are false gods and that what matters is free self-expression—usually sexual self-expression. In both cases rebellion is often a mechanism by which young people postpone recognition of the fact that life is, by and large, ordinary, and leads ultimately only to death. In the first instance, radical utopian ideologies promise the creation of a "perfect" world; in the second, the "freedom" from inhibition is psychologically a return to infancy. Both orientations provide the rebel with a sense of having mastered time and of having attained infinite power and immortality.

Whatever the psychological and sociological courses of adolescent rebellion, however, it has been partly responsible for the continued dynamism of Western society. The relative conservatism of most primitive societies was maintained because the socialization process blocked the development of new orientations. The decline of the family's role in socialization and the exposure of young people to milieus in which they learn new orientations and have the opportunity to modify or even reject parental values have been among the major factors contributing to the institutionalization of social change in Europe and the United States.

Bohemianism and radicalism as forms of rebellion have, in the past, been options open only to upper- and middle-class youth. Until very recently the young person of working-class background was initiated into adult responsibilities much earlier; and his radicalism, at least in Western Europe, was directly related to his class position and did not involve deviation from parental norms. In both the United States and Western Europe, lower-class rebellion has usually involved delinquency, and in recent years delinquency among working-class youth has increased rapidly even as this class has become more affluent. To be sure, middle- and upper-class youth can also choose the path of delinquency—and more of them are doing so.

In nations where the great majority of working-class children leave school at 15 and can look forward to a life of routine manual labor, delinquency is a form of protest. The problem has become more acute with the decline of parental authority, a decline that has been accentuated by the fact that young men can earn enough to support themselves almost from the moment they leave school. Television and other mass media, of course, have aggravated the malaise by making these youngsters aware of lifestyles that are denied them.

Adolescence and young manhood in modern society, then, are periods of strain. Even so, most young people handle their problems successfully; the proportion of those who rebel radically against parental or societal authority is small. The extent and the type of rebellion that occurs obviously depend upon many factors. It is likely to be much greater when the society is undergoing rapid changes—when traditional values are being severely attacked. It is under these circumstances that the generation gap is widest.

2. THE WESTERN EUROPEAN PATTERN

The clash in the late 1960's between university students and the larger community was not exactly a new phenomenon. In the middle ages, young scholars frequently invaded surrounding towns, raping women and engaging in other forms of mayhem. On occasion the community retaliated vigorously; for example, Oxford became the scene of a violent clash in 1354:

All night the citizens from surrounding towns and villages poured into Oxford. . . . They caught certain scholars walking after dinner . . . killing one and wounding others. Then on into the University quarter itself, where the scholars defended themselves desperately. . . . But the army of townsmen was not to be denied. The students were overwhelmed. . . . For two days the mob rioted and pillaged and slew. . . . When the pillage was over, the University had vanished, seemingly never to return.[1]

European universities during the nineteenth and early twentieth centuries were hotbeds of radical activity, and students figured significantly in many of the revolutions that occurred. Marx himself pointed to the role of students in the German upheaval of 1848. It was, of course, the radical parties of the left that were the first to take advantage of youthful enthusiasm and to establish youth auxiliaries. In Germany, a Socialist youth movement was initiated as early as 1904, although it was not given official status until 1909. Both the French and the English Socialist parties set up youth affiliates somewhat later. In all three countries, youth groups were more militant than the parent party, and were supported by the left within the party. As a consequence, the parent organization often found itself at odds with its youth groups. In France, the youth section of the Communist Party was heavily Trotskyite during most of the 1920's, and in Germany, Socialist youth groups frequently clashed with the Social Democratic Party because of what they considered its timidity.

Where more than one major party of the left existed, youth was generally drawn to the more radical. In France, the Socialist

youth groups were eclipsed by the Communists, as they were in Germany. Liberal and conservative parties in Europe attempted to create their own youth groups—but without much success. In fact, the only parties which could compete with the left were Catholic political parties, like the German Center Party, or parties of the radical right, such as the National Socialists. Youth forces and counterforces varied substantially from country to country, and they were related in each case to the nation's culture and its political and social structure.

In France, the authoritarianism of family life encouraged youthful rebellion. Further, the very fragmentation of French society and politics not only offered the university student an opportunity to choose among many ideologies, but provided the rationale for that bohemian nihilism that became the hallmark of Paris's Left Bank. For the most part, it was left-wing causes that inspired the majority of student activists. Socialist and, later, Communist parties were not only associated in the minds of these students with freedom from all the "bourgeois" restraints, they also allowed the activists to identify with the working class. In addition, the lack of employment opportunities for lower-middle-class university graduates—to whom only a few posts in traditional occupations were available—contributed to the emergence of an "intellectual proletariat." While the general movement of French university students was to the left, radical right-wing movements were not without support. At the time of the Dreyfus Affair, for instance, right-wing students fought with leftist groups at the Sorbonne, often attacking more liberal professors:

During the winter of 1908–1909 a series of public lectures was announced at the Sorbonne, to be given by a Lycée professor by the name of Thalamas, who was said to have "insulted" Joan of Arc. At the first lecture a group of newly formed Camelots du Roi (street vendors of the king) appeared, led by Maurice Pujo; they drowned out the pro-

[1] Quoted in A. H. Halsey and Stephen Marks, "British Student Politics," in *Daedalus*, 97 (Winter 1968), 116.

fessor with catcalls and bombarded him with various objects; finally one of the group jumped onto the rostrum and brutally slapped the defenseless professor. For the next few weeks the course had to be given under police protection. But the Camelots *were always finding new ways of creating a disturbance. They started brawls under the windows of the auditorium, got into fights with students who did not share their views, and bewildered the police with silent marches. Pujo made his way with some of his companions into another auditorium, dismissed the astonished professor, and gave a speech in praise of Joan of Arc. The punishments were minor—they were regarded partly as martyrdom and partly as adventures. On the next-to-last day of the course, using a strategy requiring military precision, they managed to enter the auditorium, in spite of the heavy police guard, and beat up the lecturer on the rostrum. Both state and university actually yielded: the course was not completed.*[2]

In Germany, youthful militancy was channeled more easily to the radical right. It was the sons of the peasants, the white-collar workers, and the army officers who embraced National Socialism with the most fervor and with the most genuine idealism. The Social Democrats and Communists did manage to maintain considerable support among the younger population throughout the 1920's, but in the last years of the decade they lost out to the National Socialists. For example, in 1931 only 19.1 per cent of the Social Democratic Party membership was between the ages of 18 and thirty; for the Nazi Party, the corresponding figure was 37.6 per cent.[3]

The French and German experiences differed in other ways. In Germany, a number

of nationally organized and ostensibly non-political youth movements had developed at the turn of the century. These groups stressed "direct" contact with nature through long hikes and traditional dancing, and encouraged a cult of male companionship which was not without homosexual overtones. In general, the youth who joined these movements believed they were reacting to the centralization and mechanization of bourgeois society. Strongly influenced by both Rousseau and Nietzsche, they longed for a nonrepressive society at the same time that they desired to submerge themselves in the group. They also longed for the restoration of a traditional German society—as they understood it—and emphasized the purity of the German *Volk*. In this regard there were, from the beginning, anti-Semitic overtones in the German youth movement, although these did not become dominant until the late 1920's. Indeed, in the chaos after World War I, the youth movement lost much of its drive and splintered badly into ideological factions. It recovered momentum and cohesion in the very late 1920's under the increasing influence of the Nazi Party.

While the organized youth movements were never extended to the university level, their precepts were not without support. Infatuation with the idea of the German Volk and the romantic glorification of German society were vital aspects of life within the dueling fraternities which were so important at the university. Here again there were many splits, but the general movement of university students was to the right—and to the anti-Semitic right at that. By the late 1920's, the National Socialist Party had captured the leadership of rightist groups at many institutions, where first pressures and then riots resulted in the dismissal of liberal or Jewish professors.

The various independent youth organizations throughout Germany were dissolved by the Nazis and the party's youth affiliate was designated as the sole coordinator of all youth activity. Beginning at age ten,

[2] Ernest Nolte, *Three Faces of Fascism,* tr. Leila Vannewitz (New York: Holt, Rinehart and Winston, Inc., 1966), p. 69.

[3] Data from Eric Josephson, "Political Youth Organizations in Europe, 1900–1950," unpublished Ph.D. dissertation, Columbia University, 1960, p. 210.

boys and girls were conscripted into Hitler youth organizations where they remained until they were 18. The emphasis was on indoctrination with Nazi ideals, physical fitness, and the development of future leadership cadres. Intellectuality was downgraded in favor of working with one's hands, especially on the land. Hosteling was encouraged, and an ever wider network of youth hostels constructed. Although social class distinctions were not without significance, these were muffled within the youth movement and the movement itself contributed to the spread of equalitarian values. There were those among the German youth, including many who had been members of the earlier youth groups, who resisted the Nazi regime; yet while it lasted, the Nazi movement was notoriously successful in drawing upon youthful energies to create its own version of a new and better world to replace the "decadent," bureaucratic, bourgeois culture that had preceded it.

One former member, describing her reasons for joining the Nazi youth movement in 1933, remembers that while her upper-middle-class parents were rather disdainful of the Nazis, their dressmaker was an ardent supporter of Hitler:

No catchword has ever fascinated me quite as much as that of the "National Community" (Volksgemeinschaft). I heard it first from the lips of this crippled and care-worn dressmaker and . . . it acquired a magical glow. I felt it could only be brought into being by declaring war on the class prejudices of the social stratum from which I came and that it must, above all, give protection and justice to the weak. What held my allegiance to this idealistic fantasy was the hope that a state of affairs would be created in which people of all classes could live together like brothers and sisters.[4]

On the evening of Hitler's seizure of power, she watched a huge parade of Nazi supporters march by:

Again and again amongst them we saw groups of boys and girls scarcely older than ourselves. What was I, who was only allowed to stand on the pavement and watch . . . ? Hardly more than . . . a child who was still given schoolgirl memories for Christmas. And yet I longed to hurl myself into this current, to be submerged and borne along by it.[5]

Whenever I probe the reasons which drew me to join the Hitler Youth, I always come up against this one: I wanted to escape from my childish, narrow life and I wanted to attach myself to something that was great and fundamental.[6]

Like so many Germans, she differentiated sharply between Jews as a category to be feared and hated and individual Jews whom she knew and liked. Once she attempted to convince one of her closest friends, a Jewish girl, to join the movement with her. Later, as her Jewish friends disappeared, all that remained was the category Jew. On occasion she still might recognize that behind the category were individual human beings, but these were only momentary flashes. Describing the reactions of a friend to an experience which temporarily led to this recognition, she asks herself whether she might not have changed had she witnessed the same event:

. . . No I do not think anything like that would have happened. My friend was sensitive rather than thick skinned and she remained . . . just as blind as myself. It is from such experiences that one can recognize the terrible power which so-called ideologies can exercise over young people. Once they have surrendered to them, they see without seeing and hear without hearing.[7]

[4] Melita Maschmann, *Account Rendered*, trans. Geoffrey Strachan (New York: Abelard-Schuman, 1965), p. 10.

[5] *Ibid.*, p. 12.
[6] *Ibid.*, p. 12.
[7] *Ibid.*, p. 86.

In England the pattern was quite different. Young people, and especially middle-class students, did flock to the Labor Party, especially in the 1930's, but the whole tradition of English life worked against a massive commitment of the type which characterized both France and Germany.

In the United States, the role of students in politics was even smaller, despite some activity during the 1930's. Left-wing activism did develop in a few elite colleges and universities such as Harvard and Columbia, and to a lesser extent the University of California. Student militancy was also evident at the free urban universities of New York City, where Jewish students carried on the radical tradition of Jewish intellectuals in Eastern Europe. Widespread educational opportunities were in themselves a satisfaction to most young people, however, for they provided the means by which students could rise above their parents. In the case of those from a middle-class background, the fraternity system plus institutionalized athletics provided the basis of a youth culture that encouraged the sowing of "wild oats" in ways that were nonpolitical.

Just as important, the rapid democratization of American family life, and the absence of bitter value conflicts within the society as a whole, precluded the development of either a mass party or an intellectual tradition to which young people could be drawn. For most youth in the United States, rebellion, when it came, took a highly personal form. Perhaps the most poignant breaks occurred between immigrant generations and their children; these generally meant a rejection by youth of traditional "old-country" attitudes and an acceptance of the broadly "liberal-Protestant" values of American society.

3. THE POSTWAR PATTERN

In the years following World War II, especially in the 1950's, student political activity in Europe virtually disappeared. With what had become known of the nature of the Soviet regime, the Communist Party seemed less attractive, and this was associated with a general decline in ideological fervor. Furthermore, in every European country full employment was the norm, and the economic success of mixed economies vitiated criticisms of the status quo.

The situation differed, of course, from country to country. English students had never developed a reputation for real political activism; thus the decline there was only relative. In Germany, the decline in political activity by students was so pronounced that they became known as the "skeptical generation." Their concern with postwar reconstruction and their reaction against any ideological commitments were in striking contrast with student activism during the Weimar period. In France, student activism continued during the late 1940's and declined in the 1950's, only to re-emerge with the later phases of the Algerian war.

During these years of political torpor on campus, however, forces were at work which would provide the setting for renewed—and occasionally explosive—student activism. The size of student populations was growing rapidly throughout Europe. The demand for higher education was outpacing the resources that governments were willing or able to expend in order to meet it. In France and Germany especially, the ratio of students to faculty was mounting, and overcrowding of university facilities becoming a critical problem. Moreover, the erosion of traditional patterns of authority in the society and the greater independence of young people were beginning to have implications for the structure of authority within the university. And, as the Soviet Union moved toward a policy of coexistence and new generations entered universities, ideological disillusionment became a matter of history rather than a personal experience. Finally, the growth of mass communications, particularly television, created the possibility of mobilizing students to an extent not conceivable in previous decades.

What undoubtedly crystallized all of these factors into a sudden wave of student activism in the late 1960's, interestingly enough, was the emergence of a radical student movement in the United States. The traumas associated with the racial crisis, American policy in Vietnam, the draft for military service, and, indeed, the relationship of the United States (and Western Europe as a whole) to the developing nations of the world had caused widespread repercussions on the American campus. The civil-rights movement provided a new set of tactics for American students, tactics that were further refined as student opposition to the Vietnam war grew. By way of television, the civil-rights and Vietnam demonstrations became part of a common European experience, and student activists capitalized on this experience by traveling from one country to another to foster a rebellious mood on the European campus.

Developments in the United States influenced Europe in an even more profound manner. To Europeans, as indeed to the rest of the world, the United States had come to symbolize Western political and economic institutions. Awareness that the United States had failed to solve a racial problem which, indeed, seemed to become worse, and disillusionment with American foreign policy served, for many students, to discredit the whole structure of their own societies.

The way was opened, then, for the revival of utopian radicalism—for fresh assaults upon society and upon the structure of the universities themselves, considered now as pawns of the larger, corrupt community. Identifying themselves with the Chinese Communist revolution, rather than with the Russian, and with Communist revolutions in the underdeveloped countries, some students began to think in terms of "confrontation" politics and the suppression of "reactionary" political movements.

The extent of student rebelliousness, in this extreme form at least, should not be exaggerated. Revolutionary student groups tend to be relatively small, drawing upon broader student support only on certain issues. Nor are the revolutionaries rebelling against their parents. Studies indicate that radical students generally come from radical backgrounds—the more radical the student, the more radical his parents are likely to have been. In the United States, for example, a 1966 study indicated that nearly fifty per cent of the Students for a Democratic Society were the sons and daughters of liberal or radical Jewish parents.[8]

The success of student movements in achieving at least some of their goals can be attributed to other factors, too. In Germany and England, for instance, where student activists do not command widespread enthusiasm, the larger community's ambivalence toward using force against students and its inability to cope in a less drastic way with student tactics has permitted the students to score some gains. Also, students in most societies represent a group uniquely available for mobilization on general issues; gathered together in large numbers in a comparatively unstructured environment, they can easily organize parades and demonstrations for any purpose whatsoever and sustain them fairly indefinitely. Universities as institutions are, of course, not equipped to deal with situations of this kind; their very existence has always presupposed the voluntary acceptance of the rules by the majority of students.

Students also tend to lack an extended time perspective. Even most moderate students, having become conscious of the wider world only upon entering the university, may be easily led into accepting the view

[8] See, for example, S. M. Lipset, "American Student Activism," in Philip G. Altbach, *Student Politics and Higher Education in the United States: A Select Bibliography* (St. Louis: United Ministries in Higher Education, 1968), pp. 1–14.

that a situation which has actually been changing fairly rapidly is almost static and unchanging. Nor is it easy for them to realize, even if they wished to, that the implicitly accepted premises of an earlier epoch may have differed from their own and yielded a quite different perspective. In the 1950's in the United States, many found it difficult to understand why intellectuals had supported Communist movements in such large numbers during the 1930's and early 1940's; in the 1960's, just as many found it difficult to understand how so uncritical an anti-Communist position could have achieved such widespread support in the 1950's.

It is clear from studies in the United States, and in India and Latin America, that the argument of the radical core for student power lures students who use the slogan not only as a mechanism to cover up personal problems, but as a means of lowering academic standards they know they cannot meet.[9] Mass movements also have the tendency to grow as they attract those who either want to lose themselves in a cause or want to be associated in a great and "dangerous" enterprise.

Finally, students have received both encouragement and support—less in Germany and England than in France and the United States—from those elements of the academic intelligentsia who hope to use them as a weapon to destroy a society whose values they reject, or as a way of achieving power in societies in which real authority seems to lie with businessmen, technocrats, and politicians. And as with other millenarian movements, whether of the right or of the left, some academics are attracted to the new student activism because it helps compensate for a lack of professional recognition, satisfies aggressive needs, or simply gains them popularity among their students.

Unquestionably, some of the student concerns reflect changes in Europe's culture and social structure. There is now a demand for greater equality, a shift of emphasis and concern from economic growth and personal affluence to the overall "quality" of the society. Insofar as this is true, students represent the advance guard in responding to the developments of the last twenty years and a portent of things to come, as will be noted in the last chapter of this volume. This is not to suggest, however, that students will always have their own way. It is extremely doubtful that the changes in university structure demanded by the most radical students will be institutionalized; in fact, it is probable that community reaction will eventually result in the curtailment of some of the tactics student militants have relied upon in recent years.

THE ENGLISH PATTERN:[10] All major British parties have youth affiliates. They emphasize political discussion and education as well as canvassing, and they seek to influence party policy through the publication of pamphlets. Youth groups of the Conservative and Labor parties also function as recruiting units for future party leaders. The Liberal Party's youth affiliate, however, serves mostly as a political halfway house: youngsters drift from it into one or the other of the two major parties. (See Table 8.1.)

The youth organization of the Conservative Party is by far the largest—and the most docile. In fact, its principal purpose seems to be that of a marriage bureau; as such, it is widely regarded as the best in the country. This is not to say that it does not provide a source of manpower for the party. It does, but its innovative role is minimal.

As might be expected, the Labor Party youth affiliate, the Young Socialists, is al-

9 On India see Philip Altbach, "Students and Politics in India," in *Daedalus,* 97 (Winter 1968), 254–273. On the United States, see Samuel Lubell, "That Generation Gap," *The Public Interest,* 13 (Fall 1968), 52–61.

10 Much of the background information contained in this section is derived from A. H. Halsey and Stephen Marks, "British Student Politics," *Daedalus, op. cit.,* pp. 116–137, and Philip Abrams and Alan Little, "Britain: Young Voters, Young Activists and the Irrelevance of Age," mimeographed paper presented to the Sixth World Congress of the International Political Science Association (September 21–25, 1964).

TABLE 8.1. MEMBERSHIP IN PARTY YOUTH AFFILIATES:
GREAT BRITAIN

	Young Conservatives[1]	Young Socialists[1]	Young Liberals[1]
Membership	120,000	25,000	12,000
Branches	1,600	720	400
Typical branch size	80	35	30
Age limits	15–30	15–25	15–30
Average age	19	19	19
Per cent of party's parliamentary candidates	11	6	15
Per cent decline per annum	2.5	5	20

[1]Calculated over the decade from 1954 to 1963 for the Young Conservatives but for 1963 only for the Young Socialists and the Young Liberals.

Adapted from Philip Abrams and Alan Little, "Britain: Young Voters, Young Activists and the Irrelevance of Age," paper presented to the Sixth World Congress of the International Political Science Association (September 21–25, 1964), mimeographed, p. 4. Reprinted by permission of the publisher.

together different. Indeed, as in the past, it has found itself in such constant and strident conflict with the parent organization that it has, periodically, been forced to close down. It is in persistent danger of being "captured" by militants anxious to make the party as a whole more ideologically pure and aggressive, and older Labor leaders, while they recognize its many values, often feel that the affiliate is more trouble than it is worth.

As in other European countries, however, it is among specifically student groups that youthful political action has taken place in the past several years. After considerable passivity in the postwar period, these groups have once again become active. The chief British student organization is the National Union of Students (N.U.S.); there are other student groups loosely associated with the political parties, and more recently, an array of ad hoc "revolutionary" left-wing groups has formed.

Immediately after the war, membership in the National Union of Students declined from its high in the late 1930's; a good many students felt that membership fees were not in line with services rendered. Party-affiliated groups, except for the Liberal Party youth

organization, also declined. After 1956, however, student political groups again began to increase in size and activity, particularly the National Association of Labor Student Organizations and groups associated with *The New Left Review*, a journal originally sponsored by students.

Student activism reached something of a high in 1960 and 1961 with the formation of the Committee for Nuclear Disarmament (C.N.D.), which sponsored demonstrations and marches urging England's unilateral rejection of nuclear weapons. But after a year or two, the C.N.D.'s membership dropped off and the next spurt in student activity did not come until 1966 and 1967. In the meantime, a Radical Students Alliance had been formed, whose aim it was to reshape British education by giving students more power in university decisions. While membership in the alliance remained small, its militant activism pushed the N.U.S. to the left.

By 1967 and 1968, then, English students were ripe for a new brand of activism—"confrontation" politics. The most dramatic exercise of confrontation occurred at the London School of Economics over issues that combined elements of student syndicalism

TABLE 8.2. DIFFERENCES OF OUTLOOK BETWEEN YOUNG SOCIALIST AND YOUNG CONSERVATIVE ACTIVISTS IN GREAT BRITAIN

	Capital punishment		Corporal punishment		For easier divorce
	For	Against	For	Against	
Young Conservatives	68%	11%	65%	29%	38%
Young Socialists	18	79	7	90	76

Adapted from Abrams and Little, "Britain: Young Voters," p. 24. Reprinted by permission.

with attempts to influence the larger society on "racism" and the Vietnam war. At this point, with English students clearly influenced by events in the United States and beginning to establish contact with other European student groups, their activism escalated quickly, although it has yet to reach the level of violence that has taken place in other nations.

So far as national policy is concerned, the results of the new tactics have been slight. Nevertheless, they did have some effect on the campus; in 1968, N.U.S. and the Committee of Vice Chancellors, which represents English universities, came to an agreement that would allow students some voice in university decision-making. The agreement did not mollify all activists, however. A Revolutionary Socialist Students' Federation has been organized to replace the Radical Students Alliance. The announced plans of the federation are for further militant action to end the "bourgeois" character of British university life.

The plans of the federation notwithstanding, the 1968–1969 academic year was relatively quiet on the student front, except for some disturbances at the London School of Economics and three or four other institutions. A committee of Oxford dons issued a report calling for somewhat less "paternalism" and more student participation in university affairs, and trends in this direction have continued. A select committee of the House of Commons was created to investigate student unrest, and its report may well bring Parliament into the matter of university-student relationships in a systematic way.

THE FRENCH PATTERN: Except for eruptions during the Algerian conflict, the general pattern of political activity by French youngsters during the 1950's and early 1960's was one of relative calm. The emphasis here is on the word "relative"; political activity, including fairly violent demonstrations, has always been far more typical of student groups in France than in England.

Nevertheless, the protest cycle in France immediately after the Liberation was not dissimilar to that of other European countries. Students, like other groups in the society, were far more concerned about a stable environment in which to get ahead than they were in political credos. Membership in all party youth affiliates declined, even in that of the Communist Party. Moreover, young people became more active in nonpolitical organizations having a social impact. Young businessmen formed groups to work for more progressive labor practices; young farmers banded together to push for more advanced agricultural policies. Many other youngsters in search of fresh social policies founded organizations; some of them, neo-Catholic in nature, represented a new radicalism within the Catholic Church that captured the imagination of youth.

Within the universities, students formed a specifically nonparty organization, the *Union nationale des étudiants de France*

(U.N.E.F.), although it had some prewar roots. From the beginning, the movement took on a trade-union syndicalist coloration, and its membership and activity fluctuated widely, depending almost entirely on external circumstances. In the early 1960's, there was considerable agitation over the war in Algeria, but by 1964 student activity had again tapered off. During this period the U.N.E.F. did make some demands, however, that indicated a general move to the political left; they called for the "democratization" of education and the payment of salaries to students. Partly as a result of the contagion of protests in the United States and Germany, student ferment increased in 1967, and in May 1968 it exploded into a full-scale example of confrontation politics. A sizable portion of the student population and a segment of the younger members of the working class joined in a bloody melee against the French educational and governmental establishment. The events of May and June—rioting, police bludgeoning, street fighting from behind barricades, arson, mass arrests, sit-ins—were exhilarating to some and frightening to others, as students in mass assemblies proclaimed the democratization of a university system in which students and professors would share equally in making policy, examinations would be eliminated, and decisions would be made in mass, open assembly.

The confrontation was sparked by one of the many left-wing revolutionary groups that have mushroomed in every European country. But as the situation polarized, it was the full commitment of the U.N.E.F. to the cause that turned a protest into a government crisis.

The upshot of the clash was a new national election in which the left as a whole felt the sting of a popular backlash and slipped, at least temporarily, into disarray. Nevertheless, the riots and strikes were not devoid of success. They compelled the de Gaulle regime to initiate some reforms in industry, and to outline new university programs that would permit greater decentralization of the university system and more participation in decisions by both faculty and students. They also precipitated a balance-of-payments crisis which, in turn, raised some questions about the regime's general economic policies.

The reforms, initiated by de Gaulle's Minister of Education Edgar Faure, and supported by the president himself, involved more than just greater participation by the students in certain aspects of university decision-making. They were designed to decentralize the university system somewhat by giving individual universities greater autonomy. Their objective also was to reduce the size of individual universities, to replace faculties by American-style departments, and to curb the authority of senior professors. The government tried during the 1968–1969 academic year to put some of these changes into effect, but student ferment still continued at a good many campuses, with students physically attacking teachers and each other. A number of student leaders were arrested or drafted into the armed forces. Some of the major clashes occurred between the Communists, whose student youth group has increased enormously in size and power, and the more loosely organized "left-wing" students. At many institutions, the school year was largely a waste of time from an academic point of view. The fall of de Gaulle and the replacement of Faure by Olivier Guichard could conceivably lead to new outbreaks; Guichard is less likely to sympathize with student demands.

THE GERMAN PATTERN: For German youth, the collapse of the Third Reich brought several years of intense disillusionment and passivity. It took nearly two decades for their attitudes to improve. When they did change, German youngsters demonstrated characteristics common to younger people all over Europe—traits that disapproving elders labeled "Americanization." While dueling fraternities reappeared on some campuses in the 1950's, many more adolescents were interested in the latest American dances, hot rods, and intensive heterosexual ventures on the beach, park bench, and bed.

Party youth affiliates became active again in the early 1960's, and, as might be expected, took lines to the left of parent bodies. As it did during the Weimar Republic, the Social Democratic Party found itself forced to disaffiliate its youth organization, the German Socialist Student Alliance (*Sozialistischer Deutscher Studentenbund*—S.D.S.) and to form a new one. The S.D.S. continued to exert an influence on students, however, and, especially after 1967, to grow in strength even as its successor moved to the left.

Under the leadership of "Red" Rudi Dutschke, the S.D.S. mobilized more and more students to press for the complete revamping of the university structure. Dutschke advocated not only full student participation in university decision-making, but also—going beyond the campus issue—demanded what he termed the "democratization" of German society. German student confrontations came to involve more continuous violence, including the burning of periodicals and books, over a longer period of time than did student activism in other countries. And, as in other nations, the protests resulted in at least some steps toward reforming the university structure.

Thus far, however, efforts at reform have not noticeably reduced student militancy; in some cases, violence has even escalated. The Free University of Berlin, among the most liberal in Germany, lost many members of its staff during the academic year 1968–1969, and teaching activity came to a halt for considerable periods of time during the year. In the meantime, student movements have been fragmenting and refragmenting as some groups move further to the left. In 1969, the federal government withdrew all funds from the German National Union of Students after its capture by left-wing groups, and the Social Democrats cut off all financial support for its new student subsidiary.

Unlike the situation in France, however, German students have evoked little sympathy from the trade unions, whose membership has grown more hostile to them as events have unfolded. Nor do they have the proportionate support of as many intellectuals as do students in other European nations—even of the left within the intellectual community. Yet German authorities are very hesitant to use force against student demonstrators lest they appear to raise again the specter of nazism.

4. THE RUSSIAN AND SOVIET PATTERN

Late in the nineteenth century, as the Russian people became more and more restive under the czarist regime, Russian universities became one of the major centers of intrigue and opposition. Russian national development was so slow that to the young men studying in the traditional professions, there was scant hope of finding fulfillment. As for the students of lower-middle-class background, they could foresee little opportunity to use their training as a means of social advancement, and they came to regard themselves as a kind of intellectual proletariat. To the students of upper-class background who attended universities in Western Europe, Russia appeared as a stagnant, pitifully backward nation.

Given the lack of channels through which dissent could be expressed, many students came to combine a kind of nihilism with the most utopian hopes for a new Russia, once a revolution—any revolution—was consummated. Many Bolshevik party leaders made their first contact with radical politics at universities, even though until the Revolution the Bolsheviks represented only a small portion of the student body.

Before the Revolution, the Bolshevik Party lacked a separate youth organization. Actually, it did not need one, for it was primarily a party for young people. The

Komsomol (Communist Youth League) was not created until 1918. Its members provided some of the most militant fighters against "counterrevolutionary" forces and tended to be more radical than the official party itself, presenting, almost from the beginning, a number of disciplinary problems. Some of the more militant youth committed suicide with the advent of the New Economic Policy (N.E.P.), in protest over what they regarded as a betrayal of the Revolution. For several years thereafter, membership fell off despite the efforts of the Communist Party to recruit new cadres through the establishment of a still younger party affiliate, the Pioneers, in 1922.

The Komsomol was rent by a series of schisms during the 1920's. The more radical youth were sympathetic to Trotsky and his vision of a world revolution and refused to endorse Stalin's more conservative slogan of "socialism in one country." The radicals, not surprisingly, went the way of Trotsky—they were expelled. And as it became clear that the Komsomol was becoming the road to party position and to power, a new generation began to enroll in ever larger numbers. By the eve of the first Five Year Plan, membership had reached two million. The Five Year Plan itself and the new program of collectivization and industrialization aroused immense enthusiasm among young people. Here again was the opportunity for youth to accomplish great tasks and bring about fundamental changes. Thousands of youngsters joined shock brigades to build dams and construct factories. Some went among the "backward" masses to combat religion; others were extremely effective in pressing collectivization, and were among the most righteous and brutal in eliminating kulaks.

Until 1936, membership in the Komsomol was theoretically limited to workers, and it was regarded as purely a party organization. With the new Stalin constitution, however, the Komsomol was made over into a non-party organization; admission policy was liberalized, and a mass campaign was initiated to bring in members from all strata of the population. The organization has grown continuously since then—although it, too, suffered setbacks during the great purges of the 1930's—until it now embraces about one-third of Russian youth between 14 and 28 years of age.

Membership requirements for the Komsomol today are less rigid than those of the party. The organization is designed not only to supply future party cadres but also to provide the more numerous nonmembers with an example and standard of the ideal Soviet youth. On the matter of membership, the Komsomol is unlike the Pioneers, which enrolls all youth between ten and 14 (although membership is supposed to be voluntary), or the Octobrists, an informal group that all children join on entering school.

All these organizations cooperate with the school system in socializing youth—that is, in instilling attitudes toward the "creation" of the ideal Soviet citizen. They also offer a range of activities, such as athletics, dramatics, and hiking, that are sponsored by similar organizations in Western European nations.

The organization of Komsomol is modeled after that of the Communist Party, with primary, district, regional, and national divisions. On the primary levels are the older, full-time, salaried bureaucrats who, despite recent efforts, still dominate national congresses. The entire Komsomol system is completely subordinate to the Communist Party. While it controls its own publishing house, and publishes a special newspaper, *Komsomolskaya Pravda,* pertaining to the problems of youth, the party determines policy.

Komsomol members who are to become part of future party cadres receive special training in Marxism-Leninism and undertake special duties in both secondary schools and universities. If students in secondary schools misbehave, shaming techniques are used to bring them back into line. There are, however, occasions when the demands of Komsomol membership and school work conflict, and there is evidence of occasional tension between Komsomol groups and teachers.

At universities, Komsomol membership is, for all practical purposes, compulsory, for it is impossible to get into any institution of higher learning unless one is a member. The most active Komsomol members control student standards through volunteer police patrols (*druzhina*) and comrades' courts which can recommend expulsion for improper behavior. The standards of "improper" behavior are rather vague, but they can run the gamut from improper dress (skirts which are too short) to too close association with foreigners.[11]

In general, and aside from spreading specific Marxist-Leninist doctrine, the Komsomol's educational efforts are directed at implanting values not unlike those associated with "bourgeois" morality in the West: respect for work and authority, good manners, and general helpfulness. But these efforts toward propagating and exacting party policy cause almost constant tensions—tensions resulting from the stress on individual achievement and the insistence that one submerge oneself in the group as a whole, tensions from the pressure to participate actively as a sign of "normalcy" and the increasing demands for privacy.

Within the Komsomol in the past ten to fifteen years there has been a loss of élan. The denunciations of crimes committed during the Stalin era, which in turn have produced an intergenerational conflict, have had a pervasively disquieting effect. According to the Yugoslav scholar Mihajlo Mihajlov, concentration-camp ballads are a popular form of "rebellious" behavior among youth.

It is difficult to estimate how far this type of rebellion has gone, but it was serious enough to prompt Khrushchev to remark at the Fourteenth Komsomol Congress:

> *You young people, don't become conceited; we haven't lived for nothing you know, nor did we spend our time swatting flies with our noses, as the saying goes! I am proud of my generation. . . . People of the older generation lived through hunger and devastation; they restored the economy by heroic effort.*[12]

The same points were made (albeit in a somewhat less earthy fashion) by Brezhnev in 1968 on the occasion of the fiftieth anniversary of Komsomol. Shortly afterward, the youth organization underwent a shakeup of its leadership.

Many youth now find life in the Komsomol overbureaucratized, and the constant reiteration of party slogans dull. This disenchantment is equally evident among students seriously interested in attaining professional competence and among those who are already affluent, by Soviet standards, and are developing their own youth culture. In its extreme forms, the new culture is manifested in the *stilyagi* (from the Russian word for style), youths criticized as idlers and nonconformists, addicted to decadent bourgeois values. The term, used most often in the 1956–1960 period, has been replaced by another: "crown princes"—youngsters considered idlers interested only in satisfying their narrow egotistical desires.

To what extent are Soviet youth in general affected by this kind of rebellion? All we know is that juvenile delinquency is on the rise in the Soviet Union, even among the somewhat affluent, and that "hooliganism" is also increasing. Some observers, including Mihajlov, claim that it is unsafe to walk alone at night in many parts of Moscow, despite the squads of militiamen who supplement the police.

---

[11] For the role of the Komsomol at universities see Allen Kassof, *The Soviet Youth Program* (Cambridge, Mass.: Harvard University Press, 1965), pp. 100–107, and Darrell P. Hammer, "Among Students in Moscow: An Outsider's Report," *Problems of Communism*, XIII, 4 (July-August 1964), 11–18.

[12] Quoted in Fainsod, *How Russia Is Ruled*, p. 304.

The Soviets officially deny the existence of widespread delinquency. Indirectly, however, they admit that problems with youth have developed and they seem at a loss to find official explanations for them. The juvenile gangs that roamed most Russian cities during the 1930's could be explained by poverty or the hangover of bourgeois values, but these excuses no longer suffice. When explanations are forthcoming, the official line blames pampering by parents and seduction through contacts with the "decadent" bourgeois West. The suggested remedies are usually stricter parental discipline and harsher punishment for miscreants. The following quotations are illustrative:

Bourgeois propaganda places more and more hope on its art, music and dances in trying to reach the minds of young people. . . . It stresses art that awakens animal instincts and that preaches egoism, cruelty, and a thirst for unhealthy pleasures. . . . Apologists for the bourgeois way of life stress licentious and hysterical jazz like trash, dances with pornographic overtones—hack work by artists that relieves man of the need to think. On some people here and there this creates a certain impression.[13]

In our society, in which the social causes of crime have long since been eliminated, where do thieves, hooligans, parasites and other lawbreakers come from? . . .

Soviet legal science rightly refutes the hypotheses of certain bourgeois scholars about . . . the inevitability of lawbreaking. After all each person in our country has an opportunity to labor and to earn his living in an honest way.

There has been enough coddling of vicious criminals. As a matter of fact, measures of persuasion and public influence have no effect on some of them. . . . Our humaneness should be shown to those who have slipped for the first time and have recognized their error.

In other cases it is necessary to act with all severity.[14]

There are reasons for the increase of juvenile delinquency which are not found in Soviet propaganda. For a long time, youth in the Soviet Union exercised an enormous influence on the course of the nation. The cadres of the party were young, and youth was called upon to lead the rebellion against the old society. Both the purges of the 1930's and World War II continued the process whereby youth could find itself an influential niche fairly quickly. All of this has now changed. The older generation is less willing to surrender its position of authority. Moreover, Soviet ideology increasingly sees society's goal in terms of satisfying individual needs and not as the subordination of these to other ideological ends.

In many ways it is far more difficult for Soviet authorities to recognize the problems among youth than it is for those in the West. Because of the Marxist belief that alienation and crime are merely the by-products of capitalist society, they have been forced to create a new official ideology that saves the determinism of Marxism by arguing that in a Socialist society men are *free* to choose evil, and thus it is justifiable to punish them.

There are, however, counter-trends. Soviet scholars working in the field of psychology are developing a fairly sophisticated outlook, even though they start from Pavlov rather than Watson or Freud. For example, for a long time Soviet ideology denied that adolescence was a natural stage of development. Adolescent crises, therefore, occurred only in capitalist societies. Now, however, the line has been modified:

The adolescent, just as the child, grows physically and mentally . . . but still is not aware of the extent of his strength. He can no longer live by those illusions by which the child lives. . . . The adolescent attempts to

---

[13] *Komsomolskaya Pravda*, September 15, 1960. Quoted in Kassof, *Soviet Youth Program*, p. 163.

[14] V. Tikunov, R.S.F.S.R. Minister for Safeguarding Public Order, *Izvestia*, February 6, 1965.

appear more mature than he really is; he is
likely to imagine himself to be more adult
than child [and] . . . considers himself to be
more knowledgeable than he really is.[15]

The Soviet author of the volume from
which this quotation comes sees the answer to
the adolescent's lack of self-discipline in a
more active attempt to involve him in the life
of the collective. Other Soviet social scientists,
however, relying more and more upon sociological techniques developed in the West, are
seeking to channel youthful urges into meaningful outlets, including youth centers. They
are also conducting studies of family strains
and delinquency based on Western sociological techniques. Furthermore, many Soviet
psychologists are relying on supportive ther-
apy, in which they encourage adolescents to
talk about their emotional problems. Finally, after a long period of silence, Soviet

pedagogues are considering the introduction
of a minimum of sex education for young
people.

The amount of youthful delinquency in the
Soviet Union should not be overestimated,
just as one should not overestimate the
amount of rejection of the Communist system itself. Both manifestations of rebellion
apply to only a small segment of youth, although the number of those militantly dedicated to the regime is also small. As a
poll taken in Smolensk reveals, most young
people are concerned with marriage, self-
advancement, and enjoying themselves. Very
few are rebels, and very few (only three per
cent) are activists.[16] For the great majority
of Soviet youth, as for most youngsters in
Western countries, life is ordinary. The small
percentage of Soviet youth active in Komsomol work tend to view their membership
pragmatically—as an avenue to political success.

15 G. S. Prozorov, *Heredity and Upbringing* (Moscow, 1960), p. 52. Quoted in Kassof, *Soviet Youth
Program,* p. 35.

16 As reported in *The New York Times,* June 23,
1965.

part III

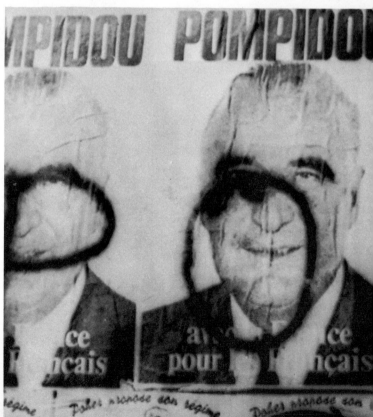

Voting in Moscow.
Willy Brandt. D.P.A.-Pictorial
French Campaign Posters. Wide World
Photos

9

The European

Pattern

1. INTRODUCTION

The political system of any society consists of those structures through which its members—or the most powerful among them—determine its goals and the manner in which they are to be implemented. These goals include decisions on such questions as the distribution of the society's resources among its members.

If it is to perform its functions, the political system must include mechanisms for recruiting political leaders and for providing them with the power to formulate rules that will bind the whole community. Except in those rare—and usually short-lived—instances in which an elite imposes its rule by force alone, a regime can mobilize power in two ways: by implementing policies that take into account the demands of at least a portion of the citizenry, and by establishing its own legitimacy.

Historically, rulers have been able to gain their legitimacy by appealing to tradition, or by relying on charisma, or by claiming special religious or ideological insights. The demands of the subjects or citizens are determined by elections, by consulting assemblies of notables, or by the perceptiveness of the rulers as to the "real" interests or needs of their people.

All societies, of course, are composed of a plurality of interests all of which cannot be satisfied at the same time. How the "real" interests of the people are to be ascertained, just which of these are to be satisfied, how political elites should be recruited, and what makes power legitimate—these questions have traditionally constituted the heart of political philosophy.

Democratic theory assumes that individuals and groups within the society be given relatively free play in urging the adoption of their demands as public policy. The major limitation placed upon the expression of such demands is that those who make them not resort to violence. The political system is viewed as an arena in which members of the society, responding to changes in their environment, compete in an attempt to translate their demands into appropriate public policy. This contest, in which the weapons are

297

persuasion and certain limited forms of pressure, is justified by the belief that the rules under which it is conducted will cause it to produce results that represent a creative response to the needs of most citizens.

Since the number of demands that can be made upon the political system by its members is theoretically infinite, one function of political parties is to aggregate these into a smaller number of more or less coherent alternatives. The political elites who staff the parties are rewarded by seeing their demands translated into programs, by the satisfaction that comes with exercising authority, by the material rewards that are often a by-product of exercising authority, and by the attention that accrues to those who hold public office. These elites compete for support on the basis of policies they have already implemented or promise to implement.

If the democratic, or, rather, the polyarchic, system is working well, political parties also serve other functions: they enable members of the society to make more rational policy choices by spelling out actual or possible consequences to different alternatives, and they also provide expressive satisfactions in the form of rhetorical combat. Thus, the whole ritual of the political campaign serves to enhance political solidarity, even as it may aggravate tensions by revealing what divides the society. The principal problem faced by a democratic polity is that the demands of its citizens may be of such magnitude or character that it is impossible to satisfy them within a reasonable time, at least without seriously alienating certain segments of the population. When the demands of a substantial portion of the population of any community cannot be satisfied by its political mechanisms, the community is faced with the threat of widespread alienation from the political system.

Again, it should be emphasized that the functions fulfilled by political parties in a democratic political order can be handled by other structures, as indeed they have been through most of recorded history; it may well

be true that a politics of parties will turn out to have been a transitory type of political order, limited in time to the nineteenth and twentieth centuries. Nor do all types of political systems have the same functional requirements. Parties emerged as instruments for legitimizing the use of authority for certain ends when it became generally accepted that political systems can and should serve as channels for satisfying freely expressed demands; only when this premise is accepted are mechanisms required for the processing of such demands.

2. PARTIES AND ELECTORAL SYSTEMS

All democratic societies characterized by competitive party systems face the problem of creating machinery for reflecting the expressed preferences of voters. Ideally, representation on decision-making bodies should accurately reflect all the opinions that exist within the society itself.

It is not too difficult to demonstrate, however, the logical impossibility of achieving this goal or even of creating an electoral system that mirrors the will of the majority, when all the various positions on all issues, as well as the intensity of feeling about particular issues, are taken into account.[1] The best any electoral system can hope for is to provide a rough approximation of the feeling of different groups on the issues that are most important to them. Historically, two systems of representation, each with a number of modifications, have been most commonly used: single-member electoral districts with election by plurality or majority, and multi-member districts with election by proportional representation.[2] Because many political scientists have believed that the type of system chosen influences the number and character of political parties in important

[1] See Robert A. Dahl, *A Preface to Democratic Theory* (Chicago: The University of Chicago Press, 1956).

[2] There are still other variations, such as two-member districts with preferential ballots, but these have not been used widely enough to merit consideration here.

ways, with very significant consequences for the ability of the political system successfully to fulfill its functions, it is worth outlining the structure of these two systems of representation in some detail. The possible impact of electoral arrangements will be discussed after they have been described.[3]

England and the United States have used a system of single-member election districts, with a *plurality* of the votes cast necessary for election. Both nations are divided into districts from which only one candidate can be elected. In each election the candidate with the largest number of votes is declared the winner, even if he receives fewer than a majority of the ballots.[4] Assume a field of four candidates receiving the following portion of the total votes:

Candidate A   35 per cent of the votes cast
Candidate B   25 per cent of the votes cast
Candidate C   20 per cent of the votes cast
Candidate D   20 per cent of the votes cast

In this example, Candidate *A* would be the victor.

In France during the Fifth Republic, as during most of the Third Republic, a system of single-member districts is combined with the requirement that a candidate receive a majority of the vote to be elected. If no candidate does so on the first ballot, a second election is held and only a plurality is necessary. Thus, in the example cited above, a second ballot would be required.[5]

3 The classic exposition is that of F. A. Hermens, *Democracy or Anarchy* (Notre Dame: University of Notre Dame Press, 1941). See also Maurice Duverger, *Political Parties,* translated by Barbara and Robert North (New York: John Wiley and Sons, 1954); and Douglas W. Rae, *The Political Consequences of Electoral Laws* (New Haven: Yale University Press, 1967).

4 Some Southern states represent a partial exception in that runoffs are held in primary elections when no candidate receives an absolute majority on the first ballot.

5 Any candidate may compete a second time provided (since 1967) he has received at least 10 per cent of the vote. More usually, however, an agreement is reached whereby some parties will withdraw their candidates in return for the promise of political favors.

A system of single-member districts with election by plurality tends to discriminate heavily against smaller political parties, to distort the result of voting, and to reduce the range of opinions represented in legislative bodies. Assume, for example, a nation with one hundred single-member electoral districts and four political parties, whose total vote is distributed more or less in the proportions listed in the example just given. Assuming further that the vote of each party is spread uniformly throughout the country, the largest party (Party *A*) would elect all of its candidates, receiving a hundred per cent of the seats in the legislature—on the basis of 35 per cent of the popular vote. The smaller the party, of course, the greater the discrimination. With almost ten per cent of the vote in the 1951 elections, for instance, the British Liberal Party received only 1.44 per cent of the seats in Parliament. In the 1922 elections, to cite another instance, the British Labor Party obtained only 142 seats, 39 fewer than it would have received under a system of proportional representation. The Conservatives, on the other hand, got 346 seats, 111 more than they would have on a proportional basis.

Provisions for a second ballot are fundamentally an attempt at "minimax." Those voters whose own candidate has no chance of being elected can vote for their second preference in the runoff election; in France, for example, a Radical voter might support a conservative candidate rather than chance the election of a Communist. Further, parties with little hope of winning on the second ballot can negotiate between elections; one party may withdraw its candidate in return for promises that the other will do the same in another electoral district, or in return for policy or other concessions. This system can, and does, distort electoral results. The French Communists in 1958 received only 1.7 per cent of the parliamentary seats even though they won some 20.7 per cent of the popular vote on the second ballot because other parties would not enter into electoral alliance with them. In 1967, however, they entered into an arrangement with other left-wing parties in which each agreed to support the strongest candidate on the second ballot. As a result, they captured 15.5 per cent of the seats in the Assembly, although their popular vote had increased by only one per cent.

Any system of proportional representation is designed to insure the "fair" representation of every possible political tendency. Basically, proportional representation involves multi-member election districts and a process by which votes are divided among the candidates participating in the election.[6] For example, let us assume that four political parties are competing for five seats in a multi-member district, and that the votes are distributed as follows:

List A   13,500 votes
List B   4,500 votes
List C   4,500 votes
List D   1,500 votes

In this example it would be easy to divide the seats among the parties. List A would receive three seats and B and C one seat each. List D would receive no seats.

As it is, List D has been discriminated against and the votes of its supporters wasted. Discrimination is likely to be greater, as will the difficulty of distributing seats, if the votes received are not in neat proportion. For example, let us assume that the following distribution of votes had occurred:

List A   8,700 votes
List B   6,800 votes
List C   5,200 votes
List D   3,300 votes

6 The description of systems of proportional representation is largely derived from W. H. M. McKenzie, *Free Elections* (New York: Rinehart and Company, 1958). In most European countries, the list system of proportional representation is used. Therefore, in a district with five seats at stake, each major party will enter a *list* of five candidates.

If five seats are again at stake, the party lists are entitled to seats as follows: List A, 1.813 seats; List B, 1.416; List C, 1.008, and List D, 0.687 seats. No matter how the seats are divided, some votes are going to be lost. One way to minimize this waste is to reduce the number and increase the size of electoral districts. Another way is to employ techniques that have been developed to insure the fairest possible distribution. Two techniques, or variations of them, are most commonly used: the *highest average* and the *greatest remainder*.

In distributing seats in terms of the highest average, the votes of each list are first divided by one; the list with the highest average (which, of course, is equal to its vote) receives the first seat. For the second seat, the votes received by each list are again divided by one plus the number of seats any of the lists may have thus far obtained. The list now having the highest average receives the second seat, and so on until the number of seats to be distributed is exhausted. List A would clearly receive the first seat. Its total vote would then be divided by two. Since the votes of all other parties would still be divided by one, List B would receive the second seat, List C the third. However, List A would receive the fourth seat and so on. The process is illustrated by Table 9.1.

In the method of the greatest remainder, the total number of votes cast is divided by the number of seats available. The seats received by any list are the result of dividing its votes by the quotient thus obtained. The remaining seats are distributed among competing lists in terms of the remainders available after the initial distribution has taken place. In this case the quotient is 4,800, and each of the three largest parties receives one seat. The largest remainder is that of List A, which gets a second seat. List D now has the largest remainder and, thus, receives the final seat. (See Table 9.2.)

In general, the method of the highest average tends to favor larger parties, while

TABLE 9.1. DISTRIBUTION OF SEATS BY HIGHEST AVERAGE

List	Calculation of first seat	Calculation of second seat	Calculation of third seat	Calculation of fourth seat	Calculation of final seat	Total seats
A	8,700	4,350	4,350	4,350	2,900	2
B	6,800	6,800	3,400	3,400	3,400	2
C	5,200	5,200	5,200	2,600	2,600	1
D	3,300	3,300	3,300	3,300	3,300	0

that of the greatest remainder favors smaller ones. Thus, the method of the highest average would allot two seats each to Lists *A* and *B*, one seat to List *C*, and none to List *D*. If the greatest remainder were used, however, List *A* would receive two seats and each of the remaining lists would obtain one seat.

The French under the Fourth Republic used the highest average, except, after 1950, in the Department of the Seine. The Germans used the method of the greatest remainder during the Weimar period. In fact, the electoral law went still further to insure accurate representation; a national constituency was established which allowed "wasted" remainders to be collected and used for the election of candidates from national party lists to the Reichstag.

The list system of proportional representation creates a number of problems. Voters choose among party lists rather than individuals, and candidates from the list are declared elected in order of their appearance on it. Thus, if Party *D* had presented a list of five candidates and was entitled to two seats, the first two candidates on its list would normally be returned to the parlia-

ment. The arrangement minimizes the role of the individual candidate, underscores the importance of party voting, and places a good deal of power in the hands of party leaders, who usually determine the order in which names will appear.

Understandably, individual candidates who might have a large following but who are, for some reason, not destined for first place consider this procedure unfair. In France, a provision was added whereby voters could change the position of an individual on the list if they so wished; but the problems were so complex that it was of little value.

Proportional representation has always been supported on the ground that it allows for a more equitable delineation of voters' preferences. Since the fall of the Weimar Republic, however, PR has fallen into some disrepute. As for plurality elections in single-member election districts, most of the proponents argue that its apparent unfairness is actually a virtue. Plurality elections and single-member constituencies reduce the number of parties competing for office.

TABLE 9.2. DISTRIBUTION OF SEATS BY GREATEST REMAINDER

List	Votes	Seats won by quotient	Remainder	Total seats
A	8,700	1	3,900	2
B	6,800	1	2,000	1
C	5,200	1	400	1
D	3,300	0	3,300	1

Eventually, the voter's choice is between two political parties, thus permitting comparatively moderate, responsible politics and the formation of a government that can work effectively.

Political parties are reduced in number when voters, finding their votes wasted on minor parties, switch to one of two major parties. The major parties, of course, attempt always to broaden their appeal to obtain these votes, and this, in turn, helps guarantee their moderation. Both the reduction to two parties and the consequent certainty of a one-party government elected to implement its program insure effective choice —because responsibility for policies is more easily allocated.

It is argued that proportional representation, on the other hand, tends to have the opposite effects. It encourages the continued fragmentation of parties. Given the inevitable multiplicity of policy differences, individual or group votes are much more likely to split into smaller and smaller political segments because no vote is wasted. Since in a multi-party system all governments are apt to be coalition governments, even a very small party may be placed in a politically strategic position. In France under the Fourth Republic, for example, the Radical Socialist Party supplied more prime ministers than any other party, even though it was one of the smaller French factions, exceeded in strength by the Communists, the M.R.P., the Socialists, the Independents and Peasants, and, while it existed, the Rally of the French People.

The encouragement of fragmentation and the fact that votes are not lost also prompts the proliferation of "crackpot" opinions, both the narrowest and the most radical. The polarization of politics is further induced by government instability, the absence of effective government policy, and the lack of real political alternatives. Government instability is the result of party fragmentation and the consequent coalitions composed of men who find it difficult to compromise without losing

their identity. When, as in parliamentary systems, the government is responsible to the legislature, the result is either the rapid change of governments or a government that remains in office by doing nothing. During the 12 years of the Fourth Republic, France was governed by 25 different cabinets, and while often a change in government meant only a slight shifting of personnel, the development of any consistent, long-range policies was difficult if not impossible. Government instability—or immobility—prevents, therefore, the political system from achieving those goals upon which all might agree, such as economic growth.

Finally, it is argued that under proportional representation citizens do not have an effective choice because there is no rational manner by which responsibility for public policy can be assigned to a particular party or regime. Voting decisions and the discussion of public policy take place in a vacuum that inspires narrowly doctrinaire, rather than more pragmatic, responses to issues.

Elections by majority and a double ballot may yield many of the same results. The possibility of a second election creates a multiplicity of smaller parties that hope to benefit through "deals," even if their candidate is not successful. Thus, both proportional representation and majority elections with a double ballot encourage party multiplicity and its attendant consequences—government instability and national inertia.

This argument makes a certain amount of sense, although some important qualifications are required. For example, while single-member plurality districts discourage third and fourth parties, these parties will develop and continue to exist if they represent an ideological or ethnic minority ignored by the larger parties. This is especially true if the minority group is geographically segregated and has its own strongholds. For example, the Communists in France during the 1920's and early 1930's retained the support of their electorate despite the discrimination of the electoral system. So, too, the

Irish Nationalists continued to receive the support of their constituency so long as they were represented in the British parliament, even though their supporters knew they could never hope to achieve majority status.

The empirical evidence, moreover, does not conclusively demonstrate that proportional representation must always lead to the progressive fragmentation of the party system. Sweden, Norway, and Denmark have all used PR in political systems that have had no more than four large parties. Their systems have not been excessively unstable, nor have they failed to take effective action toward the achievement of common goals.

The case for the moderating effects of single-member districts with plurality elections is not the most convincing. One can argue that in a country marked by sharp political divisions the effect of single-member districts is most likely to polarize the electorate around the extreme parties. Certainly the rise of the British Labor Party as a replacement for the British Liberals was not the victory of a more moderate party over a more extreme one. And it can be legitimately argued that the American electoral system, including the method of electing presidents, served to so polarize the situation in the United States in 1860 that it contributed directly to the breakdown of politics and the Civil War. Further, if a radical minority finds itself unrepresented in the political system, as with the French Communists, it is more likely to turn to violence than if it were so represented.

In sum, then, the relationship among electoral systems, party systems, and the functioning of political systems is not easy to unravel. It is probably true that proportional representation removes obstacles that might inhibit an increase in the number of parties, and, at least in a parliamentary system, somewhat reduces the possibility of stable, coherent government policies. Even so, it is difficult to believe that the politics of the United States or Great Britain would have been very different if elections had been by proportional representation, or that Swedish politics would have been notably affected by the use of single-member plurality districts. Given the strains that characterized Germany in the years between the two world wars, it is highly unlikely that another electoral system would have been enough, by itself, to yield a stable politics. It is also unlikely that another system would have materially altered French politics during the Third and Fourth Republics. Most of the important parties would have possessed sufficient strength in some areas to have continued to survive.[7]

3. THE DEVELOPMENT OF EUROPEAN PARTIES

European political parties, in the modern sense, began to take form only in the nineteenth century, with the beginnings of industrialization, the formulation of liberalism as an ideology, the gradual extension of the suffrage, and the creation of parliamentary regimes. To be sure, factions or "connexions" had existed earlier in England. In the eighteenth century, one could speak of Whigs and Tories and trace their antecedents back to the English Civil War; the Whigs were more inclined to favor commercial interests and the more radical Protestant sects, and the Tories were oriented toward the established church. The lines between them, however, were blurred, and, with England's limited suffrage and a Parliament consisting almost entirely of gentlemen, "connexions" formed and reformed, based on individual, family, regional, or religious factors.

The American and French Revolutions had an enormous effect upon the development of political parties. In the United States, commitment to a government based on the

[7] The time at which PR or other systems are introduced may be crucial. In an effectively functioning two-party system, the introduction of PR may not make much difference. Also, once a multiplicity of reasonably well-organized parties has materialized, replacing PR by single-member districts may not affect the political scene.

participation of the people resulted in a fairly rapid extension of voting rights and the early emergence of modern political parties. By 1840, American Whigs and Democrats were using most of the techniques associated with contemporary electoral campaigns. In England and on the Continent, the evolution of modern parties was much slower. During the French Revolution, an assortment of political factions surfaced, including, most importantly, the Jacobins. But the cycle of revolution and repression as well as the splintering of French political life prevented the establishment of an organized party structure until late in the nineteenth century. In most of Europe, the first attempt to form enduring factions came from liberals who wished to change the existing social order. In England, however, more conservative gentlemen saw the need for organization at about the same time; the founding of the Carlton Club in 1832 preceded by four years that of the liberals' Reform Club. In Germany, liberal political groups started to organize in 1848, and in France, again, the Jacobins of the revolutionary period were followed by numerous groups that formed throughout the nineteenth century, although political parties as such did not appear until the 1870's. The formation of "liberal" parties caused, in response, the founding of a series of "conservative" organizations dedicated to preserving the patterns of the traditional society. As the century wore on, the conservative groups found themselves forced to assume a more permanent form in order to compete for the new electorate's votes.

On the whole, conservative and liberal parties in Europe were parties of notables— men of substance who organized in order to achieve common ends or serve particular interests. And although they appealed to the electorate, their organizational efforts were always limited (especially in the case of conservatives) by a distaste, bred of their traditional values, for developing a truly mass party. Initially this was not too important; the electorate was still small, and the

practice of public voting permitted not only bribery but intimidation. By the 1880's, however, most European countries had established the secret ballot, and most were well on the way to universal manhood suffrage. Traditional political methods would no longer suffice.

The first European "mass" parties were the Socialist parties. Founded by trade unions or reformers outside the parliamentary structure, and based on a weltanschauung that demanded the total transformation of society, they appeared as organized "movements" with a highly disciplined mass membership. The impact of the Socialists and the growing need to organize a larger electorate compelled other parties to look again to their structure, although the effort to organize more conservative parties varied with national circumstances. In England, the existence of a two-party system and the acceptance of a democratic polity by the Conservatives led them to adopt a mass-membership structure of their own. In France, however, political fragmentation and the conservatives' persistent distaste for appealing to the masses inhibited such organization. The same factors operated even more strongly in Germany, and the collapse of German conservatism in the post–World War I period was due partly to its inability to come to terms with the new mass society.

Although European liberal parties were among the first to develop a modern structure, they, too, did not succeed in creating a mass base. Some of the same factors operated here that inhibited the conservatives. Their ideology notwithstanding, liberal parties were led by a class-conscious middle class that to a certain extent remained suspicious of the industrial proletariat and shied away from "demagoguery." Liberal ideology itself was an inhibiting element, especially its individualistic emphasis and its conception of the state as a broker whose function it was to facilitate negotiations among competing regional, individual, and group interests.

The only other mass parties that sprang up

in the nineteenth century were those that catered to minority ethnic or religious groups. The Irish Nationalists and the German Center (Catholic) Party, both created as mass organizations, were based on an appeal to a particular group. In a society where the reins of power were held by a hostile establishment, this was the only manner in which minorities could protect their interests.

After World War I, two other types of mass parties, which were to have a prodigious effect upon the remainder of the twentieth century, burst forth in Europe: the Fascist and the Communist. Both were, and are, highly ideological, demanding the immediate and total transformation of their society. The mass base of Fascist parties makes it clear that they were not merely "conservative" parties, and both the Communist and Fascist parties can be seen as part of a broad reaction to the tensions produced by social change.

In the case of Communists this reaction has involved a degree of discipline that far surpasses that of the Socialist tradition from which they sprang. The only parties today that approach their level of organizational capacity are a few nationalist parties in developing nations that are attempting to mobilize the population.

In the post–World War II period, Christian Democratic parties appeared in Western Europe with the aim of both uniting Catholicism—or more vaguely Christianity—with democracy and of breaking away from the traditional image of Catholic conservatism. Within a few years, however, most of them had lost their original élan and, while retaining something of a mass base, had become primarily pragmatic parties of the center or center left.

Indeed, the trend in Europe after World War II through the 1950's and the first part of the 1960's was away from mass parties and toward the cadre parties led by professional politicians. This political trend also involved the increasing bureaucratization of party structure, greater use of new publicity techniques, and the closer identification of parties, on the national level at least, with political leaders who were able to register a favorable television image. The trend toward bureaucratization and professionalization seemed to be taking place in the Communist parties of Western Europe and in the Soviet Union, reflecting the resolution of some of the strains that had produced the ideological conflicts of the nineteenth century—even as the phenomenon seemed to imply that the problems faced by technologically advanced nations were, in fact, basically "technical" rather than ideological.

Student upheavals in the late 1960's, as well as the manifestations of new local nationalisms (Welsh and Scots nationalism in England, for example), may presage new ideological divisions whose implications for political parties are difficult to predict. For the moment, however, they have not altered the basic trend of contemporary party developments.

The pattern of European party development mirrors the social and cultural conflicts that divided European societies in the nineteenth century. That the most important parties have been "ideological," and that many have been tightly disciplined mass parties, is closely related to these conflicts. In the United States, both major parties have been relatively unideological and "pragmatic" because they share a common liberal wellspring; the Republican and Democratic parties most closely resemble European liberal parties in both structure and outlook. There are, however, two important and closely connected differences. The first is that in the United States, these parties—like liberalism itself—have represented the entire political spectrum, while in Europe liberal ideology and liberal parties have represented only one segment of that spectrum, a segment that has been declining in importance since World War I. Second, the relative lack of class consciousness on the part of the American middle class permitted the swift democratization of American liberalism—especially since the middle class did not perceive the working class as a hostile mob. The result was a "populist" democracy and a system of political parties more democratic in their organization than their European counterparts. However, because of this almost total absence of a class consciousness in the United States and a culture whose premises were incompatible with specifically ethnic or religious parties, nothing comparable to the mass-membership, highly organized European parties of the left ever developed.

In Europe, liberal parties became identified with a particular set of doctrines. Their triumph was that some of these, such as the mass franchise and separation of church and state, have been accepted by most other political parties; their tragedy, that their victory left them with little more of relevance to say. Identified by a class-conscious working class with a laissez-faire, middle-class ideology, they were unable to retain mass support even as they attempted to adjust their doctrines to meet new problems. Having lost their following, they have been unable to lure back working-class voters from Socialist parties, even though the Socialists have retreated from their early radicalism.

In England, France, and Germany, liberal and conservative parties were generally created by legislators who had been elected more or less as individuals. As the electorate expanded, the parties found it necessary to form national organizations for the purposes of locating suitable candidates and conducting election campaigns. These organizations, for the most part, remained under the control of parliamentary leaders or local notables. Mass ideological parties of the Socialist type, however, were invariably first organized as extraparliamentary parties whose basis of strength was the working class. Committed to the rule of the people and to ideological purity, they insisted that ultimate authority be vested in party members meeting regularly to decide party issues. Within most of these parties, tensions developed between the growing party bureaucracies, dedicated to the maintenance of the party; the militants, dedicated to the ideal image of the party as they saw it; and the parliamentarians, dedicated to winning majorities.

The uneasy balances achieved between these forces, and the commitment to inner-party democracy, have varied, depending not only upon the nature of the party system itself, but on the particular configuration of politics within a nation.

THE BASES OF PARTY SUPPORT: The first major political conflicts in modern Europe existed between centralizing monarchies and local and regional authorities, or between monarchs and special groups, such as the Catholic Church, that wished to retain their corporate privileges. To these were added the sectional clashes between urban and rural interests. By far the most significant source of political division in Western Europe since the nineteenth century has been that of social class. Class division as a source of po-

TABLE 9.3.   WORKING-CLASS SUPPORT OF COMMUNIST AND SOCIALIST
PARTIES IN EUROPE: THE 1960'S

	Per cent of workers in the electorate	Per cent voting Communist or Socialist
England	55%	66%
France	37	44
Germany	50	43

litical differentiation is most clearly apparent in England, where both the national and the religious issues had been settled before the growth of modern parties, and where the Industrial Revolution effectively and rather quickly reduced the power of a distinct agricultural interest. Yet such factors must be considered by the major national parties. In France and Germany, for instance, the religious issue, with its historical and in some cases regional roots, continues to have an impact. In other European countries, pre-industrial variables are even more important. In Belgium, linguistic differences are still key determinants of voting behavior, and in Sweden, the Center (Peasant) Party draws its votes heavily from farmers and conceives of itself as primarily oriented to serving their needs.

Working-class voters in England, France, and Germany have tended to support Communist and Socialist parties in relatively large numbers. About 45 per cent of German workers support the German Social Democratic Party or other Socialist groups; the comparable percentage for professional men and businessmen is about 12. In France, too, about 45 per cent of working-class voters (but not their wives, who often vote far more conservatively) support the Communist or Socialist parties. Both parties received no more than seven or eight per cent of the vote of French businessmen. In England, anywhere from sixty to seventy per cent of the working class supports the Labor Party, as contrasted with ten to 16 per cent of the upper-middle class.

In the United States, the Democrats have at times obtained from 55 to 78 per cent of the working-class vote. While social class is an important variable, the Democrats are, of course, not a Socialist party in name or doctrine. As public-opinion polls demonstrate, the American worker is still overwhelmingly committed to a capitalist economic system.

Europe's farmers or peasants are more conservative than the urban working class.

In France's 1967 elections, only about 27 per cent of the peasants voted for left-wing parties, whereas some 45 per cent voted for de Gaulle's Union for a New Republic (*Union pour la nouvelle république*—U.N.R.). Earlier, many peasants had supported Pierre Poujade's semi-Fascist political organization. In Germany, only 12 per cent of farmers now support the Socialist Party, while about fifty per cent or more support the Christian Democratic Union. On the other hand, farm workers tend to vote left, and workers who have recently left the farm, where theoretically they were conservative, reveal a higher sense of class consciousness and vote more to the left than those who have lived in urban areas for some time.

There are, to be sure, other differences in working-class voting patterns. Most workers in difficult occupations, occupations subject to marked economic fluctuations, or occupations like mining, where they live and work in fairly isolated communities, tend more to the left. Also, workers in larger factories usually vote in larger proportions for left-wing parties than those in smaller factories, where the relation between employer and employee is often closer. Despite the generally leftist orientation of Europe's working class, however, there are recent indications that workers have grown more conservative in their opinions. In all Europe, they are retreating from the idea of nationalization in favor of a mixed economy. And it is partly for this reason that Socialist and even Communist parties have modified their electoral appeals.

While social class is the factor most closely correlated with voting differences, other varibles, as indicated previously, are still very important. Religious people, for instance, tend to be more conservative than the agnostics or atheists. In France, practicing Catholics vote heavily for center and conservative parties. French and German Protestants, on the other hand, while less radical than those with no religious affiliation, are more inclined to vote for left-wing parties. This undoubtedly has something to do with the minority status of Protestants in France and the fact that in Germany the Christian Democratic Union is still identified in the minds of many as a Catholic party. Religious belief, as one might expect, is also correlated with voting for Christian Democratic parties, although somewhat more so in Germany, where Catholics still are a self-conscious minority, than in France, where there were other parties besides the Popular Republican Movement (*Mouvement républicain populaire* —M.R.P.)[8] closely identified with the Catholic Church. Neither in England nor in the United States is there a Catholic or "Christian" party, which indicates something about the social patterns of the two countries; in both, for different reasons, any attempt to form such a party would be considered illegitimate by most people, Catholics as well as non-Catholics. Jews, as a third religious group in both Europe and the United States, tend to vote for parties of the left, partly because of their minority status.

Finally, women are more likely to be conservative voters than men. In the British election of 1964, only 39.7 per cent of men voted for the Conservative Party, six percentage points less than the women's Conservative vote. And in France and Germany also, women vote either for more conservative or more religiously oriented parties in larger numbers than men. For example, in 1967 only 43 per cent of those who voted for the Communist Party in France were women, while 58 per cent of the supporters of de Gaulle's U.N.R. were women.[9]

The general pattern of voter alignment is summarized in Table 9.4.

4. A TYPOLOGY OF EUROPEAN PARTIES

As an aid to understanding their political role as well as their internal dynamics, Europe's political parties can be classified in a number of ways. For our purposes, they may be categorized as follows:

Command

Ideological parties/Pragmatic parties
Parties of mobilization/Parties of representation
Mass parties/Cadre parties
Strongly articulated parties/Weakly articulated parties

In other words, in terms of their dynamics, parties may be described as having a relatively integrated ideological position, or as

---

[8] After the 1967 elections, the *Mouvement républicain populaire* re-formed itself as the Democratic Center (*Centre démocrate*).

[9] For the 1968 elections, the U.N.R. changed its name to the Union for the Defense of the Republic (*Union pour la défense de la république*—U.D.R.).

TABLE 9.4. GENERAL PATTERN OF LEFT-WING VOTING

Higher Leftist Vote	*Lower Leftist Vote*
Larger cities	Smaller towns, country
Larger plants	Smaller plants
Groups with high unemployment rates	Groups with low unemployment rates
Minority ethnic or religious groups	Majority ethnic or religious groups
Men	Women
Economically advanced regions	Economically backward regions
Manual workers	White-collar workers
Specific occupations: Miners, fishermen, commercial farmers, sailors, longshoremen, forestry workers	Specific occupations: Servants, service workers, peasants, subsistence farmers
Less skilled workers	More skilled workers

Adapted from Seymour Martin Lipset, *Political Man* (New York: Doubleday, 1960), p. 244. Copyright © 1959, 1960 by the author. Reprinted by permission of the publisher.

pragmatically seeking to achieve limited goals that are not based on a clearly articulated weltanschauung. In the latter case, party members will regard their function as one of reacting to the changing demands of the environment. Political parties may also be classified as to whether they conceive of their function as one of mobilizing the community to achieve ends they consider desirable, or of representing the diverse interests within the community in terms of their expressed goals.

Structurally, parties may consist of groups of notables or professional politicians who may or may not rely on the services of a limited number of unpaid militants at election time. Parties may also be mass organizations composed of and dependent upon large numbers of dues-paying members who are expected to work continuously for the party on a voluntary basis. Mass parties usually establish affiliated organizations such as youth groups and women's sections; these are designed to create a subculture in which members reinforce each other's loyalties, which, in turn, serve to protect them from the corrupting influences of the larger society. Finally, parties may be disciplined organizations whose members must accept and work for party policies whether they agree with them or not; or they may be loosely organized coalitions whose members are allowed, or maintain, considerable independence with regard to party policies.

Historically, ideologically oriented parties have usually been mass parties of mobilization with a strongly articulated structure. The most notable examples of such parties in recent history have been those with millennial aims—the Fascist, militant Socialist, and Communist. Moderate Socialist parties and parties based upon the desire to preserve a particular ethnic identity have rarely mustered the kind of fervor required to sustain a mass organization. In recent years, some of the non-Communist parties of African and other single-party states have approached

the Communist Party in organizational capacity, drawing their energies from elite desires to foster economic development and create a sense of national identity.

The use of the concept of ideology presents a serious problem. Certainly both American political parties share certain value assumptions that are widely diffused among the population. Their "pragmatism" operates only within the framework of these values. The difference between them and a party like the French Communist Party is that the latter is dedicated to changing in fundamental ways the normative order and the structure of society.

The emergence of mass ideological parties in any society is a reflection of fundamental cleavages that cannot be easily processed by the existing political system. In societies experiencing the emergence of nationalist aspirations and attempting to destroy the power of colonial rulers, the cleavages may be primarily political. In societies where this political question is not central, mass ideological parties usually develop only when a substantial segment of the articulate population believes that fundamental social changes are required. However, no nationalist party is likely to retain its mass ideological character unless its leadership is convinced that it must embark upon a program of fundamental social change. Contrast, for example, the experiences of the Soviet Union and India: in Russia, the seizure of power was but a preliminary step to more important revolutionary changes; in the case of India, on the other hand, independence was among the major aims, and while the Congress Party has remained wedded to vaguely Socialist goals, it has tended to become a holding company for diverse interests.

Mass ideological parties usually come to power under the leadership of a charismatic figure whose authority is based as much upon his personal magnetism as upon his party role. Once in power, the regimes established by such parties will inevitably be more or less repressive, depending not only upon how radical the changes are that they wish to make, but also upon the personalities of party leaders. Since the leadership of these parties desires to remake the society, they are likely to take responsibility for functions normally performed by governmental institutions as well as for a whole range of other activities, especially those relating to socialization. Despite their propaganda about representing the "whole people," they are likely to become elite parties, with basic decisions emanating from a small cadre of leaders. Practice here will vary, contingent upon party ideology, the character of the leadership, and the conditions prior to the acquisition of power. For example, the Nazi Party, while claiming to represent the "true instincts" of the people, was based on the concept of a racial elite that would govern the people in their own interest. The Bolshevik Party of the Soviet Union was formed as a conspiratorial group of professional revolutionaries, in part because of existing circumstances within Russia. But the Bolsheviks were also ideologically committed to the view that the party represents the most socially advanced segment of the people, and hence is the natural repository of power until such time as the ideal society has been created. The institutionalization of an elitist ideology in the Bolshevik Party was, of course, no accident, given the resistance of large portions of the population. And the fact that utopia, like the horizon, recedes even as one approaches it, provided further justification for an elitist structure.

There are, certainly, many other factors contributing to the transformation of a mass ideological party into an elitist corps. National or even regional party congresses are found to be ineffective in dealing with complicated issues of public policy. The party bureaucracy becomes jealous of its prerogatives and annoyed at those who would challenge the smooth flow of decisions. Ambitious young men who might otherwise serve

as a focus for opposition know that if they want to become co-opted into leadership positions, they must accept the decisions from on high; indeed, the upper echelons naturally look with most sympathy upon those individuals whose "understanding" of the leadership's goals is "more profound." Finally, the effort required to draw the masses into the discussion of crucial issues begins to seem wasteful—as time taken away from more "essential" tasks.

The fact of the matter is that the range of significant decisions that must be made by any national state is so great, and the decisions themselves so complex, that the only way to assume effective popular participation is to build it into the system by institutionalizing an opposition. That is, the political system must be constructed in such a way that ambitious young men and women can hope to achieve power, or at least win concessions, through the process of opposition. What this requires is, in effect, the creation of a two- or multi-party system.

It is one of history's tragic ironies that those most given to slogans about the necessity for participatory democracy have often produced the most authoritarian and oppressive political parties. One suspects that such slogans rest on the unconscious assumption that the masses naturally accept the leadership of those using them. Since the masses prove to be infinitely corruptible by false ideologies, the leadership, out of concern for the future of humanity, is forced to repress dissident elements until some future time when the masses can clearly grasp the true nature of the good society. The irony is also manifest when, convinced of the essential goodness of the "people," those urging "real" democracy often decide that guarantees of individual rights, and limitations upon the desires of the majority, are no longer necessary. The removal of such restraints and an emphasis upon decisions made in mass assemblies lead to situations in which minorities are shouted down and have no opportunity to work for policy reversals. This was the fate of Trotsky and others during the 1920's.

Once the party elite is in control, policy conflicts in one-party regimes are necessarily and most easily resolved by the purge. Rules regulating and limiting the scope of factional infighting have never existed, and so the knowledge that defeat will most probably yield removal from any position of power invariably makes the conflicts more savage. In the Soviet Union, defeated politicians have been reduced to nullities—when they have not been arrested or executed, although, as we shall see later, the nature of intra-party conflicts in the U.S.S.R. seems to be changing.

In the early stages of the development of mass ideological parties, leadership most often falls to revolutionary, "cosmopolitan" intellectuals, especially in the case of parties on the left. Once the party comes to power, however, the intellectuals are generally purged and replaced by bureaucratic manipulators, usually because the leadership of intellectuals is essentially based on verbal skills which are less effective in postrevolutionary power struggles. Often the prerevolutionary regime offered some protection to intellectual dissidents, if only because it accepted certain procedures as to what constituted legitimate political action. Revolutionary intellectuals find themselves at a disadvantage, however, when competing with those who rise in the party after the revolution, for the latter are even less willing than they to accept procedural rules as binding. Trotsky and others like him, for instance, were in a tremendously advantageous position vis-à-vis Russian liberals or Socialists, who had a "bourgeois" mentality when it came to the relationship between means and ends. Trotsky was at a distinct disadvantage when competing for power with Stalin. In the final analysis, of course, the forte of the intellectual is criticism, and his rebellion is usually directed against any bureaucratic routine. He becomes, therefore—especially if he insists upon the right to retain his independence of mind—a positive impediment to the new regime, which is anxious to set up and maintain a new bureaucratic system.

Many ideological parties in Europe have been led by members of subjugated minorities who hoped the new society they were creating would end oppression. Once in power, they discovered that old prejudices have not disappeared. The leadership of the Bolshevik Party in the prerevolutionary period contained a large number of Jews who believed that socialism would make religious and ethnic questions irrelevant. Jews also dominated the Communist parties of Rumania, Poland, and Hungary in the interwar years and immediately after World War II. In all these countries, they were either purged or executed, although anti-Semitism was not the overt reason.

In time, of course, the fervor of the party in a one-party state begins to erode, even as the requirements of an advanced society demand new technical elites and the party moves in the direction of a mediator among competing interests. Under such circumstances, one perceives the possibility of a more pluralistic society emerging once again. However, so long as the nation is divided effectively between the "clergy" (the party) and the "laity" (the people), the path of liberalization remains tortuous. It is in the party elite's interest to renew constantly its faith in those utopian goals that can never be achieved, for it is these goals that legitimize its power. That they can never be achieved can mean that authoritarian rule in one-party states, once established, may be of long duration. This is a problem to which we shall return in the concluding chapter.

Thus far, we have discussed some general categories to enable us to understand European political parties, and have outlined their overall development. Quite clearly, this development was decisively influenced by the social and ideological conflicts that emerged in Europe during the nineteenth century. Moreover, the structure and dynamics of

European political parties today cannot be understood except in terms of the factors that brought them into existence and sustained them.

The next several chapters will concentrate on how, within this general framework, European party systems evolved; why they evolved in somewhat different ways; and the consequences of these differences. The chapters will introduce each party in the order of its historical appearance, describe its development, and focus on the interplay of those forces that have resulted in the contemporary—and still changing—political scene.

For Western Europe the argument of these chapters is, very briefly, as follows: in England, the relative homogeneity of the society, and the fact that class conflict occurred well within the broader framework of an in-

clusive sense of community, resulted in a disciplined two-party system. In both France and Germany, failure to solve old societal problems before new ones appeared produced a far more complicated environment, with religious and regional issues joined to class issues as major sources of party differentiation. In both nations, for varying periods of time, the result was the fragmentation of the party system, and its inability to integrate effectively the demands of various interests.

As Part 4 of the text, "The Process of Government," will demonstrate, the nature of the party system which characterizes a society, the effectiveness with which it integrates group demands, and the manner in which it integrates these demands have important consequences for other political institutions.

10

The British

Party System

1. INTRODUCTION

Since 1931, English politics has been marked by the alternation in office of two disciplined, ideological mass parties. That is, both the Labor and the Conservative parties have campaigned on the basis of reasonably well-defined programs, and, once in office, have proceeded, by and large, to carry out their programs. Both parties have been supported by a fairly large core of dues-paying members—militants or enthusiasts—to whom party work is something of a mission. Many commentators, therefore, have spoken of British government in these years as party government.

Yet that statement must be qualified. During the period a number of smaller parties—the Liberal Party among the most important—have participated in electoral campaigns. And while it is legitimate to emphasize the ideological differences between the Labor and Conservative parties, as compared with American parties, neither was ever known for the kind of doctrinal rigidity that has been a common feature of so many Continental parties. Just as important, the Conservative Party has been far less self-consciously ideological than the Labor Party. Both have overlapping factions, and both have moved closer to each other in outlook since the end of World War II.

Nevertheless, the statement is accurate enough as a first generalization, and, insofar as it is accurate, the British party system requires explanation because it is unique. The United States has been characterized by a two-party system, but these parties have never had significant ideological disagreements. The Republican and Democratic parties have generally consisted of various interests that have formed temporary coalitions. Thus, both parties have been decentralized cadre parties and have been noted, certainly on the national level, for their relative inability to develop a coherent, disciplined organization. On the other hand, continental European countries have been characterized by multi-party systems in which three or more major parties and a number of electorally significant minor parties have competed for power. Moreover, these parties

313

have differed widely in accordance with the types described in the previous chapter.

In the past, European political scientists have attempted to explain the differences between England and the Continent in terms of certain elements in national character, the nature of the electoral system, and even the fact that the British executive can dissolve Parliament if defeated on a major piece of legislation. Americans, however, in explaining the differences between the United States and England, have emphasized the existence of a federal system in the United States and of a popularly elected president who is not dependent upon parliamentary support in order to stay in office. They have also stressed the fact that the executive in the United States is elected every four years, while senators are elected every six and congressmen every two. Consequently, while party unity may be insisted upon during presidential years, off-year elections tend to reduce the saliency of party and national issues.

The role of the electoral system in accounting for party differences was dealt with in the previous chapter. Other factors offered as explanations will be discussed after the British party system is briefly outlined.

THE DEVELOPMENT OF BRITISH POLITICAL PARTIES: Traditionally, the origin of modern British parties goes back to the conflict between Cavaliers and Roundheads—between those who supported Charles I during the Civil War (1642–1648) and stood for a high church (with leanings toward Catholicism), and those who represented the Presbyterian and dissenting sects as well as English commerce. One can, in any event, identify two reasonably coherent—although temporary— factions in the parliament of 1679. One group, again tending to represent the interests of Presbyterians and Dissenters, sought passage of an Act of Exclusion to prevent the Duke of York (later James II) from ascending the throne upon the death of his brother Charles. Those who opposed succession of the duke, their opponents

called "Whigs"—a Scots-Gaelic term meaning "cattle thieves." The second faction supported noninterference and its members were labeled "Tories," a term meaning "Irish papist outlaw." The typical Tory was described as a "monster with an English face, a French heart, and an Irish conscience. A creature of a large forehead, prodigious mouth, supple hams, and no brains."

During the next century, the names continued to refer to two loosely defined factions. The term "party," however, had as yet little significance, since real power and real differences of opinion were distributed among a multiplicity of groups and determined by a great many personal, regional, and family loyalties. A good number of parliamentary seats were controlled by the king or the landed oligarchy and many were bought and sold quite openly.

The formation of modern political parties began only after the Reform Bill of 1832 and other laws regarding suffrage had so enlarged the electorate that party organization became more and more necessary. Between 1830 and 1880, the Whigs became Liberals and the Tories Conservatives, and both parties established political machines. The transformation was slow. Even after 1832, the choice of candidates lay in the hands of notables—gentlemen who reached informal agreements as to which constituencies they would represent—and local concerns still affected these choices. In time, both parties created a more formal organization. A Liberal Registration Association was set up to promote the political task of uniting constituencies and candidates, and the Conservatives followed suit, although the authority of these organizations was limited. By the latter half of the nineteenth century, local concerns were no longer the prime issues of British politics; national issues had become decisive.

In general, the social basis of Liberal leadership was still Nonconformist, that is, non-Anglican, or relating to such Protestant sects as the Congregationalist, Methodist, or Baptist, while the Conservatives represented the establishment. Liberals were drawn increasingly from the newer commercial strata, Conservatives from the traditional landholding class. However, both party organization and party identification were still weak during the middle of the nineteenth century. The existence of Irish Nationalists further complicated matters, so that one found a variety of factions: Whigs, Conservatives, Peelites (Conservatives who accepted free trade), Radicals (those who took a more liberal line on the suffrage and tended to be anti-monarchical), and the Irish—all formed an assortment of loose and changing alliances.

The Reform Acts of 1867 and 1884, and the Ballot Act of 1872, which provided for secret voting, contributed to the modernization of party structure. The Reform Acts also more than quadrupled the electorate—to almost five million—and the Ballot Act all but eliminated the practice of buying parliamentary seats and the use of social or economic pressure by the gentry or businessmen to insure that their tenants or workers voted the "right" way. Political parties became internally more homogeneous and more sharply divided from one another. And as the parties worked to enlist the voters' support, party organization became tighter and party discipline stricter. Both the Conservatives and the Liberals created national organizations outside Parliament (the National Union of Conservative and Unionist Associations in 1867 and the National Liberal Federation in 1877), but despite attempts by some political figures to change the party hierarchy, control over both parties remained firmly in the hands of the parliamentarians.

The Labor Party, established in 1901, represented a unique departure in British politics. Here was a party founded outside Parliament and specifically designed as a mass party of the working class. Self-consciously ideological and considering itself a "movement," it created a whole host of subsidiary organizations for the sole purpose of making the party an integral part of the lives of those who supported it. It quickly attained a high degree of discipline, and its sense of unity, identity, and direction, its hostility toward the opposition, and the fact that working- and lower-middle class candidates had to rely heavily upon party financial support made this discipline effective.

With the decline of the Liberal Party in the 1920's, Conservatives and Laborites came face to face across the aisle in the House of Commons. Thus, after a short period in which three major parties competed for power, the British entered upon a period

TABLE 10.1. VOTE CAST IN BRITISH GENERAL ELECTIONS

Year	Electorate	Conservative	Labor	Liberal	Other	Turnout
1945[1]	32,836,419	39.8%	48.3%	9.1%	2.8%	73.3%
1950	34,269,770	43.5	46.1	9.1	1.3	84.0
1951	34,645,573	48.0	48.8	2.5	0.7	82.5
1955	34,858,263	49.7	46.4	2.7	0.2	76.8
1959	35,397,080	49.4	43.8	5.9	1.0	78.8
1964	35,892,572	43.4	44.1	11.2	1.3	77.0
1966	35,966,975	41.9	47.9	8.5	1.7	75.8

[1]Voting figures adjusted to allow for double-member constituencies in which electors had two votes each, and to omit university seats.

Adapted from Peter G. J. Pulzer, *Political Representation and Elections* (New York: Frederick A. Praeger, 1967), p. 96. Reprinted by permission of Frederick A. Praeger and George Allen and Unwin, Ltd., London.

TABLE 10.2.   SEATS WON IN BRITISH GENERAL ELECTIONS

Year	Total	Conservative	Labor	Liberal	Other	Overall majority
1945	640	213	393	12	22	Lab. 146
1950	625	298	315	9	3	Lab. 5
1951	625	321	295	6	3	Con. 17
1955	630	345	277	6	2	Con. 60
1959	630	365	258	6	1	Con. 100
1964	630	303	317	9	1	Lab. 4
1966	630	253	363	12	2	Lab. 97

Source: Pulzer, *Political Representation*, p. 96. Reprinted by permission.

of two-party competition. After the 1959 and 1964 elections, there was talk of a Liberal revival, but in the 1966 elections, the Liberal vote dropped once again.

The discipline of the Labor Party has been a reflection both of its quality as a movement and of the fact that it has been operating within the framework of a two-party system and a parliamentary regime. Once popular sovereignty had been accepted, the emergence of two disciplined parties implied that an effective government could be formed only by the party that possessed a majority, rather than through the intra-parliamentary negotiation of the 1850's. Thus, any prime minister who lost his legislative majority could only dissolve Parliament and call for new elections so that the nation might again be effectively governed—a recourse that all Englishmen, whatever their party, agreed was necessary. Consequently, for Labor members of Parliament—or for the members of any party—to break discipline was to open the way effectively for the opposition to come to power, a possibility that could only alienate the other party members. Recalcitrant members, therefore, might very well find themselves expelled, and under such circumstances their chances of re-election would be fractional indeed. Unlike the American pattern, where voters traditionally have been more concerned with local issues and personality, the loss of the party label, especially the Labor

label, in England has usually meant political extinction.[1]

The Conservative Party, with origins long predating those of the Labor Party, remained for more than a century a collection of local figures united under a parliamentary leadership. Given the greater tendency of the Conservative voter to support individuals, and the fact that campaign expenditures were met largely by the candidates themselves, the Conservative candidates were often able to exercise considerably more independence than their Labor Party opponents. However, once the Conservative Party came to realize that it faced, in the Laborites, members of a mass disciplined party in an era of mass parties, the Conservative organization gradually adopted some of the political techniques of its opponent. Since 1945, for instance, the amount of money a Conservative candidate can contribute to his own campaign has been strictly limited—thereby also limiting any tendencies toward independence. Furthermore, local political independence is, at least temporarily, far less pronounced than it once was.

In England, then, the existence of class and ideological conflict helps explain the emergence of disciplined parties, and the existence of an underlying consensus based on attachment to the larger community, to-

[1] This generalization is subject to some qualifications, which will be discussed in the sections on particular parties.

gether with the relatively uniform structure of English society, helps explain both the stability of the party system and the existence of only two big parties. There were other factors, of course, including electoral mechanisms that discriminated against smaller parties and a political framework in which any government was dependent upon a parliamentary majority. But these other variables were of far less significance, as should become clearer after a brief comparison with the American pattern and an examination, in Chapters 11 and 12, of the structure of party systems on the Continent.

As already noted, both American parties have traditionally been congeries of any number of special interests, political and otherwise. American parties are not mass parties. They are dominated, for the most part, by professional politicians, and except for short periods around election time, volunteer party work is at a minimum. The main function of the national organization is to provide some semblance of coordination in nominating and attempting to elect presidential candidates. The party organization in each state is comparatively autonomous; it is related only indirectly to the party organization in the congress, and even more indirectly to the national party organization. Unlike England, local issues are immensely important and personality is a far more crucial factor in selecting and electing a candidate. Further, a candidate's independence of outlook is invariably respected, and, except in extreme cases, there are few penalties for being a maverick—provided, of course, the maverick retains his local base of political support.

The United States has only two major parties—a result, in part, of the electoral system, but also of the fact that thus far the two parties have absorbed the demands of every important group within the society. They have been able to do this because they are loose coalitions of interests and because almost all groups accept the general framework of a liberal capitalistic society. Certainly the fact that the president is elected

separately and that congressmen are elected for fixed terms in nonpresidential as well as presidential years has helped significantly to reduce both national party discipline and a closer integration between the president and his party. Both parties' general acceptance of an ideology that, until the 1930's, emphasized local issues and a somewhat limited role for the national government also thwarted any drive toward tightly centralized political organizations. The fact that the United States is a federal state has undoubtedly been a factor, too. Nevertheless, if American liberals had felt the need to destroy "feudal" institutions as liberals did in Europe, or if class differences had taken on vital significance in political conflict, it is difficult to believe that the constitutional forms would have prevented both greater centralization and the emergence of a mass, tightly wrought Socialist party.

In the United States both the national parties and the president are now increasing their strength as regional differences fade and national problems become more and more a part of the citizens' everyday life. The focus of power within American parties is shifting to national headquarters. In England, on the other hand, the decline of the class-ideological issue may presage both a decline in party discipline and the surfacing of regional issues and political groups, as manifested in the recent local-election support for both Scots and Welsh nationalist parties.

SOURCES OF PARTY SUPPORT:[2] The chief variable in British voting is still that of so-

---

[2] Some good surveys of the data on the sources of support of British parties and the attitudes of supporters of each party will be found in Gabriel Almond and Sidney Verba, *The Civic Culture* (Princeton: Princeton University Press, 1963); Robert R. Alford, *Party and Society* (Chicago: Rand McNally, 1963); J. Blondel, *Voters, Parties and Leaders* (Harmondsworth, Middlesex, England: Penguin Books, Ltd., 1963); James B. Christoph, "Consensus and Cleavage in British Political Ideology," *The American Political Science Review,* LIX (September 1965), 529–543; and Richard Rose, "Class and Party Divisions: Britain as a Test Case," *Sociology,* II (May 1968), 129–162.

MAP 10.1. LABOR PARTY'S SHARE OF MAJOR PARTY VOTE, 1966, BY REGIONS

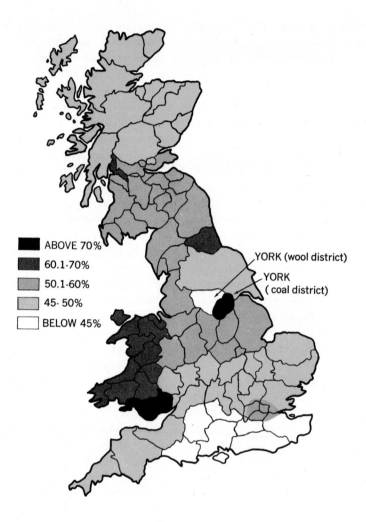

Adapted from Pulzer, *Political Representation*, p. 118.
Reprinted by permission.

cial class. The Labor Party receives from three-fifths to two-thirds of the vote of manual workers and only about one-fifth of the vote of nonmanual groups. It receives a mere tenth of the vote of managers and businessmen. In effect, this means that almost one-half of the Conservative Party vote comes from working-class voters. On the whole, workers who are religious—especially members of the Church of England—older workers, and workers in the south of England vote in larger proportions for the Con-

servative Party. As Table 10.3 indicates, workers in bigger, more modern plants are far more inclined to vote for Labor than workers in smaller, more traditional industries. And, as one might expect, workers who are in trade unions vote in greater numbers for the Labor Party than those who are not. Older working-class Conservatives are more deferential toward established authority than the older Laborites; however, pro-Conservative younger workers are differentiated from Labor supporters by their belief that the

TABLE 10.3. TYPE OF FIRM AND VOTING BEHAVIOR: GREAT BRITAIN

From survey taken in Banbury

	Manual	*Nonmanual*
Traditional firms		
Conservative and Liberal	39%	61%
Labor	81	19
Non-traditional firms		
Conservative and Liberal	71	29
Labor	93	7

Adapted from Jean Blondel, *Voters, Parties and Leaders* (Harmondsworth, Middlesex, Eng.: Penguin Books, Ltd., 1963), p. 66. Reprinted by permission of the publisher.

Conservatives are more realistic and hard-headed and that they are more likely to allow advancement on the basis of ability.

The Liberal Party draws its vote from all strata of the population. It still retains a regional base in Wales, and, in general, its supporters are those with a Nonconformist religious background. Today, the Liberals are a party of transients—voters who have left either the Conservative or Labor parties and are trying to decide what to do next. No more than one-third of the Liberal Party vote is stable.

British voters have usually been more intensely divided on issues than are American ones—and more hostile to members of the opposing party. Only four per cent of both American Democrats and Republicans said they would be displeased if one of their children married a member of the opposite party, while 12 per cent of the British Conservatives and three per cent of the Laborites indicated that political mismatching would make them unhappy.

Despite party differences and the cleavages in voter attitudes, however, nearly half of the British voters believe the opposition party would, for the most part, govern just as well as their own. And other studies have shown that both Labor and Conservative party supporters pick almost the same traits as important in a party leader: strong leadership, the willingness to make unpopular decisions, honesty, and sincerity; just as noteworthy,

TABLE 10.4. VOTING BY OCCUPATIONAL CLASS IN BRITAIN, 1964

Occupational class	*Percentage of total*	*Conservative*	*Labor*	*Other*
Professional	7	64%	21%	15%
Business	7	75	11	14
Office workers	14	56	27	17
Shop; personal service	12	46	37	17
Skilled workers	29	33	52	15
Semi-skilled workers	14	25	64	11
Unskilled workers	12	21	65	14
Unclassified	5	39	40	20

Adapted from Richard Rose, "Class and Party Divisions: Britain as a Test Case," *Sociology*, 2 (May 1968), p. 144. Reprinted by permission of the publisher and the author.

they chose them in the same order. Disagreements on policy issues are still significant, but most Britons agree that it is as important to have effective government as it is to have one's own party in power.

2. THE LIBERAL PARTY

DEVELOPMENT AND CHARACTER: The term "liberal" was first applied to the "advanced" segments of the Whigs in Parliament in the early nineteenth century by their Tory opponents, who wished to identify them with the detested "radical" ideas of the French *libéraux*. It was not, however, until the Gladstone ministry of 1868–1874 that the term came into common currency. Gladstone, who was prime minister on four different occasions, dominated the party until his death and represented, in his own person, the transition from eighteenth-century Whiggery to nineteenth-century Liberalism. Gradually, he had been converted to both full extension of the suffrage and free trade— major Liberal policies. While Gladstone generally supported a laissez-faire economic policy, he was not averse to measures of social reform designed to aid the "less fortunate"; he was also strongly anti-imperialist, and eventually came around to supporting Irish Home Rule.

It was, in fact, the question of Home Rule for Ireland that caused the first of many party splits, for it was on this issue that Joseph Chamberlain led his followers out of the Liberal camp and eventually into the Conservative. Chamberlain's critique had actually been a broader one; before the rupture he had tied the issue of more radical social reform to support for the empire, attacking the hallowed doctrine of free trade.

The split consigned the Liberals to the wilderness until 1905, when they returned to power under the leadership of Herbert Asquith and Lloyd George. In the years from 1905 to 1914 the Liberal Party moved decisively, if moderately, to the left. Income taxes were raised to finance new programs of social reform, and the secondary position

of the House of Lords was formalized by the Parliament Act of 1911. The party, however, remained committed to both free trade and liberal capitalism.

A personal rivalry between Lloyd George and Herbert Asquith again split the party during World War I—a split that continued after the war and helped speed the final eclipse of the Liberal Party. Lloyd George joined in a coalition with the Conservatives, and those Liberals who supported Asquith ran on a separate ticket. After the coalition fell apart in 1922, the Liberals united once again. In the election of that year both they and the Labor Party received approximately thirty per cent of the vote, the Conservatives having received more than 38 per cent. In the election of 1924, Liberal strength fell still further: the party received only 17.6 per cent of the votes cast and, because of the operation of single-member–district plurality elections, an even smaller proportion of parliamentary seats. After that, the party's decline continued apace amid still further splits, and in the election of 1945 the Liberals received only 9.1 per cent of the votes cast. Their share was to drop to 2.6 per cent in 1951.

The reasons for the decline of the Liberal Party are fairly obvious. It was the party of democracy, relatively free enterprise, and free trade. Its purely political program had been more or less achieved by the end of the First World War and had come to be fully accepted by all political parties. The remainder of its program, however, was not such as to continue to attract widespread enthusiasm. Larger portions of its working-class support slipped away into the Labor Party; the working class preferred either a party that represented the *working class,* or, in the case of the more traditional-minded, one which inspired deference and defended tradition. Some of the Liberal Party's more radical middle-class support turned to socialism and the Labor Party as constituting the heirs of the reform tradition, but the bulk of the middle class preferred the Conservatives. In an era of tougher competition from other industrial nations, free trade no longer held the same magic appeal it once did. Moreover, English entrepreneurs had lost a good deal of their earlier élan; they had been co-opted by the system and awarded peerages and prestige; by now their sons were attending public schools and moving in the "best" circles. The balance of political power had shifted and the commercial strata were now part of the establishment. They identified with a national tradition which had become their own and distrusted Liberal rhetoric as contributing to both an erosion of social hierarchy and the threat of working-class radicalism.

Fundamentally, then, the Liberal decline occurred because the party had nothing more to say, or, more precisely perhaps, fewer and fewer listeners. The electoral system and splits within the party itself also contributed to its decline. Failure to get votes, of course, led to the failure to attract potential talent—and that, in turn, to the failure to obtain financial support. In the last analysis, the Liberals might have remained a major party if they had adopted the program of either the Conservative or the Labor Party. But then they would have been Liberals in name only.

In the late 1950's and early 1960's, the Liberal Party experienced something of a revival. Its percentage of the popular vote rose to 5.9 in 1959 and to 11.2 in 1964. To many younger voters, both the Labor and Conservative parties seemed to be "conservative"—each wedded in its own way to outmoded doctrines that no longer corresponded to the real world. But the revival was as temporary as it was modest; in the 1966 elections, the Liberals' vote fell once again, to 8.5 per cent of the total, although their representation in Parliament rose from nine to twelve. Barring a social upheaval or a change in the electoral system, it is unlikely that the Liberals have anywhere to go but down, although they may well continue to exist on the margins of British politics for some time. The difficulties of maintaining any national political organization in the twentieth century have become enormous—

the more so for a party that is out of favor. Furthermore, both the Conservatives and the Labor Party have proven flexible enough to adjust, albeit sluggishly, to changes in the national mood. Thus, the Liberal Party finds itself unable to offer a distinctive alternative program—or an image that has broad appeal.

THE PATTERN OF DECISION-MAKING: Like the Conservative, the Liberal Party began as a parliamentary party, and until the 1920's the key decisions were made by those members of the party who were in Parliament. The party had created in 1877 a mass organization, the National Liberal Federation, which its organizers hoped would become the effective center of policy making. While the federation was not without influence, it remained for about fifty years under the control of parliamentary leadership.

The Liberal Party never developed the degree of discipline which the Labor Party achieved from the beginning, and which the Conservative Party was to emulate. This was true partly because of ideological premises that rejected a mass party of the Labor type; but added to this was a purely structural cause: the Liberal Party declined in power and size before its institutional mechanisms for party discipline could be established. As an organization with no hope of serving as a government—and hence devoid of those expedient pressures for coherence—the Liberal Party today is characterized by semi-anarchy. Its parliamentary party, its mass party, and its party leader all tend to move in several directions at the same time—and to wrangle interminably over very minor doctrinal points. Moreover, the constituency or local organizations of the party go more or less their own way, subject only to advice from the central office.[3] Their independence extends to the nomination of candidates. In the Conservative and Labor parties, the central offices have at least the theoretical right to

---

[3] For purposes of elections, Great Britain is divided into 630 constituencies, each of which elects one Member of Parliament. The basic unit of organization for all parties is the constituency.

exercise a veto, and in any event, candidate choices by local organizations must be cleared with them. In the Liberal Party, many candidates are nominated without the national organs even being notified.

The leader of the Liberal Parliamentary Party (L.P.P.) is the leader of the Liberal Party as a whole. For many years he was subject to annual re-elections, but today, because of the small size of the party, this practice has been dropped. The parliamentary leader's authority over his colleagues and over the mass party is extremely limited, however, and the mass party has been able to force his resignation when it believed him to be no longer useful.

The L.P.P. meets regularly to formulate policies on various issues, but there is little or no attempt to enforce party discipline; members are free to vote in Parliament as they please. Although the party outside Parliament has, on occasion, attempted to press its own claims as the chief policy-making body, it has had slight success. And to make the policy impasse complete, the parliamentary party has been unable to impose its views upon the mass party.

The basic national unit of the Liberal Party is the Annual Assembly, consisting of about one thousand delegates drawn from the constituency parties and the L.P.P. Policies adopted at the assembly are theoretically the policies of the party outside Parliament, and not necessarily those of the L.P.P. The assembly elects a smaller body, the council, which meets quarterly, and an executive committee, which meets at least once a month to look after routine affairs. The onus of fund raising and propaganda rests with the council, which is also responsible for the party's paid professional staff.

Interestingly enough, for complex historical reasons, the L.P.P. has its own professional staff separate from that controlled by the mass party. The Liberal Central Association predates the National Liberal Federation, and today it is concerned not only with finances but also with research and party staff. That the professional organization of the party is bifurcated has certainly contributed to its difficulties.

During and after the 1959 campaign, when for the first time since the days of Lloyd George the Liberals seemed on the verge of a comeback, an effort toward coordinating the mass and parliamentary wings of the Liberal Party was made through the creation of what became known as the Organizing Committee. Now that this comeback has proved an illusion, it is doubtful that real cooperation between the L.P.P. and the mass party can be maintained.

3. THE CONSERVATIVE PARTY

DEVELOPMENT AND CHARACTER: After a long period of decline in the first part of the eighteenth century, the Tory Party entered upon a period of predominance in English politics under the leadership of William Pitt the Younger. This lasted until 1830; after that, the party split repeatedly, and a number of its followers, including Gladstone, moved over to the Whigs. From 1830 to 1874, the Tories were seldom in office and only once in power. It was during this period that the name of the party was changed to Conservative in an attempt to mold a better public image.

The modern Conservative Party was born with the leadership of Benjamin Disraeli, who during his first and second ministries was responsible for important measures of social legislation and the Electoral Reform Act of 1867. It was during Disraeli's leadership, too, that the Conservative Party created the National Union—the beginnings of a mass party to serve as handmaiden to the parliamentary party and the party leader in the organization and financing of electoral campaigns. From the beginning, the national party organization, in contrast with that of the Labor Party, was expected to remain subordinate to the parliamentary party and the party leader. And it has. The national group, however, has not been without influence on the formation of party policy and even in the determination of the choice of leadership.

Disraeli's hope that the Conservative Party would appeal to the mass of Englishmen as a political instrument dedicated both to a hierarchical social order and to social reform was not realized. After his death, the leadership was dominated by business interests who now accepted the party as their natural habitat, and the record of the party in the late nineteenth and early twentieth centuries was essentially one of opposing social change. There were other points of view represented by Randolph Churchill and Joseph Chamberlain, but these men never obtained a dominant voice in party councils.

Not until Neville Chamberlain rose to prominence in the party in the 1930's did the Conservative government, in response to the Depression and to England's changing world position, take the lead in using the power of the state to effect social change. In fact, it was the Chamberlain government of the late 1930's that laid the foundations of the postwar welfare state and took many measures toward the nationalization of important sectors of the British economy.

The defeat of the Conservative Party in 1945 by the Laborites led to self-examination. The Conservatives not only reorganized and democratized their party structure, but, under the leadership of such men as R. A. Butler and Harold Macmillan, fully committed themselves to accepting the reforms that the Labor Party was then initiating. Butler, for instance, was instrumental in persuading party leaders like Winston Churchill and Anthony Eden to rethink both party policy and party structure in the period between 1945 and 1950. The Conservatives also endorsed the idea of an economy in which the government would not only guarantee more job opportunities but would use fiscal and monetary controls to insure full employment.

Once in power after 1951, the Conservatives put into practice all these accepted commitments. Fiscal and monetary controls were used extensively, direct taxes remained high, and welfare expenditures increased in proportion to the growth of the economy. Near the end of their tenure in office, the Conservatives moved even more directly toward the idea of a managed economy by creating, in 1962, the National Economic Development Council ("Neddy") to provide for the systematic national planning of economic growth.

By 1964, there was a general conviction that the Conservative Party, after three successive terms of office, would be defeated in the election of that year. A sex scandal involving high government officials had tarnished its reputation, and while the country was prosperous, there were signs of a growing intellectual malaise. Britain's rate of economic growth had fallen behind that of the Continental countries, and the per capita income of both France and Germany was threatening to exceed England's. There seemed to be the distinct feeling that Conservative Party leaders had failed to modernize the country or to bring it back to the center of the world stage. The resignation of Harold Macmillan as prime minister and leader of the party had not helped Conservative fortunes; his successor, Alex Douglas-Home, had been chosen—after considerable acrimony—because he had fewer enemies than any other candidate.

Nevertheless, on election day in 1964, Labor squeaked by with only a bare plurality. With the imminence of new elections, the Conservatives re-examined their structure and image once again. Lord Home stepped down, after instituting a new policy of electing the party leader, and was replaced by Edward Heath, who was formerly Lord Privy Seal. During the campaign preceding the elections in March 1966, the Conservatives, now led by newer faces, attempted to present themselves as the party that would "modernize" England. Despite their efforts, however, or rather because of Harold Wilson's rather solid performance as prime minister, their message did not get across and Labor substantially increased its parliamentary majority. England was assured of a Labor government for at least the next five years.

Since the 1966 election, the Conservative Party has made renewed attempts to adapt itself sufficiently to return to power. The party is, if anything, more flexible than it ever was. Far more than the Labor Party, Conservatives are an organization dedicated to governing; far more than the Labor Party, they are attuned to giving the public what it feels it needs. This is not to say that the Conservatives no longer have an ideological position. Increasingly, they represent the new professional business technocracy, committed to a managed economy, though with a large private sector, as the means of guaranteeing dynamic growth. The Conservatives are also fully committed to extensive welfare measures and to extending the opportunities of those who can to rise to positions of leadership. They remain, however, firm believers in social hierarchy and the need for leadership by a responsible political and social elite. There are a few Conservative politicians—most notably Enoch Powell—who have tried to develop a power base within the party by pandering to racial prejudices; thus far they have made little headway.

There was a period during the 1950's in which powerful Conservatives, resisting the pace of decolonization, seemed on the verge of causing a serious division within the party. Bitterly opposed to the rapidity with which England was relinquishing the facade of being a world power, the most extreme members of this group labeled themselves the "Empire Loyalists." They have, of course, since been reduced to a very minor position; events have passed them by, and the traditional loyalties that once moved them have little significance. Conservatives are now more fully committed to entering the European Common Market than the Laborites, despite the strains that such action will place on Commonwealth ties. They are convinced that the competition engendered by such association is far more necessary to a healthy British economy than clinging to what is left of the once formidable British Empire.

There is in the Tory party still rather more nostalgia than among the Laborites for the traditional elements of the British past, including the monarchy and the House of Lords. But, like all Englishmen, Conservatives are also eager to press forward the technological and social revolution that is remaking Europe and the rest of the world.

STRUCTURE AND DYNAMICS: The Conservative Party began as a party of notables in Parliament clustered about a leader, or leaders. In response to the gradual enlargement of the electorate and the rise of nationally organized parties, it created its own mass organization; in response to the greater democratization of British society, it has democratized parts of its own structure. Even so, the party's organization still reflects its parliamentary origins and its ties to more traditional concepts of political life. Power is lodged within the parliamentary party, and especially in the party leader who, unlike the Labor party leader, is not formally subject to annual re-elections, is personally responsible for the party's program—which is *his* program—and, moreover, is directly in charge of the party's bureaucratic apparatus.

Until 1964, Conservative leaders materialized from within the party without any formal election upon the retirement or death of the incumbent. What happened, in effect, was that the more powerful party figures would take soundings in the party and suggest to the king (or queen) the person they believed could command the loyalty of both the parliamentary and the mass parties. The monarch, relying upon his ancient prerogative, would call the person suggested to the palace and name him prime minister. He would then be elected unanimously by the parliamentary party—and, since 1922, by a number of other party notables also—as leader of the party.[4] If the leader departed

---

[4] The group responsible for this election is called the 1922 Committee, after the year in which it was created.

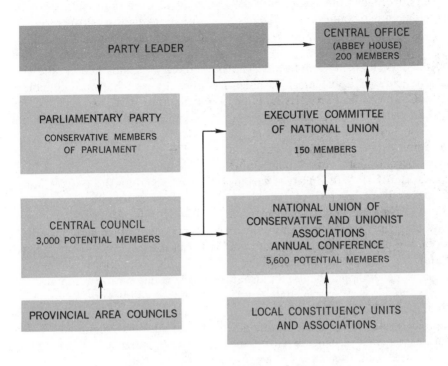

FIGURE 10.1. THE STRUCTURE OF THE CONSERVATIVE PARTY

while the party was in opposition, the post was usually left vacant until the next general election.

Most often in the past the choice of party leader has been rather clear cut because one party member has fairly well established himself as heir apparent; the case of Anthony Eden succeeding to the post of prime minister after the retirement of Winston Churchill in 1955 is such an example. On other occasions, as with the selection of Lord Home in 1963, an attempt was made to choose from among several contenders that leader who had offended the fewest people. The latter choice entailed a good amount of bitterness, and the hand-picked manner in which he was made party leader—and prime minister—contrasted vividly with the Labor Party's public election of its leader during the same year. The Home episode added further to the image of the Conservatives as essentially a party of the past. Home himself came to

share the view that the method of selecting the party leader had to be changed, and a procedure for formal elections was adopted in 1965. When Home stepped down, Edward Heath became the first Conservative leader chosen under the new procedure.

The manner in which the Conservative party leader is selected has changed, but his powers remain undiminished. He is still free to choose his own "shadow cabinet" when the party is in opposition.[5] He appoints the other party spokesmen in the Parliament and exercises those controls over the national organization which were noted previously. Further, while he appears from time to time before his parliamentary colleagues to ex-

5 The term "shadow cabinet" is applied to that group of opposition party leaders who would theoretically form the ministry if their party were in power. Each member is responsible for criticizing the government in a specific area. Thus, the shadow secretary of state for foreign affairs would have primary responsibility for attacking the government's foreign policy.

plain and discuss his policy, such appearances are not mandatory, nor are they
required at the annual conference of the mass
party.

The National Union of Conservative and
Unionist Associations is the mass organization of the Conservative Party. Its functions
include the promotion of Conservative and
Unionist Associations in every constituency,
acting as a link between the party leader and
the party organizations and maintaining
close relations between the party's various
associations and the central office. Membership in the National Union is open to all
who share the principles of the Conservative
Party, upon the payment of a small fee; total
membership today is about three million.

Each year the National Union holds an
Annual Conference for approximately two
and a half days. The conference, attended
by elected delegates from the constituency
organizations as well as members of the
party's central council, is essentially an occasion for rhetoric and expressions of party
unity. It hears the reports of the central
council and of its executive committee, but
not of the party leader, who addresses a mass
rally only after the conference has formally
adjourned.

While policy issues are sometimes discussed at National Union conferences, and
on rare occasions a policy proposal emerges,
control over the agenda, the number of delegates (well over 3,600), and the short duration of the meetings leave little room for
meaningful debate. Any views adopted by
the conference are, of course, only advisory.

The central council is theoretically the
governing body of the National Union. It
consists of the party leader and other party
officials as well as Conservative M.P.'s and
representatives from provincial area councils and each constituency. However, its large
size (about 1,200) and the infrequency of its
meetings—only one a year—limit its effectiveness and its capacity as a decision-making
body. In fact, despite its power to change

the rules of the National Union, the central
council's primary function has devolved into
serving as liaison between the parliamentary
and the mass parties. From time to time, attempts have been made by members of a
minority group within the parliamentary
party to use the central council, and through
it the mass party, to force a change in policy
or leadership. These attempts, however, have
been rare.

The executive committee of the National
Union consists of approximately 150 members, including the party leader and principal party officials as well as representatives
from provincial area councils. It ordinarily
meets every other month, and is empowered
to act for the central council between council
meetings. Functions of the committee include ruling on the acceptance or removal of
National Union constituency representatives,
and the election of representatives to the different advisory committees that serve the national organization. From time to time, the
executive committee initiates studies on public issues and makes policy recommendations
to the party leader. As is the case with other
party groups, however, its opinions are
merely advisory. Much of its work has been
allocated to a still smaller General Purposes
Subcommittee and to several national advisory committees that are concerned with
political education, trade unions, publicity,
and speakers. The advisory committees serve
as mechanisms for fostering party work, and
as organizations where different views on
party policy can be formulated and transmitted to the executive committee and the
party leader.

In addition to the executive committee,
there are national advisory committees on
which the party leader relies. Some of these
committees—among them the Advisory
Committee on Policy, the Consultative Committee on Party Finance, and the Standing
Advisory Committee on Party Finance—are
the most influential organizations in the
party, but like the party's bureaucratic apparatus, they are responsible to the party leader

FIGURE 10.2. THE SOCIOECONOMIC BACKGROUND OF BRITISH PARTY ACTIVISTS

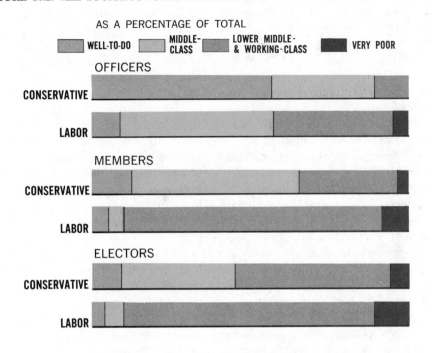

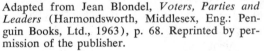

Adapted from Jean Blondel, *Voters, Parties and Leaders* (Harmondsworth, Middlesex, Eng.: Penguin Books, Ltd., 1963), p. 68. Reprinted by permission of the publisher.

rather than to the National Union. The principal officers of the Advisory Committee on Policy, for example, the chairman and vice chairman, are appointees of the party leader, while the 15 other members are selected by the parliamentary party and the executive committee of the National Union. But the entire committee is responsible solely to the party leader. It has at its disposal the resources of the Conservative Research Department, and has, on many occasions, been responsible for formulating Conservative Party policy.

On the local level, the constituency organization is the basic unit of the Conservative Party. Relatively autonomous, it is concerned essentially with spreading Conservative principles, raising money, and generating enthusiasm to elect Conservatives to Parliament. For many members, the organization serves an important social function—as well as the opening wedge for a political career. The effective head of the constituency is an elected chairman aided by a central office representative who is a paid constituency agent. Candidates for constituency chairman are either selected from a list prepared by the central office, or submitted to the central office for approval.

Although manual workers give roughly 25 per cent of their vote to the Conservative Party, they constitute a small proportion of the membership of the Conservatives' constituency organizations, which tend to have a distinctly middle-class atmosphere. An even smaller proportion of manual workers exists among party activists,[6] who are almost entirely absent from local leadership. In gen-

[6] The proportion of party activists to total membership is small. In a constituency organization of five thousand, probably no more than two or three hundred attend meetings regularly and do other party work.

eral, activists within the Conservative organization seem to represent a cross section of Conservative voters in terms of political attitudes. Unlike their equivalents in the Labor Party, their activism does not extend to militancy in political opinions.

Overlying the constituency groups are twelve provincial area councils of the Conservative Party that have both executive and advisory functions. They are supposed to express the "collective views of the party in the area" and to "utilize the financial and other resources of the area in the best interests of the constituencies." The organizations consist of a chairman, a council, an executive committee, and a range of advisory committees that parallel those of the national organization. The central office is represented in each of the twelve areas by an agent who serves as honorary secretary to the area council. The council includes representatives of every constituency organization in the area as well as special groups catering to women, youth, and trade unionists; its executive responsibilities include the organization of propaganda and educational activities. It debates and forwards resolutions to the National Union and disposes of certain funds provided for the assistance of needy constituency organizations.

While their role in party decision-making is limited, as is that of the National Union itself, the area organizations of the Conservative Party are more important than those of the Labor Party. For one thing, they are represented on both the central council and the executive committee. For this reason, the position of chairman of an area council, which is unpaid and requires a good deal of work, has, on the whole, been filled by notables. Of the 43 persons who held positions as chairmen from 1952 to 1962, 29 have appeared in *Who's Who*. Of the 28 chairmen whose occupations could be traced, 13 were in business, mostly large businesses; seven were in the professions; five in the armed services; and three in the civil service. Over

one-quarter of the chairmen during the 1950's were members of Parliament.

The Conservative Party's central office— Abbey House—was created in 1870 as part of the party's effort to reach voters enfranchised by the Reform Act of 1867.[7] Over the years it has grown in size, until today it consists of approximately two hundred administrative and clerical personnel, about one-third of whom are full-time paid bureaucrats. Like the National Union, the central office is the instrument of the parliamentary party—or more particularly of its leader. The head of the office, whose title is chairman of party organization, is appointed by the party leader, as are the vice chairmen and the treasurer. Because of its administrative functions, the chairmanship is an office of considerable importance, although it has little public authority over policy.

The central office organizes local party groups, prepares propaganda, draws up lists of recommended candidates, and oversees the general efficiency of the party structure. It works closely with area and constituency organizations, and attempts to guide them in the direction desired by the leadership.

Especially since World War II, the central office has greatly expanded its propaganda and research efforts. The Conservative Political Center concentrates on preparing special publications for activists, and the Conservative Research Department investigates and analyzes the general problems of party policy. During periods when the Conservative Party is in opposition, and, therefore, without the services of the government bureaucracy, party leadership is particularly reliant upon the central office's services.

Traditionally, the Conservative Party has spent less time than Labor on thinking or at least arguing about broad general ideological issues. Ideological nuance has been far less important than power. No group within the

---

[7] The central offices of both parties are popularly referred to by the names of the buildings in which they are located—Abbey House and Transport House.

Conservative Party, for example, was ever as influential as the Fabian Society on the left. In 1951 a group of university-trained young Conservatives formed the Bow Group, an independent organization whose job was to supply the party with ideas. Although the group's influence waned somewhat after the initial burst of enthusiasm that greeted its inception, its continued existence is indicative of the increasing importance attached to professionalization and theoretical sophistication by the present generation of Conservative politicians. The group organizes study discussions and publishes pamphlets concerning Conservative policy issues, and most of its members have represented the more modern and "technocratic" wing of the party.

POWER AND POLICY: Even the closest observers of the Conservative Party have always had difficulty tracing its dynamics of power: in the Conservative Party, even more than in the Labor, many decisions are made informally and in private. On paper at least, the position of the party leader is extremely strong and that of the mass organization quite weak when compared with the Labor Party. Yet the reality is not that simple. It is certainly true that the Conservative party leader enjoys far more power on paper than the Labor party leader, and that, until 1965 at least, he was more often than not the choice of party notables. However, the choice usually reflected an attempt to meet the wishes of the parliamentary party.

The power of the party in Parliament is indicated by the fact that, since 1922, five of the seven men who have served as leaders of the Conservative Party have left office under conditions that suggest the exercise of pressure by Conservative M.P.'s. Austen Chamberlain, for instance, resigned after the 1922 Committee passed a motion, over his opposition, urging that the party not join an election coalition with the Liberals. Neville Chamberlain quit as prime minister in 1940 after it became clear that the Labor Party would not enter into negotiations for a coalition government as long as he remained in office. Anthony Eden resigned, ostensibly for reasons of ill health, after the Suez fiasco of 1956. Harold Macmillan resigned, also for reasons of ill health, shortly before the election campaign of 1964, and Sir Alex Douglas-Home shortly after the election of that year. Neville Chamberlain had lost the confidence of a good many Conservatives in Parliament, and in the other four cases there is evidence not only that support among members of the parliamentary party had declined, but that Conservatives throughout the country were restive because they believed that the party leader was no longer an asset.

The Conservative Party, both in Parliament and throughout the nation, has always been rather more attuned to office than the Labor Party. To be sure, no Conservative leader could move too far ahead of his party. But in office or out, he is permitted a good deal of political leeway. In consultation with his cabinet—real or shadow—and various advisers, the Conservative leader formulates policies as reactions to what are thought to be the needs of the nation. There is very little direct participation in policy decisions by either the parliamentary party or the mass party. A particular policy may on occasion raise the hackles of some in the party, and their response may extend to active opposition, as, for example, the anger of the Empire Loyalists. And groups of M.P.'s, or those within the mass party, may also react stridently to policies they believe are injuring the vested interests they strongly support, as, for example, when portions of the government's tax policy in the 1950's provoked ire in some. But on the whole, provided the party leader limits himself to initiating reforms within the broad and ever-evolving social and economic system that the Conservatives seek to preserve, he will be given his head. The leader, after all, is supposed to lead. Thus, the party continues to accept the oligarchic pattern of decision-making that has been the one major characteristic of its ideological orientation. For Conservatives, the real test of leadership is whether or not policies are pragmatic, whether they preserve and enhance the national inheritance within the framework of the existing system—and, of course, whether they insure that the Conservative Party will be the party in power.

4. THE LABOR PARTY

DEVELOPMENT AND CHARACTER: The British Labor Party is the product of a number of disparate groups. The first were the Socialist organizations, most importantly the Fabian Society and the Social Democratic Federation. The federation was formed in 1881 by an English disciple of Marx, H. M. Hyndman, as a political party. It constantly split into factions, and its influence all but disappeared by World War I. But at the turn of the century, it served to introduce a whole generation of trade-union and Labor Party leaders, including such figures as Ernest Bevin, to the intricacies of Socialist theory.

The Fabian Society was and is of much more lasting importance. Founded in 1883–1884 as a small discussion society of intellectuals, the group soon turned to socialism. Its aim became twofold: to convince the middle classes that social reform and, eventually, socialism were necessary in order to provide, most efficiently, the greatest good for the greatest number; and to encourage working-class political action. The famous *Fabian Essays,* first published in 1889 and including contributions by such noted writers as Sidney and Beatrice Webb and George Bernard Shaw, had a tremendous impact upon a whole generation of British intellectuals. It was among middle-class intellectuals that the society remained most effective. The socialism it preached was, of course, a peculiarly British kind, rejecting class conflict as a leading principle and emphasizing rational administrative reform.

For many years the Fabian Society served

as the most important research arm of the Labor Party, and through it have passed most of the party's important leaders. With the development of a strictly party research organization, the society's functions have declined; given the catholicity of its membership, it never presumes to speak with a single voice. It is still an organization with considerable prestige, and it continues to examine political and social problems from sundry left-wing points of view.

The second major group that helped shape the Labor Party was the Independent Labor Party (I.L.P.), founded by James Keir Hardy, a Scots miner and former Methodist lay preacher. The I.L.P. was again ostensibly Socialist but, at its founding, not Marxist; aspects of it were reminiscent of a peculiarly Scottish Protestant type of religious revivalism. Alone, the I.L.P. could never obtain enough votes to be counted as a potent political force. But after the Labor Party was finally formed, the I.L.P. served for many years as its constituency organization, drawing to it many middle-class radicals who could not become really active in Labor Party practical politics in any other way (until 1918, individuals could only join the Labor Party as members of one of the organizations of which it was composed). Most of the important early leaders of the Labor Party, including Ramsay MacDonald, Philip Snowden, and Clement Attlee, were at one time or another members of the I.L.P.

The third major group contributing to the formation of the Labor Party was the Trades Union Congress, the loosely organized association of British trade unions. Within the congress, sentiment had been growing for an organization dedicated to electing working-class men to Parliament and the achievement of social reform. Younger union leaders and those from the newer unskilled unions wished to go further and establish a Socialist Party, but they represented a distinct minority.

In 1900, representatives of all these groups—the Fabians, the Social Democratic Federation, the I.L.P., and the trade unions

—converged to form the Labor Representation Committee. The resolution creating the committee was ambiguously worded, committing the group to no more than seeking the election of candidates who would press for legislation to aid the working man's condition. Spurred by the Taff Vale Decision of 1901, which seemed to imply that unions could be sued for financial losses incurred during strikes, the support of the trade unions for the new group grew rapidly. It took the name of the Labor Party in 1906, but until World War I it remained a minor party serving primarily as the left wing of the Liberals.

After World War I, partly as the result of the radicalism induced by the war, the Labor Party suddenly became one of the major contenders for political power in what was now virtually a three-party system. It adopted a new and avowedly Socialist program—still its fundamental statement of aims—and a new formal constitution which provided for a constituency organization and attempted to coordinate the other segments of the party.

Theoretically, the Labor Party was to be governed by an Annual Conference, at which would be represented, in proportion to membership, trade unions, Socialist societies, and constituency organizations. This conference would elect a national executive committee to run the party between meetings and develop a bureaucratic apparatus to implement the program adopted by the conference. Given the number of party members who joined through the constituency organization and the number of those who were members by virtue of their affiliation with trade unions, it was clear that the Annual Conference would be dominated by the trade unions, especially the larger unions of the unskilled. It also became obvious that the formation of a constituency organization effectively meant the end of the I.L.P., whose function had disappeared. During the 1920's, the I.L.P. slowly withered, becoming more insistently radical as it did so. In the early 1930's, it

finally broke with the Labor Party and eventually disappeared.

The Labor Party, during the 1920's, continued to grow at a rather phenomenal pace and, in fact, formed two short-lived minority governments in 1924 and 1929. The second of these was in office when the Great Depression hit, and the decision of the prime minister and party leader, Ramsay MacDonald, to form a national government with the Conservatives and the Liberals rocked the party to its core. In the election of 1931, Labor lost some two million votes, although its organization remained intact with only a very few of the more prominent members joining the new government. To many in the party, MacDonald had been an unsatisfactory "moderate," and this fact plus the ravages of the Depression and the rise of National Socialism in Germany pushed the party further to the left during the 1930's, a direction fervidly endorsed by the more articulate middle-class intellectuals who flocked to its standards.

The radicals within the Labor Party, however, remained a relatively small minority, and the party that came to office in 1945 took a moderate stance. It fulfilled its immediate nationalization promises, instituted a National Health Service, and found itself siding with the United States against the Soviet Union (albeit with some reservations) on foreign affairs.

By 1950, the Labor Party was facing a crisis; its leadership—and, indeed, the party itself—seemed to have lost its way. The social measures that it introduced had not created an ideal society; on the contrary, as many new problems had been raised as had been solved. Within the party there were those who were beginning to urge that Labor drop its Socialist ideology and become a radical party of social reform. Others called for renewal of the older faith; still others demanded an entirely new approach to solving social problems, an approach that would take into account the changes occurring in British society and the world.

The problem of program was debated by the party throughout the 1950's while it lost three elections in a row. During this period and into the 1960's, its dominant ideological faction was "revisionist." Composed largely of middle-class intellectuals, and with strong parliamentary support, the revisionists argued that capitalism had fundamentally bettered its character and that the function of the Labor Party was to work for further changes to create a more just society. Socialism might remain as a distant goal, but England would be a "mixed" economy for a long time to come, and harping on class themes and employing Socialist bombast would only lose votes.

In the late 1950's and early 1960's, the revisionists were joined by another group who may be called, for convenience, the modernizers. While agreeing in general with the revisionists, the modernizers believed that many traditional British cultural and social patterns had become outdated and dysfunctional. The Labor Party, they argued, must dedicate itself not only to greater equality among the people but also to the elimination of the fuddy-duddy quality of British society. For the modernizers, a new emphasis upon the application of science and social science to social problems was needed; so, too, was a restructuring of British economic life. In general, they wanted more government initiative on solving social problems than did the revisionists, but their approach to these problems remained self-consciously pragmatic and nondoctrinaire. Like the revisionists, the modernizers were most heavily supported by intellectuals and the new class of professionals emerging from the universities; but they obtained additional strength from trade-union leaders connected with the newer, more dynamic industries.

Opposed to both groups, but agreeing with them on many specific issues, have been what might be called the traditionalists, primarily trade unionists and older party members, who still cling to the conventional Socialist images and still proclaim that the Labor Party is a class party. For some traditionalists—usually not trade-union leaders—Marx remains the man who has spoken the final word. The majority, however, are more conservative: their commitment to socialism is largely rhetorical and emotional, for their major goal is simply to obtain more wage and pension benefits for the working class. The traditionalists' influence is declining within the party as British society itself, including the working class, modernizes.

Finally, another segment of the Labor Party took form in the late 1950's: the so-called post-revisionists or, in their own terms, the new left. Its members are committed to socialism, and while they bow to Marx they are more concerned with his humanism than with his economic analysis. Their argument is that British society is as inegalitarian as ever, and, more important yet, that the whole structure of capitalist society alienates man from himself by emphasizing competitive values. If cultural and social life is to reach new heights and produce a genuinely humane democratic society in which each man fulfills himself, new sets of community purposes, defined by the community, must be developed. For this to occur, the capitalist ethos of British society must be radically altered.

The new left's critique goes deeper than this, however, for many of its members are as opposed to the rationalization of British society as they are to what they consider its injustices. It is for this reason that while they sympathize with the Soviet Union in many ways—a good number of them are ex-Communists or Trotskyites—they reject the Soviet model as being repressive and dominated by a kind of bourgeois bureaucratic rationality. Instead, the new left conceives of its goal as a quasi-anarchic society in which social and sexual repressions will be almost completely eliminated, and a new culture based upon the free flow of all human impulses will produce a meaningful esthetic life for everyone; a society whose dominant aspects are the esthetic and the sensual. They regard the Soviet Union, despite its repressive quality, as more progressive in some ways than the Western democracies, precisely because they believe the new society will evolve more readily from a collectivized economy than from a capitalist one.

The new left has remained a minority in the Labor Party, but a minority that wields considerable influence. It has drawn the greater part of its strength from the academic community, and especially from the literary intelligentsia. It has been able to widen the base of its support on many issues, such as its campaign for England's unilateral nuclear disarmament and its opposition to American policy in Vietnam. In 1960, drawing upon a large bloc of traditionalists, the new left was able to defeat portions of the Labor Party leadership's defense and foreign-policy planks and to frustrate its attempts to modify the party constitution toward a revisionist orientation.

In the late 1950's, the party was led by Hugh Gaitskell, a revisionist who, by 1961, seemed to have beaten down a good deal of his left-wing opposition, both traditionalist and new left. When Gaitskell died in 1963, however, he was replaced as party leader by Harold Wilson, identified by many as of the left, if not completely the new left. Once in power, however, Wilson turned out to be primarily a modernizer, and while he listened to the left and even assigned some of its members posts in his government, his emphasis was upon providing England with the economic and social muscle needed to meet current and future challenges.

During Wilson's first years in office, the left found itself in a state of confusion. Much of its leadership had been brought into the government, and even when the rank and file disagreed with government policies it was difficult to organize an effective opposition. By 1969, however, the situation had altered considerably. Wilson's refusal to attack United States policy in Vietnam with sufficient sharpness alienated much of the left, and his economic policies, including wage restraints and proposals for regulating collective bargaining, brought the new left and trade unionists into a temporary alliance. The left also gained some strength from the ferment in the universities. While no direct challenge was mounted against Wilson's authority, the party once again indulged in rather noisy public acrimony.

STRUCTURE AND DYNAMICS: Like Socialist parties throughout Europe, the British Labor Party began its life as a mass organization outside Parliament. Since its ideology stressed both equality and popular participation, it attempted from the very beginning to create an institutional structure that would serve, in some sense, as a model for the kind of society it eventually hoped to create. The key decisions of party policy were to be made by a democratically elected Annual Conference; the party was to have a chairman rather than a leader,[8] party members were to address each other by their first names and as "comrade." Furthermore, those elected to Parliament under Labor Party support were to derive their policies from the mass party, which represented the most advanced segments of the working class and its allies. Even before the party had taken an official Socialist position, it was far more self-consciously ideological than the Conservative Party. Whatever may have been the pragmatic and limited aims of many of the trade unionists who supported the Labor Party, the intellectuals who joined and came to lead it were motivated much more by principle.

The Labor Party today is not the same party that formed more than a half-century ago: both its organization and the objective situation it faces are substantially different, and these changes have affected both its

8 The term "leader of the Labor Party" replaced the term "chairman" in the 1920's. The party leader is elected by the Parliamentary Labor Party. The term "chairman of the Labor Party" is now used for the chairman of the national executive committee of the mass party. The parliamentary party elects a chairman only when the party has taken office and the leader has become prime minister.

program and the dynamics of its operation. For example, the party leader and the parliamentary party now exercise far more power than do the militants or the party's Annual Conference. Tension always existed between the party's demand for discipline and its homage to democratic decision-making; nevertheless, both its ideology and its structure give the decision-making process within the Labor Party a far more open quality than that of the Conservative Party. Invariably, the Labor Party's squabbles are fought out in public. Whether the mass party actually plays a larger role in decision-making than in the Conservative Party is debatable.[9] As will become clear in the course of the following discussion, my own feeling is that it does, and that the difference is more than marginal. This does not mean, of course, that Laborites are more responsive to the electorate than are the Conservatives; that is an entirely different matter.

The structure of the Labor Party still reflects the fact that it was founded as an association of many groups, although the party now has its own constituency organization. Of the party's components, the various Socialist societies, with the possible exception of the Fabian Society, have little influence on political decisions. The influence of members of the Cooperative Societies is also slight; they have their own party, the Cooperative Party, which is loosely affiliated with Labor, but there is scant evidence that they have any real say in the formation of policy. The three key groups within the Labor Party are the trade unions, the constituency parties, and the Labor Members of Parliament. The key structural elements are the Annual Conference, the national executive committee (N.E.C.), and the Parliamentary Labor Party.

[9] For contrasting views on this issue see R. T. McKenzie, *British Political Parties* (New York: Frederick A. Praeger, 1964), and S. H. Beer, *British Politics in the Collectivist Age* (New York: Alfred A. Knopf, 1965).

The trade unions provide the party with most of its members (some 5,500,000 out of 6,400,000) and most of its money. Of course, not all British trade unions are affiliated with the party, and not all those affiliated do so in terms of full membership. Unless a union member objects, however, he contributes to a political levy that can be used by trade-union officials for political purposes. It can, for example, be used to pay membership dues to the Labor Party, thereby increasing the number of votes that the union can command at the Annual Conference. The levy can also be used to cover direct contributions to the national executive committee or to local parties, both of which allow the unions a greater degree of influence on the nomination of local-party candidates, thus helping to make sure these candidates win. In fact, many Labor Party candidates are union-sponsored, generally from heavily trade-union districts—and hence safe Labor Party districts. This has in the past given the party more of a trade-union cast in defeat than in victory.

The trade unions have tended to be more conservative and more passive than the constituency organizations. Most trade-union members are not excessively concerned with day-to-day political decisions; consequently they have permitted trade-union officials considerable freedom. The trade-union leadership, in turn, has shared this attitude and delegated a good deal of authority to the political leadership of the party with the proviso that the leadership must not contravene traditional working-class attitudes and feelings—a peculiar and hard-to-summarize combination of class consciousness, Socialist slogans, distrust of employers, and bread-and-butter concerns, added to a general conservatism toward the traditional values of British society. However, since the political passivity of trade-union members automatically places power in the hands of union officers, especially the general secretary of a union, it is their attitudes and feelings that are of essential importance. Thus, for exam-

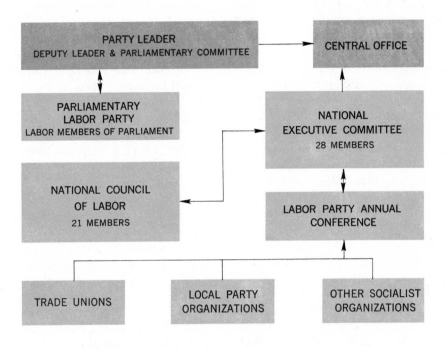

FIGURE 10.3. THE STRUCTURE OF THE LABOR PARTY

ple, the Transport and General Workers Union had, under the leadership of Ernest Bevin, been a bastion of conservatism in the Labor Party since the late 1920's. His death and that of his two successors after relatively short terms brought to power Frank Cousins, a union leader who has identified himself with the left.

The constituency organizations of the Labor Party are its basic operating units. Membership is open to all who subscribe to party principles and are willing to pay nominal dues. Individuals can also affiliate through their local trade-union branches or the local Cooperative Society or Socialist Society. As in the Conservative Party, local organizations are responsible for the general spreading of the word, as well as, theoretically, the nomination of parliamentary candidates.

The governing body of the constituency party is the General Management Committee (G.M.C.), which consists of representatives from ward committees and affiliated organizations. The G.M.C. in turn delegates its authority to a smaller executive committee. The principal officer is the secretary of the local party, especially if he is at the same time a paid election agent.

The political efforts of a large number of unpaid volunteers make the Labor Party a mass rather than a cadre party. These efforts have, in the past, been a part of an emotional commitment to party goals. The term "large" is relative; only a small percentage of constituency organization members works actively for the party.[10] What with the commitment of the volunteers deriving from a sense of mission, it is not surprising that they stand rather to the left of the ordinary Labor Party supporter. Nor is it surprising that their

10 Public-opinion polls indicate that 45 to fifty per cent of the electorate strongly identify themselves with a political party; 23 to 27 per cent are dues-paying members of a political party, and about one per cent of the electorate do unpaid work for the parties.

fervor has had its effect within the constituency parties, which generally support left-wing resolutions at Annual Conferences in greater proportions than do trade unions. Even further, members of the national executive committee, who are elected by the constituency parties, have usually been more to the left than those elected by the trade unions. There are, however, factors which limit the leftward movement of constituency parties. The national executive committee can expel—and has expelled—branches that have strayed too far from official Labor Party policy. Also, as far as nominations are concerned, a search for candidates who can command the support of the more conservative trade unions often exerts a moderating influence.

The Labor Party has also created regional offices, but they have very little power—far less than those of the Conservatives. On the other hand, the three-day Annual Conference of the Labor Party has more influence on party policy than the Conservatives' Annual Conference. Certainly it has been the focus of a good many bitter ideological battles.

The functions of the Annual Conference include the election of the national executive committee, consideration of its reports and those of other committees, and voting upon resolutions submitted by the membership. The party leader is expected to appear before the conference to express and defend his views, which can be subject to a conference vote. Votes at the conference are distributed in proportion to affiliated membership, so that the six largest national trade unions can dominate the sessions.[11] Trade-union members have traditionally cast their votes as a bloc.[12] Since trade-union leaders at the conference are without a mandate on many issues, a very few men have a very large number of votes in their pockets. It

[11] Together these unions account for about half the total votes at the conference.

[12] That is, the representatives of the union at the conference decide what position they will take by a majority vote, and then present a united front on the conference floor.

was for this reason that the constituency parties fought so hard in the 1930's to change the method of electing the national executive committee. Originally the entire conference had voted on candidates nominated by each section of the party. Today, the seven N.E.C. members allocated to the constituency parties are voted upon by the constituency section alone.

The N.E.C. is responsible for the day-to-day operation of the party and controls its growing bureaucracy. The N.E.C. consists of 28 members: the party treasurer, elected by the whole conference; 12 trade-union delegates; seven delegates elected by the constituency parties; one delegate each from the Socialist and Cooperative Societies; five women elected by the conference; and the leader and deputy leader of the party serving *ex officio*. The N.E.C. prepares the party program and issues general policy statements; it also keeps a list of prospective candidates, and its approval is required for candidates nominated by constituency organizations. Although this power has been used sparingly, the executive committee has, from time to time, rejected nominees, especially members of the Communist Party or Trotskyites. In the last analysis, it can disaffiliate constituency organizations which refuse to comply with the party rules, and it will run official Labor candidates against those of branches that have refused to accept national directives. The N.E.C. can also expel members from the party; but again, this is rarely done, and dissidents are usually readmitted upon promise of good behavior.

The N.E.C. of the Labor Party is more diverse in membership than its Conservative counterpart. The election of twelve trade-union representatives assures the presence of a sizable number of people who began life as ordinary workers. With some exceptions, most of the trade-union seats on the N.E.C. are given to unions rather than to individuals. Thus, the larger unions have a seat by right, and only within the union itself do personal or ideological considerations play any role. Those trade-union leaders who do take seats on the N.E.C. are usually of the second echelon, or, as with trade-union members of Parliament, those who have passed their prime. The first-echelon leaders of the trade unions prefer to seek power within the trade-union movement.

Constituency and women's representatives, on the other hand, invariably have a middle-class background. Between 1952 and 1963, only three of the 19 persons who served as N.E.C. representatives of the women's or constituency sections were of working-class background. The remainder represented the professions, with teachers and journalists predominating. As in the case of local Labor parties, the reasons for this have much to do with the requirements of politics itself. Political party work, especially on the national level, is quasi-professional in nature, so that professional people find an easy entry to political posts.

The national organs of both parties are similar in that they tend to be dominated by members of Parliament. In the Labor Party, almost all the constituency and women's representatives are M.P.'s, as are four or five of the trade-union representatives. This, again, is natural: delegates are likely to vote for candidates who have some sort of reputation, and within the party M.P.'s are likely to have distinct advantages. Finally, turnover on the N.E.C. is rather slow. Although elections are held annually, the average term of service is about five years. In the constituency sections at least, large-scale shifts occur only when there are overall shifts in the strengths of factions within the party. During the 1950's, for example, the more conservative representatives from the constituency section were gradually replaced by supporters of Aneurin Bevan.

The central office (Transport House) of the Labor Party, under the direction of the executive committee, is responsible for maintaining contact with and guiding local organizations. It provides speakers, arranges conferences, carries on research, edits party publications and propaganda, and examines and trains the agents who direct local campaigns. It also manages the party's funds.

The Parliamentary Labor Party consists of all Labor members of the House of Commons plus some Labor peers from the House of Lords. When Labor is out of office, the parliamentary party meets regularly to discuss general issues; its decisions are binding on the parliamentary party as a whole. Day-to-day management of party strategy is left to a parliamentary committee, elected by Labor M.P.'s, and to certain additional M.P.'s appointed by the party leader. The parliamentary committee is equivalent to the Conservative Party's shadow cabinet and is often referred to by that name.

The party leader and deputy leader, as well as the chief whip, are elected annually by the parliamentary party. Historically, not one Labor party leader has been forced from office once elected, although George Lansbury resigned in 1935 after the Annual Conference had supported policies with which he disagreed. There have, however, been a number of attempts to replace the party leader, although on only one occasion has this led to a vote—Harold Wilson's unsuccessful attempt in 1961 to unseat Hugh Gaitskell.

When the Labor Party is in office, the prime minister is less likely to attend parliamentary party meetings, although a consultative committee keeps him informed of backbench attitudes and complaints. The party has also experimented with informal specialized committees for the twin purpose of bringing together back-benchers who are interested in particular matters of public policy and of serving as liaison between the cabinet and the M.P.'s. The committees, however, have proved less important than certain interest groups, such as trade-union M.P.'s, and ideological units, such as Keep Left and Victory for Socialism, which form and reform within the parliamentary party. Most of the ideological groups have consisted of left-wing M.P.'s who attempt to counter what they consider to be the excessive timidity of the leadership.

POWER AND POLICY: In theory, the ultimate fount of policy in the Labor Party remains the Annual Conference. It is quite clear, however, that neither the parliamentary party nor the prime minister, when Labor is in power, will accept conference decisions with which they disagree. After the defeat of the N.E.C.'s resolution on national defense in 1960, Gaitskell stated quite explicitly that the party in Parliament would continue to follow those policies it considered correct—even though he admitted that failure to reverse conference policy might lead to disastrous consequences in the long run. Harold Wilson took an even stronger stand in 1967 and 1968, especially with regard to attacks on the government's incomes policy; he made it evident that he would not feel bound by any conference decision.

To set the parliamentary party or the N.E.C. apart from the Annual Conference is, however, misleading. Bitter policy differences are comparatively rare, notwithstanding the serious conflicts that split the party in the early and late 1960's. Power in the Labor Party is widely diffused, although the parliamentary party and the party leader exercise more of it than the democratic rhetoric of the party allows. The party leader, especially when he is prime minister, stands for the Labor Party in the eyes of the public. To attack him in areas that he considers important is to weaken the party. For the militant, policy attacks injure the "cause"; for those more oriented to public office, they reduce the possibility of re-election.

The parliamentary party as a whole carries with it the prestige of national office, which, as already indicated, explains its members' prominence on the National Executive Committee of the mass party. The domination of the N.E.C. by members of Parliament goes a long way toward insuring

that the committee will not adopt positions too far out of line with what the parliamentary party believes is possible, or wise.

The N.E.C., in turn, through its disciplinary powers and its control over the party bureaucracy and the agenda of the Annual Conference, commands considerable power. Given the size and short duration of Annual Conferences, the relative lack of information available to delegates, and a general unwillingness to upset the applecart, successful full-scale rebellions are rather rare. For example, in 1958 it was obvious that the conference was not happy with the N.E.C.'s proposed statement on education. However, with the executive committee pointing out that the document had been worked on for a long time, and that substitutes from the floor were, at best, hastily put together, the delegates felt forced to accept it *faute de mieux*.

It is true, of course, that the N.E.C., and indeed the party leader, often stave off conflict by seeking compromises in advance of the Annual Conference on issues they believe will encounter heavy opposition. Thus, Gaitskell's "victory" in 1961 was partially the result of restating the official position of the party in such a way as to make it less objectionable to its delegates than it had been in its original form. Most observers of the Labor Party have argued that, on the whole, the parliamentary party is more "moderate" —that is, pragmatic—than the national executive committee: apart from the M.P.'s give-and-take experience in Parliament, they are concerned with a wider constituency than the N.E.C. itself. Further, it is argued that the N.E.C. tends to take a broader view than do individual militants.

The traditional picture of the Labor Party has been one in which the parliamentary party and the party leader control both the N.E.C. and the Annual Conference, with the support of more moderate trade-union leadership. Since the late 1950's, this description has come under some attack. It has been noted, for example, that the constituency parties are not nearly so radical as some have held, and that most N.E.C. victories have been achieved by concurrent trade-union and constituency-party majorities. It is argued further that most conflicts within the Labor Party operate at all levels equally—that is, they occur simultaneously within the parliamentary party, the N.E.C., and the conference. While this portrait does offer a necessary corrective to the more traditional one, it does not completely falsify it.

The distribution of power within any political organization is difficult to measure. A party leader may remain in office because of his ability to compromise, or because the office endows him with the power to control colleagues. The measurement of power must take into account what is not done as well as what is done, and the real foci of power are often hidden from view.

The Conservative party leader, for the most part, has far more authority vis-à-vis the mass organization than the Labor party leader. However, it would be difficult to argue, despite differences in ideology and formal organization, that he has more authority in relation to his parliamentary colleagues. Rather, the difference would seem to be of another sort. As already indicated, the Conservative Party is more oriented toward power while the Labor Party is more self-consciously ideological. Within the Conservative Party, therefore, opposition to the leader's policies clusters about ad hoc responses to particular issues; these are unlikely to produce a public stir unless the party believes that its national position is being seriously weakened. In the Labor Party, on the other hand, where details of program and ideology are much more significant, policy questions are of greater importance. Furthermore, the party's organization and ideology encourage attempts to resolve policy conflicts openly; the Labor Party is, therefore, almost always engaged in acrimonious public debate. In fact, it might be argued that while the whole structure of

the Conservative Party is one that transforms policy conflicts into power conflicts, that of the Labor Party is such as to force those whose goal is power to seek an ideological justification for their actions.

5. ON THE HUSTINGS [13]

The Parliament Act of 1911 limits the life of a parliament to five years, although the party in office usually calls for an election before that time expires. To vote in Britain, one must be over 21, a British subject, and have one's name inscribed on the voting register. Aliens, hereditary peers, felons, and persons convicted of past election offenses are excluded from the franchise. Voting lists are made up once a year; a form is sent to every house in the nation and householders must state the name, age, and citizenship of those living at the residence. After the rolls are compiled, an announcement appears that the register is being prepared and everyone is invited to check to see if his name is on it.

Election campaigns are comparatively short affairs. The first step is an announcement by the prime minister that on a certain date—usually in about ten days' time—the queen will dissolve Parliament. As soon as Parliament is dissolved, a royal proclamation is published summoning a new one, and the election must be held within three weeks.

Writs are issued to all the constituencies commanding them to return a representative to Parliament. The very next day, the local returning officer must put up an announcement that there is to be an election; and within eight days of the summons to the new parliament, the nominations of the candidates must be complete. Parliamentary candidates require nominations by two voters and support by another eight. The candidate must also put down a £150 deposit, which is returned if the candidate polls more than

[13] The term is Norse in origin and refers to open-air meetings. In modern times it has been used to describe election campaigns.

one-eighth of the total votes cast; otherwise it goes to the state to help pay election expenses.

THE CANDIDATES: The national organs in both Conservative and Labor parties theoretically retain ultimate control over the nomination of candidates—despite the fact that the constituency parties are relatively autonomous.

In the Conservative Party, the preliminary work in securing a candidate is done by a local election committee appointed by the chairman of the local party in consultation with the National Union's Advisory Committee on Candidates. Local Conservative Party leaders interested in running for Parliament may make their desires known (unobtrusively, of course) to the Selection Committee, or attempt to get placed on the list of possible candidates at the central office. Since there is no residence requirement for national office in England, the local party has a far wider choice than in the United States. However, other things being equal, Conservatives prefer local people, or at least candidates who will agree to settle in the constituency and promise to give it their full attention. All names gathered by the Conservative Party's Selection Committee must be approved by its Advisory Committee on Candidates, but in only one case since 1945 has the Advisory Committee refused to allow a potential candidate to be considered.

While the Advisory Committee has had some success in placing Conservative luminaries who have lost their seats, it has by no means found the constituency parties overwhelmingly enthusiastic about accepting its suggestions in this area. The committee has had even less success in persuading local parties to consider candidates who would give the party a more representative character in Parliament. The majority of Conservative Party candidates tend to be professional men (in law, public relations, and the armed forces) or businessmen—in any event, distinctly middle class. Despite the urging of the central office, local organizations have

been extremely loath to adopt Jews, workers, or women as candidates. There were only two Jewish Conservative M.P.'s elected in 1966, and they both had the advantage of titles. More important, only two M.P.'s out of the 253 returned to office were manual workers, despite the fact that about half the Conservative Party vote comes from manual workers.

The Selection Committee generally recommends a list of three or four names to the executive council of the local party, which then invites those nominated to a special meeting. The candidates are asked to speak, usually for about twenty minutes, and to answer questions, after which a vote is taken. The council's choice is then submitted to a general meeting of the local party, where it is almost always approved.

The task of prospective candidates is not always terribly pleasant. As one M.P. described it:

It is a gala occasion for the selectors; slow torture for the candidates. So great is the strain of maintaining an amicable conversation with his rivals and their wives, that it is a relief for the applicant to leave the anteroom . . . for the ten or twenty-minute interview which may alter the entire direction of his life. The audience already knows a great deal about him, but he cannot be sure quite what they know. Normally, a candidate makes the most of all of the favourable facts which are not likely to be contradicted by the more impartial summary of his life-story which the selectors hold in their hands. They do not want a speech about party policy. They want to discover what sort of person he is, or is capable of pretending to be. . . .[14]

In fact, Conservatives are rarely concerned about ideology.

What most associations want is a man of solid character. Not necessarily a brilliant

[14] Quoted in Austin Ranney, *Pathways to Parliament* (Madison: The University of Wisconsin Press, 1965), p. 60.

*man. . . . in fact they may distrust a chap
who seems too brilliant or flashy or glib.
They want someone with the right sort of
background, someone who looks good and
sounds right. They want someone they can
count on to do the right thing. . . .*[15]

Very few incumbent M.P.'s are denied renomination by the party. A number of Conservative M.P.'s have on occasion abstained
or voted against the party on important votes
since World War II, but the national
agencies have *never* challenged their readop-
tion. Constituency parties, however, failed to
readopt twelve; half of these involved objections relating to "personal" deficiences, the
other half were related to the split in the
Conservative Party during the Suez crisis.

The process of selecting Labor Party candidates resembles that of the Conservatives
in many ways, but here again, central control
and ideological questions are more important. Prospective Labor candidates are not
permitted to raise their own names publicly
before a local party; only through private
channels can they make their political ambitions known. They must be nominated by
one of three groups: the National Executive
Committee, a ward committee, or an affiliated organization such as a trade union. The
names of proposed candidates are submitted
to the N.E.C., which may also take the initiative in suggesting names. In the latter case
special care must be taken, for local parties
are quite sensitive about pressure from
above. Labor Party militants, of course, have
a tendency to regard all authority as arbitrary.

The N.E.C. maintains two lists, one of
possible candidates who have trade-union
sponsorship, and one of those who do not.
Sponsorship is usually an important consideration, inasmuch as trade unions may pay
up to eighty per cent of the campaign expenditures. Constituency parties with their
dominant left-wing, usually middle-class,

majorities are, therefore, often torn between
their desire to find a candidate who mirrors
their views and their need to accept a super-
annuated trade unionist.

Prospective candidates appear before a
selection conference which, in spite of differences, is as forbidding as its Conservative
counterpart:

*When the first contestant is led into the
meeting hall a shock awaits him. Instead of
the kindly, compassionate faces he has come
to know so well from years of work inside
the Labour Party, there sitting before him
are several score members of the family por-
trayed in the New Yorker by Mr. Charles
Addams. In a halting voice (made more ner-
vous by immediate complaints that no one
at the back can hear) he then launches into
the subtle blend of egotism and idealism
which, with the aid of the Labour Party
Speakers' Handbook, leading articles from
the Guardian and the aphorisms of Mr. Adlai
Stevenson, he has been busy preparing for
weeks. Questions follow, each more bewil-
deringly irrelevant than the one before. The
nominee has painstakingly worked out advance replies to possible queries on nuclear
disarmament, German rearmament (yes,
still), capital punishment and Clause Four.
Now one delegate after another rises to seek
his views on street lighting, the aldermanic
system and Moral Rearmament.*

*At last the ordeal is over and, in the dead
silence that has prevailed from the moment
he entered the hall, he plods dully back to
the waiting-room where the others gaze at
him with undisguised loathing. There, while
each of his fellow contenders (on a strictly
regulated equal-time basis) goes through the
same procedure, he sits, wincing at the repeated bursts of appreciative laughter which
punctuate his rivals' performance.*[16]

Verbal attachment to ideology is a much
more important factor in the Labor Party
than it is in the Conservative, and prospec-

15 A central office official quoted in Ranney, *Pathways to Parliament*, pp. 60–61.

16 Quoted in Ranney, *Pathways to Parliament*, p.
173.

tive candidates must make at least some effort to indicate that they are spiritually part
of the "movement." G. D. H. Cole once wrote
a speech which he guaranteed would be successful in almost any selection conference.
Part of it goes like this:

*I support fully the home policies of the
Party, although I could wish for a little more
enthusiasm among certain of our comrades
for the fundamentals of our Socialist faith.
(Hear, hear—fervently.) I make no apology
for saying it, I mean public ownership.
(Applause.) In foreign affairs, I support Labour's initiative for peace, although I would
go farther than the present—I repeat the
present—policy of the movement to get rid of
the appalling weapon which . . . (cheers
drown out the end of the sentence).*[17]

Beyond this, constituency parties want
people who are forceful speakers and who
will campaign hard. They are also favorably
disposed toward the person who has already
indicated his devotion through service in the
party or a trade union. All this considered, a
local man will be given preference over an
outsider. As in the Conservative Party,
women seem to have less of a chance for
nomination than men. There seems also to
be some prejudice against Catholics, although hardly any against Jews. Of the 114
non-Anglican Labor M.P.'s elected to Parliament in 1966, about whom it was possible
to obtain information on religious background (many M.P.'s are reticent about specifying their religion), 26 listed themselves
as Jewish.

The Labor Party elects a good many manual workers to Parliament, although their
proportion of the total number of elected
Labor candidates depends upon the party's
fortune. Since a considerably larger number
of trade-union M.P.'s than non–trade-union
M.P.'s come from safe Labor districts, their
proportion of the party's representation varies

inversely with the number of seats won by
the party. Thus in 1959, when the Conservatives won a substantial electoral victory, 35
per cent of the Labor candidates elected to
Parliament came from working-class backgrounds, whereas in 1966 it was only thirty
per cent. Whatever the percentage variance
of manual workers, the proportion of trade-
union officials nominated for Parliament is
gradually dropping. Moreover, even for
trade-union–sponsored seats, middle-class
aspirants with a university education are becoming more attractive as party candidates.
They are usually professional men, predominantly lawyers, teachers, or journalists. Almost one-fourth of the new Labor M.P.'s
elected in 1966 were university teachers, and
another ten per cent were secondary school
teachers.

The control by the National Executive
over nominations is stronger than in the
Conservative Party, although, again, the
N.E.C. has not been notoriously successful in
securing good seats for favorites. Labor's
Central Office, nevertheless, has exercised
more authority than the Conservatives' Abbey House in preventing the adoption of
candidates it did not like, or in preventing
local associations from turning down candidates it found congenial. The central office
expelled four leftist M.P.'s from the party
between 1945 and 1964 and denied renomination to four left-wing, locally selected candidates who were not M.P.'s. In many cases
the local constituency organizations protested, but they were eventually forced to
bow; the deposed candidates who ran as independents were invariably badly beaten. In
two cases, local constituency parties tried to
deny renomination to right-wing M.P.'s and
were prevented from doing so by the N.E.C.
Even so, in the great majority of cases, the
N.E.C. does not interfere with the local
choice.

THE CAMPAIGN: The foundation of the
parliamentary campaign is the canvass. It is
the aim of each party to call on every voter

in the district and to learn, if possible, how he will vote. Very little effort is expended on those who uphold the other party, but supporters and marginals are flooded with campaign literature. Candidates appear at street rallies—and endure a good amount of rough heckling; national party figures concentrate their political efforts on key districts, and both parties make arrangements to get their supporters to the polls. Both are also making greater use of public-relations firms and techniques. Laborites were slower than the Conservatives in picking up this maneuver, believing it to be un-Socialist, but they have overcome their earlier qualms. Since 1959, the parties have used television more extensively, with time for television broadcasts being distributed among the parties in proportion to their votes at the last election.

Both parties have come to rely more and more on paid professional agents, whose job it is to know the intricacies of the election law, to direct the work of fighting a campaign, and, between campaigns, to maintain and build the party organization. Successful agents may be promoted to better paying constituencies, or to the party's central office. The Conservative Party's agents are generally better paid, better trained, and about twice as numerous as the Labor Party's. About four-fifths of the electoral districts in England and Wales have a full-time Conservative agent, as compared with less than half having Labor Party agents. The distribution is even more skewed when one considers the fact that a good many of the Labor Party agents are in safe seats where they can receive succor from trade-union coffers. Labor, however, can draw upon a somewhat larger pool of dedicated militants.

British law sets fairly low limits upon campaign expenditures and fairly tight restrictions upon the manner in which these funds may be used. For example, the services of bands may be accepted only as a free gift; even a cup of tea at campaign headquarters must be paid for to avoid the charge of "treating." There are, however, no limits on the amount of money that can be spent between campaigns (the Conservatives spend far more); nor are there restrictions upon expenditures by private groups such as trade unions or individual firms whose advertising, while not directly favoring a particular political party, may create a disposition to favor one against the other. Most talk about party financial advantage bogs down in disagreement as to how such expenditures can be effectively regulated.

In the nineteenth century most political campaigns were financed out of the pockets of the candidates, a practice that continued in the Conservative Party until after its 1945 defeat. As the national organization of the party grew, the Conservatives turned to industry for contributions, and there is considerable evidence that a few hundred large-scale donations met most of the party needs in the interwar period.

After World War II, the Conservative Party placed strict limitations on the amount of money candidates and prospective candidates could contribute to local associations; it stressed the need for local parties to meet their own expenses by broadening their fund-raising base. The party also initiated public appeals to raise money. Direct contributions from a few large backers are far less crucial to party finances today than they used to be. The exact distribution of financial contributions is difficult to measure, since there is no legal requirement that this be published and the Conservative Party is quite secretive. However, the party's annual income probably runs close to three million pounds a year.

From the beginning, the Labor Party has relied very heavily upon the contributions of trade unions, supplemented by individual affiliation dues, and, undoubtedly, assistance from a few angels. The total income of the party today is probably about one million pounds a year, of which the trade-union contribution is more than four hundred thousand pounds. Both the trade unions and the party have been rather penurious in their election expenditures, and both have built up sizable funds to be used in case of "emergency."

6. A FOOTNOTE ON THE FUTURE

Modern British political parties took form at a time when social-class issues of a certain type were the most significant determinants of political attitudes. The structure of the party system and the orientation of both the Conservative and Labor parties was the result of a complex interaction of cultural, socioeconomic, and political factors, some of which the British shared with other European nations, others of which were typically English. All these variables contributed to the evolution of a disciplined mass two-party system in which rather moderate political parties alternated in office with, however, the Conservatives representing the normal majority.

In the past ten years some of the major features of this system have begun to change. Class issues have become less significant. The leadership cadres of both parties include a larger number of professionally trained young men and women who are impatient with traditional political styles. Both parties now have massive bureaucratic organizations, and both are becoming catchall parties which attempt to outbid each other in promising services to voters. The mass media have placed increasing emphasis upon individual personalities, especially that of the party leader, although the importance of personal-

ity has not become nearly as great as it is in the United States.[18]

In addition to the changing aspects of the political system, new issues are emerging in British life—issues involving racial, ethnic, and regional conflicts. The race issue has been brought to a head by the migration of Pakistanis, Indians, and West Indians to England, and although, thus far, it has not become a source of intense inter-party disagreement, it well might become such a source in the future. Perhaps more significant is the emergence of Welsh and Scots nationalist parties, which in 1967 and 1968 received substantial votes in local elections. These parties seem to represent a peculiar combination of regional and cultural aspirations fused, in some cases, with radical politics and in others with more conservative ideas. In Scotland, for example, many voters have deserted the Labor Party because they believe that it has not been dealing forcefully enough with such issues as crime, and yet they have not brought themselves to vote Conservative. All these developments, coupled with the growing intransigence of students, indicate that British politics in the future may be less oriented toward problems of class than toward problems of cultural and political style. If this is to be the case, significant shifts in the structure and dynamics of the British party system can be expected.

[18] Much of the analysis of this section derives from Samuel H. Beer, "The Comparative Study of British Politics," *Comparative Politics*, 1 (October 1968), 19–36.

11

The French

Party System

1. INTRODUCTION

The French political system has always differed from the British or American not only in the often paralyzing multiplicity of its political parties but also in its continuing retention of powerful factions within it committed, at least rhetorically, to changing the system in fundamental ways—by force if necessary. Every possible ideological current that has caused a ripple of any political significance whatsoever in Europe—from the most unreconstructed conservatism, through communism, Trotskyism, anarchism, and a half dozen shades of socialism—seems, at one time or another, to have developed its own political party in France. During the Fourth Republic, for instance, ten to twenty parties competed for office at each national election. Our discussion of French parties, however, will deal primarily with those of nationwide importance.

These cleavages seriously reduced the possibilities of creating a government that could evolve and effect a coherent set of public policies. And the difficulties of the French political situation were compounded not only by the fact that until the Fifth Republic the executive was drawn from and entirely responsible to the parliament, but also by the mutual antagonism and suspicion of even political groups whose ideological positions differed only marginally, and whose interest lay more in refining their rhetoric than in finding solutions to the problems that plagued France.[1]

The French party system, then, has been far less successful than the British or American in aggregating the interests of Frenchmen. The tragedy was that for a very long time no other institution or combination of institutions could fill the vacuum; as a result, little was done either to make the populace aware of the real issues they had to face or even to approach many of these issues in a meaningful way. The best that may be said for the system is that it kept the political conflicts from exploding into civil war.

---

[1] The effect of the party system on the process of government and the formation of public policy is discussed in more detail in Chapter 16.

TABLE 11.1. FIRST BALLOT RESULTS
IN FRENCH PARLIAMENTARY ELECTIONS, 1945–1968

Voting in Metropolitan France

	1945	(Nov. 10) 1946	1951	1956	1958	1962	1967	1968
Communists	26.0%	28.6%	25.9%	25.7%	18.9%	21.8%	22.5%	20.0%
Socialists	23.8	17.9	14.9	14.8	15.5	12.7	18.8[1]	16.5
Radicals	11.1	12.4	11.2	13.4	8.3	7.6		
Gaullists	0.0	1.6	20.4	4.4	20.4	31.9	37.8[2]	43.6
M.R.P.	24.9	26.4	12.8	11.1	11.2	8.9	12.8[4]	10.3
Conservatives	13.3	12.8	12.3	14.4	22.9	13.9[3]		
Extreme right				13.3	3.0	0.9	0.9	0.1

[1]Allied in the Federation of the Left.
[2]Gaullists and Independent Republicans allied.
[3]Both pro- and anti-Gaullist conservatives.
[4]M.R.P. and anti-Gaullist conservatives allied.

Source: *Le Monde*, various editions. Reprinted by permission.

Certain other features of the French party system distinguish it from the British and American. Organizationally, for example, French parties run the whole gamut of types as described in Chapter 9. The Communists are still a good representation of a mass disciplined ideological party, while the Radical Socialists are much closer in structure to American political parties. Studies of French voting patterns also reveal vivid contrasts with the British and American and what, on the surface at least, would seem highly paradoxical behavior. The public rhetoric of French elections still deals primarily with ideological issues; the parties of the left, especially, speak in terms of social classes. Yet while class divisions are perhaps more significant than in England, no single French party comes anywhere near mobilizing the support of any group in French society. In the 1968 elections, an estimated 33 per cent of the working class voted for the Communist Party (see Table 11.2); but 31 per cent of this class also supported the Gaullists and another 18 per cent backed the Federation of the Democratic and Socialist Left, an organization largely composed of the Socialist and Radical Socialist parties. Other social strata were equally fragmented in their support of political groups.

Further, the voting behavior of Frenchmen—depending, of course, on the point of view—is a rather peculiar alternation or combination of stability and erraticism, quite unlike the British or American pattern. Both the Third and the Fourth Republics were marked by the sudden rise and almost equally sudden collapse of flash parties appealing to particular groups, or of organizations claiming to transcend ideological divisions and calling themselves "movements," "rallies," or "unions." All Frenchmen generally maintained that what was needed was a "pragmatic" approach to political and social questions, and quite often they were dominated by "heroic" leaders who relied upon personal charisma as a substitute for political programs. On the other hand, an examination of the French electoral map reveals that areas which voted left in 1849 were still voting for left-wing candidates in the 1960's, and that areas which leaned to the right were also expressing roughly the same preferences a century later. Some of France's departments with left-wing majorities are in regions that became "dechristianized" at about the time of the French Revolution, although the sources of dechristianization have earlier historical roots. The old county of Toulouse, part of the "Red Belt" of the Midi today,

TABLE 11.2. PARTY AFFILIATION BY CATEGORY, 1968

Distribution of voting interactions by sociodemographic categories

	Communists	U.D.R. and republican independents	Federation of the Left (F.G.D.S.)	Democratic Center (P.D.M.)	Others, including Unified Socialist Party (P.S.U.)
Sex:					
Men	25%	35%	18%	12%	10%
Women	18	46	16	11	9
Age:					
Under 50	23	38	17	11	11
Over 50	20	43	17	12	8
Profession:					
Farmers	12	48	20	12	8
Industrial and commercial	10	53	13	15	9
Professions and higher management	10	48	9	23	10
Lower management and employees	21	40	15	12	12
Workers	33	31	18	8	10
Unemployed	21	42	19	11	7
Size of city:					
Rural communes	14	47	20	12	7
Less than 20,000 inhabitants	23	45	11	13	8
20,000 to 100,000 inhabitants	24	35	26	5	10
More than 100,000 inhabitants	21	40	18	12	9
Paris region	32	30	10	13	15

Adapted from *Sondages*, no. 2, 1968, p. 102. Reprinted by permission of the publisher.

was noted for its radicalism as far back as the Albigensian wars of the thirteenth century. Other dechristianized areas were Jansenist in the seventeenth century, while others, for example the Vendée in western France, have been supporting the clerical right since the Revolution.

Explanations of the French party system have been legion. Some political scientists, in discussing its organization as well as its fragmentation, have stressed the effect of proportional representation during the Fourth Republic and the use of single-member districts and *ballotage* (a second ballot) during the Third and the Fifth. Others have stressed aspects of the French national character, and still others have argued that the nature of the party system reflects certain basic conflicts in

French society that are a heritage of its historical development. The analysis that follows will emphasize a social-historical approach and will parallel the interpretation developed in Chapter 2. It will be useful, however, to deal first in some detail with analyses that place emphasis on the electoral system.

The core of this argument is already familiar: both proportional representation and single-member districts requiring a second ballot if no candidate receives a majority on the first encourage an increase in the number of parties competing for office. But just how convincing is this analysis? Even if both PR and single-member districts do contribute to multiplicity, this could not explain the profusion of political parties which devel-

MAP 11.1. CONTINUITY IN FRENCH VOTING PATTERNS:
TRADITIONAL VOTING IN FRANCE

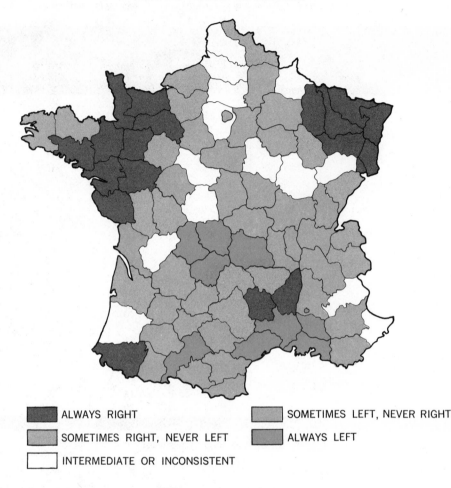

◼ ALWAYS RIGHT   ◼ SOMETIMES LEFT, NEVER RIGHT

◼ SOMETIMES RIGHT, NEVER LEFT   ◼ ALWAYS LEFT

☐ INTERMEDIATE OR INCONSISTENT

Adapted from Gordon Wright, *France in Modern Times*
(Chicago: Rand McNally, 1960), p. 478. Reprinted by
permission of the publisher.

oped. Furthermore, a double-ballot system would not necessarily result in more organized parties unless these parties could establish at least some regional constituencies willing to support them over a reasonable length of time. Primary elections in many states of the American South, such as Georgia and Alabama, are conducted under a double-ballot system, but the factions that emerge as a result have no lasting power because they have no permanent geographic base of operations. From 1848 to 1851 and

again from 1871 to 1873, France did experiment with single-member district plurality elections, but the experiment had no effect on the overall pattern of French politics.

Finally, if we examine the historical development of the electoral system in England and France, we arrive at the conclusion that the reasons for the adoption of one system over another were partially related to the societal differences between the two nations. The English saw little need to concern themselves with the representation of a whole host

MAP 11.2. CONTINUITY IN FRENCH VOTING PATTERNS:
THE DE GAULLE VOTE, 1965

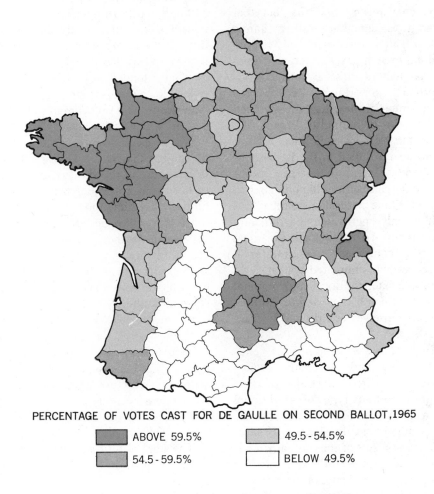

PERCENTAGE OF VOTES CAST FOR DE GAULLE ON SECOND BALLOT,1965

ABOVE 59.5%   49.5 - 54.5%

54.5 - 59.5%   BELOW 49.5%

Adapted from Wright, *France in Modern Times,* p.
479. Reprinted by permission.

of political groups. In France, on the other hand, the very multiplicity of factions led to the adoption of more complicated electoral mechanisms. Political groups have taken turns trying to bend the electoral system to further their own ideological viewpoints or to secure political advantage. In 1873, for example, the French conservatives replaced the single ballot with the double because the splits among Bonapartists, Bourbonists, and Orléanists were permitting republicans to win election after election. In 1945, the Commu-

nists, Socialists, and Popular Republican Movement pressed for a system of proportional representation because they wanted to encourage nationally oriented, disciplined, programmatic parties and because leftist mythology included the proposition that all political tendencies must be accurately represented. Of course, they also believed that the rather small size of single-member electoral districts operated to the advantage of the more traditional, conservative parties— their point being that the influence of local reputation and prestige was greater under such a system.

Electoral mechanisms, and the fact that France was a parliamentary rather than a presidential regime, were significant factors in determining French party structure. Nonetheless, social factors must also be considered of primary importance. Perhaps the most consequential of these has already been described—the fragmentation of French life, which led to the plethora of political ideologies; that, in turn, resulted in the freezing of positions already taken, so that new problems always emerged before old conflicts had been resolved. Quite naturally, political and social rigidity only aggravated the difficulty of resolving them. To this, of course, must be added the continuance of traditional social patterns that stimulated, or at least did little to alleviate, the local and regional differentiations which had existed for so long and which in themselves contributed to fragmentation.

As in England, the development of genuinely conservative and genuinely radical political groups reflected the strains of transition from a certain type of traditional society to a modern industrial one. The intensity of sociopolitical divisions in France, however, was the result of the mutual alienation of all social strata. Until well into the twentieth century, this alienation was related to a rather slow rate of economic growth that in itself contributed to the perpetuation of traditional patterns of social organization. In the French political system, then, several incompatible subcultures have existed side by side to produce what some writers have called a "stalemate society."

While the broad ideological outlines of the French party system stem, therefore, from the same factors that have influenced every European nation, the multiplication of parties differing only in ideological nuance has its roots in the fragmentation of French society. And, ironically, even the long-range stability—or rigidity—of portions of the French electorate is closely connected with the French inability to solve the crises associated with modernization. These factors are certainly partly responsible for that "individualism" that historically has made it so difficult for Frenchmen to organize for common purposes. Relationships among Frenchmen have tended to be far more formal and inflexible than those among Englishmen or Americans. The Frenchman's attitude toward authority is equally ambivalent. Often willing to see it imposed from the top because he recognizes that it is necessary if the society is to cohere at all, the Frenchman also tries to keep it at arm's length in order to protect himself. To him, those in authority are almost never to be trusted—almost never because, as further evidence of French political ambiguity, he also has a penchant for submerging his individualism in messianic mass movements that promise either to dissolve all authority or to place it in the hands of a dynamic political personality.

If most of these charismatic leaders or movements failed to transform French politics, it was because the culture and socioeconomic structure of France set limits on what could be done and reduced the possibility of any leader commanding enough support to achieve his ends.

The normal attitude of the French citizen toward politics is well illustrated by the observations of Lawrence Wylie:

[There is one] point on which everyone . . . would agree: a man with power over you is essentially evil. Except for a few supporters of the M.R.P. the voters of Peyrane say that the heads of their parties and of all other political parties "are a pile of bandits."

Thus political bitterness is more than an effect of people's bitterness. It is also a cause of their not getting along together. The existence of party labels gives them the opportunity of blaming on each other not just the evils which arise from living together but also the evils that threaten from without. It is . . . usual for people who dislike each other for personal reasons to disagree politically.

In view of the passion which politics arouses . . . one might expect the political parties to be well organized and active. This is not the case. Even the Communist Party is loosely held together. In the winter of 1950–1951, it was split with such dissension that some people thought it would *not be in a position to support its candidates in the next elections. The trouble was that some members of the party like to hunt rabbits with ferrets, and others like to hunt them with a gun. Since the ferret is more effective than the gun . . . the gun men accused the ferret men of ruining the sport. . . .*[2]

FIGURE 11.1. COMPARATIVE RATES OF POLITICAL PARTICIPATION: FRANCE AND THE UNITED STATES

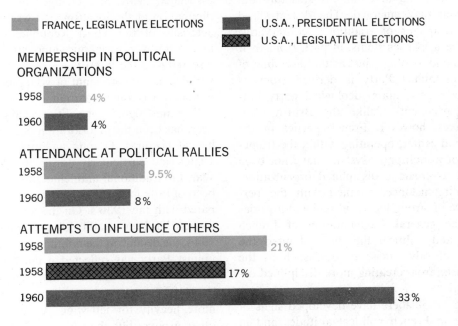

Adapted from Phillip E. Converse and George Dupeux, "Politicization in France and the United States," *Public Opinion Quarterly*, Spring 1962, p. 5. Reprinted by permission of the publisher and the authors.

The distrust in which political parties have been held by the French public is also partly the result of the political situation in which the parties have historically found themselves. Since no party was able to form a government by itself during the Third and Fourth Republics, it was always forced to compromise its program, and, in Parliament, deputies found themselves spending more time entering into deals in order to secure meager advantages than in facing the real issues. The fact that nothing could really be changed or accomplished under the French political system corrupted those who participated in politics.

It is not surprising, then, that the identification of the average French citizen with political parties has been tenuous as compared with Englishmen or Americans. Neither is it surprising that, despite large elec-

2 *Village in the Vaucluse* (Cambridge, Mass.: Harvard University Press, 1958), pp. 207–208, 211, 212.

toral turnouts, Frenchmen have expected less of politics than Americans, notwithstanding the continued existence of a core of active militants in many parties. The Frenchman's lack of involvement with parties has at times contributed to a political vacuum often filled by "flash" movements, and it also helps explain the phenomenon of Charles de Gaulle's massive victories.[3]

The organization of French parties reflects the social and cultural structure out of which they emerged. The decentralized cadre character of traditional conservative and liberal parties stems, in part, from their origins and ideology, just as the discipline of the Communist Party is derived from its character as a mass ideological party outside Parliament. Unlike the British Conservatives, however, French parties of the right and center, operating within the framework of a multiparty system, have not been forced to create a disciplined organization. This circumstance, coupled with the persistence of strong local and regional loyalties and the general fragmentation of French social and political life, has inhibited the efforts of other mass parties, such as the Socialists, from creating more disciplined organizations.[4]

Since 1958 there have developed signs of change in French political attitudes and in the party system itself. To a considerable extent the beginnings of these changes date back to the Fourth Republic, when the pace of modernization in France began to accelerate. Paradoxically, the very fragmentation of the party system as well as the resulting weakness of the executive had something of a positive influence. For in effect, the political vacuum of the years between 1945 and 1958 permitted a new generation of technocrats in the bureaucracy to set into motion a number of plans that all but revolutionized the economic structure of France. De Gaulle capitalized on and contributed to this development; he by no means initiated it.[5]

Among the more telling results of this economic renovation has been a gradual lessening of the historic variations in regional voting as France becomes more urban. Also associated with this change has been a diminution of the localism that was so characteristic of the Third Republic. Furthermore, postwar economic innovations have also reduced the importance of the religious variable as a determinant of voting behavior, although it is still important.

The most significant political change, however, has been the deterioration of rigid ideological postures. Despite an upsurge in the 1950's and particularly during the Algerian War, the traditional antidemocratic right has been of little moment in recent years as compared with the 1930's. On the left, which as a whole has been steadily losing strength since 1946, the decline in the militancy of the Communist Party has reflected a corresponding decline in the alienation of the French working class. French workers still, of course, vote more heavily for left-wing parties than do other groups, but the old divisions are not quite so incisively etched. The institutional structure of the Fifth Republic seems to command reasonably widespread support, even if the authoritarian manner in which de Gaulle manipulated these institutions resulted in the waning of his popularity. The 1968 electoral victory of his party was less a personal endorsement of the general than it was a reaction to the threatening chaos; even so, the U.D.R., providing it can hold together, is potentially a majority party that can draw votes from all sectors of the populace. The decline of political extremism may also be attributed

[3] Even those Frenchmen who consider themselves loyal party members find the intricacies of party maneuvers so complicated that they tend to ignore them; in fact, they spend less time and effort trying to accumulate political information than do Americans—although some of the differences here are attributable to the higher levels of education attained by Americans.

[4] See discussion on party discipline in Chapter 9, 303–306, and the analysis of a disciplined mass Conservative Party in England in Chapter 10.

[5] These policies and the bureaucracy's part in creating and implementing them will be discussed in more detail in Chapters 22 and 24.

TABLE 11.3. RELIGION AND PARTY PREFERENCE IN FRANCE

	Commu-nists	Social-ists	Radi-cals	M.R.P.	U.N.R.	Inde-pendent–Giscard d'Estaing	Inde-pendent–Pinay
Catholics:							
Regularly attend mass	2%	11%	7%	45%	33%	28%	32%
Occasionally attend mass	22	37	49	35	41	43	45
Seldom attend mass	44	31	28	13	17	17	13
Indifferent to or without a religion	29	17	11	3	4	5	3
Other religions	3	4	5	4	5	7	7

Adapted from *Sondages*, no. 2, 1967, p. 25. Reprinted by permission of the publisher.

to the fact that most Frenchmen now appear to accept an economic system in which the state is pre-eminent in planning the economy and in fostering economic growth. There is, moreover, some evidence that the traditional hostility toward the bureaucracy and its authority is fading; more and more Frenchmen are coming to view it as a source of individual and collective benefits.

Pressures to modify the structure of the party system have manifested themselves partly as a result of these changes in French life. The creation of a popularly elected president and the massive victories of the Gaullists have impelled the political organizations, especially the left-wing parties, to enter into alliances and federations of varying kinds. Despite the failure of the leftists to cement their relationships, however, a distinct trend in the direction of fewer parties and a streamlining of the French party system can be detected. Increasingly, too, traditional party rhetoric is beginning to appear outdated. The young activist intelligentsia has been drawn to a whole array of "nonpartisan" political clubs for the purpose of discussing and acting upon civic problems. The influence of these clubs on the parties themselves has thus far been slight, but their influence on middle-class opinion has been considerable.

The events of 1968 also indicated that a new generation is emerging in France and raising new issues—issues related to the

style of French social and political life rather than to narrowly defined economic demands. While it is hard to believe that the extra-parliamentary opposition reflected in student activism and the creation of a new quasi-revolutionary, quasi-anarchist mythology will play more than a marginal role in French politics in the next ten or 15 years, it is nevertheless obvious that French politics, like that of other European nations, is entering upon a new phase.

In an effort to provide a systematic and yet dynamic picture of the development of the French party system, the sections that follow will discuss French parties in the order of their historical appearance on the political scene. Limitations of space do not permit as full a discussion of each party as that given to the three parties of England, and some of the smaller parties will receive rather short shrift.

2. THE JACOBIN LEFT

The contemporary Radical Socialist Party of France (*Parti républicain radical et radical socialiste*) developed historically as the left wing of French liberalism. Like a number of other French parties, it has split and regrouped with sufficient frequency that any discussion of the party must, on some occasions at least, refer to the multiplicity of closely related factions which make up the

TABLE 11.4. FREQUENCY OF NEWSPAPER READING FOR
POLITICAL INFORMATION

	France 1958	United States 1960
Regularly	18%	44%
Often	10	12
From time to time	29	16
Rarely	21	7
Never	22	21

Adapted from Converse and Dupeux, "Politicization in France and the United States, p. 6. Reprinted by permission.

TABLE 11.5. FRENCHMEN'S REASONS FOR SUPPORTING A POLITICAL PARTY

	P.C.F.	S.F.I.O.	Radicals	M.R.P.	Inde-pendents	R.P.F.
Defense of one's interests	28%	24%	27%	22%	30%	11%
Desire to work for progress	7	6	11	2	9	5
Association with those who have the same ideas	1	2	3	6	3	5
Loyalty to class	2	1	4	3	2	1
To shape the future of France and of the world	4	7	11	13	24	33
To work for the country	32	28	18	27	17	23
To build a new society	19	17	13	20	9	14
No response	7	15	13	7	6	8

Adapted from Pierre Fougeyrollas, *La conscience politique dans la France contemporaine* (Paris: Éditions Denoël,
1963), p. 100. Reprinted by permission.

"radical" family rather than be limited exclusively to the Radical Party itself.[6]

The radical tradition in France traces its
origins to the Jacobins of the French Revolution. The Jacobin clubs represented in
embryo form the beginnings of an organized
political party. Throughout the nineteenth
century, however, like every other political
tendency in France, radicalism also remained
merely that—a tendency. From time to time

groups such as Masonic lodges developed the
rudiments of a political organization, but, for
the most part, the politics of radicalism revolved about personalities and parliamentary
cliques.

The term "radical" did not become an
actual part of the French political vocabulary
until about 1830, when it was used to describe opponents of the monarchy who were
unwilling to compromise with their republican ideals. These "radicals" combined a
faith in universal suffrage with violent anticlericalism, a fervent belief in education and

[6] Most commentators on the French political scene
use the terms "Radical Party" and "Radical-Socialist
Party" interchangeably.

MAP 11.3. THE LEFT IN 1849

*Proportion of Vote Cast for Democratic Socialist Candidates
to the Legislative Assembly, May 13, 1849*

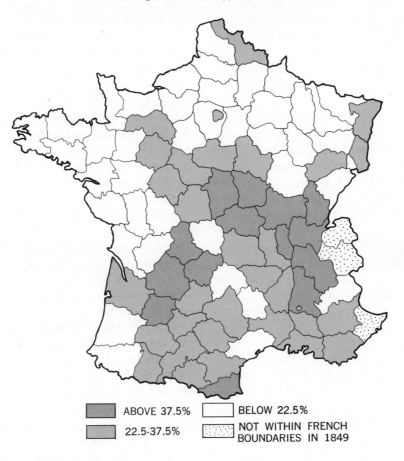

	ABOVE 37.5%		BELOW 22.5%
	22.5-37.5%		NOT WITHIN FRENCH BOUNDARIES IN 1849

Adapted from Michael Stead, "Four Elections of 1965,"
Government and Opposition, 3 (May, 1966), p. 326.
Reprinted by permission of the publisher.

science, civil liberties, and, somewhat later, strong opposition to imperialism. In essence their program was liberal; but whereas in England, Whigs and radicals remained in the same political camp and eventually transformed themselves into the Liberal Party, French liberalism split into two irreconcilable political entities. The right wing of the tradition—Orléanism and later moderate republicanism—was willing to compromise with the monarchy and the church. Such was the bitterness of the conflict over these institutions, however, that the left wing of the liberal tradition found it almost impossible to work with the right except on a de facto basis. The whigs saw radicalism as opening the way to mob violence and mob rule, and the radicals saw French whiggery as essentially a reactionary force.

From the fall of the empire in 1870 to

the beginning of the twentieth century, radicals were returned to Parliament in increasing numbers. In 1901, the two major radical groups, the Republican Radicals and the Socialist Radicals, fused to form the Radical Republican and Radical Socialist Party, thus becoming the largest political party in the Chamber of Deputies. In 1910 the Radicals received 38 per cent of the popular vote, the largest they were ever to attain, but by that time they had seen most of their program enacted into law: all forms of government censorship had been abolished, church and state separated, compulsory primary education laws passed, and a mildly progressive income tax adopted. Other parts of the program were forgotten, however, as the Radicals became the governing party. For example, their hostility to both the military and imperialism diminished, and their original commitment to abolish the Senate was abandoned. Radicals had become so entrenched in the upper house that they no longer regarded it as a threat to republican liberties.

By World War I the bases of Radical electoral strength had begun to shift. Initially, the various radical tendencies had derived considerable support from urban workers. However, the rise of Socialist parties sapped the strength of Radicals in these areas. Further, the middle classes of the large cities began to move to the right, even as workers left the Radical Party. Increasingly, the center of Radical power was to be found among the middle class of small towns and villages—schoolteachers, shopkeepers, country doctors, and lawyers who acted as the spokesmen for the inarticulate peasantry. These groups were often extremely hostile to the new industrial society; they feared and distrusted the "socialism" of the rapidly growing cities.

Thus, the Radical Party was drawn in two directions at once. Its individualism and egalitarianism, as well as its general rhetoric, led its members to want to join in coalitions with the Socialists and later with the Commu-

nists. On the other hand, its belief in the sanctity of petty-bourgeois private property and the virtues of rural peasant France pushed it to the right. During the period between the two world wars, it vacillated between these positions. Indeed, the Radical came to be described as a man whose heart is on the left but whose pocketbook is on the right; he has also been compared to a radish: red on the outside but white within, and best taken with a grain of salt. When danger from the left appeared paramount, or when Radicals believed that prudent fiscal policies were required, they allied themselves with the right. Yet in 1934, when the republic was in danger, they joined a popular front with the Socialists and Communists, only to bring the government down over its social policies. Deeply in favor of appeasement—it was the peasantry that had provided the bulk of the soldiers in World War I and that had suffered most—they supported both Munich and Pétain. The Radicals were opposed to "excessive" state intervention, either for social reform or modernization, and opposed to the new industrialized society in general; to many, the Radicals seemed to look neither to the left nor to the right, but to the past.

It is, of course, difficult to speak of the Radical Party as a unit, for it remained, throughout the whole period, a loosely organized cadre organization. Local notables dominated the regional organizations, and Radical parliamentarians accepted no discipline but that of their own consciences or interests, or those of their constituents. Every political view—from unreconstructed laissez faire to reformist liberalism, from peasant Jacobinism to acceptance of the need to modernize French life—thrived within the party. In general, however, the Radicals resembled most closely the American progressives: their small-town, antiurban attitudes could give rise to an intransigent liberalism on some issues, while on others they were extremely conservative. They were an authentic part of the liberal tradition, but

MAP 11.4. THE LEFT IN 1936

*Proportion of Vote Cast for Popular Front Candidates
to the Chamber of Deputies, April 26, 1936*

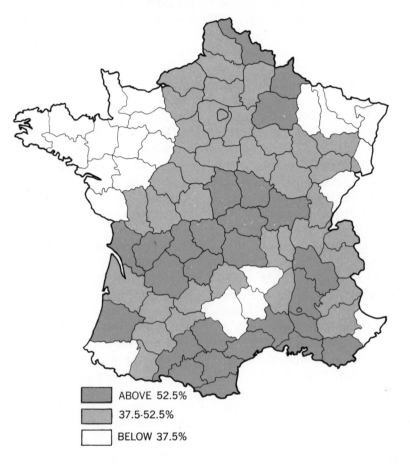

ABOVE 52.5%

37.5-52.5%

BELOW 37.5%

Adapted from Stead, "Four Elections," p. 327. Reprinted by permission.

their peasant and small-town base inhibited even a partial adjustment to changing problems.

The position of the Radicals, however, was not without its advantages, and even though their popular vote continued to fall during the interwar period, their parliamentary representation and influence remained considerable. By 1936, their proportion of the popular vote had dropped to 14.6 per cent, behind both the Socialists with twenty per cent and the Communists with 15.4 per cent. Even so, the combined representation in Parliament of the party and the various Radical splinter groups was much more substantial than either of the other two parties. As a result, the Radicals, finding it relatively easy to form coalitions with either the right or the left, participated in almost every government, and provided a far larger proportion of premiers than their strength would seem to have warranted. Not committed to a rigid ideological position, and more oriented to office than to policy, the Radical politician came to personify the deputy of the Third Republic: intelligent, sensitive, willing to listen to diverse points of view, and popular with all—a man with a sense of proportion, and the most acceptable, or least unacceptable, candidate for the premiership. The Radical was, in other words, the perfect broker in a political situation fraught with ideological discord.

It was the close identification of the party with the Third Republic that partly explains its weakness in the postwar period. In the 1945 elections, the Radicals received only 11 per cent of the popular vote. In the first elections under the Fifth Republic, their percentage dropped to less than eight on the second ballot, and in 1962 it fell to seven. The role of the Radicals in the Fourth Republic was very similar to that in the Third. Of the 19 premiers who served from 1946 to 1958, 11 came from the Radical Party or closely allied groups. And during the entire twelve-year period, Radical politicians moved back and forth among the parties, collaborating first with the Communist and Socialist parties and later with the Gaullists and the conservatives.

By 1956, however, it had become clear to many Radicals that unless they reoriented both their organization and their program, they were doomed as an effective political party. For a short time the party was led by Pierre Mendès-France, who attempted to remake it into a more modern, disciplined organization that would have a broader popular appeal. He also attempted to create an image of a party dedicated to economic modernization and social reform—in short, a pragmatic party of the left. For a time, it looked as though Mendès-France might succeed; such was the enthusiasm generated by his efforts that party membership doubled and the Radicals' vote between 1951 and 1956 jumped from 11.2 per cent to 13.4 per

cent. But the prospect of further success was foreclosed; the ultimate result of Mendès-France's campaign was a renewed split of the party, and, eventually, his own defeat. For all practical purposes, he was expelled from the party in 1958 for refusing to accept party directives. Having been converted to a pragmatic, non-Marxist socialism, he joined one of the myriad little Socialist splinter parties that forever form and re-form in France.

The Radical Party never recovered from the collapse in 1958 of Mendès-France's efforts to bind and rebuild it. A partial reconciliation between its left and right wings occurred after his expulsion, and the weight of the party came to stand somewhat left of center. But on the whole its members refused to engage in a head-on clash with de Gaulle until the Algerian question had been resolved. After 1962, however, the Radical Party came out strongly in opposition to the regime, although it continued to be in constant turmoil as to just how to oppose it. In 1964 and 1965 the Radicals appeared to be on the verge of joining with the Socialists and the Popular Republican Movement (*Mouvement républicain populaire*—M.R.P.) to support presidential candidate Gaston Defferre, the Socialist mayor of Marseilles, against de Gaulle. When this maneuver fell through, the party entered into an alliance with the Socialists to form the Federation of the Democratic and Socialist Left (*Fédération de la gauche démocrate et socialiste*—F.G.D.S.) behind the candidacy of François Mitterrand, the leader of one of those small splinter parties between the left wing of the Radical Party and the Socialist Party. The federation continued its activities through the 1967 and 1968 elections, entering into an alliance with the Communist Party whereby it was agreed that all parties would withdraw their candidates on the second ballot in favor of the strongest candidate on the left. In the 1967 elections, the tactic worked and the number of parliamentary seats won by the parties composing the federation increased from 105 to 116. The 1968 elections, however, were a debacle for the federation, which lost 61 seats. It is impossible to determine precisely how the Radicals themselves fared in either election, but there is not much doubt that many traditional Radical voters were disturbed by the alliance with the Communists and that some of them left the fold.

In the aftermath of the 1968 election, the federation collapsed under the impact of mutual recriminations. The Radicals refused to join with the Socialists in the formation of a new political party, and many supported Senate president Alain Poher's candidacy for the presidency in 1969 against Pompidou. Whatever the fate of efforts to increase the unity of the left, however, the days of radicalism are numbered. Like the liberal parties in all European countries, it belongs to the past.

STRUCTURE, POWER, POLICY: The Radicals are a loosely organized cadre party. Coordination between parliamentarians and the party outside Parliament has always been minimal. So, too, has coordination among parliamentarians and among local party federations. To the Radicals' natural distrust of discipline have been added the pressures and opportunities of a fragmented, multi-party system, and the temptations and opportunities for acquiring office through political maneuvering.

The primary local unit of the party is the committee. A number of these are grouped into departmental and regional federations; the committees are completely self-sufficient and the federations enjoy full independence in choosing candidates and determining electoral tactics. Membership is open to individuals, organizations, and newspapers that support the party's program. Both the local committees and the federations send delegates—on the basis of one per hundred members—to the National Congress, theoretically the key decision-making body for the party. Other voting delegates to the National Congress, which normally meets

every year in a city selected by the previous congress, include newspaper editors affiliated with the party and members of the National Executive Committee. Until 1959, the federations were responsible for membership lists, so that a fair allocation of seats was next to impossible. In fact, various factions always tried to hold the annual congress in cities where they were strong so that their supporters could more easily attend. Furthermore, faction leaders bought membership cards for distribution to sympathizers. The inception of a national party register in 1959 was supposed to add a bit of rationality to delegate representation, but there is little evidence that it has done so.

The National Congress writes the party program; hardly anyone, however, pays attention to it. The congress also elects the party president, but not the party's Executive Committee or its Bureau, both of which work with the party president in determining policy between congresses. The Executive Committee consists of two hundred members of the Bureau, parliamentarians, and federation chairmen. It meets six times a year and, although its influence is quite limited, the committee "decides" such issues as whether or not the party should support a particular government. The Bureau meets every week and is responsible for such activities as approving candidates for office, although it usually simply endorses nominees of the local organization.

As already indicated, the national organization has little control over the parliamentary party. Radical members of Parliament have voted on all sides of every issue; they have also been responsible for overthrowing Radical prime ministers, and they have joined parliamentary intergroups with other parties, such as the Gaullists, without fear of being disciplined. In fact, there is not really a Radical Party in Parliament in any meaningful sense of the term.

The party had a nominal membership of some eighty to one hundred thousand before World War II. During most of the postwar period, membership has ranged from 35 to fifty thousand, except for the short Mendiste period when it rose to 90 thousand, bringing into the party, for the first time, young technically trained people who represented "modern" France. By 1959, however, party membership had fallen back to twenty thousand and, once again, the Radicals were the representatives of small-town, nineteenth-century France.

3. THE TRADITIONAL RIGHT

The right in France has historically included a potpourri of political beliefs—the "ultras" of the Restoration, the quasi-Fascist leagues of the 1930's, the Orléanists of the 1850's, and the moderates of the turn of the century. Before the Third Republic was established, the moderate republicans could have been considered part of the liberal tradition. But once the Radicals emerged, and later the Socialists, they became increasingly identified with right-wing positions despite leadership and ideological differences.

Attempts were made, all of them abortive, to organize the political right during the 1920's and 1930's, but there was, properly speaking, no conservative party in France until after World War II. One reason for this was because all conservative factions tended to distrust mass organization as smacking of mob rule. In addition, old right-wing ideological nuances, and the social conditions that sustained them, did not—as they did in England—give way as new groups moved to the right. Thus, as late as the 1930's, France contained a right wing that still lamented the fall of the monarchy and had aspirations of restoring at least some elements of "traditional" France. It was this group, whose social base lay with old aristocratic families, elements of the military, and traditional commerce, that provided much of the impetus for the Vichy experiment. There was also a right that was republican, albeit not enthusiastically so: committed to economic laissez faire but also to modernization.

Further complicating the conservatives' disarray was a right closely tied to and supporting the Catholic Church as well as a right that was indifferent to the church except as it provided protection against radicalism and rule by the masses. Quite understandably, then, all the various conservative groups found it very difficult to unite except on an ad hoc basis.

Finally, with a multi-party system and a government that could not govern, most members of Parliament who conceived of themselves as being on the right could and did depend largely upon their contacts with the bureaucracy to secure favors for themselves and their constituents. In this sense, French conservatives did not organize as a party because they did not have to; so long as the nation remained politically fragmented, they could achieve their goals through other means. It was only during the Fourth Republic that circumstances prompted some real attempts to establish an organized conservative party. The effort was a failure, partly because the potential constituency of the conservatives was pre-empted by de Gaulle.

Most right-wing politicians were discredited at the time of the Liberation because of their general association with Vichy. Those remaining set about organizing what they hoped would be the great conservative party of the Fourth Republic, the Republican Party of Liberty (*Parti républicain de la liberté* —P.R.L.). However, the P.R.L. neither built up an effective organization nor acquired a popular following. Along with a number of other conservative groupings, a loose holding company was formed in 1948, the National Center of Independents and Peasants (*Centre national des indépendents et paysans*—C.N.I.P.). In 1951 the Independents received 12.3 per cent of the vote, and shortly thereafter Antoine Pinay, a conservative, was elected premier with the support of 27 dissident Gaullists who had broken with the Rally of the French People to form the Republican and Social Action

(*Action républicaine et sociale*—A.R.S.). The A.R.S. cooperated closely with the C.N.I.P. and finally joined it in 1954, after de Gaulle had dissolved the R.P.F. In the 1956 election, the new combination received 14.4 per cent of the popular vote, and formed a single conservative group in the National Assembly. Led by Pinay, this new combination represented the greatest unity the parliamentary right had ever achieved.

In 1958 the Independents reached the peak of their growth. Supporting the new regime and, thus, riding on de Gaulle's coattails, the C.N.I.P. obtained nearly twenty per cent of the vote on the first ballot and almost 24 per cent on the second. With 132 seats in the assembly, they ranked second only to de Gaulle's Union for a New Republic (*Union pour la nouvelle république*— U.N.R.). Moreover, Antoine Pinay returned to power as finance minister in de Gaulle's cabinet.

The internal unity of the conservatives and their delight with de Gaulle was not to last very long. They split with him on four crucial issues: Algeria, which they favored retaining; economic policies, which led to Pinay's resignation; the power of the National Assembly, which they did not wish to see curbed; and France's ties to the Atlantic Alliance, which they wanted maintained. The Algerian question, in fact, brought to the fore a temporary coalition of some C.N.I.P. members with ultra-rightists that might have imposed a military dictatorship had it been able to mobilize enough power.

By 1962 the C.N.I.P. had split into three factions, and in the parliamentary elections of that year, the conservative percentage of the popular vote dropped to 13.9. Only 48 Independents were returned to Parliament, largely because of Gaullist support. Most of these formed a parliamentary group called the Independent Republicans (*Républicains indépendents*) which, under the leadership of Valéry Giscard d'Estaing, supported de Gaulle on crucial issues, yet tried to retain at least some independence. For the most part,

members of this faction ran for office with the support of the Gaullists in both the 1967 and the 1968 elections; today, they are less a party than a collection of notables who rely upon local contacts for their election. The rump of the C.N.I.P. endorsed Jean Lecanuet, president of the M.R.P., for the presidency in 1965, and then effectively disintegrated as an organization, some of its members joining the Democratic Center (basically, the old M.R.P.), while others continued to run as Independents.

Some conservatives, of course, hope eventually to cash in on the expected collapse of the Gaullist movement now that the general no longer occupies the Elysée Palace. The party supported Pompidou in 1969, in return for which the Independent Republican leader Giscard d'Estaing was appointed minister of economic affairs and finance. The party's future will depend very much on its ability to work out a political relationship with the U.D.R., for traditional French conservatism, even in its somewhat modernized form, has passed into eclipse.

Despite the efforts of Roger Duchet, the founder of the C.N.I.P. and its general secretary during most of the Fourth Republic, the Independents remained, and remain still, the least organized of the major parties. After 1954 they began to hold national congresses for the purpose of formulating some sort of common program. Control of the C.N.I.P., however, was retained by its parliamentary leadership, which was composed primarily of local notables whose ties with constituents were direct. Thus, while the party label did prove of some assistance in the 1956 elections, it was never sufficient to make or break a candidate.

Before 1939, the strongholds of conservatism had been in the Catholic west, the eastern frontier departments, and the Massif Central. In the Fifth Republic, however, the M.R.P. and even the U.N.R. have drawn off many voters whose support of the Independents had been based primarily on religious conviction. In comparison with the Gaullists, the Independents have received a much larger proportion of their vote from less industrialized areas. Their leadership has also come principally from rural and small-town France, and their parliamentary representation has always included more peasants than any other parliamentary group. Traditional conservatism had never been averse to extensive government intervention in the economy; in fact, as already indicated, the social policies of the Vichy regime helped pave the way for greater participation by the state in the Fourth and Fifth Republics. However, dominated by rural and traditional bourgeois elements, the outlook of the Independents has tended to be Malthusian and defensive, conceiving the state as primarily designed to protect their vested interests; their major objective has been to hold on to what they have. Here they have been in sharp contrast with the Gaullists, who, in terms of national policy, have been dominated by technocrats dedicated to the principle of authority but also to policies that have as their purpose the modernization of France and the creation of a social-welfare state.

Traditional antirepublicanism of the Vichy stripe all but expired with the Liberation. Since then, the base for the kind of conservatism represented by the Independents has been narrowing. Although de Gaulle's Rally of the French People was considered antiparliamentary and right-wing by many on the left when it first appeared, only two really right-wing political groupings have emerged in France since World War II—and both have proved ephemeral. In 1956 the Union and French Fraternity (*Union et fraternité française*—U.F.F.) received almost 12 per cent of the vote; two years later it had all but disappeared. In 1965 Jean-Louis Tixier-Vignancour, a prominent right-wing lawyer, received some five per cent of the vote on the first presidential ballot, but he was unable to create a political organization. The votes of the U.F.F. came primarily from

peasants and shopkeepers in some of France's declining rural areas, while Tixier-Vignancour capitalized on the hostility which European refugees from Algeria felt toward de Gaulle. If a genuine conservative, non-Gaullist party is to emerge, then, it will have to take on many of the economic and social policies associated with de Gaulle. It will have to be oriented toward a dynamic rather than toward a static France. It seems unlikely that the Independents can provide the base from which such a party can grow.

4. THE DECLINE OF THE SOCIALIST LEFT

Socialist ideas and even a Socialist political faction in France can be traced back to the French Revolution. Later, Saint-Simon, Fourier, and Proudhon contributed greatly to Marx's intellectual development. An organized Socialist Party did not really begin to surface, however, until the 1870's and 1880's, when an atmosphere of relative freedom and the pace of industrialization opened the way for the political organization of the working class. In France, unlike England, revolutionary Marxism was an integral part of Socialist thinking from the very beginning, although non-Marxist elements—anarchist and syndicalist—also developed revolutionary theories. Again, unlike their English counterparts, none of these left-wing movements was able to establish a close relationship with the trade-union movement. French trade-union leaders distrusted "bourgeois" politicians and preferred to concentrate on their own programs of direct action.

By the end of the century, two Socialist groups, among the multiplicity that existed, established their predominance: a revolutionary Marxist party headed by Jules Guesde, and a reformist group, still heavily Marxist, led by Jean Jaurès. In 1905 the two factions merged, along with a number of other splinter groups, to form a unified Socialist Party, the French Section of the Workers' International (*Section française de l'internationale ouv-*

rière—S.F.I.O.). It was the first mass party to form in France. The agreements reached at the unity conference were sufficiently vague to conceal factional disagreements; they consisted primarily of a series of compromises designed to include all Socialist positions. For instance, parliamentary action was agreed to be necessary in order to please the reformers, but to please the revolutionaries it was agreed that ultimately the transition to a Socialist society would probably require violence. There was, however, general agreement that Socialists would not enter a bourgeois ministry and that bourgeois governments would be supported only under exceptional circumstances.

On the eve of World War I, the reformists in the French Socialist Party, as in the German, seemed to be winning out over the more revolutionary elements. The party now could count on some 16 per cent of the popular vote, largely concentrated among the industrial workers in the north and around Paris—but also including those peasants in the south who had traditionally voted left, and even some agricultural workers. The First World War and its aftermath, however, wrought profound changes within the Socialist movement. The number of militants in the S.F.I.O. skyrocketed and in the first postwar elections the Socialists received approximately 25 per cent of the popular vote. Once again, the mood of the party was clearly revolutionary. At its 1920 conference, despite appeals by some of its most important leaders, the majority of the militants voted to join Lenin's Third International and formed the French Communist Party. The minority delegates walked out, and it was they who took on the task of reconstructing a "Socialist" party. They had, however, lost to the Communists some of the most brilliant of the younger S.F.I.O. members, a sizable portion of the party's treasury, and control of *L'Humanité,* the party newspaper founded by Jaurès.

Under the leadership of Léon Blum, however, the job of rebuilding the S.F.I.O.

seemed to meet with a good deal of success. The Socialist proportion of the popular vote rose from eight to 18 per cent between 1924 and 1928, and the organization of the party was considerably tightened. The success of Blum's endeavors had much to do with the change in the party's appeal—and clientele. Increasingly, its strength was coming from white-collar workers and teachers, as well as peasants, who now considered the Socialists to be more advanced than the Radicals and yet reasonably safe. Simultaneously, of course, the party was losing much of its working-class support to the better organized and more actively militant Communist Party.

The shift in supporters was closely associated with the continuing reformist orientation within the Socialist Party, despite the rhetorical militancy that characterized it during the period of the Popular Front of the 1930's, a political alliance of Socialists, Communists, and Radicals devised to save the republic from what they considered to be a Fascist threat. The victory of the Popular Front in the 1936 elections led to the formation of a government headed by Blum. The front ended with the defection of the Radicals and, later, the refusal of the Communists to support the war against Germany after the Nazi-Soviet pact. The Socialists and Communists did, however, draw together again in a new "alliance against fascism" after the Nazi attack upon the Soviet Union.

Cooperation between the Socialists and the Communists continued in the early postwar period. Given the record of the Communists in the resistance movement and the prestige of the Soviet Union at that time, Blum and others were unable to get the party to reconsider its Marxist slogans in terms of contemporary realities, and the more militant cadres won control of the party's machinery. As the cold war grew in intensity, however, the Communist and Socialist alliance again fell apart, and the Communists were driven from the government with Socialist approval. By this time, however, the Communists had come to dominate the trade-union movement, forcing many workers of a Socialist but non-Communist bent to set up a rival organization.

By 1949 it was evident that, except for certain regions of France, the Socialists could no longer claim to speak for the working class. The discipline and effectiveness of Communist organization, as well as the greater capacity of the Communists to organize militant activities to satisfy immediate working-class demands, had dissipated Socialist strength among the workers.

The organizational defects and fading power of the Socialist Party eventually caused it to be confronted with a dilemma —whether or not to take part in coalition governments with bourgeois political parties. Failure to do so could have meant not only the impossibility of any government being tolerable to them, but the distinct possibility of either a Communist or Gaullist regime. Since the Socialists considered de Gaulle to be, at the very least, a semi-Fascist, they found themselves pushed into forming coalitions with parties far more conservative than themselves and taking the responsibility for conservative policies over which they had little control. Their excuse was that they had at least preserved the great reforms enacted in 1945 and 1946, including nationalization and expanded social services.[7] In 1951 the Socialists finally split with the M.R.P. and other parties over the issue of aid to religious schools and went into opposition. Yet this issue merely precipitated the break: it was the Socialists' belief that the Gaullist threat had ended that really encouraged the party to strike out on its own. Now the Socialists could safely criticize the government's "reactionary," "clerical" policies and, perhaps, pick up some of the working-class votes they had lost to the Communist Party.

The party's new position as critic of the "system," however, failed to halt the decline in the number of its militants. In eight years, the party lost two-thirds of its dues-paying

members, claiming a total of only 113,000 in 1954. Partly out of fear of losing even more working-class votes to the Communists, the Socialist Party refused to accept the argument of some of its members that what was required to stem disaffection was a more pragmatic program based on twentieth-century realities in a postcapitalist society.

In 1956, the electoral fortunes of the Socialist Party improved slightly, especially in industrial areas, but it was now subject to new strains—the Algerian conflict and, later, the re-emergence of Gaullism. After bitter internal wrangling, the party, under the leadership of its secretary general, Guy Mollet, decided in 1958 to support de Gaulle. This support continued, with growing reservations, until 1961, when the parliamentary party voted unanimously in favor of a motion of censure against the de Gaulle government. In 1962, the Socialists opposed de Gaulle on the question of the popular election of the president, and, in the legislative elections, made some local agreements with the Communists on the second ballot, although they refused the call of the Communist Party for united action in all constituencies. They received 12.7 per cent of the vote on the first ballot and 15.2 per cent on the second, and suddenly the Socialists were the largest antigovernment party in the legislature. Nevertheless, their proportion of the vote was smaller than in 1958, and the number of party militants had fallen below 85,000.

For the next three years, the Socialists searched for some basis for a new party alignment preparatory to the 1965 presidential election. After flirting with a broad alliance of every political party except de Gaulle's U.N.R. and the Communists, they seemed about to join in a coalition, including the Radicals and the M.R.P., behind the candidacy of Defferre, a leader of the party's more pragmatic wing; but they were kept from doing so by the hostility of Mollet and some of the M.R.P. leaders to such a coalition and by the rekindling of the clerical issue. The Socialists eventually aligned them-

---

[7] For a discussion of those reforms, see Chapter 24.

selves with a segment of the Radical Party—
and the Communists—behind Mitterrand.
The Federation of the Democratic and Socialist Left, which emerged out of the election, continued to function through the 1967
and 1968 legislative elections.

After the 1968 elections, the Federation
fell apart, and the S.F.I.O. and the Radicals
negotiated between themselves on a full
merger of the two parties, the Russian invasion of Czechoslovakia having dampened
relations between the Socialists and the Radicals on the one side and the Communists on
the other. The Radicals, however, refused to
merge with the Socialists, and the S.F.I.O.
then linked up with a loose federation of left-
wing political clubs in a plan to form a new
Parti socialiste. The renovation maneuver
had little effect on the fortunes of the Socialists, however; the Socialist candidate for the
1969 presidential elections, who was again
Defferre, received only five per cent of the
vote on the first ballot. In the meantime, Socialist Party militants continue to drop away,
and the average age of the party's leadership
goes on rising.

In 1958 a small group of Socialists broke
away from the S.F.I.O. on the question of
supporting de Gaulle. They were eventually
joined by others who opposed Mollet. Out
of this mélange came the Unified Socialist
Party (*Parti socialiste unifié*—P.S.U.), dedicated, again, to unity of the left. In the 1967
elections the P.S.U. won 2.2 per cent of the
vote and elected three deputies. In 1968 it
distinguished itself as the only political party
with national pretensions to give its unqualified support to the rebellious students. While
its vote in the election rose to almost four per
cent, the increase was caused primarily by its
running candidates in more districts than it
had in previous elections. Actually, its vote
per candidate dropped sharply and it lost its
three parliamentary representatives. It also
lost Pierre Mendès-France, who resigned as
the party's leader after an unsuccessful bid
to regain his seat in the assembly. Con-

stantly splintering and resplintering, the
P.S.U. is not likely to become a major political organization.

STRUCTURE, POWER, AND POLICY: Like all
European Socialist parties, the S.F.I.O. was
organized from the very beginning as a mass
party. Its basic operating unit is the section,
which may be regarded as the equivalent of
the constituency organization of British parties. However, while France is now divided
into about 470 electoral districts, the party
section is based on the commune—communes, as well as departments, being the
fundamental administrative units in France.
Theoretically, every commune has one section, but in fact there are only about eight
thousand sections in France as against 36,000
communes. A section has no fixed membership, varying in size from as few as twenty
members to more than a thousand. Membership is determined by the purchase of a permanent card, an annual voucher, and
monthly stamps. Local organizations are free
to set membership fees.

The sections of a given department form a
federation which meets annually to select an
executive and, on the basis of proportional
representation, to elect representatives to the
National Congress which meets at least once
a year. Motions to be considered at the National Congress are submitted to federations
in advance, so that members may discuss
them and be prepared to take a position.
Most federations split their votes in proportion to the sentiments expressed at federation
meetings; however, some of the larger working-class federations rely upon a bloc vote, a
device that tends to increase their influence.
In fact, the few large federations—such as
the Pas de Calais and Nord, which have
more than ten thousand members—can dominate the National Congress if they stand
together.

The congress supposedly defines the doctrinal and tactical positions of the party. Between congresses, authority to decide issues
of policy and tactics rests with the National

Council made up of one delegate from each federation who has a vote proportional to his federation's membership. The National Congress also elects a 45-member executive committee, of which no more than twenty may be members of Parliament; the committee picks a party secretariat, headed by a general secretary, from its own membership.

The executive committee is entrusted with implanting decisions of both the congress and the council, directing propaganda, keeping party members in line politically, watching the maneuvers of the party's M.P.'s, and with calling special meetings of the congress or council if the need arises. The general secretary, who has, since World War II, usually been a member of Parliament, is the single most powerful figure in the party, combining the functions of director of the party machinery and caucus leader.

The Socialists have always prided themselves on the internal democracy of their party; compared with other French parties the pride is justified. Unfortunately, this internal democracy often borders on anarchy; sections and federations are extremely jealous of their autonomy and prefer lengthy discussions, particularly at banquets, on traditional party principles to practical political work. Congresses are dominated by lower-middle- and middle-class militants who are more interested in nineteenth-century Marxist rhetoric, including anticlericalism, than they are in the real problems of the twentieth century.

As with the British Labor Party, conflicts have often developed between the mass party and the parliamentary party of the S.F.I.O. Time and time again the executive committee, prodded by militants, has threatened to discipline its representatives in Parliament for supporting governments or legislation that it opposed. Members of the assembly have on occasion been expelled from the party and departmental federations disbanded. Even so, the ability of the executive committee, or even the parliamentary party, to punish rebels has been limited both by a political system that encourages the formation of new factions and by a localism that has always granted individual deputies and federations support even when they were disowned by the national organization. Thus, for the most part the Socialists have maintained the facade of organizational unity by temporizing on important issues and by being extremely lenient with party deviants. For example, in 1954 half the parliamentary party defied the executive committee and refused to support the creation of a European Defense Community—and nothing of a disciplinary nature was done about it. On another vote a year later, 17 members of Parliament were expelled for defying party orders; they were, however, hastily readmitted in the face of a forthcoming election. In all, while party discipline has been strong enough to prevent minorities from moving in new ideological directions, the party has been unable to hold people in line when there have been major disagreements over tactics.

Since World War II, the Socialist Party has held less and less appeal for France's youth, probably because of the party's penchant for talk rather than action but also because it wants evidence of long-term loyalty before granting promotions. The average age of party members, one-third of them workers, has been increasing as youth finds the Communist Party and even the U.D.R. more attractive. To a considerable extent, the civil servants in the party—and they include a large number of teachers—have imposed their own conceptions of seniority upon the party's organization. Not only has youth been disenchanted with the Socialist Party, but the party's professional anticlericalism has reduced the number of left-wing Catholics who might join it, and an antifeminist bias has kept the number of women members at a minimum.

Like so many other French political parties, the Socialists are weighed down by a past whose battle cries are no longer applicable. Their Marxist and quasi-revolutionary slogans continue to impede them from appealing to the new professional middle classes and technocrats, and their anticlericalism reduces the possibility of cooperation from and appeal to Catholics interested in social reform. Indeed, like the Radicals, the S.F.I.O. has become essentially a conservative party. The Socialists' anticlerical dogma, their membership in Masonic lodges, and their continued attachment to nineteenth-century catchwords give them an archaic air that is unlikely to bring in new voters or militants. Furthermore, the fact that the party continually compromises its own revolutionary rhetoric for the sake of day-to-day political advantage has led many to believe that, as an organization, it is completely opportunistic. Its divorce from the trade-union movement and its general composition cause it to lack even the Communists' advantage of a reasonably effective bureaucratic machine that does something about working-class needs.

There are many in the Socialist Party who would like to change its direction. Unfortunately, too many of the militants prefer to meet in bistros where they may ruminate about the glories of the past and mistake sweeping generalizations for profound insights.

5. THE COMMUNIST PARTY

The French Communist Party (*Parti communiste français*—P.C.F.) was organized by militants who took control of the Tours Conference of the Socialist Party in 1920. Theoretically, those who joined accepted the rules laid down by the Third International and were amenable to the kind of discipline Lenin considered the sine qua non for successful revolutionary activity.

Actually, the party contained many left-wing anarchists, as well as many militants, who considered themselves disciplined left-wing Marxists but who were essentially unwilling to take orders from any party leadership, much less an international one centered in a "backward" country like Russia. The lack of discipline of party cadres, in fact, was among the most pressing problems faced by the infant organization, a problem compounded by Moscow's demand that the party bolshevize itself by setting up Communist cells in factories. Since such cells exposed workers to the danger of punitive action by employers, the suggestion was not enthusiastically received. Problems of the newly formed party were further complicated by the conflict between Stalin and Trotsky and by Trotsky's eventual expulsion from Soviet leadership; many of the early militants knew Trotsky personally and ardently supported him. And finally, many militants resented what they considered the subordination of the need for a Communist revolution in France to the requirements of Soviet foreign policy.

As a consequence, the P.C.F. split and re-split, purged and repurged itself, during the 1920's—and the number of militants dropped precipitously. Given its own unwillingness to enter into alliances with other parties on the second ballot, and the unwillingness of other parties to ally themselves with the Communists, its parliamentary influence during the decade was also quite limited. While the party received more than 11 per cent of the total vote cast in 1928, it controlled less than two per cent of the seats in the Chamber of Deputies.[8]

Despite these difficulties, the French Communist Party did survive, and strengthened both its electoral and underground organization. Because of its organizational capacity it was able to take full advantage of the movement to the left among voters during the period of the Popular Front; in the elections of 1936, in fact, the P.C.F. received 15 per cent of the popular vote. But the failure of the Popular Front, the Munich crisis, and finally the Nazi-Soviet nonaggression pact resulted

8 During the Third Republic, as in the Fifth, the French used single-member districts and a double ballot. Thus, the number of seats received by a party depended heavily on the alliances it could forge between the first and second ballot. See pp. 298–303, 385.

in considerable diminution of Communist strength—as did the party's attempted collaboration with the Nazis in the first days after the fall of France.

After the German attack on the Soviet Union, the Communist Party took an extremely active role in the Resistance. The efficiency of its underground apparatus and the dedication of its militants gave it a tremendous advantage over other Resistance groups. Its efforts have often been exaggerated, and they were not always rationally directed; nevertheless, the reputation it acquired during the war and the members it recruited while fighting the Germans enhanced both the party's postwar prestige and its strength. It also put to use the chaotic days immediately after the Liberation, eliminating a number of its enemies who were charged with being collaborators.

It is little wonder, then, that the Communists emerged as the largest party in France in the first postwar elections, with 26 per cent of the vote. Collaboration with Vichy had tainted almost all of the traditional parties, as it had, indeed, compromised large segments of the middle class. Consequently, despite its short period of flirtation with the Nazis, the Communist Party represented for a great many all that was noble in the French revolutionary tradition. The number of party militants soared, and the circulation of the party paper, *L'Humanité*, rose to a record 450,000.

The party maintained its strength through the late 1940's. The inability of the Fourth Republic to muster effective policies, the failure of working-class living standards to rise, and the continuance of prickly class differences within French society enabled the Communists to mobilize discontent. And where the party came to dominate municipal governments, its militants proved themselves to be hard workers, dedicated to civic improvement; within the trade-union movement they became effective organizers. With the Socialists functioning as part of the government, the Communists stood as the one major opposition group on the left.

No revolutionary party, however, can maintain a heady level of enthusiasm forever, and as early as 1951 and 1952 there were signs of a growing malaise. The number of militants declined, it became more difficult to organize mass demonstrations, and newspaper circulation began to slip. After 1954, the rising prosperity of the working class resulted in a further lessening of interest on the part of activists, and the party revealed the kind of creakiness that comes from domination by a static bureaucracy. Most of the party's leaders, including its general secretary Maurice Thorez, had been in power for a long time—tied to traditional slogans and outmoded ways of doing things.

All these factors, plus the shocks of Stalin's death and the Hungarian intervention, undoubtedly contributed to a decline in the P.C.F.'s vote. From a 1956 percentage of just under 26, it fell to 18.9 per cent on the first ballot in 1958, and although it rose to nearly 22 per cent of the total votes cast in 1962, it remained almost a million and a half votes shy of its earlier strength.

With the 1962 election, the Communist Party showed signs of regaining its strength—partly because of a resurgent desire by other parties of the left to form a common front against de Gaulle, partly because of the P.C.F.'s own changing image. Although it did not move as far or as quickly as the Italian Communist Party in establishing its independence from Moscow, the French party did come to assert itself on a number of minor issues. It also began, self-consciously, to revise parts of its doctrine in order to assure other political parties that it was no longer committed to the suppression of all non-Communist groups during the transition to communism.

The burnishing of a new image was aided by the general Communist process of "de-Stalinization," a process furthered by the death in 1964 of Maurice Thorez and the subsequent increase in the power of the party's new general secretary, Waldeck Rochet. From 1928 until 1953 the party had been completely subservient to Moscow; as late as 1956, in fact, it had refused to endorse Khrushchev's denunciation of the former dictator. Thorez had been Stalin's choice for the leadership of the French Communist Party and, like his hero, brooked no opposition during his tenure as general secretary. In the year following Thorez's death, the party did not put up its own presidential candidate but supported Mitterrand, and through 1966 and 1967 it worked actively to reach agreements with the Federation of the Democratic and Socialist Left on supporting the strongest left-wing candidate on the second ballot in the legislative elections.

In the elections of 1967, the Communist Party benefited tremendously from its new alliance. Although its percentage of the total vote increased only slightly, it almost doubled its parliamentary representation. Of more importance, the party's image constantly improved. Public-opinion polls indicated an increasing willingness on the part of members of other parties, especially the Socialists, to see Communists in any new government. (See Figure 11.2.) Although the party split with the Socialists and Radicals over its support of the Arabs—echoing Moscow's position during the Arab-Israeli conflict of 1967—this did not prevent continued cooperation with the F.G.D.S. and the issuance of a number of joint statements revealing substantial agreement on domestic economic reforms.

The events of May and June 1968 were as much of a surprise to the Communists as they were to other political parties. After some hesitation, the P.C.F. attacked the leaders of the student uprisings as anarchists, Trotskyites, Maoists, or worse, and argued that a revolutionary situation did not exist in France. Through its control over the C.G.T., the party was instrumental in getting the workers to end their strike once immediate economic demands had been met.

Yet the party's moderation during the 1968 crisis was of little immediate political value, as the election which followed demonstrated. Its percentage of the national vote dropped by two points and it lost more than

half its parliamentary seats. The 1968 election and the Czechoslovakian crisis precipitated a split between the Communists and other parties of the left. In the 1969 presidential elections, the P.C.F. refused to support Defferre and instead ran Jacques Duclos, an old party wheelhorse whose close identification with the Stalin period did not prevent him from doing surprisingly well in the election. The Communists also registered gains among students, but these successes notwithstanding, the party's general public standing had declined. Further, the party itself has been torn internally. While the leadership criticized the Soviet invasion of Czechoslovakia, more conservative elements in the P.C.F. opposed this move. In general, the leadership is divided between those within the party who want to move further in the direction of liberalization, those who want to retain the party's traditional Stalinist orientation, and those who want to create a brandnew revolutionary image, combining elements of anarchism and Maoism.

STRUCTURE, POWER, AND POLICY: The structure of the French Communist Party is patterned after the Soviet mold. With certain national modifications, the French organization generally operates under the Leninist principle of "democratic centralism"—that is, full discussion of all decisions, but full obedience by all elements within the party once a decision is made. The organization is essentially military in form, with control emanating from the top and the key positions filled by co-optation.

The basic unit of the party is the cell, which consists of at least three members. Ideally, a cell should function at a place of work; but the party does permit the organization of basic units by residence, strongly preferred by members, and not more than one-fourth of the urban cells are workplace cells. Directing each cell is a bureau composed of a secretary and a treasurer; the secretary is the chief official, "elected" by the membership of the cell upon the recommendation of the next higher echelon, the sec-

FIGURE 11.2. ATTITUDES TOWARD THE FRENCH COMMUNIST PARTY

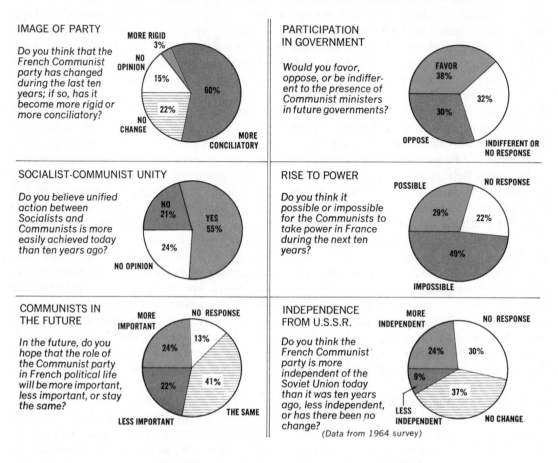

Adapted from *Sondages*, no. 1, 1966, pp. 65–67; no. 4, 1964, p. 178. Reprinted by permission of the publisher.

tion—a grouping of cells with "a common direction and a common activity." Again, the key section officer is the secretary; he is chosen by higher-level officials and is assisted by specialized party workers, such as agents for propaganda and for women's work, who share responsibility for the activities of the section.

Elected from each of the sections in a given department are federation members. These federations—one for each of France's 95 departments—are ultimately responsible for the party's activities on the departmental level and are dominated by a secretariat composed of full-time salaried bureaucrats who have made a career of party work. The party tries to recruit persons of working-class background for these posts; in order to prevent departmental sclerosis, it rotates staff members among federations.

The National Congress of the Communist Party, which usually meets every three years, is composed of delegates from the membership, usually section and federation officers. Early congresses were often characterized by bitter debate, but from 1928 until recently the party's leadership has transformed them into paradigms of dullness. The congress "elects" a central committee, which in turn selects from its own members a politburo and a secretariat. The actual direction of the P.C.F. is in the hands of the secretariat, and more particularly the general secretary—despite some recent tendencies toward liberalization.

Lines of communication in the party are hierarchical; direct contact between sections or federations, except as directed by the politburo, is discouraged. The rate of turnover at the top level has been extremely slow, and generally has been the result of purging members who for some reason broke with the party line. Thorez, for example, remained general secretary from 1936 until he was incapacitated by illness just before his death in 1964.

The politburo completely dominates Communist candidates elected to the National Assembly. It approves the parliamentary party's choice of officers, has a veto over all decisions made by the parliamentary party, and gives instructions in advance on all important matters. Every Communist candidate for election to the National Assembly must agree in advance to resign if called upon to do so by the party. He also turns his full salary over to the party and receives in return the equivalent of a skilled worker's wage. Party leaders and officials have usually found seats in Parliament, but because of the secondary importance assigned parliamentary activity, Communist parliamentarians have not been among the most dynamic people in the organization, a circumstance that has contributed to the party's ability to control its parliamentary delegation.

In addition to the General Confederation of Labor,[9] the party controls a variety of other mass organizations. One of the most vocal is the Union of French Women, which replicates the party in structure and which publishes both a weekly and a monthly journal. The Communists have, in fact, been extremely successful in recruiting female militants. Communist youth groups include Young Farmers, Young Communists, Girls

of France, and Communist Students. The party also controls a Workers' Sports and Gymnastics Federation, a National Union of Aged Workers, a Federation of Tenants, and various organizations for the "defense of peace." "Progressive" non-Communists are welcomed into all of these groups and many of the organizations are regarded as mechanisms for party recruitment. They are also part of an attempt by the party to create a "total" environment for its members, one which not only protects them from the "corrupting" influences of the larger community but which works to establish the kind of attitudes necessary for the creation of a new society.

Finally, the party maintains a number of commercial organizations that either earn money for the party or perform necessary services. One of these is La Banque Commerciale Pour l'Europe du Nord, the majority of whose personnel are party members, thus insuring secrecy with respect to the party's financial transactions. The P.C.F. also runs publishing houses for its literature, among them Editions Sociales, Le Cercle d'Art, and Le Chant du Monde, a music printing and recording company. In addition to a publicity office and a printing press for posters and political tracts, the P.C.F. operates many bookstores and a distribution center for its books and magazines. This represents an impressive array of auxiliary commercial props; by owning its own separate channels for the dissemination of propaganda, the P.C.F. is never dependent upon elements that are likely to be hostile to its program.

The Communist Party has, in the past, exhibited a great capacity for attracting a solid core of dedicated militants among both the working class and intellectuals of middle-class background. Those who have entered the party have done so for a variety of reasons, not the least of which, in the case of workers, has been the sense of comradeship offered by work in the local organization. As one ex-Communist worker put it:

[9] For a discussion of the party's relations with the C.G.T., see Chapter 5, pp. 172–173.

What makes for the cohesion of the cell is that there is no leader. It is a democratic organization of completely equal men. The secretary is really elected; he is not a superior, but the member of a homogeneous group. . . . The man who enters the Party enters a real democratic community in his cell, where he feels friendship and mutual confidence. He feels good, that is, as long as he subordinates everything to his duties as a militant. If he is curious and asks himself the whys and hows, then he quickly becomes ill at ease and sooner or later leaves the party.[10]

Very often, those of working-class background who enter the party have very little real comprehension of Marxist theory. Once they have entered, however, they gradually find themselves surrounded only by party members. They are encouraged to bring their families to party meetings, to read only party publications, and to associate primarily with party members. In a real sense they become part of a religious community, so that fairly soon, especially if they have become part of the paid bureaucracy and have entered the class of white-collar workers, a break with the party would involve a psychological wrench of considerable magnitude. Once this stage has been reached, it is possible for the leadership to take all sorts of steps without fear that a member will react negatively or question its authority, for the psychological strain of doing so would be too great. As a consequence of all these circumstances, it becomes possible for the working-class party member to retain a highly distorted picture of the society around him, to continue to insist that the living standards of his class are falling, when, in fact, the objective evidence points quite the other way.

For the intellectual, disoriented in a society that seems to lack a fundamental basis for value commitments, the Communist Party also provides a leap into faith—an escape from the terrible responsibilities of free choice. Many existentialists, including Sartre himself, have embraced the party's goals, if not the party itself. The P.C.F. also offers intellectuals the possibility of power in a society which, while it may flatter them, still tenders the most responsible positions to businessmen and technicians trained in practical spheres.

The French Communist Party has benefited in its recruitment from certain circumstances. The upheavals following World War I brought into the party thousands of people who looked upon communism as the midwife of the millennium; a second great wave of militants entered during the Depression and the period of the "fight against fascism" in the 1930's. Finally, many joined immediately after World War II, when the party appeared to be the most democratic of the left. Many of them had little idea of Marxism when they entered; once in, however, they were absorbed by the system and they passed on its values to their children. In this sense the P.C.F. has become institutionalized.

Its very size and organization have given it other advantages. Because it controls France's strongest trade union, the C.G.T., anyone interested in a successful trade-union career would be well advised to become a party member. Its intellectual cadres have dominated the movie industry, many of the scientific research centers, and, during the 1940's and 1950's, branches of the government bureaucracy—thus encouraging young men anxious to rise in these hierarchies to explore the possibility of becoming Communist militants.

The great bulk of those who vote Communist seem to do so out of a feeling that the P.C.F. is truly the party of the working class, even though many distrust it. The vast majority of its supporters today are not revolutionaries, and are not interested in importing Soviet institutions to France. They are attracted to the party because it has been, in their eyes, less compromised by the system,

[10] Quoted by Charles A. Micaud, *Communism and the French Left* (New York: Frederick A. Praeger, 1963), p. 84.

and because of the effectiveness of the party's militants. As one former Communist leader put it:

The Party multiplies inquiries about the needs and grievances of everyone—heads of families, housewives, tenants—in order to draw up a list of demands. . . . A cell newspaper busies itself with all kinds of demands concerning the factory or the neighborhood, including clean toilets and showers. . . . The Socialists do just the opposite. . . . They will never fight for small things and do not think that they are important.[11]

A study completed in early 1968 found that only 18 per cent of Communist voters want the establishment of a Communist regime in France, as against 35 per cent who vote for the party because it is "a useful opposition force" and 38 per cent who do so "in order to express a general discontent." On the other hand, the same poll also revealed that 30 per cent of the Communist voters believed that if the Communist Party joined a coalition government, it would try to seize power.[12] In another study, more than ninety per cent of Communist voters expressed agreement with the statement "There are certain institutions like inheritance and property which must not be touched without the threat of economic catastrophe."

During the 1940's and 1950's the Communist Party was strongest electorally in the industrial zone between Paris and Belgium, on the northern and western edge of the Massif Central, and along parts of the Mediterranean. In the rural areas there is a good deal of evidence that part of the P.C.F.'s strength stemmed from its annexing the traditions of the Great Revolution, from the party's record in the Resistance, and from the fact that many peasants, reacting to the onset of modernization, simply voted for a party of opposition. Within the working class, the

party's appeal was strongest with the less well paid, a group whose radicalism was purely economic.

By the late 1950's and early 1960's, however, the party had reached the limits of its expansion. It never completely recovered the votes lost to the Gaullists; its allure for intellectuals had waned rather suddenly; newspaper circulation had fallen off, as had the number of militants; and the party machinery was exhibiting bureaucratic sluggishness. At the same time, the party and its affiliated organizations, such as the trade unions, had become an integral part of the established political system; the paid bureaucratic staff of both had a vested interest in making sure that no revolutionary turmoil caused a situation in which the party might be destroyed or driven underground.

All these factors, plus the arrival of a new generation of party leaders, led to the beginnings of a re-examination of the party line for the purpose of making it more respectable. After 1962, the party became receptive to cooperation with other left-wing parties, and after a time began to project an image of itself as an organization that, despite its dedication to radical change, could be trusted to work within the framework of the parliamentary system. By and large, the effort was successful. And as the cold war became less intense and other parties also felt the need for unity against de Gaulle, the P.C.F.'s efforts at cooperation were stepped up, and its image improved even among non-Communist voters.

But this reorientation was not without its drawbacks. While the party remained attractive to many of the younger generation, its loss of revolutionary ardor began to disenchant others. Also, a slight softening of the party's discipline and authority suddenly produced demands for more democratic party deliberations. By 1966 and 1967, therefore, the party was facing attacks by both the "liberalizers," who wanted the P.C.F. to become part of a democratic left majority, and young Trotskyites and Maoists, who thought that

11 Micaud, *Communism*, p. 82.

12 *Le Nouvel Observateur*, February 21, 1968, pp. 6–7.

what was really needed was a restoration of revolutionary (nonbureaucratic) élan. It was also faced with the difficulty of reconciling a traditional Marxist ideology with a world in which such an ideology no longer seemed relevant even to those intellectuals who opposed the system, many of whom were turning to the young Marx in a search for what might appropriately be labeled "existentialist socialism."

The events of 1968 and 1969 brought some of these issues to a climax. The response of the party was to maintain its new line— cautiously conservative, post-Stalinist, but still in many ways traditionally Communist. The results of the election, however, indicated that the party had been caught in a dilemma. It had not changed its image sufficiently to attract a larger constituency, even in combination with other left-wing parties, and the changes it had made were sufficient to threaten it with the loss of the new "revolutionary" student generation.

6. THE RISE AND DECLINE OF THE CATHOLIC LEFT

The Popular Republican Movement (M.R.P.) was formed in 1944 as an attempt to transcend the divisions of French political and social life by forging a political movement that was both Catholic and leftist. It referred to itself as a movement rather than a party because it hoped to rise above the traditional party system and provide France with a new basis for political consensus. In 1945 and 1946 it was one of the nation's three major parties, commanding about 25 per cent of the vote. By the 1950's, however, its percentage of the total vote had plummeted to about 11, and it had become merely one more political party along the spectrum —without any hope of effecting fundamental social changes, without any hope of creating a new political alignment that would transcend the old cleavages. Finally, in the mid-1960's the M.R.P. transformed itself first into the Democratic Center (*Centre démo-crate*) and then into the Progress and Modern Democracy (*Progrès et démocratie moderne*—P.D.M.). The new group, while based largely on the old M.R.P., also drew to it some former Independents who did not wish to support de Gaulle, and some Radicals who were unhappy with the Federation of the Left. Billing itself as a moderate alternative to de Gaulle, the P.D.M. hoped to rally to it a sizable portion of the French electorate. In this it failed dismally. In the 1968 elections, the old M.R.P. constituency, which was the core of the new grouping, was diminished still further by Gaullist gains. Whatever the future of French politics, Christian Democracy of the M.R.P. stamp seems to be dying out as a distinctly political movement.

Since the 1790's there have been those within the Catholic Church who strongly believed that some effort must be made to come to terms with the French Revolution, although the identification of Catholicism with political and economic as well as religious conservatism persisted well into the twentieth century. After World War I, however, several lay Catholic movements emerged, dedicated to political and social reform, and, in 1919, a Catholic trade union was formed. At the same time, a number of progressive Catholic youth organizations came into existence, along with two small reformist Catholic parties—the Popular Democratic Party (*Parti démocrate populaire*) and the small Young Republic (*Jeune république*). The latter, which was more an extraparliamentary league than a political party in a true sense, took a very liberal line, joining the Popular Front, opposing Franco in Spain, and associating with left-wing causes. The newspaper *L'Aube* and the journal *Esprit* tended to serve as its intellectual organs.

It was within the Resistance, where persons associated with liberal Catholic groups established a creditable record, that the idea of a Catholic political movement of the left took firmer root. Indeed, the M.R.P. was officially founded in 1944 at Lyons, a center of Catholic resistance, and by 1945 it had established a mass organization that claimed one hundred thousand active members. In general those who constituted the core of active militants were drawn to a kind of Christian socialism, or rather corporatism; they wanted to reconstitute the traditional social thought of the Catholic Church and apply it to the modern era. Insofar as they were corporatist, their approach resembled that of fascism, one of whose central ideological elements was the desire to restore an idealized "corporate" society in which members would be organized according to occupational groups, responsible for their own behavior.

Catholic thinkers had always emphasized the role of natural associations such as the family and work groups, and had criticized liberal capitalism for its excessive individualism and its refusal to accept the idea that economic activities should be subordinated to the moral ends of the community. In this sense, Catholic thinkers conceived of society as made up of relatively autonomous groups regulating their own behavior, but ultimately responsible to the community. By organizing society in this way, they believed the class struggle could be overcome. Jacques Maritain, for instance, one of the M.R.P.'s spiritual mentors, initially felt a certain attraction to a Fascistlike state. However, as the militants' commitment to democratic procedures and their acceptance of political pluralism became more stable, they came to represent something of a quite different order.

Party doctrine condemned the outlook of both the left (Jacobin or Marxist) and the economic liberals. The left, according to the M.R.P., thought of men only in terms of masses, while economic liberals fostered unbridled individualism. Every man, however, is both a member of some social group and an individual; the goal of society is to work for the continued perfection of the individual while simultaneously recognizing his fundamental weaknesses. Party doctrine also proclaimed democracy to be a means

toward achieving the good society, a society in which no single group would impose its will upon the whole. The function of the state is to aid all groups in the realization of their goals and to coordinate their activities for a general welfare based on Christian precepts; but it must not do so at the cost of the political rights of either individuals or groups.

More concretely, the M.R.P. favored a democratic constitutional order based on both individual and collective interests. This order would include a two-house legislature, with one house representing occupational and social groups; the decentralization of the French administrative structure in order to permit greater local initiative and autonomy; and the establishment of a stronger executive power than that which had existed under the Third Republic. Indeed, the party initially looked with favor upon the idea of a regime that combined parliamentary and presidential features. In foreign policy, the M.R.P. was associated with strong support of European integration and with reconstituting the colonial system by incorporating the colonies into Metropolitan France.

The domestic economic program of the M.R.P. called for substantial economic reform, involving nationalization where necessary, and the extension of social services, including a publicly supported housing program, increases in family allowances, and extended social-security benefits. Its economic program was clearly of the left. Militants saw the party as a movement of the left willing to work with even Socialists and Communists to gain needed social reform. Thus the M.R.P. joined with the S.F.I.O. and the P.C.F. to form the first coalition government immediately after World War II.

For a time, the M.R.P. seemed likely to provide a left-wing Christian alternative to communism. In the first postwar elections in 1945, it polled almost 25 per cent of the vote. As it turned out, however, its electoral strength had, in large part, been built on sand; many had supported it *faute de mieux,* as the least dangerous of the left-wing parties at a time when conservatism was out of style. This became evident when the party split reluctantly with de Gaulle over the issue of the constitution of the Fourth Republic, thus aligning itself with the Socialists and the Communists, and again in the elections of 1951, when many of its previous supporters voted for de Gaulle or the reviving parties of traditional conservatism.[13] In 1951 its electoral strength dropped to 12.3 per cent. The M.R.P. never regained the vote it had lost. De Gaulle's Rally of the French People and the increasing respectability of conservatism continued to draw off a good part of its initial support.

At first the militants of the M.R.P. did not consider the decline of the party's electoral strength to be terribly important. The remaining supporters, they believed, would present a more homogeneous front that could help educate the population to social reform. What was important to them was that the M.R.P. continue to be part of a left-wing coalition, lest the Socialist Party be driven into the arms of the Communists. But after 1947, the growing antagonism between Socialists and Communists made saving the Socialists less necessary, and the M.R.P.'s original enthusiasm for social reform and political restructuring was fading away. Furthermore, the former harmony between the Socialists and the M.R.P. was completely disrupted by clashes, fostered in part by more conservative forces, over aid to Catholic parochial schools. There were other signs of the party's decline: the 12 per cent or so of the voters who remained faithful proved somewhat more conservative than expected; its parliamentarians began to acquire a vested interest in remaining in office; and, finally, within a multi-party system, the M.R.P. found itself continually called upon to make up a majority for essentially conservative governments—in short, it became easier and easier for the M.R.P. to accept the rewards of office by converting itself into a government party.

13 On the constitutional issue, see Chapter 2, p. 59.

After its 1951 split with the Socialists over the school issue—which some Socialists welcomed because of their general discomfort at being associated with a "clerical" party— the M.R.P. continued to take part in many of the more conservative governments that held office during much of the 1950's. Responding to the objections of the more radical militants, parliamentary leaders pointed out that to leave office would place France in the hands of either the Gaullists or the Communists, or lead to civil war. They also argued that they were, in fact, contributing to the development of a united Europe, a mission all party members considered sacred.

Between 1955 and 1958, the strength of the movement was further threatened as some militants turned to the left, out of disgust with the party's increasing conservatism, and others to the right, over its moderate policy on Algeria. However, the great bulk of its parliamentarians and militants remained loyal, and with the 1956 elections the party seemed to be moving once again to the left.

In the 1958 elections, the M.R.P. supported de Gaulle and became part of the first government of the Fifth Republic; but as the Algerian crisis drew to a close, it became more and more alienated by what it considered to be the authoritarian, technocratic qualities of the Fifth Republic. Nor was it captivated by de Gaulle's search for grandeur, involving, as it did, an emphasis upon establishing an atomic striking force and a movement away from the concept of a united Europe. In 1962, then, all the M.R.P. deputies withdrew from the government. Their convictions were not shared, however, by the French voters: the 1962 elections revealed the increasing attractiveness of de Gaulle for M.R.P. voters, and the party's strength declined by some eight hundred thousand votes. Shortly before the presidential elections of 1965 (see Table 11.6), M.R.P. militants voted to join with the Socialists and Radicals behind Defferre. However, the issue of state aid to religious schools, the problem of relations with the Communists, and the difficulties of integrating the organizations of the three parties prevented the negotiations from coming to fruition. Instead, a smaller coalition, centered around the presidential candidacy of Lecanuet, drew most of the support of M.R.P. voters. Lecanuet got less than 16 per cent of the vote, and the M.R.P. and its successors continued to lose ground in the 1967 and 1968 legislative elections. The 1969 presidential candidacy of Poher, a member of the P.D.M.'s political bureau, split the party. Jacques Duhamel, one of its principal leaders, supported Pompidou and was rewarded with the Ministry of Agriculture in the new government.

STRUCTURE, POWER, AND POLICY: At its founding the M.R.P. regarded itself as a democratic mass party, and it created a fairly complex organization with sections, federations, a national congress, and various smaller executive bodies. In actuality, the real decision-making power in the party slipped slowly into the hands of its parliamentary delegation which, beginning with youthful enthusiasm, stayed in power so long that its age and the parliamentary system itself eventually transformed it into a more conservative bloc. In the late 1940's and early 1950's the most effective recruiting grounds for the party and for the spread of M.R.P. propaganda were the Catholic action groups, particularly those with a younger membership. By the late 1950's, however, the dedication of these groups had also waned.

Among French voters the M.R.P. received considerable support from white-collar workers and from traditionally Catholic rural areas such as the Vendée. In fact, except for its very first years, it was never really a national party in terms of electoral support. Although the party no longer exists as an entity, the

TABLE 11.6. THE FRENCH PRESIDENTIAL ELECTION OF 1965

Candidate	First ballot December 5, 1965	Second ballot December 19, 1965
de Gaulle	43.7%	54.5%
Mitterrand	32.2	45.5
Lecanuet	15.9	
Tixier-Vignancour	5.3	
Others	2.9	

Source: *Le Monde*, December 30, 1965. Reprinted by permission of the publisher.

TABLE 11.7. THE FRENCH PRESIDENTIAL ELECTION OF 1969

Candidate	First ballot June 1, 1969	Second ballot June 15, 1969
Pompidou	44.0%	57.6%
Poher	23.4	42.4
Duclos	21 5	
Defferre	5.1	
Rocard	3.7	
Ducatel	1.3	
Krivine	1.0	

Source: *Le Monde*, June 17, 1969. Reprinted by permission of the publisher.

former M.R.P. organization provides most of the activists for the new P.D.M. coalition. The groups making up the P.D.M., however, are divided between more conservative and more liberal elements and divided, too, on the general problem of its future. The hope of its founders had been to create a massive center party as an alternative to de Gaulle, but the victory of Pompidou has temporarily, at least, reduced that possibility. The future of the party, therefore, depends far more on how successful Pompidou is in forging a center-right coalition than on anything the P.D.M. can do.

7. GAULLISM: THE UNION OF DEMOCRATS FOR THE REPUBLIC

The Union of Democrats for the Republic (*Union des démocrates pour la république*—U.D.R.) is the most recent name adopted by the political movement that emerged in 1947 as the Rally of the French People (*Rassemblement du peuple français*—R.P.F.).[14] The central figure in both, until 1969, was Charles de Gaulle. In the early days of the movement, left-wing intellectuals tended to identify Gaullism with the traditional right, and the antiparliamentary right at that. This was and is a mistaken view, for like all parties of its type the U.D.R. did not fit neatly on the political spectrum. De Gaulle himself seemed to believe in a vague corporatism, derived from traditional Catholic ideology and involving worker representation on boards of management; he also believed in

a parliamentary system in which representation is based on occupation as well as geography; and he always endorsed national planning and community control of economic activity.

Whatever de Gaulle's political predilections, Gaullism as a political phenomenon was not new to France. French history, like that of other fragmented societies, has witnessed time and time again the appearance of a "heroic" leader who promises to resolve the nation's problems by combining the best of both the old and the new, within a framework of ordered change. The two Napoleons were the most outstanding representatives of this tradition in France, and both left their imprint on French development. Neither, however, succeeded in establishing the conditions for lasting stability, and whether or not de Gaulle managed to do so remains to be seen. Georges Pompidou, de Gaulle's successor as president of France and leader of the U.D.R., is a conservative—albeit a modernizing conservative—whose goal is the creation of a broadly based conservative party that can effectively govern France. Whether or not Pompidou can hold the U.D.R. together, and at the same time draw upon the support of other political groups, is still an open question. The success or failure of his efforts will help determine the political course of France over the next ten years.

Charles de Gaulle was born in Lille on November 22, 1890, the second son of a philosophy professor in the Jesuit schools in the area. He was educated in Catholic schools, attended Saint Cyr—France's West Point—and embarked upon a regular army career. During the interwar years, he taught military history and theory, wrote books attacking France's Maginot mentality, and called for a mobile army of high firepower. His suggestions were almost entirely ignored by the French, although the Germans paid them avid attention. During the brief 1940 campaign, his unit distinguished itself in a number of rapid thrusts against the enemy.

After the fall of France, de Gaulle refused

14 The Gaullist party retained the name "Rally of the French People" until 1953, when de Gaulle withdrew from politics. In 1958, de Gaulle supporters created the Union for the New Republic (*Union pour la nouvelle république*—U.N.R.); in 1967 the U.N.R. became the Union for the New Republic/Democratic Union of Labor (*Union pour la nouvelle république/Union démocratique du travail*—U.N.R./U.D.T.). Just before the 1968 election, the party changed its name once again, to Union for the Defense of the Fifth Republic (*Union pour la défense de la cinquième république*—U.D.R.); it adopted its present name—same initials—when the new parliament was convened after the election.

to accept the authority of the Vichy government, fled first to Africa and then to England, and proclaimed himself and his movement—the Free French—as the legitimate heirs of the Third Republic. He took as his symbol the Cross of Lorraine, identified historically with Joan of Arc. For four years his name was synonymous with Free France, not only among millions of Frenchmen, but among people all over the world.

As World War II drew to a close, de Gaulle hoped that a new republic would rise like the phoenix from the ashes of France's experience, a new republic with a set of common social purposes and an institutional structure that would enable Frenchmen to translate those purposes into action. De Gaulle was thus willing to accept and even support extended social benefits, the nationalization of some industry, and a partially directed economy. He also envisioned a vaguely corporatist framework of economic relationships within industry, one that would bring workers into the decision-making process. His economic ideas, however, remained relatively sketchy; economics never interested him very much and he always placed primary emphasis upon political reforms. He was convinced that a parliamentary system after the British model was not suited to the French temperament, which required institutions to counteract the centrifugal tendencies always present in France. Such institutions, he argued, might legitimately include a strong, popularly elected president with the power to dissolve parliament and even to bypass it through a national referendum. The president should represent a force powerful enough to act in the name of the nation as a whole; he should be, in a sense, above partisan politics.

Since de Gaulle conceived of himself as standing above the political fray, he had little initial interest in founding a new political organization, and was glad to identify himself with the recently formed M.R.P., a movement that, in its attempt to end the traditional political conservatism of Catholics, might serve to bridge one of the many chasms inhibiting the development and implementation of sound common policies. He was also willing to work with Socialists and any other liberal factions that were anxious to create a new France. Willing though he might be, however, de Gaulle was never an easy man to work with. Stubborn, proud, convinced both of his personal mission and of the principle that authority must be exercised if anything were to be achieved, his relations with others were seldom serene. His concept of French grandeur, for instance, led him into frequent and often bitter clashes during World War II with other Allied leaders. Winston Churchill is reported to have remarked that of all the crosses he had to bear during the war, the heaviest was the Cross of Lorraine.

As head of the first French provisional government after the war, de Gaulle brought into it all the major political parties, including the Communists. His hope was to rally all Frenchmen to a common cause; but he was swiftly disabused on that premise, and on January 20, 1946, resigned his office. The wranglings of politicians and their inability to agree upon a common program discouraged and disgusted him; the unwillingness of the three major parties to accept a presidential regime convinced him that the new constitution could not succeed in remaking France. In fact, de Gaulle opposed it—thus breaking with the M.R.P. Aside from announcing his opposition, de Gaulle took no action, at least in the beginning. To those in his entourage who, like Jacques Soustelle, tended toward the idea of a coup d'etat, he replied that the future of France lay with republican institutions and that the use of illegal means to obtain his ends would be self-defeating. Rather, convinced that the Fourth Republic could not work and that he would eventually be called back to head the government, he retired to write his memoirs.

Under pressure from his supporters, de Gaulle emerged from retirement in 1947, and, in a speech at Strasbourg, announced the formation not of a new party but of a *rassemblement,* a rally of Frenchmen—a movement above parties that would unite all French people of good will into an effort to find pragmatic solutions to the ideological conflicts that kept France from achieving its "destiny." His program was vague; he spoke of the need for a strong government that would free France from the threat of domination by either the Soviet Union or the United States, and urged new forms of association between labor and capital. He also suggested that strong measures might have to be taken against the French Communist Party, which he did not consider a genuine national party.

De Gaulle's appeal met with an astonishing response. Thousands of Frenchmen joined the movement, providing a cadre of young and vigorous militants, and members of many of the other parties, especially the M.R.P. and the Radicals, joined a Gaullist parliamentary intergroup that permitted them to retain their traditional attachments. In the municipal elections of that year, the R.P.F. and its allies received some forty per cent of the votes cast. De Gaulle hoped that the mandate would force parliament to dissolve itself and that new elections would bring him to power. Parliament, however, refused to accommodate him. The center and center-left parties tightened their lines, seeing in de Gaulle a pattern of Caesarism whose tradition went back to Napoleon I; the M.R.P. and the Socialists both forbade members of their parliamentary parties to join the Gaullist intergroup, and though almost one-half of the M.R.P.'s electoral strength went to de Gaulle, the party's militants held firm.

What de Gaulle did receive as a result of the 1947 elections was the support of moderate and right-wing deputies in his parliamentary intergroup. These were men who considered him and his party the most respectable, or least dangerous, of the new political forces. For a while he hoped to use his intergroup to paralyze the work of parliament in the hope that its inability to function would result in his being called to office.

He insisted that those considering themselves Gaullists should not participate in or support any non-Gaullist government. However, the tactic did not work: the other parties drew together to preserve the republic and while divergencies among them did, in fact, prevent really effective government action, the result was a modicum of stability. As conservatism regained respectability, those drawn to de Gaulle found it difficult to resist the rewards of office and refused to accept a discipline that prevented them from partaking of these rewards.

In late 1949, de Gaulle took another step. The R.P.F., although still calling itself a rally, actively entered the political scene, forming the cadres of a mass party to participate in the 1951 elections. In these, the party received 20.4 per cent of the vote—making it the second largest in the country. Only a change in the electoral system pushed through in 1950 by the center parties prevented the Communists and Gaullists together from having enough deputies to paralyze the work of the Assembly completely.

Once again, de Gaulle's following failed to hold together. Technocrats and modernizers found themselves at odds with more traditional elements; clericals and anticlericals revived their differences; the left and the right within the R.P.F. found themselves equally uncomfortable in each other's embrace. The result was a breakdown of party discipline. The splintering of the party in Parliament weakened it among the electorate. De Gaulle came to represent less and less the figure of a powerful leader who could solve the problems of France. In the 1953 Paris municipal elections, the vote of the R.P.F. showed a marked decline. Two days later de Gaulle, having decided that for the moment further political action would only weaken his position, dissolved the R.P.F. and retired once more.

However, the last word had not been spoken. In the Algerian crisis of 1958, de Gaulle's followers, including Soustelle, pushed the general forward once again, and once again the ambiguity of his position and his prestige made him the least unacceptable alternative, this time in a deteriorating situation that brought France to the verge of civil war.

The upshot was the return to power of Charles de Gaulle, the constitution of the Fifth Republic, and a new nonparty designed to unite all Frenchmen of good will, the Union for the New Republic (*Union pour la nouvelle république*—U.N.R.). In the 1958 elections, the U.N.R. received 20.4 per cent of the vote on the first ballot and 26.4 per cent on the second. It elected 189 deputies out of the 467 seats available, and although it did not have a majority, the expressions of support for de Gaulle as the newly elected president of the republic led to the expectation that there would be little difficulty in establishing a cabinet that could command the support of a substantial part of the General Assembly. Such in fact was the case: the cabinet of Michel Debré—who had been handpicked as premier by de Gaulle—was invested by a vote of 453 to 56.

In effect, the results of the election favored conservative and rural France. The right-wing parties increased their portion of the vote, and within the U.N.R. the winning candidates were those identified with a more conservative position; most of the new deputies, in fact, seemed to be more conservative than the leader with whom they chose to associate.

In the following years the U.N.R. proved its fidelity to de Gaulle. Despite disagreements on economic and social policy, most of the deputies adhered to party discipline and supported his programs.[15] The support continued through the resignation of Debré and the investiture of Pompidou as premier, and through a number of legislative sessions during which it became evident that the government was a constitutional monarchy in everything but name.

15 The domestic and foreign policies of the regime are discussed in more detail in Chapters 24 and 25, respectively.

De Gaulle, his administration, and his party were rewarded in 1962 by an overwhelming electoral victory, largely at the expense of the M.R.P. and more conservative groupings, although the party continued to hold most of the working-class votes it had garnered from the Communists and Socialists in 1958. By 1965, however, de Gaulle's popularity was slipping, and his close victory in the presidential election (see Table 11.6, above) of that year indicated that Frenchmen were becoming politically restive. While the Gaullists continued to gain in the 1967 elections—again largely though not entirely at the expense of the center and the right—the creation of the Federation of the Left provided the Assembly with a much stronger opposition, and by early 1968 deputies were beginning to talk openly about post–de Gaulle France.

The events of 1968 seemed to belie these expectations, despite the age of the general. In the wake of student riots and widespread strikes, the Gaullists, now under the banner of the U.D.R., won another impressive electoral victory, largely at the expense of the left. The voters' verdict, however, was primarily a reaction to fears of disorder rather than a new increase in support for de Gaulle, and this was clearly confirmed by the failure of these same voters in 1969 to endorse his plans for weakening the French senate and for creating new regional political organizations. With his defeat, de Gaulle resigned the presidency and a new phase opened in the development of the U.D.R.

STRUCTURE AND DYNAMICS: The Rally of the French People was founded as a supra-party "movement," and de Gaulle was inclined to oppose the formation of organized cadres. However, as indicated earlier, his hand was forced by his inability to obtain commitments and loyalty from individuals elected by the other political parties. By the time the R.P.F. was dissolved, it had, therefore, developed a reasonably tight-knit organization under the aegis of Soustelle and others.

MAP 11.5. THE GAULLISTS IN 1968

*Geographic Distribution of U.D.R. and Republican Independents,
First Ballot, June 23, 1968*

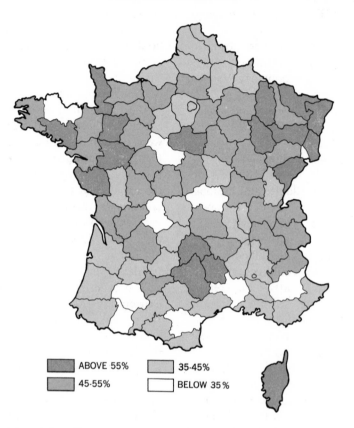

ABOVE 55%		35-45%	
45-55%		BELOW 35%	

Adapted from François Goguel, "Les élections législatives des 23 et 30 juin, 1968," *Revue française de Science Politique,* 18 (October 1968), Chart 8, p. 857. Reprinted by permission of the publisher.

Both workshop organizations, modeled after Communist cells and designed to counteract them, and local units based on French administrative divisions—communes, cantons, and arrondissements—had been formed.

The R.P.F. also built up a political structure on the regional and national level, culminating in a national congress and a national council. The congress, ostensibly the fount of the party's national policy, elected the president of the party and the national council, which met several times a year to deal with specific party problems that the congress, because of its size, could not handle. The most important organization within the R.P.F. was the executive committee, a policy group controlled by de Gaulle himself: he picked its members, convoked its weekly meetings, and even dismissed those whose attitudes displeased him.

On the lower levels, policy decisions on political matters were made by a department delegate appointed from the executive committee, although regional organizations controlled their own finances and studied measures suggested by the national organizations. All in all, then, the fundamentals of policy were decided by de Gaulle and those around him whom he trusted; disagreement with national policy could lead only to submission or resignation. Even so, there were gaps in the authoritarian nature of the party. In a good many areas it had never defined its position clearly, and departmental and local organizations as well as members of Parliament were left with considerable flexibility on particular policy matters. Nor was de Gaulle completely isolated from pressures. On a number of occasions he retreated or compromised. For example, initially the R.P.F.'s executive committee did not contain any parliamentarians. However, in 1949, de Gaulle agreed to add four deputies and three senators, bringing the committee's total membership to twenty. Later concessions increased the membership so that by 1952 the executive committee contained 29 members, the majority of them parliamentarians.

When the U.N.R. was formed in 1958, it could draw upon the talents of many of the same men who had been responsible for organizing the R.P.F. At first de Gaulle was opposed to re-creating a political party, for he believed that his job was to bring about a political transition and that the U.N.R. had no future. It was on this issue, as well as that of Algeria, that he split with the party's right wing, which was ejected from the organization. By the late 1960's, however, some of de Gaulle's animus to party organization had been overcome, although the newly formed U.D.R. had yet to sink firm roots into the countryside.

The basic unit of the U.D.R. is the electoral district committee. It elects its own executive committee, which selects a secretary general and treasurer. District units are grouped into department unions that select delegates to the National Council and to the National Congress. The departmental organizations direct their efforts toward organizing district committees, selecting candidates for local elections, and proposing candidates for national elections.

On the national level, there are five principal organs of the party: the National Congress; the National Council; the central committee; the political committee; and the

secretariat, headed by a general secretary. According to the party's bylaws, the congress is the supreme arbiter of policy, while between sessions the council carries out its mandates and probes into political issues. In practice, however, neither group has thus far had much to do with policy making. The central committee, on the other hand, does have a number of important bureaucratic functions dealing with matters of discipline, the selection of candidates, and possible alliances with other political parties. Here the general secretary, as head of the party's bureaucratic apparatus, exercises a certain degree of influence.

In terms of actual policy making, the only party organ of any significance is the political committee, a group dominated by U.D.R. members who are in the government and by the chairmen of the party groups within the National Assembly. It is in the political committee that the most important party decisions are made, and it was both through and with this group that de Gaulle determined political strategy.

From the very beginning, the Rally of the French People, while it had great appeal for traditional conservative voters, also attracted a following unlike that of older conservative parties. During its early years especially, it was supported by a higher proportion of younger voters than any party except the Communist, and it also drew a sizable vote from the working class. In fact, its center of gravity was in the newer industrial areas, not in those rural areas that had theretofore provided the main support for conservatism. In essence it was what political scientists have come to call a "catchall" party. Like the American parties it drew upon many groups for support, but its solid power base was among those elements of the middle class anxious for both reform and order and not deeply committed to other political organizations.

The R.P.F.'s constituency, of course, fluctuated from election to election, as has that of its successors, the U.N.R. and the U.D.R.; but the U.D.R. has continued to increase its working-class support, and its center of politi-cal gravity is even more obviously located in the industrial north. As the older Gaullists re-linquish power, more and more of the new party cadres and members of parliament are technocrats drawn from the bureaucracy and the more modern sector of business—a trend that heartens those who visualize the U.D.R., with the departure of de Gaulle, as continuing to develop as a pragmatic modernizing party of the center right. The problem, of course, is that the party's support is still highly dispar-ate; many of the factions that compose it have held together only because of de Gaulle him-self. Whether his successors can maintain this alliance is problematical.

If the U.D.R. does survive, it is not easy to determine what, concretely, its policies are to be. Both de Gaulle and other party spokes-men stressed the need for a strong executive, a goal that de Gaulle and the new constitution achieved. On the economic side, the general and the men around him were associated with a moderately conservative policy that com-bined respect for private property with a will-ingness to institute social-welfare measures and to engage in public enterprise and plan-ning where the need to do so was evident. What domestic policy de Gaulle's successors might choose is another matter. Many in the party are less flexible than de Gaulle in adapt-ing to social change, as indicated by the very difficult time he had in forcing proposed edu-cational reforms through party councils after the 1968 riots.

The foreign policy followed by de Gaulle has been highly nationalistic. He has never trusted ideologies, believing that they are merely rationalizations for power drives. From the very beginning, he was suspicious of both England and the United States, be-lieving that both nations wished to deny France its proper place among world powers. In the late 1950's and early 1960's he became greatly concerned about the possibility of America—aided and abetted by the English —achieving an economic hegemony over Europe. And more and more, he came to be-lieve that as Communist ideology erodes in the Soviet Union, its natural conflicts with what he has termed the "yellow masses" of China will lead it back to an accommodation with its European neighbors. He was also skeptical of European unity, believing that a looser association of nations would, as long as Germany remained divided, permit France to play a much larger—and grander—role.

But these were de Gaulle's personal poli-cies. Many supporters of the U.D.R. are much more pro-European than de Gaulle, and less suspicious of the United States, Brit-ain, and the Atlantic Alliance. Pompidou, for example, has a far less exalted view of French grandeur, and while he will move only very slowly toward a reconsideration of Britain's application to enter the Common Market, he will sharply curtail France's new military and political commitments. It is most likely that Pompidou's major emphasis will be on domestic policy—an effort to continue and accelerate the modernization of the French economy.

8. ELECTORAL POLITICS IN FRANCE

Prospective candidates for the National Assembly must send a formal application to local government authorities at least 21 days before the first ballot. Those eligible to vote are registered on permanent electoral rolls. Registration is completed by the municipal authorities on the basis of their lists of resi-dents. Each year the rolls are open for a limited period of time, to enable anyone con-cerned to check the accuracy of the voting lists. The law strictly regulates written as well as radio and television propaganda. All can-didates of national parties (those presenting candidates in at least 75 of about 470 districts) are permitted a limited amount of broadcast time, the expense of which is borne by the state. Candidates must pay for the distribution of their own campaign mate-rial, but if they poll more than five per cent of the vote on the first ballot, such expenses are refunded.

Electoral expenses in France have been far less than in England or the United States. While the finances of most parties are a well-kept secret, they are all relatively poor. Right-wing and center parties generally get most of their money from special-interest groups—and from the pockets of individual candidates. On the left, a greater effort is made to raise money through dues, raffles, and social affairs. Communists and Socialists also obtain money from elected deputies, and the Communists have used funds accruing to the party from its commercial ventures. The M.R.P. probably received some financial assistance from Christian Democratic parties in other countries, and the Socialists have been aided by the American and British trade unionists. Undoubtedly, the Communist Party has received financial support from the Soviet Union.

Ideological rhetoric has always characterized French politics. It seems paradoxical, therefore, that local interests figured so crucially in French politics during the Third Republic. But some two-thirds of the deputies elected to national office between 1870 and 1940 started out as local officials, and a good many hung on to their local offices while serving in Parliament. Just which political banner they carried made little difference; they all emphasized to voters their ability to obtain subsidies from the national government, if and when elected. Promises like this were bound to have local appeal, for almost all local funds had to come from national coffers. Party strength was further dependent upon the ability of the national organizations to find local notables willing to serve as their candidates.

French politics, then, from the end of the Franco-Prussian War to the fall of France in 1940, reflected the durability of local attachments in largely rural and small-town areas, most of whose voters cast their ballots on the basis of local interests, no matter what the citizens of Paris might do. More important, perhaps, localism was to a considerable

extent the result of the fragmentation of French politics. Since no single party was going to govern and enact its program, rhetoric and real politics were two different worlds; one might speak in general terms of the great issues of state, but except in extreme circumstances, one voted by one's pocketbook.

Many students of French politics have cited the electoral system as a source of localism. Indeed, there is something to their argument: 13 of the 16 elections held in the Third Republic used single-member districts and a double ballot. The system encouraged candidate identification with his locality and hampered party discipline; it contributed to the large number of nonparty candidacies. It also encouraged party moderation: at the second round the serious candidate nearest the political center could attract the doubtful voters. For instance, Radical Party candidates in left-wing areas could attract conservative votes to block the "more dangerous" Socialists; in Catholic areas, they could gain Socialist votes to block "the domination of the church." Since single-member districts benefited the Radical Party, both the Socialists and the conservatives came to support a form of proportional representation.

When the Fourth Republic came into existence, every party but the Radical preferred some form of proportional representation. New parties such as the M.R.P. believed that proportional representation would orient the voters to ideas rather than men, and thus weaken the power of local notables—a view also held by the Socialists and Communists. All three parties thought that a list system of PR, in which party leaders would control the position of the candidate on the list, would strengthen party discipline. But the M.R.P. and the Socialists also calculated that only PR could prevent the Communists from completely dominating the national legislature. Out of the complicated party negotiations on voting methods emerged a new election law that provided for a rigid list system of PR based on comparatively small constituencies; the law did not allow for the national pooling of votes.[16] The fact that the constituencies were small permitted local reputation to remain of some importance in campaigns, even though there is no local residence requirement for candidates in France.

The system did have the effect of encouraging discipline and favoring the larger parties, although it did not generally reduce the number of parties. While a trend toward nationalization of politics could be seen, local interests continued to be vital. Fear that the system as it stood would give a negative majority to the Communists and to de Gaulle's R.P.F. led the center parties to change the electoral law. Just before the 1951 elections, a new law was promulgated that not only allowed a preferential vote but permitted parties to form pre-election alliances in any constituency except the Paris area. If the combined list won a majority of the votes in the constituency, the list would receive all the votes; if it failed to win a majority, the seats would be divided proportionally. The law had its intended effect: in 1951 the Communists won 71 fewer seats and the R.P.F. 21 fewer seats than they would have under the 1946 law. This is not to say, however, that the result was less fair than it would have been under the 1946 law; the old law allowed the Communists one seat for every 26,000 votes, and the Radicals one for every 59,000. The new law gave the Radicals one seat for every 28,000 and the Communists one for every 52,000.

When de Gaulle swept into power in 1958, the U.N.R. was split on the question of how to elect members to the National Assembly. Some members of the party believed that

PR had distinct advantages for them; the view of the majority, however, was that a return to single-member districts with a double ballot would be more advantageous, and this was the method finally adopted. Under the new constitution, too, any deputy who joined the government had to resign his parliamentary seat. To obviate the necessity of frequent by-elections, then, each deputy was required to campaign with a substitute (suppléant) who would replace him if he entered the government. The new constitution also provided that France's president be elected for a seven-year term, and deputies for the National Assembly for five-year terms.

Perhaps the most outstanding political feature of Fifth-Republic France is the reduction in the number of parties. At the same time, election campaigns for national office are taking on a national tone, despite the return to single-member districts. These changes should not be exaggerated, for local interests and prejudices are still important; Protestants expect representation in Alsace, veterinarians are at a premium as candidates in the countryside, and doctors are in political demand everywhere. Furthermore, all candidates—including Communists—tailor their messages to the constituency. Nevertheless, the differences between today's political trends and the pre–World War II pattern are sufficient to warrant comment.

The most fundamental variable in these changes has undoubtedly been social modernization. France is becoming increasingly urbanized and suburbanized; traditional rural allegiances are breaking down, even as the mass media are making people aware of national issues. Indeed, all political parties have—within the limits imposed by the government—been relying more and more on television, public-relations campaigns, and public-opinion polls in determining their strategy. Moreover, the effects of the U.D.R. and of de Gaulle as a leader of national and international stature cannot be underestimated. De Gaulle's was a government that

---

[16] The larger the constituencies, the fewer votes wasted. In fact, the fairest system of PR, in terms of not wasting votes, would treat the entire nation as one constituency, or at least allow for the national pooling of votes "wasted" in constituencies around the country. A rigid list system is one that does not permit the voter to change the order of the names on the list (preferential vote), to distribute his vote among a number of lists, or even to compose his own list (panachage).

governed; it became identified with concrete policies for which it assumed responsibility. Voters, consequently, are coming to examine opposition parties in terms of concrete alternatives.

Beyond this, the establishment of a popularly elected presidency has served to offer the voters clear alternatives. The turnout in the 1965 elections was extremely high, and while it was much lower in 1969, studies of voter opinion have revealed a sense of tremendous satisfaction on the part of citizens who felt their vote would actually count for something in fairly straightforward terms. Indeed, the popularity of the elections indicates that the office of president may very well survive de Gaulle, even if the U.D.R. does not.

The contours of the French party system—both its general form and the ideology, dynamics, and structure of individual political parties—are a reflection of the aspirations and conflicts that characterize French life. Political parties evolved at a time when France was experiencing any number of social cleavages, and they formed along the lines of these class, religious, and local conflicts and divisions. The parties could not aggregate the interests of Frenchmen; the divisions among them were too deep and too complex. France was, indeed, a "stalemate society."

The social changes that have developed since World War II are also changing the context of political action in France. It is true, of course, that in France as in all societies institutions once established do not adapt quickly. It is to de Gaulle's credit that, coming to office at a critical time, he served to press France further along the road to modernization, even if, in doing so, his authoritarian style did little to encourage certain forms of public dialogue.

12

German

Political Parties

1. INTRODUCTION

One of the major reasons for the collapse of the Weimar Republic was that the party system failed to aggregate the multiple interests of the German people into a reasonably coherent set of pragmatic political alternatives. During the 1920's, as many as 41 parties put up candidates for seats in the Reichstag, defining their programs in narrow ideological terms and contributing to the total fragmentation of German social and political life.

Since the founding of the Bonn Republic, the political trend has been toward fewer and fewer parties competing for office. (See Table 12.1.) Today Germany has what amounts to a two-and-a-half-party system, with the two largest parties accounting for more than 88 per cent of the vote in national elections. Both parties are moderate; both appeal to a wide spectrum of the population. Although the Christian Democrats and the Social Democrats lean for support on somewhat different social groups, and still have significant differences on important policy questions, both foreign and domestic, they have unquestionably moved closer together in recent years.

The postwar alterations in the German party system for the most part mirror certain fundamental changes in German social life brought about by both the Nazi experience and World War II. As pointed out in Chapter 2, many of the particularly traumatic conflicts associated with Germany's transition from a traditional society to a modern one have been largely resolved, even though the bases for other conflicts remain and new problems are emerging, as indicated by the rise of an "extraparliamentary opposition" consisting largely of students and the appearance of a new nationalist party on the right. This chapter will describe the evolution of the German party system; as with France and England, the discussion will place that development within the general context of German social and cultural life.

The Revolution of 1848 not only brought

TABLE 12.1. CONSOLIDATION OF THE GERMAN PARTY SYSTEM

	1928	1949	1953	1957	1961	1965	1969
Number of parties presenting candidates	41	14	15	14	8	10	13
Number of parties gaining parliamentary seats	15	11	6	4	3	3	3
Percentage of votes won by three largest parties	56.1	72.1	83.5	89.7	94.3	96.4	94.6
Percentage of seats won by three largest parties	58.7	80.1	91.0	96.6	100.0	100.0	100.0
Index of overrepresentation of three largest parties (ratio of percentage of seats to percentage of votes)	1.05	1.11	1.09	1.08	1.06	1.04	1.06

Source: Gerhard Loewenberg, "The Remaking of the German Party System," *Polity*, I (1968), p. 103. Reprinted by permission of the publisher.

Prussia its first constitution and parliament, it also sparked the founding of the nation's first political parties. Organized by coalitions of notables, various liberal and conservative groupings began to appear in both Parliament and the country.

Under the empire, political organization proceeded apace and political horizons soon broadened with the emergence of Socialist groups and a specifically Catholic party, the German Center Party (*Deutsche Zentrums Partei*), organized to defend Catholic minority interests in the Second Reich. The ethnic diversity of the new German state and the enduring importance of regional ties prompted the founding of parties representing Bavarians, Danes, Guelphs, Poles, and Alsatians. Also making their appearance were small, pre-Fascist, anti-Semitic organizations.

In part, then, the large number of parties bidding for office in the late nineteenth century reflected the diversity of the national community. Other contributing factors were the use of the double ballot and the impotence of the Reichstag. Since the only popularly elected national legislative body had little power over public policy, or over the composition of an executive branch that served at the emperor's pleasure, political groups did not conceive of themselves as representing potential majorities which might form a government. Party leaders, therefore, felt free to play up the particular weltanschauung that their organizations claimed to represent.[1]

The disintegration of the German Empire in 1918 and the formation of the Weimar Republic failed to mark any decline in the number of political parties (see Table 12.2). This was partly the result of the system of proportional representation established by the republic; but more important was the fact that although some of the older regional and ethnic differences lost their immediacy, German social life had, if anything, become more fragmented. And the ideological fervor of party pronouncements increased in direct proportion to the inflexibility of ideological commitments. Rather than seek a basis for bringing new voters under their rubric, many parties stepped up their efforts to foster special little societies of their own in an attempt to isolate their members from the larger community. The Social Democrats had been the first to do so under the empire, through the establishment of newspapers, youth groups, women's auxiliaries, and housing projects in which their members might live as a community. The efforts of the Catholic-supported

[1] For a discussion of the constitution of the empire, see Chapter 2, pp. 79–80.

TABLE 12.2. REICHSTAG ELECTIONS, 1919–1933

	National Assembly Jan. 19, 1919	June 6, 1920	May 4, 1924	Dec. 7, 1924	May 20, 1928	Sept. 14, 1930	July 31, 1932	Nov. 6, 1932	March 5, 1933	Nov. 12, 1933
Majority Socialists	37.9%	21.6%	20.5%	26.0%	29.8%	24.5%	21.6%	20.4%	18.3%	
Independent Socialists	7.6	17.9								
Communist Party		2.1	12.6	9.0	10.6	13.1	14.6	16.9	12.3	
Center Party	19.7	13.6	13.4	13.6	12.1	11.8	12.5	11.9	11.7	
Bavarian People's Party		4.4	3.2	3.7	3.0	3.0	3.2	3.1	2.7	
Democratic Party	18.6	8.3	5.7	6.3	4.9	3.8	1.0	1.0	0.8	
People's Party	4.4	13.9	9.2	10.1	8.7	4.5	1.2	1.9	1.1	
Wirtschaftspartei	0.9	0.8	2.4	3.3	4.5	3.9	6.4	0.3		
National People's Party	10.3	14.9	19.5	20.5	14.2	7.0	5.9	8.8	8.0	
Christlich-soz. Volksdienst						2.5	1.1	1.2	1.0	
Landbund			1.9	1.6	0.6	0.5	0.2	0.3	0.2	
Christlich-natl. Bauern und Landvolk					1.8	3.0	0.2	0.1		
Deutsch Hannover Partei	0.2	0.9	1.0	0.8	0.5	0.4	0.1	0.2	0.1	
Deutsch Bauern Partei					1.5	1.0	0.3	0.4	0.3	
National Socialists			6.5	3.0	2.6	18.3	37.4	33.1	43.9	92.2
Other parties	0.4	1.6	4.0	2.0	4.8	3.1	0.9	2.2	0.3	

Adapted from Kopel S. Pinson, *Modern Germany* (New York: Macmillan, 1954), Appendix B, pp. 574–575. Reprinted by permission of the publisher.

Center Party were bent in the same direction. During the Weimar period, the conservatives and the liberals also created bureaucratic machines, as well as satellite organizations designed to isolate the party member. By the mid-1920's, many of the parties had also created paramilitary organizations, although few of these developed the streetfighting capacities of the National Socialists.

Weimar parties, then, never served as mechanisms for aggregating various interests into more or less comprehensive programs. If anything, they drove additional wedges into the mixed elements of German society and reinforced the mutual hostility with which each regarded the others. Even the Social Democrats—who, with the loss of their left wing, were now effectively committed to democratic institutions and moderate programs—continued to mouth Marxist slogans, thus eliminating the possibility of attracting substantial middle-class support.

Another indication of the extent to which social and political life had fragmented was the array of political parties that catered to the economic self-interest of tight little bands of people. Electoral lists included such parties as the People's Coalition of the Victims of Inflation, the Party of House- and Landowners, and the Nonpolitical List of War Victims, Work Invalids, and Welfare Recipients. These organizations put up candidates for election after election—even though many of them could not hope to be represented in the Reichstag because of the requirement that a party receive at least 60,000 votes nationally before it could attain a seat.

Many of the parties did, of course, manage to form coalitions on the national level. But their ideological rigidity, mutual suspicion, and limited definition of self-interest made these coalitions unworkable at their worst and unstable at their best. The result was political instability, with governments falling in quick succession.

The decay of social and political life fed on itself. German political culture had always emphasized the importance of developing systematic ideological positions that defined what was morally and politically right, and then taking action. Given this perspective, it was difficult for Germans to conceive of politics as representing, in part at least, a competition for power: to engage in political bargaining was to act immorally. Consequently, even under the best of circumstances, German politicians found it difficult to compromise on principle. And group self-isolation, suspicion, and self-righteousness during the 1920's only made compromises more difficult. The Weimar years were a time of intensely ideological politics, a decade in which continued calls were made for more ideological purity, and continued attacks launched against those who supposedly had sacrificed principle in the name of compromise.

The ultimate result was the rise of the National Socialist Party and the destruction of the Weimar Republic. The Nazis had built up a huge infrastructure, or party organization, that paralleled the government's; once in power, they imposed that structure upon the state apparatus, and proceeded to eliminate all other political organizations.

With the end of World War II, political activity slowly revived in West Germany. Although at first there were any number of political factions in Bonn, they eventually thinned out: between 1949 and 1969 Germany became, essentially, a two-party state. (See Figure 12.1.) In 1949, 14 parties put up candidates for public office. The two major parties, the Christian Democratic Union/ Christian Social Union (*Christlich Demokratische Union/Christlich Soziale Union*— C.D.U./C.S.U.) and the Social Democratic Party (*Sozialdemokratische Partei Deutschlands*—S.P.D.) received more than sixty per cent of the vote in the Bundestag election. Six other parties managed to obtain more than three per cent and 11 parties altogether were represented in the lower house. In 1957, the two major parties received 82 per cent of the vote between them; for the first time in German history, one party, the

FIGURE 12.1. GERMAN VOTING PATTERNS IN SIX FEDERAL ELECTIONS

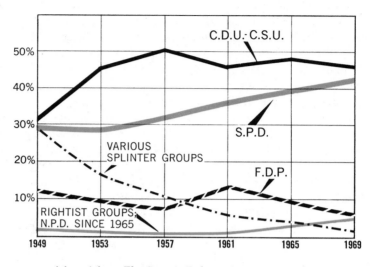

Adapted from *The German Tribune,* October 14, 1969.
Reprinted by permission of the publisher.

Christian Democrats, won a majority of legislative seats in a free election. In the election of 1965, the two major parties together again polled an even larger majority—87 per cent of the vote—and only one other political group, the Free Democratic Party (*Freie Demokratische Partei*—F.D.P.), was represented in the Bundestag.

The surge of votes for West Germany's two major parties had been at the expense of special-interest factions and extremist parties. The Communist Party, after a reasonably respectable showing in the first postwar elections, sank in strength until it was finally outlawed, and the appeal of the different right-wing parties dwindled to the point where they became of little national consequence. Furthermore, the three parties with national representation tended increasingly to soften the edges of strict ideology, thereby making broader appeals to the electorate. The isolation of various strata in the population also diminished, while at the same time the extent of overlapping membership in associations rose markedly.

There are those in Germany, primarily among intellectuals and university students,

who believe that the parties have moved so close together as to be almost ideologically indistinguishable. To them, the result has been a lack of meaningful alternative policies. They argue that many important issues—including a re-examination of the authoritarianism that they maintain continues to pervade much of German life—have been evaded. Their feelings, of course, were confirmed by the 1966 coalition government. Certainly, the formation of the Grand Coalition contributed to the emergence of a radical "extraparliamentary" opposition in the universities on the part of students who believed that the Social Democrats no longer represented a real alternative to the status quo. At about the same time, the National Democratic Party (*National Demokratische Partei Deutschlands*—N.P.D.) was able to capitalize on a resurgence of right-wing nationalism. Between 1966 and 1968, the N.P.D. managed to obtain as much as 12 per cent of the vote in some Land elections.

Despite these rumblings on the left and right, however, it is the comparative decline of "extremist" political views that is still the most significant fact about post–World War

II German politics. The reasons for this decline are fairly clear. National Socialism was destroyed in a Berlin bunker. Both the Nazi revolution and the war had succeeded in effectively eliminating traditional German conservatism by undermining the old class structure of German society. Postwar economic and social developments have continued the process. Finally, the decline of regional, ethnic, and religious variations has also blunted the edge of old political conflicts.

2. PATTERNS OF CLEAVAGE AND CONSENSUS

The Christian Democratic Union has been the Federal Republic's largest party since 1949. Officially committed to a broadly "Christian" approach to politics, it has supported policies designed, in its view, to combine a free-market economy with social responsibility, and to encourage natural associations such as the family. Aside from a few splinter groups, the C.D.U. is the nearest thing to a conservative party in Germany today.

Its major competitor is the Social Democratic Party, originally a Socialist party, but now committed to pragmatic reform, with the goal of complete socialism pushed into the distant future. The remnants of traditional German liberalism are represented by the Free Democratic Party, which seems to owe its survival to an electoral system under which votes that are cast for it will not be wasted provided it receives five per cent of the national total.[2] As a party, the F.D.P. remains vaguely anticlerical and vaguely Protestant. It was committed to a free-market economy, and for many years its economic program was difficult to distinguish from that of the C.D.U. In the past several years it has tried to establish an image as a democratic reformist party of the center-left; but

---

[2] A discussion of the German electoral system begins on p. 411.

like other liberal parties it is marked by considerable factionalism, and its leaders roam over a wide range of political terrain.

Although in more recent elections the Social Democrats have been wooing the middle class, their electoral support still comes largely from industrial workers (see Table 12.3). Social class continues to be the single most important determinant of voting behavior in Germany. The best estimates are that about 43 per cent of the industrial and rural workers support the S.P.D., while about 22 per cent back the C.D.U./C.S.U. and about three per cent the F.D.P. The major factor preventing the S.P.D. from obtaining a larger portion of the working-class vote seems to be the religious one. Polls indicate that some 14 per cent more Catholic workers than Protestant workers vote for the Christian Democrats and that the proportion of Catholic workers supporting the C.D.U. over the Social Democrats rises with the worker's religiosity, as measured by church attendance. Workers who vote for the Free Democrats tend to come from the more privileged segments of the working class, although the proportion of these voting for the Socialists is growing. As one might expect, trade-union members and workers in large modern plants in the major urban centers vote in greater proportions for the S.P.D. Primarily because of the religious question, the Christian Democrats receive more support from unskilled workers than semi-skilled ones.

The German upper middle class—including professionals, businessmen, civil servants, and white-collar employees—gives its support primarily to the C.D.U. and the F.D.P.; here again, the major variable is religion. Farmers and peasants, too, vote rather more heavily for the C.D.U. and the F.D.P. than they do for the Social Democrats, and again the question of which of the former two parties they support seems to be determined primarily by religious affiliation. Finally, the self-employed craftsmen usually give the Christian Democrats a rather lopsided en-

TABLE 12.3. SOCIOECONOMIC GROUPINGS AND PARTY PREFERENCES, 1966

Preferences expressed in opinion polls

	Proportion of adult population, 1966	C.D.U./ C.S.U.	S.P.D.	F.D.P.	Others	None indicated
Total:	100%	30%	33%	5%	2%	30%
Men	46	25	38	5	3	28
Women	54	34	27	4	1	34
Age:						
16–29	20	29	34	5	3	29
30–44	24	29	40	5	2	24
45–59	25	31	35	4	3	27
60 and over	20	37	27	4	2	30
Religious identification:						
Protestant	53	23	39	6	3	29
Roman Catholic	42	41	25	3	2	29
Others or none	5	11	33	5	1	50
Education:						
Primary (8 years)	73	29	36	3	3	28
Secondary (9–10 years)	17	33	25	7	2	33
Higher (incl. university)	10	36	22	13	3	26
Occupation:						
Industrial and agricultural workers	50	22	43	3	2	30
Salaried employees	24	33	29	5	3	30
Civil servants	7	39	26	6	2	27
Self-employed and professions	12	42	12	14	4	28
Independent farmers	7	48	12	7	3	30
Income level (monthly):						
Under $100	10	35	24	1	1	39
$100–200	38	29	30	5	2	34
Over $200	52	30	37	5	3	25

Source: Institut für Demoskopie Allensbach, January 1966. Reprinted by permission. Data supplied by the Roper Public Opinion Research Center.

dorsement, with the Socialists receiving only a very small fraction of their vote.

Whatever their party allegiances, German voters do not seem to feel their political differences as strongly as they once did. During the entire chancellorship of Christian Democrat Konrad Adenauer very few Social Democrats held intensely negative views of his administration, and the same has been true of attitudes toward his successors. Since the war, German voters have taken both a more detached and a more practical view of politics, and most of them explain their voting preferences in terms of economic self-interest. As Table 12.4 indicates, some Germans, but only a small minority, still look back with nostalgia upon certain aspects of the National Socialist regime. The fact is that democratic institutions have become more and more popular in the twenty years since the founding of the West German Federal Republic, and the elites of both major parties are strongly committed to the present system. Most important of all, perhaps, Germans now believe that a victory by one or another of the major parties would not be catastrophic. Indeed, by the early 1960's "socialism" was no longer a scare word even for middle-class Germans. (See Table 12.5.)

TABLE 12.4.   ATTITUDES TOWARD HITLER IN THE GERMANY
OF 1967

*"If you had a chance today as in 1933 of voting in an election for or against a man
like Hitler, what would you decide to do?"*

Year of survey	For	Against	No opinion
1953	12%	67%	21%
1954	15	81	4
1958	10	81	9
1963	5	77	18
1965	4	80	16
Attitude toward the National Democratic Party			
N.P.D. partisans	36	42	22
N.P.D. sympathizers	11	62	27
N.P.D. opponents	1	93	6

Source: *Polls*, III, 1 (Autumn 1967), 30. Reprinted by permission of
Emnid-Institut, Bielefeld, Federal Republic of Germany.

Yet despite high voter turnout, Germans still have a far more passive attitude toward political participation than Englishmen or Americans. They are less interested in joining voluntary associations which seek social or political reforms; they are less sanguine about the possibility of altering the direction of national policies through individual participation. Although this bias is slowly changing, most Germans still regard politics as something best left to experts.

For the older generation the Nazi experiment is a harsh reminder of the folly of becoming involved in "romantic" political experiences. For all generations there is a sense that their environment is unstable—as the bifurcation of their country testifies. And while the great mass of Germans may think that their political institutions are working rather well, they have little real pride in them. Most Germans continue to hold that Germany has not yet found its place in the postwar world, or developed a sense of purpose and self-identity—a deep uncertainty mirrored by the reactivation of the German right and the turbulent manifestations of radical student opposition.

3. THE LIBERAL TRADITION

The Free Democratic Party of Germany is the heir of the German liberal tradition that came to the fore in 1848. Like the British Liberal Party and the French Radicals, it is but a remnant of a once-powerful political force; like them, it looks both to the right and to the left in search of a position that can be publicly differentiated from those of the political giants against whom it competes. And, also like its French and British cousins, its makeup is sufficiently heterogeneous and transitory that its self-definition seems to change from year to year.

During the empire, German liberalism split into two factions. The National Liberals, who represented for the most part industrial interests and were on good terms with the Junkers, were at times among Bismarck's strongest supporters. The other faction, the Progressives, favored parliamentary democracy and showed much more concern for individual liberties. Committed to the need for social reform, the Progressives received considerable support from the commercial

TABLE 12.5.   GERMAN ATTITUDES TOWARD
THE WORD "SOCIALISM," 1961

*"If you . . . think of the word 'socialism' . . . all sorts of . . . things might enter one's
mind in connection with it. May I read a few to you? And will you please tell me
whether, on hearing the word 'socialism,' these things really could come to mind?"*

	Yes	No	No reply
Safety from disease and distress	75%	12%	13%
Security in old age	73	12	15
Prosperity for all	69	15	16
Justice	65	15	20
Progressive	63	16	21
Human dignity	63	21	16
Freedom	62	21	17
Peace-loving	60	20	20
Comradeship	55	20	25
Vigorous	35	33	32
Trade-union boss	30	48	22
Soviet zone	28	55	17
High social insurance contributions	26	53	21
Radical	25	56	19
Bureaucratic	22	51	27
Compulsion	19	64	17
Communism	18	65	17
Bleak theory	17	56	27
Undemocratic	13	66	21
Obsolete	13	68	19

Source: E. Noelle and E. P. Neumann, *The Germans: Public Opinion Polls, 1947–
1966* (Allensbach: Verlag für Demoskopie, 1967), p. 398. Reprinted by permission
of the publisher.

TABLE 12.6.   GERMAN PERCEPTION OF OBLIGATIONS
OF CITIZENSHIP, 1959

Mass opinion data in rounded-off percentages

To do one's job well, raise one's children properly; to be honest, helpful, and have a sense of responsibility in one's conduct	31%
To vote	31
To pay taxes	30
To obey laws; to respect public authorities	23
To love one's country; to be loyal and faithful to it; to speak well of it; to be a good representative of it in foreign lands	21
To defend one's country, if necessary; to serve in the armed forces	12
To participate in public and political affairs, in political discussions; to speak one's mind; to criticize the government, if necessary	4
To endeavor to understand public affairs and to keep abreast of political developments	3
Other answers	7
No obligations specified; no response to question	9

Source: Edinger, *Germany*, p. 106. Reprinted by permission.

interests believing in free trade, as well as from intellectuals and peasants.

With the end of the empire, the two parties re-formed. Most National Liberals transferred their allegiance to the German People's Party, which, under the leadership of Gustav Stresemann, was extremely influential in Weimar politics during the middle 1920's. (After 1928, most of its support was captured by the National Socialists.) The German Democratic Party, the Weimar successor of the Progressives, was committed to the democratic republic and to social reform. It had strong support from German intellectuals; one of its leaders, Hugo Preuss, helped draft the Weimar constitution. During the first years of the republic, the Democratic Party cooperated with the Social Democrats and the Center Party as the governing coalition, but in doing so it lost most of its traditional base of support, some of which moved over to the German People's Party. The Democrats received 19 per cent of the popular vote in the elections of 1919, the year the Weimar Republic was founded; in the 1920 elections, their vote dropped to less than nine per cent. In the last years of the republic, the party tried to develop a more nationalistic program—but too late: it received five per cent of the vote in 1928, and only one per cent in 1932. Progressive German liberalism died with the republic.

The Free Democratic Party was founded in 1948—a nostalgic effort to recombine the old National Liberal and Progressive traditions. From the beginning, the more liberal wing of the F.D.P. was based in southern Germany, while its more conservative candidates drew support from anticlerical, business, and professional interests in northern and western Germany. In the 1949 elections to the first Bundestag, the F.D.P. received only 11.9 per cent of the vote, and it quickly became evident that there was little chance of its developing into a major political force. It was not long, therefore, before many of its potential leaders defected to the Christian Democrats and the Social Democrats.

For the next decade, the Free Democrats continued to appeal primarily to anticlerical Protestants who could not bring themselves to join the Socialists or the C.D.U., and the party also continued to fragment. In 1953 its percentage of the vote slipped to 9.5; in 1957 it declined still further to 7.7. After that, the F.D.P. engaged in a major effort to build up its organization and create a new image with broader appeal. Like liberal parties all over Europe, however, it had small success: the electorate had no interest in nineteenth-century liberalism, and the political distance between the two major parties was getting too narrow to allow room for a moderate third to maneuver. Actually, the F.D.P. followed several strategies. On the national level it allied itself with the Christian Democrats, joining the government as the minor partner of a coalition. In a number of Länder, however, the Free Democrats joined with the Social Democrats to form coalition governments.

When the party was established, its national leadership came from its more progressive wing. By the late 1950's, however, its more conservative and nationalistic elements had come to predominate, a trend confirmed with the 1960 election of Erich Mende as party chairman. Even so, the party line was nothing if not flexible: after attacking Chancellor Adenauer for being too subservient to American interests, Mende himself supporting the pro-American Ludwig Erhard against those in the C.D.U. whom Mende considered both too authoritarian and too chauvinist. Indeed, in both 1961 and 1965 the F.D.P. campaign argued the dangers of allowing the C.D.U. to have a clear majority in the Bundestag. The Free Democrats offered themselves as a group that would support the C.D.U. but prevent it from following dangerous policies under the wrong leadership. In 1961 the strategy seemed to work; the popular vote of the F.D.P. rose to 12.7 per cent. It was, however, a negative victory, reflecting the decline in Adenauer's popularity; four years later the party's vote dropped back to less than ten per cent.

In 1966, the formation of a coalition government of the Christian Democratic Union and the Social Democrats left the F.D.P. as the only opposition party in the country, at least on the national level. The new coalition, and the emergence of the N.P.D. and student activism, led the Free Democrats to adopt a new strategy. Thus, in 1967 and 1968 the party moved from a center-right to a center-left political position. Under Walter Scheel, the new party chairman, the C.D.U. and S.P.D. were attacked as symptomatic of the staid, bureaucratic mentality that has typified German politics. Domestically, the Free Democrats urged the further democratization of German society; in foreign policy, they adopted an increasingly neutralist policy. In short, the party was cautiously trying on a new liberal image—radical but not Socialist, accepting the welfare state but desiring to humanize and "debureaucratize" it, and, above all, concerned with eliminating the authoritarian elements that persistently appear within the German community.

The strategy both succeeded and failed. In the 1969 national election, the F.D.P.'s share of the vote fell to 5.8 per cent. It was enough, however, to permit the Free Democrats to join the S.P.D. in a mini-coalition so as to secure for Scheel the post of foreign minister.

This official embrace of the Social Democrats is, even so, something of a risk. A moderate and successful regime led by the S.P.D. is likely to capture those Free Democratic voters who in the past were anti–C.D.U. but unwilling to vote for a "radical" Socialist party. At the same time, the success of the new coalition could well drive the more conservative F.D.P. members into the C.D.U. Like its French and English counterparts, the liberal Free Democratic Party is caught in a squeeze that leaves it very little room for maneuver.

4. THE DECLINE AND RE-EMERGENCE OF THE GERMAN RIGHT

Like the liberals, conservative political groupings made their appearance at the time of the 1848 Revolution and the Frankfurt Assembly. Merging into a loosely organized Conservative Party, they drew their major support during the German Empire from the Junker aristocracy, large business, and portions of the peasantry. The Conservatives were pro-Prussian, suspecting both industrialism and capitalism, which they saw as opening the way to radicalism. They also served as the first political receptacle for anti-Semitism, which later, of course, became much more rabid. While the Conservatives disliked Bismarck's endorsement of industrialization, universal suffrage, and social reform, they continued, for lack of an alternative, to back the government. For a time, a group calling itself the Free Conservatives split with the parent organization. Rather more enlightened, the leaders of the Free Conservatives were ardent supporters of all Bismarck's works. In due time, however, the Conservatives and Free Conservatives reunited.

The Conservatives eventually saw the necessity of becoming a mass party; in the 1880's they allied themselves with the Christian Social movement of Adolf Stöcker as a way of reaching the people. Stöcker later formed the Christian Social Workers' Party, which relied very heavily upon anti-Semitism as a weapon for creating mass enthusiasm. The Conservatives' embrace of Stöcker, even though they disapproved of some of his rabble-rousing, was an important ingredient in making anti-Semitism more respectable.

After World War I, the Conservatives grouped themselves around the German National People's Party (Deutsch-nationale Volkspartei), which urged the restoration of the monarchy and the empire. Recognizing the need for developing a popular political base, the leadership tried to emulate the parties of the left by creating a mass organization—the use of the word Volk in the party's name is indicative of its concern for mass support. And in an attempt to broaden its appeal during the late years of the Weimar Republic, it became stridently anti-Semitic. These efforts were of little avail, however, for the Nazi Party took away most of its support. Between 1928 and 1930, its percentage of the popular vote dropped from more than 14 to seven.

By 1921, Adolf Hitler had established himself as the leader of the National Socialist German Worker's Party (*Nationalsozialistische Deutsche Arbeiter Partei—*N.S.D.A.P.). Although the party lost much of its momentum during the relative stability of the middle 1920's, it continued to build its organization, modeled very closely upon that of the Communists. Aside from its nationalism and its anti-Semitism, the party program was vague and contradictory; it promised all things to all groups. It would, for example, nationalize industry, but only the industry of capitalists who, like the Jews, were exploiting the German people. Relying upon violence and intimidation, the Nazis promised to end the civil disorder they had helped create and offered themselves as the only viable alternative to communism.

As pointed out in Chapter 2, the Nazis were not really a conservative party; much of their rhetoric was characterized by anti-Prussian populism. They seriously undermined traditional German conservatism, however, by drawing off the only groups that might have constructed a mass base for a genuinely conservative party—and their policies, World War II, and the division of Germany after the war effectively completed the job.

When political parties formed again in West Germany, most of the more conservative Germans and most ex-Nazis gravitated to either the Free Democratic Party or the Christian Democrats. A number of right-wing parties did crop up, including the conservative German Party (*Deutsche Partei* —D.P.) and the neo-Nazi Socialist Reich Party (*Sozialistische Reichspartei*—S.R.P.), but except in a few local elections, their vote was never large. The Socialist Reich Party itself was outlawed by the Constitutional Court in 1952, although other right-wing groupings sprang up to replace it, including the German Reich Party (*Deutsche Reichspartei—*D.R.P.), but none of these were able to elect a single candidate to Parliament. For a time, a move was made to organize a party around the demands of the refugees from the East. The new group took on a glaringly nationalist coloration. By 1961, however, its vote and that of the D.P., with which it had combined to form the All-German Party, was down to 2.8 per cent; in 1965, all the right-wing parties together polled only slightly more than two per cent of the national vote.

The poor showing of right-wing parties in postwar elections was not precisely duplicated in a number of public-opinion polls taken during the 1950's and early 1960's, which demonstrated the continued existence of a good number of voters—from ten to 15 per cent—who could conceivably be mobilized by a nationalist populist party of the right. In 1966 just such a party—the National Democratic Party—was catapulted to national prominence because of its success in local elections in Hesse, where it received some eight per cent of the vote. In 1967 and 1968 the N.P.D. garnered from six to 12 per cent of the vote in Land and local elections throughout Germany.

The N.P.D. was founded in 1964 by Adolf von Thadden, a right-wing politician who had been active in rightist splinter groups during the 1950's. Studies of its leadership and sympathizers indicate that it has a great attraction for supporters of earlier right-wing parties. The party is more popular among Protestants than among Catholics; its largest constituency consists of self-employed artisans and white-collar workers, although it also includes a sizable sampling of industrial workers. The N.P.D.'s initial support came almost entirely from older age groups, but three years after its founding, many younger people were also giving it their allegiance.

Unquestionably, the success of the N.P.D. was fostered by the weaknesses of the Erhard government and the mild German recession of 1966 and 1967. Later the formation of the Grand Coalition of Christian Democrats and Social Democrats pushed some disaffected members of the C.D.U. into its ranks; and, no doubt, the weakening of Germany's international position during the 1960's and the rampages of leftist students drove still more voters to the right.

The program of the N.P.D. is, even today, somewhat vague, combining calls for order and discipline at home with a nebulous international policy not unlike de Gaulle's. Its leadership disavows any racist bias and has denied that the party is anti-Semitic, but it has urged the expulsion of foreign workers.

In some respects, the N.P.D. may be classified as neo-Nazi. Yet there is little evidence that in either intention or program it is more than a very pale imitation of the National Socialists. It is unquestionably authoritarian, although in 1968 the government was forced to drop plans for declaring it illegal for lack of evidence of undemocratic intent. Further, few observers believe that, barring an economic catastrophe, it has any hope of becoming a major political force. The fact that it is also rent by internal conflicts and may well fragment into other parties does not enhance its future prospects for national success. Indeed, in the 1969 elections it polled only 4.3 per cent of the vote and failed to elect a single representative to the Bundestag.

5. THE TRANSFORMATION OF GERMAN SOCIALISM

The Social Democratic Party of Germany was born in 1875, the official offspring of two parent Socialist organizations created in the 1860's. At its inaugural congress held in Gotha, the program adopted, while it was strongly influenced in many ways by Marx, owed a good deal to the writings and rhetoric of Ferdinand Lassalle.[3] The program was, in fact, attacked by Marx for its lack of theoretical sophistication; his main criticisms were directed against its reformist emphases

[3] Lassalle had been the founder of the older of the two parent groups, the General Association of German Workers.

and its assumption that the state would continue to have an important function in a Socialist society.

While many of the earlier leaders of the Social Democrats were imbued with the tenets of Marx, the S.P.D. did not become officially Marxist until the adoption of the Erfurt Program in 1891. By that time, a combination of factors, including the partial repression of the party by Bismarck, had given Marxist intellectuals, under the leadership of Karl Kautsky, a dominant role in defining the organization's political stance. The program was officially revolutionary, but the party did not eschew parliamentary activity designed to provide a platform for educating the proletariat and attaining social reforms.

Despite Bismarck's efforts at repression from 1879 to 1890, the Socialist Party grew with amazing rapidity. In 1877 it had received nearly nine per cent of the vote cast; by 1890 its share was twenty per cent; in 1903 it soared to roughly 32 per cent, making it the largest party in the nation, although not yet in the Reichstag.

By 1907 it had more than five hundred thousand dues-paying members. From the very beginning, the Social Democratic Party was a mass party committed to creating a new society within Germany. Thus it spawned a wide variety of groups to insulate Socialists from the larger community and re-educate them. It owned and published its own newspapers; it formed its own insurance company; it organized factories to be run by the workers; it even built its own apartment houses. The S.P.D. also developed a close working relationship with the trade-union movement—which, to an extent, was its own creation—and trade-union leaders came to assume a significant part in its councils.

Within the party, strong reformist and non-Marxist voices continued to carry considerable weight, despite the party's official adoption of a Marxist and revolutionary program. Trade-union leaders especially, while they might use revolutionary rhetoric, were more concerned with immediate gains.

And their rhetoric notwithstanding, most of the party's leaders were not about to lead the masses in a revolution. Eventually, a movement did develop among party intellectuals seeking to revamp the S.P.D.'s program. Led by Eduard Bernstein, the group wanted the party to emphasize its reformist character and enhance its appeal to other social groups by reconsidering its Marxist commitment. However, nothing came of this effort; not only did the party remain officially attached to doctrines that alienated a large portion of Germans, but they were doctrines that the party was not prepared to implement. This rigidity prevented the Social Democrats from formulating programs that would have allowed them to cooperate with German liberals for the urgent purpose of attaining more limited goals. The party leadership was not unaware of the problem, but, aside from an emotional commitment to pure Marxism, it was faced with the fact that many of its most active militants were effective because of the religious zeal that Marxism inspired. To have repudiated this rhetoric might have split the party and seriously hampered all its efforts.

During the First World War, the German Social Democrats, like Socialist parties all over Europe, supported their government. As the war continued, however, the S.P.D. began to break apart, especially after the Russian Revolution. Many of the radical Marxists within the party supported the Bolshevik effort and eventually formed the German Communist Party; others, including many reformists, left the party because of their opposition to the S.P.D.'s continued support of the war, and formed the Independent Social Democratic Party.[4]

After the war, the majority of the Socialists joined with the army to suppress a half-hearted attempt at a leftist revolution and collaborated with the Catholic Center Party and the two liberal parties to draw up

a constitution for a new German republic. Under the leadership of Philipp Scheidemann, they joined with the more moderate parties to form the first government of the Weimar Republic. In the first few years of the republic, the Social Democrats remained part of the governing coalition; by the mid-twenties, however, they were back in opposition. Part of the reason for this change in political roles lay in the creation and growth of the Communist Party, which, in dividing the working-class vote, weakened the overall influence of the left and placed the reins of government in the hands of center and center-right political groups.

In addition, the contribution of the Socialists in founding the republic and their acceptance of the Versailles Treaty saddled them with the stigma of being antinational and dominated by Jewish intellectuals. This stigma, combined with their continued anticlericalism and a rhetoric that belied their conservative actions, limited their appeal to middle-class voters; yet to surrender their rhetoric would have left them open to the possibility of being even further outflanked on the left by the Communists. The party was also handicapped by a tired bureaucracy in which, during the 1920's, there was very little turnover in personnel. Young people of talent were not given party status, and, at the end of the decade, most men in the Socialist cadres were in their forties and fifties. A good many had developed their political orientations during the empire, and they were not likely to change them very quickly.

Shortly after World War II, the S.P.D. began to reorganize itself. At its first postwar organization meeting in 1945, a number of delegates urged fusion with the Communists; others, including party leaders Erich Ollenhauer and Kurt Schumacher, managed to forestall such an option and secured a postponement of the decision until a full conference could be called the following year. By then, however, the European situation had changed considerably. Western–Soviet

4 The party dissolved in 1922, its supporters joining either the Social Democrats or the Communists.

TABLE 12.7. SOCIAL CLASS AND OCCUPATION OF SOCIALIST
MEMBERS OF THE REICHSTAG, 1903–1930

	1903	1912	1919	1930
Middle class				
Intellectuals	13	28	21	29
White collar	0	9	16	20
Working class				
Artisans, skilled workers	68	59	107	79
Unskilled workers	0	2	14	11
Occupation				
Party secretaries	35	13	22	25
Trade-union officials		20	54	31
Other officials		7	18	26
Editors and writers	17	40	33	31
Other professionals		7	6	9
Self-employed	29	22	15	3
Workers	0	1	9	3
Housewives	0	0	7	7

Adapted from Richard N. Hunt, *German Social Democracy, 1918–1933* (New Haven: Yale University Press, 1964), pp. 92, 93. Reprinted by permission of the publisher.

amity was cooling, and the compulsory merger of Communist and Socialist groups in the Soviet zone of Germany had disillusioned a good many of those Socialists who had believed in the possibility of a democratic fusion. The proposal of marriage with the Communists was, as a consequence, decisively defeated.

With the reactivation of its formal organization, the S.P.D. grew in strength very quickly—all traditional loyalties not having been destroyed by the Nazis. By 1948 dues-paying membership had reached 840,000, and the party was winning roughly 35 per cent of the popular vote in local elections. However, continued antagonism between Adenauer, the leader of the Christian Democrats, and Schumacher, who now led the Social Democrats, prevented the formation of a coalition. In the first postwar elections to the Bundestag, in 1949, the S.P.D. received a little more than 29 per cent of the popular vote, compared with 31 per cent for the C.D.U. The Christian Democrats then formed a government in coalition with some of the minor parties, and the S.P.D. came to serve as the main source of opposition.

While the Social Democratic Party no longer considered itself bound by Marxist orthodoxies, its rhetoric during the early 1950's still smacked of Marxism and its program called for the establishment of a Socialist Germany. Since the C.D.U., under the leadership of Adenauer and Erhard, was moving away from both planning and socialization, the differences between the parties in the economic area became increasingly obvious. To economic differences were added those over foreign policy: Schumacher strongly opposed German rearmament and the formation of excessively close ties between Germany and the United States, fearing that such actions would reduce the possibility of German unification. He especially opposed programs such as the European Defense Community and the European coal and steel agreements, which he believed would align Germany with predominantly Catholic nations dominated by conservative parties.

Schumacher's position was based on a number of factors. For one thing, he genuinely wished to see Germany unified, and he believed that the maintenance of a neutralist position made the achievement of that goal

TABLE 12.8. AGE DISTRIBUTION OF SOCIALIST AND
COMMUNIST REICHSTAG FRAKTION MEMBERS, 1903–1930

Age	1912 S.P.D.	1919 S.P.D.	1928 S.P.D.	1928 K.P.D.	1930 S.P.D.	1930 K.P.D.
20–30	1	1	1	2	0	8
30–40	10	19	23	33	20	47
40–50	51	71	49	17	49	20
50–60	30	59	56	1	51	1
60–70	13	14	21	0	22	0
Over 70	5	1	2	1	1	1
Under 50	56%	55%	48%	96%	48%	97%
Over 50	44	45	52	4	52	3

Source: Hunt, *German Social Democracy*, p. 89. Reprinted by permission.

more likely. A neutral West Germany, Schumacher reasoned, might lead more quickly to a détente between Russia and the West; that, in turn, would facilitate unification. Moreover, a reunited Germany would not only fulfill Schumacher's sense of nationalism; it would also, he believed, be a boon to the Socialists, who could never hope to win a majority unless they regained some of those areas in the East that had been the bastions of party support during the Weimar period. He also feared a resurgence of militarism in Germany should a new German army come into existence, even as part of NATO. Finally, by emphasizing German nationalism, Schumacher hoped to remove the taint of being "un-German" from the Socialist Party. To all these attitudes was added the Socialist leader's violent—and fully reciprocated—personal dislike for Adenauer.

Schumacher's policies, however, were notoriously unsuccessful. While the Socialists continued to make a good showing in Land elections, their percentage of the popular vote in the 1953 elections slipped to 28.8, while that of the Christian Democrats rose from 31 to 45.2 per cent. Four years later, the election results were not much more satisfactory. The S.P.D.'s share of the total vote increased to 31.8 per cent, but the C.D.U. increased its percentage to more than fifty and obtained a majority of the seats in the Bundestag.

Throughout this postwar era, of course, many changes had taken place in both the Socialist Party and German society. The economic policies of the Adenauer government had proved eminently successful, and the Federal Republic was recovering from the war at a fantastically rapid rate. In the party itself, a new generation of political figures, men who had little attachment to the more traditional slogans of power, was taking the reins. Led by people like Fritz Erler and Willy Brandt, who became mayor of Berlin in 1957, and supported by local and regional party leaders who had been elected to Land and municipal governments, they looked to a fundamental reorientation of the party. They were joined in their efforts by older leaders impressed with developments in England, and by many former Communists who had radically altered their views, including Herbert Wehner, who was to become vice chairman of the party.

Like Bernstein before them, these men argued that the fallacies of Marxist economic and social analysis had been amply demonstrated. Capitalism was capable of continued development, and the job of a Socialist party should be to urge amendments and reforms as new problems emerged—and not to champion a new economic system based upon doctrinaire goals. To the S.P.D.'s new leaders, the Soviet experience showed convincingly that socialism did not automatically usher in utopia. They also maintained that the party's devotion to and concern with democratic procedures must be at least as strong as its concern with economic reform; their aim was to transform the S.P.D. into a "people's" party rather than solely a working-class one, a party that would overcome its negative image and would appeal to the salaried middle class. Finally, they argued that the party should accommodate itself to the Catholic Church by emphasizing that it was not hostile to organized religion, that it was prepared to compromise on the issue of denominational schools, and that it would work with Catholics of the left to achieve concrete social reforms.

It was Schumacher himself who had started the party on the road to a re-examination of its doctrines and attitudes; despite the efforts of leftists within the party, the process of developing a new program continued under Ollenhauer, his successor as party chairman. By the 1957 election, the party's action program was conspicuously moderate. It stated, in part:

We Social Democrats demand a free economic development, free competition and private property conscious of its responsibilities to the general good.[5]

In 1958, the new program was presented in draft form at the party's Stuttgart convention, and one year later it was formally adopted at its Bad Godesberg convention. It was a victory for the reformers, and later emendations went even further in making the Social Democratic Party essentially a pragmatic party of social reform. The

1961 and 1965 election campaigns were conducted on the basis of these new programs, and under the new party leadership. Brandt, one of the new generation of political leaders to whom rhetoric was no substitute for the careful analysis of social problems, was designated the party's candidate for chancellor before the 1961 elections, and in 1963 he became party president. Brandt had left Germany in 1933 and emigrated to Norway; after the Nazi occupation of that country, he had fled to Sweden, returning to Germany after the war. Gathering about him two of the most important of the revisionists, Erler and Wehner, Brandt conducted an American-style campaign modeled after that of John F. Kennedy. His efforts were rewarded; in 1961, the party's share of the vote rose to 36.3 per cent, and in 1965 to 39.3 per cent—despite the defection of some of its supporters to the German Peace Union.

To many Social Democrats, however, the 1965 results were a disappointment. It was clear that while the S.P.D.'s image had improved, many Germans still could not bring themselves to vote for the "red" anti-religious party. To this must be added the natural reluctance of voters to switch during what was still an era of prosperity, and the cutting attacks leveled against Brandt because of his illegitimate birth and his "unpatriotic" behavior.[6]

Party leaders, nevertheless, persisted in their new course and, in 1966, agreed to join a coalition government with the Christian Democrats in which the S.P.D. would be a slightly junior partner. The move had mixed results. Many intellectuals, as well as university students, considered the coalition a sell-out and, in fact, agitation on the campus and rumblings within the party itself pushed the S.P.D. slightly back toward the left between 1966 and 1969. Thus, the party has moved

[5] Quoted in Peter H. Merkl, *Germany, Yesterday and Tomorrow* (New York: Oxford University Press, 1965), p. 316.

[6] For a short time he posed as a Norwegian soldier to escape the attention of the Gestapo. This has led to the spreading of rumors that he fought against Germany.

toward a somewhat more neutralist position in foreign affairs and a more conciliatory attitude with respect to East Germany. Yet the moderate stance on public issues adopted by the Social Democratic leadership and its "responsible" participation in the Grand Coalition undoubtedly so enhanced its popularity that it was able, after the 1969 parliamentary elections, to form a new coalition government, this time with the Free Democratic Party, this time with itself as the dominant partner.

Whether the mini-coalition forged by Brandt, with himself as chancellor, holds together or not, the Social Democratic Party has finally succeeded in reaching the goal toward which it has been struggling since the late 1950's. It is now clearly a major party with a broad national appeal. It is difficult to conceive of it ever again returning to nineteenth-century Marxist rhetoric.

STRUCTURE AND DYNAMICS: The Social Democratic Party began as a democratically organized mass party. Local and regional branches gradually expanded throughout the entire nation; these elected delegates to the party congresses, the party's ultimate source of policy. Between party meetings, authority rested in an elected National Executive Committee, to which the parliamentary party was supposedly subordinate. Unlike the British Labor Party, the S.P.D. maintained only an informal relationship with the trade unions, although they supported the party financially and worked closely with it.

As the S.P.D. evolved, it began to exhibit many of the customary characteristics of large-scale organizations. Increasingly, the power to make decisions seemed to be taken over by the party bureaucracy—the national executive, parliamentary representatives, and the trade-union leadership. It was, in fact, these developments that led Robert Michels to formulate his "iron law of oligarchy" after a study of the S.P.D. just before World War I. If even the most democratically organized party, in theory, became highly stratified in terms of power, what hope

was there for any political organization?[7] In the Weimar decade, the National Executive and the parliamentary party were usually dominated by both party and trade-union bureaucrats who had slowly worked their way up through the S.P.D.'s apparatus. Younger radicals migrated to the Communist Party, while the Social Democrats ossified.

When the S.P.D. reorganized after World War II, it retained its basic structure, including the revival of many of the same groups and activities that had, under the Weimar Republic and earlier, made it a state within a state. Simultaneously, between 1945 and 1969 the party continued to evolve along lines already prefigured in the Weimar period— that is, having begun its life as a mass, ideological party, it was transformed into an organization that more closely resembled a pragmatic cadre party run by professional politicians. For example, while the power of the bureaucratic apparatus declined somewhat, the S.P.D. did not return to its initial ideal of a mass democratic party. Rather, authority has fallen to political figures who can gain popular support, in either Land or national affairs, and to individuals who combine party loyalty with expertise. While the party bureaucracy is still very important, it is certainly less so than it was in previous years.

The Social Democratic Party is still a mass party, with some 650,000 members whose dues provide most of its funds. The basic unit is the local organization (*Ortsverein*), which elects its own officers and is the agency through which dues are collected. The local branches enable members to maintain contact with each other, serve as agencies for recruiting, and have a limited voice in the conduct of elections and in some cases the nomination of candidates. The level of activity in most branches, while respectable, has dropped off in recent years; for younger members at least, the party no longer

7 See Robert Michels, *Political Parties* (New York: Crowell Collier Publishing Company, 1962). His study has become a classic.

commands their total support. Nevertheless, many do join and become active, not just because of idealism but because they believe that local branches are the means to advancement within the party.

The principal territorial units are the regional and subregional branches (*Bezirke* and *Unterbezirke*). These effectively determine who the party's national candidates shall be and are largely responsible for organizing election campaigns. The regional groups hold regular congresses to which delegates are sent from local organizations. The congresses are dominated by an executive committee and council elected by the delegates with the approval of the national executive. Committees of specialists and closely affiliated groups of Socialist business and professional men assist regional executives in planning campaigns and dealing with local and state political problems.

According to its statutes, the Social Democratic Party Convention, which meets every two years, is its "highest organ." It is composed of the members of the national executive committee; the control commission, which supervises party finances; and three hundred delegates elected from the Bezirke, a good portion of whom are paid party officials. Its prime function is to listen to reports from the party executive, the parliamentary party organization (*Bundestagsfraktion*), and the party's control commission. The conventions are not without influence, but their significance in determining the direction of policy is even less than that of British party conventions. Rather, their function is primarily ritualistic.

The most important organs for declaring policy are the parliamentary Fraktion and the national executive committee. The former consists of all S.P.D. members in the Bundestag; the latter of 33 members elected by the congress. Since 1958 the N.E.C.'s work has fallen increasingly to a smaller group of nine members called the Presidium, which is elected by the executive committee. This second body is made up entirely of paid national officials and members of the Bundestag, and it meets almost every week. Since the executive, too, is dominated by Bundestag members, the parliamentary party has more and more become the policy-making power of the Social Democrats.

Traditionally, the executive committee chairman has been the candidate for party leader and chancellor in any general election, although Brandt was designated the latter when Ollenhauer still held the chairmanship. The deputy chairman of the committee has, in the past, been responsible for organizational matters; in 1968, however, a special

TABLE 12.9. SOCIAL STATUS OF S.P.D. LEADERS

Analysis on the basis of delegates to the S.P.D. Conference at Hamburg in 1950

	Workers	White collar	Professional	Party workers	Unemployed
Executive	0	13	1	8	4
Party council	1	12	0	9	5
Control commission	2	3	2	0	0
Parliamentary group	0	11	1	0	2
Main speaker	0	1	0	0	0
Subtotal	3 (4%)	40 (53.3%)	4 (5.3%)	17 (22.7%)	11 (14.7%)
Rank-and-file delegates	26	130	34	52	35
Total delegates	29 (8.2%)	170 (48.3%)	38 (10.8%)	69 (19.6%)	46 (13.1%)

Source: David Childs, *From Schumacher to Brandt* (London: Pergamon Press, 1966), p. 31. Reprinted by permission of the publisher and the author.

post of executive secretary was created to handle these problems.

The Party Council is another national organ of considerable importance. According to the 1958 party statute, it must be consulted on "basic foreign and domestic decisions, basic organizational questions, establishment of central party institutions that will represent a continuing cost to the party, [and] the preparation of Bundestag elections." It is also charged with coordinating policies at the federal and Land levels. Its membership consists mostly of Bezirke and Land representatives, and its work is largely one of coordination.

Unlike the Christian Democratic Union, which is a "catchall" party appealing to widely disparate groups, the S.P.D. still retains a sense of cohesion and discipline which not only reflects its ideological origins but also binds its members together despite the heated public debates at party congresses. Thus the transformation described earlier is not yet complete, although one suspects that the trend will not be reversed.

The German Communist Party (*Kommunistische Partei Deutschlands*—K.P.D.) grew out of the Spartakus League, founded during the First World War by a group of radical Socialists under the leadership of Rosa Luxemburg and Karl Liebknecht. Rosa Luxemburg had conceived of the Communist Revolution in Germany as occurring only when the masses were fully ready. She also thought of it as being a democratic revolution from the very beginning, and in this regard she had early made known her opposition to Lenin's tactics and approach. After her death and the defeat of her supporters, the K.P.D. quickly took on the Bolshevik pattern of organization, losing the allegiance of many of the Jewish intellectuals who had so actively helped its formation.

The party was rent by factional disputes throughout the 1920's, especially between those who wished to pursue a quasi-independent policy and those who, regarding the So-viet Union as the first "fatherland of all workers," considered their primary objective the protection of the Russian Revolution. Nevertheless, it managed to attract some ten per cent of the vote, and despite (or perhaps because of) the military quality of its organization, it drew to itself thousands of young people who considered the Social Democrats far too tame. With the beginning of the Great Depression, its proportion of the popular vote, primarily from unemployed and unskilled workers, rose to 16 per cent and its membership doubled.

Throughout most of the Weimar years, the Communist Party seemed actively to prefer the victory of conservative or even reactionary forces over candidates of the S.P.D. and the center. The Communists' argument was that the reformers merely concealed the true evils of capitalism, and that a victory for the right would reveal its naked ugliness and lead more quickly to a proletarian revolution. Their most violent hatred was reserved for the Social Democrats, whom they called "Social Fascists." In 1925 the Communist Party refused to withdraw its candidate from the presidential election and join the Socialists and other republican parties in supporting the centrist candidate; they thereby assured the election of General Paul von Hindenburg —an event that directly contributed to Hitler's ultimate victory. They followed the same tactics from 1930 to 1933, even joining the Nazis to bring down moderate governments.

In 1933 the German Communist Party was convinced that Hitler's victory would be followed almost immediately by a Communist triumph. It was shortly disabused of its optimism: thousands of Communists were slaughtered or sent to concentration camps, and the K.P.D. completely disintegrated, although many of its leaders managed to find their way to the Soviet Union. In the first Land elections after the fall of the Third Reich, the K.P.D. received eight to nine per cent of the popular vote in West Germany. By 1949, however, its vote had dropped to

5.7 per cent; in 1953 it skidded to 2.2 per cent, and three years later it was outlawed by the German Constitutional Court.

After the Social Democrats had moved toward the right in 1959, a group of dissidents, joined by some ex-Communists, formed the German Peace Union. The party, however, never received more than 1.9 per cent of the vote, and that was in 1961. In 1968 a new German Communist Party was formed, pledging itself to follow a democratic road to communism. In alliance with the German Peace Union and other left-wing groups, it ran candidates in the 1969 elections—without much success. Barring the unexpected, it is not likely to win any Bundestag seats in the foreseeable future.

6. THE CHRISTIAN DEMOCRATIC PARTY

At the 1848 Constituent Assembly in Prussia, a number of Catholic deputies met informally to discuss issues of common concern, and a Catholic Fraktion was later formed in the Prussian Diet. The impetus to create a specifically Catholic party, however, came as a result of the Austro-Prussian War, in which Catholic Austria was excluded from the empire. Once it was clear that Catholics would be a perpetual minority in the new Reich, the pressure to form a political organization intensified, and in 1870 the Center Party (*Zentrumspartei*) was officially created. Its first platform, the Soest Program, called for (1) preservation of the independence and the rights of the Catholic Church; (2) parity for all religious organizations; (3) the creation of a *Bundesstaat,* with autonomy provided for all the separate states of the Reich; (4) decentralization of administration; and (5) social reforms recognizing the legitimate demands of all groups.

The formation of the Center Party coincided with the beginnings of Bismarck's *Kulturkampf.* The proclamation of the doctrine of papal infallibility provided Bismarck with his excuse for a campaign to weaken German Catholicism, a campaign in which he was supported by the National Liberals and the Progressives. The Jesuit order was dissolved and extensive anti-Catholic legislation was passed. Clerics who failed to obey the new laws were jailed.

The struggle continued until 1878, when the death of Pope Pius IX and the election of Leo XIII offered the opportunity for a reconciliation. Bismarck was becoming increasingly agitated over the gains of the Socialists, and both he and the conservatives feared that to continue the violent attack against Catholicism might weaken Christianity in general. However, the church's strength had not flagged in the struggle—nor had that of the Center Party, whose vote had in fact risen from about 18 per cent of the total in 1871 to almost 27 per cent in 1877. In addition, it had begun to establish a mass organization with its own newspapers, and, supported by the Catholic Church, to create the kind of community that has traditionally characterized parties of the left.

The Center Party's proportion of the vote held more or less constant until 1912, and it became the second largest political party in the Reichstag. It gradually perfected its organization, and together with the church formed an array of associations in order to appeal to and aid Catholic workers. In Parliament it held the balance of power between the Socialists and the other parties, and after 1905 no government was formed without representatives of the Center.

The Center Party was never a politically homogeneous unit, however. Its left grew to favor constitutional reforms that would democratize the state and to opt for more extensive social legislation; its right wing was closer to the conservatives in its orientation. Yet in spite of these differences, the party managed to glean the votes of most Catholics, whatever their class. What held the party together, of course, was Catholicism: no matter how divided they might be on social and political issues, the crucial question for Catholics was the protection of their church and its teaching mission. Toward the end of the empire, many leaders on the left argued that the party should be more broadly based—a Christian party of social reform—but not much came of their argument.

The Center Party was also an integral part of coalition governments under the Weimar democracy, even though it was divided on social issues. In the early years of the republic, the left predominated within the party. But by 1928 the right had gained the upper hand, and it was a member of this wing, Franz von Papen, who helped pave the way for Hitler's chancellorship by contending that the responsibility of office would moderate Nazi demands. In fact, in exchange for promises by Hitler that church rights would be protected, the Center Party joined with others in voting Hitler "extraordinary" powers.

With the end of Nazi Germany, a series of groups which sprang up in the occupation zones advocated a political party that would draw its inspiration from an interdenominational Christian orientation. The leading proponents of the new party included Konrad Adenauer and Andreas Hermes, both of whom had been active in the old Center Party, and others who had been influential in the Christian trade-union movement. The proposal of an interdenominational party was not new; its origin can be traced to the empire. But the postwar era seemed a most propitious time for bridging the gap between Protestants and Catholics: old ideologies appeared to be discredited, and the churches, drawn together by the common experience of persecution, were among the few viable forces remaining in German life. An interzonal meeting of the different groups involved was held at Bad Godesberg in the winter of 1945, and out of it emerged the beginnings of a new national organization. By 1947 its development was well under way, and in 1950 the Christian Democratic Party held its first federal congress and adopted a constitution outlining its structure.

From its inception, the C.D.U. was composed of dissimilar elements, from left-wing Catholics to conservative Protestants. But in its first flush of enthusiasm, it seemed to be dedicating itself to a genuine social revolution. Under the aegis of Karl Arnold and Jacob Kaiser, the party in the British zone adopted a program in 1947 that was essentially Christian Socialist. It sought such reforms as the nationalization of basic industries and the participation by labor in management. As the party began to organize throughout West Germany, however, its leaders quickly realized that it was drawing its major support from the more conservative sectors of the population, and its political center of gravity shifted to the right. The shift was signaled by the consolidation of Adenauer's position as leader of the party.

In 1949 the C.D.U. adopted a new economic program on which it fought its first parliamentary elections—the "social market" policy of Ludwig Erhard, later Adenauer's Minister of Economics. Originally drawn to the F.D.P., Erhard, a Protestant, was also to become Adenauer's successor as chancellor and the leader of the C.D.U. In essence, Erhard's policies emphasized a freely competitive market economy, guided by government monetary policies. He pressed for returning industries owned by the state to private ownership, as well as for legislation to reduce the power of cartels. At the same time, however, he encouraged the extension of social legislation.[8] The success of his program, after a brief period of inflation and heavy unemployment, was reflected in Germany's march to prosperity—and in the party's election victories in 1953 and 1957.

Although the C.D.U. remained a coalition of groups in which the role of the left was critical, prosperity and popular endorsement of its policies encouraged the party to stand pat on its successes. Its economic policy continued to be neoliberal; its social policy, conservative. It did not, in other words, attempt to lead Germany in any new directions.

---

[8] A fuller delineation of Erhard's policies is given in Chapter 24, pages 768–769.

Adenauer's leadership and his installation as chancellor stamped the party for the 1950's. The C.D.U. was indeed an amalgamation of regional and economic interests, united primarily by antisocialism. But it was also held together by the desire to retain office, and by the personality and prestige of Adenauer. Making use of the state bureaucracy, Adenauer was able to dominate the party and play off one faction in the coalition against another, making strategic concessions when necessary.

Adenauer's chief passion, aside from being chancellor, was foreign affairs: he worked tirelessly to establish a close relation with France and to encourage European integration. A native of the Rhineland, he had always been pro-French and anti-Prussian, and he was convinced that the reconciliation of France and Germany was as important as the attainment of German unity, if not more so. He strongly believed that only by tying his nation more closely to France could he insure the future stability of German democracy. And to his mind, the source of traditional German militarism had been eastern Germany, especially Prussia. Although Adenauer had brought Germany into the Atlantic Alliance, his attitude toward the United States cooled during the Kennedy administration; he became increasingly anxious that a Soviet-American détente might leave the Germans out on a limb. Nor was he especially unhappy to see the British, whom he regarded as basically anti-German, excluded from the Common Market.

By the late 1950's, Adenauer's popularity began to dwindle, and pressures mounted for him to retire. The slip in C.D.U. fortunes in the 1961 elections was interpreted by the party as a sign that the 85-year-old chancellor had lost his appeal, and defeats in Land elections in 1962 and 1963 seemed to be further evidence. Adenauer did finally step down in 1963, to be replaced by Erhard.

From the begining, however, Adenauer's own reservations about Erhard's ability to govern turned out to be almost totally cor-

rect. Factionalism rose within the C.D.U., and the "Rubber Lion," as many of his less charitable critics called him, came under attack for being incapable of controlling either his party or the operation of the government. In the vanguard of the attackers were a number of aspirants for chancellor, including Franz Joseph Strauss, the leader of the Bavarian Christian Social Union and a former defense minister.

The C.D.U.'s victory in the 1965 elections did little to stem the criticism, and the mild recession that followed, as well as Germany's increasing difficulties in the international arena, only made it more caustic. Erhard was forced from the chancellorship in 1966, but the party factions responsible for his fall could agree on little except that they were glad he was gone. In the end, Kiesinger was chosen as a compromise candidate, a man who was not closely identified with any particular group. Kiesinger led the C.D.U. into a coalition with the Social Democrats, but he was unable to restore genuine party cohesion.

The 1969 parliamentary elections were not really a defeat for the C.D.U.; its percentage of the national vote dropped only slightly and the party itself remained united behind Kiesinger. Even so, the strains within the party following its removal from power are likely to become more pronounced in the next few years.

STRUCTURE AND DYNAMICS: Organizationally, the C.D.U. stands somewhere between the Social Democratic Party and the Free Democrats. Even though it has a membership of some three hundred thousand, it relies upon local notables and professional politicians as the nucleus of its strength. Further, it is essentially an "umbrella" party, united by a vague adherence to "Christian doctrine" and antisocialism. The relative autonomy of many of the C.D.U. groups was obscured for a while by Adenauer's stature and control over the party, but the assertion of independence has again come into the open.

Basically, the national organization of the

Christian Democrats consists of 19 Land parties, in addition to a twentieth which "represents" party members in Eastern Germany. Bavaria's C.S.U. maintains a separate organization but cooperates with the C.D.U. in national elections and in the Bundestag. Members of the four thousand C.D.U. local organizations elect their own leadership and take on responsibility for nominating candidates, campaigning on the local level, and collecting dues. The party, however, secures most of its funds from business organizations, so that dues collecting is not so important as in the S.P.D.

The party's governing body is a Federal Convention to which the Land parties send representatives. As is usually the case with such a conference, it functions mainly as a sounding board and device for rousing party enthusiasm. It does elect the party chairman and four deputy chairmen, and in that sense is not without significance. But it is not in any sense a grass-roots convention. Its membership consists almost entirely of chairmen —chairmen of the state parties and chairmen of factions in the state legislatures—and other party officials; its votes, therefore, reflect the opinion of party chiefs, not necessarily the wishes of the party's rank and file.

The two executive organs of the party are the Federal Executive Committee (*Vorstand*) and the Federal Committee (*Ausschuss*). The Vorstand contains most of the important Land and national party leaders and is dominated by the Land leadership. And as part of the executive machinery, the party has created the post of general secretary to cope with organizational affairs.

The C.D.U. also contains special organizations representing such interests as trade unions, youth, local government officials, Protestants, women, and civil servants; and a Committee for Economic Policy consults with business groups in order to obtain their opinions on policy matters. But none of these organizations, with the possible exception of the business committee, has much to say about party policy decisions. In addition to these special organizations, there are the lay groups affiliated with the Catholic Church; while these have no direct influence on party decisions, they do try to preserve an environment favorable to the C.D.U.

The two principal power groups within the C.D.U. are the Vorstand, which represents the Land parties, and the parliamentary party caucus. Both, of course, contain representatives from the states, and given the fact that the Land organizations exercise a powerful influence over party nominations, divisions consequently tend to occur within each group rather than between them. While Kiesinger has managed to smooth over these differences within the power groups, he has not been able to establish himself as a focus of authority. More than ever, policy decisions of the Christian Democrats are reached through an intricate series of touchy negotiations and under the omnipresent threat that party conflict will break out into the open.

The problem lies only in part with Kiesinger himself. Much of it is related to events occurring inside and outside the Bonn Republic. The assumptions that guided the party through the 1950's are now in question, especially West Germany's relations with the German Democratic Republic and the United States. German domestic politics seems to be entering a new phase. The very heterogeneity of the C.D.U. makes it extremely difficult for the party to confront the new era with any decisiveness. It is more important than ever that it face up to this issue soon. Its past victories have stemmed partially from the fear that the Social Democrats would not be able to govern effectively—a fear which the C.D.U. itself helped to allay. Now, even a modicum of success by the new Brandt government will make the C.D.U.'s comeback that much more arduous.

7. ELECTORAL POLITICS IN GERMANY

One of the major arguments against the list system of proportional representation in the Weimar Republic was that it gave excessive power to party bureaucracy, which chose the order in which candidates appeared on the voting lists. It was also argued that the large size of electoral districts accented ideological considerations rather than the personality or record of individual candidates.

In an effort to correct these "faults," the Bonn Republic has adopted a two-ballot system. The nation is divided into 247 electoral districts, each of which elects one member to the Bundestag; here election is by plurality. In addition, another 247 candidates are elected from party lists for each Land. The number of seats available to each state is proportional to its share of the total number of citizens eligible to vote. In effect, each citizen votes twice. On the first ballot (*Erststimme*), he chooses between two or more candidates in his electoral district. On the second ballot (*Zweitstimme*), he votes for the party lists of candidates for his Land.

Seats in the Bundestag are doled out in proportion to the percentage of the vote that a party receives on the Land list. Then the number of seats obtained in the single-mem-

ber election districts is subtracted from the total number of seats to which the party is entitled, and the remainder of the elected candidates are chosen from the state list itself. In the 1965 elections, for example, the Free Democratic Party received 9.5 per cent of the vote on its second (Land list) ballots. However, it did not elect any candidates from single-member districts. The 49 F.D.P. candidates seated in the Bundestag—just over nine per cent of the total—were all drawn from Land lists.

Election results under the German system are much as they would be under a purely proportional system of representation, with two minor exceptions. First, if any political party elects more candidates in single-member districts than it is proportionally entitled to, it is allowed to retain the seats it has won and the size of the Bundestag is enlarged accordingly (its fixed size of 494 members has, on occasion, varied from 496 to 499). Second, no party is entitled to seats from the Land lists unless it receives either more than five per cent of the total national vote or

FIGURE 12.2. A GERMAN BALLOT, 1969

elects at least three candidates from the single-member constituencies.

There are those who have argued that the five per cent minimum, by discouraging the growth of minor parties, is what has saved Bonn from the political fragmentation that characterized the Weimar Republic. This is doubtful. A fairly substantial number of parties could have easily passed the minimum requirement, and there is no proof that a minimum percentage discourages attempts to form new parties. Indeed, concern about the impact of the N.P.D. and the desire of many German political leaders to move toward a two-party system prompted the major parties to consider the establishment of a single-district, plurality election system modeled on that of the British and Americans.

Whether the present system has achieved its other objective, that of creating a closer liaison between voters and candidates, is problematical. Local organizations do have considerable power in the nominations of candidates, especially of those for safe seats, for here candidates do not need the insurance of also appearing on the Land list. But the local parties tend to be the preserve of a small group of militants or of special-interest groups; there is not much evidence that the great mass of party supporters is involved one way or another in nomination decisions. The Land organizations, of course, wield their power in nominations to Land lists, particularly the C.D.U.'s state organizations; in the C.D.U., the national party organization has little influence over the Land lists, primarily because of the party's structure. The leadership of the S.P.D., on the other hand, can sometimes make its influence felt, although most of its candidates are local or at least Land residents and take care to keep their constituency fences mended despite the absence of a residence requirement.

The Land lists are drawn up by regional party organizations. Theoretically, those chosen for the state lists take the high political road, emphasizing ideological or general policy issues, while constituency candidates concentrate on local needs. In fact, of course, there is a good deal of oratorical overlap, primarily because many, if not most, candidates seek—and get—a place on state party lists in addition to a constituency nomination. Land party lists are also places where attempts are made to balance tickets. The C.D.U., as an example, carefully allocates places for Protestants and Catholics; it also makes sure that representatives of various interest groups are on the slate. Each party tries to have some women and some younger people on its ticket, and for a long time, certain Länder saw the advantage of a candidate or two who were members of the local refugee organization.

For the Social Democratic Party, the major source of funds in the post–World War II period was membership dues. Additional money was raised through special programs and through minor commercial ventures controlled by the party. Both Christian Democrats and Free Democrats, on the other hand, relied upon a few sizable donations from business firms and trade associations for financial succor. As the party in power, the C.D.U. also benefited from special funds available to the chancellor for "educational" and "informational" activities. In 1958, however, the Federal Constitutional Court declared that individual and business donations to political parties were not tax deductible, and these sources of income began immediately to dry up. The F.D.P. suffered most severely, but the C.D.U., because its campaign expenditures were usually higher than those of all other parties combined, also found itself in difficult straits.

The Bundestag reacted to this situation by partially financing the parliamentary work of the three major parties—and the money allotted increased year by year. In 1966 the N.P.D., which was not included in the government's largess, finally brought the issue to the Constitutional Court, which ruled that general payments of party expenses by the state were unconstitutional but implied that some money might be granted to defray campaign expenses if all political parties of a reasonable size received assistance.

By 1968 a compromise had been worked out to meet the court's implicit requirement. As amended by still another court decision, the law now states that all political parties will receive the equivalent of about 62 U.S. cents for each vote obtained in a federal election, provided they win more than .5 per cent of the total national vote. The amount advanced to each party is to be based on the results of the previous Bundestag election. The legislation originally establishing the aid program also provides for public identification of large party contributions from individuals or corporations. Similar legislation applying to state elections has also been adopted by many Land governments.

Since World War II, election campaign expenses have risen steeply, as first the C.D.U. and then the Free Democrats and Social Democrats turned to public-relations firms and mass campaigning in the American style. In 1959 and 1960, for example, Willy Brandt, the S.P.D.'s candidate for chancellor, sent his campaign manager to both England and the United States to study election techniques; he also commissioned a series of public-opinion studies. In his campaign he concentrated on specific appeals rather than ideological generalities, promising concrete policies for the betterment of the little man's lot. He also adapted the American whistle-stop campaign: for three months before the election Brandt toured Germany in a cream-colored Mercedes convertible, decked out with flowers. His schedule was carefully organized; a program was even provided to entertain expectant crowds should he be late. Following the lead of John Kennedy, he challenged Adenauer to a round of television debates, which, however, the chancellor wisely spurned.

Studies of German opinion convinced Brandt that many Germans went on voting for Adenauer, not for ideological reasons, but because he was a father figure. Brandt attempted to counteract this by emphasizing his youth and dynamism. He also turned the other cheek and refused to attack the chancellor, despite the rather scurrilous attacks made upon him, especially regarding his illegitimacy. In general, every effort was made to convince the German voter that the Socialist Party had, in fact, broken with its traditional moorings. Party leaders were convinced that the rise in its 1961 vote was a direct outcome of the campaign; the same techniques were used again in 1965, but with less spectacular results. Even so, for the 1969 campaign public-relations firms were more in evidence than ever.

The party system of postwar Germany bears little resemblance to that of Weimar Germany. Instead of a multiplicity of parties defined in terms of either narrow interests or narrow ideologies, the Bonn Republic has sustained two political organizations whose differences, particularly in recent years, have become increasingly marginal. The Christian Democratic Union is a catchall party run by professional politicians whose aims now are to consolidate the gains made in the postwar years and to reflect what they see as the aspirations of the German people. The Social Democratic Party, while it retains elements of its traditional working-class background and ideology, has been edging toward the political center in the hope of becoming a majority party of moderate reform.

The new party system has provided Bonn with fairly stable government. Yet as the postwar period ends, different kinds of problems are emerging. A new generation of university students, for instance, is demanding far more rapid and fundamental changes, even as the old verities regarding West Germany's relations with her neighbors to the east and to the west seem less and less applicable. Neither the S.P.D. nor the C.D.U. has, as yet, discovered an imaginative way to respond to these new pressures. The Christian

Democratic Union is hampered by its very nature; as a coalition of varied interests, each with its own power base, the party, now that Adenauer has departed, finds it exceedingly difficult to develop a cohesive position on the issues before the nation. The Social Democratic Party does not have quite the same problems. Nonetheless, having finally jettisoned its nineteenth-century rhetoric, it has not really developed a concrete, workable set of new goals of its own. For both parties, as for the Federal Republic itself, the next ten years are likely to be characterized by considerable ferment.

13

The

Communist Party

of the Soviet Union

1. INTRODUCTION

The Communist Party of the Soviet Union began its life in the first years of the twentieth century as the "Bolshevik," or majority, faction within the Russian Social Democratic Party. By 1912 the Bolsheviks had all but completed their split with the parent organization, and in 1919 they adopted the name "Communist." Once in power, the Communists created what is best described as a one-party mobilization regime.[1]

Those who made the Revolution conceived of the Communist Party as the vanguard of the nation's most progressive elements, dedicated to the transformation of Russian society. This conception of the party still officially holds. Inevitably, therefore, the most far-reaching decisions in Soviet life came to be made by the leadership of the Communist Party as it operated through the state apparatus, for the organization of the party parallels and permeates the state at every level. Inevitably, too, the Communist Party took over a much wider range of community functions than those assumed by political parties in Western European countries, performing tasks which in England, France, or Germany are the province of other structures. Thus, the Communist Party of the Soviet Union (C.P.S.U.) plays a far more extensive role in socializing its citizens and exercises far greater supervision over the state's economic institutions than do the political parties in the other nations under study.

Even those tasks which the Communist Party does share with political parties in pluralistic societies are performed in a different manner. For example, the C.P.S.U. serves to legitimize the decisions that are made by the Soviet regime, and the party systems of England, France, and Germany have the same respective function. But whereas the Western European parties derive their legitimacy from the fact that they represent and

---

[1] For details of the split see Chapter 3. Until 1952 the party was officially the Communist Party of the Soviet Union (Bolshevik); the name "Bolshevik" was only then dropped. For a theoretical discussion of one-party mobilization regimes, which provides the essential framework of this chapter, see Chapter 9, pp. 309–311.

aggregate the interests of their citizens, the legitimacy of the C.P.S.U. is based primarily on its position as a vanguard organization. Indeed, the party still denies that it has anything to do with aggregating interests. It is still, officially at least, committed to the view that its function is not only to discover the correct road to communism in terms of Marxist-Leninist doctrine, but to keep the Soviet citizen on that road. The task of recruiting elites for important political positions is also shared by the Communist and Western parties alike. But whereas in England men compete for positions of power on the basis of their ability to carry out the public's wishes, members of the Soviet political elite are officially chosen for their ability to interpret correctly and implement efficiently the task of constructing a Communist state. The wide range of party duties in the Soviet Union also means that the technical qualifications for political success differ somewhat from those required by English, French, and German politicians.

The functional differences between the Communist Party of the Soviet Union and Western European parties can, of course, be exaggerated. Political parties in England and the United States also contribute substantially to political socialization; within the Soviet Union, on the other hand, there is increasing evidence, some of which will be discussed in Chapter 18, of factional disputes in which elites are competing for power by attempting to satisfy the interests of wider groups. Nevertheless, the differences between the Soviet and Western European party systems remain far more striking than the similarities.

Chapter 18 will describe in more detail the interrelationship between the Soviet Communist Party and the Soviet government. The remainder of this chapter will deal primarily with the development, organization, and internal dynamics of the C.P.S.U., and offer some comments on its changing role in Soviet society. Stress will be placed on its transformation from a revolutionary clique into a hierarchical, bureaucratized organization in which the cardinal decisions are made largely at the top.

Because of its ideology, the party's transformation after the Revolution has been the source of considerable controversy. Many commentators have contended that it was an aberration resulting from Stalin's victory over Trotsky—a view shared by Trotsky himself. But as both Chapters 3 and 9 have already pointed out, the analysis of this volume is quite different. The bureaucratization of the party, and its authoritarianism as well, are to be understood as a direct consequence of both the goals that the party set for itself and the organization required to achieve at least some of these goals within the context of Russian society. It follows from this that as the goals and the society change, so will the party's organization and dynamics.

2. THE DEVELOPMENT OF THE COMMUNIST PARTY OF THE SOVIET UNION

The entire spectrum of European political ideologies made its appearance in Russia during the nineteenth century, with permutations derived from the specific nature of the Russian historical experience. But except for various underground revolutionary movements, the repressive nature of the regime permitted little or no opportunity for the development of political organizations.

The Revolution of 1905 changed all this, and by the time the first Duma met in 1906, a whole series of political groups had begun to organize. On the left, the Mensheviks and the Socialist Revolutionaries (S.R.'s) came out into the open. The latter, under the leadership of Victor Chernov, called for a federal state and the socialization of all land, which would then be distributed to individual peasants on the basis of their ability to work it. In the center, two loose groupings emerged, the Octobrists and the Kadets (Constitutional Democrats). The Kadets' program included universal suffrage, full civil liberties, land reform, and a progressive income tax. The right was represented by several groups, among them the Russian Monarchist Party, which denounced Western European institutions, insisted upon the property rights of landowners, and urged the czar to resist all requests for popular participation in government. Also on the right, the strongly Slavophile and anti-Semitic Union of Russian Men, in an effort to bring czar and people closer together, advocated the re-creation of certain feudal assemblies that had met from time to time during the sixteenth and seventeenth centuries; the Union of Russian People had roughly the same ideas and was extremely active in the pogroms directed against Jews in 1905 and 1906. Finally, groups sprang up among the ethnic minorities, some seeking degrees of national autonomy, others demanding independence.

Not one of these parties, however, developed effective national organizations. The right-wing groups did not think in terms of permanent party structures, and both the Kadets and Octobrists remained loose collections of notables. On the left, the repressive policies of the regime after 1906 forced many of the Socialist Revolutionary and Social Democratic leaders (Bolshevik as well as Menshevik) to remain in exile, and both parties were plagued by bitter factional disputes. The S.R.'s and the Mensheviks did manage to engage in some organizing work within Russia, but they had only very limited success. The Bolsheviks, of course, remained a small underground group of professional revolutionaries and were not taken very seriously by the other groups—not, that is, until it was too late.

The ultimate success of the Bolsheviks ended the development of all other political parties. Right-wing and bourgeois parties, considered antirevolutionary, were suppressed; most of their leaders either fled into exile or fought the Communists. The parties of minority groups suffered the same fate. Policy toward the Mensheviks and the Socialist Revolutionaries vacillated; they con-

tinued to survive, albeit under severe political pressure, until 1921.

Both of these Socialist parties had, in fact, split into numerous factions, all with different attitudes toward the new regime. Initially, many of their members joined the Bolsheviks, or at least supported them, regarding them as less of an evil than the establishment of a right-wing militarist regime. Other Socialists eventually joined the opposition in the civil war, when it became clear that Lenin and his entourage regarded all opposition, even Socialist opposition, as "objectively" reactionary. Still others attempted to maintain a "legal opposition" by not fighting the Bolshevik regime by force, but by campaigning for change within the framework of democratic processes. All these tactics were to no avail; Lenin was convinced that only his course was the right course. All other groups represented reaction, whether they realized it or not.

Thus, Social Revolutionary and Menshevik leaders were either shot or imprisoned, or else allowed to go into exile. Both parties were officially suppressed in 1922 shortly after the inauguration of the New Economic Policy. Leading Mensheviks and S.R.'s had also been urging policies which, like the N.E.P., were designed to ease economic controls over both workers and peasants. The apparent resurgence in popularity of the S.R.'s and Mensheviks among the masses, however, made it clear to Lenin that, in a period of what he himself considered temporary "retreat," those who urged the retreat could not be allowed to continue their activities lest they succeed in seducing the masses from the correct course.

As the Communist Party became more and more powerful, it also became increasingly centralized and bureaucratized. It had begun as a revolutionary elite led largely by intellectuals. Founded for revolutionary purposes, it was organized, wherever possible, on the basis of party cells at places of work. Political coordination on the national level was extremely flexible. The principal national organ was the Central Committee, composed of Lenin, Trotsky, Stalin, and other leading Bolshevik figures; despite Lenin's domination of the group, discussion and debate were relatively free. The success of the Revolution wrought extensive changes within the party. Thousands joined it in order to share the fruits of victory—or because of a newly awakened enthusiasm for the Revolution. The immensity of the tasks involved, and the organizational role assigned to the party by Bolshevik leaders, made these thousands necessary, although there were frequent reorganizations for the purpose of weeding out the "unfit," including "opportunist" Social Democrats. By 1924, membership in the Communist Party had jumped to almost five hundred thousand; by 1928 it was more than one million. The new cadres were, of course, easily distinguished from those who had joined the party initially: in 1927, no more than one per cent had received a higher education, less than eight per cent had completed a secondary education, and 25 per cent were completely illiterate or "self-taught." The nature of these new cadres helps explain the defeat of the party's intellectual elite—of Trotsky and his supporters—during the mid-twenties.

The party's growth and the political, social, and economic functions it had undertaken called for tighter organization and a new party structure. The Central Committee was reorganized, and sections were created to parallel the structure of the government. Local party units were brought more closely under central control, especially their finances, and organized according to the newly established administrative divisions of the state.

In 1917, a seven-man political bureau (*politburo*) had been created to deal with emergency problems. It was dissolved shortly thereafter, but by the next year it had become obvious that both the Party Congress and the Central Committee had become too large and unwieldy to handle, on a continuing basis, the vast problems facing the new

regime. Thus, the Eighth Party Congress, meeting in 1919, re-established the politburo as an executive body to be elected by and responsible to the Central Committee; the Central Committee was to be elected by the Party Congress. The congressional resolution provided that the Central Committee must meet every two weeks, that even those of its members who did not serve on the politburo had the right to attend politburo sessions, and that the politburo would act only in emergencies.

The congress also authorized the creation by the Central Committee of a second executive body, the organizational bureau (*orgburo*), whose membership overlapped with that of the politburo. Vaguely defined, the work of the orgburo was primarily concerned with organizational matters of the party, while the politburo dealt with matters of policy. Yet as Lenin pointed out, the distinction was, in practice, an artificial one. Of the two, the prestige of the politburo was greater, although Stalin was to use his orgburo position to considerable advantage in establishing control over the party's bureaucratic apparatus. Almost immediately, the two new groups began to supplant the Central Committee. The committee met only six times between April and November 1919, instead of the prescribed 16 times. During the same period, the politburo met 29 times and held 19 joint meetings with the orgburo, which itself met 110 times.

Finally, the Central Committee was granted the power to establish a secretariat, whose functions were not clearly defined either. It consisted of a secretary, who was required to be a member of the orgburo, and five technical secretaries chosen from experienced party workers. Originally, the scope of the secretariat grew with the party and was determined in part by its personnel. At the Ninth Party Congress, it was given responsibility for problems of an executive and administrative character, while the orgburo remained responsible for overall organizational work. The congress also added three members of the Central Committee to the secretariat's staff. After the congress, the secretariat, as well as its functions, grew with increasing rapidity. It had been delegated responsibility for party records, and, given the need for reliable personnel, it effectively determined who would be the full-time party officials, or secretaries, at district, regional, and republican levels, despite the requirement that those officials be elected. By 1922 the party contained 15,325 full-time employees, and the staff of the secretariat, which had reached seven hundred, was already being subdivided into various departments concerned with specific personnel problems.

The integral importance of the secretariat in the Communist Party structure was outwardly confirmed in 1922, when Stalin was appointed its director with the official title of general secretary; he was the only party leader at that time who combined membership in the politburo, orgburo, and secretariat. He used the secretariat to consolidate his position, making certain that party officials who attached themselves to him were placed in strategically powerful posts. His prime tool was the Department for Organization and Assignment (*Orgaspred*), which coordinated the appointment of party secretaries on all levels and checked on party operation through a corps of "instructors."[2] As early as 1923, Trotsky had complained despairingly:

In the fiercest moment of War Communism, the system of appointment within the party did not have one-tenth of the extent that it has now. Appointment of the secretaries of provincial committees is now the rule. That creates for the secretary a position essentially independent of the local organization. . . .

The bureaucratization of the party apparatus has developed to unheard-of proportions by means of the method of secretarial selection. There has been created a very broad stratum of party workers, entering into the apparatus of the government of the party, who completely renounce their own party opinion, or at least the open expression of it, as though assuming that the secretarial hierarchy is the apparatus which creates party opinion and party decisions.[3]

The secretariat, however, eventually found the job of inspecting the party at every level far too demanding. What developed, therefore, was a process of appointment from above, with each level of the party made responsible for the one below it.

Once Stalin had completely consolidated his power within the party and had determined to push forward with his plans for collectivization, the entire nature and role of the Communist Party was transformed. It was converted into Stalin's personal instrument of power, the instrument for creating the kind of society he envisioned and in the manner which he regarded as correct. The remaining cadres who dated from the Revolution were purged; the broad policy-making role of top-level party groups became less and less significant, and their meetings less and less frequent. The Seventeenth Party Congress was held in 1934, the Eighteenth in 1939; the Nineteenth did not meet until 1952. The same was true of the Central Committee and even the politburo, both of which were purged of any possible opponents of the dictator. According to Khrushchev's secret speech at the Twentieth Congress of the Party, 98 of the 139 members and candidate members elected to the Central Committee in 1934 were arrested and shot, mainly in 1937 and 1938. Of the ten members elected to the politburo in 1934, only six were left five years later—with records of unswerving loyalty to Stalin. In fact, party position was no longer a requisite for membership in the politburo. Stalin made Lavrenty Beria, head of the secret police, a

[2] The department was formed in 1924 with the merger of the secretariat's Account and Assignment Division and Organization and Instruction Division.

[3] Quoted in Fainsod, *How Russia Is Ruled*, pp. 182–183. The term "War Communism" is explained on p. 566, note 6.

member and used others in the politburo, the government apparatus, and the party to keep tabs on one another, creating a climate of fear and suspicion such that, according to the testimony of his erstwhile colleagues, no one knew if or when his time had come.

In spite of all this, the party continued to grow in strength. Stalin remained loyal to the idea of its representing those progressive elements bent on remodeling Soviet society; at every level, members were instructed to guide, cajole, and educate the population to new efforts. The purged cadres were replaced by a technocratic middle class that had been trained by the new regime. By 1939 perhaps 45 per cent of the party members were of middle-class origin, and some fifty per cent had completed a secondary or higher education. In the army, in factories, in apartment houses, and on collective farms, the party was given responsibility for guaranteeing that policies were implemented correctly. As a consequence, not only were all important government officials necessarily Communist Party members, but they found themselves under the steady eye and constant supervision of the party apparatus.

As the party expanded, its apparatus did too, and to the secretariat were added more and more duties. Subdivisions within the secretariat were created and made answerable for various sectors of the economy, such as agriculture, transportation, industry, and trade. While the responsibility of the secretariat in these areas was theoretically restricted to problems of personnel, this of necessity meant its participation in deciding more general issues.

During World War II, there was a loosening of party discipline, and, coincidentally, a large increase in the number of party members. With the end of the war, however, controls were restored and a general purge instituted to weed out individuals who did not represent proper party material. Even so, Russians went right on joining; by 1952 membership had reached a total of almost six million.

Shortly before the death of Stalin, the politburo and the orgburo were dissolved and

TABLE 13.1. C.P.S.U. MEMBERSHIP, 1918–1967

Year	Full members	Candidates	Total
1918	390,000	0	390,000
1919	350,000	0	350,000
1920	611,978	0	611,978
1921	732,521	0	732,521
1922	410,430	117,924	528,354
1923	381,400	117,700	499,100
1924	350,000	122,000	472,000
1925	440,365	361,439	801,804
1927	786,288	426,217	1,212,505
1930	1,184,651	493,259	1,677,910
1934	1,826,756	874,252	2,701,008
1939	1,514,181	792,792	2,306,973
1952	5,853,200	854,339	6,707,539
1956	6,767,644	405,877	7,173,521
1959	7,622,356	616,775	8,239,131
1961	8,472,396	803,430	9,275,826
1966	11,548,287	809,021	12,357,308

Adapted from Thomas H. Rigby, *Communist Party Membership in the U.S.S.R.*, 1917–1967 (Princeton: Princeton University Press, 1968), pp. 52–53. Reprinted by permission of the publisher.

replaced by a single larger body, the Presidium.[4] Khrushchev later charged that this
move represented the first step of Stalin's
plans for a new bloodletting, to eliminate
those about whom the old dictator had growing suspicions. If indeed this was the case,
the purge failed to materialize. Stalin died in
1953 without assigning an heir to his power,
and this omission provoked a new struggle
over who was to lead the world's most formidable Communist state.

In the first months of the struggle, Beria,
relying upon the secret police, attempted to
secure supreme power for himself. But the
party proved too strong for him, and in the
end it was through the agency of the party,
with assistance from the military, that Khrushchev was able to consolidate his power.[5]
Khrushchev was a party man, and during his
rule the party apparatus again asserted itself
as the governing elite of Soviet society. His
reorganizations of the economy and the party
were meant to increase the function of the
cadres, even as he attempted, however timidly, to extend the range of free discussion
and criticism within the lower party ranks.
Moreover, he made a renewed effort to expand the influence of party activists and to
recruit party workers. By 1966, party membership had passed 11 million.

Even after he solidified his power, Khrushchev did not rule in the same manner that
Stalin had. Meetings of the Presidium were
marked by the tug of interests and ideas, and,
on at least one occasion, Khrushchev was
outvoted and had to turn to the Central
Committee to override his opposition. Party
congresses began to meet regularly once
again, although they still served merely as
sounding boards for the leadership. Those defeated in intra-party squabbles were no longer
imprisoned or executed, but retired or sent to
obscure posts.

Khrushchev himself was, however, an interim figure. The son of a peasant turned

coal miner, and but partially educated by the
party, he retained many of the attitudes of a
traditional Russian of lower-class rural background. To the newer generation of Russian
party technocrats, he was "uncultured." His
outbursts of vulgar sarcasm, his monumental
temper tantrums, his flamboyant style of
personal decision-making were regarded as
"harebrained" and "erratic." These attributes, plus his inability to solve a number of
crucial domestic and international problems,
led to his downfall. Many observers believe
that his opponents on the party Presidium
called a special meeting of the Central Committee, and that Khrushchev bowed to a vote
of no confidence by the larger body.

Khrushchev, like Stalin, had gathered in
his own person both political and governmental authority. He had been, despite his
attack upon Stalin's cult of personality and
his lectures on the importance of "collective
leadership," both general secretary of the
party and chairman of the Council of Ministers (premier). He had been, in other
words, far more than first among equals.

The new Soviet leadership has behaved
rather differently. The posts of general secretary and chairman of the Council of Ministers
are still divided between Leonid Brezhnev
and Aleksei Kosygin respectively, and, as
far as can be determined, the politburo is
more actively engaged in decision-making.
Whether or not the executive in a powerful
industrial state can remain split for long is
open to question. What does seem manifest,
however, is that the party, and hence the
state, are now firmly in control of a bureaucratic elite—an elite that is far more conservative in some ways than was Khrushchev,
yet far less committed to any simple interpretation of Communist doctrine. The goal of
the elite is still, vaguely, a Communist society. But for a long time to come, policy
decisions are likely to entail cautious measures that not only insure the continuance of
party control but emphasize pragmatic criteria for achieving more limited ends. While
the regime, for instance, has moved ahead

[4] The term *politburo* was restored in 1966.
[5] For details on Khrushchev's rise to power, see
Chapter 3, p. 116.

with some economic reforms, it has proceeded with great circumspection, and, unlike Khrushchev, the present leadership talks in specific terms about the possibilities of economic growth in the near future. Slogans predicting that the Soviet Union will catch up with and surpass the United States have all but disappeared—along with references to the idealized Communist society that, at times, Khrushchev seemed to believe was about to emerge at any moment. At the same time the regime, while not resorting to overt terror, has raised the status of the secret police and been less tolerant of dissent than was Khrushchev. In the realm of foreign policy, it has also demonstrated extreme caution; in fact, the Soviet invasion of Czechoslovakia in 1968 can be regarded as a purely defensive move.

Finally, within the party itself, turnover among high-level officials has dropped markedly as their average age has risen. Also, the proportion of paid party bureaucrats in primary posts has increased over even the Khrushchev era. In short, the present leadership of the C.P.S.U.—careful, pragmatic, conservative—is dedicated primarily to maintaining the status quo.

3. THE ORGANIZATION AND DYNAMICS OF THE PARTY

The Communist Party of the Soviet Union was created as a conspiratorial organization to achieve power in a revolutionary situation. Once in power, it took upon itself the task of remaking Soviet society. This task required the training of cadres dedicated to the party's program; the establishment of a vast organization to manage problems of administering the government; the socialization of its citizens in accordance with "correct" behavior; and the making of a range of political, economic, and social decisions that in more pluralistic societies would be undertaken by a whole panoply of institutions.

The immensity of its assignments, its leaders' dogmatic conviction that only they knew the true road to a new society, and the difficulty and enormity of the problems to be dealt with, all combined to give the party the semblance of a military organization run by a priesthood. The function of the party was not to help articulate the interests of all the separate groups within the society, but rather to eliminate special interests, and, in effect, to eliminate politics. The control still exercised over Soviet society by the Communist Party, despite the changes that have occurred since Stalin's death, is far greater than ever attempted even by the Nazi Party, and goes a long way toward explaining the particular features of the party's organization and dynamics.

THE PRIMARY PARTY ORGANIZATION: The basic party unit—what until 1939 was called a cell—is the primary party organization (P.P.O.), of which there are about 350,000 in the Soviet Union. A P.P.O. may be set up in any enterprise or institution in which there are not less than three party members; it may also be formed on a territorial basis or at places of residence in rural areas where an economic entity is too small to form a single P.P.O. Thus, party cells are found in factories, collective farms, universities, research institutes, stores, cultural institutions, government bureaus, schools, police departments, and the armed forces.

In primary units having less than 15 members, only a secretary and assistant secretary are "elected" as officers, with the approval of the next higher echelon of the party. In larger P.P.O.'s, bureaus are created which "choose" officers for a one-year term. If the unit contains 150 members or more, it will be served by at least one full-time paid member, although exceptions are made for smaller units under 150 in certain industries. Part-time paid secretaries are also used in the smaller units.

The P.P.O. is responsible for admitting new members to the party, instilling the membership with the spirit of Marxism-Leninism, strengthening labor discipline and increasing productivity, and agitating among the masses to make them more aware of communism. Party rules give primary units the right to "supervise the work of administration" in such areas as factories, government bureaus, and the military. In this way, party members are supposed to check for work inadequacies and to insure that the economic and social policies of the regime are being properly carried out. Not unexpectedly, their efforts often bring them into conflict with managers and other officials charged with the direct responsibility for a given operation. Soviet newspapers are filled with complaints about party members taking on too much—or too little—administrative responsibility or about so many lines of authority existing in a particular organization that it is impossible to get anything done.

Despite the rapid growth of its membership during the past several years, the Communist Party remains an elite organization. To join the party, a citizen must submit a complete life history and the recommendations of three party members of not less than five years' standing who have known and worked with the applicant for not less than one year. These recommendations must be verified by the P.P.O. secretary, and membership candidates are then permitted to serve a one-year probation. The recommendation of the district committee of the Komsomol is counted as the equivalent of the recommendation of one party member; persons under 23 can join the party only through the Komsomol.

The life of a party member is extremely demanding. He is supposed to set an example at work, and his leisure hours are filled with party meetings and special campaigns. His private life must be above reproach, by standards which remain quite puritanical. In the 1930's and even the 1940's, survival within the party required considerable ruthlessness, if not fanaticism. Today, while tough-mindedness is still important, the successful party member is likely to be one who has some of the qualities of a successful

politician anywhere—the personality of an extrovert and a capacity for organizing people without arousing excessive resentment.

Within the primary unit, the secretary is the central figure. He is not permitted to delegate either the collection of party dues or the organization of agitators. In recent years, the party has tended once again to stress self-criticism, encouraging members to bypass the secretary and appeal to higher party units if they believe he is not adequately fulfilling his job. However, there is very little sign so far that major ideas are permitted to percolate up from the bottom.

DISTRICT, REGIONAL, AND REPUBLIC PARTY ORGANIZATIONS: Above the P.P.O. level, the organization of the Communist Party follows the administrative organization of the Soviet state. The U.S.S.R. is divided into 15 union republics. The larger republics are, in turn, divided into *oblasts*—basic provincial or regional units of government—although some also include, in descending order of importance, nationality units called autonomous republics, autonomous oblasts, and national districts (*okrugs*). The oblasts are subdivided into rural districts (called *rayons*) and urban districts. Normally, the administrative chain of command is from federal government to republic to oblast to rayon or city. However, some of the smaller republics have no oblasts but are divided directly into rural and urban districts; conversely, the R.S.F.S.R., as the largest republic, contains a number of special regional administrative divisions called *krays*.

This same administrative pattern is followed by the Communist Party, whose organization proceeds upward from the P.P.O., to rayon and city district units; to oblast, autonomous republic, and kray organizations; and finally to party organizations at the republic level in all republics except the R.S.-F.S.R. Party affairs of the Russian Republic, which has lacked a separate party organization, were directed between 1952 and 1966 by a special bureau of the Central Committee. At the Twenty-third Party Congress in

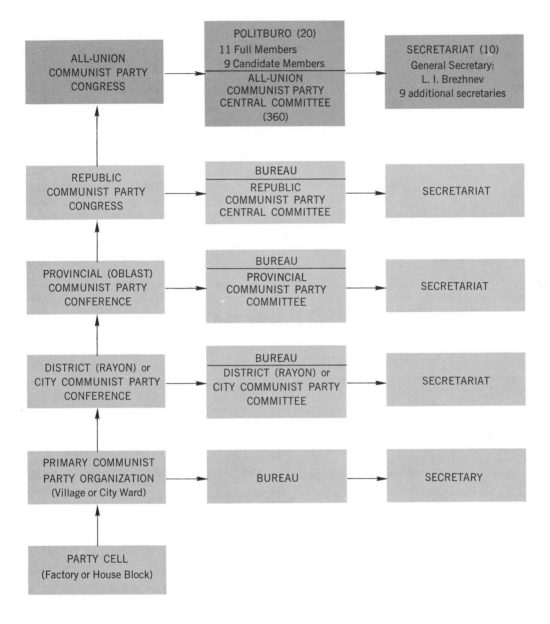

FIGURE 13.1. THE STRUCTURE OF THE COMMUNIST PARTY

1966, the R.S.F.S.R. bureau was abolished and its functions transferred to the politburo.

Between 1962 and 1964, party organizations on the provincial (oblast) and special regional (kray) levels were divided by Khrushchev into two branches—one for agriculture and one for industry. But the division ended with Khrushchev's removal from power and was criticized as being among his more ridiculous schemes. It constituted part of Khrushchev's effort to involve the party more actively in the day-to-day management of economic affairs, but it seems only to have complicated problems of coordination.

Theoretically, at the kray, oblast, rayon, and urban levels, the key decision-making body is a constituent assembly called the party conference, which consists of delegates elected from the party organization one step lower in the organizational hierarchy. For example, oblast party conferences, which are made up of delegates elected from rayon and urban party units, are supposed to make the basic decisions for the two party subgroups directly under their jurisdiction. In actuality, of course, authority moves from the top down in a complicated pattern of co-optation. Conference delegates at each level are, for the most part, members of the paid party bureaucracy from the immediate subgroup selected upon the "recommendation" of the party bureaucracy on the next higher administrative level. Thus, oblast party conferences consist mostly of party bureaucrats from district and urban organizations whose election to those units in the first place was determined by the oblast party organization. This same interlocked pattern of operation is followed throughout the party structure. Other delegates to conferences are usually government bureaucrats or local notables whose election was also "recommended" from above.

The conference is not, however, a really effective cog in the party machinery. It is usually too unwieldy to make sound decisions, and since most of its delegates have full-time jobs elsewhere, it rarely has the time to solve urgent problems. What it does, therefore, is to "elect" a smaller committee to act for it when it is not in session; the committee, in turn, "elects" a bureau to serve as an executive body, modeling itself, at all levels, on the national party organization. To complete the picture, the committee appoints a paid secretariat, made up of a first and second secretary and a staff. Again, "election" to all these posts is invariably preceded by approval from above, and on all levels, primarily because bureau and committee members have full-time responsibilities elsewhere, effective authority rests with the paid party bureaucrats in the secretariat.

Two of the major responsibilities of the party on the oblast and district levels are the selection of personnel for local party assignments and the general supervision of subordinate units in the party hierarchy. In addition, oblast and district party functionaries oversee the election and appointment of officials to various government posts, including local soviets. The district organization of the party also serves as its basic record office, maintaining record calls for all party members and candidates within its area. Finally, district organizations are, in general, responsible for supervision of the economic, cultural, and administrative life of their areas—except for the military, which has its own independent channel of command.

Both the oblast and kray organizations have jurisdiction not only over the assignment of persons to party and economic positions but also over the general guidance and direction of their region or province. In short, oblast and kray party units, working within the broad limits established by national economic planning and national laws, keep a fairly tight rein on the provincial economy. Given the vast size of the Soviet Union and the difficulties of complete control from the center, it is obvious that regional party leadership must assume a certain amount of policy initiative; it is also obvious that the post of provincial secretary has a good deal of influence.

The control of oblast and district party organizations over appointments to party and government posts is spelled out in a set of regulations on the range and nature of supervision to be exercised by each party organization. The *nomenklatura* is a list of persons and positions over which a particular party agency is expected and authorized to maintain surveillance. In this way, the Communist Party exercises complete control over which persons shall become chairmen of collective farms, factory managers, secretaries of trade unions, and regional or local government officials.

The work of executive officials on local, regional, and provincial levels is both arduous and exacting. In the past, turnover rates have been very high, for these officials are invariably caught in the cross fire of criticism from groups and individuals seeking to enhance their own positions.[6] The party also follows the practice of frequently rotating its officials, not only to give them broader experience but to avoid the creation of informal groups that might conceal deviations from the orders of higher authorities.

In the republics which boast their own party organization, party congresses usually meet every two years to elect a central committee, which in turn elects a bureau. Again, delegates to the congresses are professional party workers from the lower echelons, and congressional authority is concentrated in the secretarial apparatus—more particularly in the hands of the first secretary, who is usually appointed by the national leadership of the party. A republic's bureau consists of regional secretaries, the chairman and first deputy chairman of the republic's council of

ministers, the presidium chairman of its supreme soviet, and other influential republican officials.

The organization of a republic's central committee into a secretariat is modeled more or less on that of the C.P.S.U.'s highest echelon. The first obligation of the republic's party is to carry out decrees sent to it by the central apparatus, including the placement of key personnel as assigned to its nomenklatura. Through its staff of inspectors, the republic secretariat studies and reports on the operations and deficiencies of lower party and governmental organs.

THE CENTRAL ORGANS OF THE PARTY: The Party Congress of the C.P.S.U. is, organizationally, the highest political body in the Soviet Union. Under rules adopted in 1952, it must meet at least once every four years; since Stalin's death it has met regularly. It does not, however, seem to have any greater influence within the party than it did during the 1930's; its primary function remains that of listening to and cheering reports of leading party officials. Party rules require the congress to elect a Central Committee, which directs the work of the party between congresses.

While in recent years the committee has had some weight during succession crises, its meetings have remained rather infrequent. Its size and composition have changed over the years. The Central Committee elected in 1966, for example, contained 195 voting members and 165 alternate members; in 1952 it had only 125 voting and 122 candidate members. At least 43 per cent of the committee members elected in 1966 were party functionaries. State officials, including members of the U.S.S.R. Council of Ministers and the chairmen of the republic councils of ministers, constitute about thirty per cent of the membership; another 15 per cent or so are members who hold both party and government positions. In addition, there is a sprinkling of representatives from the mili-

6 The work was particularly dangerous under Stalin. According to Khrushchev, 1,108 of the 1,966 delegates to the Seventeenth Party Congress, held in 1934, were arrested and liquidated during the great purge of 1937–1939. Most of these men and women were regional and provincial party secretaries.

TABLE 13.2.   COMPOSITION OF PARTY BUREAUS OF THE REPUBLICS

	1954		1956		1961		1962–1964		1966	
	Member	Candidate member	Member	Candidate member	Member	Candidate member	Member	Candidate member	Member	Candidate member
Full-time party apparatus	56	10	79	6	83	12	86	13	75	20
Republican secretaries	44	0	67	0	68	2	70	1	70	1
Republican department heads	7	4	3	3	3	7	0	3	0	5
City regional secretaries	5	5	9	3	12	3	3	8	5	14
Chairmen, party state control							13	1		
Chairmen, party control committee	0	1	0	0	0	0	0	0	0	0
Republican state apparatus	62	4	55	6	56	8	33	11	48	15
Chairmen, Council of Ministers	14	0	14	0	14	0	14	0	14	0
Chairmen, Presidium Supreme Soviet	14	0	14	0	13	1	14	0	14	0
Deputy chairmen, Council of Ministers (agriculture)	5	1	8	2	4	1	1	4	5	2
Ministers (agriculture)	4	1	1	0	1	0	0	0	0	0
Deputy chairmen, Council of Ministers (industry)	9	0	6	2	9	0	1	2	6	2
Chairmen, Sovnarkhozy					9	2	1	0		
Ministers (industry)	1	1	0	0	0	1	0	0	0	0
Deputy chairmen, Council of Ministers (culture)	1	0	2	0	0	1	0	1	0	0
Ministers (culture)	1	0	0	0	1	0	0	0	0	0
Head of police	11	1	9	1	5	2	2	4	1	3
Chairmen, State (people's) Control	1	0	0	0	0	0			8	6
Miscellaneous	1	0	1	1	0	0	0	0	0	1
Other	13	15	10	17	11	24	7	17	8	14
Military	5	2	6	1	5	3	5	2	6	1
Republican Komsomol secretaries	0	9	2	7	1	8	1	6	1	5
Republican trade-union chairmen	4	1	2	3	3	8	1	9	1	8
Newspaper editors	2	2	0	6	1	5	0	0	0	0
Miscellaneous	1	0	0	0	1	0	0	0	0	0
Unknown	1	1	0	0	0	0	0	0	0	0
Totals	131	29	144	29	150	44	126	41	131	49

Source: Jerry Hough, "The Soviet Elite: I," *Problems of Communism*, XVI (January–February 1967), p. 30.

tary, as well as prominent party ideologists, intellectuals, scientists, and trade-union members. (See Table 13.4.) For the most part, the Central Committee is composed of persons of middle-class background with higher education in technical subjects. Given the fact that most committee members have full-time positions outside the party, membership is more a recognition of status than a source of real power. The flood of decrees

TABLE 13.3. GROWTH IN SIZE OF PARTY CONGRESSES

Year	Congress	Congressional membership
1918	Seventh	46
1919	Eighth	301
1920	Ninth	554
1921	Tenth	694
1922	Eleventh	522
1923	Twelfth	408
1924	Thirteenth	748
1925	Fourteenth	665
1927	Fifteenth	898
1930	Sixteenth	1,268
1934	Seventeenth	1,225
1939	Eighteenth	1,574
1952	Nineteenth	1,192
1956	Twentieth	1,349
1959	Twenty-first	1,269
1961	Twenty-second	4,408
1966	Twenty-third	4,620

Adapted from Roy C. Macridis and Robert E. Ward, *Modern Political Systems: Europe* (Englewood Cliffs, N. J.: Prentice Hall, 1968), p. 535. Reprinted by permission of the publisher.

issued in its name is largely the work of the secretariat, the politburo, and the Presidium of the Council of Ministers.

Secretaries of the party are, as in the past, formally elected by the Central Committee, after being designated by the party leadership. After Stalin's death, the term "general secretary" was temporarily replaced by "first secretary," and it was in this post that Khrushchev consolidated his power. At the Twenty-third Party Congress in 1966, the term "general secretary" was restored. The secretariat still continues to take on overall responsibility for the organization of the C.P.S.U., controlling its personnel and supervising the thoroughness with which party decisions are enforced. On its professional staff, therefore, are highly competent technical specialists who, in effect, are part of the policy-making process—not only insofar as they guide the implementation of decisions, but also as they inform important personnel within the secretariat and the politburo about the problems arising in carrying out policy.

The general secretary is the only member of the secretariat whose political strength is clearly superior to that of his colleagues. Indeed, the position is still the most powerful single office in the Soviet Union. Undoubtedly, a pecking order exists among the other ten to twelve senior officials (secretaries) who have composed the secretariat in the past ten years; those who are at the same time members of the politburo are probably the most important. But the apex of political power in the Soviet Union remains with the post of general secretary of the secretariat.

The politburo is today the principal decision-making body in the Soviet Union. In Stalin's time, its major decisions were made by the dictator himself; but now most issues are resolved by the group as a whole, despite the fact that Brezhnev and Kosygin have more power than other politburo members. Little information on the actual operation of the politburo is made public. Since most of its members also have other full-time positions, however, much of its authority is delegated to the secretariat or to various government de-

TABLE 13.4. OCCUPATIONAL STATUS OF MEMBERS OF THE
CENTRAL COMMITTEE

	Before 1953		After 1953	
	Members	Candidate members	Members	Candidate members
Party apparatus	40.0%	40.0%	54.9%	50.4%
High-level bureaucrats				
Heavy industry	13.6	7.2	12.5	11.2
Light industry	0.5	3.2	0.5	4.0
Agriculture	2.7	3.2	5.4	4.0
Low-level bureaucrats				
Heavy industry	8.2	0.0	0.0	0.0
Light industry	0.5	0.0	0.0	0.0
Agriculture	6.0	3.2	0.0	0.8
Other bureaucrats[1]	2.7	2.4	6.5	5.6
Indeterminate[2]	1.6	2.4	2.7	3.2
Military officers	8.2	7.2	7.6	8.8
Scientists	2.2	2.4	2.2	2.4
Writers	1.6	3.2	1.6	3.2
Journalists	0.5	2.4	0.5	1.6
Trade-union officers	2.2	0.8	3.3	3.2
Workers	1.6	1.6	1.1	1.6
Others	1.1	0.0	1.1	0.0
No data	6.5	16.0		

[1]Including those in the cultural, welfare, planning, and security ministries of government.
[2]Including those who spent such equal portions of their careers in both party and state work that it is impossible to place them in either category.

Source: Michael P. Gehlen and Michael McBride, "The Soviet Central Committee," *American Political Science Review*, LXII (December 1968), pp. 1234–1235. Reprinted by permission of the publisher.

partments. More and more frequently, the politburo is subject to the influence of professional and other elite groups within the Soviet Union—to the ploys of the military, of the managerial cadres of agriculture and heavy industry, and of all the other special interests competing for a larger share of the economic pie.

THE DYNAMICS OF POWER: The Communist Party of the Soviet Union took its form as a direct consequence of the tasks it set for itself. Its organization is hierarchical: its leadership is renewed by co-optation; its policies—dedicated to transforming Soviet society in accordance with certain ideological commitments—trickle down from the top.

According to official rules, the guiding principle of the party is "democratic centralism," which is defined as election of all party executive bodies from bottom to top; periodic accountability of party bodies to their party organizations and to higher bodies; strict party discipline and subordination of the minority to the majority; and the absolutely binding character of the decisions of higher bodies upon lower bodies.

The nature of democratic centralism quite clearly makes a euphemism of the word "democratic." Since Lenin insisted upon the elimination of factions within the party, there has been little or no possibility of developing organizations that would present and campaign for effective policy alternatives.

TABLE 13.5. C.P.S.U. CENTRAL COMMITTEE: AGE, LENGTH OF
PARTY MEMBERSHIP, AND OCCUPATION

	Professional function				
	Party apparatus	State apparatus	Army	Other	Total
Date of birth:					
Before 1901	4	5	6	0	15
1901–1910	25	48	7	7	87
1911–1920	46	21	1	5	73
Since 1920	3	1	0	3	7
Date not given	7	1	0	5	13
Total	85	76	14	20	195
Entry into party:					
Before 1925	6	6	5	0	17
1925–1930	10	27	5	2	44
1931–1935	8	6	0	2	16
1936–1939	18	12	2	2	34
1940–1945	31	22	2	3	58
1946–1953	2	0	0	2	4
Since 1953	0	0	0	4	4
Date not given	10	3	0	5	18
Total	85	76	14	20	195

Source: Borys Lewytzkyj, "Generations in Conflict," *Problems of Communism*,
XVI (January–February 1967), p. 38.

Nevertheless, this does not imply that discussion and debate are missing from party decision-making, or that party functionaries are free to do whatever they please. As noted previously, self-criticism is encouraged at all levels of the party, as is discussion of the means by which policy is to be carried out. Further, party members are encouraged to report incompetence or the excessive use of authority to persons higher up the party ladder. The party, in fact, has a vested interest in making sure that those who rise within it represent the best possible material and that policies are rationally implemented. In 1961 Khrushchev attempted to increase intra-party mobility by requiring that one-quarter of the members of both the politburo and the Central Committee be "renewed" at regular intervals, and that politburo members serve no more than three successive terms. The same type of rule was to apply to the lower levels of party organization. In 1966 Khrushchev's rules were amended; while turnover is still encouraged, no specific percentages are now mentioned.

Though organizational turnover is now lower than during Khrushchev's heyday, the C.P.S.U. is still fairly consistent in its efforts to discover new talent—especially talent from the working class—and bring it into the official party apparatus. Any member demonstrating exceptional capabilities may be sent to one of an elaborate network of party schools for both technical and political training. The four-year party school attached to the Central Committee in Moscow is reserved for those already well on the way up the party ladder; candidates for it must be at least forty years old and be recommended by the relevant party organization. In addition to a good dash of Marxist-Leninist theory, subjects include party and state administration, local industry, trade, finance, bookkeeping, and foreign languages.

Schools notwithstanding, the best way to reach the top of the Communist Party hier-

TABLE 13.6. CURRICULUM OF THE FOUR-YEAR PARTY SCHOOL

Subjects[1]	Instruction hours
History of the Communist Party of the U.S.S.R.	250
Dialectical and historical materialism	200
Political economy	300
History of international workers' and national liberation movements	180
History of the U.S.S.R.	150
Party and government affairs and procedures	150
Foundations of Soviet jurisprudence (civil, labor, and collective farm law)	100
Economic geography of the U.S.S.R. and foreign countries	100
Economics, organization, and planning in industry, construction, and transport	200
Economic organization and planning in agricultural enterprises	180
Power resources in industry	80
Industrial technology (in major branches of industry)	270
Industrial and civil construction	100
General agriculture, plant cultivation, and agrochemistry	240
Animal breeding	140
Mechanization and electrification of agriculture	160
Regional planning of local industry and cultural services	80
Trade, finance, and banking	80
Accounting and auditing techniques	60
Statistics	80
Mathematics	100
Total	3,200
Optional:	
Foreign language	200
Russian language	150
Automotive and driving instruction	120
Industrial practice (not included in total hours)	2 months

[1]Students who have completed the curriculum take state examinations in the history of the C.P.S.U., dialectical and historical materialism, and political and national economy of the U.S.S.R.

Source: Zbigniew Brzezinski and Samuel Huntington, *Political Power/U.S.A.– U.S.S.R.* (New York: The Viking Press, 1964), p. 145. Reprinted by permission of the publisher.

archy is still to be closely associated with a higher-ranking party member whose star is rising. Khrushchev was picked out quite early in his career by Lazar Kaganovich, then party boss of the Ukraine, and it was through him that Khrushchev came to the attention of Stalin. Leonid Brezhnev, the current general secretary, was a Khrushchev protégé. He became a party member in 1931, was sent for five years to the Metallurgical Institute, and during World War II served as a member of Khrushchev's Military Council of the Stalingrad Front. Aleksei Kosygin, the other half of the duumvirate that now dominates the party and the state, joined the Communist Party in 1927; in 1935 he began a course of studies at the Leningrad Textile Institute, later attached himself to Stalin's one-time heir apparent, Andrei Zhdanov, until his death in 1948, and finally sided with

Khrushchev against Malenkov in their struggle for power.

Of course, such attachments can be dangerous, as the liquidated supporters of Trotsky are testimony. While such violent demotions have not occurred in the postwar period, attachment to the wrong man can destroy a party career. For obvious reasons, the party officially frowns on these "family circles": time and time again, they have been condemned for frustrating the execution of policy, attempting to create centers of local power, and covering up failures. Yet it is unlikely that the party will ever be able to eliminate them. As in all organizations, informal—even surreptitious—relations are formed as a means not only of obtaining or exercising influence but of mitigating the effects of a rigorous application of party rules. Brezhnev, for instance, like his predecessors, used the post of general secretary to pack the Central Committee with his partisans. How long, then, the present duumvirate will last, and when (or if) Brezhnev will emerge as the dominant political figure, are problematical; past experience would indicate that the pattern of dual leadership is an unstable one. Unstable or not, turnover within the party echelons under the Brezhnev-Kosygin regime has been smaller than ever before—whether because Khrushchev had alienated most of the party apparatus by the time he fell from grace, or because of growing party bureaucratization, is difficult to determine.

Today, the Communist Party continues to wrestle with problems posed by the greater complexity of Soviet society. There are signs that Soviet leaders are seeking means by which succession crises may be circumvented; they are also trying to create a place for the party which preserves its status without making it dysfunctional. Theoretically, the party still has three roles: it interprets the nature and future of Soviet society, operates as the decisive instrument of political power, and intervenes directly in the practical problems of the economy.

As we have seen, the proper balance among these functions is not easy to strike. Thus, the party alternately urges that its members give more attention to production, and warns that they must not fall into the error of "practicality." Ideally, members say, the party should be like an orchestra conductor—it should strive for harmony without trying to "play the instruments." The correct emphases have yet to be achieved.

Membership in the Communist Party may be divided for convenience into three main categories. There are, first, the full-time functionaries, the apparatchiki, who are oriented to the overall direction of the party. Second, there are those distributed as leaders through the different levels of the administrative, productive, cultural, and political organizations of Soviet society. Those in the second group, while of necessity party members, are more often primarily concerned with their professional or sectional interests. Finally, there are the rank-and-file party members who do not serve in positions of authority, either in the party apparatus or in the state or other organizations. They furnish recruits for the upper echelons, disseminate party-approved attitudes and policies, and supply information to party organizations.

Of the three, the apparatchiki are, of course, the most important. Their character has changed considerably since the early days of Stalin; they are now of the middle class, on the whole rather well-educated, and professional politicians. According to scattered figures, some eighty per cent of the district party secretaries have received a higher education, and the figure for regional secretaries exceeds ninety per cent.

The party bureaucracy represents, in a sense, a priesthood. Talent, not inheritance, is still the major requirement for advancement, although well-placed parents are not a hindrance. There is some doubt, however, about whether the party continues to draw in the best people. Many observers of the Soviet scene believe that more dynamic individuals no longer wish to make the party a career, preferring professional training and commitment. If this is true, it could result in a new crisis of confidence within the Soviet system.

Indeed, there is some evidence that just such a crisis is already developing with regard to the role of the Communist Party in Soviet life. The increasing differentiation of Soviet society has brought about the emergence of new institutional structures manned by professionally trained personnel—scientists, engineers, and economists. These groups have demanded either more autonomy or a greater voice in shaping policy decisions pertaining to those areas in which they have expertise; they claim, not without reason, that the party's attempt to control the whole of Soviet society, while it may have been functional at an earlier stage of development, is non-adaptive in a society as complex as the Soviet Union is today. With the disenchantment of both the technocrats and the party bureaucracy itself over some of the more millennial aspects of Marxism-Leninism, one of the prime ideological props supporting party dominance has been seriously weakened. The professionals argue that if the main tasks of the future involve a more efficiently organized Soviet society in order to achieve concrete, clearly defined social and economic goals, such as improving the material conditions of life, why should this task not be left to those most skilled in dealing with such matters?

It seems most probable, therefore, that unless the leadership of the Communist Party is willing to return to the naked use of terror, it will have to find new ways of justifying its authority. In a sense the party has attempted to meet this challenge by changing its image, primarily through recruiting and bringing to the fore personnel who combine the two qualifications of technical training and party experience. Scholars such as George Fischer believe that the party may well be successful in this effort, and that the new "dual executives," as he calls them, will be able to justify their authority on the basis of their technical and political skills—skills that will enable them to organize Soviet society with considerable efficiency.

Other scholars argue that party authority is bound to erode as the Soviet Union gropes for new structures more in line with the requirements of the late twentieth century. They see a gradual evolution in the direction of forms which, in some ways, will come to resemble Western European concepts of pluralistic politics. Some commentators maintain a third view: that the Soviet system is too rigid to adjust and that a violent upheaval in the not too distant future will occur. For, as they point out, Marx taught us a long time ago that no ruling class ever surrenders its power willingly.[7]

7 See George Fischer, *The Soviet System and Modern Society* (New York: Atherton Press, 1968) and the discussion in *Problems of Communism,* XV, 3 (May–June 1966), and XVI, 1 (January–February 1967). For convincing evidence of tensions between party and other elites, see Milton Lodge, " 'Groupism' in the Post-Stalin Period," *Midwest Journal of Political Science,* XII (August 1968), 330–351, and Milton Lodge, "Soviet Elite Participatory Attitudes in the Post-Stalin Period," *American Political Science Review,* LXII (September 1968), 827–839.

part IV

THE PROCESS OF GOVERNMENT

14

The European

Pattern

1. INTRODUCTION

No complex social order has ever been entirely governed by the people acting in concert; in all but the simplest, most homogeneous societies, the authority to develop general rules which bind the community as a whole—that is, a public policy—is centered in institutions with certain more or less specific responsibilities. If these institutions are to exercise power for any length of time, they must be supported by a framework of values that legitimizes them. In most modern states, legitimation is provided by constitutions which outline the role various governmental structures are to play in the rule-making process.

In France, Germany, and England—and with some modifications in the Soviet Union —the authority to develop public policies is constitutionally delegated to national, and sometimes local, legislative bodies whose authority is justified by the fact that they express the wishes of the people according to fixed and generally accepted guidelines of political representation.

This chapter will discuss, primarily, the impact of constitutional forms upon governmental processes. Chapters 15 through 18 will analyze these processes for each nation under study; Chapter 19 will deal with local and regional politics. Our discussion in this chapter will also include an analysis of the role and behavior of interest groups. We have already taken up some of the more important interest groups in these countries; others, including the military, will be reviewed in later chapters. The discussion of the general nature of interest-group behavior has been placed here not only because rule-making institutions are the focus of societal pressures but because the structure of these institutions is a determining factor in the manner in which interest groups behave.

Modern parliamentary government, including the American presidential variant, is the great achievement of Western Europe, and more particularly of England. That it has been so widely adopted or proposed as an eventual goal by political societies around the world is an indication that it appeals to a fundamental sense of equity. And, indeed, it

439

is difficult to conceive of any other arrangement compatible with the idea of self-government. This is not to say that the parliamentary regime represents humanity's highest achievement; it is certainly possible that its present forms will become obsolete and will eventually be replaced by others. For as we shall see, the variations upon a common theme have been immense; parliamentarianism, even in Europe, has been constantly changing over the past century.

As we have noted earlier, parliaments sprang from a type of feudal society. Throughout Europe, with England as a partial exception, their authority declined during the age of absolute monarchy. Their revival and enhanced power was related to the emergence of new ideas and social classes. From the fifteenth through the nineteenth centuries, parliaments gradually came to the fore as political structures endowed with the authority to determine both the nation's goals and the means by which those goals should be implemented; they devised the rules by which the community would govern itself. Whether through relatively peaceful change or violent revolution, monarchs were stripped of their power. The alternative to parliamentarianism in the twentieth century is no longer hereditary monarchy but the dictatorship of one man or party.

Postfeudal parliaments differed greatly from their predecessors. In feudal society, the king and parliament discovered and implemented the law; feudal parliaments served as both courts of justice and councils through which community grievances were placed before the monarch. Modern parliaments *make* law; they are the ultimate source of legislative authority. Feudal parliaments were designed to represent the great estates of the realm; modern parliaments ostensibly represent individuals as individuals. To be sure, there are degrees of ambiguity in modern parliamentary representation. On the one hand, deputies supposedly act in accordance with the wishes of their constituents; on the other, they are expected to follow the dictates of their conscience, of their own considered judgment, even when these run counter to the popular temper.

The conflict between essentially liberal and traditional concepts of representation was clearly delineated at the time of the American Revolution. The British felt the colonists were represented in Parliament by virtue of their membership in estates that did have representation; the Americans argued that since they did not directly elect members to Parliament, their individual interests could not be adequately taken into account.

In fact, liberals have generally frowned on group representation as retrograde—that is, as something which would detract from the realization of the general will of the community. Dominated as they still are by a national liberal ideology, a good many Americans recoil with horror at any suggestion that interest groups are a legitimate part of the political process or practice. In most European countries, the direct representation of social and economic groups has continued to be regarded as at least partially legitimate. Indeed, the Catholic Church has always maintained, as did Fascist regimes and certain brands of socialism, that individual representation should be replaced by the representation of functional interests, such as agriculture, industry, and labor—thus harking back to an earlier tradition.

As European monarchs were divested of their power, some of their authority was transferred to an executive, or to executive bodies responsible to the legislature itself. While the parliament could legislate, it was thought, an executive body was needed to speak for the nation as a whole, to prepare general programs of action, to oversee administration, and to handle such matters as foreign policy. Under these premises, the British cabinet, once responsible to the monarch and now to the legislature, acquired more real power. Its authority has grown as public affairs have become more complicated, and integrated programs concerned with all aspects of the economy have become an ever greater necessity. For a time during the nineteenth century, parliaments actually legislated—that is, they were the source of most laws. Today, in all the countries under discussion, the executive—whether cabinet, chancellor, or president—is the primary source of important new legislative proposals; parliaments have come to assume the role, primarily, of critical watchdogs, even as they legitimize political decisions and serve as public forums for the discussion of these decisions.

In England the transition from parliamentary to cabinet government was a natural one, based, in some measure, on the development of a disciplined two-party system. In Germany and France, such evolution did not occur. The multiplicity of political parties during the Weimar regime, and during the Third and Fourth Republics, inhibited the development of a stable and powerful yet responsible executive. Since Parliament could not itself legislate effectively in the two nations, either very little was done, or, in emergencies, the executive was given—or seized—the power to act by decree. In both Fifth Republic France and the West German Federal Republic, attempts have been made to assure executive dominance over the legislature—in Germany, by requiring a "positive" vote of no-confidence; in France, by creating a popularly elected executive with considerable authority.

The separation of the executive and the legislature, each directly responsible to the people and each with its own sphere of authority, was, to a large extent, an American invention, generated partly by a reading of Montesquieu and partly by American perceptions of the existing pattern of English government. Whatever its values in practice, and there are many, the belief that executive and legislative functions can be neatly separated has never made any sense from a theoretical point of view. In the United States, the president does not merely execute programs legislated by Congress; he is party leader, chief executive, and, increasingly, chief initiator of legislation, all rolled into one. In the same way, Congress legislates, oversees the execution of legislation, and figures crucially in such areas as foreign policy. Yet, the myth of separation has allowed the American congress in the twentieth century to exercise more authority than its British counterpart, especially as a check upon the executive. For some time the American pattern was considered obsolete by many Europeans; today, however, at least some analysts believe that, in an age of specialization, parliaments, if they are to fulfill more than a rhetorical function, might do worse than to take a look at some of the devices that have preserved the power of the American congress, including the committee system.

2. PARLIAMENTS

While parliaments are an almost universal phenomenon in the modern world, many of them, as in the Soviet Union and other one-party states, have little or no power. Almost all functioning parliaments share legislative power with other organs of government. The executive's control over the order in which proposed legislation is to be discussed and the amount of time to be spent on particular bills, as well as over the initiation of legislation, has seriously compromised the legislative function of parliaments. Judicial interpretation of laws in some countries has also limited parliamentary authority, and both the executive and the bureaucracy make policy in the process of putting general statutes into effect. Moreover, legislators themselves are, on the whole, generalists rather than experts in many areas, and are, therefore, incapable of wielding the influence they did in the less hectic days of the nineteenth century.

The contention that parliaments have completely lost legislative authority is, of course, not completely correct. The congress of the United States still has very considerable authority over the making of public policy, and while the authority of the legislature as a body is far less significant in Germany, France, or England, it is still important. In all three nations, although to different degrees, the power of the executive is founded on the discipline of party majorities in Parliament itself, and these majorities are not entirely passive. Prospective executive actions are always examined with an eye to the reaction of legislative bodies, or at least to the reaction of those deputies who compose the parliamentary majority.

Parliaments perform other key functions. In cabinet and chancellor political systems like those of England and Germany, the government is responsible to the legislature, and while the overturn of any regime requires a split within the governing party, the possibility of such a political calamity affects decisions made by the executive. In presidential systems like that of the United States, the executive is responsible to the electorate and serves for a fixed term. But in a mixed system, such as France has, where the cabinet is responsible to the legislature, the views of Parliament can never be completely ignored. Of course, the French political scene of the 1960's has been so dominated by Charles de Gaulle that it is difficult to assess how it will function now that he has stepped down. One suspects, however, that the role of the legislature in making and unmaking French governments will again become significant.

Despite the fact that bureaucrats are formally responsible only to the executive, their activity is not above the influence of most European legislatures, which review administrative decrees, intervene in the administrative process on behalf of constituents, and question ministers on the activities of civil servants under their jurisdiction; where a committee system exists, legislatures may also conduct investigations of administrative activities. The investigatory functions of legislative committees, especially of important

ones, are becoming increasingly vital in the twentieth century. Committees are quite powerful in the United States Congress, less so in Germany, and still less so in France; with some exceptions, they are of relatively little importance in England. Yet many persons concerned with the reform of the English parliament, for instance, have urged a strengthening of committees so that M.P.'s may more competently handle important issues of public policy.

The bulk of the legislative work of most parliaments does not take place in plenary (full) sessions. Usually parliamentary chambers are fairly empty, with members delivering speeches to a few bored colleagues as others file in and out paying only a modicum of attention. To be sure, during a major debate the atmosphere can become exciting as exchanges grow keener. In fact, there have been times in the past, in England and the United States, when the exchange became so bitter that members punched, caned, or shot one another. Sessions in both legislatures have been somewhat calmer during the past century. Parliamentary bodies in other nations, however—in Germany during the Weimar Republic and in France under the Third and Fourth Republics—have witnessed considerable violence.

No matter how persuasive parliamentary speeches may sound, most members know long before the final tally is taken how they are going to vote on a piece of legislation. The issue has already been determined by their party, or as the result of either committee work or the pressure from constituents. Speeches, when not made for the purpose of delaying the proceedings, are directed primarily at the press. The real work of the parliament, then, takes place elsewhere.

Parliamentary rules set forth the procedures for introducing and considering proposed legislation. These bills may be drawn up outside the legislature, but usually they must be introduced by a member. In

TABLE 14.1. FREQUENCY AND DURATION OF PUBLIC SESSIONS
OF PARLIAMENTS

Parliament and time period	Sitting days (annual average)	Length of sitting (daily average in hours and minutes)	Length of sitting (annual average in hours)
England			
House of Commons, 1954–1958	161.6	7:54	1280
France			
National Assembly, 1954	132.0	6:02	796
Germany (F.R.)			
First Bundestag, 1949–1953	68.5	6:19	433
Second Bundestag, 1953–1957	55.8	7:37	425
Third Bundestag, 1957–1961	41.8	6:45	281
Fourth Bundestag, 1961–1965	49.0	5:33	273
United States			
House of Representatives, 1954–1958	125.8	4:13	532

Adapted from Gerhard Loewenberg, "The Remaking of the German Party System," *Polity*, I (1968), p. 513. Reprinted by permission of the publisher.

the United States, for example, many important pieces of legislation come from the executive, but the president must find a congressional sponsor. In a cabinet system, the government may introduce bills directly. In some cases, individual members of legislatures are not permitted to introduce legislation at all. In Germany, for example, all members must join a *Fraktion* consisting of at least fifteen deputies; only a Fraktion can introduce a bill and exercise certain other rights.

Once introduced, bills proceed through a series of steps, customarily referred to as "readings," a term derived from British practice. Traditionally, clerks read proposals three times in Parliament in order to insure that representatives understood their contents. Today this is no longer necessary, since bills are printed and distributed to all members, but the terminology has been retained.

The method of considering bills differs greatly. In the United States, Germany, and France, bills are sent to committees for study either immediately or shortly after being introduced. The power of these committees also varies. In the United States they are still quite important; in Germany and France, although they exercised considerable author-

ity during the Weimar period and the Third and Fourth Republics, their influence has diminished. In the House of Commons, legislative committees are of minor importance; bills are sent to committee only after they have been approved in general terms by Parliament, and committee discussions rarely result in significant changes in legislation. Where committees are powerful and political parties weak, committee chairmen and rapporteurs are men with considerable influence. When political parties are strong, especially in a two-party system, the committees, and hence committee chairmanships, are not usually foci of legislative power.

Most legislative bodies have rules permitting the cutting off of debate so that a majority can eventually push through the legislation it favors. The United States Senate remains a unique bastion of free speech in this regard, since the ending of debate requires the support of two-thirds of those voting. Other legislatures require only a majority vote to end debate. The ability of a government to make sure that its proposals receive fairly prompt attention depends upon both institutional mechanisms and its own strength. Despite the fact that the American presidency is a fairly powerful office, the combination of weakly disciplined parties, strong committees, and the separation of powers can result in extremely rough sledding for presidential legislation proposals. During Germany's Weimar Republic and France's Third and Fourth Republics, governments had very little power over legislation, primarily because they had very tenuous majorities in the multi-party legislatures. In both nations this circumstance has now changed, one reason being that the executive has been strengthened and another that the party systems are no longer quite as fragmented. In England since the end of the nineteenth century, a disciplined two-party system has insured that the government of the day will, under most circumstances, have its way.

Compensation for legislators also differs from nation to nation, although there is an increasing tendency to raise salaries and improve facilities. Members of the United States Congress are probably the best-paid legislators in the world; they also have the widest range of available services, including extensive office space, and the most liberal expense allowances. American politics, at least on the national level, has long been regarded as a profession like any other, and members are expected to receive commensurate salaries. Until recently, service in the British parliament was looked upon as a duty of the political and social elite, something that should not be remunerated. With the rise of the Labor Party, sentiment shifted, albeit slowly; in fact, many M.P.'s now supplement their salaries by part-time work, by other occupations, or, in the case of trade-union M.P.'s, by being partially subsidized.

Paid or unpaid, legislators are not necessarily the image of the population they represent. For a long time, Continental legislatures were the domain primarily of gentlemen. With the rise of Socialist parties, contingents of working-class members and middle-class and lower-middle-class radicals were added. Working-class strength in most parliaments is usually in direct proportion to the size of the Socialist or Communist vote, although not always. The French Communists, for instance, are much more concerned about having working men in Parliament than either the British Labor Party or the German Social Democrats. In both of the latter parties, many trade-union officials have been replaced by middle-class schoolteachers and journalists.

Most legislatures contain large contingents of lawyers—not only because of the nature of the profession, but also because it can more easily be resumed if a legislative career is interrupted. Lawyers are particularly prominent in the United States Congress Americans have always tended to think of politics as a process of regulating social intercourse by legal rules rather than as, say, in France, an area of ideological confrontation. British and French parliaments, on the other hand, contain substantial contingents of journalists and academics—a reflection, in part, of the greater prestige of professional intellectuals in both societies. Further, all European legislatures contain a much larger representation of business executives than does the United States congress. This can be explained by the fact that, as distinguished from the attitude in the United States, it is considered legitimate for business interests to be represented directly by businessmen, and, of course, European parliamentary schedules are often such as to permit executives to continue their professional activity while serving.[1]

The behavior of members of parliament is strongly influenced by the nation's political culture, as well as the character of the legislative body of which they are part. In England, such has been the prestige of Parliament, at least until recently, that there is a distinct sense of community in being a member of an institution having its own

---

[1] In 1964 about sixty per cent of the members of the American congress were lawyers. In 1966 between 15 and twenty per cent of British M.P.'s were lawyers. The French parliament elected in 1967 contained 71 teachers and only 34 lawyers, in a total membership of 487.

style, tradition, and rules of the game. At the same time, the strict discipline of its two-party system makes party reputation more important for political advancement than reputation in the House of Commons. In the United States, on the other hand, party ties are much weaker; reputation, indeed even power, in the legislature depends much more upon personal qualities and how these relate to the general atmosphere of the House or the Senate. In France during the politically chaotic Third and Fourth Republics, there was much less sense of community, although most deputies did develop a kind of mutual understanding which enabled them to work together. The Communists, of course, were its major exception: they remained aloof, existing in a world dominated by party discipline.

New members of most legislative bodies are expected to be seen rather than heard—and to learn appropriate forms of behavior. As in any functioning group, sanctions are available if the freshmen do not behave appropriately. New members who fail to conform will find themselves socially ostracized and deprived of the opportunity to advance politically. In countries such as England, where party discipline is strong, the norms of behavior and the political penalties are set primarily by the party. Where party discipline is weak and legislative committees are strong, as in the United States, the attitude of senior members of the legislature can be at least as important as that of fellow party members, for the passage of legislation one desires may very well depend upon their good will.

All European legislatures consist of two houses. Originally, the differentiation was between a legislative body in which the aristocracy sat (the upper house) and one that, in some sense, represented the people (the lower house). In federal regimes, such as the German Empire, the upper house tended to represent not only the aristocracy but the various Länder as well. In the United States, the Senate, whose members were initially elected by the lower houses of the state legislatures, represented both the states and, theoretically, the elite of the community. England retained an upper house based on modified aristocratic representation longer than any other European country, although the power of the House of Lords was almost nil by the end of World War II. Under the French Third Republic, the Senate served as the "conservative" upper house, and had somewhat less authority than the Chamber of Deputies. The constitution of the Fourth Republic provided for a very weak second chamber; that of the Fifth increased its power to some extent. In Germany, the Weimar regime stripped the upper house of most of its power; under the Bonn constitution, the Bundesrat—representing federal but no longer aristocratic or conservative interests—has regained some of its traditional prerogatives. In the United States, the Senate was democratized by providing for the direct election of its members, and over the years it has retained, and perhaps even increased, its power.

3. THE EXECUTIVE

The particular division of functions between the legislature and the executive that has manifested itself in Europe is a direct outgrowth of European historical experience. The development of European political institutions may be seen as a long process in which political power was stripped from the monarchy, only to be returned to an executive responsible either to a popularly elected legislature or to the electorate itself. All the European political systems with which we are concerned have divided authority between a legislature that is formally responsible for creating the rules under which the society functions and an executive whose primary function is to propose such rules, to apply those adopted by the legislature, and to represent the nation as an entity in relations with other political systems.

It has been argued that the differentiation of governmental functions into the making and the application of rules is a peculiarly European phenomenon, and that just as one cannot really speak of a separation of powers, so one cannot sharply distinguish between the functions of the legislature and of the executive. It was Lenin's contention that the separation of powers was purely a bourgeois absurdity, and that the new Soviet state would be organized along quite different lines. It is well to point out, however, that non-European nations which have adopted democratic models of one kind or another have usually organized their political systems very much like the European, and that Soviet institutions, despite differences in nomenclature, are organized in much the same manner. Further, while some parliamentary regimes vest authority in an executive body exercising collective responsibility, every major political system in the modern world that operates with reasonable effectiveness has eventually concentrated symbolic, and to a certain extent real, authority in the hands of one man. There is, therefore, good reason to suspect that the current attempt at "collective" leadership in the Soviet Union will not last very long.

In parliamentary regimes in which the executive is elected by the legislature, his power depends very much upon the party system. In France under the Third and Fourth Republics, for instance, and in Weimar Germany, the premier and chancellor were ineffective simply because the coalition governments they headed were usually based upon flimsy, transitory majorities composed of parties and politicians with widely divergent views. In England, on the other hand, the existence of a system of two parties, each tautly controlled and each taking its turn in office, has conferred considerable power upon the executive. The cabinet is, to be sure, collectively the government, but the prime minister is far more than *primus inter pares*. The mere fact of his selection as party leader and prime minister yields him a national promi-

nence that enhances his role far beyond that of any of his colleagues.

The fear of a repetition of the Weimar experience prompted the writers of the postwar Bonn constitution to institute a negative vote of no confidence and to place ultimate responsibility for governmental action in the hands of the chancellor.[2] To date, this additional authority has undoubtedly strengthened the position of the West German executive at the expense of the parliament; yet even so, his ability to govern effectively still depends to a great extent upon his ability to mobilize a parliamentary majority.

In systems like the American, in which a popularly elected president is entrusted with executive authority, his power rests to a great extent upon the fact that he is elected by the people as a whole. Since his government cannot be overturned by a congressional vote, he is less dependent upon the legislature than is either the British prime minister or the German chancellor. Nevertheless, the political independence of American congressmen does place limitations upon presidential power. In the United States a substantial segment of party members in the legislature can defy a president of their own party without serious repercussions; in England such defiance could mean the fall of the government and new elections in which the dissident members might suffer defeat. Thus, while the American president, like the British prime minister, has become the chief legislator, he cannot be nearly so certain that programs emanating from the government will receive the kind of consideration he wishes. Moreover, since his road to office and his requirements for getting elected are often quite different from those for congressmen, he rarely has the working arrangement with legislators that a British prime minister does. Lyndon Johnson, in the early years of his presidency, was a partial exception because he had worked so closely with senators as Senate majority leader. How-

2 See Chapter 2, pp. 81–87.

ever, many of the factors that made him a powerful senator were dysfunctional for other aspects of his presidential role.

The French pattern of "mixed" government adds further complications to the interrelationship between the executive and the legislature. Since 1962, the president has been elected nationally and has held wide powers; yet executive authority is shared with a premier responsible to the legislature. Under de Gaulle, the president dominated the scene, but it is not yet clear whether Pompidou will be able to do so—or even that the system will survive in its present form.

Attempts to generalize about styles of political leadership and to relate these styles to economic, social, or cultural factors have not been very fruitful. Nor is it clear what personal characteristics and qualities make for more effective leadership; these vary with circumstances.

Certainly different kinds of systems tend to produce different leadership styles. During the 1930's and 1940's, success in the Soviet Union depended upon a combination of ruthlessness and sycophancy, as Stalin's heirs have testified. More recently, both traits have become less crucial, but ability to manipulate the Communist Party organization and to translate one's own power drives into an acceptable ideological stance are still necessary to survive politically.

Negotiation and compromise are far more significant in parliamentary regimes, and overt ruthlessness can stop a political career. The constituency of any political leader is far broader than his party cadres; in effect, the leader must demonstrate a capacity to work with party and other elites, as well as an ability to project the right national image. The quality of this image is more important in a presidential system than in a parliamentary one, and more important in a parliamentary system that alternates between two major parties than in one in which governments rise and fall on the basis of intraparliamentary negoti-

ation. Mendès-France achieved great national popularity during the middle years of the Fourth Republic, but that popularity did not help him when he alienated too many special-interest groups with strong representation in the National Assembly.

Whatever the continuing differences among industrial societies, however, there are signs of a growing similarity in their leadership styles. Part of the reason for this has been the emergence of certain common problems requiring the attention of professionals, but new technologies, especially in the field of mass communications, have also had their impact. Stalin, Adenauer, Churchill, and de Gaulle clearly belong to another epoch, an earlier age in which the image of traditional authority was of paramount importance. In all four nations, a new breed of leadership is now coming to the fore; its style and image reflect its professionalism, its self-assurance, and, particularly in the West, an easy rapport with the common man. The quickness with which a number of European political leaders sought to emulate the Kennedy image is a further indication of the increasing convergence of leadership styles.

The impact of television is hard to measure. It has certainly increased public awareness of political decisions, as it has reduced the ability of any democratic regime either to manage the news or to minimize the public's awareness of governmental actions. As a medium of mass communication, it must, of course, be mastered by any aspiring politician—and to do that requires the projection of a winning image.

4. INTEREST GROUPS AND GOVERNMENTAL PROCESSES

Individuals who are linked together by common concerns, and who have an awareness of these concerns, constitute an *interest group*. Such groups are an integral part of all societies, except the smallest and the most primitive. Their character is related to the culture of a society as well as its economic and social structure. In primitive and traditional societies, the most important interest groups are usually those associated with kinship and lineage; as societies become more complicated, regional and class groups make their appearance.

One of the major characteristics of modern societies has been the proliferation of interest groups formed on the basis of the members' functional position within the society. Workers, managers, teachers—all have formed interest groups. In addition, group organization has become more and more complex and sophisticated. Most modern states contain a plethora of highly organized interest groups, which serve to express the needs of their members and compete with other groups for an increased share of their society's resources. For our purposes, we may follow Gabriel Almond and divide interest groups into two broad classifications: institutional and associational.[3]

Institutional interest groups develop from formal organizations such as churches, the police, the military, and the government bureaucracy. They are composed of professionally employed personnel with designated social and political functions in the society. Associational interest groups, on the other hand, are formed primarily to articulate the demands of specific strata of the population, whether these be workers, students, or birdwatchers. The proliferation of groups of both types is a result of the increased complexity of modern industrial societies. Insofar as the institutional structure of all modern societies is coming to have certain common features, there is a greater similarity in the kinds of interest groups and in their brand of political activity.

Even so, the behavior of modern interest

groups and their ability to articulate their members' interests and press for changes in public policy varies widely. The prevalence of both associational and institutional groups in Western Europe is partly due to acceptance of the legitimacy of their activities. The complete absence of associational groups in the Soviet Union, on the other hand, has been closely related to Communist ideology. To Stalin, the Communist Party, personified in himself, represented the real will of the people. Since the aim of the regime was a society embodying universal love and spontaneous unanimity, divergent interests and cliques representing these interests were not necessary; indeed, the desire to create "factions" was regarded as subversive.

The political style of interest groups, their degree of influence, their powers and techniques of persuasion depend upon the kind of society in which they operate. Where sharp social divisions exist, the demands of such groups are likely to be highly ideological and diffuse—that is, involving a total transformation of the society rather than the attainment of limited ends. Under such circumstances, compromise between authority and interest groups is almost impossible, and there is a greater likelihood of physical violence—as there is, also, when a group believes that its legitimate demands cannot be met within the society's existing institutional structure. But the willingness to use force is also contingent upon the cultural attitude of the society as a whole, or of its subgroups, toward violence. Fragmented societies usually contain a large number of amorphous groups with shifting loyalties, groups that define their interests in such narrow terms that the integration of aims into fewer policy alternatives becomes extremely difficult. This produces stalemates that prevent the satisfaction of any demands whatsoever; these stalemates, in turn, radicalize the demands of all groups.

A society in which most of the people accept the community's basic norms usually contains interest groups whose goal is limited

[3] See Gabriel Almond and G. Bingham Powell, Jr., *Comparative Politics: A Developmental Approach* (Boston: Little, Brown and Company, 1966), pp. 73–97. While the discussion here of interest groups draws heavily upon Almond, there are some differences in emphasis and interpretation.

simply to obtaining a somewhat larger share of the assets. Politics in such a society is more likely to be characterized by give-and-take relationships. Under such circumstances, coherent public policies are more easily formulated, and compromises with and between special-interest groups more readily facilitated. In general, the politics of the United States and England has been one of accommodation. This is not to imply that both countries have not had grave intergroup conflicts from time to time. They have: in England, the Irish question proved intractable and could be settled only by Home Rule, after a good deal of bloodshed; in the United States, the race problem has periodically taken on many of the same dimensions.

Quite naturally, almost all interest groups want access to those elites in the topmost decision-making positions, and gravitate to the centers of power. In the France of the Fourth Republic, interests concentrated their efforts upon Parliament and its specialized committees; in the Fifth, their efforts have been directed at the executive. In England, groups turn primarily to the cabinet and the bureaucracy.

Techniques for obtaining the support of strategic political elites differ. What modus operandi one interest group perceives as effective, another may not; the intensity of group feelings is also a prime factor in the determination of procedural methods. The technique used to win the decision-makers' favor may be merely the presentation of "objective" information; it may also be the threat of a loss of votes, or even violence. French peasants in 1960 and 1961, for instance, used violence with some success to prevent the government from reducing agricultural subsidies; some civil-rights groups in the United States, too, have used force. The tactic can be effective, provided it does not get out of hand and deeply antagonize those against whom it is directed. Violence as a technique can boomerang if those turning to it do not have the support of a large constituency.

Most groups attempt to identify their interests with the general welfare, or at least some abstract conception of justice. Thus, they employ the mass media in order to gain the support of a larger public, or to reduce the hostility of other groups. The success of their efforts has a good deal to do with the general norms of the society in which they operate. The acceptance by most Americans of the norm of equality, as well as a growing awareness of past and present injustices in the treatment of black citizens, was tremendously useful to civil-rights organizations during the 1960's.

The interrelationship of interest groups and political parties is keyed to the nature of group conflict in the society. In nations with a highly fragmented political system, parties will often be identified with one particular interest group; in societies that are not sharply fragmented but in which class lines are reasonably distinct and class interests and ideologies paramount, interest groups are apt to cluster about the political party that seems to represent their class. This is far more probable when the parties are rather tightly organized and have a reasonably integrated program; otherwise the major interest groups are likely to try to influence all political parties, playing off one against the other.

In a fragmented society in which governmental structures are weak, political decisions may be the outcome of direct negotiations with interest groups. This may also occur in nations whose political culture and political institutions inhibit the formation of systematic policy alternatives by either the political parties or governmental institutions.

Americans have a tendency to conceive of policy as emanating from "the people," and to distrust all organized interests because they prevent the free expression of the people's will. Yet the political culture and the structure of political institutions in the United States is such as to provide well-organized groups with excellent opportunities to veto public policy. Because political parties are holding companies for local and regional interests, congressmen frequently demonstrate greater loyalty to their districts than they do to the national party. And because they can be politically injured by the activities of a particular interest group far more easily than can M.P.'s in England, congressmen often place the demands of special interests above party loyalties. The lack of party discipline in Congress and the consequent ability of congressional committees and even committee chairmen to block or further legislation in the interests of relatively small organizations also contribute to the immensely powerful role of interest groups in the American congress.[4]

The liberal ideology which dominated American society for so long contributed to the same results, for government was not supposed to act creatively upon the social environment; its only function was to respond to limited demands for assistance by members of the community and to make sure that certain general rules of social conduct were obeyed. Creative change would come from the society itself. Political parties or candidates were not called upon to offer programs involving an appreciable amount of intervention in the economic life of the nation. Since the 1930's, these orientations have been changing slowly, but it is still the decentralization and the holding-company quality of American parties that command attention.

In England, on the other hand, with its disciplined parties and their capacity to form strong, responsible governments, interest groups have been forced to operate upon the government as a whole. Small, well-heeled groups, consequently, have been unable to establish strategic relations that could be used to block policy decisions. And while group demands are always considered by the party in power, they are more likely to be considered only within the framework of overall policy.

Interestingly enough, while in some ways

organized interest groups have had a greater influence on American politics than on English, the British, as well as the French and the Germans, have been far more willing to recognize the existence of special interest groups and to provide for consultation with them as one legitimate aspect of political decision-making. All three countries (but England and Germany more than France) have encouraged the amalgamation of groups in order to simplify the bargaining process.

The difference between the European and the American attitude toward interest groups is partly a matter of political culture. Europeans still think of the community as composed of estates, whereas Americans, under the influence of liberalism, believe more strongly that the legislature represents "the people," and that the relationship between "the people" and the government should not be impeded by the machinations of "interests." Whatever the national attitude toward special interests, however, since people desire to organize—and American society is characterized by a very active group life—interest groups have become, willy-nilly, an integral part of the political process.

5. THE GOVERNMENTAL PROCESS ON THE LOCAL AND REGIONAL LEVEL

To a considerable extent, the study of local and regional politics has been neglected in Europe. Certainly there have been few attempts to establish systematic relations between what studies we do have and analyses of national political processes. Yet even though European source material on European local politics is rather sketchy, certain features of the local government process can be adequately described.

The present division of political authority among national, local, and regional units within the European nation states is the result of a long and intricate process. In general, the trend has been toward the concentration of political authority at the national level, even when there has been a movement

4 Certain of these aspects of American political culture have already been discussed. See, for example, Chapter 1, pp. 29–31, 37.

toward the decentralization of administrative organization. There has also been a trend toward the creation of new regional and local units based less on traditional boundaries than upon the requirements of an ever-changing pattern of economic and social development—requirements that have grown even more complex since World War II, as interconnected metropolitan areas have emerged.[5]

Of the four countries we are studying, two are officially federal states and two are officially unitary. In both France and England, political power is theoretically concentrated on the national level; both the Soviet constitution and that of the German Federal Republic, however, provide for a separation of powers between the national government and the constituent units. Many factors determine why some states have federal structures and others a unitary form. The sense of England as a unified community, for instance, was such that the possibility of a federal structure was never raised, despite local nationalisms. Wales was forcibly brought into the United Kingdom, but even the official unification of Scotland with England and Wales did not produce a call for a specifically federal organization. Aside from the fact that constitution making was alien to the English experience (except for the Commonwealth period), the very sense of English nationhood permitted a high degree of local autonomy until well into the twentieth century. Local areas retained control over education, the police, and a wide variety of other functions. There seemed to exist, therefore, little need to provide officially for local autonomy. The great disparity in population between England and both Wales and Scotland also contributed to the formation of a centralized, unitary state. In France, the revolutionaries who transformed the country believed it was absolutely necessary to eliminate provincial and local rights if a French nation were to emerge. The whole thrust of subsequent na-

tion building in France, then, was toward a centralized state.

The German situation was quite different. The nation was soldered together through a sense of cultural identity and the persuasiveness of Prussian arms; but many of the petty kingdoms brought into the realm, especially Bavaria, had a long history of autonomy. A federal structure seemed to many as the most effective way of reducing potential conflict—especially to men like Bismarck, who believed that Prussia, because of its size, would dominate the federation in any event. The return to federalism under the Bonn regime, even though many of the Länder now lack any historical rationale, was partly a reaction to the centralizing tendencies of Hitler's National Socialism and partly a result of the influence of the Western Allies on the making of the constitution. In the Soviet Union, the creation of a federal structure stemmed directly from the multiplicity of nationalities within the Soviet Union and the desire of Soviet leadership to allay the suspicions of minority groups by offering de facto recognition of that diversity.

The four examples cited, as well as the American experience, indicate that the relation between a formal federal structure and local or state autonomy is not a simple one. In many ways the United Kingdom boasts more local autonomy than the Soviet Union, even though the former is officially a unitary state and the latter a federation. As for the German Empire, the principal policy decisions were made on the national level, despite the existence of a formal federal structure. Of course, insofar as a written federal constitution is taken seriously, federal regimes are more likely to allow for local autonomy than are unitary regimes. There is, however, no necessary relationship between federalism and freedom.

As we have noted previously, growing interdependence and the necessity for national planning have caused a general decline in the political privileges of regional and local units since the middle of the nineteenth

---

[5] A discussion of some of the problems involved in this development will be found in Chapter 24.

century. The trend has even affected the United States, a nation whose political system has traditionally been far more decentralized than that of any of the European countries treated in this volume. At the same time, certain counter-pressures are also being exerted in some European nations: in France, for example, the government is fashioning plans for some degree of regional autonomy, and in England the demands for Scottish and Welsh autonomy have prompted the beginnings of a re-examination of England's political structure. The problem of reconciling pressures for more direct participation in political decision-making—of which local nationalism is but one manifestation—with the requirements of planning in an increasingly interdependent environment is likely to be a major one for all European political systems during the remainder of the twentieth century.

6. EPILOGUE AND PROLOGUE

The analysis of governmental institutions in the next four chapters will demonstrate two propositions, among others: first, that the functioning of these institutions can best be understood if they are examined as part of a total system whose parts influence each other in numerous ways that have been and still are constantly changing; second, that while the institutions of each nation are unique, they fall within the framework of a common European historical experience.

The constitutional foundations of these institutions can only be understood in terms of the conceptions of legitimate authority accepted by members of the community. As we shall discover in the chapters that follow, the functioning of an organization rarely, if ever, corresponds exactly to the constitutional rules defining its operation. This is especially true of an all-inclusive organization like the modern state. Even where the formal institutions themselves once represented a balance among claims made by different groups or individuals, that balance is always chang-

ing. Furthermore, informal cliques and authority relationships develop which circumvent or modify the formal mechanisms. And, too, the organizational framework of any institution always permits some free play among the forces competing for power and for the development or implementation of decisions.

This is not to say that formal institutions are without importance. To the extent that certain ways of formulating and carrying out policy are accepted by most people in a society, formal structures do set limits on what can be done, and how. These limits vary depending upon the nature of the formal organization itself and the extent to which it is supported.

The conception of the political system as a formal compact characterized by a basic law arose, as we have seen, with the emergence of liberalism and the modern nation state. The fullest application of this idea is, perhaps, the United States, where a written constitution has taken on the quality of a sacred writ. The concept of a written constitution as the guideline for governmental action has, in fact, spread throughout most of the world. Its appeal seems to be that it represents a rational, public set of institutional structures by which all are bound; as a set of bylaws, a constitution also seems to appeal to man's sense of justice and fair play. In most modern states, the idea of "rational-legal" authority of a constitutional kind has been closely tied to popular sovereignty—to the idea that the political order should in some way reflect the desires of those individuals who compose it, each man counting as one, politically. Even in the Soviet Union and other Communist states, the existence of written constitutions theoretically based on popular sovereignty indicates the power this concept exercises over the modern mind.

The Soviet example, however, also indicates the extent to which principle can be divorced from the reality of power. To a lesser extent, this is true of all political systems; just how true, and what the relationship between formal constitutions and the actual structure of political decision-making in any society is, depend upon any number of elements, and no simple generalizations are possible. The nature of this relationship for each of the nation states with which we are concerned should become apparent as we examine the operation of their political systems.

In the nineteenth century and the first part of the twentieth, political scientists in Europe and the United States (except for Marxists) concentrated upon formal organizations, including constitutions, in their critical examination of societies. Today the emphasis has swung quite the other way, and the analysis of formal institutions has been rejected in favor of behavioral studies of the exercise of power. The point has now been reached where it is often argued that constitutions and constitutional "engineering" are relatively unimportant for understanding societies. The pendulum has perhaps swung too far, for, as will be shown, the function of these institutions is certainly not without importance.

One final caveat: the following chapters do not constitute the full and final analysis of the manner in which public policy is developed in England, France, Germany, and the Soviet Union. In all societies, government structures and the elites formally charged with making and enforcing rules are responding to demands from groups within the society; they are also operating within a culture that conceives of certain actions as illegitimate and others as reasonable. Furthermore, they are acting within the limits imposed by the resources at their command as well as by the nature of their particular environment. In some ways, the kinds of decisions that are *not* made reveal as much about a society as the kinds that are. In the United States, for example, a good many decisions on what is to be produced—decisions that can effect the lives of most members of the community—are left to the free play of market forces, subject to certain regulations; in the Soviet Union the determination of what is to be produced, how much is to be produced, and even the type and content of cultural activity, involves explicitly political decisions. Of course, the decision to allow certain matters to be determined by the market is also essentially political. A full discussion of the evolution of public policy in the United States, or any society, ultimately requires, therefore, an examination of the society as a whole, its social structure, its culture, and the power configurations that characterize it. In short, our analysis of the process of government will not be complete until the last chapter of the text. Indeed, a concern with explaining this process underlies the analysis of each topic we discuss.

15

Cabinet

Government

in England

1. INTRODUCTION

British political institutions exhibit that peculiar combination of the traditional and the modern and that peculiar continuity which characterize English life. Out of feudal structures have developed modern political forms. They retain many of their traditional customs, adding to British institutions a sense of mystery and agelessness unequaled by those of any other major European nation. Only in England can a direct line be traced from feudal patterns to the twentieth century. It is something of a paradox that the nation which has been the fount of modern representative government, and the model most copied by nations wishing to break with tradition, preserves so much of the old.

With the abrupt decline of the British Empire and the emergence of a series of seemingly intractable economic problems, British political institutions have come under attack in recent years by the intellectual establishment. What was once considered the source of greatness is increasingly seen as archaic, and more and more voices are urging a fairly radical modernization of Parliament and other governmental structures. Whatever merit the criticisms may have, there can be no denying the fact that all these institutions have been extremely creative forces, and they remain one of the great achievements of European culture.

The transfer of authority from the British monarchy to Parliament was accompanied by the development within Parliament of an increasingly powerful executive—in the form of a cabinet headed by a prime minister—that was responsible to it. The system thus created has provided the British with a stable and effective government, certainly in comparison with those of other European powers, while it has also allowed England to preserve much of the time-consuming pageantry associated with other epochs.

In Weimar Germany and in the France of the Third and Fourth Republics, governments were usually shaky coalitions which unraveled fairly quickly. In England, a cabinet could usually retain power until the next regular election, unless it decided to call for a special election. In both Germany and France, attempts by the executive to devise and effect comprehensive programs of public policy were frustrated at every turn by parliamentary factionalism or powerful committees —legislative roadblocks not uncommon in the United States. The British government's legislative program, however, generally advanced majestically through Parliament and was enacted into law without much modification. Indeed, the British have yet to create anything comparable to the legislative committees that have characterized the American and Continental legislatures.

During de Gaulle's presidency, the French executive dominated the legislature and managed to get its programs safely translated into law. The price of achievement, of course, was the emasculation of Parliament, and precisely what the relationship between executive and legislature will be with de Gaulle's retirement is an open question. For a dozen years, the postwar Bonn government also had a stable, fairly powerful executive. And, as was true of France, the linchpin of the system was a rather authoritarian, charismatic leader. The retirement of Adenauer in 1963 led to a crisis in the political system that was papered over but not solved by the coalition government of 1966–1969.

The major governmental difference between England and France, or England and Germany, or England and the United States is that the British executive (whether one emphasizes the prime minister or the cabinet) quite early established its dominance over the legislature. In comparing the English system with the French or the German, many commentators have emphasized the prime minister's power to dissolve the parliament. Others have stressed the fact that the English parliament was never, by tradition, expected to govern the country; rather, except for a short period in the nineteenth century, its role was always that of a critic of the executive.[1] Comparisons with the United States, on the other hand, point up the fact that the president and the congress are elected by different constituencies, and that the effect of presidential as against parliamentary government is to reduce the executive's effectiveness as chief legislator.

While these analyses are of some value, none of them is completely adequate. If one wished to emphasize a single factor, one would have to say that the essential characteristics of British cabinet government are traceable to the emergence of a disciplined two-party system within the framework of a parliamentary regime in which the executive is responsible to the legislature. It is only because any government taking office has been assured of the support of a cohesive majority that the English executive has been able to assert its dominance over the parliament. In France and Germany, at least until the Fifth Republic and the Bonn government, fragmented, multi-party systems have inhibited effective government; and in the United States, the local and catchall qualities of the dominant political parties have stymied the formulation of integrated legislative programs, even if the presence of a popularly elected executive has assured governmental stability. Explanations of the British system that highlight the continuity of tradition are not satisfactory, for what must be taken into account are the reasons why tradition has continued to be viable in England whereas it was broken in France and Germany. In the latter two countries, parliaments were initially critics of the executive, too; furthermore, the power of dissolution was also invested in the French and German monarchy, but it failed to serve as an effective control mechanism for a parliamentary executive. There is, in fact, little evidence that the power of the British prime minister rests on his power to dissolve the parliament.

Even this analysis, however, is not fully adequate, for any discussion of the differences among the parliamentary systems of European nations must interrelate a number of factors and involve both historical and sys-

---

[1] See, for example, Ronald Butt, *The Power of Parliament* (London: Constable and Co., 1967).

tematic analyses. This chapter will describe and explain the qualities that differentiate the process of government in England from that of other countries. The primary comparison here will be with the United States. Therefore our analysis will not be complete until we have compared the English pattern with that of the French and the German in Chapters 16 and 17; certain other differences will not be clarified until the organization of the national bureaucracy in all three countries is examined in Chapter 22.

2. THE DEVELOPMENT OF CABINET GOVERNMENT

FEUDAL ORIGINS: Anglo-Saxon England was not yet fully feudal at the time of the Norman invasion, and, indeed, the monarchy was weaker in many respects than in more highly developed political communities. Until the Norman conquest, tribal and local loyalties were so strong that hardly more than a vague fealty to the king had yet to manifest itself. The Anglo-Saxon monarch acted in concert with a witenagemot—a council consisting of the chief nobility and clergy of the realm; theoretically this body could depose him should he violate custom.

After the Norman invasion, the monarch's authority spread very quickly. The Conqueror, having divided the land among his followers, made them all swear personal oaths of allegiance to him, thereby bringing into existence a single feudal community. Subsequently, monarchs periodically summoned "royal courts" at which they sought advice on matters of common interest. They also kept a number of barons in closer attendance for the ordinary business of government, although many of these advisers later came to be professionals of nonbaronial rank.

This court of advisers became the *Curia Regis* or King's Court, which was, in effect, both a legislative and a judicial body. Out of that emerged the *Magnum Concilium* or Great Council—and ultimately, the parliament. The king also had in attendance a

smaller group of officials known as the Privy (private) Council, which eventually gave rise to the cabinet, a still smaller body, so called because of the palace room in which it met during the reign of Charles II. Such is the pervasiveness of tradition that the Privy Council still exists, and it is as a committee of the Privy Council that the cabinet derives its legal authority. The council now has none but ceremonial functions to perform; the real source of the cabinet's power lies in the House of Commons and the party system.

Initially, the Great Council was composed entirely of the upper nobility and higher clergy; it insisted upon the right to be convened before granting the king money to meet his needs. In the thirteenth century, these councils came to be called parliaments, the term being derived from *parlement,* "conversation." In the thirteenth century, too, knights and burgesses of the shires and boroughs, as well as the lower clergy, began to be invited to the parliament, one reason being that the monarchy needed additional sources of revenue.

The king's writs summoning the knights and burgesses required that local communities (communes or commons) also send a specified number of representatives. The role of the communes in the parliament was at first minimal, and many displayed a marked reluctance to be represented, recognizing that their attendance might well mean additional taxes. The lower clergy withdrew from the Great Council in the fourteenth century, and the knights and burgesses began to deliberate separately—in the "Commons House," later the House of Commons. The House of Lords did not receive its official title until the reign of Henry VIII.

Parliament was originally regarded as a body that only "discovered" the true law, through a process of adjudication. Yet in fact, legislation was continuously being enacted. The first step in the passage of laws took the form of a petition addressed to the king from the barons, or to the barons and the king from the Commons. The primary weapon used by the Commons to have its petitions heeded was a refusal to grant the king supply (money) until its grievances were heard; not surprisingly, it became customary for the consideration of grievances to precede the granting of supply. Since most of the king's funds came from the constituencies represented by the Commons, it also became customary to consider such grants—that is, financial legislation—in the lower house before they were reviewed by the barons.

Through the fourteenth and fifteenth centuries, the Commons remained much the junior partner in the parliament. Indeed, the power of both houses of Parliament actually declined under the Tudors, although by the middle of the fourteenth century it had become established that sovereignty rested with the king in Parliament, rather than with the king alone. The king could still decide when to grant titles of nobility and when to rescind them; which boroughs and counties to enfranchise; and when to convene and dismiss Parliament. Nor was he required to accept the petitions of either house. The Tudors made use of all of these devices, plus a careful husbanding of their funds and their general popularity, to avoid relying upon Parliament. The decline in the aristocracy's power was one further factor which allowed the Tudors to be much freer of control than their predecessors.

Nevertheless, forces were at work during the Tudor period preparing the way for a shift in power from the House of Lords to the House of Commons—and a general increase in the power of Parliament. One of these forces was the new commercial class that began to demand a say in the nation's affairs. The implication of these changes became apparent during the reign of the Stuarts, when the English removed two kings, beheaded one of them, and established a short-lived republic. The conflict between the Stuarts and the parliament was partly economic, partly religious, and partly constitutional. But the constitutional aspect of that conflict—whether sovereignty would reside in the king in Parliament with the emphasis on the king or the emphasis on the parliament—was what would determine for all time the balance of power in England's government. And in the struggle the Commons, using control over finance, was instrumental in precipitating the English Civil War.

THE CLASSIC AGE OF THE CONSTITUTION: The republic failed and the monarchy was restored, but not before a new balance had been established. The Bill of Rights of 1689 laid down the requirement that Parliament *must* consent to all laws involving taxation and *must* meet regularly. The Act of Settlement of 1701, by limiting the monarchy to Protestants, clearly established parliamentary supremacy.

The new power balance ushered in what has been traditionally called the classic age of the constitution. The king was never more to exercise his ancient prerogative of rejecting legislation passed by both houses of Parliament—they were now supreme in the legislative field—but he did, nevertheless, retain a broad, though not completely defined, executive authority, including the power to dissolve Parliament. Further, an independent judiciary had been created to apply the common law,[2] and the Commons and the Lords became equals, at least theoretically, with the Commons given special rights in the area of finance.

The new arrangement constituted, or seemed to constitute, a separation or balance of powers, with the executive, judiciary, and legislature each supreme in its own sphere, and with a further balance between Commons and Lords, each representing different estates within the community. This was the model constitution which was so admired by foreign observers such as Montesquieu and was used to explain English stability. It was the image of the British constitution that Americans accepted when they drew up their own, also involving a separation of powers

2 The development of the British legal system is discussed in Chapter 21, pp. 615–617.

among three branches of government and between two legislative houses. It was, finally, the pattern copied by most other European nations when the traditional political elites tried to find a stable balance between the claims of hierarchy and the demands of democracy.

In none of the European nations, including England, did the new balance last very long. The forces of democratic reform, modernization, and rationalization proved too strong. Monarchy was not in accord with the democratic principle; its authority had no rational base, and therefore it had to be either weakened or destroyed. A hereditary House of Lords, too, could not be justified; it, too, had to go or be deprived of its power. On the Continent, where the old and the new were at such extreme odds, the course most often chosen was destruction. Monarchs and lords disappeared as authority became increasingly centered in popularly elected legislative bodies. The British, of course, chose to weaken traditional institutions, retaining the fiction in many cases that their legal authority continued unchanged.

In reality the power of the king and the Privy Council slowly devolved to the cabinet, which became responsible to the parliament and, more specifically, to the House of Commons. In this manner, the cabinet provided that fusion of legislative and executive power that has come to characterize British political life. The development did not become clear until the middle of the nineteenth century, specifically after the Reform Bill of 1832. As is the case with so many things British, the changes came by degrees, almost imperceptibly, and the outward forms remained the same.

By the time of the Tudors, the Privy Council had effectively become the executive arm of the government and included most of the important crown ministers. But its size caused the Tudors to rely on a smaller group of ministers to handle particular kinds of business. The Commonwealth wiped out the old administrative system, but it reappeared

under Charles II, who relied heavily upon the council and even more heavily upon a small cabal (cabinet) of his closest advisers. These invariably included men who were members of Parliament and who could be used in efforts to manage parliamentary affairs.

The parliament resented the cabal, which it regarded as illegal, and the Act of Settlement of 1701 not only attempted to suppress it but prohibited individuals serving the king, as well as members of the House of Lords, from appearing in Parliament. The Commons soon learned, however, that this attempt to maintain a strict separation of powers reduced its ability to control or influence the nation's affairs. After a short time, the cabinet became an accepted part of the political structure, and its ministers were permitted to attend sessions of Parliament or be members of it.

During the eighteenth century the cabinet continued to serve at the pleasure of the king, although there gradually evolved the practice of retaining in office cabinets that were supported by a parliamentary majority. Thus Queen Anne, after the 1710 election had brought a Tory majority to the Commons, replaced a Whig ministry by a Tory ministry.[3] Again, the practice of having the cabinet reflect politically the results of an election was not adopted suddenly, and the development of the idea that the cabinet was completely dependent upon the Commons did not really become settled until the middle of the nineteenth century. As late as 1807, George III removed the so-called Ministry of All Talents, with only a feeble protest on the part of Parliament, and as late as 1834 William IV, on his own initiative, dismissed Melbourne and called in Peel to form a new cabinet. Peel's repeated defeats in Parliament, however, forced the king to relent, and

---

3 The term "ministry" came into use in the eighteenth and early nineteenth centuries. It referred to the prime minister and cabinet ministers who did not, at that time, constitute a government even though they were more than mere advisers to the monarch.

there was no question after that about the cabinet's dependency upon the will of Parliament—although even today the monarch is "constitutionally" responsible for appointing the prime minister and the members of the Privy Council, from which the cabinet is drawn.

THE GOLDEN AGE OF THE M.P.: The year 1832 marked a turning point in the development of parliamentary power. All during the preceding century, it had been possible for the king, or the king in league with a number of Lords, to assure a majority in the Commons through the purchase or sale of seats. Many seats simply went to the highest bidder. The suffrage was limited, and the regime controlled patronage and the influence that went with it. The management of elections, consequently, was usually not a troublesome matter, and although in many electoral districts campaigns were hard fought, in others the relation between representative and represented was, to say the least, tenuous. As one M.P. responded in 1714, when pressed by his constituents to change his vote on a proposed excise tax:

Gentlemen: I have received your letter about the excise, and I am surprised at your insolence at writing to me at all.

You know, and I know, that I bought this constituency. You know, and I know, that I am now determined to sell it, and you know what you think I don't know, that you are now looking out for another buyer, and I know, what you certainly don't know, that I have now found another constituency to buy.

About what you said about the excise: may God's curse light upon you all, and may it make your homes as open and free to the excise officers as your wives and daughters have always been to me while I have represented your rascally constituency.[4]

4 Quoted in P. G. Richards, *Honorable Members* (London: Faber, 1959), p. 157.

This attitude changed with the reform bill. The enlargement of representation meant that the exercise of such arrogance would no longer be feasible. The gradual adoption of the democratic idea as well as the new importance of a commercial middle class lessened the need to curry the king's favor.

After 1832 it was apparent not only that ministries were responsible to Parliament, but that the authority of the king had been considerably reduced. It was also clear that from this time forward the Commons was the more important house in Parliament. As long ago as 1712, when the Lords threatened to block the signing of the Treaty of Utrecht, the queen had created enough new peers to insure passage; it was William's threat to pack the House of Lords, after its initial rejection of the Reform Act of 1832, that finally secured the bill's acceptance. The Lords had long since given up the right to reject money bills; now they could no longer reject any others ardently desired by the Commons. It was also apparent that ministries—that is, cabinets—were henceforth responsible to the House of Commons. In the nineteenth century, more and more important ministers came to be chosen from that house, so that as cabinet ministers they could also participate in its legislative management. This was especially true of the king's first minister, the prime minister—a title that had originally been applied to Walpole and then to others who had the special favor of the king and who were asked to form governments.

The period between 1832 and 1867 has been called by some the "golden age" of Parliament and of the individual M.P. In fact, the years were a stage of transition, in which contradictory forces were at work; Parliament did indeed come into its own as the legitimate source of political decisions, but the cabinet was simultaneously beginning to gather unto itself certain prerogatives that would eventually strip Parliament of some of its authority. During the transition period, the cabinet was responsible to Parliament, and, increasingly, it was responsible as a team. But because of the multiplicity of loosely organized factions within the Commons, the fall of a cabinet did not necessarily result in a new election; rather, as often as not cabinet defeats were followed by intra-parliamentary negotiation, in the fashion of the French Fourth Republic or Weimar Germany. Nor did a defeat by the cabinet mean its automatic resignation. Melbourne and Peel, defeated a number of times on particular issues, continued to serve after accepting the determination of the House of Commons.

CABINET GOVERNMENT: The nature of the legislative process, however, was changing. Between the late seventeenth century and the early nineteenth, most legislation was introduced by ordinary members of Parliament in the form of private bills of a facilitative kind—pertaining, for instance, to rights of way for canal or railroad construction, or to the granting of monies to local communities for building docks and harbors or improving water supplies and other local services. Legislative timetables were usually set by the Commons, and bills were considered first by specially created committees. Almost imperceptibly, however, the cabinet came to play a larger role in legislation until, by 1884, British parliamentary government had effectively become cabinet government. The years after 1832 were a "golden age" for Parliament only in the sense that the Commons, freed from the domination of the monarchy and the House of Lords, seemed momentarily to be sovereign.

An important factor contributing to the depreciation of the M.P.'s position was the growth of government activity. As the obligations of the state in the economic life of the nation began to increase, legislative proposals introduced by the government took an ever larger share of the Commons' time. By the middle of the nineteenth century, too, English politics had become more or less national; national rather than local issues usurped the political scene, partly because of the very homogeneity of English society, but also because of the direct and continuing impact of foreign policy upon domestic affairs. Further, democracy itself was growing. With the advent of mass campaigns, the prime minister began to symbolize the government, even though he was elected by his fellow M.P.'s; as a result, his prestige and authority increased enormously as the collective influence of the M.P.'s receded.

Probably the most important factor contributing to the rising strength of the cabinet was the establishment of a disciplined two-party system, which meant that the cabinet was to be chosen from the majority party and that the cabinet's defeat really meant the defeat of the party—or at least sufficient disenchantment to inhibit effective governance. Whatever their differences, the parties were agreed that it was vital for England to have a government that could govern; the defeat of the cabinet in power, then, could signify nothing but the dissolution of the government and a new election. Only in this way could the government be assured of a stable and effective majority.

The dissolution of Parliament in the twentieth century has rarely been the result of a party split. Those chosen by their party colleagues to form a government represent a common ideological outlook; they are also the leading members of the party, men who have worked together for a long time. Because an increasing number of M.P.'s have become part of the government, the relationship between the government and the back bench has been a close one compared with either the American or French systems—certainly close enough that the average rank-and-file member would accept a cabinet decision that he did not particularly like in preference to seeing the government and his party go down to defeat. After all, no matter what the back-bencher's party did, within very broad limits, he would believe that the opposition could only be worse; besides, a new election fought by a divided party would undoubtedly spell defeat and the likely loss of his seat. On the other hand, any prime minister who contemplated a potentially disruptive measure would have to recognize that he might very well destroy his party or his own political career. Indeed, no prime minister in the twentieth century has even attempted to use the threat of dissolution as a means of insuring party discipline, so that the main advantage derived from his authority to dissolve Parliament lies in the government's ability to call for new elections at the time it considers most propitious to do so.

The possibilities of a serious back-bench rebellion against the cabinet were further reduced by the control that party leaders came to exercise over the party machinery. Rebellion could mean expulsion from the party, and with the growing preference by voters for party labels, an independent was less and less likely to be returned to Parliament by his constituents. Also, as the power of the government as a whole increased, so too did that of the prime minister. Slowly, ineluctably, he increased his authority within the party and over the other members of the cabinet. All the king's old authority to choose ministers came to rest in the hands of the prime minister, who by the very nature of his position became identified with the party, even as the party became identified with him.

All these circumstances—circumstances contributing to the greater power *of* government and the greater concentration of power *in* government—undermined the influence of the back-bench M.P. Most of the bills introduced were government bills, and most of the time of the parliament was spent discussing government measures; little need was felt for specialized committees, which might serve as threats to party leadership. Committees, then, all but disappeared, and the M.P. came to rely more and more upon the government itself for technical information. Opportunity to obtain other perspectives became restricted. By the end of the nineteenth century, what was once parliamentary government had been transformed into party government and cabinet government. The

system reached its fullest development in the decades after World War I. Some would say that since 1945 British government has become a quasi-presidential regime, dominated by the prime minister and a rather anonymous government bureaucracy. There is, as we have seen, some evidence to support this contention. Yet to call British government "quasi-presidential" rather than "cabinet" is to exaggerate the prime minister's role and to blur certain important distinctions that should become clear later in this chapter.

After 1832 the power of the monarchy faded very quickly. With the unsuccessful attempt of William IV to prevent Melbourne from becoming prime minister, it became obvious that the cabinet must always have the support of the Commons. As late as the first years of the twentieth century, the monarch might have had some say as to who was to become prime minister; today, this authority is practically nonexistent. Victoria did not want Gladstone, whom she vehemently disliked, but she had to accept him. George VI, after the resignation of Neville Chamberlain, preferred Lord Halifax to Winston Churchill in 1940, but the politicians made their own choice and he could do little but accept the results. Elizabeth II has never even considered disputing the decision of party leaders, or of a formal party vote.

It is at least possible that Victoria, because of her personal popularity and because the mystique of monarchy was still strong, influenced the government of the day on some public issues. It is difficult, however, to find an instance in which the monarch can be said to have exercised any real authority in the twentieth century, although his advice may have been accepted on occasion. A cabinet decision was a cabinet decision, and that was that. For example, King George did stress his unwillingness to receive any ambassador from the Soviet regime which, after all, was responsible for the death of his cousins. But as Arthur Henderson, then Foreign Minister, reported,

I didn't argue or interrupt. I just let him run on, And then I said: "Well your Majesty, that's the Cabinet decision . . . but perhaps the Prince of Wales could receive him for you?"[5]

This was the solution adopted.

In the meantime, the power of the House of Lords also diminished. Theoretically, the Lords still had a veto over all but financial legislation, and thus it was practically co-equal with the House of Commons. In actuality, the fact that the prime minister was being chosen more and more often from the House of Commons, and that his authority depended upon the House of Commons, was concrete evidence of what little significant power the Lords had. As Gilbert and Sullivan put it in *Iolanthe,* referring to the Crimean War:

The House of Lords throughout the War
Did nothing in particular
And did it very well.

After 1860, they were careful not to block any legislation that had a clear majority in the Commons. However, when the reform-oriented Liberal government that came to power in 1906 under the leadership of Campbell-Bannerman, and then Asquith and Lloyd George, embarked upon a broad program of social reform, the Lords bridled. Their feeling was that some of the legislation threatened the foundations of the realm, and they vetoed some 18 bills. That, as things turned out, was their last demonstration of any real power. The fight between the liberals and the Lords, which was fundamentally a fight over how much power the Lords should have, came to a climax with the introduction of the Finance Bill of 1909, legislation involving heavy land taxes which many in the Lords regarded as confiscatory. The introduction of the bill was accompanied by a cutting attack on the Lords by Lloyd George. The Lords rejected the bill, the government

resigned over the issue, and, although the Liberals actually received some two hundred thousand votes less than the Conservatives in the ensuing election and only two seats more in the Commons, the bill was introduced again and passed. This time the Lords accepted it, but it was too late. The issue had been drawn, and a measure to limit further the power of the Lords was introduced into the Commons, the government once more calling for a dissolution to test voter sentiment. In the election, the Conservatives again received a plurality of the votes; but the Liberals, forming a government with the support of the Labor Party and the Irish Nationalists, pushed through the parliamentary reform. The Lords, under threat by the king to produce a majority by creating new peers, acquiesced in their own burial. The Parliament Act of 1911 provided that the House of Lords would henceforth have only the power to delay legislation—for no more than thirty days on financial legislation and no more than three years on other matters.

In 1947 the Lords' power to delay legislation was cut to one year by a Labor government, which, during the 1930's, had threatened to abolish the House of Lords altogether. Today, despite Conservative attempts in the 1950's to restore some of its authority, the real power of the Lords is almost entirely gone. Indeed, in 1968 a new landmark was passed when the Labor government introduced legislation depriving hereditary peers of the right to vote in the House of Lords. The bill called for the house to consist essentially of life peers chosen by the government in office. The proposal had to be withdrawn in 1969 because of the growing weakness of the Wilson government, but the fact that it was introduced is a clear indication that the days of the House of Lords in its present form are numbered.

2. THE IMPORTANCE OF BEING ANCIENT

The ceremony convening a new parliament begins when an official, known as the

---

[5] Quoted in Hugh Dalton, *Call Back Yesterday* (London: Frederick Muller, 1953), p. 233.

Gentleman Usher of the Black Rod, knocks on the door of the Commons, and, being admitted, requests that the members attend the Lord Chancellor in the peers' chamber. There, after hearing the royal summons read, members of the Commons are invited by the Lord Chancellor to return to their chamber and choose a speaker.

The gentleman chosen shows some reluctance, and is escorted to his chair by two members. On the following day the speaker, wearing a bob wig and accompanied by many members of the house, announces his election at the bar of the Lords' chamber. The Lord Chancellor signifies royal approval of the choice. The speaker then demands recognition of "the ancient and undoubted rights and privileges of the Commons," an assurance the Lord Chancellor extends.

Upon returning to the Commons, the speaker retires to don a full-bottomed wig and his robes of office. He reports to the House that his election has received royal approval and that he has laid claim to the rights and privileges of the Commons. The members of the Commons then take an oath of allegiance to the monarch and sign the roll. The following day Black Rod leads the members to the upper house again to hear the speech of the monarch,[6] who usually opens the parliament in person, riding from Buckingham Palace in a state coach, surrounded by family, a bevy of officials, and an escort of household cavalry. From the throne, the queen—or, in her absence, the Lord Chancellor—reads a speech outlining the program of the government. After the speech, members of the Commons return to their chamber, where they give first reading to a Bill for the Better Suppressing of Clandestine Outlawries, a procedure which is then followed by a general debate on the Speech

from the Throne, but only after thanks have been expressed for her majesty's remarks.

Everyone knows, of course, that the monarch had little or nothing to do with writing the Speech from the Throne. Even so, the Labor Party expressed some anxiety, when it was first decided to televise the opening of Parliament, that people might mistakenly conclude that the Conservative Party program was Queen Elizabeth's program. The Bill for the Better Suppressing of Clandestine Outlawries has no real legislative import whatsoever; it dates back to 1743, when it was initiated as a means of asserting once again the right of Parliament to discuss grievances—that is, legislation—before considering the king's recommendations. Too, the fact that the monarch, rather than the government in power, presents the policy of the government, finds its source in the original raison d'etre of Parliament—a body called together by the king to consider his proposals.

And so it is with the whole pattern of British parliamentary government. While a system of specific rules—standing orders—has been developed, much of Commons' procedure is still governed by hallowed tradition, a tradition that is constantly, almost imperceptibly, changing, and yet remains the same. It is as if the British had refused to throw away any historical accretion, no matter how archaic, preferring to remake it, if at all possible, to meet modern needs. When evening falls and light in the Parliament is needed, the request is still: "Mr. Speaker, I call for candles."

The "protestations" of the speaker over his election date back to the days when he was in a politically exposed position because of the antagonism between king and Parliament. The Lord Chancellor, who presides over the House of Lords and serves as the head of the British judiciary, was once the most powerful figure in the kingdom, second only to the monarch; the office has been held by such men as Sir Thomas More and Cardinal Wolsey. Today the Lord Chancellor fulfills a number of

---

6 Traditionally, Black Rod also appeared to announce royal assent to any bill passed by Parliament. In response to the feeling of many members that the practice was "ludicrous" and time-consuming, this aspect of his functions was abolished in 1967.

functions in addition to his formal ones, but the position is no longer one of any real power. The Gentleman Usher of the Black Rod came into existence in the reign of Henry VIII, and ever since he has been sent by the sovereign, in the opening ceremonies of a new parliament, to knock on the Commons' doors—which are closed so that the Commons may continue to demonstrate that it can bar all comers if it so wishes.

Many of the traditions take an inordinate amount of time. The custom that in voting on important questions members must rise and move out of the chamber into an "aye" or "no" lobby, rather than use any of a variety of mechanical devices, is not precisely in the mold of a computerized age.[7] The House can maintain such procedures only because certain other features of British political life enable it to act with dispatch when necessary. Nevertheless, attacks on what an ever-growing band of reformers now regards as merely mumbo-jumbo have increased radically in the past few years, and a number of traditional procedures have been eliminated.

The historical tradition of which the Commons is so deeply a part pervades Westminster Palace itself. For five centuries the chief residence of the kings of England, from Edward the Confessor to Henry VIII, the palace has continued to serve as a meeting place for both Houses of Parliament even after this original justification for their location at Westminster had vanished.

The great fire of 1834 destroyed most of the palace buildings, and the Commons itself was severely damaged during World War II. When it was rebuilt, the original structure of the Commons chamber—an oblong room, small for its purpose, in which members sat facing each other in two phalanxes of rising benches—was retained despite many inconveniences. At the time, Sir Winston Churchill justified the retention on the ground that

the shape furthered a two-party system and that both the size and the shape encouraged easy exchange rather than harangue. While there is something to be said for his argument, one suspects that the real motivation lay in tradition for the sake of tradition.

In any event, today the House can seat fewer than two-thirds of its members, even providing them with neither desks nor chairs. It measures 68 by 45 feet—less than one-fourth the size of the U.S. House of Representatives, which contains more than a hundred fewer members. M.P.'s face each other on two sets of long benches, graded upward, one on each side of the speaker. This arrangement stands in marked contrast to the semicircular shape of most legislative chambers; members speak from their benches to each other, and the auditorium atmosphere that occurs in many chambers when the speaker talks from a rostrum is absent. To the right of the speaker sit the government and their supporters, ministers on the front bench and rank-and-file members grouped behind them. On the left side sit the opposition, again with the leaders of the party on the front benches and the same grouping to the rear. When important debates are held, the chamber is extremely crowded since six hundred–odd persons must then squeeze into a space designed to hold 346, and it may be true that a quality of added excitement accrues, just as it is possible that the chamber's small size and shape lend themselves to a more discursive exchange than might otherwise be the case.

The palace itself contains more than a thousand rooms—committee rooms, public rooms, office rooms used primarily by ministers and parliamentary staffs, lounges, libraries, dining rooms. Control over the allocation of this space is rather diffuse, Parliament having only part of it. A select committee investigating the use of the buildings in 1953 was, in fact, unable to identify all users of the space, although it did discover a special room for painting used by the Lords, a shooting gallery, and a mortuary.

---

[7] A special procedure committee appointed in 1966 concluded that electromechanical voting devices would not save time unless each member was provided with his own desk.

FIGURE 15.1. FLOOR PLAN OF THE HOUSE OF COMMONS

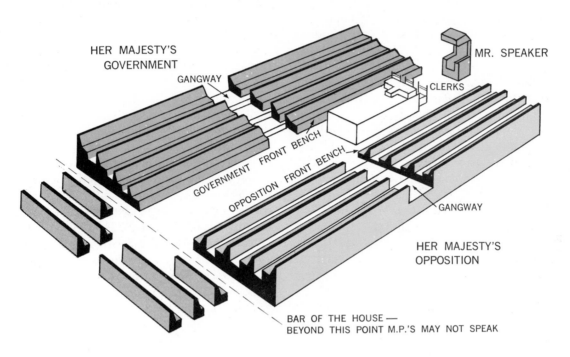

HER MAJESTY'S GOVERNMENT

GANGWAY

MR. SPEAKER

CLERKS

GOVERNMENT FRONT BENCH

OPPOSITION FRONT BENCH

GANGWAY

HER MAJESTY'S OPPOSITION

BAR OF THE HOUSE — BEYOND THIS POINT M.P.'S MAY NOT SPEAK

Compared with the services and accommodations available to an American congressman, those for an ordinary M.P. are spartan: M.P.'s do not have private offices or secretaries, or, in many cases, desks or phones. It is still difficult for them to get adequate typing or clerical assistance; many do hire secretary-typists, but they do so on their own salaries or by using funds supplied by outside groups such as trade unions. There is nothing comparable to the Legislative Reference Service of the Library of Congress, and the House of Commons library itself is quite inadequate. Members of the Commons are forced to talk to their constituents in the halls of the House, and a good many must handle their own correspondence. An American congressman is said to have collapsed with shock some years back on being shown the writing rooms and

the Library of Commons full of men writing letters in longhand. Even the new government office building, closely adjoining Westminster, is not expected to meet satisfactorily all the needs of the English M.P.

3. ALL SORTS AND CONDITIONS OF MEN

For most of the nineteenth century, parliamentary representatives were almost entirely men of property who had gone to the same schools and mixed with the same groups before entering Westminster. In a very important sense, Parliament was a club in which the members, in terms of immediate status and background, had more in common with each other than with the vast majority of their constituents. This situation, of course, has changed in recent years. More and more of the newer professions, such as teaching and journalism, are represented, as are the lesser public schools, the state schools, and the redbrick colleges and universities. The old school tie, however, remains important, especially in the Conservative Party, both in receiving the nomination and in being elected.

For example, only two workers out of the eight running on the Conservative ticket in 1966 were elected, while 55 of the 101 barristers were successful. Again, those with a more extensive or more exclusive educational background had a better chance of winning than those who had less education, or those who had gone to state schools or to universities other than Oxford or Cambridge. In 1966, 54 per cent of those Conservative candidates who had graduated from Oxbridge won their seats, compared with only 35 per cent who had graduated from other universities. The class and educational background of Conservative M.P.'s indicates either that Conservative voters are still somewhat deferential or that candidates representing more traditional attitudes usually get nominated from safer constituencies.

The background of the Labor Party representatives is slightly different. Members of more traditional middle-class groups, such as barristers and university teachers, had a better than three-to-one chance of being elected in 1966, but less than half the candidates who were secondary-school teachers were elected. Further, public-school graduates were more successful than non–public-school men. On the other hand, manual workers, who constituted only 21 per cent of the Labor Party's candidates, formed 30 per cent of the parliamentary party, a circumstance that is not surprising considering the fact that trade-union sponsored M.P.'s generally run for the safer seats.

Most Labor Party M.P.'s, then, like most Conservatives, are persons of middle-class background, although only nine per cent of the Labor M.P.'s, as compared with thirty per cent of the Conservatives, have a business

background. Of the professional people, the Labor Party boasted a smaller number of barristers and a larger number of teachers, especially secondary-school teachers. Only 66 Labor M.P.'s had gone to public schools and only 83 had gone to Oxford or Cambridge, 103 having gone to other universities. Eighty Labor M.P.'s, but only two Conservative M.P.'s, had received no more than an elementary-school education. On the whole, the "left" within the Labor Party has tended to come from the journalist and secondary-schoolteacher group, while university teachers and other professionals, as well as those of a business and working-class background, have represented the more conservative element in the Labor Party.

Nevertheless, as Table 15.1 indicates, the 1966 election figures are the latest reflection of important changes that have been taking place in the social composition of the Parliamentary Labor Party. The proportion of middle-class professionals elected to Parliament has been steadily increasing, while the proportion from working-class background has been on the decline. Among those of middle-class background, Oxford and Cambridge degrees are becoming increasingly desirable, especially for those seeking appointment to cabinet posts. As for working-class Laborites entering Parliament, they are now better educated and aspire to a parliamentary career at an earlier age than the previous generation. In the past, working-class M.P.'s were often older men who had been "retired" to political office; today, the trade-union contingent includes much larger numbers of younger men who intend to pursue a political career. These changes, as we shall see, have significantly affected the operations of the P.L.P.

The British parliament is in some ways more nearly representative of the nation than is the legislature in the theoretically more democratic and less class-ridden American system. By far the largest portion of American congressmen are middle-class lawyers, and such groups as manual workers, businessmen, and teachers are present in very small numbers, if at all. The absence of manual laborers, of course, is explained by the lack of a self-conscious working class in the United States, and thus of a mass Socialist Party. The small number of businessmen and teachers in Congress is related to the fact that, since the middle of the nineteenth century, politics has not been regarded by them as a particularly estimable career. For most American businessmen, unlike their English colleagues, business was its own justification and source enough of prestige. Those few American entrepreneurs who desired to cap a successful career with the laurels of community service turned to philanthropy. Politics, after all, represented a realm of rather squalid activity that contributed little to "production" and served primarily as an arena in which special interests fought for an ever larger share of the social spoils.

Many eschewed a public career in the United States because of the emphasis on local politics and the importance of the local political machine—factors which tended to reserve a political career for persons of middle- or lower-middle-class background who sought to raise themselves still further in social status and were not averse to the long pull of rather corrupt local political activity. In large urban areas, politics appealed especially to recent immigrants or their children who bid for political power as a means of obtaining economic gains for themselves and their particular ethnic group. In more recent years, however, the American attitude toward politics has been changing. The prestige of business activity has declined, while that of government service has risen appreciably.

THE PARLIAMENTARY PROFESSION: One of the persistent myths about the British parliament is that its members are not professional politicans, but amateurs who are engaging in politics out of a sense of civic duty. Thus, members theoretically should not spend all of their time in Parliament, but are encouraged to cultivate outside interests, including those that pay money.

It is for this reason that after the middle ages the practice of communities paying members small salaries disappeared; agitation for official salaries, primarily as a means of encouraging working-class representation in Parliament, did not develop again until the nineteenth century. Regular salaries were not paid until 1910, when members were given £400 a year; as late as 1964, they received a salary of only £1,750 ($4,900) annually, although the leader of the opposition was allowed an additional £1,250 per year. In that year, however, salaries of the rank-and-file M.P.'s were raised to £3,250 ($9,100) a year, and those of cabinet-rank ministers from £5,000 ($14,000) to £8,500 ($23,800). Parliamentary salaries are still far from adequate: compare, for example, members of the U.S. House of Representatives, who receive $30,000 a year and an additional $10,000 for expenses. Consequently many people in England who might be drawn into politics are not, and a number of M.P.'s have declined to stand for re-election or refused ministerial posts for the simple reason that they could not afford them.

Parliament is organized, therefore, to permit "gentlemen" to engage in other occupations. It convenes at 2:30 in the afternoon and sessions, while getting longer, are still well under two hundred days a year.[8] What this effectively means is that the nation's business is not receiving the attention that more and more people believe it should get. Even though parliamentarians can theoretically hold other jobs, increasing numbers are finding it difficult to do so and at the same time do a conscientious job of representing their constituents. As a consequence, there is mounting pressure for increases in both sal-

8 In 1967 the Commons experimented with holding two morning sessions a week. The practice was soon discontinued, although morning sessions can now be called under certain special circumstances.

TABLE 15.1. SOCIAL BACKGROUND OF M.P.'S ELECTED IN 1966

Occupation	Conservative		Labor		Liberal	Total	Percentage of all M.P.'s
	Number	Percentage	Number	Percentage			
Barristers, solicitors	70	27.7	54	14.9	3	127	20.3
Business, management	75	29.6	32	8.8	3	110	17.5
Workers	2	0.8	109	30.0	0	111	17.7
Teachers	4	1.6	72	19.8	1	77	12.3
Journalists, publicists	17	6.7	29	8.0	0	46	7.3
Farmers	27	10.7	2	0.6	2	31	4.9
Armed Services	19	7.5	3	0.8	0	22	3.5
Civil Service, local government	13	5.1	9	2.5	0	22	3.5
Politicians	2	0.8	9	2.5	1	12	1.9
Doctors, dentists	2	0.8	9	2.5	1	12	1.9
Other	22	8.7	35	9.6	1	58	9.2
Total	253	100.0	363	100.0	12	628	100.0
Education							
Elementary only	2	0.8	80	22.0	0	82	13.0
Secondary only	18	7.0	93	25.5	2	113	18.1
Secondary and university	29	11.4	124	34.2	3	156	24.9
Public school only	63	24.9	4	1.2	0	67	10.6
Public school and university	141	55.9	62	17.1	7	210	33.4
Total	253	100.0	363	100.0	12	628	100.0

aries and services that members consider necessary.

Because of governmental control over legislation, the importance of party labels, and the national character of British politics, British M.P.'s probably spend less time receiving delegations from interest groups or visits from constituents than do American, French, or German legislators. Yet most of them do hold "surgeries" during which they serve as combination social worker and legal adviser; British M.P.'s can and do intercede for constituents in cases where they feel that legal rights have been ignored.

4. PARTY IN PARLIAMENT

Pivotal to the genesis of cabinet government in England was the emergence of a disciplined two-party system. All members of Parliament belong to a political party, and,

TABLE 15.1 (*Cont'd*).   SOCIAL BACKGROUND OF M.P.'S ELECTED IN 1966

	Conservative		Labor				Percentage of all M.P.'s
	Number	Percentage	Number	Percentage	Liberal	Total	
Universities							
Oxford	83	32.6	54	14.8	3	140	22.3
Cambridge	61	24.0	29	8.0	3	93	14.9
Other	26	10.2	103	28.5	4	133	21.2
Total	170	66.8	186	51.3	10	366	58.4
Public Schools							
Eton	55	21.6	3	0.8	2	60	9.6
Harrow	14	5.5	0	0.0	0	14	2.2
Winchester	8	3.2	2	0.6	0	10	1.6
Other	127	50.0	61	16.8	5	193	30.8
Total	204	80.3	66	18.2	7	277	44.2
Religion							
Anglican	110	43.4	32	8.8	2	144	23.0
Other Protestant	12	4.7	54	14.9	2	68	10.4
Roman Catholic	12	4.7	23	6.3	0	35	5.6
Jew	2	0.8	26	7.2	0	28	4.5
Other	1	0.4	11	3.0	1	13	2.1
Total	137	54.0	146	40.2	5	288	45.6

Adapted from David E. Butler and Anthony King, *The British General Election of 1966* (London: Macmillan, 1967), pp. 208–209. Reprinted by permission of the publisher.

on the whole, their votes are party votes. Occasionally a maverick or two finds his way into Westminster, but the vast majority of M.P.'s are there because the party helped them get there, and the party is not about to allow a member to forget his debt of allegiance. Continual violation of party discipline can lead to sanctions of one kind or another, the ultimate sanction involving withdrawal of the whip—expulsion from the parliamentary party. Here, as in other areas, the organization of the Labor Party in Parliament differs somewhat from that of the Conservative. The differences stem primarily from the fact that the Labor Party began its life outside Parliament as a mass, ideological party committed to "democratic" procedures,

while the Conservatives started out as an aristocratic faction with close ties to traditional conceptions of hierarchy and the Establishment. However, the parties have gradually moved closer together, adjusting to each other and to the changing requirements of the political system.

THE CONSERVATIVE PARTY: In Parliament, as in the nation, the Conservative Party revolves about the party leader. Once elected by his party, he is not formally subject to re-election, nor is he formally required to report on his work to anyone. He appoints the chief party whip and, as noted, he can have the whip withdrawn from recalcitrant party members.[9] The leader also appoints his shadow cabinet, a group of M.P.'s who theoretically will take office in his government should he be called upon to form one.

The key Conservative Party organization in Parliament is the 1922 Committee, which meets once a week for an hour or so to obtain a general sense of what Conservative M.P.'s think about the issues before Parliament. The meetings are informal, and the committee operates without standing rules. When the party is in opposition, all members are eligible to attend, and the whips and members of the shadow cabinet do so, reporting results of the deliberations to the party leader, who attends only if he has a message to deliver. When the party is in power, neither ministers nor junior ministers attend. Either the whips or the committee chairman, usually a prominent M.P., report to the prime minister. The leader is also advised on policy matters by a business committee, which consists of the principal officers of the parliamentary party's main functional committees. There are about twenty of these committees, each dealing with a major field of government policy—such as foreign affairs, defense, trade and industry, finance— and their purpose is to help members develop expertise in special areas. The committees often try to influence ministers directly, and when disagreement occurs, the matter at issue may be referred to the 1922 Committee.

The ultimate disciplinary sanction of withdrawing the whip has only rarely been used by the Conservative Party leadership, although more independent-minded Conservative members have occasionally resigned from the party—refused the whip—in protest over particular policies. Thus, while the sanction is theoretically important, it is also one that the party leadership is chary about

using. A somewhat larger number of M.P.'s have not been readopted as candidates by their constituencies as the result of their policy stands; yet even here there is a reluctance to act and it is usually only after repeated disagreements that the constituency party will finally withdraw its support from the party maverick.

On the whole, the Conservative Parliamentary Party is prepared to give a Conservative prime minister a good deal of leeway on the formulation of policy, provided, of course, it does not feel he is stepping too far out of line with its sense of what Conservative voters want and expect. Occasionally, back-benchers will bridle over an issue on ideological grounds, although this happens far less frequently than in the Labor Party. Occasionally, too, the Conservative Parliamentary Party will register displeasure when it believes that it has not been brought fully into policy discussions on crucial issues. Nevertheless, Conservative M.P.'s regard it as the function of the leader to lead, and their definition of good leadership is primarily a pragmatic one: good leadership can be estimated by the party's standing among the voters.

THE LABOR PARTY: The Parliamentary Labor Party (P.L.P.) consists of all Labor members of the House of Commons and the House of Lords, although the latter do not vote on questions of special concern to the lower house. At the beginning of each session, the P.L.P. elects a party leader and a deputy party leader (or vice chairman), as well as the chief party whip. It also elects a parliamentary committee of twelve members, of which the leader, deputy leader, and whip are ex-officio members. Since 1955, the party leader has had the authority to appoint additional M.P.'s, up to a total of 39, to act as a shadow cabinet and to sit on the front bench. Finally, the Labor Party has established numerous committees for back-benchers to encourage specialized knowledge in a particular area of government.

9 The whips in each party are M.P.'s who serve many functions, the most important of which is securing membership attendance for crucial votes. The term comes from fox-hunting parlance of the eighteenth century, where the whipper-in kept the hounds from straying by using a small whip. The most pressing duties fall upon the chief whips, who are important party officials.

The P.L.P. operates according to a set of standing orders, among them provisions for disciplining members who violate parliamentary party decisions. These measures, which include withdrawal of the whip, have been suspended from time to time to encourage voluntary agreement, but the continued existence of factionalism has always led to their reimposition in one form or another. As in the Conservative Party, members can abstain on certain issues which involve a "matter of conscience."

The parliamentary party as a unit usually meets several times a month, and the parliamentary committee, when the party is in opposition, on the average of once a week to discuss the program of the coming week. Important issues are decided by a formal vote. The party leader and members of the shadow cabinet attend meetings of the parliamentary party, although they do so less frequently when Labor is in office than when it is in opposition. When in office, the P.L.P. establishes a small consultative committee to serve as liaison between the cabinet and the party in Parliament.

The Labor Party's specialized committees have always offered party members the opportunity to become fairly expert on particular subjects, but their most important contributions have been made when the party is in office, and a complicated though informal relationship of mutual assistance develops between ministers and the respective committees. In the last years of the first postwar Labor government, however, the feeling existed that the committees had slipped under the thumb of the more militant in the party, a circumstance that somewhat reduced their influence.

To a far greater extent than among the Conservatives, informal groupings tend to proliferate in the party. Trade unionists, for example, often meet together to discuss common problems. In a more controversial vein, M.P.'s to the left of the leadership have a tendency to form groups to push programs they like: the Keep Left group of the late 1940's, the Bevanite group of the early and middle 1950's, and the Victory for Socialism group of the late 1950's and early 1960's. Time and again the leadership has demanded the dissolution of such groups, believing them to hamper party unity; however, they always manage to surface again, under another name, a few years later.

In theory, the Labor prime minister takes his parliamentary party completely within his confidence; in practice, relations between the two have always been rather uncertain. The ideological commitment of many P.L.P. members automatically limits the Labor prime minister's room for maneuver more than that of his Conservative counterpart. Also, many Labor M.P.'s are more inclined than their Conservative colleagues to offer at least verbal resistance to the prime minister, even on issues on which they know he commands the support of the voters, simply because they believe his policies are wrong. While in the last analysis they may toe the line because they know a constantly divided party is likely to fare less well at the polls, the principle of harmony has never stayed the P.L.P.'s rather fractious tendencies.

The problems facing the prime minister have become more troublesome as the party has moved away from its traditional ideological moorings. In part, this situation is the result of the changing composition of the party and the new M.P.'s greater desire to participate in decision-making; in part, it stems from the economic problems facing the Wilson government. Indeed, the prime minister has been forced to retreat on some matters that he considered vital. For example, in 1969 the government dropped fairly mild legislative proposals to curb wildcat strikes, because of sizable left-wing and trade-union opposition within the party.

5. CABINET GOVERNMENT

English government is, as by now should be clear, dominated by the executive. The history of the cabinet has already been traced, but in summary the cabinet emerged out of the Privy Council and consisted at first simply of those persons most closely in attendance on the king. Individuals were responsible only to the king, and, except for his authority, went their own way. Later, as Parliament gained in power, it became advisable to select an M.P., or at least someone who could command the support of Parliament, for the cabinet, even though initially all Parliament could do about an official it did not like was to demand his impeachment, and occasionally his head.

During the reign of George I, the cabinet began to demonstrate a certain degree of autonomy and cohesion, and, in the absence of the king, a prime minister, exercising the prerogatives of an executive, moved closer and closer to the eye of authority. By the 1840's, both cabinet and prime minister were responsible to Parliament as "the Government," although the notion of collective cabinet responsibility as an operative ideal did not fully develop until later in the century.

It has always been evident that the prime minister is more than first among equals in relation to his fellow cabinet members. With the decline of the king's authority to determine who would—and would not—join the cabinet, it was the prime minister who came to be formally responsible for choosing the government, and to a very considerable extent came to personify it. Today, the prime minister represents both his party and the government in the view of the electorate. There are those who would argue, then, that his power has increased accordingly—that England, in fact, has developed a quasi-presidential system. As Lord Home pointed out before he became prime minister:

Every Cabinet Minister is in a sense the Prime Minister's agent—his assistant. There's no question about that. It is the Prime Minister's Cabinet, and he is the one person directly responsible to the Queen for what the Cabinet does.

If the Cabinet discusses anything it is the Prime Minister who decides what the collective view of the Cabinet is. A Minister's job is to save the Prime Minister all the work he can.[10]

This seems rather strong, for, as Lord Home must have realized later, there are many limitations upon the prime minister's power over his colleagues. The relationship varies, of course, depending upon the persons involved, and we can, perhaps, clarify it somewhat by a more detailed examination of the formation and functions of the cabinet.

THE FORMATION OF THE CABINET: On paper, the leader of the Labor Party would seem to have less leeway in choosing his cabinet than does the Conservative leader. He is tied to the twelve-man parliamentary committee, and in recent years the expectation has grown that those elected to the committee by the P.L.P. or appointed to the shadow cabinet are most likely to enter the government. The Conservative party leader is not bound by the possible dictates or obligations connected with any parliamentary committee. Nevertheless, the differences in appointive power between the two party officials are more apparent than real: both leaders can ignore many expectations, and both, in establishing a new government, must take into account the same kind of variables.

A government today may consist of one hundred or more M.P.'s. These include twenty or so members of the cabinet—usually, although not always, heads of departments—and approximately another twenty senior ministers who are not cabinet members; there are also some 35 junior ministers —that is, parliamentary secretaries and parliamentary private secretaries. The prime minister's power to appoint the government is, therefore, obviously a crucial source of his own strength; the number of posts available and the competition for them goes a long

[10] Cited in Bernard Crick, *The Reform of Parliament* (Garden City: Doubleday Anchor Books, 1965), p. 38.

way toward explaining the power that any prime minister can exert over his own party. It is, however, a resource that cannot be wasted, not just for his own political well-being, but for his party's survival in power as well.

If a prime minister's shoulders are broader and considerably higher than any possible contender's, he can choose men whom he simply wishes to have near him, either because he respects their opinions, because they are cronies, or because they possess some special knowledge. Ramsay MacDonald in the Labor Party and Winston Churchill in the Conservative were, at times, very much like this—they picked whom they wanted although neither could ever afford to neglect completely other party notables. On the other hand, Lord Home and Harold Wilson had to take much fuller cognizance of other party leaders. Bringing a man to the center of power, or retaining him, can give a prime minister an important call upon his loyalties, for a position in government is one few men desire to relinquish. Patrick Gordon Walker described it after having been Secretary of State for Commonwealth Relations in the Labor government from 1949 to 1951:

From being at the very heart of affairs and among the few dozen best-informed men in the world, faithfully served day and night, he suddenly reverts to obscurity. The invitations which a short time before had seemed to flow in embarrassing numbers, thin to a trickle. Workmen arrive to remove the direct line which linked him to his Private Office and by which he could control a great Department of State.[11]

The selection of who is to be in the cabinet is determined as the new prime minister appoints men to head the executive departments or ministries. There are at least forty ministerial offices—far too many to form a cohesive working body. Therefore, with due consideration to party power and party endorsement, most cabinets contain 15 to twenty ministries, although during both world wars, cabinets consisted of as few as ten members. When the cabinet has been

[11] Anthony Sampson, *Anatomy of Britain Today* (New York: Harper & Row, 1965), p. 129. One other means used by the prime minister to exact loyalty lies in his consignment of honors. Clement Attlee distributed 23 peerages and knighthoods between 1945 and 1951; between 1951 and 1957, Conservative prime ministers distributed 104.

TABLE 15.2. SIZE OF CABINETS AND GOVERNMENTS

	1900	1910	1920	1930	1940	1950	1960	1967
Cabinet ministers	19	19	19	19	9	18	19	24
Non-cabinet ministers	10	7	15	9	25	20	20	27
Junior ministers	15	22	33	27	32	35	35	58
Number of M.P.'s in government	33	43	58	50	58	68	65	92[1]
Number of peers in government	27	19	22	12	19	13	18	23
Total paid government posts	60	62	81	58	74	81	82	115[1]
Parliamentary private secretaries	9	16	13	26	25	27	36	30
Total number of M.P.'s involved in government	42	59	71	76	83	95	101	122

[1] Figures include assistant government whips who have been paid only since 1964.

Adapted from *British Political Facts, 1900–1967*, 2nd ed. (London: Macmillan, 1968), p. 57. Reprinted by permission of the publisher.

large, many prime ministers, including Wilson, have established what has come to be called the "inner cabinet," a smaller group of men that a prime minister consults regularly, either separately or together, because he finds them particularly congenial.

Traditional ministries, because of their great importance, are almost always included in the cabinet. Thus Treasury (the chancellor of the exchequer), Foreign Affairs (the secretary of state for foreign affairs), and the Home Department (secretary of state) are invariably represented. Other ministers may be included if their departments happen to be at the center of public attention. The 1945 Labor government included the Minister of Fuel and Power and the Minister of Health; they were natural choices because of Labor's decision to nationalize the coal and gas industries and to sponsor a new health program. By the end of Attlee's term of office both ministries had been dropped from the cabinet; both the coal and gas industries were being administered by public corporations, and the National Health Service was well under way. Similarly, Wilson's decision to bring the newly created Ministry of Technology into the cabinet in 1964 was based on his desire both to emphasize the "modernizing" qualities of his administration and to co-opt Frank Cousins, an important left-wing trade union leader. Indeed, the Wilson government is among the largest in recent British history, reflecting Wilson's strategy to secure party support by generously distributing the rewards of office.

The prime minister can also bring into the cabinet ministers without portfolio—men he wants to include in the government but to whom he does not wish, for one reason or another, to assign departmental responsibilities. Other appointments which do not entail ministerial duties are made to fill posts on the Privy Council, posts that once had important functions but are now little more than sinecures. The Chancellor of the Duchy of Lancaster, for example, is in charge of administering certain lands that have been owned by the crown since the thirteenth century; actually these holdings are now much reduced and the work of administration is done by a small board, leaving the chancellor free for other tasks. The same is true of the Lord Privy Seal, who was at one time a crown officer with certain important duties, especially related to the payment of money; today he has few if any functions. Nevertheless, the position has been held as a cabinet post by such men as Attlee and Conservative leader Edward Heath. Of the 18 ministers in Macmillan's government in 1962, four were reasonably important figures who had no departmental responsibilities.

THE CABINET AS A TEAM: The cabinet is a body whose members share collective responsibility for all decisions taken by the government. Meetings are officially secret, and members are not normally supposed to reveal disagreements or, should they resign, to proclaim publicly their reasons for doing so; any criticism of official policy by a cabinet member is expected to be couched in fairly mild terms, lest he be accused of injuring the party. This code of conduct has been the general tradition since the middle of the nineteenth century, and prime ministers have enforced it, in many instances, by dismissing members who have openly expressed their disagreements over the government's policy. Nevertheless, in recent years the lid of secrecy attendant upon cabinet decisions has occasionally blown off. In 1967 Douglas Jay made no secret of his opposition to Britain's application for membership in the Common Market, even after the Wilson cabinet had decided officially upon this course of action; in 1969 Home Secretary James Callaghan actively opposed, both in the Commons and in the press, a cabinet decision to push for legislation against wildcat strikes.

Ordinarily, however, the cabinet functions well as a team, largely because its members have known each other for a very long time. They have worked together in Parliament, they have dined together, and they have drunk together, developing friendships and antagonisms—both of which bind them together—that can only come after long and intimate association. Here they differ considerably from the American cabinet, which is usually composed of appointees who scarcely know each other or, for that matter, the president. One other reason why the English cabinet functions well as a team is because its members have roughly equal political status.

The prime minister does, of course, possess considerably more power than any of his colleagues; in the last analysis it is he who must decide who will and who will not be in the government, and (by setting the agenda) what will and what will not be discussed at cabinet meetings. Moreover, in some areas, such as foreign policy, where rapid decisions may be necessary, the prime minister can act almost alone; many of Anthony Eden's decisions at the time of the 1956 Suez crisis were made without consulting more than a few colleagues. Then, too, cabinet members will usually support the prime minister, despite sharp disagreements, on issues he considers crucial to his administration; Harold Wilson, for example, has received the acquiescence of his colleagues time and time again, whatever their reservations. Nevertheless, many cabinet members are men of power within the party: the prime minister can override them only with difficulty, especially on issues that do not require immediate action; and if he can dismiss some colleagues with equanimity, there are others whom he cannot, without seriously endangering himself politically. Harold Macmillan fired seven cabinet members in 1962 in an attempt to refurbish the government's image; the result was such that he damaged both himself and his party. While Macmillan's action is often cited as an example of the degree of power a prime minister can wield, there were some in his cabinet, R. A. Butler for one, whom he simply could not touch because of their own individual base of political support. This is not the situation in the American cabinet,

where the president is most often the only official present who has ever been elected to a public office, or at least the only one voted into office in a nationwide election.

When Parliament is in session, the cabinet meets about once or twice a week at 10 Downing Street, under the chairmanship of the prime minister. It may be called more frequently on special occasions, and often, depending upon the prime minister, a smaller number of cabinet cronies will gather together for a particular purpose. Churchill liked to meet with his cabinet intimates in the small hours of the morning, for he tended to work most of the night and sleep until late in the day.

In general, the cabinet's agenda has been prepared some days in advance and circulated to other members by the cabinet secretariat. Until 1916 the cabinet lacked a staff for this purpose, nor were minutes of its meetings kept. In many cases, it was difficult for members to agree on precisely what had happened. As Lord Curzon recalled it:

No record whatever was kept of our proceedings, except the private and personal letter written by the Prime Minister to the Sovereign, the contents of which, of course, are never seen by anybody else. The Cabinet often had the very haziest notion as to what its decisions were. . . . Cases frequently arose when the matter was left so much in doubt that a Minister went away and acted upon what he thought was a decision which subsequently turned out to be no decision at all, or was repudiated by his colleagues.[12]

Today the cabinet is served by a knowledgeable group of civil servants, including a permanent secretary, two deputy secretaries, an under secretary, a senior assistant secretary and five assistant secretaries. Not only does the secretariat help the prime minister draw up the agenda, it also insures that mem-

[12] Cited in Sidney D. Bailey, *British Parliamentary Democracy,* 2nd ed. (Boston: Houghton Mifflin, 1962), p. 177.

oranda on specific items of cabinet business are circulated and that ministers who are not cabinet members will be available if issues affecting their ministry are to be discussed. The secretariat occasionally serves as a fact-finding body as well.

The nature and content of cabinet meetings are never constant. They depend largely upon the issues at stake and the personal style of the ministers. In earlier days, meetings could be very casual, as indicated by the following description of a cabinet session in 1840 over which Melbourne, then prime minister, presided:[13]

The Cabinet met on Monday evening (September 27) and sat until seven o'clock. . . . There was for some time a dead silence. At length Palmerston, trying to shuffle off the discussion, but aware that he must say something, began. . . . Nothing, however, could be got from Melbourne, and there was a long pause. . . . Palmerston pulled out of his pockets a whole parcel of letters and reports . . . and began reading them through, in the middle of which operation someone happened to look up and perceived Melbourne fast asleep.[13]

Even today, when the pace of activity is far more hectic, cabinet meetings can be discursive. Churchill, for instance, liked to try ideas on his colleagues, thinking out loud before arriving at any conclusions; sometimes only the first point on the agenda was reached. Attlee followed the agenda carefully, cutting off ministers who took too much time. Macmillan seems to have run fairly tight cabinet meetings; he would introduce a subject and then let senior ministers have their say, indicating his own position only when summarizing their views. Wilson, on the other hand, has generally opened the discussion by stating his views and then, after the members have voiced their own opinions, polled the ministers in order to obtain something like a formal vote. Of course, on most issues the cabinet rarely makes policy at its full sessions. Rather, its primary concern is to ratify, at the highest levels, proposals developed by the departments under the aegis of individual ministers, or by cabinet committees, which consist of three or four ministers and a small staff. The use of cabinet committees has its precedent in the nineteenth century, but it is only in the past thirty or forty years that they have achieved any real importance. Originally, most committees were merely ad hoc groupings shaped informally to handle particular problems; today, however, they are widely used to lighten the burden of cabinet work by providing for coordination of legislative proposals that cross departmental lines at a lower level. Indeed, Wilson has enhanced the power of these committees by insisting that their public-policy decisions are final. Thus, ministers are no longer expected to appeal to the full cabinet should they disagree with a cabinet-committee decision.

It is difficult to determine with any precision the origins of much parliamentary legislation. One study of the major sources of policy concluded that of 59 bills passed by Parliament during its 1936–1937 session, only nine were initiated by the cabinet. Twenty-seven were proposed by administrative departments or interdepartmental committees; nine resulted largely from the demands of pressure groups; three could be attributed to government policy significantly doctored by outside pressure; seven had their basis in departmental policy, similarly modified; two were derived from local-government associations and two originated with M.P.'s. A review of pending legislation in *The Times of London* in October 1962 listed only one measure derived from the Conservative Party's 1959 election manifesto, and a later review of pending legislation for the 1963–1964 session estimated that 16 of the 22 bills being considered had been initiated by various departments.[14] However, it is not true, as some have argued, that cabinet gov-

13 *Ibid.*, p. 167.

14 S. A. Walkland, *The Legislative Process in Great Britain* (London: George Allen and Unwin, Ltd., 1968), pp. 22–23.

ernment in England is being replaced by bureaucratic government, for the decisions which come through departments are, naturally enough, in line with the overall policy of the government. Should a minister, for example, initiate, or permit his department to initiate, a policy that runs counter to the government's general position, he will have to satisfy his cabinet colleagues on the viability of the new policy. The use of expert administrators has removed some legislative initiative from both the cabinet and Parliament, but the ultimate political controls still operate. To be sure, the amount of cabinet activity in the area of legislation depends upon the government in power—as well as upon how long the government has been in power. During the first majority Labor government (1945–1950), which had committed itself to a program of nationalization, the cabinet was more significant as an instigator of legislation than were the Conservative cabinets that preceded or followed it, and the Wilson cabinet has certainly been more active than was Macmillan's.[15] The studies for the early 1960's cited above reflect the fact that the government in office was a Conservative government and that it had held office for more than a decade. The 1936–1937 study was also made during the tenure of Conservatives who, effectively, had held the reins of power for almost five years.

THE INDIVIDUAL MINISTER: The individual minister, if he is a member of the cabinet, has three major responsibilities. He must join with his colleagues in collective action, participate in Parliament as a member of the front bench, and supervise and—a full-time task in itself—take full responsibility for the activity of his ministry. The minister coming to a major department is faced with a vast bureaucratic apparatus run by civil servants who over a period of time have developed considerable competence. They cannot help

but try to suggest what the "facts" are to a minister who wishes to make substantial changes; but provided he is strong-minded, he is by no means helpless in the face of the "facts." It was widely argued by the left wing of the Labor Party that, in the period just after the Second World War, Ernest Bevin had become a victim of the Foreign Office bureaucracy when he was attacked for his "pro-Arab" attitude during the 1948 Israeli-Arab conflict; as we now know, however, the Foreign Office was divided, and Bevin's policies, right or wrong, were his own. For one "fact" is, of course, that government departments consist of individuals with different opinions, and a good civil servant will bring this diversity to the attention of the minister.[16]

Furthermore, the minister has probably specialized at some time in the area of the department he is now administering, and is, in general terms, familiar with its work. If the party has been in power before, he may have had some experience in the department as a junior minister; moreover, the relative stability of British governments gives him time to acquire a deeper understanding of the problems of direct concern to him. And, finally, he has several outside sources of assistance. He chooses a principal private secretary from among the younger civil servants in the department, and the personal relationship between the two permits the latter to become wholly cognizant of his chief's attitudes and to provide extremely valuable assistance. Further, the minister brings with him a number of ambitious young M.P.'s as parliamentary secretaries (who are considered junior ministers) and parliamentary private secretaries. These men aid him in his contacts with back-benchers, the public, and pressure groups; they take care of the paper work and also serve, quite tellingly, as an additional source of information.

The minister's parliamentary and departmental secretaries also brief him for his

---

15 In the 1950 general election, Labor was returned to office for its second, although sharply reduced, majority government. The party lost to the Conservatives in the 1951 election.

16 The role of the English bureaucracy will be discussed again in Chapter 22, pp. 669–681. It may be noted here, however, that to an astonishing degree it has, on the whole, served various masters impartially.

parliamentary work, and his parliamentary private secretary is with him at question time on the floor of Parliament. The cabinet minister's performance in Parliament is crucial. However good an administrator he may be, his reputation in the party is to a certain extent based upon his reputation in the house —and careers can be made and unmade on the floor.

One further onus a minister carries is the total responsibility for his department, its flaws as well as its perfections. Major blunders committed by the department have been committed by him. Though he may have been unaware of them, more than one minister has been forced out of the government because of the actions of his departmental civil servants.

Even more than the Commons itself, the cabinet was for a long time the preserve of gentlemen from good public schools and from Oxford or Cambridge. The first Labor government in 1924, however, brought to the cabinet a majority of men of working-class background. Labor regimes since then have become increasingly middle-class, and the aristocratic element in Conservative cabinets has declined (see Tables 15.3 and 15.4). This slow social coalescence of the parties reflects not only the changing structure of British politics but the more insistent demands for expertise.

Personal connections are not unimportant in a successful parliamentary career, but parliamentary performance is the key, despite the fact that ministers are occasionally drawn

TABLE 15.3.   CLASS STRUCTURE OF CABINETS, 1868–1955

Administration	Aristocrats	Middle class	Working class	Total
Gladstone (1868)	7	8	0	15
Disraeli (1874)	7	5	0	12
Gladstone (1880)	8	6	0	14
Salisbury (1885)	11	5	0	16
Gladstone (1886)	9	6	0	15
Salisbury (1886)	10	5	0	15
Gladstone (1892)	9	8	0	17
Salisbury (1895)	8	11	0	19
Balfour (1902)	9	10	0	19
Campbell-Bannerman (1906)	7	11	1	19
Asquith (1914)	6	12	1	19
Lloyd George (1919)	3	17	1	21
Bonar Law (1922)	8	8	0	16
MacDonald (1924)	3	5	11	19
Baldwin (1925)	9	12	0	21
MacDonald (1929)	2	4	12	18
National ministry (1935)	6	10	2	18
Baldwin (1935)	9	11	2	22
Chamberlain (1937)	8	13	0	21
Churchill[1] (1945)	6	9	1	16
Attlee (1945)	0	8	12	20
Churchill (1951)	5	11	0	16

[1]Churchill's wartime government has been left out, as the war cabinet was a very small body.

Source: W. L. Guttsman, *The British Political Elite* (New York: Basic Books, 1963), p. 78. Reprinted by permission of Basic Books, Inc. and MacGibbon and Kee, Ltd.

TABLE 15.4. WORKING-CLASS MEMBERSHIP OF LABOR CABINETS, 1964–1967

Year	Cabinet size	Working-class members	Percentage working class
1964	23	6	26
1966	23	4	17
1969 (October)	21	1	5

Adapted from Richard Rose, "Class and Party Divisions: Britain as a Test Case," *Sociology*, 2 (May 1968), 132. Reprinted by permission of The Clarendon Press and the author.

from outside Parliament.[17] The qualities required are an ability to comport oneself well on the floor and a willingness to subordinate personal wishes to party demands. Mavericks are, from time to time, successful, but they are few and far between. The usual ascent up the ladder is from ordinary M.P. to parliamentary secretary, to a noncabinet department, and from there to the cabinet itself. (See Table 15.5.) In general, those who sit in the cabinet are men who have been in the party for many years and gradually have established reputations. This hierarchical system has the advantage that the men finally achieving ministerial office know each other's strengths and weaknesses; on the other hand, the fact that those favored for cabinet posts are too often men who have made few

[17] In which case they must be represented in Parliament by a junior minister who is a member of that body.

enemies usually indicates that they also formed few original ideas. Some British commentators have argued that American presidents have a wider range of fresh talent to choose from in organizing administrations, and that the presidential system has, in the past fifty years, tapped a greater number of really dynamic leaders than has the British.

In summary, then, the evidence indicates—and more will be offered later—that British government is cabinet government; it is not quasi-presidential government, nor is it rule by an anonymous bureaucracy. The prime minister is more than first among equals, but the extent of his authority depends very much on his relationship to his party, and this, in part, depends upon what can only be called "the national mood." The argument that the prime minister is a quasi president became widely accepted at about the time that the

TABLE 15.5 THE ROUTE TO CABINET OFFICE

Experience of cabinet officers and prime ministers from 1918 to 1955: percentage serving in offices given.

Offices held	Labor	Conservative
Served as parliamentary private secretary, junior minister, minister, cabinet minister	22.6	24.1
Served as junior minister, minister, cabinet minister	41.9	51.7
Served as minister and cabinet minister	29.0	17.3
Served as cabinet minister only	6.5	6.9

Adapted from Philip W. Buck, "The MP's in Ministerial Office, 1918–1955 and 1955–1959," *Political Studies*, IX (October 1961), p. 305. Reprinted by permission of the publisher.

Wilson government took office in 1964. Wilson's personality and early prestige impressed many with the idea that it was his government and that he would dominate both his cabinet colleagues and the Labor Party. The results, however, have been quite different. By 1969 the Wilson government had become all but immobilized; segments of the party were in open rebellion, and the prime minister was jumping from expedient to expedient in a desperate effort to maintain the illusion of forward motion. And the argument that England's government had evolved into a quasi-presidential system had become less and less valid.

6. THE HOUSE OF COMMONS AT WORK

A legislative body, like any other group, must satisfy certain requirements in order to function effectively, or even at all. If it is engaged, as are all legislatures, in simultaneously discussing public issues and making decisions about them, mechanisms and ground rules must be set up by which its time is sensibly organized, information is funneled to its members, and personal and political differences are reduced to the point where they do not prevent the legislature from operating.

The kinds of legislative mechanisms developed and their success in permitting parliaments to function effectively depend upon several important factors, including the role of the legislature in the governmental process, the cultural norms of the society, and the nature and depth of the conflicts that divide the society (and, consequently, members of the legislature). In England, the two-party system and cabinet government have made the organization of parliamentary business a comparatively simple matter, whatever current critics of Parliament may believe. The fact that the issues which divide British society are not extremely deep has allowed easy relationships to exist between members of the parties that many other political systems have not experienced, and the

continued acceptance of certain cultural styles that are part of the national heritage has given the conduct of parliamentary business a uniquely British flavor.

THE STRUCTURE OF AUTHORITY: The organization of the Commons is the purview of two offices: the speaker of the house and the whips. The speaker, unlike speakers of most legislatures, is a man who has divested himself of party label when he assumes the post and who has, provided he discharges his duties acceptably, a lifetime tenure. Like speakers of most legislatures, he enforces the rules of debate, recognizes members who wish to speak from the floor, and, in general, is responsible for the conduct of parliamentary business. Both his responsibility and his authority are great, for his rulings and his ability to determine who should speak and when can have considerable effect upon the course of debate. Even so, the successful operation of the house as an ongoing body is contingent upon his ability to maintain a reputation for impartiality. And in line with this responsibility, the speaker, while originally a party man, drops his party identification once he assumes office. Further, it is understood that he will serve for life even if party control of the Commons changes during his tenure, and that the opposition party will not contest his seat. This tacit agreement has not always held; the Labor Party in recent years has contested the seat of the speaker from time to time and in 1951 even contested the election of the speaker when party members could not agree with the Conservatives upon a suitable candidate.

Once elected, the speaker in the Commons has a rather easy time of it. The agenda of parliamentary business is arranged in advance by the parties, and he has only to carry out their decisions. The parties themselves readily reach accord on the agenda because, given the discipline of the majority party, everyone knows it can set any legislative pace it wishes. The labors of the speaker are further lightened because, whatever the dis-

FIGURE 15.2. A TYPICAL WHIP IN THE HOUSE OF COMMONS

William Whiteley, M.P.
House of Commons

On Monday, 27 October, 1947, the House will meet at 2-30 p.m.

Continuation of the General debate on the Address.
Discussion of Germany until 8-30 p.m., then Opposition Amendment on Imperial Security. (Mr. J. P. L. Thomas).

YOUR ATTENDANCE AT 3-30 p.m. AND THROUGHOUT THE SITTING IS REQUESTED. A DIVISION WILL TAKE PLACE AT 11 p.m.

On Tuesday, 28th October, the House will meet at 2-30 p.m.

Debate on the Address.
Opposition Amendment.

YOUR ATTENDANCE AT 3-30 p.m. AND THROUGHOUT THE SITTING IS REQUESTED.

On Wednesday, 29th October, the House will meet at 2-30 p.m.

Conclusion of the debate on the Address.
Opposition Amendment.

YOUR ATTENDANCE AT 3-30 p.m. AND THROUGHOUT THE SITTING IS PARTICULARLY REQUESTED. A MOST IMPORTANT DIVISION OR DIVISIONS WILL TAKE PLACE.

On Thursday, 30th October, the House will meet at 2-30 p.m.

Consideration of the Reports from the Committee of Privileges relating to the cases of the Hon. Members for Gravesend (Mr. Garry Allighan) and Doncaster (Mr. Evelyn Walkden).

YOUR ATTENDANCE AT 3-30 p.m. AND THROUGHOUT THE SITTING IS REQUESTED. THERE WILL BE A FREE VOTE OF THE HOUSE.

On Friday, 31st October, the House will meet at 11 a.m.

Expiring Laws Bill; Committee and remaining stages.
Jersey and Guernsey (Financial and Provisions) Bill; 2nd Reading.
Motions to approve the Fish Sales (Charges) Order and the 4 Purchase Tax Orders on the Paper.

YOUR ATTENDANCE AT 11 a.m. AND THROUGHOUT THE SITTING IS REQUESTED.

Note.

During the week it is hoped to consider the Motion relating to the Parliamentary Electors (War-Time Registration) Act, 1944.
A Prayer has been tabled for consideration on Tuesday.

Source: Herbert Morrison, *Government and Parliament* (Oxford: Oxford University Press, 1954), pp. 110–111. Reprinted by permission of the publisher.

agreements of the two parties, both share a common belief in the importance of preserving certain rules of the game. It was not always thus, of course. When Charles I ordered his man, Speaker Charles Finch, to adjourn the house, Finch was held forcibly in place by some members, the doors were locked, and the house passed three resolutions the king had not wanted discussed. In 1929 several radical members of the Labor Party attempted to steal the speaker's mace so that the results of a vote suspending one of their group from Parliament for disobeying him could not be tabulated. During the Suez crisis, too, debate waxed so bitter that, at times, the speaker almost lost control and members came close to exchanging blows.

The whips are party officials responsible for informing members about parliamentary business for the coming week, and for reminding them of their voting and attendance responsibilities. Among other duties, whips supply lists for committee memberships, and arrange for pairing of members. Each party has a chief whip and several assistant whips. The opposition whips are not paid, but governmental whips are given official titles, dating from some now forgotten time, that enable them to receive salaries. The government's chief whip is usually a member of the cabinet and serves as a source of communication between back-benchers and the prime minister. He and the chief whip of the opposition constitute the "usual channels" through which the organization of weekly business is decided, including the amount of time to be permitted for debate. The chores of assistant whips are much less significant. One government whip, for instance, sends a daily summary of and commentary on parliamentary proceedings to the monarch; he also carries messages between Commons and the crown. Equipped with a white staff, he stands at the bar of the house to deliver "a message from the Queen, sir, in reply to a loyal and dutiful address from this House."

Every Friday, the whips send each member of their party a written notice, also called

a whip, outlining the program for the following week. The importance of a particular
event is indicated by the wording, "Your
attendance is requested" or "Your attendance is particularly requested," as well as by
the underlining of the phrases. One line
indicates that the matter is not of extreme
urgency, two indicate a more important item
of business, and three lines imply that the
member had better be present unless he is
able to offer an extremely good excuse.

The structure of authority in Parliament
is to be found not only in the function of particular individuals but also in historic rules
that determine how and under what circumstances debate is conducted. For example, many important issues are discussed on
"motions of adjournment" rather than on
motions having anything to do with the subject involved. Other rules of debate require
that a member who wishes to speak rise
in his seat and, if male, have his head
uncovered. All members are required to address the chair, and to refer to other members not by their names but by a standard
circumlocution, such as "My right honorable
friend the Home Secretary." New members
are expected to remain fairly silent; each
new member also, at some time, makes a
maiden speech, theoretically on a noncon-
troversial subject, which inevitably wins warm
congratulations.

By long established custom, too, members
of Parliament are prohibited from using
words calculated to incite a colleague, such
as calling him "cowardly," "bloodthirsty," or
"mendacious." Never should one M.P. say of
another that he has not kept his word. These
restrictions have taken some of the sting out
of debates, but they have not prevented members from making caustic remarks about their
fellow M.P.'s. Harold Wilson, for instance,
said of Harold Macmillan:

*The right honourable gentleman is the only
statesman of this century to claim . . . to em-
body all that is best in both Disraeli and
Gladstone. In fact, of course, he is wrong.*

*He has inherited the streak of charlatanry in
Disraeli without his vision and the self-
righteousness of Gladstone without his dedication to principle.*[18]

Sir Anthony Eden was described by one
Labor M.P., during the Suez disaster, as
"an overripe banana, yellow outside, squishy
in." Winston Churchill once said of Clement
Attlee that he was "a modest man with
plenty to be modest about," and called
Aneurin Bevan "a squalid nuisance." All in
all, invective is kept within reasonable
bounds, and the M.P. most respected is one
who can insult cleverly, with a neat turn of
phrase.

Tart tongues aside, the house does retain
something of the quality of the aristocratic
club it once was. This has many advantages:
it can be argued that the continuance of tradition inspires a sense of history in M.P.'s;
that it smooths the cutting edges of their
radicalism and blurs the lines of party conflict; and that the pageantry of Parliament and
its emphasis on wit and behavior serve certain expressive needs for M.P.'s, bolstering
their feeling of importance and softening the
hostilities that naturally materialize. All in all,
the rules and customs of the House of Commons seem to have a number of significant
functional purposes. The point, of course,
can be debated: time and time again radicals
like Bevan have criticized this very blurring
for reinforcing the Establishment and inhibiting that collision of political forces which
would produce necessary social changes. As
one disgruntled M.P. declared not too long
ago:

*It's just like being back as a new boy at
public school—with its ritual and rules, and
also its background of convention, which
breeds a sense of anxiety and inferiority in
people who don't know the rules. . . . You
don't know where you're allowed to go, and*

[18] *Hansard Parliamentary Debates,* 594 (1958–
1959), November 3, 1958, 628.

*where not—you're always afraid you may
be breaking some rule, by wandering into
the Speaker's house by mistake. . . . In the
chamber, you don't know where you're supposed to be sitting. . . . It's just like a public
school: and that's why Labor M.P.'s are
overawed by it—because they feel that only
the Tory M.P.'s know what a public school is
like.*[19]

In recent years debate in the House has
grown more waspish and, in the eyes of some
members, less witty. There are those, in fact,
who have suggested that the work of the Commons be televised, if only to help the speaker
control the language of some of the members.

THE ORDER OF BUSINESS: Today, the work
of the Commons consists largely of discussing
government measures, and it is the government, supported by the weight of its majority,
that, in the last analysis, determines in what
order these measures will be considered. Of
course, the government is always careful to
try to reach an equitable arrangement with
the opposition, through the usual channels,
on the order of parliamentary business. It
remains extremely sensitive to any charge
that it may have failed to allow the opposition sufficient time to discuss the major issues
of public policy.

An average session of the Commons may
witness the introduction of anywhere from 75
to one hundred major proposals for legislation. Of these, ninety to one hundred per cent
will be introduced by the government itself,
and 97 to one hundred per cent of them will
be enacted into law, generally without notable changes. The extent to which the legislative program is planned by the government
still hinges, to a large degree, upon circumstances, including which party is in power.
For example, the first Labor government after
World War II monopolized Parliament's
time; during the years 1945 to 1948, not a
single private member's bill was introduced.

19 Mark Bonham-Carter, quoted in Sampson, *Anatomy of Britain Today*, p. 52.

In that period, although the cabinet consulted
the departments and relied upon them for
drafting bills, it was responsible as a body for
all major pieces of legislation. Operating with
the aid of a cabinet-level Future Legislation
Committee, it not only arranged each parliamentary week but also developed detailed
schedules for each session of Parliament and
even for its full, five-year term. The Conservatives returning to power after 1951 were
more flexible, allowing more bills to be introduced by individual members; a good deal of
the proposed legislation, too, was in response
to the nation's developing needs as the government and various private interests perceived them.

Sessions of Parliament are usually organized in such a fashion as to permit ample discussion of the government's major policies.
These policies became palpable not only in
debate on particular bills, but also on such
occasions as the Speech from the Throne, and
during parliamentary consideration of appropriations. The amount of discussion time to
be allotted is settled in advance by the party
leaders who also, in the case of most policy
issues, agree upon speakers. These agreements are not always completely satisfactory;
the opposition occasionally believes that it
has not been provided with adequate time to
assess the government's proposal. Nevertheless, compared with other parliaments, the
problems of getting legislation considered
and enacted are handled with comparative
dispatch—partly because the government,
knowing it has the votes to push through its
program, can afford to be generous; partly
because it is acutely aware that riding rough-
shod over the opposition would injure it politically. The opposition, on the other hand,
knows that attempts to inhibit legislative
activity beyond a reasonable point will evoke
public criticism. But perhaps the overriding
reason is simply that both sides are convinced
that the government should always be permitted to carry out its policies.

This would not be so, of course, if the
community were split by fundamental con-

flicts, as it was in the latter part of the nineteenth century. At that time, Irish Nationalists in Parliament filibustered again and again in an attempt to block the normal operation of business. A little later, during the discussion of the Finance Bill of 1909, the Conservatives did exactly the same thing. These actions resulted in a number of standing orders, or rules of procedure, designed to limit debate: the kangaroo, by which a committee chairman selects certain amendments for discussion and leaps over others; the guillotine, by which the House of Commons sets a time limit on the discussion of certain sections of a bill; and simple cloture, by which debate is cut off after an M.P. calls for a vote. These rules were instituted because some members of Parliament did not accept the broad, established agreements on how Parliament should function; they were adopted because most members did. These standing orders are rarely used today, except in consultation with the opposition; for the most part, Parliament operates within a general consensus as to what kinds of behavior are legitimate.

LEGISLATING: About 75 per cent of the time of the House of Commons is taken up with government-sponsored "public bills" and routine financial business. A public bill is a proposed law that affects the entire nation; as previously indicated, it may originate from several sources—the party, a royal commission report, an investigation or recommendation by a particular ministry, or an interest group such as the Trades Union Congress. In any event, before the public bill is presented to the Commons, it must pass through many hands. Even if the legislation does not originate in a ministry, the ministry concerned reviews its terms and makes recommendations, suggestions, and amendments.

The bill is also assessed by any interest group it is likely to affect. Every government engages in prior consultation with private organizations to secure their approval of a public bill, wherever possible; if the group withholds its complete endorsement, it is at least offered the opportunity to suggest any modifications that do not drastically change its substance. It is hoped that any opposition to the bill outside Parliament will, in this way, be reduced. Governments are also interested in obtaining whatever information the group has to offer on the subject of the law under consideration. On the whole, the British have never felt that distrust of "interests" so common to the American experience; in fact, almost every government since the turn of the century has encouraged the formation of nationally organized interest groups so that it can, when the occasion arises, readily consult with knowledgeable persons in the various sectors of the community.

After a proposed public bill wins cabinet approval, it is given to what is called the Parliamentary Counsel for drafting. The counsel office is in the Treasury, and is manned by highly expert civil servants with legal training, whose job is not only to make sure that the wording of the bill is precise, but also to check on its relation to other legislation. Drafting is an intricate process involving the checking and rechecking of such matters as phraseology and all possible implications of the proposal's legal strictures; important pieces of legislation go through as many as twenty to 25 drafts before being submitted to the house.

All bills introduced into the house receive three readings; the first, which is simply a formality, is by title only. Publication of the complete bill follows soon after. The bill is not actually read during the second and third "readings"; it is printed and distributed to members. The second reading is held about two weeks after the first, with debate lasting about a day or two. At this time the general principles of the bill are aired. If the bill is approved in principle by members of the Commons, it is sent to either a standing committee, a select committee, or, in matters of "constitutional importance," to a Committee of the Whole House. The third reading occurs after the bill returns from committee and all amendments to it have been debated and approved or rejected (report stage); it is, in short, a discussion of the bill in its final form before the house takes a vote on it. Of course, both the discussion and the vote at this point are normally pro forma; the vote after debate on the second reading usually tells the story as to whether or not the bill will be approved by the Commons.

As noted earlier, the House of Commons lacks the specialized standing committees that have developed in the American, German, and French legislatures. Specialized select committees did spring up during the reign of Elizabeth I and continued to be created even during the nineteenth century, but they never attained permanent status because of the rise of cabinet government. Today, standing committees consist of from twenty to fifty members appointed to them in proportion to the party's strength in the Commons and on the basis of their interest in the subject matter of the legislation then under consideration by the committee; decisions on committee membership are made by the speaker, assisted by his Committee on Selection, in consultation with party whips. Theoretically, a standing committee is permanent, while a select committee is appointed for a specific purpose and dissolved after its task has been accomplished. In practice, however, there is nothing permanent about a standing committee either, except possibly its name. The composition of all standing committees (with the exception of the two dealing with laws for Scotland and Wales) changes with the legislation under consideration. A Committee of the Whole House is simply the house itself, operating as a committee under more flexible procedures and presided over by a chairman instead of the speaker. This committee dates from the seventeenth century, when it was used as a device to reduce royal influence during the discussion of crucial issues. At the time, the speaker of the house served at the pleasure of the king; when a Committee of the Whole House was formed, he simply left the chamber and thus could not report the content of debates to the monarch. In recent years, the device has been used infrequently and, until 1967, primarily during the consideration of finance bills.

English standing committees operate quite differently from those in the United States and in various European legislatures. They never conduct hearings with outside witnesses, and they cannot suppress bills or hold them up in any way. Rather, their function is to take a bill after the Commons has approved it on second reading, and go over it line by line to consider amendments which can then be recommended to the Commons. When a bill leaves the committee, it enters the report stage; it is circulated to all members of the house and then debated on the floor. Debate and votes during the report stage deal entirely with proposed amendments to the legislation. The third reading is a final review of the amended legislation. The general principles of the amended bill are debated, and a vote of the M.P.'s is taken. If it is approved, the bill is sent to the House of Lords and, when the Lords concur, to the monarch for royal assent.

In terms of the amount of time they consume, the most important public bills considered by the house each session are those relating to finance. The financial year begins April 1 with a budget statement by the chancellor of the exchequer outlining both estimated expenditure and the ways and means of meeting it. Financial bills are the result of several months' work, during which the Treasury and the cabinet, in consultation with the specialized agencies of the government, have collated the budget requests of all departments and related them to what they deem to be the general needs of the economy. Since it is obvious that the resolutions that comprise the financial program will pass into law almost as introduced, debate on the measures, which extends over several months, is primarily concerned with issues of public policy rather than with a detailed examination of specific debits and credits. As compared with the procedures in the American congress, there are no specialized committees to scrutinize the financial proposals. Nor is there, on the other hand, the possibility of the outbreak of wild confusion over budgetary matters that so often, in the United States, results in a hodgepodge of financial legislation only loosely related to the government's initial requests or needs. Traditionally, financial legislation was not even sent to a standing committee for detailed consideration. Rather, the committee stage was conducted by a Committee of the Whole House. In 1967, however, the Commons changed its procedures; finance bills are now considered by a standing committee of fifty whose sessions may be attended by the chancellor of the exchequer or other interested ministers.[20] Here individual items can be examined more easily than they could before the house as a whole.

THE OPPOSITION AND THE POWER OF PARLIAMENT: Thus far, the emphasis of this chapter has been upon the predominant role of the government in the legislative process; and, indeed, compared with other parliamentary systems, it is the English executive—the cabinet and the prime minister—that is the most significant part of the entire legislative process. Nevertheless, despite all the current talk about the decline of Parliament, the House of Commons continues to be an important part of that process.[21] It is the voice box for all varieties of opinion within the nation; it is also the arena in which the government and the opposition engage in continual debate, each striving to convince not only the other but the national electorate

of the rightness of its position. When the opposition scores points in the debate, government leaders are anxious to deal with them. They may do so by stating their own case more effectively, by accepting opposition amendments to legislation, or by introducing amendments of their own which take opposition arguments into account. Whichever course it follows, the government's action is based partly on public opinion and partly on the degree of influence exercised by the opposition.

The Commonwealth Immigration Act of 1962, for example, was one of a series of legislative moves to curb immigration from the West Indies, India, and Pakistan. The Conservative government's rather mild bill was quite popular with the electorate, which most likely would have supported an even stronger measure. The Labor opposition, however, was bitterly opposed at that time to any restrictions whatsoever, and their arguments persuaded the Conservatives to act more circumspectly than they might otherwise have done. (Ironically, the Labor Party, after it returned to power, passed far more stringent legislation on immigration.) Again, in 1963, the Conservatives reacted very quickly after the Labor opposition used a series of rent scandals to attack earlier legislation freeing rents from control; almost immediately, the government appointed committees to investigate the situation and to reconsider modifications of the law. The Labor government in 1969 was forced to withdraw its reform plan for the House of Lords for fear that it would be defeated; opposition came from a segment of the Labor Party that believed the proposal did not go far enough and from Conservative Party members who either felt it went too far or were quite content to embarrass the government on a very touchy issue.

The influence of Parliament as an institution is also apparent from the importance of legislation introduced by back-benchers during the 1950's and 1960's. Legislation to eliminate capital punishment, for instance, was among the important proposals made

[20] I have omitted a discussion of private members' bills and private bills. The former, introduced by individual M.P.'s, usually concern relatively unimportant matters, although, on occasion, significant proposals that both parties deem too controversial have been introduced as private members' bills. Private bills have a personal or local application only and originate mainly with local authorities.

[21] The best treatment of parliamentary influence is to be found in Butt, *Power of Parliament.* For a contrary view see John P. Mackintosh, *The British Cabinet* (London: Stevens and Sons, 1968).

through private members' bills during these two decades. While the Wilson government in 1964 unanimously favored such a measure, its fear of electoral consequences prevented it from introducing legislation to secure this reform. Earlier legislation reducing the number of crimes to which the death penalty could be applied was also introduced by back-benchers, and decided on "free" votes—that is, parliamentary votes in which members are not obliged to vote according to party dictates. Measures designed to lighten penalties against homosexuals and to ease restrictions on abortions were also introduced, in 1964 and 1966 respectively, by M.P.'s; once again the Wilson cabinet favored the proposals but was too fearful of voter reaction to associate itself officially with the reform measures.

7. PARLIAMENT: INVESTIGATING AND CONTROLLING

The decline of parliamentary power in decision-making. can, as we have just noted, be exaggerated. True, the House of Commons no longer legislates in the sense that it did for a short time in the late eighteenth and nineteenth centuries; nor does Parliament really overturn governments. And without question, the principal loci of power and authority are to be found in the majority party, the government, and the prime minister. Yet despite the ties of party and the power of the government, the Commons retains a sense of being a group that can and does transcend party lines and influence policy. It is this sense—of identity, of history, of importance—that today leads Parliament to fulfill, aside from its legitimizing function, the roles of critic, educator, and public spokesman. These roles are closely related to one another. Parliamentary debates over legislation, the questioning of government policy by M.P.'s, and the use of legislative devices for investigating government actions or social problems allow individuals and interest groups to express their views in the most important public forum in the nation. Further, they allow Parliament the opportunity to keep tabs on government operations and serve as part of the process by which the public is presented with alternative courses of action.

THE QUESTION PERIOD: Perhaps the most spectacular instrument used for these ends is the parliamentary question period, which lasts for about an hour at the beginning of proceedings in the Commons.[22] At this time, from Monday through Thursday, members receive oral answers to their questions on a wide range of matters that cannot effectively be handled in debate; usually these involve departmental policies in pursuance of a law and individual or group grievances. The questions either seek information or press for action, and supplementary questions arising out of the original answer may be allowed at the discretion of the speaker. The person to whom the question is addressed must be officially responsible for the subject matter; ministers, for instance, have refused to answer certain questions having to do with nationalized industries, which are operated as quasi-independent public corporations.

The questions and the supplementaries can provide some painful moments for ministers and their departments; but they can also provide the stimulus for important policy changes. A well-known case of the 1920's is described by Sir Ivor Jennings as follows:

On 17 May 1928, Mr T. Johnston, by private notice, asked the Home Secretary "whether he was aware that on Tuesday, the 15th of May, about 1:50 p.m., two police officers called at the place of business of Miss Savidge, and without affording her any opportunity of communicating with her parents or legal advisers . . . conveyed her to Scot-

[22] The practice dates from the early nineteenth century, but it did not really develop until the twentieth, when the combination of disciplined parties and the government's monopoly of parliamentary time began to seriously inhibit the back-bencher's chances to participate in the initiation of policy.

land Yard, and that there she was questioned by two police officers for a period exceeding five hours; and whether such action was authorized by the right hon. gentleman in connection with his inquiry into the Sir Leo Money Case?" The Home Secretary returned a soft answer, giving some information, and stating that he was making inquiries. Further questions followed, producing a telephoned message from Scotland Yard which, being read by the minister, was interrupted with cries of "Shame!" At the end of the questions Mr Johnston moved the adjournment of the House. . . . A debate took place the same evening . . . (and) the Home Secretary . . . consented to a public inquiry. The inquiry resulted in some criticism of the police, and a Royal Commission then examined the whole question of police powers and practice.[23]

More recently, charges by a daily newspaper in 1967 that private outgoing and incoming cables were being scrutinized by the British security services prompted a storm of questions to the prime minister. Wilson attempted to fudge the issue, but after a series of supplementary questions he was forced to concede the need for an impartial inquiry into the allegations.

Most questions do not produce quite such dramatic results. In fact, most questions are handled through written answers, and most complaints through private negotiation. Nevertheless, questions can be telling; they can also serve as an opportunity for an ambitious —or resentful—M.P. to have his say and, if he is clever enough into the bargain, to score a point. Further, they mollify the back-bencher with a feeling of having some dialectic weapons at his disposal, thus bolstering both pride in the house and self-esteem. Finally, questions can, in the hands of one well practiced in posing them, provide the necessary comic relief to start the day off right, as

in the following exchange in 1958 between Gerald Nabarro, a back-bencher, and Jocilyn Simon, then chancellor of the exchequer:

55. Mr. Nabarro asked the Chancellor of the Exchequer when the regulation was introduced laying down that doorknockers 5 inches or more in length shall be free of tax whereas doorknockers under that length carry 30 per cent. Purchase Tax. . . .

Mr. Simon: Following consultation with the trade, doorknockers over 4¾ inches long have been treated as free of tax under a relief for builders' hardware introduced in 1948. . . .

Mr. Nabarro: Why is there this invidious distinction between doorknocking nutcrackers and nutcracking doorknockers—

Mr. Speaker: Order.

Mr. Nabarro: This is an invidious distinction, Mr. Speaker.

Mr. Speaker: It may be an invidious distinction, as the hon. Member says, but I rather think he is now anticipating Question No. 56. Is not that about nutcrackers?

Mr. Nabarro: I understood the Financial Secretary to say that he was answering the Questions together. It is a quite understandable mistake, because that is how the Chancellor of the Exchequer generally rides off these difficulties. Will my hon. and learned Friend put this matter into good order?

Mr. Speaker: The hon. Member should ask Question No. 56 if he wants to get on to the subject of nutcrackers.

56. Mr. Nabarro asked the Chancellor of the Exchequer whether he is aware that, in view of the fact that a nutcracker is liable to Purchase Tax at 15 per cent. whereas a doorknocker over 5 inches in length is free of tax, there is an increasing practice of supplying nutcrackers with screw holes so that they could theoretically be used as doorknockers, with the result that with such modification these nutcrackers become free of tax; and what instructions have been issued to Customs and Excise staff with regard to this matter.

[23] Sir Ivor Jennings, *Parliament*, 2nd ed. (Cambridge: Cambridge University Press, 1957), p. 105.

Mr. Simon: No, Sir; I do not think Customs staff need instructions to help them distinguish a nutcracker from a doorknocker.

Mr. Nabarro: Now will my hon. and learned Friend apply himself to the Question that I have put to him? Why is there this invidious distinction between doorknocking nutcrackers and nutcracking doorknockers? Is he aware that this is a perfectly well known device, practiced by manufacturers? I have evidence of it in my hand. Is he aware that this ridiculous position, which was mentioned in a leading article in The Times *on 11th February, is bringing the whole of the Purchase Tax Schedules into disrepute? Is it not time that the matter was drastically overhauled by abolition of the Purchase Tax and substitution of a sales turnover tax at a very small and uniform rate over the whole field?*

Mr. Simon: My hon. Friend tempts me to reply in the words of the conductor Richter to the second flute at Covent Garden—"Your damned nonsense can I stand twice or once, but . . . always, by God, never."[24]

COMMITTEES FOR INVESTIGATING AND CONTROLLING ADMINISTRATION: It is not quite accurate to say that the British parliament has no specialized committees. The Commons has from time to time created select committees to investigate special matters of a factual nature, although for the most part these have lacked adequate staffs and the power to compel testimony. Again, governments have been loath to appoint committees because of their fear that party discipline might be subverted, preferring to use other methods of gathering information, chief among them being the research and investigation conducted by the ministries. Even so, demands for alternate sources of parliamentary information have become more and more frequent, and in recent years three new select committees have been created. In 1956 the House of Commons set up a quasi-perma-

nent select committee on nationalized industries; pressure for creating the committee stemmed from the fact that nationalized industries are more or less independent, and hence, ministers can refuse to answer questions about their operations. Further, the problem of evaluating the efficiency of those operations is sufficiently complex to inhibit Parliament's effective control over them without professional assistance. The committee was given the power of subpoena and was authorized to have a small staff. To date, it has served a very useful function, bringing to light and evaluating important information that might not otherwise have been available.

In January 1967 the house established two more select committees: one to deal with the general problems of science and technology, the other to review agricultural problems. Both committees were also given the power to subpoena persons and records, and to recruit small staffs. The creation of these two committees was regarded as an experiment which, if successful, would lead to the appointment of a number of other committees paralleling the government's departments. The purview of the science and technology committee crossed departmental lines, but it has continued to work without arousing much controversy; the agriculture committee, however, quickly came into direct conflict with the ministry it was to oversee. The upshot was that the agriculture minister and various civil servants complained about increased workloads and excessive interference, and after an extensive battle the committee was disbanded in 1969. At the same time, however, several other select committees were created, including one on race relations.

Other select committees that have been in existence for some time and oversee the expenditure of public funds are the public accounts and the estimates committees. Both are nonpartisan. The chairman of the accounts committee, which is concerned with insuring that money is spent for authorized purposes only, is usually a prominent mem-

[24] Quoted in D. N. Chester and N. Bowring, *Questions in Parliament* (London: William Collins and Co., Ltd., 1961), p. 247.

ber of the opposition. The estimates committee engages in constant spot checks on expenditures in an attempt to determine whether government economies can be made. Since both groups have the power of subpoena, they resemble in some ways the legislative committees of the American congress and are respected by the bureaucracy.

The House of Commons and the House of Lords have each created a select committee on statutory instruments. Both were formed in response to Parliament's tendency to legislate in only the most general terms, thus granting to the government and bureaucracy the authority to make legal policy through the issuance of administrative decrees in the form of statutory instruments. The annual number of such decrees increased from 986 in 1906 to more than two thousand a year in the 1960's, and it became obvious that the instruments, are, in fact, a form of legislation. As of now, all decrees must lie before Parliament for forty days, during which time a member may move a "prayer" to annul the instrument. The function of the two committees is to draw the attention of their houses to an instrument if it believes that the parliament as a whole may wish to consider its legality. Many critics, however, complain that only a small proportion of the decrees issued receive adequate attention.

CONSTITUENTS AND THE PARLIAMENTARY COMMISSIONER: The control that the government exercises over legislation, the importance of party allegiance, and the national character of British politics have all had their effect on the relationship between M.P. and constituent, and have contributed to the fact that British M.P.'s spend less time receiving delegations from interest groups or visits from constituents than do American, French, or German legislators. Most M.P.'s do, however, hold "surgeries," during which they serve as a combination of social worker and legal adviser. They can and do intercede for constituents in cases where they feel that legal rights have been ignored or abrogated by administrative bodies. And, as indicated

earlier, parliamentarians do use the Commons to raise questions brought to their attention by the public.

The increasing influence of administrative agencies and tribunals in the day-to-day life of British citizens led to the creation in 1967 of a parliamentary commissioner to deal with citizens' complaints against administrators. The commissioner is an officer of Parliament and can act only on complaints referred to him by M.P.'s. He has no executive power, and his jurisdiction extends solely to central ministries; he has no authority to investigate local officials or the nationalized industries. He informs the M.P. who asked his intercession of the disposition of cases, and he is expected to submit annual and special reports to a parliamentary committee. Thus far, the influence of the new post has been marginal; indeed, in one recent case the foreign office rejected a commissioner's report and refused to allow the committee to investigate the matter further.

ROYAL COMMISSIONS: Royal commissions are, strictly speaking, created by the crown, and hence the government—usually in response to parliamentary or public pressure. Every effort is made to secure opposition approval of the appointees, because theoretically royal commissions undertake the investigation of problems transcending party lines. They have, of course, been used by governments to avoid responsibility for dealing with potentially explosive issues. Nevertheless, during their long history royal commissions have been the source of a good deal of significant legislation, including the first factory acts of the mid-nineteenth century. They have been somewhat less important in the twentieth century, although they have been used to good advantage in clarifying problems pertaining to freedom of the press, the relation of the police to the public, the penal system, and the organization of trade unions.

The commissions are composed of members of Parliament as well as private citizens. A prominent public figure is usually named chairman, and a civil servant from a department concerned with the matter at hand almost invariably serves as secretary. An effort is made to secure the representation of a cross-section of social and professional backgrounds and political tendencies, as well as the services of men whose judgment is likely to be accepted by the community at large. Commission members are not compensated, but they may make use of a paid staff. They cannot compel witnesses to appear or give oaths, nor can they demand the submission of documents, unless the commission's charter specifically gives them that authority.

The use of tribunals of inquiry and royal commissions once again underlines the uniqueness of British political culture: their use demonstrates the willingness to accept the idea that there are disinterested citizens who can command the respect of the community and who can be called upon to investigate important matters and provide an objective answer to divisive issues. Such an attitude not only reflects the community's traditional deference to a social and cultural elite, it also reveals a continuing belief that there is a community interest that can somehow be discovered and at least partially removed from the realm of politics. More sharply divided societies have found it almost impossible to develop such persuasive instruments. In the United States there is no elite to command the national respect and deference that England's does.

This also must be said, however: royal commissions have served to maintain a sense of community by preventing irreparable alienation over highly controversial issues. Yet with the decline of that particular kind of civility hitherto so characteristic of British life, it is open to question whether such commissions can long continue to serve the same function.

8. THOSE DIGNIFIED ASPECTS

THE HOUSE OF LORDS: Although it is not totally devoid of purpose, the House of Lords has little or no political significance in contemporary Britain. The Conservatives regard it as having a certain social utility, mainly that of adding dignity to the status of the peerage itself, but many in the Labor Party believe that it is a complete anachronism. Even though they are not as hostile to the institution as they were in the more militant period of the Labor movement, they would not be unhappy to see it wither away. It was under the Attlee government in 1949, in fact, that the power of the House of Lords to delay ordinary legislation was further reduced—to about six months. Even this limited prerogative has been used sparingly by the Lords.

This is not to say that the Lords serve no function. The house has done some very useful work examining private bills and amending hastily drawn public ones. It has also conducted intelligent, leisurely debates about important matters of public policy—debates which the Commons, caught up in its more rigid timetable, was unable to hold. To be sure, there is some question whether anyone was really listening, and whether these same functions could not be performed more satisfactorily by a reformed House of Commons.

The Conservative Party attempted in 1958 to bolster the prestige of the House of Lords. With the thought, perhaps, of eventually adding to the Lords' power, the Macmillan government initiated, and Parliament enacted, legislation for the creation of life peers—men who would be rewarded for public service by being given titles and seats in the house, but who could not pass their titles to their heirs. At about the same time, all peers were granted a small allowance for each day of attendance. The creation of life peers has not really changed the composition of the House of Lords, although the proportion of Labor supporters—still a small minority—is increasing; the fact is that most of them would probably have been granted hereditary peerages in any event. It is worth pointing out that about half of the Lords' membership consists of peers of the first creation, that is, persons granted peerages for outstanding service. In 1963, as the result of the desire of one Labor

THE ROYAL WARRANT

ELIZABETH R   ⎫
                                     ⎪   Signed
                                     ⎬   on behalf
                                     ⎪   of
MARGARET   ⎭   Her Majesty

ELIZABETH THE SECOND, by the Grace of God of the United Kingdom of Great Britain and Northern Ireland and of Our other Realms and Territories QUEEN, Head of the Commonwealth, Defender of the Faith, To

Our Right Trusty and Well-beloved Counsellor Hartley William, Baron Shawcross, one of Our Counsel learned in the Law:

Our Trusty and Well-beloved:—
Sir Graham Cunningham, Knight Commander of Our Most Excellent Order of the British Empire;
  Robert Browning, Esquire, Commander of Our Most Excellent Order of the British Empire:
  William Brian Reddaway, Esquire;
  William James Percival Webber, Esquire,

                                                               Greeting!

WHEREAS We have deemed it expedient that a Commission should forthwith issue to examine the economic and financial factors affecting the production and sale of newspapers, magazines and other periodicals in the United Kingdom, including (a) manufacturing, printing, distribution and other costs; (b) efficiency of production; and (c) advertising and other revenue, including any revenue derived from interests in television; to consider whether these factors tend to diminish diversity of ownership and control or the number or variety of such publications, having regard to the importance, in the public interest, of the accurate presentation of news and the free expression of opinion:

Now KNOW YE that We, reposing great trust and confidence in your knowledge and ability, have authorised and appointed, and do by these Presents authorise and appoint you the said Hartley William, Baron Shawcross, Sir Graham Cunningham, Robert Browning, William Brian Reddaway and William James Percival Webber to be Our Commissioners for the purposes of the said inquiry:

M.P. to continue serving in the Commons, legislation was passed allowing individuals to renounce their titles. The most important effect of the law was to permit Lord Home to serve in the House of Commons as prime minister.

Today there are approximately 950 persons eligible to sit in the House of Lords. Actually, those present average about a hundred, and no more than sixty to seventy are regular attenders. In order to limit the possibility of the regulars being suddenly outflanked by "backwoodsmen" who might show up to vote on one or two issues, all peers must reply to a royal writ of summons at the beginning of each session, or be deemed to have taken a leave of absence. Since party lines are far less significant and votes are without real party significance, the House of Lords does have some corporate sense and there is less attempt to score debating points.

THE MONARCHY: Before the Norman Conquest, the power of the British monarch, as we have already seen, was comparatively

AND for the better effecting the purposes of this Our Commission, We do by these Presents give and grant unto you, or any three or more of you, full power to call before you such persons as you shall judge likely to afford you any information upon the subject of this Our Commission; to call for information in writing; and also to call for, have access to and examine all such books, documents, registers and records as may afford you the fullest information on the subject and to inquire of and concerning the premises by all other lawful ways and means whatsoever:

AND We do by these Presents authorise and empower you, or any of you, to visit and personally inspect such places as you may deem it expedient so to inspect for the more effectual carrying out of the purposes aforesaid:

AND We do by these Presents will and ordain that this Our Commission shall continue in full force and virtue, and that you, Our said Commissioners, or any three or more of you may from time to time proceed in the execution thereof, and of every matter and thing therein contained, although the same be not continued from time to time by adjournment.

AND We do further ordain that you, or any three or more of you, have liberty to report your proceedings under this Our Commission from time to time if you shall judge it expedient so to do:

AND Our further will and pleasure is that you do, with as little delay as possible, report to Us your opinion upon the matters herein submitted for your consideration.

Given at Our Court at Saint James's the fourth day of March, 1961;
In the Tenth Year of Our Reign.

By Her Majesty's Command.
R. A. BUTLER.

Royal Commission on
the Press

Mr. W. J. P. Webber was appointed a Commander of the Most Excellent Order of the British Empire in January, 1962.

Source: Great Britain, *Report of the Royal Commission on the Press,* Cmnd. 1811 (London: HMSO, 1962), pp. 2–3.

---

tenuous. The Plantagenets gradually strengthened the position of the king, and by the time of the Tudors, the throne was the focus of power in the realm. Beginning with the Stuarts, however, the emergence of new political and societal forces challenged the omnipotence of the monarch and eventually succeeded in surmounting his position of authority; by the middle of the nineteenth century, the crown's real power was a thing of the past.

By that time, too, the popularity of the monarchy had sunk to a new low. Liberal reformers who wished to rationalize the political system had little use for such an anachronistic institution, and the general conduct of George IV had certainly failed to engender mass affection. As the *Times* put it on the occasion of his death in 1830:

There never was an individual less regretted by his fellow-creatures than this deceased King. What eye has wept for him? What heart has heaved one sob of unmercenary sorrow? . . . Has not his successor gained more upon the English tastes and

*prepossessions of his subjects by the blunt
and unaffected—even should it be grotesque
—cordiality of his demeanour, within a few
short weeks than George IV—that Leviathan
of haut ton—ever did during the sixty years
of his existence? If George IV ever had a
friend . . . we protest that the name of him
or her never reached us.*[25]

The reign of Victoria brought renewed
popularity to the throne, not only because of
her image, but also because Victorian England enjoyed unprecedented prosperity and
power. Nevertheless, the prerogatives of the
sovereign were being simultaneously stripped
away. For the most part, Victoria accepted
this inevitability with grace; she did, of
course, balk from time to time, and it was
only after repeated urgings that she finally
acquiesced in relinquishing more and more
royal prerogatives. With her death, it was
clear that the monarchy had become primarily an ornament.

In the meantime, the antimonarchical sentiment of the Liberals had all but completely
disappeared. With the king at last relatively
impotent, it was hard to become overwrought
about the crown as an institution. While
there was some antimonarchical feeling in the
left wing of the Labor Party in its early years,
this, too, never amounted to much. The
working class, while it might be self-conscious about its social position, was itself
strongly attached to the institution. During
the 1936 crisis over the desire of Edward
VIII to marry an American divorcée, even
the Communist *Daily Worker* joined with
other newspapers in a self-imposed censorship, while American newspapers printed
every detail of the "scandal."

The honor with which George VI invested
the crown during the war years and the coronation of Elizabeth II brought an upsurge in
the popularity of the monarchy, and the coronation itself was a vivid emotional experience

for most Englishmen. Shortly thereafter,
however, manifestations of disenchantment
reappeared. Increasingly, the institution has
been satirized and criticized, and the royal
family has found it can no longer rely upon
the self-restraint of the fourth estate to protect its privacy. The court, with all its para-
phernalia and tradition, remains; but ever
larger numbers of Englishmen find it irrelevant.

The lasting power of the monarchy in the
first "modern" state has long been the subject
of comment and conjecture by foreign, and
especially American, observers. They have
explained its survival primarily in functional
terms: it is a symbol not only of national
unity but of the unity of the Commonwealth,
albeit a vanishing Commonwealth, and it
is a source of personal identification and
pageantry in a dull, drab world. This may all
be true, as are the counterarguments of
critics to the effect that the crown perpetuates
an archaic, class-conscious, snobbish culture.
But none of these rationalizations, either pro
or con, explains the longevity of the English monarchy. Americans, Germans, and
Frenchmen have, after all, the same socially
functional requirements as Englishmen, but
lack a king.

The United States has historically been
defined by a set of ideas: the Declaration of
Independence and the Constitution, documents that represent, in essence, the eighteenth-century liberal view of the world. The
British monarchy, on the other hand, has no
real ideological continuity with the past. At
one time it was an integral part of a feudal
society in which it combined dignity with
power. Today only the dignity remains.

If the monarchy does not, like the American Constitution, stand for a set of political
ideas handed down from the past, what does
it stand for? To raise the question in this way
is to answer it. It represents the British community *qua* community, not only at the present moment but in its total development. To
be sure, the monarchy could not have survived if it had not relinquished political

[25] Quoted in Kingsley Martin, *The Crown and the
Establishment* (London: Penguin Books, Ltd., 1963),
p. 23.

power gracefully, that is, if it had not agreed to be lifted out of the realm of politics. In this regard, its survival is, in part, an historical accident. Yet the accident could not have occurred were it not for the cultural role the English monarchy has played.

For better or for worse, the monarchical tradition seems to be proving more and more dysfunctional in the modern world. With the decline of British power, the halo that once surrounded the English crown is disappearing at a proportionate pace. When the Puritan revolution triumphed temporarily in England, both the monarchy and the House of Lords were abolished. The revolutionaries believed that both institutions were not only useless but dangerous; so, too, did the liberals of the nineteenth century. Sentiment today for the elimination of kings and lords is not very strong, and demands for their abolition are rarely heard, but one suspects that both institutions are in the incontrovertible process of simply fading away.

9. BRITISH INTEREST GROUPS AND POLITICS[26]

In the eighteenth century, parliamentary politics revolved largely about personal, regional, and economic interests. By modern standards, most of the legislation was private, local, and facultative. Even that which seemed to concern general national policies had local implications, and M.P.'s dealt with it as agents of local interests.

The two Canal Acts of 1762 and 1766 are cases in point: both set off the canal boom of the late eighteenth century, but their enactment was essentially an example of parochial interests at work in Parliament. The first act, which provided for a canal to reduce the cost of transportation between Manchester and Liverpool, was sponsored by the duke of Bridgewater and supported by the city of Liverpool and by powerful aristocratic

factions with whom the duke was associated through marriage. The opposition consisted of a few groups of traders, certain gentry whose land the canal would pass through or near, and the Mersey and Irewell Navigation Company, which had a monopoly on river transportation between Liverpool and Manchester. The bill was considered by a select committee chaired by one of the duke's allies, and was introduced into the House of Commons by the member who sat for his pocket borough of Brackley.[27] Its passage took four months; the major struggle was in the House of Commons, where numerous petitions for and against were received and pressures exerted on M.P.'s to secure their support.

The rise of liberalism and democracy and the Reform Bill of 1832 all combined to change the pattern of interest-group politics. For one thing, increased popular participation in politics resulted in the founding of mass organizations such as the Anti–Corn Law League, which attempted to whip up public support in favor of repealing protective duties on imported grain. For another, Liberals tended to frown on the direct representation of interests in Parliament; members with a direct financial interest in particular matters were excluded from private bill committees, and their votes in the house were even subject to disallowance.

Nevertheless, parliamentary activity still pivoted about group rather than party interests. One of the most powerful of these special-interest groups during the middle of the nineteenth century was the railroad clique, which was heavily represented in Parliament; of the 815 M.P.'s who sat from 1841 to 1847, 145 were railway directors. In the

---

26 Much of the historical analysis in this section is drawn from Samuel E. Beer's *British Politics in the Collectivist Age* (New York: Alfred A. Knopf, 1965).

27 The term "pocket borough" applies to constituencies which, before the Reform Bill of 1832, were "owned" by the gentry or the crown in that they contained small populations whose voting behavior could be guaranteed through bribery or coercion. Bright young men of impecunious background often sought—and were sought out by members of the aristocracy—to serve as M.P.'s from these constituencies. Naturally, they often served the interests of their benefactors.

early days of railway legislation, those proposing measures to authorize the construction of a line found themselves locked in conflict with canal and turnpike interests, and extremely expensive legislative battles ensued. The struggle over the Liverpool and Manchester Railway in 1824 to 1826 is estimated to have exacted some £80,000 in parliamentary expenses.

Later in the nineteenth century the power of the railroad interest declined as the political muscle of industrial capital and organized labor began to be flexed. But of greater importance as a cause in the changing pattern of parliamentary activity was the increasing cohesion of parties and the pressure of public business; the growing concern of M.P.'s with national problems and national policy quite naturally affected the operation of interest groups. The rise of the Labor Party was yet another factor in the changing political orientation of Parliament, since the major producer interests—that is, workers and entrepreneurs—were usually segregated into one or the other political party. Moreover, the producer groups were organizing into a small number of associations—a process encouraged by the government. At the same time, the political weight of local and religious interests declined in importance as massive industrialization further homogenized British social life. Finally, the emergence of the welfare state meant that interest-group involvement in the formation and implementation of government policy was growing apace.

Between the two world wars, and even immediately after the war period, the politics of groups was of far less importance in England than in France and the United States. Business groups settled in the Conservative Party, while the Labor Party was primarily concerned with the interests of trade unions. At least as important, the impetus of the Labor Party was ideological. Rhetorically, at least, it was less interested in aggregating the interests of diverse groups than in implementing a particular program. Since the 1950's the parties have modified their attitude toward special-interest groups. This is not to say that ideological politics has disappeared or that all groups turn equally to both major parties; rather, it is to say that most groups are concerned with and enter into negotiations with both political parties—and vice versa. Further, while it is true that the Conservatives lean more toward business for support and Labor more to the trade unions, the situation is occasionally reversed in terms of public policy. The Conservatives, for example, can call upon business groups to make sacrifices that a Labor government cannot. On the other hand, as Harold Wilson demonstrated in 1966 and 1967, Labor can sometimes make demands upon the trade unions that a Conservative government would never consider.

Today, with some exceptions, Parliament is not the central focus of interest-group activity. The relative lack of localism in English politics, the pervasive importance of party, and the dominance of the cabinet mean that groups cannot expect to accomplish very much by attempting to woo a bloc of back-benchers. The government, since it will be held responsible for the overall effects of all public policy, must evaluate the demands of any special group within a fairly broad frame of political reference. Hence, unlike the American scene, where lobbyists seek out individual congressmen, especially those on influential committees, the principal efforts of British groups are now directed at the administration and the bureaucracy.

There are other variables, too, which make interest-group activity in England somewhat different in character from that of France or the United States. Englishmen still strongly believe that there exists a public interest which overrides group interests and that individual groups should not push too hard or too raucously to achieve their ends. Their belief is augmented by a continuing general commitment to civil behavior. Of course, this commitment does not always hold, as threatened doctors' strikes and wildcat industrial strikes indicate, and some of these attitudes are obviously eroding. But in a comparative perspective, the civility of British political behavior is astonishing.

In 1948, for example, certain members of the Licensed Victuallers' Defense League were considering a huge national campaign to force the government to lower taxes on beers, wines, and other alcoholic beverages. Most of the league leadership, however, was opposed to the idea. As the *Brewers' Journal* noted:

> . . . *the* . . . *approach* . . . *can leave the* . . . *Chancellor* [of the exchequer] *under no delusion as to the spontaneity of the proposed protest against the beer tax, even though the monster petition be launched at the psychological moment appointed by the experts in these matters. The plebiscitary rejection of the financial expedients of governments, though it still appears to be* . . . *operative in France, is in this country* . . . *obsolete. A reasoned argument* . . . *could derive no added weight from the appending to it of some thousands of signatures.*[28]

Four years later, to cite another example, the British Legion was urging the Conservative government to raise disability pensions from 45 shillings a week to ninety. The government endorsed an increase to 55 shillings a week, and its bill was passed by a nonparty vote in the Commons. Sir Ian Fraser, Legion president and a Conservative M.P., was chastised at the Legion's annual conference for not pressing its case more forcefully. Some conference delegates thought Fraser should have put down a motion demanding the original figure. However, after noting that the government had a majority of only six and could have conceivably been defeated on the issue if it were pressed, Fraser declared:

> *It would be an excessive use of political power to try and bring down a Government on an issue affecting a minority of the citizens*

> . . . *unless on an issue affecting the constitution or a matter of conscience or protest arising from prolonged negligence by Government.*[29]

Group pressures, naturally enough, continue to be exerted. They are, however, less open to public view than in the United States. At all stages in its administration of public affairs, the government seeks the advice and cooperation, if not the complete acquiescence, of the groups intimately involved with a particular law, and complex negotiations take place at all levels. Some of these contacts are informal. But even so, at least five hundred advisory committees attached to government ministries have been established for the purpose of bringing together civil servants and the representatives of interested associations to consult and bargain on a formal basis. Ministries often consult organizations well in advance of making legislative proposals or taking administrative action. Groups such as the Association of Municipal Corporations and the County Councils' Association have become very closely involved with all decisions made by ministries that deal with problems of local government.

The substantive role that an interest group can assume in the fashioning, passage, and implementation of English law can be seen from an examination of the circumstances surrounding the inception of the National Health Service.[30] Plans for some form of health service had been outlined in a white paper by the wartime coalition government in 1944, and the Labor government that came to office in 1945 immediately announced its intention to ask Parliament "to approve measures to provide a comprehensive scheme of insurance against industrial

28 Quoted in John D. Stewart, *British Pressure Groups* (London: Oxford University Press, 1958), p. 34.

29 *Ibid.*, p. 186.
30 The following analysis is based on James Christoph, "The Advent of the National Health Service," in James Christoph and Bernard Brown, eds., *Cases in Comparative Politics*, 2nd ed. (Boston: Little, Brown, 1969), pp. 35–74. Details on the provisions of the legislation can be found in Chapter 24, pp. 757–760.

injuries . . . to extend and improve the existing scheme of social insurance and to establish a national health service."

The drafting and administration of the legislation were to be the responsibility of the Ministry of Health. And the minister of health was Aneurin Bevan, a radical within the Labor Party, given to fiery speeches denouncing the "exploiting" classes—and not a figure particularly beloved by the British Medical Association (B.M.A.).

It took nine months from the time of Labor's election until the actual introduction of a health bill in Parliament. In these months Bevan and his subordinates engaged in unending negotiations with members of the medical association, and others, in drawing up the legislation. Bevan allowed the B.M.A. officials to make all the points and exercise all the persuasion they cared to, but he made it clear that the final decisions on the contents of the legislation would be made by the government. Given Bevan's personality and the B.M.A.'s suspicions, the negotiations did not endear either party to the other. But to the surprise of many B.M.A. officials, the health bill did not turn out to be as fearsome as they expected. In fact, when the details of the legislation were made public, it was obvious that Bevan had accepted a good many B.M.A. proposals. During parliamentary discussion of the health bill, debate centered on those secondary aspects that continued to disturb the medical profession, aspects that many Conservative and Liberal M.P.'s with medical connections feared would "enslave" the medical profession. They attempted through amendments to alleviate these misgivings; and Bevan, too, tried to calm their fears with a show of reasonableness.

After the bill had received a second reading and been approved in principle, it was sent to a committee. Again, those supporting the view of the medical profession tried to change a number of provisions. But by and large the Labor members stood firm, and only a few concessions were made. In mid-July the standing committee passed the bill back to the house substantially as it had been received, and it passed its third reading on July 26, 1946.

The bill was taken up by the House of Lords in October, and despite the preponderance of Conservatives in the upper house, debate was relatively mild. The Lords did tack on 13 amendments, but all but one were minor. The Commons accepted all but two of the Lords' amendments, rejecting the one major change, and the Lords acquiesced. The bill became law on November 6.

This, however, was by no means the end of the matter. The health act approved by Parliament presented only a broad outline for a National Health Service; but many procedural details remained to be worked out in discussions between the government and the medical association. The prospect was for fairly lengthy negotiations—except that they almost ended before they began. Shortly after passage of the bill, the B.M.A. polled its membership on the question of whether it should "enter into any discussions on the framework to be created within the limitations of the act." Ninety per cent of the doctors replied, and of these 64 per cent said "No." Fortified by this expression of constituency support, the B.M.A.'s council voted to break off negotiations with the Health Ministry.

Bevan responded to the threat of noncooperation with uncharacteristic restraint, suggesting that wiser counsels would prevail. He also stated that he remained fully prepared to work and consult with doctors in the implementation of the law. Turning to those in the profession who supported it, he indicated that many features of the act which disturbed the profession were still open to negotiation. At the same time, the ministry made some show of getting on with the process of framing health-service regulations. Bevan's tactics paid off. The B.M.A. reversed its earlier position and entered into tough bargaining sessions with the Health Ministry. The negotiations, most of which remained secret, continued through the spring and summer of 1947. When in December of 1947 Bevan reported on their results, it became apparent that he had conceded to the medical profession on all but two points: he did not meet the doctors' demands on remuneration (although he did narrow the difference between them and the government's original provision), and he refused to accept the B.M.A.'s demand that the act be amended to preclude the possibility of an administrative decision that might transform doctors into full-time civil servants. On this issue, he argued, the profession would simply have to accept his word that it would not become an adjunct of the government.

The concessions proved unsatisfactory to the B.M.A. In the first months of 1948 attacks upon the law in the *British Medical Journal* mounted—as did the virulence of the language used. The threat of a mass boycott of the service was raised, and by spring Bevan was willing to make new concessions. He promised that the law would be amended to guarantee that a full-time, salaried service would not be imposed upon the profession by regulation. He also vowed that other concessions would be made. But it is perhaps of even greater significance that on those few points he would not accept, Bevan remained the epitome of sweet reasonableness, couching his rejection in the most conciliatory terms.

In April 1948 another plebiscite was held by the B.M.A. While the profession, by a small majority, still indicated opposition to the health service, the vote was close enough for the council to urge that its members participate provided Bevan agree to continue negotiations on a few disputed issues. A Special Representative Assembly of the B.M.A., meeting on May 28, ratified the council's decision, and on July 5, 1948, the service officially began operations.

But the formal institution of the health service was by no means the end of the story. For in the decades since it became law, a good many changes have occurred. The B.M.A. and the Health Ministry have consulted and wrangled and negotiated on any number of aspects of the law, and occasionally there have been threats of strikes by the medical profession. Most of the negotiations, of course, have involved neither Parliament nor the government as a whole; rather they have been among the B.M.A., various advisory committees, and the civil servants in the Health Ministry. In short, public policy in this area, as in so many others, is continually being revised through talks between the government and the interest group. Only in the event of a really serious crisis do most matters pertaining to the adjustment or modification of public policy become the object of parliamentary attention.

10. SOME CONCLUSIONS

In the past several years, criticism by British intellectuals of their own institutions has become more and more insistent. They have charged that Parliament has declined in importance, that the cabinet is being converted into presidential government, and that both Parliament and the cabinet have surrendered control over large areas of public policy to the bureaucracy. The studied amateurism and aristocratic tradition of the Commons has been attacked for preventing Parliament from adequately fulfilling its purpose, and the secrecy with which both cabinet and bureaucracy operate has been castigated as undemocratic.

As we have seen, many of the arguments are less than accurate. All too frequently, they are ill-disguised attempts to find a scapegoat for England's difficulties—difficulties whose sources lie elsewhere. However, given the swift demise of the British Empire and the failure of her economy to grow apace with those of other European countries, it is not surprising that institutions once credited with being the source of English greatness should now be fingered as the cause of her "decline," nor that, in a world marked by increasing prestige for professional competence and greater demand for technical expertise, amateurism and ritual have come to seem not only outdated but a serious handicap.

In a comparative perspective, however, the British parliament remains one of the most effective political institutions in the world. Its capacity to arrive at fairly consistent general policies, to create an informed public, to safeguard the liberties of its citizens, and to maintain flexibility and a sense of national unity is still unequaled.

In the United States, for example, it is still very difficult for the electorate to know just who is responsible for what. Despite the increased power of the president, most sessions of Congress enact a confused grab bag of legislative proposals that rarely, if ever, represent a comprehensive program. Could the American electorate really evaluate the success or failure of the Johnson administration's war on poverty? How could such a fair determination be made when many of the elements the president regarded as necessary to the poverty program's success were either not accepted by Congress or not provided with the funds he considered adequate? In England, at least, the government in office has the time and the opportunity to develop and administer its program. If after four or five years the voters find the program unacceptable, they can, with legitimacy, throw its sponsors out.

The past success of the British form of government is not, of course, an argument against change. Political institutions can become obsolete as the problems faced by a society alter, and there is little point in maintaining traditions that no longer serve a purpose or command respect. The politics of England—of all European nations—has entered upon a new period of uncertainty. The forces that once bound the British to their traditions are weakening, and changes in the composition and outlook of both political parties are making it more difficult to maintain party discipline in traditional ways. Understandably, therefore, back-benchers are demanding a larger voice for Parliament in the process of making policy. In an era in which the problems faced by those responsible for national policy are increasingly complex, Parliament may well need new tools if it is to retain any effectiveness; consequently, many of the suggestions for reform—including more office space, secretarial staffs, and improved library facilities—seem sensible. A case can also be made for still more specialized committees on the American, German, or French order; yet even such minor structural modifications will inevitably be associated with a shift in the nature of the party system and a loss of some of the advantages of the present arrangements.

So many groups now participate in the political process that it has become more and more difficult for any government to act decisively. Indeed, the call is for new devolutions of authority at the very time that some of England's problems require effective and decisive national action. It may be that the crucial problem in British politics over the next ten years will be that of discovering new ways to mobilize public support for the very difficult choices with which the nation continues to be faced.

16

France:

From Parliamentary

to Presidential Government

1. INTRODUCTION

It has been the argument of this text that the instability and disorder of French governmental processes during the nineteenth century and much of the twentieth reflected the fragmentation of the French community and its inability to deal constructively with the vast problems created by France's transition from a traditional to a modern society. After 1870, the French attempted to create a parliamentary regime modeled on the English one. But what resulted was an entirely different approach to the business of governing: the French were unable to duplicate the English parliamentary system simply because the institutions and attitudes that supported England's regime were absent in France. It was impossible in France both to develop a party system that could aggregate the interests of Frenchmen into a smaller number of coherent, alternative programs and to create governments that could govern. Such was the dimension of conflicts that beset French society that it was almost equally difficult to develop lasting agreement on the rules of the political game.

The advent of the de Gaulle regime in 1958 provided France with ten years of relative political stability. Basing his power on a new constitution establishing a quasi-presidential regime, on his personal charisma, and on an overwhelming popular desire for a steady hand in the Elysée Palace, Charles de Gaulle succeeded in restructuring certain aspects of French society in fairly fundamental ways. He capitalized on the social, economic, and political changes that had taken place in France after World War II, and because he was able to translate into action so many of the essential and unrealized desires of his countrymen, he was also able to preside over a nation in which the pace of modernization had suddenly accelerated.

This chapter will deal first with the governmental processes of the Third and Fourth Republics, focusing primarily upon the relation between those processes and the other aspects of the French political and social systems which have been discussed in earlier chapters. References will be made to the English pattern of government, for comparisons between the two nations can increase our understanding of both. Finally, we will examine the governmental institutions of the Fifth Republic in an effort to throw some light on the future of French politics.

2. PARLIAMENTARY GOVERNMENT

The first meeting of the Estates-General of the Kingdom of France was held in Paris on April 10, 1302. As in England, the three estates of the realm—the nobility, the higher clergy, and the people—were represented, although from the beginning the third estate met separately. However, while the English parliament commenced an existence that was to be almost uninterrupted until full sovereignty was placed in its hands, the Estates-General met only 42 times in little more than three hundred years. Agents of the king disbanded it in 1615, and no further meetings were held until 1789. The failure of the Estates-General to increase its influence and to transform itself into a genuine parliament was a direct reflection of the fragmentation of the French realm and the rise of absolutism.

At the meeting convened in 1789, the third estate demanded that all three estates meet in one assembly, and that the veto power held by the nobility and the higher clergy be abolished. Its point was quickly won, and the Estates-General was transformed into a National Assembly which drew up France's first constitution.

THE THIRD REPUBLIC: From the French Revolution to the Franco-Prussian War, the French experience with parliamentary government was, to say the least, checkered. Only with the downfall of the Second Empire was a parliamentary regime exhibiting any real stability created. The institutional structure of the Third Republic—which lasted from 1871 to 1940—superficially resembled that of England, especially after the decline of the French president's power. But in actuality the two political systems functioned quite differently. The continued existence of a mul-

tiplicity of ideological factions and parties meant that cabinets were of necessity coalitions; to become a member of the French government, therefore—and especially to become premier—one had to obtain the support of a wide range of groups rather than of a single party. Furthermore, the fragility of any French government meant that maintaining oneself in office required considerable political dexterity; it also meant that cabinet members, each hoping to use a political crisis to advantage, could never constitute a body with a sense of collective responsibility. Secrets were invariably leaked, internal dissension constantly flared, and each member of the government was continually tempted to gently knife his colleagues in order to improve his own position.

Of course, no wise man would act in such a way as to completely destroy a colleague, thus establishing the reputation for being too ruthless, which would weaken rather than strengthen his political position with fellow parliamentarians. The destruction of a government had to be accomplished with finesse and within the rules of the discordant game of musical chairs that became a regular part of the French parliamentary scene. Successful candidates for the premiership and other cabinet positions, therefore, tended to be nonideological brokers—men of balance, with sympathy and understanding for a variety of positions, but no strong commitment to any.[1] They also tended to be men capable of satisfying the fairly narrow demands of particular interests. To be sure, in times of crisis, when crucial decisions could no longer be put off, dynamic leaders such as Clemenceau might be invested with tremendous power. But such men rarely lasted beyond the immediate crisis; their power was feared and distrusted,

---

[1] A recent study of the Fourth Republic notes that former and potential French cabinet members were less likely to vote to bring down a government than were ordinary deputies. In this particular regard, the Third Republic was very much like the Fourth. See Duncan MacRae, Jr., *Parliament Parties and Society in France: 1946–1958* (New York: Saint Martin's Press, 1967), pp. 181–229.

and their actions invariably alienated too many special interests.

With the French executive a constitutional weakling, the effective locus of power was the legislature. But its disunity, as well as the cumbersome size of both the Chamber of Deputies and the Senate, uniformly resulted in chaos. It was almost impossible to establish a reasonable timetable for considering legislation, and, in many cases, to set realistic limits on debate. Yet legislation had to receive some attention, if only so deputies might engage in those minimal actions that permit the system to survive, and to satisfy— for their own survival—at least some of the demands of their constituents. Both houses, therefore, set up a complex series of committees that in many ways resembled the American pattern. Their function was to write, examine, and press for legislation— and to serve as a device for burying measures that deputies had to introduce in order to pacify special interests but were not anxious to have considered. The committees also served as watchdogs over the state bureaucracy, preventing it from stepping out of line —a task that was all the more important, since the weakness of the executive prevented it from exercising the kind of control over the bureaucracy that the English cabinet could.

Not surprisingly, the power of French legislative committees attracted men of considerable competence and ambition. The absence of effective, disciplined party organizations also enhanced the position of committees as a major source of expertise for members of the parliament, performing a function similar to that of legislative committees in the United States. Competition for committee assignments was fierce: only as a member of the right committee could one wield wide power or hope to secure passage of legislation in which one's personal interest was involved.

Government bills were first submitted to the relevant committee, which had the right to amend them or to introduce its own version of the proposed law. If the legislation

were of paramount importance, its defeat could mean the resignation of the government. Since all members of important committees were anxious to become ministers, even if only for a short time, strong pressures developed to effect precisely such a collapse. The committee *rapporteur's* role was especially popular, since it was he who delivered the committee's report, and many promising politicians entered upon their first ministerial posts as the result of a telling attack upon a particular piece of government legislation. In essence the whole legislative situation was one that encouraged impassioned speeches and opposition for the sake of rhetoric and opposition.

The deficiencies of the system were, furthermore, self-generating. The manner in which governments were made and unmade, for example, also helped to undermine party discipline. Time after time, deputies broke party lines to bring down existing governments in the hope of entering a new one— or they supported a particular government with the same end in view. Only the Communists, and to a lesser extent the Socialists, were able to maintain a semblance of party cohesion.

Many attempts were made to strengthen the executive, but all of them failed. Proposals for a quasi-presidential form of government that might afford stability were opposed by the left because they were considered reactionary. Suggestions to strengthen the prime minister's office were persistently put forth by those parties that believed they could benefit from such a change, but they were opposed by others, especially on the left, who considered a stronger premier a threat to their interests. This position was even truer of the Radicals than the Socialists; the former, aside from doctrinal considerations that caused them to be suspicious of all authority, believed that a more powerful executive would jeopardize their own position as a government broker.

Actually, the premier possessed far more potential power than he was able to exercise.

The Third Republic's "constitution" had placed the authority to dissolve the chamber of deputies in the hands of the president, and, constitutionally, the premier could have assumed this authority as he had assumed other presidential prerogatives. This was exactly what had happened in England, where the power of the monarch to dissolve Parliament had been assumed by the prime minister. Many French commentators, misreading the English scene, thought that the English prime minister's power to dissolve Parliament explained the stability of British governments, because, they argued, if deputies knew that bringing down a government would precipitate a new election, they would think twice before voting to do so.

France, however, was not England. The fragmentation of the political system, the fixity of voting patterns, and the lack of discipline in most parties meant that single elections hardly ever resulted in a fundamental shift in the balance of power in the legislature, as it usually did under a two-party system. Any premier who dissolved Parliament would only have made himself very unpopular with legislators for having forced them to fight an election for nothing. For him to dissolve Parliament, then, would have been tantamount to committing political suicide.

French governments, consequently, rose and fell without new elections being held. One set of ministers was replaced by another set on the basis of intra-parliamentary negotiations, much as had been the case in England before the rise of the two-party system. And the governments did not, on the whole, differ very much from one another. After all, there were only a limited number of politicians who could hope to secure the backing of even a temporary majority, and these "ministrables," as they were called, were potential premiers or ministers only because it was understood that they would not rock the boat too much.

The negative features of the French parliamentary system during the Third Republic should not be overstated. Differences of principle were indeed important, and many deputies did decide issues primarily on this basis. It is also true that in times of crisis the French political system often produced leaders who could make meaningful decisions. Nevertheless, the system itself corrupted those who took part in it. French politics during the Third Republic was tarnished by scandal after scandal and, perhaps more important, by the kind of cynicism within and without Parliament that could only bring the system itself into disrepute and eventually ruin it. Repeatedly, men of wisdom and courage arose only to be defeated by forces over which they had no control.

In the last analysis, of course, the weaknesses of French government lay not in the political institutions, but in the cleavages that rent French society so deeply that no one group was strong enough to overcome them. France was, in the words of one author, a "stalemate" society; its institutions reflected that fact. It should be pointed out, nevertheless, that these institutions did manage to preserve a kind of tenuous balance that prevented the renewal of civil war and a framework of order that permitted periods of reasonably rapid economic development. Before World War I, this was quite enough: France was a rather prosperous country. In the interwar period it was not sufficient, and the essential impotence of French political institutions contributed finally to the nation's inability to cope with its monumental domestic and international problems.

THE FOURTH REPUBLIC: The constitution of the Fourth Republic represented an attempt to correct some of the weaknesses of the Third. A list system of proportional representation was established to strengthen party discipline. The Senate was replaced by an almost powerless Council of the Republic in order to reduce the number of interests and combinations of interests with which French governments invariably had to contend. Moreover, the authority of the cabinet was broadened. But none of these changes worked, and within a very short time the Fourth Republic came to resemble its predecessor. Yet its internal deficiencies did not destroy it, and if it had not been for the Algerian War, the Fourth Republic might very well have survived. Even so, it was as susceptible as the Third to being destroyed by political crisis. Its failure stemmed partly from the fact that the constitutional reforms undertaken did not go far enough. Yet it also failed because constitutional reforms alone could not change the fundamental structure of the French political system.

In the Fourth Republic as in the Third, the balance of power lay fundamentally with the legislature and its committees, not with the government. In England, between eighty and one hundred bills are introduced in any session of Parliament; most are government bills and almost all of them are assured passage. Under the Fourth Republic, between 1,400 and 2,500 bills were introduced in each session. Of these, the great bulk were private members' bills and in very many cases highly specific pieces of legislation—a bill to aid the olive industry or the mushroom industry, or legislation regulating the army's wine ration. The legislative situation was not as horrendous as these figures suggest; most private members' bills were buried in committee, and others were combined into more comprehensive proposals. Of the three hundred or so bills passed during an assembly session, roughly sixty per cent were measures introduced by the government, some of which gave the executive fairly wide authority to fill in the implementing details by issuing decrees. The real problem, aside from lack of time to consider properly so many proposed laws, was that the total legislative output rarely added up to a comprehensive program. Not only did the government possess little ability to develop such a program, but even the measures it did introduce were often mangled almost beyond recognition by the legislature. These circumstances were not too dissimilar from those that prevailed at the time in the

United States. But America was a far richer country, its social divisions did not seem to run as deep, and it did possess a comparatively stable executive.

Once again, under the Fourth Republic, the result was a diffusion of responsibility. The diffusion, moreover, was encouraged by the deputies, since in any event it was fruitless to expect the adoption of an integrated legislative program. The absence of clear lines of authority and responsibility also placed tremendous power with well-heeled interest groups, which were able to block measures that would adversely affect their position.

The fate of attempts to strengthen the French executive is an indication of just how unsuccessful efforts were at instituting basic constitutional reforms. The premier's power over the cabinet was supposedly enhanced by changing the manner in which he was selected. Under the Third Republic, the president had chosen the prime minister, who then formed his cabinet and went to the Chamber of Deputies for approval of himself and his government. Only a relative majority—that is, a majority of those deputies present and voting—was required for election. The constitution of the Fourth Republic called for the prime minister to present himself and his program to the assembly for a vote of confidence first; once granted, he would then select a cabinet and return to the assembly for its approval. His investiture required an absolute majority—a majority of the total membership of the assembly. The double investiture and the requirement of an absolute majority, it was expected, would add to the premier's prestige, and also prevent deputies from abstaining and thus avoiding responsibility for the government that was formed.

Other constitutional changes made for the ostensible purpose of strengthening the government included the prevention of snap votes of confidence, and the specific placement of the power to dissolve the National Assembly with the premier. During the Third Republic, any government could be defeated on a snap vote of confidence called for during the equivalent of England's parliamentary question period. Under the provisions of the Fourth Republic's constitution, a government could be formally defeated only by a vote of censure or by a refusal to grant a vote of confidence, and a full day was required between the motion and the vote. Further, the government had to be defeated by an absolute majority. Of even greater importance was the provision that if after the first 18 months of any parliament two governments were constitutionally defeated, the premier could dissolve the assembly.

Unfortunately, the constitutional changes had little or no effect. The double investiture only complicated the forming of governments. On a number of occasions, the candidate proposed as prime minister would be approved after a long round of negotiations, only to see his proposed cabinet go down to defeat. The requirement for an absolute majority prompted the same stalemate. In 1953, for example, the cabinet fell in early May. The president consulted every party and canvassed all possible candidates for prime minister; several did obtain relative majorities, but none succeeded in obtaining an absolute one. After several weeks, prospective candidates refused to allow themselves to be considered for premier, and not until June 26 was an acceptable nominee found. Both constitutional provisions, incidentally, were eventually repealed.

The power of dissolution was used only once. First of all, despite the constitution, most governments considered defeat by a relative majority quite sufficient to close up shop, and others just fell apart. Second, as under the Third Republic, no prime minister who wanted to preserve his career dared to use the weapon of dissolution lightly. In a number of cases, potential candidates were approved only with the promise that they would not try to dissolve the assembly even if the opportunity arose to do so.

The ability of any government to work out a systematic legislative program was similarly hampered. The political division within most governments made it virtually impossible to develop an adequate internal organization for the cabinet; the French finally created a general secretariat to prepare agendas, coordinate the work of the ministers, and serve on interdepartmental meetings. Yet no sense of collective responsibility manifested itself, nor was there ever any certainty that the bureaucracy serving the cabinet would be completely loyal. Secret information would be divulged if it contained any promise whatsoever of embarrassing those in power. French military plans even found their way to Ho Chi Minh, presumably with the connivance of French bureaucrats who opposed the war in Indochina.

Even if the premier seemed to have obtained widespread popular support, he could not effectively mobilize it in order to strengthen his position in the legislature and among his colleagues. The popularity of Pierre Mendès-France, for example, was not enough to maintain him in office. Deputies were quite aware of the fact that if they played their cards right they would not be held responsible for his inability to achieve ends that the public endorsed; they turned out to be correct. Other factors were involved in the downfall of Mendès-France, but in the end he, like so many before him, found that he could not press his programs through the National Assembly; with this failure, of course, his support eventually withered away. The public seemed cognizant of the problems faced by its premier, as indicated by the fact that most Frenchmen viewed government instability and ineffectiveness as among the most important of the country's problems. But the system's almost uncanny facility for resisting all attempts to reform itself infected the public with a sense of helplessness which only further contributed to its incivism.

Thus, as under the Third Republic, the locus of power came to be the National Assembly itself. And, once again, the legislature lacked the capacity or the willingness to organize itself for effective action. The assembly's timetable was set by a conference of representatives of the political groups, and it included the presidents of the legislative committees. But securing agreement on the order of business was usually a lengthy ordeal which in itself became the subject of major clashes.

Nor could the speaker—the president of the assembly—impose any real order. Unlike his American counterpart, the French speaker was not a party man; indeed, he never could have been elected if he were. Although the center parties were careful to keep the post from falling to the Gaullists or the Communists, the person most often chosen was a man with influential connections within the assembly; his authority, however, remained limited. The power of the British speaker depends on the acceptance by the vast majority of M.P.'s of the rules of the game. But in France, even the rules were at issue. Only occasionally could the assembly, or at least its majority, agree on procedure. In November 1947, the government submitted two bills requesting authority to handle a Communist-led general strike that was then in progress. In order to block passage, the Communist Party introduced a variety of irrelevant motions and presented the assembly with continual demands that votes on each of them be held by open ballot, a time-consuming ploy. Finally, the assembly was able to switch from its discussion of the bills to amend its standing orders in such a way as to allow it to proceed with discussion and voting on the original bills. The Communists then created an uproar in an attempt to prevent action from being taken. On November 29, seventeen calls to order were administered, four of simple censure and one of censure with temporary exclusion from the assembly for incitement to violence. The deputy thus censured refused to leave the chamber, and remained all night surrounded by members of his party. At 6 A.M. the following day, he consented to be escorted from the assembly by an unarmed group of the Republican Guard.

As under the Third Republic, committees again became not only the centers of power in the assembly but the real agents in bringing down one government after another. The strategy of the government was to play one committee off against the other—with, however, scant success, for in fact the committees were, once again, the captives of special interests. Half the members on the Committee for Reconstruction and War Damage, for instance, were from Normandy and Brittany, where the Allies had landed in World War II; all members of the Committee on Merchant Shipping and Fisheries had their home towns in coastal areas. Members were unanimous only in their desire to subsidize the particular interests they represented. In one week in 1951, the Labor Committee called for larger expenditures for family allowances; Interior sought more vigorous action on slums; the Press Committee announced its opposition to proposed economies in the National Film Center; and the Pensions Committee attempted to triple war pensions. Only the Finance Committee seemed to take an overall view—in this case conservative; its emphasis, an unpopular one, was on rejecting most proposals for the expenditure of money. While the power of the Finance Committee in the Fourth Republic was not nearly so great as it was during the Third, it still exercised considerable influence.

Its faults notwithstanding, the legislature of the Fourth Republic did, after all, manage to support policies of austerity in order to promote economic growth in the crucial years after World War II. Moreover, by 1956 there were some signs that French governments were, at last, becoming a little more adept at developing integrated programs. Nevertheless, the political structure of the Fourth Republic was such as to reduce the possibilities of evolving and implementing effective national policies. The structure defied the efforts of France's most skillful politicians to overcome its limitations. It corrupted other deputies and prevented a meaningful approach to the fundamental problems of French society. If, however, we look for the reasons why

France was incapable of an operative government, it becomes quite clear that they lay not in any particular political devices but rather in the very structure of French society.

The debilitating effect of French political institutions upon attempts to deal with social and economic problems is exemplified in the rise and decline of Pierre Mendès-France, who served as premier from June 18, 1954 to February 5, 1955. By 1954, he had already established a national reputation as a political leader and was known as someone who would not play the parliamentary game. Dour, intolerant of what he considered stupidity, and committed to the view that France should face her problems realistically and pragmatically, he was an outsider in the assembly. In the normal course of events, his chances of becoming premier would have been almost nonexistent. However, with the fall of Dien Bien Phu, his chance came. He had for two years led the attack on the government's policies, and as a consequence he was the natural choice of the assembly to extricate France from Indochina and to make other decisions that could no longer be postponed.

In a speech made upon the occasion of his investiture, Mendès-France promised that he would negotiate peace in Indochina by July 20 or resign from office. He also promised a decision on the European Defense Community, a question over which France had dawdled for two years despite pressure from her allies. His main interest, however, was in economic and political reform. He strongly believed that France must develop rational economic policies if the nation's financial problems were to be resolved, and that the political system had to be restructured if the government were ever to be effective.

Once in office, Mendès-France proceeded to act with a speed and dynamism unprecedented during the Fourth Republic. A cease-fire was arranged in Indochina within his own deadline, and after seven years the war came to an end. In the meantime, however, a wave of rioting had broken out in Tunisia, and the premier was forced to turn his attention to North Africa. After a series of rapid-fire negotiations, the crisis was temporarily settled. He then took up the question of the European Defense Community, attempting first to secure modification of certain provisions in order to make the plan more acceptable to members of the assembly. When this failed, he submitted it to a vote without taking a stand. E.D.C. was defeated, only to be replaced in a short time by the so-called Paris Pacts, which permitted the Germans to enter NATO and rearm.

Having handled with dispatch the major international crises that faced him, Mendès-France turned to domestic affairs. The government began to prepare a national tax program, and, in a direct challenge to one of France's special-interest groups, issued decrees to reduce government subsidization of the "alcohol industry." Mendès-France himself started a campaign against the drinking of alcohol by imbibing—with considerable fanfare—a glass of milk. In the meantime, he had gathered about him a group of bright young technocrats who were to furnish the brainpower for future programs. He had also initiated a campaign of appealing directly to the people on national issues. The National Assembly, however, was not particularly captivated by any of his programs or maneuvers, and it was soon apparent that he was heading for a fall. In fact, his fate had already been predicted in a brilliant satirical article written for *Le Canard Enchainé* on the occasion of his Tunisian negotiations:

There is no end to the surprises Prime Minister Bang has in store for us.

The effect of the Tunisian bombshell had scarcely died down when another bombshell ... blew up with a terrific bang. ...

M. Le Troquer [president of the National Assembly], in overalls, was watering the flowers in the back garden of the Palais Bourbon, when suddenly ... a helicopter, followed by two more, landed in the lawn.

M. Le Troquer had to jump for his life. When he recovered his senses he saw M. Mendès-France and the members of the Government alighting from the helicopters; and Mendès-France cried: "Quick, quick, get into your presidential chair."

"But . . . just a moment."

"Never mind, my dear Le Troquer; let's have none of this immobilisme. *Here's the first bunch of deputies arriving. . . ."*

The meeting was opened.

"Ladies and gentlemen," said the Prime Minister,"It is time to act."

(Agitation among the M.R.P., groans from the Right, a loud snore from M. Queuille.)

"I solemnly wish to propose that you give internal autonomy—to begin with—to the people of France." . . .

"Yes, gentlemen, we must free the French people of all their fetters. I therefore table: (1) a Bill putting an end to the privileges of the following monopolies: . . . the wine trade, the milk trade, etcetera."

A member of the Right: "You mean you wish to outlaw us? You can't get away with that." (He leaves the debating hall, followed by 200 colleagues.)

PMF (unperturbed): "(2) a Bill providing for fiscal reform under which all . . . shall pay their taxes." (At this point 200 more Deputies noisily leave the hall.)

PMF (still unperturbed): "I wish to reform justice and the press. . . . I also wish to propose an electoral law. . . ." (Uproar on the last occupied benches.)

All walk out except some colonial deputies who welcome the idea of giving France internal autonomy.[2]

History, as it turned out, conformed precisely with satire. With every move he took, Mendès-France alienated some group in the assembly. His approach to the Indochina question angered the right and the M.R.P. His actions in North Africa added to the resentment of both groups. His coolness to

[2] Quoted by Alexander Werth in *France, 1940–1955* (New York: Henry Holt & Co., 1956), pp. 714–715.

E.D.C. antagonized those looking toward European unity, while his signing of the Paris Pacts raised the opposition of the Gaullists, the Communists, and many others on the left. Further, each of his economic policies produced enemies among the deputies or supporters of still another special interest. He was defeated on the alcohol issue, but the end of the drama was, like a Greek tragedy, predictable. Mendès-France had been invested because something had to be done about Indochina. Once that crisis was over, he was no longer needed. Unable to change the system, he was doomed to be defeated by it. His relative popularity in the country could not sustain him in power, and his attempt to appeal to the people above Parliament only heightened suspicions and antagonisms within the Assembly. During his final speech he was all but shouted down by his opponents. As the old French saying proved once again, the system had gobbled up the man.

3. DE GAULLE'S REPUBLIC

The essential purpose of the constitution of the Fifth Republic was to strengthen the power of the executive at the expense of the legislature. Only in this way, in the opinion of de Gaulle and those who assisted him, could France achieve a stable, workable government. In a sense, the document was partially tailored to de Gaulle himself, and during his tenure as president he used it as an instrument rather than as a framework within which he had to act. Thus, the power balance between the premier and the president, incorporated into the constitution, shifted decisively to the president, and the role of the legislature became far smaller than it almost certainly will be under other circumstances. As a consequence, Fifth-Republic France has been operating within something of a political vacuum, and it is difficult to say how many of the political precedents established under de Gaulle will survive now that he has left office. For this reason, generalizations about current French political institutions cannot be formed too easily. We can, at best, only describe what happened during the presidency of Charles de Gaulle.

THE PRESIDENCY: The constitution of the Fifth Republic stipulates that, in addition to his formal functions, the president (1) appoint the premier and, by proposal of the premier, other government ministers; (2) promulgate laws voted by Parliament; (3) be able to ask Parliament to reconsider a law within two weeks of its having been voted (he has no veto power); (4) appoint certain high civil servants and officers of the armed forces; (5) preside over the Council of Ministers and over the "high councils" of the armed forces; (6) have the power to send messages to the National Assembly; (7) negotiate and ratify treaties; (8) hold the power of reprieve; and (9) be able to dissolve the National Assembly under specific conditions.[3]

All these powers were theoretically possessed by the president of the Third Republic, and many were formally available to the president of the Fourth. Also, as was the case in the two earlier republics, many require the countersignature of the prime minister or other relevant ministers. The difference in the effect of these provisions under the Fifth Republic, however, has been a matter of de Gaulle's personality, the weakening of the legislature, and the special role of the cabinet.

The special powers granted to the president by the constitution have sufficient safeguards to prevent his free use of them for his own ends. He has, for example, the power of dissolution, unhampered by the need to secure the approval of any other individual or body; but since he cannot dissolve parliament more than once in twelve months, he cannot use dissolution against a new chamber that proves hostile. He would then have to choose either to appoint a premier who had the confidence of the National Assembly or to face a serious constitutional crisis.

[3] A brief outline of the major provisions of the Fifth Republic constitution is given in Chapter 2, pp. 64–68.

The president's constitutional power to hold a referendum also has its safeguards—even though de Gaulle twice ignored them. Under Article 11, the president has the right to refer cabinet bills to the electorate in the form of a referendum. The procedure is not universally applicable; theoretically, the bill in question must concern either the organization of public powers or the relations between metropolitan France and other members of the French community. Furthermore, according to the constitution, the president can call for a referendum only upon the request of the government, that is, the premier and the cabinet. De Gaulle, however, decided that it was up to him to make such decisions, and on two of the four occasions in which a referendum was held, he violated the relevant constitutional provisions. The first two referenda involved the Algerian question. In 1961 de Gaulle called upon the French population to support a policy of self-determination for Algeria, and in April 1962 the electorate was asked to approve the Evian agreements between the French government and the Algerian nationalist movement, establishing an independent Algeria. On both issues, it is fairly certain that the National Assembly would have supported de Gaulle; his appeal directly to the people can only be understood as a device used to demonstrate to both the military and the small group of fanatics still opposed to Algerian independence that he had the overwhelming support of the French people. (See Table 16.1.)

The use of the third referendum, again in 1962, was another matter. The issue was a constitutional change to provide for the direct election of the French president. A referendum on a constitutional proposal also requires, according to the constitution, an affirmative vote of both houses of the French parliament; but when the issue was appealed to the Constitutional Council by the president of the Senate, the council declared itself without jurisdiction in the matter.

What de Gaulle did in 1962 was to appeal to the public over the head of a parliament that seemed bent on rejecting his proposal,

TABLE 16.1. FRENCH REFERENDA UNDER DE GAULLE, 1958–1969

Date	Registered voters (in millions)	Yes: % of votes cast	No: % of votes cast	Voter turnout
9/28/58	26.61	79.25	20.74	84.94%
1/8/61	27.18	75.26	24.73	76.49
4/8/62	26.99	90.70	9.29	75.59
10/28/62	27.58	61.75	38.25	77.25
4/27/69	28.02	46.82	53.17	81.58

Source: *Le Monde*, September 30, 1958; January 10, 1961; April 10, 1962; October 30, 1962; April 29, 1969. Reprinted by permission of the publisher.

and in so doing he violated the terms of his own constitution. He did the same thing in the 1969 referendum, which grouped together constitutional proposals for superimposing 21 new regions, which would have councils with some powers of self-governance, upon France's 95 departments; supplanting the Senate with a new consultative chamber of representatives from the regional councils; and changing the order of succession to the presidency. Essentially, these were plebiscites in which, by threatening to resign, de Gaulle gave the public the choice of accepting or rejecting his leadership. In all four referenda, however, the tactic was the same: he, de Gaulle, would establish once again his bond with the people and receive the pure expression of their will, thereby strengthening his hand. As he put it at the time of his first referendum:

Frenchmen and Frenchwomen, you know that the reply you are to give is to me. For twenty years, events have made me the country's guide in the serious crises through which we have lived. Now, once again, my duty and my office have led me to choose our road. And, because it is a hard road, in order to succeed, I need the support of the nation. . . . That is why I appeal to you over the head of all intermediaries.[4]

In 1961 and 1962 the tactic worked: still fearful of the possibilities of disorder should anything happen to de Gaulle, the population supported him handsomely. In 1969 it failed.

The anxieties that had swept de Gaulle's U.D.R. to a massive victory in the 1968 elections had subsided, and Frenchmen no longer believed that de Gaulle was the only alternative to chaos. Because referenda are closely associated with de Gaulle's peculiar style of governing—and also because the last one led to his downfall—they are unlikely to be used in quite the same way by his successors.

The constitution of the Fifth Republic also allows the president to assume full powers in the case of certain emergencies, as defined in Article 16:

In a situation in which there is an immediate and serious threat to Republican institutions, national independence, territorial integrity or the application of international agreements, and in which the regular functioning of the constitutional public authorities is interrupted, the President of the Republic, after officially consulting the Prime Minister, the Presidents of the Assemblies and the Constitutional Council, takes the measures called for by the circumstances.

He informs the nation by a message.

These measures, on which the Constitutional Council is consulted, must be inspired by the will to enable the constitutional public authorities to fulfill their mission with the minimum of delay.

Parliament meets as of right. The National

[4] Broadcast of January 6, 1961 as quoted in Dorothy Pickles, *The Fifth French Republic*, 3rd ed. (New York: Frederick A. Praeger, 1966), p. 143.

Assembly cannot be dissolved during the period of the exercise of powers.

De Gaulle asserted at the time the constitution was adopted that this emergency power was to be used primarily in the event of national disaster comparable with that of 1940. He invoked it only once, in April 1961, in the wake of terrorist activities in Algeria and France led by the *Organization de l'Armée Secrète* (O.A.S.), a group committed to France's retention of full control over its former colony. De Gaulle's action met with widespread approval. But a number of deputies pointed out that because the work of the "constitutional public authorities" had not been impaired, the use of the constitutional article went, strictly speaking, beyond its meaning. Opposition was also registered to other moves made by de Gaulle during the 1961 crisis, including the extension of police controls far beyond what many thought necessary and the unpublicized revocation of tenure for certain trial judges.

Although Parliament continued to sit by right, according to the article, de Gaulle further roused the ire of opposition parties by refusing to allow it to consider any other matters except those relating to the emergency. The Constitutional Council declared itself unable to make a ruling on this issue, and de Gaulle's interpretation still stands. Many commentators believe that protections against the use of Article 16 to establish a full dictatorship are not sufficient; most likely, with de Gaulle's departure, the article will be substantially modified.

The president of France is also president of the French community. Effectively, this means that he has almost complete freedom of action with regard to problems arising from relations with former dependencies still associated in some fashion with France, as well as with those whose status is still more or less colonial.

De Gaulle's conception of the French presidency changed, at least publicly, during his tenure. Initially, he was in accord with Michel Debré, his choice as premier and the man who was largely responsible for the form of the Fifth Republic constitution. Debré had argued that the role of the president would be largely that of arbiter; he would mediate in the conflicting concerns of the various organs of government in order to insure national stability and direction. By the time of the 1962 referendum, however, it was obvious that de Gaulle conceived of himself more in the image of Rousseau's legislator: a figure whose function was to provide guidelines for Frenchmen to make the right political decisions. As a consequence, the constitution was increasingly ignored or stretched to such a degree that major policy decisions, which should have been made by a government responsible to the legislature, were made personally by de Gaulle with the advice of the bureaucracy and a few trusted companions. Indeed, de Gaulle gathered about him his own special staff, composed largely of higher-echelon civil servants whose functions were similar to those of the executive office of the president of the United States.

In the fields of foreign policy and defense, especially, it was de Gaulle's will that was determinative. It was he who decided that Algeria should become independent and that France should have a nuclear striking force. It was he who concluded that France's African colonies should determine for themselves their future association with the new French community. It was he who vetoed England's admission into the European Common Market and who, for all practical purposes, took France out of the North Atlantic Treaty Organization. On the domestic front, many important questions were handled by presidential decree, leaving the legislature and the prime minister with rather routine tasks. For example, it was de Gaulle who made the final decisions on educational reforms after the crisis of May 1968; later in the same year, he determined that France would not devalue the franc. There were, of course, a number of important domestic issues with which de Gaulle did not directly concern himself—or on which he had no fixed opinion; on these, the premier, other cabinet members, and even the Assembly exercised considerable influence.

It is not only what Charles de Gaulle did, however, but the manner in which he did it that has led many to describe him as a constitutional monarch. He stated again and again that he was France's steward, that he represented the will of France. He veiled his decisions in secrecy and effectively inhibited discussion of them before they were taken, thus leaving the public and many of his colleagues uninformed as to his intentions. When he changed his mind he often failed to inform even those closely associated with the issue, and they sometimes found themselves arguing a case that de Gaulle was shortly to repudiate. The Fifth Republic under de Gaulle was, then, largely de Gaulle's republic. It was *his* government; *he* ruled France.

THE PREMIER AND THE GOVERNMENT: The premier is, officially, the head of the French government. He chooses his ministers, whom the president appoints on his recommendation, and he can request their resignation. He is held constitutionally responsible for the work of the government—for guaranteeing that its laws are carried out and that the nation's defenses are adequate. The resignation of a premier automatically provokes the downfall of the government.

Unlike the constitution of the Fourth Republic, that of the Fifth does not require that a premier nominated by the president submit himself to the National Assembly for approval. However, Debré did so, believing that the prime minister should serve at the pleasure of the parliament because he is, under the constitution, "responsible" to it. The National Assembly may force his resignation through a vote of censure or by refusing to grant him a requested vote of confidence; aside from the fact that the government perforce resigns before each new election, the constitution provides no other way in which a premier may be discharged from office.

Debré's successor, Georges Pompidou,

also presented himself and his government to the National Assembly for approval upon his first nomination by de Gaulle and again after the 1962 elections. Pompidou did not present himself to the Assembly after the 1967 elections, nor did his successor, Maurice Couve de Murville, after the elections of 1968. A year later, however, Jacques Chaban-Delmas, Pompidou's choice for premier and a former Radical Socialist who had served under Mendès-France and de Gaulle, did present himself. Both Debré and Pompidou were forced from office by de Gaulle, although, because the president has no constitutional authority to dismiss the premier, the fiction was maintained that they had requested to be relieved of their duties. De Gaulle's hold over the premiership, of course, made its occupant little more than his agent on those matters about which he felt strongly; it seems unlikely that the office will continue to be of such minor importance in the future.

Constitutionally, the policy-making group of the French government meets as the Council of Ministers when the president serves as chairman, and as the Council of the Cabinet when the premier is chairman. Under the Third Republic, the official policy-making body was the Council of Ministers, and the Council of the Cabinet was created to prepare the ministers' meetings. As power shifted from the presidency, the cabinet council became the real policy-making group; it remained so under the Fourth Republic, even though it was not mentioned in the constitution and its authority was officially derived from the Council of Ministers.

De Gaulle reversed the pattern. Key decisions were made at meetings of the Council of Ministers, for it was at these sessions, under his leadership, that policies were initiated which he felt should be the result of collective action. The premier and other ministers were not, however, completely passive; on many issues de Gaulle simply put into effect ideas that had emerged from various departments through the ministers, and he permitted fairly wide-ranging discussions of the issue at hand. Yet in the end, it was de Gaulle and de Gaulle alone who determined the outcome of matters he considered important.

Domination of policy-making by the president was not written into the constitution, which made every effort to strengthen the prime minister and the government in their own right. Among the constitutional provisions designed to achieve this purpose, five are of particular importance. The first, which made membership in the government incompatible with membership in Parliament, was intended to eliminate the game of musical chairs that had been choreographed so frequently during the Third and Fourth Republics. De Gaulle's hope was that competition among the deputies for ministerial posts would be reduced, along with the tendency to overthrow governments for the sake of securing such posts. It was also believed that ministers free of parliamentary ties would not feel under as much pressure from both parties and constituents, and thus would more readily consider the national rather than the partisan or local interest. It is difficult to determine just how effective this provision has been. Those politicians who have entered the government have, naturally enough, retained their political connections. Initially, one of the results was an increase in the number of high-level civil servants appointed to ministerial posts, although this may simply have reflected de Gaulle's personal distrust of "politicians" and preference for technocrats. However, by 1967 members of the government were running for Parliament even if they had never served in a political office before; as candidates they declared they would continue to look out for the interests of their constituents even though they could be expected to resign from their seat in favor of their alternate once a new government was formed.[5]

5 The constitution states that each candidate for Parliament must run for office jointly with an alternate (*suppléant*) who replaces him if he takes a government post.

In Debré's government, more than a third of the ministers had never stood for a parliamentary election, most of them being career civil servants; after the 1967 elections, all but two cabinet appointees had been candidates, and a number of them had been elected to local offices. What seems to be happening, therefore, as a result of the first constitutional provision to strengthen the hand of the premier, is that a new breed of government officials is emerging in Paris—men equally at home in the higher reaches of the bureaucracy and in politics.

The second constitutional provision requires an absolute majority in the assembly to overthrow a government. A government may be brought down on a vote of censure or when the prime minister puts a question of confidence and loses, but since a motion of censure requires the signatures of one-tenth of the deputies, and since the same signatories cannot move another motion in the same session, government stability has been constitutionally enhanced. Again, it is difficult to measure the real effect of this provision because of de Gaulle's impact on French government and the majority that his ever-faithful party has enjoyed in the assembly since 1962. Yet it is well to remember that most governments under the Fourth Republic fell apart, despite the fact that the constitutional requirement for an absolute majority to unseat them had not been met. Even if governments now remain after being defeated by a simple majority, it is possible to foresee a situation in which they might face serious difficulties with a hostile assembly.

The third important provision grants the government far wider authority to issue decrees which have the force of law. The provision extends beyond matters relating to the budget, where decrees can be issued if Parliament refuses to act. Because the Third Republic parliament was so often unable to agree on the details of legislation, it allowed the government to take responsibility for filling those details in. The government was even granted authority to modify laws by decree in certain instances. This dissipation of legislative power was, however, angrily attacked, and the constitution of the Fourth Republic specifically prohibited Parliament from sloughing off its responsibilities. The same problems appeared, nevertheless, and eventually the assembly began to pass so-called "outline laws" that could be augmented by government decree. The Fifth Republic constitution specifically delegates decree-issuing powers to the government, although, as under the Third and Fourth Republics, they are subject to eventual ratification by Parliament. The difference is basically one of viewpoint: it is now constitutionally acceptable for the assembly to delegate the responsibility of legislative details to the government. Still, there are restrictions upon this authority. Every government ordinance issued under decree-delegating legislation must be laid before Parliament in the form of a ratifying bill by a date specified in the enabling act. Unless Parliament then passes the bill, the ordinances issued by the government could be challenged as being *ultra vires*—beyond the legal scope of the government. However, there is a catch here: while the constitution provides that the ordinances must be laid before Parliament, it does not provide that they must be passed by Parliament or even debated, and on a number of occasions the government has complied with the letter of the law but blocked debate. A few of the ordinances that became effective in this manner have been successfully challenged in the courts; most, however, have not.

The fourth constitutional provision to reinforce the authority of the premier and government designates the areas in which Parliament may legislate, and reserves all other matters for executive action—including the detailed application of general laws. To be sure, the powers granted the legislature are broad, but they are no longer unlimited. Unfortunately, it is not always easy to differentiate between the domain of "law," as defined by the constitution, and that of "reg-

ulations," under which the government can exercise its prerogative. Where the government and the parliament disagree, the premier or the president of either chamber of the National Assembly can bring the issue before the Constitutional Council; private citizens can also bring cases to the *Conseil d'État* on the ground that either the government or Parliament has exceeded its authority. Decisions have tended to extend the parliament's sphere of jurisdiction, although a good many issues have not been settled; the council's attitude seems to be that while Parliament can decide upon the objective of legislation, the government can decide the method of reaching the objective, except where the method determines or frustrates the objective. Thus, Parliament may pass a law setting up a new type of criminal court in Paris, Lyons, and Marseilles, but the extension of these courts to other towns would be a matter for governmental decision. One further reason for instituting this constitutional provision was to leave Parliament time to consider major legislative proposals by overcoming its tendency to preoccupy itself with a plethora of minor matters. In this connection the provision has been successful, and the number of minor bills introduced by private members has dropped from about eight hundred a year to two hundred.

Finally, the government has been given extensive control over the parliamentary timetable. Consideration of government bills takes priority, and the government now opens debate on its bills and has the right to propose amendments. Furthermore, it is the government's bill that is considered by the assembly, not the bill as amended by committee. Committee amendments must now be submitted from the floor. The government can also object to amendments from the floor once debate on a bill has begun, and ministers can, if they wish, ask that the legislature decide on the bill as a whole without taking up each amendment seriatim. Furthermore, the government can make the acceptance of a bill a matter of confidence; when that occurs, the bill becomes law unless the opposition puts down a censure motion with enough support to carry a majority of the whole house, not just those voting.

These last two weapons were frequently employed by de Gaulle's government to bring recalcitrant party members and allied groups into line and to put pressure on those who favored the legislation at hand but objected to particular amendments. By insisting on a package vote, the government forced moderates to support it, lest the entire bill fail; and by making a bill a matter of confidence, it forced deputies to make a decision on a whole series of issues solely on the basis of their attitude toward the regime. Both weapons would not have been very effective under the Third and Fourth Republics, and it remains to be seen how effective they will be under the Fifth in the post–de Gaulle era.

The government's control over the parliamentary timetable is clearly demonstrated by its new authority over financial legislation. During most of the Third Republic, deputies could introduce amendments or bills that had the effect of increasing appropriations or reducing taxes while the budget was being considered. Attempts to limit such troublesome activity were made in the final years of the republic, but they were not notably successful. The constitution of the Fourth Republic prohibited the introduction of measures involving a net increase in expenditure or a net reduction in public revenues during consideration of the budget; but that provision was easily evaded. For one thing, deputies could and did introduce amendments that *supposedly* curtailed expenditures in one area, while increasing subsidies for their own pet projects; everyone knew the curtailment was highly problematical. For another, it was still possible to introduce fiscal measures at any time during the legislative year except during budget-review periods, and deputies did so freely. Also, in order to force concessions, deputies had no qualms about threatening the government with defeat. An effort to bolster the government's position was made in 1956

by disallowing any amendment to a proposed bill if its adoption meant increased expenditures. But this availed little: all it amounted to was that such amendments had to be separate bills.

The constitution of the Fifth Republic asserts that no member of the French Parliament can introduce a legislative proposal that would either increase public expenditure or decrease public revenue. Such a provision might still be applied loosely. But the Constitutional Court has interpreted the restriction rather narrowly: quite early in the Fifth Republic, for example, a proposed law for the repression of prostitution was ruled out of order because it would require additional police. However, it is still possible to make proposals that would incur increased expenditures if they are *genuinely* compensated for in other areas, and the government has been forced to yield this point on numerous occasions.

The government's prime weapon in getting its way financially, aside from its authority to call for a package vote, is a constitutional provision which states that budgets become law automatically if Parliament fails to act on them within seventy days. This effectively prevents Parliament from delaying consideration of the budget until its demands are met, a common practice during the Fourth Republic. The upshot has been the formulation of fairly rational budget procedures in comparison with any earlier period in French parliamentary history, although frequent complaints have been heard about the government steamrolling the budget through Parliament.

The strengthening of the executive under the Fifth Republic has, without question, increased the stability of the French government and promoted cohesion among government personnel. Moreover, during de Gaulle's presidency, the cabinet finally developed an effective secretariat, as did the office of the prime minister, and something like collective responsibility became a reality. The government's ministers were also able to achieve greater control over their departments, organizing personal staffs responsive to their views.

THE LEGISLATURE: As in the past, the parliament of Fifth Republic France is also made up of two houses, the National Assembly and the Senate. The lower chamber, the National Assembly, is composed of 487 deputies elected for five-year terms by universal suffrage; the upper chamber, the Senate, contains 274 deputies elected for nine-year terms by departmental electoral colleges. Every three years one-third of the Senate is renewed by the colleges, which consist of departmental deputies and councillors as well as delegates elected by the municipal councils of the department.[6]

During the Fourth Republic, the Senate, or the Council of the Republic as it was then called, was extremely weak and largely ignored; de Gaulle, however, decided to increase its powers once again, primarily so that it could serve as a conservative check upon a National Assembly which he expected to be rather more radical in its political viewpoints. Thus, under the 1958 constitution, the two chambers were assigned equal powers except in three important respects: the assembly's traditional power of being first to examine the budget has been maintained; the cabinet is responsible only to the National Assembly; and the assembly has the final word on legislation, if the government so desires. The constitution also provides that every bill be examined by both houses with a view to the adoption of an identical text; if, however, there is continuing disagreement on the text after two readings in each chamber, the premier can convene a joint conference committee, with an equal number of members from each chamber, and ask it to write a compromise text. The government would then submit the compromise to both houses for their approval. If no agreement is

reached, the premier can ask the National Assembly to rule "definitively" on the bill, but unless he does so, a Senate veto is final.

De Gaulle originally expected to use the Senate to block National Assembly proposals which he disliked. The opposite occurred, however: the assembly, with its Gaullist majorities, proved quite tractable; it was the Senate, in which Gaullists remained a small minority, which turned out to be incorrigible so far as de Gaulle was concerned. As a result, the government was frequently forced to ask the assembly to make the final decision on legislation, and the Senate's role in legislation was progressively diminished. In the end, of course, de Gaulle decided to eliminate the Senate—or, more accurately, to replace it with a much weaker chamber of a different kind—rather than deal with it any further. And it was this decision that precipitated the 1969 referendum that led to his resignation.

Two sessions of Parliament are held each year. The first, which deals primarily with the budget, lasts eighty days; the second, which is concerned with legislative programs, lasts ninety. Although parliamentary committees can meet when Parliament is not sitting, Parliament itself is now in session a maximum of five and one-half months a year, as compared with a minimum of seven months during the Fourth Republic. The decision to shorten the time was deliberately made to allow the government more breathing space between sessions.

The basic unit of political organization in both houses is the parliamentary group. The bigger groups usually consist of members of a single political party, and bear their party's name. Members of loosely organized parties may be divided among two or more groups, and parties with less than thirty deputies—the minimum number for a group to be recognized as such—may join together to form a single group or may affiliate with one formed by a larger party. Group cohesion varies. The Communists, for instance, have acted with a good deal of unity; so have the Socialists and members of the M.R.P. much

6 A discussion of departmental and municipal councils is contained in Chapter 19, pp. 583–584.

of the time. When de Gaulle was president, the U.D.R. parliamentary group also maintained a high degree of discipline. During Pompidou's tenure as premier, the government kept in especially close contact with the group's elected political bureau, and made a number of concessions in cases where individual deputies felt that proposed measures were contrary to the interests of their constituents; the government was also inclined to favor private members' bills introduced by U.D.R. deputies as a reward for faithful service.

The official governing body of each house is known as the bureau, which in the National Assembly consists of the president and vice president of the chamber, various secretaries and several questeurs, officials responsible for certain administrative and financial matters. The function of the bureau as a collective body is to organize and supervise the different services in the assembly and to advise the president on disciplinary matters and on the admissibility of bills or resolutions. With the exception of the president, who is elected for the duration of a parliamentary session by the whole assembly, bureau officers are chosen at *Conférences des présidents*, special conferences by the leaders of the parliamentary groups; these conferences are also responsible for drawing up the parliamentary timetable and allotting membership to committees. Voting at the conferences is usually proportional to party strength, although the Communist Party suffered from discrimination during most of the Gaullist period.

Nothing better illustrates the weakness of the French parliament during de Gaulle's presidency than the fate of its standing committees. The power of such committees in controlling legislation and their stance as government watchdogs during the Third and Fourth Republics have already been described. The constitution of the Fifth Republic restricted the number of standing committees in each house to six, with the provision that ad hoc committees could be created for special purposes. The standing committees were expected to range in size from thirty to 125, and the purpose of the new constitutional criteria was to reduce their power by making them less specialized and hence less likely to be at the beck and call of particular interests. It was also believed that larger committees were less likely to develop troublesome cross-party views based on the acquired expertise of members.

As might be expected, deputies tried to get around the constitutional limitation by forming subcommittees, but these were ruled unconstitutional by the court. Informal "working groups" then sprang up, although formal decisions had to be made by the committee as a whole. Nevertheless, for a while some of the working groups took on the characteristics of the smaller, specialized committees of the Third and Fourth Republics; they became dominated by the special-interest groups concerned with particular legislation, and some ministers considered them important enough to testify before them. In the end, however, U.D.R. discipline and the broad political base of membership on the parent committees cut short the rising prestige of the working groups, although the influence of the standing committees themselves was never great during the Gaullist period.

Still another "weapon" which was used by the French parliament to maintain its preeminence over the government during the Third and Fourth Republics, but which has fallen into disuse under the Fifth, is the oral question period. In the Third Republic, interpellations of ministers could lead to a snap vote of confidence and bring down the government immediately, and the disruptive device was employed with alarming frequency. During the Fourth Republic, a period of delay was instituted before a vote could be taken; far fewer governments were destroyed, but many were weakened.

Debré wanted to save the question period, which he regarded as a useful procedure, but the Fifth Republic constitution pointedly specified that no vote could be taken on any question. Thus, deputies could gain information and challenge the government as frequently as they liked, but they could not use questions for the purpose of overturning the government. The reform, however, went too far, or perhaps it was merely that Parliament lacked the kind of unwritten rules of the game to make the question periods valuable. Ministers often sent substitutes to answer questions, and the government unabashedly used its management of the legislative timetable to control which questions would be asked and when they would be debated. Despite later attempts to revise the procedure so that the opposition might have more of a voice in what was going on, the meaningfulness of the question hour soon dwindled; absenteeism became extremely high, and questions in the assembly dealt almost exclusively with local matters. In the Senate questions remained more interesting, but even there the substance of the question hour compared very unfavorably with that of the House of Commons.

The one other weapon that previous parliaments possessed, the censure motion, became almost equally useless. Formerly, it could be introduced with comparative ease, but under the Fifth Republic's constitution, ten per cent of the assembly must now propose a censure motion and it cannot be voted upon until 48 hours after it is introduced. Only those voting for the motion are counted and a majority of the whole house is required to pass it, so that absentees and abstainers work to the advantage of the government. Further, the same signatories cannot propose another censure motion during the same session of Parliament. In sum, while Parliament could influence the government during the de Gaulle era in the sense that it could block some legislation, get other legislation modified, and raise some embarrassing issues, it became an appendage of the regime rather than a working partner.

4. ON THE GAME OF POLITICS

The French National Assembly is housed in the Palais Bourbon on the left bank of the Pont de la Concorde, its home since 1798. The palace was declared national property at the beginning of the French Revolution, and after several other buildings had been tried, it was fitted out to quarter the National Assembly. The parliamentary chamber is shaped like an antique theater—a semicircular hall with rising rows of seats broken by radial passages. The front benches are reserved for the members of the government, and the deputies fan out behind them according to political affiliation, moving from right to left. There has, on occasion, been some squabbling among parties—for example, between the Radicals and the M.R.P. at the beginning of the Fourth Republic and between the U.D.R. and the Radicals during the Fifth—as to just where they should sit, but usually such matters are settled without too much fuss. Unlike the English and American parliaments, where members usually speak from their seats, French deputies move to the rostrum to address their colleagues; the custom is also observed in the senate, located in the Palais du Luxembourg a short distance away, whose chamber is constructed along the same general lines.

A parliamentary career in France remains somewhat uncertain. During the seventy years of the Third Republic, 4,892 deputies were seated, and during the Fourth 1,112 were elected from metropolitan France. Of those elected during the Third Republic, 46 per cent served but one term and another 21 per cent only two (see Table 16.2). A mere three per cent of the deputies were elected seven or more times, many of them having more or less inherited their seats in areas of rural France still loyal to the old aristocracy.

During the Third Republic, approximately 25 per cent of the parliamentarians were members of the legal profession, but more than thirty per cent pursued other "intellectual" professions, including teaching and

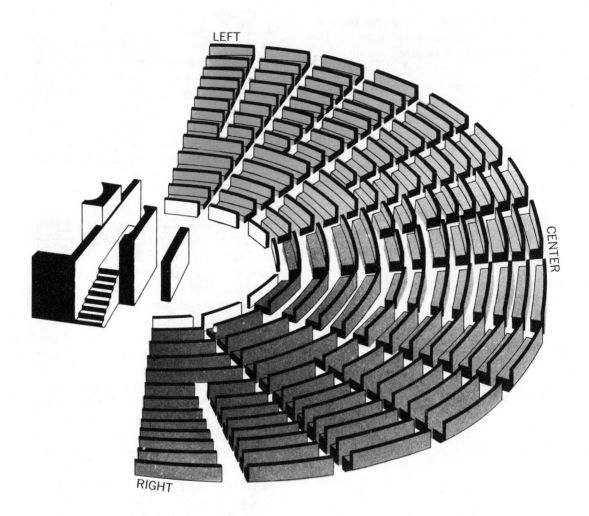

FIGURE 16.1. FLOOR PLAN OF THE FRENCH NATIONAL ASSEMBLY, 1967

journalism. During the Fourth Republic, especially at sessions in which the Communist Party representation was quite large, a substantial working-class representation was also present—21 per cent, if white-collar employees and subordinate government workers are included. In general, members of the French parliament in the years of the Third Republic came from humbler backgrounds than did their British contemporaries, for the hold of the aristocracy and upper bourgeoisie on the levers of governmental power was broken

earlier in France than in England. Moreover, if we broadly define the term "intellectual," the proportion of them—professors, secondary-school teachers, journalists, and writers —in Parliament was considerably higher in France than in England. One writer in the 1920's called post–World War I France the "Republic of the Professors," a not inaccurate appellation.

Far more than in England, too, the road to Parliament lay through local government offices. During much of the Third Republic,

TABLE 16.2. PARLIAMENT AS A CAREER: THE THIRD AND FOURTH REPUBLICS

Continuity and length of service in the French Chamber of Deputies: 1870–1940

	Number of times elected deputy							
	1	2	3	4	5	6	7 or more	Total
Deputies with continuous service	46%	18%	11%	7%	4%	2%	2%	89%
Deputies with discontinuous service	0	3	3	2	1	1	1	11
Total	46%	21%	14%	9%	5%	3%	3%	100%

Length of parliamentary mandates in the Fourth Republic: 1945–1958

	Number of times elected deputy					Number of deputies
	1	2	3	4	5	
Communists	30%	13%	20%	14%	23%	246
Socialists	33	20	14	11	22	198
Radicals	49	18	11	16	6	124
M.R.P.	32	16	21	12	19	216
Independents	51	17	13	11	8	152
R.P.F.—"Gaullists"	58	29	6	4	3	91
Extreme right—"Poujadists"	100	0	0	0	0	44
Unclassified	0	25	25	25	25	41
Total	40	17	16	12	15	1,112

Adapted from Mattei Dogan, "Political Ascent in a Class Society: French Deputies, 1870–1958," in Dwaine Marvick (ed.), *Political Decision Makers* (Glencoe, Ill.: The Free Press, 1961), p. 59. Reprinted by permission of the publisher.

more than two-thirds of the deputies had held a local office before being elevated to Parliament. The figure for the post–World War II Fourth Republic was about forty per cent, and even the 1958 (Fifth Republic) election, which produced massive political changes in parliamentary personnel, failed to alter the fact that more than three-fourths of the deputies had held local office at one time or another. The percentage remained high during subsequent elections. As for those deputies who came to Parliament by way of other routes, many of them made haste to weld local ties as soon as they could. The composition of the Fifth Republic parliament changed somewhat in other respects. The proportion of deputies with a working-class background dropped off, partly as a result of the decline in Communist Party strength; the number of lawyers also decreased, whereas the representation of other professions, especially teachers and high civil servants, rose sharply. (See Table 16.3.)

Most French deputies of the Third and Fourth Republics had to give up their occupations because Parliament took up so much of their time. Sessions normally lasted from eight months to a year, and deputies who came from areas outside Paris had to remain in the city for most of the week. The shortened sessions of the Fifth Republic have allowed more time for certain types of professional activity, but it is still difficult for most deputies to be anything but professional

TABLE 16.3.   OCCUPATION OF DEPUTIES IN THREE REPUBLICS

	Third Republic	Fourth Republic		Fifth Republic	
	1936	1956	1958	1962	1967
Farmers	13.5%	10%	11.5%	9%	7%
Workers	13.5	13	1.5	5	6.5
Clerks		9	5	8	6.5
Schoolteachers	10.5	6.5	2	4	14
Professors		8.5	8	6	
Lawyers	20	13	16	11	10
Doctors, etc.	8	5	12	12	10
Journalists	9	4.5	5	4	4
High civil servants	3.5	4	8	9	9
Officers and priests	1	1.5	2.5	4	2
Engineers, etc.	2	4.5	6	4	5
Managers	2	5	7	9	5.5
Businessmen	14	10	15.5	14.5	8
Small shopkeepers	0	6	0	0	0
Others	3	0	0	0	12.5

Adapted from Philip M. Williams, *The French Parliament, 1958–1967* (London: George Allen and Unwin, 1968), p. 34. Reprinted by permission of the publisher.

parliamentarians. Since 1910 the deputies' salaries have been reasonably adequate, and they were raised again during the Fifth Republic. In addition, they are allowed some funds for a small staff. While their remuneration is not comparable to American standards, it is fairly lavish when contrasted with the British.

Deputies in both the Third and Fourth Republics spent considerable time in contact with, and doing favors for, their constituents. If anything, the extreme centralization of France meant that every decision on local issues had to come from Paris, and this placed a greater burden on the deputy than either his British or American counterpart experienced. In the Fourth Republic, proportional representation tended to divorce deputies from constituents—but far less than those who wrote its constitution had expected. A Frenchman might vote Communist or Socialist out of a sense of resentment against the whole political system, but he did not expect anything tangible from the leftist rhetoric. He was far more concerned with a

new school or a new road or another subsidy; he knew his deputy was doing something if a school was built. The result, of course, was that deputies, already overburdened with the very time-consuming schedule of parliamentary debates, found the rest of their hours taken up with attempts to satisfy the various groups that were pressing in upon them. While he was president of the Finance Committee, Mendès-France described it thus:

I open my mail at breakfast. There are at least two to three hundred letters every morning, three-fourths of which are requests for special favors. . . . At least half come from party colleagues and other deputies forwarding requests they have received. If I help them it is understood that they will help me.

Between correspondence and [committee] hearings I must receive a stream of visitors from single favor seekers to official delegations, anywhere from five to twenty men: trade union delegates, political unions, farm groups, delegates of tax leagues . . . every conceivable private interest. Requests for anything up to forty or fifty audiences a day are quite normal.

I can't possibly see more than a dozen separate groups on any one day, so I automatically risk making three dozen enemies. I try to put them off. . . . I do what I can to dam the tide, but nothing helps. We have a fifteen or sixteen hour day, a seven day week, and on top of that the Assembly seems unable to reach a decision before four o'clock in the morning. . . .[7]

Pressures have eased somewhat during the Fifth Republic. Deputies have had less authority and, consequently, many special-interest groups seeking favors have gone straight to the bureaucracy or to the president's friends.

With the exception of the Communists and the extreme right, the parliaments of the Third and Fourth Republics had a strong sense of corporate unity. Rebels accommodated themselves to the system fairly quickly, since the alternative was to find oneself completely ineffective. Those coming to the assembly with grandiose schemes for reform soon learned to "moderate" their behavior. For those hoping to serve in the government not once but several times, it was especially important to be on good terms with one's fellow deputies. In criticizing an opponent, one only wounded him.

Even though the legislature declined in prestige during the final years of both the Third and the Fourth Republics, it continued to attract intelligent and able men. In fact, the assembly of the Fourth was remarkably free of scandal; most deputies did their best, as they saw it, within the limits imposed by the system.

Parliamentary life during the Fifth Republic under de Gaulle was far less rewarding. The sense of impotence members felt in the shadow of the de Gaulle regime resulted in heightened resentment at petty grievances. The lobbies were no longer nearly

so filled with people seeking out the representatives of the nation, and press coverage of debates was far less extensive. Parliamentarians spent even more time meeting with local constituents, fulfilling responsibilities in local offices, and negotiating with the bureaucracy to achieve local improvements. Interest groups with representatives in Paris might not seek out deputies so often, but local constituents were as anxious as ever for favors.

One of the parliamentary problems of the Fourth Republic was absenteeism—always a touchy issue in the game of politics. Deputies would take off for the provinces, leaving their mandate with friends, even friends in opposition parties. One or two Communist deputies could harass the entire government by proxy voting for sixty or seventy of their colleagues in an almost empty chamber. The Fifth Republic's "organic laws," drafted under Debré's guidance to supplement the constitution, attempted to do away with the evils of voting by proxy. No member could hold more than one proxy, and proxies were permitted for only a few specified reasons such as family illness; members who were absent too often would forfeit part of their salaries. Proxy voting was also made physically more difficult by the substitution of individual electronic voting devices for paper ballots at each deputy's bench; proxy voters would now have to leap over benches in order to do their colleagues a favor. Even so, the impediments to absenteeism proved of little avail: the deputies most in demand as proxy holders only became younger and younger and more and more agile. Cooperation on proxy voting continued to extend across party lines, and not a few Gaullists would gladly cast a Socialist vote against a government bill—in return, of course, for the same favor.

5. INTEREST-GROUP POLITICS IN FRANCE

Part of the mythology of French politics during much of the Third Republic, for the left at least, was that organized interest

[7] David Schoenbrun, *As France Goes* (New York: Harper & Co., 1957), pp. 147–148.

groups were intrinsically evil: there should
be no intermediate bodies, it was believed,
between the individual and the state. The
hostility of the French left to corporatism can
be partially explained by the heritage of the
French Revolution.

Despite the official ideology, however, interest groups proliferated during the late
nineteenth and early twentieth centuries. In
France as in England, the government turned
to some of these groups for advice or assistance as its intervention in the economy became more and more important. The Vichy
regime added considerably to the list of special-interest groups "represented" in the administration of public policy, and by the later
years of the Fourth Republic, more than two
thousand advisory groups of one kind or another were attached to government agencies.

Interest-group activity in France during the
Third and Fourth Republics was considerably different from group activity in England.
The formation of functionally specific associations is partly a product of modernization,
and insofar as France was a more traditional
nation in many ways, with a fairly large peasant and artisan base, interest-group activity
remained at a more primitive level. Organizations were relatively weak and ephemeral—
forming, dissolving, and forming again. The
fragmentation and mutual suspicion perme-
ating much of French life also made organizational cooperation difficult: the nascent
labor movement split into any number of
ideological factions, as did business groups,
the peasantry, and veterans' groups. Even
when ideological considerations did not seem
important, Frenchmen tended to define their
interests in extremely narrow terms. Sectional
as well as economic differences compounded
the difficulty of forming unified interest
groups. Large businesses and small businesses were at each others' throats; farmers
and peasants found it impossible to form a
common front; skilled and unskilled workers
seemed unable to coordinate their demands.

Moreover, when organizations did form,
the leadership found it troublesome to collect

dues or to convince members that sustained
activity was necessary for success. Workers
or peasants might riot on a particular issue,
but they would not attend meetings or actively support their organizations for any
length of time. On the whole, French personal relations were still formal and circumscribed; thus, Frenchmen never found it easy
to develop that array of durable, voluntary
associations that have been the hallmark of
Protestant countries in Europe.[8]

The left might talk of powerful business
organizations that controlled France, and the
right quake at the increasing power of the
trade unions; but in fact, both sides exaggerated the strength of their opponents, for
neither business nor labor was organized with
nearly the strength, efficiency, and intensity
of their counterparts in Germany and England. To be sure, French businessmen had
less need to organize than workers. In England, as in the United States and Germany,
business associations were formed as a reflex
to the organization of trade unions and aimed
primarily to counter working-class power as
it expressed itself in the form of direct action
or legislative pressure. In France, such strategy was considered unnecessary; the diffuseness of French social and political life made it
quite easy for businessmen to use personal
influence to block or inhibit the implementation of social policies they disapproved of.

The weakness of most special-interest
groups and the general inability of the French
political system to process their demands was
compounded by an attitude of intransigence
and a tendency toward violence. Group demands were invariably stated in the most
extreme terms, and legislative decisions,
whenever they were made, were never accepted as final. The violence and the stub-
bornness that accompanied the demands

8 Recent studies indicate that the Frenchman's associational membership is formally comparable with that
of the Englishman and American. Nevertheless, the
actual level of organizational participation in France
was and is much lower.

contributed further, of course, to the problems of the French political system.

Strikes and violent demonstrations by workers were a common feature of most European societies in the nineteenth and the early part of the twentieth centuries. But France has always exceeded Germany (with the exception of the Weimar period) and England in both regards. Almost every French organization has, historically, been willing to resort to direct action. In 1950 the Bishop for Luçon, for instance, speaking for other bishops in western France, publicly urged the faithful to "postpone" payment of taxes until their grievances on the school question were met. In the first six months of 1961, prolonged or token strikes were called by butchers, bakers, university students, student examiners, milk producers, and bank clerks.

Many other examples can be cited. In 1954 and 1955, massive resistance by shopkeepers to the more rigorous enforcement of existing tax laws resulted in tax collectors' being tarred and feathered. Peasant strikes, to cite an additional example, have a long history in France. At the turn of the century, the winegrowers of Aube and Marne resorted to burning each others' vineyards and fought government troops over the question of whose wine would be entitled to the coveted label of Champagne. Peasant strikes and violence against the government's agricultural policies were a common feature of the Fourth Republic, as well as the Fifth. And it was, finally, the French army, in rebellion against the government's Algerian policies, that brought down the Fourth Republic; it was also the army, or at least segments of it, that posed the most significant threat to the Fifth Republic in the wake of the Algerian settlement.

French politicians, more especially in the aftermath of World War II, have not been oblivious to the critically disruptive nature of interest-group activity. Robert Lacoste, a Socialist and one-time minister of labor, publicly castigated the trade-union lobby in 1952 for being responsible for the overthrow of the cabinet because its demands were not acceded to. Antoine Pinay, a conservative, warned those supporting him to be less rapacious, and the pretender to the French throne, the count of Paris, indicated that he was disturbed at the excesses of his supporters. Yet despite the politicians' public fretting, groups continued to pin the label of irresponsibility on others, not themselves; the suspicion with which each group viewed the motives of all other groups was such that none was willing to make concessions unless forced to do so.

For the simple reason that power was extremely disorganized in the French political system under the Third and Fourth Republics, members of the National Assembly and the executive, including the bureaucracy, were all targets of interest-group activity. In the assembly, deputies sympathetic to a particular special interest would form a "study group," meeting from time to time to try to load legislative committees with deputies attuned to the concerns of their interest group. They would also try to colonize the bureaucracy with supporters of their interest group.

The result was not unlike the governmental pattern in the United States: not only did various ministries fight with one another, but constant friction also existed within the ministries and the parliamentary committees. Since most governments ruled with such tenuous majorities that even the defection of a few deputies could bring them down, many special-interest groups were able to veto a bill they considered detrimental by influencing a small number of deputies. (But for the same reasons, few groups were able to push through important legislation for their own benefit.) Also, because parties were poorly organized and most deputies depended for their political survival upon establishing good constituent relations on an individual basis, they felt far more at the mercy of particular interests than did their English counterparts. They would, therefore, introduce measure after measure totally unrelated to any overall conception of government policy, though many hoped their proposals would be buried in committee—as, indeed, most of them were. Thus, the policies that emerged from Parliament often reflected the hodge-podge of unrelated group demands. In all, then, interest groups in the Third and Fourth Republics contributed to the government instability which prevented the effective consideration and implementation of public policy.

A striking example of the negative effects of lobbying can be seen in the relation between alcohol and politics in France under the Fourth Republic.[9] Most Frenchmen are either directly or indirectly concerned with the production of alcohol. France is among the most important wine-producing nations in the world, but beet, grape, and apple growers have also seen much of their product used for the production of industrial alcohol. Understandably, the French government has been actively concerned with the alcohol question for many decades. Overproduction of wine has been an intermittent problem since the turn of the century, and governments have regularly bought wine stocks to protect producers from the vicissitudes of world and domestic markets. Governments have also bought up excess stores of beet alcohol and alcohol produced from apples. Subsidization, however, has only increased production and forced more subsidization, thus increasing government expenditures. In fiscal 1953–1954 the government purchased 4,196,000 hectoliters of alcohol[10] at a cost of some 48 billion francs. Three years later, government-held stocks of surplus alcohol amounted to more than 105 million gallons.

The problem would not be quite so befuddling if something economically productive could have been done with the stocks. The government sold some to foreign countries, but generally at a considerable loss. In 1951, five million hectoliters of alcohol were sold to the United States for use in the manufacture of synthetic rubber; the alcohol had been purchased by the state at a cost of 48 billion francs—and sold at a net loss of 26 billion francs. The government also tried to use alcohol to supplement gasoline, but this did not prove particularly feasible either. For one thing, each liter purchased, at a cost of one hundred francs, replaced a liter of gasoline costing only 14 francs. For another, alcohol proved to be harmful to the engine of the automobile; it evaporated rapidly, reduced mileage, and left a deposit in the engine.

More than the problems of money and mileage were involved, however; the overproduction of alcohol had medical repercussions. It was estimated, in the mid-1950's, that Frenchmen were consuming an average of 28 liters of alcohol a year. This was not, as doctors were to point out, an average consumption to be compared favorably with the 14.2 liters for Italians, 8.8 liters each for Englishmen and Americans, 5.1 liters for Germans, and 4.9 liters for Danes. The consequences of France's somewhat excessive rate of alcoholic consumption were that deaths from cirrhosis of the liver were high, 23 per cent of all patients admitted to psychiatric hospitals were alcoholics, 17 per cent of industrial accidents were caused by alcoholism, and thirty to forty per cent of French criminals were estimated to be alcoholics. In all, it was estimated that the average family in France spent approximately nine per cent of its budget on alcohol, six per cent on medical bills and other health items, and four per cent for housing. Officials concluded in 1954 that some 15 per cent of the adult male population was in a state of "alcoholic impregnation" and that another thirty per cent "pass reasonable limits and run the risk of impairing their health." These facts had their own economic consequences: in the 1950's, the cost to the state for the care of alcoholics was approximately 7.5 billion dollars a year.

It was only natural that many public servants and ministers wanted to do something about the problem. In the postwar period, efforts were made to reduce subsidies and to

9 The following section is based on Bernard E. Brown's "Alcohol and Politics in France," *American Political Science Review,* LI (December 1957), pp. 976–995.

10 One hectoliter equals approximately 26.4 United States gallons.

regulate the home production of alcohol, and the government also mounted campaigns against excess drinking. Anyone attempting to change the status quo, however, had to contend with the fierce opposition of the vested interest involved.

Approximately one and one-half million Frenchmen were engaged in grape culture, 150,000 in beet culture, and roughly a half million were employed in subsidiary industries connected with the production and marketing of alcohol. Futhermore, another 3.5 million Frenchmen distilled alcohol at home—and home distilling of limited quantities of tax-free alcohol had long been regarded, certainly by those who engaged in it, as an inalienable right of Frenchmen. Not only had the number of *bouilleurs de cru* or *petits récoltants,* as they called themselves, grown enormously, but it was estimated that they were producing twice as much alcohol as legally permitted, thus contributing to overproduction.

The number and nature of lobbies that have been dedicated to the protection of those producing alcohol are impressive. They include the National Union of Alcohol Distillers Groups, the French Institute of Alcohol, the General Confederation of Beet Planters, and the National Syndicate of Home Distillers. Cooperation among them has not been especially noteworthy: their interests do diverge, and, moreover, insofar as any group is willing to admit that an alcohol problem does exist in France, each has tended to blame the others. Nevertheless, force of circumstance has often whipped them into a joint frenzy over the same legislation, prompting them to support each other on particularly threatening regulations.

The alcohol lobbies' efforts during the Fourth Republic to block any cutback in the production or consumption of alcohol were directed at the public, the government, and, primarily, the legislature and its committees. Producers of commercial alcohol told Frenchmen that the attempt to reduce state purchases was a plot by the American oil companies in league with the Arabs, or else a plot by the Americans to replace wine with Coca-Cola and thus to destroy French culture. Wine producers have even claimed that there is no relation between wine and alcoholism; in fact, *Le Moniteur Vinicole* discovered a correlation in 1956 between the drinking of water and cancer, and ran an editorial urging citizens to combat cancer by avoiding water and drinking wine. Finally, all groups have maintained that the attempt to end subsidies was either a Communist plot against the existence of the stalwart French peasant or a reactionary Fascist plot against the "little man."

The major focus of interest-group pressure was on the government's *Service des alcools,* which in the 1930's became a public corporation endowed with financial autonomy. Attached to the service was a *Conseil supérieur des alcools,* a group that was to be consulted on all modifications of government policy with respect to the purchase and sale of alcohol. The alcohol interests controlled the conseil and, to a considerable extent, the service during much of the Fourth Republic. In 1957, however, Paul Ramadier, then Finance Minister, named a new director of the service who tried to take an independent line. Yet even during an earlier period, public servants in the health field, as well as those in the Ministry of Finance and elsewhere, were constantly proposing plans to ameliorate the alcohol situation without much success; in many cases they managed to convince the government in office to introduce reform legislation only to have it defeated or emasculated by the assembly.

The rule of thumb in France has always been that "beets are Radical, apples are moderate, and wine is Socialist." This is an oversimplification, but the point is that the alcohol interests have supporters in all parties. During the 1950's, their best friends were the Poujadists, who denied the existence of any problem—except that of the foreign plot to cut alcohol production. Other conservative groups tended to be friendly, stressing that the real need was to maintain a strong French peasantry. The position of the left was more complicated. The Communists were utterly opposed to alcoholism, but they argued that it could never be eliminated except by revolutionizing France; until then, they claimed, efforts to limit the rights of small distillers would be reviving decrees issued by the Vichy regime. The Socialists also accepted the Marxist analysis of the causes of alcoholism, but emphasized reformist measures to relieve the human tragedy. Yet Socialist deputies from the Midi supported the grape growers. The only party that gave active endorsement to efforts to solve the alcohol problem was the M.R.P., although there were some deputies from other parties who could also be counted on to vote for reforms.

The assembly committees concerned with the problem had, of course, a heavy representation of deputies who supported the alcohol interests. Not surprisingly, 27 of the 44 members of the Beverage Committee were from wine-growing areas. The president of the Agriculture Committee was often a member of the Beverage Committee, and the chairman of the Beverage Committee was often a member of the Agriculture Committee. Both groups were in a crucial position to affect government policy on alcohol. The power of the alcohol interests and of their parliamentary supporters is illustrated by two events that occurred under the premierships of René Mayer and Mèndes-France. In 1953 Mayer was invested as premier with the support of the Radicals, the M.R.P., the Independents, some Gaullists, and most peasants. He submitted to the assembly a request for special executive powers to deal by decree with a number of economic problems, including that of alcohol surpluses. After a sustained propaganda campaign by groups within the assembly against a grant of authority to deal with the alcohol issue, he was denied a vote of confidence and was forced to resign. The alcohol interests did not themselves bring him down, but given the

flimsiness of Mayer's majority, they were an important factor in his downfall.

The efforts of the Mendès-France government in the same area are also instructive. The government asked for authority to issue decrees that would have reduced both the size of the beet crop and the number of home distillers. The government was bitterly condemned by the home distillers, who implied that the government's plan was a bureaucratic, international capitalist or Communist plot to destroy France. The Communists, too, saw in the proposals the machinations of international capitalism. As the tone of debate on the issues became increasingly shrill, the French Institute of Public Opinion conducted a national survey which concluded that 81 per cent of the population opposed subsidies to beet growers, five per cent favored subsidies, and 14 per cent had no opinion; 61 per cent supported limitations upon home distilling, 17 per cent did not, and 22 per cent had no opinion. Despite clear public support, however, most efforts of the government to master the alcohol problem—even temporarily—were overridden by the assembly.

In the later years of the Fourth Republic, the parliamentary and public activity of special-interest groups began to show signs of new attitudes. Not only were some groups developing a better organizational capacity, but, more important, they were demonstrating an increasing sense of responsibility. As distinct from the initial, violent opposition to the formation of the European Coal and Steel Community by many businessmen, for example, substantial portions of French business, including some of its more reactionary spokesmen, took a far more positive attitude toward the Common Market. Further, within the trade unions and even among peasant groups a younger generation began manifesting a more positive and pragmatic outlook. It is true, of course, that the army brought down the republic over the Algerian affair. But this was a peculiarly intractable problem and essentially a hangover from France's past. Had it not been for Algeria, it is likely that the trend toward a more constructive attitude on the part of France's pressure groups would have continued without interruption.

The trend certainly reappeared early in the Fifth Republic, as pointed out in discussions of particular interests earlier in the volume. In fact, to many Frenchmen activity in associations came to seem more meaningful than the rhetoric of the traditional parties. To be sure, there were peasant riots over grain prices and other grievances, and other interests on occasion took rather violent action. But on the whole, the trend seemed in the direction of accommodation.

The middle and late 1960's, however, witnessed a reversion to form. As the memories of former instability and crises faded under de Gaulle, and more and more groups wanted more and more concessions, the streets once again resounded with special demands. The authoritarianism of the regime itself, which had effectively blocked appeals through traditional channels, helped contribute to the clamor, warranted or extremist. The climax came in 1968 when student riots in the universities led to a nationwide general strike and a new election.

In the meantime, the nature of the de Gaulle regime had restructured interest-group activity on the political level. The basic cause of change, of course, was the expansion in the power of the executive and the bureaucratic elite at the expense of the legislature. As a result, interest groups spent comparatively less time trying to influence deputies and a good deal more upon the administrators. In doing so, they found that rational arguments seemed to carry far more weight than the traditional type of political intrigue. Bureaucrats, for their part, have now become more flexible in their disposition toward interest groups. Many agencies are still staffed with persons who sympathize with the groups in matters of government policy and, to a certain extent, act as their spokesmen. Also, as under the Fourth Republic, the groups can still exercise pressure through the advisory councils that continue to proliferate. But on many occasions the government has bypassed older, more established groups and worked with others in a particular area of interest whose members seemed more interested in rationalization and modernization; in drawing up its plans to consolidate agricultural holdings, for example, the regime worked more closely with the National Center of Young Farmers than with the older and more conservative National Federation of Syndicated Farmers.

Indicative of the changes that have taken place is the fate of the government's attempts to deal with the problems of alcohol. In 1958 and 1959, the Service des Alcools at last embarked upon a reasonably effective program of reducing the amount of alcohol distilled from apples, and in August 1960 a decree finally eliminated the tax exemption for home distillers, maintaining it as a personal right only for those entitled to it as of 1959 or their surviving mates. In addition, a decree of November 1960 limited the number of bars in the vicinity of hospitals and youth centers. The government has also initiated a campaign not only to reduce the amount of alcohol produced from beets, but also to turn land used in the production of beets to other uses as demand declines.

Some of these reform measures aroused considerable opposition. The debate over taxing home distillers was extremely raucous, and the government's proposal was defeated by the Senate the first time around. Not until a later try in 1960 was it granted the authority to issue the new regulations, which, indeed, were never ratified by or even debated by Parliament. Pressure to secure such a debate continued until 1965, with even U.D.R. deputies participating in the effort. The government, however, held firm and won its point.

It is now estimated that home distilleries are drying up at the rate of 50,000 a year. Unfortunately, the annual consumption of alcohol, after dropping in the early 1960's to an average of 26.8 liters per Frenchman, has now moved back to its present high levels.

6. RETROSPECT AND PROSPECT

The governmental process in France from the end of the Franco-Prussian War to de Gaulle's Fifth Republic reflected the fragmentation and lack of cohesion of French society. A parliamentary system in which the survival of the government was contingent upon the whim of a narrow and shifting majority could not hope to aggregate the demands of the citizenry into effective policy alternatives. All governments were based on coalitions of parties—themselves coalitions of diverse groups—and none could act decisively lest it lose the shaky majority that had put it into office. The result was a series of weak governments incapable of governing, governments that served mainly as brokers among various groups. Nor could the French government develop collective responsibility or bring the bureacratic apparatus to heel. It was not, as many have alleged, that some special group such as the bureaucracy or the "plutocrats" held power and prevented change; rather, France, divided against itself, could not generate the power to solve community problems.

With the government in almost helpless—and constant—disarray, the legislature was left to its own devices, and the complex and powerful committee system it developed was partly the result of an effort to organize its work effectively. Unfortunately, the committees themselves became the captives of limited interests and served merely to further diffuse political authority.

Indeed, the whole structure of French government, while a vivid symptom of more basic difficulties in the French community, only increased the sisyphean task of dealing with the problems facing the nation. Voters had to choose among a multiplicity of parties; not one of them could ever form a government by itself or carry through an integrated policy—and they were not expected to. Nor

could any government be judged by the consequences of its policies; most governments never bothered to develop effective policies at all, and those that did could never carry them out.

The result was a vicious political cycle. Since voters could not make judgments on the basis of policies actually carried out, they were encouraged to continue making them on the basis of an ideological rhetoric that had never had to meet the crucial test of being translated into concrete public policies. The same ideological slogans were consequently repeated year after year and decade after decade, and since no one really expected either parties or governments to promulgate policies bearing any relation to reality, most voters continued to assess their deputies on the basis of whether or not they had managed to obtain certain limited economic favors—a special subsidy, a paved road, a new school, a wage increase.

Within the assembly, ideological politics was transformed into interest-group politics; deputies mingled high-flown rhetoric with hard bargaining for specific economic objectives. And the governments most likely to remain in office for the longest time were the least ideological, and the most willing and able to act as clever brokers among the various groups. The whole process reduced the prestige of politics in the eyes of the voters and discredited the parliamentary system. It also postponed the day when France would at last have to tangle with the crucial problems that beset a modern nation.

The faults of the system should not be overstated. In times of crisis, France usually managed to establish reasonably strong governments. And the system did, on the whole, offer a framework within which political and social life remained fairly peaceful and democratic freedoms prevailed, no mean accomplishment. Charles de Gaulle is a case in point—a strong man put in office at a moment of crisis. His objective was to reform French political institutions even as he pushed through economic and social reforms to modernize and strengthen the nation. France was, at last, provided with a strong executive, established through both constitutional reforms and de Gaulle's personal leadership. The reforms remain.

It is not easy to predict the future course of French government without de Gaulle. His successor, Pompidou, appointed a government consisting of a combination of Gaullists and politicians drawn from centrist and conservative political groupings. It was clearly his hope to create a broadly based conservative—yet modernizing—coalition that would provide a stable parliamentary majority. Nonetheless, the appointments displeased some Gaullists who considered them a betrayal of the general. If Pompidou fails in his mission of conservative stability, a return to a rather more diffuse and chaotic politics can be expected, at least in the short run.

Whether Pompidou succeeds or fails, however, certain changes on the French political scene are in the offing. Most likely the presidency will not be nearly so strong as it was under de Gaulle, and some power will revert to both the premier and Parliament. Yet unless the constitution itself is changed, it is hard to envisage a National Assembly as powerful or as disorganized as those of the Fourth Republic. Of more importance, voters have experienced a government that could govern for eleven years. They have voted in elections in which they knew their decisions would make a difference, and there is clear evidence not only that they appreciated this opportunity, but that they would be extremely impatient with anything too closely resembling a return to governmental paralysis. Finally, the France of 1969 is not the France of 1958. While de Gaulle capitalized on changes that had developed earlier, his years of office witnessed some very basic modifications of French society. Small-town, rural, isolated France is quickly disappearing, and, today, the modern sector of French life is increasingly significant. A new generation has grown up that recognizes the interrelatedness of public policy and the need for integrated national policies. Many of the old cleavages have become less sharp, and much of the traditional ideology seems rather archaic.

Of course, France is not, nor has it ever been, politically somnolent. Irreconcilable cross-currents of political and social theory do exist, as represented in part by the romantic irrationalism typical of the most radical elements in the student movement. The demands of these groups for greater government concern with the style of French life will no doubt have an impact on the future of politics. Yet it is unlikely that they will persuade more than a small fraction of the citizenry that their peculiar combination of anarchy and communalism offers a solution to the problems that France will face in the immediate future.

17

Chancellor Democracy in Germany

1. INTRODUCTION

The fall of the German Empire in 1918 led to Germany's first experiment with democratic institutions—an experiment that failed dismally and was followed by the National Socialist regime of Adolf Hitler. The effort made through the Weimar constitution to establish democratic institutions came to naught because of the underlying conditions of German social life. Torn apart by tensions induced by the rapid modernization of an extremely rigid traditional society, Germans were unable to construct institutions that would have enabled them to find a peaceful solution to their problems.

The result was that a regime of reconciliation was replaced by a peculiar kind of mobilization regime, which led the nation into a devastating war and was responsible for the mass murder of millions of people. In the aftermath of that war, a second attempt was made to create a representative political order. The writers of the Bonn constitution took into account the mistakes of Weimar, and from 1949 until 1963 Germany basked

in a period of amazing political stability. Since then, however, it has once again become clear that constitutional engineering has its limits, and that the political dynamics of the Adenauer era reflected the impact of the war and reconstruction as well as the personality of Adenauer himself.

The present chapter will briefly review the evolution of governmental processes in Germany, concentrating on the post–World War II years. However, the fact that the "reign" of Adenauer was followed so closely by a coalition regarded explicitly as a temporary expedient makes it difficult to generalize. The Bonn Republic is, in a sense, still being born.

2. THE RISE AND FALL OF PARLIAMENTARY INSTITUTIONS IN GERMANY (1870–1945)

The constitution of the Imperial Reich had placed political power in the hands of the emperor, his chancellor, and the Bundesrat. Although the Reichstag's approval was required for the annual budget and other fi-

532

nancial transactions such as loans, it was unable to use this authority to wrest any real concessions, at least during Bismarck's chancellorship. Nor was its prestige very high. It became known in popular parlance as *Quasselbude,* or, roughly, chatterbox.[1]

The failure of the Reichstag to achieve greater political authority was only partially due to the nature of the constitution and the powers granted the executive: the fact was that the more important elites in German society preferred an authoritarian regime. However, after Bismarck's fall, there were indications that the Reichstag was beginning to assert itself. On several occasions between 1906 and 1914, it forced the government to backtrack on policy; more important, after 1909 the government took into account parliamentary sentiment in appointing ministers. Moreover, for the first time in German history, a Reich chancellor was forced to resign in 1909 when his program for financial reform failed to pass the Reichstag. Finally, in 1912, the newly elected Reichstag instituted a vote of no confidence against the government. But the device was used only once, in 1913—and to no effect: it was ignored. The coming of the war almost automatically eliminated the possibility of legislative reform within the framework of existing institutions.

The intention of the writers of the Weimar constitution was to place ultimate sovereignty in the Reichstag. It was given the power to overrule the upper house by a two-thirds vote, and both the chancellor and members of the cabinet were made responsible to it.[2] Further, it was given the power to establish

committees of inquiry and to question members of the government on policy and programs. It is true that the president had the power to dissolve the Reichstag—but only once on a given issue; a new lower house then had to be elected within sixty days and assembled within another thirty. It is also true that Article 48 of the constitution gave the president the right not only to rule by decree in order to maintain public order but also to suspend certain civil liberties in time of national emergency. Yet the constitutional grant was not inordinate, and was theoretically to be invoked only with the approval of the cabinet, and also only on condition that the Reichstag be kept fully informed of the actions taken by the government. Von Hindenburg used the article extensively in the last years of Weimar, because no chancellor candidate could obtain a majority in the Reichstag, much less gain support for a program dealing with the economic crisis faced by the nation. It is difficult to believe, however, that he or any other president could have exercised the power of decree so extensively had not the Reichstag been so fundamentally divided against itself.

It was the fragmentation of German political and social life, not the weaknesses of the constitution, that destroyed the Weimar Republic. The multiplicity of political parties, all of them defining their interest in a strict ideological manner, and a general unwillingness to abide by the rules of the political game, made it almost impossible to process political demands. Coalitions formed and reformed, cabinets rose and collapsed, and election after election was held without changing the hopeless impasse in the legislature. In despair, the Reichstag voted enabling legislation to permit the cabinet to act by decree on those critical, public matters that the individual deputies were too timid to consider. Finally, after 1930, power fell by default to von Hindenburg—and from von Hindenburg to Hitler. Using a combination of force and cajolery, Hitler pushed through

---

[1] The reader may wish to review the history of German political institutions in Chapter 2, pp. 78–87.

[2] The chancellor was appointed and could be dismissed by the president. Von Hindenburg used this authority between 1930 and 1932 to fire chancellors he did not like. This power accrued to him, however, because the Reichstag was unable to agree on a candidate for the office. Thus, von Hindenburg essentially ruled by the emergency powers granted him under Article 48, and his chancellor-designates did not have to receive Reichstag approval.

an enabling act that allowed him to rule by decree and to establish the Nazi dictatorship.

The regime created by Hitler was a totalitarian police state, in which the fundamental decisions were made by him, often with the advice of small groups of trusted comrades. The Reichstag continued to exist, and elections and even plebiscites were held. But in the case of elections, only one slate of candidates was permitted to campaign for office, and in the case of plebiscites, the "people" were permitted only to ratify decisions already taken. Needless to say, the plebiscites in no way represented a valid expression of public opinion.

Unlike the Soviets, however, the Nazi regime was not completely a party dictatorship. Hitler preferred to work through the traditional state machinery—after purging it of "unreliable" elements—and the party never completely permeated the armed forces. Also, a private sector of the economy remained in existence, albeit heavily controlled; but even this meant only that the Nazis were able to achieve their economic goals by exercising control rather than by wholesale nationalization.

We know now that behind the facade of unity that the Hitler regime presented to the world, incredible confusion and overlapping of jurisdictions prevailed. Hitler's subordinates used their positions to increase their power and to curry favor with the Führer, and Hitler adroitly played off one subordinate against another to make sure that no one emerged as a possible competitor. Because of the highly personal nature of the regime, and the fact that it had not succeeded in institutionalizing the Nazi Party as a source of leadership recruitment or as a policy-making body, there is some question as to whether the apparatus would have survived Hitler's death. It seems likely that even if the Nazis had not been defeated, the Third Reich would eventually have been transformed into a bureaucratic dictatorship which, itself, would probably have eroded.

3. DECISION-MAKING IN THE WEST GERMAN REPUBLIC: CHANCELLOR AND CABINET

In "correcting" the mistakes of Weimar, those who drew up the constitution of the Federal Republic of Germany downgraded the presidency and attempted to insure executive stability by creating a strong chancellor. The strength of the British prime minister, it was asserted, came from his position as the head of a powerful party within the framework of a two-party system. The writers of the Bonn constitution, knowing there was no guarantee that these conditions would apply to Germany, made an effort to create them through a number of specific provisions. For example, the unseating of a chancellor required a "constructive" vote of no confidence —the Bundestag could not overthrow a chancellor unless, at the same time, it designated a new one, a restriction intended to prevent a repetition of the Weimar experience in which the extreme left and the extreme right combined to overturn centrist governments but could not agree on any candidates to replace the officials they had dismissed. Under certain special circumstances, the new constitution also gave the government the power to enact legislation without the approval of the Bundestag. Further, the writers of the Bonn constitution had not forgotten the problems inherent in Weimar cabinets that so often were divided against themselves, with each minister attempting to strengthen his own position or that of the coalition party or interest that he represented. By clearly defining the chancellor as the leading figure in the government, they hoped that a stable focus of authority could be created.

During the regime of Konrad Adenauer, all these constitutional provisions had their expected effect, for the chancellor effectively dominated the government to the extent that commentators spoke of West Germany's system of government as "chancellor democracy." After Adenauer retired, however, and even during the last few years of his tenure, both the legislature and the political parties began to reassert their authority. It is, therefore, a little difficult to determine what relationship will develop between government and Parliament in the next few years; indeed, the Grand Coalition government gave little clue to the durability, or even viability, of the changes wrought by the authors of the Bonn constitution. However, the resignation of Chancellor Ludwig Erhard in 1966, primarily the result of splits within the Christian Democratic Union, indicated once again that institutional mechanisms alone have a limited capacity to insure governmental stability.

The German executive comprises the chancellor, the president of the republic, and the cabinet of federal ministers. Ministers are appointed by the chancellor after his election by the Bundestag, and unless they are dismissed by him, their term of office ends with his resignation. The primacy of the chancellor was thus established by the constitution despite the fact that, according to its standing orders, all cabinet decisions are to be taken by majority vote. Indeed, Adenauer regarded his ministers primarily as technical experts subordinate to him. General policies which he considered important were decided by him, and majority approval from the cabinet was usually automatic. On a number of occasions, he made personal decisions and only later informed the cabinet about them. In 1950, for example, Adenauer decided that Germany would participate in the proposed European Defense Community, but he did not so advise his cabinet until negotiations for its creation were well under way. As a result, his minister of the interior, Gustav Heinemann, resigned. It is true that Adenauer's chief concern was foreign affairs and that, by and large, he left the development of domestic policy to the cabinet and the ministries; the minister of finance and the economic minister, especially, had a great deal of leeway in making decisions.

Erhard, conversely, moved in the direction of genuine collegiality and cheerfully admit-

ted to being overruled by the cabinet on a number of occasions. Neither his temperament nor the balance of power in his party permitted him to repeat Adenauer's performance. The Christian Democrats were seriously divided over Erhard's leadership; the aura that surrounded Adenauer did not rub off on him, and he had neither the capacity nor the desire to play off faction against faction to the extent that Adenauer did. The same collegiality was manifested within the coalition cabinet headed by Christian Democrat Kurt Georg Kiesinger as chancellor and Social Democrat Willy Brandt as vice chancellor. Neither man dominated his party and the most important ministers were, in fact, leading party figures. It was, therefore, only those policies upon which substantial agreement could be reached that the cabinet could rely upon the approval of the Bundestag.

Just what relationship will prevail between chancellor and cabinet, and cabinet and Bundestag, under the mini-coalition of Social Democrats and Free Democrats formed by Brandt in 1969 is not easy to assess. More than that of previous chancellors, Brandt's relationship to his party more closely resembles that of the British prime minister to his: he has brought with him into the cabinet many first-echelon party leaders who carry their own political weight. And more than any one of them, Brandt represents the party to the nation. Yet the fact that the S.P.D. must rely on F.D.P. support to stay in office is bound to restrict Brandt's freedom of action.

During the Weimar Republic, what went on in cabinet meetings often quickly became public information, to the detriment of formulating sound policy. Even if members of the coalition wished to compromise in an attempt to achieve common policies, the publicity attendant upon their expression of views within the cabinet often forced them to maintain a rigid political stance. The standing orders of the cabinet in the Federal Republic state that remarks made at meetings are to be confidential and can be released only with the consent of the chancellor. In the first years of the Bonn regime, however, this rule was often ignored. It was only as Adenauer's power increased that he was able to insist upon strict confidence, although he was not adverse to breaking the rule himself and criticizing members of the cabinet for taking positions he did not like. Under Chancellor Erhard, the situation in the cabinet deteriorated to the extent that a few ministers were submitting proposals to the chancellor by mail, for consideration by the cabinet. The Kiesinger-Brandt cabinet was also plagued by some leaks, although the situation was kept under better control.

Seventy-five per cent or more of the bills passed by the German parliament emanate from the government, although, as we shall see, the Bundestag has more influence over the final content of legislation than the parliament of either England or France. The constitution provides that the chancellor be responsible for the general direction of public policy, and the chancellor's office, the Federal Chancellery, was created to assist him in this task. Under Adenauer, the office was an extremely powerful one; its first director, Secretary of State Hans Globke, was for many years the second most powerful man in Germany. In its coordinating capacity, the chancellery made certain that no policies objectionable to Adenauer were formed. Globke set up a staff of nearly one hundred high-level officials, organized to parallel the ministries of the federal government and to supervise the progress of legislation. In the years of his greatest authority, Adenauer relied upon the office to keep tabs on his ministries, and Globke could effectively veto legislative proposals emanating from ministries by reporting his objections to the chancellor.

The power of the chancellor's office and the technical qualifications of its personnel were such that it questioned ministries concerning issues that might eventually become legislative projects and, in conjunction with the legislative committee of the cabinet, set priorities for the government's program. It prepared cabinet agendas, insured that bills submitted by one department had received the clearance of others, and supplied the chancellor with a summary of proposed laws and the issues they raised. It also served as the channel of communication between the government and Parliament, transmitting bills approved by the cabinet to the parliament. Finally, it received all parliamentary inquiries for transmittal to the relevant ministries.

The authority of the chancellery declined somewhat during Erhard's administration and became less of a personal instrument. That decline continued under the Kiesinger-Brandt coalition. The staff was even larger and more professional than it once was, containing not only Christian Democrats but Social Democrats as well. But this pluralism prevented the chancellery from both formulating a consistent point of view and imposing it upon governmental departments as it once did.

One other agency used by Adenauer to good effect was the Federal Press and Information Bureau. Controlled directly by the chancellor, the bureau had at its disposal a special fund running to some three million dollars a year—which permitted the subsidization of favored periodicals, newspapers, and journalists. The fund was particularly effective in rural areas and small towns which had less access to different news sources. The bureau's influence, however, diminished considerably under the coalition government.

Most ministers under the German Empire were high-level civil servants and were paid accordingly. (See Table 17.1.) Even as members of the government, they were considered administrators of public policy rather than political figures. Most Weimar ministers were picked from Parliament, but they continued to be paid according to civil-service scales and received retirement benefits after four years of service.

Adenauer drew a number of his ministers from the bureaucracy, and even those who

TABLE 17.1. BACKGROUND OF GERMAN CABINET MEMBERS, 1890–1960

	Empire	Weimar Republic	Third Reich	Federal Republic
Political affiliation				
Party member	38.1%	81.8%	75.8%	100.0%
None indicated	61.9	18.2	24.2	0
Religious affiliation				
Protestant	13.2	27.9	45.5	54.5
Roman Catholic	13.2	25.4	9.1	38.6
Other (including Jewish)	1.3	15.7	0	0
None indicated	72.3	31.1	45.5	6.8
Occupational background[1]				
Civil service	64.5	48.4	48.4	27.2
Law	40.7	31.1	15.2	21.9
Business	1.3	16.4	27.3	21.9
Professional military	16.9	7.4	18.2	0
Teaching	5.2	12.3	12.1	9.1
Journalism	1.3	19.7	9.1	4.5
Engineering	0	0	9.1	11.4
Military experience				
Indicated	34.2	27.1	72.8	70.4
None indicated	65.8	72.9	27.2	29.6
Father's occupation[1]				
Civil servant	23.6	4.9	12.1	20.4
Businessman	10.4	18.9	18.2	22.3
Worker, artisan	1.3	11.5	3.0	18.2
Professional military	9.1	4.9	12.1	9.1
Lawyer	18.4	1.6	0	6.8
Teacher	0	3.3	6.1	6.8
Large landowner	18.4	6.6	12.1	9.1
Political party leader	2.6	0	0	2.3
Other salaried employee	4.0	2.4	0	6.8
Small farmer	0	0.8	3.0	4.5
Doctor or clergyman	3.9	3.3	3.0	0
Not ascertained	24.9	44.4	24.2	13.6
Size of birthplace				
Under 20,000	56.6	55.7	42.4	27.3
20,000–100,000	15.6	22.1	24.2	34.1
Over 100,000	21.6	18.9	18.2	38.6
Not available	6.2	3.3	15.2	0
Geographic origin				
Territory of Federal Republic				
Northern Germany	3.9	12.3	9.1	6.8
Southern Germany	14.4	23.9	33.4	27.2
Western Germany	14.5	26.2	18.2	43.2
Central and Eastern Germany				
(including Berlin)	63.2	34.6	24.2	22.6
Abroad	2.6	3.0	12.1	0
Not indicated	0	0	3.0	0

[1]Since one person may have engaged in several occupations during the course of his career, the columns are non-additive.

Adapted from Lewis Edinger, *Politics in Germany* (Boston: Little, Brown, 1968), pp. 182–184. Reprinted by permission of the publisher.

were party and parliamentary leaders were treated as technical experts rather than members of a political team—a policy he could follow because his stature as a political leader was so much greater than that of other party members. The manner in which ministers were chosen and Adenauer's attitude toward them also affected their relationship with Parliament. Despite the continued participation of ministers in parliamentary debates and their extended presence at committee meetings, the relations between the government and Parliament more closely resembled the American or the French pattern under de Gaulle than the British; members of the government tended not only to approach the discussion of legislation as "experts" but to impose their "expert" knowledge upon Parliament. Parliament, on the other hand, through committees and specialized parliamentary groups, regarded itself as something of an independent force. Even members of the C.D.U. did not look upon ministers as representatives or symbols of their party. As Table 17.2 indicates, a high degree of party discipline was maintained in votes on legislation, but such votes were always preceded by lengthy negotiations of a kind which made it clear that party members considered their interests and those of the government to be quite different in many areas.

With Erhard as chancellor, the C.D.U. began asserting its corporate will, and the government found itself increasingly dependent upon the party for its existence. As several strong party leaders emerged, relations between the government and the party moved closer to the British political pattern; party divisions were reflected in the cabinet, and the stability of the government became increasingly contingent upon the loyalty of the party in Parliament. It was Erhard's failure to command such loyalty that caused his downfall. Kiesinger, of course, was forced to bring into the cabinet Christian Democratic leaders representing a variety of factions, just as Brandt has sought to include within the cabinet those Socialists who can command rank-and-file support. Not only is the German cabinet today much more of an organization of "coequals," but more than ever before it must weigh the reaction of the parliamentary party in making its decisions.

Indicative of the government's greater need to take parliamentary parties into consideration was the creation in 1967 of the post, modeled after the English, of parliamentary state secretary in six of the larger ministries. These secretaries, drawn from Parliament, serve the same functions as their British counterparts. They aid the minister both in departmental coordination and in his work with Parliament. Most important, they strengthen the position of the government by bringing into it ambitious young parliamentarians who, it is hoped, will develop a vested interest in supporting cabinet decisions. The

TABLE 17.2. PARTY UNITY IN THE BUNDESTAG

Percentage of deputies voting with the plurality of the members of their parliamentary party in roll-call votes.

Party	First Bundestag 1949–1953	Second Bundestag 1953–1957	Third Bundestag 1957–1961
C.D.U./C.S.U.	93.6	95.0	97.0
Social Democrats	99.9	99.7	99.8
Free Democrats	91.3	89.5	96.3
German Party	89.8	90.2	94.0

Adapted from Gerhard Loewenberg, *Parliament in the German Political System* (Ithaca: Cornell University Press, 1967), p. 357. Copyright © 1967 by Cornell University. Used by permission of Cornell University Press.

Brandt government in 1969 expanded this practice by providing state secretaries, with increased authority, for all its ministries.

As in other parliamentary countries, ministers in Germany function in three major capacities: as part of the collective decision-making machinery of the cabinet, as heads of their own ministries, and as explicators and defenders of their policies before Parliament. But because of Germany's federal structure, their administrative duties are far less burdensome—and confer far less authority—than those of English and French ministers. Since federal programs are administered by state bureaucracies, German ministries are rather small, and ministerial decisions must always take into account the attitudes of state governments. In drawing up legislation, for example, ministers enter into negotiations with Land officials at an early stage.

Thus far, their parliamentary chores have also been less taxing than those of British ministers. Even though they are expected, as we shall see, to appear before committees, the Bundestag has yet to develop that British kind of parliamentary give-and-take that puts a minister on his mettle. The old status gap between government official and parliamentarian, derived from a time when ministers were responsible only to the emperor, still has its effect. Adenauer often refused to respond to parliamentary questions and regarded the opposition with open contempt. His high-handedness communicated itself to many of his ministers who seemed to regard themselves as standing above petty parliamentary squabbling. These attitudes continue to a certain extent, although, as already noted, the Bundestag is becoming more and more assertive.

4. THE BUNDESTAG[3]

THE PARLIAMENTARY PROFESSION: The Reichstag building in Berlin, in which the German parliament met from 1894 until the

[3] For my discussion of the Bundestag, I am much indebted to Gerhard Loewenberg, *Parliament in the German Political System* (Ithaca: Cornell University Press, 1967).

rise of Hitler, was constructed in the rectangular shape of the British Commons, but with the semicircular, rising rows of seats and radial passages of the French Chamber of Deputies and the American congress. The status of Berlin after World War II meant that it could not be used by the Federal Republic. The current legislative building in Bonn, the Bundeshaus, is located on the bank of the Rhine. Originally constructed as a teachers' training college, it was commandeered by the government in 1949 and remodeled. The semicircular design of the Reichstag has been retained, but most of the space is taken over by chairs and desks, and members wishing to speak from their seats cannot do so without turning their backs either on many deputies or on members of the cabinet. Further, the government bench was on a dais several feet above the floor of the Bundestag so that ministers literally looked down on many of their colleagues. Symbolic of changes taking place in the Bonn Republic, however, an agreement was reached in 1969 to lower the bench to the floor. In the same year, a new parliamentary building was completed which, for the first time, provides each member of the Bundestag with adequate office accommodations.

Bundestag deputies represent a fairly wide cross-section of the population, although persons of middle-class background predominate. Perhaps the largest single group in the postwar period, as was true during the Weimar decade, has been public employees; they compose about twenty per cent of the deputies, a representation far more characteristic of continental countries than of England or the United States (see Table 17.3). It is considered legitimate for members of the civil service to take a leave of absence to run for parliament. It must be remembered that in both France and Germany national unity was created by monarchs assisted by a powerful state bureaucracy; in both nations, although to a greater extent in Germany, a strong centralized bureaucracy preceded the establishment of parliamentary institutions.

Professional politicians form another large segment of the Bundestag—more of them

TABLE 17.3. OCCUPATIONAL BACKGROUND OF GERMAN DEPUTIES[1]

	All Bundestag deputies	C.D.U. deputies	S.P.D. deputies
Government officials and employees	22.3%	22.7%	23.1%
Professions: lawyers, doctors, journalists, clerics, others	20.5	17.5	25.1
Employees of political parties and labor unions	16.1	9.6	18.1
Entrepreneurs, executives, business association officials	15.5	16.7	8.4
Farmers and farm organization representatives	11.5	18.3	1.5
Small businessmen, artisans	6.0	8.0	3.5
White- and blue-collar workers	5.6	4.8	7.4
Housewives	2.5	2.4	2.9

[1] Based on data for the 1961–1965 Bundestag.

Adapted from Arnold J. Heidenheimer, *The Governments of Germany* (New York: Thomas Y. Crowell, 1967), p. 129. Copyright © Thomas Y. Crowell, 1967. Reprinted by permission of the publisher.

members of the S.P.D. than the C.D.U. because of the nature of the Socialist Party, but increasingly in both. And, of course, the professions are heavily represented. The Bundestag also contains a good many deputies who are, at the same time, representatives of trade unions and business or farm organizations. Far more than in England and France, and certainly far more so than in the United States, it is not considered unethical for a member of Parliament to retain his interest-group connections. Again, this attitude stems from a feudal tradition that regarded the political arena as one which represented all estates of the realm, and the direct representation of interests in the Bundestag, or their being consulted by the government in drafting legislation, is not thought to be suspect. Naturally enough, the interest groups most heavily represented in the S.P.D. are the trade unions, while business and agricultural interests have more influence within the C.D.U.

The percentage of blue- and white-collar workers who are deputies is rather small and has been declining even among the Social Democrats despite the fact that the S.P.D. has self-consciously been a working-class party and still gets the bulk of its support from working-class voters. Catholics predominate among C.D.U. deputies, but the opposite has usually been true of the cabinet. On the other hand, only about 15 per cent of the S.P.D. deputies have been Catholics, the remainder either Protestants or without religious affiliation.

Members of the Bundestag are well paid by European standards, and as of 1969 each deputy is provided with a special assistant. Most deputies try to maintain other sources of income and some even hold another political post such as mayor or local councillor, commuting to Bonn when Parliament is in session. A number are salaried members of interest groups. Multiple job holding is quite easy in the Bonn Republic: the Bundestag holds few plenary sessions, usually on just two days of the week. To cite comparisons: during 1954, the British House of Commons held 170 plenary sessions for a total of 1,408 hours; the French National Assembly con-

FIGURE 17.1. COMPOSITION OF THE BUNDESTAG, BY OCCUPATION, 1957–1961

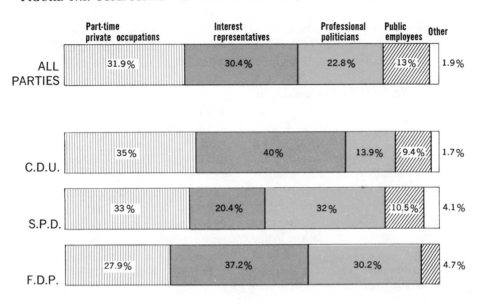

Adapted from Gerhard Loewenberg, *Parliament in the German Political System* (Ithaca: Cornell University Press, 1967), p. 122. Copyright © 1967 by Cornell University. Used with permission of Cornell University Press.

vened 132 times for 796 hours; the United States House of Representatives held 123 plenary sessions for a total of 533 hours; and the Bundestag met in only 55 plenary sessions for 273 hours. The Bonn figure remained fairly constant in the 1960's. However, to the German total must be added the many hours spent at committee and party meetings; party officials and committee chairmen generally devote themselves full-time to their jobs. Indeed, the proportion of Bundestag members who are full-time professional politicians is increasing.

Friendships in the Bundestag will cross party lines only rarely, and speeches still have that dull ponderousness so typical of German parliamentary oratory. There is little of the British witty give-and-take and still a good deal of ideological baggage in evidence, although the past few years have seen some changes in the tenor of Bundestag proceedings. Weimar sessions were enlivened by considerable uproar and an occasional punch in the nose, and similar conduct continued

through the first years of the Bonn Republic. With the disappearance of extremist parties, however, proceedings have become more sedate.

One of the major aspects of the postwar generation of parliamentarians—indeed, of most of the German elite—is the high frequency of agreement on the political rules of the game—and the strong sense of satisfaction with the operation of the new political system. This is even truer of the men now in secondary leadership positions who were children during the Nazi era. These men lack the sense of attachment to traditional subgroups in German life, including both class and church, and they share a reasonably flexible and unromantic outlook. Speaking the language of practicality, most of them are well-informed university graduates with managerial skills, and a style that tends to lack the fire of previous generations.

Some intellectuals see the emergence of this new style as a sign of the dehumanization of social life and a precursor of the faceless bureaucratic state. They are hostile to the "pragmatism" of the new men of power, who, they claim, are avoiding those fundamental human issues that require an existential commitment. The rise of an extraparliamentary opposition in Germany is partly a reflection of displeasure with the new breed of politicians. Yet despite some turbulent currents running in the other direction, political developments in Germany accord with those taking place in most other Western countries including the Soviet Union; political leadership in all of them is becoming less rhetorical in a traditional sense and more oriented toward professional concern with the intricacies of managing modern industrial societies. While the new breed may lack some of the flair of an earlier, more romantic age, one suspects that it will in the long run be associated with a more humane politics.

THE ROLE OF POLITICAL PARTIES: The parliamentary party (*Fraktion*) has had semi-official status in the German parliament since the turn of the century. From 1871 to 1933, special meeting rooms were placed at the disposal of the Fraktionen, and members of the legislative committees were chosen by each Fraktion in proportion to its membership in Parliament.

The practice is still in effect. Under the rules of the Bundestag, an officially recognized parliamentary group must consist of members of the same political party, unless an exception is specifically granted. The minimum strength of a Fraktion is fifteen. If a member of the Bundestag belongs to a party that does not have sufficient strength to form a Fraktion, he may attend meetings of an existing Fraktion as an associate, though the likelihood of his obtaining a desirable committee assignment is not very great.

Funds are appropriated by the Bundestag to support the work of the political parties, and they are used to maintain offices as well as a professional staff. In addition, parties deduct a portion of the salaries of their deputies for operational funds.

Each Fraktion is governed by a charter spelling out the rights and duties of its members. The charters are similar in terms of formal structure, with each Fraktion coordinated by an executive committee (*Vorstand*) composed of a chairman, several vice chairmen, and one or more parliamentary floor leaders who correspond to whips in the House of Commons. All Fraktionen have specialized working committees to handle substantive questions of policy. However, because of its small size, the Free Democratic Party has not carried the committee process quite as far as have the two major parties. Differences between the Fraktionen of the Christian Democratic Party and the Social Democrats are closely related to their general history.[4] The C.D.U./C.S.U.'s method of operation reflects its regional decentralization (especially the quasi independence of the Bavarian Christian Social Union), and the fact that it is a holding company for various interests; the organization of the S.P.D., conversely, reflects the homogeneity and sense of discipline which stem from its heritage as an ideological mass party.

The party Fraktion of the C.D.U./C.S.U. is a conglomeration of many organized interests. C.S.U. deputies, for example, form a separate Land group with its own chairman and deputy chairman. In each Bundestag, the association of the two parties is the result of a specific agreement, usually involving assurances that members of the Christian Social Union will be allotted a certain number of leadership and committee posts. The Christian Democratic Fraktion also contains representatives of different economic groups; the "labor group" is probably the best organized of these; it has its own executive and its own office, and meets fairly regularly. Expressing its views in regular conferences and in a monthly periodical, the labor group is a fairly cohesive force within the party.

Other economic interest groups within the C.D.U. Fraktion include the "discussion

[4] I am omitting a discussion of the F.P.D.

group on middle-class affairs," the "study group on food and agriculture," and a more informal group representing large industry. Still others speak for C.D.U. supporters who fled East Germany or were expelled from other countries.

Such groups are considered a legitimate expression of interests within the Christian Democratic Party, and they receive both official recognition and financial support from the parliamentary party. It should be noted, however, that the core of the parliamentary leadership consists of professional politicians who usually avoid too close identification with any particular interest, and who see their primary function as that of maintaining party unity.

The C.D.U. Fraktion caucuses at least once a week when the Bundestag or its committees are in session. One-half to two-thirds of the members usually attend. Meetings are semipublic and attended by the staff of the parliamentary party as well as friendly newspapermen, civil servants, and, depending on the issues discussed, members of the Bundesrat and the Land parliaments.

Because of its size and organization, the caucus is primarily a meeting in which policies are ratified and views expressed. Its success in presenting the public with a united political position, therefore, depends upon the care with which meetings are prepared. The development of an integrated party policy is one of the functions of the Fraktion's six working subgroups, which deal with legal questions, with economic, foreign and defense, financial, and social policies as well as with matters pertaining to science and publishing; they parallel the committee structure of Parliament, and their chairmen are recommended by the party's executive committee and elected by the caucus. Group chairmen within the Fraktion are experts in the fields with which they are concerned; chairmen of the relevant Bundestag committees are almost never chosen as chairmen of the working groups.

The intricate relationships among the groups that compose the parliamentary party are a ready-made source of internal rancor. The job of the executive committee, of course, is to integrate the cross pressures; the committee, which is chosen at the beginning of the parliamentary year and subject to re-election after one year, consists of the chairman of the parliamentary party, four or five deputy chairmen, two whips, the six chairmen of the working groups, 16 members elected by the caucus, and 13 co-opted by the remainder with the approval of the caucus. Every effort is made by the outgoing executive to secure a balanced representation of party interests. Within the executive committee, a smaller "council of eleven"—including the chairman, the deputy chairman, the chief whip, and the chairmen of the working groups—provides day-to-day leadership, meeting privately prior to meetings of the executive in efforts to secure agreement on important points of the agenda.

In effect, the executive and its inner body are the seat of power in the final determination of party policy: 85 to ninety per cent of the executive's recommendations are accepted by the caucus, with for the most part only desultory debate and rarely more than two-thirds of the caucus members present. This is not to say that the executive dominates the party; its primary efforts, because of the C.D.U.'s heterogeneity, are directed toward cohesion. Almost any important group within the party can veto policy proposals; this became increasingly true during Erhard's chancellorship, and it has continued to be true during the coalition period.

The job of the executive chairman, then—and of the committee itself—is that of mediator. It is extremely difficult to discipline members of the Christian Democratic Party, and in fact, deputies have been expelled from the ranks only on rare occasions. Under these circumstances, the ability of the C.D.U. to retain its cohesion is open to question.

The Social Democratic Party has remained, thus far, a more homogeneous group than the

C.D.U. Its national organization is more highly centralized; although diverse interests exist within the party, they have not developed an organizational base, at least in Parliament. The prime effort of the S.P.D. has been directed, not toward reconciling diverse interests within the party, but toward widening its appeal so as to bring in new groups.

Like the C.D.U., the S.P.D. is divided into working groups that parallel the Bundestag committees. The chairman and deputy chairman of each working group are elected by the caucus and enjoy considerable security of tenure. The Socialists' executive committee, made up of a chairman, a deputy chairman, the two parliamentary whips, and 16 additional members elected by the caucus, is, like its C.D.U. counterpart, extremely influential in the formulation of party policy. Here, too, there is a smaller group within the executive, consisting of the chairman, the deputy chairman, the chairman of the national party, and the parliamentary whips; this body meets weekly in advance of the larger one, for the purpose of securing agreement on crucial agenda issues.

Recommendations of the executive are generally accepted by the caucus, although the Socialist Party's caucus figures somewhat more importantly in the party's decision-making process than does that of the C.D.U. Attendance of deputies varies, from two-thirds to three-quarters of the nominal membership, and deliberations are less public than those of the C.D.U. caucus. Divisions of opinion are rarely between the executive and the caucus; more often, the disagreements are among the party's leaders.

Elections to the executive have often been hotly contested. The most important source of party conflict during the 1950's was between the parliamentary party and the mass party. Traditionally, the Social Democrats have not placed great stress on parliamentary ability. The office of parliamentary party chairman most often went to the party's national chairman, a man who had risen as an organizer through the party bureaucracy. With the death of Erich Ollenhauer in 1963, however, a trend which had been gathering force finally became dominant, and Fritz Erler, a leading parliamentary figure, was elected parliamentary party chairman; when he died in 1967, he was succeeded by another parliamentary leader, Helmut Schmidt, who later became defense minister under Brandt.

During the early years of the Bonn Republic, the Socialists relied upon traditional ideological appeals to maintain party unity. These slogans are now used less and less often, and discipline has been considerably relaxed. Nevertheless, members who disagree with decisions of the caucus are expected not to speak in the house against the position of the party, and, indeed, the S.P.D. remains far more unified than its rival.

THE STRUCTURE OF AUTHORITY: The key officer of the Bundestag is the president, who is elected by secret ballot at the beginning of each session. He is assisted by three vice presidents, each chosen from a different party, and a council of elders composed of officers and other representatives of the Fraktionen. The council is theoretically only advisory, but it is analogous to the British "usual channels," allocating the time for debate and choosing the chairmen of the Bundestag's standing committees. With the departure of the more extremist groups from the Bundestag, the council has been able to settle with considerable ease such matters as length of debate and the allocation of floor time to the political parties. Because party discipline is reasonably strong, and thus the question of timetables is of secondary importance, the president of the Bundestag does not have to be as partisan as the American speaker of the house, though he is somewhat more so than his British counterpart. His role is, however, not quite so important as that of the British speaker, since German deputies will often appeal to the council of elders for rulings on points of order.

Each party has its parliamentary whips, who work closely with the party chairman, although the whips of the governing party, having no access to the cabinet, lack the authority of their British counterparts. They do perform many of the same functions, and they are important members of the council of elders.

After the Fraktionen, the most important groups in the Bundestag are the specialized standing committees. They have grown more and more powerful as the Bonn regime has evolved, although they do not compare in strength with congressional committees in the United States or with the standing committees that operated in France under the Third and Fourth Republics. During the early years of the Federal Republic, there were 38 such committees, but the number has been trimmed to 19, paralleling, in general, the important ministries. Committee membership is proportional to party strength, and members are selected by the party Fraktion. Each committee chooses its own chairman, who has the service of a special assistant appointed from the Bundestag staff and that of several secretaries. Nevertheless, committee members are coming to feel that they need more professional help, and there have been suggestions that committee staffs be upgraded.

The question of which committee receives a bill can have some bearing on the final form it will take, since naturally each responds more readily to the demands of particular interests. Decisions on bill assignments are worked out by negotiation among the committees themselves, with final referral to the council of elders and the parties. To avoid extended controversy or the necessity of a vote by the whole house, one committee has often been placed in charge of reporting a given bill while several others have been permitted to consider it and offer suggestions.

Officials of the ministry initiating a proposed law have privileged access to committee meetings and can be heard at any time. Under the Bonn constitution, committees, like the Bundestag itself, may compel the attendance of ministers. Committee deliberations are usually not open to the press or the public, on the theory that open hearings reduce the objectivity of the proceedings; but on the other hand, they are not secret. Any deputy is free to attend, and permitted to report proceedings to outsiders, and persons other than parliamentarians may attend with committee permission. Many committees keep stenographic records of their discussions, and these, together with committee records, are available to the press.

On the whole, committees are creatures of the house and the parties. While a few have developed some autonomy, it would be difficult if not impossible for them to pigeonhole measures desired by the Bundestag as a whole. They have, of course, been used by the Bundestag to bury legislation, but only those proposals that party leaders had decided were best forgotten.

The committee members of each party operate as a team, led by a "foreman" who assigns responsibility for each bill to a particular deputy, and they meet regularly as a subcommittee of one of the working groups of the parliamentary party. Committee meetings generally involve a painstaking, article-by-article scrutiny of proposed legislation, with the chairman, the experts in each party, representatives of both the government and the particular ministry responsible for the bill, and the committee reporter taking over most of the discussion.

The committee chairmen are men who exercise considerable power in the Bundestag. They may determine the schedule of committee meetings and the priority of items on the agenda. Since committee meetings are limited to about nine days a month, chairmen can delay as well as facilitate deliberations. They cannot, however, block the discussion of legislation indefinitely, although they can effectively kill measures introduced late in a session by dragging their feet. Further, chairmen also appoint the reporter for each bill—the man whose task is to prepare a written report for the house on the committee's deliberations and an explanation of the changes that the committee recommends. While the analyses of individual reporters will differ

FIGURE 17.2. THE GERMAN LEGISLATIVE PROCESS

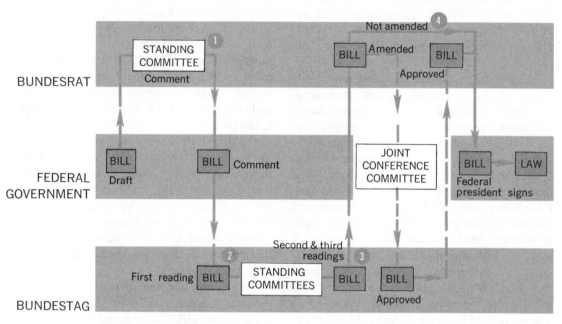

This chart illustrates the normal legislative process with respect to bills originated by the federal government; it does not depict the procedure for bills originating in the Bundesrat or Bundestag.

1 Transmits only amendatory proposals.

2 Introduced by the federal government, followed by general debate; if it is clear from the debate that the Bundestag either will approve or reject the proposal, it may not be sent to standing committee and may go directly into 2nd reading.

3 If amended in 2nd reading, 3rd reading usually is delayed 48 hours.

4 If the time period (2 weeks) elapses without the taking of amendatory action, the proposal also is sent to the federal government for promulgation. At this stage, the proposal also is sometimes sent to standing committee.

Adapted from Elmer Plischke, *Contemporary Governments of Germany,* 2nd ed. (Boston: Houghton Mifflin, 1969), p. 81. Reprinted by permission of the publisher.

slightly in nuance, the emphasis is upon objective reporting. On this, reporters have generally set a high standard, which is testimony to the lack of ideological heat that has characterized the work of the Bundestag in recent years.

Committees are beginning to develop a sense of corporate unity centered around a common command of the subject matter and identification with particular interests. This is aided by the fact that the privacy of committee meetings permits voting across party lines. On many occasions, committee members have agreed to rewrite bills and have brought their parties around to the committee's position.

Certain committees, including Defense,

Foreign Affairs, Inter-German Relations, and Internal Affairs, have authority to initiate investigations not immediately related to legislation. The Bundestag itself possesses the power to investigate matters which may not, at least initially, be related to proposed legislation. Committees to handle such investigations can be established at any time on the motion of one-fourth of the membership; they may hold open or private investigations and recommend legislative action. The Bundestag may also instigate full-scale debate on the policies of ministers, either on a motion of interpolation introduced by thirty members, or when the budget is being considered. Thus far, the Bundestag has been loath to take advantage of these powers, members feeling that they might open the way to the kind of demagoguery that characterized the Weimar Republic.

The Bundestag's lack of ample time for full-dress debates and the emphasis on committee work means that floor action is not nearly so important or so provocative as it is in the House of Commons. In 1952, to encourage participation by individual deputies, the Bundestag inaugurated a question period similar to that set aside by the British parliament. The rules originally provided for one question hour a month, and deputies had to submit their questions—which could deal only with clarification of facts—well in advance. Since then, however, the rules have been relaxed. "Urgent" questions are now allowed to be introduced as late as noon of the day before they are to be answered, and deputies are permitted to ask supplementary questions from the floor.

At first, these innovations failed to enliven the floor proceedings, primarily because not too many deputies bothered to ask questions. About three hundred were submitted at each session, as compared with twelve to fifteen thousand in the House of Commons. Also, the Fraktion dominated the question period, rather than allowing it to be used by individual deputies; nor did Adenauer's refusal to answer questions establish an encouraging precedent. Perhaps most important, the questions tended to be long and dull, the answers equally long and equally dull. There has, however, been some improvement in recent years. Questions have become briefer and acquired a certain verve, and deputies seem to be exercising some degree of independence. During the Spiegel affair, for instance, the question period was used by the opposition Social Democrats to embarrass Franz Joseph Strauss, then minister of defense; eventually the uproar led to his resignation. In 1965, questions directed against the government brought to light the fact that federal funds had been used to pay for pro-Erhard newspaper advertisements shortly before the election. The formation of the Kiesinger-Brandt coalition government made the question period somewhat less pertinent, for the obvious reason that the two major parties were loath to challenge the government publicly and the Free Democratic Party was unable to use the period effectively.

In 1965 still another innovation was introduced: on the application of fifteen members, a debate on a "definite subject of general current interest" can be placed on the agenda. The debates are limited to an hour; each speaker is required to talk extemporaneously, and for no more than five minutes. So far, the procedure has not been used too frequently because of the wariness with which the political parties look upon ill-prepared floor debates. Nevertheless, deputies are still being urged to shorten their speeches, which are invariably longer than those of British and French legislators, and there has been some talk of prohibiting the reading of speeches.

5. THE BUNDESRAT

The upper chamber of the German legislature has far more historical continuity than the Bundestag. During the empire, the Bundesrat was the repository of considerable power: its approval was required for all Reich legislation, and it could decide what legislative proposals were to be considered by the Reichstag. In addition to its legislative powers, it supervised the administration of all Reich laws.

The Bundesrat was essentially an assembly of envoys from state governments. Its conservative bias, which was partly the result of its being dominated by Prussians, was perhaps less important than its efforts on behalf of the Länder to win concessions from the federal government. German federalism, as we have pointed out, was based less on separate spheres of authority than on a distinction between policies themselves and their execution, and the Bundesrat was ruled by bureaucrats from the various states who sought to revise ordinances in order to enhance their administrative autonomy.

The Weimar constitution shifted the balance of federal power to the Reichstag, at least on paper. The upper house, now called the Reichsrat, had only a limited power of veto. If it objected to any piece of legislation, a public referendum could be ordered by the president or, alternately, the Reichstag could overrule the Reichsrat by a two-thirds majority. It was not easy to obtain such a majority in the lower house, and because referenda were not looked upon with great anticipation, governments were reluctant to press measures the Reichsrat would not accept. That the Länder were still responsible for the execution of laws was another factor abetting the continued authority of the upper house.

After the defeat of Nazi Germany, the Allies and the major German political groups were divided on how the second house should be constituted and what power it should possess. Two major proposals were made regarding the form of a new chamber. The C.D.U., the most federalist of the parties, wanted a Bundesrat, in the German tradition, to represent and be responsible to the Land governments; the Socialists wanted a senate chamber elected by the people on the basis of proportional representation. The C.D.U. also wanted a chamber that would be equal in power to the Bundestag, while the Socialists wanted the lower house to predominate. A compromise was reached which created an appointed Bundesrat, but placed it in a subordinate position to the Bundestag, even though it had considerably more power than its Weimar predecessor.

The Bundesrat consists of 41 members of the Land cabinets—five from each of the four Länder having more than six million residents, four from each of the three Länder having between two and six million inhabitants, and three each from the three small Länder having less than two million. Members are appointed by their Land governments, which may at any time recall them. According to the constitution, the votes of each Land must be cast as a bloc, and each delegation votes in accordance with instructions from its state government.

Approval of the Bundesrat is required for all constitutional amendments, and all legislation affecting the administrative, tax, and territorial interests of the Länder. On "ordinary" legislation it has only a limited veto power. If it rejects a given measure, it can be overruled by an equivalent majority in the Bundestag—that is, if it rejects a proposal by a majority of two-thirds, the bill can become law only if the Bundestag, with at least a majority of its members present, passes it by a two-thirds majority of those present and voting. It was thought initially that the great bulk of national legislation would fall into the "ordinary" category; on the contrary, bills interpreted as affecting the Länder directly have totaled fifty per cent or more of those which have become law.

This interpretation and the fact that federal ordinances require Bundesrat approval before they can take effect have considerably enhanced the power of the upper chamber. The federal government is careful to consult the Länder before introducing legislation, and the threat of a Bundesrat veto, although it has been used sparingly, has been sufficient to secure substantial modifications in government proposals. During the early years of the Adenauer administration, the chancellor's control of his party was great enough to insure him that he could usually have his own way in the upper house on matters he considered essential; by the early 1960's, however, party loyalties were being superseded by Land interests. And the problems of administration and authority became more and more difficult to resolve as events forced the government to move into areas originally considered the domain of the states.

Most of the work of the Bundesrat is done *in camera;* plenary sessions are devoted to general remarks and formal votes, and debate is rarely lively. Rather, an array of committees manned by bureaucratic experts from the Länder determines policy before any piece of proposed legislation reaches the floor. Consequently, the work of the Bundesrat has not attracted much public attention. Public-opinion polls indicate that very few Germans have any understanding whatsoever of its functions.

6. LAW MAKING

According to the constitution, bills may be introduced by the government, the Bundesrat, or the Bundestag. In practice, the Bundesrat introduces very few: preoccupied with administration, the Länder have rarely been interested in advancing legislative proposals on the national level. Their main concern has been in amending or revising legislation to serve their own interests.

The Bundestag exercises its prerogative with far greater frequency. As Table 17.4 indicates, some forty per cent of the bills introduced come from the lower house; roughly one-fourth of these are the work of individual deputies seeking to advance the cause of some interest group, and the bills are often introduced simply to pressure the government into sponsoring a particular program or to influence the details of legislation under consideration. Most of the bills introduced by the Bundestag, however, are the work of the Fraktionen.

Of course, the balance of bills introduced into the Bundestag—some sixty per cent—come directly from the government, and more than three-fourths of the measures ultimately enacted into law were originally drawn up by the cabinet or a ministry.[5] The drafting of legislation involves consultations among ministries and the chancellor's office, and between the government and Land officials and interest groups. Government ministers regularly invite members of national groups to discuss legislative proposals, in an effort to win their approval—or at least to reduce their opposition. As in England, such conferences are regarded as perfectly legitimate; the German government, also like the British, encourages the amalgamation of interest groups into more unified, national associations that can speak with one voice. Just how often the government discusses an issue with an interest group is pretty much up to the government minister concerned, but these conferences are usually fairly frequent. And the extent of rapport between the government and interest groups is indicated by the policy of the Federation of German Industries which, during the Adenauer era, addressed most of its formal statements of opinion regarding legislation to the Ministry of Economics rather than to the Bundestag.

Consultations also take place between the government and the parliamentary party lead-

[5] The constitution requires that the government submit a bill to the Bundesrat first; the government can, and frequently does, get around this stipulation by having a deputy or Fraktion introduce the measure in the Bundestag.

TABLE 17.4.   SOURCES OF LEGISLATION IN GERMANY

Percentage of total bills introduced

	Cabinet	Bundestag	Bundesrat
1949–1953	59.4	38.1	2.5
1953–1957	50.3	48.4	1.2
1957–1961	64.5	34.7	0.8
1961–1965	59.2	39.5	1.3

Adapted from Gerhard Loewenberg, *Parliament in the German Political System* (Ithaca: Cornell University Press, 1967), p. 270. Copyright © 1967 by Cornell University. Used by permission of Cornell University Press.

ers who are not in the cabinet, especially on proposals likely to yield controversy. In some cases, these party leaders have even participated in cabinet meetings, although such procedures are the exception rather than the rule. Some ministries, such as the Ministry of Labor, have established working relationships with the relevant committee chairmen in the Bundestag. Again, the extent of contact often depends upon the personalities of those involved. The Ministry of Labor established good relations with the Committee on Social Policy during the Adenauer period, but those between Interior and the Committee on Interior Affairs were severely strained for a long time, to the detriment of the government's program.

When government bills are submitted to the Bundesrat for first passage, Land ministries are under great pressure to formulate their positions quickly, for the time allotted for them to do so is not very long. The Bundesrat has only three weeks to consider a bill on "first passage" before it automatically moves on to the Bundestag. Where consultation has occurred beforehand, the problem is eased, but final decisions must still be made. The bills get most of their attention in committee session; once deliberations there have been completed, the Land cabinets decide how their Bundesrat representatives should vote. Because of the limited amount of time available, the views of committee members have considerable influence.

At this stage the Bundesrat concerns itself largely with detailed amendments to legislative proposals. The government transmits these, and its responses, to the Bundestag, along with the text of the bill.

BUNDESTAG CONSIDERATION: In the Bundestag, proposed legislation is first discussed by the parliamentary Fraktionen and their specialized subcommittees. By the time a bill receives its first reading, each party must already have determined whether or not it wishes to debate the proposed legislation, what views it will express, and who will do the speaking; it also must decide to which committee or committees the legislation should be referred, usually after working groups have expressed their recommendations at party caucuses and differences of opinion have been ironed out.

The question of which committee should receive a particular bill and which committee or committees should be allowed to comment on it has led to any number of controversies. The committees themselves, interest groups, the parties, and individual deputies all compete to obtain the committee assignment they consider most appropriate. For a while, the difficulties of reaching agreement caused a proliferation of committee assignments, such that some measures were under the simultaneous consideration of as many as eight or nine committees. More recently, efforts have been made to limit to two the number of committees considering a bill, although three or four is not unknown.

During the days or weeks preceding the floor debate, negotiations on the bill to secure support or revisions continue. Interest groups approach deputies, and members of the working parties seek out government ministers, representatives of the special interests, and other deputies who might have special concern with the measure—either for or against it. At times it is informally agreed that the bill will be revised in committee.

The debate on the first reading is invariably a staid affair. If the bill is important, this is probably the first occasion that it will be brought to the public's attention through the press. With floor discussions arranged in advance, there is little chance of surprise developments. Even so, public reaction and newspaper pressure begin to be felt at this point, and they can affect the attitudes of the government and the various parties concerned with the proposed legislation.

When the committee has completed its deliberations and prepared its report, the parties make a final determination of the stand they will take during the second and the third readings. Members of each party on the committee in charge of the bill recommend a position to the parallel working group in their party; that group, in turn, makes a recommendation to the executive committee of the party.

In general, the position the parties take on a bill is that which has been recommended by their experts, a factor that seems more and more likely to erode party differences. To be sure, such has not always been the case. During the 1950's and into the 1960's, the Socialists were split over the question of German rearmament, and the party's defense experts were not consistently able to carry the day against those Socialists who viewed the creation and maintenance of a new German army with anxiety. Furthermore, complications quite naturally occur when several committees are considering a bill and the experts on each disagree, or when Bundestag members feel that a committee or committee member has become the mouthpiece of special interests.

The second reading in the Bundestag is devoted to discussion and debate on individual sections of the bill, and the consideration of each section is followed by a vote. Different viewpoints within the parties may be expressed on the floor. The third reading is another general discussion of the bill, this time as amended. While amendments may be introduced on the floor at the third reading, such a procedure is unusual. With the showdown on the measure at hand, emphasis is now on party unity, and members are cajoled into accepting the final decision of the party —or, if they are opposed to it, at least abstaining from voting.

THE FINAL STAGES: Once a bill has passed the Bundestag, it goes to or is returned to the Bundesrat. In the case of bills introduced in the lower chamber, this may be, of course, the first opportunity the Bundesrat has had to examine it. With the Bundesrat reluctant to reject measures passed by the lower house, even if its own recommendations have not been accepted, such measures are ordinarily sent to the conference committee to iron out differences between the two houses. The com-

mittee is composed equally of members of both houses; Bundesrat members tend to be ministers of Land governments, those from the Bundestag party leaders or committee chairmen. Each Land is entitled to one member, and the Bundestag parties participate in proportion to their parliamentary representation.

Conference committee meetings are secret, although federal ministers and their assistants may attend. Often the committee will recruit special subcommittees of experts to deal with technical aspects of the bill on which it is attempting to effect a compromise. The committee addresses itself only to those matters about which the two houses differ.

The committee recommendation is first presented to the Bundestag, where it is voted without debate, and then sent to the Bundesrat. In fact, the committee has served to a considerable extent as an instrument of the Bundesrat; rarely does it accept the Bundestag's point of view without some modifications, while something like one-third of its recommendations have involved full acceptance of the Bundesrat's version of the legislation.

Finally, once a bill has won Parliament's approval, it is forwarded to the government for its formal acceptance and promulgation by the president. The president can refuse to sign a bill if he has doubts as to its constitutionality, but this has occurred in only one case of any importance.

7. THE ROLE OF INTEREST GROUPS

The rapid industrialization of Germany in the late nineteenth century produced a pattern of group behavior in which modern and traditional elements were interwoven, not always smoothly. While many traditional elements in Germany's culture and social structure remained unchanged, an increasing number of functional interest groups, representing labor, industry, and agriculture, came into existence. They operated, however, only in a context in which regional, ethnic, and religious factors were extremely important; such provincialism often prevented effective cooperation among those whose economic interests actually coincided—Socialist trade unions, for instance, found it difficult to organize Catholic workers.

The sharpness of class differences also contributed to group segregation. Workers and businessmen inhabited self-enclosed worlds. Rhetorically, at least, their contacts took on the character of a battle rather than that of a bargaining situation which would presuppose some base of common interest.

While the Reichstag and the Land legislative bodies were the focus of considerable activity, those representing industrial and landholding interests relied more heavily upon, and paid more attention to, the Bundesrat and to the federal bureaucracy. Here, after all, was where the real power lay; besides, these were men of their own social class, naturally sympathetic to their interests.

The fragmentation of German life associated with the Weimar years further exacerbated the difficulties of finding a common ground among the different interests. As sectional and purely economic differences became more complicated, by either an ideological nuance or the general malaise, groups defined their aims in terms that became more and more exacting and inflexible. Interest-group behavior, of course, had its effects upon the operation of the political party system and the Reichstag; many groups became closely identified with rigidly doctrinaire minor parties, thus reducing the possibility of effective governance. The extremism and dogmatism of the interest groups were key factors in preventing the Reichstag from fulfilling its purpose. On all too many occasions, the legislature concentrated on meaningless ideological rhetoric or wrangled interminably over extremely minor issues while, by default, the most important decisions concerning the republic were made by the president and his intimate advisers.

With the advent of the Nazi regime, independent associational life was eliminated. Some groups, including both the army and the Catholic Church, did manage to retain a modicum of organizational capacity, but most others were able to act only within the confines of "fronts" organized by the Nazi Party. The business community did get a good number of things it wanted by bribing party officials and using bureaucratic contacts; but on many occasions the party and the Nazi-organized Labor Front subjected it to demands which it considered extremely unreasonable —and about which it could do nothing. In fact, a not insignificant portion of the business community believed that the Hitler regime was far too pro-labor.

Under the Bonn Republic, the pattern of interest-group activity has shifted significantly. In Germany, as in other industrial nations, the trend has continued toward fewer and larger associations representing functional groups. Perhaps more important, the major parties, particularly the Christian Democrats, are tending more and more to be coalitions of interests whose demands have to be balanced off and aggregated into a larger political whole. The processing of group demands has become easier not only because they are now fairly specific and limited, but because the groups themselves are more willing to compromise.

Political leaders and the leaders of interest groups have, by and large, come to accept the idea that politics is a bargaining process. More and more frequently they speak the same language and understand their opponents' point of view, thereby facilitating accommodation. There is a much greater feeling today that group demands must be placed within the context of a broader general interest, and much more willingness on the part of specific interests to accept certain rules of the game as binding. The changes are, of course, partially the result of the spectacular growth of the German economy since World War II. But they also stem from memories of Weimar and the reasons for its failure.

In general, Germans have a mixed attitude toward the activity of interest groups. Many more of them speak of working through such groups to achieve political goals than do Englishmen or Americans. Nevertheless, there is still considerable suspicion of some aspects of interest-group political activity—as if, somehow, policies should simply be based on what is right and not necessarily on what interest groups want. Far fewer Germans than Americans, Englishmen—or, today, Frenchmen—join civic associations that cut across interest lines to obtain nonpolitical or even political objectives. In this sense, the strata in German society appear to be more segregated than in other European societies, although this is difficult to measure.

Interest-group activity is, of course, directed at the public, the legislature, and the executive. Because the predominant Christian Democratic Party is less disciplined than either of the British parties, and the German executive less powerful—even under Adenauer—than the executive of Fifth-Republic France, the effort expended to influence the legislature is greater in Germany than in either England or France. Furthermore, because the Länder exercise considerable power, more time is spent trying to sway local officials than in either of the other countries, although most interests naturally regard the national scene as of crucial importance.

In their attempts to influence the legislature, most important associations do not hesitate to use the front door: they encourage their members to seek parliamentary seats. Despite some concern that the interests might come to dominate the Bundestag, such a procedure is considered quite proper—an attitude which is a carry-over of a more traditional orientation toward functional representation. In addition to their efforts to gain their ends from within, interest groups also make sizable contributions to party coffers. This is most notable in business support of the Free Democrats and the C.D.U. During most of the postwar period, some 35 per cent of Christian Democratic deputies have been directly affiliated with interest associations, mostly business, and approximately one-fourth of the Social Democratic deputies have been trade-union representatives.

Germany's interest groups maintain their offices, understandably enough, in Bonn. Their methods of operation may vary slightly, but the usual form, so often employed by the business pressure organizations, is to have their friendly deputies round up others for dinner during which their point of view is "objectively" presented. Deputies representing or friendly to particular interests gravitate to the relevant intra-party working groups and are never reticent about speaking up when legislation dealing with the interests of their group is under consideration. They also often serve on the specialized committees of the Bundestag which deal with matters of concern to groups in which they have an interest. The interest groups get a hearing by the parties when legislative proposals are first made, and the policy decided upon by the Christian Democrats invariably represents an amalgam of diverse views. The Social Democrats have thus far retained more homogeneity in this regard.

Members of the Bundesrat are rarely approached directly by representatives of interest groups. From time to time, the groups may forward memoranda to Bundesrat committees when a bill is being discussed. But this action is generally pro forma, since Bundesrat members are essentially agents of state governments. Instead, groups concentrate on the appropriate Land ministries or the minister-president of a Land, and they will try to win support in Land parliaments. Members of the Bundesrat are, after all, Land officials; their mandates are derived from their state governments.

As in other European nations, there is in Germany considerable consultation between the bureaucracy and interest groups. Many government agencies in the Länder have advisory bodies, composed of interest-group representatives, attached to them. On the federal level, the cabinet discusses legislation with interest groups, and, in fact, the administrative procedures of all the principal ministries stipulate that the appropriate spokesmen of associations must be consulted during consideration of legislation. Generally, these ministries are also provided with advisory councils of nongovernmental experts who are interest-group representatives. During the early years of the Adenauer administration, even some of the upper-level bureaucrats in administrative posts were recruited from business associations. There has also been a reverse action: a tendency of civil servants to leave the bureaucracy for higher-paying positions in industry. This interchange has encouraged a community of interest and outlook among members of the bureaucracy and business groups.

The bureaucrats and the business community are perhaps more in tandem in Germany than in France, where the working relationship between them is also close. There is no question, however, that interest-group influence over legislation is greater in Germany than in either France or England. German legislators still defer to bureaucratic expertise and look for bureaucratic solutions to public issues. Yet one suspects that differences among the three countries are becoming less and less significant.

Many associations during the Adenauer administration bypassed the bureaucracy and ministries and turned to the chancellor himself. Adenauer, on his part, often turned to individual members of the business community for advice. The president of the Federation of German Industry (*Bundesverband der Deutschen Industrie*—B.D.I.) at the time, Fritz Berg, developed a particularly close working relationship with the chancellor, although they never became great friends. Under Erhard, relations were not nearly so cozy. The former economics minister was much less ready to rely upon the business community's advice; in fact, he had antagonized people like Berg on several issues. Also, Erhard's style was far less personal and authoritarian, and he preferred to use regular procedures of consultation. This lack of close rapport between the German executive and the business

community became still more evident under the Grand Coalition, and most certainly the influence of business groups will be considerably less than ever before during Brandt's tenure of office. Further, in 1969 Parliament approved a government bill requiring that interest groups wishing to be heard by parliamentary committees register on a public list which would be published annually.

German administrative courts on both the federal and the state level play a substantial role in spelling out the legitimacy of rules pertaining to federal legislation. Very frequently, lawyers attached to interests represent or advise individual claimants against the state. And whatever these federal courts decide has an effect upon the collective interests of the associations.

With the fall of the Third Reich in 1945, American, French, and British occupying authorities initiated efforts to break up German cartels.[6] It was their belief that between the two world wars the concentration of industrial control in the hands of a few wealthy and powerful German families was one of the factors that had contributed significantly to the rise of National Socialism.

As West Germany began to reassume internal sovereignty, Allied authorities requested that a law be drafted prohibiting cartels or any other restrictions on competition. Erhard, then director of the Economic Administration of the Western Zones, complied; but with the formation of the Federal Republic, the proposed legislation was filed away.

Legislation prohibiting cartels was again discussed in 1951 and in 1952. In the latter year the cabinet agreed upon a fairly tough bill and submitted it to the Bundestag for consideration. Upon learning of the details of the legislation, the B.D.I. launched a counterattack. It favored a bill which incorporated controls, registration, and the publicizing of

[6] This case study is a summary of the material presented by Gerard Braunthal in Christoph and Brown, *Cases in Comparative Politics*, pp. 187–206.

all cartel arrangements; it also favored the right of the government to take action against any firm abusing the principles of a "free economy." But it was opposed to the outright prohibition of all combinations.

The driving force behind the anti-cartel bill was Erhard himself, who, committed to the idea of a free-market economy, was committed also to the virtues of competition. To gain support for his measure among members of the business community, he began to organize groups of employers friendly to his ideas.

While debate continued, the proposals of the Adenauer government were taken up by the Bundestag's Economic Affairs Committee. The lack of unqualified support from the Christian Democratic Party and the opposition of the B.D.I., however, combined to bury it for the rest of the 1952 session. A basically unchanged bill was sent to the Bundesrat the following year, but it emerged with amendments permitting a number of exceptions to the general provisions of the law. In reviewing the Bundesrat's version, the cabinet accepted some of the amendments, thus weakening its own bill for the first time.

Erhard then deliberately postponed having the Bundestag consider the bill, partially because he was more interested at that point in tax-reform legislation, but also because he wanted to discuss the matter further with business groups. A commission was set up consisting of officials of the ministries of Economics and Justice, and of the B.D.I. Meetings of the group were held from February to October of 1954, when a statement was issued to the press announcing general agreement. In effect, Erhard had yielded to the B.D.I. on a number of points.

Interestingly enough, the Social Democrats —who for nearly a century had favored the growth of trusts, which they believed would lead more quickly to socialism—now took up the cause. They argued that the original bill with its strong prohibitions should have been defended by the government. A political imbroglio developed, with the Social Democrats and some C.D.U. members attacking Erhard

for capitulating to industry, other C.D.U. members endorsing the compromise bill, and the B.D.I. both supporting Erhard for yielding and attacking him for trying to drum up support among business groups sanctioning stronger anti-cartel laws.

As soon as the bill was submitted to the Bundestag, the B.D.I. mounted an intensive campaign to have it amended still further. The organization prepared material to be used by deputies in debates and presented their arguments to both influential government officials and sympathetic deputies on the Bundestag Economic Affairs Committee— to not much avail, as it turned out: the committee voted to support an even stronger bill than that introduced by the government.

The B.D.I. did not surrender; it continued its efforts to gain the support of some C.D.U. intra-party committees for a new bill which, as a substitute for the government's measure, called only for the regulation of cartel abuses. By this time, however, many Christian Democrats were beginning to react negatively to what they considered excessive pressures. Adenauer, albeit with no great show of enthusiasm, continued to support Erhard's watered-down bill. Debate and discussion continued through most of 1956, and finally the B.D.I. agreed to accept the government's bill—provided some additional modifications were included. Thus, somewhat further weakened, the bill was passed. In the last days before its passage, Adenauer threw his full weight behind it, but only, so it was reported, because Erhard threatened to resign if he failed to do so.

The anti-cartel bill provided that "any agreements made by business concerns or associations of business enterprises shall be invalid if their effect is to limit or reduce free competition." It authorized the Bonn government to set up federal and state agencies to administer the law. The B.D.I.'s victory lay in eight significant exceptions to the prohibition clause, exceptions which permitted the existence of cartels for setting common standards of production, for the promotion of exports, for industries in distress, and, with the assent of the newly created Cartel Agency, for price adjustments and agreements.

The main concern of the B.D.I. now was to insure that the administration of the Cartel Agency be placed in the hands of men it would describe as "reasonable." When the government announced its intention to nominate Eberhard Günther, head of the cartel section in the Ministry of Finance, to the post, the B.D.I. was somewhat less than satisfied. Günther had helped prepare the original legislation and was regarded as unsympathetic to industry. Working through a number of government ministers, the organization attempted to force Erhard to nominate someone else. The ministers did manage to delay Günther's nomination, but, unable to gain Adenauer's support, they were forced, at last, to accept defeat. Later efforts by the B.D.I. toward influencing the selection of agency staff members had as little success.

Most of the fears that the B.D.I. had displayed about the effects of the law proved unwarranted, for the Cartel Agency took a rather broad view of the exception clauses— so broad a view, in fact, that between passage of the legislation and 1965 only one firm was fined for violating its provisions and the fine was nominal. Bids to strengthen the law invariably failed while Adenauer remained in power; under Erhard and a new minister of economics, the registration provisions were tightened, and firms were required to make public all price-setting arrangements on which they had reached agreement. Efforts, primarily by the S.P.D., to prohibit any form of price fixing on brand goods came to naught in the 1968 Bundestag despite the support of the Social Democratic minister of economic affairs, Karl Schiller.

8. SOME CONCLUSIONS

Whatever its limitations, parliamentary government has proved far more successful in postwar Germany than it was during even the best Weimar years. This success is less the result of constitutional engineering than the consequence of cultural and social changes that have occurred within German society. The memory of the Nazi regime and the elimination of certain traditional and extremist sectors from the community have made the Federal Republic a more homogeneous society than its predecessor. Despite some counter-trends, German political life today is characterized by a broad consensus that has affected not only the structure of group life and the kinds of demands groups are prepared to make, but the tactics they will use in trying to obtain satisfaction.

The present period is still one of transition. Despite the many cultural and social changes, certain patterns still persist. Thus, political life, including legislative life, retains a bureaucratic character that tries to muffle disorder lest it get too far out of hand. Part of what the younger generation is protesting against is precisely this staid cultural style; in this objection, at least, they are certainly not alone. Germany, as part of Western Europe, is increasingly enmeshed in the breakdown of traditional forms of authority—a transformation that is one of the hallmarks of mid–twentieth-century European society.

The formation of a government led by Social Democrats should cause the further democratization of German social and political life. It may also cause the German political system to become more like the British. As already noted, the relationship of Brandt to his cabinet and his party is far closer to the British model than that demonstrated by previous German governments.

The major block to such a transformation is probably the continued existence of an electoral system that reduces the possibility of either of the two major parties winning a clear majority in the Bundestag. The fact that to remain in office the Social Democrats must rely on the support of a party whose continued existence requires proportional representation reduces the likelihood of their pressing for a change in the German election laws at this point.

18

Governmental

Processes

in the Soviet Union

1. INTRODUCTION

The examination of formal political institutions and how they function in polyarchic societies can yield important clues on why certain political decisions are made rather than others. Parliaments and executives become focal points for the pressures within the society, and their response to these pressures enables one to estimate the power of interest groups. Because pluralistic societies operate on the basis of more or less open group competition, it is also possible to gather a good deal of information on how political decisions are made and what the consequences of such decisions are.

In the Soviet Union, on the other hand, the relationship between the single political party and the organs of the state has never been completely clear. No regularized normative patterns of interrelationship exist, or at least none that are both publicly recognized and uniformly followed. Party rules do outline what is supposedly the process of internal decision-making, but while such rules are not completely ignored, they are not of too much

value in understanding how major policies are actually determined. Adding to the problem, of course, is the fact that political decisions in the U.S.S.R. are made through negotiations and power struggles that for the most part take place without intensive coverage by non-governmental news media. Occasionally, after the fact, reasonably reliable information is forthcoming about the processes that led to a particular policy, and one can sometimes read between the lines of official statements to discover something of the conflicts and compromises involved. Western literature on the Soviet Union is replete with analyses based on very skimpy data, attempting to unravel the complexities of the Soviet policy-making process. There has evolved a whole new discipline, popularly known as "Kremlinology," which makes use of hints and nods, deduction and induction to piece together an explanation of why particular decisions have been made or why some men have risen to or fallen from power. Often the explanations offered are quite plausible. Nevertheless, speculation on what goes on in the Kremlin never abates; one can usually find a series of

557

alternate and equally plausible explanations for the same set of phenomena. For this reason, no attempt is made here to detail the relationships among power groups in the Soviet Union. The sections that follow will offer, first of all, a description of Soviet governmental institutions and, secondly, an analysis of the *general* character of political decision-making in the U.S.S.R.

2. THE BACKGROUND

Lenin shared Marx's distrust of traditional parliamentary regimes, arguing that while they may have represented an advance over feudal autocracies, their separation of powers and the distance between the lawmakers and the people made formal democracy a sham. In the ideal state, of course, politics would disappear. But in the interim between the triumph of the revolution and the achievement of communism, Lenin believed, a new political form would have to be found to express the unique democratic features of the dictatorship of the proletariat. Although at first suspicious of them because of their "spontaneity" and disorder, Lenin came gradually to accept the view that the soviets—the workers' councils or unions that had sprung up during the 1905 Revolution and again in 1917—could provide just such a form.

In Communist theory, the weaknesses of traditional parliamentarianism would be overcome by the fact that the mandates of soviet members would be immediately revocable on demand of the citizens. Further, the people themselves would perform a wide range of administrative functions, and, in cooperation with the party and other organizations, would act as a check on and guide for formal state organizations. Representative democracy in its sham bourgeois form would, therefore, be replaced by a system in which the people participated directly. The representative assembly would be both a legislative and a real working body.

The actual results of Bolshevik rule were quite different. The soviets were quickly

stripped of power and became mere ornaments on the national and republican levels of Soviet government.[1] Real power was assumed by the Communist Party, and, in the end, by the politburo and the dictator—although since Stalin's death, the party itself has regained some of its political leverage. The failure to provide the public with any means of controlling that authority led to the growth of a power elite operating in camera, and to a system of decision-making devoid of any effective checkreins. This result can be partly attributed to the Bolsheviks' conviction that they knew the road to the true and the beautiful, and that any recalcitrance by the masses only hindered attainment of the desired goals. It is also true that the Bolshevik leadership included many whose public passion for freedom and the rule of the people disguised their personal lust for power. Yet as noted in Chapter 3, part of the explanation for the development of the Stalinist dictatorship lies in the very ideology of the party. The refusal of party leaders to accept the possibility that views other than their own deserved to be heard and their unwillingness to protect the expression of these views destroyed the possibility of their creating a truly free society.

Not all left-wing Socialists were completely blind to this. Rosa Luxemburg, for example, expressed the fears of many when she noted:

Lenin and Trotsky have shunted aside the representative bodies elected by universal suffrage and have replaced them with the Soviets as the only true representation of the working masses. But as a consequence of the stifling of political life . . . there must follow a progressive deterioration of the vitality of the Soviets themselves.

Without general elections, without freedom of press and assembly . . . the vitality of every public institution will drain away.

---

[1] This is not entirely true of local soviets, which participated actively in policy implementation. See Chapter 19, pp. 600–603.

A numbness is gradually overcoming public life. A few dozen party leaders rule and give out directives. . . . Behind them stand a dozen outstanding personalities who exercise the real leadership. . . . This is basically a government by clique. It is a dictatorship, certainly, but not a dictatorship of the proletariat. Instead it is the dictatorship of a handful of politicians.[2]

Rosa Luxemburg's assessment was totally accurate. And despite a series of constitutions establishing broadly representative institutions, the locus of power shifted more and more to a small clique and then, finally, to the dictatorship of one man. Indeed, 1936—the year in which the present Soviet constitution was adopted—was also the year Stalin launched his great purge in defiance of most of its principles. Under Stalin, then, the Soviet Union was both a mobilization regime and a totalitarian dictatorship. This is not to say that Stalin was responsible for every decision or that politics was completely eliminated from Soviet life; as we shall see, the pattern of political decision-making was fairly complex.

Today the political process in the Soviet Union is less monolithic. The regime seems to have moved in a neomercantilist direction and to be characterized by a bargaining process among elites acting in the name of various interests. Nevertheless, the constitutional organs of government, at least on the national level, are still of secondary importance in the formulation of national policy. The real political bargaining occurs—and basic policy decisions are taken—within the secretariat and the politburo of the Communist Party.

3. THE SUPREME SOVIET

According to the 1936 constitution, "the legislative power of the U.S.S.R. is exercised

exclusively by the Supreme Soviet of the U.S.S.R.," while the Presidium it elects serves as its collective president.

ELECTIONS: The Supreme Soviet is normally elected for a term of four years, although it may be dissolved by its elected Presidium. It consists of two chambers, the Council of the Union and the Council of Nationalities. After the 1966 elections, the Council of the Union consisted of 767 deputies, or one for approximately every three hundred thousand citizens. The Council of Nationalities, organized on the federal principle, contained 750 deputies, elected as follows: 32 from each of the Soviet Union's 15 union republics, 11 from each of the 20 autonomous republics, five from each of the eight autonomous regions (*oblasts*), and one from each of the ten national districts (*okrugs*). Soviet federalism is founded on linguistic differentiations, but except for the union republics, the other divisions are primarily administrative. The distinction between autonomous republics, oblasts, and okrugs is based on the size of an ethnic or linguistic group, and no unit has any greater power of self-government than another.

Deputies for each chamber are elected from single-member electoral districts, and every Soviet citizen votes for at least two deputies in each election. Those living in autonomous republics, oblasts, and okrugs, however, normally vote for three deputies, since all three of these units fall within union republics. The largest republic, the Russian Soviet Federal Socialist Republic (R.S.F.S.R.), contains within its boundaries the majority of autonomous republics and oblasts, and all ten okrugs.

Candidates for seats on the Supreme Soviet are nominated in each electoral district at open meetings of both official and quasi-official organizations, including the Communist Party, Komsomol units, trade unions, cooperatives, and even ad hoc assemblies of workers. After each group has nominated a candidate, a joint conference is held to select

[2] Quoted in Boris Meissner, "Soviet Democracy and Bolshevik Party Dictatorship," in H. W. Ehrmann, ed., *Democracy in a Changing Society* (New York: Frederick A. Praeger, 1964), p. 155.

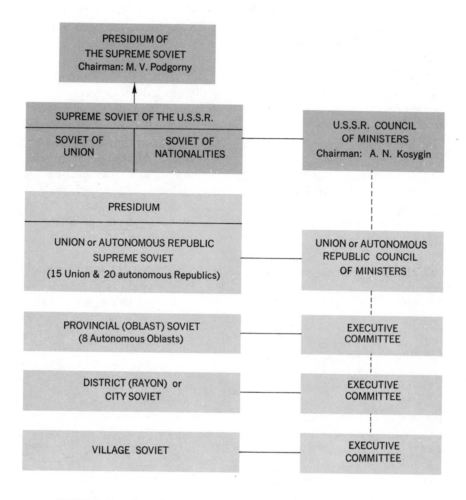

FIGURE 18.1. THE STRUCTURE OF THE SOVIET GOVERNMENT

the person who will run for office. Not surprisingly, most of the organizations choose the same candidate; in three out of four cases he is a member of the Communist Party, and about eighty per cent of the time he is a "Hero of the Soviet Union"—the winner of a medal or citation for outstanding behavior. National political figures may be nominated in any number of districts, since no residence requirement exists. However, their names are withdrawn from all but one electoral district before the election; the multiple nominations are merely an indication of their official popularity. Thus, in the 1958 Supreme Soviet elections Khrushchev was nominated by 136 districts, while in 1966, according to *Pravda,* Brezhnev was nominated by 46 districts and Kosygin by 26.

Since only one candidate is nominated for each seat, nomination is tantamount to election. Nevertheless, nominations to the Supreme Soviet are followed by a nationwide election campaign in which every effort is made to produce a large vote. The nation is inundated with brochures, newspapers cover the campaign fully, and several million agitators are sent into the field urging people to express their conviction that the Soviet regime commands their loyalty and affection. As television becomes more widespread, it, too, is giving extensive campaign coverage. The results of these election campaigns have been uniformly successful; since the 1930's, upwards of 95 per cent of those eligible have voted, and since the 1950's, more than 99 per cent—at least according to official Soviet figures.

At the polling station, voters are handed a ballot which they are "free" to mark in the privacy of a booth. Before 1936 all voting was done publicly; yet even today the voter rarely uses the booth for fear of arousing the suspicion that he had reservations about the candidate nominated. If a voter does not like the candidate chosen, he has two options: he can refuse to vote or he can cross off the name of the candidate.

The candidate is considered legally elected unless more than half the voters strike his name from the ballot. As one might expect, the number of candidates defeated is extremely small, although this does happen occasionally in elections to local and provincial soviets. Suggestions have been offered in recent years that two or more nominations be made for a single post. If the choice of the two nominees remains the prerogative of the party, such a move would be only a small step toward genuine elections; but it would be a step.

Elections, then, are almost entirely concerned with political socialization rather than with the recruitment of political elites. They provide a festive occasion on which the regime points to its achievements and maintains a sense of Socialist solidarity. They also serve as a mechanism both for informing (or reinforcing) the public about the regime's policies and for explaining, although rather ritualistically, why certain policies are being followed.

Deputies to the Supreme Soviet represent the "leading elements" in Soviet life. An earnest effort is made to recruit outstanding members of the working class and peasantry as candidates, and the party is careful to emphasize the proportion of workers who are deputies. Most often, however, figures on the representation are somewhat misleading, for members have thus far been classified in terms of social background rather than occupation. As a general estimate, about 35 per cent of the Supreme Soviet deputies are workers or peasants by occupation, 35 per cent or more are party officials or bureaucrats, and the remainder are professional personnel of one kind or another.

THE FUNCTIONS OF THE SUPREME SOVIET: The Supreme Soviet generally meets no more than sixty or seventy days a year. At the beginning of each session, the Council of the Union and the Council of Nationalities convene separately and organize themselves by electing a chairman and four deputy chairmen, a credentials commission, and other commissions (or committees) which vary in number, but usually include one each on proposed legislation, the budget, the annual economic plan, and foreign affairs. Commissions may be formed on a permanent or temporary basis, and they have the right to investigate proposed legislation as well as administrative practices. They can also introduce legislation. Their powers include the right to obtain information from government agencies and individual experts, and in recent years these powers have been used somewhat more extensively, and technical aspects of some proposed legislation have been modified as the result of committee criticisms. Committees have also criticized some administrative practices. It should be noted, however, that membership on these committees includes a disproportionate number of party bureaucrats and members of higher party organs. The chairmen of seven of the ten permanent commissions of the Council of the Union elected in August 1966 were full members of the C.P.S.U. Central Committee; only one commission (the health commission) was not presided over by a senior party functionary. Even so, as we shall see, the scope of these commissions is quite limited. In actuality, much of the organization of work by the two houses is done through a council of elders, an informal and quasi-secret body made up of senior deputies. That both chambers invariably set up almost identical agenda and commissions indicates that communication among these senior officials is fairly extensive.

When hearing proposals or reports by the government, the two chambers meet jointly; they then meet separately to discuss proposed legislation and the budget. Amendments or changes can be proposed from the floor. In case of disagreement between the two chambers, a conciliation commission can be drawn from both houses; if differences still are not resolved, the elected Presidium can dissolve the Supreme Soviet and call for new elections.

Not surprisingly, given the shortness of its sessions, little debate occurs in the Supreme Soviet. For the most part, proposals for legislation are approved by acclamation. In fact, the amount of legislation actually considered is minimal; most important matters are dealt with in the form of executive decrees. During the last years of Stalin's rule, the Supreme Soviet did not even meet for its allotted time; it held an average of only one session in a year. With his death, the constitutional requirement of two sessions a year was again observed, although the amount of time the Supreme Soviet has to examine proposals is still quite limited. Even so, the activities of the Supreme Soviet have increased somewhat in recent years. Reports have been subject to mild criticism, and deputies have requested that their committees have more time to look over the government's proposals. Nevertheless, so far as its legislative function is concerned, the Supreme Soviet remains an ornament of the realm rather than a working body to be taken seriously. It has slightly more power when it comes to overseeing the implementation of policy, and occasionally the work of a public organization will be criticized in reports of some of the Supreme Soviet's committees or speeches made during one of its sessions. Such criticisms, however,

seem to emanate either from a party decision to correct a specific abuse or from a newly dominant faction within the party that is seeking to discredit those previously in key positions.

The limited demands of legislative activity permit all deputies to the Supreme Soviet, with the exception of a few officers, to continue working at their regular jobs and thus to supplement the substantial monthly salary and generous travel allowances they receive as legislators. Deputies also may not be arrested or prosecuted—without, that is, either the consent of the Supreme Soviet while it is in session or the approval of the Presidium in the interval between Supreme Soviet sessions. The privilege of immunity is not, of course, always honored. During the great purge, many deputies who had been elected under the new constitution were removed from office and shot, necessitating new elections.

As a deputy, a member of the Supreme Soviet is supposed to explain the regime's policies to local citizens, hear their complaints, represent their grievances to government agencies, and, in general, act as their father confessor. There is not much evidence that this task weighs very heavily on the shoulders of most deputies, especially on those who are also members of the bureaucratic apparatus. Some do hold regular receptions and do intercede for their constituents; to this extent they represent local interests at the national level. And from time to time, too, the press will report how a deputy saved a marriage or rescued a young man from a life of dissipation. Most deputies, however, do not fulfill their grass-roots functions.

Whatever obligations a deputy may or may not perform on home ground, his election is in part a public recognition of his character. It is also a means of bringing constituent representatives more fully into the system, especially if they are not party members, by giving them a greater sense of participation. Further, the election campaign and the activities of those elected to office serve a socializing function by setting up deputies as models of behavior for the rest of the population. Finally, deputies serve to reduce venality and stupidity in office. The party, then, attempts to bring as many citizens as possible into the political process by providing them with the opportunity to serve on the Supreme Soviet, and turnover is, consequently, extremely high. Of the deputies elected to the U.S.S.R. Supreme Soviet in 1966, 67 per cent had not served during the previous session.

THE PRESIDIUM OF THE SUPREME SOVIET: A 37-member Presidium, consisting of a chairman, 15 deputy chairmen, a secretary, and twenty members, is elected every four years by the Supreme Soviet at its first post-election meeting. According to the constitution, the Presidium is the highest permanently functioning organ of state power in the Soviet Union. Its authority is hypothetically derived from the Supreme Soviet, to which it is responsible; in actual fact it is an autonomous body, and elections to it are preconcerted: decisions on who are to be Presidium members are made at the top echelons of the Communist Party. Invariably, the 15 vice chairmen are the chairmen of the supreme soviets of the 15 union republics; of the twenty ordinary members elected in 1967, 14, including Brezhnev and four other members of the party's politburo, were members or candidate members of the Central Committee of the C.P.S.U. Members of the Presidium may be removed at any time by the Supreme Soviet; needless to say, this has never happened.

The Presidium has no authority to delay or veto acts of the Supreme Soviet, and it acts only in accordance with powers delegated to it by the parent body. It does, however, have wide powers of appointment, including the selection and recall of Soviet diplomats and members of the military high command. It appoints the members of the Council of Ministers and may also remove them upon recommendation of the council's chairman.

Despite its formal superiority to the council, however, the Presidium clearly does not control it. In fact, the council figures far more importantly in political decision-making.

The most significant of the Presidium's powers is its authority to issue decrees. Again, theoretically, the decrees merely amplify statutes already passed by the Supreme Soviet. However, a very large proportion of the Presidium's decrees are, in effect, legislation, although they never pass through the Supreme Soviet. Further, all decrees take force immediately, and some have been submitted to the Supreme Soviet only after being in effect for several years. Nor has the Supreme Soviet ever rejected a decree as extending beyond the purview of the Presidium. It is interesting to note, incidentally, that many important decrees are issued jointly by the Presidium and the Central Committee of the Communist Party.

The chairman of the Presidium, who is elected by its members, is sometimes referred to as the president of the U.S.S.R. (See Table 18.1.) Strictly speaking, however, he has no more formal authority than any other member. He does have certain additional functions to perform, such as convening the Presidium and conducting its meetings, promulgating all official acts, and serving as nominal head of the Soviet state in its relations with other nations. While the 1936 constitution was under discussion, some had suggested that the chairman of the Presidium be invested with real authority; Stalin rejected the idea as violating the Leninist doctrine of collective leadership.

THE COUNCIL OF MINISTERS: The "highest executive and administrative organ of state power of the U.S.S.R.," according to Article 64 of the constitution, is the 84-member Council of Ministers, the final authority on the organization of Soviet ministries, and, in fact, the body responsible for the administration of all public activities. According to the constitution, the council does not legislate,

TABLE 18.1. PARTY AND GOVERNMENT LEADERS IN THE U.S.S.R.[1]

| Party | | Government | |
Politburo	Secretariat	Council of Ministers	Presidium
Members:	*General Secretary:*	*Chairman:*	*Chairman:*
L.I. Brezhnev	L.I. Brezhnev	A.N. Kosygin	N.V. Podgorny
A.N. Kosygin			(Ceremonial head of state)
N.V. Podgorny	*Secretaries:*	*First deputy*	
M.A. Suslov	M.A. Suslov	*chairmen:*	*Deputy chairmen:*
G.I. Voronov	A.P. Kirilenko	K.T. Mazurov	(The chairmen of the
A.P. Kirilenko	P.N. Demichev	D.S. Polyansky	supreme soviet presidiums
A. Shelepin	D.F. Ustinov		of the 15 republics)
K.T. Mazurov	K. Katushev	*Deputy chairmen:*	
D.S. Polyansky	B.N. Ponomarev	M.A. Lesechko	
P.Ye. Shelest	I. Kapitonov	I.F. Novikov	
A.Y. Pelshe	F.D. Kulakov	N.A. Tikhonov	
	M.S. Solomentsev	V.N. Novikov	
Candidates:		L.V. Smirnov	
P.N. Demichev		N.K. Baibakov	
V.V. Grishin		V.A. Kirillin	
V.P. Mzhavanadze		M.T. Yefremov	
S.R. Rashidov		W.E. Dymshits	
D.F. Ustinov			
V.V. Shcherbitsky			
D.A. Kunayev			
P.M. Masherov			
Yu.V. Andropov			

[1]Small capitals designate officials serving in both government and party.

Source: Radio Liberty Committee, March 10, 1969. Reprinted by permission.

and Soviet authorities have taken pains to point out that council decrees and ordinances pertain only to laws already in operation. In actuality, however, the Council of Ministers is the principal source of legislation in the Soviet Union. It has, for example, the final say in determining annual national economic plans, which assume the *form* of laws after they are passed by the Supreme Soviet, but which have the *status* of laws immediately upon their prior promulgation by the council. Further, a very large proportion of the ordinances enacted by the council are, insofar as can be determined, new laws, and although they may legally be vetoed by the Supreme Soviet or its Presidium, this has never occurred. Some of the decrees and orders are classified, and therefore not made public; they are, nevertheless, binding. As with the

Presidium, a good many of the council's decrees are issued jointly with the Central Committee of the Communist Party.

Today, the Council of Ministers consists of the heads of the most important government agencies, and, ex officio, the 15 chairmen of the councils of ministers of the constituent union republics. Its membership also includes the heads of the all-union and union republican ministries, and since the number of these changes fairly frequently, the number of council members is not always 84. The council chairman is elected by each new Supreme Soviet, and he then submits his government —that is, the other members of the council— for approval at a joint session of its two chambers. The council is ostensibly responsible to the Supreme Soviet, but in practice it appears to be responsible to no other group except, possibly, the politburo. The most important figure on the council is its chairman, and chairmanship of the council has been one of the two key posts in Soviet politics, the other being that of general secretary. Stalin combined the two posts, and so did Khrushchev; they have, however, thus far remained in separate hands under the Brezhnev-Kosygin regime.

THE PRESIDIUM OF THE COUNCIL OF MINISTERS: For some forty years, the Council of Ministers has been far too unwieldy to engage in any kind of collective decision-making. Some time during the 1930's, therefore, a smaller group of council members began to meet as the Presidium of the council. Consisting of a dozen or so members, most of whom did not carry ministerial portfolios, it became in effect the "cabinet" of the government.

Stalin later created an even smaller body, known as the "Bureau," which consisted of an intimate circle of advisers. The Soviet constitution provided for neither a Presidium nor a Bureau, and the existence of both became known only after Stalin's death, when a decree was issued by the Supreme Soviet abolishing the Bureau and "legalizing" the Presidium.

The official membership of the Presidium includes the chairman of the Council of Ministers, the two first deputy chairmen, and the council's nine deputy chairmen. The names of all Presidium members are not known outside the Kremlin's walls, and its membership fluctuates. Most officials known to be on the Presidium are, however, also high-ranking members of the Communist Party.

THE MINISTRIES: If the Presidium serves collectively as a decision-making body, the function of the ministers who make up the bulk of the council's working members— many of whom are technocrats rather than party people—is to implement policy. We may assume, however, although we know very little, that a good many policy recommendations come from individual ministers, and are derived directly from problems associated with their work.

Many of the ministries in the Soviet Union have their direct counterparts in Western nations—the ministries of Foreign Affairs and Defense, the Ministry of the Interior, and the Ministry of Finance. Other ministries or state planning commissions (or committees) are responsible for various industries, and reflect the fact that the Council of Ministers has the responsibility for managing the entire economic life of the country. The Ministry of Merchant Marine operates the commercial fleet; the Ministry of Railroad Communications runs the railroads.

The Council of Ministers has been regularly reorganized, both to reflect power and policy conflicts within the government and as a result of attempts to find more effective mechanisms for coordinating national life. Throughout the 1930's, the council increased gradually in size as the Soviet economy grew more complex and the ministries were divided and subdivided.[3] As time went on, problems of coordination grew more and more complicated, and efforts to solve them resulted in the creation of smaller groups such as the Presidium.

None of these moves seemed to be notably successful. The consolidation of certain ministries after Stalin's death seemed only to push the problem momentarily under the rug, and they were eventually to be re-created in one form or another. Thus, in 1953 the number of ministries was reduced from 51 to 25, but three years later the total had risen again to 56.

In 1957, Khrushchev won approval of a bold new scheme to ease the problem of coordination by decentralizing the entire economic apparatus of the government. The

---

[3] Until 1946 the Council of Ministers was called the Council of People's Commissars.

nature of Khrushchev's reorganization indicates that he may also have been trying to enhance the power of the party apparatus at the expense of that of the state. In any event, many of the ministries were abolished in all but name; those remaining were greatly reduced in size and their personnel transferred to regional economic councils (*sovnarkhozy*). Thus, while a few ministries in Moscow were still responsible for overall coordination of particular sections of the economy, they were, theoretically, less involved in overall management. Even before Khrushchev fell from power, however, his program was being reversed; a number of state committees began to appear which looked suspiciously like the old ministries. The chief problem was that regional authorities placed their own interests above that of the nation, thereby materially hampering economic coordination. In 1965 and 1966, the new team of Soviet leaders dropped the sovnarkhozy and restored the ministerial system.[4] At first they were anxious to keep the number of ministries down, but by 1967 there were nearly fifty once again.

Ministries in the central government are of two types: all-union and union-republic. All-union ministries are centralized in Moscow, whereas, according to the Soviet constitution, union-republic ministries handle problems in which some authority is delegated to republic governments. Soviet ministries, therefore, exist at two levels, in Moscow and in each of the 15 republics, and each union-republic ministry is legally responsible to its own council of ministers as well as to the Council of Ministries of the U.S.S.R. All types of ministries are equally dominated by the federal government with regard to general policy. However, such ministries as those of culture, health, higher education, and agriculture are marked by a genuine deconcentration of personnel and some decentralization of authority. The few state committees still in operation deal primarily with matters that cut across the jurisdictions of conventional departments, such as the Committee on Science and Technology. They are organized in much the same way as ministries, and, indeed, committee directors are often called ministers.

4. POWER AND POLICY[5]

With the consolidation of the Bolshevik regime, it became apparent that, whatever the constitutional forms, the power to make binding political decisions lay with the Communist Party, and, increasingly, with the politburo and the party's bureaucratic apparatus. Within the politburo, Lenin's prestige was such that until he became ill he could effectively determine the basic directions of national policy. This did not, of course, mean that his power was absolute; Lenin had to take into account the mood of the nation, weigh the possible resistances to his decisions, and consider carefully the resources at his disposal. The establishment of the New Economic Policy (N.E.P.) in 1921 was obviously a decision taken to counter growing opposition to the so-called policy of War Communism.[6]

Lenin also had to contend with those within the party who opposed his decisions

---

[4] At the same time, the regime explored the use of the price mechanism and the market as a means of improving the coordination of economic activities. See Chapter 24, pp. 779–780.

[5] This section has been strongly influenced by Zbigniew Brzezinski and Samuel P. Huntington, *Political Power: U.S.A./U.S.S.R.* (New York: The Viking Press, 1964), although I do not accept all of their conclusions.

[6] "War Communism" is the name by which the Bolsheviks' economic and social policy between 1918 and 1921 became known. The policy included nationalization of trade and industry, wages in kind for workers and employees, and compulsory grain deliveries by peasants. The major source of opposition came from the peasants who were refusing to deliver grain to the cities. The New Economic Policy permitted the sale of at least some grain on the open market. There were, of course, other reasons for the shift to the N.E.P.: industrial production had come almost to a halt, and Lenin was convinced that new approaches were necessary if the economy was to be revived. See the discussion in Chapter 3.

and tried to gain the support of the party's cadres. While he was usually able to overcome opposition on any point he considered essential, he found himself compromising on a number of issues. No one man, of course, could decide everything. Nor could he oversee the implementation of every policy. A good many of Lenin's decisions, therefore, came to depend upon who caught his ear— and who was appointed to carry out specific tasks. Stalin's harsh treatment of the Georgian Communist Party in 1922, for instance, was not Lenin's doing, nor was it to his liking; eventually it contributed to a break between the two men.[7] In many other cases, the implementation of policy involved, effectively, the making of policy by subordinates.

With Lenin's death in 1924, the party was racked by factional infighting until the late

[7] The Georgian Communist Party believed that it had been completely ignored by Stalin in the drafting of a new constitution for the U.S.S.R. Lenin came to agree with them on the subject of Stalin's "Great Russian chauvinism"; Stalin was a Georgian himself, and Lenin noted that assimilated Russians were usually worse in this respect than Russians themselves.

1920's. Cliques within the politburo and the party bureaucracy fought bitterly over policy and power issues. There are those who argue that as late as 1934 Stalin did not control a majority within the politburo and the Central Committee on certain issues, and that this explains at least the beginnings in 1936 of the great purge.

Between 1934 and 1953 the power of the Communist Party declined as authority was centralized in Stalin as an individual. Seeking to maintain his undisputed rule, he balanced off the state apparatus against the party, and relied for advice upon cronies who were not primarily party men, including members of his personal secretariat. He leaned especially on the secret police as a check against groups within the party that might try to conspire against him. Nevertheless, even Stalin's power was by no means absolute. Like Lenin before him, he chose courses of action that were to a certain extent dependent upon the advice of subordinates upon whom he was forced also to rely for the implementation of policy and, at times, for an interpretation and possible

TABLE 18.2. SOCIAL COMPOSITION OF THE CENTRAL COMMITTEE
1952–1966

(*Members and candidate members*)

	1952	1956	1961	February 1966	April 1966
Party apparatus	43.5%	45.8%	48.0%[1]	34.2%	43.0%[2]
State and economic officials	33.5	38.4	34.0	36.8	37.9
Military officers	11.0	7.1	9.3	9.8	9.7
Cultural and scientific			5.4		4.2
Police	3.8	1.2	0.6		0.5
Workers and peasants					2.8
Others	8.2[3]	7.5[3]	3.3[4]	19.1	2.5

[1] Includes nine trade-union and Komsomol officials.
[2] Includes ten trade-union and Komsomol officials.
[3] Includes cultural and scientific personnel.
[4] Includes a few "workers" and "peasants."

Adapted from Roy C. Macridis and Robert E. Ward, eds., *Modern Political Systems: Europe*, 2nd ed. (Englewood Cliffs, N. J.: Prentice-Hall, 1968), p. 558. Reprinted by permission of the publisher.

modification of policy. Even so, the Stalin regime came as close to being an absolute dictatorship, in terms of total range of control exercised, as any regime in history, including Hitler's.

Within the party and state apparatus, factions continued to form and re-form, but the major effort of each was directed toward getting Stalin's ear. The purpose here, of course, was to depose and replace an existing favorite. That Stalin's ear was available can be testified to by the fact that favorites did, indeed, rise and fall, and not infrequently with astonishing rapidity. As yet, we do not have sufficient information to know the precise reasons for all such shifts within the Kremlin.

The death of Stalin and the changes since wrought in Soviet society have produced another pattern of decision-making. Under Khrushchev, the party began to reassert its dominance, and groups not directly connected with the party—especially technocrats, lawyers, educators, the military, and economists—came to share more and more of the burden of the policy-making process. The changes in that process have accelerated since the replacement of Khrushchev, who was criticized for bypassing the party and making many policy decisions by himself. His successors seem to be party bureaucrats genuinely committed to bureaucratic procedures. While Brezhnev and Kosygin obviously have more authority than others within the party leadership, the most important party decisions, for the time being at least, are being made by the politburo as a group. And these decisions are, with increasing frequency, taking into account the advice of the technical intelligentsia and the demands of various strata in Soviet society.

Some observers have detected signs that the pattern of decision-making within the Communist Party is developing along lines that can be compared with a parliamentary system. The politburo could be considered the equivalent of the British cabinet, and the Central Committee the equivalent of the Par-liamentary Labor (or Conservative) Party. If Khrushchev's downfall is any indication of a new balance of forces, it can be argued that while the party leader (prime minister) still stands well above his fellow colleagues in the politburo (cabinet members), he must not step too far out of line ideologically or allow his policies to prove less than successful. If he does, politburo members will then attempt to replace him by appealing to the broader party, that is, the Central Committee as the equivalent of the P.L.P. There is something to be said for the Soviet-British comparison.

Despite the changes occurring in the Soviet Union, however, certain features continue to differentiate it markedly from pluralistic societies. The differences stem from the peculiar combination of neo-mercantilist practice and mobilization ideology that continues to mark Soviet political life. The Soviet elite remains rhetorically committed to the total transformation of Soviet life and to the elimination of all political conflict. The organization of the Soviet state is conceived of as but a means to this end. Consequently, the constitutional provisions outlining the structure of the state apparatus have never been taken very seriously. The party has changed them many times without going through the formal amending process or even bothering to indicate publicly that the constitution had been changed. This periodic sub rosa tampering with the constitution was one of the reasons why Khrushchev suggested in 1962 that a complete overhaul of the document was necessary.

In terms of the ideology by which Soviet leaders justify their power, they cannot yet publicly admit that Russian society is characterized by continuing, albeit shifting, conflicts of interests which will always have to be adjusted. The one correct course of action, when discovered, will satisfy the interests of all. Nor, of course, do the Soviets, ideologically, accept the legitimacy of political ambition or the desire for power. A politician bent on ousting another would wish to do so only because his opponent deviated from the correct party line.

In England, France, and the United States, on the other hand, the political arena is the place where conflicting interests may be reconciled through certain rules of the game. Provided they play according to these publicly accepted rules, groups and individuals may legitimately pursue their interests as far as they can. Also, while political conflicts partially involve different notions of what is right for the community as a whole, seeking political office is a legitimate ambition. The differences in Eastern and Western political life can be overdrawn, for many groups in Western European nations approach politics with a perspective which resembles in style or content that of official Soviet ideology; and, at times, American, British, French, and German political rhetoric takes on some of the qualities of a Soviet political discourse.

What effects do these ideological differences have upon the nature of political decision-making? In England political conflict, both within and between political parties, is expected and legitimated. It takes place in accordance with certain rules and within a constitutional framework that limits its intensity.

With some marginal exceptions, British Prime Minister (and leader of the Labor Party) Harold Wilson cannot deprive members of the Parliamentary Labor Party of their seats if they disagree with him; the political office (and legitimate authority) of M.P.'s derives from their own election to Parliament. Nor can the opposition simply oust Wilson should it command a majority. It can force him to dissolve Parliament and call for new elections, but it cannot deprive him of office because it disagrees with him. In short, it must follow accepted constitutional procedures.

These facts set limits to political conflicts. The English prime minister can afford to compromise in the face of strong opposition, for a defeat will not signal the end of his political career; he can usually return to fight another day. The same premise applies to his opponents. Moreover, the rules under which Parliament operates make it impossible for one side to eliminate the other politically without raising the possibility that in the process it will seriously injure itself. Both sides know they must live together, just as they also know that today's majority may be tomorrow's minority and that to press a temporary advantage too far could later cause political havoc.

While each side in a British political conflict may convince itself from time to time that it represents the good, the true, and the beautiful, it usually recognizes that the interests represented by the other side have a degree of legitimacy, too; the opposition is not, after all, evil incarnate. Such moderation is not always demonstrated, to be sure; but in all but exceptional circumstances, if absolutistic moral rhetoric begins to prevail, it means that democratic politics is on the verge of collapse, and that a pluralistic, or reconciliation, regime is about to be transformed into another type of political order.

In the Soviet system, power and interest conflicts are much more readily transformed into all-or-nothing ideological warfare, with the opposition becoming identified as "deviationist" or worse. A natural tendency exists for any conflict to become a symbolic one. It is much more difficult to compromise if one's opponent is a "reactionary, Fascist Trotskyite wrecker" who is threatening to lead the nation away from the true path to socialism by opposing the expenditure of several million more rubles on heavy industry. True, many Soviet leaders probably do not take their own rhetoric to heart; yet rhetoric has a way of creating its own reality, and individuals who constantly couch their arguments in symbolic terms of this kind are often forced to act as if they believe what they say.

The absence of publicly accepted norms limiting the power of the politburo or of the party's general secretary also exacerbates the conflict. One man in control of the bureaucracy or one faction in control of the politburo can strip its opponents of all power in an instant. Either can purge the Presidium, the Council of Ministers, or even the Supreme Soviet—as, in fact, Stalin and to a lesser extent Khrushchev did. If one decides to fight on a policy issue, the fight must be *à outrance*; to lose may spell the end of more than one's career. Justified conflicts over policy, therefore, have a tendency to be transformed into desperate conflicts over power.

The problem has been further accentuated by the highly political character of the Soviet system. For a defeated leader there is no satisfactory alternative profession; since appointments to important posts are based on both party standing and professional qualifications, the most a former political leader could hope for has been forced retirement or a minor position in the provinces.

The results are clear from the history of Soviet development. Political infighting has been extremely bitter, and, until very recently, only the most ruthless could hope to survive. It is true that since the death of Stalin the facts of political life in the Soviet Union have been somewhat less brutal. In more recent years, the loss of a leader's political power has not meant the loss of his head. Memories of the Stalin purges, the decline in power of strict ideologists, and the emergence of a bureaucratic, neo-mercantilist political order have tempered the penalty for fallen leaders. Indeed, the present leadership seems to agree that group issues should be compromised whenever possible, and that none of the contenders for power should be ejected from the political arena.

Another factor that still differentiates policy making and power in the Soviet Union from that of the pluralistic societies has to do with the kind of resources participants can draw upon in their struggle for power. As in every political system, discord and bargaining pervade every level of Soviet society. Factions within the politburo push personal advantage and pet policies; regional party organizations compete for advantage with each other and with the state bureaucracy; party subordinates vie for power with each other and their superiors; professional groups, such as the army, scientists, and teachers, contend with each other over policy questions and fight for a larger share of economic benefits. Yet, all interest groups in the Soviet Union, with the possible exception of the army and, to a certain extent still, the secret police, tend to be amorphous and shifting. They lack organizational autonomy and the capacity to bring pressure directly upon political decision-makers. This is particularly true of the great mass of workers and peasants, even when they are consulted and brought into the process of administering policy on the local level.

In the United States and England, political decision-makers can strive for changes in policy or power relations by coaxing different interests into the political arena; in the Soviet Union, the principal political battles are fought out within the politburo and the Communist Party apparatus. This is much more the case today, of course, than it was during the latter part of Stalin's reign. After the death of Stalin, Beria thought he could seize power by relying on his secret police; the party apparatus, with assistance from the army, proved far stronger. Malenkov, a little later, seems to have thought that as chairman of the Council of Ministers he might be able to use the bureaucratic apparatus to consolidate his position; but his loss of the post of first secretary of the party and Khrushchev's control of the party apparatus spelled his defeat.

In consolidating his power, Khrushchev relied primarily upon the party machinery. He did use the support of the army against the "anti-party group," and he rewarded it by promoting an officer, Marshal Zhukov, to full membership in the Presidium. But once the crisis was over, Zhukov lost not only his Presidium post but also his post as minister of defense. His support was no longer necessary and Khrushchev was not about to allow the army an opportunity to share power with the party. Nor was the military a sufficiently unified political force to insist upon the retention of its new prerogatives. In his battle with the anti-party group, Khrushchev also turned to the party's Central Committee to overcome his opposition. This was the first time since Stalin had held all the reins of power that the Central Committee had been directly involved in a power-policy fracas.

Khrushchev's fall was primarily the result of dissatisfaction within the party over many of his innovations, including industrial reorganization and the bifurcation of the party into agricultural and industrial divisions. The party was disturbed, too, by a streak of populism in his makeup: he attempted to reduce the size of the party's bureaucratic apparatus and to encourage more rank-and-file participation—albeit of a limited kind—in party decisions. Khrushchev had also aroused the hostility of other groups, including the industrial and military bureaucracies. To all this, of course, must be added his foreign-policy defeats, including what those who overthrew him regarded, at least at first, as his unnecessarily harsh attitude toward the Chinese Communists.

The emphasis on conflict within the Soviet Union should not obscure the fact that now, as in Stalin's day, most decisions are fairly rational efforts to deal effectively with current problems. Marxism-Leninism as a doctrine is flexible enough to permit both adjustments to ongoing situations and satisfactory rationalizations after the fact—which is also true of the liberal ideology that permeates American society.

The basic commitment of Soviet domestic policy—the creation of a powerful industrial state in which all the means of production are in the hands of the state—sets limits to the ways in which particular social or economic problems can be handled. Even so, the limits are extremely broad. Within the framework of state ownership, Soviet leaders have approached a good many problems through a process of trial and error. Yet in many areas professional elites have gradually come to develop what must be seen as fairly rational solutions. For example, greater heed is being paid professional educators, and professional lawyers have already played a very significant part in rationalizing the Soviet legal system. Experiments with the organization of national ministries can be viewed as a series of attempts to find better methods of coordinating economic life without stifling all local initiative. The decision to experiment in a limited way with market pricing also represents a new Soviet approach to a basic economic problem; this, together with the granting of managerial autonomy on the plant level, is a sign that professional economists are finally coming into their own.[8]

The limits imposed by Soviet ideology can be seen in the regime's attempts to increase agricultural production. Despite overwhelming evidence of the greater efficiency of small private plots, Soviet leaders have refused to consider the possibility of de-collectivization. Instead, they have tried an assortment of solutions that range from increasing the size of collective farms to employing the pseudo-scientific theories of Lysenko in an effort to increase production. Only in the last several years have they come to recognize the need to increase agricultural investment, especially in the form of fertilizer, which should provide at least a partial answer to some of their problems.[9]

Of course, the Soviet Union is not the only country in which attempts to solve problems have been hampered by ideological blinders. The British have only hesitantly come to accept the fact that they must stop acting like a great power if they are to solve some of their economic problems, and Americans have

8 On the development of Soviet education, see Chapter 7. The development of Soviet law is treated in Chapter 20, and the economy in Chapter 24.

9 See the discussion of Soviet agriculture in Chapters 5 and 24.

failed to recognize that national planning is an absolute necessity if urban decay is to be halted. It is, however, fair to say that Soviet ideology is more constricting than the beliefs and attitudes that characterize the nations of Western Europe. On the other hand, the freedom of the Soviet elite from controls by the public gives it opportunities to experiment which American leaders lack. It is impossible to conceive of the Soviet Union's sudden shifts of farm policy—or, indeed, any of the abrupt policy changes that have occurred in so many areas of Soviet life, whether law, the organization of economy, or education—being accepted with equanimity by an American or Western European public. Soviet leadership remains relatively free to manipulate its environment, to experiment with one alternative and then another, and to try a major program and then drop it. And if a major program is dropped, it usually follows that the leaders responsible for it are dropped, too—and with about the same rapidity. In the Soviet Union, a still passive population accepts the alternatives, although it is not unlikely that its patience to go on doing so is gradually growing thinner.

Policy changes in the United States tend to occur by accretion, and they require long-term alterations in public perspective. Policies involving federal intervention in the economy, for instance, and efforts to improve the position of black Americans have not developed very quickly. However, since policy shifts are, in effect, the result of broad changes in public attitudes, once the new steps have been taken they are likely to be fairly permanent. Differences between the Soviet scene and the American in this regard should not be exaggerated; important areas of stability can be found in Soviet life, and many changes that once seemed drastic have turned out not to have altered fundamental relationships very much at all. Conversely, the United States—and England, France, and Germany, as well—have been known to enter upon a period of rather free-wheeling experimentation, espe-

cially in times of crisis. Nevertheless, the difference in degree is significant.

And there are also the differences in the manner in which policies are implemented—differences primarily between a one-party state and societies in which political power is fragmented. Bureaucratic sabotage can and does occur in the Soviet Union, as individuals or groups endeavor to blunt the edge of policy. However, there are no institutions to which groups opposed to a policy can turn once it has been initiated. In most Western nations, the courts finally spell out the content of the law. In the United States, independent regulatory commissions carry out congressional mandates and subtly modify the content of legislative programs to an extent that would be impossible in the Soviet Union.

Most propositions about the nature of Soviet political decision-making must remain tentative. Not only are there limitations on the amount and quality of information available to the West, but the Soviet system itself is in a state of constant flux. The removal of Khrushchev did not involve major purges; this may mean that the new reign of the bureaucrats will henceforth separate policy from power considerations, or it may be merely a reflection of the fact that Khrushchev had alienated just about everyone. The rule of Brezhnev and Kosygin has been fairly conservative, without any startling policy innovations. Does this mean that the regime is entering an era of conservative bureaucratic stability, or that no one has, as yet, been able to consolidate a satisfactory power base? These are questions that really cannot now be answered with total satisfaction.

5. INTEREST GROUPS AND POLITICS IN THE SOVIET UNION

It was only toward the end of the nineteenth century that interest groups of the modern associational type began to appear in Russia. As industrialization progressed, trade-union organizations developed, and businessmen started to think in terms of cooperative efforts to further their interests. Yet the pattern of interest-group behavior was quite traditional. Peasants were unorganized and expressed their needs only in the form of spontaneous demonstrations or erratic, anomic violence. This was also true of the great mass of workers. The most important pressure groups were institutional associations, such as the army and the church, and ethnic minorities concerned primarily with regional autonomy or breaking away altogether from the Russian Empire.

Even after the creation of the Duma, the source of decision-making continued to be the czar and his bureaucracy. On the whole, policies reflected the influence of personal or family contacts. While many decisions were made in response to what were conceived of as the demands or expectations of interest groups, they did not involve the consultations or bargaining peculiar to advanced pluralistic societies.

The Revolution, of course, radically changed the whole structure of Soviet society. Ideologically, the Communist Party was committed to the elimination of interests; thus, any conception of politics as a process of bargaining among interest groups had no place in the Soviet scheme of things, and little or no provision was made for institutionalizing the bargaining process. For a few short years, trade-union organizations made their wishes known, but gradually they were brought under the complete control of the party and the state.

With the consolidation of the Bolshevik regime, quasi-official associations were created for a wide variety of groups, from writers to war veterans. These were perceived, however, as instruments through which the party could achieve its goals, and while the advice of professionals might be sought, it was clearly to be subordinate to the party's interest. To be sure, some institutional groups, such as the military and even the church, were not without influence on occa-

sion. But so thoroughly had party members permeated these groups, too, that it was difficult if not impossible for them to act as even semi-independent bodies that could engage in formal bargaining relations.

Under Stalin, the focus of decision-making was the dictator himself and those cliques that gathered about him. His decisions were influenced by information received from those he trusted, and, like Russia in the time of the czars, personal influence with those responsible for shaping decisions was extremely important. Like czarist Russia, too, provincial "governors"—party chiefs—wielded a considerable amount of semi-autonomous authority. The difference was that controls from the Communist center were tighter, and the general lines of national policy set more stringent limits upon personal initiative.

With Khrushchev and his successors, both party position and professional expertise became more and more significant. Economists have affected decisions on the organization of the economy; teachers have had an impact upon educational reforms; scientists have influenced the priorities of scientific research; and lawyers have helped in the determination of legal policy. All these groups still have, at best, only the status of institutional associations; it is not easy to discover the expression of a corporate will that is independent of the party or the state and that, as a consequence, might lead to any kind of negotiations between the group and the state. Certainly it is difficult to find any real organizational activity outside the control of the party, although there are some groups operating, naturally enough, either informally or under cover. Recent law reforms seem to have been derived from a general consensus on the part of some of the leading legal figures in the Soviet Union, and they came to be accepted by the party hierarchy because of the increasing respect within that hierarchy for the opinion of experts. The same may be said for the influence of teachers upon education, biologists upon the fate of Lysenko, and economists upon the decision to charge interest for the use of capital when evaluating the costs of building new plants. In the case of writers trying to achieve greater freedom from control or the military seeking budget increases, limited forms of autonomy may be developing that would enable these groups to exercise a certain amount of pressure. Yet it is impossible, because of the lack of information, to speak with absolute assurance. Other things being equal, the areas of autonomy in Soviet society should

grow, but just how quickly cannot be realistically predicted.[10]

10 For case studies of Soviet politics that try to trace the influence of interest groups, see Alexander Dallin and Allen F. Westin, eds., *Politics in the Soviet Union* (New York: Harcourt, Brace and World, 1966). For an especially useful study of Khrushchev's efforts at educational reform and the reaction of various professional groups, see Joel J. Schwartz and William R. Keech, "Group Influence and the Policy Process in the Soviet Union," *American Political Science Review*, CXII (September 1968), pp. 840–852.

19

Political Decision-Making

on the Local

and Regional Level

1. INTRODUCTION

The states of modern Europe were created through the fusion of petty kingdoms, free cities, and ethnic groups, in a process of nation building that started in about the twelfth century and has continued into the twentieth. We have already outlined the particular development of four of these countries, suggesting simultaneously some of the reasons for the differences among them. As might be expected, the differences continue to have a decided bearing on the existing divisions of political authority within each nation. The manner in which national unity was achieved, the twists and turns in the pre-industrial development of urban and local government, the circumstances of industrialization—all are phases through which each of these nations passed; but how they were experienced and how the problems concomitant with each phase were confronted and mastered help explain, for example, the enduring importance of traditions of local self-government in England as against France or the Soviet Union. They also help to explain why each of these

nations has adopted its own solutions to essentially similar problems. The present chapter will describe the patterns of regional and local government in the nations under study and discuss some of the causes for present variations.

2. THE ENGLISH PATTERN[1]

England is a unitary state. All local authorities, therefore, derive their power from the crown, and ever since the Plantagenets they have had to conform, at least theoretically, with national directives. Nevertheless, for a long period of time local authorities possessed considerable autonomy in providing public services. Even today 12 out of every 13 children attend schools operated by local authorities, the police are under local control, and between 1945 and 1965 some sixty per cent of the new houses were built by local authorities. Altogether, local authorities now employ more than a million people, including about

1 The structure of local government in Scotland and Northern Ireland differs somewhat from that of England and Wales and is omitted from this discussion.

330,000 teachers. They also have the right to raise funds through property taxes.

The increasing pace of urban growth has brought with it not only huge metropolitan areas of core cities surrounded by extensive suburbs but new problems on the organization of local government. These developments, plus demands for greater citizen participation, have accentuated the need for regional planning. Thus, with respect to local government organization, England is experiencing a period of change and reform made more complicated by the emergence, or rather the re-emergence, of nationalism in Scotland and Wales and increased tensions in Northern Ireland.

ORIGINS AND DEVELOPMENT: During the late Anglo-Saxon period, the major units of local government in England were the shires. Many of these had originally been separate kingdoms; others were carved out of newly conquered territory and rather arbitrarily divided for administrative purposes. Often the center of the shire was a fortified town (burgh) which gave the shire its name. Many of the shires were under the effective control of the barony, and the authority of the central government, which often was fairly nebulous, was exercised by a shire reeve (sheriff). Many burghs, because of their fortifications and, later, because of their economic importance, were able to obtain special governmental privileges. The ability of some burghs to obtain privileges was to grow as they became centers of important commercial activity with the revival of trade and commerce in the late middle ages.

In the years immediately following the Norman Conquest, the power of the sheriff as the king's agent in the shires (which the Normans called counties) expanded considerably. Many of the sheriffs were members of the barony and used their authority to augment their personal power at the monarch's expense. Thus, eventually, a new tier of king's officers had to be created. At the same time, many of the larger towns—now called boroughs—were winning a degree of independence because of the importance of their economic standing. Many succeeded in obtaining special charters from the king permitting them to hold their own courts and markets and to elect their own officials. According to some of the charters, the local sheriff was not permitted to enter the town. All monies due the king or the local lord were collected by chosen agents of the townsmen themselves.

Among the most effective instruments developed by the Plantagenets for checking the power of sheriffs was the creation of justices of the peace, who were originally used primarily for judicial functions but gradually became the major arm of the government in handling local affairs. Generally "men of substance" chosen from the gentry, they served without pay and heard complaints against mayors and even sheriffs in their area. By the time of the Tudors, their authority was greater than that of any other local figures.

The structure of English local government remained generally unchanged until the middle of the nineteenth century. There seemed to be until then no urgent reason for large-scale reform. On the Continent, provincial authorities and the rights that cities had obtained for themselves inhibited the development of a vital national community, and both strong monarchs and national reformers believed their power had to be destroyed if a viable national state was to be created. In England, despite some resistance during the early years of the Plantagenets, county governments were brought under the control of the central authority with relative ease; while municipal charters permitted some local autonomy, they did so within the broadly accepted framework of a national community with national institutions. In all Continental nations, the formation of national communities was closely associated with national policies designed to produce economic growth; in England, on the other hand, economic growth seemed to occur naturally—to spring, as it were, from the energies of the society itself. Thus, the central government never felt required to take on the range of responsibilities deemed necessary by other nations during Europe's mercantilist period.[2]

By the middle of the nineteenth century, however, demands for governmental reform in England were becoming more and more insistent. The Reform Act of 1832 sparked efforts to expand the franchise in local elections, and the Industrial Revolution was bringing to the fore new problems in the organization and coordination of local services. The first important reforms took place in connection with the administration of the poor law. The smallest administrative unit of local government at that time was the parish, an area derived from the basic church district committed to the care of a parson. Until 1834, provision for the poor was handled by individual parishes and was the responsibility of unpaid parish officers who were answerable to the justices of the peace. The Poor Law (Amendment) Act of 1834 created a Poor Law Commission that merged groups of parishes into "poor law unions," in each of which a board of guardians was elected to administer poor relief. The significance of the parish mergers, other than facilitating and controlling the administration of poor relief, was that they led the way to the establishment of additional ad hoc governmental organizations whose authority went beyond parish boundaries.

In the meantime, other changes were taking place. Until the mid-nineteenth century, the fifty-odd counties into which England was divided were largely administered by justices of the peace, while the urban boroughs, which had obtained royal charters, were usually governed by corporations based for the most part on a fairly restricted suffrage. The Municipal Corporations Act of 1835 provided for elected councils in the boroughs and extended the suffrage; the Local Government Act of 1888 created elected councils

[2] For a further discussion see Chapter 24.

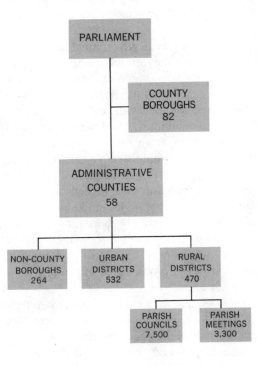

FIGURE 19.1. THE STRUCTURE OF THE LOCAL GOVERNMENT SYSTEM IN ENGLAND AND WALES

for the counties. More importantly, the 1888 law and a number of supplementary acts reorganized and rationalized English government in general. Two major types of local government units were created—administrative counties and county boroughs—and they are still the basis of English local government today. With the exception of London, the administrative counties, which often follow old county lines, are further subdivided into non-county boroughs, rural districts, and urban (small-town) districts with which they share local government responsibilities. The rural districts are divided into parishes with limited areas of jurisdiction. The county boroughs consist of urban areas large or important enough to be independent of the counties of which they are part; they exercise all local governmental prerogatives within their boundaries. Many of the boroughs created in 1888 were cities which had, in the past, obtained royal charters and a certain measure of independence.

Since 1888, local government units have continued to take on additional functions. Until very recently, however, few efforts have been made toward further structural reform —despite mounting evidence that the counties' historic boundaries had become less and less satisfactory from even a political point of view. Many administrative counties were too small; a number of cities had doubled or tripled in population and wished to become separate county boroughs, and, indeed, the division between county boroughs and administrative counties became increasingly archaic as planners began to give realistic attention to the problems of expanding metropolitan areas.

In 1958, a new Local Government Act established local-government commissions with authority to make recommendations on the reorganization and consolidation of local-government units. England alone contains 79 county boroughs, 45 counties, 227 non-county boroughs, 449 urban districts, and 410 rural districts. The changes the commissions suggested, however, scarcely met pressures for sweeping reforms, and in 1966 a royal commission was appointed with much broader authority to examine the entire question of local-government organization in England. The 1969 report of the commission (called, after its chairman, the Radcliffe-Maud Commission) recommended that English local governments outside London be regrouped into 61 new units. In 58 of these units, single authorities, called unitary authorities by the commission, would be responsible for all local services. In the remaining three units, which represent the metropolitan areas of Birmingham, Liverpool, and Manchester, the responsibility for services would be divided between the local government and a number of metropolitan district authorities.

Present county-borough and urban-district councils would continue to exist along with parish councils. The Labor government has accepted the major recommendations contained in the report; however, the report has generated strong opposition and it is as yet too early to determine how much of the plan will be put into effect. In the meantime, London itself has been reorganized on the basis of an earlier royal commission report.

Modern London traces its origins to the Roman invasion of England. The community was developed as the hub of a unified system of roads and communications that traversed as much of the island as the conqueror had seized. After the legions departed, however, the city sank back into insignificance until the late years of Saxon rule, when it again enjoyed certain special privileges and a degree of prestige. These were confirmed by William the Conqueror in a royal charter and further privileges were purchased later.

By the middle of the seventeenth century, London had developed into the cultural as well as the political and economic center of the English nation, and it has maintained this position ever since. The Industrial Revolution accelerated the city's growth, and it began to be ringed by an ever larger number of suburbs to which the well-to-do removed themselves as the inner city became more congested. It was not until the twentieth century—between the two world wars—that the population of central London declined, even as the metropolitan counties continued to expand. After World War II, the central city, like many in the United States, experienced such a vast increase in commercial employment—and to a lesser extent in residential population—that the life of the city was threatened by the growing congestion. Aside from the lack of a critical racial problem, London's postwar development parallels that of many American cities, with one other important exception: in the United States, more and more cities are competing with each other for prominence; in England,

London is beyond dispute the first city, a magnet that still draws to it the intellectual and cultural talent of the nation. It stands alone as the fount of decisions that shape England's destiny.

Until recent years, the development of adequate governmental structures did not keep pace with London's growth. The City of London Corporation, which obtained privileges from the monarchy during the middle ages, was a one-square-mile area in the heart of the metropolis. Today, it contains only five thousand residents. As the city expanded, however, no effort was made to provide it with a unified government structure; instead, a complicated network of quasi-independent local authorities sprang up. Even the reform acts of the nineteenth century did little to alleviate the confusion, although ad hoc authorities, such as the Metropolitan Police Board and the Metropolitan Board of Works, did try to handle special problems. About the turn of the century, additional moves were made to rationalize the pattern of London government without, however, getting to the heart of the matter. Until the 1960's, then, the government of the greater London area was divided among the London County Council, 28 metropolitan boroughs, the City of London Corporation, and a number of additional administrative counties, independent counties, and independent county boroughs which, while outside the County of London's boundaries, were, nevertheless, part of greater London.

A royal commission report and the London Government Act of 1963 have produced notable changes. On April 1, 1965, overall authority for the London area became vested in the Greater London Council, in effect a regional government covering 620 square miles and responsible for a population of eight million. Twelve inner and twenty outer London boroughs as well as the City of London itself continue to exercise certain autonomy, but the London metropolitan region now has, finally, a governmental structure that can deal with its problems.

SERVICE, ORGANIZATION, AND CONTROL: The services of local authorities generally fall into three classifications: environmental, protective, and personal. The environmental services pertain to, among other matters, drains and sewers, street cleaning, garbage disposal, water supply, highways, street lighting, parks and recreation. Protective services include those provided by police, firemen, and the civil-defense organization. Entertainment, housing, education, and health programs that are not part of the National Health Service are personal services under the aegis of local governments. The public schools are operated by local authorities, and even private religious schools come under local jurisdiction; teachers' salaries are determined on the national level, but teachers are appointed and dismissed by local authorities.

The structure of local authority in England and Wales is fairly uniform. The chief governing body is an elected council. In county boroughs, a mayor or lord mayor elected by the council presides over its sessions, while in the administrative counties an elected chairman serves the same function. Neither mayor nor chairman has any power, for the council has traditionally carried on its work through powerful committees, particularly the committee on finance, and with the help of full-time career officers appointed by the council. The career officers are not political appointees but rather professionally trained specialists in the operation of local government. They tend to move from a smaller to a larger authority as they ascend the ladder of local government. After several years of investigation, a 1967 report on the management of local government issued by the Ministry of Housing and Local Government recommended that the councillors limit their own work to policy-making and place more responsibility for implementing policy with the appointed officials, and a number of local-government authorities have given heed to the recommendation.

The money to run local governments comes from central-government grants and from money which local authorities themselves raise through taxation of property or borrowing. The ratio of national to local contributions is about two to one. Loans for capital improvements must be approved by the central government.

While local authorities have considerable leeway in some areas, their authority is basically delegated by the national government and is fixed by law. Local authorities can be challenged in the courts if they exceed their powers. Administratively, they must conform to departmental directives which supplement acts of Parliament, and many of their appointments and dismissals must be approved by the central government.

POLITICS ON THE LOCAL LEVEL: The general functions of local government in England have, with some exceptions, increased as local autonomy has decreased. In the pre-urban and, in a sense, pre-national era, the amateur squirearchies that determined local policy were responsible for very few services, at least by modern standards; if their functions were few, however, their freedom was considerable. The result, of course, was that the quality and extent of services provided by the gentry varied rather markedly, and, further, that some urban areas took the responsibility for certain municipal services—sewage disposal, lighting, gas—quite early. Others did so much later, if at all, but in any case the educational and health services and provisions for the poor and indigent differed from community to community during most of the nineteenth century.

In the past hundred years, the pattern has been for the national government to take on direct responsibility for many of these services or to set general standards enforced through central controls. In many cases, responsibility for a particular service was removed from local authorities in order to raise the general level of the service—only to be returned to them later for administrative convenience. In all cases, return has been accompanied by national controls. Thus, many of the problems now dealt with by local authorities involve administrative and technical matters rather than political or social issues.

The assumption by the national government of a greater responsibility for local services had important consequences for local politics. The introduction of the beginnings of local democracy did not immediately affect the gentry's position in local affairs. These families continued to dominate county government; their largess often provided community services, such as a new library building. Later in the nineteenth century, the squirearchy was joined, and to a certain extent replaced, by businessmen who shared many of their values. The complexities of the twentieth century, of course, made charity and other local problems into something more than private or provincial affairs. Such matters as welfare and street repair became public concerns—and once public they also became political. By the 1920's and 1930's, mobile, managerial personnel were beginning to figure prominently in local government; further, the Labor Party, which was rising in strength, was especially instrumental in bringing national party politics to the local scene. Council members campaigned on party platforms; when elected, they staffed committees with fellow party members and decided issues in party caucuses. In many central urban areas deserted by the middle class, more and more men from the lower middle class, as well as blue-collar workers, were elected to council positions.

Local-council politics, however, never became national politics in miniature. No matter which party was elected to local office, its responsibilities were primarily administrative. Its obligation was to exercise some control over, but to work in liaison with, professionals whose standards of conduct and ability were set either by the national government or by professional associations. While party became an important factor in the operation of local government, it was and is increasingly less important than the division between those councillors willing to take an active interest in mastering technical detail and those who prefer a more limited role.

The democratization of English local politics, then, was not followed by the emergence of democratic local politics on the American order. Elections to local office and policy questions are, on the whole, not conflicts between groups over which should get what, but "rational" discussions on the implementation of an overall policy. Furthermore, the heavy hand of the central government in local affairs minimizes political squabbling; local officials are constrained to act together if they hope to win concessions from London at the expense of other local areas. This reality tends to foster a sense of community concern. With some exceptions, the relative absence of ethnic and racial discord has also reduced the possibility of the kind of political free-for-all so characteristic of elections in many American cities.

In a very interesting way, certain traditional English attitudes have carried over to the modern period—with a new twist. The gentry, for instance, regarded it as their function to achieve a community interest; the "people" were to receive their favors passively. While the Labor Party councillors who replaced the gentry in many areas looked upon themselves as springing from the people, their general emphasis was still "collective." They did not consider either national or local politics as an arena for the expression of individual interests, but rather as an attempt to forge collective policies that would aid the working class, and, in the bargain, the population as a whole. Nevertheless, as on the national level, the feeling continued that the role of the citizenry should be limited to choosing its leaders and that public pressure upon councillors was somehow "un-English." This attitude has been reinforced by the primacy of national government and the increasingly technical nature of local problems.

Local politics, therefore, remains an area of low political saliency for Englishmen, as compared with Americans. The proportion of voters who participate in local elections is extremely small, and it has been argued that if local service did not provide an upwardly mobile political route, it would be even more difficult than it is now to obtain adequate personnel. In some ways, the lack of direct citizen participation in the American style serves a purpose. In the United States, mayors and councils often find it impossible to develop long-range plans or to take conclusive action for the general welfare simply because any action might offend one organized group or another. Indeed, the paralysis that grips many large American cities can be laid in part to an excess of citizen participation, rather than a lack of it: with each group fighting for its own "interests," the result is often that the public's best interest is compromised. In England, those engaged in planning tend to be far more insulated from the public, and their actions invariably indicate some conception of the general welfare of the community. Neither Conservative nor Labor councillors consider the public interest to be merely the sum of expressed individual or group interests. Accordingly, if ideal local government is to be equated with citizen participation rather than elite guidance, British local politics is obviously far from living up to what has long been part of the mythology of English political culture.

The debate over the proper distribution between local and national authority, as well as the correct basis for the geographic distribution of administrative authority, has, of course, exercised the British since the turn of the century—as, indeed, it has preoccupied most other nations. What the Radcliffe-Maud Commission recommended was a considerable enlargement of the authority of local-government councils. Commissioners felt that the new unitary authorities would take into account economic and geographic factors and would be large enough to make sense from an administrative point of view. For this reason, the commission strongly urged that local authorities be permitted to tap new sources

THE PROCESS OF GOVERNMENT

of revenue that would make them less dependent upon parliamentary largess.

A NOTE ON REGIONALISM: Although England is technically a unitary government in that all authority derives from the national Parliament, there has been some devolution of central authority to Northern Ireland, Scotland, and Wales. Northern Ireland, while it sends M.P.'s to Westminster, has its own Parliament made up of a Senate and a House of Commons and is largely self-governing in internal affairs. The Channel Islands and the Isle of Man are also largely self-governing in domestic matters. Scotland enjoys a considerable degree of administrative autonomy in that special departments concerned with education, development, and health are located in Edinburgh. Such devolution of authority is less true of Wales, which nevertheless is represented at Westminster by a special Minister of State for Wales, attached to the Ministry of Housing and Local Government. Wales is also represented in the cabinet by a Secretary of State for Wales. Legislative proposals especially affecting Scotland and Wales are referred to special standing committees in the House of Commons which are largely composed of M.P.'s from these two areas. The new constitutional commission appointed in 1968 by the British government is expected to recommend the still further transference of authority to both Scotland and Wales.

Pressure has also mounted for the creation of regional governments in England that would be more responsive to local needs. In 1964 the Labor government created six regional Economic Planning Boards for England; the number was later increased to eight, and separate boards were established for Scotland and Wales. The boards are composed of representatives from departments of the central government as well as delegates from local authorities and interest groups. These regional boards do not, however, constitute a new tier of government. The Radcliffe-Maud report suggested the creation of eight new provinces in England whose coun-

cillors would replace the boards and collaborate with the central government on economic and social development. Members of the provincial councils would be elected by officials representing the new unitary and metropolitan authorities, and they would be responsible for plans on effective land use and economic strategy. Provincial councils would also have some jurisdiction over educational and cultural affairs within their regional areas.

3. THE FRENCH PATTERN [3]

DEVELOPMENT: The major objectives of the Bourbon kings were the destruction of the provincial nobility's power and the creation of a national community controlled from Paris. They were only partially successful. By the reign of Louis XVI, the power of the provinces had been considerably curbed and the freedom garnered by many of the larger urban areas during the late middle ages notably reduced. But local pride and deeply etched provincial and feudal prerogatives restricted the effectiveness of the central government until 1789.

Those who made the French Revolution completed the work of the monarchy. The old patchwork of provincial and local authorities was swept away by the revolutionary National Assembly; France was divided into 83 administrative departments, roughly equivalent to English counties, which were made as geographically uniform as possible with only a modicum of attention given to historic boundaries. In order to eliminate all reminders of the old regime, the departments were named after rivers or mountains. Each department was subdivided into districts (later called *arrondissements*), which were, in turn, further split into *cantons* with the canton divided into primary units called *communes*. Unlike the departments, the communes were

---

[3] A good deal of the material for this section was taken from F. F. Ridley and Jean Blondel, *Public Administration in France*, rev. ed. (London: Routledge and Kegan Paul, 1969).

based on natural communities centering about local trade centers or the parish church; and unlike the basic English unit of local government, they embraced both urban and rural territory as well as populations that ranged from a few hundred persons to several hundred thousand.

The National Assembly also provided for a significant degree of local self-government. Each department was governed by 36 members chosen by universal suffrage and given a good deal of autonomy. The communes were governed by a popularly elected council and mayor. The results, however, were somewhat chaotic. By 1795 a reaction had set in and local areas were brought under tighter central control. The reaction continued under Napoleon. In 1800, the emperor abolished the autonomy of all local governmental units and created a system of national control that has continued more or less to the present. Elected officials were replaced by men appointed from Paris, and a direct representative of the national government, the prefect, was given overall responsibility for the management of local affairs. During the Third Republic, local offices became elective and their powers were increased slightly, but the fundamental fact of centralized authority and decentralized administration continued.

STRUCTURE AND OPERATION: Today the commune is still the basic area of local administration. France is now divided into some 38,000 communes. Their average population is 1,300; but 63 communes have a population of more than 50,000, while there are 35,000 with a population of less than 2,000. With cantons and arrondissements now of secondary importance, the only other major areas of local-government administration are the departments. These, too, have continued to differ greatly in size, for despite population shifts their boundaries have never been revised except for the recent reorganization of Paris and its environs. Thus, until 1968, the department of the Seine, including Paris and part of its suburbs, had more than five million inhabitants. The Nord, which is the second largest department, has more than two million; and Lozère, the smallest, has only 82,000.

The key official in local government is still the prefect. Assisted by various subprefects, he supervises the activities of the mayors and municipal councils as well as those of the departmental councils.

The mayor of the commune is elected by the council of the commune (generally known as the municipal council) from its own members. He serves for the duration of the council term, normally six years, and he cannot be dismissed by the council. Unlike the English mayor, he is far from a mere figurehead; like the prefect, he is the representative of the state as well as the commune, and he is entrusted with the enforcement of law and order. By and large, it is the French mayor who develops communal projects and sees to it that they are properly carried out. Many national politicians have begun their careers as mayors and retained the post even after assuming national office. The municipal council is elected by universal suffrage, and for election purposes, the entire commune constitutes a single electoral district.

Each of the departments of metropolitan France, which in 1969 totaled 95, also has a council elected by universal suffrage for a period of six years, half the councillors retiring every three years. Constituencies are based on the canton, and since cantons vary widely in size and population, rural interests are almost always overrepresented on departmental councils. In the department of Alpes-Maritimes, for example, almost half the population lives in Nice, but of the department's 31 councillors the city has only four. A departmental council, which meets twice a year for a total of about six weeks, is relatively impotent; although by law it "decides on the affairs of the department," its main power consists in reviewing and ruling on the budget prepared by the departmental prefect and representatives of the national government's ministries.

The Napoleonic scheme of local government involved strict hierarchical control from Paris. Some local autonomy came to be permitted during the Third Republic, and although there have been counter trends, local French communities today do have a certain amount of independence. There are some services that all local communities must provide, including national services administered by local authorities and specific local services which the community is legally required to maintain. All communes, for example, must supply funds for police protection, education, fire control, public health, and the construction of minor roads; but apart from these, local authorities often handle a number of other matters on which national legislation is permissive—such as parks, libraries, and child-care services. Depending on the needs of the commune and the policies of its local officials, provisions for these services do vary. Communes may regulate public services of an industrial or commercial character, or provide such services themselves; if the communes offer them, they are supposed to be economically viable and they are subject to regulation through suits brought before the *Conseil d'État*. Local services are financed in part by taxes and in part by grants from the national government. Although recent reforms have added new sources of revenue, inadequate financing continues to be one of the major problems for local authorities.

The control exercised by central authorities over local government is officially called tutelage (*tutelle*), and to the French at least, it differs in principle from direct administrative domination of local affairs by the national government. Tutelage is exercised in two main ways. First, the prior approval of central-government agents must be obtained before local authorities can initiate any programs. On the communal level it is the prefect, as the appointee of the central government, who gives the green light; on the departmental level, programs are endorsed by either the Ministry of the Interior or the cabinet. If the prefect (or subprefect) refuses to approve a decision, the municipal council can appeal directly to the Minister of the Interior. The second way in which tutelage is exercised is for the prefect to engage in certain forms of direct action. When a commune, for example, does not balance its budget, he can, after suitable warning, raise local taxes himself; if a commune fails to provide a mandatory service, he can include the item in the estimated expenditures and raise taxes to pay for it.

Legally, all French communes are equal in status. In practice, however, the size of the commune has considerable bearing on its importance. In larger communities, the mayor will have a sizable staff of trained, technical personnel who, in effect, limit his freedom of action. On the other hand, the mayor of large communes is quite likely to be a figure of some national prominence and he may, as a consequence, be able to bypass the prefect and gain his ends through political friends in Paris.

PARIS: The vital political and cultural position of Paris—and especially its historic role as creator and destroyer of French governments—has resulted in the national government exercising a more rigid control over its administration than it does over other cities. Historically, power has been divided between a municipal council, elected by proportional representation, and two executives appointed by the government. The two executives were the prefect of the Seine, with an office in the town hall of Paris, and the prefect of police; between them, they held all the powers normally exercised by a mayor and an ordinary prefect. The prefect of the Seine was responsible for economic and social matters, while the prefect of police was responsible for law and order in a very broad sense. Under the prefect of the Seine were twenty "mayors" appointed by the central government and placed at the head of the arrondissements into which Paris is divided. In effect, then, Paris was administered as part of a department, except that it boasted two prefects rather than one.

In 1964, the government introduced and Parliament dutifully passed a bill restructuring the government of Paris. As of 1968, the Department of the Seine was divided into four new departments, one of which corresponds to the present municipality of Paris, while the other three cover most of the suburban communes. The adjacent department of Seine-et-Oise was divided into three smaller departments but Seine-et-Marne remained intact.

In Paris proper, the municipal and departmental councils were superseded by a single assembly. The powers of the prefect of the Seine were transferred to the prefect of Paris, but the authority of the prefect of police has continued to extend beyond the city. At the same time, as will be discussed later, the problems Paris faces as an urban agglomeration are now the responsibility of a new regional organization, the *District de la région de Paris*.

POLITICS ON THE LOCAL LEVEL: Except for the larger cities, French local politics is rather nonpolitical. This is partly caused by the fact that the political stakes are small. The council has little power; the mayor, who does most of the work for the commune, is regarded as a figure who not only intercedes with government officials to protect the community from the unwanted encroachments of central authority, but who also attempts to pry out from them all he can get. Usually the mayor serves as both a public leader and a social one. Not only is he thought of as the commune's protector and the appropriate person to institute plans for public improvements, but in smaller communes especially he also functions as something of a father confessor when it comes to personal problems. In either case, public or social, French mayors avoid issues that might arouse public controversy; as a result, the

main purpose of most local elections is merely to indicate whether the commune endorses what the mayor is doing. Usually, he chooses a slate of council candidates and makes every effort to secure a balanced ticket representing all parties (except the Communist) and, if possible, all social groups.

Most French voters still prefer someone of substance—*un monsieur*—as mayor, someone who, they feel, can represent them effectively. Thus, despite the size of the French Communist Party, no more than four per cent of the municipal councillors are Communists (although their representation is much greater in larger cities). Indeed, it is the conservative parties that claim the largest block of councillors, about 36 per cent. The Radicals and allied groups have the second largest proportion, 21 per cent, followed by the Socialists with about 11 per cent. Many districts which give forty to sixty per cent of their vote to the Communists on the national level regularly return a conservative mayor.

The average tenure of mayors is comparatively long—about ten years—and it usually defies even large-scale changes in the national vote. More than three-fourths of the mayors of the Fourth Republic, for example, were re-elected during the first municipal elections held under the Fifth. In fact, many prominent politicians who had lost national office returned in the Fifth Republic as mayors, thus retaining a political foothold.

In attempting to obtain community services, mayors turn to the prefect, to the representatives of government ministries, and, through deputies, to the national administration. Under the Fifth Republic, contacts in Parliament have been rather less important than they were under the Third and Fourth, although mayors continue to believe that the right contact in the national legislature is extremely useful. Most observers agree that Communist mayors are probably, as a group, the best in France. They are hard workers, are technically competent, and usually push actively for local projects. They tend, too, to

FIGURE 19.2. LINKS BETWEEN CENTRAL AND LOCAL GOVERNMENT IN FRANCE

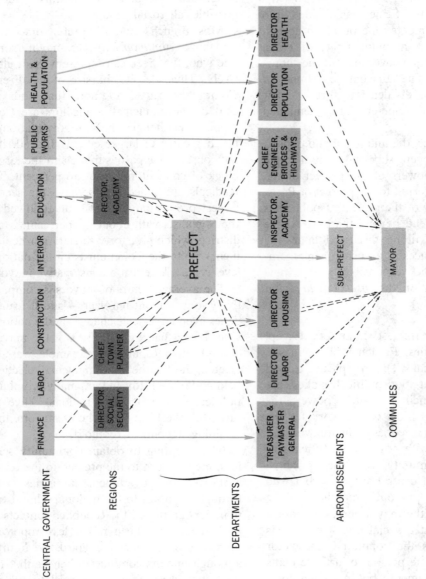

Only some ministries and some external services are shown.

Adapted from F. F. Ridley and Jean Blondel, *Public Administration in France*, rev. ed. (London: Routledge and Kegan Paul, Ltd., 1969), p. 110. Reprinted by permission of Barnes and Noble, Inc. and Routledge and Kegan Paul, Ltd.

advocate municipal ownership of services, emphasizing the problems and expense of contracting them out; finally, they tend to rely upon taxes that are progressive in form.

THE NEW REGIONALISM: It has been apparent for some time that France's 95 departments do not mirror regional realities. It has also been clear that in the Paris area, as well as other urban conglomerations, the commune does not represent the most efficient base of political organization for mastering economic and social problems. In addition, the French are particularly concerned with the relation of Paris to the rest of France. Even more than London, Paris is the center of France, draining political and economic talent from the rest of the nation—producing excessive congestion in the capital and a kind of cultural inertia or indifference in the rural provinces.

The Fourth Republic grappled with the problem on several occasions, and, indeed, the development of television, new highways, and a general increase in per capita income were starting to reduce the disparities between urban France—especially Paris—and rural France. It was only under the Fifth Republic, however, that important proposals to lessen this disparity, proposals which had been gathering dust for some time, were brought to fruition.

As early as the 1890's, French law permitted the formation of syndicates under which two or more communes could join to carry out specific projects. Communes might agree to set up, for example, a common sewage-disposal system or a water works. Originally, each syndicate was restricted to one specific purpose or enterprise; every decision pertaining to the syndicate, including being established in the first place, required the unanimous vote of each municipal council concerned, and each commune was equally represented regardless of its population. Today, syndicates may be multipurpose, and usually a decision to form one can be taken by a majority vote of the commune officials.

Furthermore, prefects may order the formation of a syndicate if they find it necessary. While thus far the prefects have rarely decreed the creation of a syndicate, their power to do so has given the central government additional leverage in encouraging the more rational allocation of resources. More than forty per cent of the intercommunal syndicates still deal with questions of water supply; joint cooperation on the problem of electricity runs a fairly close second.

In another attack on the problems of urban development, the French government in 1959 created a new institution, the urban district. Consisting of several communes, this may be formed by request of municipal councils or by order of the central government. A district automatically takes charge of fire protection and certain aspects of public housing, but it can also assume any other municipal services it chooses. The district does not, however, represent a new level of government, and the communes retain their individual identity. The districts are run by committees of delegates from the communes, with the smaller ones usually overrepresented. Only a few urban districts have been created, and they have exercised minimal authority.

In 1966 France took a further step toward solving the problems of urban growth by creating "urban communities," regional governmental units covering a city and its surrounding suburban areas. The plan was originally designed to assist Lille, Lyons, and Strasbourg, but permission to establish urban communities has now been extended to other areas with populations of more than one hundred thousand. Urban communities are governed by councils chosen by members of the communal councils. Unlike the district councils, however, the community councils are required to take responsibility for such matters as town and development planning, school building and secondary schools, housing, transportation, and roads.

Paris had begun to move in the direction of an urban community as early as 1961, under the urban district law. As revised by law in 1964 and 1966, the new Paris urban district, or community, includes all the area and communes that were within the departments of the Seine, Seine-et-Oise, and Seine-et-Marne. The result is an administrative area covering 4,670 square miles and including a population of approximately 8,500,000.

The Paris district is under the authority of a 28-member board of directors, composed half of government appointees and half of representatives of the constituent areas. Its chief executive, appointed by the government, is the regional prefect of the District of the Region of Paris, and, in general, his powers and those of the board are limited to problems of urban renewal and growth. The district is not a "supermetropolitan" government of the London type. Nevertheless, the ability of the Paris urban district to exercise some authority over so large an area has enabled it to develop reasonably sophisticated and integrated plans for the city.

To improve the organization of regional economic planning, the French government in 1960 divided the nation into 21 program regions.[4] Four years later it placed overall responsibility for each of these areas with a regional prefect who was also the prefect of the department with the largest city in the region. A series of commissions representing both the national government and local interests was also created to work out more realistic plans for regional economic development. Despite the appointment of regional prefects, the regions did not become a new level of government. Indeed, it was de Gaulle's attempt to amend the constitution in order to give these regions political status that helped bring about his 1969 referendum defeat and resignation.

4. THE GERMAN PATTERN

THE LÄNDER: CULTURE AND POLITICS: Whatever the overall cultural and linguistic

[4] A more detailed discussion of regional economic planning is to be found in Chapter 24.

unity of the German Empire that was created in 1871, it was still a nation of well-defined regional differences. The dominant orientation of Brandenburg-Prussia has already been described, but even Prussia was characterized by important socioeconomic and cultural variations. The Länder along the Rhine, for example, were and still are predominantly Catholic. Always very much under French influence, the occupation of the Rhineland by Napoleon resulted in the easier acceptance of French institutional changes. During the nineteenth century, the area was dominated by independent peasant farmers who were distinctly anti-Junker and who gave their support to the Catholic Center Party. As the area industrialized, this group was joined by a strong contingent of industrial workers who invariably voted Socialist. The cultural and social elite of the Rhineland has always been attracted to France; it is not, therefore, surprising that Konrad Adenauer, a Rhinelander who had been mayor of Cologne under the empire, regarded it as his major function to end the ancient enmity between the two countries and bring them into a mutually beneficial, working relationship.

The kingdom of Bavaria, with its long tradition of cultural and political independence, is another example of a marked regional difference within Germany. Predominantly agricultural, the land was divided among small peasant freeholders. It was also heavily Catholic, and Bavarians voted overwhelmingly for Catholic parties—Bavarian Catholic parties. Compared with the Rhineland, however, its Catholicism was far more conservative and the viewpoint of its peasants far more traditional. The separatism and rabid anti-Semitism of many Bavarians led not a few of them to support the National Socialists, although Catholic parties retained their hold on the great majority of the population.

The Nazi regime, the war, and postwar developments have helped to erode German regional differences, although they have not as yet completely disappeared. The northern Länder of the Federal Republic (Lower Saxony, Schleswig-Holstein, Hamburg, and Bremen) are still mostly Protestant. North Germany is poorer than other areas, and it now has far less influence on national politics than it enjoyed during both the empire and Weimar periods; in general, it is more conservative than other areas of Germany. Southern Germany, especially Bavaria, still has a tendency to be absorbed with local affairs—to the extent of supporting a quasi-independent affiliate of the Christian Democratic Party, the Christian Social Union. The area remains socially conservative, but with class divisions that are less distinct than those in the north. Finally, western Germany, including the Rhineland-Palatinate, is perhaps the most prosperous part of the nation and the most oriented toward working within a broader European context that includes close relations with France.

THE LÄNDER: POLITICAL HISTORY AND STRUCTURE: Most German states under the empire retained a highly conservative governmental structure with real power vested in an executive. They also reserved for themselves considerable local autonomy. With the establishment of Weimar, republican constitutions were adopted, and all the Länder except Prussia established unicameral legislatures with deputies elected by proportional representation. During the Nazi regime, Land government was completely transformed: state legislatures were abolished and each state was placed under a national governor appointed by Hitler; the governor enacted state laws with the approval of the national cabinet.

From the Franco-Prussian War to the rise of Hitler, Prussia, because of its size and population and the direction it had given to German unification, dominated the German political scene. Since the Allies blamed "Prussian militarism" for much that was wrong in Germany, they agreed that Prussia should not be re-created as a political unit in the new German state. The cold war and the division of Germany helped to solve this problem because much of what had been the Prussian state was in the Russian zone. In the western zones, each of the occupying powers followed its own inclinations as to how the Länder should be reconstructed. The Americans re-created Bavaria and combined smaller territories to form Hessen and Baden-Württemberg. The French joined part of Bavaria with parts of Hesse and Rhenish Prussia to form the Rhineland-Palatinate. The British combined other formerly Prussian areas to create the Länder of Lower Saxony and Schleswig-Holstein.

With the exception of Bavaria, then, the new postwar Länder command little historic loyalty, and it is not surprising that Germans seem to feel less and less attachment to them. In fact, most Germans would be quite happy to see the power of the states reduced, and would probably not be averse to some new form of regional organization. The Länder today are far less unequal in size and resources than they once were, but they have the virtues neither of historical identification nor, in some cases, of being regions for which logical economic and governmental plans can be made.

On the whole, Land governments closely resemble that of the West German Federal Republic, although, except for Bavaria, they are unicameral. Most of their electoral systems provide for some sort of double ballot involving elements of proportional representation, with percentage requirements in force in order to make it more difficult for very small parties to obtain seats. Several Länder also have provisions for referenda on certain issues, but these have been invoked only rarely.

With the exception of Bremen and Hamburg, the state executive is composed of a minister-president and a cabinet. The former can usually be removed only by a vote of no confidence, but his powers, by comparison with those of the chancellor of the Federal Republic, are not extensive. Land cabinets are usually fairly small, and the ministers are appointed on the advice of the parties participating in the government. Since the primary

TABLE 19.1. THE LÄNDER OF THE GERMAN FEDERAL REPUBLIC

	Area (in thousands of square miles)	Population, 1967 (in millions)	Population density (per sq. mile)	Cities with population over 100,000	1967 per capita taxable income (in dollars)	Seats in Bundesrat
North Rhine-Westphalia	13.1	16.8	1,280	34	$7,824	5
Bavaria	27.2	10.3	380	5	6,216	5
Baden-Württemberg	13.8	8.7	630	5	7,508	5
Lower Saxony	18.2	7.0	385	6	5,592	5
Hesse	8.2	5.3	645	5	7,436	4
Rhineland-Palatinate	7.6	3.6	474	3	5,464	4
Schleswig-Holstein	6.1	2.5	410	2	5,600	4
Hamburg	0.27	1.9	7,050	1	25,700	3
Bremen	0.15	0.8	5,320	2	13,636	3
Saar	1.0	1.1	1,100	1	4,536	3
Totals and averages	95.6	59.3	1,767	64	$7,572[1]	41

[1] Includes West Berlin.

Adapted from Statistiches Bundesamt, *Statistiches Jahrbuch für die Bundesrepublik Deutschland, 1963* (Stuttgart, W. Kohlhammer G.m.b.H., 1968), p. 400; and Lewis Edinger, *Politics in Germany* (Boston: Little, Brown, 1968), p. 14, copyright © 1968, Little, Brown and Company, Inc. Adapted by permission of the publishers.

function of the Land government is administrative rather than policy-making, men with administrative experience are most frequently nominated for cabinet posts. Despite Adenauer's efforts to nationalize Land politics—partly to insure control of the Bundesrat—the Land parties have resisted national party pressures. Thus, in a number of states Christian Democratic and Social Democratic governmental coalitions came into existence during the 1960's, and in others the Socialists joined with the Free Democrats to form a majority.

Many Land ministries are posts of some substance, especially in those areas of government in which the Länder have been free to assert their authority. This is especially true of state ministries of the interior, which set policies for control of the police, and of ministries of education and culture, which have jurisdiction over such problems as denominational versus integrated schooling. The bulk of the ministers' work, however, is taken up with the more mundane chores of administration.

Land governments have continued to at-

tract first-rate personnel for ministerial posts. This is partly a reflection of the fact that the formulation of postwar politics in Germany was well under way in the states before the institutions of the Federal Republic took final shape. It is also a reflection of the fact that the political power of Adenauer was so great during the 1950's that it prevented any ambitious politician from emerging on the national scene as a figure of importance. Thus, until his elevation to the posts of vice-chancellor and foreign minister under the Grand Coalition, Brandt was the mayor of West Berlin, where he made his reputation; former Chancellor Kiesinger served most of his political career in Baden-Württemberg, where he had been minister-president.

Most Land governments have experienced considerable continuity in cabinet membership. Where one party or a single coalition has been in power for some time, there is little desire to depose good men. Unlike the United States, where many governors face constitutional limitations upon re-election, German politicians can theoretically serve indefinitely; consequently, since party organization is strong and there is no system of primaries, young rebels, finding it difficult to challenge incumbents, move up in the party hierarchy only very slowly. Advancement of the younger state politicians is sometimes further stymied by the party practice of bringing in ministers from other Länder to fill posts.

Except for Bavaria, the legislatures in most Länder are organized very much like the Bundestag. The party Fraktionen exert their authority, but that authority is being increasingly undermined by a sense of common interest and need for expert guidance on the part of committee members. Most of the legislative work, because of its often fairly specialized nature, is handled in committees.

Deputies to Land parliaments, like those to the Bundestag, are elected for four-year terms. However, state election dates do not coincide. They are sufficiently scattered so that some are held each year, a circumstance that tends to contribute to lower turnouts than in federal elections and has been beneficial to the Social Democrats, in part because it is the marginal C.D.U. supporters, especially women, who vote in larger numbers in federal elections. The early success of the S.P.D. in Land elections, however, was also attributable to a greater public willingness to trust the Socialists with state problems than with national affairs. So far as minority parties were concerned, the general trend of state elections during the late 1950's and 1960's mirrored those on the national level: again except for Bavaria, the C.D.U. and the S.P.D. were taking an ever larger portion of the total vote. In 1966, the trend seemed to have been stopped with limited successes by the National Democratic Party (N.P.D.) in several Land elections. Drawing substantially from the Free Democrats and the remnants of right-wing groups, the N.P.D. did not, however, make any irreparable dent in major party bandwagons.

Land elections have not been without their impact on the national scene. It was the unmistakable decline of C.D.U. fortunes in sev-

eral 1963 Land elections that led the party to press for Adenauer's retirement; and it was the success of the neo-nationalist N.P.D. which, in 1966, was an important factor in bringing about the C.D.U./S.P.D. coalition after the fall of Erhard.

What is becoming apparent is that the present division of authority between the federal and the Land governments is proving to be more and more dysfunctional. The states have been receiving the bulk of the money derived from income and corporation taxes with the result that the amount of funds available to the federal government has been reduced and the situation in which the rich Länder become richer and the poorer Länder rely on handouts is being perpetuated. In 1967, the states had a total revenue from income and corporation taxes of \$10.5 billion; industrial North Rhine–Westphalia took in more than a fourth of the total while the Saar got less than a fortieth.

The efforts of the Bonn government to formulate a satisfactory national educational policy or to engage in worthwhile regional planning have also run into serious obstacles. Many problems faced by Germany today require governmental structures that transcend Land boundaries, yet moves by the national government to establish workable regional organizations are constantly thwarted by an unwillingness on the part of the Länder to relinquish any of their authority; the Bundesrat's power with respect to legislation is now such that Land governments are in a position to block any proposals which they feel will diminish their own prerogatives. One of the rationales for the formation of the Grand Coalition was the promise that it would carry out a reform program granting the federal government more authority to meet the nation's challenges, and, indeed, it did manage to secure some moderate changes, although the Bundesrat watered down many of its original proposals.

LOCAL GOVERNMENT: By the late middle ages, many of the larger cities in what eventually was to become Germany had attained an authentic degree of independence from their nominal overlords—including the authority to determine their own form of government. In fact, to be a member of a burg was often regarded as more important than citizenship in the larger territorial unit of which it was part. The translation of an old German rhyme ran:

No man's lord and no man's wight,
That is the freeborn Bürger's right.

In some parts of the Holy Roman Empire, thriving cities and towns merged into federations and leagues for mutual defense against predatory knights and the feudal nobility. One of the most powerful of the purely defensive leagues was that formed by the Rhenish towns in the middle of the thirteenth century under the leadership of Mainz and Worms. Even more important was the great federation of the northern trading centers, later known as the Hanseatic League, which, at the height of its power in the second half of the fourteenth century, contained nearly ninety seaport and inland towns in Germany. Hamburg and Bremen, which entered the Second Reich as free and imperial cities and the West German Federal Republic as Länder, trace their autonomy from the middle ages.

The development and consolidation of national states under absolute monarchs eventually foreclosed municipal liberties. By the middle of the eighteenth century, city self-government had been all but wiped out in most of Germany. Nowhere was the process of liquidation of home rule more thoroughly carried out than in Prussia.

During the Napoleonic Wars, however, a reversal of the trend took place. The Prussian City Government Act of 1808, sponsored by Baron vom Stein, helped restore municipal self-government in Prussia; it later became the cornerstone of municipal freedom throughout the German Empire. What vom Stein was aiming at was the reformation of German public life by combining rationalization with a return to what he considered the creative elements in the German tradition. The German tradition of local self-government, of course, was decidedly contrary to the kind of centralized political order inspired by the French Revolution as disseminated by Napoleon. In any event, during the latter nineteenth century German cities again flourished. Their administration was impeccably honest, and under the leadership of a burger aristocracy, German municipalities pioneered in city planning and in providing services, including extensive cultural facilities. It should be noted, however, that, for the most part, suffrage was restricted to property holders.

In the Weimar period, local government was democratized. Universal, equal, and direct suffrage was prescribed for all local elections, and local autonomy was guaranteed by the Weimar constitution. With the Great Depression, however, the federal and Land governments took over more and more of the responsibility for local activities, and during the Nazi regime, the organization of municipal government was fully centralized under the dual control of the party and the state.

The basic unit of local government in Germany is still the *Kreis,* or county. As in England, larger cities are organized separately, the distinction being quite similar to that between county boroughs and administrative counties in England. Traditionally, the rural counties were under the supervision of the *Landrat,* a district officer who was an appointee of the Land government, while governments of large cities were fairly independent. Local governmental structures differed from state to state, but common to all was a close relationship between the elected council and the mayor (or the mayor plus his executive associates, a body called the *Magistrat*). The mayor was elected by the council, but for a term exceeding that of the councillors, and although party affiliation had something to do with who was elected, he was generally a professional civil servant who built up a staff of competent professional officials to assist him.

Since World War II, the rural county has been reorganized in a fashion designed, theoretically at least, to permit more local autonomy. The Kreise are now governed by an elected county council and a Landrat who is usually elected or appointed on the county level. The independence of the counties, however, is more apparent than real, for they are more and more dependent upon Land grants-in-aid. In fact, many of their traditional functions are now handled by Land agencies, and the office of the Landrat is more often than not staffed by state civil servants.

Developments in urban areas have been far more complex. During their occupation, the Americans restored traditional German patterns of municipal government in their zone, while the British and French created urban governments modeled after those of their own country. While there has been a general tendency to return to older patterns in most areas, the variation in German urban government today is probably greater than it was under the empire.

German cities are still extremely active in the fields of social welfare and culture. Moreover, most of the local transportation is municipally owned, as are gas, water, and power facilities, and municipal enterprises constitute an important source of local income. In the postwar period, German cities have found themselves administering an ever wider range of activities assigned to them by the Land. Many urban governments believe they are becoming overburdened with the business of governing, and most municipalities find that larger and larger portions of their budgets come from allocations of Land and federal taxes.

But no matter how difficult it may be to find the funds for the proper operation of local government in Germany, the level of the local bureaucracy is extremely high. Officials receive training, salaries, and other benefits comparable to those serving on the state and national levels. Positions are usually filled on a competitive basis, although party or religious affiliations sometimes have a rather direct bearing on the selection of appointees. There is also a good deal of interchange among civil servants of different local units. Thus, while in a few German cities remnants of the old patrician elite still take an active interest in local affairs, most towns have become little more than the administrative arm of Land governments served by a bureaucracy that has less and less interest in traditional values.

BERLIN: The city of Berlin has its roots in the eleventh century, when the duke of Saxony established a village community on the island in the Spree River. Berlin did not assume much importance until it became the capital of Prussia in 1701, and its real growth began only in the nineteenth century. As the capital of the Reich, it became one of the world's major cities and a vital center of culture and learning.

By the turn of the century, Berlin had clearly outgrown its original boundaries, and blueprints were already being drawn up to incorporate the outlying areas. In 1920, under a law on the formation of the municipality of Berlin, no less than 95 local authorities were absorbed by the island city. The new Greater Berlin metropolitan area was detached from the Prussian state of Brandenburg and given a governmental status equivalent to that of a Land. The Berlin government consisted of a chief mayor, a mayor, a civil authority, and a municipal council elected from the city's 15 electoral districts. This central municipal administration was responsible for expenditures and taxation, utilities, transportation, parks and forests, savings banks, police and fire protection, and other activities affecting the city and its metropolitan area as a whole.

During the 1920's, the largest political party in the capital city was the Social Democratic Party, which dominated the working-class districts. As the decade wore on, however, the Communist Party grew in strength, as did the National Socialists—the

former finding most of its appeal among unemployed workers. By 1932, the Nazis and
the Communists had each captured about
one-third of the vote of the city's population.

Under the Hitler regime, the last vestiges
of local autonomy in the city were eliminated,
and the control of its affairs was vested fairly
firmly in the Nazi Party and the central state
authorities. The Battle of Berlin all but destroyed the city; its ruins were divided into
four sectors under the separate administration of the Russians, Americans, British, and
French; all four also jointly governed the
city as a unit.

As the cold war intensified, cooperation between the Western nations and the
Soviet forces became more and more difficult.
Finally, in 1948, the Russians tried to detach
Berlin from western Germany by halting all
traffic through Communist East Germany
into the city. The blockade failed, and the
city was divided between the western sectors,
continuing under joint administration, and
East Berlin, which was later to become part
of the German Democratic Republic.

In 1950, a constitution was promulgated
for West Berlin, and a political organization
similar to that of a state was established for
the isolated city. Berliners now elect a House
of Representatives (*Abgeordnetenhaus*) for
four years, and the executive consists of a
cabinet (*Senat*) and a governing mayor responsible to the house. Western Germans
wanted to incorporate West Berlin into the
Federal Republic, but Western Allies vetoed
the proposal, arguing that a change in Berlin's
status might give the Russians an excuse to
abrogate rights of free access to the city
through East German territory. In a statement
issued upon the formal granting of sovereignty to the Bonn Republic in 1955, the
three Allied commandants continued to reserve certain ultimate rights in Berlin while
granting complete freedom of administration
to the city's elected officials.

West Berlin's ties with the Federal Republic are, today, extremely close. Officially,

Berliners cannot vote in national elections,
but 22 members of the Bundestag are from
Berlin; four Berliners sit in the Bundesrat.
While deputies from Berlin cannot vote in
plenary session, they do vote on committees.
The federal government has passed laws applicable to Berlin, with the Berlin legislature
merely enacting a "covering law" incorporating the terms of the legislation. The Bonn
government has also granted extensive subsidies to Berlin—about the only basis on
which the city continues to survive.

Despite Berlin's bifurcation, its citizens
could move relatively freely between the
Western and Communist zones until 1961.
That freedom, however, resulted in the defection of many of East Germany's vitally
needed technicians and skilled workers.
Mounting desertions finally caused the Communists to erect a wall in August 1961 between the two zones; heavily patrolled and
constantly reinforced, it has achieved its purpose—furnishing the East German regime
with a sense of stability. It has also served to
demoralize those West Germans who had believed that the collapse of the German Democratic Republic and the reunion of the two
Germanies was inevitable. In the meantime,
Communist harassment of West Berliners has
continued to produce occasional crises, such
as the one in 1969 over West Germany's decision to hold its presidential election in Berlin, a practice that had been in effect for 15
years. Official Soviet and East German protests were registered, and their nettling delays
of traffic into West Berlin occurred, but the
election went off as scheduled.

5. THE RUSSIAN AND SOVIET PATTERN

DEVELOPMENT: The Romanov dynasty established in Russia a state which was, theoretically at least, as centralized as it was
autocratic. For purposes of administration,
Russia was partitioned into 78 provinces
(*guberniya*), 21 regions (*oblasts*), and one
circuit (*okrug*). Each region was headed by a

governor who was appointed by the czar and was, in effect, his personal agent. Provinces were divided into districts under the jurisdiction of chiefs of police appointed by the governor. It was the police who had primary responsibility for policy on the local level.

While ostensibly tightly centralized, the governmental system of the Russian state was, in practice, chaotic. Individual authorities had enough leeway to do pretty much as they pleased, and large landowners went right on exercising their authority over the peasantry even after the abolition of serfdom. On the village level, local assemblies did allow a degree of peasant self-government, and, in fact, many petty crimes were dealt with in village courts operating outside the regular legal system. But all of these institutions were comparatively unimportant; they could do little to withstand the pervasive authority of czarist officialdom over the activities of the "lower classes."

One of the major innovations of Alexander II, in 1864, was the creation of elective district assemblies (*zemstvos*) in the 43 provinces of European Russia. The assemblies, in turn, elected provincial zemstvos, which were originally supposed to be given extensive authority in the fields of taxation, education, public health, and roads. The original promise of these assemblies, however, was never fully realized. From the beginning, suffrage favored the nobility and the *haute bourgeoisie;* it was limited even further when local bodies later became sounding boards for critics of the regime. Since the regime was, in any event, inherently suspicious of local prerogatives, it either refused to grant any real authority to local government organs or withdrew it at the first sign of their taking any initiative. Nevertheless, the zemstvos continued to operate. Many of them evolved fairly effective programs and, in the last years of the monarchy, were beginning to assert authority of a kind which the regime probably would not have been able to suppress indefinitely.

Although Catherine II had granted Russian cities some autonomy, their charters remained more or less dead letters until the execution in 1870 of a municipal act modeled after Prussian municipal ordinances. All citizens paying local taxes were granted the right to vote and to serve on municipal boards. However, the electorate was split into three classes, in accordance with taxes paid; as a result, representation was heavily imbalanced. Furthermore, while the city was theoretically supreme within the limits of its jurisdiction, the presence of a royally appointed governor distinctly hampered the actions of municipal officials.

As with the zemstvos, many elements of the initial reform were later vitiated. The suffrage was progressively restricted to the point where no more than one per cent of the population was entitled to vote. Mayors and members of municipal boards became objects of governmental scrutiny; classified as imperial officials, they were subject to the jurisdiction of civil-service courts. As the authority of local officials was all but destroyed, the powers of the appointed governor were expanded until eventually he was able to exercise an absolute veto over municipal activity. In the period immediately preceding World War I and during the war itself, municipal councils, like the zemstvos, became centers of agitation for reform—without, however, achieving much of anything. After the success of the Russian Revolution in 1917, the provisional government issued a decree which introduced democratic principles, based on universal suffrage, in the cities; but after five months the new municipal system gave way to Bolshevik rule.

The soviets or workers' councils, which came to exercise authority on all levels of government, had a good deal of independence from Moscow in the early years of the Bolshevik regime. In fact, the situation approached anarchy in some areas. However, as the Communist Party consolidated its hold, the authority of both local and regional governing bodies dwindled. While Communist propaganda placed great emphasis upon Soviet federalism and on popular participation, it soon became evident that all local activity was subordinate to national policy decisions made in Moscow and in accordance with party plans. At the same time, the Bolsheviks tried to involve large numbers of people in the administration of local policies on a voluntary basis; their effort was part of a plan to replace state control of public affairs by "popular" control. Since the death of Stalin, further moves have been made to increase popular involvement in local government, and there are some signs that slightly more authority is being allotted to municipal officials, especially those in large cities. Even so, local government remains highly centralized and under the tight rein of the national party organization.

THE UNION REPUBLICS: The Union of Soviet Socialist Republics is composed of the federal government and 15 constituent or union republics. Each republic includes at least one preponderant ethnic group and a number of smaller minorities. Although in theory all the republics are equal, one of them—the Russian Soviet Federal Socialist Republic (R.S.F.S.R.)—contains three-fourths of the total area of the Soviet Union, as well as 55 per cent of the total population. Because of its size and location the R.S.F.S.R. has been and continues to be the dominant republic in the federal system.

The governments of the union republics follow, in general, the national pattern of the U.S.S.R. Authority is vested in a popularly elected supreme soviet, to which a presidium and a council of ministers are responsible. As with the Supreme Soviet of the U.S.S.R., candidates are nominated by the Communist Party and certain approved organizations which, after pre-election conferences, choose a single candidate. Not surprisingly, the number of negative votes cast in the election

against approved candidates is insignificant, and the proportion of those elected who are Communist Party members and hold important state or party positions is very high.

The presidium of a republican supreme soviet is elected at the first meeting of its parent body and holds office for four years. The division of authority between it and a republic's council of ministers tends to mirror that of the Union, and membership on both the presidium and council is determined by the party's *nomenklatura*.

Meetings of republican supreme soviets are infrequent, with most of the practical work of governing carried on by the presidium and, more importantly, by the ministries that compose the council of ministers.

According to the Soviet constitution, the authority of republican governments extends to the management of cultural affairs, education, public health and welfare programs, and minor industries. In Stalin's time, policies related to all these areas were determined on the federal level, and, administratively, any decree or order passed by a republic's council of ministers could be vetoed by the Presidium of the All-Union Supreme Soviet. Also, it was the Council of Ministers of the U.S.S.R. that detailed the budgets of all union republics. Moreover, the centralization and key policy-making role of the Communist Party precluded any real decentralization of authority.

In the late 1950's, however, the Khrushchev regime inaugurated what many thought would become a genuine decentralization in certain public areas. Most of the safeguards assuring ultimate national control continued in existence, but many important concessions were made to union republic authorities. Perhaps the most significant was the creation of regional economic councils (*sovnarkhozy*), which placed a great degree of authority for the control of industry under republican ministries. The All-Union Ministry of Internal Affairs was eliminated and overall responsibility for police matters was also taken over by republican ministries. The authority of the Supreme Court of the U.S.S.R. to review decisions of republican supreme courts was somewhat curbed, and republican councils of ministers were permitted more of a voice in determining the precise distribution of funds allocated to them under the annual Soviet budget.

This trend toward decentralization had been reversed by the late 1960's, however. The elimination of the sovnarkhozy and the restoration of the economic ministries reestablished federal control over most important industrial enterprises. In 1967 some of the review powers of the U.S.S.R. Supreme Court were also restored, although its authority is still less than it was before 1957. Finally, in 1968 the police forces were brought under central control once again.

The union republics today have a little more authority than they did in the 1930's and 1940's, but it remains true that whatever the formal provisions of the constitution, the Soviet Union is not a federal state in the same sense that the United States or even Germany is. There may be a limited deconcentration of administration; there has never been any lasting decentralization of authority.

The administrative structure of the U.S.S.R. also includes, as previously noted, twenty autonomous soviet socialist republics, eight autonomous regions, and ten national districts. The autonomous republics, differentiated from other administrative areas only by the right to use their own language for official purposes, have been created and abolished at the government's will.

LOCAL GOVERNMENT: At present there are about 49,000 local soviets or councils in the U.S.S.R., ranging from village soviets that exercise authority over as few as a thousand people to the Moscow city soviet with more than five million people in its territory. These local soviets are on three different administrative levels, the highest being directly subordinate to the republican governments. These

include six territorial (*kray*) soviets; 105 oblast soviets; eight autonomous oblast soviets; ten national okrug soviets; and over a score of large city soviets, including those in Moscow, Leningrad, Kiev, and Kharkov. At the intermediate level of local government are more than 2,800 rural *rayon* (district) soviets and about 1,800 town soviets. These are subject to either oblast or kray supervision. At the third and lowest level of local government are the forty thousand village soviets, 3,500 settlement soviets, and about four hundred borough soviets within cities.

Although the organization of local soviets varies considerably, a basic pattern does exist. Deputies to local soviets are elected by the public for a two-year term on the basis of single-member electoral districts. The size of soviets ranges from twenty to fifty deputies for village and settlement councils, up to six hundred or more for large city soviets. How often they meet is fixed by law, but this, too, changes from one republic to another. In the Russian Republic, for example, local soviets should meet for short sessions at least six times a year; however, the number of meetings is often fewer.

There is very little competition in local soviet election campaigns, although party dominance of local soviets is not nearly so obvious as it is on the federal or union republic levels. The proportion of local soviet members who are also members of the Communist Party may be as low as 35 to forty per cent of the total (see Table 19.2), and the turnover among party members who do serve is quite large. Of course, the party is instrumental in determining who should be nominated to the soviets, and, despite statements to the contrary, nominations are often cut-and-dried affairs that arouse little interest.

As on the national level, the elections involve armies of agitators who canvass electors and arrange for meetings to discuss problems of local government. The election does serve, therefore, as a mechanism for renewing loyalties, for boasting about achieve-

LITHUANIAN S.S.R.

ESTONIAN S.S.R.

LATVIAN S.S.R.

R.S.F.S.R.

KARELIA

Novaya- Zemlya

NENETS

Riga

Leningrad

KOMI

BYELORUSSIAN S.S.R.

•Minsk

MOLDAVIAN S.S.R.

UKRANIAN S.S.R.

Kiev•

Dnieper R.

Kharkov•

RUSSIAN

•Moscow

•Gorki

YAMAL - NENE

CHUVASHIA

MARI

UDMURT

KHANTY-MANSI

MORDOVINIAN

TATAR

KOMI-PERMIAK

BLACK SEA

Sevastopol

Don R.

Volga R.

BASHKIRIA

SOCIALIST

FEDERATED

KARACHAEV

KALMYK

ADYGEI

ABKHASIA

GEORGIAN S.S.R.

ADZHARIA

SOUTH OSSETIA

KABARDINO-BALKAR

NORTH OSSETIA

ARMENIAN S.S.R.

CASPIAN SEA

CHECHENO-INGUSH

DAGESTAN

KAZAKH S.S.R.

NAKHICHEVAN

KARA-KALPAK

ARAL SEA

NAGORNO-KARABAKH

Baku•

AZERBAIJAN S.S.R.

LAKE BALKHASH

UZBEK S.S.R.

TURKMEN S.S.R.

Tashkent •

KIRGHIZ S.S.R.

TADZHIK S.S.R.

GORNO- BADAKHSHAN

0   400
Scale of Miles

MAP 19.1. ADMINISTRATIVE REGIONS OF THE U.S.S.R.

IMYR

EVENKI

YAKUTSK

CHUKOT

KORYAK

Kamchatka

IET   REPUBLIC

Sakhalin

BURYAT

LAKE
BAIKAL

BIROBIDEZAN

KHAKASS

UST-ORDYNSKY

AGINSK

Vladivostok

TUVA

TAI

- - - - UNION REPUBLICS (15)

AUTONOMOUS SOVIET SOCIALIST REPUBLICS (20)

AUTONOMOUS OBLASTS (8)

NATIONAL OKRUGS (10)

TABLE 19.2.   PARTY CONTROL OF LOCAL SOVIETS

Percentage of Communist deputies[1] returned to local soviets in recent years

	1957	1959	1961	1963	1965
R.S.F.S.R.	45.5	44.9	45.6	45.0	45.0
Ukraine	42.5	43.9	45.8	46.5	46.3
Byelorussia	43.3	44.2	43.5	42.6	41.6
Moldavia	39.2	39.0	41.9	41.4	41.7
Lithuania	32.1	33.6	36.7	38.9	38.9
Latvia	43.0	43.3	41.6	37.8	41.5
Estonia	33.7	37.4	38.7	38.1	39.8
Georgia	48.1	44.2	43.8	48.1	47.5
Azerbaijan	54.5	51.6	52.2	51.2	49.9
Armenia	59.6	52.3	53.4	47.9	47.4
Turkmenistan	47.8	48.4	47.9	43.3	43.4
Uzbekistan	54.7	52.5	40.1	46.7	46.0
Kazakhstan	50.0	49.0	49.4	45.4	44.4
Tadzhikistan	56.1	53.9	50.1	46.2	46.1
Kirghiz	43.2	46.1	45.7	46.5	45.4

[1]Including candidate members.

Adapted from L.G. Churchward, *Contemporary Soviet Government* (London: Routledge and Kegan Paul, Ltd., 1968), p. 183. Reprinted by permission of Routledge and Kegan Paul, Ltd., and American Elsevier Publishing Company, Inc.

ments, and for gauging public reaction to the performance of the local officials.[5]

At the first meeting of a newly elected soviet, an executive committee (*ispolkom*) consisting of a chairman, vice chairman, secretary, and others is "elected." The three most important executive committee members on the district and higher levels are paid officials; all other members of the executive serve without pay. Paid or unpaid, members of the committee are all screened by higher party officials. The executive committee appoints the head of all local-government departments, and it bears the chief responsibility for carrying out the actual administrative work of local government. Apart from attending sessions of the soviet, most of the deputies work on one or another of the standing commissions, which may number upwards of a dozen in the larger soviets. The organization of the standing commissions parallels that of the local-government depart-

ments set up by the executive committee. In many cases the commissions contain, in addition to the deputies, activists who volunteer their services. Their job is essentially advisory and investigatory; they may make recommendations to the executive committee or to the soviet itself, but they do not have any authority to issue orders and their advice can be, and frequently is, ignored.

All local soviets down to the village soviet have broad powers. In fact, considering the extent of government operations in a Socialist economy, their range of duties is far greater than that of local governments in most other European countries. They supervise the economic planning for their area, they prescribe its industrial and agricultural development, and they exercise direct control over a large number of industrial, construction, and trading establishments. Theoretically, the powers of the soviets also include control over the housing, cultural welfare, health, and amenities of workers in all industrial establishments in their areas. Also, they are responsible for such conventional local mat-

[5] For a description of the 1965 elections see L. G. Churchward, "Soviet Local Government Today," *Soviet Studies,* XVII (April 1966), pp. 431–452.

FIGURE 19.3. THE ORGANIZATIONAL STRUCTURE OF A VILLAGE SOVIET

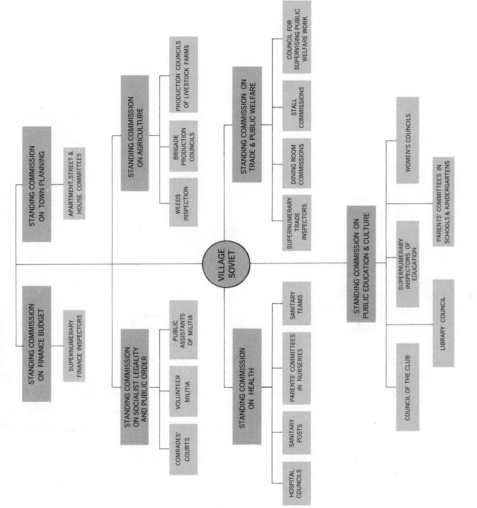

Adapted from L. G. Churchward, *Contemporary Soviet Government* (London: Routledge and Kegan Paul, Ltd., 1968), p. 178. Reprinted by permission of Routledge and Kegan Paul, Ltd., and American Elsevier Publishing Company, Ltd.

ters as roads, bridges, parks, water supply, and transportation.

In spite of these wide powers, local soviets have nevertheless lacked any real independence, at least until recently. The executive committee of each soviet has always been responsible to that of the soviet on the next higher level, and fundamental decisions on local-government policy trickle down from the top. Moreover, decisions taken by the Soviet Union's industrial ministries and implemented on the local level have been almost completely outside local soviet control, no matter what the ramifications. For example, decisions on where to establish industrial plants have come from Moscow—not the local soviets. Furthermore, the control of housing or schools or the creation of new enterprises has remained quite firmly under the control of the national ministries. Thus, the great bulk of housing construction is not handled by the soviets, nor do a great many soviets manage their water supplies or other utilities.[6] The creation of regional economic councils was supposed to have enabled the local soviets to exercise greater authority, but whatever hopes these councils might have held, they have long since faded. The re-centralization of controls after Khrushchev was deposed wrecked the experiment. It is true, even so, that greater authority is beginning to be placed with the soviets of larger cities, particularly authority pertaining to urban planning and the coordination of municipal services.

The fact that the main job of the local soviet is administrative in nature has meant that real authority has fallen to its executive committee (and in the larger soviets to the presidium) and the municipal departments staffed by trained personnel. This has been especially true since the 1930's. Time and time again, items appear in the press to the

effect that executive committees of local soviets have not reported to the full soviet or that the executive or departments have simply ignored the recommendations of standing commissions.

Since 1957, the Soviet government has tried to draw more of its citizens into the administrative process as a means of both checking the work of governmental departments and helping in the performance of certain routine, nontechnical tasks. In addition to the two to three million citizens who serve as members of the standing commissions, other millions participate in the activities of such local organizations as voluntary militia squads, street committees, house committees, and parents' committees. Some of these groups have a degree of authority. They scrutinize such things as the operation of schools, clinics, libraries, local transport, and sanitary services; or, like the people's militia (*druzhiny*) or comrades' courts, they help the authorities make sure that citizens behave properly. Other groups supplement the work of the public authorities: they complete minor housing repairs, including the planting of gardens and repainting, or take over work that was once performed by a department of local government. For example, volunteer financial bureaus have been set up to explain the tax laws; other groups acquaint citizens with their rights under the different pension laws, and still others establish volunteer fire brigades. The single largest group of unpaid workers is still the volunteer militia.

The simultaneous large-scale involvement of party and nonparty people in the administration of local-government policy indicates the continued strength of the populist elements of Soviet ideology. Without much doubt, the increase in participation, which began under Khrushchev, was a genuine effort to move closer to that day when the administration of policy would be a function of the people rather than of the official state apparatus. It is well to emphasize, however, that while volunteer groups do indeed check on administrative malfeasance and misfea-

6 Perhaps the best study of Soviet local government in English is a yet unpublished doctoral dissertation by Prof. William Taubman, *The Politics of Urban Development in the Soviet Union* (Columbia University, 1969).

sance, the citizen as yet has little or no say over policy. Further, while the government may try to enlist the services of volunteers, there is considerable evidence that their involvement in governmental affairs is closely controlled by the party. On those few occasions when volunteer groups have stepped out of line and seemed to be exerting independent and spontaneous initiative, they have been severely criticized. In most cases, those in charge of volunteers are reliable party activists who hold official positions in the state apparatus.

To assess just how voluntary mass participation is, or just how enthusiastic, is a difficult exercise. We do not know how many of the organizations exist merely on paper and how many really function effectively.[7] That they have permitted the Russians to reduce the size of their official governmental apparatus on the local level is unquestionably true. It is also true that they have enabled *some* retired people, such as pensioners, to find something to do that gives them a sense of dignity. But whether this is worth the resultant overlapping of functions and constant conflicts of jurisdiction is another matter.

Most Westerners, quite understandably, would have some reservations about the control aspects of popular involvement. The comrades' courts will be discussed further in Chapter 21, and the druzhiny will be described in Chapter 23. Other groups also exercise pressures toward conformity, and the nature of their zeal is not particularly attractive. Soviet newspapers give accounts of individuals being denounced by groups of neighbors for perfectly legal activities of which the neighbors simply did not approve. They have also printed accounts which indicate that activists, once graced with any authority whatsoever, are inclined to become officious. These negative results are criticized, but other items in the press which relate with satisfaction how individuals with

nonconformist views were brought to heel are even more disturbing.[8]

6. COMPARISONS AND CONCLUSIONS

The nature of the relationship established between national and local authorities in England, France, Germany, and the Soviet Union has evolved from a complex interplay of factors, including the society's ethnic composition, the pattern and timing of its economic development, and its ideological presuppositions. In England national unity was achieved comparatively early and did not require the elimination of local autonomy. Economic growth and modernization were generated without the kind of active state intervention characteristic of societies that industrialized later, and this, again, reduced the need for central control. Indeed, the idea that change should emanate from the people without too much intervention by the government—especially without meddling on the part of the central government—was an integral part of English social and political ideology until well into the nineteenth century. The continuance of local autonomy, as well as England's dominant position in terms of population and power, explains the lack of pressure for the construction of a British federal state, despite the fact that both Wales and Scotland retained distinctive cultural traditions.

In France, the centralization which followed the French Revolution can be seen as a reaction to that provincial particularism which had prevented France from becoming a modern nation. The reformers wished to unite the French people—to complete the work of the Bourbons. They persisted in their efforts throughout the nineteenth century, for they believed that only a strong, centralized state could enable France to regain its power and authority.

The nature of German federalism is to be understood in terms of the conditions under

[7] See David T. Cattell, "Leningrad: Case Study of Soviet Local Government," *Western Political Quarterly*, XVII (June 1964), pp. 188–199.

[8] For examples, see Robert G. Wesson, "Volunteers and Soviets," *Soviet Studies*, XV (January 1964), pp. 231–249.

which unification was achieved. Despite Prussia's pre-eminence, the other states in the union also had a distinct culture and an individual history that would seem to preclude the creation of a highly centralized government. The rapidity with which German economic development took place before World War I also seemed to indicate that a more centralized system of government was not necessary. The fact that a federal republic was re-established after World War II was largely the result of a reaction against the Nazi experience by both the Western Allies and many Germans themselves.

The creation of a federal structure in the Soviet Union is to be explained in terms of the ethnic variety of both old Russia and the new Soviet state. The ideology of the Communist Party, of course, favored giving ethnic groups the right to govern themselves, assuming, as was pointed out in Chapter 6, that

they would choose to remain within the Soviet state. Yet insofar as Soviet ideology called for the creation of a modern industrial state through forced-draft methods under a system of central planning, local autonomy was bound to suffer.

By the second half of the twentieth century, European countries were facing new problems and new choices. All had developed complicated interrelated economic systems that required some form of central control and coordination—thus, in England, the national government had gradually reduced the autonomy of local governmental units. At the same time, all were increasingly aware that the effective organization of government operations required some decentralization of authority. All were attempting to find an appropriate balance in accordance with their past experiences. None can be said to have been completely successful in finding it.

part V

Procession of Judges, London.   The Times

*Police and Demonstrators, Paris.   Wide
World Photos*

*Housing Project, Moscow.   United Press
International Photo*

Law, Society, and Politics in Western Europe

1. INTRODUCTION

The legal system of any society fulfills two principal functions. First, it permits the community to make explicit rules of behavior that it considers legitimate and that are not to be violated on pain of sanctions; the law thus serves as a means of socializing members of the community. Second, a legal system outlines the rights and obligations of community members to each other; the law thus also serves as a means of settling disputes among members of the community, including public officials. The law's function here is integrative; it enables the society to achieve its goals by reducing friction.

In a comparative and historical perspective, the development of law seems to have passed through several stages. In primitive societies organized in terms of kinship units, there is generally little or no development of legal institutions; even when legal codes do appear, they are considered to be statements on the customary rules of conduct. It is usually when kinship ceases to be the main basis of social cohesion, and when a political organization is imposed upon a society, that legal institutions are created. No longer are private wrongs left to private devices of retaliation and indemnification. In these somewhat less primitive societies, law serves primarily to maintain traditional patterns of social conduct; to that end it secures the societal status of the individual. Traditional legal systems tend to resist change, but various legal "fictions" allow a slow adjustment to new circumstances—by pretending that new rules are really restatements of customary practice.

In politically organized societies marked by extensive commercial development, individual status relationships are gradually replaced by contractual ones. Slave status is superseded by the contractual relation between servant and master; a wife's status becomes a contract between the mates. These changes in relationship are accentuated in industrial societies where the growth of science and technology hastens social change and reduces still further the importance of status and kinship ties.

Industrialization and the growth of modern science have yielded still other changes in legal institutions and in the law itself. In traditional societies, legal and religious institutions were closely interwoven and the authority of law was based either on religious sanctions or on the fact that certain rules had been handed down from generation to generation. Modernization has resulted in the substitution of "rational" authority and popular sovereignty for religious authority or traditional customs. Further, the law has become increasingly rationalized as integrated legal codes take the place of a multitude of specific rules, and as jurists apply specific legal sanctions within a framework of general principles of punishment which the community accepts. The very complexity of the legal rules that govern a society has, naturally enough, led to professionalization, and in most modern societies lawyers and judges have come to wield great influence in determining the content of law along with being the chief agents of its administration.

This is not to argue that law is merely a reflection of more basic social change. In fact, it can be maintained that the development of commerce and of modern society in the West was in part due to the West's sophisticated legal system, which was based largely on the Roman legal tradition. Nor is it to argue for a simple, unilinear pattern in the evolution of legal institutions. Even in societies that can be classified as equally modern, differences in legal institutions continue, depending upon the values emphasized by a society and the history of its legal tradition. Nevertheless, the legal structures of all industrial societies have a tendency to resemble each other, particularly in their more significant aspects. For example, aside from purely political "crimes," Soviet and American legal institutions certainly are far more like one another than either is like the law of feudal Europe. The major differences have to do with the fact that most Soviet law is public law and that the Soviet elite, dedicated to the achievement of a certain kind of society, uses the law rather more insistently than either Englishmen or Americans as a device for

socialization; or, to put it another way, in the Soviet Union the law is used as a means of instilling the citizenry with those values the regime regards as necessary for the realization of a fully Communist society.

The violation of a society's laws necessarily leaves the offender open to numerous sanctions. Traditionally, the most violent punitive action has accompanied crimes that threaten the fundamental values of the community— values that its members believe, consciously or unconsciously, are required for its survival. Sanctions vary, depending on the nature of the values. In the Soviet Union, for instance, crimes involving state property can result in the death penalty; in the United States, except for treason, execution is reserved for crimes against persons, although at an earlier period in American—and English—history, theft was punishable by torture or death.

Whatever the differences in attitudes, however, there has always been a sizable number of acts that most societies have punished severely, indicating that all human societies share at least some common concerns. From the beginning of history, these have included crimes of violence, as well as adultery and incest. In traditional societies, the severity of legal sanctions was undoubtedly connected with the fear by members of the community that unless violations of basic taboos were harshly and publicly punished, they would be unable to control their impulses.

Legal development in advanced communities has generally been in the direction of reducing the severity of criminal penalties, restricting the definition of crime to those acts that are disruptive of public order, and emphasizing rehabilitation of the criminal rather than punishment. How far such practices should go is open to dispute, but they clearly show a greater understanding of the sources of criminal action, and also a greater ability on the part of modern societies to tolerate deviations from the norms held by most of their members.

While to a large degree a legal system reflects a society's norms, the common features of all legal systems, and the general direction of their evolution, suggest the existence of common human conceptions as to what constitutes justice. Certain rules are recognized as legitimate because they are fair; certain procedures for determining guilt or innocence are considered reasonable because they are likely to get at the truth. Public rules of justice adopted by a community after carefully weighing their consequences are deemed a more satisfactory mechanism for regulating behavior than ad hoc decisions made at a time of general stress or by one or a few individuals or groups.

It is also fairly clear that the development of sophistication in legal matters has been partially independent of other social variables. Many movements for reform have come out of the legal profession itself. In the Soviet Union, the profession in recent years has gone a long way toward convincing the regime of the necessity to lessen the arbitrariness of Soviet legal practice.

Modern legal systems include the following salient features:[1]

1. *Law is relatively uniform:* The legal system consists of rules that are uniform and unvarying in their application. Laws are applied territorially rather than in terms of personal characteristics—that is, the same rules are applicable to members of all religions, tribes, and classes within the society. Legally recognized differences among persons are not intrinsic differences or differences of quality, but differences in behavior.

2. *Law is universalistic:* Particular commands regulating behavior are derived from commonly accepted and clearly specified general standards; thus, the application of law is reproducible.

3. *The structure of legal institutions is hierarchical:* A network of courts of appeal and review exists to guarantee that local action conforms to national standards.

4. *The legal system is bureaucratically or-*

ganized: In order to permit uniformity, the system must operate impersonally, following prescribed procedures in each case. In order to permit review, written records in prescribed form must be kept.

5. *The system is rationally organized:* These procedures are ascertainable from written sources by techniques that can be learned.

6. *The system is characterized by professionalism:* The legal system is staffed by persons chosen in accordance with testable qualifications for legal work. Their qualifications derive from their mastery of the legal system's techniques, not from special gifts or talents or from their eminence in another area of life.

7. *The system of legal rules is amendable:* There is no sacred fixity to the legal system. It contains methods for revising rules to meet changing needs or to express changing preferences.

8. *The legal system is functionally differentiated from others:* The task of finding law and applying it to concrete cases is assigned to institutions specifically organized to deal with such problems and it is placed in the hands of personnel specifically trained in legal techniques.

The classification of the law is a subject that has been disputed at great length by jurists. The broad differentiations that are generally accepted by Western legal scholars are between public and private law, and between civil and criminal law.

Private law governs the relationship between private citizens, or persons in their private capacity. Contracts between individuals or private corporations, marriage, and divorce are governed by private law. Public law, on the other hand, is concerned with the relation of citizens to the state or to the officials of the state. It includes criminal law, constitutional law, and administrative law. In the Soviet Union, no distinction is made between public and private law. In England and the United States, private and public law have until recently been administered almost entirely by the same courts. In France and

1 This section follows closely the categories used by Marc Galanter, "Hindu Law and the Development of the Modern Indian Legal System" (paper presented for delivery at the 1964 annual meeting of the American Political Science Association, mimeographed).

Germany, special courts deal with administrative law.[2]

The term "civil law" has historically been applied in the West to cases between private persons or organizations which involve the definition of their legal rights. Persons bringing suits under civil law seek legal redress in a personal interest, such as for breach of contract, a divorce action, or defamation of character. The deeper involvement of governments in the social life of the community has resulted in an increase in the number of civil actions—between government agencies and citizens and between government agencies themselves. In the Soviet Union, for example, public corporations enter into contracts with each other and may be sued by each other for breach of contract.

Criminal law defines crimes against the public order and provides for appropriate punishments. Actions against those accused of crimes are invariably brought in the name of the government; any payments the guilty are required to make go into the public treasury.

In this chapter and the next, we shall be concerned first with the general evolution of law in the four European nations under study, and then with the reasons for the continuing differences in their legal systems. Here, again, differences are closely related to the manner in which each nation made the transition from a traditional to a modern society.

2. THE DEVELOPMENT OF EUROPEAN LEGAL INSTITUTIONS

By the fourth century, the Roman Empire had fashioned an exceptionally sophisticated legal system. Yet with the fall of the empire, its legal edifice all but crumbled, too, and although the corpus of Roman law was never completely forgotten, it disappeared as a major social force in much of Europe. The Continent returned to local and more primitive Germanic customs.

By the late middle ages, however, Europe was once again being transformed into a highly differentiated civilization whose new commercial activity demanded far more advanced legal instruments than those available. Almost simultaneously Roman law, which universities had begun to teach, took on renewed importance with the "rediscovery," completed by the order of Emperor Justinian in A.D. 528, of its great compilation and systematization.

Thus, between 1000 and 1500, Roman law became the basis for legal science throughout Western Europe, although its importance differed in various parts of the Continent. In France, for instance, Roman influence was greater in the southern section of the nation. In the Germanies, too, there was little uniformity in its application, but it did become the foundation of almost all university teaching. Its wide acceptance in academic and commercial circles was attributable to several factors: the inability of feudal law to cope with the problems of a commercial civilization; the desire for a uniform system of law; the fact that behind Roman law stood the prestige of the Roman Empire. And not the least significant factor was the Roman Catholic Church, whose canon law was based on Roman models.

While the universities may have been persuaded of the virtues of Roman law, the goal of a unified legal system was not achieved in most Continental countries until the eighteenth and nineteenth centuries. In France, several partial codifications of the law occurred under the ancien régime, but the monarchy lacked the power to dominate completely those local, class, and guild interests that effectively blocked the organization and implementation of an integrated legal system. The provincial parlements and the Parlement of Paris were ultraconservative and sufficiently powerful to prevent innovation.[3] Germany, of course, could not develop a unified legal system until its political unifi-

---

[2] Problems of administrative law in Western European countries will be dealt with in the chapter on bureaucracy.

[3] The French parlements were aristocratic assemblies which combined legislative, administrative, and judicial functions.

cation had been achieved, although a number of the component states had codified their law as early as the first part of the nineteenth century.

England was the first European nation to develop its own system of law. As a consequence, not only was the influence of Roman law far less in England than on the Continent, but no great movement for codification manifested itself in Britain. English common law evolved from local custom. The Plantagenets, beginning with Henry I, initiated the practice of sending ministers around the country to hear cases in the local courts. Before the end of the twelfth century, the king's court, with its regular circuits, was the most powerful political institution in England. The result was the establishment of one law for the entire realm—an amalgam of local custom and a certain amount of Roman law.

The resultant system was based not on explicit general principles but rather on individual cases. It was considerably flexible, and adjusted to the changes taking place throughout the nation in a period when the pace of change was fairly slow. The officials who administered the law—lawyers and judges—founded powerful teaching guilds which emphasized practical experience and the case method. For this reason, training for the legal profession never became centered in the universities.

Throughout the modern period, the legal guilds came to dominate both the bar and the bench. It was they that decreed the general pattern of legal training and determined that the pratice of law should be a prerequisite to appointment as a judge. The judiciary, in turn, gradually established its independence from the monarchy. England was the only nation in Europe in which bench and bar were so closely related, one reason being that the nature of the common law, as distinct from an abstract code, required long experience in the courts before its intricacies could be mastered.

English common law and the English courts were very popular. They were a pro-gressive force, promoting both national unity and the adjustment of society to changing economic circumstances and ideologies. Moreover, the legal profession could count on the support of the new commercial class in its efforts not only to maintain and extend its independence from the monarchy but also to control the judiciary. Indeed, the influential and creative role of the English legal profession helped it to attract forceful men who persuasively and tenaciously urged its cause.

In France, on the other hand, the legal profession and the courts were among the more stubborn bastions of local and feudal custom. Any attempt to weaken still further the monarch's power over judicial appointments was construed as retrogressive by those forces oriented toward creating a unified nation state. This antipathy to judicial power was shared by those who made the Revolution as well as Napoleon. The Code Napoléon, which drew upon Roman law as interpreted by French universities, represented a successful attempt to create a general system of laws that would permit France to adapt to the commercial and industrial changes taking place throughout Western Europe. The code, and the legal structures created at the same time, also served to further weaken the power of the judiciary and the legal profession as a whole.

The code's aim was to eliminate those elements that prevented France from becoming a modern society. Local customs had inhibited the development of a national community; therefore the code would sweep them aside, although the break here with tradition should not be overemphasized. And because the legal profession had been conservative, the judiciary would not be drawn from the legal profession, but from the universities; after all, they had been the first to advance proposals on a modern system of national law. Moreover, the judiciary would remain part of the government bureaucracy, responsible to the government. Also, since decisions by the old French courts had undermined acts of the government, the state would establish a new set of courts to deal with public law; questions of state action would now be handled by specially trained men, who would be more sympathetic to *raison d'état* arguments.

Once again the contrast with England is instructive. The progressive character of traditional English courts caused them to be regarded as bulwarks of "liberty," and the legal profession won considerable support for its insistence that all questions of law, including those raised by actions of the government, be dealt with by the common-law courts. Indeed, under the influence of liberal ideology, English lawyers came to consider the government as merely another party to a dispute. The protection of individual rights became, if anything, more important than effective state action. Therefore, no separate system of administrative courts was founded, and a judiciary, drawn from the legal profession, continued to help specify the content— and limitations—of legislation enacted by the government.

The pattern of legal development in Germany resembled the French far more than it did the English, the major differences stemming from its self-conscious attempt to incorporate traditional Germanic law into the codes adopted at the end of the nineteenth century. In fact, most peoples establishing a modern state, including the Russians, have more or less followed the French example, creating legal codes based on abstract principles that provide a good deal of freedom for state action. The English could afford to move from precedent to precedent, and bind the government with all sorts of restrictions designed to protect the individual, because the forces making for modernization sprang from within the society itself. This option was not open to radical or revolutionary elites in most other nations in which the transition from a traditional to a modern society seemed to require an abrupt break with the past.

The historical experience of the individual European nations with which we are dealing

has significantly affected both the content of their law and their legal procedures. Yet the differences should not obscure the underlying unity that stems from the common Roman and Germanic base of all European law, from similar responses to changing economic and social circumstances, and from the logic of Western law itself. The early modern era saw the disappearance of European feudal restrictions in the wake of commercial activity and the formulation of legal mechanisms to encourage "free" economic enterprise. During the vast transition to the modern period, property rights were redefined, and the law of contract and such instruments as the corporation were established. As might be expected, English—and especially American —law came closest to institutionalizing a liberal laissez-faire ideology, while German and French law retained many more elements from a traditional past in which state regulation of economic and other activities was regarded as a legitimate function of political authority.

With the emergence of the welfare state, legal institutions have continued to undergo change in line with political decisions. The content of the law has shifted slowly in its emphasis from the economic rights of the individual to the needs of the community. More and more frequently, the law now restricts economic activity in terms of political conceptions of community requirements.

The content of the criminal law has also undergone substantial modification. In traditional law the only public crimes were those directly offending the community, such as treason or desertion to the enemy. The community was not primarily concerned with injuries to individuals; such matters were settled privately. Throughout the middle ages an extension of the "king's peace" and the "king's justice" was attempted; nevertheless, private settlement of disputes persisted. It was not until the revival of Roman law in the twelfth and thirteenth centuries that criminal law came into its own. Initially, the new criminal law was extremely brutal; maiming, branding, flogging, and death by hanging were not uncommon, and it was not until the eighteenth century, when more humane ideas on criminal sanctions made their appearance, that the severity of punishments was reduced. The trend has continued until the present day. Not only has greater stress come to be placed on the prevention of crime and the rehabilitation of the offender, but the tendency toward reduction of sentences has led to the restriction of the death penalty; in many nations it has been eliminated altogether. Further, the notion of crime has continually been redefined. Offenses by juveniles, for example, are being treated differently from those by adults, and in a number of instances medical treatment has replaced punishment. Many personal acts, especially those involving sexual morality, are no longer considered criminal. Conversely, certain types of commercial behavior once permitted are now subject to the sanctions of criminal law.

The following sections, outlining the English, French, and German legal systems, will not touch upon the substance of law. Some of the more important substantive questions of law are discussed in other chapters, but a full treatment of the corpus of the law would involve a detailed, technical discussion that goes beyond the scope of the present volume. Rather, we shall be concerned here with three matters: the structure of legal institutions, the dynamics of the legal process, and the role of the legal profession and the judiciary.

3. THE ENGLISH PATTERN[4]

THE DEVELOPMENT AND CHARACTER OF THE COMMON LAW: The origins of English law are to be found in the customs of the Germanic tribes that made Britain their home-

land. Some codification of these customs occurred during the Anglo-Saxon period, but the codes created were even less comprehensive—and more primitive—than those developed by a number of Germanic tribes on the Continent. Because of the lack of central authority, there was also a lack of consistency in customary law throughout the country, and much of the responsibility for law enforcement lay with manorial courts. National legal institutions were founded at a fairly rapid pace after the Norman Conquest: within a century, the King's Court (*Curia Regis*) under Henry II was systematically dispatching itinerant justices throughout the realm to hold court sessions. The old manorial courts were not abolished, but the royal courts offered a superior form of justice. By purchasing a writ from the king, litigants could buy the privilege of a jury trial—a more equitable arrangement for obtaining justice than the primitive methods, such as trial by combat, used in many manorial courts.

England's monarchs were seeking to expand both their sources of revenue and their political power, and the enlargement of the sphere of royal justice accomplished both ends. The law applied by the royal judges was a distillation of local practices intermingled with Roman and canon law—not surprisingly, inasmuch as most of the royal judges were churchmen. The result was that a body of national law was assembled fairly quickly. As late as the reign of Henry I, at the very beginning of the twelfth century, it was still possible to speak of district customs and regulations as existing in Wessex, Mercia, and other places, but by the time of Henry II, 25 to fifty years later, men spoke only of the laws and customs of England. Thus, by the time Roman law had been rediscovered on the Continent, and reformers in the universities were pressing for its adoption as a means of replacing feudal law with a more proficient legal system of wider application, the English had already put together a national law that seemed to

[4] This section will refer only to the legal system of England and Wales. Legal institutions of Scotland and Northern Ireland differ somewhat; Scottish law, for example, has been more strongly influenced by Roman law. For all four areas, however, the House of Lords in its judicial role is the highest court of appeal.

meet their needs. They also had a powerful·professional group in lawyers and judges, who, in fact, were continually creating new law, and who had a vested interest in retaining the English system.

Certainly, the common law could not have remained predominant had it not adjusted to the requirements of English society. This it was eminently capable of doing. The fact that the law was based on cases, and that each case differed, enabled the judiciary to make constant changes in its actual content. Indeed, until the nineteenth century the principle of *stare decisis*[5] was not consistently applied, although precedent was an important factor in legal decisions from the beginning.

There was a period early in the sixteenth century when the adaptive potential of the common law was threatened. In the first years of fashioning the new law, writs issued by the king's secretary (Chancery) were a notable source of innovation, but in the late fifteenth and early sixteenth centuries the use of this procedure declined as judges began to insist upon the limitation of the king's authority to influence the content of the law and as the development of precedent reduced the flexibility of the common law court.

However, a way of solving the conflict between judicial and royal prerogative was eventually found. The king's chancellor could dispense grace by royal prerogative; petitions to the King's Court praying for relief from conditions not included under the common law could, therefore, be dealt with as matters of grace. Eventually the Chancery became a court and the chancellor a judge, and to avoid further contention with the common law courts, the fiction was maintained that Chancery did not alter the common law but merely followed it. In theory it only granted relief in accordance with common-law rights, when for some reason this could not be obtained in the regular courts; in practice Chancery constantly modified common law with

the issuance of new writs. For example, the common law permitted the collection of damages only as the result of breach of contract. By appealing to Chancery, however, a plaintiff could sue to force the performance of a contract. The body of law created by Chancery came to be known as equity, because, it was argued, the court applied standards of fairness or justice to cases not covered by ordinary common-law courts.

The flexibility of equity proceedings permitted a far easier adjustment to changing conditions than did the traditional common law. It also promoted reforms within the common law itself. In time, of course, equity developed its own precedents and rules and lost much of its earlier pliancy; but it had already made its contribution to England's legal system. For several centuries British courts continued the practice of administering equity and the common law separately. Today, however, almost all English courts administer both kinds of law.

In the meantime, the growth of parliamentary institutions and the concept of legislation had added another dimension to the legal system, in the form of statutes. Statutory law has acquired greater and greater importance, providing as it does an additional and immediate instrument whereby the law may be adapted to changing circumstances.

There have been continued efforts to codify parts of English law, but the idea of a general code on the Continental model has never attracted much support. In 1965 Parliament did pass legislation setting up a permanent Law Commission to recommend measures leading to the consolidation, simplification, and reform of English law. While it is unlikely that any overall codification will result, appointment of the commission represents a move in the direction of bringing some consistency and rationality into the British legal system. For whatever its virtues, it is characterized by considerable confusion in a number of areas.

Unlike Continental law, then, English common law has three interrelated features. It is,

---

[5] Literally "to stand by the decided things." Under the doctrine, previous decisions of higher courts should be followed, and courts should not reverse themselves.

first of all, case law, built on particular legal decisions rather than on the basis of a unified code. This is not to say that it completely lacks underlying principles, for cases are legion and the possibilities of differentiating among them vast. But the distinction is nonetheless valid. The education of Continental lawyers embraces training in philosophy, the social sciences, and the code, although the study of cases is certainly not dismissed; the training of the English lawyer embodies the mastery of legal cases. Secondly, common law is made by judges. It has been modified and adapted through countless numbers of decisions, although legislation has become increasingly significant. Finally, it relies heavily on precedent to provide consistency, even though its continual evolution means that many decisions are ex post facto. Often, a mastery of the relevant cases permits the lawyer to make only an intelligent guess as to what a decision will be.

THE COURTS: English courts at the time of the Conquest were the communal courts of the shire and hundred, the manorial (or seignorial) courts, and the borough courts. All three lost their functions and powers to royal courts, although the process took centuries. The most majestic of the king's courts was the Magna Curia, or Great Council; it consisted of all the tenants in chief and other magnates as well as ecclesiastics whom the king might call to attend. It also included the king's personal advisers. The Great Council eventually gave birth to the British Parliament, which initially combined legislative, executive, and judicial functions.

The king's personal advisers, meeting alone, constituted another distinct court, known as the Lesser Curia. From the members of this body the king chose justices to take charge of his affairs throughout the realm; the duties of these justices slowly expanded. After 1195, the crown also appointed local citizens to aid in the administration of justice; at first their function was to take custody of prisoners until the king's

justices arrived to try them, but eventually they were permitted to try prisoners and later became known as justices of the peace.

Beginning with the reign of Henry II, the system of royal courts was expanded. Probably the most important of the newer ones was the Court of Common Pleas, which at first was primarily concerned with civil cases pertaining to ownership of land. Originally subject to the Great Council, it subsequently established its own organization and independence. The Court of King's Bench also developed out of the council for the purpose of handling criminal cases. Because of the close relationship between certain types of criminal and civil cases, and because of the continued association of the King's (or Queen's) Bench with the council, it soon became a court of review for civil cases heard in the Court of Common Pleas.

The Court of Exchequer of Pleas was the third of the new common-law courts. The exchequer was the treasury of the king, and its jurisdiction in civil cases arose originally from claims by those who owed the king money that they could not pay unless their debtors in turn met their obligations. The fourth court, Chancery, and its functions in the field of equity have already been discussed. Finally, the House of Lords, retaining its function (which originated with its position as part of the King's Council) as the High Court of Parliament, has remained the highest court of appeal in certain civil and criminal cases; in fact, until 1948, it tried all criminal cases involving peers.

Through a series of expedients and fictions, then, the British established a complex system of courts. As it took form, there was considerable overlapping and confusion of jurisdiction. Beginning with the Judicature Act of 1873, a series of reforms was initiated to rationalize the whole system, although, as usual, the British made use of existing institutions wherever they found it possible. The Court of Common Pleas, Exchequer of Pleas, and King's Bench were merged to become the King's Bench Division of a new

FIGURE 20.1. THE STRUCTURE OF THE ENGLISH COURT SYSTEM

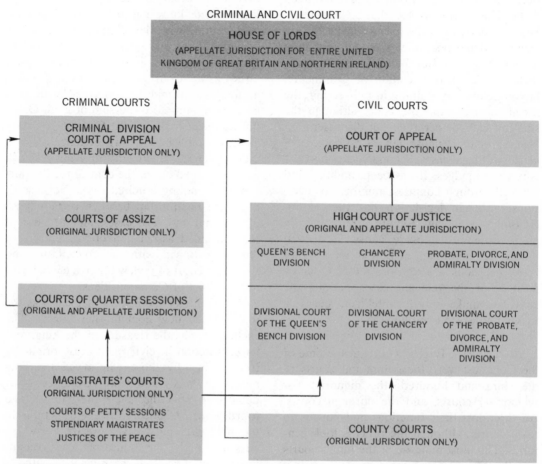

Adapted from Henry J. Abraham, *The Judicial Process,*
2nd ed. (New York: Oxford University Press, 1962), p.
257. Reprinted by permission of the publisher.

court, the High Court of Justice. Chancery also became a division of the new court.

At the base of the criminal-court system today stands the unpaid justice of the peace.[6] Approximately four thousand J.P.'s are at work in England and Wales—in rural areas and smaller cities. In the large cities, the functions of J.P.'s are performed by stipendiary magistrates, who, unlike the justices, are full-time professionals. Both J.P.'s and magistrates sit without juries and are courts of summary jurisdiction for minor criminal offenses; in other words, they can punish offenders without a formal trial. They also have the power to hold an accused for action by a higher court in the case of more serious offenses. Actually, most of their cases are traffic violations; they also have jurisdiction in matrimonial cases which on appeal go to the

[6] The criminal court and civil court systems are described separately. It is well to remember, however, that there is some overlapping of jurisdiction and considerable overlapping of personnel between the two court systems.

Probate, Divorce, and Admiralty Division of the High Court of Justice. Justices of the peace and magistrates are appointed by the Lord Chancellor after careful screening by advisory committees in each county. When two or more J.P.'s or one stipendiary magistrate sit, a Court of Petty Sessions is constituted.

The next level in the hierarchy of criminal courts is occupied by the Court of Quarter Sessions, so called because it traditionally met four times annually. It is the first British court in which an accused is entitled to trial by jury. The court rarely handles cases that call for more than five years' imprisonment, and it serves as both a court of original jurisdiction and an appellate tribunal from decisions of justices of the peace and stipendiary magistrates.

The Court of Assize is the most important court in the criminal hierarchy; its jurisdiction covers all major crimes, and its trials are always held before a jury. The criminal division of the Court of Appeal takes appeals from the Assize and Quarter Sessions courts. It is the most important tribunal of appellate jurisdiction in criminal cases. Sitting without a jury, its judges (usually three) hear the defendant's appeals on the transcripts of evidence taken at his trial; it may revise sentences if it decides they were not legally justified, were based on improper evidence, or were unduly severe. It may not, however, order a new trial. Both the Assize Court and the criminal division of the Court of Appeal are staffed by judges from the King's (or Queen's) Bench Division of the High Court of Justice—which, incidentally, can also take certain appeals in criminal law directly from Courts of Petty Sessions. At the highest level of the criminal-court system is the House of Lords which, in very restricted circumstances, may hear appeals when a point of law of "general public importance" is involved.

The court of first instance in civil matters is the County Court. Between four hundred and 450 County Courts in England and Wales are presided over by some eighty judges, who, in order to qualify, must be barristers in good standing with at least seven years of experience. Immediately above the County Courts is the High Court of Justice, staffed by three presiding officers and 45 judges who have had a minimum of ten years of experience as barristers. The High Court is divided into three sections: the Chancery Division; Probate, Divorce, and Admiralty Division; and the King's (or Queen's) Bench Division, which is the largest and busiest, partly because it also participates in the work of the criminal courts.

Appeals from any of the divisions of the High Court of Justice go to the Court of Appeal, whose members include, among others, the Lord Chancellor, all former Lord Chancellors, and eight lord justices of appeal, who must have 15 years of experience as barristers or else have been High Court judges. The court may order a new trial or reconsider the evidence itself. From the Court of Appeal, if the matter of law is deemed of sufficient significance, there remains the final path of appeal to the House of Lords. The Lords, when serving in their judicial function, do not sit as a single body; rather, the review is conducted by the legal section of the House of Lords, consisting of the Lord Chancellor and a small skilled group of judges, the law lords, who are appointed for life.

THE BAR AND BENCH: The origins of the English bar go back to at least the thirteenth century. From the very beginning, the profession was split into two categories—the pleader and the attorney. The pleaders eventually became known as barristers and the attorneys as solicitors. As early as the time of Henry I, a man was permitted to have a "pleader" speak for him during a trial. Many of these pleaders were churchmen, but as law grew more secular the church discouraged its clergy from participating in court matters. By 1250 the lay leaders were forming guilds and training apprentices, who learned through lectures and by attending court and observing procedures.

The attorney's work, on the other hand,

was basically that of lightening the burden of his client in a suit. He would attend court as his representative or draw up legal papers and engage in other routine legal work. Since the right to have an attorney was considered a great privilege in the early days, the courts supervised the system carefully. Out of this tradition arose the rule that the attorney is an officer of the court and not merely an employee of his client.

In the late middle ages, a system of Inns of Court grew up among the pleaders. The inns began as law schools, but soon became fraternities of practicing lawyers as well— with membership in an inn a requirement for legal practice. Initially, attorneys were also admitted to the Inns of Court, but by the seventeenth century they had been excluded and were forced to arrange for their own training and to regulate their own profession. They later formed a Law Society which took on these responsibilities.

Today, all barristers have had a university education, and can receive some legal training by taking law as an undergraduate major. However, the major portion of professional training still occurs in the Inns of Court. Solicitors receive their training through apprenticeship to those already practicing, and entry into the profession continues to be regulated by the Law Society. A university education is not required, and more than half the solicitors now practicing in England are not university graduates.

The traditional functional differentiation between the two professions has been retained. Solicitors prepare the cases of potential litigants for court presentation or try to arrange for an out-of-court settlement. They are also active in the general field of investment and other commercial transactions. The essential function of the barrister is to present cases in court; he has the exclusive right of audience in most courts. The barrister who is to plead a case is approached through a solicitor by a potential client.

There were no true judges outside the royal courts. In the communal and manorial

courts, laymen called "suitors" performed the judicial function, but they had no professional training; even the earliest justices of the king were amateurs. The first true judges emerged with the Court of Common Pleas; they were selected by the king and were subject to his whim. By the late thirteenth century, however, judges began to be appointed by the king from the ranks of eminent sergeants-at-law (barristers), and the training of future lawyers and judges came to be entrusted to the legal profession. The shift was undoubtedly part of a strategy by the barony to protect itself from encroachment by the king, but, as already described, it had far more lasting and important effects. Only after 1701 did the judiciary become fully independent; before, judges served only at "the king's pleasure."

Today, judges are still officially appointed by the monarch on the advice of the Lord Chancellor, who is the official head of the judicial hierarchy in England. In actuality, of course, the Lord Chancellor himself is appointed by the prime minister and is a member of the cabinet. There is little evidence that, in this century at least, political considerations have entered into the appointment of judges.

It is the judiciary, of course, that was primarily responsible for the evolution of British common law. Operating under the fiction that they were "discovering," not making, the common law, judges nevertheless adapted it with creditable speed to the changing requirements of the society. That they could do so was a reflection of the prestige they enjoyed; English judges were, and are, appointed from among the more successful, highly regarded barristers in the community. Further, the reputation of the judiciary built upon itself. Having become identified with those forces which protected Englishmen from arbitrary authority and at the same time contributed to the creation of an effectively integrated national state, the judiciary's prestige was always great. Consequently, it drew forceful and creative personalities. If it had not, or if the common law had proved less flexible, radical revision and codification would have occurred, as on the Continent.

Indeed, there were times when the common law, as it matured, became less responsive to the changing demands of society. In the earlier period, flexibility was provided by the development of equity. Equity itself, however, gradually developed its own precedents and rigidities, and the major source of legal innovation in the twentieth century has been parliamentary statutes. In fact, judges today play a far smaller role in making law than they ever did, primarily because the adoption of *stare decisis* and the full reporting of cases and opinions have limited the judiciary's options. Also, in an age in which sovereignty is thought to lie properly with elected bodies, judicial lawmaking is regarded as rather suspect. It has not, of course, completely disappeared; many statutes are stated in fairly broad terms and thus allow for considerable interpretation by the bench.

There are those who contend that the judiciary should reclaim its lawmaking prerogatives. Yet the argument does not seem to have much merit: judges are not equipped to contend with broad social questions, and the whole structure of the judicial system is ill suited to decide basic social issues. One suspects that the era of real judicial creativity in England is about over—notwithstanding the fact that in 1966 the British House of Lords announced it would no longer be strictly bound by precedent in its decisions.

THE ADMINISTRATION OF JUSTICE: Criminal litigation in common-law countries differs in important respects from that in civil-law countries, and the variances are related, in considerable degree, to the differing natures of the legal systems. Fundamentally, England relies upon an "adversary" procedure: in both civil and criminal cases, the judge acts more as an umpire between contending parties, and elaborate trial rules exist concerning the admission of evidence. On the Continent, the procedure is "inquisitorial": the state is not so much umpire as active participant in the procedure of getting at the truth, at least

in criminal cases; more reliance is placed upon the judiciary, and far greater leeway is permitted in terms of the type of evidence that may be introduced.

Although the foundations of the adversary procedure can be traced back to Germanic law, the British, like other Europeans, were very much influenced by the procedures of canon law—and hence Roman law—as the king's peace spread. Until the impact of the Puritan revolution and Protestantism, therefore, criminal trial procedure in England was not unlike that on the Continent.

It is true that jury trials had come into existence in the thirteenth century, and that by the middle of the fourteenth defendants were beginning to be granted the right to challenge jurors. However, it was only through centuries of slow, barely perceptible change that court rules came to place the defendant on equal terms with the prosecution. Indeed, until the Indictable Offenses Act of 1848, it was justices of the peace who decided in many cases whether an accused person should be indicted for a crime. Until the mid-nineteenth century, the investigations of J.P.'s were informal, and the suspect's rights were not particularly safeguarded.

In an earlier period, the same informality and abridgment of rights existed in the trial itself. As late as the seventeenth century, witnesses could be called only for the crown, there were no rules of evidence, the defendant's counsel was not allowed to cross-examine the witnesses testifying against him, judges took an active part in questioning witnesses, and members of the jury could be fined or imprisoned if they reached a verdict that the judge regarded as wrong. Increasingly, however, the trial judge came to be viewed primarily as an arbiter—a referee or umpire in a combat between the state, in the form of the prosecuting attorney, and the defendant, represented by counsel. And, also increasingly, he came to function on the basis of rules which gave the defendant every benefit of the doubt. Adversary procedures have reached their fullest development in the United States, where judges are limited to enforcing the rules of debate and charging juries solely on points of law. In England, the remnants of an older tradition remain to the extent of permitting the judge to comment on the weight of evidence and the credibility of witnesses, both during the trial and in his charge to the jury.

Among the more typical features of common-law procedure are the elaborate rules governing the conduct of the trial, especially those pertaining to the kind of evidence that may be introduced in court. For example, in criminal cases husband and wife may not be compelled to testify against each other. Hearsay evidence is excluded, as is evidence of previous crimes (except under special circumstances) or bad character. These prohibitions are not as exact in practice as in theory, since some of this information may come to light under cross-examination; nevertheless, the burden of proof of guilt is heavily upon the prosecution. The pattern in civil cases is somewhat different; here the plaintiff and the defendant are both on equal footing insofar as proof is concerned, and most civil cases in England are tried before judges without juries. Thus, the plaintiff does not have to prove his case "beyond a reasonable doubt," but must simply prove that his version of the facts is the more probable. In civil cases, unlike criminal cases, leading questions may be asked, but there are still rules against hearsay evidence and other matters which might prejudice the issue at hand. In civil cases, the court costs are borne by the litigants rather than the state, since the role of the latter is only that of an arbiter between private parties.

4. THE FRENCH PATTERN

THE BACKGROUND AND CHARACTER OF FRENCH LAW: Unlike the English, the French did not establish a fully integrated system of national law until the early nineteenth century. Until the thirteenth century, members of the landholding aristocracy were to all intents and purposes independent rulers, administer-ing justice in their own names as a corollary of sovereignty. The closest parallel to the British royal courts were the semijudicial agencies, called *parlements,* which began to appear in the fourteenth century. The term was used to designate judicial sessions of the Curia Regis of the Capetian kings. The first parlement created was that of Paris, but as the royal domain spread, provincial parlements were created by the monarchy throughout France. These came to exercise a certain amount of independence, emphasizing in their decisions traditional feudal and local law and thus limiting the effect of national legislation.

By the sixteenth century, royal legislative power in certain broad areas had begun to attain recognition throughout France, and attempts were made to further codify and reduce the diversity of local custom. These legal reforms, pushed by the universities which were very much under the influence of Roman law theories, were not completely successful during the old regime, for the monarchy was unable to overcome the conservatism of the parlements.

It was the Revolution that paved the way for the unification and codification of French law by abolishing the parlements. During the revolutionary period, commissions were appointed to draw up a unified code; but their work did not come to fruition until the creation of the First Empire, when the Napoleonic Codes were promulgated. The codes, revised and amended, provide the basis for French law today and have been copied by most nations not colonized by the English.

The codes outlined the content of the law in all fields on the basis of relatively few principles. They are an amalgam of customary law, Roman law, and conceptions of natural law regarding the character of universal justice. The natural-law theories, of course, were in many cases imbued with classical liberal ideas as to the nature of property and personal relations.

Adoption of the codes had a very profound effect upon the entire nature of French law and the legal profession. From the time of the Revolution, law was regarded, not as something to be "discovered" by the community, but rather as something to be created by it through legislative action. The English idea that judges should make law ran counter to the entire spirit of the French code, and although in practice the judiciary has been responsible for making law in France, it has never had the same recognized authority to do so that the English judiciary has. The codes themselves were a reaction to previous centuries of judicial conservatism and reflected the rather low status of the judiciary in the eyes of the community. Adoption of the codes only perpetuated that status. For one thing, lawmaking became almost entirely the special privilege of political authorities; after the Revolution, court-made law had very little impact in France. Secondly, judicial appointments, instead of honoring a man who had had an illustrious legal career, were now made from among those who had just graduated from the university. Judges became bureaucratic officials who stood, at best, on a par with members of any other legal profession, and made far less money than a good advocate; as a result not only did men of talent shy away from the judiciary, but the creative centers of legal interpretation continued to be the universities.

The suspicion with which the reformers regarded the judiciary had another consequence. Whereas in England the courts were deemed to be the major source of protection against the arbitrary exercise of public authority, in France they were regarded as major inhibitors of social reform. The whole realm of public law, therefore, was placed outside the competence of the regular courts. The August 1790 judiciary law barred the newly created courts from disturbing "in any manner whatsoever the activities of the administrative corps." Eventually, responsibility for the regulations of the executive branch of government was placed with the *Conseil d'État,* the highest court in an entirely separate court system with its own set of procedures for dealing with cases involving the relationship of the citizen to the state.

THE REGULAR COURTS: Until the reforms initiated by the de Gaulle government in 1959, the lowest of the ordinary courts in France was that of the local justice of the peace (*juge de paix*). The French J.P.'s, unlike the British, were required to have law degrees; they had the responsibility of reviewing petty, usually civil, infractions, and offered a very informal and fairly inexpensive court procedure. They were replaced in 1959 by Courts of Instance (*Tribunaux d'instance*) located in every *arrondissement*. Each of these courts has several judges, but cases are heard and decisions are rendered by a single judge. They have considerably more authority than the old J.P.'s, and they are expected to become the most important unit in the new French judicial system.

Replacing the old civil Court of First Instance (*Tribunal de première instance*) is a new Court of Major Instance (*Tribunal de grande instance*), which has both criminal and civil jurisdiction. These 172 courts now have jurisdiction throughout each of France's 95 metropolitan departments. Each department contains at least one Court of Major Instance, and more populous departments may contain two or more. In civil cases, the tribunals have unlimited original jurisdiction; they also have appellate jurisdiction from the Tribunaux d'instance. Their authority in criminal cases extends to less severe felonies and to misdemeanors such as assault, embezzlement, and theft. The Courts of Appeal (*Cours d'appel*), of which there are 27 in France, have appellate jurisdiction over all civil cases, including those emanating from special courts such as Labor Conciliation Boards, Juvenile Courts, and Commercial Courts. Each of the Courts of Appeal has from five to seven judges, and their decisions on points of fact are final. The Assize Courts (*Cours d'assises*) have appellate jurisdiction over criminal cases and original jurisdiction in all major criminal cases such as homicide.

FIGURE 20.2. THE COURTS OF THE FRENCH FIFTH REPUBLIC

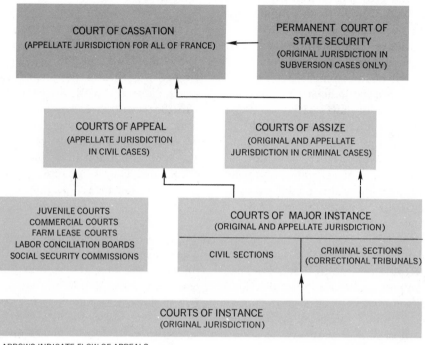

ARROWS INDICATE FLOW OF APPEALS

Adapted from Henry J. Abraham, *The Judicial Process,*
2nd ed. (New York: Oxford University Press, 1968),
p. 263. Reprinted by permission of the publisher.

As appellate tribunals, they hear cases without a jury, but a jury is normally present when Assize Courts try cases as a court of first instance.

In 1963, prompted by O.A.S. terrorism, Parliament created a special tribunal to combat "subversion." The tribunal, operating without a jury, consists of civilian judges and senior military officers; its decisions can be appealed only to the Court of Cassation (*Cour de Cassation*), which stands at the pinnacle of the regular court system in France. It is, in effect, the supreme court of appeal. The court has a membership of 83 judges plus the chief prosecutor and his staff, and its jurisdiction extends throughout France. The court is divided into three sections: criminal, civil, and a screening section to determine which cases should be reviewed.

The Court of Cassation rules only on the legal appropriateness of the decision rendered by a lower court, not on the facts of the case. It has only the power to quash (*casser* means to break or to smash) a decision and remand it below for retrial by a court of the same rank as the one from which it came.

THE BAR AND THE BENCH: The French bar and bench are far from being a duplicate of the English; the factors which set them apart relate primarily to the differences between the systems of common law and of code law. There are also, of course, the differences in the social structure and culture of the two societies. In France, the bench and the bar are quite separate. Judges are recruited directly from law school, and a young man interested in the law must determine whether he wishes to go into private practice or enter upon a judicial career. As already indicated, French judges have been far less significant as law-makers than their English counterparts; yet the differences here can be overemphasized. A considerable body of case law has been built up in France, although, in the last analysis, reference is always back to the provisions of the code. For this reason, it is not surprising that universities have at least as much authority as judges in determining the meaning of a particular section of the code.

In the middle ages, the French legal profession was composed of advocates (*avocats*) and attorneys (*procureurs*). It was the advocates who represented the parties before the courts, whereas the attorneys merely assisted them. By the fourteenth century, the profession of attorney, as well as the number who could enter the profession, was regulated by ordinance, an attorneyship became a purchasable office; the advocates also came under public regulation. Both attorneys and advocates formed orders responsible for the conduct of their membership.

The French legal profession never gained control over judicial appointments. French monarchs interested in extending the jurisdiction of royal courts had turned naturally to Roman law and to the universities. Also, the French Revolution itself and the codification of French law had firmly separated the bench from the bar. Henceforth, not only would the judiciary consist of state-appointed bureaucrats, but matters of public law would be outside the control of the regular courts. To the reformers, as to Napoleon, the lawyers as well as the traditional judiciary represented an essentially conservative, feudal force; if a modern nation was to be created, their power had to be reduced. Indeed, for a time the legal profession was abolished.

Today, the legal profession in France is organized in various associations (*ordres*), which are partially regulated by the state. There are five main orders: advocates, attorneys or solicitors (*avoués*), notaries (*notaires*), court clerks (*greffiers*), and ushers (*huissiers*). The most important are the advocates, who are roughly akin to the English barristers; the combined functions of the *avoué* and the *notaire* are approximately those of the English solicitor. Of the five orders, that of advocate is the only one to which entry is open, and such matters as fees are not regulated. The other four are considered public offices. Members receive their remuneration by way of fees, and the total number of members is limited by government decree.

The advocate can appear before any court except the Court of Cassation. He represents his clients in court but cannot draft the necessary legal documents on their behalf. This is the function of an attorney, who can also represent his client in court in minor cases. However, unlike the English solicitor, he is not a general legal adviser. The attorney is only entitled to deal with matters that reach the courts. The work of drawing up other legal documents, such as contracts and wills, is done by the notaries. Cases brought to the Court of Cassation or the Conseil d'État are handled by an elite group of *avocats aux conseils,* whose number is limited to sixty and who combine the work of the avocat and avoué. Use of a lawyer is not required by French law except before the Court of Cassation or the Conseil d'État. While the practice is discouraged, and very few elect to do so, any citizen is permitted to plead his own case before the other courts.

Although legal guilds in France never attained the power of those in England, it is true that most lawyers practicing before the medieval parlements had received their final professional training as apprentices and were members of the ordres des avocats controlled by the parlements. Since the Revolution, legal training has been entirely under the control of the universities, and professional training in the law begins at an age when American students are entering college. Because of the character of French law, the training includes a very large proportion of courses in the social sciences and philosophy; law degrees, in fact, have traditionally been acquired by young men of good family who have no particular profession in mind.

The French technique of teaching law also stresses systematic oral presentation, a reflection of the advocate's role during a trial. With the questioning of witnesses in French trials done by the court, and with rules of procedure having only minor importance, the obligation of the advocate is to demonstrate, through formal testimony, the weaknesses in his opponent's case, and, especially in criminal cases, to sway his audience through oratory. The advocate's part in a criminal trial is very similar to that of a British or American lawyer at the time of summation.

Members of the French judiciary collectively form a body known as the magistracy; they are members of a career service recruited not from the legal profession but almost always from young law graduates by means of a special examination to test their theoretical knowledge. To improve the quality of the judiciary, the de Gaulle regime in 1958 created the *Centre national d'études judiciares,* a postgraduate, three-year professional school to which entrance is by competitive examination. As soon as students enter the school, they become civil servants and receive a salary. The hope has been that the postgraduate school would broaden the base of recruitment for the French judiciary.

The magistracy consists of two parts— judges who decide cases, and the "parquet" of public prosecutors. The prosecutors act on behalf of the state in criminal trials; under very special circumstances, they may also intervene in civil cases to "defend the public interest." It is possible to move from one position to another and back again with relative ease.

The independence and status of French trial judges varied considerably during the nineteenth century. For most of the century, direct government intervention in cases with political overtones was not uncommon, and recalcitrant judges could be relegated to the provinces. In 1883 the French parliament prohibited the removal of a judge from his post without his consent, unless he had been subject to disciplinary action. Until 1946, however, control over promotions was the responsibility of the Ministry of Justice, and although intervention in judicial decisions was not common, political pressure could be—and was—brought to bear by the state in some cases. In that year the *Conseil Supérieur de la Magistrature* (High Council) was established, and it became solely responsible for promotions within the French judiciary system. Membership on the Conseil Supérieur was drawn mostly from extra-government sources. Revisions under the Fifth Republic, however, have given the president much more authority in choosing its members and have also transferred some authority over promotions from the High Council to the Ministry of Justice. Even so, the reduction of pay differentials among judges of different grades, together with the provision for automatic salary increments, has made the issue of control somewhat less urgent.

The relative lack of prestige of French judges, compounded by the nature of the recruitment process, has not helped to attract forceful, creative law graduates to the bench. A career in the judiciary is considered to be a "safe" one, provided one plays one's cards right, and it has usually enlisted only those for whom security is paramount. For these reasons, court decisions are invariably very brief; judges seldom feel compelled to spell out how or why they reached a particular decision. While the writing of dissenting opinions is not permitted, learned annotations prepared by attorneys are often appended to reported cases which discuss the issues involved, in a manner not unlike that of English common law judges. Further, law professors' discussions of points of law and their interpretation, in texts and journals, have a good deal more weight in France than in either England or the United States, although the influence of academic jurists is gaining in both. The professional who teaches law in

France moves directly from law school to a doctoral program. A few professors may practice as advocates and thus be members of the bar, but in general the law teacher does not regard his total lack of practical experience as a handicap. The emphasis of his work is upon theoretical formulations and the underlying philosophical problems of law.

THE ADMINISTRATION OF JUSTICE: In France, as in other civil-code countries, a fairly clear distinction exists between procedures in criminal and civil cases. Civil trials are rarely, if ever, conducted before a jury; they are based for the most part on written evidence. Furthermore, the role of the community or the state in a civil case is considered to be quite different from what it is in a criminal trial. In traditional Germanic law, both civil and criminal cases were adversary in nature: the community was thought of as an arbiter between individuals who came into conflict. Basically, court procedure was to preserve the peace of the community by substituting public for private means of settling disputes. On the Continent, under the impact of the revival of canon and Roman law, the approach to disputes changed. The function of the courts came to be seen as that of protecting the welfare of the community against those who violated its rules, and the adversary system in criminal cases was, by degrees, replaced by what has come to be called the inquisitorial system, in which representatives of the state actively attempt to get at the "truth." By the seventeenth century, it had become a fixed part of French criminal proceedings. Trials were often held in secret and no jury was used. Civil procedure retained its adversary character, although the court may still step directly into the case if it believes the public interest is involved.

The French Constituent Assembly in 1791, under the influence of liberal ideas, introduced an entirely new system of criminal procedure, based largely on the English system; for the most part, it was adversary in nature and made use of both public trials and a jury.

It did not work too well, partly because of the political turmoil that accompanied the Revolution. The ultimate result was the adoption under the First Empire of a new code of criminal procedure that combined traditional French court practices with some elements of the English legal system. Throughout the nineteenth and twentieth centuries the system was modified, the most recent changes occurring under the Fifth Republic. In some ways the general direction of French criminal procedure has been toward common-law practice, and yet the French approach remains quite distinctive.

Preliminary investigations of suspected crimes are conducted by public prosecutors who are part of the police hierarchy. Once an accusation is made, investigation of the evidence is conducted by an investigating judge (*juge d'instruction*), who has the right to detain any person accused of a crime by the public prosecutor. He interrogates the accused—who, since 1897, has had the right to refuse to speak except in the presence of his counsel—and he also questions witnesses, with whom the accused is finally confronted. If the investigating judge finds a case against the accused, he sends the documents to the public prosecutor for trial.

For most of the nineteenth and early twentieth centuries, the investigating judge was at least partially dependent upon the public prosecutor, who could and did influence his chances for promotion. The 1959 reforms specified that the prosecutor had no power to give orders to an investigating judge, and that the judge, in turn, has no authority over the police. Some doubt still remains, however, as to just how independent the investigating judge is. He obviously continues to find it quite difficult to resist accepting police suggestions as to the guilt or innocence of the accused, and the public prosecutor still has considerable leeway not only in dealing with suspects but in deciding which ones are to be accused.[7]

7 For a discussion of police functions, see Chapter 23, pp. 725–726.

It is the responsibility of the investigating judge to assemble the evidence. He conducts all the questioning, visits the scene of the crime, and establishes panels of experts to assist him when necessary in evaluating the evidence. He may, of course, call upon the police for assistance in the case. One of the difficulties with the assistance of the police in the past was their tendency to hold a suspect until they had a fairly complete case against him. The 1959 reforms attempted to correct this abuse by extending the right of bail, limiting the initial period of detention to 24 hours, and insuring that full records be kept of all matters pertaining to the case. But the effect of this reform has been partly nullified by the many exceptions to these procedures which have been allowed. During the preliminary investigation, too, search and seizures may be made without warrant, although once the investigating judge takes over, limitations are placed upon such permissiveness. However, even illegally obtained evidence is not excluded by the rules and will be considered by French courts in making their decisions. Furthermore, while bail may be posted during the time the investigating judge is looking into the case, those suspected of serious crimes may be detained for four months, and sometimes longer.

If a strong prima facie case is established and the crime is a major one, the dossier built up by the investigating judge is forwarded to the *Chambre d'accusation*. If the members of the chamber agree, trial is set. The dossier thus compiled is used throughout the trial by the court. There are very few exclusionary rules of evidence in French trials, so that the individual's character, including any previous crimes, is from the beginning part of the trial record. Hearsay evidence is also permitted and spouses may not refuse to testify if called upon to do so. On the other hand, neither the accused nor his relatives are compelled to testify under oath, and they may refuse to answer particular questions.

All trials in Assize Courts are held before three judges and a jury. One of the judges, the president of the court, both directs the trial and interrogates all witnesses, including the accused, after they have completed their testimony in narrative form. The prosecutor may also interrogate witnesses, as may the other judges and members of the jury with the president's permission, and the defense counsel may request that questions be addressed to particular witnesses by submitting them to the president.

The status of the jury in France has undergone many radical changes since it was introduced in 1791. After long experimentation with separating the functions of judge and jury—the judge dealing only with questions of law and the jury bringing in a verdict on the basis of the facts—judges and jury now retire together to determine both the question of guilt and the sentence. From 1941 to 1958 these determinations were made by three judges and a seven-man jury; since decisions are by majority vote, this meant that a majority could consist of three judges voting with three laymen. In 1958 the number of jurors was increased to nine and a verdict now requires a majority of eight votes out of 12.[8]

French civil procedure is quite different. Juries have never been used in civil cases, and the role of the judges is far more passive: they evoke legal or other points only where they believe the public interest is involved. Otherwise, the parties in the trial are complete masters of their case. As in criminal cases, most civil cases of any importance are heard before three judges. Finally, again except before the Tribunaux d'instance, the evidence is primarily written; the litigants cannot rely on the oral statements of witnesses. In some respects, then, the term "trial" is inappropriate in civil cases.

[8] Traditionally, jury verdicts in Anglo-Saxon countries have had to be unanimous. However, new legislation in England permits verdicts by a ten to two majority in certain criminal cases.

5. THE GERMAN PATTERN

THE BACKGROUND AND CHARACTER OF GERMAN LAW: With the end of the Roman Empire, traditional Germanic law replaced the Roman codes in vast areas of central Europe. Customary law varied from one part of Europe to another; some legal systems prevailed over large stretches of territory, while others were confined to a single city, village, or manor, or to special groups of persons. Many of these systems were privately collected and expounded in "law books," some of which, in the course of time, attained quasi-statutory force.

However, in the absence of a strong central authority, the growth and development of Germanic law were extremely slow, as compared with English common law after the Norman Conquest. In the late middle ages, the rediscovery of Roman law, and the enthusiasm with which it was met in the universities, began to have an effect upon the legal systems of German principalities. By the end of the fifteenth century, Roman law had replaced substantial portions of Germanic law throughout the Holy Roman Empire; one reason for this shift was that Roman law provided the basis of a common legal tradition over a broader territorial area. However, its increasing acceptance can also be explained on the basis of other factors, one of which was the continued existence (however shadowy) of the Holy Roman Empire. Certainly, the adoption of Roman law gave credence to the empire's myth. Just as important was the continued involvement of the different German monarchs in the affairs of south and central Europe, a circumstance that made them continually receptive to Roman law; it was, after all, in Italy that the tradition of Roman law had been most fully retained. Finally, Roman law was, on the whole, more sophisticated than German customary law and far more useful in a society in which commerce was expanding.

This is not to say that Roman law completely replaced traditional systems in Germany. Rather, the legal system that evolved was an amalgamation of Roman law and Germanic custom, and this, too, varied throughout the empire. In fact, the Roman law that took root in Germany was Roman law as reinterpreted by German scholars.

The first major attempt at large-scale codification occurred in Prussia, beginning under Frederick the Great and being completed under Frederick William II in 1794. The occupation of Germany by Napoleon's armies resulted in the adoption of the Napoleonic Code in a number of areas; other principalities, such as Saxony in 1863, later adopted codes, also. In large areas of Germany, however, a confused array of traditional laws derived partly from Germanic tradition and partly from Roman influence remained in effect until the creation of the Second Reich in 1871; then, almost immediately, efforts began toward the development of a single code for the entire empire. It was not, however, until 1896 when the German Civil Code was finally adopted, although civil and criminal procedure had been made uniform and a uniform court system had been created by 1877.

The new code attempted both to unify and to modernize German law. "Obsolete" institutions and customs which were not consonant with what were thought to be modern needs were swept away. The code differed in important ways from the Napoleonic Code, primarily for two reasons: first, the nationalism that accompanied the emergence of the Prussian Empire abetted the retention of traditional Germanic concepts wherever possible; second, the regime which united Germany was paternalistic as well as authoritarian. Therefore, classical and liberal laissez-faire ideas, as interpreted in the nineteenth century, were never incorporated into German law to the same extent that they were in the French code or even in English common law. From the beginning, the codes took care to protect weaker groups in the society and to place restrictions on freedom of contract where the public interest might be involved.

Under the Weimar Republic, the rationalization and modernization of the legal system continued. Unfortunately, however, large numbers of jurists were hostile to the republic and used every occasion they could to interpret the law in such a way as to undermine government policies. What this led to, naturally enough, was a crisis of confidence in the judiciary. Liberals pointed out that many justices were drawn from the upper classes, and schemes were proposed to counteract their influence and to liberalize the bench. But very little was accomplished, and attacks upon the judiciary by the left only intensified its sense of alienation from republican institutions.

The Nazi regime had a profound influence on the whole pattern of German law. The judiciary was purged of "non-Aryan" and politically suspect individuals. The judicial system was centralized and placed directly under the control of the Reich minister of justice, special courts were set up to rule on political crimes, and the power of the judiciary to interfere with administrative decrees was drastically reduced.

The Nazis argued that the German codes were too much influenced by Roman law concepts—which they hoped to replace with a purer "Germanic" law. They also maintained that the concept of an independent judiciary was a "bourgeois" prejudice: to them, law represented the will of the nation, as interpreted by the party and the Führer, and it must be subject to political control. Actually, in the field of civil law, the Nazi regime did not come up with too many innovations, for it was very difficult to discover principles that were indeed uniquely germanic. Even so, "honor" courts were created outside the regular judicial system to keep tabs on all professional activity, and a number of statutes further restricted property rights in the interest of the community. Ordinary criminal law was also not excessively

affected, although the trend to more humane treatment of criminals was reversed.

Nazi changes in German law were most pronounced in the greatly expanded notion of political crimes. Millions of people were arrested and imprisoned or executed without any attempt whatsoever to provide legal safeguards. Further, when ordinary courts proved reluctant to sentence "political criminals," the Nazis created a special People's Court, dominated by party members, to apply to these cases the "people's" sense of right and wrong, regardless of formalistic legal rules. Ironically, the Nazis purged far more judges than had the Weimar Republic; while the traditional German judiciary may have been anti-republican, most judges did believe in the rule of law, and the Nazis were ruthless in weeding out those who refused to conform.

With the regime's collapse and the Allied occupation, the Nazi elements in the law were completely eliminated and the status quo ante was restored. Under American and English coaching, some changes were made to bring the system into line with more advanced Western thinking, and the Germans have continued to move in this direction. Indeed, a recodification of the criminal law, which considerably liberalized it, was all but completed by 1969.

As in France, German law is code law, with all that that implies. The bench and bar are separate; *stare decisis* does not officially apply, and German judges are not supposed to make law. Criminal procedure is disposed to be inquisitorial, although today it probably provides greater protection for defendants than does the French procedure.

THE REGULAR COURTS: Even though the German Empire was federal in structure, it did not create different sets of courts—federal and state—as the United States did. Rather, it developed a single integrated system, with state courts at the lower levels and federal courts at the top. Uniformity was insured by the fact that courts, procedures, and the content of the law itself were regulated by federal codes. Indeed, because of the extensive diversity that existed in the laws of the German states prior to unification, such a structure was absolutely necessary if any kind of viable legal unity was to be achieved.

Like France and other civil-code countries, the major juristic division in Germany is between private and public law, and, again like France, cases bearing on the relationship of the citizen to the government or other matters defined as falling into the public realm are reviewed by special courts. In Germany, these include labor courts, which decide lawsuits between employers and employees arising out of collective-bargaining agreements.

The regular court system consists of four distinct levels: local, district, and appeal courts, and the Federal Supreme Court. Local courts are found in all larger cities and towns and many smaller ones. In the latter, there is often only one judge, who takes care of both civil and criminal matters. In larger cities, the local court may have several judges who divide the different categories of cases among themselves. In more important criminal cases, the judge is joined by two lay assessors—in a sense, jurors—who are chosen by lot from among local inhabitants. From 1884 to 1924, Germany experimented with the jury system, with the judge ruling on points of law and the sentence, and the jury deciding questions of fact; today, in more important cases, judges and lay assessors determine guilt and the sentence jointly as a *Schwurgericht* (literally "jury court").

District courts have both original and appellate jurisdiction. They are staffed with a larger number of judges who divide into chambers for different types of cases; they sit as collegiate bodies and their decisions are by majority. These courts have original jurisdiction in particularly grave crimes such as murder. Their appellate jurisdiction for other cases involves a review of both the law and the facts. In effect, district courts retry the case appealed to them. The appeal courts, which on the whole lack original jurisdiction, are divided into criminal and civil sections; the criminal sections decide points of law, and have the power only to confirm or to quash sentences, or to order a retrial in a lower court.

Strictly speaking, the Federal Supreme Court does not evaluate the constitutionality of legislation; its major function is to insure uniformity of legal interpretation. It has original jurisdiction in political criminal cases, such as treason, and it is divided into civil and criminal chambers.

BENCH, BAR, AND UNIVERSITY: In Germany as in France, the bench and the bar are separate, and young men graduating from law school choose one or the other as a career. The German legal profession, like the French, has never obtained the strength to dominate the bench—and for the same reasons. Germanic law was also replaced by concepts of Roman law and then by codes, and sophistication in the law did not require a long apprenticeship as a practicing lawyer. In Germany, too, the legal profession never developed sufficient status as maker of the law to establish its pre-eminence in this field.

The German judiciary, again like the French, is part of the civil service. In all Land judiciaries, the judge is appointed and promoted by state ministers of justice, and his work is supervised by these ministries. He has life tenure and cannot be transferred from one jurisdiction to another against his will, but promotions do depend upon his bureaucratic superiors far more than upon his professional peers.

The status of the German judiciary has probably always been somewhat higher than that of the French, although it has never matched that of the English. The judiciary was not regarded as a force which had blocked unification. Nor, as conservative nationalism permeated German life during the late nineteenth century, did judges come under the kind of attack from radical social re-

FIGURE 20.3. THE STRUCTURE OF THE WEST GERMAN COURT SYSTEM

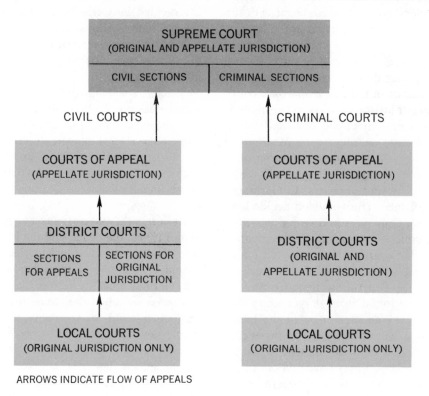

ARROWS INDICATE FLOW OF APPEALS

Adapted from Gwendolen M. Carter and John H. Herz,
Major Foreign Powers, 5th ed. (New York: Harcourt,
Brace and World, 1967), p. 450. Reprinted by permis-
sion of the publisher.

formers that their counterparts did in France —despite the Weimar and Nazi experiences.

German judges in regular (as distinct from administrative) courts do not have a tradition of "making law" to the same extent as their English colleagues. Yet as in all code countries, their role of filling in the interstices of the code by deciding cases has increased, so that both the civil and criminal code have been augmented by a significant body of case decisions. Precedent does not strictly apply, and theoretically judges are not obliged to follow the decisions of superior courts except in cases that have been set up for appeal. However, as in France, the corpus of already decided cases does carry considerable weight; judges who want to be promoted are not likely to send to the higher courts a case that will probably be reversed.

The legal profession in Germany, as in the United States, is unified—the distinction between barrister and solicitor does not apply. Court opinions are based on written evidence even more than in France, and the court participates actively in trial proceedings. Pleading before courts, therefore, is not nearly so important as in England. Legal education is primarily theoretical, with emphasis upon jurisprudence and training in the social sciences, especially economics. A law degree provides basic training, not only for those who intend to practice law but also for young men who wish to enter business or the bureaucracy; a far larger proportion of German bureaucrats, for example, have law degrees than those of any other European nation.

Academic lawyers, like those in France and other code law countries, are influential in defining the framework and content of the law. In Germany, the prestige that has always been attached to the universities gives academic jurists even more authority than their French counterparts; for instance, the commissions that drew up the codes of criminal and civil law during the empire contained many academic lawyers. Comments on the law by academics, and theoretical articles on jurisprudence, are taken quite seriously by both the judiciary and the legal profession, and academics are frequently called upon to testify as experts or to submit briefs as friends of the court.

THE ADMINISTRATION OF JUSTICE: Traditional Germanic criminal procedure, like traditional Anglo-Saxon procedure, regarded the redress of most crimes as a private matter. There was, consequently, little distinction between civil and criminal proceedings. Under the influence of Roman and canon law, inquisitorial procedures began to spread in the late middle ages, and by the sixteenth century had become common practice throughout the Holy Roman Empire. Unlike the procedure in France, however, a system of public prosecutors was never established, and the preliminary investigation was lodged in an investigating magistrate who was part of the judiciary rather than the police. The investigation itself had many of the qualities characteristic of the French: it was secret and the prisoner was denied the right of counsel, although he could eventually confront witnesses. Trials, too, were secret. The prisoner, again, did not have the right of counsel, and determinations of both fact and law were made by judges.

Among the first efforts of judicial reformers in the nineteenth century was the creation of a system of public prosecutors. Reformers hoped that the new office would prevent the

investigating magistrate from acting as an organ of prosecution. Borrowed largely from the French, the criminal codes promulgated in the German states after the middle of the nineteenth century provided for a public trial with complete liberty of defense, although the defendant's rights remained severely restricted during the preliminary investigation. Trial by jury was also established for serious cases. In 1924, however, the jury was abolished and replaced by the Schwurgericht.

After the downfall of the Nazis, traditional procedures were re-established with some modifications. The present criminal code provides that any person arrested under suspicion of having committed a criminal offense must be brought before a judge no later than the end of the day after the arrest. The judge must immediately either issue a warrant of arrest, giving the reasons for doing so, or order the release of the detained person. As in France, release on bail is difficult to obtain while the preliminary investigation is being carried out; however, the reasons for the arrest—if a person is detained—must be re-examined after one month, and every three months thereafter. In the preliminary investigation, the magistrate is under obligation to secure evidence on behalf of the defendant if so requested, and the defendant is entitled to counsel from the beginning of the investigation.

The German criminal court, again like the French, plays the leading part in questioning witnesses during the trial. There is no cross-examination of the Anglo-Saxon type, and very few rules of evidence. The question of guilt and sentence are determined by the judiciary and the lay assessors sitting together, and the code provides for a full review of both facts and evidence by appellate courts.

Civil cases differ somewhat, in that more elements of an adversary procedure are present; also, civil court judges are not quite such an integral part of the proceedings as they are in criminal court. Even so, they are supposed to intervene to insure that all pertinent facts are brought out. A good deal of reliance is placed upon written evidence, despite the fact that the code requires an oral hearing. Suits in civil law are relatively inexpensive because attorneys' fees are fixed at specific rates by statute, and impecunious parties may be entitled to free proceedings if the court believes they warrant it.

6. CONCLUSIONS

The legal systems of England, France, and Germany form part of a common European heritage. The national differences that manifested themselves from the fourteenth through the nineteenth centuries reflected—even as they influenced—the manner in which each of these countries became a modern nation state.

In the last half-century, with the exception of the Nazi period in Germany, the legal systems of all three nations have become more and more similar. This convergence can be partly attributed to a growing similarity of problems, but it is also the result of increased communication and greater economic interdependence.

All three legal systems are continuing to evolve. Demands for more adequate legal services for the poor and the far more frequent intercession of the state in the economic and social life of the community are but two factors contributing to the changes in contemporary European law. Indeed, it is becoming increasingly difficult to distinguish between private and public law, since the community as a whole is taking an ever larger interest in disputes among its members. Perhaps the major legal problem of the next twenty or thirty years will be that of finding new methods to protect the citizen from arbitrary action by the state while at the same time permitting political authorities to function effectively on matters concerning the public interest.

21

Soviet Law

1. INTRODUCTION

The structure of Soviet legal institutions and the content of Soviet law reflect many influences. Marxist-Leninist theory, traditional Russian legal patterns, and the requirements of an industrial society have all had their effect. Marx and Lenin envisaged an anarchistic society—one, that is, without a legal system. Their writings, therefore, offered no guide for constructing a legal system that would serve a Socialist community. However, the fact that the Soviet Union is a nation in which the means of production are owned by the state has had, as one might expect, important implications for the substance of the law. Furthermore, the Soviet society's goal of creating a new Soviet man who will usher in communism has had a tremendous impact on its legal system.[1] Soviet law serves both a socializing and an integrative function, and socialization—in the sense of using the law as a teacher—is stressed to a far greater

extent than in the nations of Western Europe.

The peculiar role of the Communist Party in Soviet society, including its conception of itself as the ultimate repository of truth, has also had considerable effect upon the status of the legal profession, especially upon its independence of action. Finally, the egalitarian bias of the regime, as well as its commitment to the ultimate elimination of formal organs of rule-making and compulsion, cannot help but influence the function and organization of the court structure.

Given the impossibility of establishing a society without law—at least at the present stage of human development—and the concomitant need to create a legal structure, it is not surprising that the Communist regime tried to adapt some traditional Russian institutions to its needs, and that certain traditional Russian attitudes have manifested themselves in the content of Soviet law—even though they conflict with portions of Marxist-Leninist theory. Family law is one area in which there has clearly been tension between Soviet dogma and Russian customs.

The need for order in the development of

[1] As noted in Chapter 3, the Soviet regime considers itself still only in the Socialist stage of development.

635

a modern industrial society has also forced the Soviet leadership to become engaged in creating a new body of law. Thus, the Soviet legal system bears a marked resemblance to the legal systems of other modernizing societies that have adopted codes. Most of these have turned to the French code as a model, which, indeed, the Soviets have done. Moreover, because certain social institutions and patterns of authority are typical of all complex societies, Soviet law resembles that of similarly complex societies: the Soviet system has gradually been incorporating legal procedures it once disparaged as merely a reflection of the bourgeois, formalistic approach to the law. Not unexpectedly, the legal profession has been instrumental in bringing about the acceptance of these procedures. In fact, as professional standards have risen, a certain amount of friction has occurred between lawyers and the Soviet political leadership.

2. THE DEVELOPMENT OF RUSSIAN LEGAL INSTITUTIONS [2]

The traditional law of the Slavic peoples who inhabited the western part of Russia closely resembled that of the Germanic tribes of Northern Europe. With their conversion to Christianity, they, like Western Europeans, also became heirs to the law of Rome and of the canon law of the Christian church. Nevertheless, the legal system of Russia remained far more primitive than that of the West.

This lack of development can be traced to several factors: the Tartar conquest, which was certainly not conducive to the creation of more sophisticated legal institutions; the Russians' never having come as much under the influence of Rome (or Byzantium) and its heritage as did Western Europe; and finally, the Orthodox Church never having possessed that determination to rationalize both man's thought and his institutions which so influ-

enced the development of canon law in the Catholic Church.

With the destruction of the Tartar empire late in the fifteenth century and the emergence of a Russian state, a national system of courts and a formal judiciary began to take shape. Supreme legal authority was invested in the Boyars' Duma (king's council), in which a special commission for judicial matters heard cases for which no law was known to exist, or about which there was some doubt as to the interpretation of the applicable law. This special commission supervised some forty special boards (*prikazy*), each of which was assigned jurisdiction over a particular problem—robbery or serfs or Siberia. Under the prikazy were the governors of the provinces, appointed and paid by the czar, and, next, elected judges paid by the litigants. Trial by combat was eventually eliminated, and, as in Western Europe, the adversary system came to be replaced, especially in criminal cases, by the inquisitorial. Until the eighteenth century, however, Russian legal institutions and, indeed, Russian law itself remained five hundred years or so behind the West. Jurisdictions overlapped, the law was highly primitive, the judiciary venal, and a legal profession nonexistent.

The first major attempt to bring Russia abreast of Western legal customs was made by Peter the Great. In 1722 he set up a commission charged with codifying the law, and created the procuracy, under a procurator general whose function was to check on the legality of various organs of government. His work was continued by Catherine the Great; like her predecessor, she looked to the West as a model.

In all, some ten commissions sat between 1700 and 1815, but with little result. The difficulties of the task were immense. In all Western nations there was, at the time of codification, a reasonably well-developed system of private law upon which to build. Russia lacked this. In addition, the diversity of legal custom throughout the empire and the different rights and privileges attached to var-

[2] Much of this section is based on Harold J. Berman, *Justice in the U.S.S.R.,* revised edition (New York: Alfred A. Knopf, 1963).

ious estates, as well as the absolute position of the monarch, inhibited the establishment of a rational legal structure.

Finally in 1832, as a result of the work of Michael Speransky, the first codification of Russian law since 1649 was completed. Although Czar Nicholas had forbidden him to depart from traditional Russian law, Speransky was able to incorporate elements of French law, and the structure of the Russian code itself followed the French. Still, by European standards, the code was rudimentary. The great mass of people were excluded from its provisions—the peasantry was, on the whole, still under the domination of the aristocracy—and the Russians were still without a trained legal profession and a trained judiciary. Above all, the monarchy itself continued to be outside the law.

Yet the code was a beginning. During the next thirty years, a class of jurists educated in Western Europe began to make its appearance on the Russian scene. Simultaneously, the legal status of the peasant changed, and in 1861 serfdom came to an end. Three years later Alexander II, impelled by the desire for further reform, promulgated a judiciary act designed to bring the Russian legal system still more closely in accord with that of the West. A court system, independent of administrative officials, was set up, with judges irremovable except for judicial misconduct. Most class courts were eliminated; justices of the peace, on the English model, were established; public trial by jury was instituted in criminal cases; and defendants were given the right to be represented by counsel. In all, the reforms marked an enormous improvement in the Russian legal system.

As in other areas of Russian life, however, many of the reforms were abrogated as revolutionary violence increased in the 1880's and 1890's. The acquittal in 1878 of Vera Zasulich, who had shot and killed the governor of Saint Petersburg, led the government to withdraw the right of jury trial in many cases involving political crimes. Nevertheless, the new legal profession asserted itself throughout the whole period as the defender of legal processes, even under circumstances in which its members defied the state's authority. Furthermore, in political trials, statements in which lawyers defended their clients' actions by referring in somewhat derogatory terms to the nature of the political system were reported in the newspapers. For example, during the trial in 1904 of Yegor Sazonov, who assassinated the reactionary minister of the interior, V. K. Pleve, the defense lawyer described the chain of thoughts of his client as follows:

All the horror which overtook Russia in the last years was attributed to Pleve. It was he who . . . jailed and banished thousands of innocent people, he flogged and shot peasants and workers . . . he instigated mass massacres of Jews. . . . Sazonov's imagination pictured Pleve as a fatal, sinister . . . figure. . . . It seemed to Sazonov that this monster could be annihilated only by another monster— death. And grasping with trembling hands the bomb . . . Sazonov believed, piously believed, that it was filled . . . with the tears, sorrow, and calamity of the people. . . . That is why when he regained consciousness [after the explosion], *he shouted: "Long live liberty!"*[3]

Immediately preceding World War I, a new wave of legal reforms was set in motion. A criminal code, drafted in 1903, was an exceptionally creative adaptation to Russian conditions of the best achievements of Western Europe. Although only part of it was adopted, the new criminal code was a distinct advance. And just prior to the war itself, an equally sophisticated civil code was drafted. The war, however, marked the end of the empire and the opening of a new phase in Russian history.

[3] Quoted in Samuel Kucherov, "The Legal Profession in Pre- and Post-Revolutionary Russia," *The American Journal of Comparative Law,* 5 (1956), pp. 450–451.

3. THE DEVELOPMENT OF SOVIET LAW

To Marx and Engels, law was part of that system of compulsion identified with all prehistoric societies—societies in which full human freedom has yet to be attained. The law mirrored the economic structure of those societies, whatever superficial variations might be found. What was more to the point, the law not only institutionalized the domination of one class over another, it served to perpetuate this stratification even as it held the society together. In bourgeois society, law, according to Marx and Engels, reflected the peculiar property concerns of capitalism and reduced all human relationships to contractual relationships, setting the latter up as norms which, for some reason, must command the loyalty of all. In a Communist society, of course, law would disappear even as would the state, and human relations would be governed by the voluntary acceptance of the norms of human fellowship.

Lenin's analysis of law was essentially the same; he expected, as did a great many other Bolsheviks, that soon after the success of the Revolution both substantive law and the society's legal structure would wither away. As P. I. Stuchka, first president of the U.S.S.R. Supreme Court, wrote in 1927:

Communism means not the victory of socialist law, but the victory of socialism over any law, since with the abolition of classes with their antagonistic interests, law will die out altogether.[4]

In the first flush of revolutionary fervor, steps were taken that seemed to presage just this dissolution. The previously existing system of courts was abolished, and so-called people's courts, which were to be guided by "revolutionary consciousness," were instituted. The practice of law was opened to all who enjoyed civil rights, and a series of decrees was issued with the purpose of eliminating traditional areas of substantive law, including the law of property.

Almost at the same time, however, the exigencies of organizing the Soviet state required moves in other and opposite directions. The basis for a legal profession was re-established to a certain extent, the procuracy was revived and even strengthened as an instrument of control, and decrees were promulgated covering both civil and criminal law and procedure.

This trend toward re-creating an organized legal system continued and was accelerated during the period of the New Economic Policy (N.E.P.). The hiring of labor and renting of land were legalized. Also, a judiciary act established a hierarchy of courts and a system of trials and appeals, and codes were enacted—copied from German, French, and Swiss models—that covered the traditional spectrum of "bourgeois" law.

Most sections of the codes which made concessions to "bourgeois" practices were justified as temporary expedients. The leading Soviet jurist of the period, E. B. Pashukanis, openly admitted that the law of the new regime was basically bourgeois law, which was necessary for the transition period but would, he claimed, disappear with the establishment of a truly Communist society. There was, however, Pashukanis added, one fundamental difference between Soviet law and the law of capitalist countries: in the Soviet Union law was regarded not as independent of public policy but rather subordinate to it, and the aim of public policy was still the eventual elimination of the legal order. Writing in 1935, Pashukanis declared:

The relationship of law to politics and to economics is utterly different among us from what it is in bourgeois society. . . . We require that our legislation possess maximum elasticity. . . . Accordingly . . . law occupies among us, on the contrary, a subordinate position with reference to politics.

We have a system of proletarian politics and upon it law should be oriented. . . . Revo-

4 Berman, *Justice*, p. 26.

*lutionary legality is for us a problem which
is ninety-nine per cent political.*[5]

The civil code, therefore, contained a provision that any legal transaction "directed to
the obvious prejudice of the state" was invalid, and that profits from any such transaction would be forfeited to the state. In
addition, the doctrine of analogy[6] permitted
the punishment of socially dangerous acts
that were not directly prohibited. The whole
corpus of Soviet law was pervaded by the
assumption that the law should not be applied
in accordance with formal rules, but rather
in such a manner as to further the interests
of the Revolution. As Article 1 of the civil
code noted: "Civil rights shall be protected
by law except in instances where they are
exercised in contradiction to their social-
economic purpose." A man could own a
house, but he could be forced to take in a
tenant if the state so required; a person
could be deprived of his property if—as in
the case of a farm or mill—he made use of
it for anti-social purposes.

With the end of the N.E.P. and the consolidation of the Stalinist dictatorship, the early
Communist law was modified. At first, under
the heady influence of utopian radicalism,
many once again began to believe that the
prophesied end of a formal legal system was
imminent—a feeling that gained impetus with
collectivization. In actuality, however, while
many bourgeois elements of the law were dis-
regarded or modified, the period after 1934
involved in many ways an even greater retreat from "Socialist law." Family ties were
tightened and divorce made more difficult,
personal responsibility for crime was brought
back into the law, and criminal penalties
were made harsher in an effort to combat a
rising crime rate in large cities. Inheritance
was effectively restored, and the role of con-

tract law, which was strikingly similar to that
in the West, was applied to public corporations. The new legal pattern also placed a
great deal of emphasis upon the importance
of "Socialist legality,"[7] even as this was being
violated by the secret police.

At least as important as the changes taking
place in Soviet law was the formulation of a
new legal theory to replace that of Pashukanis, who, like so many other prominent
Communists in the mid-1930's, recanted and
denounced his heresies in 1936—too late to
avoid arrest and execution the following year.
He disappeared in 1937, and the fact of his
"trial" and execution became known only in
1956. The new theory, prescribed by Stalin
and expounded in detail by Andrei Vyshinski, his chief prosecutor during the party
purges, argued that with the 1936 constitution the Soviet Union had actually achieved
a Socialist society, and this now meant, contrary to previous theories, that institutions of
the state and the law should not be weakened
or eliminated but strengthened. To be sure,
these institutions would eventually disappear
but only after being granted greater authority.
As Stalin had phrased it earlier:

*We are in favor of the state withering away
and at the same time we stand for the
strengthening of the dictatorship of the proletariat, which represents the most powerful
and mighty authority of all forms of the state
which have existed up to the present day. The
highest possible development of the government power with the object of preparing conditions for the withering away of government
power, this is the Marxist formula.*[8]

According to this argument, Russia now
had its own Socialist law, an expression of

[5] Quoted in Berman, p. 42.

[6] According to which a person could be sentenced
for committing an act not specifically prohibited by
law if the court or administrative organ of the state
decided it was analogous to a prohibited act.

[7] As formulated under Stalin, the doctrine of
"Socialist legality" emphasized that Socialist law, while
unlike capitalist law, had to be adhered to consistently.
In the post-Stalin era, those using the term were invariably pressing for the reduction of arbitrary elements
in the Soviet legal system.

[8] Quoted in Berman, p. 43.

the will of the Soviet people, who, since they had achieved socialism, could now use the law as a creative force to push Russian society further in the direction of communism. The new law was also quite different from bourgeois law, even though the techniques it used in some areas might resemble bourgeois techniques. Vyshinski openly admitted that the Revolution was still primary—Socialist legality would be applied to those areas that had been stabilized, but where the regime was threatened by "enemies," it could still rely upon extraordinary measures. Throughout the 1930's and 1940's, millions of people were taken into custody and shot or sent to concentration camps on the basis of decisions made by special boards attached to the secret police. Among the arrested were not only those accused by almost anyone of counterrevolutionary activity, but also their relatives and friends. Managers or workers who, for any reason whatsoever, were suspected of not "adequately" fulfilling their functions also found themselves sentenced by administrative fiat. One analyst of Soviet affairs estimates that between 1930 and 1953, more than twenty million people passed through labor camps. During those years, he believes, up to twenty million citizens died either from starvation, at the hand of an executioner, or because of conditions in the camps.[9]

During the Khrushchev period, Soviet law and legal theory were the subject of challenge and change. The legal system was further rationalized, and the law was, on the whole, liberalized so as to protect the right of citizens against arbitrary arrest. In the new criminal codes, for example, no law could be applied retroactively unless specifically permitted by the law itself. The special secret police boards were abolished, and the secret police put under the supervision of the procu-

racy. In addition, while the presumption of innocence was not incorporated into the new criminal codes, the burden of proof was placed on the state, and defense attorneys were given greater freedom of action. Indeed, the legal profession, although still limited in influence, took an ever more active part in the discussion and formulation of new legislation.

After a period of relaxation, however, "economic" crimes again became subject to severe penalties, including death by shooting. In some cases, the new laws were applied retroactively in violation of their provisions; in others, intellectuals accused of "anti-Soviet" writing were tried and sentenced secretly, or sent to mental hospitals by administrative action. Laws were promulgated without being published, and cases decided without being reported. Beginning in 1957, a number of vaguely worded "anti-parasite" laws were adopted in almost all Soviet republics; these permitted the sentencing of individuals to long terms of hard labor, or to mental institutions, if they were not engaged in "productive" work. Further, "parasitic" individuals could be "resettled" in camps if found guilty at trials conducted by popular assemblies or meetings of factory workers.

Tied in with these changes was the partial rehabilitation of Pashukanis's legal philosophy. Soviet Socialist law was regarded as a reflection of the will of the Soviet people in an "All-People's State," but in addition, it was expected that with the movement from socialism to communism, greater and greater authority would devolve upon the people. Theoretically, this authority was to be exercised by the "voluntary" comrades' courts, organized on such immediate levels as apartment houses and places of work, and supervised by the Communist Party. These courts could impose small fines and recommend demotion or dismissal from work or eviction from an apartment. Such decisions were not ordinarily subject to review by the regular courts, but the more severe of their penalties had to be approved by the trade-union committee or the executive committee of the local

9 Robert Conquest, *The Great Terror* (New York: Macmillan, 1968), especially pp. 276–336 and 525–535.

soviet. To a Westerner, comrades' courts were quite regressive, inducing conformity by organized social pressure and restricting the scope of individual privacy.

With Khrushchev's fall, some of the populist elements associated with his rule were eliminated. The theory of the All-People's State was gradually discarded; such a state, it was argued, was but one phase of the dictatorship of the proletariat, and official state organs rather than voluntary groups should carry the burden of decision-making responsibility. For this reason, but also because of pressure from Soviet jurists, the "anti-parasite" laws were heavily amended; the comrades' courts, however, have continued to operate.[10]

The Brezhnev-Kosygin regime has stepped up repressive measures against any dissent. In 1966, the criminal code of the Russian Soviet Federal Socialist Republic was amended to provide prison terms for disseminating material which discredited the Soviet system, insulting the Soviet flag, and participating in activities which "violate public order." These new measures and others were used to stage trials against writers whose critical books had been smuggled out of the Soviet Union, as well as against those who protested that such trials violated the Soviet constitution. Peaceful assembly and the peaceful distribution of literature objecting to such political intimidation were defined as a violation of the public order. Some of the 1967 and 1968 trials were closed to the public; others were packed by party members, with non-Soviet newspaper officials excluded. Smuggled transcripts indicate that in some instances even the legal procedures required by the new codes were violated.

The following comments on Soviet law by Harold Berman are a reasonably accurate statement of its present character:

And if one looks behind the structure to the purposes of Soviet law, it remains a totalitarian law, in the sense that it seeks to regulate all aspects of Soviet economic and social life, including the circulation of thought, while leaving the critical questions of political power to be decided by informal, secret procedures beyond the scrutiny or control either of legislative or judicial bodies. It remains the law of a one-party state. . . . It remains a law whose primary function is to discipline, guide, train, and educate Soviet citizens to be dedicated members of a collectivized and mobilized social order.[11]

4. SOME ASPECTS OF SOVIET CIVIL AND CRIMINAL LAW

With the success of the 1917 Revolution, the leadership of the Communist Party was convinced that the legal structure so characteristic of capitalist society would soon disappear—and with it such administrative and institutional apparatus as courts and the legal profession. The vision, of course, proved false—or at least premature—and during the past fifty years the Soviet Union has constructed a legal system that has been forced to borrow, in many telling ways, from the legal concepts of other nations. Nevertheless, the vision, if somewhat more ambiguously blurred, remains, and it continues to influence both the content and the implementation of Soviet law. That the society of the U.S.S.R. is one in which the means of production are controlled by the state has had a direct effect upon the content of its law. So, too, as we shall see, has the fact that Soviet jurists continue to underscore the educational or socialization aspects of law far more than non-Communist societies. A discussion of the administration of justice in the Soviet Union, therefore, must be preceded by an outline of the substance of Soviet law. To examine the entire range of the law, however,

---

[10] See Roger E. Kanet, "The Rise and Fall of the 'All People's State': Recent Changes in the Soviet Theory of the State," *Soviet Studies,* XX (July 1968), pp. 81–93.

[11] Harold J. Berman, "The Dilemma of Soviet Law Reform," *Harvard Law Review,* 76 (March 1963), pp. 930–931.

would require far too much space; hence, the sections that follow are brief, general discussions of selected aspects of both Soviet civil and criminal law. In both, the tension between Marxist-Leninist theory and the objective requirements of a modern industrial nation have prompted an uncertain series of compromises, and Soviet law is still very much in a state of flux.

SOVIET CIVIL LAW: When the Bolsheviks seized power, they issued a series of decrees abolishing property, and with it the whole corpus of traditional civil law. With the advent of the New Economic Policy, however, they recognized the need for clear and comprehensive rules of law regulating relations among citizens, and between citizens and the state. A civil code was devised for the R.S.F.S.R. in 1922; other union republics followed suit soon after. In both structure and content, the codes were strongly reminiscent of those of Western Europe; but they contained distinctive Socialist elements, especially in the limitations placed on private property and the primacy assigned to the state's interests. The official legal theory, as propounded by Pashukanis, viewed civil law as a capitalist phenomenon that would eventually disappear; nevertheless, for the present "transition stage," the codes, following Pashukanis's legal precepts, divided civil law into two spheres: an economic law applicable to legal relationships in the public sector and a civil law that would apply to the remaining private sector.

During the initial stages of the second Soviet revolution, which began in 1928 and 1929, many sections of the 1922 codes were repealed and many others simply ignored. Legal transactions within the greatly enlarged socialized sector of the economy were replaced by administrative procedures, and the civil law became applicable only to a greatly diminished private sector. By 1936, however, the political situation had begun to stabilize itself again, and new legal structures were introduced. In the public sphere, a series of statutes and decrees, as well as court decisions, re-established contractual, as against purely administrative, relations among government firms; in the narrow private sector, the state extended guarantees with respect to certain forms of personal property, including the right to pass it on to one's heirs. The legal theory of these years, detailed by Vyshinski, argued that Soviet civil law was specifically Socialist law, and the two-sector theory of Pashukanis was denounced.

After Stalin's death, there was a revival of discussion of the theoretical issues involved in the relationship between civil and economic law. It was fairly obvious that recodification was necessary, and in 1961 the U.S.S.R. Supreme Soviet laid down detailed guidelines for such action—guidelines which have served as the basis for the new codes gradually being introduced in the union republics. Following the continental European pattern of categorizing the law, these codes are divided into such sections as property, contracts, and inheritance. Legal relations within the "Socialist" or public sector are now included within the civil code, a shift from the thinking of the late 1950's when it looked as if Pashukanis's doctrines were again becoming dominant. However, the Socialist sector—within which "plan fulfillment" continues to be the overriding consideration—is heavily favored, so that in practice a two-sector view does prevail. For example, the statute of limitations which has been incorporated into the law does not apply to claims arising from the public sector.

The role of private property has undergone many modifications since the period of War Communism. In the 1920's, somewhat greater latitude was tolerated in the ownership of property. Citizens were allowed to retain ownership of buildings not nationalized by the local soviets, and furthermore were allowed to transfer their ownership. They were also permitted to construct new dwellings which would be their personal property for a fixed period, not to exceed 49 years. In

1925, the hiring of labor and the renting of land were granted in agriculture, and during most of the decade private entrepreneurship in retail trade was also authorized. Theoretically, of course, all peasant-occupied land was in the hands of the state; but, in fact, the peasant's right to use it as he wished was not questioned. The civil codes, however, did contain a provision that these rights to property could be abrogated if they were "exercised in contradiction to their socioeconomic purposes."

In the first years of collectivization, the state abolished private ownership of anything involved with the means of production. By the mid-1930's, the trend, at least in the case of personal property, had been somewhat reversed; the Soviet citizen could own his house, have personal belongings, and maintain a savings account, which collected three per cent interest in the state banks. By 1942, the right of inheritance was fully recognized; Soviet citizens were permitted to inherit most personal items, including savings, after paying a very small tax. Moreover, peasants were allowed to work private plots and to sell the produce from them in the open market. The regime remained quite firm, nonetheless, in insisting that no private property could be used to obtain additional income through renting. In 1937, for example, one Poliakov was granted the ownership of a car as a work bonus. Because he had no immediate use for it, he contracted to rent the car to a government agency. The agency later refused to pay, and, after extensive litigation, the courts ruled that the contract was void.

The issue of private ownership of houses has always troubled the Communist regime. Some loosening of controls pertaining to home ownership did occur in the 1950's; indeed, state subsidies were granted for the construction of private homes. But by 1960 there was evidence of second thoughts on the part of the leadership. Under new codes, persons who own one house and acquire a second are now required to sell one of them within a year. Further, private houses that are discovered to have been built with "unearned income" are subject to confiscation without compensation. The decrees are retroactive. During the last years of Khrushchev's power, the regime discouraged the building of private houses and emphasized the "Socialist" virtues of living in apartments constructed and owned by the state. This theme has not been stressed quite so much by Khrushchev's successors, but the proportion of private construction to new public housing remains about one in four in urban areas.

Initially, the Bolsheviks thought that the Soviet economy could be managed by a central administrative apparatus. The regime soon discovered, however, that matters were not nearly so simple. The whole system of production and distribution in the Soviet Union ground almost to a complete, and chaotic, halt. The early period of the New Economic Policy, therefore, was marked not only by the establishment of a private sector of the economy but by the reintroduction of "capitalist" laws governing contractual relations in both the private and the socialized sectors. Again, however, it was made clear that any contractual arrangements were valid only insofar as they did not interfere with the general purposes of the community.

A renewed attempt to rely upon administrative procedures for handling problems of production was made between 1929 and 1935. Virtually all state enterprises, including industrial plants, were financed directly out of the federal budget, and the state compensated for any deficits. By 1936, however, it again became apparent that a completely centralized administrative approach was highly unsatisfactory. State enterprises were given greater independence in investing funds and arranging for the purchase and delivery of raw materials and finished products. A body of case law developed to clarify and ease the relationships between enterprises, and those between enterprises and administrative authorities.

When the new civil code came up for discussion in the 1950's, some jurists argued that relations between economic enterprises should be treated as a separate category of law, for the contracts reached between enterprises in the socialized sector were of a different order from those between private parties in their private capacities. But the argument was rejected, and although the new codes do contain a few sections applying specifically to enterprises, the same general procedures govern all contractual relations. Today, contracts are an integral part of the economic system. While no precise figures are available, one scholar has estimated that during the early 1960's as many as 250 million economic contracts were concluded in the Soviet Union each year. If present trends permitting more flexibility in the operation of economic enterprises continue, it is quite likely that the number will increase.[12]

Soviet contract law today does not differ much in important respects from that of civil law in capitalist countries. A contract is deemed to be concluded when the parties have reached agreement on all essential points; in the event of a breach of contract, the obligor is required to compensate the obligee for losses caused by the breach. Also, liability for breach of contract must be founded on fault unless otherwise provided by law, and illegal contracts cannot be considered binding. A contract is invalid if one of the parties was legally incompetent, or if the contract was concluded fraudulently or under threat of violence or duress.

There are, to be sure, significant differences as well. In the Soviet Union, the state plays a direct role in contracts, even in those between private individuals, and it may intervene at any time to insure that contractual decisions are in the interest of the state. Also, while contracts between firms are concluded

at the initiative of managers, they are by and large derived from the state's overall economic plan, and the substance of the plan, and subsidiary plans, places certain limits upon their content.

SOVIET CRIMINAL LAW: Soviet criminal law has undergone a number of abrupt shifts since the Bolshevik Revolution. Once it was recognized that a structure of criminal law was necessary, if only "temporarily," Soviet jurists appropriated the most advanced European thinking on criminal matters. The 1926 code spoke not of crime but of "socially dangerous acts," and it divided them into two categories, those of a "medico-educational" nature and those of a "judicial-correctional" nature. The terms "crime" and "punishment" were excluded from the code, as was the term "prison." Under the leadership of N. V. Krylenko, an effort was made to eliminate the "moral stigma" of guilt and to "re-educate" all those who had engaged in socially disruptive acts. Crime was regarded as a hangover from bourgeois society that would disappear with the full flowering of socialism; in the interim, individual crimes that did not threaten the security of the state would receive fairly light punishment. The death penalty was abolished for all nonpolitical crimes, and the maximum sentence, for intentional homicide only, was ten years' deprivation of freedom.

However clear Krylenko's theories may have sounded, the emphasis upon "social danger" rather than upon the criminal act itself yielded a certain amount of vagueness in the standards to be applied. For example, Article 7 of the 1926 code stated:

With regard to persons who have committed socially dangerous acts or who represent a danger because of their connection with a criminal environment or because of their past activity, measures of social defense of a judicial-correctional . . . or medico-educational nature shall be applied.

---

[12] See Dietrich A. Loeber, "Plan and Contract Performance in Soviet Law," in Wayne R. LaFave, ed., *Law in the Soviet Society* (Urbana: University of Illinois Press, 1965), p. 131.

What this meant, in effect, was that a person who had committed no act whatever but whose mere connections with a criminal environment or "past activity" caused him to "represent a danger" could be sentenced to jail. Furthermore, the code contained no provision denying retroactive effect to a law, and persons could be punished for acts not specifically prohibited by the law. As Article 16 stated:

If any socially dangerous act is not directly provided for by the present code, the basis and limits of responsibility for it shall be determined by those articles of the code which provide for crimes most similar to it in nature.

Correctional measures applied to "political" crimes were more severe than for nonpolitical crimes and there was even less protection against arbitrary punishment. "Counterrevolutionary" crimes—defined as any acts "intended to overthrow, to undermine, or to weaken the power of the workers' and peasants' soviets"—were punishable by death or, under mitigating circumstances, by deprivation of freedom with strict isolation for five to ten years and loss of property. Membership in organizations engaged in counterrevolutionary crimes, even if the member was not aware of the purposes of the organization, was also subject to severe penalties; so, too, was failure to report evidence of counterrevolutionary activities. In addition to crimes against the state, certain other categories of "crimes against the administrative order"—counterfeiting and violation of the foreign-exchange regulations, for example—were subject to harsh penalties. The statute of limitations did not apply to many of these crimes. Of course, the Soviet secret police was permitted to take measures of summary justice, and it imprisoned or executed thousands of people during the 1920's. The full extent of such actions is not yet known, and many of the decrees relating to the authority of the secret police were never published.

The severity of Soviet criminal law has fluctuated rather erratically; there have been periods of leniency followed by periods of stringency in a continuing cycle, as the regime has discovered over and over again that crime was, in fact, not dying out. For example, the death penalty has been abolished and restored and its application expanded and narrowed, while the regime continues to assert that, except for extraordinary circumstances, it will eventually be abolished. Thus, too, under the 1926 code the age of criminal responsibility was placed at 16, only to be lowered in 1935 to 12. Further, the 1926 code, as well as the new codes, has been supplemented by special decrees related to immediate situations about which the regime felt a particular urgency—methods that imparted an additional element of unpredictability to Soviet law. The 1930's, in particular, were marked by an increasing severity in criminal law, a general breakdown of Socialist legality (principally with respect to crimes against the state), and the removal of more and more cases from the jurisdiction of the regular courts.

Perhaps the most significant modification in Soviet criminal philosophy was the growing assumption that individuals were personally responsible for their acts. While the regime never altered its official viewpoint that criminal acts were merely remnants of the bourgeois order, the argument was nevertheless offered that persons living in a Socialist society were morally responsible for violating Socialist norms. By 1938 the terms "crime" and "prison" had been fully restored in Soviet law. Shortly before that time, Krylenko—who was among the leading advocates of the gradual disappearance of criminal law and the elimination of the concept of guilt—had himself disappeared; although he had recanted his earlier views, he was denounced as a "counterrevolutionary" and liquidated.

For the average Soviet citizen, however, an expanded definition of "anti-state" crimes was responsible for the terror of the 1930's. Even those who came before the regular courts were victims of new decrees that broadened the meaning of such crimes. The family of a person implicated in anti-state ventures could be subject to deportation and forced labor, even if they knew nothing of the activities of the guilty party. A 1932 law created the new crime of "speculation"—"the buying up and resale of products of agriculture and mass consumption by private persons for a profit"—punishable by confinement in a "concentration camp" for from five to ten years. Later laws imposed equally stiff penalties for industrial managers believed to be responsible for the negligent release of goods of poor quality, and for persons who deceived purchasers by the use of false weights and measures.

By 1938, the harshness of sentences against those found guilty of anti-state crimes began to lessen. The doctrine of analogy, for instance, was attacked in some courts and given a more narrow interpretation than originally. Courts also began to define "negligence" by a subjective standard: a manager would be punished in terms of what he as a person could have been expected to know, not what he should have known according to an ideal standard. The imposition of less severe penalties did not, however, gain much momentum until after the death of Stalin.

Perhaps the most meaningful first step in this direction was the abolition of the special secret police boards, followed by the issuance of decrees reducing the penalties for a variety of crimes. The liberalization and rationalization of Soviet law reached its peak—although countertrends existed even then—between 1956 and the adoption of the R.S.F.S.R. criminal code in 1960. In the 1960 code the doctrine of analogy was eliminated, and, at least in regular Soviet courts, no one could any longer be punished for something not specifi-

cally prohibited by law. The age of criminal responsibility was raised from 12 to 14 for the most serious crimes and from 12 to 16 for lesser ones; the death penalty was limited to persons over 18, and was not permitted for pregnant women.

The 1960 code also eliminated the term "counterrevolutionary crimes." It was replaced by two categories: "especially dangerous crimes against the state" and "other crimes against the state." Penalties for many of the "other crimes" were reduced; for example, the crime of "wrecking," defined as the "subversion" of state industry, transport, or trade and previously punishable by death, now carried the sentence of deprivation of freedom for eight to 15 years, with a possible additional exile for two to five years.

Unfortunately, this moderating trend has been partially annulled since the mid-1960's, although elements of such reversal were apparent somewhat earlier. Some of the reasons for the backtracking lie in the continued tension between ideology and reality, and in the regime's impatience with the perpetual manifestations of criminal activity in the Soviet Union. The Kremlin still argues that criminal acts, either ordinary or anti-state, are the legacy of bourgeois society or the result of provocation by Western influences. Except for very strident criticism of Soviet parents who "coddle" their children, it has no explanation for the fact that, after fifty years, crime has not vanished.

Some signs of backtracking appeared in the discussions of the "anti-parasite" laws, which began with the publication of draft statutes in 1957. Under these drafts, "able-bodied citizens leading an anti-social, parasitic way of life" could be tried at a public meeting of their fellow citizens and be sentenced to as much as two to five years at forced labor. Discussions of the drafts and criticism by jurists led to changes in the final law, including the provision that the regular courts would take jurisdiction in most anti-parasite cases. In 1964 the poet Yosif Brodsky was punished under the statute, despite depositions by literary figures as to his talent, because he lived at home and eked out a precarious living by translating Western literature. Notes taken at the trial by Soviet spectators and smuggled abroad reveal that his sentence—five years on a state farm, only part of which he served before being released—reflected a dislike by the judge of what he considered "pornographic" and unpatriotic elements in Brodsky's poems.

In 1965, the anti-parasite laws were further amended to prevent their misuse, and little has been heard since of their application, although they remain on the books and still contain many disturbing features. In more recent years, criminology as a social science discipline has been restored, and professionals in the field are beginning to do some empirical work; they are, however, still seriously limited by official ideology, and there are only a few signs of a more knowledgeable approach to the questions of crime.[13]

In the early 1960's, the punishment for "economic crimes" was also made more stringent. In 1961 and 1962, decrees established the death penalty by shooting for such crimes as the taking of bribes and speculation. The decrees, not all of which have been published, were quite broadly worded, and a large, although undetermined, number of persons have been tried and executed for violating their terms. The trial accounts made public in the Soviet press have been far from complete, but in some cases they indicate that the decrees may have been applied retroactively. Nevertheless, in 1964 the Supreme Court of the U.S.S.R. did reverse a death sentence in an embezzlement case and implied that the death penalty should not be indiscriminately used.

Other crimes for which the death penalty may now be applied include an attempt on

the life of a police official or member of the people's militia. And new crimes have been added, among them the "criminally" wrongful use or maintenance of agricultural material and the distortion of accounts concerning plan fulfillment. Further, the definition of some crimes—and their penalties—have been broadened. By West European standards, then, Soviet criminal law remains harsh.

It is true that on occasion the regime has tried to deal somewhat gently with those who are found guilty, particularly for the first time, of what are considered minor offenses, such as stealing small items of personal property or fighting after overimbibing vodka. In these cases, emphasis upon the teaching function of law and the rehabilitation of the criminal has been most pronounced. Yet even with first offenders signs of retrenchment are evident as crime rates continue to mount. In 1966, for example, several new decrees on "hooliganism" and "malicious hooliganism" gave the local police greater authority in dealing with such offenses through administrative action. Penalties for more serious instances of hooliganism were stiffened, and it was announced that henceforth intoxication would be considered an aggravating circumstance of a crime, not an extenuating one. Also, the penalty for using or attempting to use a knife in the execution of a crime was raised from two years to seven; persons convicted of disorderly behavior can no longer receive mail in prison; and prisoners must clean streets and do other menial work without pay. Lacking theories which can explain the increasing incidence of crime in a Socialist society, Soviet lawmakers still tend to alternate between moral preachments and more rigorous penalties when a general relaxation of either indicates that a crimeless utopia has not yet arrived.

Certainly ignorance of the law is no excuse; Soviet criminal codes are widely published, and massive efforts are made in the press to educate Soviet citizens on the content of the law. Newspapers, too, give considerable attention to judicial activities in an effort to

13 See Robert J. Osborn, "Crime and the Environment: The New Soviet Debate," *Slavic Review*, XXVII (September 1968), pp. 395–410, and the summary of articles on juvenile delinquency and crime which appeared in Soviet law journals early in 1969 in *The Current Digest of the Soviet Press*, May 21, 1969, pp. 8–14.

make Russians aware of their rights and obligations.

5. THE ADMINISTRATION OF JUSTICE

In attempting to develop legal institutions that accord with the assumptions of a Communist society, the Soviet leadership has found itself facing the same conflicting pressures it has experienced in defining the substance of the law. In the days immediately after the Revolution, the entire court system as well as the legal profession was abolished, and justice was administered by revolutionary people's courts composed primarily of laymen. The methods used were barbaric in many cases, and those safeguards which are considered an integral part of any civilized legal order were almost entirely absent. Individuals were tried and sentenced on the basis of flimsy evidence, and slaughtered in any number of ways; some were burned, some drawn and quartered.

Within a very short time, however, a system of courts was inaugurated. The legal profession became active, and rules were adopted to insure that somewhat more equitable trial procedures were followed in ordinary civil and criminal cases. Again the questions arose on what role the courts should play, what function lawyers should have, and what laws and legal procedures would conform most closely with the aims of a Communist state.

The Soviets looked to Europe and to their own traditions for solutions to these issues. In creating a formal legal structure and defining the place of the court in a Communist society, they found themselves copying from both traditional Russian patterns and continental European procedures, which they found more congenial than the Anglo-Saxon. The regime, therefore, espoused "inquisitorial" procedures in criminal cases, with a full investigation conducted by the government in advance of the trial. The role of the court was conceived as that of bringing out the truth through direct judicial participation, and

not of maintaining a set of rules defining the evidence and techniques that could be used by the prosecution and the defense. Further, the court was given far more freedom than that allowed English or American judges to weigh the defendant's background and character in determining the sentence. The defendant's attitude toward the Revolution also entered into the judicial equation.

American commentators on Soviet law are less than sympathetic to such procedures; too often they assume that they are necessarily unfair and are reflections of the regime's ideological assumptions. Yet it should be remembered that the Anglo-Saxon jury trial is not very popular around the world, and that most jury trials are held in the United States. It is indeed true that the procedures adopted by the Soviets were partially related to their view of the law as essentially a political instrument—a means of serving the community's needs in the broadest sense. But most Continental countries that follow the French model also use similar techniques. The Soviets do, of course, go much further than continental Europeans in tailoring decisions to meet particular policy imperatives, and they have also tended to stress the class background of the accused, although the differences between Soviet and French or German judges can be overdrawn. In France, a man of good bourgeois background is more likely to be let off easily than someone from the slums of Paris who is a confirmed "troublemaker"; in the Soviet Union, a bourgeois background often told against a defendant in the 1920's and 1930's, although today the courts are likely to be far more lenient with someone from the middle class or "solid" working class than they are with an idler who has a poor work record.

The Soviet Union has drawn upon the experience of Western legal systems in other areas too—or, at least, arrived at the same conclusions. The initial attitude of the Bolshevik regime toward "ordinary" crimes was that the criminal was as much victim as was the person injured, and the courts magnified the importance of testimony establishing environmental conditions as a cause of criminal acts. Definitions of mitigating circumstances were extremely broad. In the 1930's, a marked increase in the crime rate and the constant repetition of criminal acts by the same "victims" of environment resulted in a return to traditional notions of responsibility. In more recent years, Soviet jurists have chosen a middle position that, however, is still far less sophisticated than the advanced thinking of Western criminologists.

The Soviet legal profession, growing in size and influence, has been among the most important groups pressing for rationalization of court procedures. It is, therefore, tempting to argue that all industrial countries are moving together; yet the situation is not quite that simple. Marxist dictum is still accepted on the deterioration of formal state structures and the active participation by the "people," as indicated by the establishment of comrades' courts. Then, too, far more explicitly than in most Western nations, the Soviet Union continues to regard the primary function of the court as social—part of the mechanism of socialization by which citizens shall be transformed into ideal Soviet men. To be sure, the United States has moved somewhat in this direction; in some phases of American life, as in the area of civil rights, the courts have served as devices for achieving social purposes. Nonetheless, Americans remain convinced that the function of a court is principally that of an arbiter and that most individual activity should be left as unfettered as possible.

THE COURTS:[14] Decree No. 1 on the courts, issued by the Council of People's Commissars shortly after the Bolsheviks seized power, eliminated the tribunals that had developed under the empire and provided instead for two new kinds of courts. The first were lower

courts of original jurisdiction, called people's courts; members were to be elected on the basis of "democratic principles." The second were workers' and peasants' revolutionary tribunals; these courts were set up to deal with crimes against the Revolution. In addition, the regime created administrative boards, under the supervision of the secret police, that also handled political crimes.

Both the people's courts and the revolutionary tribunals underwent a series of reorganizations until 1923, a year in which the legal system attained a degree of stability. In the early years, summary justice was the rule, but after 1923 more regular procedures were observed. These procedures did not, however, apply to the special boards of the secret police, which continued to adjudicate antistate activity until they were abolished after Stalin's death.

Today, all the regular courts in the Soviet Union constitute a single judicial system, the main features of which are governed by federal legislation. Only one court, the Supreme Court of the U.S.S.R., is a federal court; all others are republican courts, although they enforce both republican and federal laws.

The lowest general courts are the people's courts established in each district (*rayon*). These are courts of original jurisdiction for minor criminal cases and a large number of civil cases. The judge for each court is elected directly by the district's constituents for a period of five years. Under the 1948 statute of judicial elections, nomination of judges is reserved to the Communist Party and related organizations. In effect, judges—who today have at least some legal training—are appointed by the party; only a single slate of candidates has ever been presented at an election. And while judges are technically subject to recall, those who fall into disfavor are usually dismissed by the party or the republic's ministry of justice.

Most cases in people's courts are tried before a bench consisting of a judge and two assessors, the latter having been elected in the same manner as the judge but serving for only

[14] Soviet military courts will not be described. The State Arbitration Commissions and the comrades' courts, described on pp. 651–652, are not technically part of the regular court system.

FIGURE 21.1. THE STRUCTURE OF SOVIET COURTS

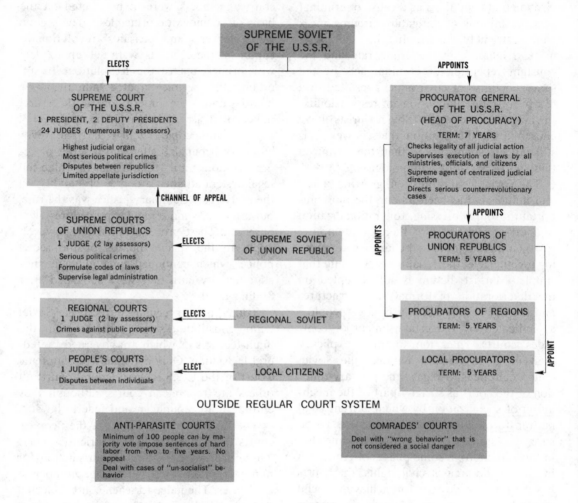

Adapted from Gwendolen M. Carter and John H. Herz,
Major Foreign Powers, 5th ed. (New York: Harcourt,
Brace and World, 1967), p. 592. Reprinted by permis-
sion of the publisher.

ten consecutive days a year. All three have equal rights and jointly decide questions of law and fact. Assessors also sit in higher courts whenever these serve as courts of original jurisdiction. It is a judicial pattern that closely resembles many Continental systems, especially the German, and there is little doubt that the opinions of the Soviet judge carry more weight than those of the two assessors combined, despite formal voting equality. Even so, most observers agree that

Soviet courts are far more informal than German courts and that the social distance between judge and assessors—and, indeed, between judge and defendant—is not nearly so great as in other European countries.

Above the level of the people's courts, the structure of the court system is not uniform throughout the Soviet Union. Where regions and provinces exist, courts have been created for these political subdivisions. In the smaller republics, however, the supreme court of the republic is the next higher echelon. Judges and assessors for these courts are elected by the highest government body of the territory, and they may be recalled.

In the R.S.F.S.R. and other large constituent republics, provincial and regional courts serve as courts of original jurisdiction for the more important criminal cases, and for all civil cases above the jurisdiction of the people's courts. Such cases are heard before a judge and two assessors. In cases that have been appealed to these courts from the people's courts, a three-judge bench makes the decision, which is final. The supreme court of a republic may, however, assume the jurisdiction of a case triable by any lower court, and thereby become a court of original jurisdiction. The supreme court decisions of the constituent republics are final. However, a case may be brought before the U.S.S.R. Supreme Court for review upon protest of the U.S.S.R. procurator general or the president of the U.S.S.R. Supreme Court; private parties cannot appeal decisions of the supreme courts of Soviet republics, but they can petition the procurator general and the president of the Supreme Court to do so for them, and this procedure has been followed.

Originally, the U.S.S.R. Supreme Court was established as a consultative body to the Central Executive Committee of the All-Russian Congress of Soviets, which, in 1922, was the highest governing body of the Soviet Union. The court could offer authoritative opinions to the supreme courts of the constituent republics on matters relating to federal legislation, but it had no authority to reverse their decisions. It could review such decisions on the motion of the procurator general, but it had to submit its opinion to the Central Executive Committee, which alone had the authority to make a final ruling.[15]

In 1935, the U.S.S.R. Supreme Court was

granted the power to quash decisions of the supreme courts of the republics, but only if, in its opinion, such decisions contravened federal legislation or interfered with the interests of other republics. The 1936 constitution and the Judiciary Act of 1938 further extended the power of the Supreme Court. It was then authorized, on the filing of protests by the procurator general of the U.S.S.R. and the president of the U.S.S.R. Supreme Court, to superintend the administration of justice by all the judicial bodies of the U.S.S.R. and constituent republics. Legislation in 1957 reduced the power of the U.S.S.R. Supreme Court somewhat, but much of it had been restored by 1967. It should be noted, however, that decisions by the U.S.S.R. Supreme Court are still constitutionally subject to review by the Presidium of the Supreme Soviet.

Today, the Supreme Court of the U.S.S.R. consists of its president, two deputies and nine justices elected by the Supreme Soviet, and the presidents of the 15 supreme courts of the individual republics, making a total of 27 judges. The number of elected assessors varies. When the court is serving as a court of original jurisdiction, the U.S.S.R. Supreme Court usually meets in plenary session for both criminal and civil cases.

Property and contract disputes between economic enterprises belonging to different ministries are handled by a number of economic courts called State Arbitration Commissions (*Arbitrazh*). Disputes arising within a single ministry are dealt with by departmental arbitrazh under the general supervision of the state group. The economic courts or commissions are hierarchically organized, with the courts on each level of authority responsible to different state administrative bodies. Councils of ministers of the various republics appoint the members of the republic arbitrazh, supervise their activities, and theoretically have the power to reverse or modify their decisions. Uniformity is maintained by the State Arbitrazh of the U.S.S.R.

---

15 The Central Executive Committee, which is not to be confused with the Central Committee of the Communist Party, was roughly equivalent to the present Presidium of the Supreme Soviet.

Council of Ministers, which may remove cases from the lower economic courts and which periodically publishes "collections of instructions" containing reports of cases, directives, and information on relevant new statutes. The national commission also convenes meetings of the republic arbitration commissions, during which common problems are discussed.

Arbitrazh personnel are not always lawyers; they are, however, invariably assisted by legal staffs, and most of them have received legal training. Originally, this was not the case: the arbitrazh were founded as arbitration agencies whose function was simply to implement an economic plan. Because of the bias against bourgeois legal concepts at the time (1931), it was clearly understood that they would not be bound by provisions of the civil code, and lawyers were specifically barred from membership. By 1938, however, it had become apparent that these commissions must operate according to standard legal techniques, and the statutes passed in the early 1960's recodifying arbitrazh procedure require that they operate in accordance with the norms established by the civil law codes.

Two types of social "courts," which are also outside the regular court system, have been created as well. The first anti-parasite laws provided for citizens' meetings of workers in a plant, or peasants on a kolkhoz, to decide upon penalties for certain social crimes, with only the remotest possibility that their verdicts would be reviewed by regular judicial authority. However, under pressure from Soviet lawyers, the law was gradually modified, and by 1965 its administration was placed with the local soviets or the regular court system.

The comrades' courts are of a somewhat different character. These courts date from 1919, but until their reorganization in 1959 they were primarily concerned with problems of labor discipline in industrial enterprises. The expansion of their functions was associated officially with the regime's desire

not only to begin transferring state functions to social organizations but also to allow these courts to act as an effective device for discouraging forms of antisocial conduct.

Today, comrades' courts are set up on either a residential basis—they are organized within an apartment building or complex of apartment buildings—or an occupational basis, within an industrial plant, commercial enterprise, or government bureau. The state does not officially require that such courts be established; the decision to do so rests with members of the collective unit. Members of comrades' courts, and each must contain at least 25 persons, are elected at a general meeting of the collective and serve for a term of one year. Those elected then choose a chairman, vice-chairman, and secretary.

Comrades' courts hear many kinds of cases —from the use of foul language to tardiness at work. Cases may pertain to violations of labor discipline, such as the poor quality of work, failure to observe industrial-safety regulations, or drunkenness or reprovable conduct including improper attire in public places or at work. The courts have also heard cases involving persons accused of unworthy behavior toward women and parents, harm done to dwellings and other premises, certain types of property disputes between citizens who are members of the same collective, and "other antisocial offenses, not entailing criminal liability."

A complaint from any citizen or the transfer of a file from the police courts, other state agencies, and civic (non-state) organizations can cause comrades' courts to be convened. Cases are heard in public after working hours, and documentation and witnesses may be required at the court's discretion, although it has no power of subpoena. The trial audience may, with the court's permission, put questions and make comments on the case. Some American observers have noted that frequently the comments from the audience are dominated by party members and other activists whose remarks appear to have been prepared well in advance. The court's decision is

FIGURE 21.2. MEMBERS OF COMRADES' COURTS: BY AGE, DURATION OF EMPLOYMENT, AND PARTY MEMBERSHIP

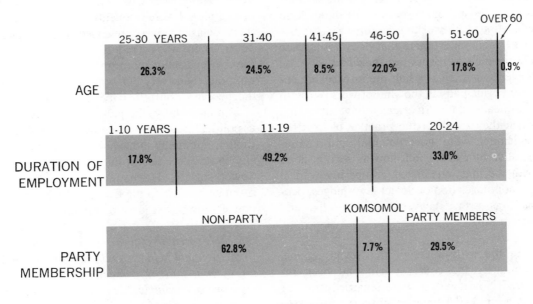

Adapted from Darrell P. Hammer, "Political Implications of Recent Trends in Soviet Legal Theory," paper presented for delivery at 1964 annual meeting of the American Political Science Association (mimeographed), p. 3. Reprinted by permission of the publisher.

by majority of the elected members participating, and it is expressed in writing.

Numerous sanctions are available. Sometimes the penalty for those found guilty is merely the evidence of sincere repentance. Sometimes voluntary compensation, a public apology, or a comradely warning is considered a sufficient sanction. Defendants have also been publicly reprimanded or fined as much as fifty rubles. The court may also recommend demotion or eviction from a housing project to appropriate agencies. Finally, a comrades' court may send a case on to a people's court. The case may also be reviewed by other groups such as the trade-union committee or the executive committee of the local soviet. Despite the variety of sanctions which comrades' courts may apply, however, it is fairly evident that their objective is not so much punishment as it is repentance, confession, and self-criticism.

Although the anti-parasite assemblies were

challenged by Soviet lawyers from the very beginning, the comrades' courts seem to have won a reasonable amount of acceptance. They were created and are sustained, of course, out of ideological considerations, and to the Western European and American, they undoubtedly appear as highly repressive mechanisms and as a means by which the community is organized to control any form of errant behavior. And, indeed, they do serve this function. But they are also a device for dealing with antisocial behavior without imposing criminal sanctions. Because of the psychological impact of the penalties which these courts have at their disposal, however, one wonders whether there are sufficient legal safeguards to insure that decisions be equitable. But whether proper safeguards exist or not, comrades' courts are likely to remain part of the scene for some time to come; as of 1967, more than 100,000 were estimated to be operating in the R.S.F.S.R. alone.

THE LEGAL PROFESSION AND PEOPLE'S AS-
SESSORS: As of 1965, roughly 100,000 persons with a higher or intermediate legal
education were working as jurists in the Soviet Union, an estimate that does not include
the people's assessors impaneled to serve on
Soviet courts. Nearly half the jurists were engaged principally in the kind of work Western
Europeans and Americans have in mind
when they speak of the practice of law; the
remainder were governmental and administrative officials. The following section deals
with the most significant groups involved in
the administration of Soviet law: judges, people's assessors, lawyers, jurisconsults, and
procurators.

In the early years of the Soviet regime,
even after the court system had been restored, Soviet judges were regarded more or
less as trained laymen. Unlike the assessors,
they had a full-time job and were paid for it;
nevertheless, it was considered that law in a
Socialist state was a relatively simple matter
which could be understood by all men if

they consulted their "revolutionary consciousness." Terms of judges were short—one year
—and judges were frequently dismissed when
their decisions were reversed by a higher
court. There was no requirement that a judge
have a legal education, and as late as 1949
no more than forty per cent of the judges of
the people's courts had been to law school.

Fundamentally, the judge was regarded as
a political worker—an individual who, although nominally independent, had of necessity to decide cases in line with the goals of
Soviet society. He had, therefore, to subordinate himself to the Communist Party. As
one leading Soviet jurist described it in 1936:

*Our judge is above all a politician, a worker
in the political field . . . and therefore he must
know what the government wants and guide
his work accordingly . . . therefore, the court
must be organized so as to make it possible
to direct the judgment in conformity with the
aim of the State policy pursued by the government. . . . We look at the court as a
class institution, as an agency of government*

"I promise to live in peace with my neighbor. I won't say another word about that
bitch!"—*Krokodil.*

*power, and we erect it as an agency com-
pletely under the control of the vanguard
of the working class . . . dependent upon and
removable by the soviet power.*[16]

The growing complexity of Soviet law,
however, and the gradual acceptance of the
idea that the effective functioning of Soviet
society required consistent adherence to established legal criteria, eventually led to a revision in the status of judges. Their terms
have been lengthened little by little and the
quality of their training has improved. A Soviet law student now begins training immediately upon graduation from secondary school.
Intermediate legal education is the equivalent
of about two years of college in the United
States, while higher legal education is equivalent to four more years of training at the
college or university level. In 1967, it was
estimated that 85 per cent of all Soviet judges
had received a higher legal education. Judges
are elected, and may be removed only by
those who voted them into office. Judges of
supreme courts, for example, are elected by
their corresponding supreme soviets, those
of regional courts by regional soviets, and the
people's court judges through general elections in their districts. However, the choice
of judicial candidates is determined in advance by the Communist Party, and the elections are merely pro forma.

Soviet jurists now argue that not only is the
Revolution best served by observing legal
norms, but inadequate laws should be formally changed rather than be constantly reinterpreted or unofficially transformed by
party or state organs. In 1963, in a rather
revolutionary statement of its own, the Supreme Court of the Soviet Union issued a set
of guiding principles specifically urging that
all legal decisions be made "under conditions
which exclude any external influence upon
the judges." It remains true, nonetheless, that

most if not all judges are members of the
Communist Party, and that both the state and
the party have violated these instructions
under certain circumstances. Yet unquestionably, the judiciary has achieved greater independence which in turn has been associated
with a larger role for judges in the lawmaking
process and with the increased importance of
precedent.

In the early years of the Soviet regime the
idea of *stare decisis* was rejected by Soviet
theorists. It was argued that:

*Judicial precedent loses its significance, be-
ing driven out by written law. The penetration
of revolutionary dialectics into the consciousness of judges is important above all in order
that their practice . . . may not become ossified through blind adherence to the letter of
precedent.*[17]

Thus, early explanations of the function of
superior courts always noted that their decisions were binding on the lower only on a
specific case and in "no way have the force
of law or of a binding interpretation of the
law."[18]

After 1936, the value of previous judicial
decisions began to be recognized. In a series
of governmental acts, the U.S.S.R. Supreme
Court, especially, was recognized as having
the authority to issue "directive rulings." As
the statute of February 12, 1957, declared:

*Section 9. The Plenary Session (full bench)
of the U.S.S.R. Supreme Court . . . (c) shall
examine the materials pertaining to the generalization of judicial practice and give directive rulings to the courts. . . .*[19]

Since 1938, the Supreme Court has issued
many comprehensive rulings in order to fill
in the details of Soviet codes. Much of Soviet
economic law in particular has become case
law. Precedent of a kind, then, has become an

---

16 N. V. Krylenko, quoted in Vladimir Gsovski and
Kazimierz Grzybowski, gen. eds., *Government, Law
and Courts in the Soviet Union and Eastern Europe,*
I (New York: Praeger, 1959), 516.

17 *Ibid.*, p. 541.
18 *Ibid.*
19 *Ibid.*, p. 542.

important part of certain areas of Soviet law—even though Soviet theorists are as yet loath to admit it. All the same, so long as the Presidium of the Council of Ministers can and does so readily issue decree laws, and so long as law and the courts still continue to be considered primarily political instruments, it is doubtful that precedent will achieve much overall value as doctrine.

From 1917 on, panels of "elected" people's assessors have been attached to all courts, including the U.S.S.R. Supreme Court. Originally, twelve assessors sat in on all court cases, but by 1922 the number had been reduced to two in all jurisdictions except that of the U.S.S.R. Supreme Court, where the number of assessors is determined by the Supreme Soviet at each election.

To be an assessor, a Soviet citizen needs only to be at least 25 years old and in full possession of his civil rights. Assessors are elected in the same manner as judges, serving for a two-year term if they are attached to people's courts and a five-year term for all other courts. They normally attend court for not more than two weeks a year, and they are paid for their services.

Together with the judge, assessors are responsible for both the verdict and the sentence, but in practice their part in the proceedings is far more passive. As one writer explained it:

Unfortunately, it is not rare for the equal rights of the assessors and judge . . . to be reduced to the active rôle played by the presiding judge alone, and this gives rise to the opinion among citizens that the 'judge passed sentence.'[20]

Suggestions for increasing the number and authority of the people's assessors were pressed at the time that new legal codes were being

[20] Quoted in Robert Conquest, *Justice and the Legal System in the U.S.S.R.* (London: Bodley Head, Ltd., 1968), p. 31. This section on assessors is based on Conquest's discussion.

considered in the 1950's and 1960's. All such proposals, however, were rejected in drafting the new legislation.

The position of the lawyer—or advocate— in the Soviet Union has changed even more radically than that of the judge. Decree No. 1 opened the practice of law to "all honest persons of either sex"—a broad policy that quickly proved unsatisfactory. Decree No. 2, issued four months later in March 1918, admitted to the practice only handpicked "legal representatives" who would act as either government prosecutors or defense counsels. These representatives were appointed by local soviets and paid by the state. But difficulties surfaced here, too, especially during the years of the N.E.P. when defendants, to assure that their trials did not go too badly, offered fees to both their attorneys and the prosecutors.

In the 1920's, lawyers were permitted to engage in private practice, although they were required to provide "legal consultation services" free of charge. The second Soviet revolution, however, resulted in the "collectivization of the bar." In fact, collectivization of the legal profession barely withstood the initial, widespread pressure for its complete abolition. Legal defense activity was centered in collectives of defense attorneys who were assigned specific cases. Some fifty per cent of the collective's income was distributed among its members, with the remainder being allocated for the administration of the collective and other never clearly defined purposes.

Today, each oblast has its own college of attorneys. They are divided into legal consultation centers established at the seats of rayons and in cities. A citizen requiring legal service applies to one of these centers, where he is assigned a lawyer upon payment of a fixed fee. In some cases he may, if the manager of the center is willing, choose his own lawyer. Lawyers still receive their compensation from the center, and their share of its income has risen to about seventy per cent of the fees paid. Since fees are still very low, lawyers are apt to respond positively to suggestions by clients that they accept additional retainers which would be paid on the sly, a practice which, if discovered, can lead to disbarment.

The public's evaluation of just what function a lawyer fulfills has also undergone a transformation. In the early 1920's, plaintiffs who relied upon lawyers in civil cases were usually considered to be out to gain private advantage through underhanded means, since, it was thought, civil suits should not occur in a Socialist country. And in criminal cases, an extensive pre-trial investigation often led to the belief that a lawyer on such a case had no really legitimate function since the defendant would not be before the court in the first place unless he were guilty. This awkward position of the legal profession was even more trying in "political" cases, where taking on the defense of an accused might place a lawyer in considerable personal jeopardy. In all of these situations, the regime argued that the first duty of the lawyer was not to defend his client but to get at the truth. No lawyer was supposed to rely on technicalities or "tricks"; on the contrary, he was expected to present the court with material damaging to his client, if he were at all aware of it.

Even before Stalin's death, however, the role of the defense attorney in criminal cases was being re-examined. As early as 1948, some Soviet jurists were arguing that he should be allowed greater latitude in the defense of his client and not be regarded merely as an acolyte of the court. More and more officials have since maintained that the belief that defense attorneys are basically disruptive is "alien" to the conception of Soviet legality. These arguments have finally resulted in the publication of instructional manuals on the conduct of the defense, and the Soviet attorney is now encouraged to bring out all the facts and circumstances favorable to his client —provided, of course, that he does not compromise his allegiance to the state. At least as important is the fact that judges are now better trained, and adhere more frequently to legal norms than to their own "Socialist consciousness."

The bulk of the Soviet advocate's work still approximates that of any capitalist country: housing and family disputes, personal-injury litigation, contractual claims (see Table 21.1). It is estimated that, in 1963, advocates gave legal advice to some 2,500,000 persons in the Russian republic alone.

But however improved their status may be, lawyers remain the cinderellas of the legal profession, and it will be many years before the Soviet Union develops a concept of the

TABLE 21.1. A TYPICAL YEAR'S CASE LOAD FOR SOVIET LAWYERS
IN A MOSCOW RAYON

Type of case	Number of cases	Percentage
Housing	2,234	25.5
Family	1,760	20.0
Criminal	1,630	18.5
Civil	860	9.8
Pension	844	9.6
Labor	642	7.3
Redress of injury	550	6.3
Inheritance	264	3.0
Total	8,784	100.0

Adapted from Robert Conquest, *Justice and the Legal System in the U.S.S.R.* (London: The Bodley Head, Ltd., 1968), p. 36. Reprinted by permission of the publisher.

rights of defendants comparable with that of Western European nations. Lawyers are still criticized by party officials for placing their client's interest above that of the community. Because of their low prestige and their relatively low salaries, the number of advocates in the Soviet Union remains extraordinarily small; the best estimates indicate that as of 1968 a mere 13,000 lawyers were serving the entire Soviet population.

Very little is known of the work of jurisconsults in the Soviet Union. Most of them are employees of the state's larger commercial and industrial enterprises, in which they serve many functions. For the most part, they give legal advice and representation to management in its relations with other organizations, and advise both management and workers on their rights and obligations toward each other. They are also responsible for reporting any legal violations by the enterprise to superior agencies.

Jurisconsults have never been subject to the same kind of ideological attacks experienced by advocates, but their status has varied with the amount of independence accorded industrial firms. The expansion of the legal profession since 1959 has been largely concentrated in the business sector, and its prestige and influence will undoubtedly continue to grow if trends toward greater independence for individual enterprises continue.

The office of the procurator general in the Soviet Union has no counterpart in Western Europe or the United States, although it might be roughly described as an office of the general prosecutor. First created by Peter the Great in the eighteenth century, its purpose was not only to bring order out of conflicting localisms but to check the tendency of subordinate czarist officials toward corruption and excessive use of their powers. In the nineteenth century, particularly after the reforms of 1864, its jurisdiction was considerably restricted, for it was justly regarded as a highly authoritarian instrument. For this reason, too, the Bolsheviks completely abolished the office in 1917.

But not for long. The Bolsheviks were establishing an administrative state, and strong forces were driving the party in the direction of centralization; thus, it was only natural that central bureaucratic controls would be created. With its roots deep in Russian history, it was not surprising, therefore, that after a number of experiments with other types of agencies, the procuracy was restored in 1922.

Article 113 of the Soviet constitution states that "supreme supervisory power over the strict execution of the laws by all ministries and institutions subordinated to them, as well as by officials and citizens of the U.S.S.R. generally, is vested in the procurator general of the U.S.S.R." Appointed by the Supreme Soviet for a term of seven years, the procurator general is responsible only to that body. He in turn appoints procurators for the republics, territories, and regions, and confirms their appointments for area, district, and city procurators. Republic procurators function independently of all local organs, being subordinate solely to the procurator general of the U.S.S.R.

The general supervisory power of the procuracy covers a vast area. Procurators keep watch over the entire system of administration to make certain that executive and administrative bodies never overstep their legal authority. They review all orders and regulations issued by regional, republican, and federal executive-administrative organs, and they sit in as consultants on sessions of local soviets. When a procurator considers an act passed by a governmental unit within his territorial jurisdiction to be in violation of the constitution of the U.S.S.R. or of the laws or decrees of higher governmental bodies, he may "protest" to the organ of government immediately superior to the one that approved the act. Procurators are also required to supervise the legality and correctness of actions by the state security organs, as well as by the police and other departments of criminal investigation.

The procuracy, as it relates to the judicial system, has the power not only to order the arrest of persons suspected of crime but to appoint the magistrates (investigators) who conduct the pre-trial examination in major criminal cases. Procurators also keep an eye on all civil proceedings, and they may initiate or enter any lawsuit at any stage on any side. Further, a procurator may "protest" any decision, civil or criminal, of any court to the next higher court, and he may move to reopen any case after a decision has been handed down. The final decision in these matters, however, resides with the court, although recommendations of the procuracy carry a good bit of weight.

Certain functions of the procurators, especially those involving pre-trial examinations, are performed by government attorneys in some Western legal systems. But in none of the other systems does the examining officer have quite so much power as he does in the Soviet Union. As one author has pointed out, the Soviet procuracy combines in one office the duties of the United States attorney general's office, congressional investigating committees, grand juries, and public prosecutors. This is an awesome aggregation of power.

CRIMINAL AND CIVIL PROCEDURE: The Soviet codes of criminal procedure adopted during the 1920's followed the inquisitorial practice of Imperial Russia and most continental European countries. They were, nevertheless, important departures. After Stalin died, the codes came more closely into accord with those of Western Europe, though significant differences still exist.

Soviet criminal codes originally provided that any arrest, to be valid, should have the approval of either a procurator or a court. It was also stipulated, however, that supervision of police inquiries—and arrests—conducted by state-security agencies would be regulated by special statutes. These statutes were never published, and it was left to the security agencies to determine whether the accused would be brought before the procuracy or the courts. The codes adopted in the post-Stalin period, on the other hand, provide that *all* police investigations shall be handled uniformly and that they shall be under the supervision of the procuracy.

The "trials" conducted by the state-security agencies during the 1920's and the 1930's were considered to be extrajudicial. So far as the regime was concerned, they involved administrative proceedings rather than judicial; consequently, they were handled by special boards. In 1956 it was announced semi-officially that these boards had been abolished; no legislative act or administrative decree has ever been issued to this effect, but all available information points to the fact that they are no longer in operation.

The special boards, like the military courts, were permitted to use summary procedures. Investigation in cases coming under their jurisdiction was to be concluded within a period of not more than ten days; the indictment was to be handed to the accused 24 hours before the "trial"; cases were to be heard without the participation of the defendant or his counsel; appeals from the judgment were forbidden; and a death sentence was to be carried out immediately upon the rendering of judgment. These laws, too, were repealed in 1956, and the 1958 statute on military tribunals limited their jurisdiction over civilians to cases of espionage or complicity in military crimes.

As in Germany, the codes of the 1920's provided for a preliminary investigation by an official from the procurator's office, whose function was to interrogate the accused and to gather all the information relevant to a possible indictment. An investigation was normally to last no more than two months, but it could be extended indefinitely; and during this time, the accused could be jailed. Under the present codes, confinement may not continue beyond nine months, although the investigation can go on thereafter. Neither the earlier nor the present codes grant the accused the right to have visitors or to send or receive letters or telephone calls during the investigation—in short, he may be held incommunicado for nine months. Suspects may also be detained for ten days without being apprised of the nature of their "crime." The decision to indict a prisoner or to dismiss the case rests with the investigator, but the procurator has the authority to overrule him.

The codes of the 1920's completely excluded counsel from the preliminary investigation. Only after the indictment was finally issued and a trial ordered did the defendant obtain the right to see a lawyer. After the death of Stalin, the whole question of lawyer participation in criminal cases was intensely debated. The result has been only a slight modification of previous regulations. The new codes permit the appearance of defense counsel after the investigator decides all the necessary measures have been taken prior to his "conclusion to indict."

Originally, defendants were permitted to appeal to the courts or to the procuracy against the improper conduct of pre-trial investigations. But after 1929, appeals could only be made to the procuracy. Thus, an accused person wishing to appeal a decision to indict can only submit his appeal to the next highest level of the procuracy hierarchy itself, although courts can, at their own discretion, decide that an indictment is not warranted after a preliminary hearing preceding the trial. The real problem here, of course, is that the courts are timid about contravening the decisions of the procuracy, and the procurators know that their reputation depends in part on the number of successful indictments and convictions they can obtain.

In an effort to curb the zeal of procurators, the new codes provide that a procurator cannot order the investigator to indict. Even so, because the advancement of an investigator's career depends upon the approval of his superiors, the reform has its shortcomings. Some Soviet jurists have contended that the authority to conduct a preliminary investigation should be taken completely out of the hands of the procurator's office and placed with the judiciary or an independent official; so far, they have not succeeded in winning their point.

The 1920 codes offered fairly satisfactory procedural guarantees for cases tried in the people's courts. However, higher courts retained extensive jurisdiction as courts of first instance in serious crimes, and they came to assume broader prerogatives in dealing with appeals. Moreover, in these higher courts, certain important guarantees were lacking; for example, the procurator and the defense counsel could be excluded from court, and decisions could be made on the basis of evidence not considered during either the pre-trial investigation or the original trial. By the 1960's, these discretionary powers had been almost entirely eliminated, and other significant changes pertaining to the codes had also been instituted. The codes of the 1920's contained no provisions regarding the burden of proof of guilt; in addition, a number of 1930 statutes went even further, all but placing the burden of proof of innocence upon the defendant. The new codes repudiate former procedures, although, despite the insistence of some Soviet jurists, the presumption of innocence is not formally written into the codes.

The early codes also gave both the defendant and the procurator the right to appeal any sentence. An appeal was always to the next higher court, and only one appeal was allowed. However, once a sentence went into effect, the procurator or the chairman of the court of original jurisdiction could bring about a review of the case by way of a procedure called "supervision," and such review appeals could be pressed as far as the Supreme Court of the U.S.S.R. In their appellate capacity, the higher courts could set aside verdicts, or remand the case to the lower court for retrial or for a reduction of sentence. But they could also find the defendant guilty after he had been declared innocent; further, they had the power to increase a sentence and even to retry the defendant under another statute that permitted more severe penalties.

The new codes have eliminated these higher-court prerogatives in the case of appeals by either the defendant or the procurator. In cases of supervisory review, the appellate court can still remand the case to the court of first instance—with instructions suggesting that the sentence was too light or that a law governing a graver crime is applicable. And, since an appeal by a defendant can, under certain circumstances, prompt judges of a higher court to suggest a supervisory review, the possibility of his appeal resulting in a stiffer sentence is not absent. The new codes, furthermore, are not always observed; in fact, Soviet courts have on occasion violated their provisions and reverted to the earlier procedures. On March 25, 1961, for example, three men were tried by the Moscow city court for illegal dealings in foreign currency and sentenced to 15 years, the maximum penalty under the new statutes dealing with economic crimes. The procurator-general appealed the sentence and the case went to the supreme court of the R.S.F.S.R. In the meantime, a new decree was issued raising the penalty to death by shooting; the defendants were tried under the new statute and executed.[21]

The new codes, like the old, place very few restrictions upon the admission of evidence, being far more relaxed on the issue of admissibility than are those in non-Communist code countries. Here the Communist regime is still in earnest about having the court serve an educational function, as the background of the defendant is examined in great detail in order to discover the reasons why he committed a criminal act. Another sign of the regime's continuing interest in the use of courts for doctrinal ends is seen in the participation of "social organizations" in the many trials held in factories or other places closely connected with the circumstances of a case. Such trials are called "visiting sessions," and any social organization may petition to have its representative appear in any criminal case as either social accuser or social defense counsel. They may present evidence and question the parties to the trial, as well as the witnesses, and they may even comment on points of law and the sentence. In 1964 and 1965 one quarter of all criminal trials were held in visiting sessions. The educational effort of such trials has, on occasion, seemed to backfire. As one observer has pointed out, trials by visiting session are usually chosen to

highlight a campaign against a common offense, and once a decision to deal with the case in visiting session is made, it is difficult for the judge or the procurator to accept less than a conviction and a fairly stiff sentence. In some cases, the trial brings out evidence which makes the spectators—and, one suspects, the judges and assessors—feel that a harsh sentence is not appropriate. The court, however, is almost forced to impose one.[22]

Many Western observers have argued that the inquisitorial system in the Soviet Union weights cases on the side of the prosecution. This criticism, especially on the part of Anglo-American lawyers, stems partially from a bias in favor of the adversary system. Yet it cannot be denied that there is more than a little truth in what they say. Even beyond the fact that Soviet society is devoid of many of the legal safeguards Western Europeans deem theirs by right, it is unquestionably true that justice depends heavily upon the goodwill of the procurator. In France and Germany, the status and authority of judges are greater than those of government attorneys, which yields a more or less effective check upon the abuse of authority by the attorneys. But the immense prestige and authority of the procurator's office in the Soviet Union, and the more extensive legal training given the procuracy, permit Soviet prosecutors to exert an influence in the courts that is far more pervasive than that plied by their Western European counterparts. In more recent years, Soviet jurists have begun to balk at the pre-eminent position enjoyed by procurators, and many have denounced the tendency of judges and assessors to assume automatically that an individual is guilty simply because he has been brought to trial. They have insisted that the presumption of innocence must hold in fact as well as in theory, even though it is not explicitly included in the new codes.

In political cases, of course, the new codes

[21] The case was reported in the June 16 and July 21, 1961 issues of *Pravda*.

[22] See the fascinating description and analysis of one such trial by Peter Juviler, "Mass Education and Justice in Soviet Courts: The Visiting Sessions," *Soviet Studies*, XVIII (April 1967), pp. 494–510.

are still openly violated. To all Western observers, the trials of dissenting intellectuals in 1967 and 1968 involved excessively lengthy pre-trial detention, stacked courtrooms, and highly selective press coverage. The presumption of guilt seemed again an obvious tenet of the Soviet courts; at least, the verdict of guilty was scarcely in doubt.

Soviet civil procedure has more of an adversary quality than criminal procedure. But here, too, the teaching role of the law, and the belief that all disputes affect the community at large, have an important bearing on a case. In a civil trial, the court is required not only to deal with the issues under litigation but also to consider any other social issues that arise during the case. Nor is the will of the parties to the court action on the disposition of the case the sole consideration: even if they choose to compromise or the plaintiff wishes to drop the case, the court may decide to render a judgment. Indeed, the court may give a remedy quite beyond that originally demanded by the plaintiff.

6. CONCLUSIONS

The Soviet Union has not succeeded in abolishing "law" or the legal profession, as those who made the Revolution had hoped it might. Neither has it succeeded in creating a completely unique system of law. Rather, what has emerged is an amalgam of diverse influences, including that manifest in the Socialist character of Soviet society. Unquestionably, the Socialist element in Soviet law will continue to differentiate it from non-Socialist countries for some time to come. Yet in a number of important areas, distinct signs of convergence are apparent, particularly in the development of common attitudes toward procedures. Soviet law still contains many arbitrary elements, especially in regard to "political crimes." Nevertheless, even the trials of 1967 and 1968, and their result, represent a distinct advance over Stalinist justice—and they must be seen in this perspective.

22

Bureaucracy

1. INTRODUCTION

The administrative structures that are such an integral part of modern societies are fundamentally mechanisms for mobilizing resources to gain specific ends. They are, in other words, tools developed by the society—or organizations within the society—to implement policies. Whether these structures be within governmental institutions, political parties, or in business organizations, they become more complex as contemporary social orders grow in breadth and intricacy.

Historically, the most efficient administrative structures have been those that approximated the model of rational bureaucratic authority described by Max Weber, for whom the essential characteristics of bureaucratic organization, either public or private, are as follows.

1. Organizations function according to sets of general, written rules, which can be learned and which save effort by reducing the need to develop a new solution for each problem. Rules facilitate standardization and equality of treatment, and create an environment in which those served by or subject to the organization can make reasonable predictions about future decisions.

2. Administrative roles are highly specialized and differentiated. Spheres of competence are well defined, and lines of authority are thoroughly understood. The administrator's authority is fixed by his office; it does not inhere in him as an individual or carry over to other spheres.

3. Service in the bureaucracy is a career for trained professionals who are paid salaries and protected from arbitrary dismissal; they are subject to discipline or removal only on specified grounds following specified procedures.

4. Recruitment for bureaucratic positions is based on achievement, as demonstrated competitively; promotion within the bureaucracy is also determined on the basis of competitive achievement.

5. Coordination is facilitated by organizing offices hierarchically; that is, each lower office is under the control and supervision of a higher one. The total organization of an

"ideal" bureaucracy, then, is by offices or bureaus, as the term "bureaucracy" suggests.

No existing administrative organization corresponds precisely in its dynamics to the Weberian model, although those of all Western European governments approach it, as do those of most large-scale private enterprises within these nations. So, too, does the bureaucracy of the Soviet Union, despite the regime's ideological presuppositions.

Bureaucratic forms of organization create a number of serious problems and can be highly inefficient under certain circumstances. Nevertheless, the general superiority of bureaucracies to other forms of administrative organization cannot be denied. As Weber pointed out:

The decisive reason for the advance of bureaucratic organization has always been its purely technical superiority over any other form of organization. The fully developed bureaucratic mechanism compares with other organizations exactly as does the machine with the non-mechanical modes of production.[1]

Complex administrative structures also developed within nations outside Europe, such as China, but it was in Western Europe that modern bureaucracies first emerged in both the private and public sphere. The reason for this lies in the cultural heritage of European society. Private as well as public bureaucratic organization requires a money economy, a certain level of literacy, and a differentiation of societal roles divorced from either territorial or ethnic groups. To a limited extent the Chinese met these requirements, but public bureaucratic organization, for instance, also demands a commitment to controlling the environment through rational modes of thought, and a sense of national citizenship that transcends family or tribal ties. Thus, the emergence of state bureaucracies in Western Europe was promoted by the general rational-

ization of European society.[2] Indeed, the first modern bureaucracy was created by the Roman Catholic Church, which served as a model for monarchs who wanted to extend their power or mobilize more effectively the resources of the community. Eventually, of course, state bureaucracies (and bureaucratic forms of business organization) contributed immensely to the early modernization of European nation states.

While all modern European bureaucracies tend to resemble the Weberian model, they continue to differ significantly in many respects. They all perform a multitude of functions, but their primary purpose is to implement governmental policies as formulated by political authorities. Even so, they also help make policy, influence policy as they implement it, aggregate public and private interests, and assist groups in the articulation of their special interests. Many factors determine how effectively they fulfill their primary function, the manner in which they fulfill it, and the extent to which they take on other roles; and the structure and dynamics of a governmental bureaucracy are without question strongly influenced by the society's political culture, its class and power structures, and the importance of its other political institutions, such as parties and parliaments.

In Germany during the Second Empire, for example, the bureaucratic official was a member of a rather closed caste in a highly stratified society. He served only the emperor and the state; his position gave him both status and authority, and he used both to influence significantly the general content of public policy. In the same period, American civil servants operated within the framework of popular, party, legislative, and executive pressures, and their status was rather low; they related to the public, therefore, far differently than did their German counterparts, and their influence on policy formulation was far less significant.

Resemblances and differences in European

---

1 Hans H. Gerth and C. Wright Mills, eds., *From Max Weber* (New York: Oxford University Press, 1958), p. 214.

2 For a discussion of the term "rationalization," see Introduction, pp. 10–11.

bureaucracies can also be observed in the example of the Soviet Union. In a limited sense, the Soviet Union is still a mobilization regime; that it also lacks a private economic sector and that political decision-making is still dominated by the Communist Party considerably affect the behavior of the bureaucracy, though not to the extent claimed in official Soviet theory.

The development of massive bureaucratic organizations has created several real dilemmas for all nations. Even if the goals of an organization can be defined and measured with reasonable ease—as, for example, in a business firm—difficulties always exist. Hierarchy and specialization permit the simplification of tasks, but they also create problems of coordination; specialists and regional offices can become so dedicated to maximizing their authority or the achievement of their own goals that overall objectives of the organization suffer.

These and other problems are magnified in a public bureaucracy. It is extremely difficult to set up clear priorities and to balance off gains and losses for an entire community. Efficiency in the achievement of a particular end may be dysfunctional with respect to the attainment of other goals. Furthermore, assuming the existence of competing social groups, most supposedly technical decisions on the implementation of policy carry important political overtones; as a consequence, high-level bureaucrats make policy imperatives as often as they fulfill them, and the problem of control and direction becomes much more pressing.

In most advanced countries, the basic source of control is, of course, political. Elected officials or party leaders have the means for checking on bureaucratic sabotage or excessive ambition. Additional controls, in Western Europe at least, are provided by the courts—either the ordinary court system, as in England, or special administrative courts, as in Germany and France. Finally, most bureaucratic organizations have internal controls of their own, based on adherence to certain professional norms.

Among the nations with which we are concerned the pattern of bureaucratic control admits of considerable variation, which will be examined and explained in this chapter. Differences notwithstanding, some critics argue that the very structure of contemporary bureaucracies is dehumanizing; they view all modern societies as overly bureaucratized, dominated by technocrats, excessively impersonal, and basically undemocratic. Their demand is for a reversal of the trend toward expanded bureaucratization; they wish to eliminate the administrative hierarchy, and to increase popular participation in administrative decision-making. Some of their arguments will be dealt with in the last chapter of the volume.

2. THE DEVELOPMENT OF THE EUROPEAN PATTERN

The Roman Empire evolved an intricate bureaucratic structure that was altogether "modern" in many of its aspects. Overall political and administrative authority was vested in the emperor and delegated by him to praetorian prefects. Eventually, military and civil jurisdictions were placed in different offices, and civil jurisdiction came to be divided into financial, judicial, and police activities; not restricted to keeping order, the last also included such duties as supervising markets and combating plagues.

With the collapse of the Roman Empire, Europe regressed, for the most part, to primitive forms of communal and tribal organization based on the notion of personal fealty. These organizations eventually became part of a fully developed feudal system, a social system in which most services were provided by local seigneurs. As the king's authority expanded during the latter middle ages, a new administrative apparatus slowly came into being and grew more complex. At first, there was no legal distinction between the private and the public personalities of the monarch. In practice as well as in law, palace officials were his personal servants, no different, except in status, from his cooks. Gradually, however, palace officials became public officials whose authority depended on royal warrants. Decisions pertaining to the national welfare were made in a council of the realm consisting of the leading nobles in attendance at court, such as the *Curia Regis* in England, while the implementation of policy devolved upon the king's scribes, or secretaries—who ultimately became secretaries of the state and, later, parliamentary ministers.

With the rise of absolute monarchs, the administration of mounting public activities became centralized. A core of national officials —*intendants* or inspectors general—was made responsible for supervising the work of provincial officials who, in turn, were made responsible to the king. Efforts were also made to recruit bureaucrats from the non-aristocratic classes and to create a group of officials whose welfare depended directly on the monarch; these efforts, of course, were directed at destroying, or at least weakening, the power of the old feudal aristocracy. However, there were limits to both the rationality of centralized administration and the extent of monarchical control. Continued localism inhibited the satisfactory implementation of national policy. Furthermore, many governmental offices were purchasable; the "owner" of the office received as his stipend a share of monies collected. These offices often became hereditary, creating a new quasi aristocracy with strong personal interests in preventing further rationalization. The development of absolutism in Russia paralleled that of France and Germany, although with a significant time lag, and the Russian czar had even less success in establishing an effective national bureaucracy. During the entire period, the Continental monarchs drew upon Roman law, which was then enjoying a renaissance, not only as a guide to action but as a means of legitimating their authority. The czar tapped the same source, albeit through Byzantium— but here, too, the Russian system remained considerably more primitive. England, as already noted, was the one exception to the European monarchical pattern of centralizing governments. By the time of the Tudors the English kings had greatly augmented the power of central authority, but they were both willing and able to leave the actual administration of local affairs in the hands of a local squirearchy.

A general rationalizing of bureaucratic organization occurred in every major European country during the eighteenth century. Perhaps the first notable attempts to create an organization approximating the Weberian model were those of the Prussian monarchy, culminating in the General Code of 1794. Under its provisions, the merit system was extended to every major administrative post. All governmental candidates were to have a university degree in cameralistics, which included training in agricultural economics, estate management, and financial and administrative law; in-service training was also provided for new employees. Needless to say, the educational requirements were such as to limit recruitment primarily to the upper classes— and the political requirements such as to exclude individuals with too liberal a turn of mind. The Prussian bureaucracy, then, developed into a caste system characterized by a highly efficient but totally aloof paternalism, which was apparent in the Prussian bureaucrats' attitude toward politics: while they were supposed to be impartial in their service to the state, it was an impartiality based on the acceptance of certain political and social premises. Not surprisingly, therefore, they often participated actively in political life as the chief ministers of the crown, for there existed, in effect, a strong tendency to reduce politics to administration.

The Napoleonic period saw somewhat similar developments in France. The entire French bureaucracy was recast along national and extraordinarily rational lines. Appointment was solely on the basis of merit, with university training in engineering and other technical subjects stressed. The École Polytechnique, once the training ground for the specialist corps of the military, became the great supplier of the best French administrative personnel, many of them from the middle classes.

Neither England nor Russia set up effective recruitment procedures at this time. In Russia, the principal stumbling blocks were a lack of facilities and the inability of even somewhat enlightened rulers to overcome the inertia of Russian society; in England, on the other hand, the comparative ease with which a viable nation state had been created inhibited effective change until after the 1860's. Before then, the small national bureaucracy was filled in a variety of ways. Many departments used at least qualifying examinations, though not competitive ones, but a very large number of appointments were filled on the basis of patronage. Moreover, a good many offices were sinecures designed to provide an income in exchange for almost no work at all. While the assertion that the English bureaucracy was filled with "the bastard and idiot sons of the aristocracy" was not entirely accurate, it did contain elements of the truth—despite the fact that a sinecure in the India Office offered John Stuart Mill the opportunity to engage in writing.

The impetus for bureaucratic reform came from the Northcote-Trevelyan Report of 1854, most of which was implemented by 1870. The report called for the creation of a merit civil service based on competitive examinations. Interestingly enough, it did not suggest the creation of a corps of technocrats trained in law or engineering. The general feeling was that the upper levels of the civil service should consist of intelligent young men of breeding—talented amateurs, in other words—who could handle many tasks well. As Lord Macaulay phrased it,

men who have been engaged . . . in studies which have no immediate connexion with the business of any profession, and the effect of which is merely to open, to invigorate, and to enrich the mind, will generally be found . . . superior to men who have . . . devoted themselves to the special studies of their calling. Indeed, early superiority in literature and sci-

ence generally indicates the existence of some qualities which are securities against vice— industry, self-denial, a taste for pleasures not sensual, a laudable desire of honourable distinction, a still more laudable desire to obtain approbation of friends and relations.[3]

In short, all that was needed to have the community operate smoothly was a corps of "superior" men to coordinate its efforts and, where necessary, to guide it.

Some years ago, when the Marxist interpretation of history was more popular than it is today, it was argued that the emergence of a merit bureaucracy coincided with the rise of the middle classes in Europe and that it was, in effect, a reflection of their general attitudes, which substituted rational economic calculation for the warrior ethic of the aristocracy. That the first modern bureaucracy came to fruition in Germany under the aegis of an aristocratic regime casts serious doubts on that hypothesis. So, also, do the nature of reform in England and the evolution of the American bureaucratic pattern.

In the early years of the American Republic, the upper levels of the bureaucracy were filled with "gentlemen" who owed their appointment to social standing. While no merit system existed, there was substantial continuity in office. It was only after the triumph of "middle-class" democracy with the election of Andrew Jackson that the spoils system was extended and justified. The Jacksonians argued that the victorious party deserved the spoils of office, and that one need not worry about merit in office since any decent citizen could serve in a public capacity. They also maintained that rotation in office was democratic, that it was conducive to the health of the republic, and, finally, that a presidential administration needed to appoint people loyal to its programs.

[3] Quoted in Herman Finer, *Theory and Practice of Modern Government*, revised edition (New York: Henry Holt Company, 1949), pp. 763–764.

It was only much later in the nineteenth century that a movement toward a merit system within a permanent bureaucracy began to take hold. Even then, Americans were inclined to consider civil-service positions ordinary jobs for which ordinary professional qualifications sufficed. The result was an extremely pluralistic civil service; it had no clearly defined hierarchy of positions, and could be entered at any age. Even with the creation of a Civil Service Commission in 1883, hiring remained in the hands of individual government departments, and employees were recruited for administrative positions on the basis of professional skill in the areas for which the agency was responsible.

The result has been a civil service much more broadly representative of the population as a whole than that of any European nation, with the exception of the Soviet Union. In recent years, more of an effort has been made to recruit younger men and women, for eventual placement in high-level administrative posts, on the basis of examinations that measure general ability and knowledge rather than specific skills. The fundamental nature of the United States civil service has not changed, however, and despite the continued extension of the merit system, America still lacks the equivalent of England's permanent secretaries; its highest-level officials usually change with each administration.

Whatever the differences among individual European countries, the state has always been regarded as a creative instrument, and a career in the state service as a highly respectable one for scions of upper-class families. In England, particularly, service to the community, as defined by the community, was looked upon as transcending personal or class interests. Although this attitude certainly did not completely eliminate class biases, British civil servants exhibited a remarkable ability to subordinate their own views to those of elected political leaders, no matter how much they disagreed with them. In the United States, however, politics has invariably been considered something of a game in which each group stuffed as many plums in its mouth as it could, within the limits of public digestion. Thus, despite the fact that the ideological conflicts which divided Englishmen in the nineteenth century were more profound than those which divided Americans, the former could more readily conceive of a bureaucracy composed of gentlemen who would serve a constantly changing national interest.

The differences in the bureaucracies of the two nations also reflect the Englishmen's continued deference to aristocratic values and the Americans' attitude that, in a plebiscitarian democracy, only differences based on skills—which could be learned—were acceptable. It must also be remembered that until very recently Americans did not believe that the national government could or should intrude upon the economic and social life of the community. The business of the community was business, and the sons of the better families went into business or the professions. Fritz Morstein-Marx, in describing the British civil servant during the late nineteenth and early twentieth centuries, put it this way:

The working doctrine of the emerging British merit bureaucracy was that of service to an "organic body politic." Although divided along party lines for purposes of responsible government, the body politic showed basic social unity. The end of patronage did not produce a social separation of the House of Commons and the competitive civil service. The new career man shared the general background of the membership of the House of Commons. . . . He was "sound" in every respect, thoroughly trustworthy, and very British. . . . As a result, an early foundation was laid for the remarkable unanimity with which the civil service is viewed by British opinion as a national asset to be guarded vigilantly against deterioration.[4]

[4] In *The Administrative State* (Chicago: University of Chicago Press, 1957), p. 86. Morstein-Marx's observations on the prestige of the British bureaucracy are no longer completely accurate.

FIGURE 22.1. CITIZENS' ATTITUDES TOWARD GOVERNMENT OFFICIALS: UNITED KINGDOM, WEST GERMANY, AND THE UNITED STATES

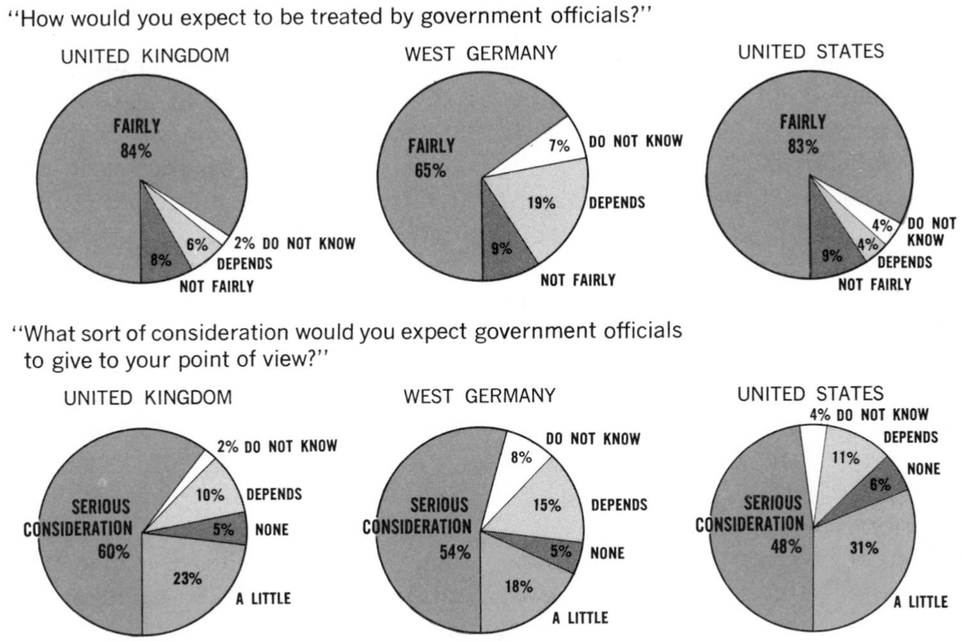

"How would you expect to be treated by government officials?"

UNITED KINGDOM   WEST GERMANY   UNITED STATES

FAIRLY 84%   6%   2% DO NOT KNOW   8% DEPENDS   NOT FAIRLY

FAIRLY 65%   7% DO NOT KNOW   19% DEPENDS   9%   NOT FAIRLY

FAIRLY 83%   4% DO NOT KNOW   4% DEPENDS   9%   NOT FAIRLY

"What sort of consideration would you expect government officials to give to your point of view?"

UNITED KINGDOM   WEST GERMANY   UNITED STATES

SERIOUS CONSIDERATION 60%   2% DO NOT KNOW   10% DEPENDS   5% NONE   23%   A LITTLE

SERIOUS CONSIDERATION 54%   DO NOT KNOW 8%   15% DEPENDS   5% NONE   18%   A LITTLE

SERIOUS CONSIDERATION 48%   4% DO NOT KNOW   DEPENDS   11% NONE   6%   31%   A LITTLE

Adapted from Gabriel Almond and Sidney Verba, *The Civic Culture* (Princeton: Princeton University Press, 1963), pp. 108, 109. Reprinted by permission of the publisher.

In these attitudes Britain also differed from both France and Germany, where the bureaucracy remained far more of a closed caste, decidedly weighted in favor of the *haute bourgeoisie* and the aristocracy. French and German bureaucrats, like their English counterparts, came to view themselves as, in some sense, representing the best interests of the nation; unlike English bureaucrats, however, many regarded it as their job to define the best interests of the community, believing that their definition was superior to any possible results of the ballot box. Some bureaucrats of the Weimar Republic and the French Third Republic, for example, tried to sabotage policies which they believed were destroying the national heritage. In the postwar era, both nations have moved toward democratization of the bureaucracy, although their educational

structure and cultural prejudices are such that they have a long way to go.

3. THE ENGLISH PATTERN

ORIGINS AND DEVELOPMENT: The most striking circumstance surrounding the evolution of the British bureaucracy is the almost total lack of thought given to the subject until the end of the eighteenth century. While Continental monarchs were striving mightily to create a satisfactory bureaucratic apparatus, the British more or less ignored the problem. Laws passed by Parliament from the middle of the sixteenth century to the end of the eighteenth were carried out not by professional agents of the central authority but by local gentry. No qualifications were required and central control was minimal; in fact, controls were handled largely by the courts. If local officials failed to deal with matters as required by law, they could be charged before a court with malfeasance or misfeasance and fined. A kind of part-time local inspectorate materialized in the person of informers who received a portion of the fine if violations were proved in court.

Most of the principal departments of government—agriculture, education, labor—date from the nineteenth century as the central government, with the beginnings of the Industrial Revolution, assumed a more active part in the regulation of the life of the community. It was only then that a national bureaucracy began to take shape, and with it the problems of reform. Impelled by liberal ideas concerned with a rationally constructed polity, the reforms were designed to create a rationalized organization on a nationwide basis. Liberals and Conservatives alike, however, agreed on the type of person who was desired—a man of character and wide-ranging interests, noted for both his wisdom and his fairness. His job, after all, was not, as in the case of France and Germany, to create a prosperous national state at the behest of a monarchy, or, for that matter, of revolutionary reformers; it was to regulate the activities of the members of society in their relations with each other by making certain that all followed the rules of community life as promulgated by legitimate political authority. The national government was, in the final analysis, the regulating mechanism whose function was to insure that the national forces of the community came into play in a reasonable and reasonably harmonious way. It was also responsible for aiding the less fortunate members of the community. While both tasks were considered to be quite important, there was little or no feeling about bureaucrats directing the nation toward any particular social or economic goals.

The pattern thus established continued well into the twentieth century; on the whole, it served England well. The British civil serv-

ice earned a reputation for impartiality, responsiveness, and general fairness unequaled by any European country. Even after the Labor Party came into office in 1945, there was little serious criticism of the civil service, except with regard to its class structure. In the past ten years, however, criticism of the British civil service has been somewhat more incisive; the argument is, fundamentally, that old conceptions are obsolete. The affairs of every modern society have become so vast that, of necessity, government itself must become a source of innovation; and this can only happen if it is reorganized and staffed with the kind of professional and technical talent that the twentieth century requires.

These criticisms led to the appointment in 1966 of a committee to study the entire structure of the civil service. Popularly referred to as the Fulton Committee, after its chairman, Lord John Scott Fulton, the committee's report was issued in 1968, and a good many of its recommendations have been accepted by the government and are in the process of implementation.

STRUCTURE: The backbone of the British administrative structure is provided by the ministries. Each is organized hierarchically under a minister who assumes responsibility before the parliament not only for general policy but for all the actions of civil servants under his authority.

Organization charts of the British government structure are always rather baroque. In the United States, all government departments are created by acts of Congress and headed by one political official, most often called a secretary; but in England, many of the older ministries evolved out of the king's household, rather haphazardly accruing all manner of functions as they went along. Others were created later as boards as the need arose; although each was subsequently reorganized under a single minister, authority is still legally vested in the parent body. The Treasury, for example, is theoretically gov-

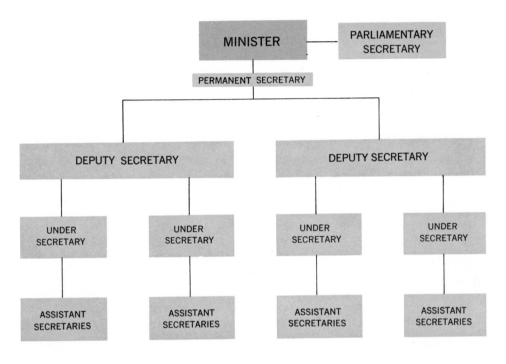

FIGURE 22.2. ORGANIZATION OF A TYPICAL BRITISH MINISTRY

erned by the Treasury Board, even though its actual head is the chancellor of the exchequer. The Board of Trade, although officially a plural body, is run by one man. Only in the ministries created as such by act of Parliament in comparatively recent times—and really only those set up since 1918—has any real attempt been made to rationalize the structure of government departments. Before then, as Walter Bagehot noted, they "grew as each could."

Despite its baroque qualities, the structure of British ministries today is nevertheless far more integrated than that of the departments of the United States government. Immediately below each minister and responsible for the management of the department is a senior civil servant, the permanent secretary, usually recruited into the administrative class of the civil service immediately upon graduation from a university. His purpose is to serve any government equally well, presumably in a nonpolitical way. The office is unique to the British: in most European nations and in the United States, those whose position is equivalent to the British permanent secretary are bureaucrats of known sympathy with the policies of the government of the day, even if they are not political appointees. The permanent secretary is normally assisted by one or more deputy secretaries, each in charge of several sections, and below them are the undersecretaries and assistant secretaries who head up the lower-echelon divisions of the department. Within these divisions, smaller units are administered by principals and assistant principals.

Attached to many ministries are one or more committees that provide expert advice or secure the representation of segments of the public. Some of these committees are established by statute; others have been created by ministers themselves. Thus, the minister of health is officially advised by the Central Health Services Council whose members include, among others, the presidents of the Royal College of Surgeons and the Royal College of Physicians, together with representatives of the medical, dental, and nursing professions. He is also advised by a number of other committees on such subjects as hospital management and the services of general practitioners.

The government of the day has almost complete control over the organization of government services, and it can rearrange departmental functions with ease. This is certainly not true in the United States, where any attempt to reorganize the executive departments becomes a major legislative issue, partly because the control of government services is a question of policy. Congressmen are anxious to make sure that bureaus or "independent" agencies serving their constituents are not placed under the jurisdiction of departments or officials who might initiate actions of which they disapprove. In England, the power to reorganize executive departments is considered part of the prerogative of the crown—and, hence, the government. In addition, the existence of a tightly controlled party system guarantees that the government can push through almost any organizational structure it considers reasonable.

Further, unlike the United States or France under the Third and Fourth Republics, the British government has complete authority over its civil servants. No civil servant can be pressured by a member of Parliament to follow a particular set of policies, nor can he turn to an M.P. in the hope of circumventing the government's general program. Again, the crucial factor here is two-party discipline within the parliamentary framework. In the United States Congress, the power of legislative committees and of the legislature itself in relation to the executive is such as to encourage the establishment of associations among bureaucrats, congressmen, and interest groups. Civil servants can be pressured by threats to reduce or even cut off appropriations, and bureaucrats can turn to Congress if they wish to circumvent the administration's efforts to reduce their appropriations, keep their activities within the perimeter of an overall program, or assign some

of their functions to another bureau or department. The Corps of Army Engineers, for example, has been extremely successful in receiving sizable appropriations, often despite the efforts of the president, because it builds harbors and bridges and engages in other activities that may benefit important groups in the constituency of a powerful congressman. French politics before the Fifth Republic was distinguished by much the same kind of interrelationships.

The British executive's control over his bureaucracy is reinforced in two ways: by the doctrine of a minister's personal responsibility for his department, and by a tacit agreement that bureaucrats must not only avoid public statements expressing personal opinions, but must also maintain complete secrecy on matters that do not have to be made public. High-level administrators, despite their role in devising public policy, rarely come to the attention of the public. Their relation with their minister is extremely confidential; leaks to the press of restricted information are prohibited by the Official Secrets Act, and rarely occur. By comparison, the business of government in Washington is conducted in a fishbowl, with administrators often baring their souls to the press and Congress alike.

The general secrecy that cloaks the operation of government business in England is partly a result of the relation of bureaucrats to the government, and the strength of the government in its dealings with Parliament. It can also be attributed to a tradition which suggests that continued participation by the population in government activity is unwise —that, in effect, governments may be selected by the people, but they govern for the people. This tradition—which applies also to Continental countries when the government in office is a strong one—has, in recent years, come under increasing attack in England. Indeed, the Fulton Committee recommended that civil servants be permitted to explain the work of departments before Parliament and the public, and that the secrecy with which the government conducts its business be lifted. Further, strong pressure has been exerted on the government to review the Official Secrets Act. The belief that civil servants should be less anonymous is shared by many permanent secretaries. Yet the government has been very cautious about taking the wraps off its operation; while it is clear that, as in all European countries, a more "open" politics is becoming the order of the day, a shift in the relationship between top-level civil servants and governmental ministers would undoubtedly have a far-reaching impact on Parliament and the party system.

For domestic policy, the most important department in the British administrative structure has traditionally been the Treasury. Until recently, it had considerably greater power than the combined authority in the United States of the Bureau of the Budget, Treasury, and, to some extent, Civil Service Commission. The British "Treasury mentality" has periodically been attacked for its unimaginativeness, and from time to time the department has been stripped of some of its functions; however, it has generally been able to recoup its prerogatives.

The Treasury is accountable for all financial transactions of the government, but it has many other functions. Until 1968 it was responsible for the recruitment, training, promotion, and salary schedule of all civil-service employees. Its supervision of the staffing and finances of other departments permitted it to investigate both their policies and their organizational effectiveness. It still has much to say about both short- and long-range economic planning. The Treasury's greatest power, however, is its effective control of the budget—a power immeasurably enhanced by the unique position in British government of the chancellor of the exchequer. The Treasury can veto departmental budgetary estimates, and while ministers can appeal to the cabinet, the chancellor can be overridden only with considerable difficulty.

Even after estimates are voted, ministries can draw money only through a requisition by the Treasury. Any increase in the number or salary of officials in a department must receive Treasury approval, despite the fact that the particular ministry may have sufficient funds to pay them. Very rarely, however, does the Treasury command departments. Rather, it works closely with them on all phases of program development and implementation, seeking to increase efficiency and, in the case of interdepartmental disputes, helping to coordinate activities. Because of its prestige, the Treasury attracts the very best minds in the civil service, a circumstance of considerable assistance to the department in carrying out its numerous functions.

The Treasury has often been reproached for what some regard as its excessive conservatism and its emphasis upon short-range manipulation instead of long-term policy considerations. Associated with this criticism has been the feeling that too few of its administrators have adequate professional training. Some of this fault-finding has, of course, been greatly exaggerated. Of the 150 men working directly on financial policy in 1964, approximately 25 were professional economists. They maintained fairly close ties with the National Institute of Economic and Social Research, a group of economists with strong leanings toward social reform and economic planning, as well as with Nuffield College, Oxford, which has become an important center of academic social scientists in England. Furthermore, opinion within the Treasury has always been pluralistic. While the overall departmental point of view has a tendency to be skeptical, there are a number of insiders with a strongly innovative bent; in fact, since the end of World War II, the Treasury has been very much under the influence of Keynesian economic doctrines.

When Labor came to power in 1945, the general prejudices against the Treasury attitudes led to the creation of a Ministry of Economic Affairs charged with producing long-range economic plans. The ministry,

FIGURE 22.3. ORGANIZATION OF THE BRITISH TREASURY TO 1964

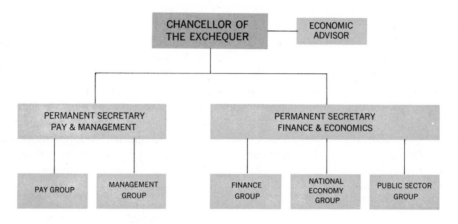

Adapted from Samuel Britton, *The Treasury Under the Tories* (Harmondsworth, Middlesex, Eng.: Penguin Books Ltd., 1964), p. 55. Reprinted by permission of the publisher.

however, was eventually absorbed by the Treasury. In 1964 Labor repeated its earlier effort to remove the responsibility for long-range planning from the Treasury by creating a Department of Economic Affairs, but four years later the Treasury was once again regaining its authority in this area. However, in 1968 the Fulton Committee recommended that responsibility for recruitment and management be taken from the Treasury and placed in a special Civil Service Department under the direct control of the prime minister. This recommendation was accepted by the Labor government.

THE CIVIL SERVICE: The Northcote-Trevelyan Report set the pattern for the modern British civil service—a pattern that has continued, although with important modifications, to the present. The implementation of the Fulton Report should cause some striking changes; indeed, it is realistic to assume that it will result in the beginnings of a fundamental reorientation of the service within the next three to five years. The nature of these changes and the reasons why they are about to take place will be discussed shortly; first, however, the structure of the service as of 1969 must be outlined. The major character-

istics of the British civil service can be summarized as follows:

1. It is made up entirely of career personnel. Once a civil servant has passed his probationary period, he holds a permanent appointment and will not be discharged except under very rare circumstances.

2. It is recruited by open competitive examinations. With the exception of scientific and technical personnel, of whom specialized knowledge is required, the concern of the service is to employ persons of general aptitude.

3. Pay scales, working conditions, and promotions are uniform for civil servants throughout the government, except for technical personnel. The service is divided into three main classes: administrative, executive, and clerical.

4. The civil service is politically neutral; neither appointment nor dismissal occurs for political reasons. Senior civil servants may not take part in any politically partisan activities, but those in the lower echelons may, and some have even become candidates for office.

The vast majority of civil servants are members of the clerical class. Usually recruited between the ages of 16 and 18, they perform largely routine services. More than two-thirds of the executive class is promoted from below: the remainder are recruited through open examination. Members of the executive class undertake preliminary investigations of governmental problems, collect data for parliamentary questions, and take on minor administrative responsibilities. They may develop specialized skills and move up the ladder in some technical grade, or they may eventually find their way into that elite of the civil service, the administrative class.

Men and women at the administrative level manage the major departments of the British government and shoulder responsibility in the making and execution of policy. A member of the administrative class has five principal obligations:

1. Overseeing the day-to-day operation of his particular departmental branch.

2. Voicing his views on the advancement of his department's policy.

3. Helping prepare legislation. From time to time he will work out the details of a bill for his minister. He also helps draft cabinet memoranda and prepares departmental rules, orders, and regulations pertaining to legislation.

4. Briefing his minister for discussions in the House of Commons and in committee. He may actually attend the debate, to provide ready information for his minister.

5. Preparing parliamentary answers for his minister and supplying him with material for speeches.

Approximately forty per cent of the members of the administrative class are recruited by promotion from below. Until 1970, the remainder invariably entered the class between the ages of 21 and 28 on the basis of competitive examinations of two types. Method I, the traditional means of recruitment, consisted of eight written examinations and a short interview. The first three examinations—which were uniform for all candidates—tested the student's ability to express himself well in the English language, his grasp of contemporary affairs, and has facility in ex-

pounding on a topic that any intelligent young man should be able to discuss. The subject matter of the other five written tests could be chosen from a list of sixty or more, and a candidate's ability to read Sanskrit counted as heavily as one in an area more relevant to immediate national concerns. Despite many changes, Method I remained largely geared to the kind of student produced by Oxbridge.

At the end of World War II, Method II was introduced as an alternate approach to recruitment. Originally designed as a temporary expedient for civil-service applicants whose academic talents had become rusty while serving in the armed forces, it was retained and eventually became the more popular means of entering the administrative class. Candidates using Method II took the three examinations required of all Method I candidates, but the selection procedure was largely based on a series of individual and group interviews that tested leadership qualities.

The Fulton Committee recommended retaining both methods of recruitment, together with revisions which would extend the appeal of the civil service to students from universities other than Oxford and Cambridge, although a strong minority on the commission urged that Method I be discarded. A continued drop in the number of candidates selecting Method I, however, decided the issue and it was eliminated at the end of 1969. Method II is now in the process of being reviewed.

The lowest post in the administrative class is that of assistant principal, and the highest office to which a member of this class can aspire by right is that of assistant secretary, a post normally reached by the age of forty. Beyond that, luck and talent determine whether a member becomes one of the select group of approximately thirty permanent secretaries, or, perhaps, achieves a post in the Treasury which, while lower in rank, carries equivalent prestige.

Members of the administrative class are considered generalists (although their critics would term them dilettantes); they are recruited on the basis of their mind and character, both of which they supposedly bring to bear upon the problems faced by the departments they serve. They enter the service at an early age and are not expected to leave it before retirement. Until recently, they received very little in-service training, either in management techniques or in the skills pertaining to the functions performed by their departments—such skills were regarded as completely unnecessary. The ideal member of this class could and would simply take advice from the professionals, and, on the basis of his mature evaluation of what the situation required, would translate this advice into cogent proposals. Technically trained professionals were considered to lack the breadth of viewpoint to determine policy; the expert was to be on tap but not on top, lest he push his own pet projects too hard. Indeed, permanent secretaries tended to be rotated regularly from department to department to prevent them from becoming too closely identified with one bureaucratic point of view. Management techniques, after all, were common-sense matters merely requiring sound judgment. As one commentator observed:

. . . the British administrator traveling abroad is shocked to discover that many countries are administered by men who read books about public administration. . . . Such people are committing the crime of learning from books something that one just does. *It is rather like venturing into matrimony only after a course of Havelock Ellis, which, for a healthy nature, should not strictly be necessary.*[5]

This view was something of an exaggeration even in 1959: aside from the need for their services in nationalized industries, technically trained personnel did perform important administrative functions in a number of ministries where special skills were required. Nevertheless, growing criticism has been leveled against the civil service for its "amateurism," and that criticism has produced improvements. Some ministries have established short-term exchanges of personnel with private industry so that civil servants might learn management techniques, and some have granted sabbaticals to enable members of their administrative class to study subjects that could be of value to the department. In 1963 a Center for Administrative Studies was opened to train assistant principals in many subjects, including economics, and its program has been gradually expanded. Also, the

[5] C. H. Sisson, *The Spirit of British Administration* (London: Faber and Faber, 1959), p. 28.

TABLE 22.1. FIELDS OF STUDY BY SUCCESSFUL CANDIDATES FOR BRITISH ADMINISTRATIVE POSITIONS

	1925–1935	*1948–1956*
Classics	35%	21%
History	25	32
History, languages and literature	7	
Modern languages	8	9
Economics and politics	7	10
Philosophy, politics and economics		10
Mathematics	6	2
English		6
Law		4
Science and technical		1
Other	12	5

Adapted from John Wilbur Price, "Education and the Civil Service in Europe," *Western Political Quarterly*, Vol. X, no. 4 (December 1957), p. 822. Reprinted by permission of the University of Utah, copyright owners.

1964 Labor government brought in some technical experts—"irregulars," as they are called—who have been placed (with mixed results) in fairly strategic administrative positions.

British civil servants are among the best paid in the world; still, as in other countries, their salaries are by no means equivalent to those paid by the business community. Since World War II especially, many top-level civil servants have resigned to take positions with industry, provoking pressures to make civil-service salaries even more attractive.

In the early part of the century, the administrative class was very much part of the British establishment. Of the permanent secretaries who served between 1900 and 1919, for instance, 64 per cent had been to the public schools. More recently—aside from the Foreign Service, which remains something of a public-school bailiwick—the links between the civil service, the public schools, and the establishment have been broken, partly because the increased emphasis on in-service promotion from the executive class has caused a greater diversity in the background of those serving in the administrative class. Then too, of course, the public schools are no longer the bastions of the establishment that they once were; the requirement that they now accept a substantial number of scholarship students has reduced their exclusiveness. Moreover, the civil service has leaned over

backwards to avoid favoring public-school graduates. By 1950, only 23 per cent of the administrative class had gone to any boarding school, and Eton supplied only two per cent of the class. Of the twenty permanent secretaries serving in 1961, only eleven had been to public schools.

It is true that a very large—although slowly declining—proportion of the administrative class is still recruited from Oxbridge. This is particularly apparent in the Treasury and it is particularly true of permanent secretaries, more than 80 per cent of whom are Oxbridge graduates. Oxford and Cambridge still attract the best students, and they still offer better training than most redbrick institutions whose civil-service aspirants are usually eliminated on the written examinations. Also, there are more recruits from Oxbridge simply because more Oxbridge graduates apply for civil-service positions; furthermore, history and the classics, which are heavily accented at Oxbridge, have until very recently been the favorite fields of applicants and recruiters alike. (See Table 22.1.) Even so, despite the establishmentarian image projected by Oxford and Cambridge, both universities since the war have become less socially restrictive than most public schools, accepting a substantial portion of lower-middle-class and working-class students.

The administrative class, therefore, no longer constitutes part of the establishment,

TABLE 22.2. THE EDUCATIONAL BACKGROUND OF BRITISH PERMANENT SECRETARIES

	1900–1919	1920–1924	1945–1963
Twenty of the best known public schools	51.0%	27.4%	26.5%
Other public schools	13.2	33.9	27.7
Private schools not classified as public schools	9.4	19.4	20.5
Schools administered by local authorities	0.0	8.1	15.7
Other schools	13.2	4.8	9.6
No attendance at secondary school	1.9	0.0	0.0
Information not available	11.3	6.4	0.0

Adapted from John S. Harris and Thomas V. Garcia, "The Permanent Secretaries: Britain's Top Administrators," *Public Administration Review*, XXVI (March, 1966), p. 33. Reprinted by permission of the publisher.

with traditional ties to Conservative Party politicians and the business community. Those recruited since World War II have usually come from fairly varied middle-class backgrounds, and recent studies indicate that the majority of them voted Labor in the 1966 elections.[6] By and large, they do not move in the same circles as the business or political communities, nor do they speak quite the same language. They do share with each other, however, a set of common orientations and connections which are based in part on their university background; this certainly facilitates their work, even as it may limit their perspective. Permanent secretaries find it quite easy to work on the whole array of interdepartmental committees that try to iron out differences and devise common policies; they accomplish a considerable amount of work rather smoothly on an informal basis.

The best minds in the bureaucracy, excluding the foreign service, are probably found among the higher officials of the Treasury. Many of them, in addition to being proficient in several languages, are highly competent mathematicians. Before the Second World War there was even a regular Treasury choir specializing in madrigals; it no longer exists, but there is still a flourishing Treasury quartet, and rumor still has it that musical competence has a bearing on promotion.

It is difficult to assess just how great an influence members of the administrative class have on policy and its execution. Despite the anxieties of the Labor Party left, however, postwar Labor ministers have found that civil servants have been loyal to the government—many, in fact, throwing themselves wholeheartedly into carrying out the new ministerial policies. Indeed, Conservatives have often complained bitterly that the bureaucracy seemed excessively committed to nationalization.

The Fulton Committee Report recommended important changes in the structure,

recruitment, training, and employment of civil servants. The government has accepted most of these recommendations in one form or another, although it will be several years before they can be completely carried out. The Fulton group urged, among other things, an end to the civil-service class system and the adoption of a uniform system of grades along the lines of those in effect in the United States. However, it was also recommended that civil-service candidates who do especially well on examinations be permitted to enter the bureaucracy at a somewhat higher grade than others, and that some even be brought into the service with the understanding that if they do well they can advance up the ladder fairly rapidly.

Another recommendation of the committee was that greater stress be placed on recruiting candidates with training in "relevant" subjects, such as political science and economics. Indeed, it was suggested not only that students trained in these areas be favored, but that prospective administrators be encouraged to choose these fields of study. In making this recommendation, the committee was not without support from administrators themselves, many of whom believed that their traditional university courses had not been very useful. The government accepted the purport of this recommendation, but indicated that it would not necessarily favor candidates with "relevant" training, since relevance was fairly difficult to define.

The establishment of a civil-service college which would provide extensive training in management techniques, as well as in substantive course work such as economics and finance, was a third recommendation of the Fulton Committee; concomitantly, it urged that the dichotomy between "specialists" and "generalists" be ended and that professionals, such as engineers, be trained in management techniques and promoted to policy-making positions upon demonstrated competence. The entire emphasis of the report was on the need for increasing specialization, and the committee advised that administrators should stop being shifted from department to depart-

6 (Fulton) Committee on the Civil Service, *The Civil Service* (London: Her Majesty's Stationery Office, Cmnd. 3638, 5 volumes, June 1968), Vol. 3, p. 9.

ment and strive to become expert in the tasks of one particular ministry. The government announced almost immediately the creation of a special civil-service college with several campuses, which would work closely with various universities in order to draft effective training programs.

Finally, while accepting the institution of the permanent secretary, the committee advocated that new ministers also recruit special senior policy advisers from the bureaucracy, the universities, or even the business community—men who more or less shared the views of the minister himself, but who, as the committee saw it, would make possible a constant interchange of ideas between the civil service and other segments of the community. The Fulton report further suggested that procedures be established to encourage men and women in their mature years to enter the service on a short- or long-term basis, thereby sidestepping the traditional rule that a civil-service career commences with graduation from a university. The government accepted these recommendations, pointing out that such procedures had already been instituted.

The effect of the Fulton Report will be to remold the British civil service somewhat in the American pattern, reducing both the gap between generalists and specialists and the distinctions among the civil-service classes. The changes will undoubtedly take time to implement, especially if the Conservatives return to power; in the interim, Britain's "talented amateurs" will continue to dominate the upper levels of the administrative class.

CONTROL AND ACCOUNTABILITY: The British civil service has often been commended for its deep sense of responsibility to both the public and its political superiors. Corruption is practically nonexistent, and bureaucrats' dealings with the public have engendered an impressive reputation for their fairness and civility. The stability and power of the British executive make the lines of bureaucratic authority clear, and responsibility reasonably easy to pinpoint. Compared with the United States, and France under the Fourth Republic, the executive branch of government can be almost certain that its programs will not be sabotaged by legislative pressures upon the bureaucracy. Even so, Parliament has manifested a growing dissatisfaction with its relationship to the bureaucracy. In the particular case of the nationalized industries, this led to the formation of a quasi-permanent select committee to oversee their operations; however, demands for reform go much deeper. Some critics believe that holding a minister accountable for the work of his entire department is anachronistic and that responsibility could be better assured by strengthening parliamentary committees. While these critics deny that inquisitive committees would vitiate executive control, their arguments are, at the very least, open to question.

The effectiveness of judicial controls upon bureaucratic action has also been a subject of greater discussion. The common-law courts in England had been among the great bulwarks against the misuse of public authority, and had also proved flexible enough to provide an adequate body of national law. These two factors, plus the efficacy of external political controls, caused the English to feel little need to create a body of administrative law applicable under a separate court system of the type instituted on the Continent. As a consequence, the only remedy to persons injured by an administrative act was to file suit for damages in the regular courts against the official or officials responsible. The state could not be sued, for the British (and the Americans) continued to adhere to the essentially feudal notion that the state as such could not be liable for the actions of its officers. The advantages claimed for the English approach were that it placed all citizens, including public officials, on the same plane; by comparison, it was argued, the so-called administrative courts, composed as they were of bureaucrats, could never render the private citizen his due because they would tend to favor the bureaucracy.

By the 1920's, however, it had become evident that the English approach was not altogether satisfactory. The state was interfering more and more directly in the lives of its citizens—with a corresponding increase in the occasions on which citizens wished to seek legal redress. And, in a good many cases, no adequate remedy was available. A fire truck responding to an alarm might injure a citizen on the road, but unless the driver had been negligent, the citizen could not collect damages. A series of legal fictions created by the courts in the 1920's and 1930's to chip away at the doctrine of state immunity, together with several parliamentary acts, expanded the number of instances in which a citizen or his family could obtain redress from the government in case of injury, death, or loss of property. Finally, in 1947, the Crown Proceedings Act explicitly opened the door to suits against the crown, "as if the crown were a fellow citizen." Nevertheless, compared with the Continental practice, the opportunities for obtaining redress are still limited, and the absence of any administrative courts to handle such suits means that efforts to do so are both time-consuming and expensive.

Administrative courts on the Continent also review allegations by citizens to the effect that officials have exceeded their authority. For a long time, both Englishmen and Americans preferred to rely upon the regular court system to handle these complaints, for the common-law courts were considered the ultimate repositories of liberty. But in actuality, it became decidedly more difficult to operate on this basis: court calendars were being overcrowded with technically complex matters, and judges were notoriously loath to interfere with actions whose rationale and implications they could understand only with difficulty. The end result was the growth of a large number of administrative tribunals; one such tribunal, for example, now has jurisdiction over workmen's compensation cases in England, and the procedures are far less time-consuming and much less expensive. There is every evidence that the rights of the plaintiff are fully protected, despite the fact that administrators are acting as judges, thus violating the classic separation-of-powers doctrine. The function of the regular courts

has been preserved by their being given authority to review decisions of the tribunals.

Some tribunals allow legal representation at hearings and keep detailed records; others follow a more informal procedure. In order to establish uniform methods and standards, an investigating committee was set up in 1955 and most of its recommendations were incorporated in the Tribunals and Enquiries Act of 1958, which created a Council on Tribunals to supervise the entire tribunal system, and stipulated that the chairman of most tribunals be appointed by the Lord Chancellor.

Yet the issues involved are by no means settled. Some commentators maintain that what is needed is a system of administrative law and courts comparable with the French model; others contend that too much authority has already been taken from the regular court system. The creation of a parliamentary commissioner for administration was an attempt to follow the Swedish example in dealing with complaints of maladministration. However, as indicated in Chapter 15, the institution has not produced any significant changes.

As the Fulton Committee pointed out, the modern British civil service is a product of the nineteenth century, and was brought into existence to create a group of public servants who would impartially advise political leaders and impartially enforce the rules established by the government for regulating English society. Those in the highest echelons of the service were to be men of judgment who would serve the nation in such a way as to balance individual rights against community needs. The civil service fulfilled its task remarkably well, and came to deserve its high reputation in England and abroad. It exercised authority without being autocratic, and acted fairly without lapsing into bureaucratic impersonality.

As with certain other English institutions, however, nineteenth-century virtues have become mid–twentieth-century weaknesses, although the current mood of the English intellectual community is such that the defects of the present structure are often exaggerated. Unquestionably, the English are faced with a series of bureaucratic problems —some of which are new, others but new forms of old dilemmas. In an age in which the state has taken on a number of tasks requiring technical knowledge and careful planning, a new balance must be found between the need for expertise and innovation in the bureaucracy and the need to keep bureaucrats subject to the authority of political leaders. In an age in which the actions of the state directly affect every aspect of a citizen's life, a new balance must be found between community needs and individual rights. And in an age in which old forms of authority are eroding and demands are being registered for "open" politics with full community participation, a new balance must be found between the requirements of effective governance and the desire of those governed to help make the decisions which affect them.

4. THE FRENCH PATTERN[7]

ORIGINS AND DEVELOPMENT: By the time of Louis XIV, the French state could boast an extensive bureaucratic apparatus scattered throughout the nation and supervised by the king's *intendants*. The creation of a bureaucracy dependent upon the throne was part of the monarchy's effort to unify the realm and give it direction. Omnipresent though the bureaucracy was, it was hardly efficient. Many important offices were either inherited or bought; since a good number of these had the power to confer titles, the ranks of officeholders burgeoned. Understandably, the methods of acquiring offices were scarcely conducive to the establishment of a well-run operation—or, usually, to the recruitment of real talent.

The French Revolution and Napoleon not

only transformed the French state, they remodeled its entire administrative apparatus. The bureaucrat was no longer the servant of the crown, but of the nation. His office and powers were explicitly defined by law. Further, the structure of the government itself was more rationally organized and grouped into a coherent set of hierarchical ministries. Provincial autonomy was swept away, and the nation was reorganized into administrative departments controlled by prefects appointed in Paris.

Just as important was the effort to create a bureaucratic apparatus staffed with able men. Napoleon's conception of the effective bureaucrat was that of a person trained in the practical sciences, especially engineering, and the highest state posts were filled by young graduates of technical schools such as the École Polytechnique. These schools were geared to turn out public officials who would be experts in particular areas of public service. Created within each ministry, therefore, was a specialized corps of men of common background trained to fulfill a specific function. The schools catered primarily to the upper middle class, but bright young men of lower-middle-class background who demonstrated talent could be subsidized by the government, especially at the École Polytechnique.

The system created by Napoleon set the guidelines for recruitment by the French administration, although they were not always followed after the collapse of his regime. Between 1815 and 1870, despite abortive efforts at bureaucratic reform, appointments and promotions were very largely contingent upon personal connections, and the upper level of the system became the province of the haute bourgeoisie and the aristocracy. To a considerable extent, however, those in the higher echelons continued to be drawn from the *Grandes Écoles* and they possessed, in many cases, an essential degree of technical proficiency. Their capabilities notwithstanding, they shared, by and large, the views of their class on social and economic questions. They were not averse to the state interceding in

---

[7] Much of the historical discussion is based on Alfred Diamant's essay "The French Administrative System: The Republic Passes but the Administration Remains," in William J. Siffin, ed., *Toward the Comparative Study of Public Administration* (Bloomington: Indiana University Press, 1957), pp. 182–218.

economic affairs from a rather mercantilist point of view, but they lacked that faith held by the British middle class in the possibilities and advantages of economic expansion. The point, of course, can be overstressed. Many in the French bureaucracy were disciples of Saint-Simon and Fourier, and were actively dedicated to applying technical knowledge to social and economic issues. The bureaucracy, then, exemplified the rest of France: the antagonistic subcultures within it coexisted uneasily and acted at cross purposes.

After 1870, programs were introduced to improve the training of bureaucratic personnel. Recruitment continued to be the province of the ministries, but they were obliged to set forth their personnel requirements in the form of public announcements. Again, the emphasis was on technical training. Yet far more than in England, the bureaucracy remained the preserve of the upper bourgeoisie —particularly for those in the so-called *grands corps,* that is, such elite groups as the Council of State (*Conseil d'État*), Finance Inspectorate (*Inspection des Finance*), and the Audit Office or Court of Accounts (*Cour des Comptes*). Loyalty to one's department and corps was the bureaucrat's prime concern; it was induced both by the decentralized nature of recruitment and by the nation's political framework.

The instability of France's regimes and the weakness of its executives made it nearly impossible to give the bureaucracy overall direction. Governments and even individual ministers were relatively short-termed, and although new administrations tried to purge themselves of those who were not sympathetic, or at least to bring in others who were, too many pressures were placed upon the national government to permit the inception of a workmanlike bureaucratic policy. The structure of departments and field services was to a large extent determined as the result of compromise between conflicting groups rather than the application of any rational criteria; departments continued to work at loggerheads not only with each other but with the government as well. Bureaucrats would

bypass their departments in order to negotiate with deputies; deputies, through their committees, would try to persuade bureaucrats to undermine social or economic programs they opposed and to provide favors for their constituents. Lines of bureaucratic authority had a baroque twist that belied the neat organizational charts which the French produced in great profusion.

The higher civil servants were, for the most part, politically conservative; their background and education inclined them to identify themselves with the upper classes, and the widespread practice of using administrative posts as stepping stones to lucrative business positions helped contribute to such identification. Even so, conservatism was not the main problem. It is true that traditional biases occasionally led civil servants to impede the implementation of more "radical" programs in the hope that a particular government would fall; from these few cases, the mythology spread that France's transient political regimes were ruled essentially by a conservative bureaucracy. Yet the actual circumstances were far more complicated. While bureaucrats might be conservative, in many instances their training and positions made them quite sympathetic to proposals for the modernization and rationalization of French social and economic life. Moreover, many of them agreed with Bismarck that the ruling social and political elites of the nation had a duty to press for the welfare of those who were ruled. There were, then, many bureaucrats interested in reform, but the very structure of the political system prevented them from obtaining the kind of practical support and direction they needed to put their ideas into practice. Further, most civil servants were imbued with the conception of obedience to legally constituted authority, a tutelage that prevented them from stepping too far out of line.

If the bureaucracy did not rule France, it did indeed run France between the governments that came and went by keeping essential public services in operation. Its conservatism, however, was at least as much a result of the stalemated quality of French political life as it was of individual proclivities.

Those who created the Fourth Republic were eager to eliminate the bureaucratic evils which they felt had been rampant in the Third. What occurred, therefore, was that broadly uniform, and more democratic, standards were set up for the recruitment of bureaucrats. Also, a general corps of administrators—that is, generalists on the British model—was established for the purpose of instilling some cohesiveness in the viewpoint of the French bureaucratic elite.

On the surface, at least, the reforms were unsuccessful. A certain amount of democratization was achieved, but the middle and upper-middle classes were still most favored as a source of bureaucratic personnel. Nor did the idea of a class of general administrators with an overall perspective really work. Graduates of the newly created École National d'Administration exhibited something of a uniform governmental viewpoint, but they were not as yet, of course, members of the higher administrative echelons. Members of the grand corps continued to dominate the bureaucracy; both they and the ministries persisted in working at cross purposes. Of greater import, the old pattern of complicated lines of authority involving the executive, the legislature, and the bureaucracy was restored with frustrating consequences. Once again the bureaucracy seemed to lack direction and intention. Superficially, at least, the Fourth Republic was the Third all over again.

Yet the outward appearance of failure conveyed by these postwar bureaucratic reforms was rather deceptive: in fact, important changes were taking place, the most significant being the rapid replacement of a much older generation of bureaucrats by young cadres. France's large loss of manpower during World War I meant that the nation had skipped a generation; the consequent absence of a sizable middle-age segment in the Fourth Republic bureaucracy, plus the purges attendant upon the Liberation, brought very quickly to the top a new

generation of skilled bureaucrats—young men trained in the social as well as the natural sciences, whose outlook was far more "modern" and less ideological than that of their predecessors. Their major concern was to renew France, to create a modern industrial state that at the same time preserved the unique features of French culture. It was during the Fourth Republic, therefore, that some of the boldest and most far-sighted plans for reform were hatched in the bureaucracy. Most of them did not see the light of day, primarily because political pressures prohibited the development of any policies that trod on the toes of powerful interests; yet a certain type of economic planning did come into its own because of the dedication of men like Jean Monnet.

It was not until the Fifth Republic that all the postwar agitation and scheming for bureaucratic reform finally culminated in vast changes in the system. The de Gaulle regime made some marginal modifications in recruitment and training patterns, but its major contribution was to provide a government that could govern. Bureaucratic technicians were brought into the cabinet as ministers, and plans for reform were brought out into the open and implemented. In short, the Fifth Republic gave fairly free rein to bureaucratic creativity, and the system has been enormously improved as a result. It is not, of course, without its negative features, which will be discussed shortly.

STRUCTURE: The principal administrative agencies of the French government are the ministries, which perform the traditional functions of government—relating to such matters as foreign affairs, justice, defense, the interior—and also participate in the control of the public sector of the economy. The formal organization of the great ministries is fairly standardized. Under the minister's leadership, the division of authority is tripartite, consisting of (1) the minister's cabinet, (2) the managerial units (*directions*) of the ministry, and (3) various organs of consultation or control.

The French never devised a post equivalent to that of the British permanent secretary, an impartial civil servant who coordinates the work of a department. Why they did not is related to the whole context of French politics. In the past, many ministries have been a hodgepodge of services whose relation to one another was determined on political rather than administrative grounds. Since the *directions* often recruited their own corps, developed their own outlook, and acquired their own powerful friends in Parliament, it became almost impossible to coordinate them.

The ministers themselves could not cope with the problem of overall coordination; as a result they habitually appointed personal political friends to bureaucratic posts and drew upon career civil servants who were not unsympathetic to their political position. These political ministerial cabinets not only aided the minister in his contacts with the legislature and interest groups, but they also tried, somewhat unsuccessfully, to coordinate the managerial staffs within the ministry.

At first the cabinets were almost entirely political, but gradually they became dominated by career civil servants, often members of the grands corps, who were sympathetic to the minister's point of view. This occurred partly because of the growing complexity of government work, but primarily because purely political figures were unable to handle the increasingly urgent problems of coordination. By the time of the Fourth Republic, some two-thirds of the ministerial cabinets consisted of civil servants. Under the Fifth Republic, of course, many of the ministers themselves have been drawn from the bureaucracy. Bureaucratic or political in their complexion, the cabinets' coordinating efforts were usually checkmated. The power of the minister's agents to make their governmental department a cohesive unit was no greater than the power of the minister himself. Line officers generally distrusted members of the minister's cabinet who, when not politicians, were often of a lesser standing and seniority than themselves. Many ministers, of course,

made efforts to "colonize" their ministries with officials who were loyal to them, thus hampering the efforts of those who came after. For example, the Interior and Education ministries remained Socialist and Radical fiefs during much of the Fourth Republic, while the Foreign Office was monopolized by the M.R.P. until 1954. Coordination of the government bureaucracy improved considerably under de Gaulle; the regime rationalized the overall structure of the government and brought into high-level posts a large number of men sharing a common outlook. Most importantly, it dominated Parliament. With de Gaulle no longer in the Elysée Palace, parliamentary influence over the administrative apparatus of the state will probably increase to a certain extent, although a return to the bureaucratic fragmentation which marked the Fourth Republic is not likely to occur.

The *directeurs* are most frequently the highest-level permanent officials in a ministry, although even they can be replaced by ministers. They have direct access to the minister, often represent him before parliamentary committees, and have the power to sign ministerial decrees falling within the competence of the minister. Below each *direction* (or the *direction générale* in some ministries), little uniformity of organization exists. Sometimes there are *sous-directions* which are genuine subdivisions. Sometimes the word *service* is used to designate a subdivision; in other instances, a *service* is a fairly autonomous unit either directly under the personal control of the minister or else comparatively independent. This organizational fragmentation is partly caused by the division of the bureaucracy into various corps, but it is also closely related to the traditional weakness of the French executive. In any event, many *directions* have had quasi-independent status. Even within ministries, directeurs have fought and negotiated with one another, members of Parliament, and ministers in order to obtain approval for particular projects.

Because of the wide responsibilities of the central government, most French ministries have established extensive field or external services. In fact, more than 95 per cent of French civil servants are located outside Paris. When the French Revolution destroyed the territorial organization of the old regime, the provinces were replaced by administrative departments which have, until quite recently, remained the major units of territorial administration. In the twentieth century, departments became too small for some administrative activities; many ministries found that a field office in each of the 95 departments was excessive and made coordination difficult.[8] Some *directions* began to develop regional rather than departmental offices or to interpose regional offices between themselves and the departments. Unfortunately, this innovation produced little uniformity, even within a particular ministry. During the 1950's, the seven external services provided by the Department of Agriculture were split up in numerous ways; water and forest conservation services, for example, administered by the *Corps des Eaux et Forêts,* were divided into 41 conservation areas. The Rural Engineering Corps (*Corps du Génie Rural*) divided its services into 61 administrative areas; the Cereal Production Office had 13 regional branches. The result was confusing both for those striving to systematize the activities of ministries or *directions* from the top, and for citizens trying to obtain services. So long as governments were weak, it was very difficult to effect reforms, although many plans for doing so were devised. Since 1959, however, considerable progress has been made in reorganizing field services to conform with the economic division of France into 21 regional areas.

All but three government ministries (justice, foreign affairs, and information) now have inspectorates to supervise field administration. Eleven have overall inspectorates, concerned with the work of the entire department, as well as specialized inspection units concerned with the activity of a corps or divi-

sion. Others have only the specialized offices. The structure of inspectorates differs from department to department, but the inspectors general usually fulfill three functions: they supervise the activities of their own department or division, take on special investigative missions at the request of a minister, and, in some cases, participate on advisory councils attached to government departments.

At first, the advisory councils themselves were composed almost entirely of civil servants. The most renowned of these was the *Conseil d'État,* which will be discussed in detail later. Advisory councils have proliferated widely in the past hundred years and have tended to draw their membership increasingly from interest groups. They may be concerned with the activities of a department or with only one of its divisions. By 1959, close to half of the ministries had a national council competent to review all aspects of the department's work. Many have councils corresponding to the different *directions* or *services*. Most advisory councils are just that; they assume no responsibility for decisions.

THE CIVIL SERVICE: From the time of Napoleon, many top-ranking positions in the civil service were filled by young men who had received their training as engineers at the École Polytechnique or other engineering schools, and then moved on to either the civil or the military bureaucracy. Training at the École Polytechnique was broadly theoretical, and graduates usually left school with not only a knowledge of the general sciences but also at least some familiarity with philosophy and other humanistic subjects. It was felt that a man so educated, although trained as a technician, could develop a general administrative capacity as he moved up the ranks of a technical corps to which he might be attached and for which he might eventually assume managerial responsibility. Members of the nontechnical corps, on the other hand, were drawn largely from major law schools; their recruitment was informal and usually based on family connections.

With the founding of the Third Republic,

8 With the recent reorganization of the Paris region, France contains 95 metropolitan departments and four overseas departments.

reforms were pushed for improving the training and recruitment procedures for higher-level bureaucrats. The École Libre des Sciences Politiques was founded in 1871 to provide for the training of administrators in public law, administration, and economics, and beginning in 1882 Parliament passed a series of laws requiring that both ministries and corps standardize recruitment methods and make them public. The reforms, however, were not particularly successful. Recruitment patterns continued to be highly undemocratic, and although the École Polytechnique did open its doors to many persons of lower-middle-class background, the fees charged at the École Libre precluded the admission of all but the well-to-do, lending a distinctly conservative caste to the bureaucracy. Indeed, the École Libre itself was considered to be archconservative and traditional; aside from courses in philosophy, student training accented formalistic rather than empirically oriented studies. Departments and corps also retained an in-group orientation that made effective cooperation and an all-inclusive governmental perspective impossible. This was especially true of such prestige services as the *Conseil d'État, Inspection des Finances,* and *Cour des Comptes,* whose members, along with those in the Foreign Service, constitute the grands corps.[9] Members of the grands corps, as noted earlier,

were often brought in over the heads of regular line officials in other ministries, creating another source of dissension and disorganization.

Critics of the system pointed to the lack of common personnel standards and central fiscal control. Departmental budgets, which included salary requirements, were not subject to central, cabinet-level review, and individual ministries pleaded for funds directly with the finance committees of the two houses of Parliament. The resultant anarchy meant that some ministries were well staffed at the expense of others.

At the beginning of the Fourth Republic, another series of reform measures was initiated to unify and democratize the civil service. The first established a *Direction générale de la fonction publique,* the top civil-service office; it was directly under the premier, who was given prime responsibility for implementing new laws on civil-service recruitment. Another 1946 law divided the civil service into classes modeled on the British system. Four government-wide categories were created—A, B, C, and D—with the first two corresponding more or less to those of the British administrative and executive classes.

The École Libre was incorporated into the University of Paris and lost its right-wing bias in the process. Of greater importance, the government created a national school of administration, the École Nationale d'Administration (E.N.A.). Henceforth, those wishing to enter the equivalent of the British administrative class, either in ministries or one of the grands corps, would have to pass through the E.N.A. Democratization of the civil service would be achieved not only because the fees charged E.N.A. entrants would be nominal but because admission to the school would be open to both university graduates and civil servants in the French equivalent of the English executive class. The E.N.A. would unify the service because, for the first time, France would have created a group of general administrators who shared a common educational

[9] Discussion of the *Conseil d'État* begins on p. 689. The *Inspection des Finances* and the *Cour des Comptes* are responsible for financial audits of all French public agencies. The *Inspection* is attached to the Ministry of Economy and Finance, while the *Cour* is quasi-independent; the work of both is largely technical, but those who serve in them, as well as those in the *Conseil,* constitute an elite group of bureaucrats who, in time, can expect to become directeurs, senior economic or financial advisers to the government, members of ministerial cabinets, or even ministers. The government formed after the 1967 election included four former members of the *Conseil d'État* and one each from the *Cour des Comptes* and the *Inspection des Finances.* The government formed in 1969, after the election of Georges Pompidou as president, included two former members of the *Conseil,* one former member of the *Cour,* and four former members of the *Inspection.* The premier, Jacques Chaban-Delmas, began his career in the Finance Inspectorate.

background. Ministries and corps would no longer be permitted to give their own examinations; rather, a common examination would be given to all E.N.A. students.

All these efforts at reform have been only partially successful. Most ministries still more or less determine their own recruitment, and once a young man enters a ministry he usually becomes part of a corps, with all that implies. Nor have the grand corps been abolished: they retain their existence, their prestige, and the loyalty of their members, who are still the mandarins of the French bureaucracy. Further, not too many members of the executive class have managed to use the E.N.A. as a means of promotion, and since most students enter the École only after graduation from a university, its success in democratizing the bureaucracy has been limited. In fact, the proportion of top-level bureaucrats of middle-class background probably has increased in recent years, while the ratio of those with a working-class origin has dropped. In 1952 and 1953, for example, the proportion of E.N.A. graduates of working-class background was 1.5 per cent; ten years later it was 0.5 per cent. On the other hand, men and women from professional backgrounds made up almost twenty per cent of the successful candidates in 1962 and 1963, as compared with a little more than ten per cent a decade earlier. As educational opportunities in France expand, however, so, too, may the civil-service opportunities for those from the working class.

The *anciens élèves* of the E.N.A. share something of a common perspective, and they are beginning to bring to the service a somewhat more comprehensive, national outlook than that which has characterized it in the past. Except for those who are already executive-class bureaucrats, candidates for the E.N.A. must pass an entrance examination and must possess a university degree. Some choice in examination subject matter is permitted, depending on a candidate's preferred branch of service, but more than 75 per cent of the grade is based on performance in such fields as economic geography, law, and history.

Much of the three years' training of successful E.N.A. applicants is aimed at creating

TABLE 22.3. FAMILY BACKGROUND OF GRADUATES OF THE
ÉCOLE NATIONALE D'ADMINISTRATION,
SERVING IN THE FOUR GRANDS CORPS, 1953–1963

Occupation of father	Council of State	Finance Inspectorate	Court of Accounts	Foreign Service	Average
Civil servant	40%	38%	43%	42%	41%
Craftsman, merchant	11	14	9	8	11
Head of industrial enterprise	0	6	10	10	6
Commercial and industrial manager	23	17	18	19	19
Industrial and commercial employee	4	4	2	6	4
Professional	16	11	18	13	14
No occupation	2	1	0	0	1
Agriculturalist	2	7	2	4	4
Worker	4	0	0	0	1

Totals exceed 100% because of rounding.

Adapted from Alfred Diamant, "Tradition and Innovation in French Administration," *Comparative Political Studies*, I (July 1968), p. 269. Reprinted by permission of the publisher and author.

a common background and orientation for the future leaders of the civil service. A student's first year is normally spent in apprenticeship within the bureaucracy, and his second at the school in Paris, where fairly technical lectures and seminars are given. At the end of the second year, he takes an examination, the results of which more or less determine the corps he will join after his third year at the E.N.A. This is a crucial point in his career. The hope of most students, of course, is to be posted to one of the grands corps; since only 15 to twenty per cent are so chosen, competition for positions with the elite group is extremely stiff. In the third year (which is often reduced to six months), the student spends time in industry and receives special training in the corps to which he will be assigned. Once a student enters his corps, he remains on probation for another one or two years.

The E.N.A. is first and foremost the training ground for French "civil administrators." Technical personnel are still recruited for the civil service from the École Polytechnique and other specialized schools. Because the French are willing to place scientific personnel in the highest levels of administration, many of these graduates achieve positions of general prominence, especially in the management of nationalized industries. Students entering the École Polytechnique and the E.N.A. do not always plan to make the state service a lifetime career. Many of the technical-school graduates go immediately into private industry; a substantial number of civil servants, including members of the grands corps, later join them, usually at about the age of forty. The large role that the French state has always assumed in the economy has placed these men very much in demand, and they can usually command higher salaries in the business world than in the bureaucratic. There has always been a far closer relationship between the *haut fonctionnaire* and the business community in France than in England. Sometimes this liaison has tended to make the bureaucracy more conservative, but

under the Fourth and Fifth Republics, it has contributed greatly to the lessening of friction between the business community and the government in the area of national planning.

Like the British, the French tend to regard the bureaucracy as a career to be entered at a fairly young age. Thus, with some exceptions, those in the administrative class are usually recruited at the time of their graduation from a university. Unlike the British, the French place scant faith in such intangibles as "character" or "experience" in determining admission to the E.N.A.—or promotion later. Until he is fairly close to the top civil-service echelons, where political connections begin to count, the French bureaucrat advances on the basis of competitive, fairly theoretical written examinations.

CONTROLS: For the seventy years following the end of the Franco-Prussian War, it was all but impossible for the French cabinet, and more especially the premier, to have effective control over the bureaucratic machinery—a result of the weakness of the French executive, not of bureaucratic sabotage. Individual ministers found themselves in the same position, although they could, if they ever remained in office long enough, "colonize" portions of their ministry with trusted subordinates.

The legislature did, in some ways, exercise a form of control over the civil service, but its efforts were directed primarily toward obtaining special favors or blocking the full implementation of particular programs. A devious interrelationship developed among the chairman of important committees (especially the finance committee and its subcommittees), special-interest groups, and the bureaucracy, under which promises of appropriations were swapped for promises of fitting bureaucratic action. And, of course, deputies could make life uncomfortable for bureaucrats gauche enough to antagonize well-placed constituents.

Executive control of the bureaucracy was strengthened under the de Gaulle regime, although the bureaucracy's continued fragmentation into various corps was still a problem. The ability of Pompidou's government to provide overall direction will depend very much on his skill in maintaining command of his own party in Parliament.

In the absence of effective political controls, the number of internal control mechanisms has proliferated. On the whole, these have been legal rather than organizational in nature—that is, they have been designed to prevent bureaucrats from exceeding their powers and to limit venality; they have not been designed for the purpose of creatively coordinating the state civil-service operation. Where bureaucratic agencies have been established for the purpose of achieving greater coordination, however, they have generally failed.

Perhaps the most important internal-control agency is the *Conseil d'État*. Under Napoleon its functions, like those of the old *Conseil du Roi* under the Bourbons, were to prepare and edit legislation, draw up decrees, and adjudicate disputes among the ministries. In fact, during Napoleon's reign it was clearly the most important legislative and administrative body in France, having, for example, the principal responsibility in drawing up the Napoleonic Codes.

Gradually, however, the *Conseil d'État* began to take on a series of other duties. Both the revolutionaries and Napoleon wished to eliminate the interference of the regular courts in the work of the government. The evaluation of administrative acts, therefore, and the protection of the citizen against the excesses of administrative authority were placed in the hands of the administration itself, primarily the Conseil. Over the years, the Conseil's authority in the judicial sphere expanded. In 1806 a special judicial section was created; in 1824 those of its members who were also active administrators were prohibited from voting on cases involving their ministries; in 1872, under the Third Republic, the Council of State was given the authority to issue final judgments in administrative litigation. Until then, its opinions had been only advisory, with final dispositions resting with the executive.

Concurrent with these shifts in its responsibilities, the reputation of the Conseil also shifted. During the middle portion of the nineteenth century, liberals, looking to England, urged the abolition of its judicial functions, arguing that only the regular courts, serviced by an independent judiciary, could protect the rights of citizens. And in the early years of the Third Republic, deputies felt that the Conseil's legislative and administrative activities were essentially political, and that both should be the immediate obligation of the executive—under parliamentary control.

By the latter years of the Third Republic, however, it had become quite clear that, as an administrative court, the *Conseil d'État* was doing an excellent job in protecting the rights of French citizens. In fact, it gradually built up a body of case law that made French administrative procedure in that area among the most advanced in the world. As its prestige continued to grow, the *Conseil d'État* attracted more of the best qualified civil-service recruits, and its members became one of the grands corps. They were often called to other departments on special missions; their placement within other ministries and the breadth of their experience gave the Conseil even more authority than it was legally allotted.

Today, the administrative functions of the Conseil involve advice on the drafting of bills and executive decrees. Actually, its legal authority in connection with executive decrees has diminished under the Fifth Republic. In both the Third and Fourth Republics, all decrees issued in pursuance of a law had to be placed before the Conseil before taking effect. This is still true, but under the constitution of the Fifth Republic the executive has acquired new powers to issue decrees which have the force of law and are not dependent upon specific legislation passed by Parliament; such decrees, which are called ordinances to differentiate them from regular decrees, do not have to be submitted to the Conseil, nor do actions taken by the president in an emergency under the powers granted him in Article 16.[10] Nevertheless, the government often consults the Conseil before issuing ordinances; since cases involving ordinances may come before the Conseil serving as an administrative court, it seems wise to secure the opinion of its members.

The Council of State also advises ministries on administrative problems. A 1963 decree formalized what had been the case for a long time: that Conseil members should be given missions to other departments and offer the government suggestions for reform. The Conseil also supervises local government by insuring that locally elected bodies operate only within their legal limits and carry out the duties they are supposed to perform. It can send investigative task forces to local areas and call the government's attention to problems requiring remedial action.

In its judicial functions, the Conseil stands at the head of a system of 23 administrative courts. It handles appeals from these lower courts, although it may act as a court of first instance in important cases. As an administrative court, the Conseil can annul actions if it finds they exceed the authority of those making them, violate proper procedures, or fail to adhere to the spirit of the law. For example, if there were evidence that an administrator had issued a regulation which seemed to benefit him to the detriment of others, or which was otherwise unreasonable, his action could be quashed even if he had acted legally. In one case, the Conseil reversed the decision of a mayor who had refused to permit a merchant to have a stall in the municipal market. The mayor could offer no good reasons for his refusal, and it was shown that the merchant had, some time previously, ignored the mayor's request that he apologize to a municipal councillor after both were involved in some local contretemps.

The *Conseil d'État* can also offer redress for damage caused by administrative actions. Here the court has gradually widened the range of the state's responsibility for the actions of its agents to a point that goes far beyond British or American practice. Today it is possible to sue a public service whenever it can reasonably be held that its agent was on duty at the time of the alleged injury, even when no fault exists on the part of the service or its agent—unless, of course, the damage was due to the complainant's negligence. For example, persons injured in a running fight between policemen and criminals are compensated. If the police official himself is adjudged partially responsible, the court may order him to share the payment of damages with the state.

There can be no gainsaying the excellent work of the Conseil in its administrative, legislative, and judicial functions. An institution that once tended to favor the state over the citizen, it has become increasingly functional, and its admiration by Anglo-Saxon commentators is not without warrant. It is true, nevertheless, that the Council of State's functions reflect a lack of political control over and coordination within the French bureaucracy. And the administrative and legislative functions of the Conseil, while technically excellent, are no substitute for an executive who can bring his authority to bear upon the entire structure of the civil service.

The problem of coordinating the work of the French bureaucracy is also complicated by the fact that the central government is totally responsible for tasks which in England would be left to local authorities. There is no decentralization of authority, only deconcentration; while various ministries have their own inspectorates for checking up on the work of field offices, one of the most important posts created for this purpose has been filled by the prefect.[11]

---

10 See Chapter 16, pp. 514 and 515.

11 The role of prefects in police matters will be reviewed in Chapter 23.

Established by Napoleon I to insure effective control of the bureaucracy by the central government, the prefecture was in some ways a carry-over from the intendancy of the old regime. With the destruction of local autonomy, however, it became far more powerful. Throughout a good part of the nineteenth century, prefects not only examined the performances of the external ministries of all departments and helped maintain internal order, they also helped incumbent politicians win re-election. The prefectures' special sphere of authority gave them a distinctly political cast, so that from time to time, changes in government brought wholesale purges. Nevertheless, because of its importance, the office drew to itself men of exceptional talent, and, in effect, it became one of the grands corps of the French state. Even after the rise of municipal councils and popularly elected mayors during the Third Republic, the prefect has remained the most powerful figure in the commune as well as in the department.

The prefect is, above all else, the representative of the state. As such he can, in time of emergency, exercise considerable powers —especially police powers—on his own initiative. He is also the representative of the Interior Ministry, which has direct responsibility for the supervision of local authorities; consequently he serves as the middle link in the chain of bureaucracy that extends from the central administration to the commune. The prefect is responsible for the coordination of all government services, and he reports on the work of field offices and the local government itself. Furthermore, requests made by mayors and local councils are funneled through him to the central government, and technicians from the ministries are required to consult with him on their improvement programs, not only to find out what is politically feasible but also to insure that someone concerned with the interests of the department as a whole has a voice in determining the value of such programs. Brian Chapman's description of the role of the pre-

fect in the Fourth Republic sums up his functions very nicely:

He is the intermediary between the Government and the population, between the politicians and the electorate. He is the administrator who is part politician, and the politician who is a first class administrator. He is the representative of the State in the Department, and the protector of departmental interests against the Ministries. He makes the Mayors obey the law and he fights other officials in the Department, and sometimes their Ministries as well, on behalf of the Mayors. He is the executive instrument of the Government, and at the same time the initiator of departmental policy. His role is partly administration, partly politics, partly social leadership.[12]

Fifth Republic France has moved toward restoring the prefect's authority, which had slipped to some extent in the postwar years. The nation's departments always were illogical from the standpoint of administering services, and this had made coordination by a departmental prefect more and more difficult. Also, despite the assistance of a technical staff, prefects were finding themselves unable to deal realistically with problems of a technological nature, with the result that they were being bypassed by both the ministerial field offices and the mayors. Under decrees issued in 1964, regional prefects, who remain responsible also for the administration of a specific department, are provided with increased technical aid and given greater responsibilities in regional economic planning. Moreover, all correspondence between ministries and their field offices relating to the affairs of a department must pass through the prefecture. In effect, the heads of the external services in a department now hold their authority from the prefect rather than from the ministry in Paris.

12 *The Prefects and Provincial France* (London: George Allen and Unwin, 1955), p. 144.

The French bureaucracy has reflected France's general historical experience. From the old regime the French inherited the idea of an administrative apparatus that would be instrumental in controlling and directing the nation's development. Napoleon carried on this tradition, augmenting it with an emphasis on a technical elite whose position would be based on merit.

Both the weakness of French political institutions and the emergence of the corps as administrative recruiter reduced the ability of political leaders to control the bureaucratic elite and provide it with direction. While the bureaucracy could maintain order as French governments quickly changed, it could not, despite the excellent training of many who composed it, channel the course of French development. Under the Fifth Republic, the bureaucracy has come into its own, and its members have been vitally helpful in modernizing French society and in lending great impetus to its economic growth. These changes were brought about because younger cadres stepped into important civil-service positions—and because the de Gaulle regime was able to exercise firm leadership over the bureaucracy.

The major problems faced by the French bureaucracy today are, in some ways, the reverse of those facing the English. The French, for example, have yet to develop an administrative organization that can curb the centrifugal tendencies of the corps, especially the grands corps. Further, the innovations developed by the Fifth Republic came largely from above, and represented technocratic solutions to what were, in many cases, political problems. Indeed, this seems always to have been the case in France; the nation alternates between periods of fairly effective authoritarian leadership and periods of administrative and political chaos. The French have never developed that capacity to balance authority and participation in policy-making which has been the hallmark of the British political system.

The two nations are moving closer together as they attempt to find procedures for insuring effective governance, the encouragement of innovation, and, at the same time, the increased participation of the citizen in decisions which affect him. Whether the Fifth Republic can produce a satisfactory balance among all these requirements without de Gaulle is an open question.

5. THE GERMAN PATTERN

ORIGINS AND DEVELOPMENT: The basis for the modern German civil service was created by Frederick William I and Frederick the Great of Prussia; it was restructured by Baron von Stein and Prince von Hardenberg in the aftermath of Prussia's defeat by Napoleon. The bureaucracy these men created was a social elite recruited on the basis of competitive examination and dedicated both to efficiency and to the principle of autocracy. In the nineteenth century, its competence and integrity brought it tremendous prestige and caused it to be emulated by other countries.

Prussia was the first European nation in which the state accepted a large measure of responsibility for seeing to it that the universities produced people with the professional qualifications needed to run a modern state. For general administration, training in law became the normal requirement. But the government also wanted officials with technical qualifications, particularly in the fields of engineering and forestry. Men with professional training, then, were brought into the public service and promoted to top-level administrative positions.

Under the firm guidance of its bureaucrats, Germany made a rapid transition to an industrial society. Theoretically, the bureaucracy was responsible to the monarch and his chief minister, but in practice it made most of the decisions on the direction of domestic policy. Prussia and later the empire were to be *Rechtsstaaten* (states ruled by law) organized in such a way as to promote general economic growth and state power. Furthermore, a Rechtsstaat was to be one in which the government looked after the welfare of the lower orders through adequate social legislation. The German bureaucracy, however, was also a force which, in treating political matters as if they were merely questions of administration, inhibited the development of the German capacity for self-governance.

The government of early nineteenth-century Germany was divided into offices responsible to the monarch and staffed at the highest echelons by civil servants. Field offices were supervised by district government officers and, on the county level, by a *Landrat,* a royal official appointed by the king on the advice of the local nobility. Until well into the century, the only checks on the bureaucracy were internal; that is, supervision came from the next higher level of administration. In fact, when a legislature was incorporated into the Prussian system, civil-service field officials took on the responsibility of guaranteeing a docile majority, and many Landräte "allowed" themselves to be elected deputies.

The formation of the Second Reich in 1871 and the subsequent industrialization of Germany created a host of new problems. German federalism involved national supremacy in the legislative field, but also left the administration of the law to the states. Thus the Länder, for instance, enforced Reich health laws, administered uniform weights and measures, and collected taxes. To the Bundesrat was given the authority to issue basic regulations (*Grundsatzvorschriften*) on the uniform execution of the law, and Berlin did retain ultimate authority—including the right of armed intervention—where local officialdom proved recalcitrant.

The division of administrative authority between the federal government and the states was a ready-made source of conflict, but the arrangement worked reasonably well under the Second Reich, which established central administrative offices to help supervise the laws. Lacking field services, these offices were compactly organized; their major functions were to draft legislative proposals and to maintain communications with Land ministries, partly in order to supervise the execution of national laws. On the whole, these relations were informal. Most of the Länder had adopted the Prussian administrative pattern and a good many of their senior civil servants were drawn from the Prussian bureaucracy. Personal contacts were, therefore, close, and in the few cases of major disagreement the Bundesrat could be counted on to iron out differences.

On the state level, the pattern of administration during the Second Reich continued almost unchanged. Authority moved downward from provincial governors to district officers and Landräte, with additional supervision by the Interior Ministry. After 1872 a certain amount of authority was delegated to self-governing bodies, especially to those on the county level. This meant that the royal official had to share some of his power with a county council and a county committee, but since the Landrat was usually a local notable, he usually dominated these bodies anyway. In 1875 there were created three tiers of administrative courts—district, county, and Land—which came to exercise a degree of independence and from time to time reversed the decisions of administrative officials. But since most court officials came from the same class and had received the same training as other bureaucrats, conflicts between them were infrequent.

The training of those bureaucrats not in charge of technical services was mostly in law, and while it pointed out the rights of individuals to equal treatment under the law, it emphasized strict obedience to the state as constituting the supreme legitimate authority. After obtaining a law degree, a prospective bureaucrat served an apprenticeship with a Landrat or district officer and fulfilled his military obligations by service in the reserve. Those admitted to the service were invariably Protestant "gentlemen" of sound "German" instincts, and their training instilled them with loyalty to the service's general ethos. The social position conferred upon them as members of the bureaucracy also contributed to an esprit de corps, and because the sons of bureaucrats so often followed in their fathers' footsteps, the bureaucracy took on the qualities of a closed caste.

The founders of the Weimar Republic moved timidly in the direction of greater centralization. The Weimar constitution provided for the creation of a national field administration for collecting taxes and, by implication, for other purposes as well. However, the constitution also declared that national laws would be executed by Land authorities whenever the federal government failed to take action. In fact, the latter created only two national agencies with their own field services, a Reich Finance Administration and a Reich Unemployment Insurance Authority. Further measures toward centralization were blocked by the fact that the Center Party, the cornerstone of most governments of the Weimar years, was strongly federalist.

It was during the 1920's that the difficulties inherent in Germany's dual system of administration became obvious. While the Reich and Prussia were, for most of the decade, controlled by moderate governments, many of the Länder came under the domination of left-wing or, more often, right-wing regimes. On many occasions, especially with regard to proposed police action against right-wing groups, the Länder refused to enforce the law despite pressures from the national government.

The problem was also aggravated by the hostility of upper-level civil servants to the republic itself. Prussia and some of the other states did try to dilute the caste orientation of the bureaucracy by broadening recruitment and lowering educational qualifications. But these reforms were not successful: educational opportunities in Germany at the time were limited, so that the changes were marginal and only resulted in further alienating the permanent officials.

The Nazis, of course, completely destroyed the federal structure of the Reich, centraliz-ing all political and administrative authority. Considerable power was delegated to the party, which was to act as both a spur to civil servants and a managerial elite. They also purged bureaucrats of Jewish background as well as those whose politics were suspect, while the more important civil servants who remained in office were forced to join the party.

Most bureaucrats went along with the new regime for numerous reasons. Even so, tensions between the party and the bureaucracy were never satisfactorily resolved. The Nazi Party had never been very successful in enlisting the membership of the administrative elite; these men came mostly from middle- and upper-class families and had spent their lives in bureaucratic security, while the Nazis were persons of petty-bourgeois or working-class background. To the bureaucratic elite, the party leaders—principally men whose lives had been marked by personal disorganization—were bohemians and upstarts. The Nazis, on the other hand, viewed the bureaucrats whom they had come to dominate with a mixture of envy and resentment. No matter how politically conservative they might have been, the traditional civil servants insisted upon regular procedures and legal forms. To the party, these forms were a sham; what was needed was dedication to the cause and an inner feeling for the spirit of the German people.

The Government Reorganization Act of 1933 gave each Land cabinet the authority to issue decree laws. As these cabinets were now appointed by Reich officials, both lawmaking and administration were, in effect, determined in Berlin. The following year, the Nazis officially divested the Länder of political autonomy and abolished the *Reichsrat,* the Land-dominated upper house of Parliament. In Prussia, all state government offices were merged with the federal equivalents. Other Länder retained their own ministries, but these were tightly controlled by the Reich governors, who were also regional party leaders (*Gauleiter*).

On all levels of the German government, Nazis were appointed, wherever possible, to strategic posts, and important personnel were put through a screening process. The party police took on the responsibility for keeping order, and Heinrich Himmler used his party position as head of the *Schutzstaffel* (protective squadron) to become ruler of a vast apparatus that included not only the SS but also the Gestapo and, in most regions, the regular police forces.

What the Nazi bureaucratic structure added up to was confusion. Rational coordination was not a forte of the regime; the multiplication of overlapping jurisdictions, as well as power struggles among party members, further complicated administrative problems. Hundreds of conflicting regulations rained down upon field offices from the party and the central ministries. Typical was the organization of civil defense. In 1939 the Reich appointed Gauleiters regional defense commissioners to coordinate the work of all agencies whose functions were relevant to civil defense. The Gauleiters also were responsible for all wartime economic controls. Unfortunately, the areas over which they exercised jurisdiction did not coincide either with the administrative regions according to which the police were organized or with the army and air force regional districts. The results were chaotic.

The Allies were convinced that it was necessary to reform and democratize the German civil service. The reform procedure, however, varied widely, depending upon the assumptions of the occupying power. In the West, the French established fairly centralized Land regimes; the British created a nonpartisan, highly professional administration that delegated considerable authority to local bodies; and the Americans emphasized democratization and decentralization. All three powers conducted de-Nazification programs, the Americans far more doggedly than either the English or the French. The Americans also placed great importance upon broadening the type of training required for upper-level bu-

reaucrats, including the teaching of social sciences.

On the whole, the Allies' programs had little lasting impact. Leading Nazis were removed from the service, but the shortage of personnel and the fact that almost every remaining administrator of any importance had been a party member vitiated the effectiveness of their programs. And as Germany regained her sovereignty, the traditional patterns of recruitment were revived.

STRUCTURE: With some significant modifications, the Bonn constitution more or less recreated the administrative structure of pre-Nazi Germany. The Länder are now again responsible for the execution of federal laws, except where the constitution specifically provides otherwise. In fact, the postwar constitution permits direct federal administration only on matters pertaining to foreign policy, tax collection, the border police and defense forces, the post office, rail and water transportation, the investigation of subversive activities, and some social-insurance programs. It also permits the federal government to execute new laws when there is an "urgent necessity" for general administration.

In practice, the federal government has established its own agencies in only one field, that of unemployment insurance, although it has also created joint federal-Land agencies for the collection of taxes. The Länder administer all other domestic programs under federal supervision. This surveillance operates through the Bundesrat, the upper chamber of the Parliament; through informal conferences between federal and Land officials; and through the administrative court system, in addition, of course, to regular political channels.

The Bundesrat has, perhaps, the key legal role in federal supervision of Land administrative activities. With its consent, the federal government may specify the field organization and the administrative procedures of those state agencies which execute federal laws. The Bundesrat also enacts general adminis-

MAP 22.1. PER CAPITA TAX INCOME, BY LÄNDER, 1967

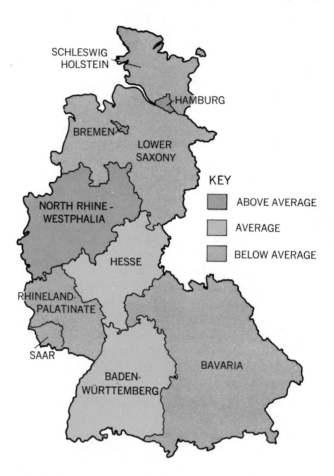

Adapted from *Statistiches Jahrbuch für die Bundesrepublik Deutsch-land, 1968,* p. 400; and Lewis Edinger, *Politics in Germany* (Boston: Little, Brown, 1968), p. 13, copyright © 1968, Little, Brown and Company, Inc. Adapted by permission of the publishers.

trative regulations and, with Bundesrat approval, the federal government may dispatch inspectors to Land field offices. In practice, the Bundesrat has been quite lenient in its supervisory capacity. If a Land refuses to comply with federal regulations, however, the federal government possesses the right to apply sanctions with the approval of the Bundesrat. Parliament may also appeal to the Federal Constitutional Court for a judgment against a state.

The West German constitution has also made the administrative court system com-

pletely independent of administrative agencies. The Supreme Administrative Court, whose judges are federal appointees, checks upon Land violations of the intent of federal law. The court is the highest body in the bureaucratic hierarchy, and its rulings on disputed questions of administration have tended to accord with the position taken by federal ministries.

Because of their extensive devolution of administrative authority, German federal offices are more compact than their French or even their English counterparts.[13] Organized along functional lines, they are headed by a political minister and permanent officials who manage the day-to-day affairs of the department. Unlike French ministers, those in Germany do not bring a "political" cabinet into office with them, although they do rely upon the services of political state secretaries who serve as seconds-in-command—men who are drawn from the bureaucracy, but are chosen either for their sympathy with the views of the minister or their contribution to the political balance of the government. A number of ministers are also now entitled to parliamentary undersecretaries to help them with both their departmental work and their parliamentary relations.

Many ministers during the 1950's did not exercise effective political control over their departments. Often themselves former bureaucrats, they tended to accept the opinions of the permanent career officials who served them, and the influence of the second-echelon officials became such that many interest groups turned directly to them. Not surprisingly, scandals occurred involving bureaucrats who had received "gifts" from private parties. Ministerial control became somewhat tighter under the Grand Coalition—the majority of cabinet members were fairly strong-minded political figures—and this trend is likely to continue under the Brandt regime. Because German administration is so decentralized, most federal ministries are concerned primarily with the preparation of legislation and of ordinances spelling out the rules for its uniform application. Since German ministries lack a substantial network of field offices, the problems of coordination that have plagued the British and the French have not arisen.

THE BUREAUCRACY: To become a permanent member (*Beamte*) of the German civil service means not only a secure life position

and an excellent pension upon retirement, it has also meant, in the past at least, being treated with considerable deference and addressed by one's title (accorded not only to a Beamte but to his wife). It should, of course, be pointed out that the term "bureaucracy" has a far wider application in Germany and France than in England or the United States. Not only has the state traditionally engaged in a broader variety of activities, but the title "Beamte" also applies to judges, teachers, and members of the state railroad and postal systems who carry out managerial functions similar to those of private employees.

In addition to Beamten, the administrative services include two other categories of personnel: employees (*Angestellten*) who lack the security of tenure and pension privileges of the Beamten, and manual workers (*Arbeiter*). The differences between the Beamten and Angestellten have steadily diminished over the years, although the Beamten still command more prestige and hold the highest positions in the civil service.

Most civil-service policy posts, especially those on the federal level, have traditionally been the preserve of those trained in the law, although now, as in the past, agencies controlling the railroads and public works are staffed at the top levels by trained engineers. In the Allied program to reform the German civil service after Hitler's defeat, the Americans especially had hoped to bring in people with a social-science background, thus breaking the stranglehold of the law faculties upon the training of bureaucrats. However, the control of social-science teaching by law faculties blocked this effort, and the Federal Career Officials Act of 1953, followed by state laws modeled closely upon it, restored the status quo ante.[14] The 1953 act and the Civil Service Act of 1961 divide the bureaucracy into three classes, roughly approximating the British and French systems.

13 Such agencies as the foreign ministry, the federal bank, the federal railways, and the federal postal service do have field services.

14 The Länder are responsible for the recruitment of their own civil-service personnel; however, the federal government, with the approval of the Bundesrat, has the authority to set general standards.

698

PUBLIC POLICY AND ITS IMPLEMENTATION

Recruitment to the higher civil service pre-supposes a university degree. Applicants are chosen on the basis of general examinations and enter a three-year program of in-service training. Success in a second examination at the end of three years leads to a lifetime position in the administrative class. It is rare, however, that entrée into these positions is gained before the age of 25. Because of this, and because of the rather limited educational opportunities and the negligible number of in-service promotions, the German bureaucracy remains very much the domain of older men from the middle and upper middle classes.

Even so, political leaders are more and more frequently calling for far more extensive training in the social sciences and foreign languages. Many ministries have complained, for example, that they have an embarrassing lack of personnel equipped to deal with other European countries at conferences on topics of common concern. Thus, courses in economics and sociology have been introduced for senior federal bureaucrats, and some states, such as Bavaria, have made arrangements to have their senior civil servants spend part of a year of in-service training at Paris's École Nationale. In 1969, the federal government opened a new academy of public administration to provide further in-service training for senior civil-service personnel.

There are other chips in the civil service's encrusted traditions. The newer generation of bureaucrats is less likely to stand solely on its dignity, and the deference with which the public once regarded the bureaucracy is slowly eroding. Moreover, Germany, like France and England, is finding that many of its best bureaucrats are being lured away from government service by attractive professional and industrial offers. As in the other two countries, concern has been registered about the growing tendency of German bureaucrats to leave the government at the height of their powers for more lucrative private positions.

CONTROL AND ACCOUNTABILITY: Political controls in Germany, exercised by the federal government through the Bundesrat, have already been described. Like most civil-law countries, Germany has established a general system of specialized administrative courts on both the federal and state levels. The Supreme Administrative Court has jurisdiction both as an appeal court from the Land supreme administrative courts and as a court of first and last instance in a few other cases.

The overall authority of these courts, however, is limited by two factors: (1) civil courts have jurisdiction in cases concerning the value of property appropriated by the government and in cases involving claims against a public authority for damages, and (2) the constitutional courts of the republic and of the various Länder have jurisdiction in areas pertaining to the violation of constitutional rights. Nevertheless, the courts have been a liberalizing force in German society; the Supreme Administrative Court, for example, decided in 1955 that the receipt of welfare was a right, and that an administrative decision to refuse welfare benefits could be appealed. It has also decided that it can review a student's grades to determine if correct examination procedures were followed, and, more importantly, it has widened the grounds on which Germans may refuse to serve in the armed forces. Germany is one of the few countries in which an individual may now gain exemption from military service on moral grounds, without having to base such refusal on a set of transcendental religious beliefs.

6. THE RUSSIAN AND SOVIET PATTERN

ORIGINS AND DEVELOPMENT: Russian bureaucracy, like that of Western Europe, began as an extension of the prince's household. Administrative tasks were initially entrusted to boyars who were in personal attendance on the czar, and eventually these aristocrats gathered around them small staffs of secretaries and clerks. As the monarchy attempted to enlarge its authority at the expense of the nobility, czars turned for support, as had many of their Western counterparts, to the lesser nobility to whom position as a member of the czar's household meant a substantial increase in both status and wealth. By the time of Peter the Great in the late seventeenth century, the bureaucracy had, in fact, become almost completely the personal instrument of the ruler.

Peter himself became passionately dedicated to the modernization of Russia—as, indeed, were several of his successors. In their efforts to transform administrative institutions, almost all of them turned to Western Europe for their models, importing foreigners to establish schools and train technicians, and sending potential servants of the state abroad for training. Progress was, nevertheless, painfully slow. Russia lacked the social and cultural patterns to support an efficient bureaucracy. More often than not, those who tried to develop a sound administrative system were either corrupted or defeated by it.

In the middle of the nineteenth century, the government entered actively upon a campaign to industrialize Russia. Railways and factories were built, mining was extended, and financial institutions were created in a program designed to pull Russia abreast of the West. With some exceptions, however, the bureaucratic talent available was unequal to the task, and the guns of World War I sounded the death knell of the old regime.

To Lenin, as to Marx, the Communist revolution would eventually replace the entire apparatus of government with some vaguely defined organization in which traditional forms of political authority would disappear and through which community decisions would be made more or less spontaneously by the people. Neither man viewed the future society as devoid of all organization, but they conceived of its structure as quite simple and marked by little if any distinctions in rewards or status.

In the years immediately following the Russian Revolution, the anarchistic strain in the Communist Party was associated with such things as worker control in factories and the proliferation of such "democratic" bodies as the workers' soviets. Indeed, many Bolsheviks went so far as to call for the immediate liquidation of both the state and the party apparatus. Needless to say, this did not occur. Under the exigencies of completing the Revolution, many who had formerly been anarchists gained power only to discover the virtues of organization and authority. And those who remained loyal to their previous commitment to anarchy quickly found themselves relegated to the margins of Soviet life, if not erased from its pages altogether.

Lenin himself wasted no time reaching the conclusion that management of the economic and political apparatus of Russian society required trained party and state cadres, and that, until these could be developed, the regime would have to draw upon the professional classes of the old regime. As he explained it:

We now have a vast army of governmental employees, but we lack sufficiently educated forces to exercise real control over them. Actually, it often happens that at the top, where we exercise political power, the machine functions somehow; but down below, where these state officials are in control, they often function in such a way as to counteract our measures. . . . Down below . . . there are hundreds of thousands of old officials who came over to us from the Tsar and from bourgeois society and who, sometimes consciously and sometimes unconsciously, work against us. Nothing can be done here in a short space of time, that is clear. Many years of hard work will be required to improve the machine, to reform it, and to enlist new forces.[15]

In fact, bureaucrats from the old regime continued to be used until the late 1930's, when the great purge probably eliminated most of them and also offered an opportunity for a new generation of young men and

---

[15] Quoted in Merle Fainsod, *How Russia Is Ruled,* rev. ed. (Cambridge: Harvard University Press, 1963), p. 389.

women, trained by the regime itself, to rise to positions of power. The regime during these years also drew upon the talents of technical personnel from the West who had been left unemployed by the Great Depression.

By the middle and late 1930's, then, the Soviet Union had created its own bureaucracy, and the nation was, in truth, fast becoming an extensively bureaucratized society. The old dreams of egalitarianism without compulsion had gone by the board to await the day when true communism arrived. In the meantime, the planning of every important aspect of Soviet life had resulted in the creation of an administrative machine more complex than that of most Western bureaucracies, and staffed by men who were both loyal to the regime and technically proficient. These officials soon received monetary and status rewards that placed them at least as far above the general population as their colleagues in non-Socialist societies.

Today, both the bureaucratic organization and the status differentials show no signs of withering away. On the contrary, the bureaucratic organization of Soviet society is in some ways becoming even more complex as the nation matures industrially and socially. This bureaucratic expansion is, of course, a governmental feature the Soviet shares with a good many modern societies, although in those that are more pluralistic the bureaucratic structure is not quite so monolithic. One observer[16] has compared Soviet society to a business corporation in capitalist nations, with the party as the owner and stockholder and the politburo as the board of directors.

STRUCTURE: The organization of the state apparatus has reflected the primary goal of Soviet leaders: the development of an advanced industrial economy. At first, the administration of economic life was placed with the Supreme Council of the National Economy, known as Vesenkha (VSNKh), under

the guidance of the Council of People's Commissars. The internal organization of Vesenkha was altered repeatedly, but it was divided essentially into two departmental sectors: functional and industrial. The former departments handled such matters as finance, economic policy planning, and research, and the latter dealt with industrial issues. The heads of all the various departments formed the actual council of VSNKh, together with representatives of the union republics, in each of which there was a similar body. Most large-scale industry was directly administered by the appropriate department of the all-union VSNKh, subject only to occasional representations from republican or provincial councils on matters of local interest. However, minor industries using local sources of materials and supplying local markets were directly controlled by republican VSNKh or by the local sovnarkhozy.

Vesenkha, again reorganized with the launching of the First Five Year Plan, was finally abolished in 1932; control over the economy was then placed directly with commissariats (ministries); the Council of People's Commissars, later the Council of Ministers, was made responsible for overall direction. As the economy expanded and became more differentiated, the number of functional ministries also grew. In 1932, for example, the council contained three industrial people's commissariats; in 1952, shortly before Stalin's death, there were 31.

Whatever political elements were involved, Khrushchev's attempts to reorganize and decentralize the administration of the economy undoubtedly represented a response to a real administrative problem—that of effectively coordinating a mature economy. The problem was far more troublesome in the Soviet Union than in nations relying heavily upon market mechanisms, because the coordination of inputs and outputs had to be determined to a much greater degree by economic planners.

Khrushchev's 1957 reforms failed to deal with the real problem faced by the leadership,

16 Alfred Meyer, *The Soviet Political System* (New York: Random House, 1965).

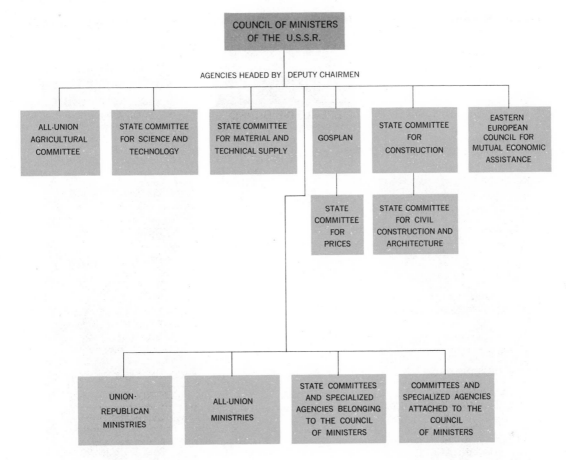

FIGURE 22.4. CENTRAL GOVERNMENTAL STRUCTURE OF THE U.S.S.R., 1967

that of reducing the overhead costs of coordination and direction. While the reforms had some advantages, they created as many difficulties as they solved and were abandoned after Khrushchev left office. The policies of his successors, especially the increasing use of market mechanisms for allocating resources, have not been in operation long enough to permit a real evaluation of their effectiveness. Despite the use of electronic computers, however, the Brezhnev-Kosygin regime has quite clearly come to the conclusion that the direct planning of all production is an impossible task. One Soviet mathematician noted in 1962 that at the rate which bureaucratic planning requirements were then increasing, the services of the entire Soviet adult population would be required by 1980.[17]

RECRUITMENT: The vast range of activities conducted by the Soviet state makes it difficult to determine whom to include or exclude as members of the state bureaucracy. For our purposes, we shall include members of state agencies as well as managerial, technical, and professional personnel who direct Soviet industrial and commercial enterprises.

Standards of employment in the Soviet bureaucracy are set largely by the Central Establishments Administration of the U.S.S.R.

17 Cited in Leon Smolinski and Peter Wiles, "The Soviet Planning Pendulum," *Problems of Communism,* XII (November-December 1963), p. 21.

FIGURE 22.5. ORGANIZATIONAL STRUCTURE OF THE U.S.S.R. MINISTRY OF FINANCE, 1965

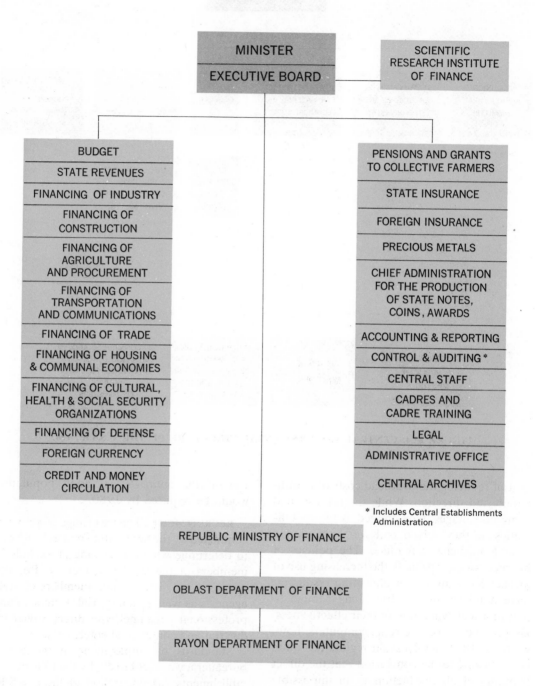

Adapted from U.S. Bureau of the Census, *The Soviet Financial System: Structure, Operation, and Statistics,* by Daniel Gallik, Cestmir Jesina, and Stephen Rapany (Washington: U.S. Government Printing Office, 1968), p. 23.

Finance Ministry. It is this agency which establishes job-classification systems and ceilings on the size of staffs. In addition, it is responsible for studies of agency efficiency. All government agencies are required to register with the Establishments Administration and to provide it with full data on their operations.

Increasingly, those who fill higher-level positions have completed a university education. Upon graduation, Soviet students are required to accept a three-year assignment, the nature and location of which are determined by state planning organs. After completing this stint, the graduate is permitted to choose his own job, and in recent years the Soviet Union has come to be characterized by considerable occupational mobility.

Most state agencies want personnel trained in the technical specializations that are the agency's responsibility, although engineering degrees are at a premium for all industrial jobs. In-service training, where it exists, is also of a technical nature. The regime holds little brief for a general education or for courses in administration; it is expected that administrative techniques will be learned on the way up the bureaucratic hierarchy. While training in economics or law is becoming somewhat more acceptable for some posts, there is little evidence as yet of interest in sociology, social psychology, or political science.

CONTROL AND ACCOUNTABILITY: The Soviet bureaucracy operates under a twin system of controls. Supplementing the authority of the state apparatus are the controls exercised by the Communist Party at every level. In some ways, the party controls are the more important.

As in any bureaucratic system, Soviet bureaucratic control is exercised hierarchically —through a formal structure of higher and lower offices. Plant managers and agency heads are responsible for hiring, firing, and disciplining personnel, and authority moves upward from plants or agencies to regional,

republican, and finally national authorities. Increasingly, too, Soviet bureaucratic organizations are guided by a plethora of procedural rules on tenure and promotion. Moreover, inspectors are dispatched from national ministries to make routine checks on agencies and enterprises, and special investigations are ordered when necessary. The chief planning agencies also have representatives throughout the Soviet Union to review the manner in which organizations are implementing national programs.

The Ministry of Finance provides a further check upon the operation of industrial corporations. Since all organizations operate on a budget determined, in the last analysis, by the national government, the ministry has the authority to question any financial operation it considers dubious. It has at its disposal a large corps of inspectors, who may drop in on plant managers at any time for an on-the-spot survey, and who have full authority to examine all financial records. Further controls are exerted by the State Bank and the All-Union Bank, which grant long- and short-term credits respectively; both are entitled to demand a detailed statement of the firm's operations. Important plants are also often kept under surveillance by the secret police, although such surveillance is certainly far less extensive today than it was in the 1930's and 1940's.

Finally, on paper at least, local soviets are granted authority to oversee the operations of industrial enterprises within their area, and from time to time they have taken it upon themselves to investigate the work of a local plant or a ministry's field office. When the decentralization of the administrative apparatus was decreed in 1957, it looked for a while as though the role of the soviets would increase considerably, for a good many local industries were placed under their jurisdiction by various sovnarkhozy. Recentralization, however, brought an end to this process almost before it had begun, and the authority of the soviets remains severely limited.

No administrative court system exists in

the U.S.S.R. to review violations of the law by administrative agencies or to process citizens' complaints. A few cases are handled by the civil courts, but these courts are not nearly so well equipped as even their European counterparts to deal with such matters. The closest thing to formal legal checks upon administrative behavior is provided by the procuracy, which is entitled to review all orders and decrees issued by administrative agencies and to investigate all complaints of violation of the law. Nonetheless, the procuracy's chief concern is not to protect citizens, but to make certain that administrative agencies conform with overall policy.

Party controls operate in diverse ways. First, the party supervises the employment of the more important personnel through the *nomenklatura*. Not all jobs, of course, require party supervision, and whether records are kept regionally or centrally depends upon how important a particular position is. Managerial posts in key plants are the responsibility of the Central Committee of the C.P.S.U.; the position of collective-farm chairman, however, is the responsibility of regional party committees, and the job of deputy chairman is the responsibility of district party committees. If a plant or ministry, for instance, wishes to appoint an individual to a responsible position, it must first secure the approval of the party, as it must if personnel are to be transferred or dismissed. Just what or how tight the actual relationship is between state organs and the party on matters of personnel is not too clear. In some cases, the party probably simply approves choices already made. In others, it obviously issues directives—as evidenced by frequent press complaints that individuals are still being assigned by the party to posts for which they have no training.

Party organizations on all levels are supposedly responsible for contributing to the successful operation of state enterprises and agencies. Yet the relationship between local party units and the directors of local agencies

and enterprises has never been worked out in a completely satisfactory manner.[18] Through the years, party officials have been criticized for either too much or too little interference in industrial or agricultural management. For the most part, the major concern of the regime in the past has been overall performance. If a plant or collective farm is overfulfilling its quotas, party leaders will be praised; if, however, things are going badly, they will share in the criticisms directed at the manager. Often, then, the secretary of a party unit in a factory or on a kolkhoz will enter into collusion with the manager to distort production records or to obtain needed supplies by illegal means. This was particularly true during the Stalin era, when highly unrealistic production goals were set and no excuse was accepted for failures.

A final organ of party control over the bureaucracy is the people's control committees. Formed originally as party-state control committees when some of the functions of the Party Control Commission and the State Control Commission were merged in 1962, they were created by Khrushchev in an effort to enlist popular support in curbing the pilfering and embezzlement of state and cooperative property. Khrushchev pointed out at the time that court cases showed that such pilfering had exceeded 56 million rubles ($61.6 million) in the first half of 1962 alone, and that numerous other instances of padded and distorted reports had been discovered.

The people's control committees, which dropped the "party-state" designation in 1964, were deprived of their authority over party units a year later and have since been concerned with public enterprises only. Controlled at the top by the Committee of People's Control of the Central Committee of the C.P.S.U. and by the U.S.S.R. Council of Ministers, thousands of these committees are located throughout the country, run by party members who, according to official state-

[18] Jerry Hough argues that the relationship is actually relatively functional. See his *The Soviet Prefects* (Cambridge: Harvard University Press, 1969).

TABLE 22.4. SOCIAL ORGANIZATIONS OF THE U.S.S.R., 1964

Type of organization	Number of organizations	Number of members
Street and house committees	170,346	919,722
Parents' committees in schools, kindergartens, public nurseries, and apartment houses	172,388	1,138,507
Councils in medical institutions	10,600	127,451
Councils of clubs and libraries	64,549	454,524
Councils for furthering the improvement of living conditions	7,174	99,537
Women's councils	32,607	297,904
Pensioners' councils	9,531	194,479
Volunteer fire brigades	38,072	707,269
Volunteer militia	85,182	3,351,078
Comrades' courts	112,372	693,434
Commissions on control of Socialist property	3,391	25,688
Technical-production councils in enterprises, state and collective farms	12,201	164,030
Councils of kolkhoz brigades	16,554	95,947
Shop and restaurant commissions	107,402	386,282
Councils of elders	1,151	13,487
Sanitary posts and brigades	90,811	485,423
Pensioners' commissions in establishments and enterprises	2,498	16,535
Other organizations	29,583	571,075
Total	966,412	9,742,372

Adapted from L. G. Churchward, "Soviet Local Government Today," *Soviet Studies*, XVII (April 1966), p. 440. Reprinted by permission of the publisher.

ments, draw upon the unpaid efforts of literally millions of volunteers. The control committees theoretically work in tandem with trade-union committees, which are engaged in the same type of activity, as well as with the local soviets.

A special note should be added on the vigilant role of the mass media. In recent years the press has been giving increased attention to the operation of state enterprises and agencies. The visit of an inquisitive reporter from *Pravda* or even one from a lesser journal can signal the beginning of a campaign of criticism or denunciation. Many such campaigns are staged by the party, but the evidence indicates that many also represent a response to spontaneous complaints.

The Soviet Union has created a complex bureaucratic apparatus which in many ways resembles that of Western European countries. The major differences lie in the role played by the Communist Party and in the proliferation and complexity of controls over Soviet bureaucratic activity. These differences are partially due to the immensity of tasks which the Kremlin has undertaken. But they are also partially attributable to its attempt to achieve its ends through direct planning rather than by relying, certainly in the case of industrial activity, upon a realistic use of price and market mechanisms. Finally, the differences stem from Soviet ideology and the crucial position of the C.P.S.U. in Soviet society. Committed to creating a powerful industrial state and a new Soviet man, the Communist Party has always regarded itself as composed of the most advanced segments of the Soviet population. Only by continuing to exercise control and direction over the state apparatus can the party be certain that the goals it has set for the Soviet Union will be attained.

The system created by the party has served its purpose in the sense that it enabled the country to concentrate its efforts on creating a powerful industrial economy. But, as we shall see, this success was related far more to the regime's ability to obtain extreme sacrifices on the part of the population than to the sophistication of its procedures. And as the economy has grown more complicated, there is mounting evidence that central domination and planning are becoming more and more dysfunctional—that they prevent the rational allocation of resources that the regime strives so hard to achieve. As the manager of a telephone-equipment factory noted in 1963:

The [plant is] *simultaneously directed by the chief administration of the* sovnarkhoz, *the* VSNKh . . . *the* Gosplan . . . *and, in addition, five state committees, two all union ministries, and so forth. They all believe that the factory should work according to their plans.*[19]

The difficulties of any operation in trying to accommodate itself to the dictates of these agencies, the relative scarcity of resources, and the hardships encountered in trying to get them led to the rise of both hoarding and influence peddlers (*tolkachi*) who used influence (*blat*) to supplement their income.

As one informant noted:

We would receive our allocation orders, and then we would send our agents out to the factory. These tolkachi were usually in a position to buy someone off with the funds they had. They would cover up these funds by writing out false receipts, usually made out in the name of loading and unloading materials. If you did not do such things you usually did not get your supply in time nor in sufficient

quantity. The accountant would quarrel with the supply department over these expenditures. The supply agent would say, "What can I do? I had to get the stuff"; the accountant would have to agree. They would then figure out ways of concealing these expenditures, often including them under "travel orders." In order to explain these expenditures they would later show receipts for overtime pay, and for loading and unloading materials. (Informant 311.)[20]

In fact the practice of blat could be fairly lucrative:

Q. *How much could you earn personally in a month by blat?*

A. *I was able to make out well on paper, glue, and tire tubes. These were the things I could buy privately on the market. These sales were made with no record. I always indicated more than I actually paid. This was the black market. Everybody knew about it, but there was nothing that could be done about it. The director did not care how I got the stuff as long as I got it. What did he care if I earned an extra 100 rubles a month? He earned 1,200 rubles. My base pay as supply agent was 400 rubles. As chief of the supply department, I earned 750 rubles. As supply agent my ability to make extra earnings depended upon the situation. If we received new tubes, I had to wait until they were worn out before I could make something on buying new ones. As agent I was usually able to make 100 to 150 rubles a month extra.*

Q. *As chief of the purchasing department did you earn more or less on the side?*

A. *More, because as chief, I would be called in directly by the director and instructed to get 300 pounds of paper. But if I couldn't get it I would send out the agents. I would say, "Boys, go out and get it." (Informant 481.)*[21]

19 Smolinski and Wiles, "The Soviet Planning Pendulum," p. 33. Gosplan is the State Planning Committee.

20 Quoted in Joseph Berliner, *Factory and Manager in the U.S.S.R.* (Cambridge: Harvard University Press, 1957), p. 216.
21 *Ibid.,* p. 218.

It can be argued that these informal arrangements of demand and supply helped enable the economic system to work. They also contributed, however, to a good deal of waste, and encouraged attitudes which could not help but dismay party leaders. That tolkachi pilfered and embezzled was one thing; that such activity was accepted as perfectly natural by many managers hard pressed for supplies only added to the leadership's consternation—and dilemma. For what was created was a vicious cycle in which an excess of rigid controls contributed to the growth of economic crimes, which, in turn, contributed to more controls, and so on and on. The extremely harsh penalties for pilfering and embezzlement which were reintroduced into Soviet law in the early 1960's indicate that the problem is by no means solved.

Those in the Soviet Union who have been pressing for economic reform have, in fact, argued the point of the cycle. They claim that a reduction of controls from the center, more autonomy for individual firms, and the use of profit as a criterion for success will enhance the rationality of the Communist economic and administrative system. They also contend that with the functions of the tolkachi eliminated, they will gradually disappear from Soviet life.

This may be so. One suspects, however, that part of the Soviet problem lies in the fact that the regime has not succeeded in eradicating certain traditional Russian attitudes toward both authority and work. Furthermore, despite notable progress in many areas, the authoritarianism of the regime probably helps foster the continuation of such attitudes. Whatever their "participation" in government, the great mass of the Soviet people regard authority as external; the party has thus failed to create an environment which would encourage that self-discipline so necessary for creating and maintaining a rational system of bureaucratic authority.

23

National Defense

and Internal Order:

The Military and the Police

1. INTRODUCTION

Whether or not men are instinctively aggressive, as Freud eventually concluded, force has been the ultimate arbiter in human relations throughout recorded history. In primitive societies, the adult male population assumed the responsibility for defense against external enemies and the maintenance of internal order. Leadership was often based on military prowess—physical strength and endurance as well as skill in handling weapons. To maintain order and defend the community was also the obligation of all adult males in more complex societies of limited size, such as the city-states of Greece. Although the Greeks developed the rudiments of military strategy, no military profession existed; all male citizens between certain ages served as soldiers, and civic education was, to a large extent, education in the arts of war.

The rudiments of a distinctive military class are to be found in the great historic bureaucratic empires—Rome, Byzantium, Egypt— that recruited slaves or "barbarians" to fill the ranks of the army. Yet because the handling

of weapons and physical stamina continued to be of prime importance and strategy was not, it is still inaccurate to refer to the existence of a military "profession." Many of these societies did begin, however, to distinguish between the task of maintaining internal order and that of dealing with external enemies, assigning ordinary, civilian police duties to special groups. Even so, the distinction between military and civilian authority was shadowy at best, with the political elite tending also to be the military elite, although there were exceptions, as China exemplifies. In the feudal societies that developed in Europe and Japan, the military and political elites were completely fused.

Not until the era of the modern commercial and industrial nation state does the problem of civil-military relations emerge: at that time came the realization not only that national well-being had to depend more upon the effective development of economic techniques than on plunder, but that the creation of a new technology required that those responsible for military affairs receive specialized training in the management of that technology. The subordination of military to political authority, then, is a relatively recent phenomenon— and, as contemporary politics should indicate, by no means a universally accepted one. Its preconditions include the development of a political order that is sufficiently complex to warrant the differentiation between military and ordinary political functions; once this dichotomy is institutionalized, of course, a professional military is established in order to carry out specific duties. The nature of subsequent civil-military relations will depend upon a number of factors, including the social background of the military, the values that characterize the society, and the degree of authority political leaders are able to command.

The military may intervene in politics if it believes that the social class from which it is drawn and with which it identifies is being threatened, if it decides that it is not being adequately rewarded for its services, or if political movements form which endanger its status. In Weimar Germany, the hostility of the military to the republic was partially based on all these factors; to the military the Weimar regime was responsible for weakening the aristocracy and for sabotaging the role of its elite. In many Latin American countries, the military, while willing to support "modernizing" movements, is unwilling to accept the political dominance of any group that attacks the prerogatives of its own middle class.

Whatever their class background, military men are likely to be conservative in certain respects. Their professional training emphasizes order, hierarchy, and discipline, and they are hostile to groups that attack or deride these values. On the other hand, they are not necessarily conservative on economic issues, for a professional military usually has little or no personal stake in any particular system of property relations. Military leaders in Burma, Egypt, and Peru, for instance, have been quite willing to initiate reforms that have drastically altered the distribution of wealth and property in their societies. They have done so because they believed that the redistribution of prop-

erty would increase the power of the community, thereby permitting economic growth and development and greater military capacity.

The most significant cause of military intervention in contemporary societies, however, is not the nature of the military but the condition of the society. The military is inevitably drawn into the political arena when political authority has broken down. For in the absence of authority, the basic issues in any society are resolved by naked force. As Thomas Hobbes phrased it: "When nothing else is turned up, clubs are trumps."[1]

2. THE MILITARY IN EUROPE [2]

With the breakup of the Roman Empire, differentiation between civil and military functions within society all but disappeared; there was a reversion to the conditions of more primitive times, for the structure of the feudal system under which Europe was governed was primarily military. One of the main tasks of the dynastic monarchies that emerged in Europe from the twelfth century through the seventeenth was to reduce the military power of their vassals. Louis XIV accomplished this through the establishment of a permanent army directly under the supervision of the French monarch. The Hohenzollerns in Prussia did the same thing. England's insular position and its early and integral national unity rendered such a policy unnecessary: the closest the British came to the institution of a national army was during the English Civil War. By the end of the seventeenth century, however, a functioning parliament had assumed control over the military —by demanding and obtaining the right to review military budgets.

In all European countries, military personnel came principally from two groups within the society: members of the aristocracy joined

[1] Quoted in Dankwart A. Rustow, *A World of Nations* (Washington, D.C.: Brookings Institution, 1967), p. 170.

[2] A good summary history of the development of the military in Europe is David B. Ralston, ed., *Soldiers and States* (New York: D. C. Heath, 1966).

because the career of military officers suited their life-style; ordinary soldiers were a mixed lot, but most of them were drawn from the lower classes through either bribery or coercion. For officer or soldier, there was little concern with military tactics and little conception of military life as a profession.

Two factors contributed to a change of this attitude: the advance of science and technology and the rise of nationalism. The advances in weaponry, which had been accumulating during the previous two centuries, had begun to have an impact even before the French Revolution. By the middle of the nineteenth century, a number of military schools had been founded to produce technically competent officers in the fields of engineering and artillery. Many of these men had a middle-class background and they brought to their work a sense of dedication and purpose that was akin to the new professionalism marking other areas of enterprise.

But the major catalysts in the development of the European military were the French Revolution and the Napoleonic conquests. The leaders of the Revolution created a mass conscript army which sought to enlist the talents of the entire French nation. The existence of states that could and did mobilize entire populations, plus the new improvements in technology, had enormous implications for the entire structure of military organization.

Armies in Western Europe became conscript armies led by professionals—men trained in the management of violence and concerned with military activity as a theoretical and professional endeavor. The first nation to execute the military reforms generated by Napoleon's march through Europe was Prussia. The excellence of the Prussian military system was revealed in the very short wars Germany fought against Austria and France in the 1860's and 1870's. Reforms in the French military followed, although not with equal success; the British, and even more so the Americans, lagged behind for several reasons, not the least of which was their distrust of a large military establishment.

What the reforms meant was the continued professionalization of the military and the increasing entry of the bourgeois, and even some of the working class, into the officer corps, although aristocratic elements retained their dominance in the corps until well into the twentieth century. This was much truer of Germany than it was of France and more so of France than of England, but it was clearly true, nevertheless, of all three countries. Also true of all three was the existence of a sizable cadre of officers who were the sons of former officers, producing a partially self-perpetuating professional elite. For example, roughly forty per cent of the officers in the German army just prior to World War I were the children of military men.

To the conservatism that reflected the class origins of a good many European officers was added that which stemmed from the nature of the military profession itself. A sound military organization required discipline, hierarchy, and respect for authority. The ideal officer was a man who could impose authority when faced with chaos and who believed in the profession of arms—therefore a man who conceived of the world as a place either threatened by violence or engaging in it.

It is little wonder that throughout the eighteenth and nineteenth centuries the military found itself at odds with the European bourgeoisie which was gradually attaining political power. In the eyes of the middle class, not only did the traditional officer corps stand as the bastion of reactionary aristocracy, its whole orientation was fundamentally opposed to the values of liberal individualism and peaceful commerce among nations. In the eyes of the military, of course, liberal individualism was breeding an unnatural pacifism, a climate inimical to authority, and a fragmented society—all of which, by breaking down the primordial ties to church, authority, and tradition, were weakening the fiber of the nation. The fact that more and more of the bourgeoisie were entering the military did not in itself produce a radical change in the political viewpoints of the officer corps. Rather, those of the middle class who chose the military as a career tended to be easily seduced by the value system of the military establishment—if, indeed, they had not picked the military in the first place because they already accepted those values.

If middle-class liberals distrusted the military, their antagonism was muted toward the end of the nineteenth century by the rise of leftist radical movements. The military, the bourgeoisie began to realize, would at least help to insure internal order against these new, uncertain elements. To Socialists, who went beyond liberals in their disapproval of military values and their identification of the military with reactionary forces, the old officer corps was anathema. The mutual antagonism between the military and both liberals and leftists exacerbated the problem of civil-military relations when reform governments came to power. In no Western European nation did the military take it upon itself to overturn a liberal or Socialist government, but officers did look longingly out of the right corner of their eyes at right-wing movements. In Russia the military, or at least part of it, attempted a half-hearted coup against Kerensky's Provisional Government—thus helping to bring the Bolsheviks into power.

Since World War II, the structure of the European military has been considerably modified—partly because of particular political events, but mostly because more general forces were also at work. In all Western European countries, the officer corps is now almost exclusively middle class, with an increasing sprinkling of men from a working-class background. The new technology and the fact that no Western European nation can seriously contemplate large-scale conventional war has placed greater responsibilities upon technically trained personnel, men who differ less and less from their nonmilitary professional colleagues. Unquestionably, the gap in orientations between the military and other elites in the community has been markedly reduced.

Areas of potential tension still exist, to be sure. The decline in power of Western Europe has weakened the military self-image and lessened the attractiveness of a military career. As military funds are cut and the prestige of the profession declines, an occasional military backlash can be expected. The rebellion of some French officers in 1960 was partially induced by their feeling that the politicians did not appreciate them and that political radicalism was again leading the nation astray; the movement to the right of a few West German officers can be largely attributed to the same factors. The Soviet Union is a somewhat different case. The revolution in military technology has undoubtedly produced significant changes in the upper echelons of the armed forces, but because the U.S.S.R. remains one of the three major military powers in the world, its officers enjoy a prestige and authority that those in West European countries lack.

THE ENGLISH PATTERN: Perhaps the two outstanding facts about England's military establishment have been the slowness with which it transformed itself from an amateur institution into a semi-professional one, and its consent, with minor exceptions, to being controlled by civilian authority since the seventeenth century. These two related characteristics are often explained by England's geographic position, which reduced the necessity of a large standing army; but the example of Japan indicates that although insularity is important, it is not in itself a sufficient explanation and must be considered in conjunction with other factors.

Certainly among the key variables in the development of the English military was the comparative ease with which England achieved nationhood. Unlike, for example, the French, the English monarchy did not have to create a permanent standing army in order to wrest power from the aristocracy. The quiescence of English social and political life and the broad acceptance throughout most of the nineteenth century of the path along which the country was moving also had their effect on the evolution of the English military. Then, too, while the military may have drawn the major portion of its officer corps from the aristocracy, it was not an aristocracy separated from middle-class liberals by incompatible interests and ideologies; or to put it another way, there existed a consensus between the military and the public on a sufficient number of questions to permit the community's political mechanisms to work effectively, and neither the aristocracy nor the military ever felt that the values it held so dear were being threatened. In short, the role of the military in English history is to be explained in terms of the same factors that caused England to generate its own kind of political and social integration, factors that have already been discussed. Of course, it must be added that for those who found the changes taking place in English life little to their taste, the existence of an empire permitted the exploitation of traditional military talents and the continuation of a certain lifestyle among the "natives."

As with all European countries, the aftermath of World War II has produced a serious crisis within the military. The major problem in Britain has been the need to adjust to the facts that the nation is no longer a first-class power and that no conceivable future war in Europe is likely to be fought along former military lines. The response of the British army has been toward more technical professionalism, although the old spirit of aristocratic amateurism lingers on and hampers innovation. Yet even with this approach, or perhaps because of its necessity, it is becoming more and more difficult for the military to provide a positive image of itself—to find a function that justifies it as a career.[3]

THE FRENCH PATTERN: The Revolution and Napoleon created a new kind of national army in France and in Europe. Although the traditional corps of officers was essential to the army's operation, it brought into posts of command men of talent from the middle

class; and, far more than had the old regime, it emphasized technical competence. The purges following the fall of the French Empire somewhat changed the complexion of the army; once again it drew most of its officers from elements in the society closely tied to the aristocracy, although it continued to retain a substantial portion from the bourgeoisie. Even officers entering the service from the middle class, however, came from groups that were invariably hostile to "radical" ideas. Its political disposition notwithstanding, the French military refrained from direct intervention in political matters and accepted the orders of those in authority, whoever they might be. The sympathies of the military undoubtedly lay with more conservative regimes, and it seems quite likely that the establishment of a truly radical government in 1848 or 1870 would have resulted in a great deal of bloodshed. As it was, in both years the army responded enthusiastically when ordered to crush revolutionary activity by the left.

The social composition of the military tended still further toward the aristocracy during the Second Empire. Many of the younger aristocrats donned a kepi simply because the income from their country estates was no longer adequate to maintain what they considered to be a decent life-style. Then, too, France offered little opportunity for the display of aristocratic virtues, while the military, especially in its colonial ventures, allowed indulgence in the grand manner. The aristocracy's hold over the French military continued through the early years of the Third Republic, and as the government came under the control of Radicals and Radical Socialists and as the Socialist Party grew more powerful, new tensions flared between the military and civilian political elites. Radicals were anticlerical, and most of the officer corps came from devout families; Radicals and Socialists had a bent toward pacifism and distrusted the army, and the officer corps felt more and more alienated in a society that treated the military profession with suspicion if not disdain. Nonetheless, throughout most

---

[3] See Philip Abrams, "The Late Profession of Arms: Ambiguous Goals and Deteriorating Means in Britain," *European Journal of Sociology,* VI (1965), pp. 238–261.

of the Third Republic, the posture of the military remained politically correct. Nor could the Radicals succeed in their efforts to purge the army of "antirepublican" officers and thus "democratize" it. The tensions and suspicions between the military and civilian leaders were, therefore, constantly ready to flare into open, bitter hostility. All that was needed was an issue, and that was not long in coming—the Dreyfus Affair, a *cause célèbre* that ripped the fabric of French society and created a climate of mutual hostility that continued until World War I. But again, no attempt was made by the military to subvert the republic, despite the urging of the extreme right.

The war itself helped for a time to heal the breach between the republic and the army. Once the armistice was signed, however, old antagonisms came again to the fore. The left still regarded the army as the enclave of right-wing "Fascist" Catholics; many army officers regarded the left as representing anarchy and the subversion of all those values they considered important. And, once again, the atmosphere of hostility continued until the eve of another world war, this time contributing to the swift defeat of France. After France's surrender in 1940, the largest segment of the officer corps accepted the Vichy regime, because Vichy represented the legitimate authority of the French state. Yet it cannot be denied that many in the military regarded the fall of France as payment for past sins—as the result of a loss of élan through the subversive wiles of left-wing propaganda and policies.

After the Liberation, the position of the French military changed subtly but significantly. Many who had supported Vichy were purged, but this did not alter the political orientation of most officers. What did alter, however, was the composition of the military —in large part a consequence of the continuing decline in prestige of military service. These changes were hastened by the high casualty rate among officers in Indochina and the difficulty of replacing them. Applications to Saint Cyr, France's West Point, had dropped off precipitously. In 1939, 2,452 candidates had applied; in 1954, the number was 360. It is true that in 1939 France declared war on Nazi Germany and 1954 was the year of Dienbienphu, the sad climax of France's unpopular war in Indochina; still, the disparity in the number of applicants is indicative of the public's overall disillusionment with military "solutions." In addition, the proportion of graduates from other Grandes Écoles—the École Polytechnique, for example—who were choosing the military as a profession had also declined. As a result, the army was recruiting more and more of its officers from within the service; the percentage of captains who had risen from the ranks in 1949 was 5.4, while in 1958 it was 35.8.[4] One commentator has referred to this phenomenon as the "proletarianization" of the French army.

The new officer corps felt cut off from a France for which it was engaged in a constant round of colonial wars. Officers believed that they were being sent into combat inadequately supplied and, to compound their bitterness, that they were being constantly subverted not only by groups within France who supported their enemies but by unstable governments that followed vacillating policies. Increasingly, they contrasted the discipline and organization of the army with the "soft" materialism and murky ideologies of bourgeois France. Increasingly, they became concerned with the "threat of world communism and internal subversion," which they believed their civilian compatriots had not recognized.

Tensions between the military and the civilian in France came to a head in Algeria. There, tough, well-trained professional soldiers found themselves called upon to undertake civil as well as military responsibilities. Developing a new theory of "revolutionary war" based in part on their own counterinsurgency experiences and the writings of Mao Tse-tung, they hoped through the use of a

---

[4] See Raoul Girardet and Jean-Pierre H. Thomas, "Problèmes de recruitement," in Raoul Girardet (ed.), *La Crise militaire française 1945–1962* (Paris: Fondation Nationale de Science Politique, 1964), pp. 11–72.

combination of military force and new techniques of psychological warfare to rally a substantial portion of the Arab population to their side. Though they identified in part with the French *colon,* especially the small farmer, their program went beyond that of the European settlers. They foresaw an Algeria completely integrated with metropolitan France, one in which Arabs were full citizens and participants. In many cases, their programs of civic welfare were reasonably effective; indeed, amidst the horror of the war, they did more for the Arab population than either the colon or the French government had ever accomplished.

Reacting against the indecisiveness of Paris's Algerian policies, a group of young officers, most of them belonging to the newer cadres that had been promoted through the ranks, were instrumental in bringing down the Fourth Republic—and in securing the return to power of Charles de Gaulle. When, to their thinking, de Gaulle betrayed them by revealing sympathy for Algerian independence, some of them turned to open rebellion. For the first time in modern French history, a portion of the officer corps tried to subvert the French state.

The attempt failed, and the subsequent purge of the army, as well as de Gaulle's liquidation of the remainder of the French empire, effectively downgraded the military's status. De Gaulle imposed stricter control upon the officer corps and moved to create an army of technicians who would direct the military's efforts toward transforming France into a nuclear power. His innovations and the decline in France's world position make it unlikely that the military will, in the foreseeable future, bring to bear as much influence on French internal affairs as it did between 1957 and 1962.

THE GERMAN PATTERN: In Germany, too, the officer corps of the army was composed of the old aristocratic elite—the Junkers, who were dedicated to the preservation and expansion of the German state. Germany's central location in Europe, the wave of nationalism that swept through Germany during and after the Napoleonic period, and the consequent failure of liberalism to take root all combined to maintain the military's status at an extraordinarily high level. It was progressive forces within the military that took the lead in modernizing the army after its defeat by Napoleon; not only did they press for a system of national conscription and a policy of promotion based on merit, but they stressed the need for creating an industrial base to support a modern army. The emphasis on merit, however, did not upset the social composition of the officer corps throughout the nineteenth century, and even those from other classes who entered the military absorbed its traditional ethos.

The military during the empire remained under the control of the monarchy, which successfully beat off most sorties by Parliament to exercise authority in this area. On the whole, the military's relationship with both monarch and legislature was completely satisfactory. It is true that the general staff occasionally attempted to bypass civilian authority in certain political and strategic matters, but these efforts were marginal and, under Bismarck at least, came to naught. It is also true that during the last days of World War I the military assumed a predominant role in the government, but this circumstance was unique and would, in any event, have terminated at the end of the war.

With the establishment of the Weimar Republic, the status of the military became another matter. The left—the Socialists and Communists as well as the republican left —bore the military a hostility which it fully reciprocated. Not only did the officer corps regard the values of the left as degenerate, but it considered Weimar foreign policy a betrayal of the fatherland. Even the military's highest officer, Hans von Seeckt, the first chief of the General Staff during the Weimar period, could scarcely conceal his animosity toward left-wing politicians.

The rancor between the army and the republic would have been much more intense had it not been for the fact that the Socialists who formed the first postwar government believed the armed forces were necessary to crush incipient revolutions on the extreme left. Von Seeckt, therefore, thought the army should remain nonpolitical and should co-operate with the new government. As he wrote to his wife:

With Herr [Friedrich] Ebert [first president of the Weimar Republic] and comrades I can perhaps co-operate, in spite of our diametrically opposed conceptions of the world and economic affairs, because I consider these people relatively honest, if ideologists and weaklings. . . .[5]

The government's need of the military to maintain order and the military's halfhearted willingness to cooperate resulted in a modus vivendi that more or less permitted the army to go its own way in return for its "neutrality." Later, because of the instability of Weimar governments and Germany's gradual movement to the right, the civilians lost virtually all control over the army, and both its organization and its control remained with the officer corps until Hitler took power.

Whatever the tacit understanding between the military and the leaders of Weimar governments, the army had never been terribly sympathetic to the republic. Many of the old-line officers were monarchists, and while they rejected the extreme right and the extreme left as being led by rabble-rousers, they could not help but have some sympathy for the rightists. In fact, the army suppressed Communist-led uprisings with extreme harshness, while its reaction to similar insurgencies by the right was much milder. The situation was complicated by the fact that during the later years of the republic many of the younger officers or those of bourgeois background collaborated actively with the Nazi

Party, seeing in it the opportunity to revive Germany, to restore old values, and to break away from the limitations imposed on their army and nation by the Versailles Treaty. They further saw the Nazis as the only real block to the Communists' coming to power.

As Major General Kurt von Schleicher, one of the officers who had developed political aspirations, described the situation in 1930:

After the events of the last days I am rather glad that in the form of the Nazis there exists a counter-weight, although the Nazis are not very honourable brethren either, and have to be treated with the utmost caution.[6]

Von Schleicher, however, failed to heed his own admonitions about the Nazis: he took the lead in bringing the power of the armed forces to bear upon the fateful political circumstances of the republic's last days, intriguing to bring down governments of which he did not approve, and trying to use the Nazis to establish a conservative government dominated by the military. In the end, he was outmaneuvered by Hitler—and became one of the first victims of the new regime.

Hitler's attitude toward the army was curiously ambivalent. His admiration for the German military tradition was counterbalanced by his awareness that, from the viewpoint of that tradition, he was an upstart. At first he was careful to secure the complete support of the army. He embarked almost immediately upon a program of military expansion; he also weakened the SA,[7] which the army regarded as a potential threat, even going so far as to arrange for the murder of many of his former colleagues.

---

[5] Quoted in Michael Howard, ed., *Soldiers and Governments* (London: Eyre and Spottiswoode, 1957), p. 86.

[6] Ibid., p. 92.

[7] The *Sturmabteilung*, or storm troops, formed in 1921 as the paramilitary arm of the Nazi Party. After the murder of many SA leaders in 1934 by Hitler's orders, it quickly declined in importance. The SS (*Schutzstaffel*—guard detachment) was an elite paramilitary group originally created in 1926 as Hitler's personal bodyguard and as a counterweight to the SA. During the Third Reich, the SS became even more powerful than the party.

Within a few years, however, harmony was replaced by tension. The officer corps not only resented the growing power of the SS, it took considerable exception to the rapidity with which Nazi officers were being promoted to positions of power. Its attitude was understandable, because the appointments speeded up the process of democratizing the officer corps; for example, 61 per cent of the generals in 1920 were aristocrats, but by 1939 the percentage had been pared to 27.[8] Nor did the officer corps appreciate Hitler's effort to destroy the caste barriers between officers and enlisted men, an effort that extended in some instances to the elimination of separate eating places.[9] Furthermore, the officer corps feared that Hitler's plans were too grandiose and too risky. The aim of the officer corps was that Germany's position as the leading military power in Europe be restored through a combination of diplomacy and threats, but the corps had no desire to go to war with the rest of Europe. Finally, the officers were not barbarians; a good many of them were horrified by the regime's blatant anti-Semitism, which led to mass brutality and murder.[10]

By this time, however, it was too late to resist. The Nazi Party had spread its agents throughout the army, and it was unsafe to express an opinion openly. In effect, the morale of the officer corps had been sapped. Moreover, it was difficult for the army to think about ousting Hitler while his policies met with one success after another, and later it was even more difficult to consider moving against him when the nation was engaged in a war. Some talk of overthrowing Hitler did circulate in 1938, but the coup failed to materialize when the French and British backed down once again at Munich. The next attempt was not made until 1944, when it was obvious that Germany had lost the war and that Hitler seemed to be comtemplating nothing less than a *Götterdämmerung*. The plot of a group of officers to assassinate Hitler and seize power, however, was badly planned; its failure was followed by widespread purges within the army, including the execution of some of its best officers.

The havoc wrought by Hitler and the war decimated the traditional officer corps, nor was it soon reconstituted: the victors saw to it that Germany remained disarmed for a number of years. By 1949, however, the cold war, the freezing of the division between East and West Germany, and finally the Korean War had fundamentally altered the viewpoint of the victors about rearming Germans. First Russia and then the Western allies began to encourage the establishment of armed forces in the sectors of Germany under their jurisdiction. Initially, Western policy called for the integration of the German army into a European Defense Community, but when this proposal was rejected by France, an alternate solution permitted the creation of a German army within the North Atlantic Treaty Organization. Thus, after 1955, West Germany began to rearm.

In creating a new army, the Germans took special care to guarantee complete civilian control. Not only was ultimate authority placed in the hands of the chancellor and a civilian minister of defense, but the Bundestag's Defense Committee was granted authority to examine all matters pertaining to the armed forces. Germany also set up an office of defense commissioner, whose director was assigned the dual task of aiding the parliamentary committee and making certain that the legal rights of persons inducted into or volunteering for the armed forces were respected. Other procedures were inaugurated to protect the individual soldier against vio-

[8] David Schoenbaum, *Hitler's Social Revolution* (New York: Doubleday and Company, 1966), pp. 247–249.

[9] H. P. Secher, "Controlling the New German Military Elite: The Political Role of the Parliamentary Defense Commissioner in the Federal Republic," *Proceedings of the American Philosophical Society*, 109 (1965), p. 76.

[10] Officers of aristocratic background were stronger in their opposition than young officers; some even brought charges against SS men who had murdered and pillaged in Poland, but the charges were dismissed or settled by amnesty. See Schoenbaum, *Hitler's Social Revolution*, pp. 208–209.

lations of his civil rights and to channel any complaints about the violation of these rights.

As recruiting for the new army began, a screening commission passed on the qualifications of all officers in order to eliminate from positions of command those who had, during the Third Reich, demonstrated excessive zeal in behalf of the regime. The screening worked well, and in recent years the problem has become less important as more and more officers with no previous military experience have been recruited. The Bonn government also introduced a comprehensive program of civic training for soldiers to imbue them with an understanding of democratic processes and the concept of the soldier as a "citizen in uniform."

Just how well these concepts and programs for a new German army have worked out in practice is open to question.[11] From the very

11 For two contrasting views see Eric Waldman, *The Goose Step Is Verboten* (New York: The Free Press, 1964), and Secher, "Controlling the New German Military Elite. . . ."

beginning, some line officers and reformers were in blunt disagreement over the extent of a soldier's civil rights, as against the right of the army to develop an adequate military force. The influence of reformers has declined in more recent years, as greater stress has been placed upon discipline.

Nevertheless, some officers continue to grumble that the German army has become too "democratic" to be an effective military force. Since the rise of the left-wing student movement, the number of young men applying for the classification of conscientious objector or moving to West Berlin to avoid service has risen sharply, as have minor acts of sabotage. Dissatisfied officers blame these events on the low status of the army and on the fact that they are hamstrung in their efforts to exert discipline. One of their major complaints is that punishments of soldiers who commit a breach of military discipline are levied by civilian courts. A few disgruntled officers have, as a consequence,

TABLE 23.1. THE SOCIAL BACKGROUND OF THE NEW GERMAN ARMY

	Enlisted men		Non-commissioned officers		Officers	
	Draftees	Volunteers	NCO	Senior NCO	Officer candidates	Officers
Semi- and unskilled laborers	6%	4%	5%	8%	0%	0%
Skilled workers, artisans	49	43	45	43	16	23
White-collar workers	7	8	7	7	8	9
Civil servants	4	9	8	9	12	16
Professional soldiers	1	3	3	1	11	12
Managers, lawyers, physicians	7	11	5	7	27	20
Self-employed, businessmen	9	9	10	6	17	10
Farmers	8	4	8	12	7	7
Other professionals	1	2	1	1	1	1
No information	8	7	8	6	1	2
Totals	100	100	100	100	100	100
Number of respondents	1,357	935	821	146	329	137

Adapted from Eric Waldman, *The Goose Step Is Verboten* (New York: The Free Press, 1964), p. 210. Reprinted by permission of the publisher.

joined the National Democratic Party, raising once again fears of a right-wing political-
military alliance.

There is little foundation for such concern.
The new German army is a far cry from the
old in terms of its structure and its relation to
both the political community and the German
people. It is a much less authoritarian institution than it has been in the past. The officer
corps no longer comes from the aristocracy;
in fact, the German army is probably the
most democratically recruited of any in the
West (see Table 23.1). Nor is the officer
corps still the bastion of conservatism that it
once was; its general political attitudes seem
to be somewhat more liberal than those of the
general citizenry. Further, although some
incidents might betoken otherwise, the German army is now as well controlled by civilian authority as the army of any Western
nation, and it is not likely to make an attempt

to re-establish its former autonomy. It is also
evident that neither the German soldier nor
the German civilian regards the military with
the awe that he once did; indeed, serious reservations persist in Germany about the desirability of having an army at all. In short,
despite some legitimate concern, the German
army is not likely ever to be again the destructive force in Central Europe that it has been
during the past century.

THE RUSSIAN AND SOVIET PATTERN: The
foundations for a "modern" Russian army
were laid early in the eighteenth century by
Peter the Great. As in the West, the officer
corps was predominantly of aristocratic origin and conservative political temper. Even
though the ethnic diversity of Russia added
a complicating factor—until the latter part
of the century, the nobility of Baltic-German
descent supplied a disproportionate percent-

TABLE 23.2. ATTITUDES OF THE NEW GERMAN ARMY
TO ORGANIZED RESISTANCE TO THE HITLER REGIME

	Positive[1]	Negative[2]	No information
Population	70.0%	19.1%	10.7%
Military rank			
Recruits	85.9	11.6	2.3
Corporals	83.0	15.3	1.5
Sergeants	78.6	19.5	1.7
Senior NCO's	80.0	17.8	2.0
Officer candidates	88.4	11.1	0.4
Officers	81.4	18.3	—
Military status			
Volunteers	80.8	17.8	1.2
Draftees	85.3	11.7	2.7
Age			
Up to 21	85.3	12.9	1.5
22 to 25	82.9	14.9	1.9
26 to 30	82.4	16.5	0.9
31 to 40	75.0	21.0	3.7
Above 40	87.7	12.1	—

[1] Either because "Hitler was a megalomaniac who led Germany into a catastrophe,"
or because "the National Socialist regime violated basic human rights."
[2] Either because "Hitler was the legal head of state," or because "Germany was
at war and needed unity."

Adapted from Waldman, *The Goose Step Is Verboten*, p. 238. Reprinted by permission of the publisher.

TABLE 23.3. ATTITUDES OF MEMBERS OF THE NEW
GERMAN ARMY TO THE ROLE OF OPPOSITION PARTIES

	Positive[1]	*Negative*[2]	*No information*
Population	58.6%	29.0%	12.1%
Military rank			
Recruits	68.4	26.3	5.1
Corporals	67.0	28.1	4.7
Sergeants	81.8	16.8	1.3
Senior NCO's	86.2	11.9	1.7
Officer candidates	94.5	4.9	0.3
Officers	95.5	4.3	—
Military status			
Volunteers	72.9	24.3	2.7
Draftees	68.1	25.5	6.2
Age			
Up to 21	72.4	23.5	3.8
22–25	74.3	21.3	4.2
26–30	84.6	14.0	1.0
31–40	84.2	13.1	2.4
Over 40	88.3	10.3	1.1

[1]"Opposition parties have to perform a very important function within a democracy."
[2]"The opposition should not be permitted to criticize in Parliament the work of members of the government"; "The opposition has the tendency to confront the government with irresponsible demands"; "The opposition usually hinders the work of the government."

Adapted from Waldman, *The Goose Step Is Verboten*, p. 221. Reprinted by permission.

age of the officers—the corps was essentially apolitical. Moreover, the lack of a corporate sense among the aristocracy reduced the officers to being, in effect, little more than military bureaucrats. It is true that in the aftermath of the Napoleonic Wars, a small group within the officer corps—the so-called Decembrists—participated in a revolutionary movement to "modernize" Russia in the image of Western Europe; but they failed in their purpose and their impact was not very great.

The latter part of the nineteenth century witnessed a gradual transformation of the armed forces. The technical necessities of war increasingly required persons with special skills, and the army became less and less the province of "gentlemen." In Russia as in the West, the proportion of officers from middle-class, worker, and peasant backgrounds steadily expanded. For children of the poor, the military became a means of social mobility. General Mikhail Alekseyev, the last commander-in-chief under the czar, was not born of the nobility; General Anton Denikin, who later became commander-in-chief of the White army, was the grandson of a serf.

The social metamorphosis of the Russian army did not immediately alter its social outlook, or, at least, the outlook of its officers. Considering themselves part of the system, they remained quite loyal to its values, an allegiance made easier by the fact that they thought very little about politics. Their loyalty was finally shaken, although not destroyed, by the war with Japan and the Revolution of 1905 and was further weakened by World War I, which exposed the incompe-

FIGURE 23.1. SOCIAL BACKGROUND OF STUDENTS ATTENDING A TYPICAL MILITARY SCHOOL IN MOSCOW

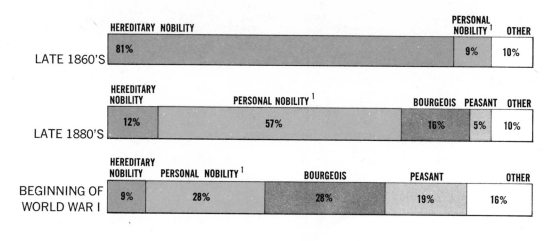

[1] All officers became personal, that is, nonhereditary, nobles upon achieving rank, and this group thus consisted in large measure of the children of former officers.

tence of the Romanov regime. Indeed, most of the officers accepted the Provisional Government without demur, and the attempted coup against that government by General Lavr Kornilov was not directed toward restoring the czar, but rather toward suppressing the soviets and the Bolsheviks who, in Kornilov's mind, constituted a fundamental threat to the Russian state.

The Bolsheviks, of course, violently distrusted the old army corps. To them, the military was an arm of the czarist regime, a mechanism by which the dominant classes retained control of the population and pursued imperial ambitions. In the end, according to the Bolsheviks' vision of the proletarian state, a Communist society would need no army; meanwhile, however, they were faced by counterrevolutionary forces and the active hostility of other nations. If the civil war were to be won and the Communist state created, visions had to be temporarily set aside and drastic military action taken. Initially, the Bolsheviks tried to draw upon the revolutionary fervor and skill of the workers to create a proletarian army—a democratic peo-

ple's army in which officers were elected, differentiations in rank minimized if not completely eliminated, and collective decisions made by the soldiers themselves. Within a short time, however, Leon Trotsky, upon whom the responsibility for this effort largely devolved, came to realize that such a procedure was visionary in the extreme; more and more frequently, he was forced to tap members of the traditional officer corps who, for whatever reasons, would fight for the Revolution and restore some degree of discipline within the ranks. To make sure that these traditional cadres would be loyal to the new regime, Trotsky, benefiting from the lessons of the French Revolution, created political officers (commissars) whose function was to prevent the old line officers from betraying their trust. The political officers were, theoretically, not to give orders but to keep watch; their authority could be enforced because the regular officers knew that defeat in a battle might be interpreted as betrayal—with consequent death not only for the officer but also for his family.

The tensions involved in such an arrangement were extreme, yet it worked sufficiently well to enable the Bolsheviks to emerge victorious from all their threats and travails. Not a little credit is due to the Bolshevik officers who, with relatively little training, acquitted themselves commendably during the civil war. Men like Frunze, Podvoisky, Voroshilov, and others represented a new military breed, and were more hostile in some ways to the new military science than the old guard of the traditional Russian army.

At the end of the civil war, the army was partially demobilized. At this point, however, Soviet leaders were faced with a dilemma. The idea of creating a quasi-permanent military establishment still repelled them; yet the Revolution had not, as they had expected, spread to the rest of Europe, and the new state was surrounded by enemies. Furthermore, as evidenced by the mutiny at the Kronshtadt naval garrison in 1921, a good many Russians remained hostile to the Revolution. The complete elimination of the armed forces would, therefore, have to await the world triumph of communism. The question now arose what kind of armed force should be maintained within the Soviet Union. Some, like General Mikhail Tukhachevsky, a former imperial officer who had accepted the Revolution, urged the creation and maintenance of a large professional army. Others, however, including Trotsky, convinced of the inherently counterrevolutionary nature of a permanent military establishment, suggested a people's militia formed on the basis of production units, such as factories. The party eventually reached a compromise decision under which both professional cadres and a militia army would be maintained, and, in addition, special security forces would be organized as a part of the police for the purpose of patrolling the borders. This plan remained in force with only slight modifications until 1934, when the militia was abolished.

The Soviet professional army—the only effective armed force aside from the police—underwent significant changes in the years following its inception. Slowly, almost imperceptibly, rank and the privileges of rank were restored. Discipline was continually tightened, and the pomp long associated with the imperial army was revived, manifesting itself even in officers' dress. The Soviet army officer today is the only representative of a modern world power to sport epaulets and velvet lapels, leather boots and a dress dirk at his side. Marshals, generals, field-grade officers, and junior officers are separated into rigid categories, with segregated messes and recreational facilities, and pay differentials are far greater than in the military forces of most capitalist nations. A field-grade officer and a company-grade officer are not social equals; personal orderlies are assigned to field-grade as well as to general officers. The existence of party cells within military units does, nonetheless, add an enforced egalitarian dimension to the armed forces.

The restoration of traditional military etiquette was accompanied by a return to professional standards. For a decade after the civil war, the regime was rather hostile to the idea of a "military science," preferring to rely upon the valor of a people's army to win over all. But in 1931, the army began to modernize and to compete with other powers in developing the newer weapons of war and training its men in their use. The regime, of course, continued to exercise strict control over the armed forces; the People's Commissariat of Defense was kept in political hands rather than military, commissars were retained to keep an eye on field commanders, and party cells within military units were charged with the duty of indoctrinating the troops. Each major army unit was also kept under surveillance by the secret police. Czarist officers and old Bolshevik cadres were replaced by a military elite trained at the new military academies. In 1918 former czarist officers constituted 76 per cent of the army's total officer corps; by 1930, the percentage had fallen to ten. The process of transition was completed in the purges of 1937–1939, during which three of the five marshals, 13 of the 15 army commanders, and 57 of the 85 corps commanders of the Red Army were eliminated—a fact of no slight importance in explaining the failure of the Russians in the Finnish campaign and the rather poor performance of the army during the first months of the German invasion.

By the end of World War II, the officer corps was completely free of prerevolutionary influences, and those who might be tainted with Trotskyism, having entered the army during the early phases of the Revolution, also were no longer in the service. Further, although most members of the officer corps still came from peasant backgrounds or were the sons of former officers, despite the regime's efforts to create a "proletarian" army of urban workers, there was little question of the corps' loyalty. More than eighty per cent of the Soviet officers were now members of the Communist Party.

Indicative of the leadership's confidence in the reliability of the army was the elimination of military commissars in 1940. Although commissars were restored briefly in 1941, they were replaced a year after the Nazi invasion began by assistant commanders for political affairs (*zampolits*), who were clearly subordinate to line officers. And since the death of Stalin, the minister of defense has invariably been a military officer, something unheard of in the early years of the Communist regime; "Bonapartism," obviously, is no longer a party concern. This is not to say that the party has granted the military full autonomy. The Main Political Administration (M.P.A.), attached to the Ministry of Defense, still sees to it that each military unit contains a party cell and that programs of education in Marxism-Leninism are provided for both officers and men. The secret police also continues to keep tabs on matters pertaining to security, although its role is now of lesser importance. While the military, therefore, may not be totally free of internal political safeguards, it now has considerable independence of action; except in extraordinary circumstances, problems of organization

and discipline are left to the military itself. This being so, it is not surprising that the military had re-established itself within Soviet society as a rather closed professional group by the end of the war. Officers once again tended to associate primarily with each other; military families intermarried and most of the new officers were the offspring of military men. It had also developed an organization and a life-style not very different from that of other traditional military establishments.

Within the Soviet Union today, members of the officer corps constitute part of the elite; their status is reflected in both their material advantages and the deference accorded them by the population. They do not, however, represent any particular, cohesive political attitude. The officer corps did support the party at the expense of the secret police after the death of Stalin, and it supported Khrushchev against the "anti-party" group in 1957. Yet its acceptance without a murmur of Khrushchev's subsequent removal of Zhukov from the Presidium, and the lack of a replacement, is fair proof that the party's dominance remains complete.

Tensions unquestionably have surfaced between military and civilian authority over specific questions of strategy. Some experts, for instance, think the military considered that Khrushchev's decision to send missiles to Cuba was as precipitous as his sudden decision to withdraw them in the face of American pressure. More broadly, the Soviet military today seems less inclined to seek accommodation through political solutions than does the Brezhnev-Kosygin leadership. Its disposition seems to be based less on ideology than on the belief, shared by the military the world over, that political détente can be forged only from a position of strength.

Whatever the differences in approach between the military and civilian elites to international problems, both have been affected by postwar technological advances. As in other countries, the importance of new technologies has brought into the army young professionals whose training and outlook resemble those of scientific personnel in other areas of the Soviet community. These officers associate in large numbers with segments of the scientific technical elite, and together they form a strong bloc which favors greater expenditures on weapons technology and related scientific research, including the space program.

The Soviet military is also, of course, not oblivious to the increasing ferment among the Soviet youth who are called upon to fulfill their military-service requirements. More and more young men not only regard military service as a nuisance but complain that the structure of army authority is excessively repressive. The attitude of youth has become of some concern to both the army, which blames "pacifist" literature for spawning troublemakers, and the party, which emphasizes the need to explain to recruits in even more detail Leninist principles of discipline.[12]

3. THE POLICE

THE EUROPEAN PATTERN: By the reign of Augustus Caesar, Rome had developed a fairly sophisticated civilian police apparatus. *Curatores urbis* patrolled the city streets, accompanied by *lictores* who carried the fasces —a bundle of rods secured around an ax—a symbol of discipline and authority. In the provinces, detachments of paramilitary police were posted in stations dotted about the countryside and towns. The police officer had the power to arrest delinquents, and his superior had authority to deal with prisoners brought to him.

With the decline of central authority, organized police forces disappeared in Europe until the late middle ages, to be replaced by the art of self-defense and the authority of an armed knighthood. Only by degrees was the police organization rebuilt. Until well into the seventeenth century, civil authority relied, for the most part, upon the military to curb civil disorder, and citizens depended upon their own prowess and private organizations of guards to protect their property.

By the nineteenth century most European nations were well on the road to developing modern professional police forces. On the Continent these were usually centralized and under the control of an interior ministry, or its equivalent; most Continental governments also established extensive secret police organizations and paramilitary units to deal with potential insurrections. England was an exception to this pattern. British police forces were decentralized and under the jurisdiction of local authorities; neither paramilitary nor secret police units were created and, in contrast with Continental police, the British bobby was unarmed. The differences, in large measure, reflected the comparative peacefulness of English society.

Both in England and on the Continent, police forces were generally recruited from peasants or workers who identified with authority and saw a police career as a way of moving a step or two up the social ladder. As with members of the military, policemen had an esprit de corps of their own, associated almost exclusively with one another, maintained a rather conservative bias, and often felt that they were unappreciated by the public.

The quality of all police forces improved steadily during the first half of the twentieth century: new methods were employed to weed out the more sadistic recruits, and new training techniques were instituted. With the exception of the Nazi period in Germany, judicial controls over the police also helped improve their public status by limiting the abuses of their discretionary power. In the postwar years, however, most European countries have had difficulty in recruiting police. As other career opportunities have opened up, that of policeman has seemed less and less attractive. In the past few years, too, the public image of the police has be-

---

12 See Thomas W. Wolfe, "The Military," in Allen Kassof, ed., *Prospects for Soviet Society* (New York: Praeger, 1968), pp. 112–142; and the article by General of the Army Aleksey Yepishev in *Kommunist*, April 1968, which is condensed in *Current Digest of the Soviet Press,* XXI (June 4, 1969), pp. 3–7.

come somewhat tarnished and their status has declined. Recruitment, of course, has not been facilitated by the kind of touchy problems faced by police in restraining student demonstrators, when policemen have not always handled themselves with an aplomb calculated to enhance their public standing. Yet it has not been easy for the police to decide how to deal with articulate middle-class student radicals against whom they are unable to use the kind of methods applied to ordinary criminals lest they incur the wrath of the mass media.

The animosity between police and students which is demonstrated in every European country is partially a class phenomenon and partly ideological. Students regard policemen as reactionary agents of the Establishment, as "Fascist pigs," and they resent taking orders from anyone of the working class; police have a tendency to regard all students as "spoiled brats" who have too much money for their own good, and find it difficult to understand why they must accept insults and bricks without cracking a few skulls. This animosity is less acute in England. While the prestige of the bobby has slipped considerably, there remains an underlying civility that has reduced the violence of police-student clashes.

THE ENGLISH PATTERN: Under Alfred the Great, every freeman was required to be a member of a group called a tithing, consisting of ten men. Each tithing member was bound by his pledge or oath to be answerable for the good behavior of the others in his group. The tithings were grouped into units of ten, known as the hundreds, and the county or shire as a whole was administered by the shire-reeve, later sheriff, responsible to his earl for the peace of the county.

The Norman Conquest did not immediately produce any drastic changes in this administrative structure, except that overall authority gradually fell into the hands of local justices of the peace. The first really major

modifications came during the Restoration, when a special force of watchmen was created for London and a special band of constables was formed to aid local authorities in emergency situations.

Not until 1829, upon the report of a select committee and over formidable opposition, did Parliament establish a paid, uniformed police force—the Metropolitan Police of London. The new force carried no weapons other than wooden truncheons, and these were concealed in order not to "inflame" the public. In 1835 all towns and cities of the kingdom were empowered by Parliament to form their own police forces, and the counties were permitted to do the same in 1839. Twenty years later, Parliament made police forces compulsory.

Initially, no rates of pay or conditions of service were prescribed, and local authorities bore the full burden of financing the police. Little by little, however, the central government began to defray a greater proportion of police expenses and to standardize the working conditions throughout the nation. But despite continued moves toward centralization since the First World War, England has not yet created a national police force. The Home Secretary is directly responsible for the metropolitan police force, and he himself is directly responsible to Parliament. He also exercises certain controls over the 49 other police forces in England and Wales with regard to training, equipment, and pay, as well as police methods and standards. Contrary to the 1962 recommendations of the royal commission on the police, however, the Police Act of 1964 permits local chief constables and police authorities to retain much of their independence.

Reaction to the new police forces in London and elsewhere was extremely hostile. However, by the end of the nineteenth century, the British police had built up an unrivaled reputation for fairness and courtesy in dealing with the public. Uniformed police still do not carry guns, although there has been some talk of providing them with weapons, and the amount of violent crime in England, although rising, remains relatively low. Most observers will argue that the British have had the kind of police force they merit because they are an orderly, law-abiding people. Since the mid-fifties, attitudes have changed somewhat, primarily because crimes of violence are on the increase, and the public image of the police is not quite so rosy. Although the disenchantment is not nearly so extreme as newspaper accounts would have one believe,[13] a royal commission did consider forming an independent police review board; the idea was finally rejected as detrimental to police morale.

Just as indicative of changing attitudes is the fact that the police are finding recruitment more and more difficult. Salary scales and work conditions are not such as to attract many, and even the new training methods and techniques have failed to keep pace with the prodigious problems of controlling traffic and combating sophisticated, organized crime. Indeed, the proportion of crimes solved in the past several years has fallen in relation to the number reported. In addition, relations between the police and "colored" immigrants, especially those from the West Indies, have been less than satisfactory, and a determined effort is being put forth to recruit more West Indians for the police force.

Concern with rising crime rates has led to a variety of reform proposals on law and order. New legislation permitting conviction on the basis of less than a unanimous jury passed Parliament in 1966, and a suggestion for the universal fingerprinting of the population is now being seriously discussed. A number of prominent jurists have suggested going even further, arguing that the privilege against self-incrimination no longer serves a useful function; under certain conditions, they maintain, prisoners should be required to answer relevant questions under pain of contempt.

THE FRENCH PATTERN: The French police institution dates back to the fourteenth and fifteenth centuries; its function has, traditionally, been defined quite broadly. Under the old regime, the police not only kept the peace, arrested criminals, and collected taxes, but also saw to it that the people were adequately provisioned at reasonable prices, that public morality was maintained, and that economic development was fostered. Deriving their authority directly from the monarch, the French police had wide powers to dispense summary justice, and they could hold suspects for long periods of time without matters being brought before the courts.

Originally part of the king's household, the police after the Revolution became centralized in the Ministry of the Interior, and police functions and powers were inextricably tied up with governmental programs of public works and education and with the regulation of economic enterprises. Indeed, much of the opposition in England to creating a metropolitan police force for the London area was based on the fear that such extensive authority would be lodged with the police. In the past hundred years, the power of the French police to regulate the nation's economic and social life has been curtailed, and many of their functions have been transferred to other departments. However, the fact that prefects are generally responsible for government services and public order in the areas under their jurisdiction is evidence that the French conception of police powers is still considerably more elastic than that of the British.

Today French police are divided into three major forces: (1) the *Préfecture de police,* covering the Paris region; (2) the *Gendarmerie Nationale,* with jurisdiction in all departments of France; and (3) the *Sûreté Nationale.*

The police force of Paris, established in

---

[13] See Frank Elmes, "The Police 1954–63," *The Criminal Law Review,* June 1964, pp. 505–520.

the fourteenth century as a quasi-military organization, did not begin to assume its modern structure until the Napoleonic era, and not until 1829 was it transformed into a uniformed civil police. The gendarmerie dates from more or less the same period, and was remodeled and modernized in the aftermath of the Revolution. It is now composed of soldiers in strictly disciplined units who are quartered in barracks. The force includes the *Gendarmerie mobile* and the *Gendarmerie departmentale,* a section of which covers each military area under a general's command. Mayors of certain communes have "communal" or "rural" policemen at their disposal, but, in general, police work in towns of less than ten thousand is performed by the gendarmerie. The mobile units are available for crisis situations and can be called into action by the prefects. From one to three of these legions are deployed in every military area; each is commanded by a colonel and is made up of eight squadrons, one of which is an armored-car unit.

With the exception of Paris, the main burden of police work in towns of more than ten thousand is handled by the Sûreté Nationale. In each town a *commissaire,* or superintendent of police, is responsible for the Sûreté's local organization; he is in constant touch with the mayor and the prefect for the purpose of complying with their orders regarding the regular police. Major decisions on working methods and other police issues are the province of the Directorate of Public Security in Paris. In addition to the regular police, the Sûreté also has control over the mobile reserve units known as republican security companies; highly trained and specially equipped for riot control, they are used to restore order in emergencies.

In comparison with England, France is policed quite heavily, a fact related in no small measure to its much higher incidence of ordinary crimes and, particularly, its long history of civic disorders. As a matter of course, the police collect dossiers of damaging material on unsuspecting citizens—material based on a whole network of spies and informers, including concierges. Nor are French police noted for their gentleness; until 1967, for example, the capes of the Paris police were lined with lead weights, and used quite freely along with firearms in dispersing demonstrators. The severity of police action has been toned down somewhat under the Fifth Republic, yet the police are still likely to seize suspects on the basis of only flimsy evidence and to abuse them with blows and kicks in order to obtain confessions. Such physical tactics are used primarily against Algerians in France and the urban lumpenproletariat rather than against the bourgeoisie, but in the student riots of 1968, many young men were severely beaten while being arrested.

The behavior of the police in 1968 can be partly attributed to student provocation. But it was in large measure a reflection of the resentment that police of working-class background felt against the middle-class students who compose France's university population. It is also true that historically the French police have been noted for their right-wing sympathies, despite efforts by the Communist Party to get their own men into key positions. On the other hand, the police did yeoman work in fighting right-wing terrorist organizations during the Algerian crisis, and they stood firmly behind de Gaulle against the threatened intervention of elements of the military in 1961.

THE GERMAN PATTERN: German states of the Second Reich retained control over their own police forces, and the central government had no police force of its own. The Reich did exercise a modicum of control over local authorities by defraying part of the cost of "efficient" police forces. This state-federal arrangement continued throughout the Weimar period. In general, the police, where they had any political sympathies at all, leaned toward the right; but even so, the situation varied from one area to the next. In Prussia, for example, police officials were considered quite liberal, and it was partly for this reason that in 1932 Franz von Papen, then chancellor, ousted the Socialist government of Prussia on the ground that it was incapable of maintaining public order.

Under the Nazis, Germany became a unitary state, and the national government took over responsibility for the regular police forces, establishing uniform conditions of pay, service, and function. A special secret state police force was also created, the notorious Gestapo (*Geheimestaatspolizei*), which was given the power of taking people into "protective custody" without having to file formal charges; its activities were protected from outside interference. Along with the SS, it was placed in charge of concentration camps and was also granted the authority to search private premises whenever necessary in the interest of state "security." Under Heinrich Himmler, the secret police became a state within a state, collecting information on all Germans of any importance; Himmler's power in the Nazi regime, and the fear with which he was regarded, were related directly to his control over the SS and the Gestapo.[14]

In re-forming the police in West Germany after World War II, the Allied High Commission directed that authority be decentralized. Jurisdiction over the police was, therefore, returned to the Land level, and this system has remained in effect. State police forces are responsible to the Land minister of the interior; they are financed by the Länder, with municipalities making cost contributions to some of them. The federal government has the right to inspect Land police forces, but it has no general authority over their organization. The Bonn government does, however, control the Frontier Police Force; organized on military lines and heavily armed, it is under the supervision of the federal Ministry of the Interior.

As under the Second Reich, the West German police today have an excellent record of

incorruptibility. Considerable care was taken to prevent the re-employment of those with Nazi sympathies, and, in general, police forces in the states seem to be almost apolitical. The German crime rate has always been relatively low (except in the 1920's and in the immediate aftermath of Hitler's defeat), and policemen have usually been accorded considerable public respect. In the postwar period, German authorities have tried to maintain this respect by giving the police a more "democratic," friendlier image; as yet the attempt has met with only mixed success.

Although student provocation in Germany has been far more serious than in France, the German police have usually reacted with far less severity than their French counterparts in handling demonstrators. Nonetheless, tensions between students and police have been mounting, and they could lead to an escalation of violence in the future.

THE RUSSIAN AND SOVIET PATTERN: Peter the Great not only established the foundations of a modern Russian army, but also created Russia's police system. The system was reconstituted in 1825 under Nicholas I, and it became the mainspring of the entire state machinery; it can be argued, in fact, that at the beginning of the twentieth century, Russia was the most police-ridden nation in the world. The police dealt with criminals, passports, hotels, boardinghouses, theaters, deaths, and marriages.

With the coming of the Bolshevik Revolution, the empire's police apparatus was dissolved, and routine police work was assigned to the "militia," which was, theoretically, responsible to the local soviets. In practice, however, the police apparatus was highly centralized under the authority of the People's Commissariat of Internal Affairs (N.K.V.D.), which also took over the responsibility for the state secret police (*Cheka*). The militia was required to place its forces at Cheka's disposal when requested.

Centralized control over the police apparatus remained in force through the Stalin

---

14 After 1939 the SS assumed almost complete responsibility for the concentration camps.

period, and for a good deal of the time the militia was also under the control of the state-security apparatus. For example, between 1946 and 1953, the coordinator of all police functions was Lavrenty Beria, who had made his reputation during the purges of the late 1930's as part of the state secret-police apparatus.[15] After Beria's execution, the secret police were transformed into the Committee of State Security (K.G.B.), attached to the Council of Ministers of the U.S.S.R.; the authority of the Ministry of Internal Affairs was limited to regular police forces only. The jurisdiction of the two groups, however, did continue to overlap in certain areas.

The organization of the regular police was decentralized by Khrushchev. The national M.V.D. was abolished and its authority transferred to local M.V.D.'s, renamed, in 1962, ministries for the preservation of public order (M.O.O.P.'s). However, recentralization set in almost immediately upon Khrushchev's fall from office. In 1966 an All-Union M.O.O.P. was created for the purpose of coordinating the work of the police, and, late in 1968, the new organ became once again the Ministry of Internal Affairs; the names of republican ministries were also changed at the same time.

As part of a system of dual control, the militia in the Soviet Union is now responsible both to republican ministries and to the All-Union Ministry in Moscow. The national ministry has been attempting to coordinate police work and to raise police standards which, as indicated by widespread comment in the Soviet Union early in 1969, are still considered too low.

The authority of the militia and the police in the Soviet Union is more extensive than that delegated to police in non-Communist European countries. They not only handle

ordinary criminal work, they also control the issuance of the internal passports required of all Soviet citizens over sixteen, except for kolkhoz members who must obtain a passport or a special certificate from the village soviet before they can visit most urban areas. The militia and the police have the authority to fine anyone for hiring or granting accommodations to persons without passports or with improper ones. They are also responsible for granting permission to persons who wish to use printing, mimeographing, typewriting, communication, or photographic equipment.

Throughout its history the Soviet regime has, from time to time, called upon party or Komsomol units to engage in "police" work. In the late 1950's, Khrushchev used this tradition as part of his plan to decentralize state functions, and he was instrumental in creating the so-called people's volunteer police (*druzhiny*). Initially, the main function of the druzhiny was the maintenance of public order, and they engaged in large-scale patrolling of the streets. In 1959 and 1960, they were organized more formally. In large enterprises, druzhiny were set up in each shop and united into a plantwide organization under the guidance of the Communist Party. And to make their position outwardly official, they were even provided with armbands.

Although Soviet literature stresses the voluntary character of the organization, the persuasive powers of the party and the Komsomol have had their effect on recruitment. In any event, a number of problems have been associated with those who do volunteer. Newspapers have on occasion criticized the organization for accepting as members individuals who joined only to feel a sense of power and who carried out their duties with so much enthusiasm that they violated the civil rights of Soviet citizens. Attempts by volunteer policemen to deal with hooliganism have been counterproductive in other ways; untrained in police methods, a number have been beaten or killed in trying to handle drunken citizens. As a result, decrees now

---

[15] During a good part of the period, regular and secret police functions were theoretically divided respectively between the N.K.V.D. and the People's Commissariat for State Security (N.K.G.B.). In 1946, both commissariats became ministries and their initials were changed to M.V.D. and M.G.B.

provide up to six months in prison for insulting a member of the druzhiny on duty, with penalties up to five years for threats or resistance; physical attacks upon volunteer policemen may now result in capital punishment.[16] The druzhiny themselves have been placed under closer supervision by the militia and given some formal police training.

The "volunteer" police experiment has not been met with the wholehearted enthusiasm of either the authorities or the public, as proved by the fact that in recent years the purely police functions of the druzhiny have been reduced and their civic functions emphasized. Today, the druzhiny are directed primarily to encourage obedience to social norms through lectures, to "shame" those who act in "un-Soviet" ways, and to check on such violations against the public as price tampering by stores. They also report to officials on other types of nonconformist behavior—including the wearing of "excessively" short skirts.

The secret police in Russia became more and more important in the last half of the nineteenth century. The "Third Section," originally set up by Nicholas I after the Decembrists' uprising, was responsible only to the emperor, and it had wide discretion in investigating, detaining, and imprisoning citizens who were regarded as a threat to the security of the state. Working through *agents provocateurs* and paid informers, it created an underworld of double and triple agents that gives the history of Russia before the Revolution an extremely bizarre character. As Sidney Monas has described it:

During the period of the 1905 Revolution and after, police agents and underground revolutionaries inhabited a common shadow world of perpetual distrust and suspicion. Almost anyone might be a police agent. Almost

any police agent might be a revolutionary spy.[17]

The Provisional Government that came to power in 1917 eliminated the secret police. The Bolsheviks, however, had no scruples about restoring them. Shortly after the Revolution, the Council of People's Commissars, at the suggestion of Lenin, created the All-Russian Extraordinary Commission to Combat Counterrevolutionary Crimes and Sabotage (*Cheka*), under the leadership of F. E. Dzerzhinski. Dzerzhinski, a son of Polish aristocrats, had studied for the priesthood and then became a revolutionary; dedicated to the cause of ending the "exploitation of man by man," he gave himself enthusiastically to the revolutionary cause and spent a good many years in prison. He was widely thought of by Communists both within and outside Russia as an incorruptible idealist, and persons as widely divergent in their views as Rosa Luxemburg and Stalin regarded him as completely selfless. A measure of the man may be obtained by one or two excerpts from a diary he kept while in prison:

What is the way out of present-day life, in which the jungle law of exploitation, oppression and force holds sway? The way out is a life based on harmony, a full life embracing the whole of society and humanity; the way out lies in the idea of socialism, the solidarity of the workers.

Here, we have felt and realized how essential man is to man, what man means to man. I think that relations between people are complex. . . . And if we may long here for flowers, it remains a fact that we have learned here to love people as we love flowers. . . .[18]

16 Dennis M. O'Conner, "Soviet People's Guards: An Experiment with Civic Police," *New York University Law Review,* 39 (June 1964), p. 608. The same penalties apply to persons who resist the militia.

17 "The Political Police: The Dream of a Beautiful Autocracy," in Cyril Black, ed., *The Transformation of Russian Society* (Cambridge: Harvard University Press, 1960), p. 180.

18 Quoted in Simon Wolin and Robert M. Slusser, *The Soviet Secret Police* (New York: Frederick A. Praeger, 1957), pp. 68, 70.

During and immediately after the Russian civil war, Cheka, under Dzerzhinski's leadership, executed several hundred thousand people without trial—either because they belonged to opposition groups like the Mensheviks or because of their "class" position. In letters to his sister, Dzerzhinski recounted the emotional turmoil he experienced in being responsible for taking these lives, but justified his actions in the name of future humanity.

Dzerzhinski did urge, once the Communists had consolidated their power, that the activities of Cheka be reduced—always assuming, of course, that new enemies of the people did not materialize. And, during the 1920's, the incidence of arbitrary arrest, imprisonment, and execution diminished somewhat. When Cheka was abolished and its authority was first transferred to the newly created State Police Administration (G.P.U.), secret-police activity was placed under the personal chairmanship of the people's commissar for the interior, and its code of operations was systemized. The G.P.U. (which became the O.G.P.U. in 1923) had full authority to search premises and make arrests on its own initiative, but henceforth persons arrested were to be supplied with an indictment within two weeks and placed on trial within two months. Although these rules were often violated, the period after the conclusion of the civil war was one of relative Socialist legality compared with what was to come.

It was, of course, the secret police—now part of N.K.V.D.—which was primarily responsible for the great purge that reached its peak in 1937 and 1938. The purge began in 1936 under Stalin's chief agent, G. G. Yagoda, who was replaced in 1937 by N. I. Yezhov. Yagoda was arrested in 1937 and executed a year later—when Yezhov himself fell victim to the purge's terrors and was replaced by Beria.

The secret police under Beria's guidance, which lasted until shortly after the death of Stalin, reached the height of their power and

influence. Beria was an intimate of Stalin and seems to have had considerable influence with the dictator who, at one time, probably considered him a potential heir. Beria established a complete hierarchy of secret-police offices that paralleled those of the Communist Party and served as a check upon party members. The N.K.V.D. also took on increasing responsibility for certain economic activities, as more and more prisoners entered labor camps; it was, for instance, responsible for the construction of Belomor, the canal connecting Leningrad and the White Sea, a job that employed more than two hundred thousand prisoners. It is still impossible to know how many people passed through forced-labor camps between 1934 and 1953. The total figure is certainly well over twenty million, as fantastic as this may seem, and memoirs by Soviet citizens who served terms in prison but have since been rehabilitated indicate that, in some of the camps at least, as many as thirty per cent of the prisoners died.

If we are to believe Svetlana Alliluyeva, Beria was the real evil genius behind her father—the man personally responsible for the tragedy of those years.[19] While the portrait she presented, like Khrushchev's portrait of Stalin, undoubtedly contains important elements of truth, it is far from being the whole story; explanations must still be provided on how a man of Beria's ilk came to power in the first place. The corruption of power is also an important element in explaining the excesses of these years. In the last analysis, however, it must be argued that the principal cause—aside from certain elements in Russian culture—was the strains put upon Soviet society by both the policies of the Communist leadership and the institutional patterns created as a consequence of these tensions.

Beria's move to seize power after Stalin's death failed, and he was executed along with many important figures in the police

19 Svetlana Alliluyeva, *Twenty Letters to a Friend* (New York: Harper and Row, 1967).

organization. Fairly quickly thereafter, the authority of the police began to be curbed; taken out of the Ministry of the Interior, it was placed with a state committee of lesser power. Further, regular police activities were removed from the K.G.B., whose chairman is now a party bureaucrat rather than a police officer. The number of forced-labor camps was cut back sharply, and they were placed under the jurisdiction of the Main Administration of Corrective Labor Colonies (G.U.I.T.K.), an agency responsible to local administrative authorities who, according to all accounts, have considerably improved camp conditions, although they continue to be quite harsh. Most of the economic functions controlled by the police were taken over by special planning agencies.

In the years since Stalin and Beria died, the K.G.B.'s power to make arrests has been drastically curtailed. Moreover, most of its authority over the determination of guilt or innocence and over the actual sentencing of those charged with political crimes has been transferred to the regular courts. Some arrests and sentencing still take place through administrative rather than court action, although the extent of these preemptory acts is difficult to pin down.

The K.G.B. remains an integral part of the Soviet system insofar as it deals with espionage and ideological deviations by Soviet citizens. It is, again, difficult to assess just how large its role is, but one suspects that agents are still placed in the armed forces, in important industrial and defense establishments, and within the party. It is probably true, too, that the organization continues to keep dossiers on a large portion of the population. On the other hand, since the fall of Beria the party has been careful to place only party men at the head of the K.G.B., and the organization is now forced to rely upon the militia for much of its manpower.

By the late 1950's, then, a good deal of the terror that had characterized Soviet life until 1953 had been dissipated. Both Stalin and the secret police had been partially discredited by the rehabilitation of former "criminals" and by the denunciation of "crimes" committed under Stalin's aegis. The denunciation, of course, was only partial; most of the leadership that was then in power, and is in power today, had taken some part in those crimes.

Soon after the removal of Khrushchev, however, a conscious effort was made to rehabilitate the secret police, and a new series of novels and plays appeared with secret agents as heroes. Trials were held of writers whose works had been published abroad, and attempts to distribute literature protesting these trials prompted beatings and arrests by K.G.B. officials. Nevertheless, it is quite unlikely that the secret police will again rise to the position of power they had under Stalin. The final reckoning for the 1930's, however, has yet to be made. Should liberalization indeed become a reality, many more Soviet citizens than we can now imagine will remind the world that they have neither forgotten nor forgiven the Stalin period.

24

Economic and Social Policy

1. INTRODUCTION

From a functional point of view, the economic system of any society consists of institutions created for the production, organization, and distribution of resources. The nature of these institutions, of course, depends to a very considerable extent upon the goals of the society or of the dominant groups within the society.

In devising economic institutions, every society is faced with at least three major problems: efficiency, allocation, and equity. When available resources are in short supply, certain methods of organizing economic life may be more efficient than others. And the organization of economic life, far from being a matter of chance, is directly related to the uses to which resources are put; a society concerned primarily with esthetic or religious values may arrange its economic activity in ways other than one dedicated to augmenting the material well-being of its members. Moreover, the manner in which the economy is organized affects the distribution of resources among members of a society; any

community concerned with equalizing distribution may create a different economic structure from one in which equity takes a secondary place.

From the middle of the nineteenth century, conflicts over the preferred way in which to coordinate an economic system have revolved about these questions. In their attack on capitalism, for example, the Socialists have contended that a society in which the means of production are in the hands of the community not only would be more efficient than one in which they are privately controlled, but also would insure a more equitable distribution of income, a more democratic society, and a social order in which esthetic goals would be more easily attained. Indeed, arguments over economic policy still focus heavily on the virtues of a Socialist economy versus a capitalist or mixed economy.

There are, however, other ways of looking at the economic organization of society. It is certainly not amiss to consider it also in terms of the mechanisms by which a community's economic activities are coordinated and to draw the usual distinction among traditional, market, and command economies.

In pre-industrial societies, the relationship among economic units was usually regulated by tradition, which on the medieval manor determined the serfs' payments to the lord in labor, produce, or money. The origins of the traditions may be traceable to certain configurations of power or initial bargains, but eventually these become crystallized into customary relationships.

In most advanced economies, until early in the twentieth century, it was chiefly the market that allocated income, adjusting production, consumption, and resources to one another. A market is essentially a place where producers exchange goods and services at prices freely agreed upon. We may speak of a market economy when three conditions are met: (1) the separate economic units (individuals, families, firms) determine for themselves what, how, where, and when they produce and consume; (2) the costs of producing goods or services are rationally calculated to maximize the financial well-being of the economic units; and (3) the prices at which items are bought and sold respond, more or less, to the forces of demand and supply.

It should be noted that this description says nothing about whether the producing units are privately or publicly owned. Nor does it take into consideration government intervention in the economy; if this occurs, it could effect all three conditions so long as the intervention is not extensive enough to eliminate the market mechanism altogether. Economic units in a market economy must, however, be largely autonomous with regard to the decisions in question.

In theory, the operation of the market mechanism insures that resources are allocated in such a way as to produce goods in an amount and quality that best fulfill the preferences of most if not all members of the society. While some regulation from outside may be necessary to serve certain social purposes, the market is largely self-regulating.

The individual determination of what to produce and consume and the haggling over costs and prices result in just that desired mix of goods and services.

The same directing, resource-allocating, coordinating, and income-distributing functions can be accomplished by means of a command principle. In such a case, the individual economic units are simply told what, when, where, how, and how much to produce and consume. The command principle implies little autonomy on the part of individual economic units; it also implies the presence of a superior authority to issue the commands and very probably a hierarchical planning structure.

No real economic system, past or present, has ever been in practice what might be termed completely "pure." Even in the United States during the nineteenth century, when the market mechanism was supposedly supreme, the government intervened in the economy in several significant ways. The Soviet Union during the period of War Communism and from about 1931 to 1966 approached the ideal type of a command economy; yet market elements were always a factor. The Soviet regime has now begun to incorporate some market principles quite explicitly.

For a number of reasons, all Western European economies in the twentieth century have moved away from exclusive reliance upon market mechanisms. Efforts to guarantee sound economic growth and pressures to allocate resources toward particular ends have both contributed to this change. Until now, the chief objective of all European nations, including the Soviet Union, has been to produce an ever greater amount and wider variety of goods with increased efficiency. Today, economic goals are shifting. Services are becoming more important than goods; the creation of a satisfying natural and social environment is beginning to have a greater appeal than the annual increase in the gross national product; and the nature of the work experience, together with its impact on the worker, is becoming far more a matter of public concern than simple considerations of "efficiency." These are issues to which we will return in the last chapter.

2. THE EUROPEAN PATTERN

POLITY AND ECONOMY: The establishment of an industrial society in Europe involved the replacement of a traditional, subsistence economic order by a market economy, one that was based on contractual associations, private ownership of property, and the growing differentiation of economic institutions from other structures within the society.

In feudal Europe, economic behavior was always subordinated to problems of community integration and organization. Production and distribution were partially regulated by religio-political norms that defined the "good" society. Even with the development of commercial capitalism and the rise of cities, the guilds regulated the price and quality of goods, and the new national states were explicitly concerned with determining the principal areas of economic policy. During the era of mercantilism, every European state engaged in important economic activities, regulating or controlling many aspects of the economy directly or through subsidiary institutions.

In France, for example, under Louis XIV's secretary of state, Jean Baptiste Colbert, the state was responsible for building canals and highways; it encouraged the export of cloth through the use of bounties and rearranged tariff schedules in order to promote economic expansion. Seventeenth-century France also supported the creation of chartered, state-controlled companies to exploit the resources of non-European areas; aided the growth of industry by subsidies and the importation of skilled craftsmen; created state industries for the manufacture of tapestries and lace; and encouraged the formation of companies—whose operations it then closely controlled—for the purpose of manufacturing such items as mirrors and tin plate. In consultation with the guilds, the state for-

mulated regulations regarding the terms of apprentices, standards of workmanship, inspection of goods, and the relationship between masters and workers. The state was also active in what today would be called "welfare" policy. During the famine of 1661 and 1662, Colbert organized relief by importing grain, distributed it below cost, and even arranged for the baking and allocation of bread in Paris; once the famine was over, he took measures to stave off its recurrence. Among other preventive policies, he directed that nationwide reports on the condition of crops be submitted; at the first sign of shortage, he forbade the export of grain from the province affected or, if necessary, from any part of the country.

Colbert was equally concerned with the poor. He renewed legislation against beggars, vagabonds, and gypsies, forcing them to work under penalty of being shut up in poorhouses or sent to the galleys. Existing poorhouses were enlarged and new ones were erected in the provinces. The administration of poor relief remained in the hands of the church, but the state took an active part in its distribution. While the results of these measures are not easy to assess, they do not seem to have been as efficacious as the system England used to provide for its poor.

These efforts by the state to add to its wealth and power and to be at once a source of integration and of authority were also characteristic of Prussia and other European nations, including England. By the beginning of the seventeenth century, however, the pattern of England's economic organization was changing: the British were not nearly so intent upon state building as were the French and the Prussians, and they lacked a centralized bureaucratic apparatus to implement the kind of policies advanced on the Continent. Also, doctrines asserting the importance of "creative" private initiative were gaining ascendancy.

As propounded by Hobbes, Locke, and, in mature form, by Adam Smith, classical liberal economic policy first achieved its full flowering in England. Its general argument placed reliance on rational self-interest and the price mechanism as the primary means by which to encourage economic and social development. The state's business was principally that of enforcing law and order, including contracts; of preventing the growth of monopolistic practices; of engaging in those necessary tasks, such as defense, with which the market system could not cope; and of aiding the poor and indigent who, for some reason not of their own doing, were unable to compete economically.

The market system worked more effectively than government enterprise or government-controlled enterprise, it was argued, because either of the latter was inevitably highly inefficient. Government enterprise or control automatically meant the misallocation of resources or the encouragement of activities that would prevent the effective distribution and maximum utilization of resources. Since individual rationality and capacity were limited, attempts by state officials to plan for the entire society inevitably led to irrationality and ineptness. On the other hand, individuals could make rational decisions about their personal preferences. The virtue of unfettered private enterprise was that these personal choices were translatable into viable public policies by the market and the price system. There was no need to plan for the economy as a whole; the economy would take care of itself. The market would also insure that rewards were proportionate to effort. In general, the market system would create a rationally oriented society which, because it was founded on human self-interest, would encourage the productive arts rather than the nonproductive ones. The search for honor or power would be replaced by the search for wealth—for commodious living—to the advantage of all concerned. To theorists such as Hobbes, the search for affluence was crucial to the sublimation of those drives to power which all men possessed. In the past, the natural combativeness of men had been given free play in societies dedicated to honor and the military arts; in the future, man's aggressiveness would be

used to further human well-being, because it would be directed toward mastering nature.

Laissez-faire doctrines became popular in England during the eighteenth century and reached the height of their influence in the first part of the nineteenth. The repeal of the Corn Laws and the Navigation Acts and the ending of export restrictions on machinery were all symptomatic of the endorsement of a policy that viewed the economy as a sphere best left to the free play of the market. Not that those embracing laissez-faire also viewed the government's role in society as totally unimportant: after all, Parliament did grant charters and rights of way for canals and railroads, and did encourage the flow of money into certain areas by legalizing limited liability companies. Further, defense expenditures were not an insignificant factor in economic growth. Then, too, the responsibility of the government for the public's welfare was not to be dismissed; indeed, England did begin in the nineteenth century to pass social-welfare measures in ever greater numbers.

It was not until the twentieth century, however, that active government intervention in the economy—for purposes that ranged from altering its general condition to controlling industrial sites—became accepted. In the 1920's the price of coal, for example, became subject to regulation, town and country planning measures were instituted, and industries were induced to locate in "depressed" areas. At the end of World War II, of course, a number of industries were nationalized, and the Labor Party continued many wartime controls and talked about comprehensive national planning. By the end of the first Labor government, however, disillusionment with government economic interference had set in, and national planning as a goal became considerably less popular even among moderate Socialists. Even so, within the Conservative Party and in the higher echelons of the bureaucracy itself, Keynesian economic analysis had been fully accepted; it was now generally agreed that the government should not only contribute

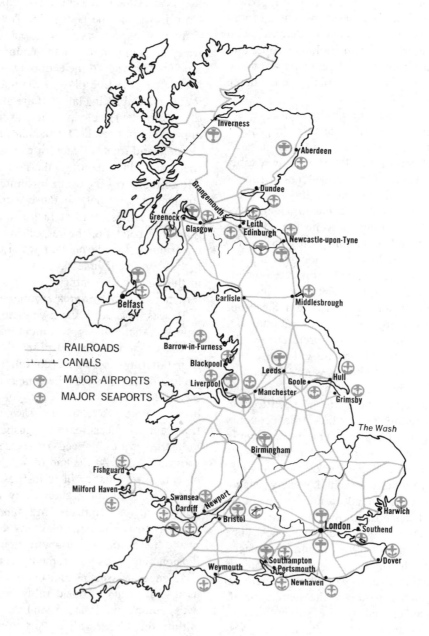

RAILROADS
CANALS
MAJOR AIRPORTS
MAJOR SEAPORTS

MAP 24.1.   TRANSPORTATION IN GREAT BRITAIN

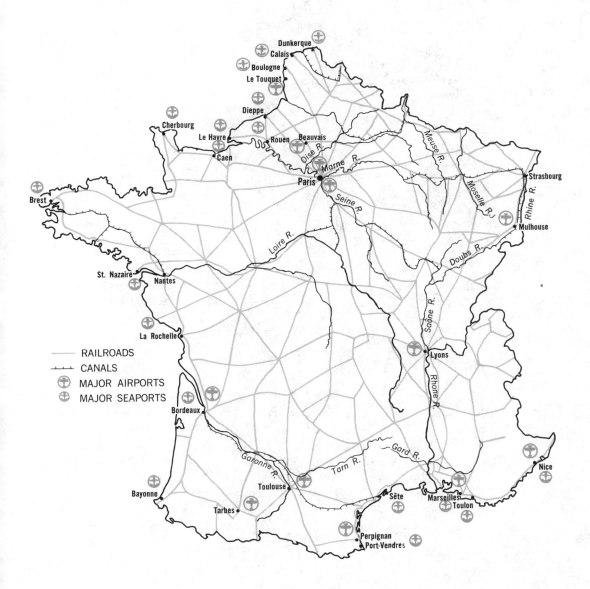

MAP 24.2.   TRANSPORTATION IN FRANCE

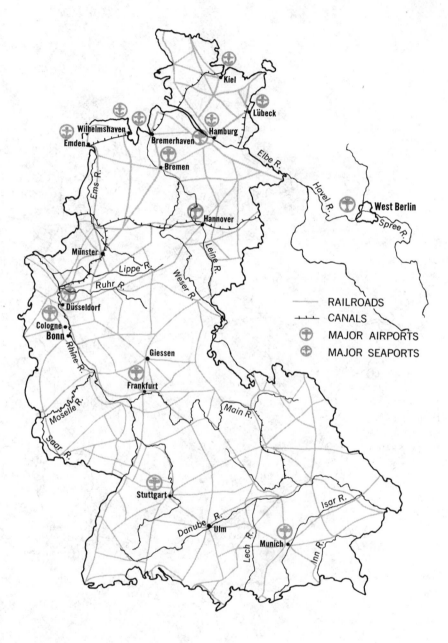

Kiel

Lübeck

Wilhelmshaven
Emden

Bremerhaven

Hamburg

Elbe R.

Havel R.

West Berlin

Bremen

Spree R.

Ems. R.

Hannover

Münster

Lippe R.

Leine R.

Ruhr R.

Weser R.

Düsseldorf

RAILROADS

Cologne

CANALS

Bonn

MAJOR AIRPORTS

Giessen

MAJOR SEAPORTS

Rhine R.

Frankfurt

Moselle R.

Main R.

Saar R.

Stuttgart

Danube R.

Ulm

Isar R.

Lech R.

Munich

Inn R.

MAP 24.3.   TRANSPORTATION IN WEST GERMANY

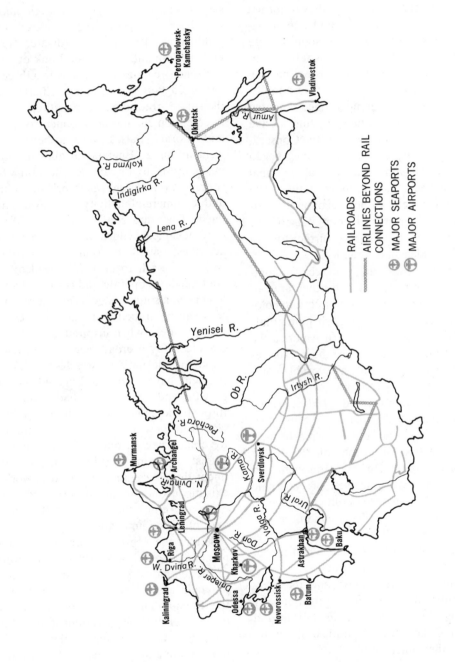

RAILROADS

AIRLINES BEYOND RAIL
CONNECTIONS

MAJOR SEAPORTS

MAJOR AIRPORTS

MAP 24.4. TRANSPORTATION IN THE U.S.S.R.

to economic growth, but should use fiscal devices to promote full employment.

The Conservatives, in fact, relied upon Keynesian mechanisms when they returned to power during the 1950's, and unemployment was kept quite low. Yet it soon became apparent that England was stagnating economically—or, rather, that it was not moving ahead at a sufficiently rapid rate; for a multitude of reasons, England's once vaunted productive efficiency seemed a thing of the past. Under these circumstances the Conservatives, inspired by French programs, began to think once again of an overall national planning agency and of more active state intervention to achieve both economic modernization and growth. Under Wilson, the Labor government has moved further toward putting these ideas into practice.

Liberal doctrines did not receive comparable predominance in any other area of the world, with the exception of certain colonies settled primarily by English immigrants —notably the United States. In America the absence of an older tradition, the pervasiveness of the Calvinist ethos, a favorable combination of land and resources, and, finally, massive immigration created an ideal setting for the application of liberal capitalist doctrines—doctrines that did not reach their fullest application until the middle of the nineteenth century. On the Continent, an older tradition that conceived of economic activity as subordinate to political concerns remained far stronger. The conditions for self-starting industrial activity were lacking, and political leaders used the mechanisms of the state to foster industrialization.

In France, the Revolution and its aftermath contributed to modernization by eliminating the vestiges of feudalism and rationalizing the nation's political structure. Early in the nineteenth century a more logical system of weights and measures was also instituted, the system of coinage reformed, a comprehensive legal code developed, and the tax system reorganized. A national system of education was inaugu-

rated, including, at the highest level, excellent technical schools. Further, Napoleon pushed the construction of an extensive road system and encouraged the development of industries, especially those related to the production of military hardware. He also laid the foundations for the Bank of France.

French regimes of the nineteenth century vacillated between economic liberalism and the more traditional conceptions of state intervention for the achievement of political and "moral" goals. France, to be sure, never went as far as England in allowing market mechanisms to direct the allocation of resources, even though most private industrial and commercial activity remained unregulated. The state continued to subsidize not only technical education but many other activities, such as railroad construction, which were felt to be vitally needed; it also continued to operate industries which had long been a source of government revenue.

It can be argued that state intervention in France—even when inspired, as under Louis Napoleon, by a broad technocratic vision of remaking the nation—was less fruitful than it might have been. In England, economic growth and innovation had come about through the emergence of an entrepreneurial class with new attitudes and with the power to create new economic institutions. The French state in the nineteenth century, as under the old regime, preferred to work with existing economic institutions and the old economic elite, thereby strengthening both and inhibiting innovation.

Under the aegis of more radical governments at the end of World War II, segments of French industry were nationalized, including railroads, electricity, gas, aviation, and the Renault automobile works. Some were taken over by the government because the then dominant political parties agreed that the "commanding heights" of the economy should be under state control. Some, such as Renault, were nationalized because their owners had collaborated during the war with the Vichy government. Along with nationalization came a program of national planning,

FIGURE 24.1. NATIONALIZATION OF SECTORS OF THE ECONOMY

Adapted from J. L. Sampedro, *Decisive Forces in World Economics* (New York: McGraw-Hill, 1967; London: Weidenfeld & Nicolson Ltd.), p. 151. Reprinted by permission of the publishers.

embarked upon under the joint impact of Socialist and Keynesian thought and buttressed by the aid of vast amounts of new information as well as new techniques. The program reflected traditional French attitudes favoring control of the economy by a technical elite—a legacy of the old regime and the peculiar characteristics of revolutionary and postrevolutionary French scientism.

The technocratic tradition has become more and more important both in the French bureaucracy and in certain areas of the business community. Combined with the French willingness to have the state direct the econ-

omy in critical areas, it has enabled France to undertake planning experiments of a kind that the British, for example, have found difficult to attempt.

In Germany, the impact of liberal economics was even less significant than in France. Feudal and mercantilist attitudes with respect to the state as an economic agent carried over into the modern era, with national and local government taking an active part in community development. German academic economics was dominated by doctrines urging that economic decisions could not be divorced from political ones, and that the state was obliged to advance economic development.

Consequently, the governments of Prussia and other German states—and, later, of the Empire—helped to create the infrastructure of economic activity by building roads, bridges, canals, and railways. They also promoted industrialization by establishing technical schools, sending people abroad to learn special techniques, encouraging the immigration of foreign craftsmen, and using taxes and subsidies to expand the economy. Moreover, they took part directly in many essential economic activities.

As early as the seventeenth century, some of the most highly developed industries in the German states, especially those producing luxuries and armaments, were owned by the local princes. This did change in the nineteenth century because private management proved to be more efficient, and many industries were sold to private companies. The public sector, however, was not ignored. Railways, for example, invariably were either built by the state or quite soon came under its control, and many states established and maintained their own financial institutions. The Prussian *Seehandlung* (overseas trading corporation) was created by Frederick II and continued to be active in economic development well into the nineteenth century; in conjunction with local entrepreneurs and banks, the organization came to own, for example, a sizable number of factories. Modern British machines were installed in some factories in the 1820's, and British artisans were imported to teach German workers how to use them. In addition, approximately one-fifth of Prussia's coal output came from state-owned mines.

From the end of the Franco-Prussian War to the end of World War I—the period of the Second Reich—many more businesses and industrial enterprises formerly owned by ruling nobles were brought under the control of state governments: the breweries of Munich, the porcelain factories of Meissen and Berlin, the tobacco factories in Strasbourg. State control of mining and agriculture became even more extensive. It is estimated that in 1907 one-tenth of all workers in industry, commerce, and transportation were employed in public services.

The early Weimar years brought a slight shift to classical liberal attitudes, but the economic chaos of the mid- and late 1920's inevitably prompted extensive government intervention in economic activities. The Nazi regime furthered the process, instituting, in line with its corporate ideology, a program of massive state intervention and control. Deficit financing was used for the extensive construction of public works, including the famed autobahns, and business activity was tightly regulated. In 1936 a four-year plan was initiated for the proclaimed purpose of guiding basic production, controlling imports and exports, allocating basic resources, overseeing orders and credit, and strengthening foreign-exchange controls. Until the war necessitated fuller mobilization, however, Nazi economic planning was very much on an ad hoc basis.

To many Germans, in their postwar reaction to the Nazi experience, there seemed to be a close parallel between active government intervention in the economic life of the nation and an authoritarian regime. Under economist Ludwig Erhard, therefore, the Adenauer government adopted what came to be known as the "social market" policy—the strategy of allowing the market itself to determine basic economic decisions while limiting the function of government to making sure that the market operated as "freely" as possible. Many economic controls were lifted and some industries, including the Volkswagen company, were denationalized. In actuality, the free-market economy involved more government intervention than the rhetoric implied, and with the formation, in 1966, of the coalition government of Christian Democrats and Social Democrats, government involvement became even more extensive. The 1969 election results, which produced the Social Democrat–Free Democrat coalition, promised still further moves in the direction of national economic planning.

As a general axiom, the later a society begins the industrialization process, the more active the role of the state in the economy. This certainly applies to Europe. In Russia, for example, the early stages of economic growth were almost entirely state-inspired. The new industries opened by Peter the Great were frequently state-owned, although they were operated by private parties for private profit. Until the emancipation of the serfs (and even later), the state owned vast manufacturing and mining properties, and when railroads began to be built on a huge scale, the state not only subsidized construction but helped in their operation. As for private enterprise, the state encouraged production through the use of tariffs and subsidies; state orders for goods were also among the major spurs to production. It is estimated that in 1899 nearly two-thirds of Russian metallurgical production was bought by the state. On the whole, the links between officials and industrialists were quite close.

Between 1904 and the beginning of the First World War, Russian rates of economic expansion were almost as high as those of the 1890's—about six per cent a year. By 1914 Russia was the fifth largest industrial power in the world. This expansion, unlike that of the earlier period, stemmed largely from the private sector, and some students of the subject think that Russia had reached an economic "takeoff point" which, had the war not intervened, would have been self-reinforcing.[1] By 1913 Russia already had passed France in the production of steel and was the world's fourth largest producer. The war and the Bolshevik Revolution, of course, reversed this trend toward a capitalist economy and opened a new era in Russian history.

When the Bolsheviks seized power, they had only a few fairly simple ideas regarding the administration of an advanced economy. Their expectation was that with the elimination of capitalism economic problems would, in effect, take care of themselves and that the use of money and the market mechanism would not be necessary in a Socialist economy. It was partly such naïveté and partly the exigencies of the immediate circumstances that led to the policy of War Communism between 1918 and 1921, a period in which the government created a command economy; ad hoc decisions regulated the production and distribution of goods, money was eliminated, factory and farm output was requisitioned, and the distribution of resources was handled through a system of rationing. The results were chaotic. Industrial production almost came to a halt, and it proved impossible to get the peasants to deliver grain to the cities. There followed mass starvation on an unprecedented scale. While exact figures are difficult to come by, the civil war and its aftermath probably caused the death of from ten to twelve million persons.[2]

It was under the impetus of this setback that Lenin instituted the New Economic Policy, which again employed market mechanisms and permitted the restoration of a considerable private sector. The N.E.P. proved quite successful in many ways. By the middle 1920's production in the Soviet Union had reached and begun to exceed prewar levels. Almost at the same time, the party and the state were creating organizations for the more effective planning of a Socialist or quasi-Socialist economy. The State Commission for Electrification (GOELRO) was established in 1920, and the State Planning Commission (Gosplan) in 1921. The latter was initially concerned with obtaining an accurate view of the economy and its trends, and it set tentative goals largely

---

[1] See Alexander Gerschenkron, "Problems and Patterns of Russian Economic Development," in Cyril E. Black, *The Transformation of Russian Society* (Cambridge: Harvard University Press, 1960), pp. 42–71.

[2] For a discussion, see William Petersen, *Population* (New York: Macmillan, 1961), pp. 415 ff. He bases his estimates on census data. A program of American famine relief in 1921, organized by Herbert Hoover, saved millions of lives.

on the basis of these trends rather than on whatever the results might be from developing a comprehensive plan. By the mid-1920's, however, there were distinct signs of a movement toward increased state domination of the economy. In 1922 75 per cent of retail trade was handled by private entrepreneurs; by 1928 the percentage had fallen to 22. Actually, the largest private sector remained the peasantry, of whom there were some 26 million in 1928.

With the advent of the First Five-Year Plan in 1928 and the beginning of collectivization a year later, Soviet economic policy veered radically once again. The new purpose was to insure the rapid industrialization of the nation while at the same time creating a Socialist society. This effort was to be made primarily at the expense of the peasants, but urban workers were also critically affected. The economy was to be entirely guided by Moscow; in other words, a command economy was re-established. Insofar as prices and interest had little bearing on determining output, the Soviet economy was at least partially demonetized. However, because wages and bonuses—as well as large-scale black-market activities—did affect the economy, none of these mechanisms was completely eliminated.

The policy thus established continued nearly unchanged until the death of Stalin, and in that period the Soviet Union was transformed into a major industrial power. To this extent, the viability of a command economy was vindicated. The regime had been able to amass huge resources of manpower in those economic areas it considered most vital and in which the returns would be most rapid. The success of the command policy, however, was only a relative one. To be sure, it is difficult to factor out losses caused by World War II, but from 1928 to 1960 the average annual growth rate of the economy was approximately seven per cent, not significantly higher than the rates achieved by the old regime in the 1890's or by some other industrializing countries for a comparable period of time. But the price in human life was staggering. Here, too, it is difficult to know what these costs were even in terms of deaths, but conservative estimates place them—if one includes the collectivization of 1932 to 1934 and the purges of the late 1930's—at anywhere from twenty to thirty million.[3]

From the point of view of economic growth, Soviet population losses were not without their benefits. Those who died during famines were primarily the old, the very young, and the weak—individuals who would have been a drain on resources without making any contribution to economic development. The chaotic conditions of the times also had their benefits by causing a sharp decline in the Soviet birth rate. Thus, the rate of growth of the Soviet population remained well under two per cent a year, and the regime never had to face the kinds of problems other industrializing nations did. Even the loss of productive, able-bodied men and women was in some ways advantageous. The Soviet Union was never short of manpower, and it is doubtful whether under conditions of normal population growth the regime, certainly in its early years, could have made effective use of most of those who died.[4]

[3] Petersen, *Population*, chap. 15. Petersen's reliance on census data makes it impossible to factor out war deaths from those which were the result of the mass deportation of ethnic groups, such as the Volga Germans and Crimean Tartars. It also makes it impossible to estimate the number who died in forced labor camps between 1940 and 1956. See, however, the analysis of census and other data by Robert Conquest, *The Great Terror* (New York: Macmillan, 1968), especially pp. 525–535.

[4] Gross figures on Soviet economic growth are quite deceptive. They do not, for example, take into account the quality of goods, an area in which, with some exceptions such as space technology, the Russians are still very backward. Further, the Russians, until the late 1950's, concentrated on producing a few standard items in large quantities rather than on the more difficult task of diversifying output in order to satisfy consumer choice. A debate, of course, continues to rage on whether comparable growth could have been achieved at less cost. My own feeling is that a moderate Socialist or even a reformist liberal regime could have achieved the same economic expansion with far less human suffering. For a discussion of the argument, see Alec Nove, *Economic Rationality and Soviet Politics* (New York: Praeger, 1964).

The structure of the Soviet Union's command economic life remained intact until the early 1960's; but even before then, there were troublesome signs. The economy was growing more and more complex, and those easy problems that could be resolved by a mass assault were no longer the ones that plagued the party. Further advances depended upon a more sophisticated allocation of resources. For a short time after Stalin's death, the regime tried to solve these problems administratively. Ministries were shifted about, and a partial administrative decentralization was undertaken. But none of these methods proved successful. Accordingly, under the impetus of a new generation of economists who have borrowed from elements of Western economics, the Soviet leaders are now turning to the use of the market mechanism and relying unashamedly upon profits, prices, and such tools as interest on capital. The changes thus far have been rather modest and nothing that has occurred leads one to believe—despite the arguments of the Chinese—that the Brezhnev-Kosygin regime is adopting some variant of capitalism. Rather, the new emphasis seems to be on the creation of a Socialist market economy, with overall central direction still very much a requirement.

SOCIAL WELFARE: The individual in primitive or static traditional societies is involved in a network of family relationships; his fate and that of his extended family group are inexorably intertwined. As traditional patterns fragment and are succeeded by a market-cum-bureaucratic society, the mutual care inherent in a family relationship is replaced by a public philanthropy and eventually by community-supported social-welfare measures. In a very real sense, therefore, social-welfare legislation is the inevitable by-product of an advanced economic system.

During the middle ages, the church was the primary source of charity for the poor. In many countries, the disestablishment of the Catholic Church in the sixteenth and seventeenth centuries placed additional heavy burdens on the state for the care of those who could not fend for themselves. In no nation on the Continent did the public authorities take as large a share of this responsibility as they did in England where, in 1601, the law explicitly recognized the right of every destitute person to receive relief. Comparable legislation was not passed in France until 1893.

The original intention of the Tudor system of poor relief was to provide work and even housing, as well as relief. Relief was to be the responsibility of individual parishes, and its actual execution fell to the local gentry. By the early nineteenth century, the mode of administration had come under serious criticism for depressing wages and reducing the mobility of labor. Therefore, the Poor Law Amendment Act of 1834, a triumph of liberal economic thought, supplanted justices of the peace as the distributors of relief with elected boards operating under a new central administrative authority. The act also sought to cut down relief payments by grouping those who could work into poorhouses, although this part of the program was never fully implemented. As the century wore on, the notion of what constituted the "poor" was further differentiated and programs were instituted that took into account special categories of persons such as the unemployed, the sick, and the aged.

With German welfare legislation in mind, the English parliament in 1897 approved a workman's compensation program requiring contributions from both employees and employers for the benefit of injured workers. In 1908 Parliament passed an Old Age Pensions Act providing men and women at the age of seventy with pensions paid entirely by the state. One year later, Parliament set minimum wages in the "sweated industries" through the Trade Boards Act and, as a culmination of its liberal reforms, approved the National Insurance Act of 1911, which combined unemployment and health insurance under a scheme in which the state, the worker, and the employer all contributed. The provisions of each of these measures were expanded in the interwar period, and, of course, they were greatly extended when Labor came to power at the end of World War II. In the meantime, factory acts of varying kinds were gradually setting maximum hours of work and minimum standards of health and sanitation in industrial enterprises.

French developments in the area of social welfare were far slower and less comprehensive than those in England. Under the old regime, the Catholic Church shouldered a good share of the burden for the care of the poor, and additional monies were distributed by the crown. The confiscation of church properties during the Revolution left a great hiatus in the financial attention accorded the poor, and while the constitution of 1793 informed the public that the community must provide its members with security and maintenance, very few practical results flowed from this edict. Bit by bit, legislation ameliorating the lot of the poor obtained approval in the nineteenth century, but as late as the 1930's, France still lacked a comprehensive welfare system.

As in England, the categorization of those who needed assistance and the endorsement of social-insurance laws gathered momentum through the nineteenth century, although in France the momentum was far more leisurely. It was not until 1905 that Parliament agreed to add to the unemployment benefits provided for workers by their trade unions, and not until 1928 that the legislature passed a comprehensive law setting up a single scheme of insurance for sickness, invalidity, and old age through contributions from employers, employees, and the state. This system served as the basis for expanded coverage after World War II.

The foundation for the German poor laws were laid in a series of imperial edicts in 1530, 1548, and 1577; they applied primarily to the Protestant areas and made each commune responsible for its own poor, although no area adopted a welfare system comparable to that of sixteenth-century England. In Prussia and later under the empire, local communities retained primary responsibility for raising funds to care for the indigent; although donors were surprisingly generous, the system, in many areas, was far from satisfactory. Whatever the inadequacies of early German poor laws, the nation in the nineteenth century became a pioneer in the development of social insurance. Under Bismarck's guidance, a series of acts were passed which granted benefits for illness, accident, and old age. The law of 1883 insured workmen against a disastrous loss of income because of illness by setting up a national fund; two-thirds of the insurance costs were to be paid by workers and one-third by employers. The law of 1884 provided injured workmen with compensation insurance paid for by their employers, who created industrial associations for their mutual protection in meeting the new liability. Finally, the law of 1889 introduced disability insurance and old-age pensions covering most industrial workers, agricultural workers, and artisans. Workers and employers contributed equally to the funds established for this purpose, and the state provided additional money.

In instituting so broad a social-welfare program, Bismarck was partly motivated by his desire to draw the teeth of the Socialists, but his willingness also grew out of the traditional view of the state as a responsible authority. The state might be governed by an hereditary elite, but this elite had a moral obligation to take care of the lower classes. Indeed, such responsibility had to be assumed if the power of the German nation was to grow.

Bismarck's welfare program, ironically, provoked violent opposition from liberals and progressives who felt that the whole idea would weaken the operation of a free market. Unemployment insurance was not inaugurated in Germany until 1927, but the program was soon overwhelmed by the Great Depression.

The National Socialist government continued and expanded social-welfare benefits, adding even stricter regulations on factory conditions, paid vacations at state-run resorts, and the quasi-compulsory collection of goods for the needy. While some of these programs have been abandoned by the Bonn regime, the postwar government has taken other significant steps toward improving welfare coverage.

In nineteenth-century Russia, responsibility for the administration of poor relief was divided between national and local authorities; despite contributions from private charity, the chief characteristic of the system was its almost total inadequacy. This fact goes a long way toward explaining the persistence of widespread begging and vagrancy until the time of the Revolution. Nor had much progress been made in other areas of social welfare. The earliest social legislation, promulgated in 1861, did not become operative until 1893; it attempted to give miners and railroad workers, as well as their beneficiaries, some protection against financial losses incurred by illness, injury, and death. Revenue was derived equally from employers and workers. A more comprehensive Health and Accident Law, finally adopted in 1912, made benefits available for work-connected accidents, illness, and death, and granted women workers maternity payments. The legislation, however, covered less than one-fourth of the work force, and the amount and duration of benefits were so small that the working class was left to face its hardships without much outside help. The regime had no time to extend welfare coverage, for the coming war with the Central Powers made other problems more pressing; with the 1917 Revolution, a new philosophy of social welfare was established.

The stated aim of the Bolsheviks was to provide full social assistance to every person as a matter of right. Their initial attempts to do so, however, collapsed in the economic chaos generated by War Communism. The unveiling of a reasonable program of social-welfare legislation had to wait until the late 1920's, when all Soviet citizens were guaranteed unemployment insurance, free medical care, old-age pensions, and disability pensions, as well as compensation for sickness. After 1930 unemployment insurance was eliminated, for the reason that unemployment did not and could not exist in a Socialist nation.

Soviet social-insurance coverage was essentially of two kinds: that which benefited workers and that which benefited peasants. Workers received payments, under the supervision of the government, from funds established by the employing industries. On collective farms, however, the money set aside was theoretically a form of "self help," and its allocation, which also was supervised by the government, was decided upon cooperatively by the collective-farm members.

From the 1930's until the early 1960's the actual amounts provided by the Soviet regime through social insurance were extremely low, and far less than adequate. Since about 1956, benefits, as well as the quality of public-health services, have been rising steadily. In the 1930's, too, the concept of equality was dropped in benefit provisions as it had been in wages, and benefits received were largely contingent upon previous income; this equation still holds, although the gap has probably been narrowed in the past several years. Also, under Stalin social insurance was geared to economic performance: a change of jobs or poor work performance could and did involve considerable losses in social-welfare benefits. This, too, has changed in the past ten to fifteen years, although work performance remains a factor in determining the kind and amount of benefits to be received. With no unemployment insurance provided by the state, workers who find themselves without jobs are, theoretically, immediately placed. Those who, for some reason, refuse to work come under the provisions of the "anti-parasite" laws and are subject to protracted visits to labor camps.

3. THE BRITISH PATTERN

THE DRIFT TOWARD PLANNING: Shortly after the British Labor government took power in 1945, it began to hone some fairly effective tools for national planning within the framework of a market economy. It set up a series of economic development councils in order to prod key industries into greater efficiency by offering technical services and financial incentives. Further, it brought the nation's finances under central control; the Bank of England, for example, was nationalized and could no longer exercise independent initiative. More importantly, the introduction of modern budget methods allowed the British chancellor of the exchequer to exercise a more sophisticated form of control over the nation's economy than had been possible before the war. The nationalization of power and transport and the planned nationalization of steel gave the government powerful levers of additional economic control. The preparation of an annual economic survey, which not only evaluated the condition of the economy but indicated the direction in which it might move, seemed to be one final piece of conclusive evidence that the government would be continuously involved in planning for economic growth.

The promises of the period immediately after the war, however, did not materialize. The nation, as well as the Labor Party, became less and less enthusiastic about the use of direct government controls over the economy. Then, too, the party itself had never really thought in national terms about integrated economic policies. Its nationalization programs and social-welfare services were basically stopgap measures to eliminate particular evils; they were not part of a comprehensive social and economic plan for the entire country. By late 1948, then, the Labor government had put down most of its planning tools and turned its attention toward attaining full employment through various Keynesian-inspired fiscal measures and a number of public-works projects. Be-

yond that, the Laborites seemed content to allow the market, with selective interference, to set the direction of the British economy.

When the Conservatives returned to power, their attitude toward national planning was even cooler. Conservative governments did continue to expand social-welfare coverage, albeit slowly, but otherwise they tended during the 1950's to rely on fiscal and monetary measures to insure full employment, assuming that the market itself would lead the way toward economic expansion.

Nonetheless, by the early 1960's even Conservatives were beginning to have some second thoughts about national economic planning. The major source of disquiet was the far more vigorous growth of other European countries in per capita income, worker productivity, and gross national product. Fiscal controls seemed able to prevent any appreciable amount of unemployment, but they were not enough to resolve long-range problems. Analyses of the sources of England's declining share of the export market and its unfavorable balance of payments were legion. Some, for instance, argued that England was overcommitted both in defense expenditures and in maintaining the pound as an international currency; while there was some truth to this analysis, it was obvious that England's predicament went far deeper and had much to do with the structure of British industry and the attitudes of management and labor.

The recognition that the problem of England's economic stability and growth could not be met by simple reliance upon the market mechanism led the Conservative government, with the example of French planning before it, to begin thinking about a more systematic approach to economic problems. The Macmillan government began somewhat tentatively, therefore, to encourage the formulation of an incomes policy that would in some way relate wage increases to the growth of productivity. The government requested a pause in pay increases in 1961 and then attempted to set guidelines for further increases, establishing, in 1962, a National Incomes Commission to which such increases could be referred. The government did not, however, seek authority to enforce its recommendations, and the unwillingness of the trade unions to accept the proposals resulted in little being accomplished.

In a second step toward espousal of an overall economic planning policy, the Conservatives reorganized the Treasury in order more effectively to obtain and process information about the economy. They hoped that on the basis of better information, sounder economic decisions could be reached.

The third step taken by the Conservatives was the establishment of the National Economic Development Council (N.E.D.C., or Neddy). The council was originally conceived as a group of representatives from the government, industry, and labor that, while independent of the government itself, would help determine public policy. In general, it would (1) examine the nation's economic performance and give particular attention to plans for the future being made by both the private and public sectors, (2) consider what the obstacles were to faster growth and what could be done to improve efficiency, and (3) seek agreement on methods to improve economic performance. Only after considerable concessions by the Conservative government would

the trade unions agree to participate in the work of the N.E.D.C., which they viewed as an instrument for curtailing wage increases. Aside from the publication of a number of reports, however, Neddy did very little between 1962 and 1964. Its members found it difficult to agree not only upon remedies, but even upon the topics to be discussed. Not until the Labor Party's victory in 1964 did national planning become more than a concept.

First of all, the responsibilities for long-range government planning were placed in a Department of Economic Affairs, which, along with the new Ministry of Technology, signified Harold Wilson's personal concern with the problem of growth. Although the N.E.D.C. was to continue in existence as a place where issues and ideas could be mulled over, long-range planning was now to be a specific function of the government. Second, the government created a group of "little Neddies," advisory committees of civil servants, industrialists, and trade unionists whose responsibility was to insure that individual industries performed properly. The Labor government also brought out a National Plan, which projected future economic developments and the part that the government would take in attempting to expand the British economy. Although the balance-of-payments crises of 1966 and 1967 were to make the plan obsolete before it even got off

TABLE 24.1. COMPARATIVE GROWTH RATES IN G.N.P., EMPLOYMENT, AND PRODUCTIVITY

Annual averages

Country	1950–1958			1958–1964		
	G.N.P.	Employment	Productivity	G.N.P.	Employment	Productivity
Great Britain	2.4	0.4	2.0	3.9	0.6	3.2
France	4.4	0.4	3.9	5.4	0.9	4.3
West Germany	7.6	2.4	5.1	5.8	1.1	4.7
U.S.S.R.	7.1	1.7	5.3	5.3	2.0	3.3
United States	2.9	1.0	1.9	4.4	1.6	2.8

Source: United States Congress, Joint Economic Committee, *New Directions in the Soviet Economy*, Part II-A (Washington: United States Government Printing Office, 1966), p. 105.

**FIGURE 24.2.   COMPARATIVE GROWTH RATES OF GROSS
NATIONAL PRODUCT, 1958–1968[1]**

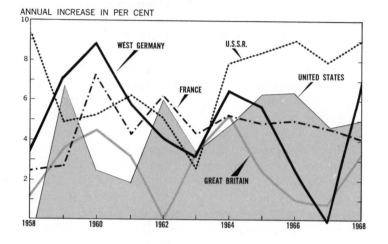

[1] Estimated figures for Russia, 1967–1968.

Source: United States Congress, Joint Economic Committee,
New Directions in the Soviet Economy, Part II-A (89th Congress, 2nd Session, 1966), p. 105; *Statistical Abstract of the
United States, 1969,* pp. 313, 837; *The Economist,* April 19,
1969, p. 99; Agency for International Development, 1969. Reprinted by permission of the publisher.

the ground, its very existence marked a new
beginning toward the solution of England's
economic woes.

The government also took action to raise
the level of productivity. Toward this end, it
enlarged the training facilities for "redundant" workers so that the manpower pool
could be enlarged for those industries in
which expansion was considered essential; in
other words, labor mobility and worker retraining were now considered a matter of
public rather than private concern. Parliament also provided lump-sum payments to
workers who lost their jobs because of technical or economic changes and increased the
benefits accruing to workers forced to move
from one area to another. In 1966 the government implemented a "selective employment" tax, the purpose of which was to shift
workers from the service to the manufacturing—and hence exporting—sector of the
economy. Under its provisions, all employers
are taxed for every worker on their payrolls,

but for some industries the tax is refunded in
part or in full, depending upon just how
important the industry is to the nation's economic health. The initial result was a considerable rise in unemployment, but some of the
expected benefits of the tax did materialize.

To improve managerial efficiency, the government has encouraged the creation of
graduate schools of business administration
and business mergers where a joint operation
is regarded as likely to be beneficial. Just as
importantly, the Ministry of Technology has
made various financial arrangements with industry to increase technological research and
innovation, especially in the field of computer
science; indeed, Great Britain is now far
more advanced in the computer field than
either Germany or France.

Plagued with an almost constant balance-
of-payments crisis, the Wilson government
has continued to rely upon and revamp an
incomes policy as perhaps its principal device
in solving the nation's general economic

dilemma. It hoped at first for voluntary compliance with government guidelines, and succeeded in partially restraining wage increases. Here it could count upon the goodwill of the trade-union movement, despite some grumbling, to support the efforts of a Labor government. By 1967, however, voluntary measures to hold down wages were proving insufficient, and the government initiated legislation which gave it the authority to freeze wages, prices, and dividends. These powers were to lapse at the end of 1969, and the government announced early that year that it would not request their renewal. Rather, Wilson indicated that he would turn once again to voluntary efforts. All prospective wage and salary increases would continue to be submitted to the National Board for Prices and Incomes (which, in 1965, replaced the old National Incomes Commission). Such increases would be delayed for three months pending a review of their "reasonableness," and the government would hope that, once again, the pressure of public opinion would prevent unnecessary increases. However, the ability of the board to secure voluntary acceptance of wage limitations is problematic, given the increased unwillingness of trade unions to accept restraints.

In conjunction with its recognition of the need for national economic planning, the Wilson government has also moved ahead with new measures in the area of regional planning. As early as 1945, the Development of Industry Act had designated several sections of England as "development areas"—regions in need of special assistance because of either high levels of unemployment or low levels of growth. The Board of Trade was authorized to offer companies special inducements to establish facilities in development areas; but in 1960 these areas were abolished by the Local Employment Act, which denoted instead smaller districts of high unemployment as needing economic revitalization. At the same time, the government tried to reduce the drift of workers to the south of England by requiring permits for the construction of office buildings and the enlargement of factories beyond certain limits in the London area.

Soon after coming to office, the Wilson government divided England into eight planning regions; Scotland, Wales, and Northern Ireland were given their own planning machinery. Regional economic planning boards and councils responsible to the Department of Economic Affairs have now been set up for the purpose of surveying regional needs and coordinating regional services. When the national plan was published, it included specific regional goals; and although it has been dropped, its general analysis is still kept in mind.

In line with proposals emanating from regional boards and councils, the government has become even more energetic in pressing industries to locate in areas of high unemployment or general economic backwardness. Tax incentives and subsidies have been expanded, and adequate housing promised. Also, the services of a number of ministries —for example, the National Health Service —are being regionalized for administrative purposes, and the government is seriously considering suggestions for regional governments possessing at least some political authority and some independent resources.

The activities of the Wilson Labor government in the area of planning have represented a new turning point in the relations between government and the economy. England is becoming a guided economy, an economy still largely sustained by market mechanisms and private ownership, but one in which the government intervenes actively in terms of its conception of national priorities.

These trends are likely to continue, for the Conservatives have given little indication that they will reverse Wilson's policies when and if they return to power. The systematic setting of national priorities is absolutely essential in a modern industrial society. Fortunately, both the information and concepts necessary to plan properly are increasingly available. The amount and sophistication of economic data are now such that planners have a much clearer understanding of the likely consequences of government policies. In England and on the Continent, a new class of technically trained personnel is committed to overall economic and social planning, and their ability to plan effectively is growing.

It should be added at this point, however, that the Wilson government has thus far failed to solve England's major problems of economic stalemate and unfavorable balance of payments. A succession of crises, beginning in 1966, has reduced the effectiveness of long-range measures and has forced the government to deal on an ad hoc basis with immediate problems, much to the detriment of overall policy. The early hopes placed in the Wilson government, then, have been replaced by disillusionment and criticism. By 1969 the government's ability to deal effectively with its problems had been seriously jeopardized by splits within the Labor Party and the intransigence of the trade unions. These political handicaps forced the government to withdraw a very mild legislative proposal for the reduction of wildcat strikes; in the bargain Harold Wilson's popularity receded to its lowest ebb.

The existence since 1967 of this so-called "credibility gap" in the Wilson government can be explained in part by excessive expectations. But the fact remains that England's economic difficulties are not the kind that can be solved within a short period of time, and no British government is in a position freely to chart its own course in a sociohistorical vacuum. For example, modernization was hampered by de Gaulle's vetoing Britain's entry into the Common Market; it was also hampered by earlier British policies to preserve the Commonwealth and create markets in underdeveloped countries. The continued traditionalism of both management and labor, as well as the deficiencies in English technical education, only add to the span of time it will take before new policies bear fruit.

NATIONALIZATION: For British Socialists, as for their Continental comrades, public ownership of the means of production represented the sine qua non of a Socialist society. When it came to office in 1945, therefore, the Labor Party brought under public ownership industries which together employed approximately eight per cent of the labor force and provided about twenty per cent of the nation's annual capital investment. The choice of which industries were to be nationalized was dictated by their effect upon the national economy and by the economic conditions prevailing within the industries themselves. In one or two cases the choice was that of a monopoly which the government deemed unwise to leave in private hands.

Public ownership, to be sure, was not a completely new phenomenon in postwar England. Telephones had been a state monopoly almost since the beginning, and in 1908 a Liberal government created the Port of London Authority. Between the two world wars, Conservative governments had set up the Central Electricity Board, which is responsible for the nationwide distribution of electrical energy; the British Broadcasting Corporation; the London Passenger Transport Board; and the British Overseas Airways Corporation. Most of the industries nationalized after World War II had been gradually coming under public control and regulation anyway; nationalization, therefore, did not represent nearly so sharp a break with the past as it might have appeared, and except for the steel industry and long-distance road haulage companies, it did not arouse excessive opposition. And with the exception of these two industries, the Conservative Party upon returning to power made no attempt to denationalize, although its handling of nationalized industries was somewhat different from that of Labor.

In nationalizing industries, the Labor Party opted against bringing them directly under ministerial control. Rather, the government created, on the model of the Port of London Authority, a group of public corporations with six interrelated features: (1) each of them is owned by the state, although it may raise all or some of its capital by issuing bonds to the public; (2) each is created by special law and is not subject to ordinary company law except as provided in the relevant statute; (3) each can sue and be sued, enter into contracts, and acquire property in its own name; (4) each is independently financed, obtaining its funds by borrowing from either the Treasury or the public and deriving its revenue from the sale of goods and services; (5) each is exempt from the forms of parliamentary control that apply to regular government departments; and (6) the employees of each corporation are not civil servants, but rather are recruited and paid on terms and conditions determined by the corporation.

The last four of these characteristics were intended to give the public corporation the flexibility of a private enterprise in the conduct of its day-to-day affairs. However, to guarantee overall public control, the "sponsoring" minister whose area of jurisdiction relates to the industry nationalized was provided with certain powers. He appoints the corporation's board or governing body, which is required to consult with him in devising capital-investment programs and in formulating plans for training, research, and education. Any capital the corporation wishes to raise externally—from the Treasury or from the public—requires the sanction of both the responsible minister and the Treasury. The minister also receives the corporation's annual report and financial accounts, which he lays before Parliament. He may require the corporation to provide him with any additional information he desires, and, after consultation with its governing board, may issue any general operating directions that appear to him to be in the public interest. A theoretical distinction is thus drawn between "day-to-day administration," over which the corporation retains its autonomy, and the industry's "general policy," over which the minister exercises more or less continuous supervision. The minister himself is responsible to Parliament only for his statutory functions in connection with the public corporation; consequently, ministers have normally refused to accept responsibility for policies and decisions that are not subject to their intervention.

The public-corporation boards differ in size according to the requirements of the industry. The discretion of the minister in making his board appointments is nearly absolute: most of the empowering laws state in only the broadest terms what qualifications members should possess. The actual organization of the boards has varied considerably from one industry to the next and even within the same industry. Although board members have been paid higher salaries than those of top-echelon civil-service personnel, their income has usually been somewhat less than for people of comparable position, qualifications, and experience in private industry.

It is difficult to evaluate the success of England's experience with nationalized industries, partly because an evaluation depends in large measure on what standards are used. Even so, most observers would agree that nationalization has not, thus far at least, radically transformed the relation of the worker to his job. Workers in nationalized industries still tend to think of themselves as workers and their employers as bosses, and relations between the two do not seem to differ materially from those in private industry. Nor have the nationalized industries been used as instruments to develop new and imaginative economic policies. It can be argued—and has been, primarily by those on the left—that this failure, coupled with the failure of nationalization to instill any new attitudes on the part of workers, lies in the fact that the industries have not been fully integrated into a comprehensive system of Socialist, or even semi-Socialist, planning; instead, they have remained subservient to economic goals formulated largely by the needs of a market economy in which the private sector predominates. Critics also note that the more radical proposals for a workers' democracy, in the form of joint consultation in the setting of policy, have not really been carried out— partly because the structures created toward this end were purposely ill-designed, and partly because the trade unions themselves have not shown any genuine interest in becoming part of management.

It is just about as difficult to determine how successful these industries have been from the point of view of economic efficiency: here, also, satisfactory yardsticks of success are hard to come by. Moreover, the industries have not been run entirely as commercial firms. Nonetheless, it seems fair to say that despite the obstacles that confronted a number of them, especially the coal and transportation industries, they have been reasonably successful.

The difficulties of evaluating performance lie in the very nature of the public corporation. Each of the nationalization acts provided that the price of the nationalized industry's product or services should be sufficient to cover its cost of production, taking into account the good years with the bad. However, no government has been able to decide exactly what this means or how closely such stipulations should be followed. After all, various sectors of the economy are closely interrelated, and industrial activities have side effects which private firms may ignore but which public ones must take into account. For example, one can argue that railroads should be profitable and that rail services running at a loss should be closed down. Yet it has been pointed out that the maintenance of an adequate rail network can promote economic expansion by fostering geographic mobility, and that closing down passenger lines only increases the number of cars on the road, resulting in more congestion, more pollution, and more noise. Some of these problems, such as congestion, could be eased by new taxes to build new roads; others, of course, could not be met at all, since they involve a deterioration in the environment which is difficult to correct.

On the other hand, if nationalized industries are operated with an eye on overall social and economic consequences rather than on mere profits, will not the result be an increase in inefficiency and irrational policies? For a long time coal prices were kept artificially low to aid other sections of the economy, prevent loss of jobs, and retain foreign markets; one consequence of this policy was that the English found themselves exporting coal at one price and importing it from the United States at a higher price.

The fact of the matter is that criteria for efficiency from the perspective of the society as a whole cannot be determined in a reasonable way until a method of national accounting and planning is devised that enables the government to assess its national priorities and the contribution of various industries— public and private—to these priorities. Thus far, no such single formula has been found. Most of the suggestions for setting up criteria do not command general agreement, and a good many generate the fear of excessive central direction and overbureaucratization.

Problems of price and efficiency have been closely tied to another issue: the relations between nationalized industries, the government, and Parliament. The balance between the day-to-day operational independence of an industry and its overall surveillance by the government has raised some touchy problems. In the years immediately following nationalization, the degree of ministerial interference in the operation of an industry was minimal, although it has always varied with the disposition of the particular minister involved, as well as with the government's general policies. Subsequently, however, ministerial intervention increased, and because the statutes did not specify the means of control, the ramifications of this increased intervention were worked out in informal conferences through the "old boy network." At the same time, ministers refused to be held accountable to Parliament for policy decisions taken by an industry's board, on the ground that they were not responsible; yet in actuality, the power of the ministers was and is considerable, especially in view of the relatively short terms of board members.

With government ministries taking the position that they were not accountable for the policy decisions of nationalized industries, more and more parliamentary voices were raised in protest. Parliament wanted some means of securing more adequate information about the industries, at least with regard to policy decisions. The eventual outcome was the formation of a select committee with a fairly broad mandate to investigate matters related to the industries' operation, but its authority was not to encroach upon those ambiguous areas of ministerial responsibility. Reaction to the committee's recommendations has been mixed. Some of its proposals have been partially accepted, but the majority seem to have been ignored. Nevertheless, the committee has served the function of pointing up the present, rather equivocal relationship between a sponsoring minister and the industries under his authority, and it has raised anew the issue of how well the nationalized industries are linked to public policy as a whole. The future seems likely to yield more rather than less ministerial control over the operations of nationalized industries, but also more rather than less acceptance of responsibility by the minister for decisions made by him.

One of the major problems to plague the nationalized industries has been their inability to recruit able managerial personnel in an economy in which such talent commands a considerably higher remuneration in private industry. Initially, the hope had been that a new type of manager would appear, someone who was a cross between the traditional civil servant, with his high sense of public duty, and an innovative American businessman; the hope, however, did not fully materialize. It was also anticipated, particularly by the left within the Labor Party, that labor would be strongly represented in top management, or, at the very least, that somehow the nationalized industries would provide an open-

end career to managerial talent from the working class; but with a few exceptions, this has not occurred either.

Many of the first board members were men who had held managerial positions in the industry prior to its nationalization. The next generation tended to consist of men taken from the top levels of the sub-board managerial staffs. While many of them were expert in their own specialties, it nonetheless began to look as if a new civil-service mentality was developing—that is, that the government was avoiding the appointment of persons who might be too imaginative, and hence too controversial at the top level.

In the 1960's the caliber of board appointees vastly improved. Lord Alfred Robens, who had spent much of his life in the labor movement, was appointed head of the Coal Boards; Sir Ronald Edwards, whose career had combined teaching economics with industrial and political experience, became chairman of the Electricity Council; and Dr. Richard Beeching was brought in from Imperial Chemicals, at the same salary he had been receiving there, to stanch the continued deterioration of British Railways. Other appointments on all levels since the return to power in 1964 of the Labor Party have reflected an effort to continue the policy of naming highly qualified men to head industrial boards. What now seems to be emerging within the nationalized industries is a new technical and managerial elite of exceptional ability. Unfortunately this, too, has caused a dilemma. Men like Beeching and Robens tend to be strong-minded and to resist ministerial pressures, sometimes even appealing to public opinion over the heads of ministers. Beeching, for example, resigned from his post in 1965 when the Labor government declined to give him the freedom of maneuver he felt he needed.

SOCIAL WELFARE: The construction of a modern welfare state in England had certainly begun by 1940. Its development had been gradual and its structure was rather baroque, but a combination of public and private initiative had created a series of institutions to provide at least minimum subsistence for those in need. The experience of the war and the politics of the first Labor government altered the structure considerably. The modifications were built on what had gone before, but they were broad enough in scope to constitute a qualitative transformation. The aims of the Labor program were threefold: (1) to extend and increase social-welfare benefits to the point where they not only provided adequate minimum care for those in need, but also helped such people to become relatively independent; (2) to restructure and reorganize various programs of public assistance in order to simplify their operation, permit long-range planning, and make them more effective; and (3) to eliminate the stigma of "welfare" by providing certain services to all citizens as a matter of right rather than basing them on "need." The Labor government attempted to model as many social services as possible on a concept of "social insurance" rather than on one of "social welfare"; that is, as many programs as possible would be financed at least partially on the basis of compulsory contributions (premiums) by all citizens.

Basic to the substantiation of this purpose were the Family Allowance Act of 1945, the National Insurance Acts passed in 1946, the National Assistance Act of 1948, and the creation of the National Health Service in the same year. The acts were considerably modified by the Labor Party during its first term of office, and later by the Conservatives, but they provided the structure of the contemporary English welfare state until 1969 when certain significant revisions began to be considered.

The National Insurance Act, applicable to almost everyone over school age, provided substantial coverage for sickness and unemployment, as well as maternity benefits, widows' allowances, and retirement benefits. A second insurance act provided permanent pensions for those incapacitated by industrial accidents. Both acts were supplemented by the National Assistance Act, which fixed on local authorities the responsibility for making accommodations available for the old, the infirm, and any others needing a place to live; it also enjoined local officials to give supplementary aid to persons requiring it, even though those in need were already receiving assistance under insurance programs. Under the Family Allowance Act, weekly benefits were paid out to each family for each child under fifteen, except the first; as amended in 1956, the age limit was raised to eighteen when the child is a full-time student.

With the exception of the National Assistance Act, all these measures theoretically dispensed with the concept of need as the basis of aid. Despite the fact that the insurance measures required considerable support from general taxes, they were to be regarded as rights accruing to all persons who paid their premiums.

The Labor government that came to power in 1964 promised to re-examine the entire welfare program with the general aim of extending benefits. Studies had revealed that the benefits actually paid were not sufficient for a good number of people and that many citizens did not even know of their rights to additional assistance. The hope was to raise the level of retirement benefits and other forms of insurance and to expand the services available to families with serious personal problems.

Although the government did increase some benefits almost immediately, economic difficulties and the uncertainty about just what kinds of revisions were necessary prevented a radical overhaul of the welfare programs. Some Laborites (and Conservatives) urged a return to the principle that aid should be contingent on need, arguing that this would raise the amount of benefits paid. The party, however, refused to consider this alternative, contending that it would revive the taint of a means test.

Finally, in 1969, the government issued a white paper announcing its intention to develop a new national-insurance plan. The

TABLE 24.2. WELFARE EXPENDITURES IN GREAT BRITAIN, 1949–1967

In millions of dollars

Government	Fiscal year	Expenditures in current $$	Expenditures in constant $$[1]
Labor	1949/50	$ 5,279.4	$ 7,149.0
Labor	1950/51	5,498.1	7,190.1
Labor	1951/52	5,977.2	6,928.3
Conservative	1952/53	5,765.1	7,500.9
Conservative	1953/54	7,091.0	7,748.6
Conservative	1954/55	7,321.4	7,672.8
Conservative	1955/56	7,845.0	7,845.0
Conservative	1956/57	8,430.5	8,106.3
Conservative	1957/58	8,881.9	8,223.9
Conservative	1958/59	9,738.1	8,852.8
Conservative	1959/60	10,411.2	9,464.8
Conservative	1960/61	11,174.2	9,977.0
Conservative	1961/62	12,359.5	10,518.8
Conservative	1962/63	13,046.0	10,811.4
Conservative	1963/64	14,798.3	12,031.0
Conservative	1964/65	16,229.1	12,565.6
Labor	1965/66	18,556.2	14,091.8
Labor	1966/67	19,855.3	14,525.3

[1] In 1955/56 dollars.

Adapted from *Monthly Digest of Statistics* (HMSO: Central Statistical Office); for the years 1949–1962 see no. 221 (May 1964), pp. vi–vii; for the years since 1963/64 see no. 257 (May 1967), p. 6.

proposal, which would supersede the scheme under which workers pay a flat fee and receive a flat pension upon retirement, called for a specified percentage of the first $4,000 of a worker's annual salary to be tapped. Upon retirement, benefits would total about fifty per cent of the wages received in peak earning years, with adjustment in payments made, after periodic reviews, to changes in the gross national product and the cost of living. The government's new plan would also permit "opting out" of the insurance program for those who wish to do so.

By 1969, too, the British were reconsidering the nature of family services in general. The government, a year earlier, had already taken steps toward a fuller integration of the health and welfare aspects of family services by merging the ministries of Health and Social Security. Now the government is re-evaluating social work as a profession, and discussing the rights of those needing assistance to receive it and to be treated with dignity. As in the United States, the argument is that social-welfare bureaucracy tends to treat those receiving family services as dependents for whom it must create appropriate rules. Measures are now being explored to give recipients of these services a larger voice in the formulation and application of these rules.

Perhaps the major innovation of the Attlee Labor government was the creation of the National Health Service. Again, the development of communal health services has a history dating back at least to 1911, and by the end of the 1930's some public care was available for most low-income groups who needed it. The dual purpose of the National Health Service was to place all existing health pro-

**FIGURE 24.3.   ORGANIZATION OF THE NATIONAL HEALTH SERVICE
IN ENGLAND AND WALES[1]**

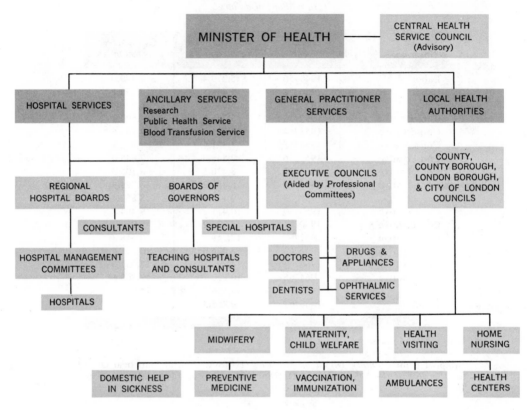

[1] In Scotland the responsible minister is the secretary of state for Scotland, and in Northern Ireland the minister of health and social services.

Adapted from Central Office of Information, *Britain: A Handbook* (London: HMSO, 1969), p. 133.

grams—private, local, and national—under one overall authority and to remove the taint of charity from health services by making them freely available to the entire community. The poor, especially, were expected to receive better health care under the program because the expansion of the service, particularly in its public-health aspects, would provide a broader range of facilities.

Responsibility for the National Health Service rests with the secretary of state for social services, who appoints an advisory Central Health Services Council consisting of some forty representatives of the medical profession and different governmental authorities. For descriptive purposes, it is easier to discuss, in order, hospitals and specialists, local-government services, and the general practitioner.

Nearly all hospitals in Great Britain are now owned by the government and managed by the minister of health. The nation is divided into twenty hospital regions, most of which have a medical school that serves as a center for research and the diffusion of knowledge. Regional hospital boards have overall responsibility for the development of hospital services in their region, and 460 hospital management committees throughout the country carry out the actual function of running the hospitals.

Individuals are referred to hospitals for treatment by general practitioners, and most services are free of charge. After a patient is admitted to a hospital, his case is taken over by the staff. Staff medical specialists receive an annual salary and are permitted to maintain a private practice outside the National Health Service; they are also permitted to bring a limited number of their own patients to the hospital on a fee-paying basis.

Local health authorities—county and county borough councils—are responsible for the medical care of children under five and the prenatal and postnatal care of mothers. The Health Service Act directed local officials to create "health centers" integrating the services of general practitioners, dentists, and oculists, in hopes of creating a form of cooperative medical center that would also educate the community in the ways of preventive medicine. For a long time, this aspect of the health-service program foundered; doctors were unwilling to congregate in a central location, and the necessary money to build the centers was not forthcoming. In 1964, however, there began to be more new centers, and if present trends continue at least four hundred will be in operation in England and Wales by 1978.

The services of general practitioners are administered by 160 local executive councils whose areas of jurisdiction are coterminous with counties and county boroughs. The councils are made up of members appointed by the secretary of state for social services and by the county and county borough councils. They also include a sizable number of representatives elected by the doctors, dentists, and pharmacists in the area. A list of available physicians is published in each local area; patients are free to choose any physician they wish, subject to his consent and to a prescribed limit on the number of patients any one doctor can have. There is no evidence that patients have found it excessively

difficult to obtain the services of a preferred physician, or that physicians have been forced to take patients they do not want. Doctors wishing to work in a particular district, however, may be refused admission if the area is considered to be "overdoctored"; even so, because the list of overdoctored locales is widely publicized and because doctors receive financial bonuses for practicing in "underdoctored" areas, the problem of a doctor's ability to practice where he wants to has not been too irksome. Furthermore, the distribution of doctors in the nation is now far more rational than it ever was in the past, although rural areas still lack sufficient doctors.

On the whole, England's National Health Service has been reasonably successful. Whatever complaints doctors may have regarding particular policies, few would care to abolish it; in fact, they find that the elimination of the cash nexus between doctor and patient has yielded more rewards than difficulties. Doctors are paid a standard fee by the government for each patient treated; they also receive an annual expense allowance. Every public opinion poll indicates that the public, too, is relatively satisfied with the program. Hardly anyone believes that the quality of medical attention has deteriorated or that doctors spend more time on the few patients who do pay fees than on those who are treated free of charge.

Nor has the Health Service proved excessively expensive. During the 1950's England spent about four per cent of its national income on health, compared with approximately 4.5 per cent for the United States and 4.6 per cent for Sweden. The percentage has risen during the 1960's, but no faster than in other countries. And despite the forebodings of the more pessimistic, visits to the doctor by "malingerers" have not increased appreciably: the average Englishman still visits a physician far less frequently than the average American.

The chief problems of the service, aside from those involving the recurrent arguments about how much doctors should be paid and

TABLE 24.3.   MEDICAL SERVICES IN EUROPE, 1963

Country	Doctors		Pharmacists		Hospital beds	
	Number	Per 100,000 population	Number	Per 100,000 population	Number	Per 100,000 population
Great Britain	56,400[1]	107	21,100[1]	40	550,700	1,022
France	52,800	110	19,800	41	455,500[2]	981
West Germany	83,000	144	18,600	32	615,700	1,064
U.S.S.R.	463,500	205	—	—	2,044,000	903
United States	289,200	149	117,400	60	1,702,000	900

[1] End of 1960.
[2] End of 1961.

Adapted from John Calmann, *Western Europe: A Handbook* (New York: Frederick A. Praeger, 1967), p. 242 (reprinted by permission of the publisher and Anthony Blond Ltd.); U.S. Bureau of the Census, *Statistical Abstract of the United States* (Washington: U.S. Government Printing Office, 1964), pp. 5, 929.

on what basis, have to do with the fact that insufficient resources have been expended upon it. In spite of its programs since 1960 to construct hospitals and upgrade medical schools, England has fallen further behind the United States and Canada in the quality of its medical education and hospital facilities. The result has been a migration of British doctors to the other side of the Atlantic, where facilities and opportunities for specialization are superior and the income a doctor can earn is larger. Unquestionably, without the migration to England of medical students from India, Pakistan, and other of the less developed Commonwealth nations, the "doctor drain" would be even more serious. There are other problems, notably the cleavage between the general practitioner and the more highly paid and prestigious specialist who has the facilities of a hospital at his disposal; but the recent increase in local health centers may go some way toward resolving this problem. An influx of funds, together with a reorganization of the traditional pattern of medical education, will be necessary in the next few years if British medicine is not to suffer a fairly serious crisis.

The Wilson government has been pressing for reforms to meet all these problems, and legislation is being prepared to rationalize the administration of the entire National Health Service. A report issued by the Ministry of Health late in 1968 recommended the replacement of the present regional boards, local health authorities, executive committees, and hospital management committees by between forty and fifty area health authorities—less parochial than local authorities, according to the report, yet less remote than regional boards. The report held that the area health authorities would also provide better coordination, linking local health authorities, general practitioners, and hospitals in a unified effort to offer more adequate medical care and a more comprehensive system of preventive medicine.

4. THE FRENCH PATTERN

A MANAGED ECONOMY: The devastation of France during World War II, coming upon the nation's failure to move ahead economically in the 1920's and 1930's, yielded a consensus among those constituting the core of the Resistance that some form of planning for national reconstruction was absolutely necessary. To the left, such planning, along with extensive nationalization, would be an integral part of a policy designed to take France further along the road to socialism;

even some conservatives, including de Gaulle and many bureaucrats, were convinced that some sort of national plan was imperative if France was to be regenerated. Government intervention in the economy and long-range planning had long been favored by many "conservative" groups; World War I had been followed by an attempt at national planning, and the Vichy government had taken more than just tentative steps in this direction. But at the end of the Second World War, the general attitude of the French toward national planning had changed. It was not merely that planning was a matter of obvious necessity; the change was also attributable to the new tools that had become available to planners, including both direct control over important sectors of the economy and new techniques of economic analysis. Also, a whole new generation of technocrats had ascended to power—men who had always been available but who, in the postwar government, assumed a far more dominant position in the bureaucratic apparatus.[5]

Two other factors were significant in changing the nature of the French economy: the Marshall Plan and Jean Monnet. The French were encouraged by the United States, during the Marshall Plan negotiations, to develop a more systematic presentation of the economic objectives toward which the aid funds would be utilized. Their response was to develop a four-year plan and a high-level planning agency, and the energy and talent of Monnet contributed greatly to the effectiveness of the General Planning Commission (*Commissariat Général du Plan*—C.G.P.), of which he was the first director. The initial plan, drawn up in 1947, was directed toward recovering from the war and expanding basic industries; it was designed to run for four years, al-

though it was in actual operation for more than five. It has been followed by four more plans (1954–1957, 1957–1961, 1962–1965, and 1966–1970), and the concept of planning has become an integral part of French economic development.

The French method of planning was once considered the last word in sophistication. Today its limitations are recognized, and it is also acknowledged that the credit given to it for France's remarkable economic expansion since World War II can be exaggerated. Nevertheless, national planning has proven a decisive factor in France's postwar recovery, and under the de Gaulle regime it became part and parcel of French economic and social life. As in most other European countries, however, planning for economic growth is slowly being replaced—or, better, supplemented—by broader considerations of the quality of life in the French society; it is becoming socioeconomic planning.

Responsibility for the elaboration and implementation of French plans is lodged with the General Planning Commission, which is under the direct jurisdiction of the premier. The commission works in close cooperation with the Ministry of Economy and Finance and with other ministries involved in the planning process. Interest groups, "modernization" committees, and the Economic and Social Council[6] are among other organizations that collaborate with the C.G.P., but decisions on the general direction of French planning rest with the government and, to a certain extent, Parliament.

The C.G.P. prepares the plan, submits it to government authorities for their approval, sees to its implementation, and assesses its results. It assigns to public and private re-

[5] A good discussion of the genesis and early development of French planning is to be found in Andrew Shonfield's *Modern Capitalism* (New York: Oxford University Press, 1965), especially pp. 71–87 and 121–175.

[6] The Economic and Social Council is a quasi-parliamentary body. Its members are chosen by private groups and the government to represent the broad interests of the nation; it includes people eminent in the economic, scientific, social, and cultural fields. It must be consulted on the preliminary and final stages of the plan. It has little or no political power, although the expertise of some of its members may influence the government.

search bodies a large part of the preliminary work, and because it also works in cooperation with government organs, its staff is rather small.

The modernization committees are each composed of from thirty to fifty persons selected from management, labor, and the government; the heads of enterprises and the leaders of industrial and trade associations; representatives of the major labor-union confederations; and officials and experts from the government ministries concerned. The participation of trade unionists has been less than fully enthusiastic; the C.G.T. refused to take part in the work of the second and third plans, maintaining that its recommendations on the first plan were largely ignored; it participated only to a limited degree in the fourth and fifth. The C.G.T./F.O. has been somewhat more active, and the attitude of the C.F.D.T. has been more or less favorable. But even the latter two unions complain that their advice is not properly taken into account, and that the French planning enterprise is weighted in favor of business. In any event, trade unionists are grievously underrepresented on the planning committees.

Physically, the French Plan is a document of some five hundred pages, divided into four sections: an assessment of the problems and potentialities of the economy; statements of government policy intentions and objectives; a statement of the necessary requirements to achieve these objectives; and discussions of the individual areas of the economy and of the government's economic and social activities. The plan is based upon a complex series of input-output tables which project the effects of different policies on segments of the economy; however, no effort is made to cover every industry in detail.

The planning procedure itself is divided into the following stages: (1) the determination of alternative schemes of economic development, accompanied by suggestions for future possibilities and potential courses to follow during the plan period; (2) the

selection of a planning strategy by the cabinet, upon the recommendation of the general commissioner; (3) the preparation of preliminary targets for output, manpower requirements, and investment; (4) review of the detailed targets for individual sectors of the economy by the relevant groups; (5) the drafting of recommendations by the modernization committees on how the plan might be carried out; (6) submission of the plan to the government and, since the beginning of the fourth plan, to Parliament; and (7) the revision of the plan as conditions warrant, after its adoption. Under the de Gaulle regime the influence of Parliament over the plan was minimal; the size of the Gaullist majority and the government's option to issue decree laws allowed the National Assembly little say. It is too early to predict what will happen to the planning process under Pompidou, although he is a vigorous supporter of long-range economic programming.

Unlike the Soviet model, the implementation of the French plan relies far more on the manipulation of an existing market economy than on governmental controls. Nevertheless, the government possesses a battery of legal weapons which enable it to put its plans into effect. Almost all private and business construction in France, for example, must be authorized by the government; by regulating the number and types of permits granted, the government can influence the volume of construction and the building industry's demand for investment capital—important levers for directing the economy toward goals the government desires. The government also essentially controls borrowing by private business; by determining which firms can and cannot borrow from banks and which may issue securities, it can exert great power over the level of private investment. Almost all bank credit facilities are nationalized or else are under the centralized control of the Bank of France.

Another legal weapon through which the French government can regulate the economy is its broad power over prices. The government can establish price ceilings as well as price formulas, and it can fix prices directly for the products of any industry or individual firm. In addition, the government helps determine the nature of collective-bargaining agreements and, consequently, the level of wages.

Finally, public enterprises in France account for perhaps one-fourth of the total capital investment in the country—an extremely important factor in the nation's economy. The government completely controls or substantially dominates the railroads, the oil industry, airlines, and the production and distribution of electricity, gas, coal, nonferrous ores, and armaments. Within other fields, such as the auto industry, its control of individual firms, such as the Renault Motor Works—the largest producer of motor vehicles in France—has a direct effect upon that particular segment of the economy. Government policies with respect to these industries understandably influence what course of competitive action the private businessman will choose.

In private business, the government has exercised a degree of control in several ways: it has subsidized firms engaged in modernization as well as those that agree to move factories into economically depressed areas, and it has reduced taxes on dividends for firms investing in activities that it wishes to encourage.

The combination of inducements and direct and indirect controls has been quite successful—partly because of the rapport between bureaucrats and the more progressive elements of the business community. While de Gaulle's search for grandeur caused, on occasion, a number of frustrating problems, national planning in France (as in all non-Socialist market economies) will probably increase in both scope and importance in the coming decades.

Perhaps the major weakness of French planning still lies in its authoritarian character, although, in one sense, this has also been a source of its strength. Despite the talk of collaboration among all sectors of the society, the participation of labor has been limited and Parliament has exercised little control over the establishment of priorities. The weakness of French trade unions and the general hostility of the C.G.T. toward "capitalist" planning have prevented full cooperation, so that in France, unlike England, the interests of labor, as conceived by labor, have not been fully accounted for. This does not mean, however, that the working class has not benefited from national planning. Though there has been less redistribution of income in France than in, say, England or Germany, the economy has grown so much that it has greatly improved the condition of the average wage earner. It can be argued, therefore, and somewhat ironically, that the very weakness of the French labor movement has contributed to economic growth and the workers' greater prosperity; on the other hand, labor's relative isolation from the mechanics of national economic planning is not calculated to encourage a sense of mutual responsibility to the community as a whole.

Paris dominated France long before the Revolution, and this pre-eminence increased during the nineteenth and the first part of the twentieth centuries, partly as a result of the political centralization of French life.[7] The railway network, for political and strategic reasons, was built like a spider's web around Paris; as late as 1938 it took less time to travel the 683 miles from Toulouse to Lyon via Paris, than to go directly, a distance of 340 miles. France's literary and intellectual life became centered in Paris. So, too, were all the big banks, and by the end of the Third Republic a very high proportion of the

---

[7] I am indebted in this section to Geoffrey Denton, Murray Forsyth, and Malcom MacLennan, *Economic Planning and Policies in Britain, France and Germany* (London: George Allen and Unwin, 1968), and Niles M. Hansen, *French Regional Planning* (Bloomington: Indiana University Press, 1968).

nation's wealth was concentrated in the Paris area, while large parts of the nation became economically and culturally stagnant. It was only after World War II that French leaders began to redress this imbalance, and only under the Fifth Republic that plans to do so have borne fruit.

The development of a comprehensive regional planning policy dates from 1950 when a *Plan nationale d'aménagement du territoire* was drawn up by the Ministry for Reconstruction and Urban Development. The plan included a detailed inventory of regional problems and outlined the needs of those areas in which human and natural resources were poorly utilized. In 1955 and 1956 the government tightened its control over industrial building in Paris and offered subsidies to businesses if they would decentralize some of their operations. Parliament also authorized development programs for the 22 economic regions into which France had been divided for planning purposes. The number of regions was cut to 21 in 1960 (see Map 24.5), and a new set of programs for each area was then drafted as part of the fourth national plan.

As work for the fifth plan got under way, regional organization was strengthened. In 1964 regional prefects were created, and *Commissions de développement économique régionale* (CODER) were established to act as official channels through which interests in a particular area could make their views known. A year earlier another institution, the *Délégation à l'aménagement du territoire et à l'action régionale* (DATAR), was founded as the coordinating body for all aspects of regional policy. French planners have tried to exercise as much care as possible in integrating regional plans with the national plan. Initially, they were anxious to extend help to the obviously less developed areas; today, policy encompasses the long-range view of the relationship between the different regional economies and between them and the national economy. The principal problem is still Paris's domination of French life, but

the government is encouraging the growth of eight cities (*métropoles d'équilibre*) to counterbalance the attraction of the Paris area.[8]

To implement regional development, outlying areas have been offered several forms of national assistance in addition to business subsidies, including new cultural facilities and new or enlarged universities. In developing regional programs, planners have also attempted to forecast the possible outcome of policies by conducting studies of the French citizenry; some of their research shows that many Parisians would be more than pleased to live in smaller communities, provided anything like the amenities available in the capital were present.

THE NATIONALIZED SECTOR: French nationalized companies of a commercial or industrial character have usually taken one of two forms of organization: the "public corporation" and the "mixed economy company." Most of the industries nationalized at the conclusion of World War II became public corporations, although the term *"établissement public"* should not conjure up images of the British model. Theoretically, French public corporations are to be run by quasi-independent boards of directors who are not part of the civil-service hierarchy. Government administrative procedures are not to be used, and the public corporation is subject, at least theoretically, to being taxed like any ordinary firm.

Whatever may have been the intention of the original statutes, however, the distinction between public corporations and ordinary government departments has all but disappeared. The financial autonomy of the corporations has ceased to exist, the power of the boards themselves has been severely circumscribed, and all important corporation decisions are subject to ministerial approval. The chief executives now wield the real

8 For a further discussion of the métropoles d'équilibre, see p. 796.

MAP 24.5.   THE 21 NEW ECONOMIC REGIONS OF FRANCE

power; they are appointed by the government and are frequently drawn from the ranks of the civil service, and the conditions under which other staff members are employed are often similar to those for civil servants.

The reasons why practice never matched theory are complicated. One of them has to do with the strong centralizing tradition of the French state; another is the belief that nationalized industries must be subordinate to national planning. Other reasons would include the political climate of France in the 1940's and 1950's and the inadequacy of the first nationalization laws. As originally conceived, the public corporation boards were to consist of representatives of labor, the government, and consumers. In the early postwar years, the Communist Party used its control over a number of ministries responsible for nationalized industries to pack the boards with party members, who then proceeded to use the industries as political weapons. After the Communist Party was ousted from the government in 1947, other political parties followed the same tack. One further reason why public corporations failed to remain independent of direct government supervision was that the representation of special interests on their boards proved not to be very effective; even when politics was not a factor, competing interests and the lack of expertise inhibited the making of necessary decisions.

Today, the boards of public corporations are primarily advisory groups. The key officials are the chairmen and the managing directors. In some industries these posts are combined; when they are separate, the chairmanship is often a part-time position and the directorship a post of considerably greater importance. The director is often a former civil servant who maintains close associations with the supervising ministry. In fact, to the ministry the status of a managing director, who is usually chosen from France's great technical corps of bureaucrats, is very much like that of a bureau chief.

The concept of "mixed economy" indus-

tries emerged from the old *concessionnaires* —companies that were partly private, partly public. In the nineteenth century, local authorities responsible for the organization and control of public-utility services, such as local transportation and the distribution of electricity, gas and water, would often entrust these services to private firms or concessionaires, but because many had to be operated at a loss, local authorities were forced to participate financially in the organization's affairs—from which it was but a short step to the acquisition of part of the capital and a voice in the management. Between the two world wars, the same practice occurred on the national level; the state became deeply involved with railways, shipping, and air transport. It now owns the majority of shares in many utilities and other large companies; as a consequence, it can effectively influence their policy. This control, however, varies: some companies are allowed ample freedom to operate as purely commercial enterprises, while others are as stringently controlled as ordinary public corporations.

Most of the nationalized industries come under the supervision of either the Ministry of Industry, the Ministry of Equipment, or the Ministry of Transport, although the Ministry of the Armed Forces is responsible for the aircraft industry, and financial institutions such as banks and insurance companies are controlled through the Ministry of Economic Affairs and Finance. Since the last ministry is also responsible for the overall financial coordination of government activity, it helps determine the policies adopted by all public enterprises.

A commissioner for each nationalized industry is appointed by its supervising ministry to represent the government as a whole. Such commissioners may be assigned to all undertakings in which the state has a financial interest; they can attend board meetings and suspend action pending ministerial intervention. In addition to the commissioners, the Ministry of Economic Affairs is represented by controllers, who may also be attached to any undertaking and seem to enjoy a good deal of autonomy; they must be consulted on virtually all financial transactions before any decision by an industry is taken. Prefects, too, have a right to information, and all nationalized industries are subject to regular auditing.

Parlimentary control over nationalized industries has fluctuated—it was rather broad during the Fourth Republic but minimal in the Fifth. Both chambers of Parliament, in the postwar years, had special committees on these industries, and the committees could bring some pressure to bear on their policies. The committees, however, were not recreated during the Fifth Republic, with the result that the authority of Parliament over nationalized industry has declined.

A WELFARE STATE: The government that came into power in 1945, in addition to instigating measures on nationalization, wrote into law a series of proposals that fundamentally altered the French social-welfare system. Supplementary laws to strengthen and rationalize the system have been passed since 1958.

The great majority of employed persons and their families are now covered by social insurance under a system that is, in principle, self-financing. The government does contribute on behalf of certain categories of persons, but essentially the social-security program is sustained by graduated contributions made according to earnings. Employers pay roughly ten per cent and employees six per cent of wages up to salaries of approximately one thousand francs a month (as of 1967). Agricultural workers come under a special, separately administered system, and some important occupational groups, such as civil servants, miners, and railway employees have more favorable, publicly regulated schemes of their own, either augmenting the national program or replacing it wholly or in part. For these groups, both employer contributions and overall benefits are somewhat larger.

The French welfare system includes sickness benefits, payments to compensate for the loss of earning power because of disablement or retirement, and widows' pensions and death benefits. Payments are usually graded in accordance with earnings; sick pay, for example, is about half the worker's ordinary wage. Medical benefits, in the form of a partial reimbursement of expenses, are available to the entire family. Pensions depend upon both the number of years worked and the average earnings during the last ten years of employment; retirement pensions total only about twenty per cent of average earnings. Social security makes no provision for unemployment benefits, but government-financed unemployment funds, averaging a little more than six francs a day, with regional variations, are granted on the basis of a "means test."

The French social-security system now provides quite generous allowances for children. The benefits are graded to favor larger families, and additional allowances are paid if the mother does not work. People with large families also receive other benefits such as income-tax rebates, reduced fares on public transportation, and increased pensions. The state also provides maternity benefits, and it may grant a small rent or home-improvement subsidy. The purpose of the family-allowance program has been to boost the French birth rate, which has indeed risen since the introduction of the program; but the birth rate has also increased in other European countries that do not have a comparable system of allowances.

In conjunction with its social-security program, France, like many other industrial societies, has an extensive system of national assistance known as "social aid." The program involves not only monetary payment to those not covered by insurance, but also government responsibility for orphanages, old people's homes, asylums, and hospitals.

France does not have a national health service, but the state contributes to medical expenses under a "fee reimbursement" plan.

The patient is free to choose the doctor he pleases and he pays the doctor directly. Under terms of the original law creating the program, the state reimbursed the patient for some eighty per cent of the cost of medical treatment upon presentation of the doctor's bill. The twenty per cent charge to the patient was made to prevent abuses; in cases of hardship, arrangements could be made for full reimbursement of the charges. In many instances, the program worked badly. Although, for example, a scale of fees was supposed to be established in each of the 95 departments by agreement between the social-security organs and the medical organizations, doctors' fees rose steadily. With the social-security agency refusing to pay what it considered inflated charges, patients were generally left to bear a fairly large portion of the cost of treatment.

In 1960 a new procedure was inaugurated. A committee of civil servants was set up to fix official scales in those departments where the social-security organs and medical units failed to reach agreement. No doctor is required to accept these scales, but they must not treat patients without first warning them that the charges will not be in accordance with the official fee schedule. A system of reimbursement also applies to prescription drugs, with the rate of compensation varying from seventy to ninety per cent.

The reforms have alleviated some former difficulties, but France has yet to put together an effective public-health program. The system is far less integrated than that of Great Britain, and the level of medical care is substantially inferior.

5. THE GERMAN PATTERN

PLANNING IN A SOCIAL-MARKET ECONOMY: In answer to those opposed to the postwar contagion of planned government intervention, West Germany's phenomenal economic growth under a "free market" system was cited time and time again as the perfect example of how a capitalist nation should function. A closer analysis, however, reveals that Germany's "free" economy was not without strings. In fact, aside from general expenditures on social welfare—which in proportion to national income are the highest of any nation in Europe—the German government since the war has intervened very actively in the economy, albeit less directly than the French or the English. It is true that market forces were given more play in Germany than, say, in France; yet it must be borne in mind that the rules according to which the market "played" were determined by the government.

The general economic policies of the Adenauer regime, as formulated by Erhard, freed the market from "unnecessary" controls but at the same time enforced stricter rules to insure free competition. Thus, in 1948 price control came to an end on a wide assortment of products, and the general wage freeze imposed by Occupation authorities was lifted. In 1949 and 1950, rationing was ended for most foodstuffs, although the government continued to regulate food prices through subsidies; by the end of the 1950's, rent controls were being removed. Of perhaps greater significance, the government initiated a program of partly denationalizing such operations as the Volkswagen Automobile Works; Preussag, a huge mining and oil company; and Veba, a state-owned coal, chemicals, and electric power company.

While all these moves were unquestionably "freeing" the economy, the government, despite its disclaimers, was intervening in other ways to give it as much direction as the self-proclaimed French plan had given to its neighbors. To achieve its goals, the Bonn government levied special taxes and distributed subsidies as it saw fit. For example, the 1951 Investment Aid Act provided for a compulsory loan from the business community of one billion marks to cover, among other things, postwar reconstruction needs in industries producing coal, iron, steel, and energy, including water power. Every business existing in January 1951 was forced to contribute to the loan. The government, through the 1949 Refugee Aid Measures and the 1953 Federal Expellee Acts, also granted businesses special tax and credit privileges to aid in the resettling of refugees.

Bonn also intervened in the economy to facilitate the reconstruction of Germany's housing. The Housing Act of 1950 provided government assistance in one form or another for three kinds of construction: public subsidized housing projects for low-income families, housing projects aided by tax preference, and privately financed building projects. To provide housing in the first category, the government contributed an essential portion of the capital in the form of interest-free or low-interest loans; in return, the government decided what rents were to be paid and required that only persons with low incomes be allowed to live in the projects. In the second category, the government gave aid by reducing taxes on the projects; in return, it retained some control over rents. In the third category, there was no rent control and no government allocation of the new apartments, but the incentive for private capitalists who financed the building projects was the tax reduction generally granted to those who saved money and to those who invested it. More than half the housing constructed in Germany until 1961 was in the first category, in which the government subsidized the rent. Altogether, one-third of the capital invested in housing construction came from public funds. If the amount of tax reductions granted to builders is added to the capital-investment figure, the public sector provided more than half the capital used for housing construction. In any event, as a result of extensive governmental interference in the housing market, some eight million new dwelling units were constructed in Germany between 1949 and 1964; more dwellings per capita were built in West Germany than in any other Western country.

Germany's postwar parliament also approved legislation giving premium allowances or tax exemptions for savings or funds reinvested in the employer's firm—measures designed, of course, to increase savings and investment and to reduce personal consumption. The government has also maintained rather strict control over the banking and insurance sectors of the economy, including interest rates.

In addition to these primarily monetary measures, the government intervened in the economy in other ways, subsidizing the production of fertilizer and certain agricultural prices, controlling farm prices by regulating imports and exports, and stabilizing these prices by assuring a government market for agricultural produce. It also worked actively, through the use of subsidies, to consolidate agricultural holdings and take marginal farms out of production.

These were only some of the measures through which the Adenauer regime intervened in postwar Germany's "free market" economy. They can be termed "neo-liberalist" only in the sense that they did postulate a market economy. Government interference was, for the most part, directed toward manipulating the market to achieve specific ends; it was not based on an overall economic plan involving, as in France, the control of an extensive public sector. The policies worked extremely well. Up to 1966, West Germany's economy remained among the most dynamic in Western Europe. A mild economic recession in 1966–1967 and the formation of the coalition government increased the amount of overt intervention in the economy, although the change was not so much one of direction as one of degree. Professor Karl Schiller, the new minister of economics, tried to find a balance between "neo-liberal" economics and Keynesian ideas of managing aggregate demand. He convinced the government to use the federal budget as an anticyclical device in 1967. The Kiesinger-Brandt government also came up with a comprehensive plan for reorganizing the ailing coal industry, and it committed itself to preparing and publishing an annual economic report and setting targets for general economic growth.

In Germany, responsibility for regional policy rests primarily with the Länder, but they have done little in this area. What serious attention has been paid to regional imbalances has come from the federal government. Even Bonn's efforts have been minimal. Starting in 1951, Germany was divided into three economic zones, and special subsidies were granted to firms establishing new enterprises in areas that were considered backward. In 1965 the Bundestag established the Council on Regional Planning, through which the Länder and the federal government can hold joint consultations on regional problems. By law, the government is now obliged to present an annual report on regional planning to the parliament.

While the Länder themselves have been very lax in meeting their planning problems, North Rhine–Westphalia did draft a comprehensive Land Development Plan—under federal prodding. Other states are now beginning to follow suit. The problem in Germany, however, is less and less one of regional imbalances in economic development—for these are quickly diminishing— than it is one of overcrowding. The prime concern of the Länder is how to deal more

effectively with such questions as the preservation of the countryside and the prevention of air and water pollution.

SOCIAL WELFARE: Germany pioneered in the field of social-welfare legislation, and as in all Western nations, both its programs and its coverage have been considerably broadened since World War II. Germany today spends a larger proportion of its national income on social-welfare measures than any other nation in Western Europe (see Table 24.4), despite the reservations expressed by Adenauer, Erhard, and others with regard to such legislation. The proponents of neo-liberal ideology reluctantly accepted the need for some forms of social legislation, but still believed that it must be instituted with care lest it reduce individual freedom as well as the individual's "sense of responsibility." As Erhard put it in 1957, the year of great pension reform in Germany:

We reject the welfare state of the socialist variety and the general collectivist maintenance of the citizen not only because this seemingly well meant tutelage of the citizen creates dependence, which in the end breeds only submissiveness and kills the spirit of free citizenship, but also because this kind of self-negation, that is, the surrender of human responsibility, cripples the individual's will to

TABLE 24.4. SOCIAL WELFARE EXPENDITURES: SOME COMPARISONS, 1962

As percentage of national income, by major types of coverage

Country	Total	Old age, sickness, disability	Sickness and maternity insurance	Unemployment insurance	Work accident insurance	Family allowances
Great Britain	10.6%	4.2%	5.1%	0.3%	0.3%	0.6%
France	13.4	3.9	4.1	0.0	1.1	4.3
West Germany	14.4	8.1	4.5	0.4	0.8	0.6
United States	4.8	3.6	0.1	0.7	0.3	—

Adapted from *European Social Security Systems* (Washington, D.C.: Joint Economic Committee of Congress, 1965).

work and must lead to the deterioration of economic performance in general.[9]

Erhard's pronouncements notwithstanding, the Adenauer government had very little option. Both the dislocation of the postwar years and the demands of the electorate impelled the extension rather than the curtailment of social-welfare measures. What the regime did try to do was to combine social welfare with what it conceived as policies that would not invalidate personal responsibility. German social welfare, therefore, differs somewhat from that which had been adopted in, for example, England prior to 1969.

One indication of this difference is the social-security legislation of 1957 for old age, permanent disability, and survivorship. A deliberate departure from the old principle of subsistence benefits, the law was intended to allow the insured person to maintain in retirement the relative economic level he had reached during his working life. To this end, the pensions were designed to reflect individual earnings as well as the growth of the national economy. Pension awards are thus made not only on the basis of a complicated computation involving an individual's lifetime earnings in relation to the earnings of others during the same period, but also, after an annual economic review, on the basis of the relation among pensions, the cost of living, and the prevailing wage levels. The aim of the pension scheme was to prevent payments from depreciating as prices rose and to allow retired workers to receive some of the benefits of increased prosperity. Accordingly, old age pensions rose in value by 57 per cent between 1957 and 1967. In 1968 they were increased by another 8.1 per cent. Retired workers today receive fifty per cent or more of their last monthly earnings, excluding special retirement plans for miners and salaried workers which pay even higher benefits. Disability insurance is calculated in

much the same way, except that payment comes to approximately two-thirds of the previous year's wages with special provisions for persons with children.

Voluntary industrial pension plans are also widespread in Germany. They are taken for granted in larger enterprises, and tight labor markets contributed to their expansion to medium and small enterprises. A 1962 survey of fifteen manufacturing industries revealed that the average private pension cost to employers was about six per cent of wages and salaries.

It is true that the public pension scheme as developed aids lower-income persons more than those in the higher-income brackets, and is far more generous than comparable programs in other countries. But it is also true that the scheme is basically a horizontal transfer of funds from the young to the old rather than a vertical transfer. It perpetuates income inequalities—and this, in view of the neo-liberal emphasis on personal responsibility, was one of the purposes of those who drafted the legislation.

Nor has the government been averse to using pensions as a mechanism for increasing the productivity of certain sectors of the economy. For example, farmers who wish to be eligible for pensions must not only withdraw from active agricultural work at retirement age, they must also transfer their enterprises through inheritance, sale, or long-term lease. The purpose of this requirement was to induce a shift of agricultural operations to younger, more efficient hands.

Family allowances have also been introduced, although payments are rather small and made regardless of family income. Unemployment insurance funds, to which employers and employees contribute equally, provide payments of from 13 to 52 weeks at about half salary. The Federal Republic has tried hard to prevent technological unemployment and to find jobs for workers. The Federal Employment Office makes payments and grants low-interest loans to workers for a variety of purposes, including travel expenses

[9] Quoted by Gaston V. Rimlinger, "The Economics of Postwar German Social Policy," *Industrial Relations,* 6 (February 1967), p. 187.

in search of a job, family relocation costs, interview expenses, the maintenance of separate households in case of jobs away from home, retraining, vocational guidance and counseling, and physical and mental rehabilitation. Legislation passed in 1969 created an advisory service to help businessmen forecast future needs and create training programs to meet them. The office also subsidizes employers who hire long-term unemployed persons.

Under specified circumstances, unemployment-insurance funds may also be used for the construction of youth and worker centers, public works, and public housing. And the government has dealt with the problem of unemployment on an even broader scale: in efforts to maintain year-round activities on the part of the building industry, employers are paid a subsidy for maintaining employment between December 1 and March 31. Construction workers are entitled to payments toward the cost of special winter clothing and are entitled to bad-weather compensation for work days lost between November and March.

German health insurance received its greatest encouragement from Bismarck, and its coverage has gone on being extended ever since. The most recent overhaul of the program occurred under the Insurance Doctors Act of 1955, and although there have been minor changes since then, moves toward major revisions of the program have thus far been blocked.

The German plan is ostensibly privately run, although regulated by law; it is a program of health insurance rather than a national health service. Its funds come from contributions by both employers and employees, with the federal government contributing only on behalf of unemployed workers. Monies for medical coverage are disbursed through two thousand welfare funds organized either on a specialized basis (for example, by craft) or else by area. The organizations administering the funds are regulated by statute. Each local fund is supervised by a board of directors and a legislative assembly consisting of representatives of employers and of those insured. State-level associations coordinate the work of local bodies and, finally, the whole program is coordinated by the Federal Association of Local Sickness Funds.

Physicians licensed to practice are paid by the local Association of Sickness Fund Physicians, not by the local funds. Membership in the association is compulsory for all doctors who participate in the national-insurance program. Patients are free to choose any doctors they wish, although doctors practice in specified geographic areas. To receive treatment, the patient presents a voucher, which he obtains each quarter and which is later submitted to the local Association of Sickness Fund Physicians. Except for certain minor charges, medical treatment is free for those insured.

The association tries to recompense doctors in accordance with a standard scale of fees set up in terms of work performed. A lump sum, based on estimated annual expenses, is given by the local sickness fund to the Association of Sickness Fund Physicians, which then pays the doctors' vouchers. Doctors police their own membership to reduce the incidence of padded vouchers. Payments do not differentiate sharply between the services of specialists and those of general practitioners—one reason the proportion of specialists to practitioners in Germany is one of the lowest in Europe. Specialists or not, doctors' salaries compare favorably with those of other professionals, and Germany has one of the highest doctor-to-patient ratios in Europe.

One of the principal weaknesses of the German health-insurance program has been the relative lack of development in group, community, and preventive medicine. In a move to correct this deficiency, the state in 1960 made it possible for insured persons to have regular checkups; it also required that medical-dental checkups be a condition for the free provision of dentures for persons over forty.

Various proposals for remodeling the structure of Germany's insurance scheme have been advanced. One involves minor changes to prevent excessive visits to the doctor (Germans go to doctors more frequently than Englishmen); another would reduce or eliminate the workers' contribution to the fund; a third would provide for a national health service. None of these proposals, however, has been able to gain the approval of the legislature.

6. THE SOVIET PATTERN

A SOCIALIST COMMAND ECONOMY: The Soviet economy is officially designated as "Socialist," not Communist. Communism is still in a state of construction, and, in theory at least, the economy of a full-fledged Communist society will be quite different. Goods and services will be dispensed solely on the basis of need. Money will probably disappear; the state and, eventually, the party apparatus will wither away; and economic activity will be coordinated by spontaneous groupings of citizens. Today's economy is termed "Socialist" because of the predominance of public ownership. The direct employment of one person by another is not permitted, except for domestic servants. Households own their personal possessions; they may also own deposits in savings banks, state bonds, and insurance policies. But all natural resources, including all land, are owned by the state; so are most capital goods. In some sectors of the economy, the position of the state is more complicated. In agriculture, retail trade, and housing, the state permits the formation of "cooperatives" under close government control, and houses and collective-farm (kolkhoz) markets can be privately owned. As a further example of a private sector in the Soviet economy, certain professions, including doctors, dentists, lawyers, and teachers, are permitted to have some private practice; so, too, are various artisans and craftsmen such as tailors, cobblers, and carpenters.

The whole Soviet economy—with the exception of the household sector—can be depicted as an enormous bureaucratic pyramid. The most far-reaching decisions are made at the very top, by members of the politburo. The bottom tier of the pyramid consists of hundreds of thousands of individual firms whose main task is to carry out orders from above. Between the bottom tier and the top exists a welter of planning, administrative, financial, statistical, and other bureaucratic hierarchies.

The most important planning agency of the Soviet government is the State Planning Commission of the U.S.S.R. (Gosplan U.S.S.R.). There is a Gosplan for each of the constituent republics, and planning offices, which are subject to higher authority, have been set up in the provinces and districts. Although the power of Gosplan has fluctuated and its functions have been subdivided on occasion among different agencies, it is responsible today for preparing both long-term and short-term economic plans and for deciding many other issues of economic policy. Gosplan does not, however, exercise a complete monopoly over planning. Other high-level planning units are concerned with construction, research and development, and the distribution of materials and equipment. Still other planning committees deal with the problems of industry, of the individual republics, and of large regions that cut across political boundaries.

The management of industries or particular sectors of the economy is handled by the ministries, each of which is in charge of a hierarchical organization, with the individual enterprises at the bottom. Between the ministry and the individual firm is another level of authority called the "chief administration" (glavk). Glavks are assigned responsibility for certain aspects of each ministry's operating activities; some are in charge of specialized branches of production, others are concerned with staff functions such as procurement, marketing, or research. Still another level of authority and control may exist beneath the chief administration: the "combines" or "trusts," which are essentially conglomerations of firms that perform interrelated functions.

Within this ministerial hierarchy, there has been little communication horizontally, even among the firms, but there has been a substantial flow of vertical information. The upward flow of messages from enterprises, combines, and glavks carries considerable data dealing with the state of the economy; these messages also contain descriptions of how past directives were executed and requests for permission to take a particular course of action. The Central Statistical Administration of the U.S.S.R. and its many regional and local offices also collect an enormous number of reports and channel this data upward to the planning authorities. The equally detailed information flowing downward consists of specific directives, instructions, and permissions or denials. Communication lines between minister and industry tend to be long, causing delays in adjustment to changing economic conditions.

Soviet enterprises work in accordance with the annual plan. Until 1965 and 1966, the production plan for industrial enterprise usually included two kinds of directives on output: a global target (gross value of output in rubles), expressed in supposedly constant prices and based on the enterprise's past performance; and production targets, usually expressed in physical terms, for specific commodities. To fulfill plans, the enterprise was assigned a maximum limit on the number of persons it could employ and on the amount it could spend on wages. It was allowed to consume no more than fixed amounts of specified materials and fuel per unit of output. Since 1966, the indicators used in the directives have changed, and enterprises have been given somewhat more flexibility.

Soviet enterprises use money and pay wages. Since the prices of all inputs and outputs are pegged and known at the time plans are drawn up, it is a simple matter to establish targets for unit cost of production and for aggregate profits and losses. Most of the planned profits go to the state, but the enterprise is encouraged to make above-plan profits, a considerable portion of which it may retain. If the profits earned and retained according to the plan are not sufficient to pay for the planned investment, the state may take up the financial slack.

Plans, of course, cannot possibly cover every detail of an industry's operation; guidance must be provided for whatever decisions management may have to take on its own. Thus, rules are laid down which enjoin the enterprise to maximize its profits within a limited range of choice.

The structure of agriculture is somewhat more complex. As we have seen, the state farm (*sovkhoz*) is organized and run like an industrial firm; it is owned by the state, its labor force is hired for wages, and it is subject to fairly rigid production plans. However, more than half of the agricultural marketing in the Soviet Union is done by collective farms, which for a long time were forced to meet delivery quotas at very low prices—in other words, were subject to central planning. In contrast to the sovkhoz, payments to collective farmers occurred only after the results of the year's production were known and the required addition to the farm's capital was deducted. The income of the kolkhoz farmer, therefore, besides being lower than that of a worker on a sovkhoz, was subject to wider variance. Kolkhoz wages are still residual, but the economic condition of collective farms has improved considerably in the past few years. A general trend toward higher payment for kolkhoz products developed under Khrushchev, as did measures to iron out income differences between poorer and richer kolkhozes. These reforms, as well as additional investment in the agricultural sector, have continued under his successors: the Brezhnev-Kosygin regime has also instituted a guaranteed minimum monthly wage below which the income of kolkhoz workers cannot fall.

Peasant households are also permitted to work a tiny plot (up to one acre), to raise what they wish, and to dispose of the produce freely, including selling it on the kolkhoz market. Khrushchev tried to reduce the number and size of such plots, but there resulted a severe shortage of meat, vegetables, and milk in most major cities. His restrictions have since been removed, and private plots now account for anywhere from thirty to seventy per cent of the production of some food staples.

All households in the Soviet Union are, of course, consumers and providers of labor services; consequently they are closely tied to the production sector of the economy via markets for consumer goods and labor. The state decides what consumer goods will be produced and in what quantities, and it places them on sale, under normal circumstances, without rationing. The consumer can take or leave the product at the quoted prices, although he is naturally limited to what the authorities choose to make available in the official stores. The regime is becoming much less indifferent to consumer tastes, but even so its efforts to cater to the public's preferences have not been extremely successful, a factor which led to the 1965 economic reforms.

In short, the economics of the Soviet worker's household is the same as that of one in any other system, with important exceptions such as the prohibition against acquiring capital goods or shares of stock. It may, however, save any portion of its income and may invest its savings in state-owned savings banks, state-issued bonds, and private or cooperative housing for its own occupancy.

The Soviet economy uses money very much like any other economy. In effect, there are two kinds, though of the same denominations: currency, which circulates almost exclusively within the household sector and in transactions between households and the state; and bank money, which circulates almost exclusively within the state sector, that is, between state enterprises and agencies. Currency and bank money are constantly being converted into each other, but only under strict controls. There are two reasons for the distinction between and careful segregation of these two kinds of money: to prevent the overissue of currency, which might lead to inflationary pressures in the household sector, and to maintain a tight surveillance of the activities of enterprises and state agencies.

The kolkhoz market is the only significant one in the Soviet economy in which prices move freely in response to demand and supply. In all other markets, prices, including wage rates, are officially fixed or "planned." In the two markets in which the state deals with the household sector and where an area of choice is open to the household—those for consumer goods and labor services—prices are fixed to balance roughly with demand and supply for individual goods and types of labor. By contrast, in the past at least, the prices which the state has paid to a kolkhoz for farm products were deliberately set below equilibrium levels.

Prices are also used within the state sector itself, mainly for the purpose of facilitating accounting. The method of price setting has been influenced by the Marxist "labor theory of value." Until 1965, for example, returns to nonlabor factors of production—rent on land and other natural resources, and interest on capital—either were not accounted for at all, or only nominally. The result was, as Soviet economists now admit, that prices were poor guides to the efficient use of resources.

THE PLANNING PROCESS: Since 1928, the Soviet Union has engaged in long-range planning, aimed primarily at achieving two interconnected goals: a very high growth rate, especially in heavy industry and weapons, and economic self-sufficiency. The overall goal, of course, has been to protect the

Soviet Union from outside attack and to prepare the way for the ultimate formation of a Communist society.

The longest-term plans for Soviet development have been for ten, fifteen, and sometimes twenty years, but none of these has had much impact upon Soviet development. The shorter five-year plans have had some effect, principally as guides for the drafting of the annual plans, but not one five-year plan has come even close to fulfilling its targets. The core of operational Soviet planning, then, is the annual plan.

The formulation of a one-year plan is an intricate process, extending over the entire preceding year; it is not really completed until well into the plan year itself. The first stage is the setting of goals by political leaders in consultation with the planners: the desired increase in the gross national product and the desired increase in both industrial output and the production of important commodities. The problems in determining these goals are highly complicated, the more so because they are always partly political. In fact, since Stalin's death some of the major political conflicts among members of the Soviet elite have revolved about which production mix should be emphasized. Once the goals have been established, it is the planner's job to translate them into detailed and consistent directives and production targets for thousands of individual enterprises. The result is an overall one-year plan for the national economy and a series of more specialized plans for individual republics, ministries, glavks, combines, and enterprises. The planners also devise parallel supply plans which determine the physical allocation of the most important materials and items of equipment.

In addition to the economic goals that the political leaders would ideally like to achieve, the central planners have two other kinds of information that permit them to proceed with their work: they know, though not always accurately, the economy's re-

sources and production capacity for the year, and they have many thousands of input-output ratios that reveal the amount of equipment, material, and labor required to produce a certain unit of a certain product. On the basis of past experience and calculations, they try to reconcile this information. The process involves a great deal of bargaining between the planners, the ministries, and the industries, as the lower echelons in the economic hierarchy try to press for targets that will be easier to fulfill and the upper echelons try to make sure that those below them are formulating estimates that accurately reflect their production capacity.

By far the most difficult task in the planning process is that of achieving internal consistency—insuring that all production requirements for individual commodities are matched by anticipated availabilities, a task that in a market economy is largely handled by the market mechanism. In performing this balancing act, the planners have not, in the past, referred to prices or profits in measuring the gap between requirement and availability, although this may now be changing. Rather, they have utilized an essentially simple form of accounting, the so-called "material balance," which lists on one side of the ledger all the anticipated availabilities of particular goods and on the other all the expected requirements.

To achieve a perfect balance, Soviet planners must be constantly on the alert to make adjustments during the year. If, for example, the requirements for copper exceed expectations, the amount of copper allotted to various users may have to be cut back or copper resources shifted in some way throughout the entire economy.

STRENGTHS AND WEAKNESSES: In fifty years, the Soviet Union has been transformed from an agricultural society into a major industrial state. In this sense, Soviet planning has worked. On the basis of Soviet statistics it is difficult to know how rapidly the country has grown, but some of the best estimates indicate a rate of some 4.8 to 11.9 per cent from 1928 to 1937 and seven per cent from 1950 to 1960. Since 1960 the rate of growth has slowed down considerably, but even so from the time the N.E.P. first went into effect it is quite impressive, though not so impressive as the Soviets would have everyone believe. As Table 24.1 indicates, Soviet growth rates in the postwar period have been exceeded by a number of non-Communist countries, and the prewar rates were equaled, during comparable periods of development, by such nations as the United States, Japan, and Australia.[10]

The reasons for the Soviet Union's comparatively rapid rate of economic expansion are not too difficult to find. First of all, the Soviets were able to invest a sizable proportion of their national income in capital goods at the expense of the Soviet consumer, especially the peasant; the best data we have indicates that per capita income in the Soviet Union did not achieve its 1928 level again until about 1950. Secondly, the regime invested in industries which promised rapid growth, postponing investment in those on which the return would be smaller. Thirdly, the Soviets could shunt labor from one place to another with much more flexibility than was possible in other countries, and could direct the nation's educational system in such a way as to secure the trained personnel they required. As previously pointed out, the Soviet Union has a good resource base, and this circumstance coupled with the fact that it has never had to face the kind of population problem that has plagued other industrializing nations has also helped it achieve a substantial rate of growth. Then, too, the Soviets avoided some of the aspects of economic waste, such as conspicuous consumption induced partially by advertising, which are

characteristic of many capitalist economies. Moreover, as an industrialized latecomer, it borrowed freely from the economic techniques of more advanced nations.

The Soviet achievement nevertheless involved a less efficient use of its resources than that made by many other nations. The command economy worked because the regime was concentrating on a few basic goals and because it was able to mobilize its human resources in a rather ruthless manner in order to achieve these goals. Yet as the economy grew more complex, highly centralized planning of the Soviet type faced mounting problems. The quality of the materials produced was not very good, the right production mix was rarely attained, innovation slackened, and even overall growth rates began to slide. Increasingly, the Soviet economy was marked by its waste of resources and energy. Three of the more obvious reasons for these difficulties have been the following:

(1) *The problem of overcentralization:* The fundamental economic decisions have been made by the planners, both political and technical; with very little leeway left for initiative on the part of individual firms, planners have been forced to make more and more decisions. Inevitably, bottlenecks have developed, and all too frequently planners have become aware of them only when they were serious. Campaigns to rectify such situations have usually been carried too far, prompting a new campaign to correct the economic imbalance created by the first one. Campaigns and counter-campaigns in the field of agriculture are a good instance of this phenomenon.

To cope with this problem, the regime tried all sorts of ways to decentralize decision-making. Between 1957 and the ouster of Khrushchev, many ministries were abolished and some authority was delegated to Councils of the Economy (*sovnarkhozy*) in the different economic regions. The effort failed partly because the regions maximized their own interests without taking national needs into account. Indeed, without the market mecha-

---

[10] For statistics, see Simon Kuznets, "A Comparative Appraisal," in Abraham Bergson and Simon Kuznets, eds., *Economic Trends in the Soviet Union* (Cambridge: Harvard University Press, 1963), pp. 333–382.

nism, decentralization had to fail because there was no device, aside from the planners, to aggregate particular interests into a general interest—not, of course, that the market mechanism does this perfectly.

(2) *The problem of indicators:* Without a free-market system to determine prices, and hence production, Soviet planners have had to use physical indicators not only to set production goals but also to ascertain whether those goals have been reached. Any item produced has certain physical characteristics; it can be described in such terms as weight, volume, diameter, or thickness. To set production plans in terms of all these physical indicators would, understandably, be impossible. Even using two or three indicators at the same time adds immeasurably to the complexity of the planning process and besides so reduces the flexibility of an enterprise's management that efficiency can be seriously impaired. In the past, therefore, planners have employed one or two indicators that seemed to provide them with a reasonable measure of productivity and a reasonable basis on which to give bonuses for fulfilling or overfulfilling production goals.

Unfortunately, none of these indicators has been completely satisfactory. At one point, for example, plants received bonuses for producing a certain number of tons of chandeliers; it turned out to be easier to achieve this goal simply by producing fewer but heavier chandeliers. According to Khrushchev, this was exactly what happened. The same criterion was used for nails, and *Krokodil* once pictured a factory which fulfilled its entire production quota for nails by manufacturing one giant nail—a tongue-in-cheek assessment of the problem, but the fact remains that it was easier to produce a few types of heavy nails than to produce the assortment that would answer the needs of consumers. When window-glass production was measured in tons, factories produced extra-thick windows because this enabled them to save on processing and handling. The planners' attempt to get

around this ruse by changing the production indicator from tons to square meters resulted only in the manufacture of extra-thin glass. The regime has used the party and administrative agencies to investigate plants in efforts to uncover just such distortions. But thus far the extension of administrative controls has brought forth only mountains of bureaucratic red tape, thereby defeating the purpose of production controls.

The lack of spare parts and the lack of innovation have been two other aspects of the Soviet production problem. Manufacturers, realizing a better return on a completed item, seldom bothered about making extra parts. Innovation has suffered under the planners' emphasis on production because enterprises have been reluctant to try new production techniques for fear of failing to fulfill or overfulfill their goals.

(3) *The problem of resource allocation and use:* The failure of the Soviet regime to accept, until recently, the fact that capital itself can be a source of value when it is scarce has created critical problems in the allocation and use of resources. The absence of a rational price system has also created allocation problems. Technical innovation has been slowed down as a consequence, and resources have been used less efficiently in a number of instances because a feedback of realistic economic information has been missing. In the 1930's, for example, Soviet planners decided that it would be wise to make iron and steel factories as large as possible in order to cut production costs to a minimum—a decision that was agreed to at the highest levels of government and carried out. Only much later did planners come to realize their error: rolling mills were designed to be so big and so specialized that a single mill could produce the total output of a particular item for the entire nation; this meant, of course, low production costs but excessive transportation costs. Not surprisingly, a campaign against "gigantomania" was well under way by the end of the 1930's.

Problems of allocation and use have also affected the electric-power industry. Power stations use a certain amount of the power they produce to run the machinery in the station. Deciding that this internal consumption was too high, the authorities made its reduction a high-priority goal and bonuses were awarded for good performance; the plant managers promptly scrapped the electric motors used to drive their equipment and replaced them with steam and internal-combustion engines—hardly efficient for the economy as a whole, since installation of the new machinery involved a huge waste of funds for advantages which were, at best, marginal.

Other instances of the faulty use of resources could be cited, but suffice it to say that while a command economy did propel the Soviet Union forward at a healthy rate of growth, the question still persists whether, given creditable leadership, the job could not have been done more efficiently and at far less cost by using other methods. To be sure, the Soviet economy has never been fully Marxist, whatever that may mean. Prices were not market prices, but money has been used much in the way it is in a capitalist economy; interest on capital was not calculated, but was, to a certain extent, brought in by the back door. Indeed, if the leadership had not so modified Marxist theory, the economy would have come to a complete standstill, as the period of War Communism proves.

In any event, by the late 1950's Soviet economists were showing signs of having some second thoughts. As the economy grew more complicated, problems of coordination were increasing geometrically, especially in the area of consumer goods, where large inventories were accumulating simply because prospective buyers refused to purchase suits that were too large or too poorly made or television sets that could not be repaired. Some economists believed that many problems would be resolved by the development of computer science, which would make possible a much more sophisticated analysis of the economy. Other economists discovered such things as the importance of interest and market prices. Suggestions for reform became closely associated with the name of E. G. Liberman, a professional economist.

The reformers came into their own with the removal of Khrushchev. Issued in the hope of reversing the declining growth rates of the early 1960's, the September 1965 edicts on economic reform were also somewhat of a reversal of standard Soviet economic dogma. The managers of enterprises were given greater autonomy: the number of plan targets assigned to each plant was reduced, sales and profits were substituted for production as measures of success, and managers were allowed more freedom to determine how to invest their funds. By the end of 1969, most Soviet enterprises were operating under the new system.

In practice, the 1965 reforms did not go quite so far as the more "liberal" economists suggested, nor have they proved as innovative as originally hoped, even though official Soviet statements claim the changes are regarded as having been successful. Supply still remains centrally allocated, restricting the freedom allowed the plant manager, and prices are still centrally administered, despite attempts to determine them in a more rational manner. Also, although sales volume as an index of production was to replace the gross-value index, many control agencies are still demanding reports on gross value, and managers seem to be of two minds about whether they should use the new yardstick. Moreover, the amount of investment funds available out of profits has been rather small; enterprises are therefore still compelled to justify most of their plans for expansion or innovation before control agencies.

In short, while the reforms have produced some short-range results, they have not solved the basic economic problems associated with the system that evolved under

Stalin. For instance, now that industries are once again organized by ministries, the old tendency of the latter to look after their own industries without regard for the national economy or regional problems is reappearing.

Soviet plant managers do not have the training and experience necessary to operate in a system of relatively autonomous enterprises. Furthermore, many enterprises are not structured to function as independent economic units. And until these inadequacies of organization and training are rectified, a long period of adjustment will be necessary before even the minimal reforms can be fully utilized.

The use of profit as a success indicator is not likely to be of much benefit to Soviet consumers under the present system. For example, as the economist V. Pereventsev has pointed out, the transportation enterprise, encouraged to maximize profits, will simply continue the present practice of jamming people into the buses like sardines. For profit criteria to serve the interest of consumers, three conditions are necessary: the absence of monopolies, competition among enterprises, and a market in which the buyer has a wide choice among competing products. None of these prevails in the Soviet Union so far.

Soviet leaders, of course, are faced with real dilemmas in this area, for such economic reforms are not merely a technical problem but a political problem as well. The Kremlin has obviously been partially convinced that more autonomy for individual firms and the use of the market mechanism, to at least a limited degree, are necessary if the Soviet Union is to resolve some of its problems. However, to transform the Soviet Union into a Socialist market economy—even with some command elements still retained—could not help but reduce the role of the Communist Party symbolically, as well as in practice, with consequences that are difficult to assay. On the other hand, the present reforms, because a rational price mechanism is still lacking, may turn out to be an untenable halfway

house, providing none of the advantages of decentralization and forsaking some of the advantages of a more centralized policy. The present situation, then, is an unstable one. Either "creeping centralization" will become evident once again, or more radical reforms will become the order of the day.

A SOCIALIST WELFARE STATE: Shortly after achieving power, the Soviet leaders announced a program of full-scale social insurance which would cover the entire population, providing benefits for retirement, sickness, the loss of capacity to work, or the inability to find work. The burden of financing the scheme was placed upon employing establishments. The Soviet Union was in such turmoil at the time, however, that the program never really got off the ground. Nonproletarian elements were usually disbarred from receiving benefits, the peasantry by and large got little or no support, and the regime soon found that it could not even meet its responsibilities to the workers.

The system was drastically reorganized during the N.E.P. period and brought into line with the regime's capacities to pay for it. From that low point in the program's history, coverage was gradually extended and increased. Nevertheless, until the end of the Stalin period, disbursals continued to be quite small, and kolkhoz members did not come under the state-insurance system until 1966.

At the present time, Soviet social insurance covers loss or decrease of earning power as the result of old age; disability, whether work-connected or not; death; pregnancy; and sickness. (See Table 24.5.) Military officers come under a separate pension system. Funeral benefits are available for all the insured, and the state makes special payments for layettes and other aspects of infant care.

Only one area covered by social insurance in capitalist welfare states is not recognized in the Soviet Union: unemployment. With unemployment considered eliminated in 1930, an unemployment-insurance program was quite naturally deemed unnecessary. There is

TABLE 24.5. SOCIAL EXPENDITURES IN THE SOVIET UNION: 1940–1963

Percentage breakdown of social expenditures as percent of total budget

	1940	1950	1955	1960	1963
Education	12.9%	13.8%	12.8%	14.1%	15.8%
Health and physical culture	5.2	5.2	5.8	6.6	6.0
Social welfare	1.8	5.3	4.7	8.9	9.4
Mothers with many children and/or no husband	0.7	0.9	0.9	0.7	0.5
Other	2.9	3.0	3.1	3.8	3.9
Total social expenditures	23.5%	28.2%	27.3%	34.1%	35.6%

Adapted from Mark G. Field, *Doctor and Patient in the Soviet Union* (New York: The Free Press, 1967), p. 193. Reprinted by permission of the publisher.

evidence that the premise of Soviet dogma on unemployment never completely corresponded to reality.[11] Today, as the economy grows more complex, some Soviet economists have suggested not only that some form of unemployment insurance be reinstituted but that special arrangements, including training programs, be made for workers released from jobs as a result of automation or the rationalization of production.

With the exception of some lump-sum payments, benefits in the Soviet system are related to previous earnings rather than to need. Thus, old-age pensions are approximately fifty per cent of average earnings in the last working year (or the best five consecutive years in the last ten years of work) if the earnings have been above a certain minimum standard. The percentage of benefits received is higher for lower-paid workers, and minimum payments have been set up for all persons entitled to old-age pensions. These pensions and other benefits are also pro-rated to reward persons who have remained in a single job, a device used to discourage excessive labor mobility. Finally, benefits are higher—and retirement can begin earlier—for workers in especially dangerous occupations such as mining.

[11] See Raymond Hutchings, "The Ending of Unemployment in the U.S.S.R.," *Soviet Studies,* XIX (July 1967), pp. 29–52.

The Soviet social-insurance program is financed entirely by contributions, based on a specified percentage of the payroll, from the employing establishments. The percentage varies from enterprise to enterprise, according to certain norms set up by the state. Disbursal of benefits, however, is centralized, and is related to the general goals outlined in the annual and five-year plans.

The Soviet Union has also created special benefit programs for permanently disabled persons and for the handicapped. The responsibility for children needing care outside their homes—orphanized, neglected, and emotionally disturbed children—is not lodged with the state social-welfare organization but with the local soviets.

Until the Russian Revolution, the medical facilities available for most Russians were elementary. Anton Chekhov, in his short story "Ward Number 6," has provided an excellent picture of the typical rural hospital, a picture of filth and stupidity. With the Revolution, the facilities deteriorated even further. The war, the Revolution itself, the civil war, the famine, and the epidemics that followed pushed the nation to the brink of economic disaster. Typhus alone caused some three million deaths. Lenin, reporting on the situation at the Seventh Party Congress in 1919, declared quite simply: "Either the louse defeats socialism or socialism defeats the louse."

The Bolsheviks' initial efforts toward creating a national-health program concentrated on preventive medicine, both because of the urgency of the situation and because some party cadres felt that disease was a characteristic of capitalist societies and would disappear with the flowering of socialism. The regime, however, was soon disabused of the latter notion, and went to work on massive programs for clinical medicine as well as preventive. In the years since the Revolution, the achievement of the Soviet Union in public health has been extremely impressive. It now has one of the highest doctor-to-patient ratios in the world; free medical service of good quality is available for the vast majority of the population; and both the overall death rate and the infant mortality rate have reached levels comparable with far more advanced industrial nations.

The organization of medicine, like that of most other Soviet public services, is highly centralized, although less so since the period of Khrushchev's reforms. Authority emanates from the Ministry of Health and proceeds downward through a hierarchy of republic, provincial, and district offices. The basic administrative unit is the medical district; each city or urban area is divided into districts of four to five thousand people, and patients requiring treatment can either go directly to a local clinic or request home treatment. The patient's files are kept at the clinic and accompany him when he moves. The Soviets do not seem to regard the personal relationship between doctor and patient as very important, and the patient has little or no freedom in choosing his doctor.

Hospitals are usually under the supervision of urban health departments, which coordinate the health services of several urban and rural districts. More specialized hospitals are located only in the larger cities. Supplementing the regular public-health service, large factories and the military maintain their own medical facilities. During the 1930's, special medical installations, superior to those provided by the regular system, were available to high-level government officials and other important persons. These facilities probably still exist, although the upgrading of the regular system of clinics has undoubtedly reduced the differences in the quality of care.[12]

Medical training in the Soviet Union is invariably downgraded by American observers because of the prevalence of formal lectures and the obsolete equipment. It consists of a six-year course which the student enters immediately after leaving secondary school. Medical school graduates are required to serve from three to five years in a location chosen by the authorities before settling down to a permanent practice. Through such coercion, eased somewhat by the payment of special bonuses, the regime improves the quality of rural medicine, which is still far inferior to that of the larger cities. While the program has had some success, its results are still far from satisfactory. The fundamental problem is twofold: the vastness of the Soviet Union and the lack of amenities in rural areas. But the nature of the medical profession itself compounds the difficulty. Soviet doctors are relatively low paid, and, except for medical professors and specialists, the profession is not one that offers any particular prestige. Doctors are, further, subordinate to the bureaucratic apparatus that regulates them and handles complaints by patients. The result of all these factors is that, except at the very top levels, most Soviet physicians are women, although their percentage has been declining in recent years.

The predominance of women in the Soviet medical profession has had two significant consequences. First, the legal workday for doctors is now about five and one-half hours, reflecting the fact that married doctors still must take care of their own households, a job that is far more complicated in the Soviet Union than it is in the United States. Second,

12 See Mark G. Field, *Doctor and Patient in Soviet Russia* (Cambridge: Harvard University Press, 1957), especially pp. 184–186.

because most women practice near where their husbands work, their choice of location is less flexible than it might otherwise be.

7. HOUSING

Estimates on the supply of housing required in any society depend upon some intricate calculations, not least of which are the expectations of those to be housed, projected population increases, and the number and size of existing households. How deeply the government gets enmeshed in housing problems has in the past been a matter of ideological considerations and the general economic situation of the country.

Today, most European nations are making comprehensive public commitments to house their entire population adequately, although their approaches differ. In the Soviet Union, the construction of housing is primarily a public concern, while in every Western European country the private sector is still reasonably important. Also, in most countries of Western Europe, the housing effort has been directed at trying to satisfy the predicted needs of the citizens as they themselves perceive these needs. England, for example, has a far higher stock of single-family dwellings than France, because Englishmen prefer their own homes. In the Soviet Union, on the other hand, more attention has been given to channeling citizen aspirations in directions which the regime itself regards as desirable; the building of individual houses, consequently, is discouraged as the earmark of a "bourgeois" mentality.

Political traditions, too, are significant in determining the structure of housing programs. In England, the existence of local governments, with their long history of independent authority, has meant that much of the responsibility for housing has devolved upon them. In France, on the contrary, policy-making has been far more centralized.

THE ENGLISH PATTERN: After World War I, and with mounting frequency during the 1930's, national and local governments took on the job of general slum clearance and housing construction, especially for lower-income groups. In the aftermath of World War II, however, public-housing programs gained new impetus. For one thing, Britain emerged from the war with some two hundred thousand houses destroyed and another 250,000 badly damaged; for another, a Labor government, committed to large-scale measures of social reform, took office.

The Attlee government asked for and received the authority to engage in the compulsory purchase of housing, and extensive subsidies were granted to local authorities for the purpose of slum clearance. An enormous number of prefabricated houses was produced, and local authorities were empowered to erect them on public land when private property could not be purchased. Tight rent control was also continued.

The program was, in large measure, a stopgap. It did not encompass in any way an overall plan, and though it scored some initial points, it soon ran out of steam. Also, with the government committed to other social services and the balance-of-payments problem casting its pall on governmental budgets, the proportion of resources devoted to housing began to diminish.

Under the Conservatives, the public component of housing shrank still further. Rent and other controls were lifted to encourage private building, which did indeed increase, but not in the areas of greatest need. For the most part, the Conservatives followed a general policy of limiting public funds to slum clearance.

Both the Labor and the Conservative governments had underestimated the scope of housing needs. Englishmen were beginning to marry younger and to have more children, and the number of separate households required was increasing more rapidly than the population. As the problems became more acute, the Conservatives found themselves forced willy-nilly to begin reimposing controls; the Labor government has continued this trend. Rent control was restored to certain kinds of housing and the government set a construction goal of five hundred thousand new housing units a year by 1970. The goal will probably be achieved, but it will still be some time before England's housing problem is solved. The best estimates indicate that as of 1967, 1.8 million housing units were unfit for human habitation, and 1,750,000 more required repairs costing more than $1,200 to meet reasonable standards.

Aside from rent controls, subsidization of rents for lower-income groups is quite common. More than half of all housing constructed since World War II has been built and is controlled by the national and local government. The extent to which rents are subsidized in this housing varies, but very

rarely are occupants obliged to pay the rent that would be required of them on the free market.

THE FRENCH PATTERN: France emerged from World War II in an even worse condition than England, and little was done immediately afterward to improve the situation. As late as 1955, almost half of the nation's dwellings had been built before 1871, and hardly more than ten per cent contained a bath or shower; only slightly more than 25 per cent contained an indoor lavatory.

In the 1950's and continuing into the 1960's, the tempo of housing construction picked up markedly. A series of urban-renewal programs was established, subsidies were extended to landlords for improving

TABLE 24.6. HOUSING AMENITIES IN EUROPE, 1963

Based on interviews with heads of households and housewives in sample surveys conducted in January and February 1963

Percentage of households with:	Great Britain	France	West Germany
Running water	98%	80%	94%
Separate bathroom	68	33	56
Private garden	72	52	48
Telephone	20	14	18
Refrigerator	30	41	52
Electric vacuum cleaner	72	37	66
Electric food mixer	5	24	23
Television set	82	27	41

Adapted from D. V. Donnison, *The Government of Housing* (Harmondsworth, Middlesex: Penguin Books Ltd., 1967), p. 56. Reprinted by permission of the publisher.

TABLE 24.7. MODERNITY OF HOUSING

Percentage of houses surveyed

Country	Date	Built or thoroughly rebuilt Before 1919	After 1945
Great Britain	1961	46%	23%
France	1960	62	17
West Germany	1960	41	38
U.S.S.R.	1960	19	—

Adapted from Donnison, *The Government of Housing*, p. 54. Reprinted by permission of the publisher.

their buildings, and tax incentives were granted to private firms to encourage new housing. Semi-public building companies were also created for the specific purpose of erecting low-cost housing for lower-income groups. The result was a striking increase in the number of dwellings constructed each year. Since 1959, more than three hundred thousand new dwellings a year have become available, and extensive urban-renewal projects have been undertaken. (See Table 24.8.) The stock of French housing, however, is still inferior to the British in both quality and quantity. The construction industry, despite improvements, remains archaic. Production costs are high, buildings take much longer to be completed, and the French have, as yet, made little use of new techniques of prefabrication. Low-cost public housing is of much higher density than in England, and shows far less imagination in construction.

THE GERMAN PATTERN: Germany had been short of housing even before World War II. During the war, one-fourth of its houses were destroyed, and this, coupled with the huge influx of refugees from other areas, produced an array of fantastically troublesome problems.

Beginning with the first Housing Act of 1950, the Germans embarked upon an accelerated program of reconstruction. As already noted, new housing construction was subsidized by the government in several ways. Rather astonishingly, approximately eight million dwelling units were constructed between 1949 and 1964—at first 215,000 a year, and since 1953 about five hundred thousand a year.

As in France and England, the rush to achieve immediate results was not without its drawbacks. Many of the low-income housing projects were below standard in quality and

TABLE 24.8.   QUANTITY OF HOUSING AVAILABLE

Country	Census date	Population in millions	Number of dwellings per 1,000 inhabitants	Number of rooms per 1,000 inhabitants
Great Britain	1961	52.7	315	1,423
France	1962	46.5	313	955
West Germany	1961	54.0	288	1,007
U.S.S.R.	1960	214.4	244	685

Adapted from Donnison, *The Government of Housing*, p. 49. Reprinted by permission.

TABLE 24.9.   DWELLINGS BY SIZE AND DENSITY OF OCCUPANCY

Percentage of dwellings

Country	Census date	Rooms			Persons per room			Average persons per room
		1–2	3–4	5 or more	Less than 1	1 but less than 2	2 or more	
Great Britain	1961	6%	40%	54%	71%	25%	4%	0.68
France	1962	39	46	15	38	47	16	1.01
West Germany	1960	10	61	29	53	44	3	0.88

Adapted from Donnison, *The Government of Housing*, p. 50. Reprinted by permission.

unimaginative in architecture; little attention was given to comprehensive city planning, a task which the Germans, like other Europeans, have now begun to consider.

THE SOVIET PATTERN: In the decade preceding Hitler's invasion, the amount of housing available for Soviet citizens dropped sharply, primarily because of the mass migration to cities and the lack of resources to build new housing. Although complete data is not available, the evidence we do have shows that the amount of living space per inhabitant decreased from 6.99 square yards per person in 1926 to 5.19 square yards in 1940. The destruction caused by the war contributed further to the shortage, and the regime's emphasis on expanding heavy industry in the postwar period meant that housing was far from the top of any priority list. As late as 1960, estimates for the average number of persons per room in the Soviet Union ran as high as 2.72, as against 1.01 in France, 0.68 in England, and 0.83 in the United States.[13]

[13] See Timothy Sosnovy, "Housing Conditions and Urban Development in the U.S.S.R.," in Joint Economic Committee, United States Congress, *New Directions in the Soviet Economy* (Washington: U.S. Government Printing Office, 1966), pp. 531–554. It is only fair to point out that other estimates for 1960 give the inhabitants per room in the U.S.S.R. as 1.5. See D. V. Donnison, *The Government of Housing* (Harmondsworth, Middlesex, England: Penguin Books, Ltd., 1967), p. 50. See also Donald Barry, "Housing in the U.S.S.R.," *Problems of Communism*, XVIII (May–June 1969), pp. 1–11.

Western experts have regarded Soviet housing as poorly equipped and poorly constructed. Soviet data itself is not likely to exaggerate the situation, and the 1967 official figures for the R.S.F.S.R., the most advanced Soviet republic, reveal that urban housing leaves much to be desired (see Table 24.10.) The average middle-class Soviet flat is still probably less soundly constructed and has fewer conveniences than the housing of most American blacks in Northern urban ghettos.

The social effects of poor housing have been a constant theme of Soviet literature: the long wait for adequate apartments, the necessity of living with in-laws. The crowded conditions are viewed as one of the prime factors in the breakup of homes and personal emotional problems.

Beginning in 1959, the regime stepped up the construction of new housing. Drawing upon new techniques of prefabrication, it has been erecting more than one hundred million square meters of new housing space a year. While early attempts to use mass-production methods were notoriously unsuccessful—and they still leave much to be desired—they appear now to be helping to relieve the housing shortage. The number of new apartment houses has multiplied, and observers report they are far more adequate than those built during the 1950's. The Soviets still have a long way to go, however, before they begin to approach Western European levels in the quantity and quality of housing.

TABLE 24.10.   URBAN HOUSING IN THE R.S.F.S.R.

Number of square meters per person	6.1
Dwellings with running water	43%
Dwellings with sewerage	40
Dwellings with central heating	38
Dwellings with hot-water supply	10
Dwellings with bath or shower	26
Dwellings with gas	26

Source: Michael Ellman, *Economic Reform in the Soviet Union* (London: Political and Economic Planning, Broadsheet 509, April 1969), p. 300. Reprinted by permission of the publisher.

TABLE 24.11. ESTIMATES OF SOVIET HOUSING CONDITIONS

*Density of occupancy per room in the urban centers in the
Soviet Union for selected years*

Years	Persons per room
1923	2.60
1926	2.71
1940	3.91
1950	3.43
1960	2.78[1]
1961	2.72

[1] As a comparison, in the United States in 1960 the average density of occupancy per room was nearly 0.60 persons.

Source: United States Congress, Joint Economic Committee, *Dimensions of Soviet Economic Power* (Washington: United States Government Printing Office, 1962), p. 332.

All rents were abolished in the Soviet Union during the three-year period of War Communism. Although they were restored in 1922, they were kept artificially low. Today the Soviet citizen pays only a very small portion of his wage or salary for rent. This percentage applies to all forms of housing, so that the difference paid in rent between good housing and poor housing is slight. The determination of who gets what housing, therefore, has had to be based on a rationing system. While it is impossible to know the precise rules governing the disbursement of apartments, it is evident from observers' reports that those who are considered to have a more important part in Soviet social and economic life have always received priority. Indeed, as much as 25 per cent of Soviet housing is administered by industrial enterprises, and housing is used both to entice workers and to reward the better employees. Workers leaving or dismissed from their jobs also lose their housing.

The maintenance of housing has always been a source of exasperation in the Soviet Union, particularly in view of the poor quality of much of it and the crowded conditions. The big apartment houses have employed managers who can exercise a degree of authority over conditions, but the fact is that the quality of such personnel has, until recently, been far from first rate. The installation of comrades' courts in housing developments, as a method of disciplining unruly or untidy tenants, has had some success in improving upkeep, but the strict penalties for defacing state property seem to prove that the Soviets have yet to solve the problem of having tenants exercise reasonable care in the maintenance of apartments.

8. A CONTINENT OF CITIES

THE URBANIZATION OF EUROPE: The pre-industrial European city, like pre-industrial cities in other parts of the world, was usually surrounded by a wall. Inside, the city was divided into sections which were, in turn, sealed off by walls, moats, or other barriers. The central area of the city contained the prominent government and religious structures and the main market. Close by stood the luxurious dwellings of the elite, often facing inward and presenting a blank wall to the streets. The distribution of population was directly related to power and wealth, the poor living farthest from the center; the city tended to be sectioned off on the basis of ethnic and occupational lines, and one's place of work was often identical with one's place of residence. The pre-industrial city was congested and generally unsanitary; death rates were in-

MAP 24.6. URBANIZED AREAS IN WESTERN EUROPE

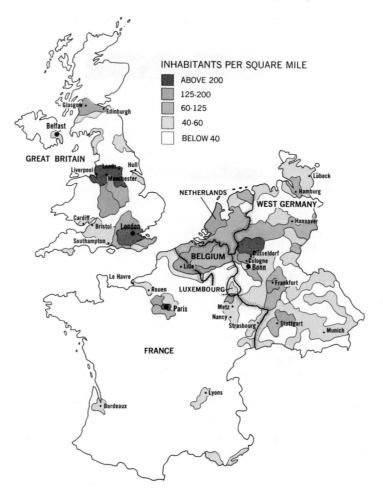

variably higher than birth rates and population growth was contingent upon migration from rural areas.

The Industrial Revolution greatly transformed the city. Walls disappeared and the city sprawled out beyond its old confines. Factories went up in or near the center of the city, drawing more and more people to the urban areas. As the heart of the city lost its attractiveness and transportation facilities improved, many of those who could afford to do so moved to the new suburbs. Nevertheless, many in the aristocracy and the haute bourgeoisie remained; to them, the city was a cultural center that should be preserved, along with the style of life associated with it.

As a consequence, certain neighborhoods continued to be highly fashionable, and in other sections the upper classes lived cheek by jowl with the poor, their privacy and goods protected by walls, fences, and watchmen. Central Paris, for example, retained its rich families while large numbers of the urban proletariat settled in districts ringing the city.

In the United States the situation was quite different. While segments of the rich remained behind for the cultural advantages the city could offer, most urban areas lacked the distinctive traditions of European metropolises; they were all post-industrial cities that had evolved in order to satisfy market needs. The urge to preserve their heritage and to keep them from decay was not nearly so strong. There was another key difference. In Europe, the middle and lower classes could live side by side because the vast differences in their status certified that the working class would exhibit deference; social segregation was not in the least compromised by close physical proximity. In the United States, social segregation could be achieved only by physical separation; the American elite, therefore, had a greater tendency to move outward with the expansion of the city, and a direct relationship came to be drawn between one's distance from the center of the city and one's social status.

Twentieth-century developments again set in motion new forces affecting the physical structure of the city. Electric power, the automobile, and the telephone generated centrifugal forces, dispersing people still farther from the central city but at the same time making possible much larger agglomerations of population than ever before. The city burst its limits and the terms "urban sprawl" and "megalopolis" were no longer a mere part of the planners' lexicon. Added to this phenomenon, of course, were the abrupt decline in the number of farmers in all European countries and the continued population growth.

The changes occurred first in the United States and, after World War II, they began to spread to the Continent. By the 1960's urban and rural areas were fusing: the expanding fringe area on the outskirts of cities was becoming partly urban. And today, from the center of the city to its outskirts, developments radiate out along highways like spokes on a Ferris wheel. Finally, the changes have wrought satellite sub-cities clustered close to the central cities, each with its own fringe area, its own roadside developments, its own service areas, and its own problems.

While much of this dispersion is caused by those who work in the city but live in the suburbs, it is also due to the establishment of factories in the rural areas which are more easily accessible by car. In the United States,

this outward movement has usually resulted in either the decay of the core area or the development of metropolises like Los Angeles, which lack a core altogether. So far such changes, if indeed they occur at all, have been less marked in European cities, primarily because of a much greater desire to preserve the central city. Yet there is little in the economic favor of the central cities; they have no edge in labor costs, and congestion limits most other advantages that might accrue. More and more, the business sector of central cities is being taken over by the headquarters of large corporations, which find communication costs lower in metropolitan areas.[14]

The new urban revolution has not only added to the volume of debates on the future of the city; it has also brought about fresh attempts to consciously plan cities in such a manner as to increase both their efficiency and the amenities they offer. In all European countries, planners are now thinking of the broader urban areas rather than the isolated unit of the city itself; they are dealing with the problems of the city as part of a larger regional complex.

As Europe enters the 1970's, debate has progressed considerably further than planning itself. Nonetheless, the questions raised have yet to produce answers which demonstrate a consensus of "expert" opinion. Should an attempt be made to preserve the central city? If so, how should transportation problems be handled? Should, for example, the automobile be excluded from the city, or should the city be redesigned in some way to accommodate the automobile? Is the contemporary city too large and too impersonal to offer people a meaningful life? Should an effort be made to draw populations away from the central city by creating independent garden cities of a limited size? Or, finally, as some have suggested, should we conclude

[14] See Melvin M. Webber, "Order in Diversity: Community without Propinquity," in Lowdon Wingo, Jr., *Cities and Space* (Baltimore: Johns Hopkins Press, 1963), pp. 23–56.

that modern trends make the city obsolete, revise our aesthetic concepts, and instead of attempting to eliminate urban sprawl, merely attempt to manage it?[15]

THE BRITISH PATTERN: Since World War II, the British have embarked upon a series of impressive urban-renewal projects, especially in their major cities. They have also pioneered in the creation of so-called "new towns" as a solution to the problem of urbanization and have looked for more effective ways to deal with the problem of London. Like Paris, London has been a magnet drawing to it talent from other portions of the nation and creating what some feel is an important regional imbalance.

In England as elsewhere, the replacement of obsolete and obsolescent housing has formed the core of the urban-renewal problem. Although the war destroyed large sections of many English cities and thereby provided the realistic basis for planning policies which considered the community as a whole, a more comprehensive commitment to such policies has come only slowly.

Under the Town and Country Planning Act of 1947, local authorities could define as an "area of comprehensive redevelopment" any section of a city which they believed had to be dealt with as a separate unit. In a number of cases, the authority granted was used with imagination—Coventry, for example, was rebuilt with a large pedestrian area, forbidden to cars, in its center. Yet on the whole, urban renewal has been disappointing. Full advantage has not been taken of the powers granted by legislation; just as important, not enough attention was paid, at least initially, to the automotive revolution. As urban-renewal problems became more acute in the

1960's, a series of studies was launched in the hope of finding some solutions. Perhaps the most important study was the Buchanan Report on Traffic in the Towns, published under the aegis of the Ministry of Transport, which predicted a serious crisis unless England did something to improve urban transportation.

In accordance with recommendations contained in that and other studies, the Labor government secured passage of the Town and Country Planning Act of 1968, intended to facilitate the acquisition of land by local governments for urban reconstruction and to broaden the authority of local officials over the manner in which privately controlled land may be used. It is also designed to encourage better planning procedures; in this connection the proposed reorganization of local government, emphasizing larger local political units, and new regional ones, will have an important bearing upon the ability of communities to devise effective plans. One of the principal handicaps in solving urban problems in England, as in other countries, has been the excessive fragmentation of local authority.

One distinctively British answer to the problems of urban life, although many other nations are engaged in similar programs, is the development of "new towns," a conception advanced by Ebenezer Howard toward the turn of the century. Howard proposed that the surplus slum population of large cities be drawn off by creating smaller, low-density, self-contained planned communities which combined the best in rural and urban living. Although two new towns were created between the wars by private corporations, largely through Howard's efforts, not much more attention was given to his idea until the postwar period, when the government started to push plans for a system of new towns. These plans were expanded and carried to fruition by the Attlee government, primarily under the provisions of the New Towns Act of 1946.

The creation of new towns is ultimately the

15 Various perspectives on these issues are contained in Wingo, *Cities and Space;* Lloyd Rodwin, ed., *The Future Metropolis* (New York: George Braziller, 1961); H. Wentworth Eldridge, *Taming the Megalopolis* (Garden City: Doubleday, 1967); and Rayner Banham, et al., "Non-Plan: An Experiment in Freedom," *New Society,* 338 (March 20, 1969), pp. 435–443.

MAP 24.7. NEW TOWNS AND MAJOR EXPANDING TOWNS IN ENGLAND AND WALES, 1968

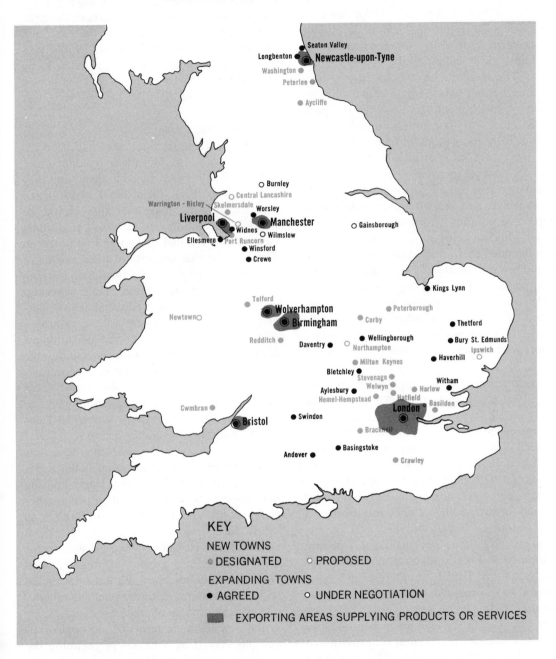

KEY

NEW TOWNS
- DESIGNATED
- PROPOSED

EXPANDING TOWNS
- AGREED
- UNDER NEGOTIATION

EXPORTING AREAS SUPPLYING PRODUCTS OR SERVICES

* For a more detailed map of the London region, see Map 24.8, p. 794.

The expanding towns shown on this map are Town Development Act schemes for 10,000 persons and over.

Adapted from "New Towns Come of Age," *Town and Country Planning,* Special Issue 36 (January–February 1968), p. 15. Reprinted by permission of the publisher.

responsibility of the minister of housing and local government. After a site is chosen, he appoints a New Town Corporation with responsibility for acquiring the land, developing a site plan, supervising the construction of facilities, and handling all the financial problems. The corporation works closely with local authorities, who remain responsible for ordinary government services once the project is under way; corporation members may include local councillors, but most are chosen for their professional qualifications rather than for their representativeness. Each step in planning a new town is accompanied by public hearings, and individuals or groups may appeal corporation decisions if they believe their rights are being infringed. Originally, it was intended that jurisdiction over the towns would revert to local authorities within a specified period of time, but legislation passed in 1959 transferred authority over any established new town to another ad hoc public body, the Commission for the New Towns, whose members are appointed by the government.

The first new towns differed in many ways, but all had common features. They were relatively small, with initial populations set at between 35,000 and sixty thousand. The residential areas, which were insulated from industrial plants, were divided into neighborhoods, all with their own schools, shopping centers, and recreation areas, and all grouped around the town center. Public transportation and pedestrian walks had first call on the planners' attention—not facilities for private automobiles. Finally, density was comparatively low by British standards, and most houses were provided with fenced gardens, some including very large yards. In short, new towns were self-contained communities built to combine the advantages of urban and rural life. All of them were separated from other communities by "green belts" to prevent urban sprawl, and the architectural design of most of them has been fairly attractive.

Because one of the chief reasons for creating the new towns is to draw off population from London, eight sites for new towns near the city were among the 15 chosen for the entire nation in the first five years of the new-towns program. The general retreat from planning that occurred in the 1950's prevented additional new towns from being started for a dozen years, except for one in Scotland. In the 1960's, the program was revived.

Meanwhile, a reappraisal of the new towns had begun. In some ways, they had been extremely successful. Despite early difficulties, industry had been attracted to them, and they were paying back their initial investments. Yet the original hope that they would be multiclass communities in which traditional class barriers would disappear had not been realized; the vast majority of the residents of the first new towns were of the upper-working or the lower-middle class. Some working-class Londoners found adjustment to a new and different environment rather painful—undergoing what came to be called "new town blues"—but they were eventually able to adapt satisfactorily to the new communities. The first new towns also had trouble holding onto the second generation, who, for somewhat different reasons, looked to London as the place "where the action is."

Many of these earlier problems have now been alleviated. A better social balance has been achieved by providing some housing that appeals to middle- and upper-middle-class people and by inducing businesses to locate their executive offices in new town communities. However, while the new towns seem to exude a greater informality than older communities, they still have not ended social segregation. Here the planners failed.

The development of greater self-sufficiency in the new towns in terms of job opportunities has served as a means of retaining the younger generation. More importantly, the second and third generation of new towns have tended to be larger: if people are to be lured from large cities, new towns must be big enough to compete with the diversity of opportunities that big cities offer. Some of the

FIGURE 24.4. SOCIOECONOMIC COMPOSITION OF LONDON'S NEW TOWNS, 1966

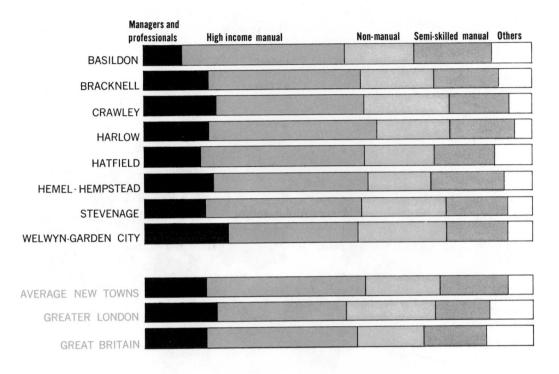

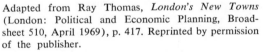

Adapted from Ray Thomas, *London's New Towns* (London: Political and Economic Planning, Broadsheet 510, April 1969), p. 417. Reprinted by permission of the publisher.

new towns, therefore, are expanding, and others are being created for populations of more than two hundred thousand.

Aside from disagreements among architects as to the aesthetic qualities of the new towns—for every two architects there seem to be at least three contrary opinions—the other major criticism of their structure is that the early towns did not take the automobile into account. The newer towns are making adjustments for cars by varying arrangements of roads and parking facilities and by constructing pedestrian shopping malls.

The reappraisal of new towns has brought with it some challenges to their basic conception. Originally, they were perceived as communities that would prevent urban sprawl; they were also expected not only to

siphon off population from London and other metropolises but to curb the general drift of population to the southeast of England and redistribute it more effectively.

Some analysts are now arguing that the initial concept was in error—that the new towns can be part of a general program of dealing with urban living, but that they are not and cannot be the answer to its problems; London and other large cities are going to continue to grow no matter how many new towns are built. These analysts also question whether an all-out effort to redistribute population makes any sense. The future of England's economic position calls for the most effective use of its resources, and this, they contend, may well turn out to mean that London and the southeast should be allowed to continue growing, simply because metro-

MAP 24.8. NEW TOWNS IN THE LONDON REGION

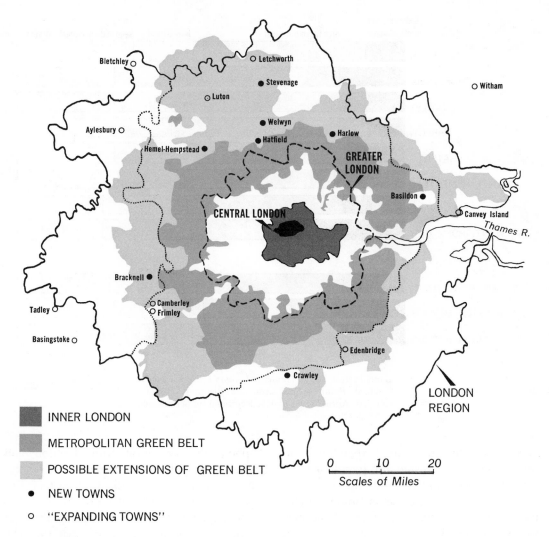

INNER LONDON

METROPOLITAN GREEN BELT

POSSIBLE EXTENSIONS OF GREEN BELT

● NEW TOWNS

○ "EXPANDING TOWNS"

······· ABERCROMBIE'S GREATER LONDON (1944)

"Greater London" is an area within 12–15 miles from the center, similar to the "conurbation" used for statistical purposes. Outside this region is the green belt, and then the new towns created after 1945. For planning purposes, the London region stretches up to 40 miles from the center; some towns receiving London's overspill population are still farther out.

Adapted from Peter Hall, *The World Cities* (New York: McGraw-Hill, 1966; London: Weidenfeld & Nicolson Ltd.), p. 34. Reprinted by permission of the publishers.

politan areas are basically more efficient in dealing with the problems posed by a new economic epoch. Furthermore, the struggle to contain urban sprawl and to retain the traditional city is a losing battle; the better part of wisdom, they argue, may lie in thinking of polycentric cities, built around the automobile rather than in defiance of it. As one writer has phrased the issue:

Instead of cordons sanitaires *of agricultural land many miles wide, protecting each town from the corrupting influence of the next, we need to think about setting the pieces of our new conurbations within a continuous country park.*[16]

By 1938, the suburbs of London had spread out to a temporary limit roughly 12 to 15 miles from the center of the city.[17] In that year, Parliament supposedly limited further urban sprawl by creating a green belt, closed to construction, around the city. The Town and Country Planning Act of 1947 introduced measures to control the land use of every acre of the nation, and the preservation and even extension of the green belt became a major objective.

London, however, went right on growing, albeit in somewhat different directions. Beyond the five-mile-wide green belt, existing towns swelled, and new towns, planned and unplanned, sprang up. The London Planning Region, therefore, as defined by the Ministry of Housing and Local Government, now embraces far more than just the city itself and its immediate environs; it is an area straddling both sides of the green belt, consisting of some 4,400 square miles and containing more than 12 million people.

Some of London's knottiest problems are

an outgrowth of the commuter's preference for the automobile, and hence they relate to the necessity of moving an ever-growing volume of traffic in and out of the central city. The result has been an increase in traffic jams, noise, and air pollution. Improvements in traffic control are for the moment just about keeping pace with urban growth, but unless drastic action is taken to remedy the traffic quandary, all these correlated problems will get worse.

Ironically, the problems of congestion, overcrowding, and urban sprawl have been compounded, in part, by government efforts to improve working-class housing. A series of urban-renewal projects has been undertaken to eliminate the East End slums and to prevent other areas from deteriorating. But these slum-clearance programs themselves, because they encourage the influx of more and more people to the city, merely create new problems.

Unquestionably, new towns have reduced the magnitude of the problems pressing upon London, and, as we have noted, the ultimate solution to its difficulties will require greater decentralization of the functions performed in the city, guided growth for the entire southeast region, and national and regional planning that encourages a more rational dispersal of population. Beyond this, more efficient systems of mass transportation, automated highway control, and the introduction of steam or electric automobiles offer possibilities for the future. In the end, however, it is hard to escape the conclusion, which will be commented upon in the last chapter, that England, like all European countries, is destined to become so overcrowded that population control of some sort must eventually be instituted.

THE FRENCH PATTERN: Although the French had done some imaginative work earlier in restoring partially bombed-out cities, they did little to deal systematically with the problem of urban renewal until the de Gaulle regime took office in 1958. One

---

[16] Peter Hall, "The Pattern of Cities to Come," *New Society*, VII, 180 (March 10, 1966), p. 10. See also R. C. Bellan, "The Future Growth of Britain's Cities," *The Town Planning Review*, 37 (October 1966), pp. 173–188.

[17] The following sections on London, Paris, the Ruhr, and Moscow are drawn largely from Peter Hall, *The World Cities* (New York: McGraw-Hill, 1966).

reason for this tardiness was the lack of capital; another was the fact that no adequate provisions existed for building control or for the implementation of urban-renewal plans.

One year after taking office, the de Gaulle government was able to issue a series of decrees setting aside zones for urban renewal in a number of major cities. Local authorities were given the power to fix purchase prices for land earmarked for renewal and to acquire it by eminent domain. They were also provided with national aid in the form of loans and subsidies, and were required to integrate their renewal operations with general plans for their city.

For the most part, progress on urban renewal has been limited, and overall planning has been notable by its absence. While some attention has been given to creating integrated, self-sufficient suburbs, housing is still often thrown up piecemeal, and the French are far behind the British in relating housing projects not only to their immediate environment but to the needs of those likely to inhabit them. This is not to say that the urban-renewal program has been a complete failure. It has not. Several provincial cities have moved ahead smartly, spurred on by a strong mayor or prefect or by national assistance. Perhaps the most significant national program has been the one concerned with the eight *métropoles d'équilibre*—cities designated for special assistance in order to counteract the magnetism of Paris. Some urban areas have also been aided by the government's decision to decentralize the university system. Finally, the efforts of André Malraux, de Gaulle's minister of culture, to establish *Maisons de la culture* in the provinces improved the quality and added to the dynamism of community life in the outlying areas.

Renewal policies have been quite successful in Toulouse, which has been transformed from a dusty provincial town into a thriving urban center. Since 1959, its population has doubled to about four hundred thousand.

Toulouse is now the main center of France's aircraft-construction industry and the headquarters of the state-run nitrogen enterprise. The government contributed to its growth by transferring the two leading aviation *Grandes Écoles* from Paris and by constructing its new national center for space research in the city. To provide for the influx of scientific personnel, Toulouse is planning and building one of the largest new suburbs in France—and designing it in a comprehensive manner. Towering blocks of flats are being built amid lakes and gardens, and whole districts are being laid out with pedestrians in mind. Similar progress is taking place in Bordeaux and Marseilles, and Grenoble, which had a population of eighty thousand in 1945, will probably reach four hundred thousand by 1972. The development of hydroelectric power and the possibility of opening new ski resorts has helped Grenoble's rejuvenation; the city has also become France's principal center for the development of nuclear power.

Paris, too, has been undergoing rapid changes, as plans have been put into motion dealing with its two main problems: congestion and poor housing. Despite all the talk about the importance of regional development, the Paris metropolitan area is still growing faster than the rest of France, and its population is expected to increase from nine to fifteen million by the end of the century. (See Table 24.12.)

The inner city today contains approximately 114 people per acre, as compared with approximately 43 Londoners per acre, and many of the working-class suburbs are much more densely populated than London's. At the 1962 census, nearly a third of the dwellings inside the Ville de Paris were classified as unsanitary or decaying. Roughly 80 per cent were built before 1914, and about 30 per cent have neither a lavatory nor a place to wash. The average size of a Paris apartment is 2.2 rooms; in London the average is 3.1 rooms and in New York 3.3.

TABLE 24.12. EVOLUTION OF THE POPULATION OF PARIS AND FRANCE, 1801–1965

In millions

	1801	1901	1921	1931	1946	1954	1962	1965
Paris region	1.40	4.82	5.77	6.80	6.69	7.42	8.60	9.12
France	27.35	40.86	39.21	41.83	40.50	42.50	46.52	48.70
Population of Paris as a percentage of the population of France	5.1%	11.8%	14.7%	16.2%	16.5%	17.5%	18.5%	18.7%

Source: Niles M. Hansen, *French Regional Planning* (Bloomington: Indiana University Press, 1968), p. 29. Reprinted by permission of the publisher.

The problem of transportation stems partially from the role Paris has historically played in French life. Some of its problems, however, can be traced to the rebuilding of the city by Baron Georges Haussmann in the nineteenth century. Haussmann transformed the inner city, replacing narrow lanes by wide boulevards. Despite appearances, however, they are not suited to the automobile. Many of them converge at traffic circles which are incapable of handling the flow. Also, until recently, very few places other than the street had been reserved for parking.

Originally, main-line railways were prohibited from entering the heart of the city, and there are still too few connections between the main business districts and the suburbs. As a consequence, travelers using public transportation between the center of the city and its suburban ring must ride both subways and buses, and the buses are placing more and more of a strain on the street system at the morning and evening rush hour.

It was only in 1960 that the first concerted effort was made to devise an integrated plan for the entire Paris metropolitan area. In that year, the government approved a *Plan d'aménagement et d'organization générale de la région parisienne* (PADOG) as the guide toward solving the problems of the city and its environs. PADOG, with its urgent objective of decentralization, called for strict control over the future growth of Paris. For the city itself, it proposed the expansion of a radial highway system; an outer-ring road to move traffic around the city instead of through it; the diffusion of the business district by creating urban "nodes" outside the central city; the construction of deep-level subways from the central city to the suburbs;

TABLE 24.13. ACTUAL AND PROJECTED POPULATIONS OF NEW TOWNS IN THE PARIS REGION

	1962	1985	2000
Noisy-le-Grand and Bry-sur-Marne	40,000	90,000	700,000 to 1,000,000
Beauchamp	12,000	60,000	300,000 to 500,000
Pontoise-Cergy	40,000	130,000	700,000 to 1,000,000
Tigery-Lieusaint	5,000	35,000	400,000 to 600,000
Evry-Courcouronnes	7,000	100,000	300,000 to 500,000
Southeast of Trappes	3,000	100,000	400,000 to 600,000
Northwest of Trappes	2,000	100,000	300,000 to 400,000
South of Mantes	1,000	5,000	300,000 to 400,000
Total	110,000	620,000	around 4,500,000

Source: Hansen, *French Regional Planning*, p. 47. Reprinted by permission of the publisher.

MAP 24.9.   THE REGIONAL PLAN FOR PARIS, 1965

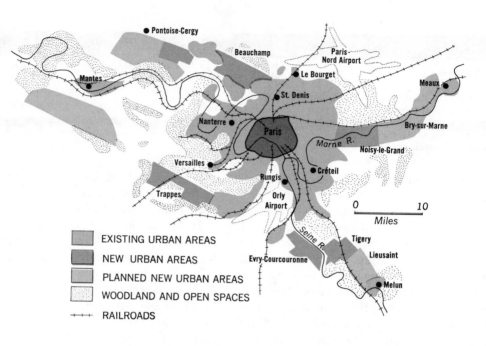

EXISTING URBAN AREAS
NEW URBAN AREAS
PLANNED NEW URBAN AREAS
WOODLAND AND OPEN SPACES
┼┼┼┼ RAILROADS

Main growth areas extend along the banks of the Seine
toward Rouen and Le Havre.

Adapted from *The Town Planning Review*, 39 (October 1968). Reprinted by permission of the publisher.

and a network of inner-city expressways and parking facilities.

By 1965, however, certain aspects of PADOG had become obsolete. Despite government efforts, Paris was continuing to expand more rapidly than anticipated; further, despite the general emphasis on regionalism, excessive decentralization was now viewed as economically inefficient. A new master regional scheme for the Paris area—*Schéma directeur d'aménagement d'urbanisme de la région de Paris*—was adopted. The new plan is concerned less with stopping than with directing the growth of Paris. This desired direction is along two axes: one follows the Seine River to the north and west, the other the Seine and Marne rivers to the east. Population will be drawn away from Paris proper by the creation of self-contained new towns along these axes; just as important, the plan

includes proposals for developing the whole metropolitan area in such a way as to insure the preservation of woodlands and recreational areas as "leisure zones."

In the meantime, work in Paris itself is moving ahead. A new business district (*la Défense*) outside the downtown area is changing the Paris skyline, and Paris's old market place, Les Halles, is finally being moved from the central city to the suburbs as a means of reducing congestion. The circular road around the city (*Boulevard Périphérique*) has been completed; new roads are being constructed through the city and old ones widened. Plans for the underground subway are proceeding, if slowly, and many new underground parking garages have already been opened.

Paris, like other big cities in the world, is still in a race with time. It remains to be seen whether the new plan is adequate and whether it can be implemented fast enough to keep pace with the city's problems.

THE GERMAN PATTERN: The main pre-occupations of West Germany during the first ten years of its existence were the rebuilding of bomb-devastated cities and the provision of adequate housing for the 12 million or so refugees who had arrived from East Germany and other areas. Authority over programs of urban reconstruction and renewal was left to the Länder and individual city governments. Germany's division and occupation delayed the beginnings of genuine urban renewal until 1949; the press of housing needs and the haste with which it was felt new housing had to be constructed shoved overall planning schemes into the background; and, finally, with the Nazi experience still raw, many communities leaned over backward to avoid exercising their powers of eminent domain in the acquisition of new land.

Thus, renewal was quite uneven. In Kiel, Kassel, Hannover, and West Berlin the results of urban planning were impressive. But in many other cities, reconstruction produced a hodgepodge of building without any general sense of community needs. By the late 1950's it was obvious that if spot planning and piecemeal renewal were to be avoided throughout the nation, active government initiative was mandatory. A building and planning law was, therefore, adopted in 1960, followed by others in 1962, 1965, and 1966, all oriented toward the promotion of a comprehensive approach to planning. One effect of the new legislation can be seen in the development of the "Rhine-Ruhr agglomeration."

As defined by a number of studies, an agglomeration consists of a population of more than ten million persons within a triangular, polycentric urban area; it is a definition that includes the three cities of Bonn, Düsseldorf, and Cologne. The agglomeration containing these cities is the industrial heart of the Federal Republic, producing more than four-fifths of its hard coal and three-fifths of its steel.

The essential problem facing the area, as with other urban agglomerations, is simple: a growing demand for limited space. Here, as elsewhere, inadequate transportation, urban sprawl, and unsatisfactory services are creating urgent problems, which are compounded by a decline in the area's coal industry and a resultant loss of taxes to many of the municipalities as firms close down.

The principal instrument for dealing with these issues is the Ruhr Planning Authority, composed of local officials and representatives of both industry and labor. It is responsible to the minister for planning, housing, and public works of the state government of North Rhine–Westphalia. The authority is supported financially by the municipalities within its jurisdiction, and it can, if it chooses, float loans and purchase and set aside land for future public development.

A draft regional plan for the Rhine-Ruhr agglomeration was published in 1966; it attempted to take into account such diverse needs as recreation, sewage disposal, and the more rational routing of traffic. Among the more important suggestions adopted was one calling for the creation of a green belt to check urban sprawl and preserve recreation areas. The authority is now working with various municipalities in order to coordinate local plans with those outlining the region's overall development.

THE SOVIET PATTERN: The Soviet Union is fast becoming a predominantly urban nation. In 1913, less than twenty per cent of the Russian people lived in cities and towns; by 1965, well over half of the population was urban. In 1926 there were 31 cities with more than a hundred thousand people; today there are almost two hundred cities with that population, and together the inhabitants of these cities amount to more than one-fourth of the total Soviet population. The growth of cities has caused not only the expansion of existing urban centers but the creation of new communities as well, especially in the east. Indeed, since the Revolution, the Soviets have built perhaps a thousand new municipalities. Many of these have been associated with the opening of Siberia and other areas to settlement; others were founded as satellite cities to help relieve the problems of urban sprawl in the larger metropolitan areas.

As in the West, satellite cities as a solution to any metropolitan problem have been far from successful. As early as 1932, the government had programs designed to limit the growth of Moscow and Leningrad, and later in the decade other cities were added to the list. Yet in every case, in spite of a rigid system of population control that even included internal passports, the major cities quickly spread beyond their boundaries. And with the subsequent loosening of controls over population movements, the difficulties, if anything, have grown greater.

In the early years of the regime, there was much debate over the optimal size of cities and what their housing policies should be. In terms of ideal size, most planners considered a city of more than two hundred thousand far too large to bring about the urban-rural unity that Marx had considered so important. It was also generally thought that the city should have communal houses serving primarily as a place to sleep, with full services for eating and the care of children provided by communal centers. This vision has not yet disappeared; some planners still see the Soviet city of the future as composed of communal socioeconomic units for two thousand to 2,500 people, with communal boarding schools for all children and communal dining rooms. Such communes would be self-contained so that members could walk easily from factory to home to other activities.

The dominant thrust among Soviet planners today, however, is rather different. Most now think of the ideal city as made up of micro-districts of four thousand to 18,000 inhabitants, with each district grouped around cultural and other special facilities in order virtually to eliminate the need for automobiles. They have come to accept as necessary some separation of industrial from residential areas, and even to acquiesce in the desirability of some individual housing, although apartments are preferred. Finally, while a wider variety of social services is acknowledged as necessary, there is far less talk of eliminating the family. Indeed, aside from the greater emphasis on apartment dwellings, the Soviets are currently establishing, as their solution to the glut of problems facing large cities, new communities not too different from the first generation of British new towns. The Soviets, however, still have hopes that they can avoid having to adjust to the private automobile by creating a flexible system of public transportation, including car rentals and car pools.

Between 1930 and 1955, very little was done to implement these plans. For one thing, industrial growth took first place, and although urban-planning agencies did possess some authority, it was the Kremlin's determination of where industries should be located that in turn determined the location of cities. Factories were constructed without much consideration for side effects such as air and water pollution, and housing was built helter-skelter without satisfactory provisions for communal services, including stores and sewage disposal. Stalin's taste for huge baroque buildings hampered architectural creativity, and even after his death the decision to solve the housing problem through the use of mass-construction techniques inhibited the execution of imaginative designs.

In the past several years, however, city planning has once again come into its own. Tensions among various agencies and among planners continue to exist, but even so some urban areas have come up with very solid plans for resolving their difficulties. A good many problems, to be sure, remain. Industrial enterprises still control much of the housing, and they are far less concerned than are planners with providing the amenities of urban living; local soviets have some authority, but not enough to counter the influence of industries. Nor have the planners themselves devised adequate programs that bring into harmony all the desired values of urban life. Most likely, the Soviet Union's urban problems will also become more, not less, complex in the future.

Moscow, of course, is now the heart of the Soviet Union, although unlike London and Paris its supremacy is challenged by other cities. As early as 1932, the Communist regime decided that Moscow's population had to be limited. Between 1935 and 1939, however, the city grew from 3.66 million to 4.14 million, eighty per cent of the planned population limit. The number of residents declined during World War II, but by 1959 the population had surpassed original estimates; by 1963, the total number of inhabitants of the extended city region had reached 6.4 million, and its growth rate was comparable to many Western European capitals. In another move not only to stem the tide but to reverse it, the government in 1966 set new population limits and prohibited new industries from coming into the city.

To limit Moscow's size, however, is an almost impossible task. The city is the transportation center of the Soviet Union, the center of all forms of entertainment, and, still, the nation's administrative center. It also

seems likely that as the Soviet economy changes and personal services and consumer goods become more and more important, the same forces that have resulted in the growth of central areas in other cities will add to the problems of Moscow.

Within the Moscow region, planning is the obligation of the Institute of the General Plan, a regional association. The broad objectives of its work have been spelled out. Within a belt motorway, opened in 1962 some 11 miles from the city center, the population is not to grow and the emphasis is to be upon urban renewal. After a false start in the 1930's, repeating many of the same mistakes that Haussmann had made in redesigning Paris, plans for express highways are now under way. Also, ever heavier investments are being made to extend the subway system and to connect it with commuter services which, today, are among the world's best.

Beyond the belt motorway, planners have set up a green belt approximately six miles wide. Some pressure to make use of the belt has been exerted in recent years, for the more affluent Russians have been building summer dachas in the area. But the regime is now trying to stop this private infiltration and to install a wide variety of public accommodations as an answer to the area's recreation needs. As in the London metropolitan area, satellite cities have mushroomed beyond the

TABLE 24.14. POPULATION FORECASTS: U.S.S.R. SELECTED CITIES

City population as planned for 1975 and as reported for 1965

City	Planned population for 1975	Actual population beginning 1965
Gorky	840,000	1,085,000
Tashkent	800,000	1,106,000
Novosibirsk	850,000	1,029,000
Kuibyshev	700,000	948,000
Minsk	450,000	717,000

Source: United States Congress, Joint Economic Committee, *New Directions in the Soviet Economy*, Part II-B (Washington: United States Government Printing Office, 1966), p. 537.

green belt, and industry is being urged to locate in these outlying cities in order to reduce commuter traffic into the central city.

Most of the Moscow regional program has thus far proved to be a disappointment, and the Soviets themselves readily admit it. Planning has lacked coordination, and the problems of effective design have been inhibited both by immediate needs and by the legacy of the Stalin era. Nevertheless, professional planners are obviously receiving greater recognition in the Soviet Union and, without doubt, their authority over establishing planning policies will increase in the future.

1. INTRODUCTION

A nation's foreign policy and its domestic politics have always been closely interrelated. Tribes, city states, empires, modern nations —all have competed for control of scarce resources in order to increase their power and the welfare of their citizens. Moreover, all have tried to impose upon others their conception of the good life for the purpose of nurturing their own sense of security and worth. Yet each of these societies has also entered into cooperative relations when it felt such arrangements would be advantageous.

The international arena can be considered in one sense as a primitive political system in that relations among states in any particular historical period are usually guided by sets of implicit, mutually accepted rules. The international system, however, lacks two prerequisites of its domestic counterpart: the social basis of a community and the political structure of a government. The establishment and maintenance of international order,

therefore, depends upon limited and conditional cooperation; when this breaks down because one or more of these states believe more is to be gained from following a policy that is not cooperative, the result is often complete chaos. Relations among political units still resemble, in some degree, Hobbes's conception of the state of nature: the individual units reserve for themselves the ultimate authority to decide what policies they will follow.

Historically, a state's policy has varied in accordance with a number of factors, including its economic power, its political culture, its institutional structure, the values and psychological equipment of its political elite, and the power and policies of other members of the international community. The interplay among these factors is so complex, and can change so radically over periods of time, that it is difficult to set down a general theory of international politics. Perhaps the most that can be hoped for is an historical sociology that may help us determine some of the principal variables operative in a particular epoch.[1] The ideological character of inter-state relations since World War I, for instance, contrasts markedly with the European international system of the eighteenth century. And who would deny that thermonuclear weapons have fundamentally restructured international relations in the latter part of the twentieth century? A factor of far greater significance in international relations is, of course, the evolution of the idea of the nation as a basic political unit—a comparatively new idea which became manifest in Europe only during the seventeenth century; from a theoretical point of view, the nation state is unlike any other form of society in the pre-modern world.[2]

This chapter will trace the development of the European international system not only as it pertains to relations among the European nations, but also as the system itself relates to the rest of the world. The chapter will also describe the development of foreign policies in the four nations that are our primary concern, analyzing some of the reasons behind the determination of their policies.

2. THE EUROPEAN PATTERN

The fourteenth and fifteenth centuries witnessed the rise of a number of powerful European monarchies, which engaged in an intensive rivalry for power within Europe and for overseas territories. Spain reached its zenith in both spheres during the sixteenth century, and for a short time, through the union of the Spanish dynasty with that of the Hapsburgs, it looked as if the Spanish throne might unite all of Europe under its leadership. Charles V had inherited the united Spanish kingdom, Spanish possessions in the New World and Italy (Sardinia, Sicily, Naples), and the hereditary Hapsburg lands in Central Europe (the duchies of Austria,

Styria, Carinthia, and Carniola, and the country of Tyrol). Through his grandmother, Mary of Burgundy, Charles was also heir to Burgundian territories, Franche-Comté, and the Netherlands. In 1519 Charles was elected Holy Roman emperor and thus became, at the age of 19, ruler of a larger territory than had been collected under one monarch since the disintegration of Charlemagne's empire seven centuries earlier.

But the dynasty could not be maintained. Others inevitably combined against it, and the continuing growth of national self-consciousness, together with the schism within Christianity, conspired to replace a politics of dynasties with a politics of nations. Furthermore, the impulses that had produced the Spanish Empire began to weaken, and before long the hegemony of Spain was being challenged by northern European nations. The defeat of the Spanish Armada in 1588 foreshadowed the shift of power in Europe north of the Pyrenees.

First Holland and then France and England extended their control over the New World and Asia. The British eventually emerged as the dominant imperial power of the period, while France under Louis XIV and Louis XV became the most powerful nation on the European continent. The aim of Louis XIV was twofold: to establish the Rhine as a "natural" boundary for France and to establish French primacy in Europe. Neither he nor his successor quite achieved either of these objectives, but only because the other European states formed a balance of power to resist the design.

Under Peter the Great, Russia in the meantime pursued its expansionist policies in Asia and began to dabble in the affairs of Europe. Peter opened the way for the first partition of Poland in 1772, and he succeeded in wresting access to the Baltic from Sweden. He failed, however, to achieve a similar success in the south, and the Black Sea was not permanently secured until the rule of Catherine the Great.

In the eighteenth century, the European

---

[1] See Raymond Aron's monumental work, *Peace and War* (Garden City, N.Y.: Doubleday and Company, 1966).

[2] Joel Larus, ed., *Comparative World Politics* (Belmont, Calif.: Wadsworth Publishing Company, 1964).

international system entered upon what has been called its "classic age."[3] The Continent was divided into a congeries of sovereign states, each of which, by and large, assumed the continued existence of the others. Conflicts among them were limited to marginal territorial and power issues, and a rough balance of power took shape, usually as a counterweight to France. It was not yet the age of the modern nation state, and Europeans were still aware that they shared a common heritage that made transfers of allegiance far easier than they were to become in later centuries; German or Swiss mercenaries could serve one country and then another without qualms, and citizens residing in nations that were at war with their own could continue to do so without the slightest inconvenience.

The diplomatic corps of many European nations often had an international character. For example, Elizabeth Farnese, queen of Spain, brought Giulio Alberoni from Parma to become the head of the diplomatic service of her country in 1714. Later another Italian, the Marquis of Squillaci, was made minister of war and finance. Baron Ripperda, a Dutchman, also figured in Spanish diplomacy, as did the Austrian count Lothar Königsegg.

The French Revolution and Napoleon ended this "classic age." Both inspired that intensive identification on the part of the people with their own nation state—a feeling, of course, that became modern nationalism. The Revolution was also the first European "ideological" upheaval since the sixteenth-century religious wars; the Napoleonic Wars, unlike the limited combats between professional armies that had been the rule since the religious wars, once again involved entire populations.

The impact of nationalism based on ethnic and cultural affiliation was to transform the map of Europe several times during the nine-

teenth century and the first half of the twentieth. Indeed, its impact is still with us. The Congress of Vienna (1814–1815) tried to limit this trend toward nationalism, but the attempt was singularly unsuccessful. In fifteen years the formation of the Low Countries into a single state was reversed, and within fifty years both Italy and Germany were emerging as new national states. Finally, nationalism helped drive the Turks from the Balkans, where a series of national and ethnic conflicts eventually supplied the spark that set off World War I.

Throughout the nineteenth century, European imperialism was entering upon a new phase prompted not only by economic motives but also by national pride and a sense of what Europe considered as its "civilizing mission." Once under way, the race for colonies built on itself with the major powers seizing new territories lest their competitors achieve dominance first and thus threaten previously acquired possessions. The French began to create a North African empire in 1830 and later expanded their control in the Middle and Far East, although their abortive effort in the New World, in Mexico, came to naught. In the Middle East and in Africa, the French at first represented the only competition to British expansion, which had reached its peak by the turn of the century; by then, however, Germany and Italy, moved primarily by conceptions of national grandeur, began to stake out their own claims. Almost simultaneously, Russia and the United States, although concerned primarily with extending their holds on contiguous, relatively unpopulated territory, became involved in imperial adventures of their own.

The defeat of Napolean had led to an attempt led by Metternich and Alexander to establish some sort of international concert—not only to prevent territorial conflicts but also to insure that the radical ideas of the French Revolution did not incite any further turmoil. It did not take them long to find out, however, that it was impossible to create an

[3] For a description of this age, see Richard N. Rosecrance, *Action and Reaction in World Politics* (Boston: Little, Brown and Company, 1963), chap. 2.

alliance of Europe's major powers which would inhibit the spread of liberal doctrines and assure the principle of dynastic legitimacy. Not all the powers accepted the importance of the principle at all times—and all were divided by conceptions of their own national interest. Nevertheless, Europe managed to avoid a major war between 1815 and 1914, and the great powers were able to engage in a modicum of cooperation; they were able to confer on their differences because each believed it had a responsibility to maintain the territorial status quo established in 1815. The great powers also believed that if the balance of power in Europe had to be modified or a problem had to be settled, changes should not be made unilaterally; gains by one nation should not be permitted without the formal and common consent of all the major powers.

The European system began to fall apart with the rise of German power under Bismarck, although Bismarck himself had no aggressive designs and considered Germany a satisfied nation once unification had been achieved in 1871. With Bismarck's dismissal in 1890, however, German foreign policy underwent significant changes. Moved by an acute sense of nationalism, a new generation of German leaders urged that their nation take its place in the world by establishing an empire; they argued that Germany's rapid economic expansion and obvious military prowess gave it the right to be the dominant power in Europe. Such expressed aspirations led inevitably to a deterioration in Germany's relations with France, Russia, and England. France had never really accepted the loss of Alsace-Lorraine in 1871, and its decline in power as Germany's grew persuaded Paris to seek new diplomatic and military alliances. Russia, on the other hand, once Bismarck had been replaced, became wary of Germany's intentions in Eastern Europe. Britain was eventually enticed into an alliance with France and Russia for three reasons: German imperial ambitions and the concomitant con-

struction of a large navy seemed to threaten England's traditional maritime supremacy, Germany had become an aggressive competitor on the world market, and German military power seemed likely to disrupt the Continental balance of power to which the British had been committed for so long. The German ambitions and French, Russian, and English fears resulted in the pervasion of suspicion and mistrust, an armaments race, and, in the end, the First World War.

The war, of course, shattered the nineteenth-century "concert of Europe"; it also marked the beginning of the end of Western Europe's domination of the world. The United States finally entered permanently upon the stage of world politics (except for a retreat into semi-isolationism in the 1920's and 1930's), and it was joined by the Soviet Union and Japan. Russian involvement in European politics initially added a new dimension to European diplomacy, for the Soviets operated, at least in part, as the self-conscious directors of a world revolution, the purpose of which was the total transformation of society.

In Western Europe, the loss of manpower and material in World War I actually hastened the decline of French and English power, and, in Central Europe, the settlement that followed the war only further complicated the problem of stability. The Versailles principle of extending self-determination to all peoples made the revival of the old Austro-Hungarian Empire an impossibility. Yet such was the ethnic composition of Europe that no settlement was conceivable which did not include a variety of nationalities within a single boundary.

The war blocked Germany's plans to secure a commanding place in Central and Western Europe; the French and the British, especially the former, were determined that Germany should never again attempt to establish its predominance. Frightened at the same time by the new Soviet regime's encouragement of revolutionary principles, the British and French first made half-hearted moves to destroy the Communist state and then to quarantine it.

French efforts to contain Germany could not succeed unless they were guaranteed and enforced by all European nations. Demographically and industrially, Germany still was potentially the most powerful nation in Western Europe; unless permanent controls were to be imposed from outside, it would eventually have to be readmitted into the European community of nations on equal terms. Some French and British statesmen recognized the realities of the situation, and, working in the late 1920's with like-minded German political leaders, they tried to pave the way toward satisfying "legitimate" German demands and establishing a new concert of European powers that would include Germany. Simultaneously, the implementation of a broader conception of international security through the League of Nations was also pursued.

All these efforts toward achieving some degree of international order in Europe came too late. The world Depression of 1929 helped bring Hitler to power, and the Nazis boldly proceeded to dismantle the Versailles settlement and rearm Germany. Hitler demanded not only the restoration of territories taken from Germany after World War I, but other territories containing German-speaking people. At the same time, the Japanese stretched their influence in Asia, first by occupying Manchuria, then, in 1937, by invading China and posing a threat to United States, British, French, and Dutch colonial possessions.

England, France, and the United States were reluctant to respond with effective sanctions to these aggressive moves. World War I and the Depression had created strong pacifistic sentiments among large segments of their populations, and, toward Germany at least, feelings of guilt. Until 1939, after all, the Nazi demands seemed almost reasonable, limited as they were to rectifying the "wrongs" of the Versailles Treaty. What was so wrong about

incorporating within the Third Reich all German-speaking peoples, who, as "plebiscites" clearly showed, wanted to be part of the new Reich anyway? Leaving aside the fantasies of Hitler's *Mein Kampf,* it could be argued that his policy was properly limited to establishing Germany's legitimate place in Europe, and that once he was satisfied he would settle down. There were others, of course, ready to argue that Nazi Germany served as a handy, formidable barrier to Soviet expansion.

When it was all but too late, the British and French tried to secure the Soviet Union's cooperation in stopping further German expansion. The effort was abortive, partly because not one of the small Eastern European states, including Poland, evinced any desire to have Russian troops cross its territory in order to protect it. The upshot was World War II, which, unlike the First World War, involved most of the nations of the world; after six years of devastation, it resulted in the defeat of Germany, Italy, and Japan.

But World War II had another, more far-reaching result: it ended the age of European world dominance. In the new international arena, which now included the whole world, power had shifted from Western Europe to both the East and the West. The Soviet Union was now a major world power—European as well as Asian. And the United States, for a time, became the single most powerful nation in the world. In Asia itself, China, after being convulsed by a Communist revolution, emerged from its self-devastation as a potentially great power.

The chief international competition immediately after the war took place between the United States and the Soviet Union. Europe was no longer in the same power league even though, for most of the 1940's and 1950's, Western Europe itself remained the center of international conflict. Responding to what it considered a threat by the Soviet Union to dominate the entire European continent, the United States engaged in a program of massive aid to help Western European nations recover from the war. The United States also served as the guarantor of Western Europe's military security and encouraged the European countries to enter into economic, political, and military agreements among themselves.

Even as Europe was recovering economically from the war, it began to lose its colonial empire. Nationalism in the Far East and in Africa had its roots in the prewar era, but it failed to reach fruition until after the Allied victory. India and Pakistan achieved independence from Britain in 1947, as the subcontinent was divided into predominantly Hindu and predominantly Muslim states. Burma became an independent nation in 1948, and Ceylon became effectively independent the same year. Malaya followed in 1957. The French colony of Indochina was divided in 1954 between a Communist-dominated regime in the north and a non-Communist one in the south, with Laos and Cambodia established as separate states. The Dutch empire in the Indonesian archipelago had crumbled even earlier. The movement toward independence in Africa started somewhat later, but by the mid-1960's, both North Africa and black Africa had broken away from their European masters, with the exception of white-dominated Rhodesia, South Africa, and the Portuguese colonies. In the Middle East, too, European influence diminished quickly.

In the first years after the war, many Europeans had expected that the United States, as the legatee of European culture, would take over the world position once held by the Western European powers in order to continue the European influence in non-Western areas of the world. To a certain extent, this was precisely the function the United States came to exercise; yet it was a function that could be assumed only temporarily, for the balance of world power had fundamentally shifted. The international system was no longer confined to Europe. Even with the United States acting as Europe's powerful

proxy, the end of the European age had come.

The Soviet Union, like Western Europe, was also undergoing profound changes. The death of Stalin and the rise to power of new leaders revealed that Russia was becoming a far less radical state. The U.S.S.R. was now accepted as a great power—a power that was more and more confident of its own military strength. It was still theoretically committed to the transformation of the world, but it was more interested in coming to terms with a pluralistic world that was still composed of independent nation states of quite different social hues.

While the Soviets were adjusting to the idea of "peaceful coexistence," they were challenged by China for leadership of the Communist world. Although the challenge was partly an outgrowth of traditional tensions between the two nations, it sprang much more from China's drawing upon the more revolutionary and apocalyptic elements of Marxism to establish its own world position. The status of its own revolutionary development was a factor, too, in China's challenge; still in the early stages of consolidation and dominated by the first generation of revolutionary leaders, the Communist Chinese continued to be dedicated not only to the fundamental remaking of their own society but to that of the world as well. In any event, the Soviet-Chinese clash accelerated a movement toward independence on the part of other Communist states and parties.

In the 1950's, the nations of Western Europe, motivated partly by uneasiness, envy, and impatience with a world dominated by two superpowers, began maneuvering toward economic and political integration. These moves were rather specifically dictated by economic considerations, military needs, and the growing recognition that they all shared a common heritage. The first real breakthrough in the direction of integration came with French Foreign Minister Robert Schuman's 1950 proposal for a coal and steel community which would integrate the coal and iron resources of France, Germany, Belgium, and Luxembourg. The European Coal and Steel Community (E.C.S.C.) was established by treaty in 1951; it was formally launched a year later with Italy and the Netherlands included as members.

A governing body for the community, the High Authority, was set up, with headquarters in the city of Luxembourg. Policy decisions were made the province of the E.C.S.C. Common Assembly, whose deputies were elected by the parliaments of member states; disputes among members were to be settled by the community's own Court of Justice. The E.C.S.C. achieved surprising success in short order: it eliminated not only all customs duties on coal and steel among community members, but all restrictions of any sort— quotas, export and import licenses, discriminatory freight rates, and price differentials —upon the two products.

The next important step toward European integration was taken in March 1957, when the six E.C.S.C. members signed two additional treaties. One established the European Atomic Energy Community (Euratom); the other, the European Economic Community (E.E.C.) or Common Market. The latter was the more important of the two new enterprises; its purpose was to extend the work of the E.C.S.C. to all goods and services by reducing all internal tariffs in specified stages until they were eliminated completely and the six nations constituted one vast trade area. Further, the Common Market specifically looked to the time when economic unity would be followed by some form of political unification.

The British were, at first, reluctant to join the Common Market. They continued to think of themselves as having a rather unique status which placed them both in Europe and outside it—a self-appraisal in which they could indulge because remnants of the old empire still existed and because of England's special relations with the United States. The British, therefore, hoped to associate with the Market through a broader trade federation of European states, whose interrelationship would be looser than that which existed among the Six. The British, therefore, sparked the founding of the seven-nation European Free Trade Association (E.F.T.A.), consisting of Austria, Denmark, Norway, Portugal, Sweden, Switzerland, and the United Kingdom.

The success of the Common Market, however, was such that by 1961 the British decided to forsake the Seven and apply for entry. Two applications and eight years later, they were still not members, primarily because of Charles de Gaulle. His ostensible reasons for blackballing the British were their ties to the United States and the sorry state of the British economy; but without much doubt, he was really motivated by his desire to maintain French leadership on the Continent, a leadership that would be threatened by British entry into the E.E.C. For the same reasons, de Gaulle brought the movement toward European political unification to a virtual halt, finding a league of nations in which France would take a leading part preferable to an amalgamation in which French identity might not be so easily distinguished. Whatever de Gaulle's reasons for excluding the British, their entry into the Common Market seems only a matter of time, not only because de Gaulle is no longer in the Elysée Palace, but because of the less rigid, less stereotyped attitudes of a younger generation of Europeans. It also seems likely that these new attitudes will help the movement toward unification gather fresh momentum.

There are, to be sure, real problems that must be overcome if England is to join the Six. The Common Market was created with the idea that ultimately its members would have a single integrated economy, an objective that can hardly be reached if the currency of one of its members, widely used for trading purposes, is subject to constant pressures. Further, the Market's agricultural policy, which places levies on imported farm products, has kept domestic food prices high; England is far less self-sufficient agriculturally than most Continental countries, and unless some accommodation is made, entering the Market would have serious negative results for the British economy. No doubt both the financial and the farm problems can be resolved if the Six determine to involve England in the Market's economy.

The independence of French foreign policy under de Gaulle was also demonstrated in other areas, including France's withdrawal, for all effective purposes, from the North Atlantic Treaty Organization. De Gaulle's rejection of N.A.T.O. seemed to express the sentiments of more and more members of the West European elite, who see the cold war as over and envisage an independent course for Western Europe. They also see Western European independence as leading to renewed ties with Eastern Europe, and these ties, they hope, would then permit the satellite nations to become more independent of Moscow.

In the meantime, the nature of the international system has been undergoing profound changes. Most importantly, a bipolar world in which the United States and the Soviet Union compete for predominance is being replaced by one in which China is beginning to wield great influence. To the major powers, it is becoming a world in which they find they have less and less control over the actions of smaller states.

3. THE BRITISH PATTERN [4]

THE HISTORICAL BACKGROUND: Since the early modern period of European history, Britain's foreign policy has been shaped by its geographic position. Between the sixteenth century and the nineteenth, England developed from a mercantile society to the world's

___
[4] Much of this section is based on the analysis of Leon Epstein in Roy C. Macridis, ed., *Foreign Policy in World Politics,* 3rd ed. (New York: Prentice-Hall, 1967).

leading industrial power. During all that time, the sea was there to protect it, setting it apart from the European continent. From the defeat of the Spanish Armada to the Napoleonic Wars, from the Battle of Trafalgar to the Battle of Britain, the country was free from the threat of invasion; since 1066 it has been spared the experience of foreign occupation that has befallen almost all Continental states. Englishmen still talk of "going to Europe" for holidays; the attitude of being *in* Europe, but not *part of* it, had a very real basis for a very long time, and it sank deeply into the British way of thinking about foreign policy.

The island position of England placed a premium on the maintenance of naval superiority over any hostile force that might be mustered, and, in addition, a commitment to deny a potential enemy control of the European coastal area from which an invasion might be launched. This meant it was important that the Low Countries and the English Channel ports not be allowed to fall into hostile hands. Even into the twentieth century, this policy was closely observed; it was the German invasion of Belgium in 1914 that made the wavering British cabinet decide in favor of war.

Linked to this policy of naval predominance and keeping a likely enemy out of the Low Countries and northern France was the desire to forestall any concentration of power on the Continent that might threaten to overwhelm Britain. This aim was to be accomplished by adherence to the concept of a "balance of power." To be able to work such a wonder, of course, meant that Britain had to hold that balance, and to hold it, Britain had to be able to shift its own weight from one scale of national alignments to the other as the power balance fluctuated. The ideal policy for England to follow was to avoid engagements in Europe which tied its hands.

Part of the basis for the formulation of its traditional foreign policy had to do with the fact that England was becoming increasingly reliant upon trade to insure its livelihood. By the late nineteenth century, it was dependent upon foreign nations for half its food supply and for most of the raw materials required by its industrial plants. England's prosperity was based upon foreign investments, upon the importance of British shipping, and, increasingly, upon its status as the world's banker.

Two world wars fundamentally altered Britain's world position. No longer is the English Channel the protective moat it once was. British military and industrial potential has slipped, and is now less than that of a growing number of other nations. The colossus of Soviet Russia in the East makes England's balance-of-power role in Europe obsolescent. The once powerful British Empire is all but a thing of the past, and the advantages that accrued to England on the world market because of its early industrialization are less and less pertinent. In sum, England's position in world affairs is now secondary. It has adjusted to its subordinate position in a reasonably satisfactory manner, although the conflicts between old traditions and responsibilities and the nation's current economic problems do not admit of easy solutions.

THE COMMONWEALTH: England knew that the end of World War II also spelled the end of its empire. Too many forces were operating which it could no longer control, even if it wanted to. Nevertheless, many English leaders hoped that the traditional empire would not merely fade away, but would gradually be revamped into a commonwealth of self-governing nations bound to each other and to England by ties of self-interest and tradition. The idea of a commonwealth of nations was formulated during the nineteenth and early twentieth centuries, and it applied first to nations that had been either settled or largely dominated by Europeans, usually of English extraction. England's hopes for a commonwealth were for the most part fulfilled. For in the postwar period, India and other former colonies in Asia and Africa joined the Commonwealth as they obtained

independence, although some members—South Africa, for instance—subsequently withdrew.

The association, however, is an extremely loose one, and the ties of its members, aside from certain elements of economic self-interest, vary with their identification with England. They are comparatively close in Australia and New Zealand, less so in Canada, and much less so in most African and Asian nations. While the idea of a commonwealth undoubtedly helped ease the strain of losing an empire, questions regarding its fundamental viability have been raised more and more frequently. The truth of the matter is that the Commonwealth does not have sufficient cohesion to lend itself to many common policies in world affairs, and Britain is not strong enough or rich enough to dominate it. Even Australia and New Zealand are looking more expectantly to the United States as their guarantor and protector than they are to England. Through the early 1960's, England continued to assume responsibilities for the protection of Asian members—Malaysia, for example—but in 1968 the Labor government decided to phase out most of Britain's military forces in the Far East. Without much question, the links that bind the British Commonwealth together will loosen with gathering speed in the next ten to fifteen years, although cultural and historical affinities will permit England to retain some influence in Australia and New Zealand.

England's loss of empire was assuaged not only by the Commonwealth, but by the special bonds that developed between England and the United States. The basic sources of this close relationship are cultural and linguistic, yet the tacit entente has been enhanced by complex economic arrangements and guarantees. The British postwar economy has weathered several serious crises only because of American aid. The United States still bears the imprint of its original English settlers, and the political elite of the United States still feels a greater identification with England than with other European countries.

From the end of World War II to the present day, the United States has taken over many of England's responsibilities, as the mother country has withdrawn from various areas of the world. While some English intellectuals have resented the predominance of a nation which in the nineteenth century largely followed England's lead, others have welcomed the extension of American power. Whatever criticisms the British may have of American foreign policy today, there are few, outside the Labor Party's extreme left, who can conceive of following courses greatly at odds with those of the United States. The reality of this circumstance was not lost upon de Gaulle, and his umbrage with "les Anglo-Saxons" was not without justification.

FOREIGN ECONOMIC POLICY: England's principal economic problem in the second half of this century has been that of maintaining a sufficient volume of exports in order to pay for the needed imports of food and raw material. During much of this period, the British have been able to bridge the trade gap only with American economic assistance.

England's balance-of-payments problem has been complicated by its being the cornerstone of the sterling bloc. Within the bloc, the free exchange of goods is encouraged, and earnings in gold and dollars are pooled for dealings with outside nations. As a unit, the sterling bloc seeks a balance of trade with the rest of the world, and England serves as its banker; this position helps London remain a center of the banking world, bolsters British prestige, and facilitates a ready exchange of English manufactured goods for raw materials produced in the Commonwealth countries. To improve its position, England has worked hard to encourage investment in bloc countries that are potential dollar earners, such as Malaysia. Yet the condition of the British economy since World War II has been such that little capital has been available for export.

To maintain its trading position, the English government has closely controlled foreign exchange and has tried in numerous ways to encourage the flow of investment into those industries that are likely to manufacture goods salable abroad. The policies of the Wilson Labor government have represented a continuation of this effort—an effort which, unfortunately, has not been fully successful. From time to time, Britain's predicament over its balance of payments has threatened the nation's entire economic and financial structure. It has certainly placed dampers on Labor Party efforts to develop new social programs.

One program designed to improve England's financial position has been the policy of Commonwealth preference. Under the arrangement, Britain and other Commonwealth nations negotiated reciprocal tariff advantages. The objective was to encourage intra-Commonwealth trade and, from the British standpoint, to establish a protected market for manufactured goods in exchange for preferential prices on imported food and raw materials from Commonwealth nations. While this program has not been a total failure, it has proved less and less attractive to its participants: Commonwealth countries, and even the British themselves, have more often than not allowed themselves greater flexibility in trading with non-Commonwealth countries than the program prescribes. Nevertheless, the relation of England to the rest of the Commonwealth has remained an impediment to its joining the Common Market; the British reluctance, for example, to surrender its advantages in obtaining food from Commonwealth nations has never been cordially supported on the Continent.

SECURITY POLICY: With Britain itself no longer capable of maintaining the balance of power on the Continent, one of the prime objectives of its postwar foreign policy was to redress that balance by insuring continued American participation in Western Europe's defense. Thus, American involvement in N.A.T.O. was considered an important diplomatic success. Even so, British attitudes toward the United States have been somewhat ambivalent: the Labor Party, especially its left wing, has always been more conciliatory toward the Soviet Union—and far less indulgent toward Germany—than has the United States. Even the Conservatives have often felt that American anxieties about the spread of communism were a bit obsessive, particularly insofar as China is concerned. The British recognized the new Chinese government almost immediately, and they have been loath ever since to support American policy in Asia.

Despite the dismantling of the British Empire, England continued to wear the trappings of a great power until the middle 1960's. When the maintenance of large-scale traditional military forces was regarded as too expensive, and not really likely to give Britain the status of a great power, it turned to nuclear weapons, exploding its first A-bomb in 1952 to become the third nuclear power in the world. It managed to produce a stockpile of atomic bombs, but before the decade ended, the significance of this achievement was undermined by the realization that it was simply going to be too expensive for Britain to fashion its own system for delivering them. To prepare for the day when ordinary bombers would no longer be sufficient, the British spent a good deal of money trying to develop a ground-to-ground missile system; when Blue Streak, their chief hope in this area, proved too expensive, they arranged to purchase a proposed air-to-ground missile, America's Skybolt, which supposedly would have extended the strategic life of military aircraft. The United States government, however, finally decided not to produce Skybolt, and agreements were then made between the two nations under which England would purchase American missiles designed for Polaris submarines; the British would manufacture the submarines themselves in accordance with American specifications.

The Wilson government has more or less continued to support American foreign policy, albeit with distinct reservations, mostly in connection with American involvement in Vietnam. In active support of United States policy, Wilson has maintained England's tie to N.A.T.O., having refused to consider seriously the alternative of an independent European security program under the aegis of Charles de Gaulle. However, primarily as a result of economic difficulties, it is now rapidly reducing its expenditures on armaments. Indeed, no British government in the immediate future will be able to solve the nation's economic problems unless military expenditures are cut drastically.

4. THE FRENCH PATTERN

THE HISTORICAL BACKGROUND: French foreign policy, like that of England, has exhibited through the centuries certain distinct elements of continuity. Its main objective has always been quite simple: that France must be the principal, if not the predominant, power in Western Europe; the model for many French governments in the nineteenth and twentieth centuries has been taken from Louis XIV or Napoleon. When Europe was the world, this policy meant the establishment of France as a world power of the first rank; with Europe now only a small part of the world, it means creating an independent Europe with France as its leading force.

The self-wrought tragedy faced by France during most of the nineteenth and twentieth centuries was that its power could never match its aspirations. The bloodletting of the Napoleonic campaigns had produced a drop in the French birth rate, and before long other European nations, including Germany, had moved far ahead of France in terms of population. The general culture and social structure of France inhibited industrial development, thereby preventing any development of the kind of muscle that lends more weight to diplomatic strokes. Finally, internal divisions and governmental instability blocked the formulation of consistent long-range policies.

Between 1814 and 1848, France pursued a policy of caution in Europe and at the same time began to build a new colonial empire overseas. To be sure, for the first few years after the defeat of Napoleon, France could have done little else without the fear of foreign intervention. But even after that threat had passed, both Bourbon and Orléans monarchies believed that France's interests were best served by working with the rest of Europe to preserve the post-Napoleonic balance of power.

Under Napoleon III, French foreign policy became somewhat aggressive. Aside from the abortive intervention in Mexico, the emperor sought to extend French influence by supporting liberal nationalist movements and by asserting France's revolutionary image as the defender of national self-determination and the rights of man. He found, however, that in abetting German unification he had helped create a new state with more resources than France. The upshot was the Franco-Prussian War, the temporary loss of Alsace-Lorraine, and the permanent end of the French monarchy. Germany emerged from the war as France's primary European rival—and enemy; that rivalry was to last through two more wars.

In the first years of the Third Republic, France found itself isolated within Europe. The British were uninterested in closer relations, the Russians and Germans had reached a mutual understanding, and the new nation of Italy seemed to be more disposed toward Germany than toward France. Yet by the 1890's, partly because of German ineptness and partly because of French diplomatic finesse, France again found itself an integral part of the European community.

Until the turn of the century, many in France hoped for a Franco-German reconciliation, although most Frenchmen continued to regard Alsace-Lorraine as part of France. By 1900, however, the re-establishment of French leadership in Europe and revenge against Germany had become the two dominant political themes of French governments, and both ideology and the desire to expand France's empire played second fiddle to concern over the German question. Thus,

France was quite willing not only to conclude an alliance with "reactionary" Russia and to encourage French investments in Russia for political purposes, but also to bow to English imperial interests in North Africa for the purpose of securing British friendship. Such would not have been the case had Germany not become France's *idée fixe;* in fact, if rival imperialisms had been the primary source of national conflict before World War I, England and France would have been enemies rather than allies.

World War I was a devastating experience for France. The French were victorious, but only with the aid of Britain and the United States and at a staggering cost in men and resources. France's urge was for revenge; Paris not only wanted to use German resources to rebuild France, it wanted a guarantee that Germany never again would loom as a threat. In the end, however, France could get neither the reparations it wanted nor the assurances it needed about Germany from either the League of Nations or her erstwhile allies, England and America. After attempting a "tough" policy of going it alone, which led to the occupation of the Ruhr in 1923, France turned to other tactics. Domestically, France enlarged its military forces and began constructing fortifications—the Maginot Line—along the German border. She also concluded a series of mutual-defense alliances with the smaller countries of Central and Eastern Europe, which also had reason to fear the Germans.

However bitter, however suspicious, France's attitude toward Germany in the interwar years was not always hostile. As in the decade following the Franco-Prussian War, there were many in France who hoped an accommodation could be reached with the Germans. Under the initiative of Aristide Briand, foreign minister from 1925 to 1932, successive French governments moved gradually toward a policy of reconciliation involving a number of important concessions. These were, on the whole, supported by the left, which hoped that the problems of

Franco-German rivalry might be solved by a new democratic Germany and by European security under the aegis of the League of Nations. Whether or not this could have been the case is difficult to say; the Depression and the rise to power of the Nazis made the question moot.

Once again France faced a Germany of greater manpower, making expansionist noises and having at its disposal an economic potential that could easily be turned into military superiority. As the intentions of the Nazis became clearer, the French became more and more desperate. They did not have the power to act alone; in fact, they were hesitant to act even with English support. The vacillation of the two allies meant, of course, that nothing was done as Germany rearmed and subverted the Versailles settlement. Although there was some awareness that the policy of alliances with the Central and Eastern European countries was largely delusionary, additional alliances were formed; the French also sought to establish a defense arrangement with the Soviet Union. To further complicate France's problem, internal ideological divisions had so rent the nation that diplomatic and defensive maneuverability was disastrously restricted.

The result was, essentially, a passive reaction to Hitler as he expanded his power, increased his territorial control, and insisted that all of Europe submit to his succession of ultimatums. When the facedown came in Poland, the French, even with British aid, were unable to stop the German army. Aside from Germany's greater military strength, France was torn by internal conflicts, sapped by a defeatist attitude on the part of large segments of its population, and hampered by conceptions of military strategy derived from the experience of World War I. As in 1870, the French crumbled before the German attack and went down to a swift, humiliating defeat.

When the war ended, France found itself in a very difficult situation: it had contributed little to Germany's downfall. True, there was

a certain symbolic participation in its own liberation under General de Gaulle, but the Free French had little power and less prestige. The Russians, for example, had no desire to see the French participate in the occupation of Germany; their occupation zone had to be carved out of the British and American zones. The Americans and British were somewhat more sympathetic, but they were inclined to decide basic policy without French advice, a practice that embittered de Gaulle. At this point, the postwar provisional government of de Gaulle returned to the traditional elements in French foreign policy: France must be assured that Germany would remain permanently powerless, and the British or Americans or Russians must guarantee France's future position.

In 1945 de Gaulle believed that the Soviets and the Americans would dominate Europe between them unless a counterforce were established. Assuming that Germany remained in a weakened condition, this counterforce, according to de Gaulle, could only be France—possibly supported by England. The two countries, as the leading nations in Europe, could then mediate between the Soviet and American superpowers. De Gaulle's strategy, however, did not work. The British were more interested in a partnership with the United States, and it very soon became clear that the Soviets were less interested in a permanently weakened Germany than in a united Germany dominated by them.

De Gaulle himself, and certainly the parties that assumed power after he left the provisional government in 1946, saw the Americans as the lesser evil at the time. For one thing, the Soviet danger seemed closer at hand; for another, only the United States could provide the massive aid necessary to get France back on its feet.

French leaders, therefore, were forced to accept American leadership in the cold war, and rehabilitation of West Germany, whether they liked it or not. They joined in the Marshall Plan and the North Atlantic Treaty Organization, and they finally accepted German rearmament, although only after protracted debate and the rejection of a plan for an integrated European Defense Community which, in fact, had first been proposed by the French themselves. Yet during this entire period, from the late 1940's to the mid–1950's, Frenchmen were divided against themselves. While French leadership gave its assent to American strategy, the powerful Communist Party remained strongly hostile to the United States, and most Frenchmen, including the French elite, continued to prefer a foreign policy that would enable France to establish its independence and neutrality against both power blocs. French support of American policy, and subordination of her own policy to it, was, in other words, extremely reluctant.

In the meantime, French relations with Germany were undergoing an extraordinary change. Konrad Adenauer, for one, was convinced that the possible unification of Germany was of less importance than integrating Germany (even as a rump state) with the West; he also believed that the traditional rivalry between Germany and France must end. His policies were oriented toward putting both convictions to practice. In the decade of the 1950's, Franco-German cooperation increased and French fears of Germany diminished, although the French still worried that Germany might come to dominate the European community. This concern mounted as German economic revival proceeded apace.

Postwar France also faced the trauma of decolonization. At the end of World War II, France's aim was the assimilation of its colonies to France itself; together they would form an empire of a hundred million Frenchmen. Such a policy might or might not have been successful if systematically carried out, but it was not; two years after the liberation of Paris, France was engaged in a long and costly conflict in Indochina. The defeat at Dienbienphu was followed by disturbances in Tunisia and Morocco and, finally, by the crisis of Algeria, which threatened to engulf France in a civil war. The leadership of the Fourth Republic tried to handle its colonies' unrest by granting them increased autonomy. In 1956, enabling legislation was passed permitting the government to extend considerable freedom to Madagascar and the African colonies, all of which became semi-independent republics with their own parliaments and executives; France retained jurisdiction over their defense, foreign policy, trade, and education. The Fourth Republic was far less successful in resolving the Algerian crisis; on this issue, in fact, it fell. It may legitimately be argued that the great failure of the Fourth Republic was the same as that of the Third: in foreign policy. In spite of the regime's inadequacies, the French economy had been moving along at a fast clip since the early 1950's; it was in the area of foreign policy, however, that the frequent shifts of governments and the inability to act decisively proved disastrous.

THE END OF THE FRENCH EMPIRE AND THE THIRD WORLD: The Algerian crisis not only led to the collapse of the Fourth Republic, it generated the return to power of Charles de Gaulle, a man who believed that the reassertion of France depended upon the skillful use of traditional (secret) diplomacy, flexibility, and a careful balancing of commitments and real power. It seems likely that when de Gaulle first returned to power he still hoped that France could retain control of Algeria; some time thereafter, however, he decided that France was no longer capable of inhibiting the development of the new nationalism. His response was to cut France loose from the burden of maintaining an empire: the African states were granted what amounted to full independence, and the Algerian conflict was settled in the same way. France, in accordance with Gaullist policy, was to continue exercising its influence in the rest of the world by relying upon cultural ties, economic assistance, and diplomatic maneuver. The possibility of such maneuvers, of course, was enhanced by the competition between the United States and the Soviet Union in the West and between the United States and China in the Far East; many nations, de Gaulle reasoned, would prefer to be assisted by a country that was not tied to either power bloc.

In Africa and Algeria, de Gaulle's policy paid off. French relations with the African states have remained good, and not only has Algeria permitted the testing of French atomic weapons, it has also encouraged French development of its oil resources. In Latin America, France has begun to replace the United States as an arms supplier, and in the Far East, de Gaulle's recognition of China has opened broad trade possibilities, although they have yet to be realized.

De Gaulle was convinced that the United States could not prevail in Vietnam and that his own policies would place France on a solid diplomatic footing in the Far East, particularly with regard to Vietnam once the United States was forced to withdraw from Southeast Asia. In the Middle East, despite strong French sympathies for Israel, he assumed a posture of neutrality between the Arabs and the Israelis, believing that in the end the position of Israel was untenable and that the better part of wisdom called for improving relations with the Arab states. To de Gaulle, the commitment of the United States—and its dependencies, including Britain—to the Israeli cause meant that France would be the only Western European country with cordial relations on both sides of the Middle East conflict.

Georges Pompidou, de Gaulle's successor, is likely to modify these policies somewhat. Moreover, less committed than de Gaulle to a policy of "grandeur," Pompidou is likely to concentrate more on domestic needs. Further, the opinion of the articulate segment of the French population is still strongly pro-Israeli; Pompidou is, therefore, apt to look a bit more benevolently on the Israeli cause. He is also more inclined than de Gaulle to maintain French ties with the United States and to

FIGURE 25.1.   FRENCH ATTITUDES TOWARD MILITARY ALLIANCES

QUESTION: Do you think that in the future France will need allies to defend her security? If so, which countries?

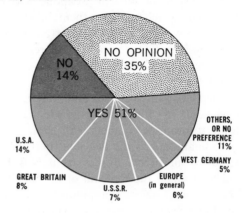

Adapted from *Le Nouvel Observateur*, 153 (October 18–24, 1967), p. 68.

renew better relations with the British. Pompidou's policy changes, however, are not expected to go so far as to compromise France's role of "broker" in the Middle and Far East.

THE NORTH ATLANTIC TREATY ORGANIZATION: As the newly installed president of the Fifth Republic, de Gaulle made it clear that France's independence of action would no longer be hindered by its membership in N.A.T.O. His feeling was that American dominance of the alliance might draw France into a conflict caused by policies over which it had no control; it was America that would ultimately decide whether, when, and how nuclear weapons would be used to protect or "liberate" Europe. And, quite obviously, France did not have the ability to use N.A.T.O. to implement its own policies. De Gaulle did suggest that France would work within N.A.T.O. if the organization were remodeled. What he meant was that N.A.T.O.'s overall world strategy should be set by a triumvirate consisting of the United States, England, and France; all three would share in the determination of such matters as the possible use of nuclear weapons.

When the United States rejected this suggestion, de Gaulle began to direct French policy away from its reliance upon the N.A.T.O. shield. He first moved to create his own stockpile of nuclear weapons and the means with which to deliver them; in addition, he withdrew the French Mediterranean fleet from the N.A.T.O. command and refused to integrate France's air defense with that of N.A.T.O.

The Cuban missile crisis and American involvement in Vietnam, plus de Gaulle's desire to promote contacts with Eastern Europe, finally led to the decision, in 1961, to withdraw all French forces from N.A.T.O. and to demand the removal of all N.A.T.O. forces from France. Pompidou has implied that France wants to continue to be part of the North Atlantic Alliance but one suspects that N.A.T.O. has outlived its usefulness and that it is only a matter of time before it becomes a mere formality. In fact, when the treaty comes up for renewal in 1970, it is quite possible that it will be abrogated, or at least fundamentally transformed.

ENGLAND, GERMANY, AND THE COMMON MARKET: De Gaulle consistently viewed the Common Market as a mechanism for establishing an independent Europe under French leadership; it was partly for this reason that he refused to agree to England's admission and stymied further plans to turn economic integration into effective political integration. In order to use the Common Market for his purposes, de Gaulle had to depend upon the willingness of the Germans to accept the lead of the French. To secure that, France supported the free status of West Berlin, and, on the whole, followed the lead of the West German government in its relations with East Germany.

But de Gaulle had very little interest in German unification, nor was he willing to support the West Germans' endeavor to that end: a divided Germany, he believed, could not easily transform its economic power into

diplomatic influence. France had not much to fear and more to gain from maintaining close relations with only a half of Germany. France's German policies are not likely to change under Pompidou.

THE FUTURE OF FRENCH FOREIGN POLICY: In his early years as president of the Fifth Republic, de Gaulle added immeasurably to French stature and maneuverability. Nonetheless, his more grandiose ambitions for France could never have been realized, and those who follow him in office will have to scale them down. France does not possess the wherewithal to become the dominant power in Europe, or even in Western Europe. All Western European countries, including France, can only hope to regain some of their lost power, especially in relation to the United States and the Soviet Union, by moving closer together. Thus, while de Gaulle did succeed in reducing American influence and in weakening N.A.T.O. almost beyond repair, some of his other policies will sooner or later be reversed: England's admission to the Common Market, for example, will eventually occur because, in general, the French political elite regards England more as a counterweight to a resurgent West Germany than as a force that would radically diminish French power.[5] As for the French public, though it is less and less enthusiastic about its American alliance, it remains attached to the idea of a European association that would include England. In a study completed in 1964, 69 per cent of French voters chose either the continuation of the North Atlantic Treaty Organization or a Western European defense pact, as against only 18 per cent who thought that France should take a neutral stance. Among Communist voters, the first two alternatives were chosen by 53 per cent of the respondents, and the neutralist alternative by only 19 per cent.

[5] See Karl Deutsch, Lewis J. Edinger et al., *France, Germany and the Western Alliance* (New York: Charles Scribner's Sons, Inc., 1967), pp. 57–122.

5. THE GERMAN PATTERN

THE HISTORICAL BACKGROUND: Germany's foreign policy has, to a very considerable extent, been determined by its geographic position in the center of Europe and by the conditions under which national unity was achieved. As a nation, the Second Reich was a latecomer. The unification of Germany had been accomplished mainly through the efforts of the conservative elements in German society, and it was these elements that dominated the nation's life until World War I. Bismarck regarded the Germany that became unified to defeat France in 1871 as fundamentally a satisfied nation; his postwar efforts were dedicated to preserving Germany's gains and the peace of Europe through the maintenance of strong military forces and a diplomacy aimed at continuing the status quo.

But Bismarck's departure from office brought to the surface national aspirations that were much more aggressive. Germany's world position seemed, at least to the new emperor and others among the German elite, poorly out of line with the growth of its population, the success of its industry, and the general flowering of its cultural life. To Kaiser Wilhelm II, Germany was destined, because of its virtues and energies, to replace France as the primary nation on the Continent and to rival England as an imperial power. These ambitions set Germany on a collision course with both France and England, the result of which was its defeat in World War I and the Treaty of Versailles.

To most Germans, the treaty was an "instrument of subjugation." They might have become reconciled to the restoration of Alsace-Lorraine to France, and of Eupen and Malmédy to Belgium. But other aspects of the treaty could not be accepted: German territory and German people in the east were turned over to Poland, and a corridor of Polish territory was created between East Prussia and the rest of the Reich. Germany was deprived of all its colonies, 13 per cent of its prewar territory, about 15 per cent of its arable land, nearly three-fourths of its iron resources, 26 per cent of its hard-coal assets, and 68 per cent of its zinc resources. The treaty also completely demilitarized the country and forced the Germans not only to accept blame for the war but also to accept the military occupation of the allied powers on six per cent of its remaining territory.

With the exception of the Communists, all the major political parties in Germany called for significant revisions of the treaty. Their ultimate objective was the restoration of Germany as a leading European nation; they also wanted the return of Germany's former colonies and the unification of Austria and Germany. The major differences among the parties lay in the techniques that each would use to restore Germany, and in the degree of violence that each employed in assailing the "injustices" perpetrated by the Allies. Almost all Germans wanted to enlarge the army, at least until European security had been attained through an international organization. Statesmen like Walter Rathenau, Karl Joseph Wirth, and Gustav Stresemann sought the goal of German revival through negotiation and compromise. In their eyes, Germany could eventually reassume its rightful place if it followed an intelligent and moderate policy; its natural power and the ultimate reasonableness of British, French, and American statesmen would lead to no other end. This was the center position. The further one moved to the political right, the greater was the distrust of other Western powers and the more fervid became the belief that Germany was surrounded by perfidious and hostile countries. On the extreme right, of course, dreams once more abounded of German hegemony in Europe—based on fantasies of German racial superiority. In the mid-1920's, partly in response to the overtures of Briand, the more moderate tendencies in Germany seemed likely to prevail. The Depression and a series of internal crises, however, led to the triumph of extremism in the person of Adolf Hitler.

In *Mein Kampf,* Hitler had listed as one of the more important objectives of his foreign policy the acquisition of land in the east to afford the German people living space. In his speeches during the 1920's, he cited as among his more immediate goals the abrogation of the Treaty of Versailles and the reestablishment of Germany as one of the ruling powers in the world. It was no surprise to the close observers of German affairs, therefore, that he wasted little time before embarking upon a program to put his ideas into action. Germany withdrew from the Geneva Disarmament Conference and the League of Nations, and rearmament began. In 1935, Hitler explicitly denounced the disarmament clauses of the Versailles Treaty, and universal military training was reintroduced. In March 1936 the German army reoccupied the Rhineland, in violation of the Versailles Treaty and without more than a waved finger from the other European nations. Concurrently, the Nazis moved to establish cordial relations with Italy. Mussolini had previously blocked the intervention of Germany in Austrian politics, but when the Nazis refused to join in sanctions against Italy during its invasion of Ethiopia and then recognized the conquest, the ice was broken and the beginnings of a Rome-Berlin axis were laid.

In 1938 the Germans marched into Austria and established an Anschluss; in the same year, after the threat of a European war, the Nazis obtained the Sudetenland of Czechoslovakia and shortly thereafter participated in the destruction of the Czechoslovak nation. Following close upon these bloodless triumphs, the Lithuanians were forced to cede the territory of Memel, which they had obtained under the Versailles Treaty, and Hitler demanded the right both to incorporate Danzig into the German Reich and to construct an extraterritorial railroad and superhighway across the Polish corridor to connect East Prussia with the rest of Germany.

Finally, after signing a pact with the Soviet Union in which Poland and the Baltic states were divided between the two countries, Hitler prepared to march on Poland. On September 1, 1939, when German troops and the German air force launched their invasion, Hitler still believed that France and England would not risk a general conflagration. His calculation was wrong, however: on September 3, 1939, England and France declared war.

GERMANY SINCE WORLD WAR II—THE ADENAUER PERIOD: In the years immediately following the cessation of hostilities, German political life was dominated by Konrad Adenauer. A Rhinelander and an admirer of France, Adenauer set the course of postwar German foreign policy, a course he adhered to despite substantial opposition. His chief purpose was to have Germany readmitted to the family of nations, more particularly those of Western Europe, with the expectation that Germany might be permitted to become an important as well as a constructive force in the redevelopment and progress of the European continent. To achieve this end, Adenauer knew that a German rapprochement with France was absolutely necessary. In fact, far more than any other European leader, he hoped to see the nations of Western Europe bound together in a supranational organization in which Germany would wield its share of influence.

Adenauer's policy also expressed the belief that Germany and Europe must retain close relations with the United States if they were to have the strength to prevent further Russian penetration. He hoped eventually to unite East and West Germany, but believed that this could be achieved only through a policy of Western unity supported by the United States. Thus, he rejected all suggestions of unification based upon a neutral Germany, believing that the end result would either be a resurgence of German nationalism, with all its well-recognized dangers, or a Communist Germany under the thumb of the Soviet Union.

To have his foreign-policy intentions succeed, Adenauer was prepared to sacrifice a variety of traditional German aspirations. For example, in 1949 he consented, in exchange for Allied agreement to curtail the stripping of German industry and other concessions, to place the Ruhr under an international authority. The Socialist opposition leader Kurt Schumacher was so enraged by this "surrender" that he labeled Adenauer "the chancellor of the Allies"; but the wisdom of the policy became even more apparent when French Foreign Minister Schuman offered the alternative plan of placing all the steel production of Germany and France under a joint authority, thus giving rise to the European Coal and Steel Community.

Later, Adenauer was willing—indeed, anxious—to participate in N.A.T.O. to the extent of rearming Germany, despite the violent opposition that this policy aroused in Germany itself. He also accepted the French plan for an integrated European army under joint command, in which national units would be no larger than regimental size. When the European Defense Community was defeated by the French parliament, however, Germany was permitted to establish an independent national army under N.A.T.O. supervision, with the stipulation that the Germans would not obtain the use of atomic weapons. In further efforts to solidify Franco-German relations, Adenauer was also prepared to sacrifice the Saar, which he agreed to place under an international statute providing for internal autonomy, rather than call for its return to Germany. When a plebiscite was held on the issue in the Saar, he urged voters to support the proposal; nevertheless, it was voted down by a two-thirds majority, and the French then accepted the reincorporation of the Saar into Germany.

The German chancellor was also one of the foremost exponents of the political integration of Europe, and accepted the Common Market with the hope that it would move Europe closer to that goal. Adenauer's conception of an integrated Europe included England, but he was willing to accept de Gaulle's ruling that England should be excluded from the Market. In pushing for European political integration, Adenauer had the endorsement of the vast majority of Germans, especially the youth who, perhaps more than young people in any other European nation, had come to see a united Europe as eminently desirable.

With regard to Berlin and East Germany, Adenauer's policies were comparatively simple. East Germany was to be isolated; Adenauer refused to recognize the German Democratic Republic and, under the so-called "Hallstein doctrine," asserted that Germany would refuse to establish diplomatic relations with any nation that recognized the Communist regime. To him, West Berlin was an economic showcase that served to remind East Germans of the presence of another Germany. The reminder, it turned out, was so vivid to the Communists that they erected the Berlin wall to stop defections; in a sense, therefore, the wall represented a policy defeat for the West German chancellor. Adenauer probably never believed that the territories lost by Germany at the end of World War II would be returned, but for political reasons he never stated his opinion explicitly; instead, his public position was that these matters would have to be disposed of by a final peace treaty.

In the closing years of his chancellorship, Adenauer's carefully constructed foreign policy came under serious strain. De Gaulle's anti-American penchant hindered the continuance of a policy based on Germany's working closely with both France and the United States. Further, evidence that the Kennedy administration was seeking a détente with the Soviet Union and Eastern Europe, which might involve the indefinite postponement or even abandonment of German reunification, raised doubts in the chancellor's mind as to the reliability of his American allies. And the stabilization of the East German regime, especially after the Berlin wall eliminated the flow of refugees, indi-

TABLE 25.1. GERMAN ATTITUDES TOWARD OTHER COUNTRIES

Question: *"With what countries listed below should Germany work closely?"*[1]

Country	1953	1954	1956	1959	1962	1963	1967
France	55%	46%	42%	48%	60%	70%	76%
U.S.A.	83	78	84	81	82	90	72
Great Britain	62	58	39	49	54	65	52
U.S.S.R.	18	22	18	31	22	27	41
Poland	11	11	17	25	22	27	27
Japan	42	35	31	32	31	31	22
Italy	44	34	30	31	36	30	22
Spain	50	42	28	27	27	20	18
Israel	15	13	9	19	18	17	16
Other or no opinion	8	14	11	13	12	3	3

[1] Percentages total more than 100 because more than one country was named.

Source: Lewis F. Gittler, "Probing the German Mind," *Interplay*, I, 3 (October 1967), p. 7. Reprinted by permission of the publisher.

cated that East Germany was not simply going to waste away.

ERHARD AND AFTER: These and other pressures have led to a constant reassessment of German foreign policy in the past several years. The Erhard regime grappled with them in a number of ways, none of which was very successful. Concerned with U.S. détente overtures, Erhard tried to fortify N.A.T.O. by opting for a multilateral nuclear force for European nations under American direction, but the proposal got nowhere. The Germans continued to uphold N.A.T.O. and European integration, although it became more and more difficult to do so without alienating the French; anxious lest its special relationship with France deteriorate and, at the same time, wishing to further European integration, Germany accepted French demands for certain concessions regarding the Common Market, and it did not press too strongly the question of British admission. Fearful that American and French moves toward closer relations with the Soviet Union and Eastern Europe might leave Germany isolated, Erhard maneuvered toward establishing relations with several East European nations, all of which had recognized the German Democratic Republic; he also indi-

cated—but did not say outright—that the settlement made at the end of World War II regarding the boundaries between Germany and Poland was, for all practical purposes, permanent.

These efforts did not allay a growing feeling of malaise at home, which was compounded by a mild economic recession. To many Germans, the slackening of interest in European integration meant the fading of hope for a larger Europe in which Germany could participate as an equal; the gestures toward détente by France and the United States meant that reunification, which the Germans had certainly delayed by joining the Western alliance, might be indefinitely postponed.[6] Within each of Germany's three major parties, more and more demands were advanced for a revision of German policy. It was argued that Germany should set its own course and engage in direct negotiations with Eastern European countries and even with the German Democratic Republic in the hope that some day German unity could be consummated.

This general disillusionment, and the re-

[6] Recent studies indicate a decline in the feeling of Germans that the United States is its most dependable ally. See Table 25.1.

emergence of the German far right in the guise of the N.P.D., helped bring down Erhard's government and open the way for the formation of the Grand Coalition between the Christian Democrats and the Social Democrats. The Kiesinger-Brandt coalition itself moved further in the direction of reconciliation with Eastern Europe's Communist countries, and it also stepped up its efforts to reach some kind of an understanding with East Germany, stopping short of recognition. Diplomatic relations were established with Rumania and Yugoslavia, despite their continued recognition of the East German regime, and the German government not only told the Czechs that the Munich Pact had been abrogated, but also offered to join any government of Eastern Europe, including the Soviet Union, in a mutual statement renouncing the use of force.

Aside from the contacts established with Yugoslavia and Rumania, the coalition's courtship of the satellite nations had scant success. The East Germans refused to respond to Bonn's blandishments; indeed, they intensified their efforts to prevent refugees from escaping to the West and were even more caustic in their attacks on West Germany. The Russian invasion of Czechoslovakia in 1968 was another blow to Germany's own efforts at détente; the Russians accused Bonn of meddling in Czech affairs and went so far as to indicate that they reserved the right to use force against any former Axis state in which the specter of fascism reappeared. Given the attacks the Russians had already leveled against the N.P.D. and their charges that West Germany was tolerating fascism, the threat was received with both anger and anxiety; and the appearance of signs that East Germans were beginning to identify more strongly with their government only added to Bonn's discomfort.

The failure of the Grand Coalition's conciliation attempts did not deter the Brandt government from immediately moving even further toward a rapprochement with Eastern Europe. It has explicitly recognized the territorial integrity of East Germany, and it has

laid the Hallstein Doctrine to rest. Moscow has responded to these initiatives with a certain cautious friendliness, but the German Democratic Republic has remained distinctly cool.

Whether Brandt will be successful in finding a basis for accommodation with Eastern Europe, while still tied to Western Europe and the United States, is open to doubt. It is a policy that is certainly dependent upon forces beyond the control of the new Bonn regime.

6. THE RUSSIAN AND SOVIET PATTERN

RUSSIAN FOREIGN POLICY:[7] Like that of other nations, Russia's foreign policy has been determined, at least in part, by its geographic position. From the fifteenth to the nineteenth centuries, Russia's rulers expanded their empire eastward until it reached the Pacific Ocean and came into direct confrontation with China and Japan. In the West, their objectives were to weaken or destroy nations that threatened their borders, such as Poland; to incorporate peoples of the same ethnic stock, such as the Ukrainians and Byelorussians; and to subjugate other smaller groups, such as the Lithuanians and Latvians, who could serve as buffers against expansionist European states. Historically, the Russians have been very much interested in making sure that the states along their western border—the modern states of Finland, Poland, Czechoslovakia, Hungary, and Rumania, as well as Bulgaria—were under the control of friendly regimes. It has also been to Russia's interest that it have access to the North and Mediterranean seas—hence Russia's activity in the Baltic area, its drive south to the Black Sea, and its traditional animosity toward Turkey.

Russia's aspirations have also included, from a very early date, the protection of other Slavic people on its borders, and of

7 The analysis in this section is based upon Cyril E. Black, "The Pattern of Russian Objectives," in Ivo J. Lederer, ed., *Russian Foreign Policy* (New Haven: Yale University Press, 1962), pp. 3–38.

Christian peoples against Moslem—especially Turkish—threats. Finally, Russia's efforts, as manifested during the nineteenth century, were aimed at establishing itself as a major European land power, the ally of other monarchies against the threat of liberalism and radicalism.

Russia entered World War I with great hopes for expansion into Europe. There were those in the czarist entourage who saw Russia replacing Germany as the leading power in Central Europe. When the Romanov regime fell, this goal was abandoned, at least for the time being. The Kerensky Socialists and many liberals were prepared to grant independence to both Poland and Finland, and they favored the transformation of the Russian Empire into a federal republic. Like liberal democrats and moderate Socialists elsewhere, they envisaged a European political system founded on national self-determination and representative government. The Russian Revolution aborted their efforts and brought about an entirely new phase in Russian foreign policy.

SOVIET FOREIGN POLICY UNDER LENIN AND STALIN: The Bolshevik Party had some very uncomplicated ideas on the future pattern of international relations—namely, that with the coming of the world Socialist Revolution such relations would cease to exist. Mutually hostile states would be replaced by a world of fraternal Communist states and, finally, by a world state. When the Bolsheviks subsequently recognized that their initial vision was, at the very least, premature, they were still determined that Russia's foreign policy would be unique in any event. The Soviet Union would not engage in traditional diplomacy; rather, it would function as the spearhead of revolution around the world. Soviet Russia was to be the dynamic motherland of socialism.

Even this vision was to undergo adjustments as time went on. Marxist-Leninist ideology for interpreting the world might be operative on the most abstract level, but it was not precisely applicable to immediate global realities. As a national state in a world of national states, the Soviet Union had to enter into diplomatic negotiations, and in order to survive economically and politically, it sometimes had to play down its support of other Communist parties. The nation still confronted the same old geopolitical problems, such as access to warm-water ports, that had faced all Russian governments since the time of Peter the Great. Further, the identification of Russian security with the Revolution was transformed by degrees into the identification of traditional Russian policy aims with the Revolution. The dialectic between ideology and historic geopolitical goals in the formulation of foreign policy is still going on in the Soviet Union, with every indication that the purely ideological component has diminished in importance, even though it continues to influence the overall direction of foreign policy. The fact of the matter is that Soviet experience in world affairs has helped erode Marxist-Leninist ideology. In the domestic sphere, the gap between ideology and reality could be papered over by stepping up the amount of force used on the population. The international arena proved much less tractable, and far more quickly than in other areas, the U.S.S.R. was obliged to adjust its behavior to some of the realities of international politics.

To Lenin and his followers, the first foreign-policy task was to take Russia out of the war. The nations fighting it were rival imperialist powers, between whom there was no real choice; whatever temporary losses of territory might result from surrendering to the Germans would soon be nullified, for revolution in the capitalist countries was imminent. The strength of the Bolshevik commitment to this ideological perspective is indicated by an event that occurred in 1918.[8] A British force had entered Murmansk to safeguard from the Germans cer-

8 The following description of the incident and the quotations are taken from George Kennan's book, *Russia and the West Under Lenin and Stalin* (Boston: Atlantic–Little, Brown, 1960), pp. 74–79.

tain military supplies that had been sent to the Russian government. The head of the local soviet, one Yuryev, cooperated with British troops as the "lesser of two evils," to the dismay and anger of Lenin and Foreign Commissar Georgi Chicherin, who charged Yuryev with being a tool of the imperialists and threatened him with dire consequences. To one of these attacks Yuryev replied manfully:

Comrade, has life not taught you to view things soberly? You constantly utter beautiful phrases, but not once have you told how to go about realizing them. . . . If you know a way out of our condition please tell it to us. . . . We ourselves know that the Germans and the Allies are imperialists, but of two evils we have chosen the lesser. . . .

Needless to say, Moscow was only further enraged, and when Bolshevik troops finally entered the city, the leader of the soviet and those who had followed him were executed.

With the relative consolidation of Soviet power and the end of the war, Lenin turned immediately to what he considered his next most pressing task, the encouragement of revolutionary upheavals in other parts of Europe. To this end, he sponsored a new international organization of Socialist parties, the Third International or Comintern. According to Lenin, the Second International had fatally compromised itself by failing to oppose the war; moreover, the traditional Socialist parties of Europe were either unable or unwilling to promote revolutionary action.

The first congress of the new international was held in 1919 and the second in 1920; at the latter a 21-point program was adopted to which all Socialist parties desiring membership had to adhere. Perhaps the two most important requirements in the program were that all members develop underground organizations to prepare for the revolution, and that all Socialist parties operate on the basis of decisions made by the Comintern centered in Moscow. In other words, the Bolshevik Party of the Soviet Union was to serve as the model and guide for other Socialist parties. The upshot of these rigid directives was the splintering of Socialist parties in most European countries, with the more radical groups joining the Third International.

Under the program adopted, the Comintern should have been the chief international policy-making body for Communist movements all over the world; indeed, at one point Lenin himself had expected that when the revolution occurred in Germany, the more advanced German party would join the Russian party in deciding Comintern policy. However, the expected revolution in Germany did not take place, and the Soviet Union thus remained the only "true" Socialist state. As such, it was natural for it to assume direction of the new international organization. Besides, the Comintern was located in Moscow, and the Soviet leaders felt unmistakable pride in their own success. Even if their prestige had not been so great, the financial support they could offer other parties and the refuge they could provide for party members in other countries would have assured their international position.

Further, the failure of the Communist revolution to spread throughout Europe led Lenin and other Bolsheviks to fear that the capitalist nations would try to destroy the new regime. To prevent this, until the Soviet Union was strong enough to defend itself, it was imperative that traditional diplomatic methods be employed. Therefore, the regime adopted a policy of playing off the capitalist countries against each other until the day when, disabled by their internal contradictions and the subversive activities of the Socialist revolutionaries, they collapsed.

George F. Kennan has summarized the attitude of the Soviet leaders toward the capitalist states as follows:

We despise you. We consider that you should be swept from the earth as governments and physically destroyed as individuals. We reserve the rights . . . to do what we can to bring this about: to revile you

*publicly, to do everything within our power
to detach your own people from their loyalty
to you . . . to subvert your armed forces, and
to work for your downfall in favor of a
Communist dictatorship. But since we are
not strong enough to destroy you today . . .
we want you . . . to finance us; we want you
to give us the advantages of full-fledged diplomatic recognition. . . .*

*An outrageous demand? Perhaps. But you
will accept it nevertheless. You will accept
it because you are not free agents, because
you are slaves to your own capitalistic appe-
tites. . . . In the blindness that characterizes
declining and perishing classes, you will wink
at our efforts to destroy you, you will compete with one another for our favor.*[9]

This is not, as Kennan points out, an extreme statement of the Soviet view, for it
can be copiously documented. Nor was it
merely a reaction to overt capitalist hostility.
The Communist attitude was formed on the
basis of internal Russian experiences and a
self-contained ideology. To the Bolsheviks,
any action by capitalist states was suspect;
their overt hostility merely confirmed Bolshevik suspicions. Capitalist policies which
seemed friendly on the surface concealed
either cupidity or impotence. No matter what
policies had been followed by other nations,
however, the Bolsheviks' faith in their own
system could never have been shaken. To
be sure, the capitalist states were hostile, but
their hostility was expressed sporadically,
and even then in a disjointed way. Most of
them were too busy with internal affairs to
mount, or to seriously contemplate mounting, a full-scale offensive against the new
regime.

The Soviet regime did succeed in establishing commercial relations with a number
of European countries in the early 1920's,
and it did receive some foreign assistance.
But this interchange was limited by the general feeling in the West, not only that the

regime would renege on its obligations (it
had, after all, canceled all war debts), but
that a system of government which ignored
the sanctity of private property could not
survive. The establishment of commercial
relations, foreign assistance aside, did create
problems for the Soviet Union. The continuance of overt hostility and subversion
could well lead to reactions so unfavorable
that the more urgent needs of the nation
would be undercut. Thus, from time to time
policies beneficial to revolutionary activity
in various countries had to be muffled; in
Germany, for instance, plans for a Communist coup in Saxony and Thuringia in 1923
were coolly received by Moscow, and the
effort failed; the lack of Soviet enthusiasm
may have resulted from a realistic estimate
of the situation, but more likely it was
prompted by a *raison d'état*. Certainly, Moscow's needs were paramount in 1927, when
a strike by German workers against arms
shipments was called off because some of
the arms were going to the Soviet Union.

It was fairly easy to justify this pragmatism, especially when Stalin came to power.
As the 1928 congress of the Comintern noted:

*In view of the fact that the U.S.S.R. is the
only fatherland of the international proletariat, the principal bulwark of its achievements and the most important factor for its
international emancipation, the international
proletariat must on its part facilitate the success of the work of socialist construction in
the U.S.S.R., and defend it against the attacks of the capitalist Powers by all the
means in its power.*[10]

Stalin put it even more strongly:

*A revolutionary is he who, without eva-
sions, unconditionally, openly and honestly
. . . is ready to uphold and defend the
USSR. . . .*

An internationalist is he who uncondi-

---

[9] *Ibid.*, p. 184.

[10] From "The Programme of the Communist International," in Emil Burns, ed., *A Handbook of Marxism*
(New York: International Publishers, 1935), p. 1022.

tionally, without hesitation and without provisos, is ready to defend the USSR because the USSR is the base of the revolutionary movement, and to defend the advance of this movement is impossible without defending the USSR.[11]

In effect, then, the interests of the U.S.S.R., as perceived by the U.S.S.R., were supreme —and indivisible from those of the world proletariat.

While Soviet foreign policy centered on Europe, events in Asia were attracting attention too. A nationalist revolution was erupting in China, where a nascent Communist Party had also come into existence. Soviet advisers and funds were sent to the Chinese Communist Party, as well as to Chiang Kai-shek's Kuomintang. The Communists were urged to cooperate with the Kuomintang, and at the same time to work within it to awaken the class consciousness of Chinese workers. In 1926, Trotsky, already virtually without power, argued against this course as opportunistic, and when Chiang turned on the Communists and massacred thousands of them Trotsky was vindicated. It did him little good, however; Stalin merely appropriated Trotsky's policies and proceeded to consolidate his own power.

The Chinese experience, together with events in Europe, produced a change in Comintern strategy. Under the slogan "class against class," Communist parties all over the world were ordered to stop collaborating with nationalist bourgeois parties and social democrats. Henceforth, they would confront them openly as tools of "bourgeois Fascist reaction." In China, the Communist Party was urged to organize the working class and to rise up against the Kuomintang. In Europe, the new policy meant collaboration with right-wing forces for the joint purpose of destroying the Weimar regime. From the Communist viewpoint, the sooner the republic was discarded, the sooner a

Communist revolution would take place; and once the workers faced naked, unadorned "bourgeois reaction," they would turn quickly to communism.

In both China and Germany, the policy had catastrophic results. The Chinese Communist Party was decimated. Only a remnant survived, fleeing to the interior and later rebuilding its cadres with peasants. By 1935 Mao Tse-tung has assumed leadership of the party and was engaged in guerrilla warfare against Nationalist Chinese forces; Stalin thought Mao's idea of relying upon peasants to achieve the Communist revolution was absolutely wrong and saw little prospect of a Communist victory in China. In Germany, the Weimar Republic had indeed fallen, but contrary to Stalin's expectations it was replaced by a National Socialist regime that instantly wiped out the German Communist Party. Fascist movements were also gaining strength elsewhere.

It was after the impact of these setbacks— and partly because of the prodding of militants in the French Communist Party, by then the leading party outside Russia—that Stalin and the Comintern executed an about-face. A new policy was inaugurated, that of the Popular Front: Communists would collaborate with the Socialists and progressive elements of the bourgeoisie in a "popular front" against the Fascist threat. At roughly the same time, fearful of the growing power of fascism in both Germany and Japan, the Soviet Union joined the League of Nations. The Popular Front, while it had elements that were sound in theory, failed to work out in practice. The Communists continued to infiltrate other groups, thereby antagonizing them, and their support of the Blum government in France helped alienate large segments of the population. The demise of the Popular Front was precipitated by the Spanish Civil War, which further polarized French politics.

Later came the setback of the Munich Agreement. Without even consulting the Russians, France and England accepted German terms for the dismemberment of Czechoslo-

11 J. V. Stalin, *Sochineniya* (Moscow, 1949), X, 61. Quoted in Vernon V. Aspaturian, "Moscow's Foreign Policy," *Survey*, 65 (October 1967), p. 44.

vakia. The two allies felt they could do little else: they were unwilling to face Germany alone, and no Eastern European nation would allow Russian troops to cross its territory to aid the Czechs. Russian promises of assistance, therefore, had little relevance. Whether Stalin was ready or even anxious to give such assistance is a moot point; evidence indicates that he saw the need of preserving what strength Russia had just then, having become more convinced than ever that both the French and the British hoped to turn Germany against the Soviet Union.

When the Polish crisis finally erupted, British and French statesmen did turn to Moscow. But by then their overtures were too late: Stalin was not interested, either in a mutual-assistance treaty or in helping the Poles, who had no real desire for Soviet aid in the first place. What he was interested in was time and space, time to continue building up the Russian army and space to serve as a buffer between Nazi Germany and the Soviet border. His interest became startlingly apparent with the signing of a nonaggression pact with Hitler. It was the end of Poland— and of peace. The pact divided Poland and the Baltic states between Russia and Germany: thus Hitler got his half of Poland and Stalin his. Latvia and Lithuania, among other territories, were also incorporated into the Soviet state. Within two years, the alliance had disintegrated. Europe, except for England, was at Hitler's feet, and he decided to extend his dominion to the East by subduing Russia. The attack brought Russia and England into alliance, and six months later the United States entered the war against the Axis powers.

For a time during the war, there was some hope that when it was over the three Allies would also collaborate on the peace. This hope, however, had been pretty well dashed by the time the war ended. Russian armies had poured into Eastern Europe and, after liquidating—or, in the case of Poland, permitting the Germans to liquidate—substantial

portions of their possible opposition, the Russians took steps to insure the emergence of Communist regimes subordinate to Moscow. Faced with what appeared to be a Soviet move to create a Communist Europe, the United States launched a policy to "contain" further Soviet expansion. The Truman Doctrine, the Marshall Plan, and the formation of the North Atlantic Treaty Organization were all a part of the strategy directed toward containment.[12]

With the United States and Western Europe joined in cooperative resistance to further Communist encroachments, the Soviet leadership moderated its actions and turned to the twofold task of consolidating its control over its satellite nations in Eastern Europe and rebuilding its ravaged country. But the prime item on the leadership's agenda was to build a nuclear deterrent, lest the temporary nuclear superiority of the United States tempt it to destroy the Soviet Union. By 1949, the Soviet Union had exploded its first atomic bomb. Then, too, the consolidation of Eastern Europe was complete; not only had non-Communist elements been weeded out of the Eastern European nations, but massive purges had eliminated the existing Communist leaders, mostly Jewish, and brought to power more "reliable" elements.

Russia's triumphs in consolidating Eastern Europe and entering the atomic age were accompanied by a swift recovery from the

---

[12] In recent years a debate over the origins of the cold war has been resumed in the United States, with some authors insisting that the American response was excessive and that, for one reason or another, Soviet intentions were misread. My own feeling is that without an American response, the Russians would have achieved in Western Europe what, in fact, they achieved in Eastern Europe. For some of the recent literature on the cold war see George F. Kennan, *Memoirs, 1925–1950* (Boston: Atlantic–Little, Brown, 1967); Louis J. Halle, *The Cold War as History* (London: Chatto & Windus, 1967); Gar Alperovitz, *Atomic Diplomacy: Hiroshima and Potsdam* (New York: Simon & Schuster, 1965); Gabriel Kolko, *The Politics of War: The World and U.S. Foreign Policy* (New York: Random House, 1969); Arthur Schlesinger, Jr., "Origins of the Cold War," *Foreign Affairs*, 46 (October 1967), pp. 22–52, and "Origins of the Post-War Crisis," *Journal of Contemporary History*, 3 (April 1968), pp. 217–252.

war—an economic success abetted by resources acquired in East Germany and other
European nations, especially Czechoslovakia
and Poland. In only one area was Soviet
policy foiled: the Yugoslav Communist
Party, which had achieved power through
its own efforts, rebelled against Soviet moves
to dominate it and, with the support of the
United States, broke away from the Soviet
bloc. Despite signs that Stalin was beginning
to think along new lines, the Kremlin made
very few adjustments in its postwar foreign
policy until after the dictator's death. The
Soviet Union indulged in a number of probes
in Europe to test the response of both Europeans and Americans, but it never pressed
them to the point of no return. Like the
United States, it also continued its buildup of
arms, particularly missiles and the more destructive forms of atomic weapons.

Under Khrushchev, Soviet foreign policy
became somewhat less rigid. Although he
engaged in adventures that Stalin might not
have contemplated, such as the Berlin wall
and missiles for Cuba, and although his
policies were marked by erratic shifts and
occasional backtracking, his actions were
the result of a new Soviet assessment of
world conditions. Obviously, the Soviets
now considered themselves strong enough to
deter an attack from the United States.

On the whole, his policy modifications demonstrated less truculence and a sharper awareness of world realities. Despite his repression
of the Hungarian uprising in 1956, Khrushchev's emphasis upon de-Stalinization at
home was eventually applied to the countries
of Eastern Europe, which gradually were
able to assert a modicum of independence.
Soviet leaders had also come to the conclusion that since a major war was unthink-
able and revolution in Europe was unlikely,
changes in the status quo were more apt to
occur through traditional diplomatic procedures. Furthermore, it was decided that
those forces within the United States which
accepted the idea of conducting the contest
between the Soviet Union and the capitalist

countries in a peaceful manner should be
encouraged. As a world power, Russia was
plainly becoming more sensitive to world
opinion and less inclined (despite the Cuban
gamble) to jeopardize its gains through precipitous action. Khrushchev and those around
him were still convinced, of course, that ultimately the world would consist of a commonwealth of Communist nations, but they
were now less prone to use force to gain that
end and more likely to tolerate minor re-
buffs, even from Eastern European nations,
without attempting repressive action. The
Khrushchev regime was also anxious to extend its influence as a great and responsible
world power, albeit a Communist power, to
non-Communist nations in the so-called
"third world" of Africa, Latin America, and
Asia; it was these nations that might some-
day become Communist, but in the meantime there was no reason not to deal with
their established governments on a regular
basis. Despite its continued willingness to
lend verbal and financial support to Communist revolutionary efforts, the Soviet Union
under Khrushchev had begun to develop a
vested interest in international order.

Complicating the change in the Soviet outlook was the developing conflict, exacerbated
by Khrushchev's personal style, with the
People's Republic of China. The schism
would have occurred even under other leadership, as Khrushchev's successors discovered, for the sources of hostility run deep.
The victory of the Communists in China
came largely through their own efforts and
in spite of Stalin's advice. The Communist
Chinese saw no reason to accept Khrushchev, or Russia for that matter, as the
leader of the Communist camp. There is,
in fact, reason to suspect that their attraction to a radical variety of communism has
been partly related to their desire to establish themselves as the most advanced nation
in the world, and, thus, to reassert their traditional superiority over the "barbarians."
In their eyes, the Kremlin's refusal to sacrifice more for a fellow Communist state and

its caution in foreign affairs are signs of bourgeois revisionism. Then, too, Russia's and China's long-standing frictions over adjacent territories have not been softened by the fact that they are both Communist states.

The Brezhnev-Kosygin regime has more or less followed the foreign policies of Khrushchev, although somewhat more cautiously. Initially, the duumvirate tried to heal the breach with China, but its efforts failed as, indeed, they were destined to do. Soviet relations with Eastern European countries have evolved in the direction of greater autonomy, despite the Czechoslovak example. What the suppression of the liberal Prague regime of Alexander Dubcek demonstrated was that this autonomy could, in Moscow's view, be carried too far—that there were limits to the Kremlin's "tolerance." Certainly the Brezhnev-Kosygin regime is more cautious than Khrushchev's; even so, the Soviet Union can no longer easily exploit the economies of the Eastern European countries for its own purpose—nor, in 1969, could it quite forbid the reception in one of them of the United States president.

The Soviet Union today is still poised between its desire to limit world violence and maintain itself as a world power and its general sympathy with revolutionary movements of the left. Its split with China has contributed to the erosion of a Marxist world view which assumed that relations between Communist states must, of necessity, be friendly. The problem is further complicated by Moscow's continued desire to be the symbolic leader of the world Communist movement; if it is not to find that

leadership seriously weakened by the Chinese challenge, it must at least appear to support foreign revolutions. As for a détente with the West, movements toward any such accommodation are hampered not only by Chinese derision and the Soviet invasion of Czechoslovakia, but by a United States that regards Communist revolutions, especially when aided by the Soviet Union, as regressive. They are also hampered by the fact that the present regime, like that of Stalin, partially justifies its function in Soviet society by claiming to be surrounded by enemy capitalist states.

Within the Soviet leadership there are undoubtedly those who urge a harder and more "revolutionary" line against the capitalist nations of the world. Undoubtedly, too, there are also those who argue for a policy of accommodation with the West, others who continue to hope that an agreement can be reached with China, and still others who would like to settle differences with the United States because of their fears of Chinese aggressiveness. The battle between these factions and the future course of Soviet policy will be affected *in part* by events within the Soviet Union itself; *in part* by American policy; *in part* by what happens in other countries, including China; and *in part* by accidental factors such as personality. It is still possible to conceive of the Soviet Union reverting to a more militant foreign policy, and even coming to terms with the Communist Chinese. It is equally possible to conceive of the Soviet Union and the capitalist nations of the West reaching an accommodation. Either way, events of the next five or ten years will have momentous consequences for all of mankind.

part VI   SOME CONCLUSIONS:

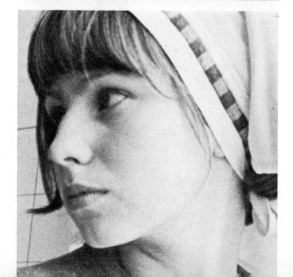

THE FUTURE OF EUROPEAN POLITICS

26

The Future

of European

Politics

Any attempt to predict the future development of European society and politics is an extremely hazardous undertaking, and the wise man, like the Delphic oracle, will couch his prognostications in language which is sufficiently ambiguous to allow several interpretations. Nevertheless, a careful examination of what is occurring today in the three Western European nations studied in this volume would have to prompt the conclusion that they are becoming more and more alike. Their cultural and structural variations are declining, and they are, increasingly, responding in the same way to the same stimuli. This convergence is partly the result of the social changes generated by advanced industrialization; yet it stems as well from the revolutions in transportation and in mass communications. And unless something happens that is as extraordinary as it is unforeseen, this trend is likely to continue; I strongly suspect that it will eventually lead to greater economic and even political unity.

Certain other trends also seem irreversible. Barring a nuclear war, poverty should be eliminated in all major European countries in the next twenty or thirty years, income inequality among the social strata will be reduced, and the state's social-welfare functions will be considerably expanded. The state will also assume far more responsibility for national and urban planning, for two reasons: new demands will force the community to reorganize its resources in order to provide for a better social environment, and the arts, education, and leisure will come to replace the production of goods as individual and community goals.[1] Trends toward income equality will accelerate because of the redistributive effects of social policies, and because the demand for unskilled labor will outreach the supply. Discussions of automation tend to assume that it will eliminate unskilled jobs; what is far more likely to happen is that it will reduce the availability of middle-level, white-collar positions and call forth sizable wage increases

[1] The need for a comprehensive set of social indicators that will enable us to engage in meaningful social and economic planning is discussed in *Social Intelligence for America's Future*, edited by Bertram Gross (Boston: Allyn and Bacon, Inc., 1969).

for the menial tasks that still have to be done by manual workers.

It is also difficult to escape the conclusion that the major productive assets of the community will ultimately come under public ownership. I do not foresee the emergence of a Socialist society in the Marxist sense in the near future. Certain forms of property —homes, for example—will undoubtedly remain in private hands; and I cannot conceive of a society without conflict and hence without the need for political authority. What I do foresee in the next one hundred years, however, is the end of a capitalist market economy in most European countries.[2]

One reason for the decline in the capitalist market system is, as I have just mentioned, not only the dwindling importance of material goods and the advancement of those sectors of the economy concerned with providing services, but the growing influence of a professional class in education, science, and the arts that has little stake in the existing system of productive relationships. A second reason lies in the need to control future technology in the interest of a rationally planned environment. In the past, technological development has proceeded largely on the basis of estimates of consumer demand and marketability by individual, privately controlled enterprises. This is still true in Western Europe, even though the governments are becoming more and more responsible for the creation of new technologies. Uncontrolled technological development is, of course, no longer feasible; the world has become too interdependent and its technology too advanced. Until recently, the negative ecological side effects of new industrial or consumer products could be largely ignored—or, perhaps, corrected after the fact. In the future, the community will have to control the development of such products, taking into account

their possible repercussions on the social organization of the community and its natural environment. For instance, the unplanned growth of automobile production and use has yielded not only high levels of air pollution but national transportation grids that are extremely inefficient. All advanced societies will have to plan transportation networks, determine what kind of vehicles will be produced and in what numbers, and control or at least direct technological innovation in this field.

A third reason for the decline of the capitalist market system is that wages and profits will eventually no longer serve as the spur for fulfilling those tasks which must be completed if the community is to survive. As recent developments have already begun to indicate, segments of the population of technologically advanced societies have ceased to be motivated by the desire for more money; this trend is likely to accelerate in those societies which guarantee at least a minimum level of welfare for all their members. Other forms of incentives, then, will have to be developed. Positions in industrial management will have to offer, for example, the promise of direct community service rather than mere income, something which is extremely difficult to do in a capitalist economic system. For the fact is that a large middle class has been created for which the acquisition of material goods is less central than it was for an earlier generation. The "dirty" jobs of the community may have to be fulfilled on the basis of compulsory requirements for public service, such as some form of compulsory national service corps. The creation of European welfare states, the products themselves of affluence, has reduced the force of economic imperatives which drove people to work at these "dirty" jobs. The decline of capitalism in Europe will stem, not as Marx thought, from its inability to deal with the problem of poverty, but rather from its success in having coped with it.

The future, in short, will require increased

[2] Some of this analysis derives from Robert Heilbroner, *The Limits of American Capitalism* (New York: Harper & Row, 1965); I should add that I disagree with Heilbroner on a number of points.

national and even international planning and control if new problems are to be dealt with effectively. New methods for gathering, processing, and communicating information, too, will become necessary, and more effective forms of organization will have to be created. Without much question, what this will entail is increasing bureaucratization.

There are some who see in these developments the threat of an increasingly dehumanized, computer-run society, in which opportunities for initiative and self-development are curtailed. They feel that this trend toward bureaucratization must and can be thwarted by restoring "community control," by decentralizing government functions. Both their assumptions and their conclusions seem dubious. In densely populated, extremely complex, technologically advanced societies, there is simply no substitute for bureaucratic organizations. However, the fact that these organizations must have a structure of authority does not mean that they must be authoritarian or highly centralized; indeed, the big bureaucracies of today are already allowing greater individual freedom. There is also ample evidence that modern societies are more tolerant of individual deviation, and that they offer a wider range of opportunities than any societies of the past.[3] This tolerance is likely to grow, although there is some question as to just how far it can go without resulting in social disorganization.

The gradual development of planned Socialist economies in most Western European nations will probably come about without major revolutionary upheavals led by workers, or any other class or group. Indeed, there is every likelihood that the transition will, on the whole, involve less ideological heat than was generated during the period of industrialization, despite the

current wave of ideological fermentation, violence, and counterviolence among students. I am rather less sanguine at this point about the capacity of the United States to deal with these emerging social and economic problems, for they are complicated by a race issue which may prove more intractable than the problem of social class has in Europe.

The dominant role that the government will come to assume in both economic planning and social planning will require the establishment of a new balance between individual rights and community needs. I see no great difficulty here. For the foreseeable future, I do not think that traditional parliamentary forms will be replaced, although they may be supplemented by other institutions. Proposals for legislative chambers based on functional representation have a long history and some form of representation of this kind may be put into effect in the future. Technocrats will come to exert more and more influence on the making of policy, but there is every reason to expect that they can be held in check; it seems likely, for instance, that legislators will seek more assistance from experts and that a greater number of lawmakers will be drawn from professions other than law. Of course, the Western European population itself is becoming more knowledgeable on public-policy matters and, as income and educational levels rise, better able to express opinions on what it wants. This trend will continue, and along with it a general rise in the level of active political participation. Our ability to educate is advancing with each new decade, and we may be on the verge of breakthroughs in the biological sciences that will revolutionize man's capacity to learn. One social scientist has spoken of the affluent society as the "knowledgeable" society,[4] and I think the appellation not unreasonable. Thus, I do not see the need for the replacement of democratic participation in Western

---

[3] Bertram Gross, *The Managing of Organizations,* 2 vols. (New York: The Free Press, 1964), pp. 280–409 and pp. 807–837, and Victor C. Ferkiss, *Technological Man* (New York: George Braziller, 1969), pp. 3–100.

[4] Robert Lane, "The Politics of Consensus in an Age of Affluence," *American Political Science Review,* 59 (December 1965), pp. 874–895.

Europe by an intellectual "meritocracy" of one kind or another.[5] Nor do I fear or hope this will happen.

I do expect continuing changes in the party systems of European nations. The age of the disciplined mass party seems to be passing. While bureaucratic party organizations will continue to fulfill certain functions, they will be more easily bypassed by candidates who can temporarily mobilize groupings of middle-class activists and effectively use the mass media. Indeed, personal charisma, albeit of a different type than we have known hitherto, seems likely to become an even more important criterion for political advancement. There are, of course, dangers in this development. Political leaders of this stamp tend to draw upon intense emotional commitments, and their failure to satisfy aspirations can lead to volatile alternations between "love" and "hate" that are hardly conducive to social stability.

On the other hand, I do not foresee the development of any pure form of "participatory" democracy, as defined by the "New Left." Modern society is too complex for a return to the kind of direct democracy that once characterized New England towns, even if such a return should be desirable. Any conceivable society, in the near future at least, will require a structure of authority if any decisions are to be made at all; the disappearance of authority would result, not in greater democracy, but in the release of anarchic violence, followed by domination by men wielding naked power until a new system of legitimate authority is created. Those intellectuals who believe that complete personal autonomy can be combined with both a heightened sense of community and the mak-

ing of more effective societal decisions in the contemporary world are deceiving themselves.

To make predictions about the Soviet Union is even riskier. I am convinced, however, that Russia will experience many of the same slow transformations that will occur in England, France, and West Germany. We can expect increasing professionalization, greater sophistication and objectivity in the social sciences, somewhat more tolerance for the expression of critical opinions, and, eventually, the evolution of a pluralistic society with democratic or polyarchic features. The transformation will not come about overnight. Nor, in all probability, will it be made smoothly; rather, it seems most likely that the Soviet political elite will experience a protracted but inexorable decay in its self-assurance, accompanied by concessions to dissenters. Probably these concessions will occur cyclically: the regime will loosen its controls ever so slightly in the hope that the people will behave "reasonably"—and then clamp down as dissent becomes far more pervasive than can be safely tolerated. At some point, the leadership's move to restore more repressive policies will backfire; the erosion of its authority will have gone too far. At that time, a period of national disorder, great or minimal, will commence as Soviet citizens learn to breathe in a more open society. The primary force behind this turn toward a libertarian direction will probably come from professional groups and students.

I do not foresee any possibility of the Soviet Union reverting to capitalism, despite Chinese polemics. It is possible that, for a time, certain forms of private initiative may be encouraged and that foreign investment may be permitted. But control over the nerve centers of the nation's economy will remain in the hands of the community at large. Yet a swing does seem likely toward a more "individualistic" orientation—one which will give citizens broader opportunities to own homes and such durables as automobiles.

[5] Both utopians and anti-utopians have viewed the future as involving rule by a technological elite. A positive view of such a society is given by B. F. Skinner, *Walden Two* (New York: Macmillan, 1962); a negative view, by Aldous Huxley, *Brave New World* (New York: Harper, 1932). A computerized, bureaucratic, dehumanized society is one of the fears expressed by the so-called New Left, in both Europe and the United States.

There is also a reasonable chance that peasants remaining on collective farms will be granted full title to those "private" plots they are now cultivating.

All this, of course, is pure speculation. Democratic forms of polity have, historically, been very fragile; when they have been successful, they have depended upon the widespread willingness of the people to exercise considerable restraint in their demands. Most men through most of history have lived under one or another form of authoritarian regime, and the most vociferous champions of "human dignity," once they are in power, have most often turned out to be disposed toward circumscribing the freedom of others; most have even been inclined to enlighten their opponents through the very trenchant device of splitting open their heads. However, I do think that we can hope for the emergence of a "modest utopia"[6] on this planet provided we can resolve three major problems:

The first is overpopulation. Most writing on this problem treats it as a dilemma faced only by the "have-not" nations, whereas in fact the problem is just as acute for the more advanced countries. Population density is not only a matter of the number of people per square mile, it also depends very much on levels of personal consumption. By comparison with India, the United States is sparsely populated, but American affluence is such that its use of irreplaceable natural resources and its pollution of the atmosphere and rivers are reaching unsafe levels.[7] The United States is in danger, as some have already pointed out, of drowning in its own effluence. Further, despite the continued existence of vast areas of open space, it is becoming more difficult for most Americans to find an environment, even for a short time, in which they can renew themselves by coming into direct contact with the natural world. With all the changes men have undergone, there is ample evidence that such renewal is still necessary, and that excessive crowding, for example, has serious social consequences.[8] Europe is beginning to encounter similar problems as the number of automobiles increases, consumption rises, and the consequent problems of waste disposal and of pollution multiply. The resort areas that were once open only to the very rich are now available to even the lower middle class, but as they become more crowded their attractiveness is quickly dispelled.

The necessity of drastically curtailing population growth in the future may require political controls, including limitations on the number of children permitted in each family —potentially an explosive issue, since such limitations will probably raise the question of who shall be permitted to have how many children. Certainly the compulsory limitation of family size will induce further changes in the family's role played in society.

The second problem in the path of a "modest utopia" is war. The possibilities of a nuclear holocaust cannot be discounted. While tensions between the Soviet Union and the United States have relaxed, the possession of nuclear warheads by the more ideologically fervid Chinese Communists is cause for dismay and anxiety; so, too, is the prospect of a battery of "mini-nuclear" powers. Short of a dramatic achievement in defense capabilities that would make nuclear warfare obsolete— a development that appears unlikely—the only permanent solution for peace would seem

---

[6] The phrase "modest utopia" is from Kenneth Boulding's *The Meaning of the Twentieth Century* (New York: Harper & Row, 1964), as is the list of major problems; but my analysis of them differs somewhat from his. Incidentally, the list does not exhaust the problems with which men will be faced in the next fifty years, although I regard them as the most salient. See also Ferkiss, *Technological Man,* pp. 101–272, a book that is among the most balanced treatments of the future that I have read, and contains an extensive and useful bibliography.

[7] Robert Rienow and Leona Train Rienow, *Moment in the Sun* (New York: The Dial Press, 1967).

[8] See William R. Ewald, Jr., ed., *Environment for Man* (Bloomington: University of Indiana Press, 1968). The essay by Professor René Dubos is especially interesting. A more optimistic view is offered in Donald J. Bogue's "The End of the Population Explosion," *The Public Interest* (Spring 1967), pp. 11–20.

to lie in some form of world order, another development that, in the short run at least, appears unlikely. For the immediate future, then, our only hope is in the prudence of our political leaders.

International tensions will not be restricted to those which exist between the present superpowers; they can be expected to mount between the have and the have-not nations as the latter steadily demand as their right a larger share of the world's resources. Whether or not the advanced nations, including the Soviet Union and Japan, will be willing or able to meet these demands in a satisfactory fashion is an open question.

Among many Western intellectuals, there is an inclination to treat the "third world" as a fount of virtue, uncorrupted by the materialistic values of the more technologically advanced nations. This myth, like that of childhood innocence, persists despite all evidence to the contrary. The truth of the matter is that rationality and humaneness generally increase with technological development, and that nations in the throes of transition from traditional to modern societies are especially prone to forms of political paranoia, only one of which is extreme nationalism.[9]

Because of the historical association of capitalism with Western imperialism, and the psychological strains connected with the changeover from a traditional society to an industrial one, many third-world countries will adopt either the Soviet or the Chinese mobilization model in undergoing the process of industrialization. I am not convinced that, insofar as economic growth is concerned, that path offers any particular advantages over one that combines elements of state direction and private initiative, but it is unlikely that decisions on this matter will be made on the basis

of a rational consideration of alternatives.[10] The choice by third-world nations of Communist industrialization blueprints is not likely to cause a broad shift in the world balance of power, because of continued rivalries between the more developed and less developed nations, and, perhaps, between ethnic and racial groups. Even so, the spread of mobilization regimes of the Soviet or Chinese variety to third-world countries will further complicate the international situation, and could conceivably trigger a series of international crises.

The third hurdle on the way to a "modest utopia," and one which is more difficult to assess, is what Kenneth Boulding has called "the problem of ennui." Broadly, it is the problem of a world in which work no longer provides the touchstone of human existence. Of course, for some the absence of work is no problem at all; those, for instance, who assume the "natural goodness" of man tend to feel that under such circumstances he would achieve higher and headier levels of esthetic creativity and humane existence. Such, certainly, was the view of Marx, and is still the view of Marxists today. Some thinkers, going even further, argue that the end of work will yield a profound metamorphosis in human nature; they maintain that genital sexuality will disappear, to be replaced by the "polymorphous perversity" of infancy. While their views of the human future are not notable for their clarity, to them man's destiny seems locked in a completely sensual world in which control over reality becomes less important than the satisfaction of those erotic impulses that will be emitted from every portion of the body.[11] It will be a world dominated by Eros,

[9] Almost all the studies we have indicate that "modern" men are less authoritarian and less punitive toward others than "traditional" men. They also tend to be less suspicious of others and more willing to try to empathize with their point of view. See the essay by Alex Inkeles in Myron Weiner, ed., Modernization (New York: Basic Books, 1966).

[10] See Stanley Rothman, "One-Party Regimes: A Comparative Analysis," Social Research, 34 (Winter 1967), pp. 675–702.

[11] The leading proponents of this view are Herbert Marcuse, Eros and Civilization (Boston: Beacon Press, 1955), One-Dimensional Man (Boston: Beacon Press, 1964), and An Essay on Liberation (Boston: Beacon Press, 1969); and Norman O. Brown, Life Against Death (New York: Random House, 1959) and Love's Body (New York: Random House, 1966).

and, consequently, free of destructive violence. I see little validity in any of these hypotheses. There is certainly nothing to indicate that societies dedicated to sensuality will be less prone to violence than more puritanical ones—in fact, the reverse is probably closer to the truth.

Still others see the problem not so much as one of ennui as one of anomie; they anticipate a world dominated by affluent societies in which more and more individuals seek only personal gratification and turn finally to drugs in their flight from reality. It seems quite probable that such societies would ultimately revert to savagery. To some analysts, the hippie movement in the United States and its European manifestations constitute a foretaste of what our future is likely to be.[12]

As might be supposed, I do not find any of these arguments convincing, although, I must admit, the forecasters of degeneration and disorder argue their case rather more cogently than those who see "sexual liberation" as providing the best of all possible worlds. I do expect a decline in the kind of work ethic that has characterized modern European society, and the gradual development in all advanced industrial communities of a greater concern with esthetic and expressive values. Indeed, this is already occurring, and constitutes part of the current generation gap. But I find it difficult to conceive of a society that is devoid of general rules governing appropriate social behavior, or of the desire to master high-level skills. Creative human art and even satisfying human games require the learning of skills; consequently they call for self-discipline.[13]

12 Herman Kahn and Anthony J. Wiener, *The Year 2000* (New York: Macmillan, 1967).

13 Max Kaplan, *Leisure in America* (New York: John Wiley and Sons, 1960).

Nor do I believe that the greater part of the citizenry of any country will willingly part with the fruits of civilization, including civil order. If the current rebellion against "civility" in the name of communal anarchy begins to lead to widespread chaos, as it inevitably would if adopted by any sizable portion of the population, order will be restored in one way or another. There runs through European history a fascination with the primitive, an undercurrent of belief that if somehow the layers of civilization are stripped away total personal fulfillment and even immortality will be achieved. Such views come to the surface periodically, especially in times of social tension, but invariably they do not get very far.

Nevertheless, I am only moderately optimistic. Freud, on whom many of the current theoreticians of the new romanticism lean heavily, was convinced that the need to work was the source of human rationality; should work cease to be a necessity, one can read the possibility of societal degeneration into his theories far more easily than one can read progress. And Hobbes, long ago, pointed out the virtues of a politics concerned with economic as against symbolic or esthetic issues. Economic differences can usually be compromised; conflicts over life-styles are far more difficult to resolve.

The idea of progress, another current of European history, had its greatest impact in the nineteenth century. But the belief that the human race will move from one triumph to another, despite temporary setbacks, may simply be a form of hubris. Plato, writing at the dawn of Europe, saw political change as a series of cycles involving growth and degeneration. His may yet turn out to have been the deeper insight.

Bibliography

I have divided this bibliography into two sections, the first listing basic research aids and the second books and articles. Only material published in English has been selected. As a matter of convenience, the section on books and articles has been further subdivided by chapter. Where I consider the material to be of particular usefulness or interest, I have added a brief comment. Some books, of course, contain information applicable to more than one chapter and are therefore listed more than once; in such instances, my evaluation, if any, is included with the first listing only. This is not meant to be a complete bibliography of all the material available on the subject of this text; it is, however, a rather extensive catalogue for further reading in English of references which I have found of special significance.

I. RESEARCH AIDS

A. ENCYCLOPEDIAS, DICTIONARIES, YEARBOOKS, BIBLIOGRAPHIES

The Annual Register of World Events. London: Longmans Green & Co. Published since 1758; a concise summary of English cultural, social, economic, and political developments, and briefer discussions of those occurring in other European countries.

Atlantic Studies. Boulogne-sur-Seine, France: Atlantic Institute. A periodical listing studies in progress on various aspects of the Atlantic community.

Banks, Arthur S., and Textor, Robert B. *A Cross-Polity Survey.* Cambridge, Mass.: M.I.T. Press, 1963. Useful compendium of statistical material on political, social, and economic questions; should be tapped with caution, however, because some of the data is dubious and some of the indices are questionable.

Beck, Carl, and McKechnie, J. T. *Political Elites: A Select Computerized Bibliography.* Cambridge, Mass.: M.I.T. Press, 1968.

Butler, D. E., and Freeman, Jennie. *British Political Facts.* 2nd ed. New York: Saint Martin's Press, 1968.

Current Sociology. A journal published regularly by UNESCO. Bibliographic essays and partially annotated bibliographies. Topics in recent years have included the military, law, urban planning, leisure, and bureaucracy.

Cutler, Donald R., ed. *The Religious Situation*. Boston: Beacon Press, 1968, 1969. This annual, which began publication in 1968, contains extremely sophisticated articles, many dealing with social as well as religious issues.

Economic Abstracts. The Hague: Martinus Nijhoff.

Florinsky, Michael T., ed. *Encyclopedia of Russia and the Soviet Union*. New York: McGraw-Hill, 1961.

Handbook of Labor Statistics. New York: International Labor Office.

Hervé, Carrier, S.J., and Pin, Emil, S.J. *Sociology of Christianity: International Bibliography*. Rome: Gregorian University Press, 1964.

Historical Abstracts. Santa Barbara, Calif.: Clio Press.

International Encyclopedia of the Social Sciences. 17 vols. New York: The Macmillan Co., 1968. Essays and articles on most of the theoretical issues with which social scientists are currently concerned.

International Political Science Abstracts. Published by UNESCO. About two-thirds of the abstracts are in English.

International Social Science Bibliography. UNESCO publishes this annual listing of almost every article and book in the social sciences. Separate volumes for sociology, political science, and anthropology.

Keesing's Contemporary Archives. Bristol, England: Keesing's Publications, Ltd. Looseleaf quarterly providing summaries of worldwide political and social events. English and Continental emphasis. Far superior to *Facts on File*, its American counterpart.

Miliband, Ralph, and Saville, John, eds. *The Socialist Register*. London: The Merlin Press, 1964. Collections of essays on British and Continental politics from left-wing points of view.

Public Affairs Information Service. New York: H. W. Wilson. The single best general listing of articles and books published in English on cultural, economic, social, and political matters. Classified by both subject and author. Emphasis is on material published in the United States, but it includes some published in England. Much better than the *Reader's Guide to Periodical Literature*.

The Statesman's Yearbook. London: Macmillan & Co., Ltd. Offers basic, annual information about every country in the world.

Szladits, C. K., ed. *Bibliography of Foreign and International Law*. New York: Parker School of Foreign and Comparative Law, Columbia University, 1955, 1962, 1968. Extensive, partially annotated.

United Nations Statistical Yearbook.

Universal Reference Service. Princeton: Princeton Research Publishing Co. Updated by Quarterly Cumulative Gazette. Computerized bibliography, compiled annually, of articles and books in the social sciences. It is fully annotated, but it will take the student a little time to learn the system of classification and abbreviations.

Wilding, Norman, and Landy, Philip. *An Encyclopedia of Parliament*. 2nd ed. London: Cassell & Co., 1967. Definitive.

World Survey of Education. 4 vols. Paris and New York: UNESCO, 1955–1966. Highly informative.

World Yearbook of Education. New York: Harcourt, Brace & World. Each volume generally deals with a special subject. Recent issues have pertained to "Church and State in Education" and "Educational Planning."

Yearbook of International Communist Affairs. Stanford: Stanford University Press, 1966, 1967, 1968. General information on Communist parties throughout the world and a chronology of important political events. Also provides translations of significant documents.

B. ACADEMIC PERIODICALS

American Political Science Review

American Slavic Review

American Sociological Review

British Journal of Sociology

Comparative Education Review

Comparative Local Government

Comparative Political Studies

Comparative Politics

European Education

Gazette. Articles on journalism, radio, and television in different languages.

Government and Opposition

International Migration Review

International Press Institute Reports

International Review of Education

Journal of Comparative Administration

Journal of Contemporary History

Journalism Quarterly

Law and Society

Minerva (British). Articles on higher education, with a chronology of developments.

Parliamentary Affairs (British)

Political Quarterly (British)

Political Studies (British)

Polls. Summaries of public-opinion polls around the world.

Problems of Communism. Published by the U. S. Information Agency, it is anti-Soviet, but nevertheless relatively balanced and scholarly.

Public Opinion Quarterly

Race (British). The most useful source of articles on race and ethnic relations.

Science and Society. Marxist, pro-Soviet.

Social Research

Sociological Review (British)

Sociology (British)

Sociology of Education

Soviet Studies (British). Perhaps the best academic journal on Soviet affairs.

Studies in Comparative Communism

Survey (British). Formerly *Soviet Survey.*

World Politics

C. OTHER PERIODICALS AND WEEKLIES (For additional British weeklies, see bibliography for Chapter 7)

Atlas. Translations from newspapers and periodicals from all over the world.

Commentary

Dissent. Eclectic, Socialist.

Encounter. Liberal left, anti-Communist.

The German Tribune. Selections from German newspapers.

Interplay. Liberal American establishment viewpoint on European and American affairs.

Le Monde. A weekly selection of articles, in English, from the French daily, with additions designed to clarify matters for American readers.

The New Leader. Menshevik in outlook. Good Soviet coverage.

The New Left Review. Left-wing Socialist.

The New Politics. Socialist.

The New Republic

New Society (British). Short, popular articles on sociological questions. The focus is mostly on England.

D. MISCELLANEOUS

The following publications contain translations from Soviet newspapers and periodicals:

Current Abstracts of the Soviet Press

Current Digest of the Soviet Press

Problems of Economics

Soviet Sociology

Soviet Statutes and Decisions

Soviet Studies in Philosophy

Both Radio Free Europe and Radio Liberty publish commentaries, including extensive translations from Soviet sources, on events in the Soviet Union and Eastern Europe. Both are anti-Soviet but reasonably objective. Both also turn out special studies from time to time.

II. BOOKS AND ARTICLES

INTRODUCTION

Almond, Gabriel A., and Powell, G. Bingham, Jr. *Comparative Politics: A Developmental Approach.* Boston: Little, Brown & Co., 1966. A systematic presentation of comparative politics from a functionalist and developmental perspective. Rather turgid, but essential for the serious student.

Apter, David E. *The Politics of Modernization.* Chicago: University of Chicago Press, 1965. Overextended, but contains a number of important insights.

_____, ed. *Ideology and Discontent.* New York: The Free Press, 1964. Includes an excellent essay by Clifford Geertz on the nature of ideological systems.

Beer, Samuel H., ed. *Patterns of Government.* 2nd ed. New York: Random House, 1962. Analytic and empirical essays on European government, with separate sections on England, France, Germany, and the U.S.S.R. The introduction and Harry Eckstein's essay on England are especially valuable.

Bell, Daniel. *The End of Ideology.* Glencoe, Ill.: The Free Press, 1960.

Bendix, Reinhard. *Max Weber: An Intellectual Portrait.* New York: Doubleday & Co., 1960. The best introduction to Weber's thought available in English. It has the added merit of being lucidly written.

_____. "Tradition and Modernity Reconsidered," *Comparative Studies in Society and History,* 9 (1966–1967), pp. 292–346. Extremely valuable.

_____, and Lipset, Seymour Martin, eds. *Class, Status, and Power.* 2nd ed. New York: The Free Press, 1966. Instructive.

Bienen, Henry. *Violence and Social Change.* Chicago: University of Chicago Press, 1969. A concise study of current theories which points up how little we really know.

Black, Cyril E. *The Dynamics of Modernization.* New York: Harper & Row, 1966.

Black, Max, ed. *The Social Theories of Talcott Parsons.* Englewood Cliffs, N. J.: Prentice-Hall, 1961. Essays summarizing and criticizing Parsons's theories; most of them assume some familiarity with his writing.

Brinton, Crane. *The Anatomy of Revolution.* 3rd ed. New York: Random House, Vintage Books, 1965. A classic work on revolution. Most studies written today start with it. Unfortunately, like so many classics, it tends to be discussed more than read.

Buckley, Walter, ed. *Modern Systems Research for the Behavioral Scientist.* Chicago: Aldine Publishing Co., 1968. Provocative essays on various systems approaches to the study of social and political life.

Dahrendorf, Ralf. *Class and Class Conflict in an Industrial Society.* Stanford: Stanford University Press, 1959.

Demerath, N. J., III, and Peterson, Richard A., eds. *System, Change and Conflict.* New York: The Free Press, 1967. A discussion and critique of system theories, with particular attention given to Parsons and those influenced by him.

Deutsch, Karl W. *Nerves of Government: Models of Political Communication and Control.* New York: The Free Press, 1963. The social system treated as a complex network of communications. Deutsch builds a general theory on this approach, incorporating the work of Parsons and others. A stimulating book.

Dray, William H., ed. *Philosophical Analysis and History.* New York: Harper & Row, 1966. Essays on how to analyze historical events from varying perspectives. Many of the contributions are fairly technical, but almost all keep the mind alert.

Easton, David. *A Systems Analysis of Political Life.* New York: John Wiley & Sons, 1965.

Eckstein, Harry. *A Theory of Stable Democracy.* Princeton: Princeton University Press, 1961.

_____, ed. *Internal War.* New York: The Free Press, 1964.

_____. "On the Etiology of Internal Wars." *History and Theory,* 4, 2 (1965), pp. 133–163. Good summary of theories of revolution and their limitations.

_____, and Apter, David, eds. *Comparative Politics: A Reader.* New York: The Free Press, 1963. The best introduction to the discipline of comparative politics for the mature student.

Eisenstadt, S. N. *Max Weber on Charisma and Institution Building.* Chicago: University of Chicago Press, 1968.

_____. *Modernization: Protest and Change.* Englewood Cliffs, N. J.: Prentice-Hall, 1966. A functional analysis in the tradition of Parsons and Almond; vocabulary might be somewhat rarefied for the uninitiated.

_____. *The Political Systems of Empires.* New York: The Free Press, 1963. Imaginative, scholarly study of historic bureaucratic empires. Brilliantly done.

Freund, Julien. *The Sociology of Max Weber.* Translated by Mary Ilford. New York: Pantheon Books, 1968. Excellent supplement to Bendix's study of Weber. Concentrates, with remarkable clarity, on key methodological issues.

Geertz, Clifford W. "Ideology as a Cultural System." In *Ideology and Discontent,* edited by David E. Apter. New York: The Free Press, 1964.

Giddens, Anthony. "Power in the Recent Writings of Talcott Parsons." *Sociology,* 2 (September 1968), pp. 257–272. Admirable summary and critique of Parsons's conception of political power.

Huntington, Samuel P. *Political Order in Changing Societies.* New Haven: Yale University Press, 1968. Lively discussion on the nature of political development which has the additional merit of avoiding jargon. The only caveat is that the author is a little too taken up with the conditions of order.

Jackson, J. A., ed. *Social Stratification.* New York: Cambridge University Press, 1968.

Johnson, Chalmers A. *Revolutionary Change.* Boston: Little, Brown & Co., 1966. A functional analysis of revolutions, their causes, and their consequences. Very useful.

Johnson, Harry. "Ideology and the Social System." *International Encyclopedia of the Social Sciences,* 7 (1968), pp. 76–85.

Kaplan, Abraham. *The Conduct of Inquiry: Methodology for Behavioral Science.* San Francisco:

Chandler Publishing Co., 1964. Among the best introductions to the methodology of the social sciences.

Krader, Lawrence. *Formation of the State*. Englewood Cliffs, N. J.: Prentice-Hall, 1968. Basic straightforward examination by an anthropologist of the origins of our more complex political systems.

Langton, Kenneth P. *Political Socialization*. New York: Oxford University Press, 1969.

La Palombara, Joseph. "Microtheories and Micro-applications in Comparative Politics: A Widening Chasm." *Comparative Politics,* 1 (October 1968), pp. 52–78. A poke at the uncritical use of functionalism as a substitute for close analysis of political systems.

Lewy, Guenter. "Historical Data in Comparative Political Analysis." *Comparative Politics,* 1 (October 1968), pp. 103–110.

McCoy, Charles A., and Playford, John, eds. *Apolitical Politics: A Critique of Behavioralism.* New York: Thomas Y. Crowell, 1967. A critical look at contemporary work in the social sciences by a group of political scientists who criticize the "pseudoscientism" of the profession.

Macridis, Roy C. "Comparative Politics and the Study of Government: The Search for Focus." *Comparative Politics,* 1 (October 1968), pp. 79–90.

————, and Brown, Bernard E., eds. *Comparative Politics: Notes and Readings.* Homewood, Ill.: The Dorsey Press, 1968. An excellent introduction to comparative politics, mostly European. Second only to Eckstein and Apter in sophistication, and perhaps better suited to the beginner.

Mannheim, Karl. *Ideology and Utopia*. New York: Harcourt, Brace & Co., 1936. A classic study of the nature of ideology. Mandatory for the industrious student.

Meehan, Eugene J. *Contemporary Political Thought.* Homewood, Ill.: The Dorsey Press, 1967. Aside from the author's discussion of Parsons, which is weak, his summaries are reliable and his criticisms trenchant. Dry, but should be read.

Merton, Robert. *Social Theory and Social Structure.* Rev. and enl. ed. Glencoe, Ill.: The Free Press, 1956. Contains, among others, an invaluable essay on functionalism and several on the relationship between religion and science.

Mitchell, William C. *Sociological Analysis and Politics: The Theories of Talcott Parsons.* Englewood Cliffs, N. J.: Prentice-Hall, 1967. Excellent summary of Parsons's ideas, especially as they apply to politics.

Moore, Wilbert E. *Social Change*. Englewood Cliffs, N. J.: Prentice-Hall, 1966. A sensitive, erudite introduction to theories on the subject.

Nagel, Ernest. *The Structure of Science: Problems in the Logic of Scientific Explanation.* New York: Harcourt, Brace & World, 1961. Wonderfully intelligible presentation of the methodology of science and social science.

Natanson, Maurice, ed. *Philosophy of the Social Sciences: A Reader.* New York: Random House, 1963.

Nisbet, Robert A. *Social Change and History.* New York: Oxford University Press, 1969. A rather devastating attack upon evolutionary theories of political development—done with style and verve.

Parsons, Talcott. *Essays in Sociological Theory.* Rev. ed. Glencoe, Ill.: The Free Press, 1954. The examination of the sources of German National Socialism is still one of the best short essays on the subject ever published. Unlike most of Parsons's work, this collection is exceptionally readable.

————. *The Social System*. Glencoe, Ill.: The Free Press, 1951. An early statement of Parsons's approach to the subject. Still useful, but not for the uninitiated.

————. *Societies: Evolutionary and Comparative Perspectives.* Englewood Cliffs, N. J.: Prentice-Hall, 1966.

————. *Sociological Theory and Modern Society.* New York: The Free Press, 1967. The essays on power and influence are particularly good.

————. *Structure and Process in Modern Societies.* Glencoe, Ill.: The Free Press, 1960.

————. "Evolutionary Universals in Society." *American Sociological Review,* 29 (June 1964), pp. 339–357.

————, et al., eds. *Theories of Society*. 2 vols. Glencoe, Ill.: The Free Press, 1961.

Pennock, J. Roland, and Smith, David G. *Political Science: An Introduction.* New York: The Macmillan Co., 1964.

Pye, Lucian W., ed. *Communications and Political Development.* Princeton: Princeton University Press, 1963.

————, and Verba, Sidney, eds. *Political Culture and Political Development.* Princeton: Princeton University Press, 1965.

Rapoport, Anatol; Parsons, Talcott; Mitchell, William C.; Kaplan, Morton A.; and Gochman, David S. "Systems Analysis." *International Encyclopedia of the Social Sciences,* 15 (1968), pp. 452–459.

Rose, Richard. "Dynamic Tendencies in the Authority of Regimes." *World Politics,* 21 (July 1969), pp. 602–628.

Rothman, Stanley. "Systematic Political Theory: Observations on the Group Approach." *American Political Science Review,* 54 (March 1960), pp. 15–33.

Runciman, W. G. *Social Science and Political Theory.* Rev. ed. Cambridge: Cambridge University Press, 1969. Sprightly discourse on most of the questions raised in this introduction. Its style is deceptive, however; most beginners will find the going rough.

Smelser, Neil J. *Theory of Collective Behavior.* New York: The Free Press, 1963.

Strauss, Leo. "An Epilogue." In *Essays on the Scientific Study of Politics,* edited by Herbert J. Storing. New York: Holt, Rinehart & Winston, 1962. A commentary on contemporary political science from a natural-law perspective. Good.

Swartz, Marc J.; Turner, W. Victor; and Tuden, Arthur, eds. *Political Anthropology.* Chicago: Aldine Publishing Co., 1966. The introductory essay on power and decision-making is exceptional.

Toulmin, Stephen. *The Philosophy of Science: An Introduction.* London: Hutchinson's University Library, 1953. Cogent, clear, with important implications for the social sciences. Highly recommended.

Truman, David. *The Governmental Process: Political Interest and Public Opinion.* New York: Alfred A. Knopf, 1951. A statement of the "group" approach to political science by one of its leading contemporary exponents.

Weber, Max. *Economy and Society: An Outline of Interpretive Sociology.* 3 vols. Translated by Ephraim Fischoff et al. Edited by Guenter Roth and Claus Wittich. New York: Bedminster Press, 1968. Essential.

————. *From Max Weber.* Translated and edited by H. H. Gerth and C. Wright Mills. London: Routledge & Kegan Paul, Trench Trubner and Co., 1947. An excellent selection of Weber's writings.

Weinberg, Ian. "The Problem of the Convergence of Industrial Societies: A Critical Look at the State of the Theory." *Comparative Studies in Society and History,* 11 (January 1969), pp. 1–15.

Wolfenstein, Victor. *The Revolutionary Personality.* Princeton: Princeton University Press, 1966.

Young, Oran R. *Systems of Political Science.* Englewood Cliffs, N. J.: Prentice-Hall, 1968.

Part I The European Inheritance

CHAPTER 1. THE DEVELOPMENT OF MODERN EUROPE

Anderson, Eugene N., and Anderson, Pauline R. *Political Institutions and Social Change in Continental Europe in the Nineteenth Century.* Berkeley and Los Angeles: University of California Press, 1967.

Andrews, William G., ed. *Constitutions and Constitutionalism.* 2nd ed. Princeton: D. Van Nostrand, 1963.

————, ed. *European Political Institutions.* 2nd ed. Princeton: D. Van Nostrand, 1966.

Baldwin, Summerfield. *The Organization of Medieval Christianity.* New York: Henry Holt, 1929.

Beer, Samuel H., ed. *Patterns of Government.* See comment, Introduction.

Bendix, Reinhard. *Nation Building and Citizenship.* New York: John Wiley & Sons, 1964. A developmental examination of European political systems, with some Asian comparisons. Combines scholarship with clarity.

————, ed. *State and Society: A Reader in Comparative Political Sociology.* Boston: Little, Brown & Co., 1968.

Bloch, Marc. *Feudal Society.* Translated by L. A. Manyon. Chicago: University of Chicago Press, 1961. A classic work by one of the great historians of our time.

Bloom, Solomon F. *Europe and America.* New York: Harcourt, Brace & World, 1961. The historical development of the New and Old Worlds, with similarities and differences highlighted.

Borkenau, Franz. *European Communism.* New York: Harper & Bros., 1953. Communism in Western Europe during the 1930's and immediately after the war, as seen by an ex-Communist. Highly readable, although it is impossible to verify some of the assertions.

Bottomore, T. B. *Elites and Society.* New York: Basic Books, 1965. Good summary and analysis of the work done in the study of social stratification and political power, despite careless use of data to support his presuppositions.

Calmann, John, ed. *Western Europe: A Handbook.* New York: Frederick A. Praeger, 1967. Brief descriptions of every European country and general articles on such topics as education, agriculture, and parliaments. Helpful as a reference, but most of the essays are too brief to add much.

The Cambridge Economic History of Europe. 6 vols. Cambridge: Cambridge University Press, 1941–1965. Most of the essays in these volumes are important for anyone anxious to acquire a broader knowledge of European history.

Carsten, F. L. *The Rise of Fascism.* Berkeley and Los Angeles: University of California Press, 1969.

Carter, Gwendolen M., and Herz, John H. *Major Foreign Powers.* 5th ed. New York: Harcourt, Brace & World, 1967. Standard, country-by-country text, strong on the description of institutions. The chapters on England and Germany are the best.

Caute, David. *The Left in Europe Since 1789.* World University Library Series. New York: McGraw-Hill, 1966.

Cheyette, Frederick, ed. *Lordship and Community in Medieval Europe.* New York: Holt, Rinehart & Winston, 1968.

Clapham, J. H. *The Economic Development of France and Germany, 1815–1914.* 4th ed. Cambridge: Cambridge University Press, 1936. A classic that still rates attention.

Clough, Shepard B.; Gay, Peter; and Warner, Charles K., eds. *The European Past.* 2 vols. New York: The Macmillan Co., 1964. A collection of diverse interpretations.

Coulborn, Rushton. *The Origin of Civilized Societies.* Princeton: Princeton University Press, 1959. The role of religion in the emergence of "civilization." First-rate.

————, ed. *Feudalism in History.* Princeton: Princeton University Press, 1956. A comparative study which throws new light on the European variant.

Deutsch, Karl W., and Foltz, William J., eds. *Nation-Building.* New York: Atherton Press, 1963.

Duchacek, Ivo D. "National Constitutions: A Functional Approach." *Comparative Politics,* 1 (October 1968), pp. 91–102.

Eisenstadt, S. N. *Modernization: Protest and Change.* See comment, Introduction.

————. *The Political Systems of Empires.* See comment, Introduction.

————, ed. *The Protestant Ethic and Modernization.* New York: Basic Books, 1968.

Fieldhouse, David K. *The Colonial Empires.* New York: Dell Publishing Co., 1967.

Friedrich, Carl J. *Constitutional Government and Democracy.* 4th ed. Waltham, Mass.: Blaisdell, 1968. Topical approach to the study of European political systems. A splendid analysis, but presupposes some knowledge of the European scene.

Ganshof, François L. *Feudalism.* Translated by Philip Grierson. London: Longmans Green & Co., 1952.

Gerschenkron, Alexander. *Economic Backwardness in Historical Perspective.* Cambridge, Mass.: Harvard University Press, 1962.

Gillispie, C. C. *The Edge of Objectivity.* Princeton: Princeton University Press, 1960. On the rise of modern science and the nature of the scientific method. Straightforward, worthwhile.

Green, Robert W., ed. *Protestantism and Capitalism.* New York: D. C. Heath, 1959. Essays on Weber's hypothesis concerning the relationship between Calvinism and capitalism. An excellent collection.

Greene, Nathaniel, ed. *Fascism.* New York: Thomas Y. Crowell, 1968.

Hall, A. R. *The Scientific Revolution, 1500–1800.* Rev. ed. Boston: Beacon Press, 1966.

Hartz, Louis. *The Liberal Tradition in America.* New York: Harcourt, Brace & Co., 1955. What the major differences are between European and American politics and why the Lockean tradition caused them. Important.

————, ed. *The Founding of New Societies.* New York: Harcourt, Brace & World, 1964. Essays on European settlers in Australia, Latin America, and other areas. Hartz calls them "fragment" societies and explains their character in terms of the nature of the immigrants.

Hazard, Paul. *The European Mind: The Critical Years 1680–1715.* Translated by J. Lewis May. London: Hollis & Carter, 1953.

————. *European Thought in the Eighteenth Century: From Montesquieu to Lessing.* Translated by J. Lewis May. New Haven: Yale University Press, 1954.

Heilbroner, Robert. *The Making of Economic Society.* 2nd ed. Englewood Cliffs, N. J.: Prentice-Hall, 1968. A description of Europe's economic evolution and the problems of the developing countries. Very well done.

Hobsbawn, E. J. *The Age of Revolution, 1789–1848.* New York: New American Library, 1965.

Holt, Robert T., and Turner, John E. *The Political Basis of Economic Development.* Princeton: D. Van Nostrand, 1966.

Hoselitz, Bert F. "Entrepreneurship and Capital Formation in France and Britain Since 1700." In *Capital Formation and Economic Growth.* New York: Columbia University Press, 1955.

Kitch, M. J., ed. *Capitalism and the Reformation.* New York: Barnes & Noble, 1968.

Krader, Lawrence. *Formation of the State.* See comment, Introduction.

Landauer, Carl. *European Socialism.* 2 vols. Berkeley: University of California Press, 1959. Standard history.

Landes, David S. *The Unbound Prometheus.* Cambridge, Mass.: Harvard University Press, 1969. An outstanding, beautifully written survey of European industrialization in the nineteenth century. Essential.

————, ed. *The Rise of Capitalism.* New York: The Macmillan Co., 1966.

Laqueur, Walter, and Mosse, George L., eds. *International Fascism: 1920–1945.* New York: Harper & Row, Harper Torchbooks, 1966.

Larus, Joel, ed. *Comparative World Politics.* Belmont, Calif.; Wadsworth Publishing Co., 1964. Interesting comparisons between the modern European nation state and other political systems.

Lenski, Gerhard. *Power and Privilege.* New York: McGraw-Hill, 1966. An extensive—rather too extensive—presentation of an evolutionary theory of social stratification, arguing that societies became more unequal as civilization progressed from the primitive hunter but that the trend has been reversed by industrial societies. Some interesting ideas and much useful data.

Lipset, Seymour Martin. *The First New Nation.* New York: Basic Books, 1963. Combines the work of Hartz and Parsons and offers an interpretation of American history that emphasizes its anticolonial past. Attempts at comparisons between the United States and the newly independent nations of Asia and Africa are somewhat strained, but the book presents sound descriptions of the American experience.

Lopez, Robert S. *The Birth of Europe.* London: Phoenix House, 1967. Medieval Europe from the perspective of Spain and Italy.

Lubasz, Heinz, ed. *The Development of the Modern State.* New York: The Macmillan Co., 1964.

McNeill, William H. *The Rise of the West: A History of the Human Community.* Chicago: University of Chicago Press, 1963. Outstanding history of the development of Europe within the context of world history. McNeill manages to synthesize a great deal of material without falling into recondite philosophic speculations.

Merton, Robert. *Social Theory and Social Structure.* See comment, Introduction.

Moore, Barrington, Jr. *Social Origins of Dictatorship and Democracy.* Boston: Beacon Press, 1966. A scholarly effort to formulate a "neo-Marxist" theory of economic and political development which can be applied equally to Europe and Asia. There is a certain diffuseness of style and some carelessness in the use of sources, but the book is an exciting achievement nonetheless.

Mosse, George. *Calvinism: Authoritarian or Democratic?* New York: Holt, Rinehart & Winston, 1957.

The New Cambridge Modern History. 12 vols. Cambridge: Cambridge University Press, 1957–1960. Basic for anyone seriously interested in modern European history. The essays, both topical and chronological, are uniformly of high quality.

Nolte, Ernest. *Three Faces of Fascism.* New York: Holt, Rinehart & Winston, 1966. A scholarly work defining the philosophic underpinnings of European fascism.

Palmer, R. R. *The Age of the Democratic Revolution.* 2 vols. Princeton: Princeton University Press, 1959–1964. A brilliant study of the French Revolution and its impact on other European countries.

————, and Colton, Joel. *A History of the Modern World.* 2nd ed. New York: Alfred A. Knopf, 1965. One of the better single-volume histories of Europe.

Parsons, Talcott. "Christianity." *International Encyclopedia of the Social Sciences,* 2 (1968), pp. 425–447.

Reichmann, Eva G. *Hostages of Civilization.* London: Gollancz, 1950. Excellent study of anti-Semitism in Central Europe, with the emphasis on Germany.

Rogger, Hans, and Weber, Eugen, eds. *The European Right.* Berkeley and Los Angeles: University of California Press, 1965.

Ruggiero, Guido de. *A History of European Liberalism.* Translated by R. G. Collingwood. Oxford: The Clarendon Press, 1927.

Sabine, George H. *A History of Political Theory.* Rev. ed. New York: Holt, Rinehart & Winston, 1961. A classic in the field. Lucid presentation and commentary on European political thought.

Singer, Milton; Bidney, David; White, Leslie A.; Carneiro, Robert L.; and Vogt, Evon Z. "Culture." *International Encyclopedia of the Social Sciences,* 2 (1968), pp. 527–568.

Southern, R. W. *The Making of the Middle Ages.* New Haven: Yale University Press, 1953.

Strachey, John. *The End of Empire.* New York: Random House, 1960.

Strayer, Joseph. *Feudalism.* Princeton: D. Van Nostrand, 1965.

Strong, C. F. *A History of Modern Political Constitutions.* New York: G. P. Putnam's Sons, 1964.

Talmon, J. L. *The Origins of Totalitarian Democracy.* London: Secker & Warburg, 1952.

————. *Political Messianism: The Romantic Phase.* New York: Frederick A. Praeger, 1961.

Urwin, Derek W. *Western Europe Since 1945.* New York: Humanities Press, 1968. A good, sound general history.

Wahlke, John C., and Dragnich, Alex N., eds. *Government and Politics.* New York: Random House, 1966.

Watkins, Frederick M. *The Political Tradition of the West.* Cambridge, Mass.: Harvard University Press, 1948. A penetrating examination of Europe's major ideological trends. Hard to fault.

Weber, Max. *General Economic History.* Translated by Frank H. Knight. Glencoe, Ill.: The Free Press, 1950.

————. *The Protestant Ethic and the Spirit of Capitalism.* Translated by Talcott Parsons. New York: Charles Scribner's Sons, 1930.

Williams, Raymond. *The Long Revolution.* New York: Columbia University Press, 1961.

Wilson, Edmund. *To the Finland Station.* New York: Doubleday & Co., Anchor Books, 1963. A study of European socialism through biographical sketches of some of its leading figures. Well worth reading.

Woodhouse, A. S. P., ed. *Puritanism and Liberty.* 2nd ed. Chicago: University of Chicago Press, 1951.

Wuest, John J., and Vernon, Manfred C., eds. *New Source Book in Major European Governments.* Cleveland: World Publishing Co., 1966. A standard collection of documents.

CHAPTER 2. ENGLAND, FRANCE, AND GERMANY

Acomb, E. M., and Brown, M. L., Jr., eds. *French Society and Culture Since the Old Regime.* New York: Holt, Rinehart & Winston, 1966.

Albinski, Henry S., and Pettit, Lawrence K. *European Political Processes: Essays and Readings.* Boston: Allyn & Bacon, 1968.

Amery, Leopold. *Thoughts on the Constitution.* 2nd ed. New York: Oxford University Press, 1964.

Angress, Werner T. *Stillborn Revolution.* Princeton: Princeton University Press, 1963.

————. "The Political Role of the Peasantry in the Weimar Republic." *The Review of Politics,* 21 (June 1959), pp. 530–549.

Bagehot, Walter. *The English Constitution.* Introduction by Richard H. Crossman. London: Collins, Fontana Library, 1963. A classic. Crossman's introduction argues that the British political system is now "quasi-presidential."

Balfour, Michael. *West Germany.* New York: Frederick A. Praeger, 1968.

Barraclough, Geoffrey. *The Origins of Modern Germany.* 2nd ed. New York: Barnes & Noble, 1966. A scholarly yet exciting book on the medieval foundations of German politics. Essential for the serious student.

Beer, Samuel H. *British Politics in the Collectivist Age.* New York: Alfred A. Knopf, 1965. A historical interpretation of modern British politics, perceptively interweaving ideological, social, and economic changes.

Benewick, Robert, and Dowse, Robert. *Readings on British Politics and Government.* London: University of London Press, 1968.

Billington, James H. *The Icon and the Axe.* New York: Alfred A. Knopf, 1966. A controversial "cultural" interpretation of Russian history.

Bindoff, S. T. *Tudor England.* Baltimore: Penguin Books, 1959.

Birch, A. H. *The British System of Government.* New York: Frederick A. Praeger, 1967.

————. *Representative and Responsible Government.* Toronto: University of Toronto Press, 1964.

Blachly, F. F., and Oatman, M. E. *The Government and Administration of Germany.* Baltimore: Johns Hopkins Press, 1928. Encyclopedic discourse on government in Weimar Germany. Dry as sawdust, but useful for reference.

Blondel, Jean, and Godfrey, E. Drexel, Jr. *The Government of France.* 3rd ed. New York: Thomas Y. Crowell, 1968. Standard text; traditional coverage.

Bolling, Klaus. *Republic in Suspense.* Translated by Jean Steinberg. New York: Frederick A. Praeger, 1964.

Briggs, Asa. *The Making of Modern England, 1784–1867.* New York: Harper & Row, 1965. Standard, balanced text on the period.

Brown, Bernard. "The French Experience of Modernization." *World Politics,* 21 (April 1969), pp. 366–391.

Bullock, Alan. *Hitler: A Study in Tyranny*. Rev. ed. New York: Harper & Row, 1962. The best study of Hitler available in English.

Cantor, Norman F., and Werthman, Michael S., eds. *The English Tradition*. 2 vols. New York: The Macmillan Co., 1967. Essays by historians with differing perspectives on English history. Excellent.

Carsten, F. L. *The Origins of Prussia*. New York: Oxford University Press, 1954.

Caves, Richard E., ed. *Britain's Economic Prospects*. Washington: The Brookings Institution, 1968.

Chapman, Guy. *The Dreyfus Case: A Reassessment*. New York: Reynal & Co., 1955.

Cobban, Alfred. *A History of Modern France*. Rev. ed. New York: George Braziller, 1965. Imaginative study, just a bit diffuse for those without a basic knowledge of France.

_____. *The Social Interpretation of the French Revolution*. Cambridge: Cambridge University Press, 1964. A revisionist critique of Marxist and neo-Marxist views that it was essentially a bourgeois revolution. Indispensable.

Cole, Taylor C. "The Constitutional Courts: A Comparison." *American Political Science Review*, 53 (December 1959), pp. 963–984.

Dahrendorf, Ralf. *Society and Democracy in Germany*. New York: Doubleday & Co., 1967. Many fascinating insights, but a poorly written book.

De Gaulle, Charles. *War Memoirs*. 3 vols. Vol. 1 translated by Jonathan Griffin; vols. 2 and 3 translated by Richard Howard. New York: Simon & Schuster, 1955–1959.

Desai, A. V. *Real Wages in Germany, 1871–1913*. New York: Oxford University Press, 1968.

Dicey, Albert V. *Introduction to the Study of the Law of the Constitution*. 10th ed. New York: St. Martin's Press, 1959.

Dickinson, Robert Eric. *Germany: A General and Regional Geography*. 2nd ed. London: Methuen & Co., 1953.

Edinger, Lewis J. *Politics in Germany*. Boston: Little, Brown & Co., 1968. A behavioral analysis, very strong on political culture, interest groups, and political communication; not as strong on institutions.

Ehrmann, Henry W. *Politics in France*. Boston: Little, Brown & Co., 1968. A behavioral study of French politics. Especially good on political socialization, interest groups, political parties, and political leadership. Well-written, but likely to be somewhat confusing for the beginner.

Finer, Herman. *The Theory and Practice of Modern Government*. Rev. ed. New York: Henry Holt, 1949. Classic study of European political systems on a topical rather than a national basis. Dated, but still offers historical material of great value.

Gay, Peter. *Weimar Culture: The Outsider as Insider*. New York: Harper & Row, 1968.

Gimbel, John. *A German Community Under American Occupation*. Stanford: Stanford University Press, 1961.

Golay, John Ford. *The Founding of the Federal Republic of Germany*. Chicago: University of Chicago Press, 1958.

Greenlaw, Ralph W., ed. *The Economic Origins of the French Revolution*. Boston: D. C. Heath, 1958.

Hadrill, J. M. W., and McManners, John M., eds. *France: Government and Society*. London: Methuen & Co., 1957. A short political history. The essays are uniformly good.

Halévy, Elie. *The Growth of Philosophic Radicalism*. Translated by Mary Morris. Boston: Beacon Press, 1955. Two classic works by a great French historian.

_____. *A History of the English People in the Nineteenth Century*. 6 vols. Translated by E. I. Watkin. New York: Barnes & Noble, 1949–1961.

Hamerow, Theodore S. *The Social Foundations of German Unification*. Princeton: Princeton University Press, 1969.

Hammond, J. L., and Hammond, Barbara. *The Village Labourer, 1760–1832*. London: Longmans Green & Co., 1913.

Harrison, J. F. C., ed. *Society and Politics in England, 1780–1960*. New York: Harper & Row, 1965.

Harrison, Martin, ed. *French Politics*. Boston: D. C. Heath, 1969. Superior collection of essays on French political behavior, many translated from the French.

Hartwell, R. M. *The Causes of the Industrial Revolution in England*. London: Methuen & Co., 1967.

Havighurst, Alfred F. *Twentieth Century Britain*. 2nd ed. New York: Harper & Row, 1966. A competent history.

Hilberg, Raul. *The Destruction of the European Jews*. Chicago: Quadrangle Press, 1961.

Hill, Christopher. *Reformation to Industrial Revolution*. New York: Random House, 1968.

Hiscocks, Richard. *Democracy in Western Germany*. New York: Oxford University Press, 1957. Standard, thorough treatment. Leaden and a bit outdated, but eminently useful.

Hobsbawn, E. J. *Industry and Empire: An Economic History of Britain Since 1750*. London: Weidenfeld

& Nicolson, 1968. Knowledgeable, readable interpretation of modern English history by a Marxist.

Holborn, Hajo. *A History of Modern Germany*. 3 vols. New York: Alfred A. Knopf, 1959–1969. Probably the best general history of Germany available in English. Scholarship served appetizingly.

Holborn, Louise; Herz, John H.; and Carter, Gwendolen M., eds. *Documents of Major Foreign Powers*. New York: Harcourt, Brace & World, 1968.

International Council for Philosophy and Humanistic Studies. *The Third Reich*. London: Weidenfeld & Nicolson, 1955. A massive collection of essays on every aspect of Nazi Germany. As in all collections, the contributions are uneven, but some of them are indeed brilliant.

Jarman, T. L. *The Rise and Fall of Nazi Germany*. New York: New York University Press, 1956. A short history, ably done.

Jaspers, Karl. *The Future of Germany*. E. B. Ashton, trans. and ed. Chicago: University of Chicago Press, 1967. Some very pessimistic, and generally overstated, views on the "bland" character of German politics by the noted philosopher.

Kafker, Frank A., and Laux, James, eds. *The French Revolution: Conflicting Interpretations*. New York: Random House, 1968. A representative selection of some of the newer, detailed analyses on the Revolution by historians with sociological training. Most of the contributions are intelligent and exciting.

Kaufmann, Walter H. *Monarchism in the Weimar Republic*. New York: Bookman Associates, 1953.

Keir, David Lindsay. *The Constitutional History of Modern Britain Since 1485*. 7th ed. Princeton: D. Van Nostrand, 1966. Good standard text.

King, Anthony, ed. *British Politics*. Boston: D. C. Heath, 1966. Some fairly vigorous essays on British political life.

Kogon, Eugen. *Theory and Doctrine of Hell*. New York: Farrar, Straus, 1950. Description of German concentration camps by a former inmate. Unforgettable.

Lijphart, Arend, ed. *Politics in Europe: Comparisons and Interpretations*. Englewood Cliffs, N. J.: Prentice-Hall, 1969.

Litchfield, Edward H. *Governing Postwar Germany*. Ithaca: Cornell University Press, 1953.

Lowell, A. Lawrence. *The Government of England*. 2 vols. 3rd ed. New York: The Macmillan Co., 1919. A classic study that holds up very well.

Lowie, Robert H. *Toward Understanding Germany*. Chicago: University of Chicago Press, 1954. An analysis by an anthropologist who succeeds in destroying a good many of the highly simplistic myths about pre-Nazi German social structure and culture. Some of the points are stretched rather thin.

Macridis, Roy. *The De Gaulle Republic: Quest for Unity*. Homewood, Ill.: The Dorsey Press, 1960.

_____, ed. *Modern European Governments: Cases in Comparative Policy Making*. Englewood Cliffs, N. J.: Prentice-Hall, 1968.

_____, and Brown, Bernard, eds. *Comparative Politics: Notes and Readings*. See comment, Introduction.

_____, and Ward, Robert E., eds. *Modern Political Systems: Europe*. 2nd ed. Englewood Cliffs, N.J.: Prentice-Hall, 1968. England, France, Germany, and the U.S.S.R. under scrutiny. Somewhat more "behavioral" than Carter and Herz. The German and Soviet sections are the strongest.

McWhinney, Edward. *Constitutionalism in Germany and the Federal Constitutional Court*. Leyden: A. W. Sythoff, 1962.

Mann, Golo. *The History of Germany Since 1789*. New York: Frederick A. Praeger, 1968. An excellent, one-volume history with the perspective primarily political.

Marwick, Arthur. *Britain in the Century of Total War: War, Peace and Social Change, 1900–1967*. Boston: Little, Brown & Co., 1968. How two world wars produced social and political changes. A good analysis.

Merkl, Peter. *The Origin of the West German Republic*. New York: Oxford University Press, 1963.

Mingay, Gordon E. *English Landed Society in the Eighteenth Century*. London: Routledge & Kegan Paul, 1963.

Moore, Barrington, Jr. *Social Origins of Dictatorship and Democracy*. See comment, Chapter 1.

Mosse, George, ed. *Nazi Culture*. New York: Grosset & Dunlap, 1966.

Muller, Steven, ed. *Documents on European Government*. New York: The Macmillan Co., 1963.

Neumann, Franz L. *Behemoth: The Structure and Practice of National Socialism, 1933–1944*. New York: Harper & Row, Harper Torchbooks, 1966.

Parsons, Talcott. *Essays in Sociological Theory*. See comment, Introduction.

Peterson, Edward N. *The Limits of Hitler's Power*. Princeton: Princeton University Press, 1969.

Pinson, Koppel S. *Modern Germany: Its History and Civilization.* 2nd ed. New York: The Macmillan Co., 1967. The best single-volume account, with intelligent attention given to social, economic, and political factors.

Plumb, J. H. *The Growth of Political Stability in England: 1675–1725.* Baltimore: Penguin Books, 1969.

Pollock, J. K., and Thomas, Homer. *Germany in Power and Eclipse.* Princeton: D. Van Nostrand, 1952. Impressive political and social history, done topically and by region.

Pulzer, P. G. J. *The Rise of Political Anti-Semitism in Germany and Austria.* New York: John Wiley & Sons, 1964.

Reichmann, Eva G. *Hostages of Civilization.* See comment, Chapter 1.

Rémond, René. *The Right Wing in France from 1815 to De Gaulle.* Translated by James M. Laux. 2nd American ed. Philadelphia: University of Pennsylvania Press, 1969. A detailed study of French conservatism which makes all the appropriate distinctions.

Rodnick, David. *Postwar Germans.* New Haven: Yale University Press, 1948.

Rose, Richard. *Politics in England.* Boston: Little, Brown & Co., 1964. Especially good on political culture and political behavior.

Rothman, Stanley. "Barrington Moore and the Dialectics of Revolution." *American Political Science Review,* in press.

Sauer, Wolfgang. "National Socialism: Totalitarianism or Fascism?" *The American Historical Review,* 73 (December 1967), pp. 404–424.

Schaffner, Bertram. *Father Land: A Study of Authoritarianism in the German Family.* New York: Columbia University Press, 1948. The origins of National Socialism explained through an examination of the German family. There is something to the argument, but it is much too simple and ahistorical.

Schoenbaum, David. *Hitler's Social Revolution.* New York: Doubleday & Co., 1966. Focuses quite clearly on the populist features of the Nazi regime.

Seton-Watson, Hugh. *The Russian Empire, 1801–1917.* New York: Oxford University Press, 1967. Comprehensive, instructive, dry.

Sharp, Walter Rice. *The Government of the French Republic.* Princeton: D. Van Nostrand, 1938.

Smellie, Kingsley Brice. *Great Britain Since 1688.* Ann Arbor: University of Michigan Press, 1964.

Smith, Paul. *Disraelian Conservatism and Social Reform.* London: Routledge & Kegan Paul, 1967.

Snell, John L., ed. *The Nazi Revolution: Germany's Guilt or Germany's Fate?* Boston: D. C. Heath, 1959.

Stern, Fritz. *The Politics of Cultural Despair: A Study in the Rise of the Germanic Ideology.* Berkeley and Los Angeles: University of California Press, 1961.

————, ed. *The Path to Dictatorship, 1918–1933.* Translated by John Conway. New York: Doubleday & Co., 1966. Uniformly excellent essays by German historians which explore the reasons for the collapse of the Weimar Republic.

————. "The Political Consequences of the Unpolitical German." *History,* 3 (September 1960), pp. 104–130.

Stone, Lawrence. *Crisis of the Aristocracy, 1558–1641.* Abr. ed. New York: Oxford University Press, 1967. Scholarship handled gracefully in a new attempt to understand the social and cultural changes that led to the English Civil War.

Thomson, David. *Democracy in France Since 1870.* 4th ed. New York: Oxford University Press, 1964. A model study integrating economic, social, and political variables. Beautifully written. It does, however, presuppose some familiarity with French history.

Tilford, R. B., and Preece, R. J. C. *Federal Germany.* London: Oswald Wolf, 1969. Dull, but with some interesting data.

Tocqueville, Alexis de. *The Old Regime and the French Revolution.* Translated by Stuart Gilbert. New York: Doubleday & Co., 1955. The classic study of the origins of the French Revolution.

United States Department of the Army. *Area Handbook for Germany.* 2nd ed. Washington: Government Printing Office, 1964. Pedestrian general survey.

Von Klemperer, Klemens. *Germany's New Conservatism.* Princeton: Princeton University Press, 1957.

Webb, R. K. *Modern England.* New York: Dodd, Mead & Co., 1968. Knowledgeable, balanced, one-volume history, extremely useful for the beginning student.

Werth, Alexander. *The De Gaulle Revolution.* London: Robert Hale, 1960. Lively and insightful introduction to the background and first years of the de Gaulle regime by a journalist with a deep knowledge of France.

Williams, Philip M. *Crisis and Compromise.* New York: Doubleday & Co., 1966. This is *the* study of politics in Fourth-Republic France. Flawless in its scholarship, sophisticated in its judgments, and superbly written.

————, and Harrison, Martin. *De Gaulle's Republic*. London: Longmans Green & Co., 1960.

Wilson, Charles Henry. *England's Apprenticeship*. New York: St. Martin's Press, 1965. The economic life of seventeenth-century England under scrutiny. Excellent.

Wright, Gordon. *France in Modern Times*. Chicago: Rand McNally, 1960. The best one-volume study available in English. The bibliographical essays which accompany each chapter, though already somewhat dated, still have much to recommend them.

CHAPTER 3. RUSSIA AND THE SOVIET UNION

Albinski, Henry S., and Pettit, Lawrence K. *European Political Processes: Essays and Readings*. Boston: Allyn & Bacon, 1968.

Andrews, William G., ed. *Soviet Institutions and Policies: Inside Views*. Princeton: D. Van Nostrand, 1966.

Arendt, Hannah. *The Origins of Totalitarianism*. New York: Harcourt, Brace & Co., 1951. The first statement of the "totalitarian model" of Soviet politics which became so popular in the 1950's. Also includes a valuable discussion of European anti-Semitism.

Avineri, Shlomo. *The Social and Political Thought of Karl Marx*. Cambridge: Cambridge University Press, 1968. A reinterpretation of Marx which stresses his eclecticism and denies that he was a materialist in the narrow sense. Suggestive and well-written, but does not really prove its central thesis.

Barghoorn, Frederick C. *Politics in the U.S.S.R.* Boston: Little, Brown & Co., 1966. An interesting but perhaps oversophisticated attempt to develop a behavioral approach to the study of Soviet politics. Useful data and some stimulating ideas.

Bell, Daniel. "Ten Theories in Search of Reality: The Prediction of Soviet Behavior in the Social Sciences." *World Politics*, 10 (April 1958), pp. 327–356.

Berdyaev, Nicolas. *The Origin of Russian Communism*. Translated by Richard and Clara Winston. London: Geoffrey Bles, 1948. The origins of the Soviet regime are traced—impressionistically—to certain peculiarities of Russian culture.

Berlin, Isaiah. *Karl Marx*. Oxford: The Clarendon Press, 1949. Still the best short intellectual biography on the market.

Billington, James H. "Six Views of the Russian Revolution." *World Politics*, 18 (April 1966), pp. 452–473.

Black, Cyril E., ed. *The Transformation of Russian Society*. Cambridge, Mass.: Harvard University Press, 1960. Essays on aspects of Soviet society and politics in their historical context. Wonderfully helpful.

Carr, Edward H. *A History of Soviet Russia*. 7 vols. New York: The Macmillan Co., 1951–1960. The most detailed examination of the Soviet revolution and its aftermath. Essential for students, although the author's biases somewhat tarnish the overall excellence.

Chukovskaya, Lydia. *The Deserted House*. Translated by Aline B. Werth. New York: E. P. Dutton, 1967. A novel describing the terror of the great purge.

Churchward, L. G. *Contemporary Soviet Government*. London: Routledge & Kegan Paul, 1968.

Clarkson, Jesse. *A History of Russia*. New York: Random House, 1961. A balanced, well-written, one-volume account, particularly suitable for the novice.

Conquest, Robert. *The Great Terror: Stalin's Purge of the Thirties*. New York: The Macmillan Co., 1968. A definitive account with documentation from Western and Soviet sources. The author, a poet as well as a Soviet expert, graphically conveys a feeling of the times.

————. *The Soviet Political System*. London: The Bodley Head, 1968.

Dallin, Alexander, and Larson, Thomas B., eds. *Soviet Politics Since Khrushchev*. Englewood Cliffs, N. J.: Prentice-Hall, 1968.

————, and Westin, Alan F., eds. *Politics in the Soviet Union: Seven Cases*. New York: Harcourt, Brace & World, 1965.

Daniels, Robert V. *The Conscience of the Revolution*. Cambridge, Mass.: Harvard University Press, 1960. On the "left" opposition during the 1920's in the Soviet Union. Good.

————. *A Documentary History of Communism*. New York: Random House, 1960.

————. *Red October: The Bolshevik Revolution of 1917*. New York: Charles Scribner's Sons, 1967.

Deutscher, Isaac. *The Prophet Armed: Trotsky, 1879–1921*. New York: Oxford University Press, 1954.

————. *The Prophet Unarmed: Trotsky, 1921–1929*. New York: Oxford University Press, 1959.

————. *The Prophet Outcast: Trotsky, 1929–1940*. New York: Oxford University Press, 1963. Written by a sympathizer who was not blind to Trotsky's failings, these three volumes were a labor of love. The first two, especially, are indispensable for an understanding of Soviet politics in the 1920's.

————. *Stalin: A Political Biography*. New York: Oxford University Press, 1949. The best available political biography of Stalin, written from the perspective of one who sympathized with Trotsky.

————. *The Unfinished Revolution: Russia 1917–1967*. New York: Oxford University Press, 1967. Deutscher argues that the authoritarianism of the Soviet regime is the result of the Revolution having taken place in a backward nation faced by a hostile capitalist world. Now that the Soviet Union has industrialized, he expects that the original Communist ideals of the Revolution will be put into practice. A stimulating analysis.

Easton, Lloyd D., and Guddat, Kurt H., eds. and trans. *Writings of the Young Marx on Philosophy and Society*. New York: Doubleday & Co., 1967. An excellent collection of the early writings of Marx with a very helpful commentary.

Fainsod, Merle. *How Russia Is Ruled*. Rev. ed. Cambridge, Mass.: Harvard University Press, 1963. A shade outdated, but fascinating and complete.

————. *Smolensk Under Soviet Rule*. Cambridge, Mass.: Harvard University Press, 1958. This skillful use of the archives of the Smolensk Communist Party provides an exciting and lifelike portrait of Soviet politics during the late 1920's and 1930's.

Fischer, George. *Russian Liberalism: From Gentry to Intelligentsia*. Cambridge, Mass.: Harvard University Press, 1958.

Fischer, Louis. *The Life of Lenin*. New York: Harper & Row, 1964. A long, rather discursive biography, but knowledgeable nonetheless.

Florinsky, Michael T. *Russia: A History and an Interpretation*. 2 vols. New York: The Macmillan Co., 1954. Skillfully written, faultlessly researched.

Friedrich, Carl J., and Brzezinski, Zbigniew K. *Totalitarian Dictatorship and Autocracy*. Rev. ed. Cambridge, Mass.: Harvard University Press, 1965. Aside from Arendt, the most influential exposition of a "model" of totalitarian societies. Far more empirical and far less speculative. Brzezinski did not participate in the revision.

Ginzburg, Eugenia S. *Journey into the Whirlwind*. Translated by Paul Stevenson and Max Hayward. New York: Harcourt, Brace & World, 1967. The harrowing experiences of a Communist Party member sent to a labor camp during the 1930 purges.

Grey, Ian. *The First Fifty Years: Soviet Russia, 1917–1967*. New York: Coward-McCann, 1967.

Haimson, Leopold H. *The Russian Marxists and the Origins of Bolshevism*. Cambridge, Mass.: Harvard University Press, 1955.

Hendel, Samuel, ed. *The Soviet Crucible*. Princeton: D. Van Nostrand, 1967. A nicely balanced collection of provocative opinions.

Jordan, Z. A. *The Evolution of Dialectical Materialism*. New York: Saint Martin's Press, 1967. Marxist thought and its transformation by Engels, Lenin, and Stalin. Drab and rather diffuse, but a book of solid scholarship.

Kassof, Allen, ed. *Prospects for Soviet Society*. New York: Frederick A. Praeger, 1968. Essays on recent Soviet developments. The contributions are uniformly top-notch.

Katkov, George. *Russia, 1917*. New York: Harper & Row, 1967.

Keep, J. L. H. *The Rise of Social Democracy in Russia*. New York: Oxford University Press, 1963.

Koestler, Arthur. *Darkness at Noon*. Translated by Daphne Hardy. New York: The Macmillan Co., 1941. A fine novel by an ex-Communist which captures the mood of the Soviet purge trials during the 1930's and explains why many of the defendants confessed to crimes they had not committed.

Lane, David. *The Roots of Russian Communism*. New York: Humanities Press, 1969. A careful, scholarly examination of the social composition of the Social Democratic Party up to 1906. Also differentiates between the Menshevik and Bolshevik factions in terms of class and ethnic background. Excellent.

Lenin, V. I. *Selected Works*. 2 vols. Moscow: Foreign Languages Publishing House, 1959.

Lichtheim, George. *Marxism: An Historical and Critical Study*. New York: Frederick A. Praeger, 1961. An imaginative, penetrating discussion of Marxist thought, placing it in historical context. Assumes some familiarity with Marx's writings.

Little, Richard R., and Riemer, Neal, eds. *Liberalization in the U.S.S.R.: Façade or Reality*. Boston: Raytheon Education Co., 1968.

Macridis, Roy, ed. *Modern European Governments: Cases in Comparative Policy Making*. Englewood Cliffs, N. J.: Prentice-Hall, 1968.

————, and Brown, Bernard, eds. *Comparative Politics: Notes and Readings*. See comment, Introduction.

————, and Ward, Robert E., eds. *Modern Political Systems: Europe*. See comment, Chapter 2.

Marcuse, Herbert. *Reason and Revolution: Hegel and the Rise of Social Theory*. Boston: The Beacon Press, 1960.

Marx, Karl, and Engels, Friedrich. *Selected Works*. 2 vols. Moscow: Foreign Languages Publishing House, 1951.

Maynard, John. *Russia in Flux*. New York: The Macmillan Co., 1948. Superb study of pre–1917 Russia and the impact of the Revolution. Especially good in evoking the mood of the peasantry.

Meyer, Alfred G. *Leninism*. Cambridge, Mass.: Harvard University Press, 1957. Absolutely the best intellectual biography of Lenin available in English.

Moore, Barrington, Jr. *Soviet Politics: The Dilemma of Power*. Cambridge, Mass.: Harvard University Press, 1950. Probably the first valuable theoretical study of Soviet politics written in the United States. Still worth reading.

Nettl, J. P. *The Soviet Achievement*. New York: Harcourt, Brace & World, 1968.

Nicolaevsky, Boris I. *Power and the Soviet Elite*. New York: Frederick A. Praeger, 1965. Essays by the former "dean" of Kremlinologists. Nicolaevsky maintained many contacts in the U.S.S.R. after he left and educated a generation of American scholars in the intricacies of Stalin's Russia.

Parker, W. H. *An Historical Geography of Russia*. Chicago: Aldine Publishing Co., 1969.

Payne, Robert. *Marx*. New York: Simon & Schuster, 1968. The author is philosophically illiterate, but the book contains a good deal of information about Marx not available elsewhere.

Pipes, Richard. *The Formation of the Soviet Union*. 2nd ed. Cambridge, Mass.: Harvard University Press, 1964. A definitive study of the nationalities question just after the Revolution.

————, ed. *Revolutionary Russia*. Cambridge, Mass.: Harvard University Press, 1968.

Plamenatz, John. *German Marxism and Russian Communism*. London: Longmans Green & Co., 1956.

Radkey, O. H. *The Agrarian Foes of Bolshevism*. New York: Columbia University Press, 1958.

Riha, Thomas, ed. *Readings in Russian Civilization*. 3 vols. Chicago: University of Chicago Press, 1964.

Rothman, Stanley. "Marxism and the Paradox of Contemporary Political Thought." *The Review of Politics*, 24 (April 1962), pp. 212–232.

Schapiro, Leonard. *The Communist Party of the Soviet Union*. New York: Random House, 1960. Without much question, the best history of the party in English. It is really a history of the Soviet Union from the Revolution. Exceptional.

————. *The Origin of the Communist Autocracy: First Phase, 1917–1922*. Cambridge, Mass.: Harvard University Press, 1955.

————, and Reddaway, Peter B., eds. *Lenin: The Man, The Theorist, The Leader: A Reappraisal*. New York: Frederick A. Praeger, 1967.

Solzhenitsyn, Alexsandr. *Cancer Ward*. Translated by Nicholas Bethell and David Burg. New York: Farrar, Straus, & Giroux, 1969.

————. *The First Circle*. Translated by Thomas P. Whitney. New York: Harper & Row, 1968.

————. *One Day in the Life of Ivan Denisovich*. Translated by Max Hayward and Ronald Hingley. New York: Frederick A. Praeger, 1963. All three Solzhenitsyn books capture the mood of the postwar Stalinist period. Each is a superior work of art.

Sorlin, Pierre. *The Soviet People and Their Society: From 1917 to the Present*. New York: Frederick A. Praeger, 1969.

Swearer, Howard R. *The Politics of Succession in the U.S.S.R.* Boston: Little, Brown & Co., 1964.

Swianiewicz, S. *Forced Labor and Economic Development*. Oxford: The Clarendon Press, 1965. A bit tiresome, but helpful.

Tomasic, Dinko. *The Impact of Russian Culture on Soviet Communism*. Glencoe, Ill.: The Free Press, 1953.

Trotsky, Leon. *The Russian Revolution*. New York: Doubleday & Co., 1959. Edited selections by F. W. Dupee from Trotsky's *History of the Russian Revolution*.

Tucker, Robert C. *The Soviet Political Mind*. New York: Frederick A. Praeger, 1963.

————, and Cohen, Stephen F., eds. *The Great Purge Trial*. New York: Grosset & Dunlap, 1965. Documents on the trial with a rather dramatic commentary.

Ulam, Adam. *The Bolsheviks*. New York: The Macmillan Co., 1965. A first-rate study of the Bolshevik Revolution and its leaders, combining fine scholarship with wry humor. Supplements but does not quite replace Bertram Wolfe.

_____. *The Unfinished Revolution.* New York: Random House, 1960. Argues that Socialist revolutions erupt at a certain stage of industrialization because of strains upon the transformation of traditional societies. Some interesting insights.

Venturi, Franco. *Roots of Revolution.* New York: Alfred A. Knopf, 1961.

Von Laue, Theodore. *Why Lenin? Why Stalin? A Reappraisal of the Russian Revolution, 1900–1930.* Philadelphia: J. B. Lippincott Co., 1964.

Walkin, Jacob. *The Rise of Democracy in Pre-Revolutionary Russia.* New York: Frederick A. Praeger, 1962. Walkin's contention is that the czarist regime might very well have taken a democratic direction had not World War I and the Revolution intervened.

Wetter, Gustav A. *Dialectical Materialism.* Translated by Peter Heath. New York: Frederick A. Praeger, 1959.

_____. *Soviet Ideology Today.* Translated by Peter Heath. New York: Frederick A. Praeger, 1966. Two commendable studies of Soviet Marxism, in all its ramifications.

Wolfe, Bertram D. *Three Who Made a Revolution.* 4th ed. New York: Dial Press, 1964. Early analysis of the Russian Revolution through biographical studies of Lenin, Trotsky, and Stalin. Although partially superseded by other works, it remains one of the outstanding books on the Bolshevik upheaval.

Part II The Social and Cultural Bases of European Politics

CHAPTER 4. INTRODUCTION

Anderson, Robert T., and Anderson, Barbara Gallatin. *Bus Stop for Paris.* New York: Doubleday & Co., 1965. Throws considerable light on the culture of rural France and the changes taking place there.

Bendix, Reinhard. *Work and Authority in Industry.* New York: John Wiley & Sons, 1956. On managerial ideologies in Western Europe and the Soviet Union.

_____. "Tradition and Modernity Reconsidered." See comment, Introduction.

Bottomore, T. B. *Elites and Society.* See comment, Chapter 1.

Dahrendorf, Ralf. *Society and Democracy in Germany.* See comment, Chapter 2.

Edinger, Lewis J. *Politics in Germany.* See comment, Chapter 2.

Gorer, Geoffrey, and Rickman, John. *The People of Great Russia.* London: Cressett Press, 1949.

Graubard, Stephen R., ed. *A New Europe?* Boston: Houghton Mifflin, 1964. Informative essays on all phases of European social life and politics, outlining the transformation of Europe since World War II.

Harrison, Martin, ed. *French Politics.* See comment, Chapter 2.

Heidenheimer, Arnold J. *The Governments of Germany.* 2nd ed. New York: Thomas Y. Crowell, 1966. Splendid introduction to German politics. Fairly behavioral in its orientation but with good discussion of institutions.

Hindus, Maurice. *The Kremlin's Human Dilemma.* New York: Doubleday & Co., 1967. Russia revisited, 1965, by an author who was born there and has returned many times. Superior to most such commentaries because Hindus knows the country intimately and offers some carefully weighed judgments.

Hoffmann, Stanley, et al. *In Search of France.* Cambridge, Mass.: Harvard University Press, 1963. Unusually illuminating essays on French culture, social structure, and politics.

Hollander, Paul, ed. *American and Soviet Society.* Englewood Cliffs, N. J.: Prentice-Hall, 1968. An exciting collection of essays on these two nations.

Inkeles, Alex. *Social Change in Soviet Russia.* Cambridge, Mass.: Harvard University Press, 1968.

_____, and Bauer, Raymond. *The Soviet Citizen.* Cambridge, Mass.: Harvard University Press, 1959. A description of the Soviet citizen's life based on interviews with refugees. Inkeles draws a fantastic amount of information from these. Unfortunately, most of the data is from the 1930's and early 1940's.

_____, and Geiger, H. Kent, eds. *Soviet Society: A Book of Readings.* Boston: Houghton Mifflin, 1961.

Keller, Suzanne. *Beyond the Ruling Class.* New York: Random House, 1963. Argues that in contemporary industrial societies power is distributed among a series of strategic elites rather than merely among social classes.

Kerr, Clark; Dunlop, John T.; Harbison, F. H.; and Meyers, Charles A. *Industrialism and Industrial Man.* Cambridge, Mass.: Harvard University Press, 1960.

Klein, Josephine. *Samples from English Cultures.* 2 vols. New York: Humanities Press, 1965. A discussion of life-styles among different strata of the population.

Leites, Nathan. *On the Game of Politics in France.* Stanford: Stanford University Press, 1959.

_____. *The Rules of the Game in Paris.* Translated by Derek Coltman. Chicago: University of Chicago Press, 1969. Two provocative books on French political culture.

Lowie, Robert H. *Toward Understanding Germany.* See comment, Chapter 2.

McClelland, David C. *The Roots of Consciousness.* Princeton: D. Van Nostrand, 1964. Includes a stimulating dissection of the German "national character."

McKenzie, Robert T., and Silver, Allan. *Angels in Marble.* Chicago: University of Chicago Press, 1968. Working-class political attitudes in England and how they are changing.

Macridis, Roy. *The De Gaulle Republic: Quest for Unity.* Homewood, Ill.: The Dorsey Press, 1960.

_____, and Ward, Robert E., eds. *Modern Political Systems: Europe.* See comment, Chapter 2.

Mead, Margaret. *Soviet Attitudes Toward Authority.* New York: William Morrow, 1955. An intriguing attempt to explain Soviet behavior by an examination of certain aspects of Russian culture.

Merkl, Peter. *Germany: Yesterday and Tomorrow.* New York: Oxford University Press, 1965. A popular introduction to contemporary German social and political life. The writing is sometimes a little cute, but the book contains much useful information and many sound observations.

Miller, Wright. *Russians as People.* New York: E. P. Dutton & Co., 1961. A refreshing, sympathetic discussion of the Russians, with politics merely incidental.

Moore, Wilbert E. *The Impact of Industry.* Englewood Cliffs, N. J.: Prentice-Hall, 1965. Moore writes concisely and well about the central issues of this chapter.

Pye, Lucian, and Verba, Sidney, eds. *Political Culture and Political Development.* Princeton: Princeton University Press, 1965.

Rodnick, David. *Postwar Germans.* New Haven: Yale University Press, 1948.

Rose, Richard. *Politics in England.* See comment, Chapter 2.

_____, ed. *Studies in British Politics.* New York: St. Martin's Press, 1966.

Runciman, W. G. *Relative Deprivation and Social Justice.* Berkeley and Los Angeles: University of California Press, 1966.

Salisbury, Harrison E., ed. *The Soviet Union: The Fifty Years.* New York: Harcourt, Brace & World, 1967. Essays by reporters of *The New York Times.* While lacking scholarly rigor, they convey an accurate "feel" for the present pattern of Soviet social life.

Sampson, Anthony. *Anatomy of Britain Today.* New York: Harper & Row, 1965. Excellent survey of English social and political life by a journalist; detailed, imaginative, well-written.

_____. *The New Europeans.* London: Hodder & Stoughton, 1968. Sampson tries to do for the Continent what he did for England—and fails. Some interesting information, but on the whole too thin to be of much value.

Schaffner, Bertram. *Father Land: A Study of Authoritarianism in the German Family.* See comment, Chapter 2.

Servan-Schreiber, Jean-Jacques. *The American Challenge.* Translated by Ronald Steel. New York: Atheneum, 1968. On American enterprise and Old World lethargy. Interesting, but with an unfortunate reliance upon adjectives instead of analysis.

Smelzer, Neil J., and Lipset, Seymour Martin, eds. *Social Structure and Mobility in Economic Development.* Chicago: Aldine Publishing Co., 1966.

Sorlin, Pierre. *The Soviet People and Their Society: From 1917 to the Present.* New York: Frederick A. Praeger, 1969.

Tannenbaum, Edward R. *The New France.* Chicago: University of Chicago Press, 1961.

Turgeon, Lynn. *The Contrasting Economies.* 2nd ed. Boston: Allyn & Bacon, 1963.

United Nations Secretariat of the Economic Commission for Europe. *Incomes in Postwar Europe.* Geneva: United Nations, 1967. The only really detailed study of trends in income distribution.

Vakar, Nicholas P. *The Taproot of Soviet Society.* New York: Harper & Row, 1962.

Vladimirov, Leonid. *The Russians.* New York: Frederick A. Praeger, 1968.

Weinberg, Ian. "The Problem of the Convergence of Industrial Societies: A Critical Look at the State of the Theory." *Comparative Studies in Society and History,* 11 (January 1969), pp. 1–15.

Wylie, Laurence. *Chanzeaux: A Village in Anjou.* Cambridge, Mass.: Harvard University Press, 1967.

_____. *Village in the Vaucluse*. 2nd ed. Cambridge, Mass.: Harvard University Press, 1964. These two studies are easy to read and vividly portray some of the major features of French small-town culture.

CHAPTER 5. SOCIAL CLASS AND POLITICS

Acomb, E. M., and Brown, M. L., Jr., eds. *French Society and Culture Since the Old Regime*. New York: Holt, Rinehart & Winston, 1966.

Anderson, Evelyn. *Hammer or Anvil: The Story of the German Working Class Movement*. London: Gollancz, 1945.

Angress, Werner T. "The Political Role of the Peasantry in the Weimar Republic." *Review of Politics*, 21 (June 1959), pp. 530–549.

Annan, Noel G. "The Intellectual Aristocracy." In *Studies in Social History*, edited by J. H. Plumb. London: Longmans Green & Co., 1955. A vigorous discussion of English intellectuals and why they have been so different from their European counterparts.

Ardagh, John. *The New French Revolution*. New York: Harper & Row, 1969. Diffuse and prolix, but nevertheless the most balanced and complete treatment of recent changes in French culture and social structure.

Aron, Raymond. *The Opium of the Intellectuals*. Translated by Terence Kilmartin. London: Secker & Warburg, 1957. A biting critique of French intellectuals. Aron maintains they are more concerned with destroying the existing order than with creating a new one, preferring grandiose ideological schemes to practical policies.

Azrael, Jeremy R. *Managerial Power and Soviet Politics*. Cambridge, Mass.: Harvard University Press, 1966. Denies that managers represent a distinct interest or that they can be regarded as a force for liberalization. Worth reading, though a little too pessimistic.

Banks, J. A., ed. *Studies in British Society*. New York: Thomas Y. Crowell, 1968.

Barber, Bernard, and Barber, Elinor G., eds. *European Social Class*. New York: The Macmillan Co., 1965. Essays concerning historical changes in the European class structure. The introductory essay is particularly useful.

Bauer, Raymond A., with Wasiolek, Edward. *Nine Soviet Portraits*. New York: John Wiley & Sons, 1955. Studies of life-styles based on interviews of Soviet refugees.

Ben-David, Joseph, ed. "Professions in the Class Systems of Present-Day Societies." *Current Sociology*, 12, No. 3 (1963–1964). Scholarly review of European educational systems and their relation to the evolution of professions. The introductory essay pulls together a mass of useful data in a very tidy manner.

Bendix, Reinhard. *Work and Authority in Industry*. See comment, Chapter 4.

_____, and Lipset, Seymour Martin, eds. *Class, Status, and Power*. See comment, Introduction.

Berliner, Joseph S. *Factory and Manager in the U.S.S.R.* Cambridge, Mass.: Harvard University Press, 1957.

Bill, Valentine T. *The Forgotten Class*. New York: Frederick A. Praeger, 1960. A discussion—rather more favorable than most—of the Russian bourgeoisie in the nineteenth century.

Black, Cyril E., ed. *The Transformation of Russian Society*. See comment, Chapter 3.

Bloch, Marc. *French Rural History*. Translated by Janet Sondheimer. Berkeley and Los Angeles: University of California Press, 1966. A basic work on the subject.

Blum, Jerome. *Lord and Peasant in Russia*. Princeton: Princeton University Press, 1961. Splendid account of rural Russia under the old regime. Impeccable scholarship.

Bolling, Klaus. *Republic in Suspense*. Translated by Jean Steinberg. New York: Frederick A. Praeger, 1964.

Braunthal, Gerald. *The Federation of German Industry in Politics*. Ithaca: Cornell University Press, 1965.

Broderson, Arvid. *The Soviet Worker*. New York: Random House, 1966. Reasoned discussion of the worker's place in the Soviet system.

Brombert, Victor. *The Intellectual Hero*. Philadelphia: J. B. Lippincott Co., 1961.

_____. "Toward a Portrait of the French Intellectual." *Partisan Review*, 27 (Summer 1960), pp. 480–502.

Brown, Emily Clark. *Soviet Trade Unions and Labor Relations*. 3rd ed. Cambridge, Mass.: Harvard University Press, 1966. A more optimistic view than is usual for American or English commentators.

Bullock, Alan. *The Life and Times of Ernest Bevin*. 2 vols. London: William Heinemann, 1960–1967. Excellent biography of one of England's outstanding trade-union leaders, with a skillful depiction of the movement and English society during the inter-war period.

Burks, Richard Voyles. *The Dynamics of Communism in Eastern Europe.* Princeton: Princeton University Press, 1961.

Caute, David. *Communism and the French Intellectuals, 1914–1960.* New York: The Macmillan Co., 1964.

Chambers, J. D., and Mingay, G. E. *The Agricultural Revolution: 1750–1880.* New York: Schocken Books, 1966.

Clark, James M. *Teachers and Politics in France.* Syracuse, N. Y.: Syracuse University Press, 1967.

Clarke, Robert H. "The Politics of French Agrarian Syndrialism." Ph.D. dissertation, Princeton University, 1965.

Clements, R. V. *Managers: A Study of Their Careers in Industry.* London: George Allen & Unwin, 1958.

Conquest, Robert. *Industrial Workers in the U.S.S.R.* New York: Frederick A. Praeger, 1967. A well-put-together summary of the workers' position, relying heavily upon official documents. Slight anti-Soviet bias.

Coser, Lewis A. *Men of Ideas: A Sociologist's View.* New York: The Free Press, 1965.

Cranston, Maurice. "The Paradox of the French Intellectual." *New Society,* 5, 119 (January 7, 1965), pp. 12–14.

Cyriax, George, and Oakeshott, Robert. *The Bargainers.* New York: Frederick A. Praeger, 1961. Discussion and analysis of English industrial relations.

Dahrendorf, Ralf. *Society and Democracy in Germany.* See comment, Chapter 2.

Deak, Istvan. *Weimar Germany's Left-Wing Intellectuals.* Berkeley and Los Angeles: University of California Press, 1969.

Deutscher, Isaac. *Soviet Trade Unions.* London: Royal Institute of International Affairs, 1950.

Dinerstein, Herbert, and Goure, Leon. *Two Studies in Soviet Controls: Communism and the Russian Peasant* and *Moscow in Crisis.* Glencoe, Ill.: The Free Press, 1955.

Dovring, Folke. *Land and Labor in Europe in the 20th Century: A Comparative Survey of Recent Agrarian History.* 3rd ed., rev., of *Land and Labor in Europe 1900–1950.* The Hague: Martinus Nijhoff, 1965.

Dunn, Stephen, and Dunn, Ethel. *The Peasants of Central Russia.* New York: Holt, Rinehart &

Winston, 1967. Relies heavily upon the writings of Soviet anthropologists. Extremely useful.

Edinger, Lewis J. *Politics in Germany.* See comment, Chapter 4.

Ehrmann, Henry W. *Organized Business in France.* Princeton: Princeton University Press, 1957. Massively documented, beautifully done.

_____. *Politics in France.* See comment, Chapter 2.

Farmer, Richard N., and Richman, Barry M. *Comparative Management and Economic Progress.* Homewood, Ill.: Richard D. Irwin, Inc., 1965.

Fischer, George, ed. *Science and Ideology in Soviet Society.* New York: Atherton Press, 1967.

Fyvel, T. R. *Intellectuals Today.* London: Chatto & Windus, 1968.

Galenson, Walter, ed. *Comparative Labor Movements.* Englewood Cliffs, N. J.: Prentice-Hall, 1952.

Glazer, Nathan. *The Social Basis of American Communism.* New York: Harcourt, Brace & World, 1961.

Goldthorpe, John H., and Lockwood, David. "Not So Bourgeois After All." *New Society,* 1 (October 18, 1962), pp. 18–19.

Goldthorpe, John H.; Lockwood, David; Bechhofer, Frank; and Platt, Jennifer. *The Affluent Worker.* 2 vols. New York: Cambridge University Press, 1968.

Grana, Cesar. *Bohemian vs. Bourgeois: French Society and the French Man of Letters in the Nineteenth Century.* New York: Basic Books, 1963.

Granick, David. *The European Executive.* New York: Doubleday & Co., 1962.

_____. *Management of the Industrial Firm in the U.S.S.R.* New York: Columbia University Press, 1954.

_____. *The Red Executive.* New York: Doubleday & Co., 1960.

_____. *Soviet Metal-Fabricating and Economic Development.* Madison: University of Wisconsin Press, 1967.

Grass, Günter. *Speak Out.* Translated by Ralph Manheim. New York: Harcourt, Brace & World, 1969.

Graubard, Stephen R., ed. *A New Europe?* See comment, Chapter 4.

Great Britain, Royal Commission on Trade Unions and Employer's Associations, Report and Research Papers. 6 vols. London: HMSO, 1968.

Grebling, Helga. *History of the German Labour Movement.* Oxford: O. Wolff, 1969.

Gruen, Walter. "Soviet Psychology's Concept of Personality as Represented at the 1966 Moscow Conference." *Soviet Studies,* 20 (April 1969), pp. 499–510.

Guttsman, W. L. *The British Political Elite.* New York: Basic Books, 1964. A close, statistical survey of the changing nature of the British elite in the nineteenth and twentieth centuries. An intriguing book that is required reading for any student of British politics.

Haffner, Sebastian. "An Intelligentsia of Demolition Men." *New Society,* 5, 142 (June 1965), pp. 24–25.

Hamilton, Richard F. *Affluence and the French Worker in the Fourth Republic.* Princeton: Princeton University Press, 1967.

Harbison, Frederick, and Myers, Charles A. *Management in the Industrial World: An International Analysis.* New York: McGraw-Hill, 1959.

Harrison, Martin. *Trade Unions and the Labour Party Since 1945.* London: George Allen & Unwin, 1960.

Hartmann, Heinz. *Authority and Organization in German Management.* Princeton: Princeton University Press, 1959.

Heidenheimer, Arnold J. *The Governments of Germany.* See comment, Chapter 4.

Himmelfarb, Milton. "Negroes, Jews and Muzhiks." In *The Ghetto and Beyond,* edited by Peter Rose. New York: Random House, 1969.

Hiscocks, Richard. *The Adenauer Era.* Philadelphia: J. B. Lippincott Co., 1966. A fairly standard history of the period with an emphasis on political developments. Competent, sober, balanced, and a little dull.

————. *Democracy in Western Germany.* See comment, Chapter 2.

Hoffmann, Stanley, et al. *In Search of France.* See comment, Chapter 4.

Hoggart, Richard. *The Uses of Literacy: Changing Patterns in British Mass Culture.* New York: Oxford University Press, 1957.

Hollander, Paul, ed. *American and Soviet Society.* See comment, Chapter 4.

Hough, Jerry F. *The Soviet Prefects.* Cambridge, Mass.: Harvard University Press, 1969. Exhaustive study of the relationship between the local party organization and the bureaucracy, including industrial management. Interesting insights into Soviet economic and political organization.

Huszar, George B., ed. *The Intellectuals: A Controversial Portrait.* Glencoe, Ill.: The Free Press, 1960. Stimulating collection of essays attacking, defending, and defining the role of intellectuals in society, with a number of studies of their position and influence in various countries. Unfortunately, no common theme is developed.

Inkeles, Alex. *Social Change in Soviet Russia.* Cambridge, Mass.: Harvard University Press, 1968.

————, and Bauer, Raymond. *The Soviet Citizen.* See comment, Chapter 4.

————, and Geiger, H. Kent, eds. *Soviet Society: A Book of Readings.* Boston: Houghton Mifflin, 1961.

Jackson, Brian. *Working Class Community.* New York: Frederick A. Praeger, 1968.

————, and Marsden, Dennis. *Education and the Working Class.* London: Routledge & Kegan Paul, 1962. An original analysis of some of the social factors that reduce the capacity of the working-class child to take full advantage of educational opportunities.

Jackson, J. A., ed. *Social Stratification.* New York: Cambridge University Press, 1968.

Janowitz, Morris. "Social Stratification and Mobility in West Germany." *American Journal of Sociology,* 64 (July 1958), pp. 6–24.

Jenkins, Clive, and Mortimer, J. E. *British Trade Unions Today.* Oxford: The Pergamon Press, 1965.

Karcz, Jerzy F., ed. *Soviet and East European Agriculture.* Berkeley and Los Angeles: University of California Press, 1967.

Kassalow, Everett M. "White Collar Unionism in Western Europe." *Monthly Labor Review,* 86 (July 1963), pp. 765–771.

Kassof, Allen, ed. *Prospects for Soviet Society.* See comment, Chapter 3.

Keller, Suzanne. *Beyond the Ruling Class.* See comment, Chapter 4.

Kerr, Clark; Dunlop, John T.; Harbison, F. H.; and Myers, Charles A. *Industrialism and Industrial Man.* Cambridge, Mass.: Harvard University Press, 1960.

Klein, Josephine, *Samples from English Cultures.* See comment, Chapter 4.

Laird, Roy D., and Crowley, Edward L. *Soviet Agriculture: The Permanent Crisis.* New York: Frederick A. Praeger, 1965.

Lamar, Cecil. *Albert Ballin: Business and Politics in Imperial Germany.* Princeton: Princeton University Press, 1966.

Landes, David S. "French Entrepreneurship and Industrial Growth in the Nineteenth Century." In *The Experience of Economic Growth,* edited by Barry E. Supple. New York: Random House, 1963.

Lapping, Brian, and Radice, Giles, eds. *More Power to the People.* New York: Humanities Press, 1968. Suggestions for reform of British political institutions designed to encourage greater public participation in decision-making. Very good, although the rhetoric in the essays is at times more telling than the analysis.

Laqueur, Walter, and Mosse, George L., eds. *The Left Wing Intelligentsia Between the Wars, 1919–1939.* New York: Harper & Row, 1966.

————. *Literature and Politics in the Twentieth Century.* New York: Harper & Row, Harper Torchbooks, 1967.

Lewin, Moshe. *Russian Peasants and Soviet Power.* Evanston, Ill.: Northwestern University Press, 1968.

Lewis, Roy, and Stewart, Rosemary. *The Boss.* London: Phoenix House, 1958. A pithy account of the life and times of the British businessman, by two authors who are sympathetic to the class and somewhat hostile to moves in the direction of socialism.

Liebman, Charles. "Toward a Theory of Jewish Liberalism." In *The Religious Situation,* edited by Donald R. Cutler. Boston: The Beacon Press, 1969.

Liggett, Eric. *British Political Issues.* 2 vols. New York: Pergamon Press, 1965.

Lockwood, David. *The Blackcoated Worker.* London: George Allen & Unwin, 1958.

London, Kurt, ed. *The Soviet Union: A Half-Century of Communism.* Baltimore: The Johns Hopkins Press, 1968. Excellent essays on Soviet life.

Lorwin, Val R. *The French Labor Movement.* Cambridge, Mass.: Harvard University Press, 1954.

————, ed. *Labor and Working Conditions in Modern Europe.* New York: The Macmillan Co., 1967.

Lowie, Robert H. *Toward Understanding Germany.* See comment, Chapter 2.

McCauley, Mary. *Labor Disputes and the Soviet Enterprise.* New York: Oxford University Press, 1969.

McGivering, Ian C.; Mathews, D. G. J.; and Scott, W. H. *Management in Britain: A General Characterization.* Liverpool: Liverpool University Press, 1960.

McKenzie, Robert T., and Silver, Allan. *Angels in Marble.* See comment, Chapter 4.

Macridis, Roy, and Ward, Robert E., eds. *Modern Political Systems: Europe.* See comment, Chapter 2.

Maynard, John. *Russia in Flux.* See comment, Chapter 3.

Merkl, Peter. *Germany: Yesterday and Tomorrow.* See comment, Chapter 4.

Mills, C. Wright. *The Power Elite.* New York: Oxford University Press, 1956. Contemporary analysis of the American power structure which maintains that in capitalist industrial societies, the military, economic, and political elites are fusing and dominating the "masses." The only hope would seem to lie with the intelligentsia. Well-written, but its facts and interpretations are somewhat dubious. Even so, basic for any student of politics.

Mingay, Gordon E. *English Landed Society in the Eighteenth Century.* London: Routledge & Kegan Paul, 1963.

Muhlen, Norbert. *The Incredible Krupps: The Rise, Fall, and Comeback of Germany's Industrial Family.* New York: Henry Holt, 1959.

Navasky, Victor R. "Notes on a Cult, or How to Join the Intellectual Establishment." *The New York Times Magazine,* March 27, 1966, pp. 28ff.

Nettl, J. P. "Consensus or Elite Domination: The Case of Business." *Political Studies,* 13 (February 1965), pp. 22–44.

Nordlinger, Eric A. *The Working-Class Tories.* Berkeley and Los Angeles: University of California Press, 1967.

Parry, Geraint. *Political Elites.* New York: Frederick A. Praeger, 1969. Succinct survey of elite theories with an attempt at synthesis that comes off rather well.

Pelling, Henry. *A History of British Trade Unionism.* New York: St. Martin's Press, 1963. A capable, scholarly job.

Pierce, Roy. *Contemporary French Political Thought.* New York: Oxford University Press, 1966.

Podhoretz, Norman. *Making It.* New York: Random House, 1968. Autobiographical light on the New York (largely Jewish) intellectual community in the 1950's and early 1960's.

Poggioli, Renato. *The Theory of the Avant-Garde.* Translated by Gerald Fitzgerald. Cambridge, Mass.: Harvard University Press, Belknap Press, 1968.

Political and Economic Planning. *Attitudes in British Management.* Harmondsworth, Middlesex, Eng.: Penguin Books, 1966.

Postan, M. M. *An Economic History of Western Europe, 1945–1964*. London: Methuen & Co., 1967. Thorough, well-written examination of postwar economic and social changes.

Potter, A. M. *Organized Groups in British National Politics*. London: Faber & Faber, 1961.

Problems of Communism. Special issues, "In Quest of Justice," 17 (July–August 1968 and September–October, 1968). Essays and documents on the current travail of Soviet intellectuals.

Reader, W. J. *Professional Men*. New York: Basic Books, 1967.

Rieff, Philip, ed. *On Intellectuals*. New York: Doubleday & Co., 1969. A few of the essays are exceptional, but the collection as a whole lacks bite.

Ringer, Fritz K. *The Decline of the German Mandarins*. Cambridge, Mass.: Harvard University Press, 1968.

Roberts, B. C. *Trade Union Government and Administration in Great Britain*. Cambridge, Mass.: Harvard University Press, 1956.

Robinson, Geroid T. *Rural Russia Under the Old Regime*. New York: The Macmillan Co., 1949.

Rose, Richard. *Politics in England*. See comment, Chapter 2.

————, ed. *Studies in British Politics*. New York: St. Martin's Press, 1966.

Runciman, W. G. *Relative Deprivation and Social Justice*. Berkeley and Los Angeles: University of California Press, 1966.

Salisbury, Harrison E., ed. *The Soviet Union: The Fifty Years*. See comment, Chapter 4.

Sampson, Anthony. *Anatomy of Britain Today*. See comment, Chapter 4.

Schwartz, V. A. *A History of Soviet Literature, 1917–1964*. New York: Doubleday & Co., 1964.

Self, Peter, and Storing, Herbert. *The State and the Farmer: British Agricultural Policies and Politics*. Berkeley and Los Angeles: University of California Press, 1963.

Servan-Schreiber, Jean-Jacques. *The American Challenge*. See comment, Chapter 4.

Shanks, Michael. *The Innovators*. Baltimore: Penguin Books, 1968.

Shils, Edward. "Intellectuals." *International Encyclopedia of the Social Sciences*, 7 (1968), pp. 399–414.

Slicher, van Bath B. H. *The Agrarian History of Western Europe, A. D. 500–1850*. Translated by Olive Ordish. New York: St. Martin's Press, 1963.

Smelser, Neil J., and Lipset, Seymour Martin. *Social Structure and Mobility in Economic Development*. Chicago: Aldine Publishing Co., 1966.

Sorlin, Pierre. *The Soviet People and Their Society: From 1917 to the Present*. New York: Frederick A. Praeger, 1969.

Strauss, Erich. *Soviet Agriculture in Perspective: A Study of Its Successes and Failures*. New York: Frederick A. Praeger, 1969.

Sturmthal, Adolf Fox. *The Tragedy of European Labor*. New York: Columbia University Press, 1951. The movement in the 1920's and 1930's, with an emphasis on Germany. Slightly exaggerated, but instructive nevertheless.

————. *Unity and Diversity in European Labor*. Glencoe, Ill.: The Free Press, 1953.

————, ed. *White-Collar Trade Unions: Contemporary Developments in Industrialized Societies*. Urbana: University of Illinois Press, 1966.

Tannenbaum, Edward R. *The New France*. Chicago: University of Chicago Press, 1961.

Thompson, Edward P. T. *The Making of the English Working Class*. New York: Random House, Pantheon Books, 1964. A powerfully written book on the impact of industrialization. Slightly overstated but compelling even so.

Thompson, Francis M. L. *English Landed Society in the Nineteenth Century*. London: Routledge & Kegan Paul, 1963.

Tracy, Michael. *Agriculture in Western Europe*. New York: Frederick A. Praeger, 1964.

United Nations Economic and Social Council, Department of Mass Communications. *Professional Training for Mass Communications*. Paris: United Nations, 1965.

United Nations, Secretariat of the Economic Commission for Europe. *Incomes in Postwar Europe*. See comment, Chapter 4.

Vollmer, H. M., and Mills, Donald L. *Professionalization*. Englewood Cliffs, N. J.: Prentice-Hall, 1966.

Warner, Charles K., ed. *Agrarian Conditions in Modern European History*. New York: The Macmillan Co., 1966.

Webb, Sidney, and Webb, Beatrice. *The History of Trade Unionism*. London: Longmans Green & Co., 1920. The classic history of the English trade-union movement in the nineteenth and early twentieth centuries.

Williams, Francis. *Magnificent Journey: The Rise of the Trade Unions*. London: Odhams Press, 1954. A popular history.

Wood, Neal. *Communism and the British Intellectual.* New York: Columbia University Press, 1959.

Wright, Gordon. *Rural Revolution in France.* Stanford: Stanford University Press, 1964.

Wunderlich, Frieda. *Farm Labor in Germany, 1810–1945.* Princeton: Princeton University Press, 1961.

Wylie, Laurence. *Chanzeaux: A Village in Anjou.* See comment, Chapter 4.

————. *Village in the Vaucluse.* See comment, Chapter 4.

Zweig, Ferdynand. *The Worker in an Affluent Society: Family Life and Industry.* New York: The Free Press, 1962. How the "affluent" society has changed working-class attitudes. The Goldthorpe studies are a necessary corrective, for Zweig stretches his point that workers are "going bourgeois."

CHAPTER 6. RELIGIOUS AND ETHNIC GROUPS

Ardagh, John. *The New French Revolution.* See comment, Chapter 5.

Armstrong, John A. *Ukrainian Nationalism.* 2nd ed. New York: Columbia University Press, 1962.

Baldwin, Summerfield. *The Organization of Medieval Christianity.* New York: Henry Holt, 1929.

Banton, Michael. *White and Coloured: The Behavior of British People Towards Coloured Immigrants.* New Brunswick, N. J.: Rutgers University Press, 1960.

Bellah, Robert N. "Religious Evolution." *American Sociological Review,* 29 (June 1964), pp. 358–374. On the stages of religious development, as derived largely from the work of Parsons. Well done.

Benz, Ernst. *The Eastern Orthodox Church: Its Thought and Life.* New York: Doubleday & Co., Anchor Books, 1963.

Birnbaum, Norman, and Lenzer, Gertrud, eds. *Sociology and Religion.* Englewood Cliffs, N. J.: Prentice-Hall, 1969.

Black, Cyril E., ed. *The Transformation of Russian Society.* See comment, Chapter 3.

Bordeaux, Michael. *Religious Ferment in Russia.* New York: St. Martin's Press, 1968.

Bosworth, William. *Catholicism and Crisis in Modern France.* Princeton: Princeton University Press, 1961. Detailed survey of the role of the Catholic Church in Fourth-Republic France, with extensive discussion of the M.R.P. Rather dry, but very useful.

Bull, George. *Vatican Politics.* Oxford: The Clarendon Press, 1966.

Burrell, Sidney A., ed. *The Role of Religion in Modern European History.* New York: The Macmillan Co., 1964.

Casey, Robert P. *Religion in Russia.* New York: Harper & Row, 1946.

Collins, Ross William. *Catholicism and the Second French Republic, 1848–1852.* New York: Columbia University Press, 1923.

Conquest, Robert. *The Soviet Deportation of Nationalities.* New York: St. Martin's Press, 1960. Complete and comprehensive.

————, ed. *Soviet Nationalities Policy in Practice.* New York: Frederick A. Praeger, 1967. Brief and straightforward, although somewhat anti-Soviet in tone.

Curtiss, John S. *The Russian Church and the Soviet State, 1917–1950.* Boston: Little, Brown & Co., 1953.

Dahrendorf, Ralf. *Society and Democracy in Germany.* See comment, Chapter 2.

Dansette, Adrien. *Religious History of Modern France.* Vol. 1: *From the Revolution to the Third Republic.* Vol. 2: *Under the Third Republic.* Translated by John Dingle. New York: Herder & Herder, 1961. Both books are a reasoned, readable account by a liberal Catholic.

Deakin, Nicholas. *Color and the British Electorate.* New York: Frederick A. Praeger, 1965.

Drummond, Andrew L. *German Protestantism Since Luther.* London: Epworth Press, 1951.

Edwards, Maldwyn. *After Wesley: A Study of the Social and Political Influence of Methodism in the Middle Period 1791–1849.* London: Epworth Press, 1935.

Elkins, Stanley. *Slavery: A Problem in American Institutional and Intellectual Life.* 2nd ed. Chicago: University of Chicago Press, 1968.

Ferris, Paul. *The Church of England.* New York: The Macmillan Co., 1963.

Fitzsimmons, M. A., ed. *The Catholic Church Today: Western Europe.* Notre Dame, Ind.: University of Notre Dame Press, 1969.

Fletcher, William C., and Strover, Anthony, eds. *Religion and the Search for New Ideals in the U.S.S.R.* New York: Frederick A. Praeger, 1967.

Fogarty, Michael P. *Christian Democracy in Western Europe, 1820–1953*. Notre Dame, Ind.: University of Notre Dame Press, 1957.

Franklin, John Hope, ed. *Color and Race*. Boston: Houghton Mifflin, 1969. A collection of many outstanding essays.

Freyre, Gilberto. *The Masters and the Slaves*. 2nd ed. Translated by Samuel Putnam. New York: Alfred A. Knopf, 1956. A basic study of Brazilian slavery. While the author may be too kind in describing it, his analysis provides interesting contrasts with the United States.

Garbett, Cyril F. *Church and State in England*. London: Hodder & Stoughton, 1950.

Glazer, Nathan, and Moynihan, Daniel Patrick. *Beyond the Melting Pot*. Cambridge, Mass.: M.I.T. Press and Howard University Press, 1963.

Goldhagen, Erich, ed. *Ethnic Minorities in the Soviet Union*. New York: Frederick A. Praeger, 1968.

Gordon, Milton M. *Assimilation in American Life*. New York: Oxford University Press, 1964.

Hales, E. E. Y. *Revolution and Papacy: 1769–1846*. New York: Doubleday & Co., 1960.

Hanham, H. J. *Scottish Nationalism*. London: Basil Blackwell, 1969.

Helmreich, Ernst C. *Religious Education in German Schools*. Cambridge, Mass.: Harvard University Press, 1960.

————, ed. *A Free Church in a Free State*. Boston: D. C. Heath, 1964.

Heubel, E. J. "Church and State in England." *Western Political Quarterly*, 18 (September 1968), pp. 646–655.

Inglis, K. S. *Churches and the Working Classes in Victorian England*. London: Routledge & Kegan Paul, 1963.

Inkeles, Alex. *Social Change in Soviet Russia*. Cambridge, Mass.: Harvard University Press, 1968.

————, and Bauer, Raymond. *The Soviet Citizen*. See comment, Chapter 4.

————, and Geiger, H. Kent, eds. *Soviet Society: A Book of Readings*. Boston: Houghton Mifflin, 1961.

Jackson, John A. *The Irish in Britain*. London: Routledge & Kegan Paul, 1963.

Kassof, Allen, ed. *Prospects for Soviet Society*. See comment, Chapter 3.

Laqueur, Walter, and Mosse, George L., eds. "Church and Politics." *Journal of Contemporary History*, 2 (October 1967), entire issue.

Latourette, Kenneth Scott. *Christianity in a Revolutionary Age*. 5 vols. New York: Harper & Bros., 1958–1962. A massive, meticulous study, not terribly original but invaluable as a reference.

Lessa, William A., and Vogt, Evon Z. *Reader in Comparative Religion*. 2nd ed. New York: Harper & Row, 1965.

Lewy, Guenter. *The Catholic Church and Nazi Germany*. New York: McGraw-Hill, 1964.

London, Kurt, ed. *The Soviet Union: A Half-Century of Communism*. See comment, Chapter 5.

Martin, David. *A Sociology of English Religion*. New York: Basic Books, 1967.

————, ed. *A Sociological Yearbook of Religion*. London: SCM Press, 1968. Informative readings on the English religious scene.

Mathew, David. *Catholicism in England 1535–1935; Portrait of a Minority: Its Culture and Tradition*. London: Longmans Green & Co., 1936.

Mayer, Carl. "The Crisis in German Protestantism." *Social Research*, 12 (November 1945), pp. 397–432. Religious and social variables employed to describe the evolution of German Protestantism and its relation to the rise of National Socialism. A tour de force.

Moody, J. N., ed. *Church and Society*. New York: Arts, Inc., 1953.

Mörner, Magnus. *Race Mixture in the History of Latin America*. Boston: Little, Brown & Co., 1967. The author seems to have read just about every monograph on the subject and summarizes many of them. Short, thorough, cautious, invaluable, and somewhat dull.

Patterson, Sheila. *Dark Strangers*. Bloomington: Indiana University Press, 1964. A sensitive account of the plight of England's "colored" immigrants.

————. *Immigration and Race Relations in Britain, 1960–1967*. New York: Oxford University Press, 1969. A review and analysis of the literature on English race relations. Competent, but less useful than Rose.

Paul, Harry W. *The Second Ralliement: The Rapprochement Between Church and State in France in the Twentieth Century*. Washington, D. C.: Catholic University of America Press, 1967.

Pickering, W. S. F. *Anglican Methodist Relations*. London: World Congress of Churches Press, 1961.

Problems of Communism. "Nationalities and Nationalism in the U.S.S.R.," 16 (March-April 1967). Special issue.

Rose, E. J. B., ed. *Colour and Citizenship*. Oxford: The Clarendon Press, 1969. The single best review of race relations in England. Incorporates information contained in other studies.

Rose, Peter. *Americans from Africa*. 2 vols. New York: Atherton Press, forthcoming. Perceptive essays on the black experience in the United States.

Rywkin, Michael. *Russia in Central Asia*. New York: Crowell-Collier, Collier Paperbacks, 1968.

Salisbury, Harrison E., ed. *The Soviet Union: The Fifty Years*. See comment, Chapter 4.

Sampson, Anthony. *Anatomy of Britain Today*. See comment, Chapter 4.

Schneider, Louis, ed. *Religion, Culture, and Society*. New York: John Wiley & Sons, 1964.

Schram, Stuart R. *Protestantism and Politics in France*. Paris: Alençon, 1954.

Shanahan, W. O. *German Protestants Face the Social Question*. Notre Dame, Ind.: University of Notre Dame Press, 1954.

Stalin, Joseph. *Marxism and the National and Colonial Question*. New York: International Publishers, 1942.

Sullivant, Robert S. *Soviet Politics and the Ukraine, 1917–1957*. New York: Columbia University Press, 1962.

Troeltsch, Ernest. *The Social Teaching of the Christian Churches*. Translated by Olive Wyon. 2 vols. New York: The Macmillan Co., 1950. The basis for most of the work done by contemporary social scientists on the subject. Not easy going, but the rewards are considerable.

Vagn, Aage, and Christensen, Canisus. "The Godesberger Socialists and the German Catholic Church." Ph.D. dissertation, University of California, 1966.

Vakar, N. P. *Belorussia: The Making of a Nation*. Cambridge, Mass.: Harvard University Press, 1956.

Vidler, Alec R. *The Church in an Age of Revolution*. Baltimore: Penguin Books, 1964. On the Christian churches since 1789—done with fairness and distinction.

Wallace, Anthony F. C., ed. *Religion: An Anthropological View*. New York: Random House, 1966.

Ward, Conor K. *Priests and People*. Liverpool: Liverpool University Press, 1961.

Wearmouth, Robert Fetherstone. *Methodism and the Working-Class Movements of England, 1800–1850*. London: The Epworth Press, 1937.

_____. *The Social and Political Influence of Methodism in the Twentieth Century*. London: The Epworth Press, 1957.

Weber, Max. *The Sociology of Religion*. Translated by Ephraim Fischoff. Boston: Beacon Press, 1963. Weber's scholarship in this field is unsurpassed.

Weinstein, Allen, and Gatell, Frank Otto, eds. *American Negro Slavery*. New York: Oxford University Press, 1968. Perhaps the best introduction to the subject.

Wheeler, Geoffrey. *Racial Problems in Soviet Muslim Asia*. 2nd ed. New York: Oxford University Press, 1962.

Wickham, E. R. *Church and People in an Industrial City*. London: Lutterworth Press, 1964.

Wilson, Bryan R. *Religion in Secular Society*. London: A. C. Watts, 1966.

World Yearbook of Education, 1966. *Church and State in Education*. New York: Harcourt, Brace & World, 1966.

Zenkovsky, Serge A. *Pan-Turkism and Islam in Russia*. Cambridge, Mass.: Harvard University Press, 1960.

CHAPTER 7. POLITICAL SOCIALIZATION: FAMILY, EDUCATION, AND MASS MEDIA

Alston, Patrick L. *Education and the State in Tsarist Russia*. Stanford: Stanford University Press, 1969.

Ardagh, John. *The New French Revolution*. See comment, Chapter 5.

Aries, Philippe. *Centuries of Childhood: A Social History of the Family*. Translated by Robert Baldick. New York: Alfred A. Knopf, 1962.

Armytage, W. H. G. *Four Hundred Years of English Educational History*. Oxford: The Clarendon Press, 1965.

Ashby, Eric. "The Future of the Nineteenth Century Idea of a University." *Minerva*, 6 (Autumn 1967), pp. 3–17.

Banks, Olive. *Sociology of Education*. New York: Schocken Books, 1968.

Bantock, Geoffrey H. *Education in an Industrial Society*. New York: Humanities Press, 1963.

Baron, G. *Society, Schools and Progress in England*. Oxford: Pergamon Press, 1965.

Bauer, Raymond A. *The New Man in Soviet Psychology*. Cambridge, Mass.: Harvard University Press, 1952.

Ben-David, Joseph, ed. "Professions in the Class Systems of Present-Day Societies." See comment, Chapter 5.

————, and Zloczower, Awraham. "Universities and Academic Systems in Modern Societies." *European Journal of Sociology*, 3, 1 (1962), pp. 45–84. A seminal analysis.

Bereday, George Z. F. *Essays on World Education*. Oxford: The Clarendon Press, 1969.

————.; Brickman, William W.; and Read, G. H. *The Changing Soviet School*. Boston: Houghton Mifflin, 1960.

Black, Cyril E., ed. *The Transformation of Russian Society*. See comment, Chapter 3.

Blumler, J. G., and McQuail, Denis. *Television in Politics*. Chicago: University of Chicago Press, 1969.

Bromhead, Peter. "Parliament and the Press." *Parliamentary Affairs*, 5, 13 (Summer 1963), pp. 363–373.

Buzek, Antony. *How the Communist Press Works*. New York: Frederick A. Praeger, 1964.

Central Advisory Council for Education in England. The Newsom Report. *Half Our Future*. London: HMSO, 1963.

————. The Plowdem Report. *Children and Their Primary Schools*. London: HMSO, 1967.

Christoph, James B. "The Press and Politics in Britain and America." *Political Quarterly*, 34 (April-June 1963), pp. 137–150.

Clark, Burton C.; Anderson, C. Arnold; and Halsey, A. H. "Education." *International Encyclopedia of the Social Sciences*, 4 (1968), pp. 509–533.

Clark, James M. *Teachers and Politics in France*. Syracuse, N. Y.: Syracuse University Press, 1967.

Clausen, John, ed. *Socialization and Society*. Boston: Little, Brown & Co., 1968.

Conquest, Robert. *Politics of Ideas in the U.S.S.R.* New York: Frederick A. Praeger, 1967.

Cramer, John Francis, and Browne, George S. *Contemporary Education: A Comparative Study of National Systems*. 2nd ed. New York: Harcourt, Brace & World, 1965. A standard text, well done.

Dahrendorf, Ralf. *Society and Democracy in Germany*. See comment, Chapter 2.

Davison, W. Philips, ed. *International Political Communication*. New York: Frederick A. Praeger, 1965.

Dawson, Richard E., and Prewitt, Kenneth. *Political Socialization*. Boston: Little, Brown & Co., 1969. Excellent, concise, and to the point.

Deutsch, Karl W., and Edinger, Lewis J. *Germany Rejoins the Powers*. Stanford: Stanford University Press, 1959.

Dizard, Wilson P. *Television: A World View*. Syracuse, N. Y.: Syracuse University Press, 1966.

Dodge, Norton T. *Women in the Soviet Economy*. Baltimore: Johns Hopkins Press, 1966.

Easton, David, and Dennis, Jack. *Children in the Political System: Origins of Political Legitimacy*. New York: McGraw-Hill, 1969.

Eckstein, Harry. *A Theory of Stable Democracy*. Princeton: Princeton University Press, 1961.

Edinger, Lewis J. *Politics in Germany*. See comment, Chapter 2.

Ehrmann, Henry W. *Politics in France*. See comment, Chapter 2.

Eisenstadt, S. N. *From Generation to Generation*. Glencoe, Ill.: The Free Press, 1956. Basic appraisal of the problem of generations in primitive and modern societies. Tough going, but exceptionally rewarding.

Emery, Walter. *Five European Broadcasting Systems*. Austin, Tex.: Association for Education in Journalism, 1966.

Erikson, Erik H. *Childhood and Society*. Rev. ed. New York: W. W. Norton, 1964.

————. *Identity, Youth, and Crisis*. New York: W. W. Norton, 1968.

Fagen, Richard. *Politics and Communication*. Boston: Little, Brown & Co., 1966. As an introduction to the subject, this is hard to beat.

Fisher, Ralph Talcott, Jr. *Pattern for Soviet Youth: A Study of the Congresses of the Komsomol, 1918–1954*. New York: Columbia University Press, 1959.

Fraser, William R. *Education and Society in Modern France*. London: Routledge & Kegan Paul, 1963.

————. "Reform in France." *Comparative Education Review*, 11 (October 1967), pp. 300–310.

Gazette 5, 1 (1959). Special issue on the German press.

———— 8, 2 (1962). Special issue on the French press.

Geiger, H. Kent. *The Family in Soviet Russia*. Cambridge, Mass.: Harvard University Press, 1968. The best book available on the subject.

————, ed. *Comparative Perspectives on Marriage and the Family*. Boston: Little, Brown & Co., 1968.

Goode, William J. *World Revolution and Family Patterns.* New York: The Free Press, 1963. Synthesis of studies on the family in different cultures. Among the best books on the subject.

—————, ed. *Readings on the Family and Society.* Englewood Cliffs, N. J.: Prentice-Hall, 1964.

Goody, Jack, ed. *Literacy in Traditional Societies.* New York: Cambridge University Press, 1969. Several of these essays deal in an engaging way with a topic which is, unfortunately, too often neglected.

Grant, Nigel. *Soviet Education.* Baltimore: Penguin Books, 1964.

Hale, Oron J. *The Captive Press in the Third Reich.* Princeton: Princeton University Press, 1964.

Halls, W. D. *Society, Schools, and Progress in France.* New York: Pergamon Press, 1965.

Halsey, A. H., ed. *Education, Economy and Society.* Glencoe, Ill.: The Free Press, 1961.

Herd, Harold. *The March of Journalism: The Story of the British Press From 1622 to the Present Day.* London: George Allen & Unwin, 1952.

Himmelweit, Hilde T.; Oppenheim, A. N.; and Vince, Pamela. *Television and the Child.* Oxford: The Clarendon Press, 1958.

Hoffmann, Stanley, et al. *In Search of France.* See comment, Chapter 4.

Hoggart, Richard. *The Uses of Literacy: Changing Patterns in British Mass Culture.* New York: Oxford University Press, 1957.

Hollander, Paul, ed. *American and Soviet Society.* See comment, Chapter 4.

Hood, Stuart. *A Survey of Television.* London: William Heinemann, 1967.

Hornby, Nathan. *The Press in Modern Society.* London: F. Muller, 1965.

Huebener, Theodore. *The Schools of West Germany.* New York: New York University Press, 1962.

Inkeles, Alex. *Public Opinion in Soviet Russia.* 2nd ed. Cambridge, Mass.: Harvard University Press, 1962. A detailed, scholarly study of how opinion is shaped in the Soviet Union, from newspapers to wall posters.

—————. *Social Change in Soviet Russia.* Cambridge, Mass.: Harvard University Press, 1968.

—————, and Bauer, Raymond. *The Soviet Citizen.* See comment, Chapter 4.

—————, and Geiger, H. Kent, eds. *Soviet Society: A Book of Readings.* Boston: Houghton Mifflin, 1961.

Jackson, Brian, and Marsden, Dennis. *Education and the Working Class.* See comment, Chapter 5.

Jensen, Jay, and Bayley, Richard. "Highlights of the Development of Russian Journalism." *Journalism Quarterly,* 41 (Summer 1964), pp. 403–415.

Kaser, Michael. "Soviet Boarding Schools." *Soviet Studies,* 20 (July 1968), pp. 94–105.

Kassof, Allen, ed. *Prospects for Soviet Society.* See comment, Chapter 3.

Kazamias, Andreas, and Massialas, Byron G. *Tradition and Change in Education.* Englewood Cliffs, N. J.: Prentice-Hall, 1965.

Kerr, Anthony. *Universities of Europe.* London: Bowes & Bowes, 1962.

King, Edmund. *Education and Development in Western Europe.* Reading, Mass.: Addison Wesley Press, 1969.

—————, ed. *Communist Education.* Indianapolis: The Bobbs-Merrill Co., 1963.

Klein, Josephine. *Samples from English Cultures.* 2 vols. See comment, Chapter 4.

Kolarz, Walter. *Religion in the Soviet Union.* New York: St. Martin's Press, 1962. The best account available in English, although now slightly dated. Detailed.

Kruglak, Theodore E. *The Two Faces of Tass.* Minneapolis: University of Minnesota Press, 1962.

Laqueur, Walter, and Mosse, George L., eds. "Education and Social Structure in the Twentieth Century." *Journal of Contemporary History,* 2 (July 1967), entire issue.

Lazarsfeld, Paul, and Katz, Elihu. *Personal Influence.* Glencoe, Ill.: The Free Press, 1955.

Lerner, Daniel, and Schramm, Wilbur, eds. *Communication and Change in Developing Countries.* Honolulu: East-West Center Press, 1967.

Litchfield, Edward H. *Governing Postwar Germany.* Ithaca: Cornell University Press, 1953.

London, Kurt, ed. *The Soviet Union: A Half-Century of Communism.* See comment, Chapter 5.

Lowie, Robert H. *Toward Understanding Germany.* See comment, Chapter 2.

McQuail, Denis, and Trenaman, Joseph. *Television and the Political Image.* London: Methuen & Co., 1961.

Macridis, Roy, and Ward, Robert E., eds. *Modern Political Systems: Europe.* See comment, Chapter 2.

Male, George A. *Education in France.* Washington, D. C.: U. S. Government Printing Office, 1963.

Markham, James. *Voices of the Red Giants*. Ames: Iowa State University Press, 1967.

Martin, David, ed. *Anarchy and Culture: The Problem of the Contemporary University*. London: Routledge & Kegan Paul, 1969. Some wonderful and witty essays on English higher education.

Matthews, T. S. *The Sugar Pill*. New York: Simon & Schuster, 1957. History and critique of the English popular press.

Mayne, Richard. "At the French Kiosk." *Encounter*, June 1968, pp. 79–85.

Merrill, John C. *The Elite Press*. New York: Pitman Publishing Corp., 1968.

————. *A Handbook of the Foreign Press*. Baton Rouge: Louisiana State University Press, 1959.

Muuss, Rolf E. *Theories of Adolescence*. 2nd ed. New York: Random House, 1968.

Organization for Economic Cooperation and Development, Study Group in the Economics of Education. *Social Objectives in Educational Planning*. Paris: OECD, 1967.

Osborn, Robert J. "Crime and Environment: The New Soviet Debate." *Slavic Review*, 27 (September 1968), pp. 395–410.

Paulu, Burton. *Radio and Television Broadcasting on the European Continent*. Minneapolis: University of Minnesota Press, 1967.

Peterson, A. D. C. "Educational Reform in England and Wales, 1955–1966." *Comparative Education Review*, 11 (October 1967), pp. 275–287.

Political and Economic Planning. *Citizenship and Television*. London: Political & Economic Planning, 1967. A useful, general discussion of television's political impact.

Pye, Lucian W., ed. *Communications and Political Development*. Princeton: Princeton University Press, 1963.

Raison, Timothy. *Youth in "New Society."* London: Hart-Davis, 1966.

Robbins Report. *Higher Education*. 5 vols. Cmnd. 2154. London: HMSO, 1963.

Robinsohn, Saul B., and Kuhlman, J. Caspar. "Two Decades of Non-Reform in West German Education." *Comparative Education Review*, 11 (October 1967), pp. 311–330.

Rodnick, David. *Postwar Germans*. New Haven: Yale University Press, 1948.

Rose, Richard. *Politics in England*. See comment, Chapter 2.

————, ed. *Studies in British Politics*. New York: St. Martin's Press, 1966.

Rosen, Seymour. *Significant Aspects of Soviet Education*. Washington, D. C.: U.S. Department of Health, Education, and Welfare, 1965.

Rudman, Herbert C. *The School and State in the U.S.S.R.* New York: The Macmillan Co., 1967.

Rugh, William A. "Radio and Television in the German Federal Republic." Ph.D. dissertation, Columbia University, 1967.

Russi, Bernard A. "The History and Development of German Broadcasting as an Instrument of Social Control." Ph.D. dissertation, Wayne State University, 1963.

Salisbury, Harrison E., ed. *The Soviet Union: The Fifty Years*. See comment, Chapter 4.

Sampson, Anthony. *Anatomy of Britain Today*. See comment, Chapter 4.

Samuel, Richard, and Thomas, R. H. *Education and Society in Modern Germany*. London: Routledge & Kegan Paul, 1949.

Schaffner, Bertram. *Father Land: A Study of Authoritarianism in the German Family*. See comment, Chapter 2.

Schoenbaum, David. *The Spiegel Affair*. New York: Doubleday & Co., 1968.

Seymour-Ure, Colin. *The Press, Politics and the Public*. London: Methuen & Co., 1968. Standard academic discussion.

Siebert, F. S.; Peterson, Theodore; and Schramm, Wilbur. *Four Theories of the Press*. Urbana: University of Illinois Press, 1958.

Tannenbaum, Edward R. *The New France*. Chicago: University of Chicago Press, 1961.

Thomas, Harford. *Newspaper Crisis*. Zurich: International Press Institute, 1967. On the problems facing the English press.

Ulich, Robert. *The Education of Nations*. Rev. ed. Cambridge, Mass.: Harvard University Press, 1967.

Vaizey, John. *Education in the Modern World*. New York: McGraw-Hill, 1967. A popular survey particularly suited to the beginning student.

Wedall, E. G. *Broadcasting and Public Policy*. London: Michael Joseph, 1968.

Weinberg, Ian. *The English Public Schools*. New York: Atherton Press, 1966. How the public schools train the British elite.

Wilkinson, Rupert. *Gentlemanly Power: British Leadership and the Public School Tradition*. New York: Oxford University Press, 1964. A good supplement to Weinberg.

————, ed. *Governing Elites.* New York: Oxford University Press, 1969. Comparisons of educational systems and how they train social and political leaders.

Williams, Francis. *Dangerous Estate.* London: Longmans Green & Co., 1957. A popular history of the English press.

Williams, Raymond. *The Long Revolution.* New York: Columbia University Press, 1961.

Wilson, John. *Public Schools and Private Practice.* London: George Allen & Unwin, 1962.

World Yearbook of Education. *Church and State in Education.* New York: Harcourt, Brace & World, 1966.

————. *Educational Planning.* New York: Harcourt, Brace & World, 1967.

————. *The Education Explosion.* New York: Harcourt, Brace & World, 1965.

Yanowitch, Murray, and Dodge, Norton. "Social Class and Education: Soviet Findings and Reactions." *Comparative Education Review,* 12 (October 1968), pp. 248–267.

CHAPTER 8. POLITICAL SOCIALIZATION: YOUTH AND POLITICS

Abrams, Philip, and Little, Alan. "Britain: Young Voters, Young Activists and the Irrelevance of Age." Paper presented at the Sixth World Congress of the International Political Science Association, September 21–25, 1964, at Geneva. Mimeographed.

Ali, Tariq, ed. *The New Revolutionaries.* New York: William Morrow & Co., 1969. Essays by European student radicals.

Ardagh, John. *The New French Revolution.* See comment, Chapter 5.

Aries, Philippe. *Centuries of Childhood: A Social History of the Family.* Translated by Robert Baldick. New York: Alfred A. Knopf, 1962.

Bettelheim, Bruno. "Obsolete Youth." *Encounter,* 33 (September 1969), pp. 29–42.

Daedalus, 7 (Winter 1968). Special issue on "Students and Politics."

Eisenstadt, S. N. *From Generation to Generation.* See comment, Chapter 7.

Erikson, Erik H. *Childhood and Society.* 2nd ed. New York: W. W. Norton, 1963.

————. *Identity, Youth, and Crisis.* New York: W. W. Norton, 1968.

Feuer, Lewis S. *The Conflict of Generations.* New York: Basic Books, 1969. A sweeping view of student rebellion which does not ignore historical and comparative perspectives. The author's premises and prejudices, stemming from his own involvement, detract from the book's overall merit, but there is so much good material here, and the quality of writing is so superior, that Feuer deserves careful attention.

Fisher, Ralph Talcott, Jr. *Pattern for Soviet Youth: A Study of the Congresses of the Komsomol, 1918–1954.* New York: Columbia University Press, 1959.

Glazer, Nathan. "The Jewish Role in Student Activism." In *Youth in Turmoil,* by the editors of *Fortune.* New York: Time-Life Books, 1969.

Gould, Julius. "Politics and the Academy." *Government and Opposition,* 3 (Winter 1968), pp. 3–22.

Himmelfarb, Milton. "Negroes, Jews and Muzhiks." In *The Ghetto and Beyond,* edited by Peter Rose. New York: Random House, 1969.

Hollander, Paul, ed. *American and Soviet Society.* See comment, Chapter 4.

Josephson, Eric. *Political Youth Organizations in Europe, 1900–1950.* Ann Arbor, Mich.: University Microfilms, 1960.

Kassof, Allen. *The Soviet Youth Program.* Cambridge, Mass.: Harvard University Press, 1965. The best source on the Komsomol and Soviet youth.

Keniston, Kenneth. *The Uncommitted.* New York: Harcourt, Brace & World, 1965.

————. *Young Radicals.* New York: Harcourt, Brace & World, 1968. Two studies of alienation and radicalism among American youth by a sympathetic psychiatrist critical of many features of American society. Highly impressionistic.

Klein, Josephine. *Samples from English Cultures.* See comment, Chapter 4.

Laqueur, Walter. *Young Germany.* New York: Basic Books, 1962.

Liebman, Charles. "Toward a Theory of Jewish Liberalism." In *The Religious Situation,* edited by Donald R. Cutler. Boston: Beacon Press, 1969.

Lipset, Seymour Martin, ed. *Student Politics.* New York: Basic Books, 1967. An excellent, iconoclastic collection of essays on student politics around the world.

————, and Altbach, Philip G. *Student Politics and Higher Education in the United States: A Selected Bibliography.* St. Louis: United Ministries in Higher Education, 1968.

Lubell, Samuel. "That Generation Gap." *The Public Interest,* 13 (Fall 1968), pp. 52–61.

Martin, David, ed. *Anarchy and Culture: The Problem of the Contemporary University.* See comment, Chapter 7.

Maschmann, Melita. *Account Rendered.* New York: Abelard-Schuman, 1964. A German woman's autobiographical explanation of why she was so "blind" as to join the Nazi youth movement. Compelling and highly relevant.

Matza, David. "Position and Behavior Patterns of Youth." In *Handbook of Modern Sociology,* edited by Robert E. Lee Faris and H. Warren Dunham, pp. 191–216. Chicago: Rand McNally, 1964.

Meek, Dorothea L., ed. and trans. *Soviet Youth: Some Achievements and Problems.* London: Routledge & Kegan Paul, 1957. A selection of articles in the Soviet press, plus useful commentary.

Muuss, Rolf E. *Theories of Adolescence.* 2nd ed. New York: Random House, 1968.

Parkin, Frank. *Middle Class Radicalism.* Manchester: Manchester University Press, 1968.

Sontheimer, Kurt. "Student Opposition in Western Germany." *Government and Opposition,* 3 (Winter 1968), pp. 3–22.

Spender, Stephen. *The Year of the Young Rebels.* New York: Random House, 1968. A warmly sympathetic (although not uncritical) overview of student rebellion in Europe and the United States.

Taubman, William. *The View From Lenin Hills.* New York: Coward-McCann, 1967. Some rather incisive opinions on the new generation of Soviet youth by an American who spent a year at Moscow University as an exchange student.

Part III Political Parties

CHAPTER 9. THE EUROPEAN PATTERN

Almond, Gabriel A., and Verba, Sidney. *The Civic Culture: Political Attitudes and Democracy in Five Nations.* Princeton: Princeton University Press, 1963. Cross-cultural comparisons of political attitudes and the factors affecting them, based on public-opinion polls. Weak in some respects, but contains much useful information.

Andrews, William G., ed. *European Political Institutions.* 2nd ed. Princeton: D. Van Nostrand, 1966.

Aron, Raymond, et al. "The Dead End of Monolithic Parties." *Government and Opposition,* 2 (February 1967), pp. 165–180.

Borkenau, Franz. *European Communism.* See comment, Chapter i.

Caute, David. *The Left in Europe Since 1789.* World University Library Series. New York: McGraw-Hill, 1966.

Dahl, Robert A., ed. *Political Oppositions in Western Democracies.* New Haven: Yale University Press, 1966.

Deutsch, Karl. "Social Mobilization and Political Development." *American Political Science Review,* 55 (September 1961), pp. 493–502.

Duverger, Maurice. *Political Parties.* 2nd rev. ed. Translated by Barbara and Robert North. London: Methuen & Co., 1959. A work, now classic, that has generated considerable reaction. Limited by the fact that the categories developed are derived primarily from the European experience, but still useful.

Eckstein, Harry. "Party Systems." *International Encyclopedia of the Social Sciences,* 11 (1968), pp. 436–453. As careful as it is erudite.

Ehrmann, Henry W., ed. *Democracy in a Changing Society.* New York: Frederick A. Praeger, 1964.

Epstein, Leon. *Political Parties in Western Democracies.* New York: Frederick A. Praeger, 1967. Worthwhile.

Finer, Herman. *The Theory and Practice of Modern Government.* See comment, Chapter 2.

Fogarty, Michael P. *Christian Democracy in Western Europe, 1820–1953.* Notre Dame, Ind.: University of Notre Dame Press, 1957.

Friedrich, Carl J. *Constitutional Government and Democracy.* See comment, Chapter 1.

Geertz, Clifford W., ed. *Old Societies and New States.* New York: The Free Press, 1963. A number of excellent essays on mobilization regimes.

Graubard, Stephen R., ed. *A New Europe?* See comment, Chapter 4.

Griffith, William E., ed. *Communism in Europe.* 2 vols. Cambridge, Mass.: M.I.T. Press, 1966.

Hermens, F. A. *Democracy or Anarchy?* Notre Dame, Ind.: University of Notre Dame Press, 1941. A formidable attack on proportional representation as contributing to the delinquency of government and the rise of extremist political movements. Overstated and slightly shrill.

————. *The Representative Republic.* Notre Dame, Ind.: University of Notre Dame Press, 1958.

Holborn, Louise; Herz, John H.; and Carter, Gwendolen M., eds. *Documents of Major Foreign Powers.* New York: Harcourt, Brace & World, 1968.

Jacobs, Dan N., ed. *The New Communisms.* New York: Harper & Row, 1969.

Janowitz, Morris, and Segal, John. "Social Cleavage and Party Affiliation: Germany, Great Britain, and the United States." *American Journal of Sociology,* 72 (May 1967), pp. 601–618.

Landauer, Carl. *European Socialism.* See comment, Chapter 1.

La Palombara, Joseph, and Weiner, Myron, eds. *Political Parties and Political Development.* Princeton: Princeton University Press, 1966.

Lijphart, Arend, ed. *Politics in Europe: Comparisons and Interpretations.* Englewood Cliffs, N. J.: Prentice-Hall, 1969.

Lipset, Seymour Martin. *Political Man: Essays in the Sociology of Democracy.* New York: Doubleday & Co., 1959.

————. *Revolution and Counterrevolution.* New York: Basic Books, 1968. Both of these books are collections of Lipset essays on contemporary politics. As usual, the author exhibits his knack for assembling a mass of fugitive statistical evidence to make his points. Invaluable.

————, and Rokkan, Stein, eds. *Party Systems and Voter Alignments.* New York: The Free Press, 1967.

MacKenzie, W. J. M. *Free Elections.* New York: Rinehart & Co., 1958.

Macridis, Roy, ed. *Modern European Governments: Cases in Comparative Policy Making.* Englewood Cliffs, N. J.: Prentice-Hall, 1968.

————, and Brown, Bernard, eds. *Comparative Politics: Notes and Readings.* See comment, Introduction.

————, and Ward, Robert E., eds. *Modern Political Systems: Europe.* See comment, Chapter 2.

Marvick, Dwaine. *Political Decision-Makers.* Glencoe, Ill.: The Free Press, 1961.

Michels, Robert. *Political Parties.* Translated by Eden and Cedar Paul. New York: Crowell-Collier, 1962. First-rate study of the German Social Democratic Party just before World War I; raises some significant theoretical issues.

Milnor, Andrew J., ed. *Comparative Political Parties.* New York: Thomas Y. Crowell, 1969.

Muller, Steven, ed. *Documents on European Government.* New York: The Macmillan Co., 1963.

Munger, Frank, ed. *Studies in Comparative Politics.* New York: Thomas Y. Crowell, 1967.

Neumann, Sigmund, ed. *Modern Political Parties.* Chicago: University of Chicago Press, 1956.

Ostrogorski, M. *Democracy and the Organization of Political Parties.* 2 vols. Edited and abridged by Seymour Martin Lipset. New York: Quadrangle

Books, 1964. Classic study of English and American political parties in the late nineteenth century. Lipset's introduction to this edition is also commendable.

Pitkin, Hanna F. *The Concept of Representation.* Berkeley and Los Angeles: University of California Press, 1967.

————, ed. *Representation.* New York: Atherton Press, 1969.

Rae, Douglas W. *The Political Consequences of Electoral Laws.* New Haven: Yale University Press, 1967.

Rogger, Hans, and Weber, Eugen, eds. *The European Right.* Berkeley and Los Angeles: University of California Press, 1965.

Rokkan, Stein. "Mass Suffrage, Secret Voting and Political Participation." *European Journal of Sociology,* 2, 1 (1961), pp. 132–152.

Rose, Richard. *Politics in England.* See comment, Chapter 2.

————, ed. *Studies in British Politics.* New York: St. Martin's Press, 1966.

————. "Dynamic Tendencies in the Authority of Regimes." *World Politics,* 21 (July 1969), pp. 602–628.

————, and Heidenheimer, Arnold J., eds. "Comparative Political Finance." Reprinted by and from *Journal of Politics,* August 1963.

————, and Mossawir, Harvey. "Voting and Elections: A Functional Analysis." *Political Studies,* 15 (June 1967), pp. 73–120.

————, and Unwin, Derek. "Social Cohesion, Political Parties and Strains in Regimes." *Comparative Political Studies,* 2 (April 1969), pp. 7–67.

Rothman, Stanley. "One-Party Regimes: A Comparative Analysis." *Social Research,* 34 (Winter 1967), pp. 675–702.

Sampson, Anthony. *The New Europeans.* See comment, Chapter 4.

Tucker, Robert C. "The Dictator and Totalitarianism." *World Politics,* 17 (July 1965), pp. 555–583.

————. "Towards a Comparative Study of Movement Regimes." *American Political Science Review,* 55 (June 1961), pp. 281–289. One of the first essays to point up the limitations of the "totalitarian" model of Soviet politics in the post-Stalin era—and to suggest an alternate approach. Still worth reading.

UNESCO. *Decisions and Decision Makers in the Modern State.* Paris: UNESCO, 1967.

Wuest, John J., and Vernon, Manfred C., eds. *New Source Book in Major European Governments.* See comment, Chapter 1.

CHAPTER 10. THE BRITISH PARTY SYSTEM

Alford, Robert. *Party and Society: The Anglo-Saxon Democracies.* Chicago: Rand McNally, 1963.

Beer, Samuel H. *British Politics in the Collectivist Age.* See comment, Chapter 2.

————. "The Comparative Study of British Politics." *Comparative Politics,* 1 (October 1968), pp. 19–36.

Benewick, Robert, and Dowse, Robert. *Readings on British Politics and Government.* London: University of London Press, 1968.

Birch, A. H. *The British System of Government.* New York: Frederick A. Praeger, 1967.

————. *Representative and Responsible Government.* Toronto: University of Toronto Press, 1964.

Blondel, Jean. *Voters, Parties, and Leaders.* Baltimore: Penguin Books, 1964. Sociological analysis of the composition of local parties, the bases of party support, and patterns of leadership. Well-written and informative.

Bulmer-Thomas, Ivor. *The Growth of the British Party System.* 2 vols. 2nd ed. New York: Humanities Press, 1967–1968. Standard discussion.

Butler, D. E. *The Electoral System in Britain Since 1918.* 2nd ed. New York: Oxford University Press, 1963.

Crick, Bernard, ed. *Essays on Reform.* Oxford: The Clarendon Press, 1967.

Epstein, Leon. *British Politics in the Suez Crisis.* Urbana: University of Illinois Press, 1964.

Guttsman, W. L. *The British Political Elite.* See comment, Chapter 5.

Harrison, Martin. *Trade Unions and the Labour Party Since 1945.* London: George Allen & Unwin, 1960.

Hoffman, J. D. *The Conservative Party in Opposition, 1945–1951.* New York: Humanities Press, 1964.

Holt, Robert T., and Turner, John E. *Political Parties in Action.* New York: The Free Press, 1968. The study of an election in a London constituency, conveying the excitement of a political campaign.

Janosik, Edward G. *Constituency Labour Parties in Britain.* New York: Frederick A. Praeger, 1968.

Jennings, Sir William Ivor. *Party Politics.* 3 vols. New York: Cambridge University Press, 1960–1962.

King, Anthony, ed. *British Politics.* See comment, Chapter 2.

Lapping, Brian, and Radice, Giles, eds. *More Power to the People.* See comment, Chapter 5.

Leonard, Richard Lawrence. *Elections in Britain.* Princeton: D. Van Nostrand, 1968.

Lowell, A. Lawrence. *The Government of England.* See comment, Chapter 2.

McKenzie, Robert T. *British Political Parties.* 2nd ed. New York: St. Martin's Press, 1963. Remains the definitive work, although the stress on essential similarities between the Conservative and Labor parties is overdone.

————, and Silver, Allan. *Angels in Marble.* See comment, Chapter 4.

Nordlinger, Eric A. *The Working-Class Tories.* Berkeley and Los Angeles: University of California Press, 1967.

Ostrogorski, M. *Democracy and the Organization of Political Parties.* See comment, Chapter 9.

Parkin, Frank. *Middle Class Radicalism.* Manchester: Manchester University Press, 1968.

Pelling, Henry. *Social Geography of British Elections: 1885–1910.* New York: St. Martin's Press, 1967.

Pulzer, P. G. J. *Political Representation and Elections: Parties and Voting in Great Britain.* New York: Frederick A. Praeger, 1967. Political behavior and the electoral process in England. Useful.

Punnett, R. M. *British Government and Politics.* London: Heinemann Educational, 1968. An excellent general text. Makes commendable use of behavioral materials, but also good on institutions.

Ranney, Austin. *Pathways to Parliament: Candidate Selection in Great Britain.* Madison: University of Wisconsin Press, 1965. Exhaustive and solid, yet written with style and humor. The definitive study to date of the English process of choosing a party candidate.

Rasmussen, Jorgen Scott. *Retrenchment and Revival: A Study of the Contemporary British Liberal Party.* Tucson: University of Arizona Press, 1964.

Rose, Richard. *Influencing Voters: A Study in Campaign Rationality.* New York: St. Martin's Press, 1967. An analysis of campaign strategies based primarily on Britain's 1964 elections.

————. "Class and Party Divisions: Britain as a Test Case." *Sociology,* 2 (May 1968), pp. 129–162.

Runciman, W. G. *Relative Deprivation and Social Justice.* Berkeley and Los Angeles: University of California Press, 1966.

Stacey, Frank. *The Government of Modern Britain.* Oxford: The Clarendon Press, 1968. Standard text.

Stankiewicz, W. J., ed. *Crisis in British Government.* New York: The Macmillan Co., 1967. Critical essays on all facets of the British political system. Uneven in quality.

Vincent, J. R. *Pollbooks: How Victorians Voted.* Cambridge: Cambridge University Press, 1967.

Watkins, Alan. *The Liberal Dilemma.* London: MacGibbon & Kee, 1966.

Weiner, Herbert. *British Labour and Public Ownership.* London: Stevens & Sons, 1960.

Wilson, Trevor. *The Downfall of the Liberal Party, 1914–1935.* Ithaca: Cornell University Press, 1966.

CHAPTER 11. THE FRENCH PARTY SYSTEM

Aron, Robert. *An Explanation of de Gaulle.* Translated by Marianne Sinclair. New York: Harper & Row, 1966.

Blondel, Jean, and Godfrey, E. Drexel, Jr. *The Government of France.* See comment, Chapter 2.

Brown, Bernard. "Elite Attitudes and Legitimacy in France." *Journal of Politics,* 31 (May 1969), pp. 420–442.

Campbell, Peter. *French Electoral Systems and Elections Since 1789.* 2nd ed. London: Faber & Faber, 1965. Good, short history which also discusses the development of parties.

Converse, P. E., and Dupeux, George. "Politicization of the Electorate in France and U. S." In *Comparative Politics: Notes and Readings,* edited by Roy Macridis and Bernard Brown. 3rd ed. Homewood, Ill.: The Dorsey Press, 1968.

De Gaulle, Charles. *War Memoirs.* 3 vols. Vol. 1 translated by Jonathan Griffin; vols. 2 and 3 translated by Richard Howard. New York: Simon & Schuster, 1955–1959.

De Tarr, Francis. *The French Radical Party From Herriot to Mendès-France.* Oxford: The Clarendon Press, 1961.

Ehrmann, Henry W. *Politics in France.* See comment, Chapter 2.

Einaudi, Mario, ed. *Communism in Western Europe.* Ithaca: Cornell University Press, 1951.

Fejtö, François. *The French Communist Party and the Crisis of International Communism.* Cambridge, Mass.: M.I.T. Press, 1967.

Goldey, David B. "The Events of May and the French General Elections." *Parliamentary Affairs,* 21 (Autumn 1968), pp. 307–337; 22 (Spring 1969), pp. 116–133.

Graham, B. D. *The French Socialists and Tripartism, 1944–1947.* London: Weidenfeld & Nicolson, 1965.

Greene, Thomas H. "The Communist Parties of Italy and France." *Studies in Comparative Communism,* 21 (October 1968), pp. 1–38.

Harrison, Martin, ed. *French Politics.* See comment, Chapter 2.

Hoffmann, Stanley, et al. *In Search of France.* See comment, Chapter 4.

Hunt, William H. "Careers and Perspectives of French Politicians." Ph.D. dissertation, Vanderbilt University, 1966.

Lacouture, Jean. *De Gaulle.* Translated by Francis K. Price. New York: New American Library, 1966. A first-rate biography, probably the best in English.

Larmour, Peter J. *The French Radical Party in the 1930's.* Stanford: Stanford University Press, 1964.

Leites, Nathan. *On the Game of Politics in France.* See comment, Chapter 4.

_____. *The Rules of the Game in Paris.* See comment, Chapter 4.

Lichtheim, George. *Marxism in Modern France.* New York: Columbia University Press, 1966.

MacRae, Duncan. *Parliament, Parties, and Society in France: 1946–1958.* New York: St. Martin's Press, 1967. A close analysis of political and parliamentary behavior during the Fourth Republic, relying on complicated statistical techniques. The author destroys, or at least weakens, many myths about French politics. Tough going, but worth serious attention.

Macridis, Roy. *The De Gaulle Republic: Quest for Unity.* Homewood, Ill.: The Dorsey Press, 1960.

Mandel, Arthur P. "Why the French Communists Stopped the Revolution." *Review of Politics,* 31 (January 1969), pp. 3–27.

Mendès-France, Pierre. *A Modern French Republic.* Translated by Anne Carter. New York: Hill & Wang, 1963. A rousing effort to outline needed social and political reforms in France, by a leading political figure of the Fourth Republic.

Micaud, Charles. *Communism and the French Left.* New York: Frederick A. Praeger, 1963.

Osgood, Samuel M. *French Royalism Under the Third and Fourth Republics.* The Hague: Martinus Nijhoff, 1960.

Pickles, Dorothy. *The Fifth French Republic: Institutions and Politics*. 3rd ed. New York: Frederick A. Praeger, 1965. Quite traditional, but with meticulous attention to detail.

Pierce, Roy. *French Politics and Political Institutions*. New York: Harper & Row, 1968.

Rémond, René. *The Right Wing in France from 1815 to De Gaulle*. See comment, Chapter 2.

Rosenthal, Howard. "The Electoral Politics of Gaullists in the French Fourth Republic: Ideology or Constituency Interest?" *American Political Science Review,* 63 (June 1969), pp. 476–487.

Sharp, Walter Rice. *The Government of the French Republic*. New York: D. Van Nostrand, 1938.

Simmons, Harvey G. "The Crisis in French Socialism Since 1956." Ph.D. dissertation, Cornell University, 1967.

————. "The French Socialist Opposition in 1969." *Government and Opposition,* 41 (Summer 1969), pp. 294–307.

Thomson, David. *Democracy in France Since 1870*. See comment, Chapter 2.

Werth, Alexander. *The De Gaulle Revolution*. See comment, Chapter 2.

Williams, Philip M. *Crisis and Compromise*. See comment, Chapter 2.

————, and Harrison, Martin. *De Gaulle's Republic*. London: Longmans Green & Co., 1960.

Wilson, Frank. "The French Left and the Election of 1968." *World Politics,* 21 (July 1969), pp. 539–574.

CHAPTER 12. GERMAN POLITICAL PARTIES

Alexander, Edgar. *Adenauer and the New Germany: The Chancellor of the Vanquished*. Translated by Thomas E. Goldstein. New York: Farrar, Straus & Cudahy, 1957.

Bald, Richard H. "The Free Democratic Party and West German Foreign Policy, 1949–1959." Ph.D. dissertation, University of Michigan, 1963.

Balfour, Michael. *West Germany*. New York: Frederick A. Praeger, 1968.

Berlau, A. Joseph. *The German Social Democratic Party, 1914–1921*. New York: Columbia University Press, 1949.

Bolling, Klaus. *Republic in Suspense*. Translated by Jean Steinberg. New York: Frederick A. Praeger, 1964.

Burden, Hamilton. *The Nuremberg Party Rallies*. New York: Frederick A. Praeger, 1967.

Chalmers, Douglas A. *The Social Democratic Party of Germany*. New Haven: Yale University Press, 1964.

Childs, David. *From Schumacher to Brandt: The Story of German Socialism, 1945–1965*. Oxford: Pergamon Press, 1966. Solid. Leftist.

Deutsch, Karl W., and Edinger, Lewis J. *Germany Rejoins the Powers*. Stanford: Stanford University Press, 1959.

Dittmer, Lowell. "The German N.P.D.: A Psycho-Sociological Analysis of Neo-Naziism." *Comparative Politics,* 2 (October 1969), pp. 79–110.

Dowell, Jack D. "Party, Caucus, and Chancellor." *Research Studies,* 36 (June 1968), pp. 131–142.

————. "The Politics of Accommodation: German Social Democracy and the Catholic Church." *Journal of Church and State,* 7 (Winter 1965), pp. 78–90.

Edinger, Lewis J. *German Exile Politics: The Social Democratic Executive Committee in the Nazi Era*. Berkeley and Los Angeles: University of California Press, 1956.

————. *Kurt Schumacher: A Study in Personality and Political Behavior*. Stanford: Stanford University Press, 1965. A penetrating sociological, political, and psychoanalytical view of the man and the period. Stimulating.

————. *Politics in Germany*. See comment, Chapter 2.

Gittler, Lewis F. "Probing the German Mind." *Interplay,* 1 (October 1967), pp. 4–8.

Heberle, Rudolf. *From Democracy to Nazism*. Baton Rouge: Louisiana State University Press, 1945. An engrossing ecological study of the social bases of National Socialism. One of the few detailed studies of its type available in English.

Heidenheimer, Arnold J. *Adenauer and the C.D.U.* The Hague: Martinus Nijhoff, 1960.

————. *The Governments of Germany*. See comment, Chapter 4.

Hiscocks, Richard. *The Adenauer Era*. See comment, Chapter 5.

————. *Democracy in Western Germany*. See comment, Chapter 2.

Hunt, Richard N. *German Social Democracy*. New Haven: Yale University Press, 1964.

Kitzinger, Uwe W. *German Electoral Politics: A Study of the 1957 Campaign*. New York: Oxford University Press, 1960.

Lehmbruch, Gerhard. "The Ambiguous Coalition in West Germany." *Government and Opposition,* 3 (Spring 1968), pp. 181–206.

Linz, Juan. "The Social Basis of German Politics." Ph.D. dissertation, Columbia University, 1958.

Litchfield, Edward H. *Governing Postwar Germany*. Ithaca: Cornell University Press, 1953.

Loewenberg, Gerhard. "The Remaking of the German Party System." *Polity*, I (Fall 1968), pp. 87–113.

Merkl, Peter. *Germany: Yesterday and Tomorrow*. See comment, Chapter 4.

————. *The Origin of the West German Republic*. New York: Oxford University Press, 1963.

Michels, Robert. *Political Parties*. See comment, Chapter 9.

Naegle, John. "Right Radicalism in the German Federal Republic." Ph.D. dissertation, Harvard University, 1968.

Nettl, J. P. *Rosa Luxemburg*. 2 vols. New York: Oxford University Press, 1966. A monumental biography that tells much about post–World War I German politics. The author's admiration for his heroine is quite apparent—and so is the beauty of the prose.

Noelle, Elisabeth, and Neumann, Erich Peter. *The Germans: Public Opinion Polls, 1947–1966*. Allensbach, Bonn: Verlag für Demoskopie, 1967.

Nyomarkay, Joseph. *Charisma and Factionalism in the Nazi Party*. Minneapolis: University of Minnesota Press, 1967.

Plischke, Elmer. *Contemporary Governments of Germany*. 2nd ed. Boston: Houghton Mifflin, 1969. Standard text.

Pollock, J. K., et al. *German Democracy at Work*. Ann Arbor: University of Michigan Press, 1955.

————, and Lane, John. *Source Materials on the Government and Politics of Germany*. Ann Arbor, Mich.: George Wahr Publishing Co., 1964.

————, and Thomas, Homer. *Germany in Power and Eclipse*. See comment, Chapter 2.

Roth, Guenter. *The Social Democrats in Imperial Germany*. Totowa, N. J.: Bedminster Press, 1963.

Schellinger, Harold Kent. *The S.P.D. in the Bonn Republic*. The Hague: Martinus Nijhoff, 1968. A judicious examination of the party's change in outlook and the reasons for it. Well done.

Schorske, Carl E. *German Social Democracy, 1905–1917*. Cambridge, Mass.: Harvard University Press, 1955.

Stern, Fritz, ed. *The Path to Dictatorship, 1918–1933*. See comment, Chapter 2.

Tauber, Kurt P. *Beyond Eagle and Swastika*. 2 vols. Middletown, Conn.: Wesleyan University Press, 1967. Right-wing movements in Germany in the postwar period. Recommended.

Tilford, R. B., and Preece, R. J. *Federal Germany*. See comment, Chapter 2.

United States Department of the Army. *Area Handbook for Germany*. See comment, Chapter 2.

Vagn, Aage, and Christensen, Canisus. "The Godesberger Socialists and the German Catholic Church." Ph.D. dissertation, University of California, 1966.

Verkade, Willem. *Democratic Parties in the Low Countries and Germany*. Leiden: Universitaire Pers, 1966.

Von Klemperer, Klemens. *Germany's New Conservatism*. Princeton: Princeton University Press, 1957.

CHAPTER 13. THE COMMUNIST PARTY OF THE SOVIET UNION

Andrews, William G., ed. *Soviet Institutions and Policies: Inside Views*. Princeton: D. Van Nostrand, 1966.

Armstrong, John A. *The Soviet Bureaucratic Elite: A Case Study of the Ukrainian Apparatus*. New York: Frederick A. Praeger, 1959.

Barghoorn, Frederick C. *Politics in the U.S.S.R.* See comment, Chapter 3.

Black, Cyril E., ed. *The Transformation of Russian Society*. See comment, Chapter 3.

Brzezinski, Zbigniew, and Huntington, Samuel P. *Political Power: U.S.A./U.S.S.R.* New York: The Viking Press, 1964. Instructive comparison of Soviet and American politics. The first major break with the totalitarian model, which Brzezinski had done so much to advance in an earlier work with Friedrich.

Burks, Richard Voyles. "The ACLS Summer, 1968 Workshop on the Comparative Study of Communism: A Report." *Comparative Studies of Communism*, 2 (June 1969), pp. 2–11. A summary of current thinking on mobilization regimes by students of comparative communism.

Churchward, L. G. *Contemporary Soviet Government*. London: Routledge & Kegan Paul, 1968.

Dallin, Alexander, and Larson, Thomas B., eds. *Soviet Politics Since Khrushchev*. Englewood Cliffs, N. J.: Prentice-Hall, 1968.

————, and Westin, Alan F., eds. *Politics in the Soviet Union: Seven Cases*. New York: Harcourt, Brace & World, 1965.

Deutscher, Isaac. *Stalin: A Political Biography*. See comment, Chapter 3.

Ellison, Herbert J. "The Socialist Revolutionaries." *Problems of Communism,* 6 (November-December 1967), pp. 2–14.

Fainsod, Merle. *How Russia Is Ruled.* See comment, Chapter 3.

————. *Smolensk Under Soviet Rule.* See comment, Chapter 3.

Fischer, George. *Russian Liberalism: From Gentry to Intelligentsia.* Cambridge, Mass.: Harvard University Press, 1958.

Fleron, Frederick J. "Toward a Reconceptualization of Political Change in the Soviet Union: The Political Leadership System." *Comparative Politics,* 1 (January 1969), pp. 228–244.

Friedrich, Carl J., and Brzezinski, Zbigniew K. *Totalitarian Dictatorship and Autocracy.* See comment, Chapter 3.

Gehlen, Michael P. *The Communist Party of the Soviet Union.* Bloomington: Indiana University Press, 1969. A functional approach.

Getzler, Israel. "The Mensheviks." *Problems of Communism,* 16 (November–December 1967), pp. 15–29.

Hendel, Samuel, ed. *The Soviet Crucible.* See comment, Chapter 3.

Hough, Jerry F. *The Soviet Prefects.* See comment, Chapter 5.

Kassof, Allen, ed. *Prospects for Soviet Society.* See comment, Chapter 3.

Keep, J. L. H. *The Rise of Social Democracy in Russia.* New York: Oxford University Press, 1963.

Lane, David. *The Roots of Russian Communism.* See comment, Chapter 3.

Linden, Carl. *Khrushchev and the Soviet Leadership, 1957–1964.* Baltimore: Johns Hopkins Press, 1966.

Lodge, Milton. "Soviet Elite Participatory Attitudes in the Post-Stalin Period." *American Political Science Review,* 62 (September 1968), pp. 827–839.

London, Kurt, ed. *The Soviet Union: A Half-Century of Communism.* See comment, Chapter 5.

Meyer, Alfred G. *The Soviet Political System: An Interpretation.* New York: Random House, 1965. Meyer argues that the system is best compared with that of a highly bureaucratized corporation, the Communist Party serving as the board of directors. Interesting hypothesis, almost convincing.

Radkey, O. H. *The Agrarian Foes of Bolshevism.* New York: Columbia University Press, 1958.

Rigby, Thomas Harold. *Communist Party Membership in the U.S.S.R., 1917–1967.* Princeton: Princeton University Press, 1968. Massive. Invaluable.

Schapiro, Leonard. *The Communist Party of the Soviet Union.* See comment, Chapter 3.

Shaffer, Harry G., ed. *The Soviet System.* New York: Appleton-Century-Crofts, 1965.

Swearer, Howard R. *The Politics of Succession in the U.S.S.R.* Boston: Little, Brown & Co., 1964.

Tatu, Michel. *Power in the Kremlin.* Translated by Helen Katel. New York: The Viking Press, 1969. Tatu comments on Soviet and East European politics for *Le Monde.* His study is a fine example of "Kremlinology."

Tucker, Robert C. *The Soviet Political Mind.* New York: Frederick A. Praeger, 1963.

Venturi, Franco. *Roots of Revolution.* New York: Alfred A. Knopf, 1961.

Part IV The Process of Government

CHAPTER 14. THE EUROPEAN PATTERN

Anderson, Eugene N., and Anderson, Pauline R. *Political Institutions and Social Change in Continental Europe in the Nineteenth Century.* Berkeley and Los Angeles: University of California Press, 1967.

Andrews, William G., ed. *European Political Institutions.* 2nd ed. Princeton: D. Van Nostrand, 1966.

Aron, Raymond. *Democracy and Totalitarianism.* Translated by Valence Ionescu. New York: Frederick A. Praeger, 1969.

Carter, Gwendolen M., and Westin, Alan F. *Politics in Europe: Five Cases in European Government.* New York: Harcourt, Brace & World, 1965.

Castles, Francis G. *Pressure Groups and Political Culture: A Comparative Study.* New York: Humanities Press, 1967.

Christoph, James B., and Brown, Bernard. eds. *Cases in Comparative Politics.* Boston: Little, Brown & Co., 1969.

Dahl, Robert A., ed. *Political Oppositions in Western Democracies.* New Haven: Yale University Press, 1966.

Edinger, Lewis J., ed. *Political Leadership in Industrialized Societies.* New York: John Wiley & Sons, 1967. Though the book lacks a common focus, many of these essays are interesting either as case studies or for their theoretical insights.

Ehrmann, Henry W., ed. *Democracy in a Changing Society*. New York: Frederick A. Praeger, 1964.

Finer, Herman. *The Theory and Practice of Modern Government*. See comment, Chapter 2.

Frank, Elke, ed. *Lawmakers in a Changing World*. Englewood Cliffs, N. J.: Prentice-Hall, 1966.

Friedrich, Carl J. *Constitutional Government and Democracy*. See comment, Chapter 1.

Graubard, Stephen R., ed. *A New Europe?* See comment, Chapter 4.

Hermens, F. A. *The Representative Republic*. Notre Dame, Ind.: University of Notre Dame Press, 1958.

Holborn, Louise; Herz, John H.; and Carter, Gwendolen M., eds. *Documents of Major Foreign Powers*. New York: Harcourt, Brace & World, 1968.

International Political Science Association. *Interest Groups on Four Continents*. Edited by Henry W. Ehrmann. Pittsburgh: University of Pittsburgh Press, 1958.

Jacobs, Dan N., ed. *The New Communisms*. New York: Harper & Row, 1969.

Lijphart, Arend, ed. *Politics in Europe: Comparisons and Interpretations*. Englewood Cliffs, N. J.: Prentice-Hall, 1969.

Macridis, Roy, ed. *Modern European Governments: Cases in Comparative Policy Making*. Englewood Cliffs, N. J.: Prentice-Hall, 1968.

_____, and Brown, Bernard, eds. *Comparative Politics: Notes and Readings*. See comment, Introduction.

_____, and Ward, Robert E., eds. *Modern Political Systems: Europe*. See comment, Chapter 2.

McWhinney, Edward. *Comparative Federalism: States' Rights and National Power*. Toronto: University of Toronto Press, 1964.

Marvick, Dwaine. *Political Decision Makers*. New York: The Free Press, 1961.

Muller, Steven, ed. *Documents on European Government*. New York: The Macmillan Co., 1963.

Munger, Frank, ed. *Studies in Comparative Politics*. New York: Thomas Y. Crowell, 1967.

Parry, Geraint. *Political Elites*. See comment, Chapter 5.

Pitkin, Hanna F. *The Concept of Representation*. Berkeley and Los Angeles: University of California Press, 1967.

_____, ed. *Representation*. New York: Atherton Press, 1969.

Riemer, Neal. *The Representative: Trustee, Delegate, Partisan, or Politico?* Boston: D. C. Heath, 1967.

Riker, William H. *Federalism: Origin, Operation, Significance*. Boston: Little, Brown & Co., 1964.

Rose, Richard. "Dynamic Tendencies in the Authority of Regimes." *World Politics*, 21 (July 1969), pp. 602–628.

Sawyer, Geoffrey. *Modern Federalism*. London: C. A. Watts, 1969.

Tucker, Robert C. "The Dictator and Totalitarianism." *World Politics*, 17 (July 1965), pp. 555–583.

Wheare, K. C. *Federal Government*. 4th ed. New York: Oxford University Press, 1964. Standard introduction.

_____. *Legislatures*. Rev. ed. New York: Oxford University Press, 1968. Traditional discussion; useful, but rather flat.

Wuest, John J., and Vernon, Manfred C., eds. *New Source Book in Major European Governments*. See comment, Chapter 1.

CHAPTER 15. CABINET GOVERNMENT IN ENGLAND

Amery, Leopold. *Thoughts on the Constitution*. 2nd ed. Oxford: The Clarendon Press, 1956.

Bagehot, Walter. *The English Constitution*. See comment, Chapter 2.

Beer, Samuel H. *British Politics in the Collectivist Age*. See comment, Chapter 2.

_____. "Interest Groups in Great Britain and the United States." *Academy of Political and Social Science*, 319 (September 1958), pp. 130–140.

Benewick, Robert, and Dowse, Robert, *Readings on British Politics and Government*. London: University of London Press, 1968.

Berkeley, Humphrey. *The Power of the Prime Minister*. New York: Random House, 1969.

Birch, A. H. *The British System of Government*. New York: Frederick A. Praeger, 1967.

_____. *Representative and Responsible Government*. Toronto: University of Toronto Press, 1964.

Birnbaum, Norman. "Monarchs and Sociologists." *Sociological Review*, 3 (July 1955), pp. 5–23. Reply to the Shils and Young essay, in which Birnbaum stresses the negative aspects of the British monarchy.

Brittan, Samuel. *The Treasury Under the Tories*. Harmondsworth, Middlesex, Eng.: Penguin Books, 1964.

Butt, Ronald. *The Power of Parliament.* London: Constable & Co., 1967. Excellent study of Parliament, by an author who denies that its power has declined as much as some critics assert.

Chapman, Brian. *British Government Observed: Some European Reflections.* London: George Allen & Unwin, 1963. A sharp, readable critique of the functioning of British government—weakened by overstatement.

Chester, D. N., and Bowring, Nona. *Questions in Parliament.* New York: Oxford University Press, 1962.

Christoph, James B. "The Study of Voting Behavior in the British House of Commons." *Western Political Quarterly,* 41 (June 1958), pp. 319–340.

Coombes, David. *The Member of Parliament and the Administration.* London: George Allen & Unwin, 1966.

Crick, Bernard. *The Reform of Parliament.* 2nd ed. London: Weidenfeld & Nicolson, 1967. Instructive critique with some concrete suggestions for reform.

————, ed. *Essays on Reform.* Oxford: The Clarendon Press, 1967.

Dicey, Albert V. *Introduction to the Study of the Law of the Constitution.* 10th ed. New York: St. Martin's Press, 1959.

Eckstein, Harry. *Pressure Group Politics: The Case of the British Medical Association.* Stanford: Stanford University Press, 1960.

Epstein, Leon. *British Politics in the Suez Crisis.* Urbana: University of Illinois Press, 1964.

Finer, Samuel E. *Anonymous Empire.* 2nd ed. New York: Humanities Press, 1966. The role of interest groups in British society. Highly sophisticated.

Galloway, George. *Congress and Parliament.* Washington, D. C.: National Planning Association, 1955.

Grainger, J. H. *Character and Style in English Politics.* Cambridge: Cambridge University Press, 1969.

Great Britain, Select Committee on Nationalized Industries. *Ministerial Control of the Nationalized Industries.* 3 vols. H. C. 371–I, II, III. London: HMSO, 1968.

Guttsman, W. L. *The British Political Elite.* See comment, Chapter 5.

Hanser, Charles J. *Guide to Decision: The Royal Commission.* Totowa, N. J.: Bedminster Press, 1965.

Hanson, A. H., ed. *Nationalization: A Book of Readings.* London: George Allen & Unwin, 1963.

————, and Wiseman, H. V., eds. *Parliament at Work: A Case Book of Parliamentary Procedure.* London: Stevens, 1962.

————. "Ministers and Boards." *Public Administration,* 47 (Spring 1969), pp. 65–74.

Heasman, D. J. "Parliamentary Paths to High Office." *Parliamentary Affairs,* 16 (Summer 1963), pp. 315–330.

Jackson, Robert J. *Rebels and Whips.* New York: St. Martin's Press, 1968.

Jennings, William Ivor. *Cabinet Government.* 3rd ed. New York: Cambridge University Press, 1959.

————. *Parliament.* 2nd ed. New York: Cambridge University Press, 1957.

Johnson, Nevil. *Parliament and Administration.* London: George Allen & Unwin, 1966.

King, Anthony, ed. *British Politics.* See comment, Chapter 2.

Lapping, Brian, and Radice, Giles, eds. *More Power to the People.* See comment, Chapter 5.

Liggett, Eric. *British Political Issues.* 2 vols. London: Pergamon Press, 1964.

Lowenstein, Karl. *British Cabinet Government.* New York: Oxford University Press, 1967. Traditional historical treatment by a noted European scholar.

Lowell, A. Lawrence. *The Government of England.* See comment, Chapter 2.

Mackenzie, Kenneth. *The English Parliament.* Baltimore: Penguin Books, 1950.

MacKintosh, John P. *The British Cabinet.* 2nd ed. London: Stevens & Sons, 1968. Readable, well-researched introduction to the evolution and structure of contemporary cabinet government; it also notes the decline of parliamentary influence on public policy. Open to argument, perhaps, but worth reading.

Martin, Kingsley. *The Crown and the Establishment.* Baltimore: Penguin Books, 1963. Highly irreverent history of the English monarchy, by a former editor of *The New Statesman.* Enjoyable, but not to be swallowed whole.

Morrison, Herbert Stanley. *Government and Parliament: A Survey from the Inside.* 3rd ed. New York: Oxford University Press, 1964.

Nicholson, Max. *The System.* New York: McGraw-Hill, 1967. An impassioned assault upon most British institutions. Overstated and occasionally wrong-headed, but always fascinating.

Pollard, A. F. *The Evolution of Parliament.* London: Longmans Green & Co., 1920. A durable classic.

Potter, A. M. *Organized Groups in British National Politics*. London: Faber & Faber, 1961.

Punnett, R. M. *British Government and Politics*. See comment, Chapter 11.

Ranney, Austin. *Pathways to Parliament*. See comment, Chapter 10.

Richards, Peter G. *Honourable Members: A Study of the British Backbencher*. 2nd ed. New York: Hillary House, 1964.

Robson, William A. "Ministerial Control of the Nationalized Industries." *Political Quarterly*, 40 (January–March 1969), pp. 103–111.

Rose, Richard. *Politics in England*. See comment, Chapter 4.

_____, ed. *Policy Making in Britain*. New York: The Free Press, 1969.

_____, ed. *Studies in British Politics*. New York: St. Martin's Press, 1966.

Shils, Edward, and Young, Michael. "The Meaning of the Coronation." *Sociological Review*, December 1953, pp. 64–67.

Stacey, Frank. *The Government of Modern Britain*. See comment, Chapter 10.

Stankiewicz, W. J., ed. *Crisis in British Government*. See comment, Chapter 10.

Stewart, John D. *British Pressure Groups*. Oxford: The Clarendon Press, 1958. Standard but colorless.

Taylor, Eric. *The House of Commons at Work*. Baltimore: Penguin Books, 1963.

Thomson, David. *Democracy in France Since 1870*. See comment, Chapter 2.

Thornhill, William. *The Nationalized Industries*. London: Thomas Nelson & Sons, 1968. Standard, rather tedious, but serves well as a reference.

UNESCO. *Decisions and Decision Makers in the Modern State*. Paris: UNESCO, 1967.

Walkland, S. A. *The Legislative Process in Great Britain*. London: George Allen & Unwin, 1968. A brief, behavioral treatment of Parliament.

Wheare, K. C. *Government by Committee*. New York: Oxford University Press, 1955.

Wilson, H. H. *Pressure Group: The Campaign for Commercial Television*. New Brunswick, N. J.: Rutgers University Press, 1961.

Wiseman, H. V., ed. *Parliament and the Executive*. New York: Humanities Press, 1966.

Young, Roland. *The British Parliament*. Evanston, Ill.: Northwestern University Press, 1963. A little out of touch, but still very interesting.

CHAPTER 16. FRANCE: FROM PARLIAMENTARY TO PRESIDENTIAL GOVERNMENT

Blondel, Jean, and Godfrey, E. Drexel, Jr. *The Government of France*. See comment, Chapter 2.

Bosworth, William. *Catholicism and Crisis in Modern France*. See comment, Chapter 6.

Brown, Bernard. "Alcohol and Politics in France." *American Political Science Review*, 51 (December 1957), pp. 776–791.

_____. "Pressure Politics in the Fifth Republic." In *Comparative Politics: Notes and Readings*. 3rd ed. Edited by Roy Macridis and Bernard Brown. Homewood, Ill.: The Dorsey Press, 1968.

De Gaulle, Charles. *War Memoirs*. 3 vols. Vol. 1 translated by Jonathan Griffin; vols. 2 and 3 translated by Richard Howard. New York: Simon & Schuster, 1955–1959.

De Lamothe, A. Dutheillet. "Ministerial Cabinets in France." *Public Administration*, 43 (Winter 1965), pp. 365–381.

Ehrmann, Henry W. *Politics in France*. See comment, Chapter 2.

_____. "Bureaucracy and Interest Groups in the Decision-Making Process of the Fifth Republic." *Factoren der politischen Entscheidung, Festgabe für Ernst Fraenkel*. Berlin: Gruyter, 1963.

_____. "French Bureaucracy and Organized Interests." *Administrative Science Quarterly*, 5 (March 1961), pp. 534–555.

Harrison, Martin, ed. *French Politics*. See comment, Chapter 2.

Hoffman, Stanley, et al. *In Search of France*. See comment, Chapter 4.

Hunt, William H. "Careers and Perspectives of French Politicians." Ph.D. dissertation, Vanderbilt University, 1966.

King, Jerome B. "Ministerial Cabinets of the Fourth Republic." *Western Political Quarterly*, 13 (June 1960), pp. 433–444.

Lacouture, Jean. *De Gaulle*. Translated by Francis K. Price. See comment, Chapter 11.

Leites, Nathan. *On the Game of Politics in France*. See comment, Chapter 4.

_____. *The Rules of the Game in Paris*. See comment, Chapter 4.

MacRae, Duncan. *Parliament, Parties, and Society in France: 1946–1958*. See comment, Chapter 11.

Macridis, Roy. *The De Gaulle Republic: Quest for Unity*. Homewood, Ill.: The Dorsey Press, 1960.

Melnik, Constantin, and Leites, Nathan. *The House Without Windows: France Selects a President.* Evanston, Ill.: Row, Peterson & Co., 1958.

Mendès-France, Pierre. *A Modern French Republic.* See comment, Chapter 11.

Pickles, Dorothy. *The Fifth French Republic: Institutions and Politics.* See comment, Chapter 11.

Pierce, Roy. *French Politics and Political Institutions.* See comment, Chapter 11.

Sharp, Walter Rice. *The Government of the French Republic.* New York: D. Van Nostrand, 1938.

Werth, Alexander. *The De Gaulle Revolution.* See comment, Chapter 2.

Williams, Philip M. *Crisis and Compromise.* See comment, Chapter 2.

————. *French Parliament, 1958–1967.* London: George Allen & Unwin, 1968. Short, penetrating look at the parliament in Fifth-Republic France. Easily the best thing available in English.

————, and Harrison, Martin. *De Gaulle's Republic.* London: Longmans Green & Co., 1960.

CHAPTER 17. CHANCELLOR DEMOCRACY IN GERMANY

Alexander, Edgar. *Adenauer and the New Germany: The Chancellor of the Vanquished.* Translated by Thomas E. Goldstein. New York: Farrar, Straus & Cudahy, 1957.

Blachly, F. F., and Oatman, M. E. *The Government and Administration of Germany.* See comment, Chapter 2.

Bolling, Klaus. *Republic in Suspense.* Translated by Jean Steinberg. New York: Frederick A. Praeger, 1964.

Carsten, F. L. *Princes and Parliaments in Germany: From the Fifteenth to the Eighteenth Century.* New York: Oxford University Press, 1959.

Dahrendorf, Ralf. *Society and Democracy in Germany.* See comment, Chapter 2.

Dowell, Jack D. "Party, Caucus, and Chancellor." *Research Studies,* 36 (June 1968), pp. 131–142.

Frye, Charles E. "Parties and Pressure Groups in Weimar and Bonn." In *Politics in Europe,* edited by Arend Lijphart. Englewood Cliffs, N. J.: Prentice-Hall, 1969.

Heidenheimer, Arnold J. *The Governments of Germany.* See comment, Chapter 4.

Hiscocks, Richard. *The Adenauer Era.* See comment, Chapter 5.

————. *Democracy in Western Germany.* See comment, Chapter 2.

Johnson, Nevil. "Questions in the Bundestag." *Parliamentary Affairs,* 16 (Winter 1962), pp. 22–34.

King-Hall, Stephen, and Ullman, Richard K. *German Parliaments: A Study of the Development of Representative Institutions in Germany.* London: Hansard, 1954.

Lehmbruch, Gerhard. "The Ambiguous Coalition in West Germany." *Government and Opposition,* 3 (Spring 1968), pp. 181–206.

Loewenberg, Gerhard. *Parliament in the German Political System.* Ithaca: Cornell University Press, 1967. The definitive work in English on the Bonn parliament. It has the added value of offering interesting comparisons with other countries.

Merkl, Peter. *Germany: Yesterday and Tomorrow.* See comment, Chapter 4.

————. *The Origin of the West German Republic.* New York: Oxford University Press, 1963.

Pinney, Edward L. *Federalism, Bureaucracy, and Party Politics in Western Germany: The Role of the Bundesrat.* Chapel Hill: University of North Carolina Press, 1963.

Plischke, Elmer. *Contemporary Governments of Germany.* See comment, Chapter 12.

Pollock, J. K., and Thomas, Homer. *Germany in Power and Eclipse.* See comment, Chapter 2.

————, and Lane, John, eds. *Source Materials on the Government and Politics of Germany.* Ann Arbor: George Wahr Publishing Co., 1964.

Safran, William. *Veto-Group Politics: The Case of Health Insurance Reform in West Germany.* San Francisco: Chandler Publishing Co., 1967.

Tilford, R. B., and Preece, R. J. C. *Federal Germany.* See comment, Chapter 2.

United States Department of the Army. *Area Handbook for Germany.* See comment, Chapter 2.

Zundel, Rolf. "West Germany: The Grand Coalition and Its Consequences." *The World Today,* 24 (September 1968), pp. 367–374.

CHAPTER 18. GOVERNMENTAL PROCESSES IN THE SOVIET UNION

Adams, Jan S. "Soviet Inspectors General: An Expanding Role?" *Soviet Studies,* 5, 20 (July 1968), pp. 106–111.

Andrews, William G., ed. *Soviet Institutions and Policies: Inside Views.* Princeton: D. Van Nostrand, 1966.

Barghoorn, Frederick C. *Politics in the U.S.S.R.* See comment, Chapter 3.

Black, Cyril E., ed. *The Transformation of Russian Society*. See comment, Chapter 3.

Brzezinski, Zbigniew, and Huntington, Samuel T. *Political Power: U.S.A./U.S.S.R.* See comment, Chapter 13.

Burks, Richard Voyles. "The ACLS Summer, 1968 Workshop on the Comparative Study of Communism: A Report." See comment, Chapter 13.

Churchward, L. G. *Contemporary Soviet Government*. London: Routledge & Kegan Paul, 1968.

Conquest, Robert. *The Soviet Political System*. London: The Bodley Head, 1968.

Dallin, Alexander, and Larson, Thomas B., eds. *Soviet Politics Since Khrushchev*. Englewood Cliffs, N. J.: Prentice-Hall, 1968.

————, and Westin, Alan F., eds. *Politics in the Soviet Union: 7 Cases*. New York: Harcourt, Brace & World, 1965.

Deutscher, Isaac. *Stalin: A Political Biography*. See comment, Chapter 3.

Fainsod, Merle. *How Russia Is Ruled*. See comment, Chapter 3.

————. *Smolensk Under Soviet Rule*. See comment, Chapter 3.

Fischer, George. *The Soviet System and Modern Society*. New York: Atherton Press, 1968. Fischer contends that a new type of politician is emerging in the Soviet Union—one who blends political with managerial skills; thus, the party should be able to adjust to the requirements of a more complex society while simultaneously retaining its dominant position.

Fleron, Frederick J. "Toward a Reconceptualization of Political Change in the Soviet Union: The Political Leadership System." *Comparative Politics*, 1 (January 1969), pp. 228–244.

Friedrich, Carl J., and Brzezinski, Zbigniew K. *Totalitarian Dictatorship and Autocracy*. See comment, Chapter 3.

Hendel, Samuel, ed. *The Soviet Crucible*. See comment, Chapter 3.

Hough, Jerry F. *The Soviet Prefects*. See comment, Chapter 5.

Juviler, Peter H. "Functions of a Deputy to the U.S.S.R. Supreme Soviet, 1938–1959." Ph.D. dissertation, Columbia University, 1960.

Kanet, Roger E. "The Rise and Fall of the 'All People's State': Recent Changes in the Soviet Theory of the State." *Soviet Studies*, 20 (July 1968), pp. 81–93.

Kassof, Allen, ed. *Prospects for Soviet Society*. See comment, Chapter 3.

Linden, Carl. *Khrushchev and the Soviet Leadership, 1957–1964*. Baltimore: Johns Hopkins Press, 1966.

Lodge, Milton. "Soviet Elite Participatory Attitudes in the Post–Stalin Period." *American Political Science Review*, 62 (September 1968), pp. 827–839.

London, Kurt, ed. *The Soviet Union: A Half-Century of Communism*. See comment, Chapter 5.

Meyer, Alfred G. *The Soviet Political System: An Interpretation*. See comment, Chapter 13.

Morton, Henry W., and Juviler, Peter H., eds. *Soviet Policy-Making: Studies of Communism in Transition*. New York: Frederick A. Praeger, 1967.

Ploss, Sidney. *Conflict and Decision-Making in Soviet Russia*. Princeton: Princeton University Press, 1965. A prime example of "Kremlinology" at work, as the author tries to unravel power configurations during the Khrushchev period.

Schapiro, Leonard. *The Communist Party of the Soviet Union*. See comment, Chapter 3.

Schwartz, Joel J., and Keech, William R. "Group Influence and the Policy Process in the Soviet Union." *American Political Science Review*, 62 (September 1968), pp. 840–851.

Shaffer, Harry G., ed. *The Soviet System*. New York: Appleton-Century-Crofts, 1965.

Swearer, Howard R. *The Politics of Succession in the U.S.S.R.* Boston: Little, Brown & Co., 1964.

Tatu, Michel. *Power in the Kremlin*. See comment, Chapter 13.

Tucker, Robert C. *The Soviet Political Mind*. New York: Frederick A. Praeger, 1963.

CHAPTER 19. POLITICAL DECISION-MAKING ON THE LOCAL AND REGIONAL LEVEL

Benham, Hervey. *Two Cheers for the Town Hall*. London: Hutchinson & Co., 1964.

Brecht, Arnold. *Federalism and Regionalism in Germany: The Division of Prussia*. Oxford: The Clarendon Press, 1945.

Carter, Edward J. *The Future of London*. Harmondsworth, Middlesex, Eng.: Penguin Books, 1962.

Cattell, David T. *Leningrad: A Case Study of Soviet Urban Government*. New York: Frederick A. Praeger, 1969.

Chapman, Brian. *Introduction to French Local Government*. London: George Allen & Unwin, 1953.

Churchward, L. G. "Soviet Local Government To-day." *Soviet Studies,* 17 (April 1966), pp. 431–452.

Clarke, John Joseph. *A History of Local Government of the United Kingdom.* London: Herbert Jenkins, 1955.

Cole, Taylor. "New Dimensions of West German Federalism." In *Comparative Politics and Political Theory,* edited by Edward L. Pinney. Chapel Hill: University of North Carolina Press, 1966.

Conquest, Robert. *The Soviet Political System.* London: The Bodley Head, 1968.

Crick, Bernard, ed. *Essays on Reform.* Oxford: The Clarendon Press, 1967.

Cullingworth, J. B. *Town and Country Planning in England and Wales.* 2nd ed. London: George Allen & Unwin, 1967. Comprehensive, basic source of information.

Dawson, William H. *Municipal Life and Government in Germany.* New York: Longmans Green & Co., 1914.

Garner, J. F. "The Role of the Mayor in Great Britain." *Journal of Local Administration Overseas,* 2 (January 1963), pp. 16–23.

Great Britain. *Report of the Committee on Local Authorities and Allied Services.* London: HMSO, 1968.

Great Britain. *Royal Commission on Local Government in England.* 3 vols. London: HMSO, 1969.

Griffith, J. A. G. *Central Departments and Local Authorities.* London: George Allen & Unwin, 1966.

Gunlicks, Arthur B. "Representative Role Perceptions Among Local Councilors in Western Germany." *Journal of Politics,* 31 (May 1969), pp. 443–464.

Heidenheimer, Arnold J. *The Governments of Germany.* See comment, Chapter 4.

Hodnett, Grey. "The Debate Over Soviet Federalism." *Soviet Studies,* 18 (April 1967), pp. 458–481.

International Union of Local Authorities. *Local Government in the Twentieth Century.* The Hague, 1964.

Jackson, Eric W. *The Structure of Local Government.* 5th ed. New York: Longmans Green & Co., 1966.

Jackson, Richard M. *The Machinery of Local Government.* 2nd ed. London: Macmillan & Co., 1967. Comprehensive.

Jones, G. H., et al. "Regionalism and Parliament." *Political Quarterly,* 38 (October–December 1967), pp. 403–410.

Kesselman, Mark. *The Ambiguous Consensus.* New York: Alfred A. Knopf, 1967. About the only good study in English on French local politics.

Lapping, Brian, and Radice, Giles, eds. *More Power to the People.* See comment, Chapter 5.

Lee, John Michael. *Social Leaders and Public Persons.* New York: Oxford University Press, 1963.

Litchfield, Edward H. *Governing Postwar Germany.* Ithaca: Cornell University Press, 1953.

MacKintosh, John P. *The Devolution of Power: Local Democracy, Regionalism, and Nationalism.* Harmondsworth, Middlesex, Eng.: Penguin Books, 1968.

McWhinney, Edward. *Comparative Federalism: States' Rights and National Power.* Toronto: University of Toronto Press, 1964.

Mote, Max E. *Soviet Local and Republic Elections.* Stanford: Stanford University Press, 1965.

Mumford, Lewis, et al. "City." In *International Encyclopedia of the Social Sciences,* 2 (1968), pp. 447–472.

Osborn, Robert J. "Public Participation in Soviet City Government." Ph.D. dissertation, Columbia University, 1963.

Piquard, Michel. "Organization and Planning of the Paris Region." *Public Administration,* 43 (Winter 1965), pp. 383–394.

Plischke, Elmer. *Contemporary Governments of Germany.* See comment, Chapter 12.

Pollock, J. K., and Thomas, Homer. *Germany in Power and Eclipse.* See comment, Chapter 2.

Preece, R. J. C. *Land Elections in the German Federal Republic.* London: Longmans Green & Co., 1968.

Rasmussen, Steen Eiter. *London: The Unique City.* Cambridge, Mass.: M.I.T. Press, 1966.

Rees, Anthony, and Smith, Trevor. *Town Councillors: A Study of Barking.* London: Acton Society Trust, 1964.

Riker, William H. *Federalism: Origin, Operation, Significance.* Boston: Little, Brown & Co., 1964.

Robson, William A. *The Development of Local Government.* London: George Allen & Unwin, 1968. Standard history. Not terribly exciting, but very little in this field is.

————. *Local Government in Crisis*. London: George Allen & Unwin, 1966. Popular treatment. Overstated.

Sirjamaki, John. *The Sociology of Cities*. New York: Random House, 1964.

Sjoberg, Gideon. *The Preindustrial City*. Glencoe, Ill.: The Free Press, 1960.

Smallwood, Frank. *Greater London: The Politics of Metropolitan Reform*. Indianapolis: The Bobbs-Merrill Co., 1965.

Smith, Brian Able. *Regionalism in Britain*. 3 vols. London: Acton Society Trust, 1964–1965.

Stacey, Frank. *The Government of Modern Britain*. See comment, Chapter 10.

Stankiewicz, W. J., ed. *Crisis in British Government*. See comment, Chapter 10.

Steed, Michael; Keith-Lucas, Bryan; and Hall, Peter. "The Maud Report Examined." *New Society*, 13 (June 1969), pp. 951–955.

Stewart, Philip D. *Political Power in the Soviet Union: A Study of Decision-Making in Stalingrad*. Indianapolis: The Bobbs-Merrill Co., 1968.

Taubman, William. *The Politics of Urban Development in the Soviet Union*. Ph.D. dissertation, Columbia University, 1969. Perhaps the best study in English of Soviet local politics.

Walsh, Annmarie Hauck. *The Urban Challenge to Government: An International Comparison of Thirteen Cities*. New York: Frederick A. Praeger, 1969. The first real attempt to develop a comparative approach to the study of urban political systems. Its major weakness lies in the fact that it does not relate political to social variables.

————. *Urban Government for the Paris Region*. New York: Frederick A. Praeger, 1968.

Weber, Max. *The City*. Translated and edited by Don Martindale and Gertrude Neuwirth. New York: Collier Books, 1962. The best study of the occidental city.

Wells, Roger H. *German Cities*. Princeton: Princeton University Press, 1932.

————. *The States in West German Federalism*. New York: Twayne Publishers, 1961.

Wesson, R. G. "Volunteers and Soviets." *Soviet Studies*, 15 (January 1964), pp. 231–249.

Wheare, K. C. *Federal Government*. See comment, Chapter 14.

Wiseman, H. Victor. "Regional Government in the United Kingdom." *Parliamentary Affairs*, 19 (Winter 1965–1966), pp. 56–82.

Part V Public Policy and Its Implementation

CHAPTER 20. LAW, SOCIETY, AND POLITICS IN WESTERN EUROPE

Abel-Smith, Brian, and Stevens, Robert. *Lawyers and the Courts*. Cambridge, Mass.: Harvard University Press, 1967.

Abraham, Henry J. *The Judicial Process*. 2nd ed. New York: Oxford University Press, 1968. Does not break any new ground, but comprehensive, detailed, and reliable nonetheless. The emphasis is on American material.

Allen, Carleton. *Law in the Making*. 7th ed. New York: Oxford University Press, 1964.

Barkun, Michael. *Law Without Sanctions*. New Haven: Yale University Press, 1968.

Bedford, Sybille. *The Faces of Justice: A Traveller's Report*. New York: Simon & Schuster, 1961. A popular and readable account of trials in England, France, and Germany. The author is not trained in the law, however, and the book is sometimes misleading.

Blom-Cooper, Louis. "Essays in Law Reform: The Judiciary in an Era of Law Reform." *Political Quarterly*, 37, 4 (October-December 1966), pp. 378–384.

Carlton, K. S. *Law and the Structures of Social Action*. London: Stevens & Sons. Helpful study of law and legal systems from a functionalist point of view.

Conquest, Robert. *Justice and the Legal System in the U.S.S.R.* New York: Frederick A. Praeger, 1968. Concise, instructive.

David, René, and Brierley, John E. C. *Major Legal Systems in the World Today*. New York: The Free Press, 1969. Fairly traditional, but extremely useful for the beginning student.

————, and de Vries, Henry P. *The French Legal System: An Introduction to Civil Law Systems*. New York: Harcourt, Brace & Co., 1958.

Davis, Floyd James, et al. *Society and the Law: New Meanings for an Old Profession*. Glencoe, Ill.: The Free Press, 1962. Not easy, but worth the effort.

Davitt, Thomas E. *The Basic Values in Law*. Transactions of the American Philosophic Society, vol. 58, no. 5. Philadelphia: American Philosophic Society, 1968.

Devlin, Patrick. *Criminal Prosecution in England.* New Haven: Yale University Press, 1958.

Diamond, A. S. *The Evolution of Law and Order.* London: Watts, 1951.

Ensor, R. C. K. *Courts and Judges in France, Germany, and England.* Oxford: The Clarendon Press, 1933.

Evan, William M., ed. *Law and Sociology: Exploratory Essays.* Glencoe, Ill.: The Free Press, 1962.

Freedeman, Charles E. *The Conseil d'État in Modern France.* New York: Columbia University Press, 1961. A standard, well-written history and analysis.

Friedmann, Wolfgang. *Law in a Changing Society.* Baltimore: Penguin Books, 1965.

Galanter, Marc. "Hindu Law and the Development of the Modern Indian Legal System." Paper presented at the 1964 meeting of the American Political Science Association at Chicago. Mimeographed.

Great Britain Foreign Office. *Manual of German Law.* 2 vols. London: HMSO, 1950–1952.

Hamson, C. J. "The Prosecution of the Accused— English and French Legal Methods." *Criminal Law Review,* 1955, pp. 272–282.

Harding, Alan. *A Social History of English Law.* Baltimore: Penguin Books, 1966.

Jackson, Richard M. *The Machinery of Justice in England.* 4th ed. Cambridge: Cambridge University Press, 1964.

Keeton, George W. *The Norman Conquest and the Common Law.* New York: Barnes & Noble, 1966.

Kempin, Frederick G. *Legal History: Law and Social Change.* Englewood Cliffs, N. J.: Prentice-Hall, 1963. Brief history of common law in England.

Lawson, Frederick Henry. *A Common Lawyer Looks at the Civil Law.* Ann Arbor: University of Michigan Press, 1953.

Lloyd, Dennis. *Idea of Law.* Baltimore: Penguin Books, 1964.

McRuer, J. C. *The Evolution of the Judicial Process.* Toronto: Clarke, Irwin, 1957.

Mueller, Gerhard O. W., ed. *The French Criminal Procedure Code.* Translated by Gerald L. Kock. South Hackensack, N. J.: Fred B. Rothman, 1964.

————, ed. *The French Penal Code.* Translated by Jean F. Moreau and G. O. W. Mueller. South Hackensack, N. J.: Fred B. Rothman, 1960.

————, ed. *The German Criminal Procedure Code.* Translated by Hurst Niebler. South Hackensack, N. J.: Fred B. Rothman, 1965.

————, ed. *The German Draft Penal Code.* Translated by Neville Ross. South Hackensack, N. J.: Fred B. Rothman, 1966.

————, ed. *The German Penal Code of 1871.* Translated by G. O. W. Mueller and Thomas Buergenthal. South Hackensack, N. J.: Fred B. Rothman, 1961. Introductory essays in these five books edited by Mueller are quite helpful.

Pound, Roscoe. *The Lawyer from Antiquity to Modern Times.* New York: International Publishing Co., 1953.

Reich, D. R. "Court, Comity, and Federalism in West Germany." *Midwest Journal of Political Science,* 7 (August 1963), pp. 177–228.

Rheinstein, Max. "Approach to German Law." *Indiana Law Journal,* 34 (January 1959), pp. 546–558.

Robinson, Cyril D. "Arrest, Prosecution and Police Power in the Federal Republic of Germany." *Dusquesne University Law Review,* 4 (Winter 1965), pp. 225–301.

Schubert, Glendon, and Danelski, David J., eds. *Comparative Judicial Behavior.* New York: Oxford University Press, 1969.

Schwartz, Bernard, ed. *The* Code Napoléon *and the Common–Law World.* New York: New York University Press, 1956. A useful comparison.

Schweitzer, C. G. "Emergency Powers in the Federal Republic of Germany." *Western Political Quarterly,* 22 (March 1969), pp. 112–121.

Smith, Munroe. *The Development of European Law.* New York: Columbia University Press, 1928. Classic, one-volume history from the primacy of medieval legal institutions down to the "reception" of Roman law. Still helpful.

Sowle, Claude R., ed. *Police Power and Individual Freedom.* Chicago: Aldine Publishing Co., 1965. Various opinions about the legal limitations on Europe's police. Authors and editor alike raise the hoary question about the conflict between the need for protecting the accused and the requirements for preserving order. However, since the essays do not explore the realities of police behavior, much of the analysis is academic—in the worst sense of the term.

Street, Harry. *Freedom, the Individual and the Law.* Baltimore: Penguin Books, 1954.

United States Department of the Army. *Area Handbook for Germany.* See comment, Chapter 2.

Von Mehren, Arthur T. *The Civil Law System: Cases and Materials for the Comparative Study of Law.* Boston: Little, Brown & Co., 1957. Possibly the best analysis in English of German and French law.

————. "The Judicial Process in the U. S. and France." *Revista Juridica de la Universidad de Puerto Rico,* 22 (September 1952), pp. 235–265.

Wigmore, J. H. *A Panorama of the World's Legal Systems.* 3 vols. St. Paul, Minn.: West Publishing Co., 1928.

Zander, Michael. "Reforming the English Legal Profession." *Political Quarterly,* 37 (January–March 1966), pp. 33–45.

CHAPTER 21. SOVIET LAW

Barry, Donald D. "The U.S.S.R. Supreme Court: Recent Developments." *Soviet Studies,* 20 (April 1969), pp. 511–522.

————, and Berman, Harold J. "The Soviet Legal Profession." *Harvard Law Review,* 82 (November 1968), pp. 1–41. The best appraisal available in English.

Berman, Harold J. *Justice in the U.S.S.R.* New York: Random House, Vintage Books, 1963. A general introduction to Soviet law, with an eye on traditional and Marxist influences; marred somewhat by excessive emphasis on the "teaching function" of Soviet law.

————, ed. *Soviet Criminal Law and Procedure: The RSFSR Codes.* Translated by Harold J. Berman and James W. Spindler. Cambridge, Mass.: Harvard University Press, 1966. The introduction is especially helpful.

————. "The Dilemma of Soviet Law Reform." *Harvard Law Review,* 76 (March 1963), pp. 929–951.

David, René, and Brierley, John E. C. *Major Legal Systems in the World Today.* See comment, Chapter 20.

————, and de Vries, Henry P. *The French Legal System: An Introduction to Civil Law Systems.* See comment, Chapter 20.

Davitt, Thomas E. *The Basic Values in Law.* Transactions of the American Philosophic Society, vol. 58, no. 5. Philadelphia: American Philosophic Society, 1968.

Feifer, George. *Justice in Moscow.* New York: Simon & Schuster, 1964. Commentary on the quality of Soviet justice based on personal observation. The book's many merits more than compensate for a predilection to lean over backwards in order to be fair.

Gsovski, Vladimir and Grzybowski, Kazimierz, eds. *Government, Law, and Courts in the Soviet Union and Eastern Europe.* 2 vols. New York: Frederick A. Praeger, 1960. Well and massively documented; somewhat anti-Soviet.

Hazard, John N. *Law and Social Change in the U.S.S.R.* London: Stevens & Sons, 1953.

————. *Settling Disputes in Soviet Society.* New York: Columbia University Press, 1960.

————, and Shapiro, Isaac, eds. *The Soviet Legal System.* 2nd ed. New York: Oceana, 1969. Documents on the system, with a commentary.

Juviler, Peter H. "Mass Education and Justice in Soviet Courts: The Visiting Sessions." *Soviet Studies,* 18 (April 1967), pp. 494–510. A fascinating study.

Kassof, Allen, ed. *Prospects for Soviet Society.* See comment, Chapter 3.

Kucherov, Samuel. *Courts, Lawyers and Trials Under the Last Three Tzars.* New York: Frederick A. Praeger, 1953.

————. "The Legal Profession in Pre- and Post-Revolutionary Russia." *American Journal of Comparative Law,* 5, 3 (1956), pp. 443–470.

La Fave, Wayne R., ed. *Law in the Soviet Society.* Urbana: University of Illinois Press, 1965.

Morgan, Glenn G. *Soviet Administrative Legality.* Stanford: Stanford University Press, 1962.

O'Connor, Dennis M. "Soviet People's Guards." *New York University Law Review,* 39 (June 1964), pp. 579–614.

Problems of Communism. Special issues, "In Quest of Justice." See comment, Chapter 5.

————. Special issue, "Law and Legality in the U.S.S.R.," 14 (March-April 1965).

Tay, Alice Ehr-Soon. "The Law of Inheritance in the New Russian Civil Code of 1964." *International and Comparative Law Quarterly,* April 1968, pp. 472–500.

CHAPTER 22. BUREAUCRACY

Armstrong, John A. *The Soviet Bureaucratic Elite: A Case Study of the Ukrainian Apparatus.* New York: Frederick A. Praeger, 1959.

Armstrong, William. "The Tasks of the Civil Service." *Public Administration,* 47 (Spring 1969), pp. 1–12.

Barker, Sir Ernest. *The Development of Public Service in Western Europe, 1660–1930.* Oxford: The Clarendon Press, 1944.

Bendix, Reinhard. "Bureaucracy." *International Encyclopedia of the Social Sciences,* 2 (1968), pp. 206–219. Short, sound discussion of modern bureaucracy and theories of bureaucracy. Weberian approach.

Birch, A. H. *The British System of Government.* New York: Frederick A. Praeger, 1967.

Blachly, F. F., and Oatman, M. E. See comment, Chapter 2.

Blau, Peter, and Scott, W. Richard. *Formal Organizations.* San Francisco: Chandler Publishing Co., 1962.

————. "Critical Remarks on Weber's Theory of Authority." *American Political Science Review,* 57 (June 1963), pp. 305–316.

————; Perrow, Charles; Argyris, Chris; Wilensky, Harold L.; and Barton, Allen H. "Organizations." *International Encyclopedia of the Social Sciences,* 2 (1968), pp. 297–343.

Blondel, Jean, and Godfrey, E. Drexel, Jr. *The Government of France.* See comment, Chapter 2.

Brecht, Arnold, and Glaser, Comstock. *The Art and Technique of Administration in German Ministries.* Cambridge, Mass.: Harvard University Press, 1940.

Brittan, Samuel. *The Treasury Under the Tories.* Harmondsworth, Middlesex, Eng.: Penguin Books, 1964.

Campbell, G. A. *The Civil Service in Britain.* 2nd ed. London: Duckworth & Co., 1965.

Chapel, Yves. "Conditions of Employment of the Staffs of Government Departments in Western Europe." *International Labor Review,* 87 (April 1963), pp. 328–360.

Chapman, Brian. *British Government Observed: Some European Reflections.* See comment, Chapter 15.

————. *The Prefects and Provincial France.* London: George Allen & Unwin, 1955.

————. *The Profession of Government: The Public Service in Europe.* 3rd ed. London: George Allen & Unwin, 1966. Fairly orthodox approach, but the product of scrupulous scholarship and extremely well written.

Chapman, Richard A. "The Fulton Report: A Summary." *Public Administration Review,* 46 (Winter 1968), pp. 443–451.

Chaput de Saintonge, R. A. *Public Administration in Germany.* London: Weidenfeld & Nicolson, 1961.

Churchward, L. G. *Contemporary Soviet Government.* London: Routledge & Kegan Paul, 1968.

Coombes, David. *The Member of Parliament and the Administration.* London: George Allen & Unwin, 1966.

Crick, Bernard, ed. *Essays on Reform.* Oxford: The Clarendon Press, 1967.

Crozier, Michel. *The Bureaucratic Phenomenon.* Chicago: University of Chicago Press, 1964. French, English, and American public and private bureaucracies compared, together with some interesting observations about the impact of political culture on the functioning of bureaucratic systems.

Dean, Maurice. "Accountable Management in the Civil Service." *Public Administration,* 41 (Spring 1969), pp. 49–64.

De Smith, S. A. *Judicial Review of Administrative Action.* New York: Oceana, 1959.

Diamant, Alfred. "The Bureaucratic Model: Max Weber Rejected, Rediscovered, Reformed," and "The French Administrative System: The Republic Passes but the Administration Remains." In *Toward the Comparative Study of Public Administration,* edited by William J. Siffin. Bloomington: Indiana University Press, 1957. The latter is a classic essay on the French bureaucratic system.

————. "A Case Study of Administration Autonomy: Controls and Tensions in French Administration." *Political Studies,* 6 (June 1958), pp. 146–166.

————. "The Department, the Prefect and Dual Supervision in French Administration: A Comparative Study." *Journal of Politics,* 16 (August 1954), pp. 472–490.

Dobb, D. H. "Recruitment to the Administrative Class, 1960–1964." *Public Administration,* 45 (Spring 1967), pp. 55–80.

Dunnett, James. "Equipping the Civil Service for Its Tasks." *Public Administration,* 47 (Spring 1969), pp. 13–32.

Dunnill, Frank. *The Civil Service: Some Human Aspects.* New York: The Macmillan Co., 1956.

Ehrmann, Henry W. *Politics in France.* See comment, Chapter 2.

————. "Bureaucracy and Interest Groups in the Decision-Making Process of the Fifth Republic." *Factoren der politischen Entscheidung, Festgabe für Ernst Fraenkel.* Berlin: Gruyter, 1963.

————. "French Bureaucracy and Organized Interests." *Administrative Science Quarterly,* 5 (March 1961), pp. 534–555.

Etzioni, Amitai, ed. *A Sociological Reader on Complex Organizations*. 2nd ed. New York: Holt, Rinehart & Winston, 1969. Excellent.

Evans, Roger Warren. "French and German Administrative Law with Some English Comparisons." *International and Comparative Law Quarterly*, 14 (October 1965), pp. 1104–1124.

Fainsod, Merle. *How Russia Is Ruled*. See comment, Chapter 3.

Finer, Herman. *The Theory and Practice of Modern Government*. See comment, Chapter 2.

Fischer, George. *The Soviet System and Modern Society*. See comment, Chapter 18.

Fisher, James W. "French Field Administration: The Beginnings." *Comparative Studies in Society and History*, 1 (October 1962), pp. 60–76.

Friedrich, Carl J. *Constitutional Government and Democracy*. See comment, Chapter 1.

Gladden, Edgar N. *An Introduction to Public Administration*. 3rd ed. London: Staples, 1961.

Granick, David. *Management of the Industrial Firm in the U.S.S.R*. New York: Columbia University Press, 1954.

Great Britain, Committee on the Civil Service, 1966–1968. *The Civil Service*. Cmnd. 3638. 5 vols. London: HMSO, 1968.

Great Britain, Select Committee on Nationalized Industries. *Ministerial Control of the Nationalized Industries*. 3 vols. H.C. 371–I, II, III. London: HMSO, 1968.

Gross, Bertram. *The Managing of Organizations*. 2 vols. New York: The Free Press, 1964.

Hamson, C. J. *Executive Discretion and Judicial Control*. London: Stevens & Sons, 1954.

Hanson, A. H., ed. *Nationalization: A Book of Readings*. London: George Allen & Unwin, 1963.

_____. "Ministers and Boards." *Public Administration*, 47 (Spring 1969), pp. 65–74.

Harris, John S., and Garcia, Thomas V. "The Permanent Secretaries: Britain's Top Administrators." *Public Administration Review*, 26 (March 1966), pp. 31–44.

Harris, Richard L. "The Effects of Political Change on the Role of the Senior Bureaucrats in Ghana and Nigeria." *Administrative Science Quarterly*, 13 (December 1968), pp. 386–401. Some stimulating theories on how social and political conditions influence the role of bureaucrats.

Harris, W. G. "The Role of the Professional in the Civil Service." *Public Administration*, 47 (Spring 1969), pp. 33–48.

Heady, Ferrel. *Public Administration*. Englewood Cliffs, N. J.: Prentice-Hall, 1966. The focus is comparative. Short and sharp.

Heidenheimer, Arnold J. *The Governments of Germany*. See comment, Chapter 4.

Heussler, Robert. *Yesterday's Rulers: The Making of the British Colonial Service*. Syracuse, N. Y.: Syracuse University Press, 1963.

Hochschwender, Karl A. "German Civil Service Reform After 1945." Ph.D. dissertation, Yale University, 1961.

Hough, Jerry F. *The Soviet Prefects*. See comment, Chapter 5.

International Review of Administrative Sciences, "Public Administration in France," 31, no. 1 (1965), pp. 1–51.

Jacob, Herbert. *German Administration Since Bismarck*. New Haven: Yale University Press, 1963. Easily the best recent study in English of the German bureaucracy.

Johnson, Nevil. *Parliament and Administration*. London: George Allen & Unwin, 1966.

Jumper, Roy. "Recruitment Problems of the French Higher Civil Service: An American Appraisal." *Western Political Quarterly*, 10 (March 1957), pp. 38–48.

Kelsall, Roger K. *Higher Civil Servants in Britain*. New York: Humanities Press, 1955.

Kingsley, John D. *Representative Bureaucracy*. London: George Allen & Unwin, 1938.

La Palombara, Joseph, ed. *Bureaucracy and Political Development*. Princeton: Princeton University Press, 1963.

Lapping, Brian, and Radice, Giles, eds. *More Power to the People*. See comment, Chapter 5.

Lijphart, Arend, ed. *Politics in Europe: Comparisons and Interpretations*. Englewood Cliffs, N. J.: Prentice-Hall, 1969.

MacKenzie, W. J. M., and Grove, J. W. *Central Administration in Britain*. 2nd ed. London: Longmans Green & Co., 1969.

Macridis, Roy, and Brown, Bernard, eds. *Comparative Politics: Notes and Readings*. See comment, Introduction.

_____, and Ward, Robert E., eds. *Modern Political Systems: Europe*. See comment, Chapter 2.

March, James G., ed. *Handbook of Organizations*. Chicago: Rand McNally, 1965.

Merton, Robert, ed. *Reader in Bureaucracy*. Glencoe, Ill.: The Free Press, 1952.

Meyer, Alfred G. *The Soviet Political System: An Interpretation.* See comment, Chapter 13.

Meynaud, Jean. *Technocracy.* Translated by Paul Barnes. New York: The Free Press, 1969.

Montgomery, John D., and Siffin, William. *Approaches to Development: Politics, Administration and Change.* New York: McGraw-Hill, 1966.

Morgan, Glenn G. *Soviet Administrative Legality.* Stanford: Stanford University Press, 1962.

Morstein-Marx, Fritz. *The Administrative State.* Chicago: University of Chicago Press, 1957. Traditional analysis of the nature of bureaucracy, in which the author carries his immense erudition lightly. Still serves the reader well.

_____. "The Civil Service in Germany." In *Civil Service Abroad,* edited by Leonard White et al. New York: McGraw-Hill, 1935.

Mouzelis, Nicos P. *Organization and Bureaucracy.* Chicago: Aldine Publishing Co., 1968. A review of theories of bureaucracy. It reads like the Ph.D. dissertation it obviously was, but it is useful.

Neunreither, Karlheinz. "Federalism and the West German Bureaucracy." *Political Studies,* 7 (October 1959), pp. 232–245.

Nicholson, Max. *The System.* See comment, Chapter 15.

Pakuscher, Ernst K. "Administrative Law in Germany: Citizen vs. State." *American Journal of Comparative Law,* 16, 3 (1968), pp. 309–331.

Parris, Henry. "The Conseil d'État in the Fifth Republic." *Government and Opposition,* 2 (November 1966–January 1967), pp. 89–104.

Pickering, J. F. "Recruitment to the Administrative Class, 1960–1964: Part II." *Public Administration,* 45 (Summer 1967), pp. 169–200.

Plischke, Elmer. *Contemporary Governments of Germany.* See comment, Chapter 12.

Public Administration Review. Special issue, "Alienation, Decentralization, and Participation," 29 (January–February 1969).

Punnett, R. M. *British Government and Politics.* See comment, Chapter 10.

Raef, Marc. "The Russian Autocracy and Its Officials." In *Russian Thought and Politics,* edited by Hugh McLean, Martin A. Malia, and George Fischer. Harvard Slavic Studies, 4. The Hague: Mouton & Co., 1957.

Raphaeli, Nimrod, ed. *Readings on Comparative Public Administration.* Boston: Allyn & Bacon, 1967.

Reich, D. R. "Court, Comity, and Federalism in West Germany." *Midwest Journal of Political Science,* 7 (August 1963), pp. 177–228.

Ridley, F. F. *Specialists and Generalists.* London: George Allen & Unwin, 1968.

_____, ed. "French Technocracy and Comparative Government." *Political Studies,* 14 (February 1966), pp. 34–52.

_____, and Blondel, Jean. *Public Administration in France.* 2nd ed. London: Routledge & Kegan Paul, 1969. Extraordinary scholarship and scope of coverage have so overshadowed a fairly routine approach to the subject matter that the book is required reading for the earnest student.

Riggs, Fred W. *Administration in the Developing Countries.* Boston: Houghton Mifflin, 1964.

Robson, William A. "Ministerial Control of the Nationalized Industries." *Political Quarterly,* 40 (January–March 1969), pp. 103–111.

Rosenberg, Hans. *Bureaucracy, Aristocracy, and Autocracy: The Prussian Experience, 1660–1815.* Cambridge, Mass.: Harvard University Press, 1958. The origins of the German bureaucracy and its impact upon Prussian and, later, German politics. Basic.

Self, P. J. O. "Reform of the Civil Service." *Political Quarterly,* 38 (April–June 1967), pp. 132–139.

Sharp, Walter Rice. *The Government of the French Republic.* New York: D. Van Nostrand, 1938.

Siffin, William J., ed. *Toward the Comparative Study of Public Administration.* Bloomington: University of Indiana Press, 1957.

Sisson, C. H. *The Spirit of British Administration and Some European Comparisons.* London: Faber & Faber, 1959.

Stacey, Frank. *The Government of Modern Britain.* See comment, Chapter 10.

Stankiewicz, W. J., ed. *Crisis in British Government.* See comment, Chapter 10.

Stinchcombe, Arthur L. "Social Structure and Organizations." In *Handbook of Organizations,* edited by James G. March. Chicago: Rand McNally, 1965. A seminal essay on the social conditions underlying the rise, fall, and restructuring of bureaucratic organization.

Thomas, Hugh, ed. *Crisis in the Civil Service.* London: Anthony Blond, 1967.

Thompson, Victor A. *Modern Organization.* New York: Alfred A. Knopf, 1961.

Thornhill, William. *The Nationalized Industries.* See comment, Chapter 15.

Tilford, R. B., and Preece, R. J. C. *Federal Germany.* See comment, Chapter 2.

United States Department of the Army. *Area Handbook for Germany.* See comment, Chapter 2.

Warnecke, Steven. "Reform, Codetermination and the German Bureaucracy." Ph.D. dissertation, Columbia University, 1967.

Williams, Philip M. *Crisis and Compromise.* See comment, Chapter 2.

Willson, F. M. G. *Administrators in Action.* London: George Allen & Unwin, 1961.

CHAPTER 23. NATIONAL DEFENSE AND INTERNAL ORDER: THE MILITARY AND THE POLICE

Abrams, Philip. "The Late Profession of Arms: Ambiguous Goals and Deteriorating Means." *European Journal of Sociology,* 6, 2 (1965), pp. 238–251.

Banton, Michael. *The Policeman and the Community.* New York: Basic Books, 1965.

Bramson, Leon, and Goethals, George W., eds. *War.* Rev. ed. New York: Basic Books, 1968.

Browne, Douglas. *The Rise of Scotland Yard.* London: Harrap & Co., 1956.

Carsten, F. L. *The Reichswehr and Politics: 1918– 1933.* New York: Oxford University Press, 1966.

Chukovskaya, Lydia. *The Deserted House.* See comment, Chapter 3.

Coatman, John. *Police.* Oxford: The Clarendon Press, 1959.

Conquest, Robert. *The Great Terror: Stalin's Purge of the 30's.* See comment, Chapter 3.

————, ed. *The Soviet Police System.* New York: Frederick A. Praeger, 1968.

Craig, Gordon A. *The Politics of the Prussian Army, 1640–1945.* Oxford: The Clarendon Press, 1956.

Cramer, James. *The World's Police.* London: Cassell & Co., 1964. Good descriptive material, but little analysis of any interest.

Critchley, T. A. *A History of Police in England and Wales, 900–1966.* London: Constable & Co., 1967.

Delarue, Jacques. *The History of the Gestapo.* Translated by Mervyn Savill. London: MacDonald, 1964.

Demeter, Karl. *The German Officer Corps, 1650– 1945.* New York: Frederick A. Praeger, 1964.

Dinerstein, H. S. *War and the Soviet Union.* New York: Frederick A. Praeger, 1959.

Elmes, Frank. "The Police 1954–1963." *Criminal Law Review,* July 1964, pp. 505–520.

Erickson, John. *The Soviet High Command.* New York: St. Martin's Press, 1962.

Fainsod, Merle. *How Russia Is Ruled.* See comment, Chapter 3.

————. *Smolensk Under Soviet Rule.* See comment, Chapter 3.

Finer, Samuel E. *The Man on Horseback: The Role of the Military in Politics.* New York: Frederick A. Praeger, 1962. A useful typology of conditions under which the military is likely to intervene in politics.

Friedrich, Carl J. *Constitutional Government and Democracy.* See comment, Chapter 1.

Furniss, Edgar S. *De Gaulle and the French Army: A Crisis in Civil-Military Relations.* New York: Twentieth Century Fund, 1964.

Ginzburg, Eugenia S. *Journey into the Whirlwind.* See comment, Chapter 3.

Goerlitz, Walter. *History of the German General Staff: 1657–1945.* Translated by Walter Millis. New York: Frederick A. Praeger, 1953.

Hewitt, William H. *British Police Administration.* Springfield, Ill.: Charles C. Thomas, 1965.

Howard, Michael, ed. *Soldiers and Governments.* Bloomington: University of Indiana Press, 1959.

Huntington, Samuel P. *The Soldier and the State: The Theory and Politics of Civil-Military Relations.* Cambridge, Mass.: Harvard University Press, 1957.

————, ed. *Changing Patterns of Military Politics.* Glencoe, Ill.: The Free Press, 1962.

————. "Civil-Military Relations." *International Encyclopedia of the Social Sciences,* 7 (1968), pp. 487–495.

Janowitz, Morris. *The New Military: Changing Patterns of Organization.* New York: Russell Sage Foundation, 1964.

————. *The Professional Soldier.* Glencoe, Ill.: The Free Press, 1960.

Kassof, Allen, ed. *Prospects for Soviet Society.* See comment, Chapter 3.

Kelly, George Armstrong. *Lost Soldiers.* Cambridge, Mass.: M.I.T. Press, 1965. The crisis in the military during the last years of the French Fourth Republic.

King, J. C. *Generals and Politicians: Conflict Between France's High Command, Parliament and Government, 1914–1918*. Berkeley and Los Angeles: University of California Press, 1951.

Koestler, Arthur. *Darkness at Noon*. See comment, Chapter 3.

Kolkowicz, Roman. *The Soviet Military and the Communist Party*. Princeton: Princeton University Press, 1967. A careful, very careful, study.

McWilliams, Wilson C., ed. *Garrisons and Governments: Politics and the Military in New States*. San Francisco: Chandler Publishing Co., 1967.

Menard, Orville D. *The Army and the Fifth Republic*. Lincoln: University of Nebraska Press, 1967.

Monas, Sidney. *The Third Section: Police and Society in Russia Under Nicholas I*. Cambridge, Mass.: Harvard University Press, 1961.

O'Connor, Dennis M. "Soviet People's Guards." *New York University Law Review*, 39 (June 1964), pp. 579–614.

Omond, J. S. *Parliament and the Army, 1642–1904*. Cambridge: Cambridge University Press, 1933.

Osborn, Robert J. "Crime and Environment: The New Soviet Debate." *Slavic Review*, 27 (September 1968), pp. 395–410.

Preston, Richard A.; Wise, Sydney F.; and Werner, Herman O. *Men in Arms*. New York: Frederick A. Praeger, 1969.

Ralston, David B., ed. *Soldiers and States: Civil-Military Relations in Modern Europe*. Boston: D. C. Heath, 1966. A judicious collection of essays mortised with intelligent commentary. Probably the best anthology of its kind.

Rapoport, David C. "Military and Civil Societies: The Contemporary Significance of a Traditional Subject in Political Theory." *Political Studies*, 12 (June 1964), pp. 178–201.

Rosinski, Herbert. *The German Army*. New York: Frederick A. Praeger, 1966.

St. Johnston, T. Eric, and Chapman, S. G. *The Police Heritage in England and America*. East Lansing: Michigan State University Press, 1962. Standard history.

Schweitzer, C. G. "Emergency Powers in the Federal Republic of Germany." *Western Political Quarterly*, 22 (March 1969), pp. 112–121.

Secher, H. P. "Controlling the New German Military Elite. . . ." *Proceedings of the American Philosophical Society*, 109 (1965), pp. 63–84.

Solzhenitsyn, Alexsandr. *Cancer Ward*. See comment, Chapter 3.

————. *The First Circle*. See comment, Chapter 3.

————. *One Day in the Life of Ivan Denisovich*. See comment, Chapter 3.

Sowle, Claude R., ed. *Police Power and Individual Freedom*. See comment, Chapter 20.

Stead, Philip John. *The Police of Paris*. London: Staples Press, 1957.

Swianiewicz, S. *Forced Labor and Economic Development*. See comment, Chapter 3.

Tucker, Robert C., and Cohen, Stephen F., eds. *The Great Purge Trial*. See comment, Chapter 3.

Vagts, Alfred. *A History of Militarism*. Rev. ed. New York: The Free Press, 1967.

Van Doorn, Jacques, ed. *Armed Forces and Society*. The Hague: Martinus Nijhoff, 1968. A first-class collection of essays which pinpoints the changing nature (and problems) of the military in contemporary Europe.

Waldman, Eric. *The Goose Step Is Verboten: The German Army Today*. New York: The Free Press, 1964. A rather favorable view of the structure of the new German army and of the attitudes of the men in it.

Wheeler-Bennett, John W. *The Nemesis of Power: The German Army in Politics, 1918–1945*. New York: Oxford University Press, 1954. Comprehensive.

Whitaker, Ben. *The Police*. London: Eyre & Spottiswoode, 1964.

Wolin, Simon, and Slusser, Robert M. *The Soviet Secret Police*. New York: Frederick A. Praeger, 1957.

Young, Peter. *The British Army*. London: William Kimber, 1967. A standard history, short on analysis.

CHAPTER 24. ECONOMIC AND SOCIAL POLICY

Aldcroft, Derek H. *British Railways in Transition*. New York: St. Martin's Press, 1969.

Arndt, Hans-Joachim. *West Germany: Politics of Non-Planning*. Syracuse, N. Y.: Syracuse University Press, 1966.

Bailey, Richard. *Managing the British Economy*. London: Hutchinson & Co., 1968.

Balinky, Alexander, ed. *Planning and the Market in the U.S.S.R.: The 1960's.* New Brunswick, N. J.: Rutgers University Press, 1967.

Banham, Rayner; Barker, Paul; Hall, Peter; and Price, Cedric. "Non-Plan: An Experiment in Freedom." *New Society,* 13 (March 20, 1969), pp. 435–443. The argument: that planned attempts to preserve the distinction between country and city are bound to fail. The plea: integrate the two by guiding, rather than restricting, development. Nicely done.

Barry, Donald D. "Housing in the U.S.S.R." *Problems of Communism,* 18 (May–June 1969), pp. 1–11.

Barry, E. Eldon. *Nationalization in British Politics.* Stanford: Stanford University Press, 1965.

Beaujeu-Garnier, J., and Chabot, G. *Urban Geography.* New York: John Wiley & Sons, 1967.

Beckinsale, R. P., and Houston, J. M., eds. *Urbanization and Its Problems.* Oxford: Basil Blackwell, 1968.

Bellan, R. C. "The Future Growth of Britain's Cities." *The Town Planning Review,* 37 (October 1966), pp. 173–188.

Bergson, Abram, and Kuznets, Simon, eds. *Economic Trends in the Soviet Union.* Cambridge, Mass.: Harvard University Press, 1963.

Beyer, Glenn H. *Housing and Society.* New York: The Macmillan Co., 1965.

Black, Cyril E., ed. *The Transformation of Russian Society.* See comment, Chapter 3.

Blacksell, M. "Recent Changes in the Morphology of West German Townscapes." In *Urbanization and Its Problems,* edited by R. P. Beckinsale and J. M. Housten. Oxford: Basil Blackwell, 1968.

Blaug, Mark. *Social Services for All?* Fabian Tract no. 383. London: The Fabian Society, 1968.

Boarman, Patrick M. *Germany's Economic Dilemma.* Translated by Jean Steinberg. New Haven: Yale University Press, 1964.

Briggs, Asa. "The Welfare State in Historical Perspective." *European Journal of Sociology,* 2 (1961), pp. 221–259.

Brooke, Rosalind. "Civic Rights and Social Services." *Political Quarterly,* 40 (January–March 1969), pp. 90–102.

Burns, Wilfred. *New Towns for Old: The Technique of Urban Renewal.* London: Leonard Hill, 1963.

Butler, J. R., and Pearson, R. J. C. "The Future of the National Health Service." *Political Quarterly,* 40 (January–March 1969), pp. 35–46.

Campbell, Robert W. *Soviet Economic Power: Its Organization, Growth and Challenge.* 2nd ed. Boston: Houghton Mifflin Co., 1963. Clear and concise.

Cartwright, Ann. *Patients and Their Doctors: A Study of General Practice.* New York: Atherton Press, 1967.

Caves, Richard E., ed. *Britain's Economic Prospects.* Washington, D. C.: The Brookings Institution, 1968.

Coates, R. J. *The Making of the Welfare State.* New York: Longmans Green & Co., 1966.

Council of Europe. *Social Aspects of Regional Development: Urban Areas.* Strasbourg, 1967.

Cullingworth, J. B. *Town and Country Planning in England and Wales.* See comment, Chapter 19.

Dahl, Robert A., and Lindblom, Charles E. *Politics, Economics and Welfare.* New York: Harper & Bros., 1953. A basic work on the political economy of planning. Difficult going for the beginning student.

Denton, Geoffrey; Forsyth, Murray; and MacLennan, Malcolm. *Economic Planning and Policies in Britain, France and Germany.* New York: Frederick A. Praeger, 1969. An excellent, comparative study for the intelligent layman.

Dickinson, Robert Eric. *The West European City: A Geographical Interpretation.* 2nd ed., rev. London: Routledge & Kegan Paul, 1963.

Dobb, Maurice. *Soviet Economic Development Since 1917.* Rev. ed. New York: International Publishers, 1968. Marxist perspective on Soviet economic development. Scholarly and readable.

Donaldson, Peter. *Guide to the British Economy.* Baltimore: Penguin Books, 1965.

Donnison, D. V. *The Government of Housing.* Harmondsworth, Middlesex, Eng.: Penguin Books, 1967. Sophisticated discussion of European housing policy, coupled with an attempt to set forth a theoretical model for understanding the problems involved.

————, and Chapman, Valerie. *Social Policy and Administration.* London: George Allen & Unwin, 1967.

Dunning, J. H., and Thomas, C. J. *British Industry: Change and Development in the Twentieth Century.* London: Hutchinson & Co., 1961.

Eckstein, Harry. *The English Health Service.* Cambridge, Mass.: Harvard University Press, 1958.

Eisenstadt, S. N. *Comparative Social Problems.* New York: The Free Press, 1964.

Eldredge, H. Wentworth, ed. *Taming Megalopolis.* 2 vols. New York: Doubleday & Co., Anchor Books, 1967.

Ellman, Michael. *Economic Reform in the Soviet Union.* London: Political and Economic Planning, 1969. Brief, enlightening.

Erhard, Ludwig. *The Economics of Success.* Princeton: D. Van Nostrand, 1963.

Erlich, Alexander. *The Soviet Industrialization Debate, 1924–1928.* Cambridge, Mass.: Harvard University Press, 1960.

Farndale, James, ed. *Trends in Social Welfare.* Oxford: Pergamon Press, 1965.

Fava, Sylvia Fleis, ed. *Urbanism in World Perspective.* New York: Thomas Y. Crowell, 1968.

Field, Mark G. *Doctor and Patient in Soviet Russia.* Cambridge, Mass.: Harvard University Press, 1957.

—————. *Soviet Socialized Medicine.* New York: The Free Press, 1967.

Finer, Herman. *The Theory and Practice of Modern Government.* See comment, Chapter 2.

Foley, Donald L. *Controlling London's Growth.* Berkeley and Los Angeles: University of California Press, 1963.

Friedrich, Carl J. *Constitutional Government and Democracy.* See comment, Chapter 1.

Galbraith, John Kenneth. *The New Industrial State.* Boston: Houghton Mifflin, 1967. Galbraith sees all industrial societies as dominated by large corporations; this is necessary, he maintains, but these organizations must be controlled if the public interest and the quality of public life are not to suffer. Not quite as stimulating as his earlier work.

Gerschenkron, Alexander. *Economic Backwardness in Historical Perspective.* Cambridge, Mass.: Harvard University Press, 1962.

Gilpin, Robert G., Jr. *France in the Age of the Scientific State.* Princeton: Princeton University Press, 1968.

Goldman, Marshall J., ed. *Soviet Marketing.* New York: The Free Press, 1963.

Grebler, Leo. *Urban Renewal in European Countries.* Philadelphia: University of Pennsylvania Press, 1964.

Gregg, Pauline. *The Welfare State.* Amherst: University of Massachusetts Press, 1969.

Greve, John. "Housing Policies and Prospects." *The Political Quarterly,* 40 (January–March 1969), pp. 23–24.

Gross, Bertram. *Social Intelligence for America's Future.* Boston: Allyn & Bacon, 1969.

Grossman, Gregory. *Economic Systems.* Englewood Cliffs, N. J.: Prentice-Hall, 1966. An introduction to comparative economics combining sophistication with clarity. Even students with a block against economic theory can read Grossman with attention and profit.

Hackett, John, and Hackett, Anne-Marie. *The British Economy.* New York: Humanities Press, 1968.

—————. *Economic Planning in France.* Cambridge, Mass.: Harvard University Press, 1963.

Hagen, Everett E., and White, Stephanie F. T. *Great Britain: Quiet Revolution in Planning.* Syracuse, N. Y.: Syracuse University Press, 1966.

Hall, Peter. *The World Cities.* New York: McGraw-Hill, 1966.

—————. "The Pattern of Cities to Come." *New Society,* 7 (March 1966), pp. 6–10.

Hanson, A. H., ed. *Nationalization: A Book of Readings.* London: George Allen & Unwin, 1963.

Hanson, Philip. *The Consumer in the Soviet Economy.* Evanston, Ill.: Northwestern University Press, 1969.

Harvey, Audrey, *Casualties of the Welfare State.* Fabian Tract no. 321. London: The Fabian Society, 1960.

—————. *Social Services for All.* Fabian Tract no. 384. London: The Fabian Society, 1960.

Hauser, Philip M., and Schnore, Leo F., eds. *Study of Urbanization.* New York: John Wiley & Sons, 1965.

Hendel, Samuel, ed. *The Soviet Crucible.* See comment, Chapter 3.

Hogarth, James. *The Payment of the General Practitioner: Some European Comparisons.* New York: Pergamon Press, 1963.

Hughes, John. *Nationalized Industry in the Mixed Economy.* Fabian Tract no. 328. London: The Fabian Society, 1960.

Hunter, Holland. *Soviet Transport Experience.* Washington, D. C.: The Brookings Institution, 1968.

Hutchings, Raymond. "The Ending of Unemployment in the U.S.S.R." *Soviet Studies,* 19 (July 1967), pp. 29–52.

_____. "The Weakening of Ideological Influences on Soviet Design." *Slavic Review,* 27 (March 1968), pp. 71–84.

Jewkes, John, and Jewkes, Sylvia. *The Genesis of the British National Health Service.* London: Basil Blackwell, 1961.

Johnson, Walford; Wyman, John; and Wykes, George. *A Short Economic and Social History of Twentieth-Century England.* New York: Augustus M. Kelley, 1967.

Joint Economic Committee, Congress of the United States. *New Directions in the Soviet Economy.* 4 vols. Washington, D. C.: Government Printing Office, 1966. Some very instructive essays.

Jones, Emrys. *Towns and Cities.* Oxford: The Clarendon Press, 1966.

Karcz, Jerzy F., ed. *Soviet and East European Agriculture.* Berkeley and Los Angeles: University of California Press, 1967.

Kassof, Allen, ed. *Prospects for Soviet Society.* See comment, Chapter 3.

Kidron, Michael. *Western Capitalism Since the War.* London: Weidenfeld & Nicolson, 1968.

Kindleberger, Charles P. *Economic Growth in France and Britain, 1851–1950.* Cambridge, Mass.: Harvard University Press, 1964.

Laroque, Pierre. *Social Welfare in France.* Translated by Philip Gaunt and Noël Lindsay. Paris: La Documentation Française, 1966.

Liggett, Eric. *British Political Issues.* New York: Pergamon Press, 1965.

Lindsey, Almont. *Socialized Medicine in England and Wales.* Chapel Hill: University of North Carolina Press, 1962.

Lutz, Vera. *Central Planning for the Market Economy: An Analysis of the French Theory and Experience.* London: Longmans Green & Co., 1969.

Lynch, Matthew Joseph, and Raphael, Stanley S. *Medicine and the State.* Springfield, Ill.: Charles C. Thomas, 1963.

Maddison, Angus. *Economic Growth in the West: Comparative Experience in Europe and North America.* New York: The Twentieth Century Fund, 1964.

Madison, Bernice Q. *Social Welfare in the Soviet Union.* Stanford: Stanford University Press, 1968. The first systematic study of the subject in English. Well-written and reliable.

Marsh, David C. *The Future of the Welfare State.* Baltimore: Penguin Books, 1965.

Marshall, T. H. *Social Policy.* London: Hutchinson University Library, 1965. Short, sharp discussion of the "welfare state" and the changing conceptions of social welfare. The primary concern is with the English experience, but extensive comparisons are made with other countries.

Millar, James R. "On the Merits of the Convergence Hypothesis." *Journal of Economic Issues,* 2 (March 1968), pp. 60–68.

Millikan, Max F., ed. *National Economic Planning.* New York: Columbia University Press, 1967.

Mumford, Lewis, et al. "City." *International Encyclopedia of the Social Sciences,* 2 (1968), pp. 447–472.

Nove, Alec. *An Economic History of the U.S.S.R.* Harmondsworth, Middlesex, Eng.: Penguin Books, 1969.

_____. *Economic Rationality and Soviet Politics, or, Was Stalin Really Necessary?* New York: Frederick A. Praeger, 1964.

_____. *The Soviet Economy: An Introduction.* New York: Frederick A. Praeger, 1968. This analysis and the history listed above are basic for an understanding of the Soviet economy. Clear and thoughtful, they are easily comprehensible to the interested layman.

Osborn, Frederic J., and Whittick, Arnold. *The New Towns: The Answers to Megalopolis.* London: L. Hill, 1963.

Oxenfeldt, Alfred, and Holubnychy, Vsevolod. *Economic Systems in Action: The United States, The Soviet Union, and France.* New York: Holt, Rinehart & Winston, 1966.

Owen, David. *Social Services for All.* Fabian Tract no. 385. London: The Fabian Society, 1968.

Parkins, Maurice F. *City Planning in Soviet Russia.* Chicago: University of Chicago Press, 1953.

Peterson, Wallace C. *The Welfare State in France.* Lincoln: University of Nebraska Press, 1960.

Postan, M. M. *An Economic History of Western Europe, 1945–1964.* See comment, Chapter 5.

Rasmussen, Steen Eiter. *London: The Unique City.* Cambridge, Mass.: M.I.T. Press, 1966.

Redden, Miles. "Universality Versus Selectivity." *Political Quarterly,* 40 (January–March 1969), pp. 12–22.

Rimlinger, G. V. "The Economics of Postwar German Social Policy." *Industrial Relations,* 6 (February 1967), pp. 184–204.

Robson, William A. "Ministerial Control of the Nationalized Industries." *Political Quarterly,* 40 (January–March 1969), pp. 103–111.

Rodwin, Lloyd, ed. *The Future Metropolis.* New York: George Braziller, 1961. Good essays on the past, present, and future of the city.

Roemer, Milton I. *The Organization of Medical Care Under Social Security.* Geneva: International Labor Office, 1969.

Rose, Richard, ed. *Policy-Making in Britain.* New York: The Free Press, 1969.

Rosovsky, Henry, ed. *Industrialization in Two Systems.* New York: John Wiley & Sons, 1966. Comparisons between Japan and the Soviet Union as two nations which industrialized late. Japan comes off somewhat better.

Rostow, W. W. *The Stages of Economic Growth.* New York: Cambridge University Press, 1960. A "non-Marxist" theory of economic growth which caused some stir in the early 1960's. Like Marx, however, the author excludes cultural variables from his scheme.

Safran, William. *Veto-Group Politics: The Case of Health Insurance Reform in West Germany.* San Francisco: Chandler Publishing Co., 1967.

Salisbury, Harrison E., ed. *The Soviet Union: The Fifty Years.* See comment, Chapter 4.

Sargent, J. R. *Out of Stagnation.* Fabian Tract no. 343. London: The Fabian Society, 1963.

Schorr, Alvin L. *Social Security and Social Services in France.* Washington, D. C.: U. S. Government Printing Office, 1965.

Schroder, Gertrude E. "The 1966–1967 Industrial Price Reform: A Study in Complications." *Soviet Studies,* 20 (April 1969), pp. 462–477.

————. "Soviet Economic 'Reforms': A Study in Contradictions." *Soviet Studies,* 20 (June 1968), pp. 1–21.

Schwartz, Harry. *Russia's Soviet Economy.* 2nd ed. New York: Englewood Cliffs, N. J.: Prentice-Hall, 1954. Standard, reliable, but not too imaginative.

Servan-Schreiber, Jean-Jacques. *The American Challenge.* See comment, Chapter 4.

Shaffer, Harry G., ed. *The Soviet System.* New York: Appleton-Century-Crofts, 1965.

Shanks, Michael. *Is Britain Viable?* Fabian Tract no. 378. London: The Fabian Society, 1967.

————. *The Stagnant Society.* Baltimore: Penguin Books, 1964. A telling critique of those features of British economic life that inhibit innovation.

————, ed. *The Lessons of Public Enterprise.* London: Jonathan Cape, 1963. Essays on the major issues facing the nationalized industries. Excellent.

Shonfield, Andrew. *Modern Capitalism: The Changing Balance of Public and Private Power.* Oxford: The Clarendon Press, 1965. How the role of the state in European capitalist societies is shifting, together with some modest proposals for reform. Uphill most of the way, but worth the trip.

Sorlin, Pierre. *The Soviet People and Their Society: From 1917 to the Present.* New York: Frederick A. Praeger, 1969.

Stevens, Rosemary. *Medical Practice in Modern England.* New Haven: Yale University Press, 1966.

Stolper, Gustav; Hauser, Karl; and Borchardt, Knut. *The German Economy, 1870 to the Present.* Translated by Toni Stolper. New York: Harcourt, Brace & World, 1967.

Strauss, Erich. *Soviet Agriculture in Perspective: A Study of Its Successes and Failures.* New York: Frederick A. Praeger, 1969.

Swianiewicz, S. *Forced Labor and Economic Development.* See comment, Chapter 3.

Taubman, William. "The Politics of Urban Development in the Soviet Union." See comment, Chapter 19.

Tetlow, John, and Goss, Anthony. *Homes, Towns and Traffic.* 2nd ed. New York: Frederick A. Praeger, 1968.

Thomas, Ray. *London's New Towns.* London: Political and Economic Planning, Broadsheet 510, April 1969. Solid analysis of achievements and prospects.

Thornhill, William. *The Nationalized Industries.* See comment, Chapter 15.

Townsend, Peter. *Poverty, Socialism, and Labour in Power.* Fabian Tract no. 371. London: The Fabian Society, 1967.

Tracy, Michael. *Agriculture in Western Europe.* New York: Frederick A. Praeger, 1964.

United Nations, Economic Commission for Europe, Housing Committee. *The Housing Situation and Perspectives for Long-Term Housing Requirements in European Countries.* Geneva: United Nations, 1968.

United Nations, Economic Commission for Europe, Housing Committee. *Major Long-Term Problems of Housing Development and Related Policies.* 2 vols. New York: United Nations, 1966.

United Nations, Economic Commission for Europe, Housing Committee, *Regional Physical Planning.* 2 vols. New York: United Nations, 1966, 1967.

Walsh, Annmarie Hauck. *The Urban Challenge to Government: An International Comparison of Thirteen Cities.* See comment, Chapter 19.

_____. *Urban Government for the Paris Region.* New York: Frederick A. Praeger, 1968.

Weiner, Herbert. *British Labour and Public Ownership.* London: Stevens & Sons, 1960.

Wiles, Peter J. D. *The Political Economy of Communism.* Cambridge, Mass.: Harvard University Press, 1962. An innovative, theoretical analysis of the Soviet economy.

Wingo, Lowen, Jr. *Cities and Space.* Baltimore: Johns Hopkins Press, 1963.

CHAPTER 25. FOREIGN POLICY

Alperovitz, Gar. *Atomic Diplomacy: Hiroshima and Potsdam.* New York: Simon & Schuster, 1965. An analysis of the origins of the cold war, placing much of the responsibility on the United States.

Aron, Raymond. *Peace and War.* Translated by Richard Howard and Annette Baker Fox. New York: Doubleday & Co., 1966. A sweeping, historically oriented study of international politics. Lucid, intelligent, and essential for anyone really interested in the subject.

Bramson, Leon, and Goethals, George W., eds. *War.* Rev. ed. New York: Basic Books, 1968.

Brandt, Willy. *A Peace Policy for Europe.* Translated by Joel Carmichael. New York: Holt, Rinehart & Winston, 1969.

Brzezinski, Zbigniew. *The Soviet Bloc.* Rev. ed. Cambridge, Mass.: Harvard University Press, 1967.

Burton, J. W. *Systems, States, Diplomacy, and Rules.* Cambridge: Cambridge University Press, 1968.

Calleo, David. *Britain's Future.* New York: Horizon Press, 1969.

Calvocoressi, Peter. *International Politics Since 1945.* New York: Frederick A. Praeger, 1968.

Camps, Miriam. *European Unification in the 1960's: From Veto to the Crisis.* New York: McGraw-Hill, 1966.

Clark, William Hartley. *The Politics of the Common Market.* Englewood Cliffs, N. J.: Prentice-Hall, 1967.

Craig, Gordon A. *From Bismarck to Adenauer: Aspects of German Statecraft.* Baltimore: Johns Hopkins Press, 1958.

Degras, Jane, ed. *The Communist International, 1919–1943.* Oxford: The Clarendon Press, 1956.

_____, ed. *Soviet Documents on Foreign Policy.* 3 vols. Oxford: The Clarendon Press, 1951–1953.

Dehio, Ludwig. *Germany and World Politics in the Twentieth Century.* New York: Alfred A. Knopf, 1959.

Deutsch, Karl W. *The Analysis of International Relations.* Englewood Cliffs, N. J.: Prentice-Hall, 1968. Sound introduction to the study of international politics, based on a communications model.

_____; Edinger, Lewis J.; Macridis, Roy C.; and Merrit, Richard. *France, Germany, and the Western Alliance.* New York: Charles Scribner's Sons, 1967.

Feld, Werner. *The European Common Market and the World.* Englewood Cliffs, N. J.: Prentice-Hall, 1967.

Gitler, Lewis F. "Probing the German Mind." *Interplay,* 1 (October 1967), pp. 4–8.

Grosser, Alfred. *French Foreign Policy Under De Gaulle.* Boston: Little, Brown & Co., 1967.

Gulick, Edward Vose. *Europe's Classical Balance of Power.* New York: W. W. Norton, 1967.

Hanrieder, Wolfram F. *West German Foreign Policy, 1949–1963.* Stanford: Stanford University Press, 1967.

Kaiser, Karl. *German Foreign Policy in Transition.* New York: Oxford University Press, 1968.

Kennan, George F. *Memoirs, 1925–1950.* Boston: Atlantic–Little, Brown & Co., 1967.

_____. *Russia and the West Under Lenin and Stalin.* Boston: Little, Brown & Co., 1961. An authoritative, stimulating account of Soviet foreign policy by an American scholar-diplomat.

Kolko, Gabriel. *The Politics of War: The World and U. S. Foreign Policy, 1943–1945.* New York: Random House, 1968. Anatomy of the cold war, with much of the blame on American policy.

Labedz, Leopold, ed. *International Communism after Khrushchev.* Cambridge, Mass.: M.I.T. Press, 1965.

Laloy, Jean, et al. "Origins of the Postwar Crisis." *Journal of Contemporary History,* 3 (April 1968), pp. 217–252. A symposium on the causes of the cold war. Useful for the wide variety of opinions expressed.

Laqueur, Walter. *Russia and Germany: A Century of Conflict.* London: Weidenfeld & Nicolson, 1965.

Larus, Joel, ed. *Comparative World Politics.* See comment, Chapter 1.

Lederer, Ivo, ed. *Russian Foreign Policy: Essays in Historical Perspective.* New Haven: Yale University Press, 1962.

Lindberg, Leon N., and Scheingold, Stuart A. *Europe's Would-Be Polity.* Englewood Cliffs, N. J.: Prentice-Hall, 1969.

Lowenthal, Richard. *World Communism: The Disintegration of a Secular Faith.* New York: Oxford University Press, 1964.

Macridis, Roy, ed. *De Gaulle: The Implacable Ally.* New York: Harper & Row, 1966.

————. *Foreign Policy in World Politics.* 3rd ed. Englewood Cliffs, N. J.: Prentice-Hall, 1967. Very instructive collection of readings on the foreign ploys and policies of the major powers.

Northedge, F. S., ed. *The Foreign Policies of the Powers.* New York: Frederick A. Praeger, 1969.

Oliva, Lawrence J., ed. *Russia and the West from Peter to Khrushchev.* Boston: D. C. Heath, 1965.

Pethybridge, Roger W., ed. *The Development of the Communist Bloc.* Boston: D. C. Heath, 1965. An excellent assortment of opinions on how the Soviet Union came to dominate Eastern Europe immediately after World War II.

Pickles, William. *Britain and Europe: How Much Has Changed?* Oxford: Basil Blackwell, 1967.

Renouvin, Pierre, and Duroselle, Jean-Baptiste. *Introduction to the History of International Relations.* Translated by Mary Ilford. New York: Frederick A. Praeger, 1967.

Richardson, James. "Germany's Eastern Policy: Problems and Prospects." *The World Today,* 24 (September 1968), pp. 375–386.

Robertson, Charles L. *International Politics Since World War II: A Short History.* New York: John Wiley & Sons, 1966. An irreproachable, readable account of postwar politicking in the international arena. Especially instructive for the uninitiated.

Rosecrance, Richard N. *Action and Reaction in World Politics.* Boston: Little, Brown & Co., 1963.

Rosser, Richard F. *An Introduction to Soviet Foreign Policy.* Englewood Cliffs, N. J.: Prentice-Hall, 1969.

Rougemont, Denis de; Spinell, Altiera; Mayne, Robert; Butt, Ronald; Lambert, John; Sidjanski, Dusan; and Zellentin, Gerda. "The Politics of European Integration." *Government and Opposition,* 2 (April–July 1967), pp. 321–426.

Schlesinger, Arthur J. "Origins of the Cold War." *Foreign Affairs,* 46 (October 1967), pp. 22–52.

Seabury, Paul. *The Wilhelmstrasse.* Berkeley and Los Angeles: University of California Press, 1954.

Senn, Alfred E., ed. *Readings in Russian Political and Diplomatic History.* Homewood, Ill.: The Dorsey Press, 1966.

Seton-Watson, Hugh. *From Lenin to Khrushchev.* New York: Frederick A. Praeger, 1960. A cursory run through the cold war by way of an examination of Soviet foreign policy. Covers too much ground too hastily.

Strachey, John. *The End of Empire.* New York: Random House, 1960.

Strang, William. *Britain in World Affairs.* New York: Frederick A. Praeger, 1961.

Ulam, Adam. *Expansion and Coexistence: The History of Soviet Foreign Policy, 1917–1967.* New York: Frederick A. Praeger, 1968. Perhaps the best one-volume study of Soviet foreign policy.

Urwin, Derek W. *Western Europe Since 1945.* See comment, Chapter 1.

Wesson, R. G. *An Introduction to Soviet Foreign Policy.* Homewood, Ill.: The Dorsey Press, 1969.

Wilkinson, David, ed. *Comparative Foreign Relations: Framework and Methods.* Belmont, Calif.: Dickenson Publishing Co., 1969.

Willis, F. R. *France, Germany, and the New Europe, 1945–1967.* Rev. ed. New York: Oxford University Press, 1968.

Younger, Kenneth. *Changing Perspectives in British Foreign Policy.* New York: Oxford University Press, 1964.

Part VI Some Conclusions

CHAPTER 26. THE FUTURE OF EUROPEAN POLITICS

Aron, Raymond. *Progress and Disillusion.* London: Pall Mall, 1968.

Arvill, Robert. *Man and Environment.* Rev. ed. Baltimore: Penguin Books, 1969. The ecology of the English landscape, with suggestions on what should be done if the quality of English life is not to deteriorate.

Baier, Kurt, and Rescher, Nicholas, eds. *Values and the Future.* New York: The Free Press, 1969.

Boulding, Kenneth. *The Meaning of the Twentieth Century.* New York: Harper & Row, 1964. Prospects for the future by an economist turned social theorist. Gracefully written and intelligent.

Brown, Norman O. *Life Against Death*. New York: Random House, 1969.

_____. *Love's Body*. New York: Random House, 1966. Both books fashion a critique of modern society based on an extrapolation of Freud. The second is more radical than the first, but Freud would spin in his grave if he read either.

Deutscher, Isaac. *The Unfinished Revolution: Russia, 1917–1967*. See comment, Chapter 3.

Drucker, Peter. *The Age of Discontinuity*. New York: Harper & Row, 1969. What the contours of postindustrial society look like. Some engaging insights are interpersed with dubious analyses, but all of it is set down with style.

Ewald, William R., Jr., ed. *Environment for Man*. Bloomington: Indiana University Press, 1967.

Ferkiss, Victor C. *Technological Man: The Myth and the Reality*. New York: George Braziller, 1969. One of the best of the current crop of books scanning the future. Ferkiss writes nicely, respects the facts, and is balanced in his judgments.

Galbraith, John Kenneth. *The New Industrial State*. See comment, Chapter 24.

Gross, Bertram. *Social Intelligence for America's Future*. Boston: Allyn & Bacon, 1969.

Heilbroner, Robert. *The Limits of American Capitalism*. New York: Harper & Row, 1966. Enlightening comments on the future of capitalist industrial societies, with particular emphasis on the United States. Suggestive, although Heilbroner sometimes pushes his argument beyond the evidence.

Kahn, Herman J., and Weiner, Anthony. *The Year 2000*. New York: The Macmillan Co., 1967. A grim look at the future.

Kaplan, Max. *Leisure in America*. New York: John Wiley & Sons, 1966.

Little, Richard R., and Riemer, Neal, eds. *Liberalization in the U.S.S.R.: Facade or Reality*. Boston: Raytheon Education Co., 1968.

Marcuse, Herbert. *Eros and Civilization*. Boston: The Beacon Press, 1955.

_____. *An Essay on Liberation*. Boston: The Beacon Press, 1969.

_____. *One-Dimensional Man*. Boston: The Beacon Press, 1964. A leading critic of "industrial" society who taps Marx and Freud. Although Marcuse is extremely popular with the New Left both in Europe and the United States, it is doubtful whether most of those who quote him really understand him.

Meynaud, Jean. *Technocracy*. Translated by Paul Barnes. New York: The Free Press, 1968.

Moore, Barrington, Jr.; Wolf, Robert; and Marcuse, Herbert. *A Critique of Pure Tolerance*. Boston: The Beacon Press, 1966. An attack on liberalism as a viable basis for organizing the community. Marcuse argues for "repressive" measures against the enemies of progress.

Public Administration Review. Special issue. "Alienation, Decentralization, and Participation." 29 (January-February 1969).

Rienow, Robert, and Rienow, Leona Train. *Moment in the Sun*. New York: The Dial Press, 1967. A pessimistic look at the state of the natural environment in the United States. Well worth some thought.

Index